THE AMERICAN PEOPLES ENCYCLOPEDIA

A MODERN REFERENCE WORK

PRINTED IN U.S.A.

ISBN 0-7172-0302-6

Library of Congress Catalog Card Number: 71-118651

MIRA, the Wonderful, in the constellation Cetus, was the first star observed to vary periodically in brightness, although Tycho's Nova of 1572 was an earlier known variable star. (See VARIABLE STAR, *Intrinsic Variables.*) When discovered in 1596 by the Dutch astronomer David Fabricius (1564–1617), Mira was at third magnitude (see MAGNITUDE) and fading. Johann Bayer (1572–1625) had listed it in his catalogue (1603) as *o* Ceti; but J. K. Holwarda, who rediscovered it in 1638, was apparently the first to note its disappearances and reappearances. Mira is a red long-period variable with a magnitude range of 9.2 to 3.4 and a period of 330 days. These are average values: the period ranges from 320 to 370 days, the magnitude at the brightest and faintest maxima from 1.5 to 5.5, respectively, and the magnitude of the minimum brightness from 8 to 10.

These magnitudes are photovisual—that is, they are determined photographically. Infrared photography gives a much smaller range, there being a magnitude difference of only about 1.5 between maximum and minimum; and from radiometric measures of the total radiation the range is still less. The changes in radiometric and infrared magnitudes are so much less than those in visual magnitude because the total amount of radiation that Mira emits varies much less than that part of the radiation that is in the visible range. At minimum the star's effective temperature is about 1900°C (3400°F) and the peak of the energy in its spectrum is then far out in the infrared, with very little energy in the visible region. At maximum, however, when the temperature is about 2600°C (4700°F) the whole energy curve is higher and the peak, though still in the infrared, is enough nearer the visible that the energy in the visible region is increased enormously. (See BLACK BODY; SPECTRUM.) At minimum brightness, the star Mira is spectral type M9, with an absorption spectrum of metallic lines and strong titanium oxide bands in the visible region which further reduce the radiant energy coming from that part of the spectrum. As the temperature rises the titanium oxide bands become markedly less strong, and bright emission lines of hydrogen appear. This stage is followed by bright lines of some of the metals, thus effecting by another means an increase in the radiation from the visible region, an increase that is relatively greater than for the whole spectrum. Paul Willard Merrill (1887–) suggested that, as the temperature drops on approaching the minimum light phase, clouds or veils might form toward the outer levels of the star's atmosphere, thus blocking some of the radiation from lower levels. See STAR.

Mira is about 250 light-years distant, and its luminosity (intrinsic brightness) at maximum is about 180 times that of the sun. That it is a giant in size as well as in luminosity, several hundred times the diameter of the sun, was shown by Francis Gladheim Pease's (1881–1938) direct measurement with the interferometer. (See GIANT AND DWARF STARS.) The average density of the star must be exceedingly low. The dark (absorption) lines of the spectrum exhibit a radial velocity variation of the same period as that of the light variation, with maximum recession at the maximum light phase. The emission lines exhibit a greater range of radial velocities, but they indicate a maximum velocity of approach at maximum light. The success of the pulsation theory of Cepheid variables suggested that Mira, and more than 1,000 other long-period m variables of which it is the type star, might also be pulsating, but the atmospheric motions indicated by the complicated radial velocities could not be reasonably accounted for. Roderich MacDonald Scott (1916–) used the bright hydrogen lines as the basis for a pulsation hypothesis; because they are known to have their origin at lower levels than do the band lines, they presumably represent more closely the actual behavior of the main body of the star. In 1923 Alfred Harrison Joy (1882–), in studying the spectrum of Mira, discovered a companion star, although Mira is not a spectroscopic binary. (See DOUBLE STAR.) This companion is a white star (type B8), perhaps as luminous as the sun, and thus markedly different from Mira in temperature, color, size, and brightness. See CETUS; CONSTELLATION.

MIRABEAU, HONORE GABRIEL VICTOR RIQUETI, COMTE DE, 1749–91, French revolutionary leader, was born in Bignon near Nemours. As a young cavalry lieutenant, he was involved in several scandals and imprisoned several times, usually through a *lettre de cachet* obtained by his father, the marquis de Mirabeau. In 1776 young Mirabeau eloped from the Castle of Joux (where he was imprisoned) with Marie Thérèse de Monnier. They went to Amsterdam, where he lived by hack writing until he was rearrested and jailed in the Château de Vincennes, 1777–82. He spent this incarceration in writing the famous letters to "Sophie" (Marie), published in 1793, and the political work *Lettres de cachet* (1782). Shortly after his release he intervened in the lawsuit between his father and mother and was exiled to Holland and England. He was a French secret agent in Prussia, 1786–87, an experience resulting in *De la monarchie Prussienne sous Frédéric le Grand* (1788) and *Histoire secrète de la cour de Berlin* (1789).

In 1789 Mirabeau was elected to the estates-general, and led the movement that turned the third estate into the national assembly, in which he became known as an exponent of constitutional monarchy. He made several memorable orations in the assembly and founded the *Journal des Etats Généraux* (1789–91). Becoming increasingly conservative, Mirabeau quarreled with Marie Joseph Lafayette and Jacques Necker, and while still president of the Jacobin Club, 1790, negotiated secretly with Louis XVI and Marie Antoinette. He asked Louis to appeal to the people in an attempt to save the monarchy, but Louis did not follow the advice. Mirabeau died in 1791, shortly after being elected assembly president.

MIRACLE, an event or effect in the physical world that is attributed to direct and special divine intervention because it seems to be unexplainable according to the laws of nature. In the orthodox view of Christianity, Judaism, and Islam only God can work miracles, but men may at times be God's agents in performing them. The "laws of nature" describe the normal workings of the physical world and are viewed as God's laws because He is the creator of the universe. By a miracle God makes a temporary change in the normal workings of the universe He created.

Dr. James R. Kaye, editor of the New Analytical Bible, lists 54 miracles recorded in the Old Testament and 57 in the New Testament. To the latter he adds the miracles performed by Stephen and Philip the Evangelist, the account of whose miracles suggests that they were multiple. The same is true in many recorded instances of miracles by Christ and the disciples. Thirty-six separate miracles are attributed to Christ, and 21 to the Holy Spirit, angels, the disciples, and Paul. Irenaeus in the second century affirmed the occurrence of miracles in the churches of his day. Martin Luther asserted that the miracle of grace in the heart, when a person experiences regeneration, is far greater than any physical miracle. From this statement proponents of the miraculous element in human experience argued that miracles were not only possible but probable.

With the increasing advances of science in the eighteenth and nineteenth centuries there came, however, a more vocal expression of men's doubts as to the possibility of miracles. This was in line with the scientific tendency to regard the world as operated within inflexible laws of nature that allow no interference. Later developments in science caused some scientists and theologians to see the possibility of reconciling to an increasing extent the viewpoints of Christian tradition and modern scientific research.

JULIUS R. MANTEY

BIBLIOG.–J. H. Newman, *Two Essays on Biblical and Ecclesiastical Miracles* (ed. 1901); S. J. Case, *Experience with the Supernatural in Early Christian Times* (1929); C. S. Lewis, *Miracles* (1947); R. C. Trench, *Notes on the Miracles of Our Lord* (ed. 1953).

MIRACLE PLAY, or mystery play, a medieval religious drama. Originally a miracle play was based on the legend of a saint and a mystery play was adapted from Bible stories. Later both types were regarded as miracle plays. Miracles and mysteries became immensely popular during the fourteenth and fifteenth centuries throughout the Christian world and were the beginning of modern drama as distinct from Greek and Roman, which, partly because of Christian proscription, ceased to be public entertainment after about 500.

Scarcity of data makes difficult more than an outline of the course of this spontaneous Christian drama. In the fifth century there was mention of a trope (a turning aside) inserted into the Easter Mass—probably the addition of a special antiphonal. Later, clerics costumed as actors chanted bits of dialogue in Latin at the beginning (introit) of the Mass. The earliest trope known is one in the tenth century manuscript of Saint Gall. In it three clerics clad as the three Marys approach Christ's sepulcher, simulated near the altar. They find it empty, but are confronted by a fourth cleric in raiment of an angel. Chanting in Latin, they exchange only three brief, obvious lines, the angel explaining: "He is not here, but is risen as He foretold." Such tropes were enlarged to plays, but retained in the church celebrations of Easter and Christmas. In the thirteenth century these and many others, more mundanely composed and acted, became more popular and were moved out of the church into the yard. Finally they were renounced by church and clergy. By then (thirteenth century) they were in vernacular and were taken over by the trade guilds that presented them at Whitsuntide—apparently as good publicity (water carriers, for instance, chose Noah's flood; bakers, the harrowing of hell; shipwrights, the building of the ark). The tradesmen had the further good luck of a new Maytime festival, Corpus Christi day, appointed by papal decree of 1264. At Chester, York, Coventry, Wakefield, and many other towns, guilds entered pageants in the festive processions, presenting plays in one square after another. A typical pageant was a six-wheeled wagon with an upper, roofed platform for stage, reached by ladder and trap door from a curtained space below for costuming. The tinker-actors provided themselves with amazing properties: "A link to set the world on fire. . . . Two yards of buckram for the Holy Ghost's coat. . . . Hell mouth with jaws worked by two men, out of which devil boys ran. . . ."

On the Continent, in London—where parish clerks were the producers—and in some other English towns, scaffolds or (as at Clerkenwell) "plots" (*platea*) provided acting space with entrances from appropriate booths or "mansions."

In his monumental *Masks, Mimes, and Miracles* (1931), Allardyce Nicoll remarks that it was not primarily the edifying matter of the Scriptures that appealed, but the realistic, humorously human scenes and characters, invented for sheer entertainment, that insured popularity and a lasting influence in English drama. Sheep stealing Mak of a Towneley shepherd play, Noah's vixen of a wife, Herod's leap from the pageant to rant in the square—such colorful characters and business created an audience eagerness that grew through the following centuries until it drew from William Shakespeare the immortal Bottom (a superbly realistic lampoon of the tinker-actor), and also Corin, Trinculo, Autolycus, Dogberry, and Falstaff—all examples of this peculiarly British vein of theater art.

Processional acting results in cycles—plays in sequence from Creation to Resurrection. Forty-eight from York, the oldest, have survived; 32 from Towneley (or Wakefield), the most entertaining; 42 from Coventry; 25 of French influence from Chester; and a few separate plays like the beautiful *Sacrifice of Isaac* of the Brome manuscript. Most notable is the eight-hour Passion play of Bavaria's Oberammergau; but this pales by comparison with the 25-day Passion play at Valencienne of sixteenth century France, with its endless lurid action on a vast stage exhibiting simultaneously heaven, Nazareth, Jerusalem with temple and palace, the golden gate, limbo, and hell with a yawning dragon's mouth. See DRAMA, Medieval Drama.

E. BRADLEE WATSON

BIBLIOG.–E. K. Chambers, *Medieval Stage* (1903); P. E. Kretzman, *Liturgical Elements in the Earliest Forms of Medieval Drama* (1916); A. Nicoll, *Masks, Mimes, and Miracles* (1931); K. Young, *Drama of the Medieval Church* (1933); H. C. Gardiner, *Mysteries' End* (1946); G. Frank, *Medieval French Drama* (1954); H. Craig, *English Religious Drama of the Middle Ages* (1955); M. Hussey, ed., *Chester Mystery Plays* (1957).

MIRAGE, an optical illusion wherein distant objects may be seen elevated or depressed, frequently inverted, and often so distorted that the image appears quite different from the object that is its source. The elevation may at times be great enough to make objects that are below the horizon visible to an observer, and similarly the depression may be sufficient to hide an object from view.

Mirages are caused by refraction of light through air layers that are not homogeneous. Ordinarily light travels in a straight line from the object to the eye of an observer. If the temperature, and therefore the density, of the air at various heights above the ground varies sufficiently, however, a light ray will be bent continuously as it encounters air of different densities. If there is a warm layer near the surface and a colder layer above it, a light ray is refracted concave upward (Fig. 1a) so that it appears to come from below the ground, an appearance that suggests that the object is reflected in water. This concept is aided by the fact that the image shimmers in a way reminiscent of water, because the density of the air layers is constantly changing. The same explanation may be given from a slightly different point of view, that is, one may think of a wave front of light that originally was perpendicular to the ground but has become distorted because of varying air density. From

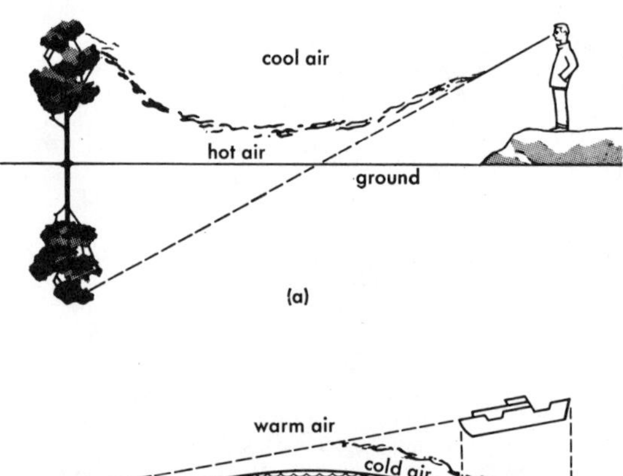

Mirage. In example *a*, light rays are bent along a concave curvature in passing across a stratum of hot air; the resulting image is inverted and seems to come from below ground level. In example *b*, the air near the surface is cooler than the air above, causing light rays to reflect downward so that the image appears to come from the sky.

each point of the wave front a ray of light emerges that travels at right angles to the front; the rays leaving a distorted wave front are consequently not parallel, and light will therefore appear to come from a different level than it actually does. In such a case all or parts of an image may be inverted. A mirage that appears below the object that has given rise to it, such as that of a lake in the desert, is an inferior image. A more commonly seen inferior image is the apparent presence of puddles on a road on a hot summer day. A superior image may arise if a cold layer of air is beneath a warm layer. Under such conditions the light will be reflected convex downward, and the image will appear to be in the sky, Fig. 1b.

A particularly famous mirage is the Fata Morgana, seen in the Strait of Messina near Italy, in the Toyama Bay near northwest Japan, and other places. It occurs when conditions are such that both inferior and superior mirages may form. Double mirages then appear, made fantastic by the fact that the intermediate layer acts somewhat like a magnifying lens. See REFRACTION.

MIRAMICHI RIVER, Canada, N central New Brunswick; a system of several rivers originating in the W highlands and proceeding E into Miramichi Bay of the Gulf of St. Lawrence at Chatham. The chief river of the system, the Main Southwest Miramichi, starts near Juniper and follows a northeasterly course for 135 miles. Several tributaries empty into it along the way. The Southwest Miramichi and the Northwest Miramichi begin independently farther north, join near Redbank, then flow east to merge with the Main Southwest Miramichi near Newcastle. The Micmac Indian word *miramichi* means happy retreat.

MIRAMÓN, MIGUEL, 1832–67, Mexican general, was born in Mexico City. In 1856 he joined the revolutionary forces against Ignacio Comonfort. When Félix Zuloaga became president, Miramón assumed the leadership of the reactionary forces. He was elected provisional president by the *junta de notables*, 1859, but in 1860 he was defeated by the Liberals at Calpulálpam and fled to Europe. Having returned to Mexico in 1866, he offered his services to Emperor Maximilian, with whom he was subsequently condemned to death and executed.

MIRANDA, FRANCISCO ANTONIO GABRIEL, 1750?–1816, Spanish American revolutionist, was born in Caracas, Venezuela. He saw service with the Spanish army and fought with the French in the American Revolutionary War. In France Miranda fought with the revolutionary forces and commanded a division at the defeat of Neerwinden. He was accused of treachery, but was acquitted, was later arrested, and took refuge in England. In 1806, having returned to America, he fitted out an expedition to free Venezuela from Spain, but the effort failed. After the Revolution of 1810 he was made dictator, 1812, but was arrested by the royalists and sent to Cádiz, where he died in prison.

MIRANDA, state, N Venezuela; bounded by the Federal District and Caribbean Sea on the N and by the states of Anzoátegui on the E, Guárico on the S, and Aragua on the W; area 3,070 sq. mi.; pop. (1950) 276,273. Except for the Tuy River valley, the region is mostly mountainous. Bananas, corn, cacao, cotton, sugar, and tobacco are grown in the lowlands and coffee is a product of the highlands. Main industries are sawmilling and sugar refining. Los Teques is the capital of Miranda. Other towns are Río Chico, El Guapo, Carenero, and Ocumare del Tuy.

MIRBEAU, OCTAVE HENRI MARIE, 1850–1917, French writer, was born in Trévières. He worked as a journalist in Paris and in 1882 was one of the founders of *Les Grimaces*, a satirical journal. He was at first a Roman Catholic royalist, but became a radical and attacked all forms of social organization. He first won attention as an author with his short stories *Lettres de ma chaumière* (Letters from My Cottage), 1886. Other works include the novels *Le Calvaire* (The Tribulation), 1886, *Les Mémoires d'une femme de chambre* (Memoirs of a Chambermaid), 1901, and *Les Vingt-et-un jours d'un neurasthénique* (The 21 Days of a Neurasthenic), 1902, and the plays *Les Mauvais Bergers* (The Bad Shepherds), 1897, and *Les Affaires sont les affaires*, 1903 (*Business Is Business*, 1905).

MIRIAM, sister of Moses and Aaron (Num. 26:59). She watched the infant Moses when he was left for safety by his mother in an ark in the bulrushes (Ex. 2:4–10). She led the women who celebrated, with timbrel and dancing, the crossing of the Red Sea by the Israelites (Ex. 15:20–21). When she and Aaron spoke against Moses' marriage to an Ethiopian (Cushite) woman, she was stricken with leprosy (Num. 12:1–10). Because of Aaron's entreaty, Moses prayed for her healing and she was restored to health (Num. 12:11–15). Miriam was buried at Kadesh (Num. 20:1).

MIRÓ, JOAN, 1893– , Spanish painter, was born in Montroig, studied at the Academy of Fine Arts, Barcelona, and at the Gali Academy, and had the first exhibit of his works in 1918. He went to Paris where he was associated with the dadaists, and in 1925 participated in the first exhibition of the surrealist group. Miró's art is personal and natural, and his work possesses a plasticity, unexpectedness, and whimsey that make it independent of any school or group. Among his paintings are *Landscape with a Donkey*, *The Farm*, *Turned Soil*, *Harlequin's Carnival*, *Person Looking at the Sun*, and *Snob Evening at the Princess'*. He also designed ballet costumes and settings and illustrated books. In 1958 a ceramic mural executed by Miró for the new UNESCO headquarters buildings in Paris was awarded a $10,000 prize by the international jury of the Solomon R. Guggenheim Foundation. The mural, *Night and Day* (1958), is in two parts, "The Wall of the Moon" and "The Wall of the Sun," and appears on two perpendicular walls (24½ and 50 ft. long) on the UNESCO grounds. In all, the mural embodies 585 tiles. The following is a statement prepared by Miró especially for THE AMERICAN PEOPLES ENCYCLOPEDIA; although this statement deals largely with the creation of the ceramic mural, Miró's remarks also reveal much as

SOLOMON R. GUGGENHEIM MUS.

Miró's "The Wall of the Moon" is part of the 1958 Guggenheim International award-winning mural *Night and Day*.

to the state of mind, purposes, and methods of this important twentieth century artist:

Art Derives from the Whole Universe, and upon being commissioned, by UNESCO in 1955 to do a large mural for the decoration of the UNESCO buildings in the Place Fontenoy, Paris, I found it appropriate to make a journey through the history of art. With the great ceramist José Llorens-Artigas, who worked with me on this large ceramic mural, I went from Paris to Santillana del Mar, in Santander Province, Spain, where we contemplated once more the world's first mural art—the paleolithic rock paintings in Altamira. After meditating on these great elemental works we discovered, quite unexpectedly, a sublime beauty in the walls of the ancient Romanesque church of Santillana, "La Colegiata." We were especially attracted to a wall long corroded by dampness, whose slow destruction had brought about a spontaneous, unforeseeable beauty: that wall was to be of use to us in the future!

It then seemed indispensable that, as Catalan artists, we place ourselves under the sign of Romanesque Catalan art and the extraordinary Barcelonian art of Antonio Gaudí. In the museum of Barcelona we learned once more the great lesson of the Romanesque frescoes—exemplary paintings on which I have meditated since my first days as a painter. Our UNESCO mural, especially its rhythm, owes much to them. Communing with the Gaudí of Guell Park, we took special note of a large disk on the wall that allowed the stone to show through in a manner similar to the circle for our mural, which I had already been tracing in my imagination. It was a good omen.

From Barcelona we returned to that old city of stone, Gallifa, where Artigas' studio and kiln are located. There, against the rock precipice that dominates the town, I laid out my maquette. Such direct confrontation with nature is always a sound practice for art, for nature is the ultimate creator, and I have never produced any art in which nature was forgotten or excluded. I cannot understand, and I regard it as an insult, that I should be called an abstract painter—as though the symbols I transcribe on canvas, whenever they correspond to a concrete representation of my spirit, did not possess a profound reality, did not form part of reality!

I do not have a very favorable opinion of the intelligence now in evidence among painters; the majority appear too preoccupied with themselves and their work. I have associated more with poets. But there are exceptions among the painters. El Greco and Goya, for example, go beyond mere plastic considerations. I consider Francisco Zurbarán the most remarkable of artists. And the Flemish are wonderful painters! José Gutiérrez-Solana is very authentic. And there is Picasso, for whom I have unlimited admiration. He is a world to himself. He is like the earth: very, very old. And that is what all great painting must be—like the earth: always old, always new. (Translated from the Spanish.) JOAN MIRÓ

MIRROR, an object whose surface has been polished so that it reflects light in a regular manner. In ancient times mirrors were made of polished gold, steel, or bronze. Glass mirrors with reflecting coatings appeared in the thirteenth century, and for two centuries Venice had a monopoly on them. Silvered mirrors were manufactured after 1840 and evaporated aluminum mirrors came into use after 1932. Commercial mirrors have generally been made by a chemical process in which the silver from silver nitrate is deposited on glass and protected from tarnish by shellac or paint. The reflectivity of a fresh silver mirror reaches 95 per cent; the front glass surface produces a weak second reflection of about 3 to 10 per cent. Thin coats of metals such as gold, chromium, and aluminum can also be deposited on glass. Such hard thin coats of aluminum reflect about 90 per cent of the light incident upon them and resist tarnishing for years. Unlike silvered mirrors, they have the additional advantage of reflecting ultraviolet as well as visible light.

Image Formation. The angle that the ray leaving the mirror makes with the normal, or a line perpendicular to the mirror at the point at which the light strikes the mirror, must equal the angle that the ray that reached the mirror made with the normal. In other words, the angle of incidence equals the angle of reflection. See REFLECTION.

If the rays of light actually cross in front of the mirror, after they are reflected from the mirror, the image formed is real; if they seem to cross behind the mirror, but do not actually cross, the image formed is virtual. Plane and convex spherical mirrors always form virtual images; concave spherical mirrors may give rise to either real or virtual images, depending on the location of the object.

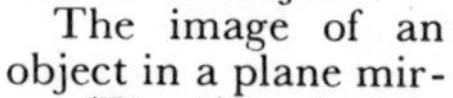

Figure 1

The image of an object in a plane mirror (Fig. 1) is virtual, upright, the same distance from the mirror as the object, and reversed—that is, left appears to be right and right appears to be left.

Image formation by spherical mirrors, mirrors that are a portion of a sphere, is somewhat more complex. The center of the sphere of which the mirror is a part is known as the center of curvature C (Fig. 2). From

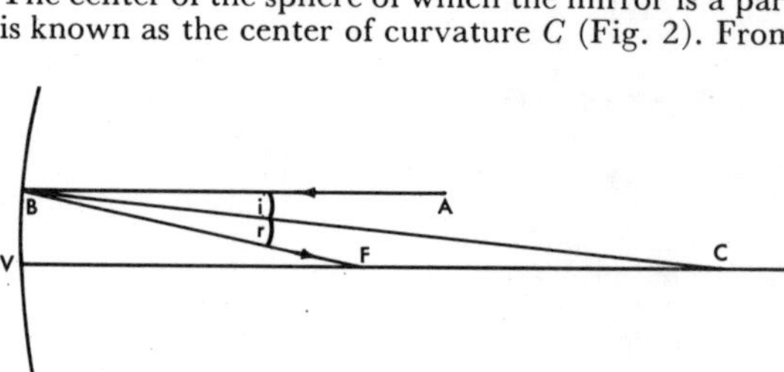

Figure 2

geometry it can be shown that a line drawn from C to any point on the mirror is a normal. The midpoint V of the mirror is known as the vertex, and line CV is the optical axis or the principal axis of the mirror. If a light ray AB parallel with CV strikes the mirror and makes an angle i with CB, it will after reflection make angle r with CB and cross the optical axis at F, the principal focus of the mirror. Triangle CFB is an isosceles triangle, CF being equal to FB, and if the arc BV is small compared with the circumference of the circle of which it is a part, then FB is approximately equal to FV, so that the focal length, or the distance of the principal focus from the vertex, is equal to half the radius of curvature of the mirror. All rays of light that are parallel with and fairly close to the principal axis of a concave spherical mirror meet at the principal focus. Rays that are fairly far from the principal axis do not quite meet at the principal focus; in this case the phenomenon of spherical aberration arises and images tend to be blurred. Large astronomical

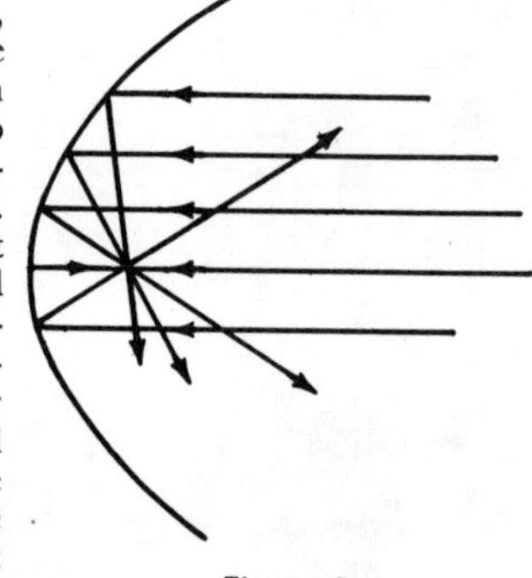

Figure 3

telescopes, therefore, are equipped with parabolic rather than spherical mirrors, because the former tend to give a sharper image (Fig. 3).

The location of an image may be easily determined with the aid of ray diagrams, at least two rays of light going from each important point of the object to the mirror. Rays that are convenient to use are a ray that is parallel with the principal axis, a ray that passes through the principal focus, and a ray that passes through the center of curvature. If an object is placed beyond the center of curvature of a concave spherical mirror, the image will be real, inverted, smaller than the object, and between the center of curvature and the principal focus (Fig. 4a). If the object is at the center of curvature, the image will likewise be at the center of curvature and will be the same size as the object, but inverted. If the object is between the center of curvature and the principal focus (Fig. 4b), the image will be beyond the center of curvature, inverted, real, and larger than the object. If the object is at the principal focus (Fig. 4c), there will be no image, the reflected rays being parallel with each other and with the principal axis. Finally, if the object is between the principal focus and the vertex (Fig. 4d), a virtual image will be formed that is erect and larger than the object. If the object is in front of a convex mirror, the image will always be virtual, erect, and smaller than the object, rays parallel with the optical axis appearing to cross at the virtual focus F (Fig. 5).

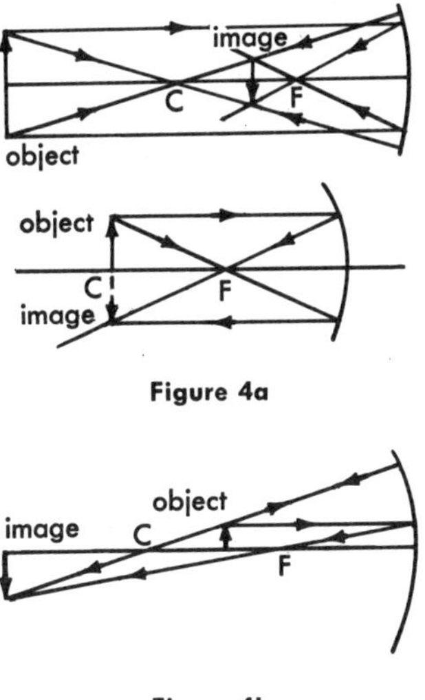

Figure 4b

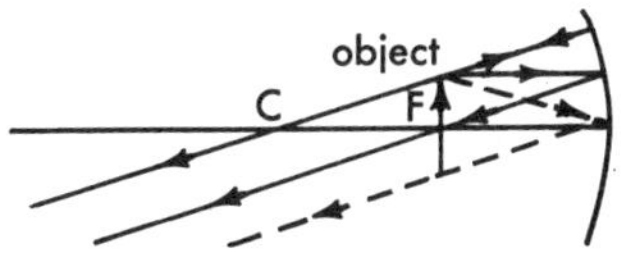

Figure 4c

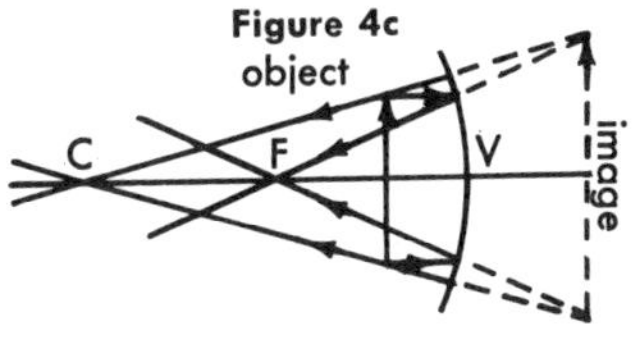

Figure 4d

The location of the image could also have been determined from the formula $1/f = 1/p + 1/q$, where f is the focal length of the mirror, p is the distance of the object from the mirror, and q is the distance of the image from the mirror. Distances measured to real objects and images are considered positive, those to virtual images and objects negative. Likewise, focal lengths of concave mirrors are considered positive, those of convex mirrors negative. The size of the image may also be predicted; it can be shown that the ratio of the size of the image to that of the object is equal to the ratio of the object distance to the image distance.

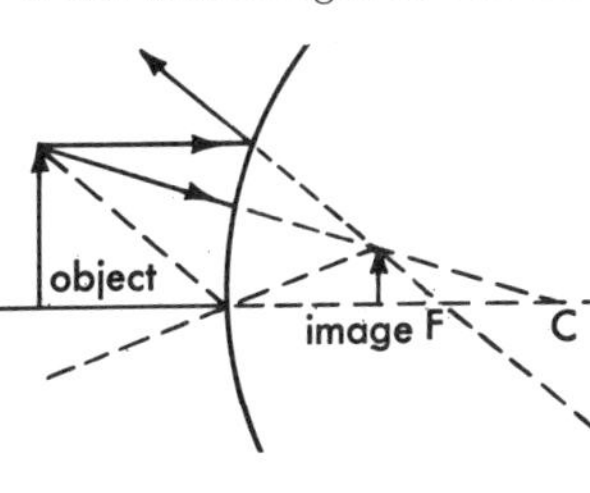

Figure 5

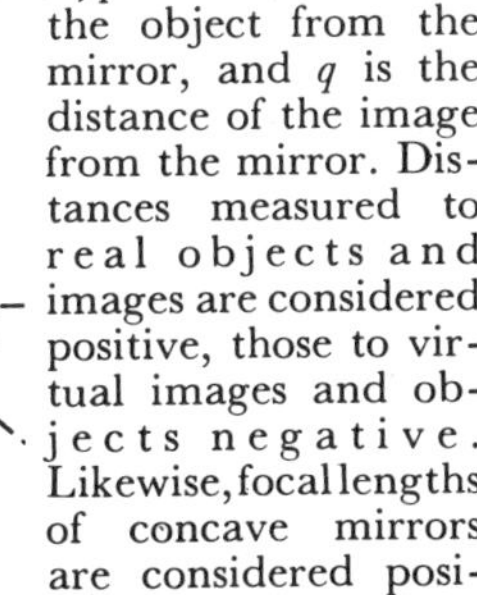

Astronomical Mirrors. The construction of a large astronomical mirror requires work of the highest precision; the front mirror surface must not deviate from the mathematically perfect paraboloid of revolution by more than one millionth of an inch. The final polishing process may take three to five years. The glass used is a special type of Pyrex which expands only very slightly when heated.

MIRZAPUR, city, N India, SE Uttar Pradesh, capital of Mirzapur District; on the Ganges River; 33 miles SW of Benares. Along the river front are ghats (stone stairs), Hindu temples, mosques, and homes of wealthy merchants, but the city's interior consists largely of mud huts. Mirzapur is an important market and distribution center for cotton, grain, and cloth. Main manufactures are brass utensils, shellac, and woolen rugs. Bindhachal, an important pilgrimage center in Mirzapur, contains Kali Temple, once a meeting place for the Thugs. Pop. (1951) 85,528.

MISAMIS OCCIDENTAL, province, Philippines, NW Mindanao Island; bounded by the Mindanao Sea on the N, Iligan Bay on the E, and the province of Zamboanga on the S and W; area 802 sq. mi.; pop. 207,575. The highest elevation is 7,965 feet at Mt. Malindang. Coconuts and corn grow along the coast. The capital of Misamis Occidental is Oroquieta. Ozamiz City lies within the province but is independent of it.

MISAMIS ORIENTAL, province, Philippine Islands, N Mindanao; bounded by the Mindanao Sea on the N, by the provinces of Agusan on the E and Bukidnon on the S, and by Macajalar and Iligan bays on the W; area 1,512 sq. mi.; pop. 369,671. Main products are grain, coconuts, and fish. Misamis Oriental includes Camiguin Island. The capital of the province is Cagayan.

MISCEGENATION, intermarriage between members of different racial groups. The Grimaldi skeletons of the Aurignacian period indicate mixture of Negroid and Cro-Magnon at least 20,000 years ago. (See CRO-MAGNON MAN; GRIMALDI SKELETONS.) European contact with other races increased after the age of exploration. The relationship, however, was generally one of conqueror and slave or servant. When areas of America and Africa were settled, the mother countries generally tried to prevent miscegenation. Spain in the sixteenth century at first forbade miscegenation but later approved it as a means of encouraging settlers to remain in the colonies permanently. After the French Revolution of 1789 there was no discrimination in French colonies, although previously there had been restrictions on marriages between Negroes and whites. British policy was traditionally against legislation banning miscegenation, but public opinion acted as a strong check. The United States from earliest colonial times had restrictions on intermarriage. In 1691 Virginia enacted legislation that made unlawful any marriage of a white person with a Negro, mulatto, or Indian. Some states still maintain restrictions on marriages between persons of different races. See MARRIAGE, *Restrictions*.

In the late nineteenth and early twentieth centuries attempts were made to test the results of miscegenation scientifically. The Norwegian biologist Jon Alfred Mjöen, on the basis of animal experimentation, concluded that mixture of diverse races was equivalent to race suicide since the fifth and succeeding generations were said to be sterile, and that such mixture might result in monsters—for example, a large Swede with a tiny Lapp might produce offspring with the body of a Swede but with the small heart and lungs of a Lapp. The American geneticist William Ernest Castle repeated Mjöen's experiments and showed conclusively that sterility did not follow race mixture. Castle also proved that such organs as heart, liver, and lungs were not inherited independently of body size. Later, cases were cited of hybrid vigor resulting from the mixture of Boers and Hottentots in South Africa and of increased fertility in Indian-white and Tahitian-white crosses. The modern American anthropologist Melville Jean Herskovits dealt at length with the results of Indian-Negro-white mixtures in the United States and did not find physical deterioration resulting. Long-continued intermarriage among the various Caucasoid races was breaking down racial lines to such an extent in mid-twentieth century that it was thought it soon would be impossible to classify existing peoples as Alpines, Nordics, and Mediterraneans. Mixture with Mongoloid or Negroid races continued at a slower rate. See RACE. FAY-COOPER COLE

BIBLIOG.–M. J. Herskovits, *American Negro, A Study in Race Crossing* (1928); G. Myrdal and others, *American Dilemma* (ed. 1944); J. F. Doherty, *Moral Problems of Interracial Marriage* (1951); E. C. McDonagh and E. S. Richards, *Ethnic Relations in the United States* (1953); O. Handlin, *Race and Nationality in American Life* (1957).

MISDEMEANOR, a criminal law offense, of lesser degree than a felony, that is punishable by fine or by imprisonment other than in a penitentiary. Petty crimes, disorderly conduct, and violation of game laws, municipal ordinances, and health regulations are usually classed as misdemeanors. Punishment usually consists merely of a fine, with imprisonment only upon nonpayment of the fine. Conviction for a misdemeanor does not involve civil disability as in the case of conviction for a felony. See FELONY.

MISENO, cape in southern Italy, between the Gulf of Gaeta and the Bay of Naples. Nearby are the remains of the harbor and town of Misenum, which Marcus Vipsanius Agrippa made, in 31 B.C., the major Roman naval station in the Mediterranean, as Ravenna was in the Adriatic. The Emperor Tiberius died in Misenum A.D. 37. The harbor was abandoned about 400 and the town was destroyed by the Saracens in 890.

MISERERE, "have mercy," Psalm 51 (50 in the Vulgate), so called from the first word in its Latin version. It is the fourth of the penitential Psalms and is regarded as the lament of David for his sin with Bathsheba. Esteemed as one of the best examples of penitential prayer, it is frequently used in Roman Catholic liturgy. It is part of the Anglican service (the Book of Common Prayer), read on Ash Wednesday. The Hebrew ritual still uses this Psalm in the ceremony observed on the Day of Atonement.

MISHAWAKA, city, N Indiana, St. Joseph County; on the St. Joseph River, the New York Central and the Grand Trunk railroads, and U.S. highway 33; 5 miles E of South Bend. Main manufactures are rubber, wool, canvas, and leather goods, power transmission machinery, foundry equipment, and metal products. In 1833 the St. Joseph ironworks was laid out on the south side of the river, and three years later Indiana City was founded on the north side. The two settlements merged in 1838, and Mishawaka was incorporated in 1899. According to legend, the name of the city is that of an Indian princess who lived there before 1800 and means swift water. Pop. (1960) 33,361.

MISHMI, a group of tribes living in the Mishmi Hills in the Northeast Frontier Agency of India, a division of Assam with a special administration. The Mishmi, who are of Mongoloid race, practice slash-and-burn agriculture, clearing and burning forest areas, which they cultivate for a few years at a time. Their social organization, based on the house rather than on the village as in other tribes in the area, is little known. There are three main groups—the Idus, the Kamans, and the Taraons. When India gained its independence in 1947, it established the Northeast Frontier Agency to administer the Mishmi Hills frontier area, which had been claimed by China for centuries.

MISHNAH, derived from the Hebrew verb *shanah*, to repeat or to learn, is the title of a collection of Jewish oral laws made by Rabbi Judah ha-Nasi (the patriarch) at the beginning of the third century. Smaller collections of the oral law were made earlier by other tannaim (teachers)—the title by which rabbis of the Mishnah are known—but this collection forms the basic text and first part of the Talmud. The other part, the Gemara, is an Aramaic commentary on the Hebrew Mishnah. The six orders into which the Mishnah is divided are (1) Zeraim (seeds), agricultural laws; (2) Moed (festivals), laws of the Sabbath and holidays; (3) Nashim (women), laws of marriage and divorce; (4) Nezikin (damages), civil and criminal laws; (5) Kodoshim (holy things), laws of sacrifices; and (6) Taharoth (purity), laws of purity and impurity. Each of these divisions is divided into parts (tractates), which are further subdivided into chapters and paragraphs. The Mishnah derives its authority from the belief (originally held only by the Pharisees) that the oral law was given to Moses on Mt. Sinai at the same time as was the written law and is therefore of divine origin. See TALMUD.

MORRIS A. GUTSTEIN

MISIONES, province, extreme NE Argentina; bounded by Brazil on the N, E, and S, Paraguay on the W, and Corrientes Province on the SW; area 11,514 sq. mi.; pop. (1958 est.) 370,900. Misiones is drained by the Iguassú, Uruguay, and Paraná rivers. Principal products are maté, citrus fruits, livestock, tung oil, tobacco, and lumber. Iguassú Falls are at the Brazilian border. The first European settlers in Misiones were Jesuits who fled hostile Indians of the Brazilian Alto Paraná and established missions in the seventeenth and eighteenth centuries. The capital of Misiones is Posadas.

MISKOLC, city, NE Hungary, capital of Borsod-Abaúj-Zemplén County but independent of it; at the confluence of the Sajó and Hernád rivers, at the foot of the Bükk Hills; a railroad and highway junction; 85 miles NE of Budapest. Miskolc is Hungary's second largest city and the center of the Borsod industrial district; it has ferrous metallurgy, cement, building materials, and food processing industries. An institute of technology and mining and electrical engineering schools were established there after World War II. Pop. (1957 est.) 150,000.

MISPICKEL. See ARSENOPYRITE.

MISREPRESENTATION. See FRAUD.

MISSAL, a liturgical book in Latin, containing the prayers and Bible passages used in the Mass. It comprises the Ordinary (invariable) and the passages and prayers proper to the Masses of the church year and of the saints' feast days. The Mass rites were first brought together in one book late in the Middle Ages and a standard form, the Roman missal, was established by Pope Pius V, 1570. Missals for the laity, with vernacular translations of the Latin text, are also available.

MISSION, city, S Texas, Hidalgo County; near the Rio Grande, on the Missouri Pacific Railroad and U.S. highway 83; 128 miles SSW of Corpus Christi. Main manufactures are brick, tile, and concrete pipes. Bentsen–Rio Grande Valley State Park is nearby. The city was founded in 1908 near La Lomita (Chapel of the Little Hill), which was completed in 1824 and is the oldest Texas mission in use. Mission was incorporated in 1910. Pop. (1960) 14,081.

MISSIONARY RIDGE. See CHATTANOOGA CAMPAIGN.

MISSION INDIANS, the North American Indians who came under the control of the Spanish Franciscan priests after the establishment of missions on the coast of California between 1769 and 1823. The Mission Indians belonged to many different tribes of food gatherers and spoke Shoshonean or Yuman languages. Before the coming of the Franciscans they formed small bands that lived in villages during the winter but wandered the rest of the year and gathered plant food and sea food. They were in contact with tribes in the interior with whom they traded their surplus of fish, clams, and shell money. Some bands were divided into moieties (halves), and all were divided into a number of clans membership in which was reckoned in the father line. Members of the same moiety or clan were not allowed to intermarry (see EXOGAMY).

The first mission was established by the Franciscans at San Diego in 1769 and the last at San Francisco in 1823. The Franciscans were devoted missionaries and converted the Mission Indians to Christianity, but many of the Indians, accustomed to greater freedom, fell sick and their number declined rapidly. In 1834 the Mexican government withdrew its support of the California missions and distributed land to the Indians. The gold rush that started in 1848, when the United States acquired California from Mexico, had disastrous results for the Mission Indians; they were almost exterminated. Some of the survivors were placed in reservations and others settled as farmers, largely around Los Angeles and San Diego.

MISSIONS

The expansion of world religions has been one of the direct fruits of missionary activity.

MISSIONS are both the efforts made by adherents of any given religion to spread its teachings and the countries or places where such work is attempted. Christian missionary activity, for example, arises from belief in the universal nature of the Christian religion and from Christ's explicit command that His disciples preach the Gospel to the ends of the earth to all creatures. It is the belief of Christians that Jesus Christ is the Saviour of all mankind and that acceptance of Him and His teaching is necessary for eternal salvation. Up to the beginning of the Christian Era other religions seem not to have considered themselves universal, with the obligation to extend themselves among all peoples; but Christianity from the beginning has been missionary in teaching and in practice. (For the history of the expansion of other religions, see the concluding section of this article.)

Apostolic Age and Early Expansion

The Apostles. The first Christian missionaries were the apostles, who began their preaching of the Gospel in Palestine and its confines. They then spread throughout the Mediterranean area, setting up centers of their faith in the Middle East, Egypt, Greece, and Rome. Their practice was to preach in Jewish synagogues, to which Gentiles also came. After a number of converts were won in a given locality, spiritual leaders (understood by some to be bishops) were usually appointed to organize and care for the young church. Christianity radiated out into the surrounding territory from these established centers. The new religion was spread not only by the apostles and those appointed by them but also through the missionary zeal of converts from all stations in society. By the end of the first century the church had grown throughout Palestine, Asia Minor, Greece and the adjacent islands, Egypt, and Italy.

Christianity continued to extend itself in the East and the West, generally following the trade routes of the Roman Empire. By the beginning of the fourth century the church had advanced into Arabia, Armenia, Persia, northern Africa, Gaul, and Britain. In spite of many persecutions by imperial Rome, Christianity became firmly established. A new era for Christianity came with its recognition by Constantine and his decree of freedom and favor, called the Edict of Milan, in 313. In the ensuing period, heresies—especially the Arian, Nestorian, and Donatist—made important advances, challenging orthodox teachings. See Arianism; Donatist; Nestorians.

The Middle Ages

Medieval Europe. From the fourth to the eleventh century Christianity advanced slowly throughout western and eastern Europe. Evangelization was carried on principally by missionary monks and bishops. The usual procedure was to seek the conversion of the chieftains of the pagan tribes; when they were converted, their people generally followed.

After Palladius, first bishop of Ireland, left that country, Patrick went there in 432 and established the church on a lasting foundation. Augustine of Canterbury, first missionary to the Anglo-Saxons, was sent to England from Rome in 596. Soon a strong monastic life flourished in Britain and Ireland, even overflowing onto the continent of Europe. In many areas where monasteries were founded in the midst of pagan tribes, centers of Christianity grew up around them. The missionary monks carried the faith to Holland, Denmark, Germany, Norway, and eventually to Sweden. Missionaries from the Scandinavian countries set up Christianity in Iceland and Greenland.

Missions to the Slavs. Conversion of the peoples in eastern Europe was accomplished by missionaries both from the church at Constantinople and the church at Rome. German bishops (Passau, Ratisbon, Salzburg) were responsible for spreading the faith in the adjacent areas among the Croats and Slovenes. Cyril and Methodius, two Greek monks, brought Christianity to the Moravians, beginning in 863. These monks put the language of the people into writing and formed a liturgy. In the ninth century Bohemia became Catholic and the church spread thence into Poland, 966. The duchy of Kiev in Russia received Christianity through Constantinople at the beginning of the eleventh century. The people of northwest Europe long resisted Christianity, but once they were subdued by the Teutonic Knights, conversions began. Hungary became Christian in the reign of St. Stephen I, king of the Magyars (997–1038).

Islam and the Crusades. During these centuries, difficulties had arisen in the East. Islam was founded by Mohammed in 632 and spread rapidly, principally by military conquest, through the Middle East, across northern Africa, even to the south of Spain. The churches in the East, cut off from contact with the church in the West, put up a brave fight simply to survive. Moslem domination and the formation of schismatic churches considerably weakened Christianity in the East. The Crusades, which began in the eleventh century, aimed at recovery of the holy places in Palestine. The failure of the Crusades resulted from the disunion of the Christian leaders, the intrigues of the Byzantine emperor, and the harsh cruelty of the Crusaders; the Crusades, nevertheless, consumed Christian energy in the West for two centuries. With the West sealed off by the power of Islam, missionary work beyond Europe became impossible. The Crusades did bring to the Western church a concern for Christians of the East and for Moslems. See Islam.

Missions to the Mongols. The impulse to missionary activity by the church in the thirteenth century came from the founding of the Franciscan and Dominican orders. These new societies gave to the church numerous missionaries to accept the challenges that arose at the time. The great political event of the century was the development of the Mongol Empire. Genghis Khan united the nomad tribes in central Asia and began his campaigns of conquest. First he was successful in northern China, then he defeated the Kharezm Empire in central Asia, and passed on through Persia, Armenia, and the Caucasus to the Dnepr, where he died in 1227. The empire was then divided. Conquest continued into South China. Moscow and Kiev fell to the Mongol arms. Hungary was defeated and the hordes advanced through the Carpathians and Transylvania to the Adriatic. The popes of the time sent three legations to the khans, two Franciscan groups and one Dominican band. The Dominicans were sent back by the khan in northeast Persia. Giovanni de Piano Carpini, a Franciscan, went north through Russia to the Khan Kuyuk (1246) and had little success. William of Ruysbroeck, a Franciscan, made another diplomatic journey to the khans (1253). But these overtures achieved nothing. The Mongols, after hesitating between Christianity and Islam, turned to Islam. It was then decided to undertake missionary work in the Mongol Empire.

The Dominicans and Franciscans began to evangelize in Persia and had relative tranquillity for almost a century. The combination of the black death and invasions by the Mongol Tamerlane destroyed this effort in the fourteenth century. The Franciscans unsuccessfully took up missionary work in Kipchak, another Mongol kingdom, controlling Russia. The Polo brothers reached the court of Kublai Khan in Kanbalik (Peking) and brought back an invitation for missionaries. Giovanni di Monte Corvino was eventually assigned to this mission and, after a journey of more than two years, arrived in Peking about 1291. He was made archbishop of Peking and had success in winning converts. Others were sent to assist him, and several dioceses were established in China. When the Ming dynasty took over from the Mongols (1368), however, the Catholic missions disappeared, for reasons unknown. Many of the missionaries who went to China spoke of their experience in India. Giovanni di Monte Corvino stayed in Mylapore, preaching and baptizing.

The Moslems. Franciscans evangelized the Canary Islands in the fifteenth century. Before the thirteenth century not much was done in the way of preaching the Gospel to the Moslems. When the power of Islam was broken in Spain at the Battle of Navas de la Tolosa, the Dominicans and Franciscans began to preach among the Moslems. Schools for the study of Arabic were established to prepare missionaries. Efforts were made in Tunis and Morocco to approach the Moslems; but proselytism was banned. Thereafter the efforts of the missionaries were directed toward Christian soldiers, captives of war, and Catholics who had apostatized. Many of the missionaries were martyred by the Moslems. The most important figure in this apostolate was probably Raymond Lull, who inisted on adequate training of missionaries in Arabic studies and who, himself, prepared many studies. He was killed by the Moslems in 1315. These were difficult centuries for the church.

WADSWORTH ATHENEUM

In the mid-sixteenth century St. Francis Xavier, "Apostle to the Indies," toured the Far East, seeking converts to Christianity. The above painting is by Bartholomé Murillo.

Catholic Missions Since the Sixteenth Century

Africa and the Orient. The modern missionary movement in the Catholic church began with the discoveries made by the Spaniards and Portuguese in the sixteenth century. Missionaries went to the Congo in the 1480's and their success was variable. Angola saw its first missionaries in 1560. Pedro Alvares Cabral, on his trip around Africa, left missionaries in Mozambique in 1500. Efforts were made to establish the Christian faith in Madagascar. Dominicans, Franciscans, Trinitarians, and Jesuits accompanied the Portuguese ships to the East. Convents were set up along the east coast, and the winning of converts began. Francis Xavier, the Jesuit apostle of the Indies, came in 1542. He worked on the southwest and southeast coasts of India. He traveled to Ceylon, Malacca, the Moluccas; he spent a little more than a year in Japan, laying the foundation of the later missions. Death came to him on the island of Sancian off the coast of China as he was waiting to gain entrance to the mainland in 1552. There was a steady growth of missionary work in India despite the difficulties caused by excessive Europeanization of converts. Japan had a century of flourishing Christianity, with more than 600,000 Japanese Christians, before persecution almost extinguished the faith in the middle of the seventeenth century. Matteo Ricci finally entered China in 1583; he was succeeded by many Jesuits. The Philippines were evangelized shortly after they were discovered by Ferdinand Magellan in 1520. Many of the Spanish missionaries went on to China and Japan. Efforts were made by the French to reinvigorate the coastal missions in Africa and on the island of Madagascar. New attempts were made among the Moslems in the Middle East, Africa, Egypt, Abyssinia, Morocco, and Tunis.

The Americas. Missionaries accompanied Christopher Columbus on his second voyage to the new world and established their first center in Hispaniola. From there they extended to the other islands of the Antilles. Mexico became a mission land with the conquest by Hernán Cortés in 1519. Soon missionaries increased, spreading to the west and north and into the southern parts of present United States.

The French occupied Canada, and missionary work among the Indians began in 1603 under Samuel de Champlain. The missionaries established centers among the different tribes, coming even into Maine and northern New York State.

The advance of the faith throughout the continent of South America began with Francisco Pizarro's conquest of Peru in 1532. From there the faith spread into Chile. Missionaries began work in Argentina in 1534. Missions were established in Brazil under the Portuguese as early as 1503.

Decline and Revival. In the latter part of the eighteenth century the missions began to decline for many reasons. The power of Spain and Portugal was challenged by the Dutch and English. The church, under assault in Europe, was dispossessed of the material means of helping the missions. Missionary vocations lagged because of persecutions, revolution, and the growth of anti-Christian ideas. Suppression of the Jesuits removed from the fields several thousand missionaries not to be replaced by other groups.

In the nineteenth century, however, the church began with new vigor its most energetic missionary activity. New congregations of religious men and women (priests, sisters, brothers) were founded, many with a purely missionary objective. The Jesuits were restored. The loss of material means occasioned by the decay of the earlier Catholic empires was remedied by the wider distribution of the burden among all believers. The number of priests increased. Religious women (nuns) for the first time began to undertake missionary work. New missionary congregations were founded. Many societies of the laity were established to supply the material means. The nineteenth century became a century of restoration and advance.

In the middle of the century Africa was opened up to the world. The White Fathers began their remarkable work in the Moslem areas of northern Africa shortly after their founding in 1868; they worked in Tunis, Algiers, and Morocco. Missionaries started in the Guineas under Msgr. Edward Barron, an American, in 1843. As more missionaries came to the west coast of Africa, stations were opened in Sierra Leone, Nigeria, the Gold Coast, the Ivory Coast, and the Cameroons. The missions in the Congo and Angola were restaffed. The Belgians were made responsible for the interior of the Congo. Up to 1914 German missionaries worked in Ruanda and Urundi. Missions in South Africa started in Natal in 1851 and spread through the Transvaal and Basutoland. Rhodesia and Zambesi received their first missionaries in 1879. The Catholic missions were extended successively to Madagascar, Réunion, Mozambique, and Zanzibar. Work was begun in the lake region of Uganda, Nyasa, and Tanganyika in 1878.

The missions in India were revived considerably, with constantly growing personnel. Missionaries extended their work in Burma, Siam, Indochina, and China. Japan was opened to foreigners once again in 1844. The law against Christians was revoked in 1872, but missionary work expanded slowly in Japan. The missions among pagan aborigines in the Philippine Islands were multipled during the twentieth century. Catholic missionary work in Indonesia did not begin to thrive until after 1874. The ecclesiastical jurisdiction of Oceania was erected in 1833 and there followed progressive evangelization of the islands of the Pacific. The church further had to establish itself in Australia and New Zealand. Missionary works were established in most of the countries of the Middle East. Although missionaries were allowed into Nepal to operate a school in the late 1950's, they still were excluded from Communist China, North Korea, Mongolia, Afghanistan, Tibet, and Bhutan, as well as from those countries of the Orient under the control of the U.S.S.R.

Social Services. In spite of expulsion from China and restriction in other countries, Catholic missions continued to show great vigor. Works undertaken by missionaries for the development of the peoples to whom they are sent have been responsible for the cultural elevation of millions, chiefly through education from the primary school to the university. Hospitals, dispensaries, and clinics, often conducted by nuns, have brought help to the sick. Leper colonies are staffed by nuns and priests. Economic improvement of mission areas has been fostered by the missionary church through agricultural schools, trade schools, credit union movements, and co-operative societies. The status of most missions has constantly improved with the development of the local priesthood and hierarchy. A reinvigoration of Catholic life in Central and South America has taken place through increased missionary activity in the twentieth century.

The modern mission movement in the Catholic church began to recruit lay personnel for work in the missions, priests and nuns having been almost the only missionaries. In 1922 the Catholic Medical Missionary Institute (*Missionsarzliches Institut*) was founded in Würzburg, Germany, and during the next 35 years sent more than 175 doctors to the missions. Begun in 1929 in Holland, the Grail Movement had more than 100 laywomen working in mission areas by 1948. The group maintained teams of workers in Africa, Asia, and South America, and in Brooklyn, N.Y., operated a training program for overseas service. The *Ad lucem* Movement, founded at Lille, France, in 1931, to foster the mission spirit among students, had more than 500 members in the missions by mid-twentieth century. In 1937 the International Catholic Auxiliaries were founded in Brussels, Belgium, to train teams of laywomen for permanent assignments to the missions; in 1953 they opened, in Chicago, their first training center for American personnel. Their members work as teachers, social workers, doctors, nurses, and in other occupations in Korea, Vietnam, Formosa, India, Syria, Jordan, Lebanon, and the Belgian Congo. In 1957 the Association for International Development began its work of sending men or married couples to the missions for temporary periods of work or for permanent assignment. Forty years after World War I more than 3,000 lay personnel were assigned to foreign missions by some 20 Catholic groups.

The worldwide missions of the church are under the supervision of the Congregation of the Propagation of the Faith, one of the 12 congregations or administrative departments of the Holy See. Only since the latter part of the nineteenth century have Catholics in the United States sent priests, brothers, nuns, and lay workers to the foreign missions. In 1957 there were 134 American groups (54 of men, 80 of women) sending out missionaries; more than 5,000 Americans were working the foreign missions. The first exclusively missionary society in the United States was the Catholic Foreign Mission Society of America (Maryknoll fathers), founded in 1911, which in 1958 had more than 500 priests and brothers in its mission territories in Asia, Africa, and South America. The Maryknoll sisters (founded in 1912) had approximately 475 on foreign assignments (see MARYKNOLL FATHERS). The largest religious order, the Jesuits, had 750 of its 6,000 American members on foreign mission assignments (see JESUITS). EDWARD L. MURPHY, S.J.

PROTESTANT MISSIONS SINCE THE SIXTEENTH CENTURY

The Early Period. Protestant missions were not well under way until late in the eighteenth century—largely because Protestant nations, in contrast to the Catholic countries, were slow in establishing commercial and colonial contacts with non-Christian peoples. Where such contacts were made, however, Protestant missions developed. They arose among the Indians in the thirteen colonies in North America through several denominations, notably Puritans (John Eliot and the Mayhew family in early New England), the (Anglican) Society for the Propagation of the Gospel in Foreign Parts, and the Moravians. The Great Awakening in the mid-eighteenth century gave them a marked impulse. The Dutch Reformed church had missions in the Dutch possessions in the East Indies and Ceylon. In India German Pietists began Protestant efforts in 1706 under the auspices of the Danish crown. Although that enterprise was Lutheran, as it continued it received financial assistance from the (Anglican) Society for Promoting Christian Knowledge. The Norwegian Lutheran Hans Egede inaugurated a mission in Greenland. Although few in number, the Moravians, in the eighteenth century with Herrnhut as their center, had missions in many parts of the world—among the Lapps and the North American Indians, in Greenland, Labrador, the West Indies, Russia, India, Ceylon, the Nicobar Islands, the Gold Coast, Central America, and Surinam.

Beginnings of the Modern Era. In the 1790's and early in the nineteenth century what may be called the modern era of Protestant missions began. It was marked by a rapid expansion which by the mid-twentieth century had planted that branch of faith in all the continents, in most of the islands, and among the large majority of the peoples and tribes of the earth. At the outset the new era arose chiefly from the evangelical awakening in the British Isles and the United States and from Pietism in Europe (see AWAKENING, *The Great Awakening;* PIETIST). Protestant missions continued to spring mainly, although by no means entirely, from the successors of those two closely related movements. The Baptist Missionary Society, British organized in 1792 at the instance of William Carey (see CAREY, WILLIAM), is usually regarded as the pioneer undertaking. It was soon followed by a number of other societies in Great

Britain, on the Continent, and in the United States. Prominent among them were the (undenominational, latterly Congregational) London Missionary Society (1795), the (Anglican) Church Missionary Society (1799), the (undenominational) British and Foreign Bible Society (1804), the Netherlands Missionary Society (1797), the Basel Missionary Society (1822), the Rhenish Missionary Society (1828), the (undenominational, eventually Congregational) American Board of Commissioners for Foreign Missions (1810), the (undenominational) American Bible Society (1816), and the (undenominational, mainly Congregational) American Home Missionary Society (1826). See BAPTISTS; CHURCH OF ENGLAND; CONGREGATIONALISM, *Development of Congregationalism;* PURITANISM; DUTCH REFORMED CHURCH; LUTHERANISM.

In the nineteenth century existing societies mounted in strength and many new ones were organized. Most of them were denominational, but a number—often called faith missions—drew from similarly minded constituencies irrespective of denomination, generally warmly evangelical or pietistic. One of the oldest and largest was the China Inland Mission, begun in England by James Hudson Taylor in 1865. A major impetus to Protestant missions was given by the Student Volunteer Movement for Foreign Missions, which arose in the United States in 1886 and was the means of recruiting several thousand for missions. It inspired the formation of similar movements in several other countries.

Worldwide Expansion. In the nineteenth and twentieth centuries Protestant Christianity became worldwide. Much of the spread was through the migration of peoples traditionally Protestant. Millions poured into the United States and hundreds of thousands into Canada, South America, Australia, New Zealand, and South Africa. For the most part they held at least a nominal allegiance to the Christian faith, and strong churches sprang up—partly on the initiative of the settlers themselves and partly through assistance from societies organized for that purpose in Great Britain, Germany, and the older sections of the United States.

Much of the spread was by conversions from non-Christian peoples. In the United States Protestantism grew rapidly among the Negroes, especially after their emancipation, and among the Indians it won about as many converts as did the Catholics. In the British and Danish West Indies gains were made among the Negroes. In several of the island groups in the Pacific the large majority of the population accepted the Protestant faith, and some from their number became missionaries to other islands. Many of the Maoris in New Zealand and hundreds of the aborigines of Australia were baptized. Protestantism was introduced to Japan in 1859. There its growth was irregular and was chiefly in the cities and among the middle classes. Its members outnumbered both the Roman Catholic and members of the Eastern Orthodox faith, but all three together after a hundred years constituted less than one half of 1 per cent of the population. Protestantism was taken to Korea by American missionaries in the 1880's. It had a much more rapid growth than in Japan. In the 1950's the Communist occupation of North Korea greatly reduced the numbers of Protestants in that region, but Protestantism continued to flourish in the south.

Robert Morrison (1782–1834), the first Protestant missionary to China, reached that country in 1807. In the succeeding century thousands of missionaries from several lands and from many different denominations followed. Growth was fairly steady in the second half of the nineteenth century, was rapid after the Boxer outbreak (1900), and was slowed by the first wave of communism in the 1920's and by the Japanese invasion, which assumed large-scale proportions in 1937. It revived after the defeat of Japan (1945), but suffered seriously in the first stages of the Communist control of the mainland. In spite of the withdrawal or expulsion of the missionaries, it persisted and after a time revived. In the Philippines Protestants were chiefly converts from Roman Catholicism, beginning soon after the American occupation (1898). In Indonesia Protestantism made rapid strides among the animistic peoples, especially in Celebes, the Moluccas, and Sumatra, and won a few thousand from Islam. Protestants were a small minority in Thailand. In Burma their chief strength was among converted animistic folk, notably the Karens. In India Protestant Christianity had a marked growth mainly among the depressed classes and the animistic hill tribes. It was embraced by minorities in Ceylon. Protestantism won very few from the Moslems in the Middle East; there it gathered small minorities from the Eastern churches. Protestantism made great strides in Africa south of the Sahara, notably in South Africa, the British possessions, and the Belgian Congo; to a lesser extent it was represented in all other sections. Since 1830 the Mormon faith has been carried throughout the world by missionaries serving at their own expense (see MORMON, *Church Tenets, Organization, and Activities*).

Increasingly, Protestant missions gave rise to self-governing and self-propagating churches, with decreasing financial support from their fellow Protestants in Europe and America. More and more, especially with the prominence of anticolonialism and anti-imperialism in the non-Occidental world, the churches in those areas wished to be independent. Missionaries continued to go to them, but as fraternal workers subordinate to them.

The Protestant missionary enterprise did not confine itself to spreading the Christian faith and nourishing Christian churches. In a wide variety of ways it sought to aid the peoples served. Protestant missions founded and conducted schools and colleges, maintained hospitals and dispensaries, trained physicians and nurses, helped to improve agriculture, and in other ways sought to relieve and prevent human suffering and to aid those among whom they labored in adjusting to the revolutionary age brought about by the impact of the Occident.

Co-operative Organizations. As the years passed, Protestants—divided though they were into many denominations—devised methods and created organizations for co-operation. In the countries from which missionaries were sent, national agencies for co-operation were developed. In countries where Protestantism was new, national Christian councils were brought into being. In 1921, as an outgrowth of the World Missionary Conference held in Edinburgh in 1910, the International Missionary Council was organized. In it the several national co-operative bodies were represented. The International Missionary Council worked in close association with the World Council of Churches, which was formally inaugurated in Amsterdam in 1948. In the mid-1950's the two were in process of integration. In a few countries actual unions of churches founded by Protestant missions were being achieved. Examples were the Church of Christ in Japan, the Church of Christ in China, and the Church of South India—all of them dating from the twentieth century. See WORLD COUNCIL OF CHURCHES.

NON-CHRISTIAN MISSIONARY EFFORTS

Efforts to win others to a particular religion have not been confined to Christianity. A number of other faiths have been ardently missionary. Some, such as Manichaeism (once widespread), have completely disappeared (see MANICHAEISM). Others have survived. Chief among them are Judaism, Hinduism, Buddhism, and Islam. See JUDAISM; HINDUISM; BUDDHISM; ISLAM.

Judaism. For some centuries Jews have not been especially active in winning others. Yet for several hundred years around the time of Christ and later they reached out to Gentiles and sought to bring them to their faith. In the Roman Empire, before the extensive spread of Christianity, many non-Jews were attracted by the monotheism and high ethical standards of Judaism. Some centuries later a Turkish folk, the Khazars, who controlled an extensive area in what is now south Russia, adopted Judaism.

Hinduism spread beyond India chiefly through migrations, merchants and rulers of that faith. Its major expansion was into southeastern Asia and the East Indies. In the early centuries of the Christian Era Indians of Hindu faith went as merchants to Cambodia, the Malay Peninsula, and Java. There, too, Hindu rulers created kingdoms and many of their subjects conformed to their religion. At one time or another Hinduism was widely extended in the areas that much later became Cambodia, South Vietnam, and Java; eventually it disappeared. It has persisted, however, in the island of Bali, east of Java. In the past hundred or more years Indian laborers and settlers have carried Hinduism to Burma, Malaya, the Fiji Islands, British Guiana, and Trinidad, but they have not sought or made many converts. From time to time in the nineteenth and twentieth centuries representatives of one or another form of Hinduism attracted a few converts in Europe and America.

Buddhism was much more missionary and had a far wider expansion than Hinduism. It began in India as an outgrowth of Hinduism. Starting in the north and at first purely regional, it eventually spread throughout India, south and east Asia, and the fringing islands. It owed much of its early expansion to Asoka, a monarch of the third century B.C. who inherited a kingdom that covered much of India and who later extended his domains. He declared in an edict that his experience with the horrors of war through which his conquests were effected led to his conversion to Buddhism. He became as active in the propagation of his new faith as he had been in adding territory to his realms. To that end he traveled widely, encouraging his subjects to follow the way of the Buddha. He sent missionaries to parts of India where his rule did not reach, to Ceylon, to the Hellenistic kingdoms that arose in the wake of Alexander the Great in Syria, Macedonia, and Egypt, and to the west of Egypt.

Of the several forms that Buddhism developed, two—the Mahayana, or Greater Vehicle, and Hinayana, or the Lesser Vehicle—survived and spread. Mahayana Buddhism, which had as its objective the salvation of all living beings, expanded northward, first into what became Afghanistan and then into China. It reached China partly by the overland caravan routes, possibly as early as the second century before Christ. Impetus was further given by missionaries and by Chinese pilgrims to India who returned, zealous, bringing with them sacred books. Buddhism did not displace the native faiths of China—Confucianism and Taoism—but existed side by side with them. It reached the acme of its popularity in the forepart of the T'ang dynasty (618–907). It then began a slow decline, caused in large part by hostile measures of the state. From China Buddhism spread to Korea and there seems to have been strongest in the tenth, eleventh, and twelfth centuries. It was carried to Japan from China and Korea in the sixth century and later was espoused by the court and the aristocracy; it gradually spread to the masses and for centuries was the dominant religion. Beginning about the eighth century, Lamaism, a development from Mahayana Buddhism, entered Tibet, mainly through missionaries from Nepal, Bengal, and Kashmir, but it was several centuries before it prevailed in the form that it eventually took. It was to this form that the Mongols were converted, chiefly in the sixteenth century. Hinayana Buddhism had its major spread in Ceylon, Burma, Thailand, Cambodia, and the East Indies.

For several centuries Buddhism lost ground. It almost completely disappeared from India, partly through the Hun and Moslem invasions and partly by absorption into Hinduism. In the East Indies and central Asia it was displaced by Islam. It declined in China and Korea and had hard going in Japan. In the twentieth century Buddhism experienced something of a revival, especially in Ceylon and Burma. Buddhist missionaries also went to Europe and America and made a few converts in both places.

Islam, the youngest of the great missionary religions, began in the seventh century of the Christian Era in Arabia and ever afterward continued to have its heart in the Arab world. Its wide spread was accomplished partly by force of arms, partly by cultural contacts, and partly through commerce. It had few professional missionaries. In its early period Islam won most of its converts in Arabia, which became almost solidly Moslem, from Christianity on the eastern and southern shores of the Mediterranean, and from Zoroastrianism in Mesopotamia and Persia (see ZOROASTRIANISM). Pagans were given the choice of Islam or death. Christians and Jews were not compelled to accept Islam but were placed under social, political, and economic handicaps. Gradually, in lands dominated by Moslems, the Christian communities dwindled. In some places they disappeared, notably in Arabia and north Africa. In some other areas, especially in the Iberian Peninsula and Sicily, they recovered and Islam disappeared. Extensive accessions came from peoples of central Asia, notably Turks and Mongols. Islam was planted firmly in India, partly by invasion and immigration and partly by conversion, until Moslems constituted about a fifth of the population. Immigration and conversion accounted for several millions of Moslems in China, mainly in the northwest and southwest. Through contacts with Moslem merchants, chiefly Arabs, Islam became dominant in the Malay Peninsula, in large sections of the East Indies, and in the southern islands of the Philippines. The Ottoman Turks carried Islam into Asia Minor, Constantinople, and the Balkans. Chiefly through traders and commerce, Islam penetrated the east coast of Africa and west Africa immediately south of the Sahara. There it continued to spread in the twentieth century. In that century some converts were made in Europe and America, in the United States mainly by the Ahmadiyyah form of Islam and through Baha'ism, a nineteenth century offshoot of Islam (see BAHA'ISM).

KENNETH SCOTT LATOURETTE

BIBLIOG.–St. Luke, *Acts of the Apostles;* M. K. Gandhi, *Mahatma and the Missionary* (1949); W. O. Carver, *Course of Christian Missions: A History and an Interpretation* (ed. 1939), *Missions in the Plan of the Ages* (ed. 1951); W. R. Hogg, *Ecumenical Foundations: A History of the International Missionary Council and Its Nineteenth-Century Background* (1952); L. M. Outerbridge, *Lost Churches of China* (1952); K. S. Latourette, *History of the Expansion of Christianity* (7 vols. 1937–45), *Christian World Mission in Our Day* (1954); E. A. Nida, *Customs and Cultures* (1954); F. W. Dillistone, *Christianity and Communication* (1957).

MISSISSAUGA, one of the four major divisions of the Chippewa or Ojibwa, a North American Indian tribe of the Algonquian linguistic stock. The Mississaugas were called the people of the large river mouth, since they lived near the mouth of the Missisagi River and on Manitoulin Island in Lake Huron. They gathered wild rice, maple sirup, and berries to supplement the food they caught by hunting and fishing. They were subdivided into numerous small bands, each with its own territory and its own leader who was usually also its war chief. Each band was composed of a number of exogamous totemic clans (see EXOGAMY). In the eighteenth century many Mississaugas, profiting from the decline of the Hurons, moved into Huron territory between Lake Huron and Lake Erie. By the beginning of the twentieth century, many had settled as farmers in Ontario, especially in Brant County. See OJIBWAY.

The Great Seal of the state of Mississippi consists simply of an American eagle which holds in one talon an olive branch symbolizing peace and in the other three arrows symbolizing war. The seal was officially adopted in 1817.

BIRD	**Mockingbird**
FLOWER	**Magnolia**
TREE	**Magnolia**
CAPITAL	**Jackson**
MOTTO	**Virtute et Armis** (By Valor and Arms)
ENTERED THE UNION	**Dec. 10, 1817**
ORDER OF ENTRY	**20th**

MISSISSIPPI, state, S central United States; bounded on the N by Tennessee, on the E by Alabama, on the S by the Gulf of Mexico and Louisiana, and on the W by Louisiana and Arkansas; maximum north-south and east-west distances 330 and 180 miles respectively; area 47,716 sq. mi., including 493 sq. mi. of inland water; pop. (1967 est.) 2,348,000. The Mississippi River forms most of the western boundary, the Pearl River flows along the southern Louisiana border, and Pickwick Lake of the Tennessee River forms the tiny northeast boundary of the state. Mississippi was the 20th state to enter the Union. It ranks 32nd among the fifty states of the Union in area. The state takes its name from the Mississippi River—a name derived from an Indian word meaning father of waters. It is nicknamed the Magnolia State, the magnolia being the state tree and the magnolia blossom the state flower. Mississippi's motto is *Virtute et Armis* (by valor and arms) and the mockingbird is its official bird. Jackson is the capital and largest city. See map in Atlas, Vol. 20. For state flag in color, see FLAG.

Physical Features

Topography. Except for the region bordering the Mississippi River in the northwest, Mississippi lies in a coastal plain of sedimentary deposits formed during the Paleozoic and Mesozoic geologic eras. The Mississippi alluvial plain is formed of more recent flood deposits. Generally hilly with a few scattered prairies and plains, Mississippi slopes gently from a maximum elevation of 806 feet in the northeast to sea level along the coast. Its surface is broken into 10 major regions. In the northern half are several north-south belts of hills and plains: from west to east the alluvial plain, the loess hills, the north-central hills, the flatwoods, the Pontotoc Ridge, the Black Prairie, and the fall line hills. The southern half of the state consists of three east-west belts: the northernmost Jackson Prairie, the Piney Woods, and the Gulf Coastal Meadows. Swamps fringe the Mississippi floodplain, the river bottoms, and the coast.

Coasts, Rivers, and Lakes. Mississippi has 44 miles of coastline along Mississippi Sound, separated from the Gulf of Mexico by several offshore islands. Major indentations along the coast are Biloxi and St. Louis bays, and the chief ports are Pascagoula and Gulfport. Mississippi is drained by a number of rivers flowing south to the Gulf of Mexico. In the north the Pontotoc Ridge constitutes the state's main watershed, dividing the Alabama River system on the east from the Mississippi River system. The western half of the state is drained by the Mississippi, Coldwater, Yocona, Tallahatchie, Yalobusha, Yazoo, and Big Black rivers; the northeast by the Tombigbee and Noxubee rivers; and the southern half by the Pearl and Pascagoula rivers. There are several oxbow lakes along the Mississippi River, and in the north are five reservoirs made by damming the Tennessee, Coldwater, Tallahatchie, Yocona, and Yalobusha rivers.

Climate. Mississippi has a humid subtropical climate. Average temperatures are 64.6°F (mean), 81° (summer), and 48° (winter). Annual rainfall varies from 49 inches in the north to 60 in the coastal area. The precipitation is well distributed throughout the year, although autumn is slightly drier. Snowfall is rare. The growing season lasts from mid-March to mid-November—250 days in the south, 200 in the central region, and less than 200 in the north.

Soils and Natural Vegetation. Most Mississippi soil is composed of sand loam and is generally fertile. Extremely fertile clay loam is found in the Black Belt. The color of these soils is either black or gray. The Mississippi alluvial plain, also called the Yazoo Basin or the Delta, contains rich soil due to the silt deposited by floodwaters of the Mississippi River. Mississippi has 18 million acres of forested land, which is 59.5 per cent of the total land area. Loblolly and longleaf pine grow in the Piney Woods area, and shortleaf pine in northern and central Mississippi. Cypress predominates in swamps, and in the uplands of the north there is an abundance of hardwood such as poplar and hickory.

Animals. A few deer and foxes remain in scattered

Population Density Map (below left). White areas indicate 10–40 persons per square mile; light gray, 40–80; and dark gray, 80–225.

Precipitation Map (below right). White areas indicate 40–50 inches per year; light gray, 50–60; and dark gray, 60–80.

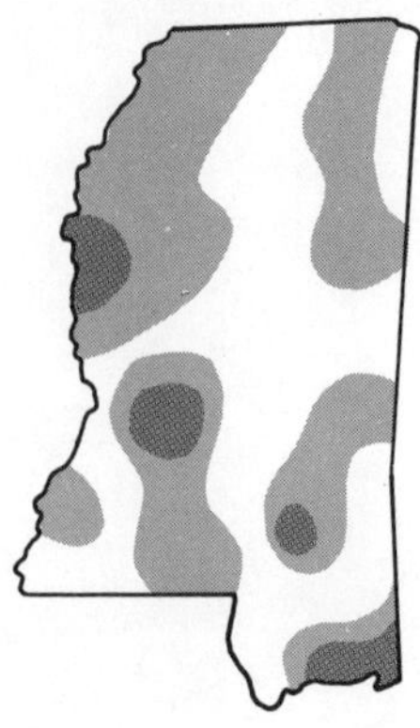

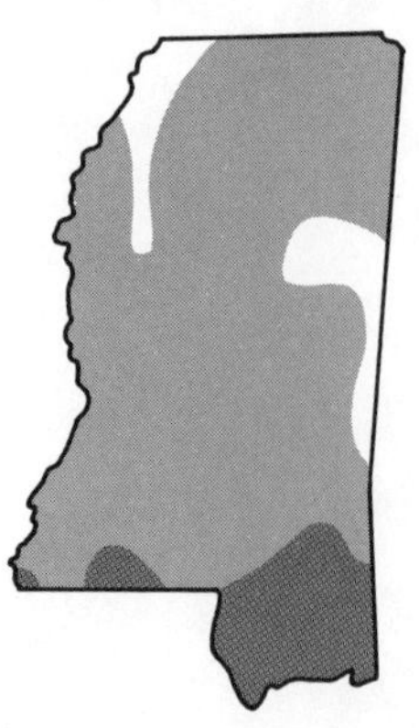

The State Capitol at Jackson

FRANK NOONE

MISSISSIPPI AGRICULTURAL & INDUSTRIAL BOARD

Perhaps the best-known landmark on the Mississippi Gulf coast is the pre-Civil War Biloxi lighthouse.

THE UNIVERSITY OF MISSISSIPPI

The Lyceum, the oldest (1848) building on the Oxford campus, is seen from the university library.

areas. Common small game animals include the cottontail rabbit, gray squirrel, raccoon, and opossum. Brown pelicans, gulls, terns, plover, and several varieties of sandpipers inhabit the Gulf coast. Herons and bitterns live in the salt marshes. Wild turkeys, partridges, quail, ducks, and geese are popular game birds. Freshwater fish such as bass, trout, perch, and bream are plentiful in Mississippi streams and lakes, and oysters and shrimp abound in the Gulf of Mexico.

Social Features

Population. In 1967 there were an estimated 2,348,000 people living in Mississippi. From 1960 to 1966 the population increased by 120,859. According to the 1960 census Mississippi ranks 29th among the states in population and has a population density of 46.1 people per square mile. The urban population is continuing to increase, as demonstrated by the 1950 and 1960 censuses. In 1960 there were 1,257,546 whites, 915,743 Negroes, and 4,600 persons of other races.

PRINCIPAL CITIES

City	Population 1950 Census	Population 1960 Census
Jackson (capital)	98,271	144,422
Meridian	41,893	49,374
Biloxi	37,425	44,053
Greenville	29,936	41,502
Hattiesburg	29,474	34,989
Gulfport	22,659	30,204
Vicksburg	27,948	29,130
Laurel	25,038	27,889
Natchez	22,740	23,791
Greenwood	18,061	20,436

Education. Mississippi has a state board of education composed of three ex-officio members: the secretary of state, attorney general, and state superintendent of education. The compulsory school law was repealed by the state legislature in 1956. State-supported teacher-training institutions are Delta State College (1924) at Cleveland, the University of Southern Mississippi (1910) at Hattiesburg, Mississippi State College for Women (1884) at Columbus, and Jackson State College (1877). State institutions for higher learning are Mississippi State University (1878) at State College, Alcorn Agricultural and Mechanical College (1871) at Lorman, Mississippi Valley State College (1946) at Itta Bena, and the University of Mississippi (1844) at University.

Public Welfare. The board of public welfare administers the state welfare institutions. These include hospitals for the mentally ill at Whitfield and Meridian; a school for the feeble-minded and epileptic at Ellisville; schools for the blind and deaf at Jackson; charity hospitals at Vicksburg, Meridian, Natchez, and Laurel; a partially self-supporting tuberculosis sanatorium at Magee; training schools at Columbia and Raymond, and a penitentiary at Parchman. Near Biloxi, Beauvoir, the home of Jefferson Davis, president of the Confederacy, was maintained as a home for Confederate veterans and their wives and widows. In 1925 the Mississippi legislature passed a law permitting, under legal safeguards, sterilization of insane and feeble-minded persons.

Economic Features

Agriculture. In 1964 there were 109,000 farms in Mississippi, the average farm being 163 acres in area and valued at $25,000. Tenant farms constitute a high percentage of the total farms. In 1965 cash income from crops and livestock amounted to $812 million. Mississippi's chief agricultural product is cotton, grown throughout the state, especially in the Yazoo Basin. The state is a major cotton-growing region, noted for production of long-staple cotton. Corn, barley, wheat, oats, hay, rice, potatoes, sweet potatoes, sugar cane, pecans, peanuts, soybeans, peaches, and garden vegetables are also grown. Livestock and poultry raising is an important occupation. Mississippi leads the states in production of tung oil.

Forestry and Fisheries. All but 32,000 acres of Mississippi's 18,008,000 acres of forested land are commercial, and 90.4 per cent of the latter is privately owned. After agriculture, forestry is the state's largest source of income, accounting for more than $700 million annually. Mississippi's stands of pine, cypress, and hardwoods such as oak, hickory, and gum supply the raw material for the many forest-products manufacturing plants in the state.

Mississippi's commercial fishing industry is generally limited to the Gulf coast, with Biloxi as its center. In 1966 the total catch amounted to 272,981,000 pounds with a value of $9,502,000. Shrimp, crabs, and oysters were caught in the Gulf as well as smaller quantities of mullet, red snapper, spotted sea trout, and redfish.

PRINCIPAL CROPS

Crop	Unit	1956	1966
		thousands	
Corn	Bushel	39,150	15,645
Cotton	Bale	1,595	1,350
Cottonseed	Short ton	660	552
Hay	Short ton	908	1,074
Oats	Bushel	15,345	3,420
Potatoes	Cwt.	370	298
Rice	Bag	1,254	2,365 (Cwt.)
Sorghum grain	Bushel	144	516
Sweet Potatoes	Cwt.	880	1,190
Wheat	Bushel	504	7,480

Mining and Manufacturing. In 1966 the mineral production of Mississippi was valued at $211 million. Mississippi was ranked 25th among the fifty states in mineral production. Crude petroleum, natural gas, and natural gas liquids accounted for approximately 85 per cent of production. Other mineral products included sand and gravel, clay, stone, and cement.

Mississippi has cotton, cottonseed, flour, and grist mills; clothing, paper, wallboard, furniture, railway equipment, and plywood factories; fertilizer, meat, turpentine, and tung oil plants; milk condenseries; and shipbuilding yards. Timber and cotton products are the leading manufactures. In 1965 Mississippi had 1,974 manufacturing establishments employing 151,761 workers who earned $635 million. The value added by manufacture was $1,199 million. Mississippi's abundant hydroelectric power resources are important.

THE INGALLS SHIPBUILDING CORP.

A trim cargo vessel is launched at Pascagoula, an important shipbuilding city in the state.

Transportation. Mississippi's transportation facilities include Gulf and river ports, an extensive highway system, and national rail and air carriers. The entire length of the Mississippi River rimming the state is navigable and there are terminal docks at Greenville, Vicksburg, and Natchez. Partially navigable are the Pascagoula, Pearl, and Yazoo rivers. Ocean steamers dock in the deepwater harbors of Gulfport and Pascagoula on the Gulf of Mexico. Numerous railway lines serve the state. Mississippi also has an extensive highway system. There are more than 60,000 miles of surfaced highways. National air service is supplied to Greenwood, Gulfport, Hattiesburg, Jackson, Meridian, and Natchez.

Tourist Attractions. The large cotton plantations of Mississippi attract visitors even though the traditional cotton picker has been largely replaced by mechanical devices. Barge and steamboat traffic on the Mississippi River ranks high among tourist interests. The state has many Civil War landmarks. In Vicksburg National Military Park are preserved the fortifications of the 47-day siege of Vicksburg, 1863, which gave the North control of the Mississippi region.

Trailers of cotton wait to be ginned off. Cotton remains Mississippi's chief agricultural crop.

GRANT HEILMAN

Petroleum is Mississippi's chief mineral. Natchez is important for its oil refineries.

STANDARD OIL CO. (N.J.)

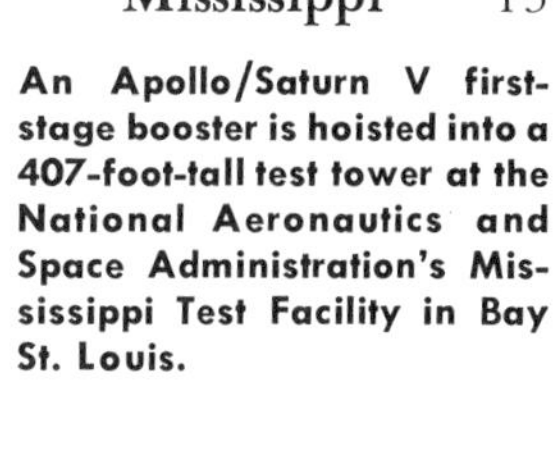
An Apollo/Saturn V first-stage booster is hoisted into a 407-foot-tall test tower at the National Aeronautics and Space Administration's Mississippi Test Facility in Bay St. Louis.

NASA-MISSISSIPPI TEST FACILITY

Vicksburg National Cemetery in the park contains graves of more than 17,000 Union and Confederate soldiers who died in the vicinity during the war. In Brices Cross Roads and Tupelo National Battlefield sites, near Tupelo, are the sites of battles in 1864. Other historical landmarks are Ackia Battleground National Monument, also near Tupelo, which preserves the site of an Indian village where the Chickasaw and English defeated the French and their Choctaw allies in 1736; and Natchez Trace Parkway, which follows the route of the Old Natchez Trace from Nashville, Tenn., to Natchez, an Indian trail and pioneer highway important in nineteenth-century travel. In Jackson are the old and new capitol buildings and the century-old governor's mansion. At Natchez, Holly Springs, and Columbus antebellum homes are open to the public during annual spring festival periods known as pilgrimages. On these occasions Natchez also presents programs of historical pageants and Negro spirituals. The Old Spanish Trail, now U.S. highway 90, unwinds across the Gulf coast through the resort cities of Pascagoula, Ocean Springs, Biloxi, Gulfport, Long Beach, Pass Christian, and Bay St. Louis. Mississippi has national forests at Holly Springs, Delta, Bienville, Homochitto, Tombigbee, and De Soto. Mississippi's 15 state parks are Tombigbee, Wall Doxey, John W. Kyle, Hugh White, Carver Point, J. P. Coleman, and Tishomingo in the north; Leroy Percy, Holmes County, Roosevelt, Golden, and Clarkco in the central section; and Magnolia, Paul B. Johnson, and Percy Quin in the south.

Government

The constitution of Mississippi was adopted in 1890. Proposed amendments must first be approved on each of three different days by a two-thirds vote of all members elected to each house of the state legislature and later by a majority of voters at a popular election. Requirements for voting include residence in the state for two years and in the same electoral district for one year and registration. In order to register, the resident must be able to read any section of the constitution or to understand it when it is read to him.

The chief executive officers are the governor, lieutenant governor, secretary of state, attorney general, auditor, and treasurer, who are elected for terms of four years. The governor and the treasurer are not eligible to succeed themselves. The governor's veto extends to items in appropriations bills; it may be overridden by a two-thirds vote of the legislature.

The legislature consists of a senate of 52 members and a house of representatives of 122, all of whom are elected for four years. Sessions of the legislature are held every other year.

The judicial system is headed by the supreme court of nine justices elected for eight years. There are 18 circuit courts and 18 chancery courts, with judges elected for four years; below them are the county courts and the magistrates courts.

One of the largest paperboard machines in the world, in Vicksburg, produces over 1,000 tons a day.

INTERNATIONAL PAPER COMPANY

HINMAN FROM MONKMEYER

An aerial photograph of Gulfport shows a portion of the longest man-made sand beach in the world.

Mississippi is represented in the national Congress by two senators and five representatives. Jackson is the state capital.

History

Spanish Exploration. The history of Mississippi begins with the search for gold. Seeking to repeat the successes of Hernán Cortés in Mexico and Francisco Pizarro in Peru, the Spaniards sent men into the interior of the North American continent in quest of the fabulous Seven Cities of Cibola (see CIBOLA, SEVEN CITIES OF). Hernán Núñez de Guzmán and Francisco Vásquez de Coronado led fruitless expeditions, but Hernando de Soto, a former companion-in-arms of Pizarro in the conquest of Peru, entered the country in 1541 and dispelled the legend of El Dorado in that region with his own disillusion and death. The rich culture and abundant wealth that the Spaniards found in the southern continent had no counterpart in the north, where the aboriginal American Indians, the Chickasaw, the Choctaw, and the Natchez, gained a meager living by agriculture.

French Colonization. In the seventeenth century there began exploration from the north. The French, expanding their colonial empire in Canada and the Great Lakes region, pushed southward. Exploration of the area now occupied by Mississippi was initiated in 1673 when Father Jacques Marquette and Louis Jolliet penetrated down the Mississippi River to the mouth of the Arkansas. In 1682 Robert Cavelier de La Salle followed the course of the Mississippi to its mouth, claiming the surrounding territory for the French crown under the name Louisiana, in honor of the king. Further exploration was carried out by Louis Hennepin, Antoine de la Mothe Cadillac, and

An aerial view of the Biloxi waterfront shows the pleasure craft basin and yacht club. U.S. Highway 90, the Old Spanish Trail, runs along the coast.

HINMAN FROM MONKMEYER

MISSISSIPPI
Highlights of History

CHICAGO HIST. SOC.

La Salle explored the Mississippi River to its mouth early in 1682 and claimed the entire Mississippi Valley for France.

LIB. OF CONGRESS

Hernando de Soto discovered the Mississippi River in 1540. Two years later he was buried in its waters near Natchez.

REEVES, BILOXI C. OF C.

One of Mississippi's oldest buildings, built by the French at Fort Pascagoula in 1718, is now a historical museum.

ILLINOIS CENTRAL R.R.

The *Mississippi*, one of the first locomotives in the south, was built in 1834 for the Natchez and Hamburg Railroad.

Union forces, which compelled the surrender of Vicksburg in 1863 after five months of siege, were led by Gen. Ulysses S. Grant.

Lorenzo Tonti. Colonization from the south began with the founding of Fort Maurepas in 1699 by the French-Canadian Pierre Lemoyne d'Iberville, who regarded the colonization of the southern territories as an essential part of the larger strategy in the struggle between France and England for supremacy in North America. Until the founding of New Orleans in 1718, Fort Maurepas was the seat of government of an empire that stretched to the north as far as modern Pennsylvania and west into what became Wyoming. The rivalry between England and France emerged as open hostility in 1702, when war was declared between the two powers. The effect on the southern colonies was immediate, for English settlers from the Carolinas began moving westward under protection of the Carolina Grant of 1630, which included the Mississippi region. France in turn removed the seat of government to Mobile and established additional forts and colonies.

If the French based their colonial enterprises on economic development rather than the acquisition of raw gold, they were no less sanguine than the Spaniards as to the commercial value of the colonies. A scheme for the development of the Mississippi Basin, known as the Mississippi Bubble, was started in 1717 by John Law, a Scottish financier operating in France. Such was the demand for shares that the company increased its stock, and the French government printed and circulated paper money unbacked by gold reserves, all in anticipation of the wealth to come from the colonies. It never came. The resulting financial crash of 1720 and the consequent disruption of the French fiscal system produced a chaos in France that was an indirect cause of the French Revolution and had the immediate effect of suspending French activities in the Mississippi region. See MISSISSIPPI BUBBLE.

Other difficulties resulted. Pressed by French expansion, the Natchez descended on Fort Rosalie in 1729, massacring and enslaving the colonists; but the tribe was itself exterminated the following year in retaliation. The British, renewing their old claims to the territory in 1732, allied with the Chickasaw, whose fortified villages blocked French expansion into the northern part of the state, thus preventing the French of Louisiana from uniting with the French of Ohio to curtail the British westward movement.

The United States and Spain. The great eclipse of the French colonial empire in the Seven Years' War cast its shadow over French dominion in Mississippi. (See SEVEN YEARS' WAR.) Canada and India were lost, the territory west of the Mississippi River was ceded to Spain, and by the Treaty of Paris in 1763 England acquired the lands east of the river and Protestants settled in the country. Mississippi could not remain for long uninfluenced by outside events. During the Revolutionary War the Natchez district remained neutral. Spain, however, taking advantage of British commitments in the north, moved troops into the Gulf region and took Natchez in 1781. For the next 30 years the aim of U.S. policy with regard to the area was the eviction of Spanish rule. Conflicting territorial claims between the United States and Spain led to the second Treaty of Paris in 1783, but the territory was not evacuated by the Spaniards until 1798. The Mississippi Territory, corresponding to modern Alabama and southern Mississippi, was organized the same year. Spain, however, retained control of the coastal region along the Gulf of Mexico up to 31°N lat. as part of its Territory of Florida. By agreements in 1810 and 1813 following border warfare, portions of Spain's western Florida possessions were ceded to the United States and incorporated into Louisiana. In 1817 the western portion of Mississippi was admitted to the Union, the remainder being constituted the Territory of Alabama. See FLORIDA, Administration and History, *Spanish Florida, Conflicting Claims.*

NATCHEZ ASSN. OF COMMERCE
Frederick Stanton, an Irish immigrant who became a wealthy Natchez cotton broker, built this mansion in the 1850's and furnished it with rich imports brought in by chartered ship.

Economic Growth. The economic foundations of the state were laid with the boom in cotton, beginning the "great migration" that lasted from 1817 to 1832. The demand for land drove out the Indians, who up to that time had owned large tracts of the state. The Choctaw moved west of the Mississippi after 1820, and the Chickasaw gave up their lands in 1832.

Civil War and Reconstruction. The news of Lincoln's election was the signal for the calling of a state convention, which on Jan. 9, 1861, passed an ordinance of secession, and Mississippi became the second state to join the Confederacy (see SECESSION). Among important episodes of the Civil War were the operations around Corinth in 1862 and the siege and capture of Vicksburg (see CORINTH; VICKSBURG CAMPAIGN). When the 14th amendment came up for a vote in 1867, it was rejected, whereupon the state was placed under military rule. The ratification of the 14th and 15th amendments in 1869 was followed by readmission to the Union. (See RECONSTRUCTION.) For a quarter of a century after the Civil War the energies of the state were expended in recuperation and readjustment to the new economic conditions and in a struggle with the race problem. By the constitution of 1890 an education test was introduced and suffrage was restricted to persons able to read the constitution or to interpret a section read to them.

Economic Changes. With the Jim Crow Law of 1904 and the voting restrictions imposed by the new constitution, white supremacy was re-established, but the structure of society had changed. Impoverished by the war and the lack of slave labor, the old planters gave way in economic and political influence to the small farmers, who gained control of the legislature. The emergence of the small farmer was an economic regression, preventing the use of large-scale agricultural methods.

The decline in value of cotton as a result of disease, and competition from other countries had an adverse effect on the state. In 1924 a law limiting the capital and real estate of corporations was repealed and the way was open for industrialization. In three years the amount of outside capital invested in the state leaped from $3 million to $586 million. Mississippi's economy, once almost entirely dependent on timber and cotton, was marked by a further increase of both industrialization and urbanization after 1936. During the postwar period there was increasing diversification of agriculture, and livestock-rearing became of considerable significance.

Movements to block the integration of schools, following the Supreme Court injunction of 1954, continued through the early 1960's. In both the 1948, and 1960 presidential elections the state's electoral votes went to minor Democratic candidates, in protest against the civil rights plank of the Democratic platform.

BIBLIOG.–D. Rowland, *History of Mississippi, the Heart of the South* (4 vols. 1925); Federal Writers' Project, *Mississippi: A Guide to the Magnolia State* (1938), *Mississippi Gulf Coast* (1939); C. S. Sydnor and C. Bennett, *Mississippi History* (1939); J. K. Bettersworth, *Confederate Mississippi* (1943); A. D. Kirwan, *Revolt of the Rednecks* (1951); P. V. Guyton, *Our Mississippi* (1952); R. B. Highsaw and C. N. Fortenberry, *Government and Administration of Mississippi* (1954); F. E. Smith, *Yazoo River* (1954).

MISSISSIPPI, UNIVERSITY OF, a coeducational, state-controlled institution of higher learning located at University, Miss. The school was chartered in 1844 and instruction was first offered in 1848.

Divisions of the university include the college of liberal arts (1848); schools of law (1854), engineering (1900), education (1903), medicine (1903), pharmacy (1908), and commerce and business administration (1917); graduate school (1927); and university extension (1953).

Degrees offered are the bachelor's, the master's by most departments, and the doctor's in the social and the biological sciences. Distinctive educational programs include annual summer sessions in France and Mexico for foreign language students and special instruction for superior students. The University of Mississippi is a co-operating member of the Oak Ridge Institute of Nuclear Studies and the Gulf Coast Research Laboratory.

Special university library collections include the Deavours collection of Mississippiana and the James Wilford Garner library containing political science and international law materials. See COLLEGES AND UNIVERSITIES.

MISSISSIPPIAN, a geologic period that was part of the Paleozoic era and is believed to have originated about 310 million years ago and to have ended about 280 million years ago. Like the Pennsylvanian and Permian periods that followed it, the Mississippian is often classed as part of the Upper Paleozoic or Carboniferous period.

During the Mississippian much of what now is the United States and western Canada were under water and marine life was prominent. The crinoids, a group of invertebrates related to the starfish (see CRINOIDEA), were particularly abundant. Among the fishes, sharks were prominent and the species apparently belonged to two main types, one resembling the sharks of today and the other having large, flat, crushing teeth rather than sharp, tearing ones. Amphibians also existed. Plants grew abundantly and included huge club mosses and ferns as tall as trees, but no true seed-bearing plants existed during this period in geologic time.

The early layers of the Mississippian are largely clastic rock (see CLASTIC ROCK) but later deposits, made up to a considerable extent of the skeletons of protozoa, or tiny one-celled animals, and of crinoids, are primarily limestone; in many parts of the world the Mississippian deposits have been the chief source of limestone and building stone. Numerous caves and sinkholes formed in this limestone, and these sites became important ore deposits—some of the ore accumulating during the Mississippian itself, some being deposited during the Pennsylvanian and later periods. The zinc ores found in the most important zinc producing region in the world, the tristate district of southwestern Missouri and adjacent areas of Oklahoma and Kansas, were laid down in the Upper Paleozoic. Some coal was deposited in the United States during the Mississippian, but the deposits are small as compared with those of the Pennsylvanian. The period is responsible for important coal beds in Belgium and the U.S.S.R., however. Oil-containing shale and salt domes also were formed during this time. Toward the close of the period the oceans receded and land was exposed; and unconformities (see CONFORMITY, GEOLOGICAL) between the Mississippian and the Pennsylvanian indicate that widespread erosion took place toward the end of the former period. See PALEOZOIC; GEOLOGIC TIME.

MISSISSIPPI BUBBLE, or Mississippi Scheme, the financial operation of John Law that ended in failure in 1720. Law, a Scot who had gained a reputation as a financier in France, in 1717 organized the Compagnie de l'Occident, or Western Company, also known as the Mississippi Company, absorbing the Canada Company and Antoine Crozat's rights in the Territory of Louisiana. The company bought the tobacco monopoly in 1718, and in 1719 consolidated with the East India Company to form the Compagnie des Indes, with virtual control of the colonial trade. Its association with Law's banking enterprises and his power in French national finances gave the company great opportunities and an even greater public reputation. Its shares sold, partly for depreciated paper, at continually rising prices, with little relation to actual operations in the colonies although the company was still generally known as the Mississippi Scheme. The speculation in the shares was one of the largest to that date, and among the most notable in history. Law's attempt to amalgamate the company and the bank, in 1720, brought on the collapse of public confidence, and shares were sold as eagerly as they had been bought, while Law's other enterprises also failed. Law fled to Italy; the company continued in control of Louisiana until 1731.

MISSISSIPPI COLLEGE. See COLLEGES AND UNIVERSITIES.

MISSISSIPPI CULTURE, a mound-type prehistoric Indian culture most developed in the southeastern United States, but also found in certain northern areas. The culture is divided into two periods —Middle Mississippian (about 1000 to 1400) and Upper Mississippian (about 1400 to 1650).

Mississippi culture was characterized by the building of groups of mounds, which served as ceremonial centers. The large size of some of the mounds indicates the exercise of organized control by chiefs. Pottery was modeled, sometimes polished and engraved, and in the Arkansas-Tennessee area occasionally painted. Shell disks were sometimes incised and copper plates were embossed. During the seventeenth century the prehistoric Mississippi culture was replaced by historically known tribes encountered by the Spanish, French, and English. See ARCHAEOLOGY, American Archaeology, *The Mississippi Valley, Mound Builders, Mississippi Cultural Pattern.*

MISSISSIPPI RIVER, central United States, which it almost intersects from N to S. The headwaters of the Mississippi drain into Lake Itasca in northwest central Minnesota and from there the river flows 2,330 miles to its mouth in the Gulf of Mexico. The Mississippi receives more than 40 important tributaries from 31 states and Canada, the longest being the Missouri (2,465 mi.), Arkansas (1,450 mi.), Red (1,018 mi.), Ohio (981 mi.), and Illinois (272 mi.) rivers. The combined erosional force of these streams brings 750 million cubic yards of silt annually to the mouth of the Mississippi. The origin of the Mississippi's most easterly tributary is 250 miles from the Atlantic Ocean, and that of its most westerly 500 miles from the Pacific. The area of the drainage basin is 1.24 million square miles, of which 13,000 are in Canada.

Physical Characteristics. The Mississippi rises in the lakes and densely wooded regions of north Minnesota, near the geographic center of the North American continent, south of Lake Itasca at 1,466 feet above sea level. Little Elk Lake drains through the short Excelsior Creek into Lake Itasca, then emerges as the Mississippi River, 12 feet wide and 2 feet deep. It meanders 60 miles north in the direction of Hudson Bay, reaching its northernmost point at Lake Bemidji. The Mississippi then flows east and beyond Lake Winnibigoshish takes a southward direction. The Crow Wing, Rum, and Minnesota river tributaries add to its volume, and after a drop of 80 feet at the Falls of St. Anthony the Mississippi becomes navigable to large vessels at Minneapolis. From Minneapolis to the point of confluence with the Wisconsin River, the Mississippi flows between loess cliffs in a narrow valley. South of that area the Mississippi forms the Iowa-Wisconsin, Iowa-Illinois, and Illinois-Missouri state boundaries. The middle Mississippi is the stretch from the mouth of the Illinois River to the mouth of the Ohio at Cairo, Ill., where the Mississippi becomes 4,500 feet wide. Major tributaries entering the river in this section are the Missouri and the combined Ohio-Tennessee. Below the middle section the valley broadens. It is thought that about 50,000 years ago the area of the lower Mississippi was a vast inland sea. The river now meanders over the sedimentary lowland that was once the floor of the sea and deposits thick layers of alluvium, frequently changing its course to leave cutoffs that form lakes and bayous.

The Mississippi is joined by several west-bank tributaries below Memphis, and then trends in a south-southwesterly direction through the Yazoo Delta. A major tributary, the Arkansas, enters the river north of Greenville. The Mississippi swings southwest after confluence with the Red River. Below the Red River lies the Atchafalaya Basin, which serves as a route for high-water runoff to the Gulf of Mexico. From confluence with the Red to the gulf, the river is sluggish and its flood plain is dotted with oxbow lakes.

The delta of the Mississippi has been built up by five distributaries, and natural levees called passes have been deposited along each of the channels. Many places on the delta are below sea level; in some, salt water has been replaced by fresh water, forming Lakes Salvador, Cataouatche, and Maurepas and the Lac des Allemands.

Ports, Bridges, and Locks. A navigable channel 9 to 12 feet deep is maintained along the Mississippi from Minneapolis and St. Paul to New Orleans. The main cities along the river are also ports: Minneapolis and St. Paul, Dubuque, Rock Island, Burlington, St. Louis, Cairo, Memphis, Vicksburg, Baton Rouge, and New Orleans. Chicago is a port with access to the Mississippi through the Illinois Waterway. Between Minneapolis and St. Louis the channel is maintained by 30 federal locks and dams, 24 of which—with locks 110 by 600 feet—were built between 1930 and 1939 at a cost of $160 million. In the 1950's the Falls of St. Anthony at Minneapolis were scaled by two locks, navigable waters were extended north, and the port channel was enlarged. In 1953 the $40 million Chain of Rocks Canal and Locks, within a mile of the confluence of the Mississippi and Missouri rivers near St. Louis, were opened to navigation. Extending for more than 8 miles, this installation eliminated the last serious navigation obstacle on the river. Dimensions of the main lock at Chain of Rocks exceed those of the Panama Canal. In 1957 New Orleans announced plans for a 70-mile tidewater channel to give the city a direct eastern outlet to the Gulf and triple the city's tonnage capacity. Excavation on the Cal-Sag project at Chicago was started in 1955 in connection with the St. Lawrence Seaway to enlarge the passageway connecting the Mississippi waterway system with the Great Lakes and expand direct connections with ocean traffic.

Towboating along the Mississippi River between Cairo and New Orleans is responsible for greater tonnage each year than that passing through the Suez or the Panama Canal.

FAIRBANKS, MORSE & CO.

The first bridge (1856) across the Mississippi linked Rock Island, Ill., and Davenport, Iowa. Most important of the many bridges, mostly toll, spanning the Mississippi are the Dubuque, the four-lane Rock Island–Davenport, the Lewis and Clark from St. Louis to Alton crossing the Missouri and the Mississippi, and the Eads at St. Louis—the world's first (1874) steel-truss bridge.

History. Hernando de Soto of Spain is usually credited with being, in 1541, the European discoverer of the Mississippi. The Chippewa or Ojibway Indians called the river beside which they lived Mee-zee-see-bee, Father of Waters, and from this Indian word comes the modern name. Little attention was paid to the North American mid-continent by west European settlers until the French penetrated to the Mississippi from the Great Lakes. In 1673 Jacques Marquette and Louis Jolliet, starting from Green Bay, Wis., paddled up the Fox River and down the Wisconsin to the Mississippi, which they explored as far south as modern Arkansas. In 1680 the Louis Hennepin expedition reached the Falls of St. Anthony. Robert Cavelier de La Salle in 1682 claimed the whole Mississippi region for France and named it Louisiana. France lost its American empire through defeat in the French and Indian War; the region west of the Mississippi was transferred to Spain, while that to the east went to Britain. In 1783 the river became the boundary between Spanish territory and the United States. Louisiana was retroceded to France in 1800, and three years later, through the Louisiana Purchase, was transferred to the United States. Finally under undisputed political control, the Mississippi quickly developed into the great inland waterway of the new, expanding nation. The flatboats and keelboats of the early nineteenth century were supplanted by steamboats, the first of which, the *New Orleans*, traveled from Pittsburgh to New Orleans in 1812. The source of the Mississippi was discovered in 1832 when Henry Schoolcraft traced it to Lake Itasca. The golden age of river transportation was 1840 to 1870, after which the steamboat slowly gave way to the railroad. The Mississippi played a strategic role in the Civil War, and although it declined in prominence afterward, it continued as one of the world's great inland waterways. In the early 1950's annual cargo tonnage exceeded 80 million tons.

The Mississippi River floods of 1913, 1927, and 1937 prodded the U.S. government to build levees and inaugurate other flood-control projects.

Bibliog.–E. Coues, *Expedition of Zebulon Montgomery Pike* (1895); H. E. Chambers, *Mississippi Valley Beginnings* (1922); F. E. Williams, *Geography of the Mississippi Valley* (1926); L. Saxon, *Father Mississippi* (1927); W. J. Petersen, *Steamboating on the Upper Mississippi* (1937); H. Carter, *Lower Mississippi* (1942); W. Havighurst, *Upper Mississippi: A Wilderness Saga* (1944); E. and L. Rosskam, *Towboat River* (1948); J. P. Kemper, *Rebellious River* (1949); F. Pratt, *Civil War on Western Waters* (1956); Mark Twain, *Life on the Mississippi* (1833, ed. 1957).

MISSISSIPPI STATE COLLEGE. See Colleges and Universities.

MISSOLONGHI. See Mesolóngion.

MISSOULA, city, W Montana, seat of Missoula County; on the Bitterroot and Clark Fork rivers, the Northern Pacific and the Milwaukee railroads, and U.S. highways 10 and 93; 99 miles NW of Butte. Missoula has lumber mills, beet sugar and oil refineries, and plants manufacturing wood products, tents, and awnings. Copper, lead, and gold are mined. Missoula is the seat of Montana State University and headquarters of Region 1 of the U.S. Forest Service. Missoula was established in 1865 and incorporated in 1889. Pop. (1960) 27,009.

TWA

Mark Twain's native state—a producer of transportation equipment, lead, and hogs.

MISSOURI, state, central United States, one of the west north central states; bounded on the N by Iowa, on the E by Illinois, Kentucky, and Tennessee, on the S by Arkansas, and on the W by Oklahoma, Kansas, and Nebraska; maximum east-west and north-south distances 305 and 285 miles respectively; area 69,674 sq. mi., including 448 sq. mi. of inland water; pop. (1960) 4,319,813. The Mississippi River marks the eastern boundary of the state, and the Missouri River forms part of the western boundary and flows west to east across the state. Missouri ranks 19th in area and 13th in population among the states. Missouri is an Indian name meaning muddy water. The state's nickname, "Show Me" state, is an expression attributed to the skeptical attitude of Missourians. It originated in a political address given by Willard D. Vandiver, a state representative to the U.S. Congress. *Salus Populi Suprema Lex Esto* (The Welfare of the People Shall Be the Supreme Law) is the state motto. The state flower is the hawthorn, the official bird is the bluebird, and the official tree is the flowering dogwood. Jefferson City is the capital. See map in Atlas, Vol. 20. For the state flag in color, see FLAG.

PHYSICAL FACTORS

Geology. Missouri's geologic history dates from the Archeozoic and Proterozoic eras when igneous rocks were formed by solidification of molten magma. These rocks are exposed to the surface only in the southeastern part of the state. During the latter part of the Proterozoic the Ozark Mountains were formed. In the Paleozoic era that followed, rock strata above the igneous formations were deposited when a series of submergences by great inland seas occurred. These deposits include stratified limestones, dolomites, cherts of organic and chemical origin, conglomerates, sandstones, and various types of shales. The coal deposits of Missouri and the immense amounts of lead, zinc, and barite ores were formed during the Pennsylvanian period of the Paleozoic era. The present land characteristics were formed during the Cenozoic era when uplifting and faulting actions took place. During the Quaternary period of the Cenozoic, called the Pleistocene epoch, glaciers advanced as far south as the Missouri River, forming rolling prairies and wide stream valleys and depositing a rich soil.

Topography. The surface of Missouri is divided into four topographic divisions: the glacial and loessial region in the north, the prairie region in the west central portion, the Ozark highland region in the south and southwest, and the Mississippi lowland region, a small area in the southeast corner, or "boot heel," of the state. The glacial and loessial region includes all of the state between the Mississippi and Missouri rivers—a rolling terrain that is almost devoid of trees except for small stands of timber in valleys and along streams. The prairie region extends south from the Missouri to the Osage River and west from Jefferson City to the Kansas border; it is an area broken by many hills. The Ozark highland region rises gradually from the Illinois border near St. Louis to southwest Missouri, where it reaches an elevation of 1,658 feet near Seymour. Its surface is broken and hilly but lacks the ruggedness of mountain areas. The hills rise in peaks and knobs that are rounded at the summit as a result of heavy erosion. Taum Sauk Mountain (1,772 ft.) in Iron County is the highest elevation in Missouri. The Ozark highland region has many deep gorges and underground streams forming numerous sinks and subterranean caverns. The Mississippi lowland's surface, once a flood plain of the Mississippi River, is diversified by cypress swamps, lagoons, and lakes.

Rivers and Lakes. The Mississippi River, flowing southeast, forms the eastern boundary of the state. Its principal tributary, the Missouri, forms the western boundary as far south as Kansas City, a distance of 144 miles, and crosses central Missouri to a point 14 miles north of St. Louis. The courses of the St. Francis and White rivers, both affluents of the Mississippi, lie partly within the southern counties of the state. The chief tributaries of the Missouri are the Grand, Chariton, Platte, Nishnabotna, and Modaway rivers in the north and the Gasconade, Big Sniabar, Blue, Lamine, and Osage rivers in the south. These southern tributaries, with the White River, drain the Ozark highlands. In the Ozarks are many large springs and swift streams that furnish water power for mills and factories. Dams on the large rivers furnish hydroelectric power for the state.

Missouri has five major artificial lakes. The Lake of the Ozarks, formed by Bagnell Dam on the Osage River, is 129 miles long, covers 65,000 acres, and is one of the world's largest man-made lakes. Other artificial lakes are Lake Taneycomo on the White River, Lake Wappapello on the St. Francis River, Lake Clearwater on the Black River, and Lake Norfork on the north fork of the White River. Throughout the state are a number of smaller lakes, many of glacial origin.

Climate. Missouri has a humid subtropical climate characterized by brief hot summers, long mild falls, short cold winters, and long mild springs. The state has an average annual temperature of 55.1°F, with recorded extremes of 118° and −40°; July is the warmest month and January the coldest. The average precipitation varies from 36.68 inches in the north to 41.37 in the southwest and 43.27 in the southeast; the state average is 40.44. Snowfall annually exceeds 17 inches. Thunderstorms are frequent and droughts occasionally occur. The prevailing winds are from the south in summer and from the northwest in winter. Tornadoes occur in April, June, and July, often causing considerable damage. The average number of cloud-free days is 170 and the growing season lasts from April to October.

Soils and Natural Vegetation. Missouri has a variety of soils including those common to mountain areas. The north is covered with loess, the most fertile soil in the state. The Mississippi and Missouri River areas are characterized by productive alluvial soil. More than one-third of the state is within the Ozark region, which has soils of low fertility—lithosols, that are rocky and extensively eroded. Other soils include gray-brown podsolic and red-yellow podsolic groups.

Among the trees that grow throughout the state are the black willow, red cedar, oak, hickory, ash, walnut, and maple. Flower- and fruit-bearing shrubs include dogwood, redbud, sumac, honey locust, persimmon, hackberry, papaw, wild plum, cherry, and crab apple. Among the well known wild plants are blackberry, strawberry, raspberry, grape, gooseberry, elderberry, violet, milkweed, sweet William, bergamot, May apple, pennyroyal, snakeroot, and jack-in-the-pulpit.

The Great Seal of Missouri depicts two grizzly bears holding a shield surmounted by a helmet, on which are the emblems of the United States and Missouri. The date in Roman numerals is 1820, the year the state's first constitution was adopted.

BIRD	**Bluebird**
FLOWER	**Hawthorn**
TREE	**Dogwood**
CAPITAL	**Jefferson City**
MOTTO	**Salus Populi Suprema Lex Esto** (Let the Welfare of the People Be the Supreme Law)
ENTERED THE UNION	**Aug. 10, 1821**
ORDER OF ENTRY	**24th**

The stream banks of the prairie areas abound in cottonwood, box elder, quaking aspen, chokecherry, and black haw trees. Witch hazel, red oak, elm, chittamwood, and hawthorn are common in the Ozark highland region. The lowlands of the southeast are noted for cypress, ash, wormwood, cottonwood, water locust, and tupelo trees; mistletoe and holly grow in abundance; several kinds of orchids are found; and blue indigo, wisteria, and swamp rose are common.

Animals. The principal animals of Missouri are the fox, squirrel, opossum, muskrat, raccoon, and mink. Gray wolves are found in the south; weasels, jack rabbits, and coyotes on the plains of the northwest; and quail and ring-necked pheasant on the prairie and in the Ozark uplands. Other common birds include the bullfinch, cardinal, mockingbird, whippoorwill, hawk, owl, crow, buzzard, and bluebird. Water turkeys are sometimes found in the southeast swamp areas. Game birds besides quail and pheasant include migratory ducks.

Social Factors

Population. The 1966 population of Missouri—4,508,000—was 188,187, or 4 per cent, greater than that of 1960. More than one half of the population is classified as urban. Missouri has a density of 64.6 persons per square mile. St. Louis is the largest city, followed by Kansas City and Springfield.

GRANT HEILMAN

Missouri's fertile soils make the state a major producer of such crops as corn, soybeans, wheat, and sorghums.

PRINCIPAL CITIES

City	Population 1950 Census	Population 1960 Census
St. Louis	856,796	750,026
Kansas City	456,622	475,539
Springfield	66,731	95,865
St. Joseph	78,588	79,673
Independence	36,963	62,328
University City	39,892	51,249
Joplin	38,711	38,958
Columbia	31,974	36,650
Webster Groves	23,390	28,990
Jefferson City (capital)	25,099	28,228

Education. The state board of education supervises Missouri's public school system. The board is comprised of eight members appointed by the governor to eight-year terms. The state board and county and district boards make up the administrative system. School attendance is compulsory for children aged 6 to 16. Courses in education are provided in summer institutes, in the normal departments of a number of colleges, and in state teachers colleges at Kirksville, Cape Girardeau, Warrensburg, Springfield, and Maryville.

St. Louis's 630-foot Gateway Arch on the Mississippi River levee overlooks Busch Memorial Stadium (foreground).

ANHEUSER BUSCH, INC

The state university is the University of Missouri at Columbia with its associated School of Mines and Metallurgy at Rolla. Other collegiate institutions include St. Louis University, Harris Teachers College, Washington University, and Fontbonne College at St. Louis; University of Kansas City, College of St. Teresa, and Rockhurst College, Kansas City; Westminster College, Fulton; Lincoln University, Jefferson City; Tarkio College, Tarkio; Park College, Parkville; Lindenwood College, St. Charles; William Jewell College, Liberty; Missouri Valley College, Marshall; Drury College, Springfield; Culver-Stockton College, Canton; Central Methodist College, Fayette; and Webster College, Webster Groves. Stephens College at Columbia, Wentworth Military Academy at Lexington, and Kemper Military School at Boonville are two-year institutions.

Missouri's fine art institutions include the St. Louis City Art Museum and, in Kansas City, the William Rockhill Nelson Gallery of Art and the Mary Atkins Museum of Fine Arts.

Public Welfare. A number of charitable and correctional institutions are controlled by state boards. These institutions include hospitals for the mentally ill at Fulton, St. Joseph, Farmington, Nevada, and St. Louis, and for the epileptic and mentally retarded at Marshall, Carrollton, and St. Louis; a tuberculosis sanatorium at Mt. Vernon; the Ellis Fischel Cancer Hospital at Columbia; the Missouri Trachoma Hospital at Rolla; a school for the blind at St. Louis and for the deaf at Fulton; a correctional training school for boys at Boonville, one for girls at Chillicothe, and another for Negro girls at Tipton; and a penitentiary at Jefferson City. There is a federal home for war veterans and their wives and widows at St. James.

Economic Factors

Agriculture. The most important natural resource of Missouri is its agricultural land, particularly in the north and in the Missouri and Mississippi River valleys. The major economic activity of the state is agriculture. In 1964 there were 147,315 farms totaling 32,691,618 acres. In 1966 cash income from crops and livestock was $1.4 billion. Corn, the principal crop, is grown on 24.8 per cent of crop acreage and accounts for 49 per cent of crop income. Other major crops include wheat, oats, soybeans, cotton, flax, hay, rye, and tobacco. Missouri is an important stock-raising state. Hogs are the chief commercial product. In the south, sheep graze in the highlands where there is an abundance of water. The state is noted for its mules. Dairying is a major industry, especially in the St. Louis region and the southwest. Eggs, poultry, and cream are marketed through well organized co-operatives.

Forestry. More than a third of the total land area of Missouri is forested and 15 million acres are classified as commercially productive forest land.

PRINCIPAL CROPS

Crop	Unit	1956	1966
		thousands	
Apples	bushel	550	1,050
Barley	bushel	11,826	714
Corn	bushel	189,408	176,328
Cotton	bale	448	165
Grapes	pound	3,400	3,400
Hay	ton	3,523	4,873
Oats	bushel	40,393	9,840
Rye	bushel	884	462
Sorghums	bushel	5,984	10,472
Soybeans	bushel	36,420	85,425
Tobacco	pound	3,930	5,269
Wheat	bushel	50,630	41,140

ANHEUSER BUSCH, INC.

At the Anheuser Busch brewery in St. Louis, hops, rice, and barley malt are mixed together in these brew kettles.

WASHINGTON UNIVERSITY PHOTO SERVICE

Researchers use a cyclotron at Washington University, one of more than 30 Missouri colleges and universities.

Jet fighter planes are arrayed in the final assembly line in the St. Louis plant of the McDonnell Douglas Corp.

MCDONNELL DOUGLAS CORP.

The largest forested region lies within the Ozark highland. Forests are composed primarily of hardwoods including oak, hickory, maple, ash, walnut, and elm. In the southeast cypress, willow, sycamore, and cottonwood trees are found. Short-leaf pine forests thrive in some areas of the Ozarks.

Mining. The state is a leading producer of lead, barite, tripoli, and lime. Lead is produced principally in the southern counties. The ores are deposited in layers often 100 feet thick and 500 feet deep. Most barite comes from Washington County where it is found in residual clays covering dolomitic formations. Barite is used in the manufacture of paints, heavy-drilling sludge, linoleum, rubber goods, and paper products. Missouri is a leading coal-producing state, Barton and Bates counties being the principal coal areas. Before 1840 coal was located under about 25,000 square miles in northwest Missouri, and was first mined in St. Louis County. Coal is obtained primarily from shaft mines and in lesser quantities from outcrops and strip pits. Sandstone is quarried in St. Peter, La Motte, and Roubidoux counties, and sand from Ozark streams is used in sandblasting. Sand from St. Peter County, a nearly pure silica, is used in glassmaking, and other Missouri sands are used in manufacturing sandpaper and glazing pottery. Burlington limestone, quarried near Carthage, Louisiana, and Hannibal, is used as building material and for production of quicklime. The highest quality of limestone, suitable for the manufacture of lime, outcrops in Sainte Genevieve County. Pike County limestone is used in production of rock wool. Deposits of marble, manganese, cobalt, bismuth, and tungsten are found throughout the state but are mined in small quantities. In 1954 Missouri ranked 22nd among states in mineral production. Mineral output in 1960 was valued at $157.2 million.

MINERAL PRODUCTION

Mineral	Unit	1950	1956	1960
			thousands	
Barite	short ton	213	381	181
Cement	barrel	9,780	12,013	12,183
Clay	short ton	1,533	2,657	2,540
Coal	short ton	2,963	3,282	2,890
Copper	pound	5,964	3,780	1,087
Lead ore	short ton	135	123	112
Sand and gravel	short ton	6,232	9,585	10,207
Stone	short ton	10,300	24,578	27,180

Manufacturing. Because of diversity and abundance of resources and its location favorable to inland water transportation, Missouri ranks high among states in manufacturing. Much of the industrial activity centers in the St. Louis and Kansas City metropolitan areas. One of the largest U.S. stockyards and meat-processing centers is in Kansas City, a market for much livestock from the southwest. The manufacture of transportation equipment, chiefly motor vehicles, is the most important industry of Missouri. Other important industries include the production of glass, tile and brick, concrete blocks, plastics, heating and air-conditioning equipment, electronics equipment, electrical appliances, communications equipment, iron and steel products, foundry and machine-shop products, hardware, aircraft and aircraft parts, shoes and leather goods, textiles and clothing, sporting equipment, munitions and armaments, fireworks, awnings, toys, chemicals, books, paper products, farm machinery, food products, and malt beverages. Springfield, Joplin, Independence, Jefferson City, Hannibal, and Sedalia are other important industrial cities. In 1958 there were 6,447 manufacturing establishments employing 381,000 persons who received $1.8 billion in wages. The value added by manufacture was $3.2 billion.

Transportation. Missouri's railroad facilities are excellent in the north half of the state, along the west border, and in the southeast corner. St. Louis and Kansas City are among the most important railroad centers in the United States. The principal lines serving Missouri are the Alton, the Baltimore and Ohio, the Burlington, the Chicago and Eastern Illinois, the Chicago Great Western, the Frisco, the Gulf, Mobile, and Ohio, the Illinois Central, the Kansas City Southern, the Louisville and Nashville, the Missouri-Kansas-Texas, the Missouri Pacific, the New York Central, the New York, Chicago, and St. Louis, the Pennsylvania, the Rock Island, the Milwaukee, the St. Louis Southwestern, the Southern, the Santa Fe, the Union Pacific, and the Wabash. River traffic on the Mississippi is heavy from St. Louis to New Orleans. Extensive improvements on the Missouri River have made it navigable for river traffic between Kansas City and the mouth of the river. Both St. Louis and Kansas City are headquarters for air traffic. Other scheduled airline stops include Cape Girardeau, Columbia, Hannibal, Independence, Jefferson City, Joplin, St. Joseph, Springfield, and Webb City. U.S. highways crossing the state from east to west are 24, 36, 40, 50, 54, 60, 66, and 136, and those from north to south are 59, 61, 63, 65, 67, 71, 169, and 275.

Tourist Attractions. The most picturesque sections of Missouri are the uplands of the Ozarks, the delta region in the southeast, and the White River country in the southwest. Rustic cabins dating from the pioneer days of Missouri are found throughout the state. Watermills still grind meal as they have for more than a century. There are eight remaining covered bridges in Cape Girardeau, Jefferson, Linn, Monroe, Pettis, and Platte counties. Missouri has 25 state parks, most near springs in woodland regions, with facilities for camping, fishing, and picnicking. Big Spring Park in Carter County is reputed to have the largest spring in the country. The state has 21 caves, all commercially operated and open to the public. In south Missouri 1.37 million acres of woodland are included in Clark and Mark Twain national forests. The state has three national wildlife refuges at Puxico, Mound City, and Sumner. Lakes Taneycomo and Norfork and the Lake of the Ozarks are among the most popular summer resorts.

The Mark Twain Museum and Home may be seen in Hannibal where are also many other relics associated with characters in the books of Missouri's famous author. In St. Louis are the Jefferson National Expansion Memorial, the botanic and zoological gardens, and the St. Louis Municipal Opera and open-air theater with summer productions. The George Washington Carver National Monument is at Diamond, birthplace of the great Negro scientist. One of Missouri's oldest villages is Sainte Genevieve,

Picturesque old mills are found along many of the 10,000 streams running through the valleys of the forest-covered Ozarks. Turner Mill, below, is located in Shannon County.

MASSIE-MISSOURI RESOURCES DIV.

MISSOURI

WALKER-MISSOURI RESOURCES DIV.

The annual grape crop is harvested at Rosita. Missouri is seventh among U.S. states in production of grapes.

Veneer plant is part of the important wood products industry at Caruthersville in the state's southeast, or "boot heel," section.

MASSIE-MISSOURI RESOURCES DIV.

MASSIE-MISSOURI RESOURCES DIV.

Lake Taneycomo, in the popular Ozark resort area, is formed by Powersite Dam at Forsyth on the White River.

MASSIE-MISSOURI RESOURCES DIV.

Kansas City is the largest U.S. market in stock and feeder cattle, horses, and mules. The city stockyards straddle the Kansas-Missouri border.

Chief products of Missouri's highly diversified mineral industry are lead, cement, stone, lime.

WALKER-MISSOURI RESOURCES DIV.

MASSIE-MISSOURI RESOURCES DIV.

Built of Carthage marble, the capitol at Jefferson City stands on a bluff overlooking the Missouri River. It was erected in 1918 after fire leveled two earlier capitols.

an early French settlement with homes built before 1785; it has a museum, old churches, convents, and cemeteries. Missouri is the seat of many important military installations including Fort Leonard Wood, one of the largest U.S. military training bases, in Pulaski County, and Whiteman Air Force Base, a Strategic Air Command field, at Knob Noster in Johnson County.

GOVERNMENT

In 1945 Missouri adopted its fourth constitution. Amendments to the constitution are proposed by a majority vote of the legislature and ratified by a majority vote of the electorate. Voting qualifications include residence in the state one year, and in the same county and district 60 days.

Legislative power is vested in the general assembly, which consists of a senate of 34 members elected from districts for four-year terms and a house of representatives elected from counties for two-year terms, the number from each county being determined by its population. Regular sessions begin in January of odd-numbered years and are limited to 150 days. There is a permanent joint committee on legislative research selected by and from the members of the two houses. The electors have power of direct legislation through initiative and referendum.

The elected state officials are the governor, lieutenant governor, secretary of state, treasurer, attorney general, and auditor, all of whom serve four-year terms. The governor and treasurer are ineligible for immediate re-election. The constitution provides for five other administrative departments—finance, education, highways, conservation, and agriculture—and authorizes the general assembly to establish up to five more. The governor submits the proposed budget to the legislature and may veto legislation, including items in appropriation bills, subject to possible overriding action by a two-thirds vote of the elected members of each house.

The judicial system is headed by the supreme court, which has seven justices elected for 12 years. There are also courts of appeal, each with three judges; circuit courts, each with at least one judge, elected for six years; a probate court for each county with a judge elected for four years; a magistrate court for each county with a varying number of judges elected for four years; and the St. Louis courts of criminal correction, courts of common pleas, and municipal corporation courts.

The state is divided into 114 counties. Any county with a population of more than 85,000 may draft a charter for its own government. The constitution provides that the general assembly may classify counties into not more than four groups and may provide alternative forms of government for the counties of any particular class. Municipal home rule has been extended to permit cities with a population of 10,000 or more to frame and adopt their own charters. Missouri is represented in Congress by two senators and 11 representatives.

HISTORY

Exploration and Settlement. The territory embraced in the state of Missouri formed a part of Louisiana, the extensive region in the Mississippi Valley acquired by France as a result of the exploration of Jacques Marquette, Louis Jolliet, Robert Cavelier de La Salle, and others.

In 1705 a party of French explorers ascended the Missouri River to the site of modern Kansas City, and later an expedition explored the Ozark country for 100 miles into the interior. The first white settlement was the mission of St. Francis Xavier established in 1703. Exploration of the territory had as its object not the conversion of the Indians, however, but the location of mineral resources. The French searched for silver but they found lead, which they decided to exploit. Early settlements were at Mine La Motte in 1714, Sainte Genevieve about 1735, and at St. Louis in 1764—the latter early becoming an important fur trading post.

Louisiana was ceded by France to Spain by the Treaty of Fontainebleau in 1762 but was returned to France in 1800. Immigration from the Northwest Territory to St. Louis was considerable, as was also the immigration from south of the Ohio, owing largely to the Ordinance of 1787, which excluded slavery from the region north of the Ohio and east of the Mississippi. In 1799 Daniel Boone moved from Kentucky into Missouri and participated in the pioneer development of the state. At the time of the Louisiana Purchase in 1803, there were upward of 9,000 settlers in the region. French influence was still dominant, but was soon submerged by the tide of American immigrants.

Territory and State. In 1804 the territory acquired under the Louisiana Purchase was divided along 33°N lat. The southern part was constituted the Territory of Orleans and the northern part the Territory of Louisiana, which was organized as Missouri Territory in 1812. Heavy immigration during the next two decades swelled the population from 10,800 in 1810 to 140,000 in 1830. The principal occupations of the time were mining, fur trading, and agriculture.

The application of the Territory in 1818, to be admitted into the Union as a state, was the subject of a series of heated debates in Congress. The Missouri Compromise, approved Mar. 6, 1820, provided for the admission of Missouri as a slave state. A constitution was drafted by a convention in June, 1820, but when Missouri submitted this constitution to Congress it was found to contain a paragraph requiring the legislature to pass laws prohibiting the migration of free Negroes into the state. After another protracted debate, Congress approved the constitution on Mar. 2, 1821, with the proviso that the obnoxious paragraph be left inoperative. Missouri became a state on Aug. 10, 1821. In 1837 the six counties in the northwestern part of the state were added under the Platte Purchase. See MISSOURI COMPROMISE.

The period from 1820 to the Civil War was marked by rapid settlement and great increase in wealth and social unity. Immigrants of Mormon faith arrived in great numbers, prepared to make Independence the site of a New Jerusalem. Social disturbances led to the expulsion of the Mormons from Jackson County. They settled in Caldwell and Daviess counties, where animosity grew, and the Mormons were driven from the state in 1839. See MORMONS.

The Slavery Question and the Civil War. The extreme position taken by the Abolitionists intensified the proslavery feeling in Missouri, and led to

MISSOURI

Highlights of History

ANHEUSER-BUSCH
In 1764 Pierre Laclède built a trading post at St. Louis, and in 1765 the town became the capital of Upper Louisiana.

GEORGE DORRILL
Ste. Genevieve, settled by Creoles from Illinois, became the first permanent settlement in Missouri.

GEORGE DORRILL
The old Rock House in St. Louis was constructed in 1818 as a warehouse to accommodate the growth of the fur trade.

MISSOURI PACIFIC R.R.
"Pacific No. 3," the first locomotive to run west of the Mississippi River, arrived at St. Louis in 1852.

MISSOURI PACIFIC R.R.
The railroad reached Tipton, Mo., by 1858. Passengers and mail transferred there to the Overland Mail stagecoach.

The Louisiana Purchase Exposition at St. Louis in 1904 observed the centennial of the territory's acquisition from France.
MISSOURI HIST. SOC.

agitation for measures favoring the extension of slavery. The Jackson Resolutions, adopted by the legislature in 1849, declared that authority to regulate slavery in the territories belonged not to Congress but to the settlers in the territories. In the years preceding the admission of Kansas into the Union the rougher element among the extreme proslavery people in Missouri played a disgraceful role by their efforts to make Kansas a slave state.

The election of 1860 resulted in the choice of proslavery officers, but a convention called to consider the relation of the state to the Union voted against secession in 1861. The governor refused to accede to Pres. Abraham Lincoln's call for troops, and instead summoned the militia to arms in opposition to Union troops under Gen. Nathaniel Lyon. The governor and legislature were forced to flee and a spirited military campaign ensued. The first important engagement, the Battle of Wilson's Creek, August, 1861, resulted in defeat of the Union forces. The convention established a provisional pro-Union government and supporting Union troops drove the principal Confederate force from the state after the Battle of Pea Ridge, March, 1862. Missouri was saved to the Union, but the large population with Southern sympathies was a cause of constant and anxious vigilance throughout the war. See Civil War, American.

Reorganization of the state government was completed before the close of the war. In 1865 a convention drafted a new constitution, providing for the immediate emancipation of slaves, imposing political disability upon those who had actively engaged in hostilities against the Union, and exacting oaths of loyalty from all office holders and professional men. Most of these exactions were removed in 1871, and four years later the third constitution was adopted. Succeeding years witnessed a great advance in material wealth and prosperity, an immense development of agricultural, mining, and manufacturing resources, and marked progress in the provision of education facilities.

Twentieth Century. During the twentieth century the economy of Missouri underwent considerable expansion with the introduction of new industries and the growth of urban life. Transportation kept pace with growing production; the railroads were extended and highway networks were authorized in 1921 and 1928. Air service was pioneered in Missouri, beginning in 1920 with the establishment of the St. Louis–Chicago run.

State legislation during this period reflected the problems inherent in growth and change. In industrial legislation much was accomplished during the Joseph Wingate Folk administration of 1904–08; antilobby, public utility, child labor, antitrust, and factory inspection laws were passed. In 1908 the Standard Oil Company was convicted of violating the antitrust laws and expelled. A contested state tax on the capital, surplus, and undivided profits of national banks voted in 1923 was upheld by the state supreme court in 1927.

In the interests of good government a statewide primary law was passed in 1904, and a law was enacted in 1925 prohibiting public officers from appointing relatives to render services to the state; in 1939 the Kansas City Police Department passed under state control as a result of the exposure of the Pendergast political machine (see Pendergast, Thomas Joseph). Constitutional reform was attempted in 1921, when nine amendments were passed, and again in 1922–23 when a convention was called. The governmental problems raised by World War II, however, rendered reform imperative, and in 1945 the constitution was completely rewritten.

Bibliography

General: C. H. McClure and M. Potter, *Missouri: Its Geography, History and Government* (1940); F. Grierson, *Valley of Shadows* (1948); M. K. Morgan, *New Stars* (1949); N. P. Gist and others, eds., *Missouri: Its Resources, People, and Institutions* (1950); H. C. Hart, *Dark Missouri* (1957).

History: W. Williams and L. C. Shoemaker, *Missouri, Mother of the West* (5 vols. 1930); A. P. Nasatir, ed., *Before Lewis and Clark* (2 vols. 1952); E. M. Violette, *History of Missouri* (ed. 1955); D. P. Stockwell, *Land of the Oldest Hills* (1957).

Politics and Economics: E. A. Collins and A. F. Elsea, *Missouri: Its People and Its Progress* (1945); J. N. Primm, *Economic Policy in the Development of a Western State: Missouri, 1820–1860* (1954); M. E. Ridgeway, *Missouri Basin's Pick-Sloan Plan* (1955); R. F. Karsch, *Missouri Citizen* (1956).

Geography: O. E. Rayburn, *Ozark Country* (1941); Federal Writers' Program, *Missouri* (ed. 1954); R. N. Saveland, *Geography of Missouri* (1954); E. A. Collins and F. E. Snider, *Missouri: Midland State* (1955); W. A. Browne, *Missouri Geography* (ed. 1957).

MISSOURI, UNIVERSITY OF, a coeducational state-controlled institution of higher learning located at Columbia. The Missiouri School of Mines and Metallurgy, which is a branch of the university, is at Rolla. The school was created in 1839 by legislative act, with instruction first offered in 1841.

Divisions of the university include colleges and schools of agriculture (1870), arts and science (1841), business and public administration (1914), education (1868), engineering (1877), graduate study (1910), journalism (1908), law (1872), medicine (1845), mines and metallurgy (1870), and veterinary medicine (1949).

Distinctive educational programs include a university-owned TV station offering students experience in that field and a daily newspaper conducted by the school of journalism. Special library collections include the State Historical Society Library and Western manuscripts. See Colleges and Universities.

MISSOURI COMPROMISE, the legislation in 1820 providing for the admission of Missouri as a state of the Union and attempting to settle the controversies over slavery. In 1819, with the admission of Alabama, there were 11 free and 11 slave states, with equal representation in the U.S. Senate. The maintenance of this equality seemed important, as the northern states grew in population and as hostility to slavery became stronger.

The inhabitants of Missouri Territory, the portion of the Louisiana Purchase centered on St. Louis, applied for admission as a state in 1818. When the bill enabling them to write a constitution was before the House of Representatives, James Tallmadge of New York offered an amendment prohibiting the further introduction of slavery into Missouri and providing that children subsequently born of slave parents should become free at the age of 25. The amendment and the enabling act passed the House, but failed in the Senate.

The proposal was the subject of public discussion during 1819 and considerable alarm was aroused by the bitterness displayed over slavery. When the next Congress met in December, 1819, it received a petition for admission from Maine, which had separated from Massachusetts. After considerable debate, bills were adopted for the admission of Missouri and Maine as slave and free states respectively, with the additional provision, proposed in the Senate by Sen. Jesse B. Thomas of Illinois, that slavery be prohibited in the Louisiana Purchase territory north of 36°30′, the southern boundary of Missouri—Missouri itself excepted. For the successful passage of these bills, Henry Clay, then speaker of the House, was given much credit and won a reputation as compromiser and peacemaker. President James Monroe signed on Mar. 3, 1820, the act for the admission of Maine and on March 6 the act enabling Missouri to submit a constitution.

Further difficulties arose when the constitution of Missouri was submitted. As drafted, the constitution enjoined on the state legislature, passage of a bill to prevent free Negroes and mulattoes from entering and settling in Missouri. Northerners objected to this as violating the rights of free Negroes and the constitutional requirement that each state respect the rights of citizens of the other states. Southerners defended the right of the state to fix such a clause in its constitution. Again under the influence of Clay, a second Missouri Compromise was adopted; the resolution admitting Missouri was passed Mar. 2, 1821, with the stipulation that Missouri was to agree that nothing in her constitution should be interpreted to abridge the privileges and immunities of citizens of the United States. The Missouri legislature accepted the stipulation, and admission was formally proclaimed on Aug. 10, 1821.

The controversy alarmed many Americans; Thomas Jefferson wrote that it came "like a fire bell in the night." The settlement was regarded as important not only for Missouri, but because it established a line between future free and slave territory. Together with the existing lines, the Mason-Dixon's line and the Ohio River, it divided all U.S. territory and, it was hoped, would end the possibility of controversy. The acquisition of Mexican territory in 1848 reopened the question. One suggestion for the new territories was the extension of the Missouri Compromise line of 36°30′ through the new land to the Pacific, but the proposal was not adopted. The Kansas-Nebraska Act of 1854, providing territorial government for portions of the Louisiana Purchase north of the line, explicitly repealed the Missouri Compromise, and the Dred Scott Decision in 1857 declared congressional prohibition of slavery in the territories unconstitutional.

BIBLIOG.–P. O. Ray, *Repeal of the Missouri Compromise* (1909); F. Shoemaker, *Missouri's Struggle for Statehood, 1804–1821* (1916); W. Plumer, *Missouri Compromises and Presidential Politics* (1926); G. Moore, *Missouri Controversy, 1819–1821* (1953).

MISSOURI PACIFIC RAILROAD, the first railroad constructed west of the Mississippi River, was organized in 1849 as the Pacific Railroad Company of Missouri. In 1876 it was reorganized and its property purchased by the Missouri Pacific Railway. The latter firm merged with the St. Louis, Iron Mountain and Southern Railway in 1917 to form the Missouri Pacific Railroad. The line was declared bankrupt in 1933 but was successfully reorganized in 1956. The Missouri Pacific Railroad derives most of its income from freight. Total revenues in 1957 approximated $300 million, of which about $260 million was derived from freight. The firm operated nearly 1,300 miles of track and the freight hauled consisted largely of minerals, grain, lumber, and refined petroleum. The Missouri Pacific is the sole or major stockholder of several small rail lines, truck freight companies, and the American Refrigerator Transit Company. Headquarters are in St. Louis, Mo.

MISSOURI RIVER, central United States, longest tributary of the Mississippi, formed by union of the Jefferson, Madison, and Gallatin rivers at Three Forks, Mont.; flows N and E through Montana, SE through North and South Dakota to form parts of the South Dakota–Nebraska, Nebraska–Iowa, Nebraska–Missouri, and Kansas–Missouri boundaries, then E through Missouri to join the Mississippi River 15 miles N of St. Louis. The Missouri is 2,465 miles long (2,713 miles with the Red Rock River), drains 529,000 square miles, and falls 3,628 feet between Three Forks and its mouth.

Physical Characteristics. The Missouri begins in the Rocky Mountains. It is known as the Big Muddy, from the large amount of sediment carried by the river. Sixteen miles downstream from Helena, Mont., the river enters the Gate of the Mountains, a gorge 6 miles long, 450 feet wide, and 1,200 feet deep that has been cut through the Big Belt Mountains. After leaving the canyon the Missouri flows 40 miles northwest before forming the Great Falls, cascades that were measured in 1805 by the Lewis and Clark

Location Map of the Missouri River

Expedition: Black Eagle, 26 feet; Colter, 6 feet; Rainbow, 47 feet; Crooked, 19 feet; Great Falls, 87 feet.

Eleven miles above the mouth of the Milk River is Fort Peck Dam, one of four large earth-filled dams on the Missouri—a multipurpose project for irrigation, flood control, power production, and navigation regulation. Near the Montana–North Dakota border the Yellowstone River joins the Missouri. Flowing east and then south across the plains of the Dakotas, the Missouri forms a reservoir behind Garrison Dam, 55 miles north of Bismarck, N.D. In South Dakota the Grand, Moreau, and Cheyenne rivers join the Missouri north of Oahe Dam, near Pierre. As the Missouri turns to the southeast the White River flows into the reservoir behind Fort Randall Dam, fourth of the large multipurpose dams, just before the Missouri turns east to form the South Dakota–Nebraska border. Midway between Fort Randall Dam and Gavins Point Dam—lowest of the main-stream dams, immediately west of Yankton, S.D.—the Niobrara River joins the Missouri.

The James, Vermillion, Big Sioux, and Little Sioux rivers, between Yankton and Omaha, Neb., are the first major tributaries to drain the land north and east of the Missouri in the Dakotas, southwestern Minnesota, and western Iowa. The Platte River, largest of the lower tributaries, drains the prairies of central and western Nebraska and the adjacent areas of Colorado and Wyoming. As the Missouri turns east at Kansas City it receives the Kansas River, which drains the prairies of northern Kansas and adjacent Nebraska and Colorado. In Missouri the rolling wooded area of the northern Ozarks is drained by the Osage and Gasconade rivers from the south, while the Grand and Chariton rivers enter the Missouri from the north before it joins the Mississippi.

The first bridge across the Missouri was completed in 1869 at Kansas City. The Omaha–Council Bluffs Bridge, completed in 1873, was the last link in the first transcontinental rail route. In 1878 at Glasgow, Mo., Gen. William Smith completed the world's first all-steel railroad bridge.

History. The mouth of the Missouri was first sighted by Louis Jolliet and Jacques Marquette in 1673. In the following decades French traders began to ascend the Missouri in search of furs, and by 1705 had reached the site of Kansas City. They gradually pushed farther up the river. Pierre de La Vérendrye is believed to have been the first to explore the upper Missouri; his expedition in 1738 was made overland from the Lake Superior region to the Mandan Indian villages not far from the site of Minot, N.D. Other French expeditions followed, hoping to reach the "western sea" by way of the Missouri. In 1762 the region west of the Mississippi was transferred to Spain. Two years later St. Louis was founded and became a focal point for most later expeditions up the Missouri. Immediately after the Louisiana Purchase, 1803, the Lewis and Clark Expedition on its way to the Pacific Northwest followed the Missouri to its source. The first steamboat to ascend the river was the *Independence* in 1819. The *Yellowstone* reached Fort Union at the mouth of the Yellowstone in 1832, and the *Chippewa* and the *Key West* reached Fort Benton in 1860. Traffic on the lower Missouri grew rapidly before 1860; Glasgow, Mo., recorded 312 steamboat arrivals in 1841. In 1858 about 60 regular packets docked at Kansas City in addition to almost 40 transient craft. After the Civil War, however, the construction of western railroads brought about a decline in river trade although the boats continued to play an important role in the Fort Benton trade until 1869.

A great political controversy raged around the so-called Missouri Valley Authority, proposed by Pres. Franklin D. Roosevelt and modeled after the Tennessee Valley Authority. Following the floods of 1943 and 1944, which caused damages estimated at $100 million, President Roosevelt recommended creation of the MVA; his plan was pigeonholed by Congress although there was general agreement that something had to be done to tame and harness the Missouri. Action was delayed by differences between the Bureau of Reclamation, interested in the possibilities of irrigation in the upper basin area, and the U.S. Army Corps of Engineers, concerned with improvement of navigation and flood control in the main valley of the lower river. A compromise, the Pick-Sloan Plan, was passed as the Flood Control Act of 1944. The chance of floods on the lower Missouri was greatly reduced by the completion of Fort Peck (1938), Garrison (1954), Fort Randall (1954), Canyon Ferry (1954), and Gavins Point (1955) dams on the main stream. See DAM, Uses of Dams.

BIBLIOG.–E. Harris, *Up the Missouri with Audubon* (1952); A. P. Nasatir, ed., *Before Lewis and Clark* (2 vols. 1952); M. Lewis and W. Clark, *Journals of Lewis and Clark* (ed. 1953); M. E. Ridgeway, *Missouri Basin's Pick-Sloan Plan* (1955); H. C. Hart, *Dark Missouri* (1957).

MISSOURI VALLEY AUTHORITY. See MISSOURI RIVER, *History*.

MISTASSINI, LAKE, Canada, SW central Québec, near the watershed that separates the waters flowing into the St. Lawrence River from those emptying into Hudson Bay. Lake Mistassini has a maximum length and width of 100 and 20 miles respectively and joins James Bay through its outlet, the Rupert River.

MISTI. See EL MISTI.

MISTINGUETT, real name probably Jeanne Bourgeois, 1874–1956, French entertainer, was born near Paris. She first appeared at the Folies-Dramatiques in Paris, 1907, and two years later became the dancing partner of Maurice Chevalier at the Folies-Bergère. She achieved international fame during World War I when she became a favorite entertainer with the troops. Mistinguett appeared in several motion pictures, including *Rigolboche, le film de Paris* (1938).

MISTLETOE, a woody parasitic shrub of the mistletoe family, *Loranthaceae*. Mistletoe has thick conspicuous leaves and small yellow flowers. The fruit is a shiny white berry that has only one seed and contains a sticky pulp. Birds disseminate the seeds as they try to clean the gluey material from their bills by wiping them on the tree branches. Many kinds of deciduous trees are parasitized by mistletoe, which retards the growth of the host. The green parasite is especially noticeable after the leaves have fallen from the host tree; the growth may then be seen hanging in large bunches from the tree. Control is effected by pruning the mistletoe or by pruning the damaged areas of the tree. There are more than 500 species of mistletoe. The common Old World species, *Viscum album*, has often been mentioned in literature. The druids, a group of ancient priests, believed the mistletoe to be sacred. The popular New World species, *Phoradendron flavescens*, is sold in the United States as a Christmas decoration. See DRUID; PARASITE.

MISTRAL, FRÉDÉRIC, 1830–1914, Nobel prize-winning Provencal poet, was born in Maillane, Bouches-du Rhône. Together with Joseph Roumanille he was a prominent founder of the *Félibrige* organization that re-established Provençal as a literary language. He eventually became leader of the movement and was recognized as its greatest artist. He published a modern Provençal dictionary and several long poems, notably *Mirèio* (1859), a rustic epic that is a rich source of Provençal customs and legends. His best poems, *Mirèio*, *Calendau* (1867), *Lis Isclo d'Or* (1876), and *La Rèino Jano* (1890), are characterized by tropical sensuousness of language and imagery and by a nostalgia for the prestige of medieval Provence. In 1904 he shared the Nobel prize for literature with José Echegaray and gave his portion to purchase an old palace at Arles to house a Provençal museum.

MISTRAL, GABRIELA, pseudonym of Lucila Godoy y Alcayaga, 1889–1957, Nobel prize-winning Chilean poet, who was born in Vicuña. She began teaching at the age of 15, directed various provincial schools, and in 1922 assisted in planning a new program for Mexico's rural schools. From 1933 she was in the Chilean consular service and held posts in Madrid, Lisbon, Brazil, Nice, and Los Angeles. She earlier won recognition as a poet, and in 1914 her *Sonetos de la muerte* won first prize in a Santiago poetry contest. Her poetry, collected in *Desolación* (1922), *Ternura* (1924), and *Tala* (1938), deals chiefly with simple themes such as childhood and motherhood, and has a strong religious sentiment and an intense lyricism. Long recognized as one of Chile's greatest poets, she was awarded the Nobel prize for literature in 1945.

MISTRAL, a violent north wind that blows from the cold, snow-covered plateau of central France down the valley of the Rhone to the northwestern Mediterranean coast, particularly the Gulf of Lions. The accompanying weather conditions are commonly clear skies and sunshine. This cold, dry wind owes its origin to the simultaneous presence of a low atmospheric pressure in the Gulf of Lions or Genoa and a high-pressure area in the north. The unseasonable cold that sometimes prevails on the Riviera is the result of this wind.

MISURATA, town, NW Libya, Tripolitania Province; on Cape Misurata, on the Mediterranean Sea, at the west entrance to the Gulf of Sidra; 118 miles ESE of Tripoli, with which it is connected by coastal highway. Misurata is a commercial center with manufactures of carpets and mats. Its port, Misurata Marina, lies to the east. Pop. (1954) 5,000.

MITCHAM, town, Australia, S South Australia State, 5 miles S of Adelaide. Mitcham is primarily an agricultural trade center. Pop. (1954) 33,783.

MITCHAM, municipal borough, SE England, Surrey County; 7 miles SSW of London, of which it is a residential suburb. It is noted for cultivation of aromatic herbs, especially lavender, which are used in the manufacture of perfumes. Mitcham was the home of the poet John Donne in the seventeenth century. Pop. (1951) 67,273.

MITCHEL, JOHN, 1815–75, Irish revolutionist, was born in Camnish, Londonderry, and was graduated from Trinity College, Dublin, in 1834. In 1845 he became assistant editor of *The Nation*, and in 1848 started a weekly paper, the *United Irishman*, as an organ of the Young Ireland party. Mitchel was tried for sedition, sentenced to 14 years transportation, and sent to Van Diemen's Land (Tasmania). He escaped in 1853 and settled in the United States, publishing in New York his *Jail Journal, or Five Years in British Prisons* (1854). During the Civil War he edited the Richmond (Va.) *Enquirer* as a partisan of the Confederacy. Returning to Ireland in 1875, Mitchel was elected to parliament but was declared ineligible; he was re-elected but died shortly afterward. He published *Life of Hugh O'Neil, Prince of Ulster* (1845), and *History of Ireland from the Treaty of Limerick* (1868).

MITCHELL, DONALD GRANT, 1822–1908, U.S. writer, was born in Norwich, Conn., and educated at Yale University. His first books, *Fresh Gleanings* (1847) and *The Battle Summer* (1850), were the fruit of two trips to Europe, the latter volume containing an account of Paris during the 1848 Revolution. *The Lorgnette, or Studies of the Town, by an Opera Goer* (1850), a series of mildly satiric sketches, was followed by his most popular book, *Reveries of a Bachelor* (1850), a collection of musing and wistful essays. *Dream Life* (1851) was written in the same vein. He was consul in Venice, 1853–54, then settled on a farm near New Haven, Conn. *My Farm of Edgewood* (1863), *Wet Days at Edgewood* (1865), and *Rural Studies* (1867) give his impressions of country life. He also wrote *Fudge Doings* (2 vols. 1855), a satire on New York society; *Dr. Johns* (1866), a novel about life in a small New England town; and two collections of essays on English and American literature, *English Lands, Letters and Kings* (4 vols. 1889–97) and *American Lands and Letters* (2 vols. 1897–99). Most of Mitchell's earlier works were written under the name Ik Marvel, originally a misprint for J. K. Marvel.

MITCHELL, JOHN, 1870–1919, U.S. labor leader, was born in Braidwood, Ill., and at the age of 12 went to work in coal mines in Illinois. He joined the Knights of Labor, 1885, and became one of the first members of the United Mine Workers of America, 1890. He served as secretary and treasurer of a union subdistrict, 1894–97, became a member of the state executive board, and was vice-president of the UMWA, 1898, and president, 1899–1908. He organized strikes of the anthracite miners, 1900–02, and obtained for them shorter hours and better wages, at the same time averting a strike of the bituminous miners. In 1914 Mitchell became a member of the Workmen's Compensation Commission of New York State, and was chairman of the industrial commission of the state, 1915–19. He wrote *Organized Labor, Its Problems, Purposes, and Ideals* (1903) and *The Wage Earner and His Problems* (1913).

MITCHELL, MARGARET, married name Mrs. John R. Marsh, 1900–49, U.S. author, was born in Atlanta, Ga. She was a feature writer and reporter for the Atlanta *Journal*, 1922–26. After devoting 10 years of research and writing to it, she published her only novel, *Gone with the Wind* (1936), story of a Georgia family during the Civil War and Reconstruction. The novel was awarded the 1937 Pulitzer prize and was made into a motion picture in 1939.

MITCHELL, MARIA, 1818–89, U.S. astronomer, was born on the island of Nantucket. She became interested in astronomy at an early age, studying and working with her father. She studied especially the sun, Jupiter, and Saturn, and in 1847 her discovery of a telescopic comet won her a gold medal from King Frederick VI of Denmark. In 1865 she was appointed professor of astronomy at Vassar College and director of the Vassar Observatory. She was the first woman to be elected to the American Academy of Arts and Sciences, and in 1922 was elected to the Hall of Fame.

MITCHELL, SILAS WEIR, 1829–1914, U.S. physician, poet, and novelist, was born in Philadelphia, was graduated from Jefferson Medical College, 1850, and after further study in France, practiced in Philadelphia. Mitchell was noted for his research on physiology, toxicology, pharmacology, and neurology. He wrote *Roland Blake* (1886), *A Psalm of Deaths, and Other Poems* (1890), the Revolutionary War novel *Hugh Wynne, Free Quaker* (1898), *Constance Trescott* (1905), and *Westways* (1913).

MITCHELL, WILLIAM DE WITT, 1874–1955, U.S. lawyer, was born in Winona, Minn. He was U.S. solicitor general under Pres. Calvin Coolidge, 1925–29, and was attorney general in Pres. Herbert Hoover's cabinet, 1929–33. He became chairman of the U.S. Supreme Court's Committee on Federal Rules of Procedure, 1935, and was chief counsel of the congressional committee that investigated the Pearl Harbor disaster of 1941.

MITCHELL, WILLIAM LENDRUM, called Billy, 1879–1936, U.S. Army officer, was born in Nice, France, and reared in Milwaukee, Wis. After studying at Racine College and George Washington University, he entered the Army as a private, 1898, and advanced to the rank of brigadier general, 1920. He served in the Spanish-American War, in the Philippines campaign, on the Mexican border, and after the United States entered World War I he commanded the air branch of the American Expeditionary Forces, 1917–18. He headed U.S. Army of Occupation Air Forces in Germany, 1918–20, and in 1920 became U.S. chief of air service. Mitchell, the author of *Our Air Force* (1921), *Winged Defense* (1925), and *Skyways* (1930), believed that future wars would be settled by air power and that the United States needed a strong permanent air force. In spite of a demonstration of the ability of airplanes to sink battleships, Mitchell's recommendations for an independent air force and a unified department of defense were little heeded in his own day. In 1925 he was court-martialed, suspended from the army, and reduced to the rank of colonel for criticizing government management of aviation. The importance of his beliefs was tardily recognized in World War II, and in 1946 Congress voted him a posthumous medal "in recognition of his outstanding pioneer service and foresight in the field of American military aviation." In 1947 he was posthumously granted a major general's commission. In 1958 Sec. of Defense Neil McElroy declined to reverse Mitchell's court-martial conviction on the grounds that although Mitchell had clearly been right about air power and his detractors wrong, he had been insubordinate in criticizing his superiors.

MITCHELL, city, SE South Dakota, seat of Davison County; on Firesteel Creek, the North Western and the Milwaukee railroads, and U.S. highway 16; 66 miles WNW of Sioux Falls. Mitchell, an important trade center and shipping point for livestock and grain, has meat- and poultry-processing industries and butter and cheese manufacturing. It is the site of Dakota Wesleyan University (1885) and the Corn Palace, in which a six-day harvest festival has been held annually since 1892. Founded in 1879, Mitchell was incorporated in 1883. Pop. (1960) 12,555.

MITCHELL, MOUNT, W North Carolina, Yancey County; in the Black Mountains; 22 miles NE of Asheville. With an elevation of 6,684 feet, Mount Mitchell is the highest point in the United States east of the Mississippi River. Its summit and a portion of its slopes constitute Mount Mitchell State Park.

MITCHILL, SAMUEL LATHAM, 1764–1831, U.S. scientist, was born in North Hempstead, N.Y., and studied at the University of Edinburgh. He served as professor of natural history, chemistry, and agriculture at Columbia College, 1792–1801, was a founder of the New York *Medical Repository*, and was its editor, 1797–1820. Mitchill served in the House of Representatives, 1801–04, 1810–13, and in the U.S. Senate, 1804–09. He taught at the New York College of Physicians and Surgeons, 1807–26.

MITE, a minute insect-like animal belonging to the order Acarina of the class Arachnida. The thick oval body of the mite is covered with sensory hairs or scales and usually consists of two parts: an unsegmented cephalothorax and an abdomen. There are six pairs of appendages: two pairs comprise mouth parts and the remaining four pairs are legs. The legs usually have five joints and each leg terminates in two claws. Most species of the order Acarina lay eggs, from which hatch six-legged young known as larvae. The larvae molt, become eight-legged nymphs, and mature; life cycles vary widely.

About half of the known species are parasitic and many of them infest man. The itch mite, *Sarcoptes scabiei*, causes human itch or scabies, and many varieties of this mite attack man and domestic animals. The itch mite is white and about 0.01 inch long. The female burrows into the skin and causes severe irritation. The larva of the chigger or harvest mite, *Eutrombicula alfreddugesi*, is a bloodsucker and is a carrier of rickettsial diseases such as typhus. A mangelike infection of the hair follicles and sebaceous glands of man and domestic animals frequently results from infestation by the hair follicle mite, *Demodex*. Chemicals are used to treat infestation of man and animals. Treatment must often be repeated to be effective.

Many mites are parasitic on plants, sucking the juices from leaves and flower buds. Perhaps the most common of these is the red spider, *Tetranychus telarius*, which infests shrubs, trees, and flowers. The European red mite, *Panonychus ulmi*, attacks fruit trees. Plant mites may be controlled by spraying or dusting with substances such as rotenone, pyrethrum, and sulfur. See ARACHNIDA; CHIGGER; GALL.

BIBLIOG.–T. E. Hughes, *Mites or the Acari* (1959); J. A Naegele, ed., *Advances In Acarology* (2 vols., 1963, 1965).

MITFORD, MARY RUSSELL, 1787–1855, English author, born in Alresford, Hampshire. At the age of 10 she won £20,000 in a lottery, but her father squandered it. She began to write to support him, and from 1819 her sketches entitled *Our Village* appeared in *The Lady's Magazine;* they were reprinted in five volumes (1824–32). Among her other works are four tragedies, *Julian* (1823), *Foscari* (1826), *Rienzi* (1828), and *Charles I* (1834); a novel, *Belford Regis* (1835); *Recollections of a Literary Life* (1852); and *Atherton and Other Tales* (1854).

MITHRA, or Mithras (in the Latin and the Greek), the Indo-Iranian god of light, heat, and fertility. He was at first a minor god in the Zoroastrian religion, but by the fifth century B.C. he was recognized as the chief Persian god.

Mithraism, the cult of Mithra, had its origin at the time when the Indians and the Persians were one people. Adopting certain practices of Chaldean astrology, the worship of Marduk, and the Phrygian cult of Attis and Cybele, Mithraism spread rapidly. By its extension into Mesopotamia and Armenia, Mithraism became a world religion and in the second century A.D. was one of the strongest in the Roman Empire. It had been carried into the West after Roman armies invaded Asia Minor about 133 B.C. The growth of Mithraism was such that it ceased to be a threat to Christianity only after the execution of drastic laws against it during the reign of Theodosius I, about 385.

The most powerful and important god in Mithraism was Infinite Time, who was responsible for the creation of Heaven and Earth, who in turn gave birth to Ocean. Infinite Time also brought forth Incarnate Evil, called Pluto, who carried on wars against Heaven with his army, Darkness. This army of evil spirits brought afflictions on insignificant man, who had to be content with worshiping the four elements of Fire, Earth, Air, and Water. The central myth of this religion was the killing of a bull by Mithra, who became known as the protector of man and the mediator between man and Infinite Time. He maintained his abode halfway between Heaven and Earth.

Followers of Mithraism believed in the immortality of the soul, eternal punishment for the wicked, and everlasting happiness for the good. Women were not permitted membership in Mithraism. Great stress was laid on high moral character, required of all Mithraites, and on brotherly charity. The highest of seven degrees of initiation into Mithraism was that of Father, the title bestowed on rulers of the cult whose leader lived in Rome. Those who had attained to the six lower degrees, disregarding any social distinction, called each other Brother. R. M. LEONARD

BIBLIOG.–Samuel Laeuchli, ed., *Mithraism in Ostia: Mystery Religion and Christianity In the Ancient Port of Rome* (1967); M. J. Vermaseren, *Mithras: The Secret God* (1963).

MITHRADATES, also Mithridates, or Mithradates VI Eupator, called the Great, 131?–63 B.C., king of Pontus in Asia Minor, born in Sinope. He was a man of extraordinary powers, both physical and mental, and was said to have spoken 25 languages. He became king at the age of 11, but little is known of the early part of his reign. About 114 B.C. he added to his dominions the kingdoms of Bosporus, Cappadocia, Paphlagonia, and Bithynia. Conflict with the kings of Bithynia instigated by the Romans led to the first Mithradatic War in 88 B.C. After seizing the Roman provinces in Asia Minor and causing 80,000 Italians to be massacred on one day, Mithradates sent a force into Greece; but his general, Archelaus, was defeated by Sulla at Chaeronea, and he himself was defeated in Asia by Fimbria. He made peace in 84. The second war, in 83 and 82, resulted from the aggressions of Murena, Sulla's lieutenant, who invaded Pontus and was defeated by Mithradates. The third war (74–63) grew out of Mithradates' attempt to regain Bithynia, which had been bequeathed to Rome. Lucullus overpowered Mithradates and expelled him from Pontus. Owing to the mutiny of Lucullus' soldiers, Mithradates recovered Pontus in 68. In 66 Pompey the Great defeated Mithradates, who took refuge in the Crimea and ultimately committed suicide.

MITO, city, on the E coast of Japan, central Honshu, Ibaraki Prefecture; a railroad junction on the Naka River; 60 miles NE of Tokyo. Mito is a major commercial center in an area where tobacco, grain, and livestock are raised and fishing is an important occupation. The city has food processing, flour milling, and cloth and paper industries. The suburbs draw tourists to their seaside resorts. The memorial hall in the city houses a statue of Emperor Meiji (1867–1912). In the seventeenth century Mito was the seat of the Tokugawa family. (For population, see Japan map in Atlas.)

MITOSIS, an organic process of division whereby cells increase their number, with the daughter cells receiving, quantitatively and qualitatively, the hereditary constitution possessed by the mother cell from which they arise. It is a process that occurs only in eucaryotic cells, that is, those whose hereditary apparatus is enclosed within a nuclear membrane. In its classical sense the term mitosis is equivalent to karyokinesis, or nuclear division, which together with cytokinesis, or division of the cytoplasm, constitutes the two major aspects of somatic cell (cells other than germ cells) division. Through common usage, however, mitosis has come to embrace the entire process of cell division; this usage is followed here.

Although the process of mitotic division is a continuous affair, it has been divided into five morphologically recognizable stages—interphase, prophase, metaphase, anaphase, and telophase—each of which is characterized by physical or chemical changes in the nucleus and/or cytoplasm.

The cell in interphase has a nebulous internal nuclear structure (except for the nucleoli and occasional clumped masses of chromatin), an intact nuclear membrane, and nuclear material that readily stains with basic dyes. When a cell in interphase is preparing to divide, the nucleus generally swells and the G_1 (G = gap) stage of interphase is initiated. The chemical events taking place in G_1 are not fully known, but they are clearly preparatory to the succeeding S (synthetic) stage during which the DNA (deoxyribonucleic acid) of the chromosomes is being replicated. Thymidine, labeled with a radioactive isotope, tritium, serves as an indicator of synthetic activity, since it is incorporated only into DNA; its presence can be detected by means of autoradiography at any later period of the cell cycle. The S period falls generally in the middle of interphase and occupies approximately one third of the entire cell cycle. It is completed in about 6 hours in human cells grown in tissue culture at 37°C and in about the same length of time in root-tip cells of the broad bean grown at 22°C. As a result of replication the DNA content of the nucleus is doubled and each chromosome, which was previously single, now consists of two longitudinal halves, or chromatids. A basic protein, histone, which is intimately associated with the DNA of the chromosome, is also synthesized during the S period. See DNA; PROTEIN.

The process of replication does not involve all chromosomes in the nucleus simultaneously. Some are replicated early in the period, some toward the end of the period. As a general rule, heterochromatin is replicated later in the period than is euchromatin. This is particularly evident in human cells where the Y chromosome in male cells and one of the X chromosomes in female cells are among the last of the 46 chromosomes to undergo replication. See CHROMOSOME;

The G_2 stage of interphase follows the period of synthesis and just precedes the initiation of prophase. The chemical events taking place in G_2 are not known, but the entire interphase is obviously a necessary preparation for the more dramatic and microscopically visible events to follow. Blockage of the S period, for example, causes a cessation of all the subsequent events.

Prophase is said to be initiated when the chromosomes become distinctly visible entities, each chromosome consisting of two longitudinal halves, or chromatids. Condensation of the chromosomes from the tenuous state in interphase to the increasingly more compact state seen in prophase is brought about by each chromosome being thrown into a series of coils or folds. In large chromosomes such as those found in amphibians, grasshoppers, and the plants *Trillium* and *Tradescantia*, the arrangement of coils is much the same as that found in a coiled door spring, but at lower levels of resolution the compaction may be in the form of coils of smaller dimensions, or of folds. For example, it is believed that DNA in the haploid set of chromosomes of the newt *Triturus* reaches a length of nearly 10 meters, but the length of the chromosomes at the end of prophase is only about 200μ (1μ [micron] = 0.001 mm [millimeter] = 10,000A [Angstrom units]). The ratio of these two lengths is about 50,000 to 1. A reciprocal change in diameter also occurs; the extended DNA, with its associated proteins, is about 40 A in diameter, the compacted chromosomes about 5μ; this ratio is about 1 to 1,000. The mechanism of compaction is not known, but it presumably begins at molecular levels and proceeds through several orders of folding or coiling. The result is the conversion of a long, extremely slender molecular structure to a compact one that is much more maneuverable within the limited confines of the cell.

During prophase the nucleoli can be seen to be attached to specific chromosomes at a specific region, the nucleolar organizer. In a human cell there are five pairs of chromosomes possessing nucleolar organizers; thus, a cell may have a total of ten nucleoli. However, nucleoli have a tendency to coalesce with each other, so that fewer than ten are more commonly seen in a late prophase cell. As prophase ends the nucleoli diminish in size, become detached from their respective chromosomes, and usually disappear by metaphase.

Metaphase is characterized by the absence of the nuclear membrane, by the appearance of a new cellular structure, the spindle, and by the congression, orientation, and attachment of the chromosomes on the spindle. Immediately prior to metaphase the centrioles, tiny paired structures found in the perinuclear cytoplasm of animal cells, divide and migrate to opposite sides of the nucleus. Through the action of the centrioles a single class of cytoplasmic proteins containing about 5 per-cent RNA is organized into a biacuminate spindle, with the centrioles positioned at its two poles. Other proteinaceous fibers not included in the spindle also radiate out from the centriolar region and form the astral rays seen in many animal cells.

Prior breakdown of the nuclear membrane during prophase releases the chromosomes into the cytoplasm and allows them to interact with the centrioles during spindle formation; additional fibers are formed which connect the chromosomes to the two poles. The chromosomes contact and attach to the fibers at the centromere, a special region of each chromosome concerned with movement during cell division. The half-spindle fibers, which in structure are really minute tubules, extend from the centromeres to the poles, and since each chromosome is connected to both poles the fibers orient the chromosomes at a point midway between the two poles.

Although animal cells possess centrioles that are intimately involved in spindle formation and chromosome orientation at metaphase, many plant species, especially the angiosperms, lack such a structure. However, they form a spindle that does not differ appreciably in appearance from those found in animal cells; the mechanism of spindle formation in these forms is unknown.

Anaphase is the stage of chromosome movement. Although the centromere of each chromosome replicates earlier along with the remainder of the DNA, functional separation does not occur until anaphase, when the two chromatids begin their migration to the opposite poles of the spindle. The spindle fibers connecting each centromere with the poles shorten, and it appears that anaphase movement is accomplished, at least in part, by a pulling action of the fibers as they shorten. In animal but not in plant cells the spindle tends to elongate in its mid-region, thus forcing the already separated chromatids farther apart. Termination of movement and of the anaphase stage occurs when the chromatids form densely clumped masses of chromatin at the two poles.

The position of the centromere in the chromosome determines its general shape and provides a means of classifying all chromosomes into several categories. When the centromere is centrally located, the chromosome at metaphase is divided into two arms of equal length (metacentric chromosomes); at anaphase, such a chromosome would move to the poles as a V-shaped structure. When located sub-terminally, the arms are of unequal length (submetacentric chromosomes) and movement at anaphase is as a J-shaped structure. When terminally located, the centromere does not divide the chromosome into identifiable arms (acrocentric chromosome) and movement is as a rod. Since the karyotypes of various species are useful in a cytotaxonomic sense, each chromosome of the haploid set can be characterized by its metaphase length, position of the centromere, and the ratio of the length of one arm to the other, thus providing a basic set of information from which variations can be determined.

During telophase, nuclei form at the polar regions and fragments of the endoplasmic reticulum appear to contribute to the rapid formation of a nuclear membrane around the mass of chromatin. The chromosomes relax their tightly compacted structure and assume the diffuse state characteristic of interphase as the nucleus swells and enlarges, and the nucleoli appear at specific regions of the chromosomes. In animal cells the partitioning of the cytoplasm is accomplished by a process of furrowing; an indentation, encircling the cell and caused by a change in the gel characteristics of the cytoplasm, appears midway between the two newly formed nuclei, and as it moves inward it cuts the mother cell into the two daughter cells. In plant cells the rigid cell walls prevent the formation of a furrow; instead a vesicular membrane, the cell plate, cuts the cell in halves. This membrane forms first within the spindle and from membranes and fragments of vesicles derived from the Golgi complex. The cell plate then grows outward as an ever-enlarging circle until it meets the cell wall. Subsequently it becomes the middle lamella shared by adjoining cells.

Viewed within the framework of inheritance, mitosis can in its entirety be considered a conservative process; it generates a succession of genetically identical individuals; in a multicellular organism, mitosis provides a mass of similar cells that can then be acted upon by the processes of differentiation to bring about the diversity of cells needed for the variety of functions carried out by the body. Meiosis, by comparison, is the primary source of genetic diversity injected into a population and subsequently acted upon by the processes of natural selection. See MEIOSIS. For illustration, see transvision insert in the article CELL. CARL P. SWANSON

BIBLIOG.–Ralph Alston, *Cellular Continuity and Development* (1967); L. Goldstein, ed., *Control of Nuclear Activity* (1967); Carl P. Swanson, *Cytogenetics* (1967); George Wilson, *Cell Replication* (1966).

MITRE, BARTOLOME, 1821–1906, Argentine political leader and writer, born in Buenos Aires. Fleeing the dictatorship of Juan Manuel de Rosas, he settled in Montevideo, Uruguay, in 1836. There he studied at a military academy (1836–37). He served in the Uruguayan army (1838–46) and in the Bolivian army (1847), and lived for a time in Chile, where he did editorial work for newspapers in Valparaiso and Santiago. He joined the movement against Rosas in Argentina in 1851, and as chief of artillery assisted at Rosas' defeat at the Battle of Monte Caseros in 1852. Mitre founded the influential journal *La Nación* in 1852, and became a member of the Buenos Aires legislature and an ardent supporter of the independence of the state of Buenos Aires from the Argentine Confederation. After Buenos Aires became part of the Argentine republic, Mitre served as president of the republic (1862–68). He conducted the War of 1865 against Paraguay (with the aid of Brazil and Uruguay). As a member of the senate (1868–1906), he continued to take a leading part in Argentine political affairs. His works include *Historia de Belgrano y de la independencia argentina* (1858, 5th ed. 1902), *Historia de San Martín y de la emancipación sudamericana* (1888), and several books of essays and poems.

MITROPOULOS, DIMITRI, 1896–1960, U.S. orchestra conductor, born in Athens, Greece. He studied at the Athens Conservatory of Music and in Belgium and Germany. He went to the United States in 1936. He was conductor of the Minneapolis Symphony (1937–49), and in 1950 he became conductor of the New York Philharmonic, a post he held until 1958. Mitropoulos was especially renowned for his conducting of nineteenth- and twentieth-century music.

MITSCHER, MARC ANDREW, 1887–1947, U.S. naval officer, born in Hillsboro, Wis. He was graduated from the U.S. Naval Academy in 1910. Mitscher pioneered in naval aviation and was pilot on the Navy's first transatlantic flight, in 1919, from Newfoundland to the Azores. During World War II he commanded the aircraft carrier *Hornet* (1941–42), from which James H. Doolittle took off for the first bombing of Tokyo. In 1944 Mitscher took command of Task Force 58, which spearheaded the American advance across the central Pacific. In 1945 he was named deputy chief of naval air operations, and in 1946 became a full admiral and was made commander in chief of the Atlantic fleet.

MITSCHERLICH, EILHARD, 1794–1863, German chemist, born in Neuende, near Jever. He became a professor at the University of Berlin in 1821. Most noted for discovering the principle of isomorphism, Mitscherlich also did important research on benzene and its derivatives and on artificial minerals.

MIXTEC, one of a tribal group of American Indians in Mexico, living mostly in the state of Oaxaca and parts of the states of Guerrero and Puebla. The Mixtecs are generally considered as forming a distinct linguistic stock. They seem to have had an advanced culture before the arrival of the Toltecs in the Anahuac Plateau of central Mexico. About the tenth century they came to their present habitat in Oaxaca, displacing the Zapotecs. The following centuries were characterized mainly by their struggles against the Zapotecs and the Aztecs. They resisted the Spanish conquest in the sixteenth century, but were finally defeated by Pedro de Alvarado. There were 155,000 Mixtec-speaking individuals in Mexico in the 1960's.

BIBLIOG.–R. E. Longacre, *Proto-Mixtecan* (1957); P. J. C. Dark, *Mixtec Ethnohistory* (1958).

MIXTURE, a material that consists of at least two pure substances that retain their individual properties and whose proportions can be varied. Mixtures are classified according to uniformity of composition. Mixtures in which the particles of the different components can be distinguished from each other either with the naked eye or with the aid of a microscope are called heterogeneous (nonuniform)—for example, a coarse mixture of sugar and sand. Those in which the particles of the different components cannot be distinguished from each other, even with the aid of a microscope, are called homogeneous (uniform)—for example, a solution of sugar in water.

One way in which a mixture differs fundamentally from a compound is that in the former the proportions of the components may be varied, whereas in the latter the proportions are fixed. For example, in a solution of sugar in water, the proportions of sugar and water can be varied over a wide range, but in the compound water (H_2O), the material is always fixed at 12.5 per-cent hydrogen and 87.5 per-cent oxygen by weight.

Another fundamental difference between a compound and a mixture is that the components of a mixture retain their original properties and can be separated from each other by physical means, whereas the components of a compound do not retain their original properties and cannot be separated by physical means. For example, a mixture of iron filings and powdered sulfur can easily be separated into the original components by removing the iron filings by means of a magnet, leaving the unmagnetized sulfur particles behind. By way of contrast, in the compound iron sulfide, where the iron and sulfur are not merely mixed but are chemically combined, the iron does not retain its magnetism, and it cannot be removed in this manner.

Other differences in properties that aid in separating mixtures into the pure components are differences in particle size, utilized in the processes of sifting and filtration; differences in density, used to float light particles away and leave heavy particles behind, and also to separate gases from each other by the process of diffusion; differences in solubility, which permit various processes of extraction and crystallization; and differences in volatility, or boiling point, which make it possible to separate components by distillation or by simply evaporating off one component and leaving the other component behind.

MIYAZAKI, city, Japan, SE Kyushu, capital of Miyazaki Prefecture; on the Hyuga Sea and the Oyodo River; 75 miles SE of Kumamoto. Principal industries are the production of silk, chinaware, and decorative trays and the cultivation of subtropical plants. Miyazaki is the site of an archaeological museum, a feudal castle, and the great Shinto shrine Miyazaki-jinju, dedicated to Jimmu, the first emperor of Japan. (For population, see Japan map in Atlas.)

MIZAR, the bright, second magnitude star, also known as ζ Ursae Majoris, that lies at the handle of the Big Dipper. Actually Mizar is not a single star; a telescope easily resolves it into Mizar A, a second magnitude star, and Mizar B, a fourth magnitude star. A and B are about 14 seconds of arc apart and may have been the first double star to be discovered telescopically. The brighter of the pair is itself a spectroscopic binary—the first such star to be discovered. In some photographs of its spectrum ordinary single spectral lines appeared; in others each line seemed to have been split in two. This phenomenon could be explained if it was assumed that Mizar A really consists of two equally bright stars close together and rotating about each other; that if one star approaches while the other recedes, the spectral lines of the first are shifted slightly toward the violet and those of the second toward the red end of the spectrum so that double lines appear; and that when both are moving across the line of sight, no shift occurs and only a single line appears. Later it was learned that the two components of Mizar A revolve about each other in a period of 20.5 days, and that they are half as far from each other as Mercury is from the sun. Mizar B is also believed to be a spectroscopic binary.

Nearly 50 times the distance from Mizar A to Mizar B is a fainter, fourth magnitude star, Alcor, whose name means "the test," although, being about a third of a full moon's width away from Mizar, it is much too easily seen to be the test of acute vision that it has been reputed to be. Alcor also is a spectroscopic binary and both Alcor and Mizar are members of the great Ursa Major moving cluster. See CLUSTER; MULTIPLE STAR.

MIZPAH, any one of several towns in Palestine mentioned in the Bible. The most important was Mizpah of Benjamin, which was probably located north of Jerusalem, although its exact site is doubtful. In biblical times it served as a base against the Philistines and became the capital of Judah after the fall of Jerusalem. Other towns bearing this name were Mizpah of Gilead, Mizpah of Judah, and Mizpah of Moab, whose exact sites have not been definitely ascertained.

MLADA BOLESLAV, city, Czechoslovakia, N central Bohemia; 30 miles NE of Prague; 754 feet above sea level. The city is a railway junction on the Jizera River. Metalworking, food processing, and the manufacture of farm implements, automobiles, and chemicals are principal industries. Founded in 995, Mladá Boleslav became a center of the Bohemian Brethren. (For population, see Czechoslovakia map in Atlas.)

MNEMONICS, a general designation for various techniques and devices to aid the memory. The basic principle of mnemonics is the setting up of a mechanical scheme, which by association connects a series of dissociated ideas. A famous example of verbal mnemonics is the verse "Thirty days hath September, April, June, and November . . ."

MNEMOSYNE, in Greek mythology, the goddess of memory, a daughter of Uranus, and by Zeus the mother of the Muses.

MOA, an extinct, flightless bird that lived in New Zealand during the Pleistocene epoch. More than 20 species of moas comprised the family Dinornithidae. Superficially, moas resembled ostriches, but were related to the flightless kiwis of New Zealand. Moas were 3 to 11 feet high and had extremely powerful legs and large four-toed feet that were probably used in defense and in digging for roots. The head was small in proportion to the body, and the beak was short and broad. Many species were entirely wingless, others had vestigial wings, but all were unable to fly. The soft, downy feathers were similar to those found on flightless birds and appeared to be double, resembling those of the emu, a bird native to Australia.

MOAB, an ancient country east of the Dead Sea, corresponding to part of modern Jordan. It was a well watered plateau, producing grains, fruits, grapes, and cattle in abundance. According to the Bible it was originally settled by the gigantic Emim, who were later displaced by the Moabites, a people closely related to the Ammonites and the Israelites. The Bible says that the Moabites were the descendants of Lot by his daughters and contains numerous references to their relations with Israel and Judah. The Israelites were originally not allowed to intermarry with the Moabites, but later the rabbis permitted Israelite men to marry Moabite women (Ruth 1:22). Moab was forced by David to pay tribute to Israel, but revolted under the leadership of Mesha in the time of Ahab and reached its apogee probably about 700 B.C.

BIBLIOG.–A. H. Van Zyl, *The Moabites* (1960).

MOABITE STONE, an ancient memorial stone erected by King Mesha of Moab to commemorate the success of his rebellion against the Israelites about 850 B.C. The stone bears a long inscription in the language of the Moabites, which is closely related to Hebrew. The stone was unearthed at Dhiban, in modern Jordan, but was later broken. It was restored and placed in the Louvre.

MOBERLY, city, N central Missouri, Randolph County; 61 miles NNW of Jefferson City. Moberly has poultry-processing plants and manufactures of brake levers, flue expanders, fans, electrical cooking appliances, cheese, butter, dried eggs, shoes, and hosiery. It was settled in 1866 and incorporated in 1868. (For population, see Missouri map in Atlas.)

MOBILE, city, SW Alabama, seat of Mobile County; on the Mobile River and Mobile Bay of the Gulf of Mexico; approximately 160 miles SW of Montgomery. A port of entry and the only seaport in Alabama, Mobile has one of the largest and most complete systems of docks, loading facilities, and warehouses on the Gulf. It is one of the top ten Gulf ports in tonnage handled and a major U.S. port. Although there are some privately owned docks and terminals, most port facilities are part of the Alabama state docks, the first docking facilities in the United States to be completely owned and operated by a state. Conducting trade with many foreign ports, Mobile has an especially large South American trade. Its exports are cotton, lumber, coal, naval stores, steel, and grain, and its principal imports are nitrates, sugar, bananas, crude rubber, iron ore, and coconuts. Mobile has shipbuilding and woodworking industries and manufactures of cement, textiles and clothing, insulation materials, foundry products, newsprint, paper, canned goods, and chemicals.

Mobile is the site of Spring Hill College (1830), Brookley Air Force Base, numerous ante-bellum buildings, and Bienville Square Park. Annual events include the Mardi Gras, celebrated just before Lent; the Azalea Trail Festival, a flower-lined drive through the city, held in spring; and the Alabama Deep Sea Rodeo, climax to the fishing season held in midsummer. Spanning Mobile Bay is Cochran Bridge, and under the Mobile River is Bankhead Tunnel.

The original settlement of Mobile was founded by the French under Jean Baptiste Lemoyne, sieur de Bienville, in 1702 at Twenty-Seven Mile Bluff, some 27 miles north of Mobile. In 1710 the settlement was moved to its present site and served as capital of Louisiana until 1719. In 1763, by the Treaty of Paris, the city came under English domination. It was taken by Spain in 1780, captured by the Americans under Gen. James Wilkinson, and attributed to the Mississippi Territory in 1813. It was incorporated as a town in 1814 and as a city in 1819. In 1817 Mobile became part of the Alabama Territory which became a state two years later. During the Civil War, Union ships blockaded the port and in August, 1864, the Confederate fleet was defeated at the Battle of Mobile Bay. Mobile was not taken by Union forces until April, 1865. After the war the city regained its importance as a port. Pop. (1960) 202,779.

MOBILE BAY, inlet of the Gulf of Mexico, SW Alabama; maximum N-S and E-W distances 31 and 24 miles respectively. Including Bon Secours Bay in the southeast, Mobile Bay is crossed by the Gulf Intracoastal Waterway in the southern portion. A dredged channel extends south from the port of Mobile to the bay's entrance between Fort Morgan and Dauphin Island. The bay receives the Mobile River at Mobile. Formed by the confluence of the Alabama and Tombigbee rivers, the navigable Mobile River flows south for 5 miles and then separates into two channels, the Mobile and the Tensaw. These channels continue south for 25 miles and then empty into Mobile Bay a few miles apart.

Battle of Mobile Bay, a naval battle of the Civil War, was fought on Aug. 5, 1864, between a Union fleet of 7 sloops of war, 7 smaller wooden vessels, and 4 ironclad monitors, under Adm. David Farragut, and a Confederate fleet of 1 large ironclad ram, the *Tennessee*, and 3 gunboats under Adm. Franklin Buchanan. After the fall of Vicksburg (see VICKSBURG CAMPAIGN), Farragut determined to take Mobile from the Confederates to prevent its use as a port of entry for munitions and materials of war. The town lay at the head of the bay, 20 miles broad at its lower end but full of shallows. The town was defended by two forts that had been strengthened by the Confederates —Forts Morgan and Gaines; a line of piles in the ship channel of the bay; and a triple line of mines, then called torpedoes.

As Farragut advanced with his fleet in line ahead, Fort Morgan opened fire and soon the whole line was engaged. The Union ship *Tecumseh* went out of her course and, passing through the mine field, was blown up and sank almost immediately with the loss of 100 of her men. The leading ship, *Brooklyn*, then paused without warning, and for a moment it appeared as though the entire battle line would collide under the direct fire of the fort. Farragut ordered his flagship, the *Hartford*, to proceed with a command that was to become famous, "Damn the torpedoes! Captain Drayton, go ahead! Jouett, full speed!"

The *Hartford* reached the open water above the fort and engaged the Confederate vessels. The three Confederate gunboats were quickly eliminated and the remainder of the engagement was between the Union fleet and the Confederate ram *Tennessee*, which surrendered after a stubborn fight. A few days later the forts surrendered and the usefulness of Mobile as a Confederate supply base came to an end, although the city itself did not surrender for some time. See CIVIL WAR, AMERICAN, *Importance of the Navy*.

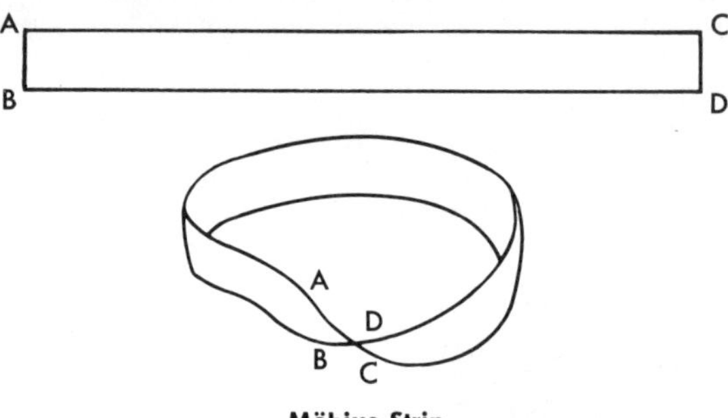

Möbius Strip

MÖBIUS STRIP, a figure that has only a single surface and can be constructed by giving a narrow rectangular sheet of paper a 180° twist and joining the ends together. In rectangle *ABDC*, after joining, *A* would lie on *D* and *B* would lie on *C*. A Möbius strip has some rather surprising properties. If a line is drawn down its center and extended until the starting point is reached, and if the strip is then cut so that it resumes its original flat rectangular shape, it is found that the line appears on both surfaces. If instead of being separated the strip is cut lengthwise along the line that has been drawn, the result is not the two separate Möbius strips that might be expected, but rather a single closed strip twice as long as the original strip. If a line is drawn down its center it is evident that this strip has two surfaces and is equivalent to a sheet twice the length and half the width of the original, which has been given a full 360° twist before joining. If the new strip is cut along the center line, two interlocked, twisted, two-surfaced rings result. The process can be continued with more and more complex interlockings appearing, but all new rings will have two surfaces. In general, a single surface can be obtained from a rectangular strip by twisting the strip through $360n + 180$ degrees, where n is zero or a whole number, and joining the edges in the manner indicated. See MATHEMATICS FOR RECREATION; TOPOLOGY.

MOBY DICK, a novel by Herman Melville (1819–91). First published in New York in 1851, the book has been variously titled *Moby Dick;* or *Moby Dick; or, The Whale;* or *Moby Dick; or, The White Whale;* and (in England) *The Whale. Moby Dick* was neglected during Melville's lifetime and for a time afterward —partly because of the preference of the public for Melville's more sensational South Sea romances *Typee* and *Omoo* and partly because the publisher's stock of the novel and the original plates were destroyed by fire in 1853. Raymond Weaver's biography of Melville, published in 1921, revealed the novelist as a genius of great power and originality and brought about a revival of interest in *Moby Dick*, which soon won acceptance as one of the world's great novels. The story, which deals with the voyage of a New Bedford whaler, the *Pequod*, in search of a white whale, was probably based on the legend of Mocha Dick, a white whale celebrated in the tall tales of whaling men of the period. Aside from the final chapters, which describe a titanic struggle between the whale and its pursuers, the book is taken up with character portraits of the captain, Ahab, and his crew and with minutely detailed descriptions of life aboard a whaler. The monomaniacal Captain

Ahab, who is determined to kill the whale that previously had destroyed one of his legs, is variously regarded as representing man's demoniac pursuit of an evil chimera; man's heroic struggle with evil, as corporealized in Moby Dick; and man's revolt against inescapable fate—among many interpretations. Whatever symbolism may be found in it, *Moby Dick* retains its stature at any level of interpretation.

MOCA, city, N Dominican Republic, capital of Espaillat Province; on the S slope of the Cordillera Setentrional, on a railroad and a highway; 13 miles ESE of Santiago. Moca is the center of an area where cacao, coffee, and tobacco are grown. Pop. (1950) 9,589.

MOCCASIN, or water moccasin, a thick-bodied snake with retractable fangs, belonging to the pit viper family, *Crotalidae.* The moccasin, *Agkistrodon piscivorus,* is about 4 feet long. The adult has brown or olive skin with patterns formed by 10 to 15 dark bands that sometimes unite to form a line down the middle of the back. The patterns become obscure in old individuals, whose color becomes slate black. The young are pink with yellow tails and have distinct white-edged transverse bands. The moccasin is sometimes called the adder, but is also known as the cottonmouth because its white mouth lining is conspicuous when the snake is alerted. The moccasin has no eyelids and the pupils of its eyes are positioned vertically, giving the snake an evil appearance. Like other members of the pit viper family, the moccasin has a depression, or pit, between its nostrils and eyes. Moccasins reproduce readily and their offspring are born live in broods of 5 to 15. Moccasins move slowly on land but are excellent swimmers. They hunt primarily at night, preying upon fish, frogs, small mammals, and birds. Moccasins are found in swampy areas of southeastern United States, where they may often be seen sunbathing on floating logs. They are not belligerent but may become vicious when attacked.

L. W. BROWNELL

Water Moccasin

MOCCASIN, a type of footwear, common among most North American Indian tribes. The two major varieties were the soft-soled moccasins and the hard-soled moccasins. Those of the soft-soled type consisted of a single piece of buckskin and were most widespread in the Mackenzie, Plateau, Eastern Woodlands, and Southeast culture areas. Hard-soled moccasins were made of a piece of buckskin sewed to a rawhide sole and were most common in the Arctic, Great Basin, and Southwest culture areas. Both kinds were worn by the Plains Indians. The Eskimo had hard-soled boots which they may have originally obtained from northeast Asia. Moccasins were also worn by tribes on the Mosquito coast of Nicaragua, where they seem to have developed independently. Since details in the ornamentation of moccasins varied from tribe to tribe, it was possible to determine the tribal affiliation of a person by examining his moccasins.

MOCCASIN FLOWER. See LADY'S-SLIPPER.

MOCHA, or Mokha, also Mukha, town, SW Yemen, Taiz Province; on the Red Sea; 125 miles WNW of Aden. Formerly the main port of Yemen, Mocha was noted in the sixteenth and seventeenth centuries for its export of Mocha coffee. It declined in the nineteenth century because of the rise of the ports of Hodeida and Aden. Pop. 5,000.

MOCKINGBIRD, mocking thrush, or mocker, a plain bird of the mimic family, *Mimidae,* distinguished for its lovely song and for its accuracy in imitating various sounds, such as the croak of frogs or the notes of a piano as well as the songs of other birds. The mockingbird, *Mimus polyglottos,* is about 10 inches long, slender, and has wide feathers with rounded tips. The long wings and tail are mostly dull black, but showy white patches appear during flight. The upper parts are brownish gray; the under parts are gray and white. The black bill is slightly shorter than the head. The bird eats insects and berries and prefers living in thick shrubbery or hedges about 10 feet from the ground. The nest is often close to houses and is made of coarse twigs and grass, with some soft lining such as moss. The female lays four to six brown-speckled, blue-green eggs. The mockingbird's song, an unconfined melody employing a wide range of notes, usually consists of several phrases with a few repetitions of one phrase before the beginning of the next. The mockingbird sings during flight, and can often be heard during the night. The bird is a permanent resident of several of the southern United States.

MASLOWSKI & GOODPASTER, NATL. AUDUBON SOC.

Mockingbird

MOCK ORANGE, any deciduous ornamental shrub of the genus *Philadelphus,* belonging to the saxifrage family, *Saxifragaceae.* The mock orange is sometimes classified with the hydrangea group, a subdivision of the family. The cream or white flowers of the mock orange, either solitary or grouped in small showy clusters, are often fragrant. The leaves are simple and opposite. Most of the 40 species of the shrub are found in North America and Eurasia. The common mock orange, *P. coronarius,* grows to 10 feet; its flowers are extremely fragrant. *P. grandiflorus* grows to the same height but has larger leaves and flowers than do most of the other species. *P. inodorus* is an attractive bush with stately arching branches. The mock orange blossoms regularly in June. It may be propagated by seeds and cuttings. Pruning is done after flowering, since the flower buds grow from the wood of the previous year.

MOCK SUNS AND MOONS, images that appear on both sides of the sun and the moon, generally at the same altitude as that of these bodies; also known as sundogs or parhelia and as moondogs or paraselenae respectively. They are associated with halos (see HALO) and are most frequently seen at 22° but may also appear at other angular distances. Like halos, white sundogs are caused by the reflection, and colored ones by the refraction, of light by ice crystals. Colored sundogs range from red nearest the sun to violet farthest away from the sun, but blue and violet ones generally are too indistinct to be seen. The 22° and 46° parhelia are caused by refraction, the parhelia of 120° by total reflection. Sometimes bright spots are the result of intersections of halos or parhelic circles that have been caused by various reflections and refractions, and such spots are also considered mock suns or moons. The parhelic circles are white circles parallel with the horizon that pass through the sun and cross the positions of the sundogs.

MOCKSVILLE, town, central North Carolina, seat of Davie County; on the Southern Railway and U.S. highways 64, 158, and 601; 23 miles SW of Winston-Salem. Mocksville has manufactures of furniture, clothing, and animal feeds. Settled in the mid-eighteenth century, the town was incorporated in 1839. Pop. (1960) 2,379.

MODE, theoretically any arrangement of musical tones in scales of whole and half steps such as may constitute the basis of the melodic—and sometimes the harmonic—organization of a musical composition (see SCALE). More specifically, mode—derived from the Latin for measure or form—is any such grouping of notes as used in medieval European music and, earlier, in the music of ancient Greece. In modern usage, the concept of mode is usually restricted to the major and minor modes that are part of the system of keys employed by most composers since the time of Johann Sebastian Bach (see ATONAL MUSIC; KEY). Many composers, however, have utilized various of the medieval modes for purposes of lending color and variety to compositions whose basic orientation is in terms of the key system. Moreover, many twentieth century composers, rebelling against the key system, have made use of the medieval modes, as have composers of church music virtually without interruption since the fourth century.

The Greek Scales, from which the modes of the medieval period were derived, were based upon tetrachords, which consisted of four notes each, the outside tones being a perfect fourth apart (see CHORD; INTERVAL). These tetrachords formed the basis for the tuning of the Greek four-stringed lyres. Although there were three types of tetrachords (the diatonic, the chromatic, and the enharmonic—the last employing quarter tones), the diatonic were the most important. Two superimposed tetrachords produced an octachord similar to the later octave scale, and these combinations produced the various scale forms named after the different provinces of Greece, as Lydian, Phrygian, and Dorian. Greek musical theorists assigned various psychological moods to the various modes; for instance, the Lydian mode was thought to be suggestive of "ecstasy," the Dorian "manly."

Medieval Modes. The Greeks "thought" their scales in descending order; in contrast, medieval church modes were thought in ascending order. Considerable confusion of the two systems of modes resulted from the fact that the medieval theorists gave Greek names to the modes they conceived. What was known to the Greeks as Phrygian (descending) was later known as Dorian (ascending) and vice versa. Beyond the names, no connection exists between the Greek and medieval systems, and it is to the latter forms that the names usually refer in modern usage.

There are several classifications of the medieval modes. The first grouping was made late in the fourth century by Bishop Ambrose of Milan, who named them as follows (slurs indicate half steps): Dorian (D $\frown{EF}$ G A $\frown{BC}$ D); Phrygian ($\frown{EF}$ G A $\frown{BC}$ D E); Lydian (F G A $\frown{BC}$ D $\frown{EF}$); and Mixolydian (G A $\frown{BC}$ D $\frown{EF}$ G). The motive for this classification was the desire to preserve in their purity a great number of plain chant melodies which were then in danger of being lost or corrupted. About two centuries later St. Gregory I, the Great, added four more modes to this list. These are known as the plagal modes to distinguish them from the previously named authentic modes. They were known as Hypodorian, Hypophrygian, Hypolydian, and Hypomixolydian, and each ranged a perfect fourth lower than its companion authentic mode (*hypo* meaning under), although the final tones for each pair were identical. The authentic modes were later numbered 1, 3, 5, 7, and the plagal modes were designated by the numbers 2, 4, 6, 8. These eight modes are known as the plain-song or ecclesiastical modes. See GREGORIAN CHANT.

Later, as polyphonic music developed, several other modes were added as follows: 9. Aeolian (A $\frown{BC}$ D $\frown{EF}$ G A); 10. Hypoaeolian (E to E, final A); 11. Locrian ($\frown{BC}$ D $\frown{EF}$ G A B); 12. Hypolocrian (F to F, final B); 13. Ionian (C D $\frown{EF}$ G A $\frown{BC}$); 14. Hypoionian (G to G, final C). Since the Locrian and Hypolocrian modes were purely theoretical and (insofar as is known) were never used, there were 12 modes actually employed during the polyphonic era culminating in the music of Bach. In the course of time the reasons for distinguishing between the authentic and plagal forms gradually disappeared in contrapuntal music; and, with the increasing use of accidentals (according to the rules of *musica ficta*), so did the differences among all the modes—as was observed by the Italian theorist Giuseppe Zarlino as early as 1570 (see HARMONY). The advent of homophonic music and of harmony finally brought the realization that the Ionian mode overshadowed all the others in importance, the Aeolian mode running a distant second. These two modes survived as the major and minor modes, the latter being usually found with raised seventh step (the harmonic form) or with raised sixth and seventh steps (the melodic ascending form—the melodic descending being identical with the unaltered Aeolian mode).

IRWIN FISCHER

MODE, the most typical value of a set of data, that is, the value that occurs most frequently. If the data are grouped in a frequency distribution (see FREQUENCY DISTRIBUTION), the mode is found by first locating the group, or class interval, that occurs most frequently, and then locating the central value of that group.

In a normal frequency distribution (see NORMAL CURVE) the mode coincides with the median and the mean (see MEDIAN; MEAN). Most frequency distributions have only one mode, but bimodal and even trimodal distributions are known. For example, if men and women wore the same style of shirt, it is probable that a curve drawn by plotting shirt sizes against the number of people wearing each size would show two peaks, one indicating the size most frequent among men and the other indicating the size most frequent among women.

Unlike the median and the mean, the mode is significant only when there is a pronounced grouping of values. For example, in the items 4, 6, 8, 8, 8, 9, 10, 10, 12, and 15, 8 is the mode because it is the number occurring most frequently. A single change of an 8 to a 10, however, would change the mode to 10, a considerably different figure in this set of items.

MODELMAKING, constructing a representation of a thing, usually in miniature. Besides its popularity as a hobby, modelmaking has been put to practical use in the fields of education, commerce and industry, and science and technology.

The art of modelmaking dates from earliest antiquity. The ancient tombs of the Egyptian kings have yielded highly artistic models of furniture, vehicles, and ships. For centuries the Japanese have been famous for their miniatures of gardens and landscaping effects. Since the early nineteenth century, models and miniatures have reflected achievements of the engineering age. In developing the first practical steam engine, James Watt found that the least expensive method was the use of models for experimentation. William Murdock, an associate of Watt, is credited with building the first model steam locomotive in 1786.

MODELMAKING AS A HOBBY

The principal models made for pleasure are miniature airplanes, ships, railroads, and automobiles. As distinguished from toys, which are purchased complete and require little or no skill to operate, models require varying degrees of skill in construction and assembly. Some modelmaking kits are so simple that assembly can be made with little more than a screw driver; others are more demanding of skills and manual dexterity. Much of the satisfaction of railroad modelmaking, for example, is derived from the actual construction of the cars, locomotives, track, switches, controls, buildings, and scenery.

MODELMAKING

CHAS. P. MILLS & SON

An Army technical school instructor employs scale-model railroad and steamship systems to explain involved transportation methods that affect military situations.

CHICAGO PUBLIC SCHOOLS

The building of model airplanes is a test of manual ability and mechanical understanding.

GENERAL MOTORS

A detailed scale model of an automobile body plant helps executives plan and review the processes of production.

LOS ANGELES BOARD OF EDUCATION

Simple model building at the grammar school level affords the children an opportunity to work on specific applications of mathematics.

Architectural models enable the architect to show his plans in miniature for consideration before construction begins.

MODELS INC.

Perhaps the most completely organized of the scale-model hobbies is that of model railroading, probably because of the opportunity that the railroad offers for incidental equipment and scenery not afforded to such an extent by airplanes, ships, and motorcars. Model railroads are built in several sizes, varying according to the scale of reduction from full-size railroad equipment. Scale is based on the gauge of track used. The standard gauge for most prefabricated toy railroad equipment is O; the preferred gauge for model railroads is HO (half O). For the miniature model railroads there is also a TT (table top) gauge. Six of seven model railroad hobbyists use the HO gauge, which measures 5/8 inch between tracks and is 1/87 full size. A 1955 survey indicated that there were 75,000 model railroad hobbyists in the United States who spent $15 million to purchase material for 127,000 locomotives, 630,000 cars, and other equipment.

Although railroad modelmaking is the most popular of the scale-model hobbies, others such as shipbuilding, airplane making, the construction and assembly of model automobiles and racing cars, and building miniature furniture also attract many thousands of enthusiastic participants. The result is a multimillion-dollar business in the United States.

Practical Aspects

A notable example of the use of models by the United States in the military field occurred during World War II when thousands of plastic scale models were made of every style of airplane used by every nation of the world. These were distributed by the armed services to military and civilian centers concerned with the identification of planes. The models were extremely accurate in scale and contour. Similar models were used in combat areas for the identification of naval and land combat equipment.

Modelmaking as an industry has developed an extremely diversified range of products. Some model companies specialize in construction of working models of machinery. These may serve many purposes. The working model of a large metal forming press, for example, may be used by a salesman to show to a prospect at less expense than would be incurred by taking the prospect to the home factory or to another company's installation for demonstration. The model press may be used in trade shows as the principal exhibit piece instead of a full-size prototype that would be expensive and difficult to transport. Complete process plants in three-dimensional miniature are often displayed at trade shows for purposes of prestige or, with the use of symbols, to demonstrate the actual flow process through the plant. Although the working model may represent a substantial initial investment, its repeated use and the results it produces in sales often make the first cost appear insignificant.

Small-scale models of real estate developments are used to give the prospective buyer an over-all view. If the development is a new subdivision, for example, the prospect may determine from the three-dimensional model the most advantageous locations in relation to shopping centers, schools, and churches.

One of the earliest commercial uses of modelmaking was that of John Brown Herreshoff (1841–1915), who designed his early sailing vessels after producing and testing models of them. For many years after the early 1860's, Herreshoff yachts won the America's Cup in international competition. A practical application of ship and airplane models is to test them in towing tanks and wind tunnels. This practice is widely used in selecting designs of both government and commercial ships and planes.

At one time the most extensive model museum in the world was the U.S. Patent Office in Washington, D.C., which for many years required that models be submitted with most patent applications. Because of expense and space limitations, however, it became the practice of the patent office to rely almost exclusively on patent drawings rather than models. An exception is made in the case of applications for patents on perpetual motion machines, which must still be accompanied by working models.

Bibliog.–B. Reeve, and P. W. Thomas, *Scale Model Ships: Their Engines and Construction* (1951); D. K. Foote, *Aerodynamics for Model Airplanes* (1952); H. S. Coleman, *Modelmaking* (1953); H. Zarchy, *Model Railroading* (1955); W. A. Musciano, *Building and Operating Model Cars* (1956); F. J. Camm, *Model Engineering Practice* (1957); T. W. Hendrick, *Modern Architectural Model* (1957).

MODENA, province, N Italy, Emilia-Romagna Region; bounded by the provinces of Mantova on the N, Ferrara and Bologna on the E, Pistoia and Lucca on the S, and Reggio nell'Emilia on the W; area 1,038 sq. mi.; pop. (1958) 505,665. Grain and livestock are the chief products. The northern half of the province is in the Po Basin and the southern half in the Etruscan Apennines. The Panaro River traverses the province from south to northeast, and the Secchia crosses the northwest corner. Modena is the capital; other main centers are Capri and Mirandola. The Modena area in ancient times was under Etruscan rule.

MODENA, city, N Italy, Emilia-Romagna Region, capital of Modena Province, 24 miles NW of Bologna. Modena is an agricultural center with manufactures of farm machinery, food products, glass, silks, and leather. Modena has a Romanesque cathedral dating from 1099, a seventeenth century ducal palace that became a military school, a university founded in 1678, and a museum and library containing archaeological and art exhibits. The city, founded by the Etruscans, became a Roman colony under the name Mutina in the second century B.C. Under the Romans the city fell into decay and suffered attacks by the Goths and the Longobardi. Modena prospered under the rule of Countess Matilda of Tuscany and became a free city after her death in 1115. In 1288 it came under control of the Este family of Ferrara. The duchy of Modena was created in 1452 and the city became the capital of the duchy in 1598. Modena became part of Italy in 1860. It was bombed in World War II. Pop. (1954) 78,500.

MODERN ART AND ARCHITECTURE, the art and architecture of any period seen by its practitioners and patrons as embodying important elements and principles not characteristic of earlier artistic and architectural production. *Modern* in this sense does not refer to work of a specific era, but to a concept the artistic expressions of which are in perpetual flux. The most rebellious modernism of one period in art history may well constitute the tradition against which the modernists of the next generation rebel. At mid-twentieth century *modern* was generally associated with those artists who had rebelled, and who continued to rebel, against certain artistic conceptions that were dominant during most of the nineteenth century. In their efforts to achieve a radical break with earlier practice, modern artists in some

Administration and Research Center of S. C. Johnson & Son at Racine, Wis., Designed by Frank Lloyd Wright.

S. C. JOHNSON & SON, INC.

MUS. OF MODERN ART, NEW YORK
Study for Hot Still-Scape, by Stuart Davis

cases sought inspiration in the remote past (cave paintings, Oriental art) and in medieval and (less often) Renaissance culture. Others derived inspiration from such distinctly contemporary factors as the machine, new materials (plastics), and new techniques (motion pictures).

In the nineteenth century the impressionists (Camille Pissarro, Claude Monet, Pierre Auguste Renoir, and others) reacted against realism (see IMPRESSIONISM), but the postimpressionists, by rejecting nature as such and thus intensifying the process of abstraction, effected an even more startling break with the past (see POSTIMPRESSIONISM; ABSTRACT ART). The fauves (Henri Matisse, Georges Braque, Georges Rouault, Raoul Dufy, among others) made a violent and astonishing denial of impressionism (see FAUVISM), and the cubists (including Fernand Léger, Juan Gris, and Pablo Picasso) carried the revolt against impressionism still further (see CUBISM). A number of "expressionisms," all emphasizing the inner essence of the subject, appeared in the twentieth century (see EXPRESSIONISM). They ranged from the humanistically oriented paintings and drawings of George Grosz through the fantastic, often demonic inventions of Paul Klee to the completely dehumanized, denatured abstract expressionism or "tachism" of Jackson Pollack.

Other Isms. Among the many movements that appeared during the first half of the twentieth century several others were especially noteworthy. The futurist movement, which included such figures as Gino Severini, Giorgio de Chirico, and Umberto Boccioni, contributed to modern art the idea of psychic simultaneity (see FUTURISM). Constructivism, associated with Naum Gabo and El Lissitsky, among others, eventually merged in Germany with the neoplasticism of De Stijl, a school whose principal figures were Piet Mondrian and Theo van Doesburg (see CONSTRUCTIVISM; DE STIJL). The highly rational De Stijl has been related to the two most famous irrational movements, dadaism and surrealism, with which such important artists as Max Ernst, Joan Miró, and Salvador Dali were associated (see DADAISM; SURREALISM).

While the objective of modern artists was to raise painting and other arts to the "pure" level of architecture and music (both construed as existing *in* and *for* themselves), such twentieth century architects as Frank Lloyd Wright, Le Corbusier, Miës van der Rohe, and Walter Gropius concluded, paradoxically, that architecture had fallen to a low level because buildings no longer existed in themselves—were merely copies of earlier buildings—and sought to restore architecture to its earlier pure state. See ART; AESTHETICS; ARCHITECTURE; FORM; PAINTING; SCULPTURE; DESIGN; articles on national arts and architectures, such as GERMAN ART AND ARCHITECTURE; biographies of individuals mentioned.

BIBLIOGRAPHY

ART: P. C. Mondriaan, *Plastic Art and Pure Plastic Art* (1945); W. Kandinsky, *Concerning the Spiritual in Art, and Painting in Particular* (1912, ed. 1947), *Point and Line to Plane* (ed. 1947); L. Moholy-Nagy, *New Vision* (ed. 1947); S. W. Cheney, *Expressionism in Art* (ed. 1948); M. Ernst, *Beyond Painting* (1948); G. Apollinaire, *Cubist Painters* (ed. 1949); P. Klee, *On Modern Art* (ed. 1949); A. Malraux, *Twilight of the Absolute* (1951, vol. 3, *Psychology of Art*); R. B. Motherwell, *Dada Painters and Poets* (1951); A. Ozenfant, *Foundations of Modern Art* (ed. 1952); D. B. W. Lewis, *Demon of Progress in the Arts* (1955); M. Raymond, *From Baudelaire to Surrealism* (ed. 1955); H. E. Read, *Art Now* (ed. 1948), *Philosophy of Modern Art* (ed. 1955); S. Dali, *On Modern Art* (1957); W. Haftmann and others, *German Art of the Twentieth Century* (1957); C L. Kuhn, *German Expressionism and Abstract Art* (1957); J. T. Soby, *Modern Art and the Past* (1957).

ARCHITECTURE: N. Pevsner, *Pioneers of Modern Design, from William Morris to Gropius* (ed. 1949); T. F. Hamlin, *Forms and Functions of Twentieth-Century Architecture* (4 vols. 1952); W. A. G. Gropius, *New Architecture and the Bauhaus* (ed. 1955), *Scope of Total Architecture* (1955); A. Whittick, *European Architecture in the Twentieth Century* (3 vols. 1955); E. R. De Zurko, *Origins of Functionalist Theory* (1957); C. E. Jeanneret-Gris (Le Corbusier), *Oeuvre Complète* (*Complete Works*, 6 vols. 1952–57); L. H. Sullivan, *Autobiography of an Idea* (ed. 1957); F. L. Wright, *When Democracy Builds* (1945), *Future of Architecture* (1953), *Natural House* (1954), *American Architecture* (ed. 1957), *Testament* (1957); B. Zevi, *Towards an Organic Architecture* (1950), *Architecture as Space: How to Look at Architecture* (1957).

MODERNISM, a movement of the late nineteenth and early twentieth centuries that aimed at making religion conform to modern knowledge by expunging from religion those doctrines that appeared to contradict the scientific or critical position. Developing along analogous lines in Protestantism, Roman Catholicism, and Judaism, the movement stemmed from the conflict modernists thought they perceived between traditional beliefs and practices of their respective religions and what were understood to be the definitive findings of modern science and literary criticism.

In Protestant churches, modernism was occasioned in large part by Darwinism and higher literary criticism of the Bible. The latter led modernists to deny the inspiration of the Scriptures (see INSPIRATION), and the former—along with allied scientific positions in geology and anthropology—induced in them the attitude that religion in general, and Christianity in particular, is in a continuous state of development and change. While retaining the names of their respective denominations, Protestant modernists tended to minimize biblical beliefs and established creeds and practices of worship in favor of stress placed upon humanitarian aspects of Christianity, especially in the matter of social reform. In the United States, Protestant modernism provoked a reaction that became known as fundamentalism—a movement which drew a sharp line between its own "biblical gospel" and the "social gospel" of the modernists (see FUNDAMENTALISM).

Roman Catholicism experienced a similar movement aimed at making the beliefs of that religion conform to the positions of modern science. Men like Alfred Loisy, Lucien Laberthonnière, and Édouard Le Roy in France, George Tyrrell in England, and Ernesto Buonaiuti in Italy engaged simultaneously in an attempt to adapt Catholicism to the modern mentality. Although they differed in many ways, Catholic modernists agreed in denying the divine inspiration and the inerrancy of Scripture. Similarly they were highly skeptical of ever achieving any certain knowledge of Christian origins; following Friedrich Schleirmacher, they put a religious sense—a personal, subjective feeling—at the basis of all religious activity. They rejected Catholic dogmas as intellectual propositions that describe extramental reality, holding that dogmas were nothing more than changeable symbolizations of the impulses of the religious sense. Catholic modernism was formally condemned in 1907 by Pope Pius X in the encyclical letter *Pascendi*; since then the movement has ceased to be a prominent factor in the Catholic scene.

The modernist trend is also apparent in Reform Judaism. This branch of the Jewish faith refuses to acknowledge the Mosaic religion as definitive, does not accept the authority of the Talmud, and has abandoned some traditional Jewish customs and practices. R. F. SMITH, S.J.

BIBLIOG.–J. Lebreton, *The Encyclical and Modernist Theology* (1908); P. Sabatier, *Modernism* (1909); D. Philipson, *Reform Movement in Judaism* (1931); A. R. Vidler, *Modernist Movement in the Roman Church* (1934); D. E. Roberts and H. P. Van Dusen, eds., *Liberal Theology* (1942); N. F. Furniss, *Fundamentalist Controversy, 1918–1931* (1954).

MODERN LANGUAGE ASSOCIATION OF AMERICA, an organization founded in 1883 for the advancement of research in modern languages and their literatures. Membership is open to anyone on payment of a nominal annual fee, which includes a subscription to the quarterly review *PMLA* (Publications of the Modern Language Association of America). The association's headquarters are in New York, N.Y.

MODERN WOODMEN OF AMERICA. See MUTUAL BENEFIT SOCIETY; FRATERNAL ORGANIZATION, *History*.

MODESTO, city, central California, seat of Stanislaus County; in the San Joaquin Valley; on the Tuolumne River, the Southern Pacific Railroad, and U.S. highway 99; a scheduled airline stop; 77 miles ESE of San Francisco. Modesto is the trade center for the agricultural region irrigated by the Don Pedro Dam. Dairies, meat-processing plants, canneries, quick-freezing plants, and farm machinery factories are in the city. Modesto was laid out in 1870 and incorporated in 1884. Pop. (1960) 36,585.

MODICA, town, Italy, SE Sicily, Ragusa Province; 33 miles SW of Syracuse. The main products of Modica are olive oil, wine, cheese, and livestock. Near the town is the Cava d'Ispica, a limestone ravine with grottoes containing Byzantine tombs. Modica was originally a Phoenician settlement called Motyca. Pop. (1954) 30,400.

MODIGLIANI, AMEDEO, 1884–1920, Italian artist, was born in Livorno. After studying at the Accademia delle Belle Arti in Florence, he went to Paris, 1906, where he associated with the leaders of the revolutionary art movements and created sculpture that was influenced by African wood carvings. He began oil painting later and first exhibited in the Salon des Indépendents in 1909. His work is expressionistic, but his linear emphasis recalls the Italian primitives. Modigliani died at 36 of tuberculosis. His lifetime output of paintings was meager but powerful, and included portraits of the poets Jean Cocteau and Arthur Rimbaud as well as portraits of the painters Soutine and Bakst.

LOS ANGELES COUNTY MUS.

Portrait by Amadeo Modigliani of the French Writer Jean Cocteau

MODJESKA, HELENA, 1844–1909, Polish actress, was born in Kraków. At the age of 17 she married Gustav Modrzejewski, with whom she acted in stock companies. After his death she married Count Bozenta Chlapowski in 1868, by which time she was an established actress in Poland. In 1876 she and her husband settled in the United States and tried unsuccessfully to establish a Polish colony in California. Modjeska made her American debut in San Francisco in an English version of *Adrienne Lecouvreur*, 1877. She later toured the United States, England, and Poland, gaining distinction as an actress excelling in Shakespearean tragedy. Her son, Ralph Modjeski (1861–1940), was a leading designer and builder of bridges in the United States.

MODOC, a North American Indian tribe of Shapwailutan linguistic stock, of which it forms, together with the Klamath tribe, the Lutuamian division. The Modocs lived along the rivers of southern Oregon and northern California in villages of low plank houses with conical roofs. Gathering, hunting, and fishing yielded sufficiently abundant food to insure a fair level of existence. The Modocs were not in contact with Europeans until after the gold rush in the middle of the nineteenth century. When the pioneers started to seize their lands, the Modocs resisted and bloody conflicts marked by many atrocities ensued. In 1864 the United States seized the territory of the Modocs, as well as that of the Klamaths, and both tribes were sent to the Klamath reservation in Oregon. Kintpuash, a Modoc chief called Captain Jack by the whites, led a group of Modocs that escaped from the reservation in 1870. This episode led to the Modoc War of 1872–73. The Modocs entrenched themselves in northern California and were defeated only after several months of repeated assaults by U.S. troops—at first commanded by Gen. Edward R. S. Canby, who was killed in April, 1873. When the Modocs were finally defeated, in October, 1873, Kintpuash and some of his followers were hanged and the survivors sent to the Quapaw and Klamath reservations. The tribe, which numbered several hundred persons before the Modoc war, was greatly reduced. The 329 Modocs left in 1945 had almost completely lost their original culture.

MODULATION, a change of musical key or mode, usually done in one of three ways, in order to permit transition without creating an unpleasant effect. The first method makes use of a chord that is shared by both the old and new key or mode (a pivot chord). In the second, one note that is prominent in a given key or mode may be repeated frequently and then incorporated into the pivot chord that is used in modulating into that key. In enharmonic modulation, the third method, the pivot chord in the old mode or key may be considered as so altered in notation that it becomes, itself, a chord in the new key or mode. A device sometimes used is the so-called false modulation, in which the listener is led to expect a change of key that actually never takes place.

MODULUS, a quantitative expression of some property, function, or effect, such as distance, elasticity, efficiency, or strength. Moduli are useful for a variety of purposes in such branches of science as astronomy, physics, engineering, and mathematics.

In Astronomy the distance modulus of a star is the difference between its apparent magnitude (brightness), m, and its absolute magnitude, M. (See MAGNITUDE.) The greater the modulus, the greater the star's distance from the observer. This relation is expressed in the following equations:

$$\log p = 0.2(M-m)-1$$
$$\log D = 0.2(m-M)+1.513$$

where p is the parallax of the star in seconds of arc and D is its distance in light-years. See PARALLAX.

In Mathematics moduli are employed in many ways such as in connection with logarithmic systems, complex numbers, proportionate or uniform scales, elliptic integrals, and the theory of numbers. The modulus of a system of logarithms whose base is the number a is the logarithm of the Napierian number e (2.71828) to that base number. Thus $M = \log_a e$ and, if $a=10$, $M = \log_{10} e = 0.434294 \ldots$, the factor by which natural logarithms are multiplied to obtain common logarithms. More generally, the number $\log_a b$ is the modulus of the system whose base is a with respect to the system of base b. See LOGARITHM.

The modulus of a complex number is the absolute value of that number. The polar form of a complex number z is $z = r(\cos\theta + i\sin\theta)$, and here the modulus is r. (See COMPLEX NUMBER.) A scale modulus is the length m used to represent a unit segment of a scale whose equation is $x=mf(u)$, where $f(u)$ means a function of u. (See FUNCTION.) A uniform scale, such as used by an architect, may represent 1 foot by a distance of ¼ inch; the scale markings then stand for feet and fractions of feet. In the equations for this scale, $x=mu$, the modulus $m=¼$ inch represents the unit segment, 1 foot; and the distance x from the origin of the scale to the mark u, which we will assume is 5.5 feet, is then $x=¼\times5.5=1.375$ inches.

In the theory of numbers, two numbers, a and b, are said to be congruent for the modulus m if there is the same remainder on dividing each of them by the number m, or if their difference is exactly divisible by m. The divisor m is the modulus of the congruence. Thus 25 and 49 are congruent for the number 8 because, if both numbers are divided by 8, there is a remainder of 1, and their difference, 24, is exactly divisible by 8.

In Engineering and Physics modulus denotes a quantitative ratio that exists as a property of or as an effect on a material. These moduli relate to such properties as elasticity, resilience, rigidity, and tension. The modulus of elasticity of a structural material is a constant ratio that exists between the unit stress and the unit strain or deformation of the material, as long as it is not stressed beyond its elastic limit. This relationship between stress and strain within the elastic limit is expressed in Hooke's law, and Young's modulus relates to elasticity in straight tension and compression. (See ELASTICITY; ELASTIC LIMIT.) When a body is subjected to stress from all sides, as in the case of hydrostatic pressure, the stress-strain constant is the bulk modulus of that material; and when the deformation results from shearing or twisting, the constant is known as the shearing modulus.

MOE, JORGEN INGEBRETSEN, 1813–82, Norwegian folklorist, poet, and clergyman, was born in Höle, Ringerike, studied theology at Christiania (Oslo), became a pastor in 1853, and was made a bishop in 1875. He published *Samling af Sange, Folkeviser og Stev i norske Almuedialecter* (1840), a collection of Norse ballads, songs, and staves; and *Norske folkeeventyr* (Norwegian Folk Tales), 1841, the latter with Peter Christian Asbjörnsen.

MOERIS, LAKE, ancient artificial body of water, NE Egypt, in Faiyum Province; immediately N of the city of Faiyum and about 38 miles SW of Cairo. The basin of Lake Moeris is now partially occupied by Birket Qârûn (Birket el-Kurûn), a shallow lake 25 miles long and 4 miles wide. The lake was described by ancient travelers such as Herodotus, and was used to control the flow of the Nile.

MOERS, town, NW Germany, in the West German state of North Rhine-Westphalia; near the Rhine River, 17 miles W of Essen. Main products are coal, metal goods, and building materials. Moers was chartered in 1300, was the seat of the Moers dukes until 1600 when it fell to the duchy of Nassau-Orania, and in 1702 joined Prussia.

MOESIA, the country of the Moesi, a Thracian tribe, was located south of the Danube and corresponded approximately to modern Serbia, northern Bulgaria, and the Dobruja. Moesia was conquered by the Romans in 29 B.C. and became a Roman province. In A.D. 86, it was divided into the provinces of Upper Moesia, corresponding largely to modern Serbia, and Lower Moesia, covering most of modern northern Bulgaria and the Dobruja. After the conquest of Dacia by the Emperor Trajan, Moesia was extended to the north. Moesia suffered greatly when it was invaded by the Goths and other Germanic tribes in the third century, but remained a military borderland of the Roman Empire until its division in 395.

MOFFAT TUNNEL, N central Colorado, passes through James Peak of the Rocky Mountains at an elevation of 9,094 feet; 36 miles WNW of Denver. It was started in 1922 and completed in 1928 at a cost of $18 million. It is 6 miles long and consists of a railroad tunnel 24 feet high and 18 feet wide with a parallel water tunnel that is 8 feet in diameter and that transports water from the Fraser River to Denver. Upon completion of a related engineering work in 1934, the Moffat Tunnel shortened the rail distance between Denver and Salt Lake City by 176 miles.

MOGADISCIO, or Mogadishu, formerly Mogadoxo, city, E Africa, capital of Somalia; on the Indian Ocean; 640 miles ENE of Nairobi, Kenya. A seaport and commercial center, Mogadiscio is connected by highway with Kenya and Ethiopia and by airline and steamship with European and other African cities. Taken by the sultan of Zanzibar in 1871, it was leased in 1892 and sold in 1905 to Italy. It was occupied by the British in 1941 during World War II. (For population, see southern Africa map in Atlas.)

MOGADOR, city, SW Morocco, Marrakech Region; on the Atlantic Ocean; 109 miles W of Marrakech. A domestic port, Mogador is connected by highway with Marrakech and Casablanca. Chief items of trade are wool, olive oil, and sheep and goat skins. The city's beaches and pleasant climate make it a popular resort. Formerly known as Souirah, Mogador was founded in the 1760's by Sultan Mohammed XVI on the site of a Portuguese fort. (For population, see northern Africa map in Atlas.)

MOGILEV, region, U.S.S.R., a subdivision of the Byelorussian Soviet Socialist Republic; bounded on the N by Vitebsk Region, E by Smolensk and Bryansk regions of the Russian Soviet Federated Socialist Republic, and S and W by Gomel and Minsk regions respectively; area 10,600 sq. mi.; pop. (1959 est.) 1,130,000. From the north, where a portion of the Orsha upland rises more than 700 feet above sea level, the terrain gently descends southward, drained by the Dnepr River and its tributaries the Berezina, Drut, and Sozh. Peat is found in abundance throughout Mogilev. The growing of rye, oats, potatoes, and flax and the raising of hogs are the main agricultural activities; lumbering, sawmilling, food processing, and metalworking, the leading industries. Mogilev is the capital of the region.

MOGILEV, city, U.S.S.R., Byelorussian Soviet Socialist Republic, capital of Mogilev Region; on the upper Dnepr River, at the junction of the Vitebsk-Zhlobin and Baranovichi-Krichev railways, on four major highways; 113 miles E of Minsk. Mogilev's industries include metalworking, pipecasting, automobile and engine repair, food processing, and manufacture of leather, textiles, and wood-chemical products. Mogilev has a teachers college, several vocational and general schools, and an eighteenth century Byzantine Orthodox cathedral. The city was taken by Lithuania under Gedimin in the fourteenth century and thus saved from Mongol domination. It belonged to the Polish-Lithuanian commonwealth from 1569 to 1772, when it was seized by Russia in the first partition of Poland. During Napoleon's advance on Moscow, Mogilev became a site of a Russian defeat, July, 1812. In World War I the city served as the Russian general headquarters. During World War II it was held by the Germans from 1941 to 1944 and suffered considerable damage. It was rebuilt within a decade after the war. (For population, see U.S.S.R. map in Atlas.)

MOGUL, in Western usage, any one of the rulers of the Muslim Empire that was established in India in 1526 and ended in 1857. Westeners referred to the Muslim emperor as the Mogul or the Great Mogul in the same way as they referred to the sultan of Turkey as the Great Turk and to the shah of Persia as the Sophy. Mogul means Mongol in the Arabic and Persian languages, but the Mogul emperors were in fact Turkish speaking.

The Mogul Empire was founded in 1526 by Baber and consolidated by Akbar the Great. It reached its apogee under Shah Jahan and his son Aurangzeb in the seventeenth century, when its territory corresponded approximately to that of modern Afghanistan, Pakistan, and India. Under this empire Muslim art and architecture attained their greatest peak as shown by the masterpieces located in the ancient capitals of Delhi, Agra, and Fatehpur Sikri. See INDIA, Early History.

MOHÁCS, city, S Hungary, Baranya County; on the W bank of the Danube River opposite Mohács Island, at the terminus of a branch of the Pécs-Osijek Railroad; 23 miles ESE of Pécs. Machines, farm implements, linen and woolen textiles, and food products are the city's chief manufactures. In 1526 Mohács was the scene of a devastating defeat of a small Hungarian army under Louis II by overwhelming Turkish forces under Suleiman the Magnificent. The period of Turkish rule that followed in central Hungary was ended in 1687 by a Hungarian victory under Charles Leopold, duke of Lorraine, near the same battlefield. Relics of the two battles are kept in the Mohács cemetery chapel. Pop. (1956 est.) 19,500.

MOHAIR, a soft, smooth, lustrous, and durable fiber made from the fleece of the Angora goat. After being processed, the long silky fibers can be easily and permanently dyed. Kid mohair is the best quality and comes from the fine, soft fleece that grows under the heavy top coat. Mohair is usually woven with other fibers such as wool and silk and is used in materials for draperies, upholstered furniture, and high-fashion coats and suits. Mohair is included in the category of wool and both fibers are subjected to similar manufacturing processes. (See WOOL.) In 1957 the United States produced slightly more than 19 million pounds of mohair, valued at almost $17 million, from a goat herd of approximately 3.2 million animals. About two-thirds of this amount was exported, primarily to Great Britain. Texas continued to produce more than nine-tenths of the domestic output. See GOAT, Domestic Goats.

MOHALL, city, NW North Dakota, seat of Renville County; on the Great Northern Railway; 48 miles NNW of Minot. The chief products are dairy goods, livestock, poultry, and wheat. Mohall was platted in 1903. Pop. (1960) 956.

MOHAMMED, in Arabic Mohammad, 570–632, founder of the religion of Islam, was born in Mecca (in modern Saudi Arabia) to a Hashemite family of the Koreish tribe. His father died before he was born, and his mother died when he was six. In his youth Mohammed was employed as a shepherd, but later engaged in trade. Early in life, because of his love for honesty and truth, he was called Al-Amin, or the Trustworthy.

At 25 he married Khadija, a rich and noble widow 15 years his senior who provided the necessities of life, thus enabling him to give much time to meditation—a full month each year at the cave of Hira near Mecca. It was during one of those periods of prayer and fasting, at the age of 40, that Mohammed received his first revelation and began his mission to preach of the unity of God, the condemnation of idol worship, the brotherhood of man, and the necessity of a virtuous life. See ISLAM.

At first the Koreish mocked and sneered at him, and only his wife and closest friends accepted his message; but later, as he gained more adherents, the Koreish found a definite threat to their vested interests in his message and began to persecute him and his followers. The persecution was so severe that many of his followers, acting upon Mohammed's advice, migrated to Ethiopia (Abyssinia). A deputation sent by the Meccans to demand the extradition of the refugees failed and the Meccans continued their persecution with added fury. They tried to lure Mohammed with wealth, prestige, and power, but he resisted, later saying "Even if they put the sun on my right hand and the moon on my left hand, to force me from my undertakings, verily I would not desist therefrom until the Lord made manifest my cause or I should perish in the attempt." Persecuted in Mecca, and hoping to find a less tyrannical city, Mohammed journeyed to Taif, but was stoned and forced back to Mecca.

The Hejira. During the next three years, however, Islam took root in Medina and Mohammed was offered hospitality and protection. He advised his followers to migrate from Mecca to Medina, and on July 16, 622, after having narrowly escaped assassination, Mohammed followed them. His flight, or Hejira, was the turning point in the history of Islam and marked the beginning of the Moslem era. See HEJIRA.

In Medina Mohammed established brotherhood between the immigrants and the residents and became the supreme judge of the different tribes and the ruler of the Moslem community. The Koreish, continuing to tyrannize the Moslems, compelled Mohammed to meet their marauding expeditions with force. The Moslems grew in number and strength and Mohammed entered Mecca with 10,000 of his followers, destroyed the idols, forgave his Meccan enemies, and became the undisputed leader of Moslem Arabia. Even at the height of his glory he lived a simple and unpretentious life; he died June 8, 632.

The Koran, held sacred by the Moslems, is a holy book containing the words that were revealed to Mohammed throughout the 23 years of his mission. His everyday sayings and actions are recorded in minutest detail in what is called *The Traditions*. (See KORAN.) His message brought a complete transformation to the life of the Arabs and out of warring tribes created a nation. ADNAN JAWDAT MARDINI

MOHAMMED I, 1387?–1421, Ottoman sultan, 1413–21, was the son of Bajazet I. He consolidated the empire, which had fallen apart as a result of Tamerlane's victory over Bajazet I at Ankara, 1402.

MOHAMMED II, called the Conqueror, 1430?–81, Ottoman sultan, was born in Adrianople, and succeeded his father, Murad II, in 1451. In 1453 he captured the Byzantine capital Constantinople, and made it his capital. He also conquered Greece, Albania, Bosnia, Trebizond, the Crimea, and some of the Aegean islands. He was a patron of the arts and education.

MOHAMMED III, 1566–1603, Ottoman sultan, succeeded his father Murad III in 1595, fought an inconclusive war in Hungary, and in 1603 fought against Persia, losing Tabriz.

MOHAMMED IV, 1641?–91, Ottoman sultan, 1648–87, succeeded his father Ibrahim I. His reign was marked by internal disorders until the Kuprili gained power, 1656. He was deposed after Turkish defeats at Vienna and Mohács.

MOHAMMED V, 1844–1918, Ottoman sultan, was born in Constantinople, the son of Sultan Abdul-Medjid. For 33 years he was a palace prisoner of his brother, Sultan Abdul-Hamid II, but succeeded to the throne when the revolution of the Young Turks, 1909, deposed Abdul-Hamid. Lacking experience in statecraft, he was a tool in the hands of the Young Turks during the Balkan wars and World War I. During his reign Turkey lost most of its European possessions.

MOHAMMED VI, 1861–1926, Ottoman sultan, 1918–22, was born in Constantinople and succeeded his brother Mohammed V. He tried but failed to suppress the Turkish nationalists who, after their victory over the Greeks, deposed Mohammed in 1922, forcing him into exile.

MOHAMMED AHMED. See MAHDI.

MOHAMMED ALI, 1769?–1849, Turkish viceroy of Egypt and founder of the royal house of Egypt, was born in Kavala, Macedonia. He fought against Napoleon Bonaparte in Egypt, 1799, gained control of Cairo, and in 1805 became pasha, a position he strengthened by annihilating the Mamelukes, 1811, long-time rulers of Egypt. He was successful in military conquests, 1811–18 and 1820–22, which made him the most powerful governor in the Turkish Empire. He supported the Turkish sultan against the Greeks with a fleet that was destroyed by the Allied powers of Great Britain, France, and Russia at Navarino, 1827. When the reward promised for his aid in Greece was not forthcoming, and because he feared the sultan would soon move against him, Mohammed Ali invaded Syria, 1831. Intervention by the Western powers resulted in the loss of his conquests, 1841, and he retired to the viceroyalty of Egypt.

MOHAMMED RIZA PAHLAVI, 1919– , shah of Iran, was born in Tehran, was educated in Switzerland, and succeeded his father, Riza Khan Pahlavi, as shah in 1941. He and Premier Mohammed Mossadegh nationalized the Iranian oil industry, 1951–52. In 1953 the shah put down Mossadegh's attempts to restrict the ruler's powers, and in 1955 he entered into the Baghdad Mutual Defense Treaty with Great Britain, Pakistan, Turkey, and Iraq. The shah divorced his first wife, Princess Fawzia, sister of King Farouk of Egypt, in 1948 and his second wife, Soraya Esfandiari-Bakhtiari, in 1958 because neither had borne him a male heir. His third wife, Farah Diba, bore him a son, Riza, 1960.

MOHAVE, a North American Indian tribe of the Yuman linguistic stock, living on both sides of the Colorado River, from Needles to the Black Canyon, in Arizona. The Mohaves were primarily an agricultural people, growing maize, squash, and beans. They were first contacted by the Spaniards about 1600. Control of the area in which the Mohaves were living passed from Mexico to the United States in 1848. The Mohaves were later relocated in the Colorado River Reservation together with the Chemehuevi and the Kawia. The Mohaves numbered about 4,000 in 1848, but were reduced to a few hundred by the end of the nineteenth century. There were 575 Mohaves in the Colorado River Agency and 343 in the Fort Mojave Reservation in 1945.

MOHAWK, a North American Indian tribe of Iroquoian linguistic stock and one of the five tribes united in the Iroquois League. The Mohawk occupied the upper valley of the Mohawk River in the modern state of New York.

An agricultural people, the Mohawk cultivated maize, squash, and beans. They lived mostly in long-houses accommodating several families under one roof. The status of the women, who owned the houses and the fields, was very high. The tribe was divided into three matrilineal clans and residence was matrilocal—that is, a husband lived in his wife's house.

The Mohawk united with the four other Iroquois tribes under the leadership of Dekanawida and Hiawatha after 1570. The Iroquois League, formed primarily to establish peace among the tribes, became powerful. The Mohawk, like the other Iroquois, remained loyal to the British during the American Revolution and their villages were destroyed by Gen. John Sullivan in 1779. The survivors were sent to a reservation on Grand River, in Ontario, except a few who went to Oklahoma. There were only 368 Mohawk left by 1910. See CAYUGA; IROQUOIS; ONEIDA; ONONDAGA; SENECA.

MOHAWK RIVER, central New York; rises in Oneida County and flows generally S and SE through Delta Reservoir to Rome, then SE to Cohoes to meet the Hudson River; length 130 miles. The river is paralleled by the New York State Barge Canal, several railroads, and excellent highways. Important cities along its route include Rome, Utica, Little Falls, and Schenectady. The Mohawk River was of strategic importance in colonial wars.

BIBLIOG.–N. Greene, *History of the Mohawk Valley, Gateway to the West, 1614–1925* (1925); T. W. Clarke, *Bloody Mohawk* (1940); C. Hislop, *Mohawk* (1948); J. J. Vroomin, *Forts and Firesides of the Mohawk Country* (ed. 1951).

MOHEGAN, a North American Indian tribe of Algonquian linguistic stock, which was settled mainly along the upper Thames River in Connecticut. It was probably a branch of the Mahican that became independent (see MAHICAN). When they first came into contact with Europeans, the Mohegan formed a single tribe with the Pequot under the leadership of a Pequot chief. In the seventeenth century, Uncas, a Mohegan chief, rebelled against the Pequot and gained control of both the Mohegan and the Pequot. At the end of King Philip's War (1675–76) the Mohegan were the most powerful of the surviving tribes in southern New England. During the following century, however, their numbers were greatly reduced. Many were killed by settlers and others were absorbed into other tribes, especially the Scaticook and the Brotherton. A few continued to live at Mohegan, Conn., where they intermarried with whites.

MOHENJO-DARO, or mound of the dead, an ancient city in Sind Province of modern Pakistan. Mohenjo-Daro was built about 2500 B.C. Excavations began in the early twentieth century and disclosed a high level of culture, with skillfully engineered sanitation systems. The people of Mohenjo-Daro produced pottery, jewelry, gold, alabaster, and marble sculptures and seal carvings. They were the earliest people known to have used the toothed saw. They had a written language, which has not been deciphered. See HARAPPA; INDUS CIVILIZATION.

MOHL, HUGO VON, 1805–72, German botanist, was born in Stuttgart and studied at the University of Tübingen where he became professor of botany, 1835. He proposed the name protoplasm for the plastic substance found just under the cell membrane, and studied the movement of tendrils. He published more than 90 papers on botanical subjects and edited the *Botanische Zeitung*, 1843–73.

MOHOLE, a major scientific project initiated by the National Academy of Sciences in 1957 to drill completely through the earth's crust, beneath deep ocean, to sample the interior. This new, direct method of exploring our planet is expected to give more specific data about the structure, composition, and history of the earth than indirect, inferential methods of geophysics could yield. To understand why deep penetration is planned beneath the ocean and what it may achieve, it is necessary to know something of the earth's structure and crust. See EARTH; GEOLOGY; GEOPHYSICS; OCEAN; OCEANOGRAPHY.

Most of the earth (85 per cent by volume) is a rigid rocky material called the *mantle.* Beneath the mantle is a molten nickel-iron *core*; above it is a relatively thin rocky *crust.* The boundary between crust and mantle is the "Moho," or Mohorovičić seismic discontinuity, named for a Yugoslavian geophysicist, A. Mohorovičić, who discovered it when examining earthquake records in 1909 (see EARTHQUAKE). A drill hole to penetrate that boundary, at which earthquake waves abruptly change velocity, is called a "Mohole."

There are two kinds of crust. *Continental crust* averages twenty miles in thickness of light granitic rocks and is too thick to drill through. *Oceanic crust,* of relatively heavy basaltic rock as thin as three miles in some places, is covered by about three miles of water and sediment. Even though this means a drill must reach six miles down, drilling oceanic crust is the easiest route to the mantle.

In 1957 after Walter Munk, a U. S. geophysicist, proposed the project, the National Academy of Sciences established the AMSOC committee to set scientific objectives and propose drilling sites. Willard Bascom was named Project Director. With funds supplied by the National Science Foundation, work began on an experiment to demonstrate the feasibility of drilling into deep ocean bottom to obtain continuous core samples of strata. Using CUSS I, a floating oil drill vessel originally designed for shallow water work, five holes were drilled in March and April, 1961, off Guadalupe Island, Mexico. The drill bit penetrated 601 feet of sediment and hard rock beneath 11,700 feet of water. The ship was not anchored, but was maneuvered with four large outboard motors which held the ship in position after sensing deep-moored buoys with radar. In the course of experiments, samples of the entire soft-sediment section of the ocean floor were obtained. The upper part of the second layer was sampled for the first time and found to be basalt. Sediment temperature was taken deep within the bottom, and geophysical measurements were made of the hole walls.

Phase I experimental drilling, a scientific and engineering achievement of the first magnitude, left no doubt that the earth's interior could be penetrated by drill, but in 1966 work on the project was suspended due to lack of funds. Before the cutoff date the National Science Foundation had spent $38 million, some of which may be recovered. WILLARD BASCOM

BIBLIOG.–W. Bascom, *A Hole in the Bottom of the Sea* (1961); National Academy of Science Publications: No. 717 *Drilling Through the Earth's Crust* (1959), No. 914 *Experimental Drilling in Deep Water* (1961), No. 984 *Design of a Deep Ocean Drilling Ship* (1962).

MOHOLY-NAGY, LASZLO GYORGY, 1895–1946, Hungarian painter, photographer, designer, educator, writer and founder of German constructivism. In Chicago he directed the New Bauhaus (1937) and founded the Institute of Design (1939). Among his writings are *From Material to Architecture* (1928), *The New Vision* (1930), and *Vision in Motion* (1947).

MOHS, FRIEDRICH, 1773–1839, German mineralogist, born at Gernrode, Anhalt. He was a professor at the universities of Graz (1811), Freiberg (1816), and Vienna (1826 onwards). In 1822 Mohs devised what has come to be known as the Mohs' scale for determining the hardness of minerals. See HARDNESS.

MOIETY, a form of social organization employed by preliterate societies, whereby each half of a given society is set off to form two basic, complementary tribal subdivisions. A moiety may be based upon marriage—that is, a society may be grouped according to whether the mother or father is followed in reckoning descent and residence, or according to whether marriage is required inside or outside the group; upon totemism, using animals or other objects as symbols for each moiety; or upon age or given names. Moieties usually compete in games and ceremonials. See CLAN; TOTEMISM.

MOISSAN, HENRI, in full Ferdinand Frédéric Henri Moissan, 1852–1907, Nobel prize-winning French chemist, was born in Paris and studied at the municipal college in Meau and with Edmond Frémy at the Natural History Museum, Paris. Moissan became professor of chemistry and toxicology at the Paris School of Pharmacy, 1886, and after 1900 was professor of chemistry at the University of Paris. His principal contribution was the isolation of fluorine from an electrolytic solution of potassium hydrogen fluoride and anhydrous hydrofluoric acid, 1886. He developed the electric arc furnace whose high temperature of 4100°C enabled such uncommon metals as uranium, chromium, tungsten, vanadium, and manganese to be reduced from their ores. In 1893 he prepared small artificial diamonds from carbon that had been dissolved in molten iron. He was elected a member of the Academy of Sciences, 1891, and received the 1906 Nobel prize in chemistry.

MOJAVE DESERT, or Mohave Desert, SE California, mostly in San Bernardino County; crossed by U.S. highways 66, 91, 395, and 466; area 15,000 sq. mi. It is a barren tableland with an annual rainfall of 2 to 5 inches. There are deposits of silver, tungsten, gold, iron, borax, potash, salt, and granite. Edwards Air Force Base is near Muroc. Barstow, Victorville, and Mojave are major cities of the Mojave Desert.

MOKPO, or Moppo, also Mokp'o, seaport, SW Korea, Cholla Province, on the Yellow Sea; 200 miles S of Seoul. Mokpo is a center of trade for marine products, rice, and cotton. Main industries include canning and cottonseed oil refining. (For population, see Korea map in Atlas.)

MOLASSES, most commonly a sweet, dark-colored viscous sirup that is the principal by-product in the manufacture of cane or beet sugar; less commonly a sirup derived from citrus fruit peels, sorgo, and celluloses. See ALCOHOL; SUGAR.

MOLASSES ACT, a British law of 1733 imposing a prohibitive duty of 9 pence a gallon on rum, 6 pence a gallon on molasses, and 5 shillings a hundredweight on sugar imported from the foreign colonies in the West Indies into the English colonies of North America. Since the northern colonies needed exports to counteract their adverse trade balance with the mother country, they had developed the triangle trade. See TRIANGLE TRADE; NAVIGATION ACTS.

MOLAY, JACQUES DE, 1243?–1314, last grand master of the order of Knights Templars, was born in Molay, Jura Department, France, joined the order in 1265 and became grand master in 1298. After the Templars were defeated by the Saracens in Jerusalem, he withdrew to Cyprus, but Pope Clement V ordered him back to France, 1306. In 1307 King Philip IV, resenting the Templars' affluence, had them all arrested for heresy. De Molay made a partial confession of guilt, probably under torture; he recanted, 1314, and was burned at the stake.

MOLD, a fungous growth, usually of woolly appearance, that occurs on many kinds of organic matter, especially on damp and decaying substances. They are non-photosynthesizing plants belonging to the phylum Mycophyta. Their basic unit of structure is a hypha that consists of a cylindrical wall containing a mass of cytoplasm and hundreds of nuclei not separated by cross walls. The collective mass of hyphae constituting a fungal growth is called a mycelium.

Molds reproduce asexually by spores that float in the air until they land on a suitable medium for growth. They then develop into vegetable bodies, which themselves become spore-bearing organs.

Many molds are responsible for serious diseases of domestic animals and crops; some infect man. Some molds cause spoilage of food and deterioration of wood, leather, fabrics, paper, and even plastics. Others are edible and considered delicacies, although their nutritional value is low. See DERMATOMYCOSES; FUNGI; FUNGOUS DISEASES OF MAN.

Water molds, of the order Saprolegniales, live in fresh and salt water and usually feed on decaying organic matter. Some parasitize fish and constitute a major problem in fish hatcheries; the gray mold grows profusely about the gills of the fish and usually causes death. The black molds, of the order Mucorales, grow on many common foods. A representative species, *Rhizopus nigricans*, frequently grows on bread. See BREAD MOLD.

Among the most widespread fungi are the blue, green, and yellow molds of the order Aspergillales. Besides decaying foodstuffs, some species of *Aspergillus* cause diseases of the ears and lungs of man and of animals. *A. fumigatus* is the cause of a lung infection among domestic animals that sometimes reaches epidemic proportions. This mold also causes brooder pneumonia in chicks. In man, *A. fumigatus* usually causes an infection of the external ear, although the organism is also capable of causing a lung disease that resembles tuberculosis. Some species of *Aspergillus*, however, are useful in the production of organic acids, and others are important in producing a rice alcohol that is used in sake, a Japanese beverage. *Penicillium* causes spoilage of foods and fabrics, but it is also the source of the antibiotic penicillin.

USE IN RESEARCH

Molds, especially species of Ascomycetes and Basidiomycetes, have been highly useful in genetic research for several reasons. In contrast to the situation in higher plants and animals, all of the four products of meiosis derived from a single diploid nucleus can be recovered for genetic analysis. In this way it can be shown that the two parental types from a monogenic hybrid appear in the expected 2:2 ratio for each set of meiotic products. Thus in a cross between a normal reddish-orange strain of *Neurospora crassa* and an albino mutant, the eight spores of a single ascus give rise to four yellow and four white offspring. These are haploid, so there is no complication due to dominance. In this species each meiotic product is duplicated by a third nuclear division in the spore sac, which is mitotic in nature. In this and several other ascomycetes, the spores are linearly arranged in the spore sac in such a way that by removing them in order and germinating them, one can distinguish segregations that occur in the first of the two meiotic divisions from those that occur in the second such division. This is important in constructing genetic chromosome maps.

For investigations of the biochemistry of gene action, molds are especially useful because many of them can be grown in pure culture on a chemically defined medium consisting of inorganic salts, a source of carbon and energy such as sugar, plus in some cases, one or more of the known vitamins. One therefore knows all the chemical materials with which growth and metabolism begin. This is not ordinarily true with higher plants and animals. Using such defined media it has been possible to produce large numbers of so-called biochemical mutants. These require growth factors such as vitamins and amino acids, in addition to those needed to support growth of the original "wild-type" strain. Thus there are mutant strains unable to make vitamin B-1, others that cannot make the amino acid tryptophane, and so on. Such biochemical mutants have been of great value in investigations on the manner in which genes act, through enzymes as intermediaries, in controlling specific chemical reactions. They have also played a key role in showing that the bacterium *Escherichia coli* may undergo a sexual cycle.

George W. Beadle

MOLDAU RIVER. See Vltava River.

MOLDAVIA, an historical region in eastern Europe, limited by the Dnestr River to the N and E, the Danube Delta and the Walachia Plain in the S, and the Carpathian Mountains to the W. Because of its position as one of the gates leading from the steppes of central Asia to the plains of central Europe, Moldavia was overrun by many waves of invaders beginning early in the Christian Era. In the third century came Germanic tribes, notably the Goths and the Gepidae. They were succeeded by the Huns, the Avars, the Bulgars, and the Slavs. The Magyars invaded the area in the ninth century and were followed by the Petchenegs and the Cumans. Moldavia became part of the Mongol Empire in the thirteenth century. The bulk of the population was then composed of Slavs and Tatars, soon joined by the Vlachs, who are considered the ancestors of the modern Rumanians.

About the middle of the fourteenth century Moldavia became an independent state under native princes. The ensuing period was characterized by struggles among the boyars, or great landowners, and the peasantry was reduced to a state of virtual slavery that lasted until the nineteenth century. Moldavia was threatened by the encroachment of Turkish, Magyar, and Polish nobles. Prince Stephen the Great, who reigned from 1458 to 1504, repeatedly defeated his enemies, his greatest victory being that of Racova, where he crushed the Turks in 1475.

After his death the Moldavian princes, threatened from all sides, were compelled to pay tribute to the Turkish sultans, and the southern part of Bessarabia, an eastern province between the Prut and the Dnestr, was ceded to the khans of Crimea, themselves tributary to the Turkish sultans. A major rebellion against Turkish overlordship occurred in 1572 under Prince Ion the Terrible, but it was put down in 1574. Prince Michael the Brave of Walachia succeeded in establishing an independent state uniting Walachia and Moldavia in 1600, but he was murdered and Moldavia fell to the Poles. In 1618 the Turks expelled the Poles and set up the Phanariot regime during which Moldavia was ruled by princes mostly of Greek origin. Prince Demetrius Cantemir in 1711 failed in an attempt to conclude a treaty with Peter the Great whereby Moldavia would become a vassal of Russia instead of Turkey. From then on, the Turkish sultans simply rented out the governorship of Moldavia to wealthy Greeks from the Phanar quarter in Constantinople. Austria annexed Bukovina, the northernmost Moldavian province, in 1774.

After the Russo-Turkish War of 1768–74 Russian influence began to challenge Turkish suzerainty in Moldavia and Walachia. The Treaty of Paris, 1812, gave Bessarabia to Russia. Alexander Ypsilanti, son of the Phanariot governor of Walachia, rose in 1821 against the Turks, who defeated him and replaced the Phanariots by native governors. The struggle between the czars and the sultans for the control of the two principalities continued, but when the French Revolution of 1848 sparked an uprising in Moldavia and Walachia the czar and the sultan co-operated to put it down. The Treaty of Paris, concluding the Crimean War in 1856, returned southern Bessarabia to Moldavia and in 1859 Moldavia and Walachia were united under a single prince, Alexander Cuza.

The subsequent history of Moldavia became that of Rumania, except for Bukovina and northern Bessarabia, which remained parts of Austria and Russia, respectively. During the Russo-Turkish War of 1877–78 Rumania sided with Russia and was granted full independence by the Congress of Berlin, which also provided for the return of southern Bessarabia to Russia. In 1918 Rumania seized Bessarabia, but Ukrainian and Moldavian refugees from Bessarabia established in 1924 the Moldavian Autonomous Soviet Socialist Republic east of the Dnestr. In 1940 the U.S.S.R. regained northern Bukovina and Bessarabia, but the area was invaded by the Germans in 1941. During World War II Moldavia suffered greatly until the Germans were expelled in 1944. The Rumanian Peace Treaty of 1947 recognized the status of Bessarabia as the Moldavian Soviet Socialist Republic, northern Bukovina as part of the Ukrainian Soviet Socialist Republic, and the remainder of the area as part of Rumania.

MOLDAVIAN SOVIET SOCIALIST REPUBLIC, or Moldavia, constituent republic, SW U.S.S.R.; bounded on the N, E, and S by the Ukrainian S.S.R. and on the W by Rumania, from which it is separated by the Prut River; area 13,200 sq. mi.; pop. (1959 2,880,000. Kishinev is the capital city. The Moldavian S.S.R. consists of cultivated and pasture steppes in the north and south separated by low hills covered with oak, birch, and beech. Moldavia is drained by the Prut and Dnestr rivers. It has a moderate continental climate favorable for diversified agriculture. Chief products are grapes, corn, wheat, sunflowers, fruit, sugar beets, tobacco, and hemp. Livestock includes cattle, pigs, sheep, and goats. In 1955 there were 800 collective farms embracing 98 per cent of the peasant households, 108 machine and tractor stations, and 66 state farms. By the mid-twentieth century industry had replaced agriculture as the chief source of income, contributing 65 per cent of the total output in 1954. Principal Moldavian manufactures are wine, sugar, textiles, and shoes. Stone and other building materials are the chief mineral resources. Railroads and highways link the main centers: Kishinev, Bendery, Tiraspol, Beltsy, and Soroki. Moldavians constitute 70 per cent of the population, the remainder being Ukrain-

Location Map of Moldavian S.S.R.

ian, Russian, Jewish, and Bulgarian. There are a state university and nine other institutions of higher learning.

MOLDING, a continuous receding or projecting surface used for decorative effect (principally) in architecture and furniture design. Moldings are classified according to their profiles. Those of classical Greece, which became the basis of later molding profiles, were of three general types: slightly projecting (fillet and fascia moldings), single curved (cavetto and ovolo moldings), and compound (*cyma recta*, *cyma reversa* moldings). Moldings are further divided as to carved decorations. Among these the egg and dart and the bead and reel are standard designs. Romanesque moldings were simpler than the Greek, but Gothic moldings became increasingly complex, adorned with vines, leaves, and animal and human figures; during the Renaissance there was a return to Greek forms. In the twentieth century some architects spurned moldings as nonfunctional.

MOLDING. See FOUNDING.

MOLE, an insectivorous mammal of subterranean habits that belongs to the mole family, *Talpidae*, as do desmans and shrew moles. The mole has a cylindrical body, usually between 5 and 9 inches long, and a short tail. Its powerful forelimbs are armed with huge claws that make effective digging implements. Usually the animal has no external ear and its minute eyes are nearly blind. Its nose is an elongated rooting snout and the mole has an acute sense of smell. It has numerous small, sharp teeth. The fur, which may be grayish or blackish, is of commercial value. Moles are found throughout the temperate zones of the Northern Hemisphere; they are plentiful in Europe, where they are the basis of a large fur trade.

The mole feeds voraciously on insects, worms, and grubs. It lives almost entirely underground where it digs tunnels at a rate of about 15 feet an hour. Occasionally it pushes excavated earth to the surface, forming molehills. Although the mole thus damages fields and lawns by upheaving the turf and making runways for water, its habit of devouring wireworms and other insects that feed on the roots of plants is beneficial. The mole usually comes to the surface in the spring to gather grass for a nest. The nest is built underground and a litter of two to six young is born there. The mole is short-lived.

The common garden mole of the western United States is *Scapanus; Scalopus* lives in the eastern part. Their normal life span is only three years. *Condylura*, the star-nosed mole, a remarkable North American species, has a disk of sensitive fleshy tentacles surrounding its snout which probably help it to find its way about. Its fat, scaly tail is 3 inches long, as is its body, which is covered with thick, black, lusterless fur. It makes its home in marshes and spends much of its time in water, being an expert swimmer and diver. The common European mole, *Talpa europaea*, lives in the temperate parts of the Old World, where it has been the subject of many superstitions.

MOLE, a birthmark. See TUMOR.

MOLE, a harbor work constructed so as to serve the two purposes of breakwater and quay. See HARBOR.

MOLE, mol, or gram-molecular weight, the weight in grams that is numerically equal to the molecular weight of a substance. (See ATOMIC AND MOLECULAR WEIGHTS.) Thus the molecular weight of carbon dioxide is 44, and a mole of carbon dioxide weighs 44 grams. A mole of any substance contains Avogadro's number of molecules (see AVOGADRO'S LAW). Because a mole of any element or compound contains exactly the same number of molecules as does a mole of any other element or compound, comparisons of the properties of various substances are frequently based on gram-molecular weights rather than on quantities of equal weight. For example, the concentration of solutions is often given on a gram-molecular rather than on a percentage basis; thus a molar solution is one containing 1 mole

L. W. BROWNELL
Mole, an Insectivorous Mammal

of the dissolved substance in 1 liter of solution, and a molal solution is one containing 1 mole of the dissolved substance in 1000 grams of solvent. See METRIC SYSTEM.

MOLECH, or Moloch, tribal god of fire worshiped by the Ammonites. He is also known as Milcom (I Kings 11:5, 33) and Malcam (Jer. 49:1–3; Zeph. 1:5). The Israelites were expressly forbidden, through Moses, to practice what appears to be a distinguishing feature of his worship, the sacrifice of children as burnt offerings (Lev. 18:21). Molech had a place of worship in the Valley of Hinnom (Jer. 32:35). Both Solomon and Ahaz are said to have introduced the worship of Molech among the Israelites.

MOLECULAR WEIGHT. See ATOMIC AND MOLECULAR WEIGHTS; MOLECULE.

MOLECULE, a unit of matter composed of an atom or groups of atoms that are capable of separate existence as gas, or that are identifiable in liquids or solids. The molecules of some of the elements in free form are monatomic, or composed of single atoms. In this category are the inert gases of Group O of the periodic table, such as helium, He; neon, Ne; argon, A; krypton, Kr; Xenon, Xe; and radon, Rn; and those of most metals in vapor form. (See ATOM; ELEMENT; PERIODIC TABLE.) Diatomic molecules, or those composed of two atoms, are common to such elements as hydrogen, H_2; oxygen, O_2; nitrogen, N_2; fluorine, F_2; chlorine, Cl_2; bromine, Br_2; and iodine, I_2. When heated to sufficiently high temperatures, these molecules break apart into monatomic types. For example, iodine is 80 per cent dissociated into atoms at 900°C (1652°F) and 1 atmosphere pressure. Molecules of ozone contain three atoms of oxygen, O_3; those of phosphorus vapor, four, P_4. Sulfur dissolves in carbon disulfide and other liquids as S_8, or molecules containing eight atoms.

Molecules of compounds may also be multiples. For example, a molecule of hydrogen peroxide, H_2O_2, is composed of four atoms, two of hydrogen and two of oxygen; a molecule of benzene, C_6H_6, is composed of 12 atoms, six each of carbon and hydrogen.

MOLECULAR WEIGHT

Gases and Vapors. The weight of an oxygen atom, O, has been arbitrarily set at 16 and is the unit in which the atomic weights of all other atoms are expressed. (See ATOMIC AND MOLECULAR WEIGHTS.) The molecular weight of oxygen gas, O_2, is accordingly 32; that of ozone, O_3, 48. Sixteen grams of oxygen is a gram-atom of oxygen, and 32 grams of oxygen is a gram-molecule, or mole, of oxygen. The number of molecules in a mole is 6.023×10^{23}, or 602,300 quintillion, Avogadro's number (see AVOGADRO'S LAW). A mole of gas at 0°C (32°F) and 1 atmosphere pressure occupies very nearly 22.4 liters (approximately 0.79 cu. ft.). This relation is illustrated in the accompanying table.

GAS	Weight in Grams of 1 Liter, at 0°C and 1 Atmosphere Pressure	Grams per Mole	Liters per Mole
Oxygen.........	1.4291	32	22.39
Hydrogen.......	0.08988	2.016	22.43
Nitrogen........	1.2507	28.02	22.40

The atomic weights, and therefore the number of grams per gram-atom of these elements, are as follows: oxygen, 16; hydrogen, 1.008; nitrogen, 14.01. In some cases molecular weight can be obtained by vaporizing a known weight of a substance and measuring its volume at a known pressure and temperature. Suppose, for example, that a substance has been analyzed and found to contain two gram-atoms of hydrogen for every gram-atom of carbon. Its formula must be CH_2 or some multiple thereof. (See ATOMIC THEORY.) Let us suppose that when heated to 100°C (212°F) at 1 atmosphere pressure 1.68 grams of this substance vaporize to occupy 0.612 liters. In terms of the absolute scale, the temperature of the vapor would be 373°K (see ABSOLUTE ZERO, *Absolute Temperature*). Now 22.4 liters at 273°K becomes $22.4 \times \frac{373}{273}$ or 30.6 liters, and contains 1 mole of vapor. Since 30.6 liters is 50 times 0.612 liters, 50×1.68 grams, or 84 grams, is the weight of 1 mole of the substance tested. Furthermore, a gram-atom of carbon weighs 12 grams, and two of hydrogen weigh 2 grams. The molecular weight of 84 corresponds, therefore, to the formula C_6H_{12}.

Dissolved Substances. The molecular weight of a substance that cannot be vaporized without decomposition may be determined from the effect of that substance upon the freezing point or the boiling point of an appropriate solvent. One mole of a substance that dissolves in water without undergoing any chemical change lowers by about 1.86°C the temperature at which ice begins to separate in 1,000 grams of water. For example if 100 grams of water with 1.8 grams of glucose dissolved in it begin to freeze at −.186°C (30°F), it would take 180 grams of glucose in 1,000 grams of water to lower the freezing point to −1.86°. The weight of a mole of glucose is accordingly 180. Since analysis shows glucose to be composed of carbon, hydrogen, and oxygen combined in the ratio $(CH_2O)_n$, the formula for glucose is $C_6H_{12}O_6$. The corresponding effect of a nonvolatile solute upon the boiling point of water is 0.51°C (32.9°F) per mole per 1,000 grams of water. The magnitudes of these effects of solutes upon freezing and boiling points of solvents are governed by their heats of fusion and vaporization.

fluorine atom — hydrogen atom

A fluorine atom and a hydrogen atom combine to form a single molecule of hydrogen fluoride.

Macromolecules. The molecules of such substances as albumin, casein, starch, and rubber are large and either cross-linked or long straight flexible chains that look like strings of beads. The molecular weight of egg albumin is near 44,000; that of pepsin, 35,000; that of tobacco mosaic virus, 20 million. Such molecules are called macromolecules. A solution of 100 grams of albumin in 1,000 grams of water would contain only about 0.0025 mole and lower the freezing point of the water only about 0.004°C, too small for accurate measurement. The effect of macromolecules on osmotic pressure is therefore used to determine molecular weight. First, a membrane, such as an animal bladder, that allows the solvent but not the dissolved substance to pass through is filled with a solution of the test substance dissolved in water. The bladder is then immersed in pure water. To prevent the water outside the bladder from passing into the solution, pressure must be applied. That pressure just sufficient to balance this tendency of the solution to become more dilute is its osmotic pressure. For a solution of albumin, this pressure is more than 4 centimeters of mercury, or a column of the solution about 60 centimeters high.

Certain small molecules can be made to link together end to end to form linear high polymers. The repeating unit in neoprene rubber, for example, is

```
  H         H
  |         |
—C—C═C—C—
  |   |   |   |
  H  Cl  H  H
```

Natural rubber is vulcanized by adding sulfur, which cross-links the chains, altering the sticky material to the familiar elastic solid.

POLARITY OF MOLECULES

Atoms consist of very small nuclei that are positively charged to a degree that depends upon the number of protons they contain. (See ATOM.) In orbits outside the nucleus an equal number of negatively charged, rapidly moving electrons neutralize the charge of the protons. The hydrogen atom, for example, consists of one proton and one electron. Two atoms combine to form a molecule in which the electrons are equally shared—that is, they move equally with respect to both atoms. The atoms of other elements have more protons and electrons, but in any case in which atoms of the same elements form molecules they do so by sharing equally certain of their outermost electrons, just as two atoms of hydrogen do. When, however, two different kinds of atoms form a molecule these outer electrons are more or less unequally shared; the electrons are displaced, so that one part of the molecule becomes negatively charged with respect to the other. Such a molecule is said to be polar. The degree of polarity is indicated by dipole moment. Moments of several diatomic molecules are as follows: hydrogen gas, H_2, 0; chlorine gas, Cl_2, 0; hydrogen iodide, HI, .4; hydrogen chloride, HCl, 1; hydrogen fluoride, HF, 2. In these molecules the electrons shift away from the hydrogen atom toward the atoms I, Cl, and F, in that order. Based on dipole moments the atoms of various elements arranged in order of increasing negativity are boron, B; arsenic, As; hydrogen, H; phosphorus, P; iodine, I; sulfur, S; carbon, C; bromine, Br; chlorine, Cl; nitrogen, N; oxygen, O; and fluorine, F.

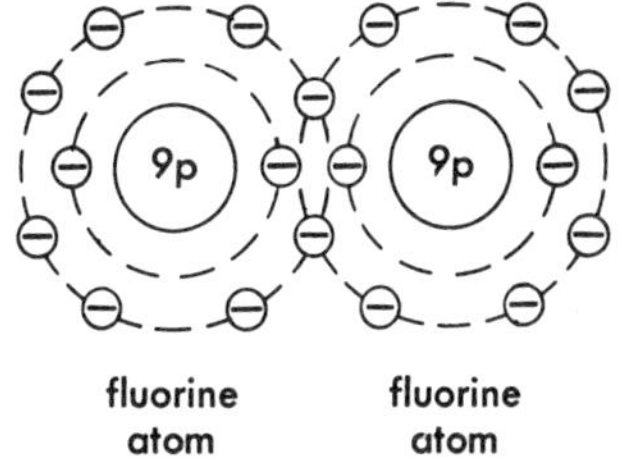

Two atoms of fluorine combine to form a single fluorine molecule.

Hydrogen Bonding Molecules. Molecules containing H bonded to F, O, or N, such as hydrogen fluoride, HF, water, H_2O, ammonia, NH_3, and alcohol, C_2H_5OH, have an attraction for each other far in excess of the electrostatic attraction between other dipoles. This phenomenon seems to result largely from the small size of the hydrogen atom, permitting exceptionally close approach. The substances composed of these hydrogen-bonded molecules have higher boiling points and are good solvents for each other. Conversely, they are poor solvents for nonpolar substances, such as carbon tetrachloride, carbon disulfide, and gasoline.

Molecular Shapes

The shapes of molecules can be inferred from several independent properties, one of which is dipole moment. There are, for example, three dichlorobenzenes:

```
      Cl              Cl              Cl
      |               |               |
      C               C               C
    /   \\          /   \\          /   \\
  HC     CCl      HC     CH       HC     CH
  ||      |       ||      |       ||      |
  HC     CH       HC     CCl      HC     CH
    \   //          \   //          \   //
      C               C               C
      |               |               |
      H               H               Cl
    ortho            meta            para
```

These pack differently in crystals and have different melting points. Their dipole moments afford a simple means of deciding the configuration of each. The three dipole moments for the ortho, meta, and para forms are 2.70, 1.56, and 0, respectively. The chlorine, Cl, atom is negative with respect to carbon, C. In the ortho form these moments point nearly in the same direction; hence the one with the largest moment, 2.70, is ortho, the one with 0 moment is para (because the dipoles cancel each other), and the one with moment 1.56 is the intermediate meta.

Carbon dioxide, CO_2, has zero dipole moment; water, H_2O, has 1.84, indicating that molecules of the former are linear, OCO, but those of water are not.

The structure of water molecules has been revealed by subjecting steam to radiation of lower than visible frequencies, and finding those that set the molecules in vibration. The possible modes of vibration of a linear molecule such as carbon dioxide, CO_2, are three:

$$O\leftarrow C\rightarrow O,\quad O\leftarrow C\leftarrow O,\quad \overset{\uparrow}{O}-\underset{\downarrow}{C}-\overset{\uparrow}{O}.$$

Those of water are different, and indicate a bent structure in which an angle of 105° is formed by the two hydrogen atoms and the intermediate oxygen atom. The molecule of carbon tetrachloride, CCl_4, in which the carbon atom is surrounded by four chlorine atoms, has the four modes of vibration of a regular tetrahedron; that of selenium tetrachloride, $SeCl_4$, has additional modes, indicating that the four chlorine atoms are not equidistant from the central selenium atom.

The structures of molecules in solids can be determined by the angles at which X rays of known wave lengths are scattered by crystals. Molecules that may exist in the gaseous state may lose their identity upon forming crystals. Graphite consists of parallel planes of carbon atoms arranged in continuous hexagons like the surface of a honeycomb. In diamonds every carbon atom is surrounded tetrahedrally by four others at equal distances in a network extending throughout the crystal. There are no discrete molecules in either. See Crystallography.

Sodium chloride, common salt, yields highly polar molecules of NaCl when vaporized at high temperatures, but its crystals consist of positive sodium ions, Na^+, and negative chloride ions, Cl^-, alternating along each of the three crystal axes. (See Ion.) Each ion has six equidistant nearest neighbors of ions of the opposite charge; they are not paired off as NaCl molecules.

The water molecules in ice are tied together by hydrogen bonds, in which every hydrogen atom is situated on a line between but not equidistant from two oxygen atoms. The hydrogen atoms shift back and forth along this line; hence an oxygen atom could come off the surface of melting ice with two hydrogen atoms different from the ones with which it originally went onto the surface. See Chemistry.

Joel H. Hildebrand

Bibliog.–L. C. Pauling, *Nature of the Chemical Bond* (1940), *General Chemistry* (1947); T. G. Cowling, *Molecules in Motion* (1950); H. I. Schlesinger, *General Chemistry* (ed. 1950); I. A. K. Syrkin and M. E. Diatkina, *Structure of Molecules and the Chemical Bond* (1950); L. N. Ferguson, *Electron Structures of Organic Molecules* (1952); P. J. Flory, *Principles of Polymer Chemistry* (1953); J. A. A. Ketelaar, *Chemical Constitution* (1953); O. W. Nitz, *Introductory Chemistry* (1956); F. W. Billmeyer, *Textbook of Polymer Chemistry* (1957).

MOLEY, RAYMOND CHARLES, 1886– , U.S. educator, journalist, and public official, was born in Berea, Ohio. He was professor of public law at Columbia University, 1928–54. Moley served on the New York crime commission, 1926–27, and on the New York commission on the administration of justice, 1931–33. He was one of the original brain trust, Pres. Franklin D. Roosevelt's unofficial cabinet of economic and political experts, and was assistant secretary of state, 1933. Moley later became an anti-New Dealer and, as editor of *Today*, 1933–37, and contributing editor of *Newsweek* after 1937, bitterly attacked Roosevelt. Among his books are *The Hays Office* (1945), *Twenty-Seven Masters of Politics* (1949), and *What Price Federal Reclamation* (1955).

MOLFETTA, city, SE Italy, Apulia Region, Bari Province; on the Adriatic Sea; 16 miles NW of Bari, with which it is connected by a highway and a railroad. Molfetta has exports of wine, almonds, and olive oil. It is the site of two cathedrals; one dates from the twelfth century, the other from the eighteenth. Pop. (1954) 57,500.

MOLIÈRE, pseudonym of Jean Baptiste Poquelin, 1622–73, French dramatist and actor, who was born in Paris, the son of an upholsterer who in 1631 became *valet de chambre tapissier du roi* (an honorary title whose bearer's duties consisted of helping to make the king's bed) with the right to transmit the position to his son. Molière received a classical education at the Jesuit Collège de Clermont.

In 1643 he relinquished his right to succeed his father as *valet tapissier*, and with Madeleine Béjart (his mistress for many years) and her two brothers formed a theatrical company in Paris known as the Illustre Théâtre. At this time he adopted the pseudonym Molière, a French word meaning millstone; the reasons for his taking this name are unknown. The Paris venture ended in failure and Molière was imprisoned briefly for debt. In 1645 the troupe reorganized and began a 13-year tour of the provinces. During this period Molière became director of the group and wrote his first plays, *L'Étourdi* (produced at Lyons, 1655) and *Le Dépit Amoureux* (produced at Béziers, 1656). In 1658 Molière returned to Paris and appeared before King Louis XIV and his court. Favorably impressed, Louis gave the company permission to perform at the theater of the Petit Bourbon. In 1659 Molière enjoyed his first great success with *Les Précieuses ridicules*, a comedy of manners whose satirization of gilded verbiage and false elegance offended the elite but pleased Louis. *Les Précieuses* was followed by *Le Cocu imaginaire* (1660), *Don Garcie* (1660)—his only tragedy and a failure—and *L'École des maris* (1661), a satire on the education of women.

In 1662 Molière married Armande Béjart, a 19-year-old actress who was either the daughter or sister of Madeleine Béjart; the marriage was an unhappy one, and Armande did little to aid him in the ensuing troubles with his enemies. Molière's next play, *L'École des femmes* (1662), treated the question of marriage between a young girl and an older man, and was the object of bitter attacks led by the *cabale des dévots*—members of the Compagnie du Saint Sacrement who in the name of religion attacked all forms of public entertainment. Public performance of *Tartuffe* (1664), a character comedy of a master hypocrite who corrupts love and honor and degrades a whole family, was forbidden (although Louis XIV liked the play personally), and it was not presented until five years later, slightly revised to appease the religious and civil authorities. *Don Juan* (1665), a character study of remarkable depth, reveals hypocrisy as the dominant vice of Don Juan, the satanic *grand seigneur*, and those like him. *Le Misanthrope* (1666), generally considered Molière's greatest comedy, depicts the sublime frustration of an idealist, Alceste, at odds with a frivolous world. In *L'Avare* (1668) Molière achieved the quality of universality in creating Harpagon, the archmiser of all time. Among Molière's last plays were *Le Bourgeois gentilhomme* (1670), a comedy-ballet, *Les Fourberies de Scapin* (1671), and *Le Malade imaginaire* (1673), a satire of the medical profession, written when Molière was in chronically failing health. During the fourth performance of *Le Malade*, Molière, playing the title role, was seized with a convulsion; he finished the performance and died a few hours later.

As a moralist and philosopher Molière continued the tradition of François Rabelais and Michel de Montaigne. In morals, nature was his guide; he saw moderation and good sense as the fundamental principles of human happiness. His subject was man in society, and his finest scenes are those in which aberration places its victim at odds with society. Molière knew human life thoroughly, and consequently his comedy is often mingled with sadness, as the foibles of man frequently lead to tragedy. There were many imitators of Molière, but no true successor.

MOLINA, LUIS DE, 1535–1600, Spanish Jesuit theologian, was born in Cuenca, entered the Jesuit order at 18, and taught in Portuguese schools— philosophy at Coimbra and theology at Évora. He was summoned to the Jesuit School of Moral Philosophy at Madrid in 1592, but died soon after accepting the post. Molina made many notable contributions to speculative, dogmatic, and moral theology, and the name Molinism was given to one of his theological systems. Molinism is explained in his chief work, *Concordia,* in which he tried to reconcile the Roman Catholic doctrines of grace and free will. His theory (which is opposed to the Thomistic doctrine of grace) asserts that the efficacy of grace has its foundation in God's foreknowledge of how man will act in any conceivable circumstances. Thus God knows before the giving of grace that some will respond freely to it while others will resist it. The gift of grace is freely given to all, but the consent of the will is necessary for grace to be efficacious. A form of Molinism is accepted by many theologians, while others, especially the Dominicans, prefer a theory that views grace as intrinsically efficacious. See GRACE.

MOLINE, city, NW Illinois, Rock Island County; on the Mississippi River, the Burlington, the Milwaukee, and the Rock Island railroads, and U.S. highways 61 and 150; a scheduled airline stop; adjacent to Rock Island, opposite Davenport, Iowa, and 74 miles NW of Peoria. Moline, East Moline, Rock Island, and Davenport comprise a metropolitan area called the Quad Cities. At Moline in 1847 John Deere, inventor of the steel plow, inaugurated development of one of the world's great farm implement industries. Moline has manufactures of machine tools, toys, heavy machinery, foundry equipment, metal products, elevators, furniture, paint, and heating and ventilating equipment. Black Hawk State Park is nearby. Moline was settled in 1829 and incorporated in 1872. Pop. (1960) 42,705.

MOLINO DEL REY, BATTLE OF, an engagement of the Mexican War that occurred near Chapultepec Hill, on the edge of Mexico City, between U.S. and Mexican forces on Sept. 8, 1847. General William Jenkins Worth, commanding the U.S. forces, ordered the capture of the group of buildings known as Molino del Rey, in the mistaken belief that it contained a gun foundry. Molino del Rey was taken after severe fighting that caused heavy casualties on both sides.

MOLINOS, MIGUEL DE, 1640?–?96, founder of quietism, was born in Muniesa, Spain. He was ordained a priest in Valencia and in 1663 went to live in Rome, where he spent most of his life. Because the Dominicans and Jesuits accused him of error in his writings, the Inquisition examined his books, especially his *Guida spirituale,* but acquitted him. In 1685, however, the Holy Office ordered his arrest. Although Molinos recanted, he was convicted of immorality and sentenced to life imprisonment; he received the rites of the church at his death. In 1687 Pope Innocent XI condemned his teachings and prohibited their being read. These teachings, known as quietism, reflect Molinos' theory concerning the annihilation of the will. Molinos believed that the soul should avoid all activity and remain entirely passive so that it might become completely absorbed in God. In this annihilation of the will the soul was not to be concerned with worldly matters, nor was it to strive to develop virtues, to perform good works, or even to avoid temptation. Molinos maintained that once the will was completely passive the individual was incapable of sinning, no matter what deeds he might perform. The principles of quietism had appeared earlier among the Gnostics, the Beguines, the Fraticelli, and the Brethren and Sisters of the Free Spirit, and were later evident in the teachings of François Fénelon.

MOLISE. See ABRUZZI E MOLISE.

MOLLET, GUY, 1906– , French political leader, was born in Arras, taught school for a number of years, took part in the resistance movement during World War II, and after the war became secretary-general of the Socialist party. He was vice-premier in Henri Queuille's cabinet, 1951, and premier for 15 months, 1956–57. He fell from office because he insisted on pursuing a social welfare program in spite of the cost of the Algerian War.

MOLLUSCA, a phylum of soft-bodied, unsegmented, bilaterally symmetrical animals, many having a calcareous shell. Included within the phylum are such familiar forms as snails and slugs (class Gastropoda), oysters and mussels (Pelecypoda or Lamellibranchiata), squids and octopuses (Cephalopoda), tooth shells (Scaphopoda), and chitons (Amphineura). Mollusks are for the most part marine animals, three of the five classes—Amphineura, Scaphopoda, and Cephalopoda—containing only salt-water forms. The Pelecypoda, however, has both fresh- and salt-water species, and a few terrestrial gastropods are known. More than 45,000 known living species and numerous fossil species comprise the phylum. See CHITON; MUSSEL; OYSTER; SLUG; SNAIL; SQUID.

The body of the typical mollusk is divided into four parts: head, foot, mantle, and visceral mass. The visceral mass, composed of the internal organs, lies dorsally. Beneath it is the muscular foot, which is the primary means of locomotion; and covering the foot is a soft, skinlike structure, the mantle, which extends down on each side of the visceral mass as a fold. The space between the mantle and visceral mass is known as the mantle cavity and contains the gills as well as

Fresh-water clams usually lie partly buried in the sandy bottoms of lakes and streams. They move about by means of a foot that protrudes from the anterior end of the shell.

LYNWOOD M. CHACE

the openings from the digestive, excretory, and reproductive organs. The calcareous shell, secreted by the mantle, may be separated into three layers: an inner nacreous or mother-of-pearl layer, secreted by the entire mantle; a middle prismatic layer of calcite or arragonite; and an outer layer, the periostracum, composed of conchiolin. Both outer and middle layers are secreted by the edges of the mantle. In some mollusks the shell is absent; in others both mantle and shell are lacking.

Internal Anatomy. The molluscan digestive system includes mouth, pharynx, esophagus, stomach, digestive glands, intestine, and anus. Contained within the pharynx may be a radula, a chitinous ribbon equipped with calcareous teeth. This works back and forth over a horny jaw located in the roof of the mouth and constitutes an efficient rasping device, capable in the case of some carnivorous forms of boring a hole through the shell of another mollusk. As the food is passed along the digestive tract it is broken down by enzymes in the esophagus and stomach and absorbed in the intestine, waste matter being eliminated from the anus. Wastes are removed from the blood by the paired kidneys, which open into the mantle cavity. Some species of mollusks are herbivorous, others carnivorous, and a few feed as scavengers. Some are parasitic.

Mollusks breathe by means of gills (ctenidia), lungs, or other respiratory organs. Both aquatic and terrestrial pulmonate snails have lungs. Other gastropods, amphineurans, pelecypods, and cephalopods possess gills. The scaphopods have neither gills nor organs of respiration, the mantle apparently serving their purpose.

The circulatory system of mollusks includes a heart with a ventricle and a variable number of auricles, and a system of tubules—the arteries and veins. Blood from the gills and mantle is received into the auricles and pumped through the ventricle into the arteries. Part of the blood is then sent directly to the mantle, where it is oxygenated and returned to the heart; the remainder flows through the arteries to the lacunar spaces in the tissues. From there it is collected by the veins and taken to the kidneys for the removal of waste products and to the respiratory organs for the gaseous exchange of carbon dioxide and oxygen, finally returning to the auricles. The circulatory system serves to transport nutrients and oxygen to the tissues and to remove carbon dioxide and other wastes from the body.

Most mollusks have separate sexes but many hermaphrodites occur, chiefly among the gastropods, pelecypods, and amphineurans. In hermaphroditic forms, however, cross-fertilization rather than self-fertilization is the rule. The reproductive organ, known as the ovotestis, is usually single and produces both eggs and sperm.

Economic Importance. Members of the phylum Mollusca have proved both beneficial and detrimental to man but their usefulness far outweighs their destructive activities. That mollusks have been used as food from the beginning of civilization is known from the shells found around kitchen middens (see KITCHEN MIDDEN). Oysters, clams, and scallops are especially popular and used for food in all parts of the world. The pearls formed within certain kinds of oysters are extensively cultivated (see PEARL). Mother-of-pearl buttons and other ornaments are made from shells, and the shells themselves serve many decorative purposes. In addition, the shells may be pulverized to provide calcium used in poultry feed. The scavenging mollusks help to purify the oceans by eating debris.

Among the most injurious mollusks are those that serve as intermediate hosts for animals that parasitize man and his domestic animals. These include such forms as the Oriental snails that harbor the Chinese liver fluke, *Clonorchis sinensis*, and the lung fluke, *Paragonimus westermani*. Other destructive mollusks are the shipworm, *Teredo navalis*, which tunnels into wooden ships and pilings; the oyster drill, *Urosalpinx cinerea;* and the common garden slugs. See AMPHINEURA; CEPHALOPODA; GASTROPODA; SCAPHOPODA; BIVALVE.

BIBLIOG.–R. Buschsbaum, *Animals Without Backbones* (1943); L. A. Borradaile and F. A. Potts, *Invertebrata* (1946); R. R. Allyn, ed., *Animal World of the Waterfront* (1955); H. Dodge, *Historical Review of the Mollusks of Linnaeus* (1957).

MOLLY MAGUIRES, a secret organization of workers of Irish origin, active in the mining districts of Pennsylvania from 1854 to 1877. It derived its name from a similar organization founded in Ireland in 1843. The main purpose of the organization was to combat oppressive living and working conditions; its members were at the same time members of the Ancient Order of Hibernians, an Irish organization founded for benevolent purposes. Since the law enforcement authorities were under the control of the mine owners, the Molly Maguires often resorted to violence and active resistance to the police. They organized strikes, notably in 1875. The organization was disbanded in 1877 as the result of the activities of James McParlan, a spy in the employ of Franklin B. Gowen, president of the Philadelphia and Reading Coal and Iron Company. McParlan had become an officer in the organization and obtained lists of members, many of whom were hanged or jailed.

MOLNÁR, FERENC, 1878–1952, Hungarian playwright and novelist, was born in Budapest and studied law at the universities of Budapest and Geneva, but never practiced. He wrote novels and short stories, such as *Eva and the Derelict Boat* (1901) and *The Paul Street Boys* (1907), but was best known for such dramatic fantasies and sophisticated comedies as *The Devil* (1907), *Liliom* (1909), *The Guardsman* (1910), *Carnival* (1917), *The Swan* (1922), *The Red Mill* (1923), and *The Play's the Thing* (1925). Among his later, relatively unsuccessful plays were *Olympia* (1928), *The Good Fairy* (1930), and *Delicate Story* (1940). A novel, *Farewell My Heart*, appeared in 1945; and the autobiographical *Companion in Exile*, 1950.

MOLODECHNO, region, U.S.S.R., a subdivision of the Byelorussian Soviet Socialist Republic; bounded by Latvia on the N, by the regions of Vitebsk on the E, Minsk on the SE, and Grodno on the SW, and by Lithuania on the NW; area 9,154 sq. mi.; pop. (1956 est.) 853,200. The terrain includes a portion of the Lithuanian-Byelorussian uplands, drained by the Viliya and Disna rivers; it abounds in moraine hills, boulders, marshes, and lakes—the largest being Lake Naroch. Lumbering, sawmilling, food processing, and the growing of rye, oats, buckwheat, and potatoes are chief activities in Molodechno. Before World War II the region formed the northernmost part of Poland. It was seized by the U.S.S.R. in 1939, occupied by the Germans in 1941, and retaken by Soviet forces in 1944. Molodechno is the capital of the region.

MOLOKAI. See HAWAII.

MOLOTOV, VYACHESLAV MIKHAILOVICH, born Skryabin, 1890–   , Soviet government official, was born in Kukarka, Viatka Province (later Sovetsk, Kirov Region). The son of a store clerk, he became a revolutionary at 15, was first arrested as a student, and was exiled to north Russia for two years. In 1911 he moved to St. Petersburg (Leningrad), entering an engineering school and continuing his underground work, in the course of which he first met Joseph Stalin, 1912, and adopted Molotov (of the hammer) as a revolutionary pseudonym. After the Bolshevik Revolution, 1917, he held posts in north Russia, the Volga area, and the Ukraine; was

FACES OF DESTINY, BY YOUSUF KARSH (ZIFF DAVIS)
Molotov

recalled to Moscow, 1921, and entered the politburo of the Communist party, serving first as a junior member (candidate), and becoming a full member in 1926. He was secretary of the party's central committee, 1926–30, and premier of the Soviet government, 1930–41. When Stalin became premier, Molotov became vice-premier. He became minister of foreign affairs, 1939. After World War II he headed the Soviet delegation to the United Nations until 1949 when he was replaced by Andrei Vishinski and returned to the Soviet Union, continuing as vice-premier and as a member of the politburo. In 1953 Molotov again became foreign minister. He resigned in 1956, becoming minister of state control and supervisor of Soviet cultural affairs. In 1957 Molotov was expelled from the politburo and from his posts as first deputy premier and minister of state control. He was ambassador to Outer Mongolia, 1957–60. In 1960 he became the Soviet representative to the International Atomic Energy Agency in Vienna.

MOLOTOV. See PERM.

MOLT, the process by which many groups of animals shed their exoskeletons, cuticles, hair, scales, or feathers, mostly for the purpose of allowing growth or replacement of worn-out outer coverings. Arthropods such as insects and crustaceans are incased in a hard exoskeleton, or shell, which serves as a protective armor. Although it is an efficient means of protection, the exoskeleton is inexpansive and thus prevents the young animal from growing. The animal must shed its armor as it grows and does so by its special form of molting called ecdysis. In the process a new epidermis is formed under the exoskeleton, and the hypodermis secretes a molting fluid that causes the shell to split. The animal is then able to make its way through the opening and rid itself of the old skin. At first the new exoskeleton is soft and the animal may grow for a short time, but once it has hardened, growth is again restricted. Molting is usually limited to the larval and nymphal forms in insects. Many crustaceans, however, continue to molt throughout their lives, the molting being less frequent in adults than in young forms. Snakes and lizards also undergo periodic molts. Many mammals undergo gradual molting of their coats, or pelages, particularly in the fall, and some mammals such as deer also molt during the spring. A complete molt, or shedding of feathers, by birds generally occurs in the autumn, and a partial molt may be observed in the spring, when the breeding plumage is assumed. Usually the feathers are not all shed simultaneously, as the bird would then be unable to fly and would be defenseless.

MOLTKE, COUNT HELMUTH KARL BERNHARD VON, called the Great Strategist, 1800–91, Prussian general, was born in Parchim, Mecklenburg-Schwerin. After training at the Danish Royal Military Academy, he served in the Danish army, then transferred to the Prussian army as a second lieutenant, 1822. He was appointed to the general staff, 1832, and on a leave of absence, 1835–39, was an aide to Sultan Mahmud II of Turkey, reorganizing the Turkish army and making geographical surveys. He returned to Berlin when the sultan died and published *The Russo-Turkish Campaign in Europe, 1828–29* (1845). In 1855 Moltke became adjutant to Prince William, and when the latter was made prince regent, 1858, Moltke was appointed chief of general staff, a position he held until 1888. With the help of Chancellor Otto von Bismarck and Minister of War Albrecht von Roon, he reorganized the Prussian army, increasing its numbers by compulsory military service and modernizing armament and communication systems. The army showed its power in Denmark, 1864, in the Seven Weeks' War with Austria, 1866, and in the Franco-Prussian War, 1870. Moltke planned the general strategy of all three campaigns. He was created count in 1870 and field marshal in 1871.

MOLUCCA ISLANDS, or Moluccas, or Spice Islands, Indonesian Maluku, an archipelago of the Republic of Indonesia, comprising Maluku Province; SW Pacific Ocean, in the Molucca, Ceram, Banda, and Arafura seas; 2°38′N to 8°12′S lat. and 124°20′ to 134°50′E long.; between the Philippines on the N, New Guinea on the E, Nusa Tenggara (formerly the Lesser Sunda Islands) and Australia on the S, and Celebes on the W; area 32,301 sq. mi.; pop. 683,416. The Molucca Islands lie in two main groups: Halmahera (largest of the archipelago), Batjan, Morotai, and Obi in the north; and Ceram, Buru, Amboina, Roma, Wetar, and the Banda, Kai, Aru, Tanimbar, Babar, Sermata, Leti, and Damar Islands in the south. The capital city is Amboina on the island of that name. The northern islands are volcanic and have frequent eruptions and tremors; those of the southern group are mainly of coral composition. The Molucca Islands have an equatorial climate tempered by cool sea breezes or monsoons. Elevations average more than 3,000 feet; the maximum is 10,023 feet on Ceram Island. Annual rainfall exceeds 40 inches. Mammals, except for bats, are rare; tropical evergreen forests prevail; and there are many colorful birds and insects, especially butterflies. Paganism has been limited to the inland regions by spread of Christianity and Islam. Malay is the principal language. Spices were once the leading export product, and nutmeg from Banda is still exported in large quantities but has been replaced by copra as the leading export. Other exports include pearls, hardwoods, petroleum, mace, and cloves. The islanders derive their food staples from the sago palm (flour), the pandanus tree, rice, and fish.

Portugal exploited the islands in the sixteenth century, but the Dutch, beginning with the Boungay Contract (1667) with the sultan of Ternate, gradually gained control of the islands. Early in World War II the Japanese seized the Molucca Islands, fortifying Morotai and Halmahera. They were invaded and recaptured by U.S. troops in 1944. After the war the Moluccas were made a part of the state of East Indonesia, and in 1950 became the province of Maluku. In April 1950 a Moluccan declaration of independence created the Republic of the South Moluccas, but Indonesian government military forces placed the Molucca Islands under a state of siege, refusing to recognize the declaration. The issue was still unresolved in 1957 when the self-declared republic appealed to the United Nations for help and recognition. See INDONESIA.

MOLYBDENITE, a mineral resembling graphite in appearance, and an important ore of molybdenum. Chemically the mineral is molybdenum sulfide, formula MoS_2; it is very soft, having a hardness of 1 to 1.5. It has a greasy feel, a metallic luster, and is lead gray with a somewhat blue tinge that distinguishes it from graphite, which is slightly brown. Molybdenite is about 4.6 to 4.7 times as dense as water. The crystals are hexagonal but may occur in formless masses, can often be separated into thin plates, and are easily cut into shavings with a knife. Molybdenite occurs as a minor mineral in pegmatites (see PEGMATITE) and other granitic rocks. The greatest single source of the mineral has been Climax, Colo., where it is found in small quartz veins.

MOLYBDENUM, a hard, tough, silvery white metallic element that together with chromium and tungsten belongs to group VI B of the periodic table (see PERIODIC TABLE). The periodic number of the element is 42 and its atomic weight, 95.95. Molybdenum is 10.2 times as dense as water, and it melts at about 2620°C (4748°F). The ductility of the metal varies appreciably with its method of preparation; if molybdenum powder is converted to a solid mass by arc melting or powder metallurgy, the result is a brittle product that becomes ductile only after being worked at temperatures between 1000 and 1300°C (1832–2372°F).

Molybdenum does not react to any great extent with the oxygen of the air at room temperature but at higher temperatures, particularly above 500°C (932°F), it reacts vigorously with oxygen to form molybdenum trioxide, MoO_3. The metal is attacked only slowly by most acids, although nitric acid, if not too concentrated, attacks it vigorously.

Occurrence and Metallurgy. Molybdenum does not occur free; it is obtained commercially from molybdenite, a molybdenum sulfide, its most important ore, and from wulfenite, a lead molybdate. Climax, Colo., the most important source of molybdenite, has in the past also been the chief producer of molybdenum; after World War II, however, molybdenum obtained from low-grade ores as a by-product of copper production became increasingly important. Utah, Arizona, and New Mexico have produced significant amounts of molybdenum from such ores; wulfenite has been mined extensively at Questa, N.M., and Knaben, Norway.

Molybdenite is easily concentrated by the flotation process. (See FLOTATION PROCESS.) After this treatment the molybdenite is roasted, thus being converted from molybdenum sulfide into molybdenum trioxide. The oxide may then be leached with ammonia to form ammonium molybdate, or it may be purified by distillation, the ore being heated in rotating silica drums until the oxide distills off and is collected in suitable containers. The oxide is then reduced to molybdenum, generally by the use of hydrogen, and the resulting powder is consolidated by sintering or electrolysis.

Uses as Metal. Most of the molybdenum produced is used as an alloying element in steelmaking. Molybdenum increases the hardness of steel at high temperatures, makes it more uniform, reduces brittleness, and increases resistance to corrosion by sea water and by hot sulfuric acid. In most steels the amount of molybdenum used is small, but high-speed steels commonly contain 6 to 7 per cent of molybdenum. Molybdenum is also used to improve the mechanical properties of cast iron.

Molybdenum, sometimes by itself and sometimes alloyed with tungsten or other elements, has been used extensively as the filament support in incandescent lamps, in other places where a good glass-to-metal seal is important, and in the radio and electronics industries. It has also been used as a heating element in electric furnaces.

Compounds and Uses. Molybdenum forms compounds in which its valence ranges from 2 to 6. Because many of these compounds decompose into others of different valence and because complexions of molybdenum occur so frequently, the exact composition of molybdenum-containing substances is at times uncertain. The same characteristics that make molybdenum chemistry so complicated, however, also cause the element and its compounds to have excellent catalytic properties, and molybdenum compounds have become important in oxidation-reduction reactions, in hydrogenation processes, in polymer formation, and in other forms of organic synthesis. Molybdenum also has been employed in the form of molybdates to dye hair, fur, and other protein substances, in lake and mordant dyeing, and—in the form of molybdenum orange obtained by precipitating lead chromate and lead molybdate together—as an orange pigment. Molybdenum pentachloride, $MoCl_5$, acts as an intermediate in the manufacture of molybdenum carbonyl, $Mo(CO)_6$, used to plate metallic molybdenum on metals, glasses, and ceramics. A decorative and protective coating has also been prepared by electrolyzing a slightly acid solution of a molybdate. The metal to be plated is made the cathode, and is soon covered by a firmly adhering smooth black deposit of $Mo(OH)_3$.

Molybdenum sulfide, MoS_2, acts as a lubricant similar to graphite, and, unlike the latter, can be used without the presence of a moistening agent. Molybdenum compounds are also used in ceramics and as chemical reagents, and a trace of molybdenum seems essential for the proper development of plants.

MOMBASA, city and seaport, Coast Province, Kenya; on the Indian Ocean, located on a coralline island 3 miles long by 2½ miles wide and on the mainland, which is connected to the island by causeways, ferries, and a bridge.

Mombasa is the chief port for Kenya, Uganda, and northeastern Tanzania. It is Kenya's second-largest city. Mombasa Harbor, on the east side of the island, is used mainly by small boats and sailing vessels. Kilindini Harbor, the modern port on the west side of the island, is considered to be the finest sheltered harbor on the east coast of Africa.

Mombasa has a warm, humid climate tempered by sea breezes. Chief industries are coffee curing, boatbuilding, brewing, oil milling, and the manufacture of lime, cement, glass, soap, metal drums, windows and bricks. Mombasa is also a market for the area's agricultural produce. Local products include coconuts, sisal, cotton, sugar, kapok, rice, maize, millet, and fruits and vegetables. Mombasa's main business district is in the central part of the island. The city has Anglican and Roman Catholic cathedrals and several mosques and temples. Fort Jesus, built at the entrance to Mombasa Harbor during 1593–95, is used as a prison.

There was an Arab settlement on Mombasa Island in the eleventh century. Vasco da Gama visited the city in 1489 and found it to be a thriving seaport. In 1505 the town was captured and burned by the Portuguese, under Francisco de Almeida. It was twice more sacked by the Portuguese, in 1529 and 1587. In 1631 all of the Portuguese on the island were executed by Arabs led by Yusuf ibn Hasan. In 1696 Arabs besieged the Portuguese defenders of Fort Jesus. The siege lasted until December, 1698, when the fort was captured and the Portuguese were killed. The city was placed under British protection in 1823 but was captured by the Sultan of Oman in 1837. Fifty years later the area became a British protectorate and Mombasa was made the capital of the East African Protectorate. The capital was moved to Nairobi in 1907 when the British Protectorate ended. Mombasa was owned by the sultan of Zanzibar, who leased a 10-mile strip to the British government, which included it in the Kenya protectorate. Kenya became independent in 1963. (For population, see Southern Africa map in Atlas.)

MOMENTUM, the dynamic quantity that is the product of the mass, m, of a body, and its velocity, v. Momentum, mv, is a vector quantity that, like a force, can be added and resolved by the use of parallelograms and polygons. See MECHANICS.

In the case of a system of several bodies, the momentum of the whole is equal to the vector sum of the momentum of all of the parts. (See VECTOR.) Also, as implied in Newton's third law of motion, the momentum of a material system cannot be changed by the action of the forces among its several parts.

Momentum is either linear or angular. The linear momentum of a body is the product of the mass of the body and its straight-line velocity. Inasmuch as velocity is expressed in units of the distance divided by the time, linear momentum (in the foot-pounds-seconds system) is expressed in foot-pounds per second. For example, if a man with a mass of 150 pounds is running in a straight line at a speed of 25 feet per second, his linear momentum, M, is $M = mv$, or 150 pounds × 25 ft./sec. = 3,750 foot-pounds per second. The time rate of change of momentum of a body is proportionate to the force acting upon that body and is in the direction of the resultant force. Expressed as an equation, $F = \frac{\Delta(mv)}{\Delta t}$. If a const nt mass is involved, the equation may be written $F = \frac{m\Delta v}{\Delta t} = ma$, where a is acceleration equal to $\frac{\Delta v}{\Delta t}$, (see ACCELERATION). If a force F acts on a body for a time period t, the product of the force and the time in which it acts, Ft, is the impulse. Impulse is equal to the difference between the product of mass times the final velocity, v, and that of mass times the initial velocity, v_0, or $Ft = mv - mv_0$. In other words, impulse is equal to the change in momentum.

The momentum that results in rotational motion is angular momentum. The equations for angular motion are analogous to corresponding equations for linear or translational motion. The angular momentum of a rotating body, therefore, is the product of the moment of inertia of that body, I, and its angular velocity, ω, expressed in radians per second. (See INERTIA.) Since $I = MR^2$, where M is the mass of a rigid body and R is the average perpendicular distance of the body from the axis of rotation, the angular momentum must equal I or MR^2 times ω. Expressed in another way, angular momentum can be thought of as the moment of momentum. In terms of the foot-pounds-seconds system, angular momentum is expressed in foot-pounds squared per second.

MOMMSEN, THEODOR, 1817–1903, Nobel prize-winning German historian, was born in Garding, Schleswig-Holstein, and was educated at the University of Kiel. He collected Roman inscriptions in France and Italy, 1844–47, and became professor of Roman law at Leipzig, 1848, but was forced to resign, 1850, because of his participation in the political movement of 1848–49. He taught Roman law at Zürich, 1852–54, and Breslau, 1854–58; and from 1858 was professor of ancient history at the University of Berlin. He was editor of a *Corpus inscriptionum latinarum*, a collection of Roman inscriptions begun in 1854 for the Berlin academy. His *History of Rome* appeared in three volumes, 1854–56 (ed. 1911); a fourth, *Provinces of the Roman Empire*, followed in 1885. In 1902 Mommsen received the Nobel prize in literature "in recognition of his being the greatest living master of historical narrative, with special mention of his monumental history." Distinguished in scholarship and style, Mommsen's history is remarkable for its novel interpretations of Julius Caesar, Cicero, and other leading Romans. He wrote also *The History of Roman Coinage* (1860) and two works on Roman law: *Römisches Staatsrecht* (1871–76) and *Römisches Strafrecht* (1899). He was a Liberal member of the Prussian parliament, 1873–79.

MONACA, borough, W Pennsylvania, Beaver County; at the confluence of the Beaver and Ohio rivers; on the Pittsburgh and Lake Erie Railroad; 23 miles NW of Pittsburgh. Monaca has manufactures of glass, iron, steel, and enamelware. It was settled in 1813. Monaca was incorporated in 1839. Pop. (1960) 8,394.

MONACO, an independent principality in S Europe, comprising a rocky peninsula and coastal strip on the Mediterranean Sea; bounded on the N, E, and W by the French Alpes-Maritimes Department; 9 miles ENE of Nice, France, and 6 miles SW of the Italian border; area 368 acres; pop. (1961) 22,300. Monaco is divided into three sectors or communes: Monaco-Ville, La Condamine, and Monte Carlo.

Monaco-Ville, situated on a high cliff overlooking the sheltered harbor, has many winding streets and narrow medieval alleys. It is considered the most beautiful section of Monaco, and is the site of the royal palace and government offices. Since 1887 the sector has been the seat of a Roman Catholic bishop; it has a Romanesque-Byzantine cathedral built during 1876–1911. A museum of oceanography, founded by Prince Albert I in 1910, stands opposite the cathedral overlooking the sea.

La Condamine, on the isthmus below Monaco-Ville, is the commercial section of the principality. It contains the central market, harbor facilities, and Monaco's office buildings, shops, and factories. La Condamine has manufactures of liqueurs and perfume.

Monte Carlo, the most famous sector, occupies the northern commune of Monaco. It contains the world-famous gambling casino; the opera and theater; and the principal restaurants, night clubs, and hotels.

WIDE WORLD

The palace square in Monaco is decked for a civil ceremony with the royal standard of Ranier III, sovereign prince of Monaco. Flags bear coat of arms of the House of Grimaldi.

Monaco was known to the Romans as Portus Herculis Monoeci. In 1215 the Genoese built a fort overlooking the harbor. During the fourteenth century the Genoese family of Grimaldi established its control over Monaco. In 1450 Monaco came under Spanish rule, and in 1641 was taken under the protection of France. In 1793 France annexed the principality, but the Treaty of Paris, 1814, returned it to the Grimaldi family. Monaco was under Sardinian protection from 1815 to 1861. During World War II it was occupied by the Germans.

French is spoken in Monaco. Fewer than 3,500 of its inhabitants are citizens (Monégasques). Citizens of Monaco are exempt from taxation but are not permitted to gamble. Each commune is administered by an elected municipal body. In 1911 a national council of 12 members, elected for four-year terms, was established. In 1959 it was dissolved upon Prince Rainier III's suspension of the constitution. In 1962 a national council of 18 members and a communal council of 16 were formed, and a new constitution was announced. The government is a constitutional monarchy and is conducted by a ministry, assisted by the national council, under the authority of a prince. The judicial system is patterned after that of the French. In 1949 Prince Rainier III of the Grimaldi house succeeded Louis II as reigning prince. In 1956 the prince married Grace Kelly, U.S. motion picture actress. In 1957 Princess Caroline and in 1958 Prince Albert, heir apparent to the throne, were born.

MONADNOCK, a solitary outcrop of hard rock that remains standing distinctly above the level of its surroundings in a region elsewhere reduced by erosion almost to base level. The name comes from Mt. Monadnock, N.H., a classic example of this sort of elevation. Clusters of notable monadnocks left standing above the general level of the Kittatinny peneplain occur in North Carolina and Tennessee. Plugs of igneous rock frequently are much more resistant to erosion than are the sedimentary strata flanking them and result in the formation of monadnocks.

MONADNOCK MOUNTAIN, or Grand Monadnock, isolated mountain, SW New Hampshire, Cheshire County; 11 miles SE of Keene, altitude 3,165 feet. Monadnock Mountain is a tourist attraction in a summer resort area.

MONAGAS, JOSÉ TADEO, 1784–1868, Venezuelan soldier and public official, was born near Maturín. He served under Simón Bolívar in the war of independence, 1812–21. In 1846 Monagas was elected president. He was succeeded by his brother José Gregorio Monagas, 1851, but returned to the presidency, 1855. There was a revolt against Monagas' rule in 1858 and he was forced to resign. In 1868 he led a successful revolt against Pres. Juan Falcón but died shortly after regaining power.

MONAGAS, state, NE Venezuela; bounded by the state of Sucre on the N, the Gulf of Patria on the NE, Delta Amacuro Territory on the E and SE, and the states of Bolívar on the S and Anzoátegui on the S, SW and W; area 11,158 sq. mi.; pop. (1950) 175,560. Monagas is mountainous in the north with elevations rising to 8,517 feet. Most of the state lies within the llanos of the Orinoco River—a sparsely settled tableland in which cattle grazing is the most important industry. Monagas is drained chiefly by the Orinoco, which forms the eastern boundary, and the Guanipa which flows through the central part of the state. There are extensive petroleum deposits in the state, especially in the north and west; crops include rice, corn, beans, cotton, and cassava. Maturín is the capital and principal city.

MONAGHAN, county, NE Ireland, Ulster Province; bounded by the Northern Irish counties of Fermanagh on the NW, Tyrone on the N, and Armagh on the E, and by the Irish counties of Louth on the SE, Meath on the S, and Cavan on the SW and W; area 498 sq. mi.; pop. (1956) 52,013. Northern Monaghan is part of the Irish central plain; the south is hilly and contains many small lakes. The Fane and Blackwater rivers provide drainage, and water transportation is facilitated by the Ulster Canal which crosses Monaghan from east to west. The chief agricultural products are livestock, oats, and potatoes. Limestone, slate, gypsum, and clay are extracted; high-grade gold ore was discovered in 1957. Monaghan has manufactures of shoes, clothing, and linens. There are a number of round towers and Danish forts and a sixth century abbey (at Clones) in the county. The capital and principal city is Monaghan.

MONAHANS, city, W Texas, seat of Ward County; on the Texas and Pacific and the Texas–New Mexico railroads and U.S. highway 80; 36 miles SW of Odessa. Monahans is in an oil-producing region and has manufactures of carbon black and oil field supplies. Hayes Museum there contains a collection of fossil remains and pioneer relics. The city was incorporated in 1928. Pop. (1960) 8,567.

CAISSE NATIONALE DES MONUMENTS HISTORIQUES
Leonardo da Vinci's *Mona Lisa*

MONA LISA, also called *La Gioconda*, a portrait by Leonardo da Vinci, in the Louvre, Paris. Leonardo began the painting in 1500 and worked on it intermittently for four years. According to tradition it is the portrait of the third wife of Francesco del Giocondo, a Florentine. The work was extensively restored several times. The *Mona Lisa* is noted for its enigmatic smile.

MONARCH, a nearly cosmopolitan, brilliantly colored butterfly, *Danaus plexippus*, that belongs to the milkweed butterfly family, *Danaidae*. The monarch has black-veined, orange-brown wings with black margins interspersed with white spots. The monarch caterpillar is yellowish green with black bands; the chrysalis is green with gold dots. Milkweeds form the main diet of monarchs and apparently help impart a bitterness to their body fluids that makes this species of butterfly inedible (see BUTTERFLY AND MOTH, *Mimicry*). Although the flight of the monarch is slow, it is, nevertheless, powerful. The monarch is one of the few species of butterflies that displays as a characteristic the habit of migration. See MIGRATION OF ANIMALS.

MONARCHY, a state ruled by a king or his equivalent who is vested with public powers either by election or by inheritance. A monarchy may be either absolute or limited. In an absolute monarchy there are few restrictions upon the monarch's power. (See ABSOLUTISM.) In a limited monarchy royal powers are limited by a constitution or shared with others, such as a cabinet, legislature, or court. In some limited monarchies, such as Great Britain, the powers of the monarch are so limited that he is only a titular authority who serves as a symbol of unity.

Ancient Greek tribes were originally governed by kings. Although Rome was at first a republic, it was later ruled by emperors. (See EMPEROR.) The Germanic tribes, who destroyed the western Roman Empire in the fifth century, had kings whose main function was to lead the tribe in battle. In peacetime, free men acted in common. Most early European monarchies were elective. Popular leaders in war were often elected as heads of state. Eventually, however, the monarchy became hereditary. In Europe during the fifteenth and sixteenth centuries hereditary monarchs wielded absolute power over their subjects but their rule was seldom tyrannical. In nearly every country the king took an important role in the unification of his realm, often allying himself with the rising commercial classes of the towns against the feudal lords. As the developing political forces began to threaten monarchic power during the seventeenth and eighteenth centuries the theory of the divine right of kings was advanced, according to which the king's right to rule was based upon the law of God. In England the absolute power of the king was undermined by the defeat of Charles I (1600–49) in a civil war that broke out in 1642 and ended in a victory for Oliver Cromwell (1599–1658), who established the Commonwealth. Absolute power was completely destroyed in England by the Glorious Revolution of 1688 whereby the parliament became supreme. (See ENGLAND, History, *The Civil War*, *The Glorious Revolution*.) In France absolute monarchy was brought to an end by the French Revolution of 1789.

The number of monarchic states decreased after World War I. Bulgaria, Egypt, Germany, Italy, Rumania, the U.S.S.R., Spain, and Yugoslavia abolished their monarchies. Most remaining monarchies became constitutional and limited. Among the countries that maintained monarchies after World War II were Belgium, Denmark, Ethiopia, Great Britain, Greece, Iran, Japan, the Netherlands, Norway, Saudi Arabia, and Sweden. See KING.

MONASTICISM, a form of religious life based on withdrawal from the world. Its origin is not clearly determined, but at a very early date—before Christianity—there were groups of religious devotees who lived apart. The great Oriental religions, especially Buddhism, have numerous monasteries. In the early centuries of Christianity, recluses began to shut themselves off from the world and live in solitary retirement. These recluses followed the practice, old as the church itself, of certain individuals of both sexes who consecrated themselves to God through a vow of perfect chastity. Ecclesiastical authorities soon established strict norms and regulations for the protection of these *continentes*, which included their way of life, special church worship, and devotional exercises in common. Then these ascetics began to live in religious communities. About 270 St. Anthony of Egypt placed his sister in a convent.

The Hermits. But a large body of the *continentes* continued to live a solitary existence apart from organized society, often on the outskirts of cities, and then in desert huts or caves. They were called hermits, and the earliest of their number to stand out with distinctness was St. Paul of Thebes. St. Anthony, best known of Paul's disciples, was the first to organize hermits into loose communities. See ANTHONY, SAINT.

Around such hermits, especially those who were saints, disciples rapidly gathered, and by the time of the Council of Nicea (325) there were thousands of solitaries in the desert lands south of Egypt, in the wastes of Nitria and Scetis. At first they did not have established rules for spiritual exercises and penance; each hermit monk worked out his own practices, sustained himself by manual labors, and gathered on Sundays to assist at mass and receive the Eucharist with his fellow solitaries.

Establishment of the Common Life. The second stage in the development of Christian monasticism was the establishment of a common way of life with all living according to the same rule of worship, penance, and work, but under the direction of a superior. Obedience to the superior's decisions became the basic virtue of all involved. This was the beginning of monasticism in the strict sense of the word. The first monastery of this character was established by St. Pachomius at Tabennisi around 320. Disciples of St. Anthony introduced the movement into Palestine, and there it took the form of the laura. In this development from the solitary to the common life, anchorites built their cells about that of a famed ascetic, subjected themselves to his common rule, but lived alone, each in his own hut. Such a collection of huts was called the laura, and these villages of monks could be counted by the hundreds in the Holy Land.

From Palestine monasticism spread through Syria to Asia Minor, and during the fourth century there emerged in the Middle East great monastic leaders who influenced the character of monasticism through their written rules, which still are observed by thousands of men and women. St. Basil (died 379) was the leader at this stage, and his rule of monastic life was a real code of living, not simply a collection of wise general directions. See BASIL, SAINT.

St. Athanasius is credited with the introduction of monasticism into Italy about 340; St. Martin of Tours (died 397) established the first monastery of Gaul. Thus monasticism was brought to the West, while the eremitical life continued in both the West and the East. By the time of the Council of Ephesus (431) monasticism had developed to such a degree in the East that it may be said to have been the most distinctive and popular feature of the individual churches. Monastic life was no longer confined to the desert or to waste places; monasteries flourished in towns. The monks of leading communities such as Alexandria, Antioch, and Constantinople were numbered by the thousands and were an integral part of the ecclesiastical life of their times. See ATHANASIUS, SAINT; MARTIN OF TOURS, SAINT.

The Father of Western Monasticism. Of all monastic founders and leaders, St. Benedict of Nursia, Italy (died 547), is perhaps the best known. He has often been called the father of Western monasticism. His early life was patterned on the Eastern models, first as a solitary, then as a reformer of an existing monastery, and lastly and most important as a religious founder at Monte Cassino. His rule for monks, written about 527, is the major outline of monastic life in the Christian world. It became and remains the principal rule for Western monks. St. Gregory the Great, one of his followers and his biographer, explains why this came to pass. The practical moderation and lucidity of this rule, its code that can be followed by the average man who wills to give himself to God, made it possible for the monastery to become a school for beginners where nothing less than perfection is the aim and design.

The permanency that Benedictine monasticism brought to Europe during the unsettled period of the decline of the Roman Empire and the coming of the barbarian tribes became one of the prime stabilizing forces of the early Middle Ages. The monk's vow of stability, his common observance in the monastery, and his devotion to following Christ, set the pattern of medieval piety. The worship of God in common through public recitation of the official prayer of the church, combined with social works as needed in the regional environment, became and remains the characteristic of Benedictine life. From Italy followers of St. Benedict spread across Europe, converting to Christianity a large number of the early nationality groupings and establishing centers of Christian life which were Roman and Catholic in emphasis. Nearly all the Western monastic bodies are offshoots or modifications of the Benedictines.

A striking exception were the famed Irish monks who, following the example of St. Patrick, were apostolic missionaries, zealous and ascetic. These scholarly Irish monks moved across Europe in the sixth and seventh centuries, restoring Christian life and evangelizing the barbarian tribes. Among their number St. Columbanus (died 615) is especially well known; wherever he passed, monasteries sprang up and generations later Irish monasteries on the Continent remained centers for Catholic missionaries.

Middle Ages and After. The medieval monastery played a most beneficent part in the preservation of light in the midst of gross darkness. It afforded a home for the saint, a place of retirement for the scholar, and a means of succor for the poor, and taught the ways of peace and order to a strife-torn and lawless world. The peaceful, the gentle, and the feeble found their only refuge in the monastery. The itinerant monks played a large part in Christianizing Europe.

The Cluniacs represent the first great reform of the Benedictine order; they originated at Cluny in Burgundy (910). In 1098 St. Stephen Harding founded a stricter type at Cîteaux, the Cistercians (see CISTERCIANS). Another type enjoining absolute silence and solitary retirement was that founded at Chartreuse, the Carthusians (see CARTHUSIANS, ORDER OF). In the twelfth century William of Corbeil introduced into England the Austin canons, or black monks, who produced offshoots known as Premonstratensians. At Sempringham in Lincolnshire originated the Gilbertine canons, the only order of English origin. The Crusades developed military orders—the Knights Templars and the Knights Hospitallers. See TEMPLARS; HOSPITALLERS.

During the French Revolution the monastic establishments of France were suppressed; but with the downfall of Napoleonic rule monasticism was revived, and under the Bourbons and Louis Philippe they again flourished. The Association Laws of 1905 caused the suppression in France of nearly all religious orders and the confiscation of their property. In 1835 Spain suppressed 900 monasteries, and the rest soon thereafter; Portugal dissolved all its religious houses in 1834. In Italy, Sardinia put an end to the monasteries in 1866, and the same measure was extended to the whole kingdom after 1870. In 1875 Prussia dissolved all orders except those devoted to nursing, but in 1887 readmitted those engaged in pastoral duty, charity, and contemplation. Twentieth century monasticism, although not so prevalent as it once was, forms an important part of Catholic religious life and, to a certain extent, that of the Anglican communion also.

United States. Organized monasticism was brought to the United States in the mid-nineteenth century after the restored European monasteries were in a position to establish new foundations. These American houses cared for European immigrants and did missionary work among Indian tribes. Among the larger and better known U.S. monasteries are St. Vincent Archabbey in Pennsylvania and St. John's Abbey in Minnesota. The nearly 50 monasteries in the United States conduct seminaries and institutions of higher education in connection with their establishments, and have extended their work to the Caribbean, Central America, and Far East regions.

Benedictine monasteries in modern times have been leaders in the liturgical revival of the Catholic church. There has also been a strong revival of Cistercian (Trappist) monastic life in contemporary society with emphasis upon silence and contemplation. The oldest and largest of the Trappist monasteries is that of Gethsemani in Kentucky. See TRAPPIST.

Officers. The life of each monastery differed not only according to its rule, but also according to national temperament and the character of the abbot who, in a general way, was at the head of each community. Theoretically he was chosen by the brethren; practically he often was nominated by high outside patronage. He exacted implicit obedience. Next in rank came the prior, who was sometimes the head. An important officer was the cellarer, who managed the domestic affairs of the house. There was also sometimes a treasurer, if the cellarer did not undertake the duties of the post. The sacristan had charge of the sacred vessels and kept the keys of the church. The almoner was an important functionary, whose duty was to find cases of poverty and to relieve them. The kitchener, infirmarian, and porter all had their respective duties clearly defined. The refectioner had care of the plate, and the chamberlain, dormitories, clothing, and household matters.

Similar establishments for women are convents or nunneries, and at the head of each community is the abbess or mother superior. See RELIGIOUS ORDERS; ABBEY; ABBOT; AUGUSTINE, SAINT; AUGUSTINIANS; BENEDICT, SAINT; BENEDICTINES; CLOISTER; DOMINIC, SAINT; DOMINICANS; FRANCIS OF ASSISI, SAINT; FRANCISCANS; IGNATIUS OF LOYOLA, SAINT; JESUITS; SIMEON STYLITES, SAINT; and articles on other monastic orders.

COLMAN J. BARRY, O.S.B.

BIBLIOG.-I. C. Hannah, *Christian Monasticism* (1925); J. Ryan, *Irish Monasticism* (1931); D. H. S. Cranaye, *Home of the Monk* (ed. 1934); G. Morin, *Ideal of the Monastic Life Found in the Apostolic Age* (1950); W. Dirks, *Monk and the World* (1954); P. Pourrat, *Christian Spirituality* (4 vols. ed. 1953-55); C. J. Barry, *Worship and Work: St. John's Abbey, 1856-1956* (1956); T. Merton, *Silence in Heaven* (1957), *Silent Life* (1957).

MONASTIR. See BITOLJ.

MONAZITE, an important thorium mineral, is a phosphate whose formula may be expressed as (Ce, La, Y, Th)PO_4, indicating that it may contain various amounts of thorium and of the rare earth elements cerium, lanthanum, and yttrium. Some thorium may exist as thorium silicate rather than thorium phosphate. Monazite has a specific gravity of 5 to 5.3 and hardness of 5 to 5.5. It is yellowish to reddish brown, has a resinous luster, and is translucent. The mineral is comparatively rare; it occurs in the form of small grains and crystals in granites and gneisses, and in larger masses in pegmatites (see GRANITE; GNEISS; PEGMATITE), as well as in the sands produced by the erosion of these rocks. Most of the mineral has been obtained from sands on the seacoasts of the provinces of Minas Gerais and Bahia, Brazil, and from the seacoast of India. In the United States it has been found in North Carolina and Florida.

MÖNCHEN GLADBACH, city, W Germany, in the West German state of North Rhine–Westphalia; a railroad and highway junction on the Niers River; immediately N of Rheydt and 16 miles W of Düsseldorf. Mönchen Gladbach, with Rheydt, is the chief center of the Rhenish cotton industry. Other products include textile machinery, paper, and armatures. The city is the seat of an academy of philosophy and theology and a textile engineering college. Mönchen Gladbach, until 1950 München Gladbach, grew up around a Benedictine monastery built in 972 which now serves as the city hall. From 1929 to 1933 the city with Rheydt and Odenkirchen was incorporated in Gladbach-Rheydt. Since 1954 the city has been the headquarters of north central European NATO forces. Pop. (1957) 148,410.

MONCK, GEORGE, 1st duke of Albemarle, 1608–70, British military and political leader, was born in Potheridge, Devonshire. He was a lieutenant colonel under Charles I in the Scottish War, 1639, fought against the Irish rebels, 1642–43, and in the English Civil War fought in the king's service. He was taken prisoner, 1644, and sent to the Tower, 1644–46. On his release he assumed a parliamentary command in Ireland, 1646–47, but was censured for making terms with the rebels. Under Cromwell, he distinguished himself at Dunbar, 1650, and was left as commander in chief to complete the conquest of Scotland. In 1653 he served as admiral against the Dutch. After Cromwell's death, Monck entered England, Jan. 1, 1660, with 6,000 men, and restored Charles II in May. Monck was made duke of Albemarle, and entrusted with the highest offices in the state. He remained in London throughout the plague, 1665, maintaining order. As admiral of the fleet he defeated the Dutch, 1666.

MONCKS CORNER, town, SE South Carolina, seat of Berkeley County; on the Atlantic Coast Line Railroad and U.S. highway 17A; 28 miles N of Charleston. An agricultural community, Moncks Corner is the headquarters of the Santee-Cooper hydroelectric project. Pop. (1960) 2,030.

MONCKTON, ROBERT, 1726–82, British colonial governor, was born in England. Sent to Nova Scotia as a lieutenant colonel, 1752, he was made provincial councilor, 1753, and in 1755, in reward for capturing Fort Beauséjour (ending French control of Nova Scotia), he was made lieutenant governor of that province. He was second in command to James Wolfe at Québec, 1759. In 1761 he became governor of New York, and in 1762, commanded the expedition that took Martinique for the British. Returning to England in 1763, he became a lieutenant general, 1770, and governor of Portsmouth, 1778.

MONCTON, city, Canada, SE New Brunswick, Westmorland County; on the Petitcodiac River; 87 miles NE of St. John. A highway, railroad, and airline junction, Moncton is an important distributing center with products of textiles, metals, woodenware, and natural gas. A local phenomenon is the daily 5-foot tidal wave (see BORE) in the Petitcodiac River. Moncton was settled as The Bend in 1763. It became a city, 1890. Pop. (1956) 40,084.

MONDAY. See WEEK.

MONDRIAN, PIET CORNELIS, 1872–1944, Dutch painter, was born in Amersfoort, and lived in the Netherlands until 1911 and from 1914 to 1919, in Paris, 1911–14 and 1919–38, in London, 1938–40, and in New York City, 1940–44. He abandoned the Dutch spelling of his name (Pieter Mondriaan) in 1912. Mondrian at first painted in a naturalistic style, then began to experiment with the figurative abstraction current in Paris during his first residence there, and finally carried non-figurative abstraction to its limits in the severely geometric paintings for which he is famous. His writings, as well as his paintings, exerted a profound influence on contemporary painting, architecture, and design. See DE STIJL.

MONEL METAL, a trade name of an alloy containing 63 to 70 per cent nickel and the following maximum percentages of other elements: iron, 2.5 per cent; aluminum, 0.5 per cent; manganese, 2 per cent; carbon, 0.3 per cent; silicon, 0.5 per cent; sulfur, 0.02 per cent; and copper, 25 to 35 per cent. It is a strong, relatively hard alloy, having a tensile strength of 80,000 to 110,000 psi and a Rockwell hardness (B scale) of 75 to 98 in the as-rolled condition for hot-rolled plate. Monel can be cast, forged, hot- or cold-rolled, drawn, spun, welded, soldered, and machined, and it has a bright blue-silver luster when polished. Monel strongly resists the corrosive action of sea water, strong caustics, and dilute sulfuric acid, but is not recommended for use in the presence of strong nitric acid or in sulfide atmospheres at temperatures above 700°F. Furnaced atmospheres for heating and annealing should be sulfur-free to preserve corrosion resistance. Monel metal may be alloyed artificially or may be reclaimed directly by smelting Canadian copper-bearing nickel ores found in Canada. Monel is widely used for food service equipment, water heaters, home laundry machines, steam turbine blades, and ship propellers.

MONESSEN, city, SW Pennsylvania, Westmoreland County; on the Monongahela River; on the Pittsburgh and Lake Erie and the Pittsburgh and West Virginia railroads; 21 miles SSE of Pittsburgh. Chief products are steel, tin, and glass. Bituminous coal mines are in the vicinity. Monessen was laid out in 1897 and incorporated in 1920. Pop. (1960) 18,424.

MONET, CLAUDE OSCAR, 1840–1926, French painter who was the leader of the impressionist revolt against the academic tradition of painting, was born in Paris and spent his childhood in the port of Le Havre. An exhibit of the 15-year-old Monet's sketches in a Le Havre store attracted the attention of the artist Eugène Boudin, who offered to teach Monet; master and pupil sketched together on the wharves of Le Havre. The success of his first painting, exhibited in Rouen in 1856, strengthened Monet's resolution to become a painter in spite of the opposition of his parents. After serving two years with the army in Algeria, he went to Paris to study in the academy of Gleyre, where he met Pierre Auguste Renoir, Alfred Sisley, and Jean Bazille.

Early Painting. Monet had been investigating new techniques in painting, but it was not until he saw Édouard Manet's famous *Déjeuner sur l'herbe* that his painting took the direction that was later to be called impressionist. His friends Renoir, Sisley, Bazille, Paul Cézanne, and Camille Pissarro were equally impressed with the light tones and lifelike technique of Manet, and together they formed the nucleus of a group that fought the conservatism of Parisian art circles. In 1865 the Salon accepted two of Monet's paintings, traditional in style. At this time he began to draw his inspiration directly from nature, and his fascination by the ephemeral qualities of light and air became evident. His first painting to exhibit the delicate quality that was to mark his future work was *Women in the Garden*, rejected by the Salon in 1867. This work, exhibited in a private gallery, attracted the attention of Manet, who arranged to meet the young painter. These two great artists remained friends throughout their lives.

During the Franco-Prussian War of 1870 Monet lived for a time in England, where he came under the influence of Joseph Turner, and from then on he painted landscapes almost exclusively. On his return to Paris the impressionists held an exhibition of their work which astounded the Parisian public. Even Monet's landscapes (which seem far from revolutionary by later standards) were denounced as mere daubs. From 1874 to 1888 Monet worked at his paintings of light and air, ignoring the scorn that greeted his work.

Recognition. By 1889 the public began to appreciate the work of Monet and other impressionists, and the struggle for bare existence was over. At Giverny, where he had gone to paint the landscape, he began his *Meules*, 15 studies of a harvest scene in every aspect of sunlight. These studies, the first in a series of such works, were followed by his most ambitious undertaking, paintings of the façade of the Rouen Cathedral. Begun in 1893, the *Cathedral at Rouen* series represents the façade at 20 different times of the day, from gray dawn to colorful sunset. Monet subordinated the detail of the façade to the air that surrounded it; and they appear less paintings of a building than picturizations of sun and light reflecting on a surface.

This series received an acclaim that stimulated Monet, and he continued his studies in London and Venice. He was particularly interested in painting water; the gray Thames River in the London fog is the subject for his *London: The Parliament*. In the first decade of the twentieth century he at last received the recognition that had been denied him in his early years, and his paintings hung in many museums of Europe. His last great work was a series of studies of a lily pond, *Nymphéas*, begun in 1916, when Monet's garden was just 40 miles distant from the western war front. Monet, then 73, was threatened with blindness, but he continued to work on the painting for 12 years until he had completed it; at the end he was virtually blind and he died soon after.

Beach at Sainte Adresse, Oil Painting by Claude Monet
ART INST. OF CHICAGO

MONETA, ERNESTO TEODORO, 1833–1918, Nobel prize-winning Italian pacifist, was born in Milan. He took part in the Milanese revolt against Austria, 1848, and later joined the forces of Giuseppe Garibaldi. He edited *La Libera Parola* (Turin), 1860–61, and *Il Secolo* (Milan), one of the leading Italian dailies, 1867–96. After 1880 he founded the Lombard Peace Union and several other peace societies in northern Italy. He edited the pacifist organ *La Vita Internazionale*, and in 1906 presided at the 15th International Peace Conference in Milan. He set forth his views in *Le Guerre, le insurrezioni, e la pace nel secolo XIX* (3 vols. 1903). Moneta was co-winner with Louis Renault of the 1907 Nobel peace prize.

MONETARY CONFERENCES. See INTERNATIONAL MONETARY CONFERENCES.

MONETARY UNION, an agreement between two or more independent countries to regulate their currencies, especially for the purpose of encouraging trade through a stabilization of monetary rates of exchange. A monetary union may have as its basis a common coinage, a common monetary unit, or free circulation in each member country of the currencies of all countries belonging to the union. In some instances one country will relinquish its currency function in favor of that of the other country.

The first monetary unions were founded by the city-states of ancient Greece. Such agreements were common in central Europe after 1200. In 1857 the Vienna Union established a single currency for Austria and Germany. The Latin Monetary Union was created in 1865, the Scandinavian Monetary Union in 1873. See LATIN MONETARY UNION; SCANDINAVIAN MONETARY UNION.

MONETT, city, SW Missouri, Barry and Lawrence counties; in the Ozark Mountains; on the Frisco Lines Railroad and U.S. highway 60; 35 miles ESE of Joplin. Principal products are berries, clothing, feeds, dairy goods, and shoes. Settled in 1871 and known successively as Billings, Plymouth, and Monett, the city was incorporated in 1888. Pop. (1960) 5,359.

MONEY, any medium of exchange that is generally acceptable as payment for goods, services, debts, and taxes. In modern times money consists almost universally of government coins (metallic money), bank and government notes (paper money), and demand or checking deposits of commercial banks (checkbook money). Early forms of money included a great variety of commodities such as cattle, grain, tobacco, sea shells, and uncoined common and precious metals.

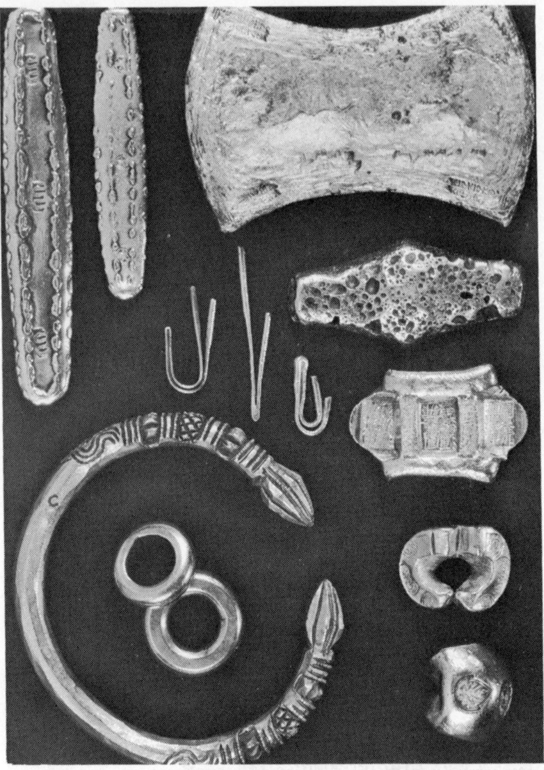

CHASE MANHATTAN BANK MUS. OF MONEYS OF THE WORLD

The types of money used in different places and different times have varied greatly. Bars, wires, coins, bracelets, rings, and ingots have been used as mediums of exchange.

FUNCTIONS OF MONEY

Medium of Exchange. The primary function of money is to serve as a medium of exchange so that cumbersome and time-consuming barter transactions can be avoided. Barter, which is the exchange of goods for other goods, is difficult when it involves only a few items and becomes impossible with many items. For example, a producer of grain who wants cloth may without much difficulty find a cloth producer who wants grain. If, however, a cloth producer wants leather and a leather producer wants lumber and a lumber producer wants grain, a series of roundabout exchanges is necessary to enable the grain producer to obtain cloth. A medium of exchange, on the other hand, converts an exchange of goods into a sale of goods for money. This money can then be used to purchase other goods. Barter is not usually employed in the modern world. See BARTER.

Measure of Value. Another function of money is to serve as a measure of value or as a unit of account. When individuals are exchanging goods and services for money with which to buy items they want, all market prices are expressed in monetary terms. Each item, instead of being subject to many rates of exchange as would be the case under a barter system, is valued at a single exchange rate or price.

Money as a measure of value or unit of account also enables individuals, business firms, and governments to keep practical records of economic transactions on both a current and future basis.

Store of Value. Money also serves as a store of value. People accept money in exchange for work or commodities, because they expect to obtain goods and services from others in exchange for this money. Anyone receiving money payments has a claim against goods and services. If such claims are made immediately, money serves primarily as a medium of exchange and only momentarily as a store of value. Many people, however, prefer to save some of their income. Although the major portion of such money savings is usually exchanged for producer goods (construction installations, equipment, and the like), promissory notes, and bonds, a minor part of these savings is held as money—either in the pocket, at home, or in a bank as demand deposits. In such circumstances money serves as a convenient store of value and makes savings economically feasible.

EVOLUTION OF MONEY

Early Forms of money were an outgrowth of barter and other special transactions such as religious sacrificial offerings, tribute, and compensation to blood relatives of a slain person. Eventually a commodity desired by members of a primitive society became the medium of exchange. Grain, cattle, and wool were used for this purpose by pastoral people; seafarers used shells and fishhooks; and skins, furs, and weapons were accepted by hunters. Ornaments, particularly metallic ones, were popular types of primitive money. The authority of a tribal chief probably reinforced—rather than initiated—the general acceptance of a particular commodity as money.

Coinage. Eventually metals, particularly the precious metals gold and silver, became the favorite commodities used as money. At first gold and silver were circulated in the form of nuggets, dust, ingots, and ornaments that presumably were weighed before changing hands. In the seventh century B.C. a notable development occurred when the kings of Lydia in Asia Minor, and soon afterward the rulers in other countries of the Mediterranean world, began to issue coins. The coinage adopted in Lydia consisted of punch-marked or stamped ingots of mixed gold and silver. The identifying marks (mottoes, seals, and the likenesses of rulers) were a guarantee of the weight and worth of the coinage. Such coins were accordingly accepted at their face or marked value without being tested or weighed, and the process of payment was greatly simplified.

Gold and silver coins remained important forms of money in most countries for many centuries. As money, these metals were superior to copper, lead, and iron in several respects. Both were desired and widely used for making personal ornaments, religious objects, and tableware and household decorations. With the exception of a few major discoveries, gold and silver remained relatively rare and therefore provided the added advantage of insuring a high value per unit of weight.

Although coinage became an important monetary improvement that facilitated the expansion of production and trade, the system was sometimes abused. Rulers in ancient and medieval times and some governments up to the seventeenth century frequently debased coins to realize additional income when tax revenues failed to meet expenditures. Debasement consisted of substituting a base metal, such as brass or tin for part of the precious metal in a coin. Such recoinage enabled the government to increase appreciably the quantity of coins in circulation at relatively small expense. But the government's financial gain in such cases was only temporary. Debasement undermined confidence in the coins and not only made necessary the burdensome practice of weighing coins before accepting them as payments, but also raised the general price level. Since a greater amount of money was thus required to purchase goods, the result of this inflation was a corresponding decrease in the country's real wealth and an even greater need for gold and silver. Clipping of coins as well as counterfeiting by private persons also created some difficulties in the use of metallic money. See INFLATION.

Paper Money as a supplement to gold and silver coins became important in many countries during the eighteenth and nineteenth centuries. This form of money was issued partly by government-chartered private banks and partly by government-operated banks. It developed primarily from the practices of professional money-changers in the Italian city-states during the fourteenth and fifteenth centuries, and of goldsmiths in London and several other commercial centers during the sixteenth and seventeenth centuries. These predecessors of banks accepted precious metals and coins from merchants and others for safekeeping in strongboxes. For this service they received a fee and issued a note or receipt to the depositor. In time such notes were used by depositors to pay for commodities. Recipients of the notes in turn came to use them for making similar payments instead of withdrawing the deposits of precious metals or coins represented by the notes.

Experience disclosed that depositors wished to store their metallic money for varying periods and that not all of them withdrew their money at any one time. Thus money-changers and goldsmiths began to lend part of the money entrusted to them, charging interest on such loans. Eventually depositors were paid for the use of their money for this purpose.

In imitation of these practices, early private banks paid a rate of interest to attract and hold deposits of metallic money while making loans at higher interest rates. Such a loan was mainly in the form of a bank note, a promise to pay an indicated amount of coin to the bearer. The notes, however, were no longer only receipts for previous deposits of coin. People who received such loans gave some collateral as security and used the notes to pay for various commodities. The notes tended to circulate in lieu of coins as long as banks kept sufficient coins on hand to redeem a portion of their notes. Converting some notes into coins on demand promoted confidence and lessened the over-all demand for conversion. Government banks issued noninterest-bearing notes.

Bank and government notes furnished a convenient form of money for many transactions, and were an inexpensive substitute for gold and silver coins. The expansion of production and trade in many countries during the first half of the nineteenth century, a period of moderate increases in the output of gold and silver, was aided by the expansion of the money supply in the form of bank notes. On the other hand, these gains were sometimes offset by losses from depreciated paper money. In some instances paper money became worthless and resulted in losses even greater than those experienced by nations because of the debasement of coins. In the United States before the Civil War, some private banks chartered by the states made more loans and issued more notes than they were able to convert into coins. Holders of such notes sustained heavy losses. Notes issued by the Continental Congress to meet expenditures during the Revolutionary War became practically worthless. Greenbacks issued by the federal government during the Civil War circulated at an appreciable discount until the Treasury began to redeem them in gold in 1879. In France notes of the Banque Royal issued in large loans to the government during 1718–20 and assignats of the revolutionary government, 1789–96, became worthless. In addition, the counterfeiting of paper money posed a more difficult problem than counterfeiting of coins.

Demand Deposits or checking accounts in banks in the late 1800's became the major part of the money supply in the United States, the United Kingdom, and other nations with advanced banking systems. This money represented liabilities on the part of banks to pay certain amounts of coin or paper money on demand. Depositors of coins in the early English banks sometimes wrote an order or check directing their bank to pay an indicated amount to the person named in the order. Demand deposits transferable by check became of still greater consequence when banks began to make loans or advances to borrowers by crediting their deposit accounts instead of issuing bank notes to them. This was a popular practice in the United States after 1865 because of a prohibitive tax imposed on the issue of notes by state banks. By the early 1900's most countries restricted the right to issue notes to a single central bank controlled or owned by the national government. Basically, however, demand deposits became more popular than coins and paper money for two reasons: the ease and safety of transferring large amounts as exact payments and the added convenience of having a check endorsed by the payee as a receipt for payment.

Despite its popularity, the use of demand deposits was responsible for substantial losses because some banks, although maintaining legally required reserves, extended too much of their capital for loans and were unable to meet depositors' demands for cash. A general inability of almost all banks to convert deposits into cash existed in the United States during the depression of the early 1930's, despite the existence of a central banking system that had been established in 1913 to assure the full convertibility of demand deposits in commercial banks. See FEDERAL RESERVE SYSTEM.

MONETARY SYSTEMS

Gold Standard. A significant attempt to maintain the convertibility of all forms of money into gold was made in most of the countries engaged in extensive international trade from the late 1900's to the early 1930's. This was the period of the unrestricted gold standard. The currency or monetary unit established by a national government was defined by law as representing a definite weight of gold. Money in any form was convertible or redeemable at that rate. For example, the U.S. dollar was equal to 23.22 grains of pure gold or the equivalent of 25.8 grains of gold 9/10 fine as used in gold coins. The U.S. Treasury was accordingly obligated by law to buy and sell gold at $1 per 23.22 grains or the equivalent of $20.67 per ounce. The bullion value of gold coins that were not appreciably worn and did not weigh less than their original weight was equal to their face value. Paper money (one-dollar notes and higher denominations), silver dollars, and subsidiary coins were redeemable in gold coin or bullion. Holders of demand deposits in banks could convert them into paper money and coins, including gold coins and bullion.

The money of one nation was similarly convertible into that of another nation with little or no loss. The pound sterling in the United Kingdom was equal to 113.0016 grains of pure gold; hence £1 was equal to $4.867. If Americans sold more to Britishers than they purchased from them, the surplus could be either left as pound sterling deposits in British banks or converted into gold and transferred to U.S. banks for dollar deposits at the current rate, with minor allowances for shipping costs.

The gold standard, with unrestricted convertibility of a nation's money into gold at a fixed rate, greatly facilitated international trade and placed some restraint on governmental use of paper money. It could not, however, be maintained in times of great national stress such as wars and depressions. Such crises usually witnessed a widespread and concerted demand for the conversion of money into gold, either for domestic hoarding or for transfer to another country. The gold reserves of governments, central banks, and commercial banks were nearly always much less than the amounts of nongold coins, paper money, and demand deposits in circulation. As a result, conversion demands during World War I and the depression of the 1930's could not be met and all nations finally abandoned the unrestricted gold standard. See GOLD STANDARD.

Restricted Gold Bullion Standard. The United States has maintained a restricted gold bullion standard since 1934, when gold coinage and the domestic convertibility of money into gold was discontinued and the private holding of gold coins and bullion by individuals and banks was made illegal. The U.S. Treasury was authorized to acquire ownership of all monetary gold in the country in exchange for gold certificates issued to the federal reserve banks. The price of gold was fixed at $35 an ounce, the value of the dollar thus being reduced from 23.22 to 13.71 grains of pure gold—a devaluation of 40.94 per cent. The U.S. Treasury was also required to (1) make gold available to licensed domestic users in industry, the arts, and the professions; (2) buy all gold domestically mined, melted from scrap, or shipped to the United States in exchange for dollar currency; and (3) make gold bullion available for the convertibility of dollar currency and bank deposits that were transferred abroad. At the end of 1962 the gold holding of the U.S. Treasury amounted to $15.98 billion. This represented about 39 per cent of the world's monetary reserves of gold excluding those of the U.S.S.R.

Managed Currency Standard. Other nations with few exceptions have adopted a managed currency standard since the 1930's. Under such a standard there is no fixed obligation on the part of a government to convert its money into gold, either domestically or internationally. On the other hand, all transactions involving payments to and receipts from foreigners are so controlled that an official price or par value for the nation's monetary unit is maintained relative to the price of other nations' monetary units.

The British government, for example, maintained a price of £12.5 per ounce of gold after 1949; in terms of gold one British pound was equal to $2.80. The government maintained this dollar rate by requiring that individuals and firms selling to Americans transfer their claims (to dollar receipts) to British banks at the official rate, and that individuals and firms buying from Americans obtain government permission before laying claims to dollars. Purchases from the United States were thus restricted to approximately the level of sales and other dollar receipts. As a result, conversion of pounds sterling into gold for transfer to the United States for the purpose of making up a deficit in the balance of trade occurred largely at the discretion of the British government. Similar controls regulated transactions with other nations—except those co-operating with the United Kingdom in the maintenance of the pound sterling–dollar rate—and permitted some transfer of claims to pounds sterling from one nation to another. However, only a limited and discretionary conversion of such claims to gold or dollars was allowed.

The official gold par value of a monetary unit under a managed currency standard is maintained primarily by restricting foreign purchases and only in a limited way by international convertibility. Many nations had to adopt a managed currency standard after World War II because of relatively high domestic prices, the urgent need for imports, and the lack of gold reserves. As an emergency and transitional arrangement, this standard prevented frequent and chaotic fluctuations in the exchange rates of currencies; but it entailed substantial administrative costs and disrupted international trade.

Convertibility of currencies, with gold serving as an international money for settlement of trade balances, enables a nation to use its net credits with one country for settlement of its net debits with another country. To achieve this objective the International Monetary Fund, a short-term loan agency, was put into operation in 1947. Its membership by 1960 numbered more than 60 nations. The fund seeks to establish convertibility of currencies at stable rates without control of international payments except in certain emergencies. It provides a basis for co-operation among nations in moving toward the general use of a restricted gold-bullion standard. It also provides a basis for an orderly adjustment in the par value of a member's currency unit when other measures fail to eliminate a persistently adverse balance and an ensuing loss of gold reserves. See BANKS AND BANKING, International Banking; UNITED NATIONS, Specialized Agencies.

MONEY SUPPLY OF THE UNITED STATES

Types of Money. Money in the form of coins and paper currency or notes is issued by the U.S. government or by the federal reserve banks acting as agencies of the government. Subsidiary coins—half dollar, quarter, dime, nickel, and penny—and silver dollars are made available by the treasury in response to the public need. Coins currently in circulation are worth about $3 billion. Since gold is no longer minted, coins are merely token money; that is, their face value is greater than the bullion value of the metal in them. Paper currency in circulation consists of U.S. notes or greenbacks (about $300 million) and silver certificates (about $2 billion), which are issued by the treasury, and federal reserve notes (about $28 billion), which are issued by the federal reserve banks. Total currency in circulation in 1962 was approximately $33.8 billion. Money held by the public in the form of demand deposits in commercial banks (about $148 billion) composes the largest portion of the total money supply.

These coins and notes are lawful money and since 1934 have been legal tender for payment of all debts contracted in terms of money, including payments made to the government. (See LEGAL TENDER.) They are not redeemable in gold for domestic monetary use. Demand deposits transferable by check are not legal tender and have limited acceptability. Nonetheless 90 per cent of the dollar volume of transactions in the United States is in the form of check payments and demand deposits are counted as part of the money supply, since a refusal to accept payment by check is met by an immediate withdrawal from the bank of cash with which to make the payment. Time or savings deposits, the withdrawal of which technically requires 30 to 60 days' notice, and some kinds of government bonds that can be readily converted into money are usually not classified as money.

Expansion of Money Supply. The supply of money in the United States increased about fourfold in the two decades following 1939. Federal reserve notes showed a slightly greater increase than did demand deposits. The money expansion was primarily a result of government borrowing from the federal reserve banks and commercial banks during World War II. Whenever taxes and the sale of government bonds to individuals and firms failed to yield sufficient income for war expenditures, the government sold its bond to the banks, thus creating additional money for government spending. The banks usually paid for the bonds by providing the government with demand deposits. When the government paid its bills by check, these new bank deposits were transferred to the general public. The new deposits were also exchanged for additional cash furnished by the federal reserve banks, mostly in the form of federal reserve notes.

Business borrowing from commercial banks during that period contributed in a similar fashion to the money expansion. Loans made to business firms and secured by promissory notes and other collateral were largely in the form of demand deposits. Some of these were additional deposits and not merely transfers of deposits made available by saving.

Control. Expansion of the money supply in the form of demand deposits in commercial banks and outstanding federal reserve notes is subject to control by the board of governors of the federal reserve system. The board may fix the average reserve requirements against demand deposits of commercial banks belonging to the system at not less than 10 or more than 20 per cent. Member bank reserves are maintained in the form of deposits with the federal reserve banks. When commercial banks increase their loans and hence their demand deposits, any need for increased reserves and additional cash may be met by borrowing from the federal reserve banks at interest rates set by the board. The member banks borrow by using their own promissory notes secured by collateral accepted on customer loans, government securities, or any other sound asset. They increase their reserves by leaving the borrowed funds on deposit. If cash is needed to meet the demands of depositors, the borrowed funds may be drawn out in the form of federal reserve notes. The federal reserve banks are required to hold minimum reserves of at least 25 per cent against their own deposits and issues of federal reserve notes. These reserves are in the form of gold certificates issued by the U.S. Treasury in payment for gold. The board, however, may suspend this requirement. As a matter of policy during the 1950's the board held the volume of federal reserve banks' deposits and outstanding notes far below the level that would have been permitted by their holdings of gold certificates.

The board may encourage member banks to increase loans at low interest rates to business borrowers and others by lowering the requirement for their reserve deposits at the federal reserve banks as well as the interest rate on borrowings to maintain such reserve deposits. This action tends to expand the supply of money. Raising reserve requirements and the interest rate tends to contract the supply of money. Expansion and contraction are influenced by the purchase and sale of government securities by the open market committee (see OPEN MARKET OPERATION). The objective of these and other federal reserve measures is primarily to promote stability in the purchasing power or value of money.

THE VALUE OF MONEY

No form of money has ever proved completely satisfactory in providing a stable measure of value. Over a period of years its value changes inversely with general price changes. The dollar purchased less than half as much in the mid-1960's as it did in 1939 because the general price level more than doubled. This drop in the purchasing power or value of the dollar occurred despite the fact that the U.S. Treasury maintained the convertibility of the dollar into gold internationally at the rate of $35 for an ounce of gold. In other words, the amount of goods and services that $35 or an ounce of gold will buy depends on the average price of other goods and services rather than on the fixed dollar price for gold. See INFLATION.

IMPORTANT CURRENCIES OF THE WORLD*

Country	Currency	Value in U.S. Currency
Aden	East African Shilling	$ .1409
Afghanistan	Afghani	.0222
Albania	Lek	.0200
Algeria	Franc	.2041
Argentina	Peso	.0068
Australia	Pound	2.2400
Austria	Schilling	.0384
Bahamas	Pound	2.8000
Barbados	Dollar	.5833
Belgium	Franc	.0200
Bermuda	Pound	2.8000
Bolivia	Peso boliviano	.0850
Brazil	Cruzeiro	.0540
British Guiana	Dollar	.5833
British Honduras	Dollar	.5833
Bulgaria	Lev	.8600
Burma	Kyat	.2100
Cambodia	Riel	.0286
Canada	Dollar	.9250
Ceylon	Rupee	.2100
Chile	Escudo	.3400
Colombia	Peso	.5128
Costa Rica	Colón	.1509
Cuba	Peso	1.0000
Cyprus	Pound	2.8000
Czechoslovakia	Crown or Koruna	.1400
Denmark	Krone	.1447
Dominican Republic	Peso	1.0000
Ecuador	Sucre	.0555
El Salvador	Colón	.4000
Ethiopia	Dollar	.4025
Finland	Markka	.0031
Formosa (Taiwan)	Dollar or Yuan	.0250
France	New Franc	.2025
French Guiana	Franc	.0020
Germany (East)	Deutsche Mark	.4500
Germany (West)	Deutsche Mark	.2500
Ghana	Pound	2.8000
Great Britain	Pound	2.8000
Greece	Drachma	.0333
Guatemala	Quetzal	1.0000
Haiti	Gourde	.2000
Honduras	Lempira	.5000
Hong Kong	Dollar	.1750
Hungary	Forint	.0429
Iceland	Króna	.0233
India	Rupee	.2100
Indonesia	Rupiah	.0222
Iran	Rial	.0132
Iraq	Dinar	2.8000
Ireland (Eire)	Pound	2.8000
Israel	Pound	.3333
Italy	Lira	.0016
Japan	Yen	.0028
Jordan	Dinar	2.8000
Kenya	East African Shilling	.1409
Korea (South)	Won	.0077
Lebanon	Pound	.4563
Liberia	Dollar	1.0000
Libya	Pound	2.8000
Liechtenstein	Franc	.2317
Luxembourg	Franc	.0200
Malaya	Dollar	.3266
Mexico	Peso	.0800
Monaco	New Franc	.2041
Morocco	Dirham	.1976
Netherlands	Guilder	.2762
New Zealand	Pound	2.7809
Nicaragua	Córdoba	.1429
Norway	Krone	.1400
Pakistan	Rupee	.2100
Panama	Balboa	1.0000
Paraguay	Guarani	.0081
Peru	Sol	.0375
Philippines	Peso	.5000
Poland	Zloty	.0418
Portugal	Escudo	.0348
Puerto Rico	Dollar	1.0000
Rumania	Leu	.1666
Saudi Arabia	Rial	.2222
South Africa	Rand	1.4100
Spain	Peseta	.1666
Sudan	Pound	2.8715
Sweden	Krona	.1933
Switzerland	Franc	.2317
Syria	Pound	.4563
Tanganyika	East African Shilling	.1409
Thailand	Baht	.0478
Trinidad	Dollar	.5833
Tunisia	Dinar	2.4100
Turkey	Lira	.1111
Uganda	East African Shilling	.1409
Union of Soviet Socialist Republics	Ruble	1.1100
United Arab Republic	Pound	2.8720
Uruguay	Peso	.1351
Venezuela	Bolívar	.2985
Vietnam	Piaster	.0137
Yugoslavia	Dinar	.0333
Zanzibar	East African Shilling	.1409

SOURCES: *International Monetary Fund; First National City Bank of New York*

*1963 figures

Over a period of years, variations in supply and demand cause the prices of some items to fall and the prices of others to rise. If the average price change remains the same after being statistically weighted according to the importance of various items in trade, the price level is constant and the purchasing power or value of money is stable. A special kind of price average known as the wholesale price index of the United States shows the weighted average of prices for nearly 2,000 basic commodities on a monthly and yearly basis. The average of prices for 1947–49 is used as the base for comparisons and equals 100. An index of 125 would designate a price level that is 25 per cent higher than the price level in the base period. The purchasing power of money is the reciprocal of the price index. Thus an index of 125 (125/100) has as its reciprocal 100/125 or 80 per cent. See INDEX NUMBER.

Quantity Theory. Determining the causes of variations in the value of money is a complex and controversial aspect of monetary theory. One of several popular concepts is the quantity theory, which asserts that the purchasing power of money depends on the quantity of money relative to the available goods that can be purchased with it. There is no fixed and automatic relationship, however, between the quantity of money and its value. Actually the factors involved are money expenditures and the price level. The number of times that existing money units are used is as significant as the number of units of money that are available. A high velocity of turnover of an existing stock of money would have the same effect upon the price level as an additional supply of money.

A third determinant of the value of money is the physical volume of trade. This takes into account stocks of goods, services, and property rights, each item of which must be counted every time its title is transferred. The less physical volume of trade performed with the existing stock of money, the higher the general prices.

The general price level varies directly with the quantity of money and its velocity of circulation and inversely with the volume of goods, services, and property rights to be obtained in exchange for money. Since the value of money is the reciprocal of the general price level, the theory may be stated as follows: the value of money varies inversely with its quantity and its velocity of circulation and directly with the volume of trade. In other words, when either the supply or the circulation of money increases, prices rise and in effect the value of money is decreased—each unit of that money buys less than before. But if supplies of goods and services increase or become more available, prices fall and in effect the value of money is increased—each unit of that money buys more than before.

For purposes of detailed analysis of the factors determining the value of money, quantity theorists frequently employ an equation of exchange, or $MV=PT$. In this equation M is the average quantity of all money used as a medium of exchange in a given period of time; V is the velocity of money—that is, the average number of times each unit of M is spent for some item of trade in the given period; T is the total number of items for which money is spent during the period; and P is the average price per unit paid for the components of T. The resulting equation $MV=PT$ is an elementary mathematical truism indicating that the total value of all the money paid in a given time for goods, services, and property rights is equal to the money value of the items purchased.

These factors are not regarded as independent forces but are the resultants of many determinants of their own, and variations in the value of money may be traceable to any one or more of the determinants underlying M, V, or T.

Cash Balance Theory. A variation of the quantity theory is known as the cash balance approach. Its adherents, in discussing the demand for money or its velocity of circulation, stress (1) the subjective evaluations made by individuals as they determine what proportion of income they will hold and (2) the effect of cash balances on people's willingness to spend. Emphasis is thus shifted from the amount of money spent to the amount of money held.

In terms of this analysis, changes in the supply of money affect the price level in some cases but not in others. If the economy is operating at approximately full employment of the labor force and if the velocity of money remains constant so that cash balances have a steady ratio to income, an increase in the supply of money will raise prices. This is pure inflation because a rise in prices is taking place without an appreciable increase in output. Since output T does not increase, the impact is on the price level P.

On the other hand, the same increase in money under conditions of less than full employment, such as during a depression, results in either (1) an increase in employment and output with little or no price increase or (2) a decrease in the velocity of spending V since the money is added to idle cash balances. The latter is likely to occur if interest rates are low and bond prices are high. Under such circumstances, individuals may prefer to hoard cash and use it as a store of value rather than to invest it.

Changes in the price level may occur without a change in money supply if there is a rise in expenditures in the form of an increase in velocity or a decrease in cash balances. A large increase in expenditures and income probably cannot be maintained over a long period of time without an increase in the money supply. Short-run increase in expenditures or velocity, however, can take place and increase prices without any change in the money supply.

Income Expenditure Theory. Another explanation of price level changes is the income expenditure approach. Analysis is concerned with (1) the nature of the decisions to spend money and (2) the main sources of expenditures that determine the level of income and employment in the economy. Changes in the money supply are considered a passive rather than an active factor.

For instance, in discussing pure inflation, the emphasis is placed on the decision by the government to increase expenditures by means of paper money or bank loans rather than on the resulting increase in the supply of money. Similarly, the interest rate is only one of several items influencing investment decisions; businessmen may decide to increase business investment expenditures solely because of improved profit prospects. Lastly, consumer spending is largely influenced by changes in net personal income. If such income increases, more money is spent although a relatively stable proportion of the increase tends to be used for savings. See INVESTMENT; SAVING.

Thus an expansion of total expenditures or of aggregate demand for output usually depends initially on increased business investment expenditures or government expenditures or both. The effects of rising total expenditures and income on the price level and value of money depend to a considerable extent on whether or not full employment exists. Falling total expenditures and income, usually initiated by a decrease in business investment or government expenditures, are likely to have much less effect on the price level than on output and employment. Prices of items in highly competitive markets will decline rather quickly without a substantial decline in output. Prices and wage rates in monopolistic markets tend to be maintained by a reduction of output and employment.

GOVERNMENT POLICY

Both monetary and fiscal controls are needed to curb inflation. Monetary controls are those exercised by the central banking system when it raises its interest rate on loans to commercial banks, increases reserve requirements, and reduces commercial bank reserve deposits by selling government securities to discourage business investment and consumer expenditures. Fiscal measures include reduction of government expenditures to curtail government contribution to aggregate demand, and tax increases to decrease business investment and consumer expenditures. These measures may eliminate government borrowing, produce a budget surplus, and halt inflation but they consequently create unemployment.

A severe deflation involving mass unemployment and greatly reduced output requires for its elimination both monetary and fiscal measures, particularly the latter. Although the central banking system can reverse the controls used to counteract inflation, the resultant lower interest rates and greater availability of credit money does not assure an appreciable increase in business borrowing and spending or stimulate consumer spending. Usually a direct increase in government expenditures and borrowing is needed to raise aggregate demand. These expenditures—for public works, social services, and the like—are more effective if accompanied by a reduction in taxes. Tax reductions make available private income for additional business investment and consumer expenditures.

Since World War II many governments have tried to maintain a high level of employment and at the same time to stabilize the price level. Such a program involves many difficulties especially in areas of administrative action, forecasts of economic trends, and selection of the appropriate time to change controls and a determination of the degree of change necessary.

CLIFFORD L. JAMES

BIBLIOG.–W. Ridgeway, *Origin of Metallic Currency and Weight Standards* (1892); A. Marshall, *Money, Credit and Commerce* (1923); I. Fisher, *Purchasing Power of Money* (1926); D. H. Robertson, *Money* (ed. 1929); R. G. Hawtrey, *Currency and Credit* (1930); J. L. Laughlin, *New Exposition of Money, Credit and Prices* (1931); E. W. Kemmerer, *Money* (1935); J. M. Keynes, *Treatise on Money* (1930), *General Theory of Employment, Interest and Money* (1936); L. V. Chandler, *Introduction to Monetary Theory* (1940); A. H. Hansen, *Monetary Theory and Fiscal Policy* (1949); A. G. Hart, *Money, Debt, and Economic Activity* (1953); G. M. Halm, *Economics of Money and Banking* (1956); R. Triffin, *Europe and the Money Muddle* (1957); A. Nussbaum, *History of the Dollar* (1958).

MONEY ORDER, a credit instrument that provides written authorization for payment of money to a payee usually in another place. Use of a money order involves three parties: the remitter, the drawee, and the payee. The remitter, or payer, deposits with the drawee, or seller of the money order, an amount of money equal to the value of the order. The remitter also is charged a small fee by the drawee, the fee varying with the amount of the order. The drawee may be a government agency, such as a post office in the United States, or a private organization such as a bank, currency exchange, or express company. The remitter usually sends the money order to the payee by mail; Western Union money orders, however, are telegraphed or cabled. Some money orders can be cashed only at places specified by the drawee, but bank and currency exchange money orders are not so restricted and usually can be cashed anywhere if the payee produces credentials to identify himself.

The U.S. Post Office issues both domestic and international money orders, and money orders drawn by some private organizations are accepted throughout the world. In 1956 the U.S. Post Office issued almost $6 billion worth of domestic money orders and more than $31 million worth of international money orders. See POST OFFICE, *Money Orders.*

MONEYWORT, a perennial creeping and trailing herbaceous plant of the genus *Lysimachia*, belonging to the primrose family, *Primulaceae*. The creeping Jennie, or creeping Charlie, as the moneywort is also known, has smooth stems, with small, roundish short-petioled leaves. The solitary yellow flowers bloom from June to August. Introduced to the United States from Europe as a garden plant, the moneywort, *L. Nummularia*, has since become a weed. It is found throughout the eastern United States.

MONGE, GASPARD, 1746–1818, French mathematician, was born in Beaune. In 1765 he entered the artillery school at Mézières, where he invented a method of applied geometry that became known as descriptive geometry. He became professor of mathematics at Mézières, 1768, professor of physics, 1771, and professor of hydrodynamics at the Paris Lycée, 1783. During the French Revolution he was minister of marine, 1792–93, and later had charge of manufacturing plants supplying republican France with arms and munitions. He was a founder of the École Polytechnique, 1794. In 1796 Monge went to Italy to superintend the removal of the captured art treasures to France, and there met Napoleon Bonaparte, whom he accompanied to Egypt, 1798, becoming director of the newly founded Egyptian Institute. He became a senator, 1805, and received the title Comte de Péluse, 1806. He wrote *Traité elémentaire de statique* (1788); *Leçons de géométrie descriptive* (1795); *Application de l'analyse à la géométrie* (1795), and other works.

MONGHYR, city, NE India, Bihar province, capital of Monghyr District; on the Ganges River; 225 miles NNW of Calcutta, with which it is connected by railroad and highway. Monghyr is noted for the manufacture of firearms and cigarettes and for its ebony work. The city has the remains of an old Mogul fort to which Nawab Mir Kasim moved his capital in 1762. Nearby are sacred hot springs. The British captured Monghyr in 1763, and three years later Robert Clive put down the "white mutiny," a rebellion of English army officers. The city suffered considerable loss of life and property damage from an earthquake in January, 1934. Pop. (1951) 74,348.

MONGOL, one of a people widely distributed throughout central Asia. The Mongols include (1) the Khalkha Mongols, the dominant people of the Mongolian People's Republic; (2) the tribes collectively known as Eastern Mongols, including the Barguts, the Chahars, and others, who live in the Inner Mongolian Autonomous Region and in the Chinese provinces of Suiyüan and Ningsia; (3) the Tsaidam Mongols, who inhabit the Chinese provinces of Kansu and Tsinghai; (4) the tribes collectively known as Western Mongols, including the Dzungars in the Chinese province of Sinkiang, the Kalmucks in the region of the lower Volga in the U.S.S.R., and others; (5) the Buryat Mongols, settled mainly in the

EASTFOTO

The Mongolian champion of kneeling archery demonstrates his skill at an interregional contest in Inner Mongolia.

Buryat A.S.S.R.; and (6) the Hazara Mongols and other Mongol groups of Afghanistan. Members of the Mongoloid racial stock are not necessarily related to the Mongols. Most Mongol tribes speak closely related languages, except the Hazara Mongols who speak an Indo-Iranian language. The Mongols number about 2 million in China, 1 million in Afghanistan, 900,000 in the Mongolian People's Republic, and 500,000 in the U.S.S.R.

Although some Mongol tribes continued to depend on hunting until comparatively late times, the economic system of the Mongols is based primarily on pastoralism. Among the animals raised, the horse was long foremost for military reasons, but the sheep is most important economically. The Mongols also keep goats, cattle, yaks, and camels. From their herds they obtain most of the material goods necessary to their way of life. Meat and dairy products form the basis of the diet. Wool is used extensively for clothing, and hides for boots and riding equipment. Most Mongols live in yurts—dome-shaped, felt-covered tents that are easily transportable. Since the Revolution of 1921 most yurts, which formerly contained little but carpets, are furnished in the Western style.

The government of the Mongolian People's Republic has encouraged agriculture, and the practice of storing hay has limited the need for periodic migration. Some groups have settled to grow wheat, rye, and barley. Mining and industry have also been developed, scientists and technicians being trained by modern methods.

The original religious system of the Mongols was a form of shamanism, similar to that of the Siberian tribes. Lamaism, first introduced in the thirteenth century, became the state religion in the sixteenth century and the monasteries took a major part in the political and economic life. Some tribes came under the influence of Islam. In practice the religion of the Mongols, whether it is nominally Lamaism or Islam, retains many features of shamanism.

The Mongols acquired four different scripts, based on the Uigur, Chinese, Tibetan, and Russian scripts. The written literature consists mainly of translations of Tibetan religious works, but the oral literature includes epic poems and folk tales. See MONGOLIA, Administration and History.

MONGOLIA, an extensive mountain-fringed tableland, customarily bounded by the Great Wall of China on the S, the Greater Khingan Mountains on the E, the border mountains of Siberia on the N, and the Nan Shan and Altai Mountains and their associated ranges on the W. So defined it has an area of about 850,000 sq. mi. and a population of more than 5 million.

Politically the area is divided between the Mongolian People's Republic, China, and the U.S.S.R. The Mongolian People's Republic, also known as Outer Mongolia, is an independent country with an area of 580,158 sq. mi. and an estimated population of 1 million in 1962. The capital is Ulan Bator.

In 1954 the Chinese portion of Mongolia, commonly referred to as Inner Mongolia, was incorporated in two administrative units of China, the Inner Mongolian Autonomous Region and the province of Kansu. The Inner Mongolian Autonomous Region, with Huhehot (Ulan Hoto) as its capital, major part of the former provinces of Suiyuan and Chahar, as well as smaller sections of the former provinces of Heilungkiang, Liaoning, and Jehol. Kansu, with Lanchow as its capital, includes the former province of Ningsia, one of the traditional divisions of Inner Mongolia.

PHYSICAL FACTORS

Topography. The Mongolian Plateau extends from 88° to 123°E long. and from 38° to 55°N lat. Its altitude varies from 3,000 to 6,000 feet, cupping slightly toward the center, and it is rimmed by mountains reaching elevations of 10,000 to 15,000 feet in the Khangai and Altai. Most of Mongolia consists of a series of broad structural basins known as talas, flat and featureless except for the dissected edges of the terraces that divide them into a series of at least three erosional surfaces. Within the lowest level of each tala are playas, or intermittent lakes. Wind erosion has left most of the tala surfaces gravelly and pebbly. Occasionally, especially on the lee side of the basins, wind-blown material has formed sand dunes, but these cover no more than 5 per cent of the total surface. The larger basins of Mongolia are the Dalai Tala in the northeast adjoining the Greater Khingan Mountains, with a series of lakes to the north and lava flows to the south; the Iren Tala in central Mongolia; and the Gashuin Tala in the southwest between the Nan Shan and Altai. The Gobi Desert is composed largely of these areas. To the northwest are two large mountain-rimmed basins, the Valley of the Lakes and the Tannu-Tuva Basin, separated from each other by the Tannu-Ola mountains. To the central north the basins give way to a series of highlands ranging from mountains in the west to hills in the east. To the south in Inner Mongolia is another series of hill lands, the Ala Shan.

EASTFOTO

Camel caravans are still essential in the Gobi Desert, although supplemented by more modern means of transportation. Here camels carry supplies to a depot on the Lanchow-Paotow Railway.

Hydrography. The northwest is drained by rivers some of which—as the Tes and the Kobdo—flow into salt or brackish lakes. A noteworthy aspect of the hydrography is the arrangement of the upland basins in terraces where a lake fed by the streams of its own system in turn may, through a canal-like river, send its overflow to a lower level. Khubsugul, 5,320 feet above sea level, gives rise to the Egin Gol which, after junction with the Selenge and the Orhan, leaves the plateau through a gap in the rim, and ultimately empties into Lake Baykal. The Kerulen is an important stream in the northeast. The headwaters of the Yenisei River are found in the Tannu-Tuva Basin. The northern marginal Gobi has a few short rivers ending in intermittent ponds or disappearing in the sands. In central Gobi and in the Chahar steppe water is obtained from wells; in the steppe, because of proximity to the Greater Khingans which retain the moisture of the southeast monsoon, water is found in abundance at depths of 15 to 25 feet. In the southwest the Etsin Gol, originating in the Nan Shan, is the largest river of southern marginal Gobi. The northern bend of the Yellow River drains Suiyuan in western Inner Mongolia.

Climate, Plants, and Animals. The climate of Mongolia is harsh, characterized by aridity, long cold winters, and great temperature extremes. Rainfall averages less than 10 inches per year in the basin-like interior and seldom exceeds 15 inches even in the surrounding highland rim; nearly all of it comes during the summer months. Winters are long and extremely cold. Midwinter monthly averages are much below 0°F and icy Siberian winds frequently bring extremes of −40° to −60°. In contrast the summer season, because of the clear, dry air and intensive radiation from the barren surface, often has daytime temperatures well above 100°. Much of the natural vegetation of Mongolia is adapted to drought and temperature extremes. In the heart of the Gobi grow much thorn scrub and some sparse grasses. On the margins of the desert are the short grass steppes, the true home of the pastoral Mongols. To the north the flora is related to that of Siberia, with pine, beech, larch, and cedar forests occupying the northern slopes of hills and mountains. The indigenous fauna, largely restricted to the mountainous tracts of the north and northwest, includes wolf, bear, deer, and various fur-bearing animals.

Social and Economic Factors

People. Mongols, belonging in large part to the Khalkha group and speaking various Mongol dialects, form the bulk of the population of the Mongolian People's Republic. With few exceptions they profess Lamaist Buddhism. Besides Ulan Bator and Altan Bulak, the Mongolian People's Republic has few large cities. There are small Soviet and Chinese minorities. Most of the inhabitants of Inner Mongolia are Chinese, many of whom are Moslem. The Mongol minority lives mostly in the uncultivated areas. The Communist regime encouraged mass education in the Mongolian People's Republic and illiteracy had greatly declined by mid-twentieth century. In 1955 a total of 80,000 students were enrolled in some 400 schools. The University of Ulan Bator, opened in 1942, had 2,500 students in 1957.

Economy. The Mongols are traditionally pastoral nomads raising sheep, goats, cattle, horses, and camels. In the second quarter of the twentieth century this nomadic existence evolved toward a collective economy with increased dry farming in the steppe lands. Animals and their products remain, however, the most important trade items of Mongolia. The dry farming areas of the steppe lands to the north produce wheat, rye, millet, and barley. Those to the south produce in addition such crops as rice, kaoliang, indigo, cotton, and opium. The Mongolian People's Republic has become self-sufficient in grain. Because of precarious and erratic rainfall, agriculture has always been a risky venture in Mongolia and the history of the area is replete with periods of expansion and contraction of the limits of cultivation.

The limited amount of manufacturing carried on in Mongolia is largely confined to the larger cities. Ulan Bator has meat, wood, and metalworking plants, a brick kiln, a steam power plant, saddleries, and felt rug factories. The area has considerable mineral wealth with coal, iron, copper, gold, silver, lead, zinc, and salt. Gold mining and salt extraction are old industries. Coal deposits near Ulan Bator are exploited to supply local needs. Trapping and hunting are important in the area along the northern boundary and furs are one of the chief export items. There is also lumbering in northern border areas.

A mixed goods and passenger train on the Tsining-Erhlien Railway crosses Inner Mongolia's western grazing regions.
EASTFOTO

The trade of the Mongolian People's Republic is oriented toward the Soviet Union. Wool, hides, meat, and fur are exchanged for oil, cement, chemicals, textiles, and other manufactured products. The most important transportation route of Mongolia is the railroad line from the Trans-Siberian Railroad through Ulan Bator across the Gobi to Kalgan in China proper. Most of Mongolia is crossed by ancient caravan routes some of which have been improved for use by motor vehicles. Ulan Bator is the center of an air transportation system as well as the key point in the communications system of the Mongolian People's Republic. Alfred W. Booth

Administration and History

Government. The constitution of the Mongolian People's Republic was adopted on June 30, 1940, and has been amended several times. The legislative power is vested in the great people's khural, whose members are elected for the three-year terms on the basis of one deputy per 2,500 inhabitants. All male and female persons more than 18 years of age are qualified to vote. The great people's khural may amend the constitution by a two-thirds vote. The executive power is vested in the presidium of the great people's khural, composed of a chairman, a vice-chairman, a secretary, and four other members, all elected by the great people's khural. The council of ministers consists of the prime minister, the deputy prime minister, the president of the government planning commission, the president of the committee for cultural affairs, and several other ministers. The judicial system includes the supreme court, whose members are elected by the great people's khural; special courts set up by the great people's khural; provincial courts and city courts with members elected by universal suffrage; and district courts, elected by the population of the district. The political capital is Ulan Bator and the country is divided into 18 provinces, 322 districts, and 2,700 household groups.

Early History. During the Neolithic age and the Bronze Age the Mongols had a mixed economy not unlike that of the Chinese, but after about 500 B.C. they became increasingly dependent on extensive pastoral nomadism, causing dispersal of population, whereas the Chinese became more and more dependent on intensive irrigated agriculture, which favored concentration of population. Consequently, the subsequent histories of the two peoples were in sharp contrast.

The Hsiung-nu, probably a Turkic people, sometimes identified with the Huns, used Mongolia as a base for raids in North China where they established an empire that lasted from the third to the sixth century. The Uigurs, a people of Turkic affiliations, founded an empire in Mongolia in the eighth and ninth centuries. The Mongols themselves, settled in eastern Mongolia and western Manchuria, are first mentioned in the annals of the Tang dynasty, (618–907).

Mongol Empire. The Mongols, being a nomadic pastoral people, developed no system of land ownership; the right to use a specific territory belonged to a tribe as a whole. The tribal chiefs who administered tribal territory on behalf of the tribe gradually gained personal power. The Mongols were economically self-sufficient, since their sheep and other animals provided them with all the necessities of life in the steppes, including food, clothing, shelter, fuel, and transport. As the Mongols perfected a way of life adapted to a steppe environment, they began to produce a surplus available for trade. The tribal chiefs exchanged their surplus goods for tea, sugar, silk, furs, and other luxuries from China, Siberia, Turkistan, and Persia. The resulting process of social stratification and feudalization was completed by the end of the twelfth century.

At that time a tribal chief, Genghis Khan, succeeded in defeating all his neighbors in turn and be-

TRIANGLE PHOTO SERVICE

This circular felt hut, called a yurt, is more elaborate than most yurts since it belongs to a shaman, or priest. The poles are decorated with plumes symbolizing his rank.

came the ruler of all the Mongols in 1206. Genghis Khan made Karakorum his capital and consolidated Mongolian unity by undertaking the conquest of other nations. By the time of his death in 1227 he had extended his empire eastward to the Japan Sea and westward to the Black Sea.

Among his four sons—Juji, Jagatai, Ogadai, and Tului—Genghis Khan chose Ogadai as his successor. Ogadai completed the destruction of the Kin dynasty in North China, taking Kaifeng, the Kin capital, in 1234. During the reign of Ogadai, Batu, son of Juji, led an army into eastern Europe, capturing Kiev in 1240 and Budapest in 1241, and became khan of the western Kipchaks, whose empire extended from Siberia to Hungary. The western Kipchaks, who adopted Islam, were the overlords of Russia for the next century. In 1381 Toktamish became khan of both the western Kipchaks (Golden Horde) and the eastern Kipchaks (White Horde), but he was defeated and his empire destroyed by Tamerlane. Muscovy, under Czar Ivan IV, the Terrible, annexed the khanate of Kazan in 1552 and the khanate of Astrakhan in 1554. The khanate of the Crimea, however, was not definitively annexed until 1783.

The house of Ogadai was displaced by the house of Tului in 1251, when Mangu, son of Tului, was elected khan of all the Mongols. Mangu sent his brother Hulagu to quell a revolt in Persia. Hulagu took Baghdad in 1258 and Damascus in 1260 and became the ruler of an empire covering the area between Baluchistan and Anatolia. His dynasty ruled until 1353, although power was divided after 1335. A second Mongol dynasty was established over the same general area, stretching from Turkistan to Armenia, by Tamerlane, who made Samarkand his capital from 1370 to 1405.

Mangu sent another brother, Kublai, to complete the conquest of China. Kublai advanced south to Tonkin. After Mangu's death in 1259, Kublai was elected khan of all the Mongols. In China the Mongols made efforts to create an upper class of Mongols distinct from the mass of Chinese. To avoid relying on the Chinese gentry, they brought in Nestorian Uigurs and Moslem Turks and Persians to administer the country. Later, connections with Turkistan and Persia weakened and the Yuan (Mongol) Dynasty was overthrown by the Ming Dynasty in 1368.

The empire founded by the house of Jagatai in Turkistan, with its capital first at Samarkand, later at Yarkand, and finally at Aksu, was destroyed by the Uzbeks in the sixteenth century. The Uzbek Empire, founded by Abulkhair Khan in the fifteenth century, ruled over Samarkand and Bukhara for centuries. Baber, founder of the Mogul Empire in India, also claimed descent from Genghis Khan.

Chinese Rule. Tibetan Lamaism, nominally Buddhist but strongly influenced by Nestorian Christianity and Manichaeism, had been introduced in Mongolia in the thirteenth century, but Christianity and Islam were tolerated in the Mongol Empire. In the sixteenth century Altan Khan established Lamaism as the state religion. The consequences were important, for fixed property became an institution with the building of temples and monasteries and the pastoral nomadism of the Mongols became less extensive. The Chinese were thus in a better position to divide and rule.

Mongolia came under the control of the Manchu Dynasty which ruled China from 1644 to 1911. The Manchus, enriched by their loot from China, were able to give economic aid to and claim allegiance from the eastern Mongols who lived in Inner Mongolia and western Manchuria. Later the Khalkhas requested Chinese assistance against the western Mongols, or Ölöts, who attempted to create a new Mongol Empire in central Asia. The Manchus seized the opportunity to intervene and impose their suzerainty over the Khalkhas. The western branch of the Ölöts migrated westward, but the eastern branch, the Dzungars, accepted Chinese suzerainty. Some of the western Ölöts came back in 1711, while the Kalmucks remained in the region of the lower Volga. Outer Mongolia was officially annexed in 1691.

The Manchus were able to perpetuate a Mongolian church looking toward Lhasa and a Mongolian nobility looking toward Peking. The higher clergy accumulated great wealth, while the standard of living of the common people fell sharply.

Around 1900, Chinese farmers started to colonize Inner Mongolia and, after the completion of the Trans-Siberian Railroad, Russians began to settle in Buryat-Mongolia and Tannu-Tuva. Upon the outbreak of the Chinese Revolution in 1911, Mongolia declared itself independent with the hutukhtu, the highest religious dignitary, as ruler. Russia, China, and Mongolia in 1915 signed a treaty recognizing Mongolian autonomy under Chinese suzerainty, but Russian influence prevailed. Taking advantage of the civil war in Russia, China regained control in 1919. Mongolia was invaded in 1921 by Alexander von Ungern-Sternberg, the "Mad Baron," who claimed descent from Genghis Khan and emulated his alleged ancestor by massacring everyone in his way. The "Mad Baron" was defeated and captured by the Bolsheviks after a campaign of several months and Outer Mongolia became independent.

Independent Mongolia. In 1924 an agreement among the U.S.S.R., China, and Mongolia recognized Outer Mongolia as an integral part of China, but actually granted it independence. After the death of the hutukhtu in 1924, Outer Mongolia adopted its first constitution, becoming the Mongolian People's Republic. Its independence was recognized by the U.S.S.R. in 1926. After the Japanese conquest of Manchuria in 1931, border incidents occurred frequently. A short undeclared war was won in 1939 by the Soviet and Mongolian forces over the Japanese. A new constitution was adopted in 1940. Following a plebiscite held in 1945, China recognized the independence of the Mongolian People's Republic and a treaty was signed in 1950 by which China and the U.S.S.R. guaranteed the independence of the republic. Parts of Inner Mongolia, Jehol, and western Manchuria were constituted the Inner Mongolian Autonomous Region within China.

Agriculture was encouraged in Mongolia and, as storage of hay became the general practice, the need for nomadism decreased. Gradually the movements of the pastoral nomads became restricted to seasonal movements only. At the same time the mineral resources of Mongolia, including gold and coal, were developed and roads, railroads, and airlines were established. Great importance was given to education, and illiteracy, which was almost general in 1921, was drastically reduced. See MONGOL.

BIBLIOGRAPHY

DESCRIPTION AND TRAVEL: D. Carruthers, *Unknown Mongolia* (1913); S. Hedin, *Jehol, City of Emperors* (1932), *Across the Gobi Desert* (1933), *Riddles of the Gobi Desert* (1933); *Flight of Big Horse* (1936), *Silk Road* (1938); O. Lattimore, *Mongols of Manchuria* (1934), *Mongol Journeys* (1941); H. Haslund-Christensen, *Mongolian Journey* (1949); S. V. Cammann, *Land of the Camel* (1951).

POLITICS AND GOVERNMENT: G. M. Friters, *Outer Mongolia and Its International Position* (1949); H. Ma, *Chinese Agent in Mongolia* (1950); O. Lattimore, *Nationalism and Revolution in Mongolia* (1955).

HISTORY: O. Lattimore, *Inner Asian Frontiers of China* (1940); M. Prawdin, *Mongol Empire: Its Rise and Legacy* (1940); H. Lamb, *Genghis Khan* (1931), *March of the Barbarians* (1940), *Earth Shakes* (1949); G. Vernadsky, *Mongols and Russia* (1954); C. H. Dawson, ed., *Mongol Mission* (1956).

MONGOLISM, a congenital defect characterized by mental deficiency and certain peculiar physical traits. Until recently the causes of Mongolism were unknown. However, recent research has uncovered causes for some cases of Mongolism. The condition may often be recognized at birth. The baby has a small head sparsely covered with rather coarse hair, a short nose with a flat bridge, roundish ears, and an unusually dry skin. Its tongue seems large and often protrudes slightly. Children with Mongolism are often small of stature and have thick, fleshy hands and feet. The thumb and little finger may be extremely short and a transverse line across the palm is characteristic. A cleft may exist between the first and second toes. Unusually relaxed ligaments permit great flexibility of the joints and the afflicted child may assume positions that appear awkward and uncomfortable. The capabilities of children with Mongolism only in rare instances exceed those of a seven-year-old. Their abilities to learn and understand vary; their mental potential remains at the same level throughout life. These children are generally happy and have sweet dispositions; usually they enjoy music. Many live in institutions; they are obedient and present few behavior problems.

MONGOOSE, a small carnivorous mammal of the family *Viverridae*. The mongoose is a long, slender animal covered with stiff, erectile, grayish-brown hair. The tail is tapered and bushy. The over-all length of the animal is usually about 2½ feet. The legs are short and the feet rather large with long claws for digging. The face is small and pointed, the ears short and rounded. Two to three litters may be raised each year with two to three young born each time. The family makes its home, in a den on the ground, in a protected spot. The life span of the mongoose is approximately eight years. One of the best known habits of the mongoose is killing and eating poisonous snakes. Its diet also includes rodents, insects, and other vermin. There are several genera of mongoose living in Asia and Africa; *Herpestes*, the most common, is the only European genus. One of the largest mongooses is *H. ichneumon*, found in Africa. This gray animal, about 44 inches long, likes especially to eat crocodile eggs, which it hunts tirelessly. *H. urva*, the crab-eating mongoose of Asia, is large also and may weigh up to 6 pounds. The Indian mongoose, *H. edwardsii*, usually weighs only about 3 pounds. This animal was imported by the West Indies and Hawaii to help rid the islands of rats. The mongoose also kills poultry and some other desirable animals; therefore it may not be brought into any other part of the United States. This animal makes a most affectionate pet if obtained when young.

CHICAGO NATURAL HIST. MUS.

Mongoose Attacking a Cobra

MONICA, SAINT, more properly Monnica, 333–87, mother of St. Augustine of Hippo, was born in Tagaste, North Africa. Brought up a Christian, Monica was married to a pagan. She watched her son drift into an evil life, but continued to pray for the conversion of her family to Christianity. After many years her patience was rewarded when husband, son, and grandson Theodore became Christians. St. Monica's feast day is May 4.

MONISM, the philosophical theory that the cosmos, however multiverse it may appear to be, is in reality a unity (universe)—a whole, one in substance. The word derives from the Greek *monos* (alone, one). According to Parmenides (fifth century B.C.) this unitary substance is being. For if anything comes to be, then it comes to be either out of being or out of nonbeing. But if it comes out of being then it already is, and in that case it does not come to be; if it comes out of nonbeing then it is nothing, since from nothing, nothing comes. Reality, therefore, is being; "becoming" having been shown to be an illusion. Being must be one, since nothing apart from being can be conceived. Because one is determinate, being must be finite, since the determinate is the finite. Because the finite is the material, this view is usually classified as materialistic monism. If, on the other hand, the one substance is conceived as mind or spirit, the viewpoint is called spiritual monism. Thus according to Plotinus (203–270) the universe is unity radiating into plurality, and emanation in successive stages from the One (God) through mind, world-soul, souls, souls-in-matter, to matter, which is pure nonbeing. The return passage, from nonbeing back to the One, is at once a passage from appearance to reality, a flight of the alone to the Alone. Another type of monism, combining the material and the spiritual into a unity as attributes of the one substance (God) is that taught by Baruch Spinoza (1632–1677). In this view the spiritual (mind) is conceived as the material (body), conscious of itself as a finite modification of the one infinite substance, God.

Although monism properly includes only philosophies (like those mentioned) that hold reality to be one in substance or in kind, the concept is usually extended to those doctrines which, admitting the existence of a plurality of things, find these things to be reducible to, or modifications of, some one type of unity. Thus Thomas Hobbes (1588–1679) holds everything in the universe, however diversified, to be describable in terms of matter-in-motion. Conversely, Georg W. F. Hegel (1770–1831) finds the process of the universe to be mind (spirit) coming to consciousness of itself in time. For Arthur Schopenhauer (1788–1860) everything in nature is a manifestation of cosmic will struggling to realization through individuals as idea. Conceptions of unity vary widely among philosophers, but the quest for unity is characteristic of every age, for man is a unifying animal, and this being so, monism is a perennial philosophy. See DUALISM; PLURALISM.

ROBERT C. WHITTEMORE

MONITOR, the largest lizard extant, and the only genus in the family *Varanidae*. The monitor's brown-

CHICAGO NATURAL HIST. MUS.

The monitor, which lived in North America 6 million years ago, now inhabits only Africa, Australia, and south Asia.

ish-black body is covered with small scales. Its neck is as long as its tail, which is used in fighting and swimming. Unlike that of most other lizards, the monitor's tail cannot regenerate. The animal's brain is almost completely enclosed in a bony case that guards it against injury from the pressure exerted by large food items in its mouth. The monitor apparently sees and hears well. It has large, pointed teeth. The smooth, deeply forked protrusible tongue is in almost constant motion and seems to serve as an organ of smell. Monitors eat greedily and include birds, rats, insects, and small mammals in their diet. Fossil beds show that these lizards inhabited parts of North America about 6 million years ago, although they now live only in Africa, southern Asia, and Australia. The largest species, *Varanus komodoensis*, or Komodo dragon, grows to about 10 feet, weighs more than 250 pounds, and inhabits the Dutch East Indies. *V. salvator* grows to 8 feet and lives in India. *V. niloticus*, or the Nile monitor, largest four-footed African reptile, grows to 6 feet. *V. gouldii*, or Gould's monitor, is the common monitor in Australia. See Lizard.

MONITOR AND MERRIMAC, a naval battle of the Civil War. At the opening of the war the Confederates converted the captured wooden 40-gun frigate *Merrimac* into an ironclad and renamed it the *Virginia*. On Mar. 8, 1862, it entered Hampton Roads with five other vessels and gave battle to the Union fleet of five ships, disabling the *Congress*, whose magazine afterward exploded, and ramming the *Cumberland* so that it sank. The next day the *Virginia* encountered the *Monitor*, an iron turret ship, constructed from the design of John Ericsson and commanded by John L. Worden. The action began at 8:30 A.M. and, after a long combat, ended in a drawn battle, but the *Virginia* withdrew, and the rest of the Union fleet was saved. The battle demonstrated the uselessness of wooden against armored ships and the advantage of the turret system of housing naval guns.

An obsolete class of armored turret vessels of light draft lying low in the water took its name from the *Monitor*. Because of the low freeboard, ships of this type were unsuited to duty on the high seas and were confined to coastal and river defense. The length of the original *Monitor* was 172 feet; beam, 41.5 feet; mean draft, 7.5 feet; inside diameter of turret, 20 feet; height of turret, 9 feet; and displacement, 776 tons. Its offensive weapons were two 11-inch, smooth-bore guns mounted on a revolving turret and the defensive armor was 8-inch laminated plate. The maximum speed was 7 knots. The importance of the *Monitor* lay in its functional design, use of armor, and revolving gun turret. These innovations had appeared before the Civil War, but their advantages were emphasized in the battle between the *Monitor* and the *Merrimac;* wooden vessels soon became obsolete. The British Navy used Monitors in the North Sea during World War I and had a few in service at the outbreak of World War II.

MONIZ, ANTONIO CAETANO DE ABREU FREIRE EGAS, 1874–1955, Nobel prize-winning Portuguese physician, was born in Avança, and studied at the University of Lisbon, where he became professor of neurology, 1911. He shared with W. R. Hess the 1949 Nobel prize in medicine for devising and perfecting a new brain operation—a prefrontal leucotomy in which a portion of the frontal lobes of the brain is removed.

MONK, MARIA, 1817?–50, Canadian impostor, was born near Montreal and appeared in New York City in 1836, asserting that she had escaped from a convent in Montreal. In *Awful Disclosures by Maria Monk* (1836) and *Further Disclosures* (1836) she claimed to reveal the frightful conditions prevalent at the convent, the Hôtel-Dieu. The books aroused strong anti-Roman Catholic feeling among prominent individuals, ill will that persisted in part even after a New York newspaperman, William Leete Stone, revealed in *Maria Monk and the Nunnery of the Hôtel-Dieu* (1836) that both the supposed nun and her books were fraudulent. She was arrested for theft, 1849, and died in prison.

MONK, THELONIUS SPHERE, 1920– , U.S. Negro jazz pianist, was born in New York, N.Y. In the early 1940's he was an habitué of the "after hours" saloon known as Minton's, and with Charlie Parker, Dizzie Gillespie, Kenny Clarke, Bud Powell, and others contributed to the musical ferment out of which developed the unusual approach to playing jazz that later came to be known as bop. Most of Monk's professional career consisted of work with small assemblages of musicians under his own direction. Although he was not technically a proficient pianist his playing was praised as direct, highly personal, and influential upon style.

MONKEY, a tree-inhabiting or terrestrial mammal belonging to the order Primates and suborder Anthropoidea. Monkeys occur throughout the tropical and subtropical world. In the Western Hemisphere they may be found from Mexico well into South America, and in the Eastern Hemisphere from Spain south and east through Africa, southern Asia, the Malay region, and the Philippine Islands. They vary in size from the foot-long pygmy marmoset, *Cebuella pigmaea*, of Brazil to the howling monkey, the size of a large dog. They are most commonly gray or brown, although they may be black or red, and many frequently have considerable white in their fur or display bare white skin. They are as diverse in form as in color and there seems to be an almost endless variety of types from the stocky, doglike baboons to the thin, long-legged spider and leaf monkeys.

In general monkeys exhibit some basic characteristics of the primates. All are covered with hair and have well developed limbs, five fingers, five toes, and usually nails rather than claws. Since many are distinctly arboreal, there is a decided tendency within the group for strong development of the forelimbs and shoulders. The brain is well marked with folds, indicating a high degree of specialization.

Two distinct groups are recognized, the platyrrhine monkeys of the New World and the catarrhine monkeys of the Old World. The platyrrhines are characterized by a broad nasal septum which widely separates the nostrils, causing them to open outward rather than downward. They have 32 to 36 teeth, with three premolars on each side of the jaw. The tail is frequently of the grasping or prehensile type. New World monkeys have neither cheek pouches nor ischial callosities (hairless rump calluses). The group includes such diverse monkeys as the howler, night monkey, spider monkey, capuchin, titi, tamarind, and marmoset. In the Old World or catarrhine monkeys the nasal septum is narrow and the close-set nostrils open downward as in man. There are always 32 teeth with only two premolars on each side of the jaw. The tail, unlike that of the New World monkey, is never prehensile. Prominent rump calluses and large cheek pouches are commonly, though not invariably, present. The Barbary ape, which is the only living European monkey, the baboon, black ape, macaque, langur, loris, leaf monkey, and others are members of this group.

CHICAGO PARK DISTRICT

Diana Monkeys

Many monkeys are distinctly gregarious and roam the forests in bands, keeping in contact by calling back and forth. The habit of play is perhaps more highly developed in monkeys than in any other group of animals, both the old and young taking part in many different types of games. Their many almost human characteristics, social behavior, and ability to learn simple tricks have long made monkeys a favorite group of mammals in zoo collections. See MAMMAL; PRIMATE. JOHN D. BLACK

BIBLIOG.–F. M. Duncan, *Monkey Tribe* (1946); W. Felce, *Apes* (1950); E. P. Walker, *Monkey Book* (1954).

MONMOUTH, JAMES SCOTT, DUKE OF, 1649–85, claimant to the English throne, was born in Rotterdam. He was alleged by his mother, Lucy Walter, to be the illegitimate son of Charles II, but was possibly the son of Lucy Walter and Robert Sidney (son of the second earl of Leicester), whom James closely resembled. When the boy was brought to England, 1662, he was lodged in the royal palace. In 1663 he was acknowledged by the king as his son, created duke of Monmouth and, after his marriage to Anne Scott, countess of Buccleuch (whose name he adopted as his own), created count of Buccleuch. Military, civil, and academic honors were heaped upon him, and in 1670 he was appointed captain-general of the army. He became the tool of Anthony Cooper, the earl of Shaftesbury, who opposed the succession to the throne of Charles' brother, the duke of York (later James II) because of the duke's pro-Roman Catholic sentiments, and hence found it advantageous to promote the Protestant duke of Monmouth's claims to the throne. Monmouth was implicated in the Rye House plot to kill the king and the duke of York, 1683. He was exiled to Holland in 1683 but returned in 1685, asserting his right to the throne. His rebellion was suppressed and he was executed. Monmouth's intrigues are described in John Dryden's satirical poem *Absalom and Achitophel*.

MONMOUTH, city, W Illinois, seat of Warren County; on the Burlington and the Minneapolis and St. Louis railroads and U.S. highways 67 and 150; 58 miles WNW of Peoria. Pottery, farm implements, metal goods, clothing, dairy foods, and beef cattle are the principal products of Monmouth; coal and clay are mined nearby. Monmouth College is located in the city, which was founded in 1831 and incorporated in 1836. Pop. (1960) 10,372.

MONMOUTH, municipal borough, SW England, capital of Monmouthshire; at the confluence of the Wye and Monnow rivers; 26 miles N of Bristol. Monmouth is a railroad and highway junction and an agricultural trade center. There are remains of the ancient town walls, of a twelfth century castle that was the residence of John of Gaunt and the birthplace of Henry V, and of a Benedictine monastery said to contain Geoffrey of Monmouth's study. A thirteenth century gateway on the bridge over the Monnow and an adjoining Norman chapel are other features of interest. Pop. (1961) 5,505.

MONMOUTH, BATTLE OF, a battle of the American Revolution fought on June 28, 1778, at Monmouth Court House, Freehold, N.J., between the Americans under Gen. George Washington and the British under Gen. Henry Clinton. The British, under orders to proceed to New York and then to the defense of the West Indies, which were threatened by the French, had evacuated Philadelphia 10 days previously. On receiving the news, Washington and his army set out in pursuit across New Jersey in a sweltering sun, overtaking the British rear guard of 8,000 men at Monmouth Court House. The attacking force of 5,000 Americans was led by Gen. Charles Lee, who ordered a retreat shortly after battle was joined instead of pressing his attack. Washington rode up, rallied the bewildered troops, and re-formed the American lines. The resulting battle was tactically indecisive, although strategically a victory for the Americans. The Americans suffered 360 casualties and the British 416. Lee was later court-martialed for his retreat and dismissed from the army. See REVOLUTIONARY WAR

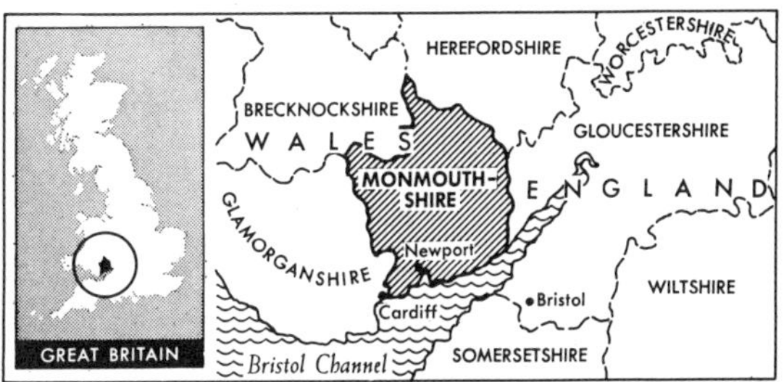

Location Map of Monmouthshire

MONMOUTHSHIRE, or Monmouth, county, SE Wales, on the English border; bounded by the English counties of Herefordshire on the N and Gloucestershire on the E, by the Severn River estuary on the S, and by the Welsh counties of Glamorganshire on the W and Brecknockshire on the NW; area 546 sq. mi.; pop. (1961) 443,689. The hilly country of north and northwest Monmouthshire contains the foothills of the Black Mountains and the Brecon Beacons. In the south and east the land becomes low and flat. The principal rivers—the Wye, Monnow, Usk, and Rhymney—drain south to the Severn. Chief centers besides Monmouth, the capital, are the port of Newport, Ebbw Vale, Pontypool, and Tredegar. Fruits are grown, but the chief agricultural occupation is the raising of sheep and cattle. Coal and iron ore are mined, chiefly in the northwest, limestone is quarried, and there are iron, steel, and tin industries. Monmouthshire has a number of historical and religious sites, including Tintern Abbey.

MONNET, JEAN, 1888– , French economist, was born in Cognac. He first developed his lifetime interest in international economic problems as a young man representing his family's brandy business in Canada. Monnet was on the Inter-Allied Maritime Commission in World War I, and later served with the League of Nations. During World War II he was a member of several Allied economic councils. In 1950 he drafted the plan which led to the establishment of the European Coal and Steel Community (ECSC), forerunner of the European Economic Community (Common Market). Monnet was president of ECSC, 1952–55, and subsequently chairman of the Action Committee for a United States of Europe, a position he still held in the early 1960's.

MONOCEROS, the unicorn, an equatorial constellation that contains no star brighter than the fourth magnitude and whose stars are thus far outshone by those of its neighbors Orion, Canis Major, and Canis Minor. The constellation contains some famous variable stars, some double stars, and a number of star clusters and nebulae. A remarkable object is Hubble's variable nebula, too faint to be shown in the diagram; its nucleus surrounds a variable star, R Monocerotis, which has a maximum brightness of 9½ magnitudes and may be the cause of the variations in the nebula. A nova appeared in Monoceros in 1918; it had a brightness of 8½ magnitudes when first observed but grew more and more faint in succeeding months. Among the numerous clusters are Messier object 50 (NGC 2323), a fine open cluster containing a red star; NGC 2244, a beautiful open cluster visible to the naked eye and containing a sixth magnitude yellow star; and NGC 2506, a fine cloud of faint stars. See CONSTELLATION.

MONOCOTYLEDON, any one of the plants containing a single cotyledon, and comprising one of the two subclasses of flowering plants, or angiosperms. See COTYLEDON; SEED.

There are about 50,000 species of monocotyledons. Their flower parts are generally in multiples of three; leaves are usually narrow and long, and have parallel veins running lengthwise. Because most stems lack cambium, they do not have secondary growth. Among the important monocotyledons are cattails, grasses, palms, lilies, onions, bananas, and orchids. Many useful products are obtained from the monocotyledons, including fibers for brushes, mats, fabrics, and rope; oils for soaps, shortenings, and cosmetics; and light wood for construction. See BOTANY; FLOWERING PLANT.

Highly Magnified Portion of a Cross Section of a Corn Stem: *A*, Epidermis; *B*, Sclerenchyma; *C*, Parenchyma; *D*, Vascular Bundle—*a*, Xylem; *b*, Phloem; *c*, Bundle Sheath

GENERAL BIOLOGICAL SUPPLY HOUSE

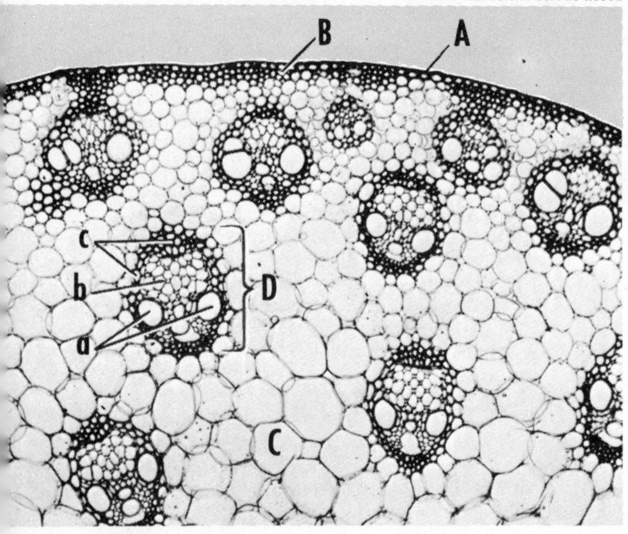

MONOGAMY, a form of single marriage whereby a person has only one wife or one husband at a time. Monogamy does not mean, however, that the two individuals must remain married permanently. In most countries they may legally dissolve the marriage through divorce or annulment, although this practice is not accepted by all religious denominations. Monogamy has been the most common form of marriage throughout the history of Western civilization and is the only legal form in most countries. In the United States plural marriages were declared illegal by an act of Congress in 1887. See BIGAMY; FAMILY; MARRIAGE; POLYGAMY.

MONOLOGUE, in drama, originally an uninterrupted recitation of some length made by one actor. In this sense monologues, later called soliloquies, have been employed as a dramatic convention from the time of the ancient Greek dramatists. In twentieth century usage a monologue usually was an entertainment by one actor who assumed the role of one or more characters. Among the best known monologists were the Canadian actress Beatrice Lillie, the U.S. entertainers Cornelia Otis Skinner and Ruth Draper, and the French singer Yvette Guilbert, who often combined monologues with her songs. The monologue in this sense was akin in many respects to dramatic readings of published works such as Charles Dickens performed (using his own works); this tradition was revived with great success after World War II by Charles Laughton and others, by the Welsh actor Emlyn Williams impersonating Dickens reading aloud, and by the American Hal Holbrook portraying Mark Twain reading his work.

MONOMETALLISM, a monetary system in which there is free coinage of only one metal, usually gold. This coinage is considered full legal tender. See BIMETALLISM; GOLD STANDARD; LEGAL TENDER.

MONONGAHELA RIVER, N West Virginia and SW Pennsylvania, formed near Fairmont, W.Va., by the confluence of the Tygart and West Fork rivers; flows NE to Morgantown, W.Va., and N into Pennsylvania to Pittsburgh where it joins the Allegheny River to form the Ohio River; length 128 miles. It receives the Cheat and Youghiogheny rivers at Point Marion and McKeesport, Pa., respectively. The Monongahela is an important freight thoroughfare that has been made navigable by means of a series of locks.

MONONUCLEOSIS, or glandular fever, a disease of unknown cause, characterized by fever, sore throat, and enlargement of the spleen and lymph glands, especially those in the neck. The number of lymphocytes in the blood increases and the blood usually contains special types of antibodies.

The disease typically affects children and young adults, presumably after an incubation period of about 5-15 days. It may occur in epidemic form and appears to be more prevalent in the spring. At the onset there is a general feeling of distress, loss of appetite, malaise, headache, and irregular fever. Sometimes nausea, pains in the abdomen, or vague pains throughout the body are experienced. The liver may become enlarged and skin eruptions or jaundice may occur.

Because of the variability of symptoms of mononucleosis, laboratory tests have proved valuable in the diagnosis of this disease. One such test involves the microscopic examination of blood. If the disease is present the blood usually reveals an increased number of leukocytes, or white cells, in general and mononuclear cells in particular. These mononuclear cells are of three types: small lymphocytes, monocytes, and large mononuclear leukocytes. The first two types are normally present in the blood but the last type is abnormal. This abnormal cell has a kidney-shaped nucleus surrounded by nongranular dark blue vacuolated cytoplasm of foamy appearance. Nucleoli are absent. Another distinguishing laboratory test for mononucleosis is the heterophile antibody test, which measures the power of the blood serum to agglutinate the red cells of sheep. Most persons recover from mononucleosis in three to six weeks without aftereffects, but there have been rare cases of fatalities because of rupture of the spleen or other complications. A person who has suffered from mononucleosis may feel run down and may not be completely normal physically for several weeks or even months after the disease has subsided. No specific treatment for this disease has been found, but rest is usually advisable. The symptoms are also treated.

MONOPHYSITES, a fifth century sect condemned for heresy at the Council of Chalcedon (451) for holding the belief that in Christ there was only one nature; this they contended was the divine nature only, as opposed to the orthodox teaching that Christ in His earthly life had both a divine and a human nature. Although the Council of Chalcedon decided against them, the sect became extremely powerful in Palestine, Egypt, and Syria. Basic Monophysite doctrines had been taught by Apollinaris of Laodicea, who died about 390, but it was Eutyches (died 454) who gave them the formulation that was expressly condemned at Chalcedon. Many attempts were made to heal the schism, perhaps the most significant being that of Justinian I who called the second Council of Constantinople in 553 partly with that end in view. But the Monophysites refused to be reconciled, and their teaching continued dominant in Armenia, Abyssinia, and Mesopotamia. The break appeared final in the sixth century when the Monophysite doctrine consolidated its position in three churches—the Copt and Abyssinian, the Syrian Jacobite (after its leader, Jacob Baradai), and the Armenian. Monophysitism still exercises considerable influence in some of the Eastern churches. See EUTYCHES.

MONOPLANE. See AERONAUTICS.

MONOPOLY, a market situation in which a single seller, because of his control of supply or distribution, can set the price of a commodity or service arbitrarily and without fear of adverse consequences from competition. A pure monopoly is essentially a theoretical concept since, by definition, it exists only when there is but one seller in the field, no possibility of competition, and no substitute for the monopolist's product or service. According to modern concepts monopoly exists when a seller has effective control of the price of a commodity; this market position is actually one of near monopoly and is more appropriately called monopolistic competition. See COMPETITION.

Monopolistic competition exists when one firm (or several firms as is the case in an oligopoly) controls the market but the threat from existing or potential competition requires that consideration be given to competitors when determining the market price. For example, although one large steel corporation may dominate the steel industry, it cannot ignore other steel producers when establishing price policies. See OLIGOPOLY.

Another example of monopolistic competition is the situation in which a seller is sheltered from other sellers in the market, as when a retailer is located miles from competition. Such a seller is in a position to demand comparatively higher prices; however, he cannot afford to set so high a price that his customers will prefer to deal with a distant seller.

Neither the size of a company nor the price of a company's product is the significant factor in determining whether a monopoly exists. The significant factor is the position of the seller relative to that of all other suppliers in the field.

Economics of Monopoly. Whereas the seller in an openly competitive market is forced by the economic mechanisms of that market to sell at a price relatively near the cost of producing each unit, the monopolist is able to set a price calculated to yield the greatest profit per unit. Thus almost without exception the price fixed by the monopolist is higher than it would be if established by a seller in a truly competitive market. (See PRICE; PROFIT; PRODUCTION, *Costs of Production;* SUPPLY AND DEMAND.) Based upon the plans of the monopolist, the price he establishes may be much greater than the cost of producing each unit, or it may approximate the cost of production as in a competitive market. If the monopolist creates an artificial shortage by limiting production, the price per unit will be high; if he wants to expand his market, however, he will produce a greater number of units to sell at a price yielding a smaller profit per unit. That portion of the monopolist's profits in excess of the amount of profit that would have been realized in a competitive market is monopoly gain.

The monopolist ordinarily will not increase his production beyond the point where marginal cost (the cost of producing one additional unit) equals marginal revenue (the amount of money received from the sale of one additional unit) since it is at this point that his total net profit is at the maximum level and would decline with further production. (See MARGINAL COST.) Up to the point at which marginal cost equals marginal revenue, increased production usually results in a lower cost of production per unit and thus the average cost of producing an individual unit decreases. However, unless there exists sufficient scarcity of the commodity after the rise in production, the demand for the product will drop and the monopolist will have to decrease his price in order to sell all the units produced. This decline in revenue may offset appreciably the savings realized from the lowered cost of production, and possibly even produce a loss.

Detrimental Effects. Most monopolies other than public monopolies prove harmful to society in many ways. The high level of prices generally set by a monopolist enables some firms, that for reasons of inefficiency and other shortcomings could not survive in a competitive market, to remain in business. Monopolies also tend to retard progress because monopolists are not inclined to finance innovations or changes unless they expect profits from such new capital investments to equal or exceed those derived from their current capital investments. Monopoly causes an unequal distribution of income since the monopolist gathers a greater share of wealth than would otherwise be his. The monopolist often creates distortion in the allocation of natural resources by gaining control over vast quantities of property or mineral rights. The existence of a monopoly price during a depression tends to retard recovery, keeps the employment level down, and generally makes the economy rigid and inflexible.

Classifications and Devices. Numerous devices are used to establish monopolies. A monopoly is often formed by horizontal or vertical integration. Horizontal integration is the unification of companies engaged in the same manufacturing process or venture; an outstanding example occurred during the late nineteenth century when Standard Oil owned approximately nine-tenths of the U.S. oil refineries. Vertical integration is the unification of an entire manufacturing process, from raw material to finished product. Vertical integration is especially prevalent in basic industries such as iron and steel.

A legal monopoly, which may be either public or private, often arises from a government grant of exclusive privileges or unusual consideration. A public monopoly originates when a franchise or license is granted by the government to an agency to prevent competition that would conflict with the public interest. Utilities are franchised and regulated primarily to avoid waste from such duplication as would result from competition among several telephone companies within a city. Because of their unique characteristics, most industries concerned with communication—including the Post Office Department—are regulated by the government.

A protective tariff is in effect a form of public legal monopoly for, by eliminating foreign competition, the government establishes a monopolistic situation for domestic industries.

A private legal monopoly is established by the government through the issuance of patents, copyrights, trade-marks, licenses, and other similar bars against entry into a given field. In many cases a legal monopoly is responsible for the creation of an economic monopoly. For example, a man possessing patent rights may include conditions in any licenses he grants to manufacturers that effectively control the sale or use of the product.

The cartel and the pool are agreements under which potential competitors reduce competition among themselves and thus increase their profits. Both of these devices are informal combinations whose members maintain their individual existence and operations but agree to co-operate in such matters as prices, trade practices, output, patents, and selling agencies. Because of its informal nature, a pool is highly unstable and individual members frequently have taken advantage of one another. See CARTEL.

Although trade associations are generally concerned only with the marketing and advertising of products, they are used occasionally to achieve uniformity in production, cost accounting, purchasing, and other business procedures with the result that at times a monopolistic market price becomes established. See TRADE ASSOCIATION; MARKETING, Development of Marketing.

The form of combination known as a trust became popular in the latter part of the nineteenth century until the Sherman Antitrust Act (1890) was passed to protect the public against abuses resulting from such combinations. The Standard Oil Trust of 1879 was an organization of this type. See TRUST.

Intercorporate relationships such as holding companies and common directorates also have enabled individuals to gain monopolistic control over a particular market by the simple means of setting similar policies for the several firms controlled. (See HOLDING COMPANY.) Mergers and consolidations are modern devices used to dominate the market. A consolidation is the union of two firms of comparable strength to form one larger, completely new organization. A merger is usually formed by a larger and stronger firm absorbing a smaller or weaker one, the smaller firm losing its identity. (See COMBINATIONS AND MERGERS; MERGER.) In addition to these devices, there are some indirect methods of monopoly formation. For example, a firm subject to minimum wage laws may find that the cost of competing with a firm under no such restrictions is prohibitive, or a competitor may be prevented from increasing production by an unfavorable union contract. See MINIMUM WAGE.

Limitation and Regulation. Economic conditions in themselves serve to limit the monopolist's control of the market. If the price becomes excessive, consumers will forego the use of a product or service, or even use inferior substitutes. Moreover, the high price level and lucrative profits resulting from a monopoly often attract competitors to the monopolist's field.

The possibility of the introduction of potential substitutes is always present, especially in an era of rapid technical innovations. A new process or invention can immediately restore competition to the monopolistic market, even to the point of replacing the monopolist's product entirely. Consumer attitudes and preferences may change so that there is no longer any demand for a particular product. When two or more firms control a market, the monopolist must be wary of his oligopolistic rivals who may, by cutting prices or forming countervailing power groups, attempt to drive him from the market.

Certain forms of taxation limit or regulate a monopoly. Although a tax imposed on net profits will not affect either the level of production or price, it may remove much of the monopoly gain and with it the incentive to establish a monopolistic price. On the other hand, a fixed tax or even a variable tax based upon the units of production does not constitute a limitation since it will eventually be passed on to the consumer without affecting the profits of the monopolist.

The United States, in contrast to most European countries which have chosen to permit private monopolies to exist under government regulation, is opposed to practices that result in a restraint of trade. Since the government maintains a program of investigation into the operations of firms apparently endeavoring to establish monopolies, the threat of government interference in itself constitutes an effective restriction because of the possibility of legislation to remedy a situation found to be inimical to the public welfare. As was demonstrated in 1890 with the passage of the Sherman Antitrust Act, and again in 1914 with the adoption of the Clayton Antitrust Act and the Federal Trade Commission Act, government regulation is the most effective form of limitation upon monopolies in the United States. See GOVERNMENT REGULATION OF BUSINESS; SHERMAN ANTITRUST ACT; CLAYTON ANTITRUST ACT; FEDERAL TRADE COMMISSION; COMPETITION; RESTRAINT OF TRADE; FREE ENTERPRISE.

BIBLIOG.–J. Robinson, *Economics of Imperfect Competition* (1933); G. M. Modlin and A. M. McIsaac, *Social Control of Industry* (1938); R. A. Triffin, *Monopolistic Competition and General Equilibrium Theory* (1940); C. Wilcox, *Competition and Monopoly in American Industry* (1941); D. Lynch, *The Concentration of Economic Power* (1946); P. Drucker, *New Society* (1949); Labor Research Association, *Monopoly Today* (1951); G. W. Stocking and M. W. Watkins, *Cartels in Action* (1947), *Monopoly and Free Enterprise* (1951); F. Machlup, *Political Economy of Monopoly* (1953); International Economic Association, *Monopoly and Competition and Their Regulation* (1955); W. Adams and H. N. Gray, *Monopoly in America* (ed. 1956); J. K. Galbraith, *American Capitalism: Theory of Countervailing Power* (ed. 1956); D. Lilienthal, *Big Business* (1956); E. H. Chamberlin, *Theory of Monopolistic Competition* (ed. 1957); E. S. Mason, *Economic Concentration and the Monopoly Problem* (1957).

MONOPSONY, a market situation in which there is a single buyer for a commodity or service but many sellers. The buyer may be an individual or an organized group acting in concert. The economic significance of monopsony is that the price of the commodity or service is set by the buyer rather than by the forces of competition. See COMPETITION; MONOPOLY.

Monopsony in the United States has existed in two major areas. The first is the marketing of agricultural products where farmers producing similar crops such as wheat or corn are forced to accept the storage charges set by the owner of the local grain elevator. The second is the labor situation in a community dominated by a single company that has the power to hire and discharge personnel as it chooses. As a result of this control over the demand for labor, the company can set whatever wage rates it wishes and can hire a sufficient labor supply at those rates.

Attempts to combat monopsony have usually been made by legislation and by the organization of sellers into groups such as labor unions and marketing co-operatives. See CO-OPERATIVE, Co-operatives in the United States, *Agricultural Marketing Co-operatives;* LABOR MOVEMENT, The United States; TRADE REGULATION.

MONORAIL, a transportation system consisting of a single track used as the support for cars or other wheeled carriers. Monorail systems fall into two classes: those used in industry for materials handling (see MATERIALS HANDLING); and those used to transport people over substantial distances.

The first successful monorail system was an 8¼-mile line built between 1901 and 1903 in the Ruhr Valley at Wuppertal, near Cologne, Germany. This system consists of two-car trains each of which is suspended from a single rail. The cars, each of which seats 50 passengers, are driven by two 36-hp motors that deliver the correct operating speed through re-

A new two-car, monorail-system train runs along a beamway supported by pylons at Cologne, Germany. Pneumatic tires, especially designed for train, allow smooth running.
CONSULATE GENERAL, FEDERAL REPUBLIC OF GERMANY

duction gears. In its first half century of operation this system carried nearly a billion passengers without fatal accident.

Another example of practical monorail design and operation is to be found in the Alweg System, developed by Axel L. Wenner-Gren, also erected near Cologne, Germany. Started in 1901 as a short experimental system, it was expanded to a complete 1½-mile line in 1956. The Alweg monorail consists of cars straddling a boxlike concrete beam approximately 25 feet above the ground. The track is supported at intervals by reinforced concrete pylons. An Alweg type of monorail is in operation in Disneyland, at Los Angeles, Calif. Houston, Tex., early in 1956 installed a 970-foot experimental section of a monorail system patterned after the Wuppertal installation.

MONOTHEISM, the acknowledgment and worship of a single, personal, transcendent God on whom all other existence depends for its reality. Monotheism differs from polytheism, the worship of many gods, even when these are arranged in a hierarchy headed by a god who is regarded as greatest of the deities; it is likewise distinguished from monolatry, the worship of only one god when the existence of other gods is admitted.

In both historic and modern times monotheism is found as a stable institution in only three religious groups: Christianity, Judaism, and Islam (see CHRISTIANITY; JUDAISM; ISLAM). As a historical phenomenon monotheism, however, is linked with the Judaeo-Christian tradition, since Islam derives its conception of God from that tradition. This fact is significant in the comparative study of religions, because monotheism thus appears as linked exclusively with a religious tradition that has always emphasized insistently its dependence on a divine revelation. It has been estimated that 46.47 per cent of the human race (the percentage represented by Christians, Jews, and Moslems) professed monotheism in the late 1950's.

Egyptian religion was markedly polytheistic except during the reign of Ikhnaton, who attempted to induce his people to worship only the god Aton (see IKHNATON). After his death polytheism was immediately restored. Far Eastern religions, such as Buddhism, have not professed monotheism but have been joined to an elaborate system of polytheism. Zarathustra, or Zoroaster, who lived in Persia during the latter half of the seventh century B.C., has been regarded by some as a monotheist; but his doctrine was not entirely free from a dualism of good and evil, and after his death the religion he founded immediately evolved into such a dualism. See BUDDHISM; ZOROASTRIANISM.

Up to the eighteenth century the Western world accepted the doctrine that monotheism was the first religion of mankind, revealed by God to the first members of the race. David Hume in that century asserted that polytheism must have been the first religion and that it had gradually evolved into monotheism. This teaching of a gradual and unilinear evolution of religion toward monotheism became the accepted position of the majority of ethnologists and anthropologists of the nineteenth century. Advocates of monotheism point out, however, that monotheism always appears not as a development from polytheism but in opposition to it; existing polytheistic religions manifest no tendency toward monotheism. This last fact is not regarded as constituting scientific proof that monotheism was the original human religion; but advocates of monotheism assert that it does disprove the evolutionary theory of religion, and also shows that findings by students of the history of religions do not necessarily contradict the traditional Christian doctrine that monotheism was the initial and revealed religion of the human race.

R. F. SMITH, S.J.

BIBLIOG.–R. Pettazzoni, *Essays on the History of Religions* (1954); S. Freud, *Moses and Monotheism* (ed. 1955); J. B. Noss, *Man's Religions* (ed. 1956); W. F. Albright, *From the Stone Age to Christianity* (ed. 1957); E. O. James, *History of Religions* (1956), *Prehistoric Religion* (1957).

MONOTHELETISM, the doctrine that Christ in His earthly life had only one will. Monotheletism originated in the seventh century as the result of efforts by the Byzantine Emperor Heraclius and Pope Honorius of Rome to find a formula acceptable both to the Monophysites and the Western church, which accepted the Council of Chalcedon's rejection of the Monophysite doctrine that in Christ's earthly ministry He had only one nature—the divine (see MONOPHYSITES). Whereas Heraclius had gone no further than producing a formula that asserted two natures in Christ but only "one energy," Honorius used the expression "one will" in correspondence with Patriarch Sergius of Constantinople. In the Ecthesis, probably drawn up by Sergius and issued by Heraclius in 638, the expression "one will" is used to the exclusion of "one energy" or "two energies." Successors of Pope Honorius condemned monotheletism, and Emperor Constans II, seeking religious peace, withdrew the Ecthesis and replaced it with another edict (Typos), forbidding use of either "one will" or "two will" formulas. The Typos was condemned at the Lateran Council in 649, and the controversy was finally settled by the Council of Constantinople in 680, which condemned monotheletism and its followers and asserted that the orthodox faith recognizes two wills in Christ, both the divine and human, during His earthly life.

MONOTREMATA, or egg-laying mammals, the most primitive order of living mammals, belonging to the subclass Prototheria. The duck-billed platypus and the spiny anteater, each about 1½ feet in length, represent living forms of monotremes. The young hatch from eggs which have large yolks and tough flexible shells, much like those of the reptile. Like reptiles, the adult monotreme has special bones in its shoulder girdle that are not present in most mammals. The monotreme also resembles a reptile in that its oviducts, intestine, and urethra open into a cloaca with a single ventral opening to the exterior. Adults have leathery beaks, but no teeth or external ears. The monotreme's blood is not as warm as that of most other mammals. Although the female monotreme, like a mammal, suckles her young, no teats are present; the milk exudes through several pores on the abdomen. Monotremes are native only to Australia and nearby islands. These include a few species of spiny anteaters and only one species of duckbills. See ECHIDNA; PLATYPUS.

MONOTYPE. See PRINTING.

MONREALE, town, S Italy, Sicily, province of Palermo, 4 miles SW of Palermo. The town is a market center for the surrounding valley, which produces mainly citrus fruits and olives. Monreale contains one of the most famous Norman cathedrals, dedicated to the Assumption of the Virgin Mary. The church was begun in 1170 and became the metropolitan cathedral of Sicily in 1182. It was damaged by fire in 1811, but was well restored. It contains 70,400 square feet of magnificent mosaics entirely covering the inner walls. Monreale also has a Benedictine abbey (1174), whose cloisters are among the largest and finest in the Italian Romanesque style. Pop. (1958) 20,623.

MONROE, HARRIET, 1860–1936, U.S. poet, was born in Chicago and was educated at Visitation Academy, Washington, D.C. She was founder and first editor, 1912–36, of *Poetry: A Magazine of Verse*, which published early works of such writers as T. S. Eliot, Robert Frost, Vachel Lindsay, William Carlos Williams, and D. H. Lawrence. Her works include *Valeria and Other Poems* (1892), *Poets and Their Art* (1926), and *A Poet's Life: Seventy Years in a Changing World* (1938). With Alice Corbin Henderson she compiled *The New Poetry: An Anthology* (1917, 1932). Among later editors of *Poetry* were George Dillon, Peter De Vries, Jessica North, Karl Shapiro, and Henry Rago.

MONROE, JAMES, 1758–1831, fifth president of the United States, born in Westmoreland County, Va. His father, Spence Monroe, was a small landholder, but his mother's brother, Joseph Jones, was of the Virginia aristocracy and served his nephew as a patron for many years.

As a boy James rode through the forests to the school of Rev. Archibald Campbell, where one of his fellow pupils and close friends was John Marshall, later to be chief justice of the United States during Monroe's presidency and a bitter political opponent. At the age of 16 Monroe entered the College of William and Mary, but left in 1775 to serve in the Virginia militia, first as a cadet, then as a lieutenant.

Monroe's military career spanned most of the Revolution. Early in 1776 he joined the Continental Army under Washington and fought in the battles of Harlem Heights and White Plains. He led the scout patrol that crossed the icy Delaware on Christmas Eve, 1776, in advance of the main American force. The next day at the Battle of Trenton he was wounded in the shoulder. Promoted to captain, he became aide-de-camp to Lord Stirling and fought in the battles of Brandywine and Germantown during the 1777 campaign. At Valley Forge the next winter he served on Washington's staff along with Alexander Hamilton, John Marshall, and Aaron Burr.

After the campaign of 1779, armed with a strong letter of commendation from Washington, Monroe returned to Virginia hoping to receive a command of his own. He was commissioned a lieutenant colonel, but lack of finances prevented the state from raising his regiment. Monroe then began to read law under the direction of Gov. Thomas Jefferson, serving at the same time as a confidential agent of the governor in the struggle against the British in the Carolinas. At the end of the war he was among the Virginia officers at the Battle of Yorktown.

Political Life. Monroe's political career began even before the war was officially over. In 1782 he was elected to the Virginia House of Delegates and by that body to the governor's executive council. The following year he was elected delegate to the Congress of the United States and served a 3-year term. During that period Monroe participated in the ratification of the peace treaty with Great Britain, took an active part in legislating for the western territories, and in 1784 made a hazardous journey across New York and Canada to Detroit and back along a northern route to Albany and New York City by way of Lake Champlain. In 1786 he married Eliza Kortright, a popular New York belle. The Monroes had two daughters, and a son who died in infancy.

Monroe attended the Annapolis Convention (1786), which was charged with revising the Articles of Confederation. When a quorum failed to develop, he was among the majority who voted to hold a convention at Philadelphia in 1787. He was not a delegate to the Constitutional Convention, however, since his term had expired. When the draft Constitution was sent to the states, Monroe was elected delegate to the Virginia ratifying convention. At that time he made an exhaustive study of republican and constitutional government from early times to his own, a study that convinced him that there must be a separation of powers in a national government, firm guarantees of civil liberties, and protection of local governments against the encroachments of national government. Though he favored a strong central government for the United States, he voted against the draft Constitution, finding it unsatisfactory in several respects, including the absence of a bill of rights.

Shortly after the adoption of the Constitution, Monroe ran unsuccessfully against James Madison for a seat in the First Congress. This was the only defeat he ever sustained in elective politics. The following year, 1790, he was elected to the U.S. Senate to fill a vacancy.

METROPOLITAN MUSEUM OF ART
James Monroe

As a senator, Monroe joined forces with the Jeffersonian Republicans against the Hamiltonian Federalists. Because he was an ardent party man and supporter of the French Revolution, President Washington sent him to Paris in 1794 as U.S. minister, hoping that he could persuade the French government to accept without serious protest an American treaty of commerce with England (Jay's Treaty). While Monroe succeeded in mollifying the French for 2 years, he felt himself betrayed by his own superiors, especially Secretary of State Timothy Pickering, and he adopted an increasingly pro-French attitude. He was recalled "in disgrace" by Pres. John Adams.

Returning to the United States in 1797, Monroe immediately took a leading place in the Jeffersonian opposition to Adam's administration and wrote a controversial pamphlet in defense of his own mission to France. Elected governor of Virginia in 1799, he worked vigorously for the election of Jefferson as president in 1800. When Jefferson and the Republican party came to power, Monroe remained as governor of Virginia but was everywhere understood to be one of the top leaders of the Republicans.

In 1803 Monroe accepted Jefferson's request that he go to France again to negotiate the purchase of New Orleans. Arriving in Paris at the court of Napoleon, he found that Minister Robert R. Livingston had been offered an opportunity to purchase not only New Orleans but the whole of the vast Louisiana Territory. Relying on his close relations with Jefferson and Secretary of State Madison, Monroe accepted the offer on behalf of the United States and signed the articles for the Louisiana Purchase. He spent the next 4 years in less successful diplomacy at London and Madrid. He failed in his negotiations with Spain for the cession of Florida and with Great Britain on maritime questions, negotiating a treaty which President Jefferson could not accept. Monroe then returned to the United States.

His relations with Jefferson and Madison had deteriorated during his absence, chiefly because he felt that they should have approved his work in London. The Republican party was split, in 1808, over the succession to Jefferson. Monroe was approached—and tempted—by the faction opposed to Madison. He did not, however, become a candidate, and Madison was elected. Monroe was deeply hurt when Madison did not ask him to become secretary of state. But before the end of 1809 he was reconciled with Jefferson.

In 1809 and 1810 a number of important posts were offered to Monroe, including the governorship of Upper Louisiana and a seat in the U.S. Senate. He rejected the former because he felt it would put him in "political exile" and the latter because he could not afford it financially. However, when the legislature again elected him governor of Virginia, he accepted and took office on Jan. 1, 1811.

Meanwhile U.S. relations with Great Britain were worsening and war seemed likely. Under these circumstances President Madison urged Monroe to forget his grievances and enter the government as secretary of state. After some weeks of consultation and negotiation, he accepted. Monroe became secretary of state on Apr. 6, 1811, and remained in that office until he became president in 1817. At first he differed from Madison on policy toward England, believing that peace with that country could be preserved. But with the outbreak of the War of 1812 the breach was finally and permanently healed. Monroe was a unifying force in the government during the dark days of the war, and for 2 years (1814 and 1815) he personally took charge of the war effort as secretary of war. He was thus the only man ever to hold two cabinet posts at once. His success in organizing the armed forces after the burning of Washington (1814) left him in high popular favor when the war ended and guaranteed his succession to Madison.

The Presidency. Elected president in 1816 by a large margin, Monroe, the former partisan Democratic-Republican, bent his efforts to healing party divisions. He toured the North and East in 1817 and the South and West in 1819 to unprecedented acclaim as the "last of the founding fathers." In all his speeches he stressed the theme of national unity and harmony. His policy as president was to maintain a climate of confidence in which private business, commerce, and agriculture could flourish. He encouraged industrial development and low tariffs to favor trade. As party feelings subsided and public affection for Monroe increased, the period of his administration came to be known as the "Era of Good Feelings."

In domestic matters Monroe's administration was noteworthy more for escaping disaster than for positive achievement. Monroe feared the growing pressures of the North against the extension of slavery and the pressures of the South to extend it into the West. Though he deplored the necessity for the Missouri Compromise (admitting Missouri as a slave state, Maine as a free state, and excluding slavery north of 36°30′), Monroe supported it and signed its measures into law in 1820. The country was struck by its first severe economic depression in 1819, and though hard times continued until 1821 Monroe was never held responsible by the people. He was re-elected in 1820 without opposition. His second term (1821–1825) was the only U.S. experiment in one-party national government.

So bitter were the factional and regional disputes arising within the country and reflected within the Democratic-Republican party in the struggle for succession to Monroe that the president turned most of his attention to foreign affairs. In 1819 he succeeded in purchasing Florida from Spain and continued to conduct a policy favoring the development of republican government throughout Latin America. While observing diplomatic correctness in relations with Spain, Monroe nevertheless gave quiet encouragement to the Washington agents of the South American revolutions and quickly recognized independent governments when Spanish troops were forced to withdraw.

The Monroe Doctrine. President Monroe's greatest achievement was undoubtedly the proclamation of the doctrine that bears his name. Resting on an unwritten understanding with Great Britain, the Monroe Doctrine set forth in Monroe's annual message to Congress in 1823 declared that (1) the United States would not permit further colonization in the New World by any European power, (2) the political system of the Americas was and would remain different from the monarchical systems of the Old World, (3) the United States would consider it a threat to its own safety if any effort were made to introduce the European system into the Americas, and (4) the United States would not interfere with existing European colonial possessions in the Americas and would not intervene in European affairs. This statement of policy was more than a pious expression. Since it was acceptable to Great Britain, as Foreign Secretary George Canning made clear, both the British navy and the U.S. army stood behind it. It had been Monroe's first thought that the policy should be set forth in the form of a treaty with Great Britain, but he was persuaded by Secretary of State John Quincy Adams to put it instead in the form of a unilateral declaration rather than "to come in as a cockboat in the wake of a British man-of-war."

VICE-PRESIDENT AND CABINET

VICE-PRESIDENT	Daniel D. Tomkins	1817–25
SECRETARY OF STATE	John Quincy Adams	1817–25
SECRETARY OF THE TREASURY	William H. Crawford	1816–25
SECRETARY OF WAR	John C. Calhoun	1817–25
ATTORNEY GENERAL	Richard Rush	1814–17
	William Wirt	1817–25
POSTMASTER GENERAL	R. Jonathan Meigs, Jr.	1814–23
	John McLean	1823–29
SECRETARY OF THE NAVY	Benjamin W. Crownshield	1814–19
	Smith Thompson	1819–23
	Samuel L. Southard	1823–25

In the twentieth century, after a succession of "strong presidents," James Monroe is not much admired. He did not believe that the executive branch of the government should have a strong positive program or should endeavor to assert its primacy over the states. He was restricted in some areas by his own strict interpretation of the Constitution. He would not, for example, approve legislation to bring about internal improvements with federal tax money and federal planning without a constitutional amendment, even though he personally favored such improvements. He approved federal funds for repair of the Cumberland Road only because the road was already in existence. Other major projects of his presidential administration were accomplished only as measures of national defense.

His attitude toward foreign affairs was quite different, owing both to his own deep involvement throughout a long career and to the constitutional delegation of authority in this field to the president. It is not remarkable, therefore, that his greatest impact should have been on foreign policy, in which, as Jefferson wrote to him, he "sets our compass and points the course which we are to steer through the oceans of time opening on us."

After completing his second term as president, Monroe retired to his home "Oak Hill" in Virginia. He served as a trustee of the University of Virginia and was a delegate to the state constitutional convention of 1829. In 1830, with failing health, he went to live in New York with one of his daughters. He died July 4, 1831, and was buried in New York but later removed to Virginia. See ERA OF GOOD FEELINGS; LOUISIANA PURCHASE; MONROE DOCTRINE.

STUART GERRY BROWN

BIBLIOG.–Stuart Gerry Brown, ed., *The Autobiography of James Monroe* (1959), *The First Republicans* (1954); W. P. Cresson, *James Monroe* (1946); George Dangerfield, *The Era of Good Feelings* (1952); Daniel C. Gilman, *James Monroe* (1898); S. M. Hamilton, ed., *The Writings of James Monroe* (8 vols., 1898–1903); Dexter Perkins, *A History of the Monroe Doctrine* (1955).

MONROE, city, NE Louisiana, seat of Ouachita Parish; on the Ouachita River, near Cheniere Lake; on the Arkansas and Louisiana Missouri, the Illinois Central, and the Missouri Pacific railroads and U.S. highways 80 and 165; a scheduled airline stop; opposite West Monroe and 96 miles E of Shreveport. Monroe is situated near one of the largest natural gas fields in the United States. Carbon black, wood pulp, paper, lumber, cotton, and cottonseed oil are major products of the city, which is the site of Northeast Louisiana State College (1928). Settled in 1785 as Fort Miro, Monroe was renamed in 1819 and incorporated in 1900. Pop. (1960) 52,219.

MONROE, city, SE Michigan, seat of Monroe County; on the Raisin River 3 miles from its mouth at Lake Erie; on the Baltimore and Ohio, the Chesapeake and Ohio, the Detroit and Toledo Shore Line, the New York Central, and the Pennsylvania railroads and U.S. highway 25; 34 miles SSW of Detroit. Monroe has nurseries, fisheries, limestone quarries, and factories for the manufacture of paper boxes, paperboard, and automotive parts. Settled in 1784 by the French as Frenchtown, the city was the site of the Raisin River Massacre during the War of 1812, in which American troops were defeated by Indian allies of the British. Monroe was incorporated as a village in 1827 and as a city in 1837. It was the home of Gen. George A. Custer for part of his life. Pop. (1960) 22,968.

MONROE, city, S North Carolina, seat of Union County; on the Seaboard Air Line Railroad and U.S. highways 74 and 601; 24 miles SE of Charlotte. Cotton yarn, clothing, bedding, locks, tools, lumber, plastic, metal products, poultry, and marble are the principal products of Monroe. Settled in 1844, the city was incorporated in 1947. Pop. (1960) 10,882.

MONROE, city, S Wisconsin, seat of Green County; on the Illinois Central and the Milwaukee railroads; 35 miles SSW of Madison. Monroe, an important Swiss cheese-making center, also has manufactures of other dairy products, cheese-making equipment, burners, loud-speakers, and hearing aids. The city was settled in 1832 and incorporated in 1858. Pop. (1960) 8,050.

MONROE DOCTRINE, a fundamental principle of American foreign policy designed to prevent outside interference in the Western Hemisphere. The doctrine has never been clearly formulated, and has received many modifications and interpretations.

Origin of the Doctrine. The Monroe Doctrine was enunciated in 1823 because of a threat to the Latin American countries that had recently revolted from Spain. The threat arose in 1822 when the Concert of Europe discussed plans at the Congress of Verona for the reconquest of the former Spanish colonies. Since British sentiment was opposed to the project because of trade interests in the area, the British foreign secretary George Canning proposed to the American government a joint declaration against reconquest. Secretary of State John Quincy Adams opposed joint action for reasons of national prestige, advocating instead a declaration by the United States alone. Accepting this point of view, Pres. James Monroe declared in his annual message to Congress on Dec. 2, 1823, that "the American continents, by the free and independent condition which they have assumed and maintained, are henceforth not to be considered as subjects for future colonization by any European powers."

He added: "In the wars of the European powers in matters relating to themselves we have never taken any part, nor does it comport with our policy so to do. It is only when our rights are invaded or seriously menaced that we resent injuries or make preparation for our defense. With the movements in this hemisphere we are of necessity more immediately connected, and by causes which must be obvious to all enlightened and impartial observers. The political system of the allied powers is essentially different in this respect from that of America. . . . We owe it, therefore, to candour and to the amicable relations existing between the United States and those powers to declare that we should consider any attempt on their part to extend their system to any portion of this hemisphere as dangerous to our peace and safety. With the existing colonies or dependencies of any European power we have not interfered and shall not interfere. But with the governments who have declared their independence and maintained it, and whose independence we have, on great consideration and on just principles, acknowledged, we could not view any interposition for the purpose of oppressing them, or controlling in any other manner their destiny, by any European power in any other light than as the manifestation of an unfriendly disposition toward the United States."

The declaration met with approval in England as a fulfillment of British foreign policy and as assistance to trade in an area long dominated by Spanish monopolistic practices. Implementation of the policy devolved in practice upon Great Britain. Because of the power of the British navy, no attempts were made to reconquer the former Spanish colonies.

Polk's Restatement. The first restatement of the doctrine came more than 20 years later at a time when the belief in "manifest destiny" was running strong in the United States. Great Britain and France, concerned over U.S. expansionism, attempted to establish a balance of power in the New World similar to that which regulated Europe. President James K. Polk, mistrustful of what he conceived to be European intervention in Argentina, Oregon, the Republic of Texas, and California, stated in 1845 that the United States could not view with indifference the attempt of European powers to "interfere" with the independent action of the nations of this continent. In condemning the balance of power, Polk was objecting to European diplomatic intrigue in the New World. The doctrine was thus extended to include diplomatic as well as military interposition. See BALANCE OF POWER; CALIFORNIA, History; OREGON, History; TEXAS, History, *The Texas Republic*.

Empire in Mexico. The attempt in 1861 by France, and halfheartedly by Great Britain and Spain, to establish an empire in Mexico under the Austrian Archduke Maximilian was interpreted as a serious challenge to the Monroe Doctrine. The episode firmly established the doctrine in the public consciousness, but of greater importance is the fact that the doctrine, with all its implications, had come to be recognized by the governments of Europe as the mainspring of U.S. foreign policy. See MEXICO, History, *Nineteenth Century*.

The "No Transfer" Addition. In 1869 Pres. Ulysses S. Grant, persuaded that the Germans eyed Santo Domingo with an imperialistic gleam, attempted to thwart this menace to Dominican independence by acquiring the island for the United States. On May 31, 1870, he accordingly enunciated the "no transfer" principle, according to which "no territory on this continent shall be regarded as subject to transfer to a European power." The treaty of annexation was rejected by the U.S. Senate, but the corollary was not, and became an accepted part of the doctrine.

International Law and the Doctrine. In 1895 a long-standing dispute between Great Britain and Venezuela, concerning the boundary between British Guiana and Venezuela, came to a head. The United States insisted on acting as arbiter in the matter in a strong and undiplomatic note sent to Great Britain by Sec. of State Richard Olney. Public opinion in England was friendly toward the United States and arbitration was eventually accepted, but in so doing, the foreign secretary, Robert Gascoyne-Cecil, 3rd marquis of Salisbury, denied that the doctrine had the force of international law, thus expressing a view generally shared by the governments of Europe. The

United States recognized international law, but insisted that diplomacy in the New World should be conducted under the auspices of the Monroe Doctrine. This position was further affirmed at the first Hague Conference of 1899, when U.S. representative Andrew D. White included a proviso that the United States should not be required to "abandon its attitude toward questions purely American." The ambivalent position adopted by the United States established a precedent with far-reaching consequences. See HAGUE CONFERENCES.

The Roosevelt Corollary. The period from 1900 to 1917 was one of U.S. expansion in the Caribbean area. The contributing causes included a popular mood of nationalism, the political and financial instability of many of the Central American republics, and the concern of European governments over their trade interests in the area. The United States used armed intervention in an effort to promote peace in the area, such action being sanctioned by an extension of the Monroe Doctrine by Pres. Theodore Roosevelt in 1905. There were two parts to the Roosevelt corollary. The first claimed the right of international policing whereas the second prohibited loans by European powers to the Caribbean countries. The policy that resulted from the corollary established U.S. officials in Cuba in 1901 and in the Dominican Republic in 1904; the U.S. Marines peacefully supervised Nicaragua and Honduras from 1911, Haiti from 1914, and the Dominican Republic from 1916. This interpretation of the doctrine was bitterly resented in South America. See DOLLAR DIPLOMACY; PLATT AMENDMENT.

The League of Nations. The efforts of Pres. Woodrow Wilson in 1919 to promote the League of Nations met with severe resistance. The arguments both for and against the league were based on different interpretations of the Monroe Doctrine, a situation made possible by its lack of formal definition. In its strict interpretation, and in a broad sense as well, the Monroe Doctrine did not conflict with the aims of the league. It was President Wilson's contention that the adoption of the aims of the league would in fact mean the application of the doctrine to the whole world. Opposition to the League of Nations rested on the division of the world into two hemispheres and was isolationist in aim. The isolationist position was that the Monroe Doctrine was not to be universally applied, but was to be interpreted by the United States alone; with the election of a Republican president, Warren Harding, in 1920, the United States refused to join the League of Nations and ratified a separate treaty with Germany. See ISOLATIONISM; LEAGUE OF NATIONS; VERSAILLES, TREATY OF.

Modification and Disuse. The following decades of the twentieth century saw four main developments of the doctrine: the extension of the doctrine to the entire Western Hemisphere, the abandonment of the Roosevelt corollary, the reaffirmation of the "no transfer" principle, and the ultimate lapse of the doctrine as an instrument of policy.

The Good Neighbor policy developed by Pres. Franklin D. Roosevelt resulted in a series of Pan American conferences that gradually moved toward solidarity and mutual defense. The conferences at Montevideo in 1933 and Buenos Aires in 1936 placed the American republics on an equal footing in multilateral agreements, whereas the Conference of Chapultepec in 1945 provided for joint diplomatic, economic, and military action against external aggression, thereby ignoring the (Theodore) Roosevelt corollary. Defense agreements with Canada and Greenland were negotiated under the provisions of the Monroe Doctrine, and ratified by the Treaty of Rio de Janeiro in 1947. The "no transfer" principle was reaffirmed when Germany laid claim to the West Indian colonies of France and the Netherlands after having conquered the mother countries in 1940. Their transfer was vigorously opposed, and the colonies were administered by a joint council set up for the duration of the war.

The doctrine lapsed in two ways. At the end of World War II, the United States was unreservedly committed to NATO and to interests beyond the New World. To that extent the Monroe Doctrine was no longer applicable. South American memories of "imperialism" died hard and the doctrine was no longer mentioned, although hemispheric defense and the Organization of American States remained important.

In 1962 the Monroe Doctrine was challenged by a Soviet military build-up in Cuba. When, in October, Soviet missile sites were discovered there, the United States, with the unanimous approval of the OAS, decided on a blockade against further weapons and strategic material for Cuba. The embargo proved effective; the U.S.S.R. agreed to dismantle its bases and withdraw its missiles. Thus, the Monroe Doctrine's interdiction of European interference in the western hemisphere was upheld. See GOOD NEIGHBOR POLICY; NORTH ATLANTIC TREATY ORGANIZATION; ORGANIZATION OF AMERICAN STATES; UNITED NATIONS.

BIBLIOG.–A. B. Hart, *Monroe Doctrine* (ed. 1920); A. Alvarez, *Monroe Doctrine* (1924); W. P. Cresson, *Diplomatic Portraits: Europe and the Monroe Doctrine One Hundred Years Ago* (1924); G. Nerval, *Autopsy of the Monroe Doctrine* (1934); D. Perkins, *Monroe Doctrine* (3 vols. 1927–37); *History of the Monroe Doctrine* (1956).

MONROEVILLE, borough, W Pennsylvania, in Allegany County; on U.S. highway 22 and the Pennsylvania Turnpike; 12 miles E of Pittsburgh. Monroeville's main industry is a steel research plant. The borough was incorporated in 1951. Pop. (1960) 22,446.

MONROVIA, city, S California, Los Angeles County; at the foot of the San Gabriel Mountains, on U.S. highway 66; 29 miles NE of Los Angeles, of which it is a residential suburb. Fruit packing and the manufacture of water heaters, aircraft and electronic components, pottery, draperies, hardware, and plastics constitute the chief industries of Monrovia. Settled in 1885, the city was incorporated in 1887. Pop. (1960) 27,079.

MONROVIA, city, W Africa, capital of Liberia; on the Atlantic Ocean, at the mouth of the St. Paul River, on Cape Montserrado; 242 miles SE of Freetown, Sierra Leone. Monrovia is connected by highways with interior and other coastal Liberian cities, by a railroad with the interior iron-ore mines, and by air service with European and other African centers; it is Liberia's chief port and commercial center. Principal exports are rubber, iron ore, palm kernels, and piassava fiber; manufactures include brick, tile, and soap. Monrovia was founded in 1822 under the sponsorship of the American Colonization Society as a settlement for freed American slaves and was named for U.S. Pres. James Monroe. Liberia College was established there in 1851. During World War II, when U.S. forces had bases there, the city's modern harbor on Bushrod Island, which is connected with Monrovia by a bridge, was extensively developed, largely with lend-lease aid from the United States. In 1948 Monrovia was opened as a free port. In 1961 Monrovia was host to a 19-nation African conference, resulting in the formation of a new African bloc. The Monrovia Conference Powers agreed to work together on various projects. (For population, see northern Africa map in Atlas.)

MONS, town, SW Belgium, capital of Hainaut Province; 34 miles SSW of Brussels. Situated on a railroad, a canal, and several highways, Mons is an important industrial town, a center of the cloth trade, and the shipping point for the Borinage coal-mining district. In addition to cloth and coal, its products include sugar, leather, metals, and soap. Mons is the site of a polytechnical and two commercial institutes, and is noted for its Gothic town hall and

Church of Sainte-Waudru, both dating from the fifteenth century. The city was made the capital of Hainaut by Charlemagne in 804. It prospered under the rule of the houses of Burgundy and Austria in the fifteenth and sixteenth centuries but suffered repeated attacks by the French and other European powers during the seventeenth and eighteenth centuries. In August, 1914, the first battle of World War I between the Germans and the British took place at Mons. In World War II the town was occupied by the Germans and was subjected to a number of bombing raids. Pop. (1955 est.) 25,567.

MONSERRAT. See MONTSERRAT.

MONSON, town, including Monson village, S Massachusetts, Hampden County; on the Central Vermont Railroad; 13 miles E of Springfield. Monson is a market for dairy, poultry, and truck farm products and the site of woolen mills and a granite quarry. Settled in 1715 as part of Brimfield, Monson was incorporated as a town in 1775. Pop. (1960) town 6,712, village 2,413.

MONSOON, a wind that changes in intensity and direction with the seasons. Monsoons blow from large continental land areas to the ocean in winter, and in the reverse direction in summer. As winter approaches, land areas cool to a greater extent and more rapidly than does the ocean, and in summer this situation is reversed. These temperature variations give rise to winds of different intensities that reverse their direction with the changes of the seasons. The direction of the monsoon winds is also greatly influenced by the direction of the earth's rotation. In the Northern Hemisphere monsoons blow in a clockwise direction in winter and counterclockwise in summer. In the Southern Hemisphere the wind directions are reversed.

The winds prevailing in the Indian Ocean, which blow with varying degrees of violence from the southwest during the period April to October and from the northeast during the rest of the year, were formerly the only winds commonly known as monsoons. Toward the end of May the southwest, or wet, monsoons of India, blowing from the tropical sea to the Himalayas, occur in a succession of tremendous thunderstorms, the rainy season continuing for two or three months. In October the northeast, or dry, monsoon sets in, the reversal in the direction of the wind being caused by the marked increase of pressure in central Asia, where the barometer shows pressures up to 30.20 inches, while in the Bay of Bengal the readings may be only 29.80 inches. The northeast monsoons that prevail from October to April bring very little rainfall to most of India. See METEOROLOGY.

MONTAGU, LADY MARY WORTLEY, 1689–1762, English author, was born in London, the daughter of Evelyn Pierrepont, later duke of Kingston. She married Edward Wortley Montagu and in 1716 accompanied him to Constantinople where he served as ambassador. She was impressed by the effectiveness of the Turkish custom of inoculating against smallpox, and on her return did much to promote the practice in England. She was a close friend of Alexander Pope until they quarreled in 1722, reputedly because she laughed at his declaration of love. Her literary reputation rests on the amusing *Turkish Letters,* written during her residence in Constantinople, and on her letters to her daughter, Lady Mary Bute. She also wrote the sophisticated *Town Eclogues* (1716).

MONTAGUE, town, including the villages of Turners Falls, Millers Falls, Montague, Montague City, and Lake Pleasant; NW Massachusetts, Franklin County; on the Connecticut and Millers rivers, on the Boston and Maine and the Central Vermont railroads; 30 miles N of Springfield. Manufactures include fishing tackle, dyes, and machinery. Montague City is the site of a large hydroelectric station; and the first dam built over the Connecticut is in Turners Falls. The town of Montague was settled in 1715. Pop. (1960) town, 7,836; Turners Falls, 4,917; Millers Falls, 1,199.

MONTAGUE, village, N central Texas, seat of Montague County; 50 miles ESE of Wichita Falls. Montague is a market center of an area that is important for its livestock, fruit, and oil. Nearby are an old Spanish fort once used by French traders in the Red River valley and a Texas Agricultural and Mechanical College fruit experiment station. Montague was settled in 1859. Pop. about 300.

MONTAIGNE, MICHEL EYQUEM DE, 1533–92, French essayist, was born in Périgord, near Bordeaux. Michel's father, veteran of the Italian wars and councilor at court, encouraged his son's taste for the classics by ordering that his entire household speak only Latin to the boy ("without books and without tears") until he was six. No less unusual was his order that the boy should be awakened by the strains of sweet music. At the Collège de Guyenne in Bordeaux, where Michel was graduated in 1546, the regent let him indulge his fancy in Latin poetry. Michel proceeded to the study of law, probably at Toulouse, and at length became councilor at the parliament of Bordeaux, where he met his most devoted friend, Étienne de La Boétie, the pamphleteer against monarchies and dictatorships (*Le contr'un*), whose early death, 1568, deeply affected Montaigne. In 1565 Montaigne married Françoise de la Chassaigne, who bore him six daughters, of whom only one survived him.

He resigned his office as councilor, 1570, and retired to an ivory-tower existence in his château at Périgord, where he might (as he said) "leaf through books" and compose essays. During this period he wrote his *Apologie de Raimond Sebond*. In his *Natural Theology* (translated earlier by Montaigne) Sebond, a Spanish theologian of the fifteenth century, had opposed the idea of faith over reason. Montaigne's essay is more a censure of Sebond's enemies than an endorsement of Sebond himself. The first two books of Montaigne's *Essais* appeared in 1580 and were approved by the church authority, for although Montaigne did not uphold the validity of faith, he did not directly attack the institution of the church. Between June, 1580, and November, 1581, Montaigne traveled through Switzerland, Germany, and Italy. Although the trip was ostensibly taken for reasons of health, it was more nearly a humanist's pilgrimage to Rome, the center of antiquities, which Montaigne considered the great "sepulcher." In his *Journal de voyage* he evinced inexhaustible interest in the ways of men.

During his absence Montaigne was elected mayor of Bordeaux, 1581, and he was re-elected in 1583. Toward the end of his second term a plague broke out in the town. Absent at his château at the time, Montaigne prudently stayed away from the pest-ridden town; this "prudence" has been roundly criticized by some. As mayor, Montaigne was noted for his moderation in dealing (on the whole successfully) with opposing factions. He served Henry III, but also favored the king of Navarre, whom he received in his château in 1584 and 1587. After 1585 Montaigne composed a third book of *Essais* (1588) and revised the first two books. In 1588 he accompanied Henry III to Rouen, and attended the estates-general at Blois. During his last years he enjoyed the companionship of Mlle. Marie de Gournay, who aided in preparing a new edition of the *Essais* (1595). Montaigne died in 1592 from quinsy, devoutly receiving the last rites of the church.

The Essays. It has been said that Montaigne's thought went through three stages: Stoicism, skepticism, and Epicureanism, the latter in the sense of a search for happiness through the moderate and harmonious exercise of all one's faculties. If it is true that he underwent these phases, sometimes allowing them to coexist in his thought, his skepticism was the dominant note. In a prefatory statement, Montaigne makes it clear that the book will be entirely about himself: "I wish people to see me in my simple, natural, and ordinary state, without study or artifice; for it is myself I paint. My faults will be clearly read here as real as life." Throughout the essays are found the elements for a detailed portrait of a Renaissance gentleman: his health, education, diet, clothing, pastimes, family life, his various likes and dislikes, his strengths and weaknesses. "Others look before them; I look within myself."

The basis for his skepticism is clear. He studied the behavior of men, from the ancient Greeks to the American Indian, and found their politics, morals, laws, religions, and customs so apparently divergent and contradictory that the only conclusion possible for him was to doubt the ultimate validity of any and all. If history can provide no clear-cut distinctions between right and wrong, who can claim to have the right on his side? And if no one has the right to make this claim, then tolerance must be the necessary rule of life. One must avoid excesses of opinion and behavior and live tranquilly with one's fellow men. This was the lesson of the classic philosophers, Montaigne concluded; later it was to be the lesson of Voltaire.

Influence. The opportunities of the essay form exploited by Montaigne became evident to many great writers who came after him: Francis Bacon, who acknowledged his debt to Montaigne, Pierre Bayle, Denis Diderot, and a host of others. After John Florio's masterful translation of Montaigne's works into English, 1603, Montaigne became extremely influential in England, and even William Shakespeare apparently borrowed from him. If the French Renaissance produced its share of moral and reflective sermons in print, it also contrived the counterpart of the Christian sermon in Montaigne's humanistic essays. To the certainty of Christian dogma, the *Essais* counterposed the skepticism of ancient Pyrrho and the disturbing question, "*Que sçay-je?*" (What do I really know?). To the authority of the church fathers Montaigne opposed the declarations of the multitude of classic historians and moralists which are, as he says, "piled up" in his prose. To faith he opposed reason ("We must accompany faith with all the reason which is within us") and to organized religion he counterposed nature. As a humanist he centered his attention on the microcosm, man ("Every man bears the entire form of mankind's lot"), and left speculation about the macrocosm to theologians and priests. The objectivity and detachment that he preached made him inevitably an apostle of tolerance and, in the seventeenth century, free thinkers adopted him as one of their precursors. In 1674 Montaigne's works were placed in the Index of forbidden books by the Roman Catholic church, although Montaigne was throughout his life a devout Roman Catholic.

ROBERT J. CLEMENTS

BIBLIOG.–A. M. Boase, *Fortunes of Montaigne* (1935); Donald M. Frame, *Montaigne's Discovery of Man* (1955), *Montaigne* (1965); André Gide, *Montaigne* (1939).

MONTALE, EUGENIO, 1896– , Italian poet, born in Genoa. From 1929 to 1938 he was director of the Florentine literary organization Gabinetto Vieusseux, and later was literary editor of the Milan newspaper *Corriere della sera.* Antinationalist and antifascist, Montale's poetry reflects the disillusionment shared by many poets in Italy following World War I. He was a leader of the "hermetic" movement, which sought to communicate emotional experience with complete immediacy and stylistic simplicity. It therefore opposed the florid poetical manner of Gabriele D'Annunzio and was greatly influenced by the French symbolists. Montale often uses the desolate Ligurian landscape in his poetry to express his disenchantment with life. His most noted works include *Ossi di seppia* (1925), *Le Occasioni* (1939), and *La bufera* (1956).

MONTALEMBERT, CHARLES FORBES DE TRYON, COMTE DE, 1810–70, French political figure, was born in London, the son of a French émigré. With Félicité Lamennais he founded in Paris the newspaper *L'Avenir* (1830), which was condemned by the pope as too liberal (1832). He entered the chamber of peers in 1835, and as a member of the national assembly (1848–57) was one of the leading representatives of Catholic liberal opinion and a champion of the church against secular and anticlerical tendencies. His opposition to the policies of Napoleon III brought about his political defeat in 1857, and he spent the rest of his life writing and traveling. His most important works include *Catholic Interests in the 19th Century* (1852); *The Free Church in the Free State* (1863); and *The Monks of the West* (7 vols. 1861–79), which was finished from notes after his death.

MONTANA, state, NW United States; bounded on the N by the Canadian provinces of British Columbia, Alberta, and Saskatchewan, on the E by North Dakota and South Dakota, on the S by Wyoming, and on the W by Idaho; maximum east-west and north-south extents 556 and 322 miles respectively; area 147,138 sq. mi., including 1,402 sq. mi. of inland water; pop. (1960) 674,767. Montana ranks 42nd among states in population and fourth in area. Its name is Latin in derivation and means mountainous. Its nickname, Treasure State, is based on Montana's valuable mineral deposits. The state motto is "*Oro y Plata*" (Gold and Silver); the state flower is the bitterroot; the state tree is the ponderosa pine; and the official bird is the western meadowlark. Helena is the capital. See map in Atlas, Vol. 20. For state flag in color, see FLAG.

PHYSICAL FEATURES

Topography. The surface of Montana shows the effect of most geologic periods. There is much intermingling of rock types, from Pre-Cambrian sedimentary sandstone, shale, and limestone to relatively recent glacial drift. Extensive folds and faults further complicate the geologic structure.

Montana is divided into two physical sections: the eastern plains, comprising three fifths of the state, and the western mountain region. More than 20 ranges of the Rocky Mountains extend from Yellowstone National Park at the Wyoming boundary across Montana in a northwesterly direction. Among these are the Beaverhead and Bitterroot ranges and the Cabinet and Purcell mountains that mark the western boundary of the state. The continental divide enters Montana from Canada at Glacier National Park and roughly parallels the Idaho border. The highest peaks lie east of the continental divide and culminate in Granite Peak (12,799 ft.) in the Absaroka Range near Yellowstone National Park. The plains, interrupted in central Montana by several isolated mountain ranges, vary in elevation from 4,000 feet at the base of the Rockies to 2,000 feet in the east. The lowest point in the state is 1,800 feet on the Kootenai River

The Great Seal of the State of Montana was adopted in 1893. In the foreground are depicted a miner's pick and shovel and a plow. The great falls of the Missouri River are shown on the right. Mountains rise on the left.

BIRD	Western meadowlark
FLOWER	Bitterroot
TREE	Ponderosa pine
CAPITAL	Helena
MOTTO	Oro y Plata (Gold and Silver)
ENTERED THE UNION	Nov. 8, 1889
ORDER OF ENTRY	41st

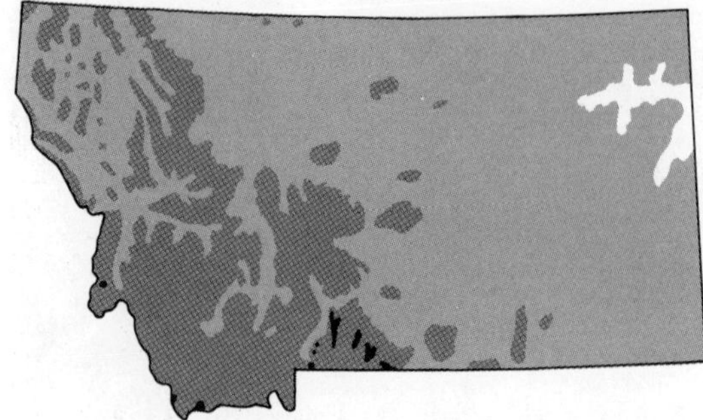

Elevation Map of Montana. White, 1,000-2,000 feet; light gray, 2,000-5,000 feet; dark gray, 5,000-10,000 feet; black, over 10,000 feet.

near the northwestern Idaho border. The average elevation is 3,400 feet.

Rivers and Lakes. The portion of Montana lying east of the continental divide is drained by the Missouri River, which is formed by the Jefferson, Madison, and Gallatin rivers near Three Forks. The principal tributaries of the Missouri in Montana are the Musselshell, Milk, and Yellowstone rivers, the latter merging with the Missouri near the Montana–North Dakota border. The Kootenai and the Clark Fork rivers—the latter having as tributaries the Flathead, the Bitterroot, and the Blackfoot rivers—drain the area west of the continental divide. The Missouri is navigable for 120 miles to Fort Peck Dam, and at seasons of high water the Yellowstone may be ascended for 260 miles to the mouth of its chief tributary, the Big Horn River. The Flathead River is navigable as far as Kerr Dam, immediately southwest of Flathead Lake. Most of the state's natural lakes are in the Rockies and, with the exception of Flathead, are quite small.

Climate. The weather pattern of Montana is determined by the continental divide. West of the divide winters are milder and summers cooler, and the rainfall is more abundant. The climate of Montana is characterized by instability and by wide ranges in annual and daily temperatures. Average January and July temperatures are 19° and 68°F respectively, and the average annual temperature is 43°. Extremes of 117° and −70° have been recorded. The average annual precipitation is 15 inches. The summer rainy season frequently brings thunderstorms and crop-damaging hailstorms. Yearly snowfall averages 52 inches. Prevailing winds are from the west, and during winter the periodic chinook has a warming effect upon the eastern regions. The growing season is May to September.

Soils and Natural Vegetation. The soils of eastern Montana are fertile but those of the western mountain region are thin, poorly developed, and subject to erosion. Large areas of fertile alluvial soils lie along the Missouri and Yellowstone rivers and their tributaries. Montana has more than 2,000 species of wild flowers and nonflowering plants, classified in three categories—subalpine, montane, and plains. The subalpine plants grow in mountain areas and include glacier lilies, alpine poppies, columbines, violets, asters, and Rocky Mountain laurel. The montane group thrives in mountain foothills and valleys and comprises great coniferous forests of ponderosa pine, lodgepole pine, western larch, Douglas fir and spruce, many varieties of shrubs, and such flowers as dogtooth violet, Mariposa lily, beargrass, and bitterroot. Plants of the plains type grow throughout eastern Montana and include species of grasses, four kinds of cacti, and bluebells, golden asters, and daisies. Hardwoods such as aspen, cottonwood, box elder, green ash, willow, birch, and elm grow along stream banks on the plains.

Animals. The state fish and game department operates 70 game ranges, bird farms and development areas, game and bird preserves and refuges, and fish hatcheries and spawning stations for development of Montana wildlife. There are more than 90 species of mammals, 30 of amphibians and reptiles, 60 of fish, and 300 of birds. Common game animals are the deer, black and grizzly bear, elk, mountain goat, antelope, and moose. There are also rabbit, skunk, weasel, mink, otter, raccoon, fox, and coyote. Principal game birds are Chinese and Mongolian pheasants, Hungarian partridge, grouse, sage hen, and wild ducks and geese. Hawks, owls, crows, woodpeckers, thrushes, and meadowlarks are common in the state and rattlesnakes are found throughout. In lakes and streams are trout, grayling, bass, pike, catfish, sturgeon, perch, whitefish, and salmon.

Population Density Map of Montana. White, 1-3 inhabitants per square mile; light gray, 3-10; dark gray, 10-20; black, 20-65.

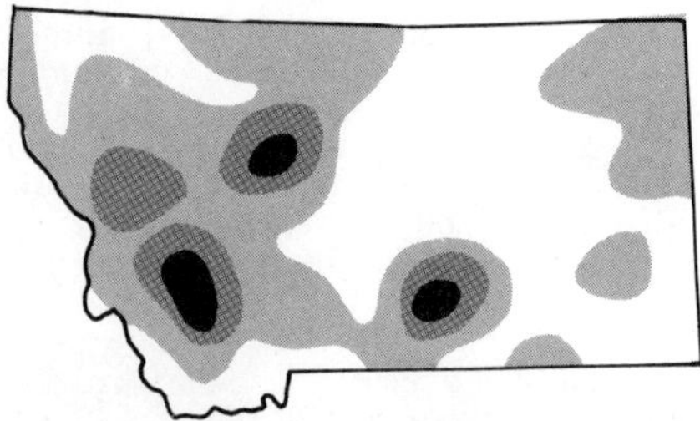

Precipitation Map of Montana. Area with diagonal lines, less than 10 inches annually; white, 10-20 inches; light gray, 20-30 inches; dark gray, 30-50 inches; black, 50-80 inches.

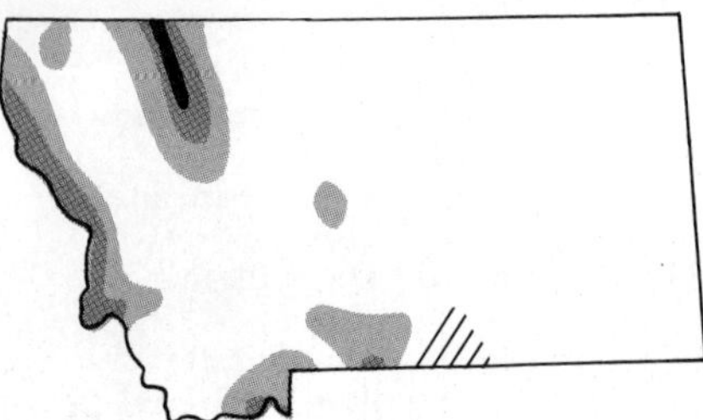

Social Features

Population. In 1960 the population of Montana was 674,767, an increase of 14.2 per cent over the 1950 figure of 591,024. Montana ranked 42nd among the states in population in 1960. In that year, 50.2 per cent of the population was classed as urban, an increase of 6.3 per cent over the 1950 figure, and the average density in the state was 4.6 persons per square mile. Of the total 1960 population 650,738 were white, and 23,929 were non-white. The latter group included 1,467 Negroes and 21,181 Indians.

PRINCIPAL CITIES

City	Population 1950 Census	1960 Census
Great Falls	39,214	55,357
Billings	31,834	52,851
Butte	33,251	27,877
Missoula	22,485	27,090
Helena (capital)	17,581	20,227
Bozeman	11,325	13,361
Anaconda	11,254	12,054
Havre	8,086	10,740
Kalispell	9,737	10,151
Miles City	9,243	9,665

Education. Montana has a state board of education composed of the governor, state superintendent of public instruction, attorney general, and eight others appointed by the governor. Each county has a superintendent of schools. Schools must be open at least 24 weeks each year. Public education is free. Attendance at a public, private, or parochial school is compulsory for children aged 8 to 16. The training of teachers is provided in the two state normal schools, the state university, the state college, and a private college at Great Falls. The state maintains the University of Montana system, which comprises Montana State University (1893) at Missoula, Montana State College (1893) at Bozeman, Montana School of Mines (1893) at Butte, Western Montana College of Education (1893) at Dillon, and Eastern Montana College of Education (1925) at Billings. Carroll College (1909) at Helena is under Roman Catholic administration, as is the College of Great Falls (1932) at Great Falls. Rocky Mountain College (1883) at Billings is sponsored by several Protestant denominations.

Public Welfare. The state board of examiners supervises most Montana state institutions. The state board of education, however, has certain control over the Montana School for the Deaf and Blind at Great Falls, the state industrial school at Miles City, the state vocational school for girls at Helena, the state training school at Boulder, and the state orphans' home at Twin Bridges. Other state institutions include a hospital for the mentally ill at Warm Springs, a prison at Deer Lodge, a soldiers' home at Columbia Falls, a tuberculosis sanatorium at Galen, and a home for aged men and women at Lewistown. The state department of public welfare, created in 1937, administers old age assistance and aid to dependent children.

HERB AND DOROTHY MCLAUGHLIN

Kerr Dam, at the south end of Flathead Lake in northwest Montana, is an important source of power.

Economic Features

Agriculture. Agriculture is Montana's major source of income, the annual gross averaging $420 million. In 1966 the income from crops was $225.6 million and from livestock and livestock products $274.9 million. Wheat accounted for 33.4 per cent of farm income, cattle for 40.7 per cent. Montana also has crops of barley, oats, rye, corn, mustard seed, peas, beans, flaxseed, sugar beets, cherries, apples, alfalfa seed, potatoes, sweet clover, and hay. In 1966 there were 2.84 million cattle, 1.39 million sheep, and 128,000 hogs. Water supplies for dry areas are available from 658 dams and reservoirs constructed on Montana rivers and streams.

Four general types of farming are carried on in Montana; irrigation, dry-land, ranch, and specialized. In 1964, 1.9 million acres were devoted to irrigation farming, the main crops being sugar beets, peas, potatoes, corn, oats, and barley. Dry-land farming, centered largely in central and northeastern Montana, produces wheat, oats, barley, rye, flaxseed, mustard seed, and hay. Ranching is common on plains and mountain foothills, where cattle and sheep are grazed. The specialized farm stresses dairy ranching, poultry raising, or seed, fruit, or truck farming. In 1964 there were 27,020 farms in Montana totaling 65.8 million acres. In 1964 the average farm, 2,437 acres, was valued at $105,230.

PRINCIPAL CROPS

Crop	Unit	1955	1965
		thousands	
Barley	bushel	40,620	50,700
Beans	cwt.	230	209
Hay	short ton	3,054	3,801
Oats	bushel	10,840	11,176
Potatoes	cwt.	1,350	1,360 ('66)
Sugar beets	ton	724	745
Wheat	bushel	109,350	101,212 ('66)

Cattle graze on a ranch in Livingston. Agriculture is the chief occupation in the state.

HERB AND DOROTHY MCLAUGHLIN

Glacier National Park in the Northern Rockies provides spectacular scenery.

HERB AND DOROTHY MCLAUGHLIN

HERB AND DOROTHY MCLAUGHLIN

Helena, the state capital, sits 4,000 feet above sea level, in the center of a mining region.

HERB AND DOROTHY MCLAUGHLIN

The Montana State Historical Museum at Helena contains a large collection of Western art.

Mining and Forestry. In 1965 the value of Montana's mineral production was $211 million. The principal mineral products in order of total value were oil, copper, zinc, sand and gravel, silver, phosphate rock, lead, chromite, natural gas, and stone. Montana is a leading U.S. producer of chromite, manganese, silver, zinc, and vermiculite and commercially produces 10 metal minerals, found chiefly in the southwest, and 16 nonmetal minerals. Copper is mined in the vicinity of Butte. The best bituminous and lignite coal beds are in the south central portion of the state. The Montana oil industry was begun in 1915. The largest fields are the Cut Bank and Kevin-Sunburst in the north and the Elk Basin in the south. The Cut Bank field is also the largest producer of natural gas. Other minerals produced in Montana are aluminum, iron ore, uranium, barite, cement, clay, fluorspar, gypsum, lime, pyrite, sulfur, and talc.

MINERAL PRODUCTION

Mineral	Unit	1956	1966
		thousands	
Coal	short ton	846	346 ('65)
Copper	short ton	96	130
Gold	troy ounce	38	29 ('65)
Lead	short ton	19	4.5
Manganiferous ore	short ton	5	20 ('65)
Natural gas	million cu. ft.	25,847	25,188 ('65)
Oil	barrel	21,760	35,380
Sand and gravel	short ton	10,024	13,816
Silver	troy ounce	7,386	5,290 ('65)
Stone	short ton	1,247	4,150
Zinc	short ton	71	29

Lumbering is the third major industry of Montana, following agriculture and mining. One fourth of the state's total land area, about 22 million acres, is forested, 58 per cent of it west of the continental divide. Nearly 16 million acres are classified as commercial forests. Almost 70 per cent of the forest lands, including 11 national forests and 7 Indian reservations with forests, are government owned or managed. Ponderosa and lodgepole pine, western larch, Douglas fir, Engelmann spruce, white fir, and Idaho white pine are the most common trees. The annual value of Montana forest products exceeds $100 million, the main items being lumber, pulpwood, fuel wood, poles, posts, timber for the mining industry, and Christmas trees.

Montana has 22 million acres of forest. The state university has an important forestry school.

HERB AND DOROTHY MCLAUGHLIN

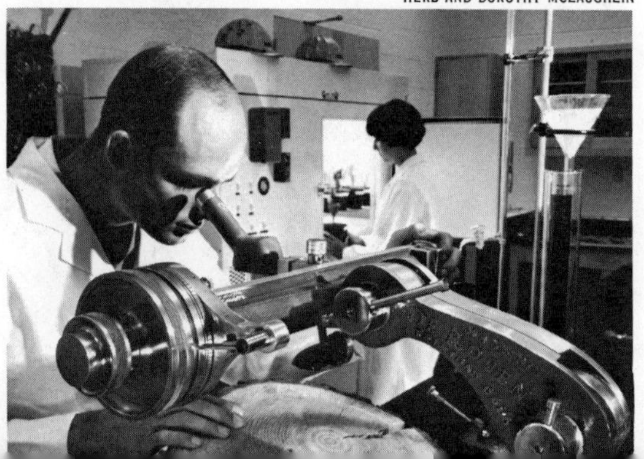

Manufacturing and Transportation. Montana industry centers in the processing of farm, mine, and forest products. Leading industries include flour milling, sugar-beet processing, vegetable and fruit canning, butter and cheese making, copper smelting, lead and oil refining, phosphate and aluminum reducing, metal fabricating, lumber milling, printing and publishing; the manufacture of copper and aluminum wire, chemicals and fertilizer, cement, insulation, machinery; and wood, stone, clay, glass, oil, and coal products. Chief manufacturing centers are Butte, Great Falls, Billings, Missoula, Helena, and Anaconda. In 1964 Montana had 976 manufacturing establishments employing 20,000 persons and paying $115 million in wages. The value added by manufacture was $272 million.

In 1964, there were 4,940 miles of railroad operated by the six railroad companies serving the state. The federal government maintained 7,535 miles of highway; the state, 11,383; and local communities, 53,369. In 1965 there were 186 airports, all of which were publicly owned. Airlines serve the cities of Bozeman, Wolf Point, Butte, Sidney, Cut Bank, Missoula, Glendive, Miles City, Great Falls, Lewistown, Helena, and Kalispell.

Tourist Attractions. Montana has abundant opportunities for hunting and fishing, camping, hiking, mountain climbing, skiing, swimming, boating, prospecting, and rock and fossil hunting. There are more than 1,500 lakes, 32,000 miles of fishing streams, and 7 state and 11 national forests in the state. Part of Yellowstone National Park is in southwestern Montana and can be approached by way of Silver Gate, Gardiner, and West Yellowstone. Glacier National Park, established in 1910, is a primeval wilderness in northwestern Montana on the Canadian border. Much of the park is accessible only by trail. Nestled among its higher peaks are more than 60 glaciers and 200 lakes. The park forms part of Waterton-Glacier International Peace Park, established in 1932. Montana has more than 15 state parks, recreational areas, and state monuments. Of special interest are the Lewis and Clark Cavern, the largest limestone cavern in the northwest; Bannack State Monument, first territorial capital of Montana and now a ghost town; Maco Sica State Park, in the Bad-

MONTANA

NORTHERN PACIFIC RY.

Large herds of sheep fatten on a slope of the Beartooth Range near the north entrance to Yellowstone National Park.

LIB. OF CONGRESS

A cattle hand on a ranch near Birney ropes a calf during an early summer roundup. The calf will be branded with the symbol of the ranch.

One of Montana's most productive natural gas fields is at Cut Bank in the northern part of the state. Here a gauger measures the contents of a tank at the large oil refinery.

STANDARD OIL CO. (N.J.)

Preparatory to blasting, workers in a copper mine at Butte cut dynamite holes in the face of a stope, using a pneumatic drilling rig.

ANACONDA COPPER MINING CO.

A combine threshes and harvests a grain crop on a northern Montana farm. Wheat is the leading cash-crop of the state. In the distance an oil derrick stands against the horizon.

STANDARD OIL CO. (N.J.)

SANTA FE RY.

One of Montana's many natural wonders is the Paradise Room in Morrison Cave near Three Forks. Paradise Room, 160 feet high and 75 feet across, is ¾ mile from cave mouth.

lands area of east Montana; and the Missouri River Headwaters State Monument, where Capt. Meriwether Lewis and Lt. William Clark discovered the beginning of the Missouri River. Big Hole Battlefield National Monument is on the site where the Nez Percé Indians were defeated in 1877 by U.S. soldiers, and the Custer Battlefield National Monument is a cemetery for those who died in the famous Battle of the Little Big Horn in 1876. The seven Indian reservations within Montana are popular because of the colorful celebrations held by the various tribes. Northwest of Missoula on the Flathead Indian Reservation is the national bison range, where buffalo, elk, deer, and antelope live. Relics of Montana's colorful past may be seen in Virginia City and other ghost towns. Mines in Butte and smelters in Anaconda and Columbia Falls are open to the public. Other attractions are the state capitol at Helena and the numerous state and federal dams, historical forts and museums, and rodeos and dude ranches.

GOVERNMENT

The constitution of Montana was adopted in 1889. Amendments require the approval of two-thirds of the elected members of both houses of the legislative assembly and of a majority of the voters at a popular election. A minimum age of 21 and residence in the state for one year and in the same county for 30 days are prerequisites for voting. An amendment in 1906 instituted the initiative and referendum.

The legislative assembly consists of a senate and a house of representatives. The senate is composed of one senator for each of the 56 counties, elected for four years. Members of the house of representatives are elected for two-year terms on the basis of one representative per county plus one representative for every 7,000 persons in each county in excess of 3,500. Regular sessions are held biennially, beginning in January of odd-numbered years with a limit of 60 days.

The executive officials include the governor, lieutenant governor, secretary of state, attorney general, treasurer, auditor, and superintendent of public instruction, all elected for four years. The governor with the advice and consent of the senate appoints many administrative officials. He has veto power extending to items in appropriation bills, but this may be overridden by a two-thirds vote of the members present in each house.

Judicial power is vested in a supreme court consisting of a chief justice and four associate justices, elected for six years by popular vote; 18 district courts with judges elected for four years; justice of the peace courts; and municipal and police courts.

Montana is represented in the U.S. Congress by two senators and two representatives.

HISTORY

Exploration and Settlement. Most of the area corresponding to modern Montana was included in French Louisiana. The area was first explored in 1742–43 by Pierre de La Vérendrye, but was long neglected by white men other than fur trappers. Following the Louisiana Purchase in 1803, the Lewis and Clark Expedition crossed the region and in 1805 followed the Missouri and Yellowstone rivers to their junction (see LEWIS AND CLARK EXPEDITION, LOUISIANA PURCHASE). A fort was built at the mouth of the Big Horn in 1807, and most of the area was incorporated in the Missouri Territory in 1812. The first settlements, founded along the Yellowstone River between 1809 and 1829, were little more than trading posts, many of the settlers being employees of the Hudson's Bay Company and other fur trading companies. The American Fur Company in 1828 established Fort Floyd, which was later renamed Fort Union and became the major trading post on the Missouri River, and in 1846 Fort Lewis, which was later renamed Fort Benton and served as a base for miners during the gold rush. In 1841 Jesuits led by Father Pierre Jean de Smet established a permanent mission among the Flathead Indians of the Bitterroot Valley. Much of the exploration of the area was accomplished by the "mountain men," such as the famous Jim Bridger. See FUR TRADE; MOUNTAIN MEN.

Development and Statehood. Gold was first discovered near Hell Gate River in 1852, and more promising discoveries in 1857 and 1860 in the Deer Lodge Valley caused a gold rush. Mining settlements sprang up on Grasshopper Creek, Big Hole River, North Boulder River, and other places. Upon the discovery of gold at Alder Gulch in 1863, Virginia City was founded, and the population of the district increased by 10,000 within a year. The period was characterized by lawlessness, but order was restored by the vigilantes. See VIGILANTES.

Most of the area became part of the Nebraska Territory in 1854, then of the Dakota Territory in 1861, and all of it was incorporated in the Idaho Territory in 1863. On May 26, 1864, Montana was organized as a separate territory, with its capital at Bannack. The territorial government was moved to Virginia City in 1865 and to Helena in 1875. Frequent conflicts occurred between the Indians and the settlers, culminating in the disastrous battle of June 25, 1876, on the Little Big Horn River between the army, led by Gen. George A. Custer, and the Dakotas. See CUSTER, GEORGE ARMSTRONG; LITTLE BIG HORN BATTLE.

Copper and silver mining, begun around 1880, soon surpassed gold mining in importance. The promotion of mining interests in Montana led to a struggle among mine owners such as William A. Clark, Marcus Daly, and F. Augustus Heinze. The Northern Pacific Railway, surveyed in 1853, partly through the stimulus of mining activity and partly as a result of the competition between England, Russia, and the United States for trade in the North Pacific area, was completed in 1883. In 1889 the territory adopted a constitution and applied for admission to the Union, becoming a state on Nov. 8, 1889. Montana voters participated in their first presidential election in 1892 and supported the People's party. In 1916 Montana elected Jeanette Rankin, the first woman ever sent to Congress.

MONTANA

Highlights of History

GREAT NORTHERN RY.
Some dormitory cars had to be sawed down to pass tunnels during the construction of a new Montana railroad in 1887.

NORTHERN PACIFIC RY.
The discovery of gold at Last Chance Gulch in 1864 made a boom town out of what became Helena, Montana's capital.

NORTHERN PACIFIC RY.
While leading their expedition along the Missouri River in 1805, Lewis and Clark camped at Black Eagle Falls in Montana.

NORTHERN PACIFIC RY.
Joseph, Nez Percé chief, surrendered to federal troops in 1877 after leading his tribe on a bitter retreat into Montana.

NORTHERN PACIFIC RY.
Ill-fated Gen. Geo. A. Custer and Indian scouts guarded track laying operations during the Indian Wars.

This painting by Charles Russell shows Flathead Indians meeting the expedition of Lewis and Clark in Montana in 1805.
HIST. SOC. OF MONTANA

This home in Redwater Valley is typical of the first Montana ranch houses along the Northern Pacific Railway in the 1880's.
NORTHERN PACIFIC RY.

Twentieth Century. Between 1917 and 1921 Montana suffered from a severe drought which aggravated the difficulties of the farmers. Improvement in the price of copper, development of the oil and natural gas industries, federal programs for soil conservation, insect control, irrigation, and rural electrification eased the economic situation. Cities Butte and Kalispell became eligible for federal aid as chronically depressed areas under the Areas Aid Bill, 1961. Montana supported Republican presidential nominees Dwight D. Eisenhower, 1956, and Richard M. Nixon, 1960, although the state elections in those years were split between Republicans and Democrats.

BIBLIOG.–R. G. Raymer, *Montana: The Land and the People* (3 vols. 1930); E. Thane, *High Border Country* (1942); J. K. Howard, *Montana: High, Wide, and Handsome* (1943); Federal Writers' Project, *Montana* (1949); R. W. Poston, *Small Town Renaissance* (1950); H. J. Hoflich and M. M. Johnson, *Economy of Montana* (1951); W. G. Browder and H. J. Hoflich, *Population and Income in Montana* (1953); N. C. Abbott, *Montana Government* (1937), *Montana in the Making* (ed. 1954); P. F. Sharp, *Whoop-up Country* (1955); M. G. Burlingame and K. R. Toole, *History of Montana* (3 vols. 1957); J. M. Hamilton, *From Wilderness to Statehood* (1957).

MONTANA SCHOOL OF MINES, a technological land-grant, coeducational, state-controlled institution of higher learning located at Butte. It was established in 1893, with instruction first offered in 1900. The state bureau of mines and geology is a part of the school. Distinctive educational programs include a plan whereby all physically qualified juniors and seniors are permitted to work occasionally in nearby mines, mills, or smelters to provide experience in engineering practice. The school offers the bachelor's degree, with the master's degree being offered in geology, mining, metallurgy, and petroleum engineering. See COLLEGES AND UNIVERSITIES.

MONTANA SERIES, a series of rock strata belonging to the Upper Cretaceous system in America. It follows the Colorado series and is succeeded by the Laramie series. The Montana series is composed of two subdivisions, the Fox Hills beds and the Pierre shales. Some of the sandstone layers of the Montana series are rich in oil deposits. See GEOLOGIC TIME.

MONTANA STATE UNIVERSITY, a coeducational state-controlled institution of higher learning located at Missoula. The school was chartered as the University of Montana in 1913, with instruction first being offered in 1895. In 1913 the name was changed to State University of Montana. The shorter name was adopted in 1935.

Divisions of the university include colleges of arts and sciences (1895) and fine arts (1954); and schools of pharmacy (1907), law (1911), forestry (1913), music (1913), journalism (1914), business administration (1920), and education (1930).

The university offers the bachelor's degree, with the master's degree being offered by most departments and the doctor's degree by the school of education. Distinctive educational programs include institutes and workshops concerned with teaching, business, journalism, music, and other subjects. See COLLEGES AND UNIVERSITIES.

MONTANISM, second century schismatic religion, was named after a Phrygian, Montanus, who was converted to Christianity (about 156) and immediately declared himself a prophet. Montanistic doctrine, as proclaimed by its high priest, demanded that spiritual things be rapidly set in order in preparation for the second coming of Christ which was approaching. Montanus stated that he was specifically the prophet of the Holy Spirit, and that the Spirit was guiding him to supplement the revelation that Christ had made. This claim was considered dangerous by the Roman Catholic bishops; the Montanistic prophecies were soon condemned as heresy by the Church and its followers were excommunicated. Although its teaching spread widely, and even counted the great lawyer Tertullian among its devotees in Africa, Montanism was short-lived. A few followers still existed in Africa at the time of St. Augustine, but they turned over their basilica to that saint and gave up their doctrines (about 400); after that time nothing further is known of them.

MONTAUBAN, city, SW France, capital of Tarn-et-Garonne Department; at the confluence of the Tarn and Tescou rivers; 29 miles N of Toulouse. Montauban is a trade and transportation center for the surrounding region which produces wheat, corn, oats, potatoes, and grapes. The city has manufactures of textiles, hats, processed food, furniture, flour, and decorative earthenware. Of interest are the Church of St. Jacques, built in the late fourteenth and early fifteenth centuries; the museum (1659) which contains paintings by Jean Auguste Ingres, born in Montauban; and the brick bridge (1303–16) of seven arches that spans the Tarn connecting Montauban with the suburb of Villebourbon. Montauban was founded in 1144 by the count of Toulouse, Alphonse Jourdain. During the Reformation it became a stronghold of Protestantism and was often besieged by royalist forces. In 1629, after the fall of La Rochelle, the city surrendered to Cardinal Richelieu, who razed its fortifications. After the repeal of the Edict of Nantes in 1685 imposed further hardships upon the Protestants, Montauban rapidly declined in importance. Pop. (1954) 24,258.

MONTAUK, a North American Indian belonging to any one of a group of tribes of the Algonquian linguistic stock. The Montauks lived in the central and eastern parts of Long Island, New York, and grew maize by simple methods. They numbered about 6,000 in 1600, but were nearly decimated by epidemics and wars against the Narraganset. The survivors took refuge at Easthampton, N.Y., in 1759. Most of them joined the Brotherton Indians in 1788. A few mixed-blood descendants of the Montauks remain on Long Island.

MONTAUK POINT, easternmost point of New York, at the E extremity of Long Island, on the tip of the S peninsula, fronting Block Island Sound of the Atlantic Ocean; at the terminus of the Montauk Highway; 112 miles ENE of New York City. It is the site of Montauk Point State Park and of a U.S. lighthouse built in 1796. Montauk Point is a popular fishing and recreational area.

MONTBÉLIARD, town E France, Doubs Department; at the confluence of the Luzine and Savoureuse rivers, on the Rhône-Rhine Canal; 8 miles W of the Switzerland border and 9 miles SSW of Belfort. Montbéliard is the center of an industrial region noted for the manufacture of automobiles and automobile parts, hardware, clocks, and watches. It is built around a tenth century fortified château belonging to the house of Bar-le-Duc, a member of which in the twelfth century founded the countship of Montbéliard. The château, rebuilt in 1751, has two intact towers dating from 1425 and 1594. Other features of interest include a seventeenth century market place, a town hall, and the Church of St. Martin; there is a statue of Georges Cuvier, French naturalist born in Montbéliard. The town, awarded to Lorraine by the Treaty of Verdun (843), was the scene of many battles for ownership of the countship. It was officially incorporated into France in 1801 by the Treaty of Lunéville. Pop. (1954) 17,023.

MONTCALM DE SAINT-VÉRAN, MARQUIS LOUIS JOSEPH DE, 1712–59, French soldier, was born near Nîmes. In 1756, during the French and Indian War, he became military commander of Canada. For some time he was successful against the British and Americans, capturing Fort Ontario at Oswego, 1756, Fort William Henry in 1757, and turning back Gen. James Abercromby's army at Ticonderoga in 1758. In the latter year, however, the French lost Louisburg and forts Frontenac and Duquesne. Montcalm successfully defended Québec until the British forced an open battle on the Plains of Abraham, which resulted in the surrender of the city. Montcalm fell, mortally wounded, in battle against Gen. James Wolfe, who also was killed.

MONT CENIS PASS, Alpine Pass, SE France, in the department of Savoie; in the Graian Alps; NW of the Italian border; highest point 6,833 feet. The pass is paralleled by the Mont Cenis Tunnel, 12 miles to the southwest.

MONTCLAIR, city, S California, San Bernardino County; on the Southern Pacific and the Union Pacific railroads and U.S. highways 60, 70, and 99; 33 miles E of Los Angeles. The city was incorporated in 1956 as Monte Vista; the name was changed in 1958. Pop. (1960) 13,546.

MONTCLAIR, town, including Upper Montclair, NE New Jersey, Essex County; on the Erie and the Lackawanna railroads; residential suburb 6 miles NNW of Newark. Montclair is situated on the slopes of the Orange Mountains. Manufactures include paints, chemicals, and metal products. A state teachers college and the Montclair Art Museum are located in the town. The summit of nearby Eagle Rock Reservation offers a view extending from the Passaic-Hackensack valleys east to New York City. Montclair was settled in 1669 and incorporated in 1868. Pop. (1960) 43,129.

MONTEBELLO, city, S California, Los Angeles County; on the Hondo River, on the Santa Fe and Union Pacific railroads; 9 miles ESE of Los Angeles, of which it is a residential suburb. Oil wells are in the vicinity. Montebello was incorporated in 1920. Pop. (1960) 32,097.

MONTE-CARLO, town or commune, in the principality of Monaco; on the Mediterranean Sea; 11 miles ENE of Nice, France. Monte-Carlo is the northernmost of the three communes of Monaco. The Riviera town is noted for its flowers, trees, and shrubs, its pleasant climate, and the lavishness of its residences. It is famed primarily for its nineteenth century gambling casino, where such games as roulette, baccarat, and trente-et-quarante are played. Monaco derives most of its revenue from these gambling concessions, which were first granted in 1861 by the prince of Monaco to François Blanc of Homburg. The casino, first opened in 1856, was moved to the present site in 1862. The opera, the theater, and the principal hotels, restaurants, and night clubs of Monaco are in Monte-Carlo. Pop. (1956 est.) 9,500. See Monaco.

MONTECRISTO, island, Italy, Livorno Province; in the Tuscan archipelago of the Tyrrhenian Sea, midway between the W coast of Italy and Corsica; 28 miles S of Elba; area 3.5 sq. mi. The island is rocky and rises to an elevation of 2,116 feet in the center. It is widely known through Alexandre Dumas *père's* novel *The Count of Monte Cristo.*

MONTECUCCULI, COUNT RAIMONDO, also Montecuccoli, 1609–80, Austrian general, was born near Modena. He entered the imperial army in 1625 and took part in the Thirty Years' War. In 1658 he defeated the Swedes, who had invaded Denmark, and between 1660 and 1664 the Turks, who had invaded Transylvania. He commanded the imperial troops on the Rhine, 1672–76, against Henri, viscomte de Turenne, and Louis II, prince de Condé. He wrote *Memorie della guerra* (1703).

The famed gambling casino of Monte Carlo is an elaborate structure decorated with statues and paintings. Roulette and *trente-et-quarante* are the casino's principal games.
EWING GALLOWAY

MONTELLO, city, central Wisconsin, seat of Marquette County; at the E end of Buffalo Lake, at the confluence of the Fox and Montello rivers; 50 miles N of Madison. Montello has granite quarries and manufactures of machined parts. It was settled in 1849 and incorporated in 1938. Pop. (1960) 1,021.

MONTEMAYOR, JORGE DE, 1520–61, Spanish poet, was born in Montemôr, Portugal. After 1543 he was a chapel singer at the Spanish court. His pastoral romance *Diana Enamorada* (1559?) became famous throughout Europe and Bartholomew Young's English translation (1598) may have inspired Shakespeare's *Two Gentlemen of Verona.* Montemayor's lyrics also appeared in a *Cancionero* published in Antwerp (1544–58).

MONTENEGRO, Serbian Crna Gora (Black Mountain), a people's republic of S Yugoslavia; bounded on the NE and E by Serbia, on the SE by Albania, on the SW by the Adriatic Sea, and on the W and NW by Bosnia and Hercegovina; area 5,394 sq. mi.; pop. (1957 est.) 465,000, composed predominantly of Montenegrins, with an Albanian minority.

Location Map of Montenegro

Physical Factors. The Montenegro uplands, separated from the Adriatic by the Karst limestone ridge, are cut by river valleys. Mount Lovćen in the coastal ridge rises to 5,737 feet above sea level; in the rugged interior are Durmitor (8,294 ft.) and Sinjajevina (7,331 ft.). The Morača River drains Montenegro into the picturesque Lake Shkodër. The north and northeast are drained by the Tara, Piva, and Lim, headstreams of the Drina, a tributary of the Danube. The climate is continental except for the coastal strip within the Mediterranean zone. The mean temperature in the Titograd area is 43°F in January and 82° in July. The annual precipitation in the lowlands varies from 62 to 71 inches; the mountain slopes turned toward the Adriatic receive up to 118 inches. The coastal ridge has sparse maqui vegetation; and there are beech and oak groves and conifer forests in the interior. One-third of the area is covered by forests and another third by pastures; farm land, mostly in the river valleys, amounts to 6.6 per cent of the total area; and the rest consists of wasteland. There are deposits of lead, zinc, chromium, bauxite, and lignite and the country is rich in water power resources.

Economic Factors. The livelihood of some 75 per cent of the people is based on agriculture, the area

EWING GALLOWAY
Peasants pause with their loads on the road to Cetinje, former capital of Montenegro. Montenegro is one of the six people's republics composing modern-day Yugoslavia.

adjacent to the Lake Shkodër being the main farming region. Corn, wheat, barley, oats, rye, potatoes, tobacco, olives, grapes, fruit, rice, and cotton are the chief crops. Sheep breeding is an important occupation in mountain pasture areas. An electric power station operates at Kotor and four hydroelectric power plants were built on the Zeta River after 1955. In 1953 lead and zinc mines and an ore concentrating plant were put in operation at Suplija-Stena. In 1956 metallurgical works began production at Nikšić. Kotor has a naval arsenal; Titograd has furniture and tobacco factories; Rijeka Crnojevica, a fish processing plant; Bar, oil and soap industries. There are breweries at Kotor and Nikšić. A railway line connects Plavnica on Lake Shkodër with Dubrovnik in the Croatian People's Republic by way of Titograd and Nikšić. The highway system consists of a road linking the Adriatic coast with Cetinje and Titograd, a road from Ulcinj along Lake Shkodër to Titograd and up the Albanian border, and two roads running roughly north to south through the center of the country and along the Piva River in the east. Titograd has an airport with service to Belgrade. Kotor is a naval base. Herceg Novi, Budva, Bar, and Ulcinj are local fishing and commercial harbors. The Adriatic coast of Montenegro is of interest to tourists, and some of its architectural relics date from the Romans and the Venetians. Ulcinj with its sulfur springs, a pirate haven in Roman times, is also known as a health resort.

History. The coastal portion of the country formed part of Greek and, later, Roman Illyria. Serbian tribes arrived in the seventh century and organized the kingdom of Zeta. After Serbia's conquest by the Turks in the fifteenth century, Montenegro was cut off from the sea but it retained autonomy under Serbian princes. After 1516 it was ruled by prince-bishops, who at first were elected by popular assemblies. In 1696 Danilo Petrović made the office hereditary in his family. Revolts against the Turks flared up periodically but the country preserved its autonomy. In 1851 Danilo II dropped the ecclesiastical title. His successor, Nicholas, joined Bosnia and Hercegovina in revolt against the Turks, and in 1878 the Berlin treaty recognized the country's independence (see BERLIN, CONGRESS OF). In 1910 Nicholas assumed the title of king. Montenegro fought in the Balkan Wars of 1912 and 1913 against Turkey. During World War I it fought on the side of Serbia, Russia, and France, and was occupied in 1915 and 1916 by the Germans and Austrians. In 1919 the country was included in the Kingdom of Serbs, Croats, and Slovenes, renamed Yugoslavia in 1929. During World War II it was occupied by the Germans and the Italians in 1941 and placed under Italian rule. The Montenegrin partisans carried on a strong resistance against much better equipped forces. Montenegro reverted to Yugoslavia in 1945 and became autonomous as the Montenegrin People's Republic in 1946. In the following decades extensive projects for modernization were undertaken.

MONTEREAU, or Montereau-faut-Yonne, town, N central France, Seine-et-Marne Department; at the confluence of the Seine and Yonne rivers; 43 miles SE of Paris. The town has manufactures of boots and shoes, bricks, farm tools, and varnish. There is a statue of Napoleon I, who in 1814 near Montereau defeated combined European forces under Marshal Karl von Schwarzenberg. Pop. (1954) 10,119.

MONTEREY, city, W California, Monterey County; on Monterey Bay of the Pacific Ocean; on the Southern Pacific Railroad; a scheduled airline stop; 85 miles SSE of San Francisco. An excellent climate, many scenic attractions, and historic associations make Monterey a popular tourist resort. The city has fishing industries and fish, fruit, and vegetable canneries. There are many old buildings, including the customhouse, an adobe building of 1814, which contains collections of manuscripts by George Sterling and Ambrose Bierce, and of Robert Louis Stevenson, who lived there in 1879; and the state's first brick house (1847) and theater (1843). Fort Ord, a U.S. Army camp, is in the northeastern part of the city. Monterey was named by Sebastián Vizcaíno who sailed into the bay in 1602. The settlement was founded in 1770 by Gaspar de Portolá with the establishment of the Spanish Mission of San Carlos de Monterey. Under both the Spanish and the Mexicans it became a thriving trading post and was capital of Alta California, 1775–1846. U.S. forces occupied the city in 1846 during the Mexican War, and three years later the California constitutional convention and the first state legislative meeting were held in Monterey. Pop. (1960) 22,618.

MONTEREY, town, NW Virginia, seat of Highland County; in the Allegheny Mountains, near the Jackson River; on U.S. highways 220 and 250; 74 miles NW of Lynchburg. Monterey is a popular fishing resort. Agriculture and lumber milling are the main local industries. Pop. (1960) 270.

MONTEREY PARK, city, S California, in Los Angeles County; on the Pacific Electric Railroad; a residential suburb 13 miles E of Los Angeles. Monterey Park has manufactures of food and metal products. It was founded in 1910 and incorporated in 1916. Pop. (1960) 37,821.

MONTERREY, city, NE Mexico, capital of Nuevo León State; in a valley (1,765 ft.) at the foot of the Sierra Madre Oriental; third largest city of Mexico; on the Pan American Highway and a railroad and airline junction; 138 miles SSW of Laredo, Tex. Monterrey, one of Mexico's major industrial centers, has manufactures of iron and steel, glass, furniture, paints, beer, cement, soap, textiles, flour, cigars and cigarettes, plastics, electrical equipment, lead, and

Saddle Mountain dominates the beautiful landscape around the city of Monterrey. Once an old-fashioned Mexican town, Monterrey has become one of Mexico's most modern cities.
EWING GALLOWAY

refined metals such as silver, gold, copper, bismuth, antimony, and arsenic. The city is popular as a resort and is the site of the state university, a technological institute, and a cathedral and a bishop's palace, both built in the eighteenth century. Monterrey was founded in 1596. Its industrial development began during the U.S. Civil War when the South used it as a shipping point for cotton exports. Pop. (1959) 563,547.

The Battle of Monterrey was fought in the city during the Mexican War. A force of about 6,000 Americans under Gen. Zachary Taylor attacked Monterrey on Sept. 21, 1847. The hills protecting the city were captured by the U.S. troops, and after a short siege the city itself fell. The Mexicans capitulated on September 24, the surrender being carried out on the following day. Taylor signed an eight-week armistice, pledging that his troops would not penetrate farther south, but Pres. James K. Polk disclaimed the armistice and insisted on continuing the war. The estimated losses in the battle were 488 killed and wounded on the American side and 367 on the Mexican side.

MONTE SAN GIULIANO. See Erice.

MONTESANO, city, W Washington, seat of Grays Harbor County; at the confluence of the Wynoochee and Chehalis rivers; on the Milwaukee, the Northern Pacific, and the Union Pacific railroads and U.S. highway 410; 56 miles WSW of Tacoma. Canned peas, lumber, and dairy products are processed in Montesano. Lake Sylvia State Park is nearby. The city was incorporated in 1883. Pop. (1960) 2,486.

MONTES CLAROS, city, E Brazil, Minas Gerais State; on the NW slope of the Serra do Espinhaço; a scheduled airline stop; 222 miles N of Belo Horizonte, with which it is connected by railroad and highway. Montes Claros is primarily a trading center for sugar, rice, and livestock. Pop. (1950) 71,736.

MONTESPAN, FRANÇOISE ATHÉNAÏS DE ROCHECHOUART, MARQUISE DE, 1641–1707, mistress of Louis XIV, was born in Tonnay-Charente. She became maid of honor at Versailles, 1661, and in 1663 married the marquis de Montespan. In 1668 she became the favorite of Louis XIV. She bore the king seven or eight children, the eldest of which was legitimized in 1673, and all of whom were educated by Françoise de Maintenon who replaced her in the king's affections. Her *Mémoires* appeared in 1829.

MONTESQUIEU, CHARLES LOUIS DE SECONDAT, BARON DE LA BRÈDE ET DE, 1689–1755, French political theorist and man of letters was born at the château of La Brède, near Bordeaux. The son of Jacques de Secondat, a member of the Montesquieu family, and his wife, Marie Françoise de Penel, Charles Louis was reared in a family distinguished by a long line of lawyers and military leaders. He began his formal education at the age of 12 in the college of the Oratorian priests, Juilly, where he remained until 1701, when he took up the study of civil law at Bordeaux. In 1715 he married the daughter of a lieutenant colonel of the Régiment de Maulevrier, Jeanne de Lartique—a woman said to have possessed few personal attractions, but who brought to her husband a sizable fortune.

In 1714 Montesquieu became a councilor in the parliament of Bordeaux, and upon the death two years later of his uncle, Jean Baptiste de Secondat, inherited the important office of *président à mortier* in the court of justice and a large amount of property, on the condition that he assume the old family title of Montesquieu. The new baron of Montesquieu, little interested in the routine of legal procedure, devoted the greater part of his time to study, travel, and observation. He was especially attracted by the Latin classics, history, philosophy, and metaphysics—in particular the doctrines of Stoicism and the writings of Michel Eyquem de Montaigne. As a result of these studies Montesquieu wrote several essays on politics, philosophy, and the natural sciences for the academy at Bordeaux. His attention soon centered, however, on the study of man in relation to politics and society, rather than as a psychological phenomenon. In 1721 his *Lettres Persanes* appeared, published anonymously in Amsterdam. The *Lettres* were followed by *Dialogue de Sylla et d'Eucrate* (1722) and *Le Temple de Gnide* (1725). In 1728, after overcoming the objections of government and church officials to his satirical *Lettres Persanes*, he was accepted for membership in the French Academy. Shortly after his election Montesquieu visited England, 1729–30, where he became an admirer of the English political system and customs. On his return to France he published *Considérations sur les causes de la grandeur et de la décadence des Romains* (1734), a history of the Roman Empire and a study of the moral issues involved in Rome's decline. In 1748 *De L'Esprit des lois*, a work that had occupied Montesquieu for about 20 years, was published at Geneva. The book was placed on the Roman Catholic Index of forbidden books in 1751. In 1754 Montesquieu wrote the article "L'Essai sur le goût" for the *Encyclopédie*. He spent most of his last years at La Brède, and died in Paris.

Montesquieu's Significance rests on his *Lettres Persanes* and *De L'Esprit des lois*. The *Lettres* are a satire, written with humor and acumen, on the religious, political, social, and literary life of France. The satire is veiled in the framework of what purports to be a novel of harem life. Two Persians, Rica and Usbek, visit Paris and write home their apparently naïve and innocent impressions of French customs. In *L'Esprit des lois* Montesquieu analyzes different forms of government, which he classifies in three categories (monarchy, despotism, and republic), that existed in European and ancient nations. Montesquieu attempts to show the relation between the laws of a country and its customs, climate, religion, economics, and the like. His position is that of a relativist and the work expresses a spirit of moderation. For the existing European governments of his day he favored the constitutional monarchy, following John Locke in urging the conservation and moderation of monarchy by the balance and separation of powers in legislative, judicial, and executive branches of government. *L'Esprit des lois* is divided into 31 books and it is often disconnected, but the excellence of style has caused it to be valued as a literary work as well as a classic of political science. Montesquieu's theories had great influence in Europe, and his doctrine of the separation of powers became one of the basic principles of the Constitution of the United States.

Bibliog.–J. C. Collins, *Voltaire, Montesquieu and Rousseau in England* (1908); C. Morgan, *Liberty of Thought and the Separation of Powers* (1948).

MONTESSORI, MARIA, 1870–1952, Italian educator, was born in Chiaravalle. She was the first woman to receive a degree in medicine from the University of Rome, 1894. While working as an assistant in the university's psychiatric institute, she became interested in the methods of teaching mentally defective children introduced by Édouard Séguin (1812–80) and in 1898 founded the Orthophrenic School, Rome, to teach handicapped children. Dr. Montessori lectured on pedagogy at the university, 1900–07, and in 1907 opened her first *casa dei bambini* (children's house), a school in the tenement district of Rome that applied her teaching methods to normal children. Her method, applicable to all children, spread rapidly through Italian schools and schools in other countries. She established a research institute in Barcelona, Spain, 1917, and in 1919 gave teacher

CONSULATE GENERAL OF ITALY
Maria Montessori

training courses in London. She was appointed government inspector of schools in Italy, 1922. Although she was honored by Benito Mussolini's government, she objected publicly to the Fascists' "warping of youth in their own brutal pattern," and left Italy in 1934 when her schools were closed. She spent several years in Barcelona, founded a training center at Larens in the Netherlands, 1938, and went to India to establish another training center, 1939. She was interned as an enemy alien in India during World War II and after the war returned to Italy in 1947 to help reorganize schools and to resume lectures at the University of Rome. Doctor Montessori wrote *The Montessori Method* (1912), *Pedagogical Anthropology* (1913), *The Advanced Montessori Method* (2 vols. 1917), *The Secret of Childhood* (1936), and other works.

The Montessori Method assumes that children learn best by discovering things by themselves; that sense training and muscular co-ordination, accomplished by handwork, is of primary importance; that the teacher should guide rather than instruct and should encourage self-discipline; and that marks, penalties, and rewards should not be used. Perhaps the most striking aspect of the method is the didactic apparatus used which includes large colored blocks, cylinders, sounding boxes, threads and cloths of various textures and colors, and other materials. Children engage in such occupations as tying knots, building, folding, sewing cards, weaving, and cutting forms. They are encouraged to carry on such work exercises with interest and concentration so that satisfaction rather than weariness follows the completion of each task. The system teaches them to read, write, count, and work simple sums before they are six years old. The method was criticized for its lack of opportunity for creative work and imaginative expression in the child. Its self-corrective principle and emphasis on the physical well-being of the child usually were considered the method's strongest features. During the 1960's, there was an enormous revival of interest in the Montessori method.

Bibliog.–E. M. Standing, *The Montessori Method: A Revolution in Education* (1962).

MONTEUX, PIERRE, 1875–1964, French-American conductor, was born in Paris, and studied at the Paris Conservatory. He began his career as a viola virtuoso, later acting as a guest conductor for European and U.S. orchestras. He conducted the Metropolitan Opera Orchestra, 1917–19, the Boston Symphony Orchestra, 1919–24, the Paris Symphony Orchestra, 1930–38, and the San Francisco Symphony Orchestra, 1936–52. He became a U.S. citizen, 1942. In 1952–53, he toured with the Boston Symphony Orchestra, and afterward conducted at the Metropolitan Opera for two years. In 1961 he was made the conductor of the London Symphony Orchestra.

MONTEVERDI, CLAUDIO, 1567–1643, Italian composer, was born in Cremona. He studied counterpoint under Marco Antonio Ingegneri and at the age of 16 he published his first works, a book of *Canzonetti a tre voci*. Between 1587 and 1605 he published five collections of madrigals, some of extraordinary beauty, and many containing musical innovations for which he was severely criticized. These innovations consisted in the employment of unprepared dissonances, that is, the use of chords such as the dominant seventh as essential combinations—a practice that all composers since have followed and built upon. In 1590 Monteverdi entered the service of Vincenzo Gonzaga, duke of Mantua, and in 1602 succeeded Ingegneri as the duke's *maestro di cappella*. In 1607 he was called upon to produce an opera, *Orfeo*, to celebrate the marriage of the duke's son. Opera was to prove the ideal field for the exploitation of Monteverdi's musical discoveries. The freer use of dissonances fitted perfectly the expression of passion and poignant sorrow. Monteverdi's genius was better suited to the new dramatic style than to the older polyphonic one, and the overwhelming success of his early operas *Orfeo* and *Arianna* (1608) established the new style and spelled the doom of the old.

In 1613 Monteverdi went to Venice as *maestro di cappella* at St. Mark's where he remained the rest of his life, directing the magnificent choir, composing much sacred music (most of it lost), and such operas as *Proserpina rapita*, *L'Adone*, *Le nozze di Enea con Lavinia*, and *Il ritorno d'Ulisse in patria*. In 1632 Monteverdi joined the priesthood, but he wrote at least four more operas, the last (*L'incoronazione di Poppea*) in 1642.

Although Monteverdi's operas were important to the development of music, only *Orfeo* was published in his lifetime and many of the rest are lost. His madrigals are both beautiful and interesting, and the estimate of their worth has risen through the years.

As a musical innovator, Monteverdi is today recognized as one of the great revolutionaries—as radical an inventor in his time as Beethoven, Wagner, and Debussy were to be in the nineteenth century. In realizing his conception of opera, Monteverdi's innovations included an enlarged orchestra, music that contained *arioso* passages from which evolved directly the *bel canto* style of Alessandro Scarlatti, the development of the art of thorough bass practice, and the invention of the tremolo and pizzicato for the orchestra. Though he never wrote any purely instrumental music, his church music was the first to be conceived orchestrally and the first to use a full operatic orchestra. Irwin Fischer

Bibliog.–Denis Arnold, *Monteverdi* (1963); G. F. Malipiero, *Claudio Monteverdi* (1930); Hans Redlich, *Claudio Monteverdi* (1952); Leo Schrade, *Monteverdi: Creator of Modern Music* (1950).

MONTEVIDEO, city, SW Minnesota, seat of Chippewa County; at the confluence of the Chippewa and Minnesota rivers; about 120 miles W of Minneapolis. Montevideo is a trade center for a grain, livestock, and poultry area; agricultural products are processed there. Camp Release State Park is nearby. (For population, see Minnesota map in Atlas.)

MONTEVIDEO, city, S Uruguay, capital of Uruguay and of Montevideo Department; on the N shore of the Rio de la Plata estuary; on the Pan American Highway; 130 miles ESE of Buenos Aires, Argentina; pop. (1963 est.) 1,173,114. The city is one of the largest and most notable cities in South America. Having one of the best harbors on the continent, with inner and outer breakwaters, modern wharves and loading facilities, and extensively dredged channels, it is Uruguay's chief port and industrial and cultural center. It contains about one third of the country's population and handles about 90 per cent of its foreign trade. Montevideo is the terminus for almost all of Uruguay's railroads and highways, and has air and sea connections with most major South American, and European cities. The climate of the city is temperate with a mean annual temperature of about 60°F.

Commerce and Industry. Meat processing is Montevideo's main industry. Cattle and sheep received from the interior are slaughtered, processed, and exported in large quantities. Other exports are meat products and by-products—canned meats, meat extract, tallow, hides, skins, wool—and flour, cereals, flax, linseed, fruits, and vegetables. Montevideo is also a major manufacturing city with products of wine, cigarettes, paper, textiles, shoes, cement, soap, pharmaceuticals, glass, and enamelware.

Setting. Montevideo is a modern cosmopolitan city. In the older section, which occupies a peninsula that partially encloses semicircular Horseshoe Bay, are concentrated the city's shipping, commercial, and financial interests. The new city, stretching eastward along the estuary and northward along the eastern shore of the bay, contains beautiful government buildings, shops, and modern residences. On the west side of the bay is the Cerro, a hill, 388 feet high, topped by an old fortress, now a military museum and the oldest lighthouse in the country (1804). At the base of the hill is Cerro, one of Montevideo's industrial suburbs.

Sites. The old city, once fortified by walls, contains the Plaza Constitución, oldest square in the city, which is flanked by the archiepiscopal cathedral (1790) and the *cabildo*, or town hall (1804), now housing a government ministry. Also in the old city are the stock exchange and the customhouse. Extending from this section of Montevideo eastward to the suburbs is one of the finest boulevards in South America, the Avenida 18 de Julio, named in commemoration of the adoption of the Uruguayan constitution on July 18, 1830. At the junction of the old and new cities is the Plaza Independencia, which serves as the city's social and political center and is notable for the colonnades fronting the buildings that surround the square. Among these buildings is the Salvo Palace, a skyscraper hotel and the tallest building in Uruguay. In the new city are many government and public buildings: the legislative palace; the new municipal palace; the University of the Republic (1849); the national library; the Centennial Stadium; and fine museums and hospitals. Among Montevideo's many outstanding parks are the Prado, famous for the 800 varieties of roses from which Montevideo takes its popular name, the City of Roses; and the Rodó, containing a summer open-air theater and amusement area. Many of the city's museums are located in its parks.

Its temperate climate and excellent beaches have made Montevideo one of South America's leading resorts. Along the coast of the estuary east of the city lie a string of beaches and resorts, including Ramirez, Pocitos, Malvin, and Carrasco, the latter also serving as the airport for the city.

History. Although the site of Montevideo possesses many natural advantages, it was not settled until 1726 when the Spaniards under Bruno Mauricio de Zabala, governor of Buenos Aires, established a colony there after capturing the Portuguese fort that had been established on the nearby Cerro in 1717. From then on the history of the city is essentially that of Uruguay. The development of Montevideo as a commercial center began in 1770 with the lifting of the trade restrictions imposed by Pedro Ceballos, first viceroy of la Plata, which had subordinated the city to Seville. The early nineteenth century was marked by a long struggle between the Spaniards and the Portuguese for control of the Montevideo area. When the independence of Uruguay was recognized in 1828, Montevideo became the capital of the new republic and thereafter suffered a long series of civil and foreign wars lasting until 1899. In the first half of the twentieth century the city gained importance as a port and as a resort, and was the setting of several international conferences.

MONTE VISTA. See MONTCLAIR.

MONTEZ, LOLA, real name Maria Dolores Eliza Rosanna Gilbert, 1818–61, Irish adventuress, was born in Limerick. In 1837 she married a Capt. Thomas James, went to India with him, but left him, 1842, and became a dancer and singer in Paris. At Munich, 1846, she met Louis I of Bavaria, who made her his mistress and countess of Landsfeld. For a time she virtually ruled Bavaria, but she was driven out in the Revolution of 1848. In 1851 she appeared in the United States as an actress and lecturer. She settled in New York and engaged in charity work.

MONTEZUMA I, 1390?–?1464, Aztec emperor, succeeded to the throne about 1436, but was not crowned until 1440. He extended his rule from the Pacific to the Gulf of Mexico, protected his capital, Tenochtitlān (later Mexico City), by a dam and dikes, rebuilt and beautified the city, and codified Aztec law. His court displayed great luxury.

MONTEZUMA II, 1479?–1520, Aztec emperor, was selected ruler in 1503 because of his great reputation as a warrior. In expeditions against the Tlascalans and Tarascos he ravaged lands south to Honduras. He permitted Hernán Cortés to visit him in his capital, receiving him with honors and gifts, November, 1519, but was imprisoned and held as hostage by Cortés, who feared an uprising of the people who opposed Montezuma's conciliatory policy toward the Spaniards. When the Aztecs attacked, Montezuma appeared upon the palace roof to beg them to cease all resistance, and was met with a shower of stones and arrows from his own people. He either died from the wounds or was killed by the Spaniards.

MONTEZUMA, town, SE central Iowa, seat of Poweshiek County; on the Rock Island Railroad and U.S. highway 63; 58 miles E of Des Moines. Montezuma is a minor industrial town with manufactures of wood products and chemicals. It was incorporated in 1868. Pop. (1960) 1,416.

NATL. PARK SERVICE

Montezuma Castle in Arizona, occupied probably from late in the twelfth century to the end of the fourteenth, was a perfect natural fortress set in a high vertical cliff.

MONTEZUMA CASTLE NATIONAL MONUMENT, central Arizona, Yavapai County; 41 miles SSW of Flagstaff. Montezuma Castle National Monument, established in 1906, is an area of 738.09 acres in which are preserved the ruins of prehistoric Pueblo Indian cliff dwellings. The best known of these is Montezuma Castle, 90 per cent of which is still intact, a five-story, 20-room structure located more than 45 feet from the base of a vertical cliff. In a detached part of the monument is Montezuma Well, a crater-like lake with cliff dwellings just below its rim.

MONTFERRAT, a historical region in N Italy, E Piedmont, corresponding to parts of the modern provinces of Alessandria, Asti, Cuneo, and Vercelli. Montferrat was organized during the tenth century as a marquisate and then later it became a county and then a duchy. The Aleramo family, who ruled it originally, distinguished themselves in the Crusades. Marquis Conrad of Montferrat successfully defended Tyre against Sultan Saladin and became king of Jerusalem in 1190. His younger brother, Count Boniface, succeeded him. He led the Fourth Crusade, taking part in the capture of Constantinople in 1204, and was awarded Macedonia, Thessaly, and Crete. His son Demetrius became king of Thessalonica in 1207, but lost his eastern kingdom in 1222. The county of Montferrat passed to the Palaeologus family in 1305 when Theodore Palaeologus inherited it through his mother. It was acquired by the Gonzaga family in 1533, but the dukes of Savoy coveted it and annexed part of its territory in the seventeenth century. In 1708 Savoy annexed the whole of the duchy of Montferrat, its action being recognized by the Peace of Utrecht in 1713.

MONTFORT, SIMON DE, 1160?–1218, leader of the Albigensian Crusade, was the son of Comte Simon III de Montfort and the heiress to the English earldom of Leicester. In 1198, and again in 1203, he crusaded in Palestine. In 1208 he led a crusading army into southwestern France to exterminate the Albigensian heresy. On Sept. 3, 1213, he inflicted a crushing defeat on Comte Raymond VI de Toulouse at Muret; in consequence he himself became count of Toulouse. Nevertheless the country remained unpacified, and on June 25, 1218, while besieging the city of Toulouse, Montfort was killed.

JOHN R. WILLIAMS

MONTFORT, SIMON DE, earl of Leicester, 1208–65, was the third son of Simon IV de Montfort. In 1229 he went to England to claim the earldom of Leicester inherited from his grandmother. In this he was successful, although it was not until 1239 that he was formally invested with the title. Meanwhile, in 1238, he had married Eleanor, sister of King Henry III. With Henry his relations proved stormy and on several occasions Montfort had to flee from England. Nevertheless in 1248 the king made him governor of Gascony. His administration of the province led only to new quarrels, and in 1252 Montfort resigned the post. By 1258 he had become one of the leaders of the baronial opposition to the crown, playing a conspicuous role in the imposition of the Provisions of Oxford on the king. When Henry repudiated the Provisions, 1261, Montfort led the barons in civil war. His victory over Henry at Lewes on May 14, 1264, made him the most powerful man in the kingdom. In the parliament that he called in January, 1265, representatives of the towns as well as of the counties were invited to attend. In the same year Henry III's son, Edward, escaped from captivity and reopened the civil (Barons') war. On August 4 Edward defeated the barons at Evesham. Among the slain was Montfort. JOHN R. WILLIAMS

MONTGOLFIER BROTHERS, Joseph Michel (1740–1810), and Jacques Etienne (1745–99), French inventors of the first man-carrying balloon, were born in Vida-lon-lez-Annonay, where they engaged in paper manufacturing. In 1783 they built a balloon whose spherical linen bag was covered with paper, but called a hot-air (or fire) balloon because air used to inflate the bag was heated by burning wool and slightly moistened straw in an iron grate in the balloon's basket. On the test flight at Annonay, June 5, 1783, the balloon ascended to a height of 6,000 feet and was aloft 10 minutes. A few months later another successful demonstration was given at Versailles before Louis XVI and Marie Antoinette. The king authorized a grant of 40,000 francs to enable the Montgolfier brothers to continue their research in aerial navigation. The hot-air balloon was renamed the montgolfier in their honor. See BALLOON, History of Ballooning.

MONTGOMERIE, ALEXANDER, 1556?–?1610, Scottish poet, was born in Hessilhead, Ayr. He held an office at the court and received a pension from the Scottish crown. His major work was the *Cherrie and the Slae* (1597) whose peculiar alliterative 14-line stanza with six rhymes, probably invented by him, was used by Robert Burns.

MONTGOMERY, BERNARD LAW, 1st Viscount Montgomery of Alamein, 1887– , British military leader. Montgomery was born in London, educated at Sandhurst, and entered the army as a second lieutenant in 1908. In World War I, as a captain, he was severely wounded. He was promoted to major general, 1938, and in 1939 led the 3rd Division to France and commanded it throughout the campaign of 1940, including the period of evacuation at Dunkirk. In 1941 he took charge first of the 5th Corps and then of the southeastern command in England. In 1942, having been promoted to lieutenant general, he was put in command of the British 8th Army in Egypt under the middle eastern command of Gen. Sir Harold Alexander.

After careful preparations Montgomery attacked the German Afrika Korps of Field Marshal Erwin Rommel at El Alamein, Oct. 23, 1942. British tank forces broke through November 2, and Rommel's army was driven back to the borders of Tunisia. The 8th Army broke the Mareth Line in southern Tunisia. made a junction with American forces, and took Tunisia May 7, 1943. German forces in Africa surrendered May 13. Montgomery then led the 8th Army in the invasions of Sicily and Italy. For his victory at El Alamein Montgomery was knighted and made a full general.

BRITISH INFORMATION SERVICES
Montgomery

At the end of 1943 he was recalled from the Mediterranean, promoted to field marshall, and given command (under the supreme Allied commander Gen. Dwight D. Eisenhower) of Allied forces in the invasion of Normandy, June, 1944. In August, 1944, he was given command of the 21st Army group, and in the Battle of the Bulge, December, 1944–January, 1945, he commanded all troops north of the German breakthrough in the Ardennes. In final attacks beginning in March, 1945, Montgomery's forces swept across the Rhine and on to Hamburg and Bremen. He commanded British occupation forces in Germany, 1945–46; was chief of the imperial general staff, 1946–49; was named permanent chairman of the Western European Union's defense organization, 1948; and was made deputy supreme commander of the North Atlantic Treaty Organization forces in Europe, 1951. After that, as a self-appointed ambassador of good will, he received numerous honors and decorations all over the world. Montgomery wrote about his experiences in *Normandy to the Baltic* (1947), *El Alamein to the River Sangro* (1948), and *The Memoirs of Field-Marshall the Viscount Montgomery of Alamein* (1958); *An Approach to Sanity: A Study of East-West Relations* (1959) and *The Path to Leadership* (1961).

MONTGOMERY, COMTE GABRIEL DE, 1530?–1574, French soldier. He was an officer in the Scottish Guard from 1547, but in 1559 accidentally killed Henry II of France in a tourney, and was an exile in England for some years. On the outbreak of the Huguenot Wars, 1562, Montgomery became a Protestant leader under Louis I de Bourbon, Prince de Condé. He was captured at Domfront, Normandy, in 1574, and executed in Paris.

MONTGOMERY, RICHARD, 1738–75, American revolutionary soldier, was born in Swords, County Dublin, Ireland. He entered the British army, 1756, and distinguished himself at the siege of Louisburg in the French and Indian War. During 1763–65 he was stationed in New York. On his return to England he sold his captain's commission, 1772, and returned to New York to settle. He served in the first provincial congress, 1775, was commissioned brigadier general in the Continental Army the same year, and soon replaced Maj. Gen. Philip Schuyler in command of the Northern Department. Montgomery captured forts Chambly and St. Johns, entered Montreal, and joined the forces of Benedict Arnold to lay siege to Québec. On December 31 Montgomery was killed during an assault on the town.

MONTGOMERY, city, SE central Alabama, capital of Alabama and seat of Montgomery County; on the Alabama River and U.S. highways 31, 80, 231, and 331; a scheduled airline stop; 85 miles SSE of Birmingham.

Montgomery, the state's third largest city, is situated in the heart of Alabama's fertile cotton belt. The city is one of the leading cattle markets in the southeast as well as an important trade center for cotton, poultry, and dairy products. Principal manufactures include fertilizers, food products, cotton fabrics, work clothes, glass, plumbing and heating supplies, and creosoted wood products.

Places of interest include the Alabama state capitol building, architecturally a fine example of the Greek revival style; the first "White House of the Confederacy," so called because it was the residence of Jefferson Davis (1861); the state Archives and History Building; the Montgomery Museum of Fine Arts; and the Alabama State Coliseum. Just outside Montgomery are Maxwell and Gunter Air Force bases. Maxwell was the site of the Wright brothers' flight school before World War I, and in 1946 an advanced air training school was established there. Montgomery is the seat of Huntingdon College and the Alabama State College (for Negroes). A federal prison camp is nearby.

The towns of New Philadelphia and East Alabama were laid out on the present site of Montgomery in 1817; in 1819 they were consolidated with Alabama Town as Montgomery, which was named for the Revolutionary War figure Gen. Richard Montgomery. Montgomery became the state capital in 1846 and the first capital of the Confederacy in 1861. It was captured by Union troops on Apr. 12, 1865. Pop. (1960) 134,393.

MONTGOMERY CITY, city, E central Missouri, seat of Montgomery County; on the Wabash Railroad; 75 miles WNW of St. Louis. Montgomery City is a market center for an area that produces grain, dairy products, cattle, and poultry. The city was laid out in 1853 and incorporated in 1859. Pop. (1960) 1,918.

MONTGOMERYSHIRE, or Montgomery, county, central Wales; bounded by Merionethshire on the W and N, Denbighshire on the N, Shropshire on the E, Radnorshire on the S, and Cardiganshire on the S and W; area 797 sq. mi.; pop. (1961) 44,228. Montgomery is generally a region of hills and mountains with some fertile valleys. It is drained by the Severn, Wye, Dovey, and Vyrnwy rivers. Montgomery is the capital; other main centers are Newtown and Welshpool. Chief agricultural products are oats, sheep, and dairy cattle. Slate and stone are quarried, and some lead is mined. Montgomery became a county in 1535.

MONTGOMERY WARD AND COMPANY, second largest mail order house in the United States, developed out of the activities of Aaron Montgomery Ward and his brother-in-law, George R. Thorne. In 1872 the two men launched sales of a general line of merchandise advertised by a single-sheet circular and backed by a capital of only $2,400. By 1887 the firm had attained a sales volume of more than $1 million. Montgomery Ward and Company, Inc., organized in 1913, succeeded the original mail order business founded in Chicago. In addition to its 415 catalogue mail order offices, the firm operates 562 retail stores, most of them located in communities catering to a predominantly rural population. Net sales for their fiscal year ending Jan. 31, 1958, exceeded $1 billion and the number of employees approximated 58,000. Headquarters are in Chicago. See MAIL ORDER BUSINESS.

MONTH, a natural division of time and of the calendar, based on the average interval between two consecutive new or full moons, a period of about 29½ days.

The Astronomical Month is the period of eastward revolution of the moon from some arbitrary point in its orbit back to that same point. In the sidereal month the interval is between consecutive alignments of the earth and moon with the same star, and averages 27.32166 mean solar days. The mean nodical or draconitic month, important in eclipse calculations, is 27.21222 days, from one node of the orbit back to the same node. It is shorter than the sidereal month because the two nodes, the points where the moon's orbit intersects the plane of the earth's orbit, are moving westward, opposite in direction to the moon's motion; the nodes complete a circuit in about 18.6 years. The anomalistic month, from perigee to perigee, averages 27.55455 days (see APOGEE). Its greater length is caused by eastward revolution of the major axis of the moon's orbit, and hence of the perigee and apogee points, in a period of about nine years; since the perigee point is moving forward (eastward), the moon has to go a little farther than a sidereal revolution to catch up to it. For a similar reason the synodic month of the phases averages 29.53059 days; the sun has an apparent eastward motion among the stars because of the earth's eastward motion in its orbit; hence the moon, after completing a sidereal revolution following new moon, still requires an additional two days to catch up to the sun and come into alignment again with it and the earth at the next new moon. The solar month is, by definition, just one-twelfth of the solar year, or just less than 30½ days in length.

The Calendar Months used by most of the modern world for civil, if not for religious, purposes were derived from the old Roman calendar. According to the historian Theodore Mommsen, March continued to be the first month of the Roman calendar year until the reform instituted by Julius Caesar, although January 1 was the beginning of the consular year. Until 1752 the first day of the legal year in England was March 25; in the American colonies the change to January 1 was made about 30 years earlier. Most peoples of the world have used other dates and seasons for beginning the new year; even today there is great variety in the new year dates of the various religious calendars. See CALENDAR; DAY; MOON; ORBIT; YEAR.

BIBLIOG.–R. A. Parker, *Calendars of Ancient Egypt* (1950); W. Y. Darling, *Book of Days* (1951); E. Achelis, *Of Time and the Calendar* (1955); A. A. McArthur, *Evolution of the Christian Year* (1955); H. S. Bellamy and P. Allen, *Calendar of Tiahuanaco* (1956); W. G. Branch, *All the Year Round* (1957).

MONTI, VINCENZO, 1754–1828, Italian writer, was born in Fusignano, near Ravenna. He went to Rome, 1778; became secretary to Prince Luigi Braschi, the pope's nephew; and gained a literary reputation with various odes and the tragedies *Aristodemo* (1787) and *Galeotto Manfredi* (1788). He is chiefly remembered as the author of a Dantesque epic, the *Bassvilliana* (1793), based on the assassination of Hugo de Bassville, French ambassador to Rome. Monti's antirevolutionary sentiments (in *Bassvilliana*) changed to pro-Napoleonic, and under Napoleon Bonaparte he became court historiographer and professor of oratory at Pavia, 1802. He later supported the restoration of Austrian rule. His works include a translation of the *Iliad*, the poems *Mascheroniana* (1801), and *Sermone sopra la Mitologia* (1825), an attack on romanticism.

MONTICELLO, city, SE Arkansas, seat of Drew County; on the Ashley, Drew and Northern and the Missouri Pacific railroads; 82 miles SSE of Little Rock. Monticello's industries include cotton processing, textile manufacture, and lumber milling; the city is a market center for a cotton, fruit, corn, livestock, and truck farm area. Monticello is the seat of the Arkansas Agricultural and Mechanical College. Pop. (1960) 4,412.

MONTICELLO, town, NW Florida, seat of Jefferson County; on the Atlantic Coast Line and the Seaboard Air Line railroads and U.S. highways 19 and 90; 26 miles ENE of Tallahassee. The town is a farm trade center and plywood is manufactured there. Monticello was settled by planters in the early 1800's. Pop. (1960) 2,490.

MONTICELLO, city, central Georgia, seat of Jasper County; on the Central of Georgia Railroad; 50 miles SE of Atlanta. Manufacturing products include clothing, lumber, bobbins, and canned foods. Jackson Lake is nearby. Monticello was incorporated in 1810. Pop. (1960) 1,931.

MONTICELLO, city, NW central Indiana, seat of White County; on the Tippecanoe River, on the Monon and the Pennsylvania railroads and U.S. highways 24 and 421; 75 miles NNW of Indianapolis. Monticello's products include flour, furniture, and packaged meats. Monticello was settled in 1831 and incorporated in 1853. Pop. (1960) 4,035.

MONTICELLO, city, S Kentucky, seat of Wayne County; in the foothills of the Cumberland Plateau; 85 miles S of Lexington. Monticello is in an area whose main products are corn, Burley tobacco, wheat, coal, oil, timber, and stone. Monticello's industries include oil refining, flour and feed milling, and the manufacture of wood products, tanks, trailers, and log carts. The town was settled before 1800. Pop. (1960) 2,940.

MONTICELLO, town, S central Mississippi, seat of Lawrence County; on the Pearl River, the Gulf, Mobile and Ohio Railroad, and U.S. highway 84; 52 miles S of Jackson. Monticello's products include clothing and lumber. The town was founded in 1798. Pop. (1960) 1,432.

MONTICELLO, village, SE New York, seat of Sullivan County, 72 miles NW of New York City. Manufactures include paint, perfumes, bedding, lumber and wood products, lighting equipment, and food products. Monticello was settled in 1804 and incorporated in 1837. Pop. (1960) 5,222.

MONTICELLO, town, SE Utah, seat of San Juan County; on U.S. highway 160; 195 miles SE of Provo. Monticello's main industries are uranium and vanadium ore processing and flour milling. The Abajo Mountains in La Sal National Forest are immediately west of the town. Monticello was settled in 1810 and incorporated in 1911. Pop. (1960) 1,845.

MONTICELLO, estate, central Virginia, Albemarle County, 65 miles NW of Richmond. Monticello was the home for 56 years and the burial place of Thomas Jefferson, its architect. Situated at the top of a hill, Monticello offers an excellent view of the Blue Ridge crest and much of the Virginia Piedmont. Architecturally, Monticello is an early example of American classic revival; Jefferson designed it according to the Greco-Roman principles of Andrea Palladio (1518–80). Construction began in 1770 and in 1772 Jefferson with his bride occupied Honeymoon cottage, which stood on the site now occupied by the south pavilion. When finally completed in 1809, the estate included a dairy, servants' rooms, a smokehouse, a summer kitchen, a law office, an outchamber, and two promenades. All materials used, even nails and bricks, were made on the property. After Jefferson's death the ownership of the estate changed hands five times and Monticello gradually fell into ruin. After the Civil War the estate was restored and enlarged to 2,000 acres by Jefferson Levy, who sold it in 1923 to the Thomas Jefferson Memorial Foundation for $500,000. On July 4, 1926, Monticello was dedicated as a national shrine.

MONTIGNAC, town, SW France, Guyenne, Dordogne Department, on the Vézère River, 24 miles ESE of Périgueux. Near the town is the cave of Lascaux, one of the most important prehistoric sites in the world, discovered in 1940. The walls and ceilings of the cave are covered with numerous drawings and paintings in iron and manganese oxide pigments depicting animals such as bison, boars, deer, and horses. Remarkably well preserved, they belong to the late Aurignacian period—about 15,000 to 20,000 B.C.—and illustrate the development of an art that reached its highest expression in the paintings of the Magdalenian period as represented at Altamira. See ALTAMIRA.

MONT JOLI, village, Canada, S Québec Province, Rimouski County; at the base of the Gaspé Peninsula, near the St. Lawrence River; on the Canadian National and the Canada and Gulf Terminal railways; a road junction 187 miles NE of Québec City. Mont Joli has manufactures of hosiery, mining accessories, furniture, cement blocks, and soft drinks. It was settled in 1880. (For population, see southern Québec map in Atlas.)

MONT LAURIER, village, Canada, SW Québec Province, seat of Labelle County; in the Laurentian Mountains, on the Lièvre River and the Canadian Pacific Railway; 79 miles N of Ottawa. The village is in a lumbering and agricultural area; Plywood is manufactured. The village was incorporated in 1909. (For population, see southern Québec map in Atlas.)

MONTLUCON, city, central France, Allier Department; at the edge of the Massif Central, on the Cher River, at the mouth of the Berry Canal; a highway and railroad junction; 46 miles NNW of Clermont-Ferrand. Montluçon has manufactures of steel and steel products, chemicals, rubber goods, and glass. The Commentry coal field is nearby. The city has many examples of fifteenth and sixteenth century architecture. (For population, see France map in Atlas.)

MONTMAGNY, town, Canada, SE Québec Province, seat of Montmagny County; on the St. Lawrence River, at the mouths of the South and St. Nicholas rivers, on the Canadian National Railway; 33 miles ENE of Québec city. Montmagny is situated in a farming, dairying, and market gardening region and has textile mills, lumber mills, woodworking plants, foundries, creameries, and furniture factories. The town was founded in 1678 and incorporated in 1845. (For population, see southern Québec map in Atlas.)

MONTMARTRE, district, also the hill that it occupies, N Paris, France. The highest point in Paris (more than 330 ft.), Montmartre, meaning martyrs' mount, is famous as the site of the martyrdom of St. Denis, St. Eleuthère, and St. Rustique. The Basilica of the Sacré-Coeur (1875) is situated at the summit of the hill, and there is a cemetery containing the tombs of many famous men. A Benedictine abbey was founded on the hill in the twelfth century, and during the late nineteenth century the district became dotted with night clubs and artists' studios. Today it is a tourist attraction noted for its night life.

MONTMORENCY, DUC ANNE DE, 1493–1567, French soldier, the friend and military companion of Francis I, was born in Chantilly. He was made a marshal of France, 1522, was taken prisoner with Francis at Pavia, 1525, and helped to negotiate the Treaty of Madrid. He became grand master of the royal household and governor of Languedoc, 1526, and in 1538 became constable of France, but, falling into disgrace, was banished from court, 1541. He was recalled in the reign of Henry II, 1547, and in 1557 was defeated at St. Quentin and made prisoner by the Spaniards. In 1562, while in the command of the royal army against the Huguenots, he was defeated and captured at Dreux. At the Battle of Saint-Denis, 1567, he was wounded fatally.

MONTMORENCY, or Montmorency Village, village, Canada, S Québec Province; on the St. Lawrence River, at the mouth and near the Falls of the Montmorency River, on the Canadian National Railroad; 7 miles NE of Québec city. Montmorency has a hydroelectric plant that supplies power for Québec. (For population, see southern Québec map in Atlas.)

MONTPARNASSE, quarter of Paris, France; on the left (S) bank of the Seine and centering on Montparnasse and Raspail boulevards. Many intellectuals including writers, artists, and political exiles live in Montparnasse and meet at the Dôme, Rotonde, Coupole, and other famous cafés. In the quarter are the Church of Notre-Dame-des-Champs; the Pasteur Institute; the Montparnasse Cemetery where numerous famous Frenchmen are buried; and the catacombs, formerly a burial place, which served as headquarters for the resistance movement that assisted Gen. Jean Leclerc in the liberation of Paris from German control in 1944.

MONTPELIER, city, central Vermont, state capital and seat of Washington County; in the Green Mountains; on the Winooski River, the Central Vermont Railway, and U.S. highways 2 and 302; a scheduled airline stop; 36 miles ESE of Burlington. Montpelier has large granite quarries; from them came the material for the rebuilding of the capitol in

1857 after the original structure had been destroyed by fire. Other principal industries are woodworking and the production of sawmill traveling derricks, machinery, and flour. Several large insurance companies have their home offices in Montpelier. Besides the capitol, which houses a museum of natural history and the Vermont Historical Society, interesting features of the city include Wood Art Gallery and Hubbard Park. Montpelier was the birthplace of Adm. George Dewey. The city was settled in 1787, made the state capital in 1805, and incorporated in 1894. Pop. (1960) 8,782.

MONTPELLIER, city, S France, Languedoc Region, capital of Hérault Department; on the Lez River and 7 miles from the Mediterranean Sea; 29 miles SW of Nîmes. Montpellier lies in one of the world's major vineyard areas. It is a production and trade center for wine, brandy, liqueurs, macaroni, biscuits, fruit, chocolate, silk, linen, hosiery, soap, fertilizers, vineyard equipment, marble, and metal parts. The city is also a cultural center and has been called the "city of art and science." The University of Montpellier, founded in 1180 and reconstituted in 1289, includes faculties of letters, sciences, law, medicine, and pharmacy. The school of medicine, founded in the eleventh century, is the oldest in the world; and the department of law and Romance philology are considered outstanding. Many famous men studied or taught at the university, including Petrarch, François Rabelais, and Paul Valéry. The city also has schools of agriculture, commerce, military administration, fine arts, music, and Catholic and Protestant theology and noteworthy theaters and concert halls, libraries, and art galleries and museums, including the Fabre museum of painting. The city contains many beautiful examples of seventeenth and eighteenth century architecture. The Place du Peyrou, overlooking the city, affords magnificent views of the surrounding region and of the Mediterranean. There is a triumphal arch erected by Louis XIV. Near an old Benedictine abbey is the Cathedral of St. Pierre, built in 1364 in Cistercian Gothic style. The botanic gardens were established by Henry IV.

Montpellier first gained importance in the eighth century and several ecclesiastical councils were held there in the twelfth and thirteenth centuries. The city belonged to the kingdom of Majorca from 1204 to 1349, when it was purchased by Philip IV of France. Later it belonged temporarily to the kingdom of Navarre. In 1567 Montpellier became a Huguenot stronghold, but it was captured by Louis XIII in 1622. Until 1791 it was the capital of Languedoc Province. (For population, see France map in Atlas.)

MONTPENSIER, ANNE MARIE LOUISE D'ORLEANS, DUCHESSE DE, called La Grande Mademoiselle, 1627–93, French noblewoman, daughter of Gaston d'Orléans, was born in Paris. She commanded an army in the Fronde of the Princes, and at Faubourg St. Antoine, July 2, 1652, gave the order to open the gates of Paris to Louis II, prince de Condé. She lived in retirement till 1657, and is believed to have married Antonin Nompar de Caumont, duc de Lauzun, a political prisoner, about 1681, after buying his freedom. The marriage was short-lived, and she spent her later years writing her *Mémoires* (1729) and books of religious devotions (1908).

MONTREAL, city, Canada, S Québec, Montreal Island County, on the SE section of the island of Montreal in the St. Lawrence River near its confluence with the Ottawa River, where Canadian inland navigation begins and at the head of ocean navigation; about 1,000 miles from the Atlantic on the course of the St. Lawrence, about 160 miles SW of Québec city, and 384 miles by rail from New York City. Montreal is the largest city in Canada and the largest North American port near Europe, lying 2,747 miles from Liverpool, England. Pop. (1961) city proper 1,191,062; metropolitan area 2,109,509.

CANADIAN PACIFIC RY. CO.

Montreal, situated at the head of navigation on the St. Lawrence River, is one of the world's great grain-shipping ports. The harbor operates from April to early December.

PHYSICAL AND SOCIAL FACTORS

Setting. Montreal occupies an area of about 50 square miles, stretching approximately 13 miles along the shore of the St. Lawrence and across a part of the island that is about 30 miles long and 7 to 10 miles wide. The city takes its name from the mountain that dominates the area, Mount Royal (Mont Réal), named by Jacques Cartier in 1535 (see CARTIER, JACQUES). The peak rises to an elevation of more than 700 feet above sea level. The summit and slopes of Mount Royal are a public park of more than 450 acres; the business district lies south on the plain below; and on the slope and to the north of the mountain is a fashionable residential district. Among the suburban municipalities on the island are Verdun, St. Laurent, Lachine, Outremont, Montreal North, Westmount, Côte St. Michel, Lasalle, Mount Royal, and Dorval.

Climate. The climate is humid, with warm summers. Average temperatures range from 13°F in January to 69°F in July. Average annual precipitation is 38.39 inches. The city's harbor is icebound from early December until mid-April.

Points of Interest. The panorama of Montreal may best be seen from the lookout at the top of Mount Royal, reached by an encircling drive. A 100-foot illuminated cross is set on the crest of the mountain to commemorate the day in 1643 when Paul de Chomedey, sieur de Maisonneuve, the founder of Montreal, carried a wooden cross up the mountain. Among the landmarks is the Place d'Armes, over which towers a monument to Maisonneuve facing Notre Dame de Montreal (1656; completed 1929), one of the city's most picturesque churches. Behind the church is the Treasure of Notre Dame, a museum of religious art; and adjoining is the city's oldest building, the Seminary of St. Sulpice (1683). A famous landmark in the old French part of the city is the Château de Romezay, now a museum. Erected in 1705, it was the residence of French and British governors of Canada; and in 1775–76 during the American Revolution it was used by representatives of the American colonies seeking support from Canada. Other famous churches in Montreal are St. James Cathedral (1870) on Dominion Square, a smaller replica of St. Peter's in Rome; St. Joseph's Oratory on the north slope of Mount Royal; and the Church of St. Andrew and St. Paul (Presbyterian). In the lower city, facing the St. Lawrence, is the sailor's shrine Notre Dame de Bon Secours (Our Lady of Good Help), founded in 1657. Adjoining is Bon Secours Market, the largest open-air market in Montreal, over which towers Horatio Nelson's monument. Among other noteworthy places are the Canadian Historical Museum, the art center, McGill University, and the University of Montreal. The

G. HUNTER, NATIONAL FILM BOARD

La Place Ville Marie, surmounted by the 42-story cruciform building, successfully harmonizes modern skyscrapers and historic edifices of downtown Montreal.

Champ de Mars has been a parade ground since the French regime.

Montreal has more than 100 parks, the largest of which is Mount Royal. The city is famous for its winter sports and its facilities for curling and hockey. There are year-round concerts, exhibitions, and dramatic plays organized by local and sometimes foreign artistic groups. In the summer the city offers baseball, golf, horse racing, and yachting. Near Montreal in the St. Lawrence is St. Helen's Island, which is reached by the Jacques Cartier Bridge. Once a fort, it is now a park with a restaurant and swimming pool.

Population. Although Montreal has the second largest French-speaking population of any city in the world, it is also bilingual; business and social relations are carried on in both French and English. More than 64 per cent of the population are of French descent and Roman Catholics, most of whom live in the east and northeast sections of the city.

Education. The public schools of Montreal are controlled by separate boards of Catholics and Protestants. A large number of children, including boarding students from other localities, are educated in schools maintained by religious orders. McGill University (nondenominational), opened in 1829 on property bequeathed in 1813 by James McGill, offers study in the arts and sciences, engineering, law, and medicine. Incorporated in the university are McDonald College at Sainte Anne de Bellevue and Royal Victoria College for women at Montreal. Affiliated theological colleges include Presbyterian College, United Theological College of Canada, and Diocesan College of Montreal. (See McGill University.) The University of Montreal, founded in 1876, developed from a branch of Laval University and is Roman Catholic. It offers study in the arts, law, medicine, and science. See Montreal, University of.

Economic Factors

Montreal is one of the greatest inland ports in the world. Its pre-eminence as a seaport is attributed to the Lachine Rapids, which, before completion of the St. Lawrence Seaway in 1959, blocked most ocean vessels from going upstream. The city is also an outlet of an inland navigation system that extends 1,200 miles into the continent and serves as a funnel through which the agricultural, mineral, and forest products of Canada pass to Europe. Montreal Harbor, with a water area of 12,000 acres, contains about 10 miles of high-level concrete piers and wharves, extensive grain elevators, cold-storage warehouses, and floating dry docks. The Harbor Terminal Railway, which serves the harbor, is largely electrified. Ocean steamship lines link Montreal with European as well as other American coastal cities. The port is linked to the Great Lakes by the St. Lawrence Seaway, whose

first lock, the St. Lambert, is at Victoria Bridge. Other waterways include the Ottawa River canals, which connect the city with the Canadian hinterlands; and the waterway to New York City by way of the Richelieu River; Lake Champlain, Lake George, and the Hudson River.

As the railroad center of Canada, Montreal has the chief repair shops and administrative offices of the Canadian Pacific, which reaches the island at Lachine, and the Canadian National. East of the city the Jacques Cartier Bridge—completed in 1930—serves motor travel between Montreal and cities on the south side of the St. Lawrence. West of the city the Victoria Bridge—built in 1860—is used for both railroads and motor vehicles. Montreal is connected by air with every part of Canada and many foreign countries through Dorval Airport, the Canadian terminal of many overseas airlines.

Petroleum and coal products are the leading manufacturing industries of Montreal. Other important industries and manufactures are clothing, electrical supplies, meat processing, tobacco products, aircraft, railway cars, sheet metal products, furniture, pharmaceuticals, publishing, structural steel, bakery products, paper products, footwear, primary iron and steel, paint and varnish, wire, confections, and fur goods. Montreal's financial district includes banks, investment houses, and insurance companies.

Government

The municipal government is headed by a mayor, elected biennially by popular vote, and an executive council of six, who are members of and responsible to the municipal council. The municipal council consists of 99 councilors who represent 11 electoral districts and whose term of office is three years. One-third are elected by property owners and one-third by voters otherwise qualified; the other third are selected by recognized public bodies such as the board of trade, the chamber of commerce, and the Conseil Central des Syndicats Catholiques. The mayor presides over council meetings, and may vote only when a majority of 51 council votes is required. The authority of the council to pass laws and ordinances is subject to the Québec municipal code of 1916.

History

Founding of Montreal. The site of the modern city was visited in 1535 by Jacques Cartier, who found a village of Hochelaga Indians on the island. In 1611 Samuel de Champlain built Place Royal—a trading station—on the site of the present customhouse (see Champlain, Samuel de). The site of Montreal was chartered by France in 1640, and two years later a small group of clergy and laymen led by Maisonneuve established a settlement there. The activity of these settlers was at first restricted to converting the Indians to Christianity, since the French authorities at Québec, jealous of their monopoly of the fur trade, sought to prevent the new settlement from engaging in that industry. There were also political and religious rivalries between the settlements of Montreal and Québec, although the constant menace of the Iroquois united them in emergencies. In 1660 the heroism of Adam Dulac (also known as Dollard des Ormeaux), who with a few other young Frenchmen had formally consecrated himself to the purpose, withstood a force of Iroquois at Long Sault Rapids and saved Montreal. A massacre at Lachine in 1689 in which 400 whites perished was the culmination of the Indian wars affecting settlers in the area. In the seventeenth and early eighteenth centuries the city was enriched by the fur trade and became the starting place for French expeditions that explored North America. At different times Montreal was the home of Antoine de la Mothe Cadillac, Daniel Greysolon Duluth, Pierre Lemoyne d'Iberville, Isaac Jogues, and Robert Cavelier de La Salle.

Canada's pavilion at Expo 67 was dominated by a 108-foot-tall inverted pyramid, the Katimavik. Below this structure were the pyramidal roofs of the exhibit areas.

After the French and Indian War. The struggle between the English and French for control of North America was decided in favor of England by the capture of Québec in 1759. Montreal surrendered in 1760 without opposition to British forces under Jeffrey Amherst, who was governor general of British North America, 1760–63. At the beginning of the American Revolution an attempt was made by the American colonists to enlist the co-operation of Canada, and in 1775 Montreal was captured and briefly held by American forces under Gen. Richard Montgomery. During the War of 1812 severe weather and inadequate means of supply prevented Gen. James Wilkinson from launching a U.S. attack on Montreal.

In 1837 Montreal was the center of a rebellion by the French in Lower Canada against the administration of Great Britain, which was settled in 1840 by the union of Upper and Lower Canada, in which both regions were given limited autonomy in administrative and judicial matters. In 1844 the capital of Canada was moved from Kingston to Montreal. Rioting in the city in 1849, provoked by the Rebellion Losses Bill, compensating some French Canadians for losses incurred in the 1837 rebellion, led to the destruction of the parliament buildings. In the same year the seat of government was moved to the city of Québec.

Twentieth Century. Among the many harbor improvements made from 1900 to 1910 were the building of a flood wall, high-level piers, and steel sheds, the installation of a grain elevator system, and dredging to a depth of 35 feet. By 1926 Montreal had become one of the most important grain harbors of the world.

After World War II Montreal underwent considerable modernization and physical expansion, mainly attributed to increased commerce and the development of the St. Lawrence Seaway. New buildings throughout the city transformed some older parts of the city into modern quarters devoted to business and commerce. In 1956 modern buses replaced streetcars as a means of public transportation. In 1962 the Place-Ville Marie, a tourist and business center similar to New York City's Rockefeller Center, was completed. Montreal's new Place des Arts opened in 1963. In 1966 a new 16-mile subway opened, and early in 1967, Canada's new trade center, the 3.1-million-square-foot Place Bonaventure, was completed. The Universal and International Exhibition of 1967 (popularly known as Expo 67) was opened in Montreal in April, 1967, its opening coinciding with the 100th anniversary of Canada's confederation. The exhibition lasted for 6 months. Its theme was "Man and His World." Sixty-two nations were represented. JEAN-GERARD AUMONT

BIBLIOG.–J. M. Gibbon, *Our Old Montreal* (1946); Victor Morin, *Historical Records of Old Montreal* (1944); W. P. Percival, *Lure of Montreal* (1946); C. M. Wilson, *Commandant Paul and the Founding of Montreal* (1966).

MONTREAL, UNIVERSITY OF, a Catholic coeducational institution of higher learning in Montreal, Qué., Canada. It was founded in 1876 as a branch of Laval University and acquired its present name and independence in 1919. It is a French-language university and has two charters—civil and pontifical—under which it can grant civil and canon degrees.

The faculties of the university consist of theology, law, medicine, philosophy, letters, sciences, dental surgery, pharmacy, social sciences, arts, music, nursing, science of education, and school of hygiene. These, plus many annexed and attached schools, make up the corporation of the university. Numerous other affiliated schools and institutes are supervised by the university while remaining financially independent.

The university is administered by a board of trustees, eight of whose members are appointed by the Québec provincial government. Its library receives all documents published by Québec's government and is also recognized as an official depository of the Canadian government's publications. The library also contains special collections on medical history, Canadian history, ancient and modern philosophy, law, literature, political science, and fine arts, as well as many original and important manuscripts of outstanding writers.

MONTREUIL, or Montreuil-Sous-Bois, town, N central France, Seine Department, Sceaux Arrondissement; suburb, 5 miles E of Paris. Montreuil is noted for its peaches; other products include processed skins and hides, distilled spirits, biscuits, porcelain, metal containers, and chemicals. (For population, see France map in Atlas.)

MONTREUX, resort, W Switzerland, Vaud Canton; on the E shore of Lake Geneva; 14 miles ESE of Lausanne. Montreaux comprises three communities—Le Châtelard, Les Planches, and Veytaux. Its popularity as a tourist center is based on its mild climate, its situation on the lake and at the foot of the Alps, and the variety of vegetation that exists in the area because of differences in elevation. Chillon Castle is nearby (see CHILLON). Industries include printing and the manufacture of metal and wood products, wearing apparel, and chocolate. (For population, see Switzerland map in Atlas.)

MONTROSE, JAMES GRAHAM, 5th **EARL** and 1st **MARQUIS OF,** 1612–50, Scottish Royalist general, succeeded his father to the earldom in 1626. He joined the national Covenanting movement, 1637, won victories at Aberdeen and the Bridge of Dee, 1639, and at Newburn, England, 1640, but was imprisoned at Edinburgh Castle, 1641, after turning against Argyll. Freed by Charles I, Montrose became a Royalist. When the Covenanters invaded England in 1644, the king appointed Montrose lieutenant general in Scotland and made him a marquis. Montrose defeated the Covenanters at Tippermuir and Aberdeen, 1644, and after driving Argyll from his castle at Inverary he wheeled north, routed the pursuing Argyll at Inverlochy, 1645, and continued victories over the Covenanters until Sept. 13, 1645, when he was surprised and hopelessly defeated by David Leslie near Selkirk; he escaped to the continent. In 1650, while attempting an invasion of Scotland he was captured and hanged.

MONTROSE, city, W Colorado, seat of Montrose County; a scheduled airline stop; 175 miles SW of Denver. Montrose is a market center for peaches, potatoes, and sugar beets grown in the surrounding area. Water for irrigation comes through Gunnison Tunnel from the Gunnison River. Meat, dairy products, and flour are processed in Montrose, and radium, uranium, and vanadium are mined nearby. (For population, see Colorado map in Atlas.)

MONTROSE, burgh, E Scotland, Angus County; on a peninsula between the North Sea and Montrose Basin, a tidal lake at the mouth of the South Esk River; a highway and railroad junction; 33 miles SSW of Aberdeen. Montrose is an important trade center, fishing port, and resort, with industries that include textile mills, shipyards, flour mills, canneries, and fertilizer plants. The city was an important seaport in the thirteenth century. It was the scene of John de Baliol's surrender to Edward I in 1296 and the birthplace of James Graham, 5th earl and 1st marquis of Montrose, in 1612. (For population, see Scotland map in Atlas.)

MONTS, PIERRE DU GUAST, SIEUR DE, 1560?–1630?, French explorer and colonizer, was born in Saintonge, of Roman Catholic parents. He became a Protestant, and in 1603 Henry IV made him governor of the French Company of Canada. He sailed in the following year for America, and with Samuel de Champlain explored the coast of New Brunswick and New England to Cape Cod. In 1605 he founded Port Royal, later Annapolis Royal, the first French colony in Canada.

MONT-ST.-MICHEL, islet, NW France, Manche Department, Avranches Arrondissement; on the Bay of Saint-Michel of the English Channel; connected with the mainland by a mile-long granite causeway; 38 miles NNE of Rennes; area of the islet, 3 acres. The bay, noted for its rapid tidal waters, is left dry during ebb tide. The islet is a solitary cone of granite ½ mile in circumference at the base and 256 feet high, topped by a Benedictine abbey and fortress dominating a village of a few houses and shops. The buildings of the abbey-fortress, one of the leading tourist attractions in France, include buttresses, crypts, cloisters, spires, and gargoyles; on the tallest spire stands a figure of St. Michael (Michel) weighing nearly two tons. In the Hall of Knights Louis XI founded the Order of St. Michael in 1469. La Merveille, the monastery proper, dates from the thirteenth century. On the summit high above the other structures is the church.

The abbey was founded in 708 by St. Aubert, bishop of Avranches, who built it according to instructions he is said to have received from St. Michael in a vision. The islet was besieged by the English during the Hundred Years' War, but was not taken. After the French Revolution the abbey was used as a prison until 1863, when the buildings were designated a national monument and restored. The structure has been pictured as a symbol of the strength and unity of medieval civilization. (For population, see France map in Atlas.)

BIBLIOG.–Henry Adams, *Mont-Saint-Michel and Chartres* (1904); Rene-Jacques, *Mont-Saint-Michel* (1963).

MONTSERRAT, one of the Leeward Islands of the Lesser Antilles; 34 miles NW of Guadeloupe; 11 miles long and 7 miles wide; area of the island totals 32.5 sq. mi. Montserrat consists of a series of forest-covered volcanic peaks, the highest of which is Soufrière (2,999 ft.). Plymouth is the principal town. Chief exports are limes, lime juice and oil, tomatoes, carrots, fruit, hides and skins, and cotton lint, seed, and cake. Discovered by Columbus in 1493, the island was settled by the Irish in 1632. From 1958 to 1962 Montserrat was a member of the West Indies Federation. (For population, see West Indies map in Atlas.)

Mont-St.-Michel, an islet connected with the mainland by a mile-long granite causeway, is a solitary granite cone crowned by an impressive Benedictine abbey and fortress.

PHILIP GENDREAU

MONTSERRAT, or Monserrat, mountain (4,054 ft.), NE Spain, Catalonia Region, Barcelona Province; 24 miles NW of Barcelona. On Montserrat's slope, at an altitude of 2,400 feet, is a Benedictine monastery founded in 888, one of the great religious shrines in Spain. In a sixteenth-century church among the monastery buildings is a black wooden image of the Virgin that is supposed to have been carved by St. Luke.

MONTT, MANUEL, 1809–80, Chilean government official, was born in Petorca and educated at the National Institute, Santiago. He was president of the house of deputies, minister of foreign affairs, minister of justice and education, minister of interior, president of the republic for two terms, 1851–61, and president of the supreme court, 1861–80. His administration brought industrial improvement, progress in education, and legal reform.

MONTT, PEDRO, 1848–1910, Chilean government official, son of Manuel Montt, was born in Santiago. He was admitted to the bar, 1868, and elected to congress, 1876. He was president of the chamber of deputies; minister (successively) of justice, public instruction, the treasury, and the interior; minister to the United States; and president of Chile, 1906–10.

MONZA, town, N Italy, Lombardy Region, Milan Province; on the Lambro River; 8 miles NNE of Milan. Monza is a rail junction and an industrial center; manufactures include hats, carpets, textiles, machinery, glass, furniture, organs, plastics, and paints. The cathedral, built in the thirteenth and fourteenth centuries on the site of a church founded by Theodelinda, queen of Lombardy, contains the Iron Crown of the Lombards, used at coronations of Holy Roman Emperors. Monza has a thirteenth-century town hall and an expiatory chapel erected on the site of Humbert I's assassination in 1900. (For population, see Italy map in Atlas.)

MOODY, (ARTHUR EDSON) BLAIR, 1902–54, U.S. journalist and senator, born in New Haven, Conn., and educated at Brown University. A longtime Washington correspondent for the Detroit *News*, he was appointed in 1951 to fill the unexpired term of Sen. Arthur Hendrick Vandenberg. He was subsequently chairman of the Senate Small Business Subcommittee and chairman of the rules committee at the 1952 Democratic National Convention. Moody was also the publisher of two newspapers and the author of *Boom or Bust* (1941). He died while campaigning for re-election to the Senate.

MOODY, DWIGHT LYMAN, 1837–99, U.S. evangelist, was born in Northfield, Mass., one of nine children reared by a widowed mother. He left school when he was 13 and eventually made his way to Chicago, where he became a traveling shoe salesman and opened a mission Sunday school. He gave up his job at the age of 23 to become a city missionary; three years later, 1863, he organized a nondenominational church, but he spent most of the Civil War years with the Christian Commission giving spiritual attention to the sick and wounded. He became president of the Chicago Young Men's Christian Association, 1866, and was active in Sunday school conventions. In 1870 Moody became associated with Ira D. Sankey, singer and chorister; in 1873 the two began evangelistic work in Great Britain, attaining great success. Returning to the United States, 1875, they repeated their success in many cities. They revisited Great Britain, 1881–84, then continued their evangelistic work in the United States and Canada, 1884–91; Moody returned alone to Great Britain in 1891–92. During the World's Columbian Exposition in Chicago in 1893, Moody organized an evangelistic campaign in numerous churches of the city. Meanwhile he had organized the Northfield Seminary for girls (1879), the Mount Hermon School for boys (1881), and the Chicago Bible Institute (1889), later renamed the Moody Bible Institute.

Moody was never ordained a minister, and throughout his career he remained a lay preacher. He spoke a simple colloquial language and displayed a remarkable personal magnetism. His creed was nonsectarian and his theology was strongly fundamentalistic. Included among his numerous volumes, chiefly hymnbooks and sermons, were *The Second Coming of Christ* (1877), *Secret Power, or the Secret of Success in Christian Life and Work* (1881), and *Notes from My Bible* (1895).

BIBLIOG.–Richard K. Curtis, *They Called Him Mister Moody* (1966); J. C. Pollock, *Moody* (1963).

MOODY, JOHN, 1868–1958, U.S. financial analyst, born in Jersey City, N.J. After working with Spencer, Trask and Company, bankers (1890–1900), he founded *Moody's Manual of Railroads and Corporation Securities* in 1900. He also founded and edited *Moody's Magazine*, an investor's monthly, and *Moody's Analyses of Investments*, an annual. In 1903 he established Moody's Investors Service. He wrote *The Truth About the Trusts* (1904), *How to Analyze Railroad Reports* (1911), *Profitable Investing* (1925), *The Long Road Home* (1933), *Fast by the Road* (1942), and *John Henry Newman* (1945).

MOODY, WILLIAM HENRY, 1853–1917, U.S. legislator and jurist, born in Newbury, Mass. He was district attorney for the eastern district of Massachusetts from 1890 to 1895, when he entered Congress as a Republican. He served until 1902, when he was appointed secretary of the navy in Pres. Theodore Roosevelt's cabinet. He became U.S. attorney general in 1904. In 1906 he became an associate justice of the U.S. Supreme Court. In 1910 Congress passed a special bill allowing him to retire on full pay.

MOODY, WILLIAM VAUGHN, 1869–1910, U.S. educator, poet, and dramatist, born in Spencer, Ind., the son of a river steamboat captain. He was graduated from Harvard University, traveled in Europe, served a year as assistant in the English department at Harvard (1894–95), and taught at the University of Chicago from 1895 to 1907. Moody's first book was a lyric drama, *The Masque of Judgment* (1900), upholding the right of the individual to "rebel." This was followed by *Poems* (1901), *History of English Literature* (with Robert M. Lovett, 1902), and the plays *The Fire-Bringer* (1904), *The Great Divide* (1906), and *The Faith Healer* (1909).

MOON, the natural satellite of the earth. In a general sense, a moon may also be any other satellite, as for example the moons of Jupiter. The moon revolves around the earth at a mean distance of 238,857 miles in a period of 27 days 7 hrs. 43 min. 11.5 sec., the sidereal month. Hence the moon's average daily motion, eastward among the stars, is 360° divided by 27.32166, or 13.176358°. Since the sun's eastward daily motion averages 0.985609°, the moon's motion exceeds that of the sun by 12.190749° per day. This corresponds to the synodic month of 29 days 12 hrs. 44 min. 2.8 sec., which is the average interval between successive new moons or full moons and the period in which the moon's phases pass through a complete cycle. The moon shines by reflected sunlight, the intensity at full moon being about 1/500,000 that of the sun. On each side of the full phase the brightness falls off so sharply that at first quarter and at last quarter it is only about 10 per cent of that of the full moon. To some extent this contrast results from the fact that the angle of reflection of the sun's rays is much smaller at full moon than it is at quarter phase, but the roughness of the moon's surface is the more significant factor. See MONTH; PHASE; SATELLITE.

Lunar Atmosphere. The moon's diameter is 2,160 miles, or 0.2723 times the earth's diameter; the mass is 1/81.5 (0.01227) that of the earth. It follows that the moon's mean density is 3⅓ times that of water and that the acceleration of gravity at the moon's surface is ⅙ that on the earth. The velocity of escape, or the velocity a body at the moon's surface must have to escape the moon's pull of gravity, is 1.5 miles per second, a value so small

LICK OBSERVATORY

The phases of the moon are shown in these reversed photographs taken through a 36-inch refracting telescope: (a) at 4.6 days; (b) at 7 days, first quarter; (c) at 10.35 days, gibbous; (d) at 13.83 days, full; (e) at 22 days, third quarter; and (f) at 26.4 days.

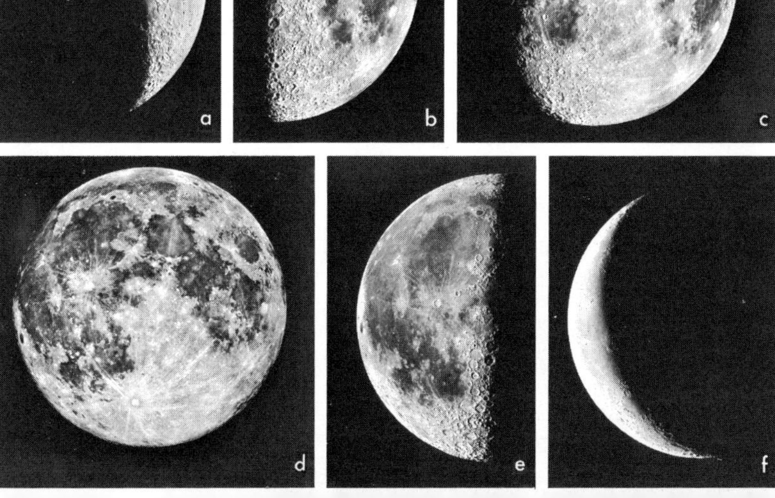

Mountains and craters can be seen most easily along the terminator at quarter phase, when the angle of the sun's rays is greatest. Maria and rays are most evident at full moon, when the angle is smallest. The effects of libration can be seen by comparing (b) and (c).

that the moon cannot retain an atmosphere made up of relatively light molecules such as those of the earth's atmosphere. The conclusion that the moon has no appreciable atmosphere, drawn from the kinetic theory of gases, is confirmed by observation in many ways. Stars occulted by the moon disappear and reappear suddenly without gradual dimming, and without any observable time errors that might be ascribed to the refraction of light in a lunar atmosphere. At times of solar eclipses, no phenomenon that could be ascribed to an atmosphere on the moon has been observed. The absence of an atmosphere also excludes the presence of water on the moon's surface. See ATMOSPHERE; OCCULTATION.

The absence of a protecting atmosphere exposes the moon's surface to extensive changes of temperature. The surface temperature is obtained by measuring and analyzing the total radiation received from the moon. Of the solar radiation received by the moon, only about 7 per cent is directly reflected; the remainder is absorbed as heat and eventually reradiated as invisible, infrared radiation in wavelengths determined by the surface temperature of the moon. The sunlit side of the moon apparently has a temperature of more than 100°C (212°F); the dark side is extremely cold, only a few degrees above the absolute zero of −273°C (−460°F). Measurements at Mount Wilson Observatory show a drop of 210°C (378°F) in the moon's temperature while a lunar eclipse is in progress.

Surface Features. The most typical feature of the moon's surface is its abundance of craters, the largest of which are more than 100 miles in diameter. These craters, tens of thousands of which have been counted, are distributed most irregularly over the visible surface of the moon, but there are relatively smooth areas that are more or less free from craters. These are the darker regions, or *maria* (seas), so named before it was understood that large bodies of water do not exist on the moon. Long mountain ranges, so common on the earth, are not much in evidence. The longest is the lunar Apennines, extending for about 400 miles. Many of the craters have received names of prominent astronomers and philosophers of the past: Aristarchus, Kepler, Plato, Tycho (Brahe), and innumerable others. The *maria* have fanciful names such as Mare Tranquilitatis and Mare Serenitatis.

The best time to view the moon through a telescope is near quarter phase, when the shadows near the terminator bring out the relief of the surface. At full moon the contrast has disappeared but the systems of rays from some of the larger craters are visible. Rays connected with the crater Tycho are particularly prominent. They are about 10 miles wide, and the longer ones extend many hundreds of miles over the moon's surface, crossing all other features. Their nature is not clearly understood; since they cast no shadows they cannot be elevations or depressions. Of a totally different nature are the narrow crevices, called rills, which also extend for hundreds of miles.

The first photographic information to be obtained regarding the topography of the moon's hemisphere that is hidden from the earth came in October, 1959, following the October 3 launching by the U.S.S.R. of the satellite, Lunik III. In its orbit within 5,000 miles of the moon, satellite cameras made photographs showing the moon's surface on the hidden hemisphere as less rugged. Launched on Jan. 31, 1966, the Soviet spacecraft Luna IX made the first soft landing on the moon. Photographs indicated that the lunar surface was covered with porous material and that it did not have a thick dust layer. The first U.S. spacecraft to make a soft landing on the moon was Surveyor I, launched from Cape Kennedy on May 30, 1966. Mounted within the structure of Surveyor I was a sophisticated 22-pound camera unit for transmitting pictures of the lunar surface to the earth. The pictures revealed the moon's surface near Surveyor I to be rough and strewn with pebbles. Surveyor I landed in the Ocean of Storms, just south of the lunar equator on the western side of the moon. Surveyors V, VI, and VII carried alpha-particle spectrometer equipment; it indicated a chemical composition similar to basalt, and dissimilar from more basic dunite and from acidic granite. The result implies that some degree of differentiation has taken place on the surface of the moon. See GEOLOGY; SPECTRUM.

Maps and Atlases. Although photographs of the moon taken by satellites and astronauts have revealed close-up features of the moon, maps and atlases dating back to the seventeenth century have been largely instrumental in determining its overall topography. Among the earlier photographs of the moon, those by Lewis M. Rutherfurd, about 1860, were long unexcelled in quality. Toward the end of the nineteenth century Lick Observatory produced an excellent photographic map of the moon and the Paris Photographic Atlas was constructed. In 1903 the Harvard Observatory issued an atlas by William Henry Pickering; and one edited by Gerard P. Kuiper of Yerkes Observatory was issued in 1960. A photographic atlas of the moon was also edited by Zdenek Kopal and published in 1965. Volumes of pictures taken by the Ranger and Orbiter spacecraft have been compiled by the National Aeronautics and Space Administration.

Manned Exploration of the Moon. The U.S. Apollo program, designed to land men on the moon, met with spectacular success. Apollo was made possible by the success of the Saturn V launch vehicle. The first manned Apollo flight, Apollo 7, was launched on Oct. 11, 1968; Apollo 11 was launched on July 16, 1969; 4 days later, on July 20, 1969, Neil Armstrong and Edwin Aldrin were the first men to set foot on the moon. They spent 9½ hours on the lunar surface before returning. During their moon walk, they collected samples of lunar surface material for analysis on the earth and set up several experiments. Charles Conrad and Alan Bean, the astronauts of Apollo 12, launched Nov. 14, 1969, set up a nuclear-powered scientific station and brought back parts of Surveyor III. See SPACE EXPLORATION.

Analyses of Apollo 11 Samples. The first samples of the moon, brought back by Apollo 11, consisted of rocks and of fine material. The rocks and fine particles are generally similar chemically. Some rocks are fine-grain and medium-grain crystalline, indicating formation by reasonably rapid cooling (hours to weeks) of originally molten matter. Although the word "volcanic" is used, the melting may be local and produced by high-energy impacts. Other rocks are breccias, mixtures of fragments, indicating a complex history of breakups and shocks. The rocks are basaltic and resemble in composition earth mantle material; they seem to have undergone some differentiation. The rocks are unlike either terrestrial rocks or meteorites in detailed chemical composition and in mineralogy. Hydrated minerals are absent. The alkalis (e.g., K) and some volatile elements are depleted; some refractory elements (e.g., Ti and Zr) are enriched. The rocks appear to be sandblasted and rounded on the exposed upper side. They also show surface pits. Both may be caused by the impact and erosion of micrometeorites. There is no evidence of erosion by water. There is no evidence of biological material, and only a very low upper limit can be given to organic material. The fine material and breccias contain large amounts of noble gases, which appear to have come from the solar wind. Radioactive dating of the rocks, using the argon-potassium method, shows that they crystallized 3 to 4 billion years ago. Their exposure to cosmic rays near the

NASA

THE IMPOSSIBLE DREAM

The impossible dream of landing men on the moon was realized at 4:17 P.M., Eastern Daylight Time, July 20, 1969. On July 16, after 8 years of planning and testing, the Apollo 11 space team of Neil Armstrong, Edwin Aldrin, and Michael Collins was launched from Cape Kennedy for its 500,000-mile, 8-day journey to the moon and back. After hurtling through space for 4 days, the astronauts fired the main rocket of the spacecraft to slow it so that it would be caught up in the moon's orbit. Then, leaving Collins to guide the command module, Armstrong and Aldrin boarded the small, spindly legged lunar module *Eagle* (shown above), which swept them 300 miles across the face of the moon to touch down in the Sea of Tranquility.

ONE SMALL STEP

Descending the ladder from the lunar module Neil Armstrong's booted left foot made the first human impression on the moon's surface, and Armstrong uttered the historic words, "That's one small step for a man; one giant leap for mankind." Nineteen minutes later, Armstrong was joined by Edwin Aldrin. They erected a wire-stiffened flag and exposed a plaque commemorating five pioneer spacemen—2 Russian and 3 American—whose lives had been lost. Then, for more than two hours, they explored the lunar terrain, while the world watched via television. The astronauts took photographs, set up a sheet of aluminum foil to catch rare solar gases; and left behind a seismometer and a laser reflector designed to redirect a beam of light back to earth. Most important, they collected nearly 50 pounds of lunar rock and soil.

NASA

MOONSCAPE

The Apollo 11 astronauts found thc lunar surface around their craft to be fine, powdery, and dark gray, resembling somewhat the desert of the United States, and pocketed with thousands of craters varying in width from one or two feet to 50 feet. Shown at right and below are photographs taken from the lunar module. The bottom photo was taken 63 miles above the moon's surface, as the module approached the landing site. The top photo is of the moon's far side. Despite the impediment of their 185-pound spacesuits, the astronauts found walking on the moon to be less difficult than had been expected. They were able to perform the tasks required of them with relative ease, including the gathering of rocks and soil to be brought back to earth for analysis. It was certain that these rocks would provide valuable new clues as to the origins of the moon and of the earth itself.

NASA

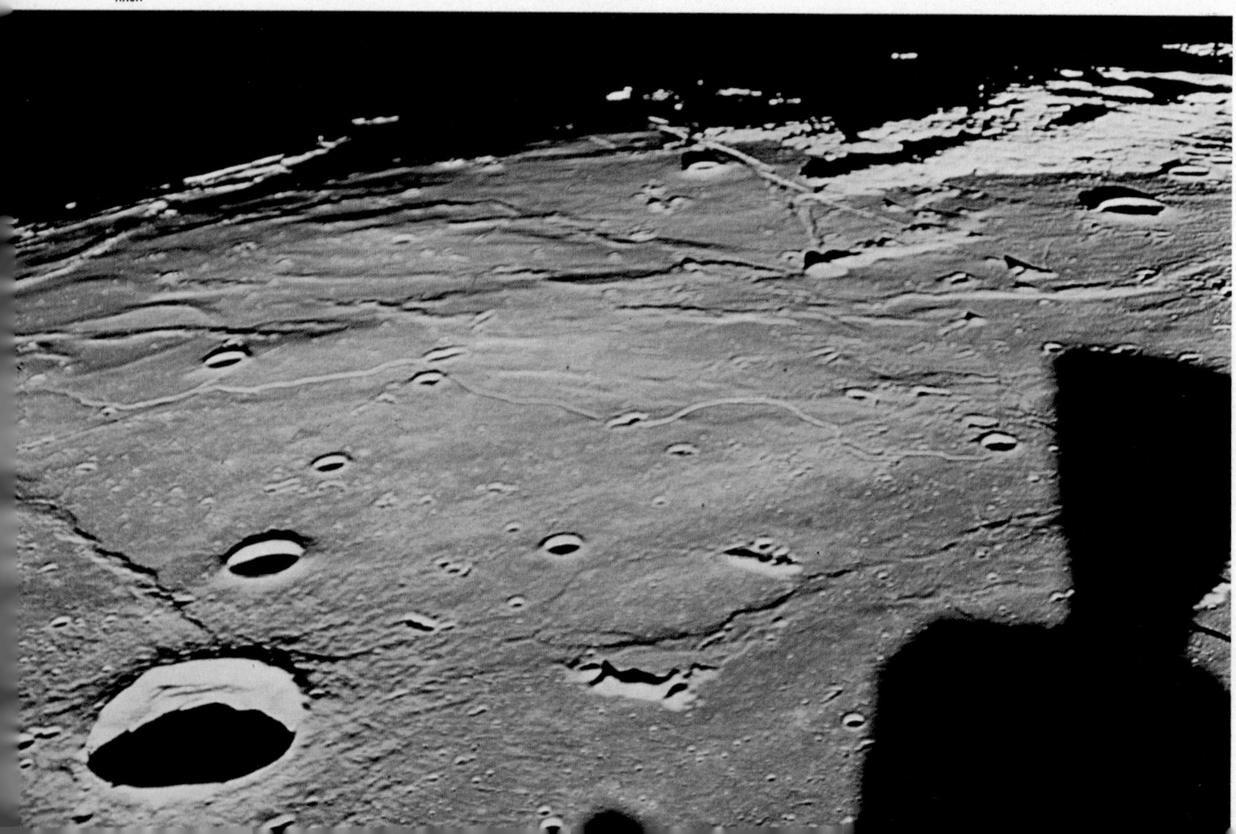

surface ranges from 20 to 160 million years. The strontium-rubidium method and the lead-lead method of dating both give the date of the formation of the rock material as 4.6 billion years; this "age" corresponds to the age of meteorites and to what is generally held to be the age of the solar system. See METEOR; SOLAR SYSTEM.

Lunar Theory. The motion of the moon has been the subject of many investigations during the past 2,000 years or more. Until 1687, when Sir Isaac Newton established the laws of motion and of universal gravitation, this study was based upon observation alone. In a first approximation, the orbit of the moon may be described as an ellipse with an eccentricity of 0.0549 and an inclination with respect to the ecliptic of 5°8′. If the earth's attraction alone were active, the orbit would remain unchanged in size, shape, and in orientation. The variable attraction exerted by the sun upon the earth-moon system is primarily responsible for the deviations from undisturbed elliptic motion. This causes the ellipse to revolve in its own plane in the direction (eastward) of the moon's motion at the rate of one revolution of the line of apsides in 8.85 years, and causes the line of nodes to revolve in the opposite direction in 18.61 years. In addition, the sun's attraction causes further deviations from elliptic motion that may be described as periodic perturbations. See APSIDES, LINE OF; NUTATION; ORBIT.

The inclination to the ecliptic and the revolution of the line of nodes must have been known in ancient times, because these properties of the orbit are directly accessible to observational determination and because they are important factors in solar and lunar eclipses. The oldest known determination of the eccentricity and the motion of the line of apsides is that by Hipparchus in the second century B.C. The evection, the largest periodic perturbation in the moon's orbital longitude, was discovered by Ptolemy about A.D. 150. This inequality has a period of 31.8 days and a coefficient of 1°16′; hence, in this period the moon's position oscillates between 1°16′ ahead of and 1°16′ behind its position in a stable elliptic motion. The next largest periodic inequality, the variation, with a coefficient of 39′ and a period of one-half synodic month, is more elusive because it vanishes at new and full moon and at first and last quarters. It was perhaps known to the Arabian astronomer Abul Wefa toward the end of the tenth century; it was established by Tycho Brahe, who also discovered the annual inequality with a coefficient of 11′. See ECLIPSE.

Newton succeeded in accounting for all the known inequalities in the moon's motion on the basis of his gravitational theory, but did not develop a complete theory. Some of the great mathematical astronomers of the eighteenth century—Alexis Claude Clairaut (1713–65), Leonhard Euler (1707–83), Joseph Louis Lagrange (1736–1813), Pierre Simon de Laplace (1749–1827)—contributed to progress in this field. In one respect, improved tables of the moon's motion were desired for the purely theoretical purpose of using the lunar theory to test the law of gravitation. From a practical point of view, accurate knowledge of the moon's motion was important for determination of longitudes on the earth's surface. In the nineteenth century highly significant contributions were made by Peter Andreas Hansen (1795–1874), whose improved lunar tables were used for construction of the national ephemerides from 1862 until 1922; Charles Eugène Delaunay (1816–72), who constructed a magnificent lunar theory of great mathematical interest; George William Hill (1838–1914), whose original work formed the basis of the exhaustive theory created by Ernest William Brown (1866–1938). Brown completed his monumental lunar tables in 1919. In 1923 they replaced those of Hansen for the construction of the moon's ephemeris. See EPHEMERIS.

Changes in the Rate of the Earth's Rotation. Since 1925 it has further been established that the observed apparent deviation of the moon's motion, predicted from gravitational theory, can be accounted for by the nonuniformity of the time determined by the rotation of the earth. It seems that tidal friction, especially in shallow seas, accounts for a gradual slowing down of the rate of rotation of the earth. This causes an apparent secular (continuing; nonperiodic) acceleration of the moon's motion, in addition to a real secular acceleration caused by the decrease of the eccentricity of the earth's orbit. The increase of the length of the day by tidal friction, approximately 0.001 second per century, is cumulative and amounts to a discordance of two hours in the calculated time of an eclipse 20 centuries ago. Records of ancient eclipses were first used in 1693 by the English astronomer Edmund Halley to establish the secular acceleration in the moon's motion. In addition, observations of the moon have established that there are irregular fluctuations in the rate of rotation of the earth. During the past three centuries the time determined by the rotation of the earth has been as much as 30 seconds fast and 30 seconds slow compared with uniform time. See TIDE.

Possible History and Future. The origin of the moon is not clear, but three theories have been widely accepted: that the earth and the moon originated from one mass at the same time; that the moon originated from the earth not long after the earth's formation; or that the moon was formed apart from the earth but was later captured. Objections have been raised to all theories of origin; however, dynamical studies and the results of Apollo 11 provide strong support for a particular version of capture. In any case, on evidence based on the lengthening of the day and the month and the acceleration of the moon's motion, astronomers have concluded that at one time the moon must have been quite close to the earth, perhaps at a distance of 8,000 or 10,000 miles; that a month at that time was about a quarter of the present month; and that a day was less than a quarter of the present day. It has also been estimated that the day and month will continue to increase until both reach a length of 47 of our present days; and that at that time the earth will always present the same side to the moon, just as the moon does toward the earth. Because of disturbances caused by solar tides, however, such a condition would not be permanent; the moon would again soon start moving closer to the earth.

S. FRED SINGER

BIBLIOG.–A. C. Clarke and others, *Man and Space* (1964); J. Holmes, *America on the Moon* (1962); Zdenek Kopal, *An Introduction to the Study of the Moon* (1966), *Exploration of the Moon by Spacecraft* (1968); Fred L. Whipple, *Earth, Moon and Planets* (1963 ed.); H. P. Wilkins and P. A. Moore, *Moon* (1955.)

MOONEY, EDWARD FRANCIS CARDINAL, 1882–1958, U.S. Roman Catholic prelate, born in Mount Savage, Md. After studying at St. Mary's Seminary in Maryland and the North American College, Rome, he was ordained a priest in 1909. In 1926 he was appointed apostolic delegate to India and titular archbishop of Irenopolis. He was apostolic delegate to Japan (1931–33) and then returned to the United States to become bishop of Rochester, N.Y. In 1937 Mooney became first archbishop of Detroit and in 1946 he was created a cardinal.

MOONFLOWER, a twining perennial herb belonging to the genus *Calonyction* and comprising subtropical and tropical American plants of the morning-glory family, Convolvulaceae. The foliage of

Calonyction (from the Greek for night beauty) consists of large heart-shaped or arrow-shaped leaves growing alternately. Two important species are *C. aculeatum*, or common moonflower, a plant with white trumpet-shaped flowers that may be 6 inches across; and *C. muricatum*, which has purplish blossoms that may grow to 3 inches across. Moonflowers usually open at dusk and close in the forenoon. They are propagated by seeds that are notched to hasten germination. The flowers are fragrant and quite decorative.

MOONSTONE, a variety of feldspar that has an opalescent reflection and sometimes a delicate play of colors. Milky in appearance, it ranges from a grayish white to a grayish blue, and is transparent to opaque. The finest specimens of moonstone come from Ceylon, although they are also found in Switzerland and Burma. Cut in the cabochon shape, they are widely used for jewelry, expecially rings. SEE GEM, *Semiprecious Stones*.

MOONWORT, any plant of the genus *Botrychium*, the fleshy ferns belonging to the adder's-tongue family, *Ophioglossaceae*. *Botrychium* derives from Greek and means grapelike. Moonwort, or grape fern, bears short underground stems that send up two stalks. A compound leaf with several triangular leaflets grows on one stalk; on the other, usually taller stalk appears a small panicle of sporangia arranged like grapes in a cluster. The larger stalk constitutes the fertile frond. Approximately 40 species exist and most are hardy in temperate regions. *B. virginianum*, or rattlesnake fern, grows to 2 feet and is large enough to be decorative. Moonwort requires shade and much moisture; and is little cultivated because it is not generally showy. See HONESTY.

MOOR, Spanish *More*, in modern times a member of one of several peoples called Moors living in such diverse regions as Mauritania, Ceylon, and the Philippines; during the Middle Ages either a Moslem in North Africa or Spain, any dark-skinned Moslem, or a Moslem generally. *Moor* is derived from the Latin *Maurus*, meaning an inhabitant of Mauritania, a region corresponding in Roman times to modern Algeria and Morocco, and the region from which Islam spread into southwestern Europe after the seventh century. Although the Moors of North Africa and Spain were notably light skinned, many medieval Europeans considered a Moor to be a dark-skinned Moslem as portrayed in William Shakespeare's *Othello*.

The 450,000 Moors of modern Mauritania are Moslems of Berber stock who formerly spoke Zenaga, a Berber dialect of the Hamitic language, but most of whom later adopted Arabic. Many are nomads who raise livestock and subsist mainly on agriculture and hunting. They ruled Morocco from the eleventh to the mid-twelfth century, after which they became politically obscure in that country. See BERBER; MAURITANIA; MOROCCO, Administration and History, *The Almaravides*, *The Almohades*.

MOOR, a tract of open, flat, or gently rolling unarable land, especially common in western Europe. The moors of southern England are areas of low watery ground whereas those of Scotland are at higher elevations. They bear little vegetation other than moss and heather. Wastelands overlaid with peat are also referred to as moors.

MOORABBIN, municipality, SE Australia, Victoria State; adjoining Melbourne, of which it is a suburb. Moorabbin is situated in a truck gardening area. Pop. (1954) 65,337.

MOORE, CLEMENT CLARKE, 1779–1863, U.S. educator, son of Bishop Benjamin Moore, was born in New York, N.Y., and studied at Columbia University. Possessed of considerable means, he made a large gift to the N.Y. General Theological Seminary on its organization, and was professor there, first of biblical learning and then of Oriental and Greek literature. His *Hebrew and Greek Lexicon* (1809) was the first such work published in the United States. He contributed many articles and poems to periodicals. His most famous poem, *A Visit from St. Nicholas*, which begins "'Twas the night before Christmas," first appeared in the Troy *Sentinel* in 1823.

MOORE, DOUGLAS STUART, 1893–   , U.S. composer and teacher, was born in Cutchogue, N.Y. He studied music at Yale University and the Schola Cantorum in Paris. He taught music at Columbia University, 1926–62, and was chairman of the music department, 1940–62. As a composer, Moore is chiefly famous for his operas, which are imbued with an American flavor derived from folklore and regional melodies and rhythms. Among them are *The Headless Horseman* (1936), *The Devil and Daniel Webster* (1938), *The Emperor's New Clothes* (1949), *Giants in the Earth* (1950; Pulitzer Prize, 1951), *The Ballad of Baby Doe* (1955), and *The Wings of the Dove* (1961). Moore was president of the National Institute of Arts and Letters, 1946–53. He became president of the American Academy of Arts and Letters in 1960.

MOORE, GEORGE, 1852–1933, Irish novelist, was born at Moore Hall, county Mayo, and was educated at Oscott, near Birmingham, England, and by a private tutor in London. On the death of his father in 1870, he was assured of an income of some £500 and went to Paris to study art. In time he became convinced that he could not paint, and turned to literary pursuits instead, frequenting the circles of Villiers de l'Isle Adam, Stéphane Mallarmé and Emile Zola. After 10 years of Bohemianism, later recorded in his *Confessions of a Young Man* (1888), Moore returned to England and began an arduous apprenticeship in the art of fiction writing, striving to acquire a vigorous native English style. After two volumes of verse, *Flowers of Passion* (1877) and *Pagan Poems* (1881), he published the novel *A Modern Lover* (1883), a fictional exercise in imitation of the French naturalists. This was followed by *A Mummer's Wife* (1885), *Esther Waters* (1894), *Evelyn Innes* (1898), and *Sister Teresa* (1901). Settling in Dublin in 1901, Moore associated himself for a number of years with Edward Martyn and William Butler Yeats in the Irish literary revival. His experiences during these years furnished the material for the trilogy *Hail and Farewell* (1911–14). Among his later works are a play, *The Making of an Immortal* (1928), and novels, *Héloise and Abélard* (1921), and *Aphrodite in Aulis* (1930).

MOORE, HENRY, 1898–   , British sculptor, was born in Yorkshire, the son of a Castleford coal miner. He served in World War I, and then studied at the Leeds School of Art and at the Royal College of Art, London. He became recognized as an outstanding sculptor and received great acclaim in the United States after a one-man show at the Museum of Modern Art, New York, 1947. Working in the mediums of wood, marble, and stone, he often emphasized the basic form or natural pattern of the material used, such as the wood grain or the marble texture. He sought to represent vitality as such in his art, apart from the ostensible subject matter. His work includes *Reclining Figure*, *Family Group*, *Bird Basket*, and *Madonna and Child*. See MADONNA.

MOORE, JOHN BASSETT, 1860–1947, U.S. jurist and educator, was born in Smyrna, Del. He was professor of international law and diplomacy at Columbia University, 1891–1924. He served on The Hague tribunal, 1912–28, and as a judge of the Permanent Court of International Justice at The Hague, 1921–28, resigning to devote himself to writing. Perhaps his greatest work was his *Digest of International Law* (8 vols. 1906).

MOORE, MARIANNE CRAIG, 1887–   , U.S. Pulitzer prize-winning poet, was born in St. Louis, Mo. She taught at Carlisle Indian School, 1911–15, was a librarian in New York City, and was editor of the literary magazine *The Dial*, 1925–29. Her first volume, *Poems*, was published in 1921, and was followed by *Selected Poems* (1935), *The Pangolin and Other Verse* (1936), *What Are Years* (1941), *Nevertheless* (1944), a translation of the fables of Jean de La

PICTORIAL PARADE

Marianne Moore

Fontaine (1954), *Like a Bulwark* (1956), *O To Be a Dragon* (1959), *The Absentee: A Comedy in Four Acts* (a play, 1962), and *Tell Me, Tell Me: Granite, Steel, and Other Topics* (1966). Her *Collected Poems* (1951) won the 1952 Pulitzer prize. She also won numerous other awards. Her poems are tightly written, highly intellectual, and compact with irony, and make use of unconventional metrical patterns.

BIBLIOG.–B. F. Engle, *Marianne Moore* (1964); Jean Garrigue, *Marianne Moore* (1965).

MOORE, THOMAS, 1779–1852, Irish poet, was born in Dublin, and studied at Trinity College, Dublin, and Middle Temple, London. His personal charm gained him influential friends in London and in 1803 he was appointed admiralty registrar in Bermuda. After a year he tired of the work, entrusted it to a deputy, and went to the United States, where he traveled extensively during 1804. Apart from verses published in 1801 under the pseudonym Thomas Little, Moore's first publication was *Epistles, Odes, and Other Poems* (1806). This and later verses, *Corruption and Intolerance* (1808) and *The Sceptic* (1809), were too imitative of existing models to give real scope to his powers; but in 1807 Moore began the *Irish Melodies* (1807–34), which contain his best work and which made him the national lyricist of Ireland. *Lalla Rookh*, an "Oriental" poetical romance, appeared in 1817, and ran through six editions. Moore was also successful with political squibs such as *The Fudge Family in Paris* (1818), *Fables for the Holy Alliance* (1823), and *Odes upon Cash* (1828); but he was obliged to live on the Continent to avoid arrest on account of the defalcations of his Bermuda deputy; through the help of Moore's friends the matter was eventually settled. *The Epicurean*, a prose romance, appeared in 1827; a life of Richard Brinsley Sheridan in 1825; an edition (with a biography) of George Gordon Byron's *Letters and Journals* in 1830; a life of Lord Edward Fitzgerald in 1831; and a *History of Ireland* (4 vols.) during 1835–46. His *Poetical Works* were published in 1840; his *Memoirs, Journals, and Correspondence* were edited by Earl Russell (8 vols.) between 1853 and 1856.

BIBLIOG.–H. M. Jones, *The Harp that Once* (1937); L. A. G. Strong, *The Minstrel Boy. A Portrait of Tom Moore* (1937).

MOOREA, formerly Eimeo, island, S Pacific, French Oceania, Society Islands, Windward group; 12 miles NW of Tahiti; area of the island 50 square miles. Moorea is a volcanic island of triangular shape, largely mountainous, and is surrounded by a reef and its lagoon. Mount Tohivea (3,976 ft.) is the highest point. Cook and Papetoai bays, on the north coast, have excellent anchorages for vessels. Copra and coffee are the main products. The London Missionary Society has its South Sea College there. In 1903 a tidal wave killed many of the inhabitants, who are mostly Polynesians. Afareaitu, on the east coast, is the principal town. (For population, see Pacific Ocean map in Atlas.)

MOORE'S CREEK, BATTLE OF, a skirmish of the American Revolution fought at Moore's Creek, N.C., on Feb. 27, 1776, between a force of 1,600 North Carolina Loyalists under Gen. Donald McDonald, and about 1,100 North Carolina Whigs led by Col. Richard Caswell. The Whigs won a decisive victory that helped prevent the British from regaining North Carolina. Casualties were 1 killed and 1 wounded on the Whig side and about 50 killed and wounded on the Loyalist side.

MOORESTOWN, town, SW New Jersey, Burlington County; 7 miles ENE of Camden. It is a residential town in a farming region. Manufactures include wood and metal products, fungicides and insecticides; a guided missile and surface radar plant is located there. Moorestown, laid out in 1722, has a few eighteenth-century buildings. (For population, see New Jersey map in Atlas.)

MOORHEAD, city, W Minnesota, seat of Clay County; on the Red River of the North, just E of Fargo, N.D. Moorhead is a market center for a potato, onion, and grain area; products include farm machinery and refined sugar. The city is the seat of Concordia and Moorhead State colleges. Moorhead was settled in 1871 and incorporated in 1881. (For population, see Minnesota map in Atlas.)

MOOSE, the largest member of the deer family, Cervidae, and the American form of the rare European elk, *Alces machlis*. The moose, *Alces americanus*, is found in the Western Hemisphere from the Rocky Mountains to Maine and is abundant in Canada; the genus *Alces gigas* is found in Alaska. The moose is found in forested regions of Eurasia. It is a huge, ungainly, long-legged animal with a blackish brown coat and lighter colored face, legs, and belly. Its neck is so short that it can graze only by kneeling. An average bull usually stands 6 feet high, weighs about 1,400 pounds, and has a growth of skin and hair, known as "the bell," hanging from his neck. The long, narrow head ends in an overhanging flexible proboscis, and the head of the bull moose bears a pair of large, many-pointed antlers that may have a spread of more than 6 feet. The cow has no bell or antlers and is smaller than her mate.

The moose is an animal of the forest, especially where water is abundant. In rough country it will crash through brush like an elephant. The moose is fond of wading in marshy rivers and ponds in summer, feeding on aquatic herbage or going completely under water for bulbous lily roots. Its principal diet in winter, however, consists of leaves and twigs. Moose keep open certain trails, known as mooseyards, when the ground is covered with snow. In autumn the bull moose ranges the woods in search of a mate, bawling out invitation and challenge night and day and often engaging in terrific combats with rivals. It is in prime condition as to both venison and robe at this season. A bull is a dangerous adversary when cornered or wounded, for he will charge and kill a hunter who cannot evade

Bull Moose

TOM MC HUGH—PHOTO RESEARCHERS

him or stop him with a bullet. In the spring the cows hide away to bear their young, which resemble the mother in having a uniformly colored coat. A favorite lying-in place is an island, and the cow will stay there until her calf is two weeks old. Calves brought up in captivity become pets, and remain gentle even as adult moose. They have been trained to draw sledges and work like horses. See DEER; ELK.

MOOSE, LOYAL ORDER OF, an international fraternal organization founded in 1888. Activities include sponsorship of community affairs as well as social functions. In 1913 the order founded Mooseheart, Ill., about 40 miles west of Chicago, as the site of a home and school for children of deceased members. In 1922 the organization founded Moosehaven, a home for aged and dependent members and their wives at Orange Park, Fla. The Moose are active in the United States and possessions, Canada, and Great Britain. Membership in 1958 exceeded 1 million men. There were also approximately 300,000 women in the auxiliary known as the Women of the Moose. The total number of lodges and auxiliaries was 3,268. Headquarters are at Mooseheart.

MOOSEHEAD LAKE, W central Maine, lies mainly in Piscataquis County, with Somerset County on the western shore; maximum E-W and N-S distances 10 and 35 miles respectively; elevation 1,023 feet; area 120 sq. mi. Moosehead Lake, the largest in Maine, is the source of the Kennebec River. The lake has several islands and there is shore-to-shore steamer service. Moosehead Lake is a popular fishing (trout) and hunting (moose and deer) resort.

MOOSE JAW, city, Canada, S Saskatchewan; at the junction of Thunder Creek and Moose Jaw River; on the Canadian Pacific and the Canadian National railways; 40 miles W of Regina. Major industries include oil refining, meat processing, flour milling, clothing manufacturing, dairying, and the manufacture of clothing and bricks. Moose Jaw Bible College is located in the city. Settled in 1882, Moose Jaw became a town in 1884 and a city in 1903. Pop. (1956) 29,282.

MOPPO. See MOKPO.

MOQUEGUA, department, S Peru; bounded by the departments of Puno on the N and E and Tacna on the S and by the Pacific Ocean and Arequipa Department on the W; area 4,716 sq. mi.; pop. (1958 est.) 49,497. Moquegua is traversed by the Cordillera Occidental of the Andes, and elevations exceed 10,000 feet in the north and east. The narrow coastal plain is dry and subtropical. The Moquegua and Tambo rivers, rising in the Andes, flow to the Pacific. The Pan American Highway parallels the seacoast. Moquegua ranks second among Peruvian departments in the production of olives, grapes, and wine; among other products are corn, figs, cotton, sugar, and livestock. There are important copper deposits near the capital city, Moquegua (1953 pop. 5,091), an agricultural processing center on the Moquegua River.

MORA, village, E Minnesota, seat of Kanabec County; near the Snake River; on the Great Northern Railway; 62 miles N of Minneapolis. Mora is a market center in an area of dairy, cattle, poultry, and grain farms. An Izaak Walton League Museum is there. Named after a town in Sweden, Mora was platted in 1881 and incorporated in 1891. Pop. (1960) 2,329.

MORA, village, N New Mexico, seat of Mora County; on the Mora River; 39 miles NE of Santa Fe. Mora is a resort and irrigated fruit-growing center in the Sangre de Cristo Mountains. The Sante Fe National Forest and the Fort Union National Monument are nearby. Mora was settled in 1835. Pop. about 300.

MORADABAD, city, N India, Uttar Pradesh State, capital of Moradabad District; a railroad and highway junction on the Ramganga River; 97 miles E of Delhi. Moradabad's industries include the engraving of plated ornamental tin and brass articles and cotton spinning. The city was founded in 1625 by Rustam Khan, who built a fort and the Jama Masjid Mosque (1634). Pop. (1951) 154,018.

MORAES BARROS, PRUDENTE JOSÉ DE, 1841–1902, Brazilian political leader, was born in Itú, São Paulo. He studied law and became a member of the national legislature, 1885, and a leader of the republican party. In 1889 he became governor of the state of São Paulo, and was the first civilian president of Brazil, 1894–98.

MORAINE, an accumulation of rock debris carried along or deposited by a glacier. Materials heaped up along the sides of a valley glacier, derived largely from the fall of rock from valley walls, constitute lateral moraines. When two glaciers merge, two of the lateral moraines unite to form a medial moraine, which may or may not be near the middle of the main glacier. A glacier may have several medial moraines as a result of the confluence of several tributary glaciers. Ground moraines result from material that is carried along by the lower layers of valley glaciers. Much of this material is derived from the beds of the glaciers by scouring action. Ground moraines may also consist of the relatively thin but widespread deposits left by receding ice sheets. Such deposits, commonly unsorted gravel, pebbles, and boulders, cover most of southern Canada and the northern part of the United States. Terminal moraines are made up of debris deposited at the front of valley glaciers and ice sheets. When well defined and ridgelike, they indicate that the terminal margin of the ice remained in one location for a considerable time. See GLACIER.

MORALES, LUIS DE, called El Divino, 1509?–86, Spanish artist, was born in Badajoz. His work, mostly religious in subject (hence his nickname The Divine), is intensely emotional and executed with great devotion. Themes of persecution and suffering give his paintings a harshly melancholy quality. His favorite subjects were the *Pietà*, *Virgin and Child*, *Ecce Homo*, and *Christ Carrying the Cross*.

MORALITY in its most general sense consists of the customs, habits, aims, and values adopted by a given society, or the quality of rightness or wrongness the society attributes to the acts and attitudes of an individual as these conform or fail to conform with prevailing custom. The English word derives from the Latin *moralis*, from *mos*, meaning custom or habit. Some identify morality with the forms that a social group observes in expressing praise or blame, the individual's acts and attitudes that are singled out for praise or blame, and in general the set of values toward which society expects loyalty and respect. This view, current among anthropologists and sociologists, makes morality amenable to a purely descriptive or empirical investigation. According to some philosophers and spokesmen for religious groups this view is in error. For them morality is not a matter of what various societies do, in fact, value or despise;

A moraine, deposited by the large glacier on Mt. Lyell in Yosemite National Park, is mute evidence of the power of glaciers that can crush mountain walls into rock splinters.

NATL. PARK SERVICE

rather, morality is concerned with what all men *ought* to praise or blame—morality should be normative rather than descriptive.

Most philosophers at mid-twentieth century, even those identified with organized religion, generally accepted the descriptive meaning of morality, conceding the empirically established fact that different societies have different moralities or sets of values. But apart from this empirical issue remained the philosophical problem of finding (if possible) both a basis and a general content for a set of values that all men ought to accept. Anthropologists objected that no universal set of values ever existed or could exist, and that there could be no critique of value (if, as they contend, all value is "culturally relative," no man and no culture can criticize the values of another). Finding the value that has a right to criticize all customary moralities was at mid-century the task of a study known as axiological ethics. Do we "intuit" it (Plato, G. E. Moore, W. D. Ross, N. M. Hartmann), do we see it in being as developing (Aristotle, St. Thomas Aquinas), or is it a natural quality open to empirical study (R. B. Perry, John Dewey)? See ETHICS. EDWARD B. COSTELLO

MORALITY PLAY, or simply morality, a type of medieval allegorical drama which existed from the late fourteenth through the sixteenth centuries. The characters in the play usually personified various abstractions of good and evil. Also called Paternoster plays, the most celebrated morality was *Everyman*, in which Everyman summons his friends Beauty, Worldly Goods, and Kindred to accompany him to Death, but only Good Deeds responds. Moralities differed from miracle plays in that the latter drew their characters from the Bible or from the lives of the saints.

MORAL RE-ARMAMENT (MRA), an international movement aimed at reforming the character of individuals and hence of society. It was previously called Buchmanism, after its founder, U.S. Lutheran minister Frank N. D. Buchman, or the Oxford Group, after Oxford University, in England, where the movement had its beginning. It is based on "universals of conscience and faith" and "aims to achieve throughout society a revolution of character and motive, so that the non-Communist world is regenerated and united, the Communist world won to a greater ideology, and science and technology used to serve and not destroy the human race." The movement maintains a number of centers throughout the world (the one in the United States is at Mackinac Island, Michigan) and, to enlist support for its program, sponsors traveling lecturers, films, and plays. See BUCHMAN, FRANK N. D. JOHN McCOOK ROOTS

MORAN, EDWARD, 1829–1901, U.S. painter, older brother of Thomas and Peter Moran, worked as a weaver and cabinetmaker before studying painting in Philadelphia, under Paul Weber and James Hamilton, and in England. Among his more notable works is a series of 13 paintings depicting major marine events in American history.

MORAN, PETER, 1841–1914, U.S. painter, studied painting under his brothers Edward and Thomas, and became noted for his etchings and his paintings of animals, such as *Pasture Land* and *The Stable Door*.

MORAN, THOMAS, 1837–1926, U.S. painter and etcher, was born in Bolton, England, went to the United States with his family in 1844, and studied painting in Philadelphia with his brothers and abroad in England, France, and Italy. During 1871–73 he visited the Yellowstone region and the canyons of the Colorado, regions he later depicted in such monumental canvases as *The Grand Canyon of the Yellowstone* and *The Chasm of the Colorado*.

MORATIN, LEANDRO FERNANDEZ DE, 1760–1828, Spanish poet and dramatist, was born in Madrid. In 1787 he became secretary to Francisco de Cabarrús, head of the Spanish embassy in Paris, and later took part in diplomatic missions in England, Holland, Germany, and Italy. During the French occupation of Spain he was royal librarian to Joseph Bonaparte. When the French were defeated he emigrated to France. His lyric poetry, although charming, is overshadowed by his plays—such as *La Comedia nueva* (1742), and *El sí de las niñas* (1806), sparkling, satiric comedies in the tradition of Molière.

MORATORIUM, a postponement, by legislative action or executive proclamation, of the date when debts or contract obligations have to be paid. Its effect may be domestic or international.

In Rome under Justinian I (483–565), moratoria were granted for five-year periods by written permission of the emperor if a stipulated number of creditors agreed. During the Middle Ages kings often granted moratoria without consulting those to whom payments were due. In the modern period moratoria have been occasioned by natural calamities, monetary panics, or political or industrial upheavals. In 1910 France declared a moratorium following severe floods in Paris. During World War I moratoria were declared in almost all the belligerent countries. In 1933 the United States halted banking activity from March 4 through March 14 after runs on banks had become widespread.

The most striking international moratorium was the one-year suspension of reparations and war debt payments in 1931. It was suggested by U.S. Pres. Herbert Hoover on June 20 and accepted on July 6 by all the countries involved. SEE REPARATIONS.

The U.S. Constitution (Art. I, Sec. 10) prohibits states from passing laws impairing the obligation of contracts. In 1934, however, in the case of *Home Building and Loan Assn.* v. *Blaisdell* (290 U.S. 398), the Supreme Court upheld state moratorium legislation on the grounds that it constituted part of a state's police power that could be lawfully exercised during an economic emergency.

MORAVA RIVER, German March, main river of Moravia, Czechoslovakia; rises on the S slope of the Kralícký Sněžnik, flows generally south through a fertile valley, forms a portion of the Czechoslovak-Austrian boundary, and joins the Danube 10 miles upstream from Bratislava; length 227 miles. The Morava flows past Olomouc, Kroměříž, Otrokovice, and Uherskè Hradiště. From Hodonín the river is navigable in its lower course for about 80 miles.

MORAVA RIVER, Serbian Velika Morava (the Great Morava), Yugoslavia; formed by the junction of the Western Morava and the Southern Morava at Stalać in central Serbia; flows 227 miles N through the fertile Pomoravlje Valley and enters the Danube 28 miles ESE of Belgrade. It is navigable for about 75 miles downstream from Cuprija. Including the Southern Morava, which rises in southern Serbia 45 miles northeast of Skoplje, the river is 353 miles long.

MORAVIA, ALBERTO, 1907– , pseudonym of Alberto Pincherle, Italian author, born in Rome. He gained acclaim with his first novel, *The Indifferent Ones* (1932), which portrayed the decadence and emptiness of contemporary Roman life. In this and later works Moravia depicted society with compelling realism and treated man with a detached and almost quizzical irony. His characters, both high and low, are often denizens of a great city, epitomized by Rome, with its particular blend of sophistication and spiritual boredom. Moravia married the novelist Elsa Morante. His works include *Wheel of Fortune* (1937), *The Fancy Dress Party* (1947), *The Woman of Rome* (1949), *Two Women* (1958), and *The Empty Canvas* (1961), and several collections of short stories, including *More Roman Tales* (1964) and *The Fetish and Other Stories* (1965).

MORAVIA, Czech Morava, German Mähren, historic region, central Czechoslovakia; bounded on the NW by Bohemia, on the NE by Poland, on the SE by Slovakia, and on the S by Austria; area of the region about 10,350 square miles. Moravia occupies the basin of the Morava River, a traditional trade and

Location Map of Moravia

strategic route between the Oder-Vistula and Danube River basins, and is enclosed by the Bohemian-Moravain Heights on the west, the Jeseníky Ridge with Praděd Mountain (4,887 ft.) on the north, the White Carpathians on the east, and the Little Carpathians on the southeast. The climate is generally moderate and mild; the mean annual temperature in the Brno area is 48°F, the average precipitation 22 inches. Some 55 per cent of the area is fertile plowland; 27 per cent is forested. Agriculture is well developed; wheat, corn, oats, rye, sugar beets, grapes and other fruits, and flax are the main crops. Owing to its rich mineral resources, which include iron, lead, copper, coal, graphite, clay, and limestone, Moravia is highly industrialized. The Ostrava Basin alone supplies 80 per cent of the total Czechoslovak coal output, nearly all of the country's coke, 80 per cent of its pig iron, and 72 per cent of its steel. Brno, the former capital of Moravia—near the historical site of Slavkov, formerly Austerlitz—is a machine-building center with manufactures of arms, tractors, diesel engines, and turbines; it also produces textiles. Ostrava, the "steel hearth" of Moravia, is the leading center of the coal and metallurgical industries. Automobile works are located at Kopřivnice, and Gottwaldov is one of the world's leading centers of footwear manufacture. Olomouc, in the fertile Háná Plain, has metallurgical, machine-building, and food-processing industries. Jihlava is an important rail junction and a center of textile and other consumer goods manufacture.

Moravia received its name from Slavonic tribes who occupied it in the sixth century. In the ninth century its inhabitants were converted to Christianity. Moravia belonged to the Holy Roman Empire from the end of the eighth century to 1029, when it was made part of Bohemia, and in 1526 passed to Austria. In 1918 it became part of Czechoslovakia and in 1927 was merged with Czech Silesia into the province of Silesia and Moravia. Upon German seizure of Czechoslovakia in March, 1939, the region became part of the protectorate of Bohemia and Moravia, but was returned to Czechoslovakia in 1945. On Jan. 1, 1949, it was divided into the provinces of Brno, Gottwaldov, Jihlava, Olomouc, and Ostrava.

MORAVIAN CHURCH, a body of Christians tracing their origin to the Bohemian Brethren, or Unitas Fratrum, originating in Moravia in the fifteenth century.

The Moravians have no formal creed apart from the Holy Scriptures, which they accept as the only rule of faith and practice. Their main points of doctrine are the total depravity of human nature; the love of God; the real Godhead and the real humanity of Jesus Christ; the atoning power of the sacrifice on the Cross; justification by faith and sanctification by the power of the Holy Spirit; good works as the expression of faith; the fellowship of believers; the second coming of the Lord; and the supreme headship of Christ in the Kingdom of God. They maintain fraternal relations with other churches, and are known for their catholicity of spirit and for their educational and missionary zeal.

The form of worship is in general liturgical, though not universally so. Holy communion is celebrated periodically, and love feasts are observed. Infant baptism is practiced, but children may not become full members until they voluntarily confirm their baptismal vows. The standards of membership and church discipline are high, only those who give evidence of their faith by Christian living being admitted to communicant membership.

Organization. The government of the church is democratic although its orders are strictly episcopal. The entire body is organized in four provinces—Continental, British, North American, and South American. A general synod, meeting every six years and consisting of bishops, delegates from the provincial synods, and representatives from the mission fields, is the highest governmental body. Provincial synods exercise supervision over the spiritual interests of their respective provinces; the congregations, though subject to the general laws of the synods, are in the main self-governing. Pastors are appointed by conferences of elders named by the provincial synods, with the advice and consent of individual churches. Provincial synods elect their own bishops. Bishops of missionary provinces are elected by or under the authority of the general synod. In 1957 the general synod provided for the gradual development of missionary provinces into self-governing synodical provinces.

In 1957 the Moravians in the United States, including a small body known as the Bohemian and Moravian Brethren, reported 191 churches and a total membership of 61,741. An extensive missionary work is carried on and various educational institutions are maintained. Among these are Moravian College (coeducational) at Bethlehem, Pa.; Salem College for Women at Winston-Salem, N.C.; and Linden Hall, a junior college for women, at Lititz, Pa. The Moravians of Continental Europe also carry on an extensive home mission or "inner mission" enterprise known as the Diaspora, having as its object the promotion of spiritual life within the state churches.

History. The Council of Basel in 1433 caused a complete separation between the two parties of Hussites: the Calixtines and the Taborites. The former drew toward the Roman Catholic church while the latter formed themselves into a distinct community under the name of the Bohemian and Moravian Brethren (see HUSSITES). Michael Brandacius, the first bishop of the Bohemian and Moravian Brethren, was chosen by lot in 1467, and the union rapidly increased under the leadership of Lucas of Prague (died 1528) until at the opening of the sixteenth century it numbered some 400 congregations. It suffered great persecution in the Schmalkaldic War (1546), and in the Jesuit Counter Reformation it was overthrown as a visible organization in Bohemia and Moravia (1627). About 100 years later the remnants of the brotherhood were led by Christian David into Silesia, where they received a habitation from Count Nikolaus Ludwig von Zinzendorf. There they built a town known as Herrnhut (the Lord's Watch) and there, in 1727, was organized the first church of the modern Moravians. The movement prospered under the leadership of Count Zinzendorf, who became a bishop; similar settlements were founded elsewhere in Germany as well as in Holland, Denmark, Switzerland, Russia, Great Britain, and the United States.

In the United States the first Moravian settlement was in Georgia in 1735, but that field was soon abandoned for Pennsylvania, where settlements were made at Bethlehem, Nazareth, and Lititz. The early U.S. towns, like those of Europe, were of the exclusive type, where only church members owned property; but this system was ended in 1844. IRVIN E. DEER

MORAVIAN COLLEGE. See COLLEGES AND UNIVERSITIES.

MORAVIAN GATE, Czechoslovakia, a broad mountain pass or gap between the Carpathians and the Sudetes at an elevation of 1,017 feet. The Moravian Gate, part of an ancient trade and strategic route connecting the Oder-Vistula and Danube basins, is traversed by highways, the Oder-Danube Canal, and the Ostrava-Přerov Railroad.

MORAVSKÁ OSTRAVA. See OSTRAVA.

MORAY, a heavy-bodied eel of the family *Muraenidae* found about rocks and coral reefs in all warm seas. There are more than 100 kinds of morays, many of them savage and spectacularly colored. The largest, the green moray, or *Gymnothorax funebris*, may be 6 feet long and weigh 30 pounds. Its green color results from a mucous covering on the leathery bluish gray skin. Sharp teeth, strong jaw muscles, and a pugnacious disposition make the green moray a dangerous adversary, particularly of the smaller fishes that serve as its food. The common speckled moray, *G. moringa*, is abundant in the West Indies where it is used for food. Another species of moray, *G. mordax*, is a food fish of minor importance found in California waters. See EEL; FISH.

MORAY FIRTH, inlet of the North Sea, NE Scotland; maximum SW-NE and SE-NW distances 39 and 15 miles respectively. Moray Firth contains Cromarty, Inverness, and Beauly firths. Apart from many fishing ports, chief cities on its coast are Inverness, Nairn, and Dingwall.

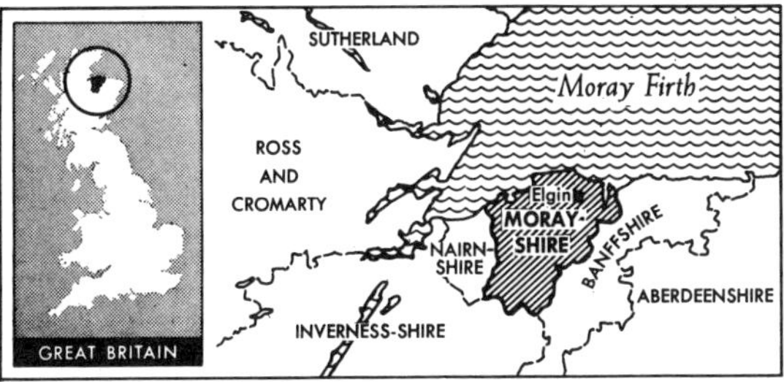

Location Map of Morayshire

MORAYSHIRE, or Moray, county, NE Scotland; bounded on the N by the Moray Firth, on the E by Banff, on the S by Inverness, and on the W by Nairn; area 476 sq. mi.; pop. (1961) 49,156. The surface of Moray is about equally divided between hills of more than 2,000 feet elevation in the south and sandy lowlands along the coast. The area is drained by the Lossie, Findhorn, and Spey rivers, the latter forming the boundary with Banff; all are famed salmon streams. Chief centers are Elgin, the capital, and Rothes, Lossiemouth, Forres, and Grantown-on-Spey. Sea and river fishing, farming, and cattle and sheep raising are the main occupations. Industries include woolen mills, whisky distilleries, shipyards, fruit and vegetable canneries, and granite, sandstone, and slate quarries. Besides Sweno's Stone at Forres, other antiquities are Elgin Cathedral (1224), Kinloss Abbey (1150), and Pluscarden Abbey (1230). The ancient county of Moray was considerably larger than the present county, which was formerly known as Elgin or Elginshire.

MORBIHAN, department, W France, Brittany; bounded by the departments of Finistère on the W and NW, Côtes-du-Nord on the N, Ille-et-Vilaine on the E, and Loire-Inférieure on the SE, and by the Bay of Biscay of the Atlantic Ocean on the S; area 2,738 sq. mi.; pop. (1954) 520,978. Morbihan includes Belle-Île and several smaller islands off the much indented coast. The department is drained by the Blavet, Scorff, and Oust rivers, rising in the Armorican massif to the north and flowing generally south. The chief crops are cereals, vegetables, cider apples, and wine grapes. Sardine fishing and cattle raising are important. Industries include fish canning, tanning, furniture making, and metalworking. There are quarries of granite, slate, and kaolin and deposits of iron ore. The tourist centers of Carnac and Locmariaquer contain prehistoric monuments. Principal cities besides Vannes, the capital, are Lorient, Hennebont, and Pontivy.

MORDANT, a compound capable of uniting with dyestuffs to form insoluble pigments. The principal functions of a mordant are to form colored compounds with the dyes, to combine with the dye molecules and thereby give color fastness to light and moisture, and to act as a catalyst for the dyes. Mordants may consist of compounds of iron and copper, including ferrous and copper sulfates; aluminum compounds, such as alum and aluminum sulfate; chromium compounds, such as chrome alum and sodium and potassium dichromate; and nickel and other metallic salts.

Mordants are used in the dyeing of silk, wool, cotton, and furs. Mordanted dyestuffs are used most frequently for worsted suitings where fastness of color is more desirable than brightness. Before mordants were used, the dyeing of cotton was an uncertain and difficult process because the natural dyes had little or no affinity for the cotton fibers.

Among the more common of the mordant acid dyes are anthraquinone, momoazo, disazo, triphenylmethane, and xanthene. See DYEING.

MORDEN. See MERTON AND MORDEN.

MORDOV AUTONOMOUS SOVIET SOCIALIST REPUBLIC, U.S.S.R., a subdivision of the Russian Soviet Federated Socialist Republic; bounded on the N by Gorkiy Region, NE by the Chuvash Autonomous Soviet Socialist Republic, and E, S, and W by Ulyanovak, Penza, and Ryazan regions, respectively; area 16,159 sq. mi.; pop. (1956 official est.) 1,000,000. Most of the people are Russians (57 per cent) and Mordvinians, a Finno-Ugrian strain (37 per cent), the rest being Tatars and Chuvash. The republic occupies the northeast fringe of the central Russian black-earth belt and agriculture is the chief activity. Rye, wheat, oats, corn, and potatoes are the leading crops; hemp, tobacco, sunflowers, and sugar beets are also grown. Dairying and food processing are major occupations; other industries include sawmilling, woodworking, paper milling, and the manufacture of prefab houses and wood-chemical products. Saransk, the capital, has a large peat-fueled electric power station and an electrical engineering works; and at Ruzayevka, which is located 14 miles southwest, are railway rolling stock repair shops and metalworking industries.

MORE, HANNAH, 1745–1833, English poetical and ethical writer, was born in Stapleton, Gloucestershire. During her early career in London she became the friend of Sir Joshua Reynolds, Samuel Johnson, Edmund Burke, and especially of the actor David Garrick; the latter friendship led to two of her plays being produced at Covent Garden—*Percy*, 1777, and *The Fatal Falsehood*, 1779. Following Garrick's death she turned against the stage. *Sacred Dramas* (1782) is a link between her earlier writings and the pious works that followed: *Slavery* (1788), *The Religion of the Fashionable World* (1790), *On Female Education* (1799), *Coelebs in Search of a Wife* (1809), *Practical Piety* (1811), *Christian Morals* (1813), *On the Character of St. Paul* (1815), *Moral Sketches* (1818), *The Spirit of Prayer* (1825).

MORE, HENRY, 1614–87, English philosopher, was born in Grantham, Lincolnshire, and studied at Christ's College, Cambridge, where he became a teaching fellow, 1639. He took holy orders, but refused preferments and lived his life quietly in Cambridge. He was influenced for a time by the doctrines of René Descartes, but soon became one of the Cambridge Platonists. His mystical tendencies became more and more evident in his writings, and the lucidity that distinguished his early work was gradually replaced by the elusive radiance of poetic rapture. Representative of his 24 volumes of prose and verse are *Psychozoia Platonica: or a Platonicall Song of the Soul* (1642), *The Second Lash of Alazonomastix* (1651), *Enthusiasmus Triumphatus* (1656), and *Divine Dialogues* (1668).

MORE, PAUL ELMER, 1864–1937, U.S. literary critic, was born in St. Louis, Mo., was educated at Washington and Harvard universities, and taught at Harvard, 1894–95, and Bryn Mawr, 1895–97. He was literary editor of the *Independent*, 1901–03, the New York *Evening Post*, 1903–09, and *The Nation*, 1906–14, and later was a lecturer in Greek philosophy at Princeton University. He became identified as a leading proponent (with Irving Babbitt) of the so-called new humanism—an eclectic philosophical system incorporating elements of Christianity, Neoplatonism, and Oriental philosophy. More's works include *Shelburne Essays* (14 vols. 1904–35), *Hellenistic Philosophies* (1923), *The Christ of the New Testament* (1924), *The Demon of the Absolute* (1928), *The Catholic Faith* (1931), and *Pages from an Oxford Diary* (1937).

MORE, SIR THOMAS, also Saint Thomas More, 1478?–1535, English statesman, was born in Cheapside, London, the son of a London barrister, Sir John More. Part of his early education was in the household of John Morton, archbishop of Canterbury (later cardinal). His father discouraged him from his humanistic studies at Oxford, and in 1494 he entered New Inn as a law student, and later, 1496, studied at Lincoln's Inn. The public career upon which he subsequently embarked did not prevent him from cultivating his interest in the classics and the new humanism, and neither career nor learning inhibited his profound and ascetic piety. During four years before entering parliament in 1504 (the year in which he married Jane Colt, who bore him four children) he subjected himself to the discipline of a monk, wearing a hair shirt, scourging himself regularly, and sleeping on the ground with a log for his pillow. In parliament and on various foreign official missions his leadership and ability commended him, after 1509, to the favor of Henry VIII. He held a number of offices in succession, including those of undersheriff of London from 1510, master of bequests from 1514, treasurer of the exchequer from 1521, and speaker of the house of commons from 1523. His wife died, 1511, and he married widow Alice Middleton the same year. More's public career reached a peak in 1529 when Henry appointed him to succeed the disgraced Cardinal Thomas Wolsey as lord chancellor. In his judicial capacity More was noted for painstaking fairness and harshness toward heretics.

GALLERY OF PORTRAITS
Sir Thomas More

The king's quest for a male heir, which so changed the course of English history, eventually martyred Sir Thomas. Disapproval of the king's divorce proceedings and the widening rupture with the Roman Catholic church caused the lord chancellor to resign. When More refused to recognize the king as head of the English church, 1534, Henry caused his arrest on a charge of high treason. Before a biased jury and on perjured testimony More was accused and found guilty. He was beheaded July 6, 1535.

More's life, with its varied interests, reflected the transition of his country from an essentially medieval polity to a Renaissance state. A devout upholder of the hallowed concept of a universal church, More also looked far ahead, contemplating reforms beyond his time. His shrewd wit, gentle humor, and literary genius earned him the esteem and friendship of such great contemporaries as John Colet and Desiderius Erasmus. More's most famous work, *Utopia* (1516), gave civilization a word (meaning "nowhere") and an idea. More's ideal commonwealth, where reason and toleration regulate life, is remarkable for the social justice of its people and the broad theism of their beliefs. More was beatified by Leo XIII, 1886, and canonized by Pius XI in 1935. St. Thomas More's feast is celebrated July 6. See UTOPIA.

MICHAEL FIXLER

BIBLIOG.–R. Ames, *Citizen Thomas More and His Utopia* (1949); R. W. Chambers, *Saga and Myth of Sir Thomas More* (1927); *Thomas More* (1949); W. E. Campbell, *Erasmus, Tyndale and More* (1950); J. H. Hexter, *More's Utopia* (1952); J. Farrow, *Story of Thomas More* (1954).

MORÉAS, JEAN, pseudonym of Ioannes Papadiamantopoulos, 1856–1910, French poet, was born in Athens, Greece, but lived most of his life in Paris, where he was associated first with the decadent poets and symbolists and later with the École Romane of Ernest Raynaud and Charles Maurras. His best poems, classical in form and inspiration, include *Stances* (1899–1901) and *Iphigénie à Aulis* (1903). He also wrote criticism, *Les premières armes du symbolisme* (1889), *Esquisses et souvenirs* (1908), and *Réflexions sur quelques poètes* (1912); and (with Paul Adam) two novels, *Le Thé chez Miranda* (1886) and *Les Demoiselles Gaubert* (1887).

MOREAU, GUSTAVE, 1826–98, French painter, was born in Paris. His paintings are romantic and mystical and are characterized by exotic subjects and brilliant color. He treated biblical subjects in an Oriental (specifically Persian) manner. His house in Paris (which he gave to the city for the Musée Moreau) contains most of his works, including *Prometheus; Hesiod and the Muses;* and *Leda*.

MOREAU, JEAN VICTOR, 1763–1813, French military figure, was born in Morlaix and educated in law at Rennes. Joining the revolution in 1789, he became general of division, 1794, and succeeded Charles Pichegru as head of the Army of the North, 1795, and in command of the Army of the Rhine, 1796, he drove the Austrians beyond the Danube, then led an "admirable" French retreat. In 1799 he commanded the French army in Italy, and after helping Napoleon Bonaparte overthrow the *Directoire* led the Army of the Rhine to victory at Hohenlinden, 1800. He was banished, 1804, when Napoleon accused him of complicity in a royalist plot. He lived in the United States, 1805–13, but returned to Europe, 1813, joined the Russian service, and was mortally wounded at Dresden.

MORECAMBE AND HEYSHAM, municipal borough, NW England, Lancashire County; on Morecambe Bay of the Irish Sea; 4 miles W of Lancaster, with which it is connected by railroad and highway. The borough consists of the seaside resort of Morecambe and the port of Heysham, the latter containing an eighth century Norman chapel. Pop. (1951) 37,000.

MOREHEAD, city, NE Kentucky, seat of Rowan County; in Cumberland National Forest; on the Chesapeake and Ohio Railroad and U.S. highway 60; 58 miles E of Lexington. It is the seat of Morehead State College. Clay, timber, and Burley tobacco are products of the area. Morehead was incorporated in 1869. Pop. (1960) 4,170.

MOREHEAD CITY, town, E North Carolina, Carteret County; on the SW shore of Beaufort Harbor, on the Southern Railway and U.S. highway 70; 32 miles SSE of New Bern. The town is a fishing center and coastal resort. It is near the Hanes-Lassiter State Game Refuge and Park. Morehead City was settled in 1857 and incorporated in 1860. Pop. (1960) 5,583.

MORELIA, city, central Mexico, capital of Michoacán State; in a valley of the central plateau; on the National Railroad; 132 miles WNW of Mexico City. Industries include the processing of corn, beans, sugar, fruit, flour, coffee, vegetable oil, and beef and the manufacture of wood, wearing apparel, tobacco, textiles, candy, and chemicals. The municipal palace and the state museum and capitol are fine examples of colonial architecture; a Spanish aqueduct, built in 1789, is at the city's gates. Morelia is the seat of San Nicolás College, founded in 1540, and of a cathedral constructed between 1640 and 1744. The city, founded in 1541 as Valladolid, was renamed Morelia in 1828 for José María Morelos y Pavón (1765–1815), hero of the Mexican war for independence, who was born there. Pop. (1950) 63,245.

MORELOS, state, central Mexico; bounded by the states of Mexico on the W and N, Puebla on the E and SE, Guerrero on the SW, and the Federal District on the N; area 1,917 sq. mi.; pop. (1957 est.) 359,679. It is situated mainly on the south slope of the central plateau; the land dips noticeably from north to south with an average elevation difference of about 10,000 feet. It is drained by tributaries of the Balsas River. The climate varies from the tropical savanna to the cool upland type; summer is the rainy season. Morelos, primarily an agricultural state, produces corn, rice, wheat, sugar, coffee, wine, oranges, tropical fruit, and vegetables. Cattle raising, the making of wood products, and food processing are important. Hernán Cortés conquered the region in 1530; the state of Morelos was organized in 1869. Cuautla and the capital, Cuernavaca, are the principal cities.

MORENA, SIERRA. See Sierra Morena.

MORENCI, village, SE Arizona, Greenlee County; on the S tip of the Blue range; 107 miles NE of Tucson. The village is on a steep hillside at an altitude of 4,836 feet. Its major industries (since 1872) are copper mining and smeltering. Morenci was founded in 1871. Pop. (1960) 2,431.

MÖRE OG ROMSDAL, county, W Norway; bounded by the counties of Sör-Tröndelag on the N and E and Opland and Sogn og Fjordane on the S, and by the Atlantic Ocean on the W; area 5,820 sq. mi.; pop. (1958 official est.) 208,754. The east section of the county is traversed by the Dovrefjell and Trollheimen Mountains. Numerous rocky islands lie offshore and deep fiords cut the rugged coast; the largest fiords are the Sunndals, Molde, Volds, and Stor. Agriculture is limited to the low islands, the narrow coastal strips, and the level land about the fiords; livestock is raised on lower mountain slopes. Barley, hay, oats, and potatoes are the chief crops and cod fishing is the principal industry; Kristiansund, the county seat, has Norway's largest trawler fleet. The fiords and valleys attract an important tourist trade. Before 1918 the county was named Romsdal; it then became Möre; finally it was renamed Möre og Romsdal, 1935. Principal cities besides the county seat are Alesund, Andalsnes, Molde, and Orstavik.

MORETON BAY, inlet of the Pacific Ocean, E Australia, SE Queensland; partially enclosed by Bribie, Moreton, and North and South Stradbroke Islands; maximum N-S and E-W distances 71 and 23 miles respectively. Moreton Bay receives the Brisbane River at the port of Brisbane.

MORETO Y CAVAÑA, AGUSTÍN, 1618–69, Spanish dramatist, was born in Madrid. He was a friend and disciple of Pedro Calderón, whom he equaled in stagecraft and surpassed as a humorist. His masterpiece, *El Desdén con el Desdén*, is a skillful rehandling of Lope de Vega's *Milagros de desprecio.*

MORETTO, IL, real name Alessandro Bonvicino, 1498?–1554, Italian painter, was born in Brescia. His masterpiece is the *Assumption*, in the Church of San Clemente, Brescia. Other works are *Christ in the Desert*, *The Vision of Moses*, and *Christ in the House of the Pharisee.* Il Moretto fasted and prayed before beginning a sacred subject.

MORGAGNI, GIOVANNI BATTISTA, 1682–1771, Italian anatomist, was born in Forli and studied under Antonio Valsalva at Bologna. He became assistant professor of theoretical medicine, 1711, and professor of anatomy, 1715, at the University of Padua. Morgagni has been called the founder of pathological anatomy because of his classic work on diseases and their effect on the body: *De sedibus et causis morborum per anatomen indagatis* (5 vols. 1761).

MORGAN, DANIEL, 1736–1802, American revolutionary army officer, was born probably in Hunterdon County, New Jersey, and moved to Virginia in 1753. A veteran of the French and Indian War, he raised a company of Virginia riflemen for the Continental Army, 1775. He assumed command when Benedict Arnold was wounded in the Quebec campaign, and was taken prisoner, Dec. 31, 1775. He was exchanged in 1776 and joined the operations that led to John Burgoyne's surrender at Saratoga, 1777. In 1780 Morgan resigned in protest against the army's promotion system, but rejoined Horatio Gates later in the year with a brigadier general's commission, and led the 2nd Division of Nathanael Greene's Southern Department to victory at Cowpens, Jan. 17, 1781. He commanded the Virginia militia during the Whiskey Rebellion, 1794, and served a term in Congress, 1797–99.

MORGAN, GIB, folkloric hero of American oil drillers. As the result of the careful study by folklorist Mody C. Boatright, Gib's place in oral occupational folklore is far more accurately known than that of his more famous rivals, such as Paul Bunyan. Gib actually lived and followed the oil booms most of his life, reaching the height of his fame as a teller of whoppers about 1900. Among Gib's more notable deeds were his strikes of buttermilk, champagne, quinine, and whisky; his use of Strickie, a monster boa constrictor, as a drilling cable; and his building of a giant derrick, so high it had to be hinged in two places to let the moon pass by, and took two weeks for an agile tool-dresser to climb to the top to grease the crown pulleys. Richard M. Dorson

MORGAN, SIR HENRY, 1635?–88, English pirate, was born in Wales. He was kidnaped from Bristol and shipped to Barbados, where he was sold as a slave; arriving eventually at Jamaica, he threw in his lot with the buccaneers. He succeeded Edward Mansfield as the pirates' "admiral" about 1666, and from that time, working under commission of Sir Thomas Modyford, English governor of Jamaica, Morgan conducted a reign of terror on the Spanish main, capturing Porto Bello, 1668, plundering the Cuban coast, Maracaibo, and Gibraltar, 1669, and taking Santa Catalina, 1670, and Panama City, 1671. He was summoned to England for trial in 1671, a treaty having been concluded between England and Spain the previous year. But Morgan won the favor of Charles II, was knighted, and in 1674 was appointed lieutenant governor of Jamaica. Accused of drunkenness and supporting privateering, he lost his position in 1683.

MORGAN, JOHN HUNT, 1825–64, Confederate army officer in the U.S. Civil War, was born in Huntsville, Ala. He served as a U.S. cavalry officer during the Mexican War and in 1861 joined the Confederate army as a scout. In 1862 and 1863 "Morgan's Raiders" executed a number of daring attacks on Union supply lines in Kentucky, Mississippi, Tennessee, and Ohio. Morgan was killed while raiding Greenville, Tenn.

MORGAN, JOHN PIERPONT, 1837–1913, U.S. financier, was born in Hartford, Conn., son of Junius S. Morgan, a prominent banker. After schooling that included two years at Göttingen University in Germany (where he specialized in mathematics), young Morgan in 1861 entered the banking business in New York, establishing the firm of J. P. Morgan and Company. He prospered from the start, and developed a number of important alliances with other bankers, such as Anthony J. Drexel of Philadelphia.

In the 1870's Morgan began to assume a position of real prominence in his profession, but only in the 1880's did he become known as an important industrial organizer. He was dismayed by the cutthroat competition prevalent in the railroad industry, where every business downturn produced a wave of bankruptcies. In 1885, using his financial influence, he forced the New York Central and Pennsylvania railroads to buy up competing lines in order to forestall rate wars. Thereafter his power grew rapidly, and after the Panic of 1893 he was able to force reorganizations (Morganizations, as they were called) of the Erie, Southern, Northern Pacific, and several other railroads. In each case he or one of his partners became a vital force in management of the line.

The Panic of 1893 also led to a financial crisis for the government itself, and in 1895 Pres. Grover Cleveland asked Morgan (who with August Belmont had marketed $260 million in U.S. bonds, 1878–79) to underwrite a $65 million issue of U.S. gold bonds. Morgan found the necessary gold and disposed of the issue at a good profit—for which he was much criticized in spite of the enormous risk he took.

By 1900 Morgan had become almost a legend in Wall Street. Disturbed by the threat of competition in the steel industry, he organized the vast United States Steel Corporation, capitalized in 1901 at nearly $1.5 billion. Much of this was watered stock, but the huge monopoly prospered, adding to Morgan's immense prestige. In 1902 he successfully reorganized the farm machinery industry, creating the International Harvester Company.

Not all of Morgan's activities were so successful. His consolidation of the shipping industry was a failure, and his attempted expansion of the New Haven Railroad System was a disaster that crippled the road for more than a generation. His "war" with Edward H. Harriman for control of western railroads resulted in a draw and led to a revival of antitrust activity under Theodore Roosevelt.

Morgan's last great financial operation occurred during the Panic of 1907. By tireless negotiation and sheer force of character he persuaded the leading New York bankers to band together to save institutions threatened by runs. In the process he arranged to have United States Steel absorb Tennessee Coal and Iron, thus strengthening still further the dominant position of U.S. Steel in the steel industry.

By 1907 Morgan had practically retired from business. His time and energy were devoted chiefly to travel and the collection of his vast store of art treasures. He gave lavishly to many churches, educational institutions, and other worthy causes. At his death he left about $68 million, a relatively small fortune considering the extent of his influence and the lavishness of his way of life.

Morgan did not fully understand the socioeconomic problems that developed in the modern industrial society he helped to create. Even in his own day he was something of an anachronism. He was commonly portrayed as a symbol of the grasping power of the nineteenth century corporation, and it is true that through interlocking directorates he and his partners exerted a strong influence over most of the large American corporations of their day. But his real influence was personal and moral. He had a basic integrity and an overwhelming faith in himself.

JOHN A. GARRATY

J. P. Morgan, Sr.

CULVER

BIBLIOG.–J. K. Winkler, *Morgan the Magnificent* (1930); H. L. Satterlee, *J. Pierpont Morgan* (1939); R. G. Wasson, *Hall Carbine Affair* (ed. 1948); F. L. Allen, *Great Pierpont Morgan* (1949).

MORGAN, JOHN PIERPONT, 1867–1943, U.S. financier, was born in Irvington, N.Y., studied at Harvard University, became a member of his father's banking firm, J. P. Morgan and Company, 1891, and succeeded him as head of the bank, 1913. At the outbreak of World War I the firm became a fiscal and purchasing agent for the British and French governments, organizing and financing the purchase in the United States of food and munitions for these governments. Morgan organized the syndicate that arranged large wartime loan issues to Great Britain and France, and after the war issued loans to other nations under the Dawes Plan. He was active in the reparations conferences of 1922 and 1929 and, in addition to heading the Morgan Company, was a director of the United States Steel Corporation and the Pullman Company. Like his father, Morgan was a noted art collector and philanthropist.

MORGAN, LEWIS HENRY, 1818–81, U.S. ethnologist, was born near Aurora, N.Y. Educated at Union College, he was admitted to the New York bar, and served in the state assembly, 1861–68, and senate, 1868–69. Morgan's amateur interest in American Indian culture developed into a serious career. Aided by the Seneca leader Ely Parker (1828–95), he studied Iroquois customs and wrote *League of the Ho-dé-no-sau-nee or Iroquois* (1851), one of the first competent studies in Indian ethnology. Becoming interested in the parallel development of kinship systems among Indian tribes, he wrote "Systems of Consanguinity and Affinity of the Human Family" (*Smithsonian Contributions to Knowledge*, 1871). Morgan's most notable contributions to anthropology were *Ancient Society* (1877), which developed the theory that all societies go through stages of savagery, barbarism, and civilization; and *Houses and House-Life of the American Aborigines* (1881).

MORGAN, SYDNEY (Lady Morgan, nee Sydney Owenson), 1776–1859, Irish author, born in Dublin. Her father was an actor. In 1801 her first volume of poems was published, and five years later there appeared the novel that made her immediately famous, *The Wild Irish Girl*, a lyrical, nationalistic paean to Ireland. In 1812 she married a distinguished surgeon, Sir Thomas Morgan. In 1814, she published *O'Donnell*, considered by many to be her finest achievement in fiction for its vivid description of the life of the Irish working class. A critical travel book, *France* (1817), aroused great political controversy when it was published.

MORGAN, THOMAS HUNT, 1866–1945, U.S. Nobel prize-winning biologist, was born in Lexington, Ky. He was professor of experimental zoology at Columbia University, 1904–28, and director of the Kerckhoff Laboratories of Biological Sciences at the California Institute of Technology, 1928–41. He formulated the theory of the gene as a carrier of inheritable characteristics and was awarded the 1933 Nobel prize in physiology and medicine for his discoveries regarding mutations and the hereditary functions of the chromosomes. He wrote *Evolution and Adaptation* (1903), *Heredity and Sex* (1913), *Critique of the Theory of Evolution* (1916), *The Physical Bases of Heredity* (1919), *The Theory of the Gene* (1926), and *Embryology and Genetics* (1933).

MORGANATIC MARRIAGE, a union between a man of royal blood and a woman of lower rank. Morganatic is derived from the Old German *Morgengeba*, meaning morning gift, which was presented to the wife by the husband on the morning after the marriage was consummated. The distinctive characteristic of the morganatic marriage was that the wife did not take the rank of her royal husband, and the children, although considered legitimate, had no right of succession to the dignities or property of the royal parent. The wife and children, however, usually received an allowance assigned to them by the marriage contract. The morganatic marriage originated among the royal families of the German states during the Middle Ages, where a necessary condition for a perfect marriage was equality of birth. Morganatic marriages were later adopted by other European countries.

MORGAN CITY, city, S Louisiana, St. Mary Parish; on Berwick Bay; about 70 miles WSW of New Orleans. An important port, Morgan City handles lumber, sulfur, iron and steel products, petroleum, chemicals, and canned sea food. Agriculture, fishing, hunting, and fur trapping are carried on commercially in the area. Morgan City was settled in 1850, incorporated as Brashear City, 1860, and renamed in 1876. (For population, see Louisiana map in Atlas.)

MORGAN LE FAY, also Morgana or Morgaine, the sister of King Arthur. Legends concerning her seem to have evolved from those dealing with various Brythonic and Old Irish goddesses. She was often represented as a temptress living at the bottom of a lake and as the ruler of Avalon, the earthly paradise in the seas of the west that figures in the Arthurian legend. In Sir Thomas Malory's *Morte d'Arthur* (fifteenth century) she is an evil figure who attempts to have her brother killed but is thwarted by her son, Sir Uwaine.

BARBARA NAGELSMITH

The Morgan Library

MORGAN LIBRARY, officially the Pierpont Morgan Library, is located in New York, N.Y. It was originally the private collection of incunabula, manuscripts, coins, paintings, and art objects of the elder John Pierpont Morgan (1837–1913). His son added materially to the collection and in 1924 organized it as a free public library for research students under a New York state charter. The library contains approximately 50,000 books and manuscripts and is particularly strong in incunabula, illuminated manuscripts, autographed manuscripts, historical and literary letters and documents, bookbindings, and first editions of American and English classics. The library has an important collection of books from the press of William Caxton (1431?–91), the first English printer. The library also contains paintings and art objects, etchings by Rembrandt (1606–69), and original drawings by great European artists from the fourteenth to the nineteenth century.

MORGANTON, town, W central North Carolina, seat of Burke County; 58 miles NW of Charlotte. Morganton's principal products are furniture and textiles. A state hospital for the mentally ill and the North Carolina school for the deaf are located there. The town was established in 1774 and incorporated in 1885. (For population, see North Carolina map in Atlas.)

MORGANTOWN, city, N West Virginia, seat of Monongalia County; on the Monongahela River; 55 miles S of Pittsburgh, Pa. It is the site of West Virginia University and the West Virginia Medical Center. The city is situated in an area rich in limestone, bituminous coal, and glass sand. Its manufactures include handblown glassware, plumbing fixtures, chemicals, and textiles. Cooper's Rock State Forest is nearby. Morgantown was settled in 1767 and incorporated in 1785. (For population, see West Virginia map in Atlas.)

MORGENTHAU, HENRY, 1856–1946, U.S. government official, was born in Mannheim, Germany, and came to New York in 1865. He practiced law in New York, 1879–99, then made a fortune in the real estate business. A supporter of Woodrow Wilson, he headed the Democratic finance committee in the 1912 and 1916 presidential campaigns. He was ambassador to Turkey, 1913–16; vice-chairman of Near East Relief, 1919–21; ambassador to Mexico, 1920; chairman of the Greek Refugee Settlement Commission of the League of Nations, 1923; and U.S. technical expert at the London Monetary and Economic Conference, 1933. He was also a philanthropist, and helped to establish the American Red Cross. He wrote *Ambassador Morgenthau's Story* (1918), *All in a Lifetime* (1922), and *I Was Sent to Athens* (1929).

MORGENTHAU, HENRY, 1891–1967, U.S. cabinet officer, was born in New York, N.Y., the son of Henry Morgenthau. After studying agriculture at Cornell University, he became a farmer in New York, published the *American Agriculturist*, 1922–23, and was appointed chairman of the New York Agricultural Advisory Commission by Gov. Franklin D. Roosevelt, 1929. When Roosevelt became president, Morgenthau was named chairman of the Federal Farm Board and governor of the Farm Credit Association, 1933, and in 1934 secretary of the treasury, an office he resigned in 1945. In *Germany Is Our Problem* (1945) Morgenthau proposed that defeated Germany be stripped of heavy industry and that part of her territories be given to Russia, Poland, and France—a plan Roosevelt was dissuaded from adopting by Cordell Hull and Henry L. Stimson. A prominent Zionist, Morgenthau was chairman of the American Financial and Development Corporation for Israel, 1951–54.

MORGHEN, RAFFAELLO SANZIO, 1758–1833, Italian engraver, was born in Florence. In 1781, while studying in Rome, he helped engrave Raphael's figures *Poetry and Theology* in the Vatican and later reproduced the principal works of Guido Reni, Titian, Antonio Correggio, Nicolas Poussin, and Bartolomé Murillo. Morghen became professor at the Academy of Arts, Florence, 1793. He did engravings of Leonardo da Vinci's *Last Supper* and Raphael's *Transfiguration.*

MORIGUCHI, town, Japan, S Honshu, Osaka Prefecture; immediately E of Osaka. Moriguchi is the center of an agricultural community where rice, wheat, radishes, and poultry are produced. (For population, see Japan map in Atlas.)

MORIKE, EDUARD, 1804–75, German writer, was born in Ludwigsburg, Württemberg. At first a pastor, after 1851 he was professor of literature at Stuttgart. His idyls and lyrics, written in free verse, hexameters, and antique forms, are marked by tenderness and musicality, and many were set to music by Hugo Wolf. His unfinished novel *Maler Nolten* (1832) is in the tradition of Johann Wolfgang von Goethe's *Wilhelm Meister*, and his romance *Mozart auf der Reise nach Prag* (1856) reveals the love of nature characteristic of his poems.

HARRY SLOCHOWER

MORIOKA, city, Japan, N Honshu, capital of Iwate Prefecture; on the Kitakami River; a railroad junction 100 miles NNE of Sendai. Morioka is a commercial and manufacturing center, especially noted for its pharmaceuticals and its artistic cast-iron kettles. Other industries include sake brewing, toy making, and horse trading. The city is the home of

Iwate and Morioka universities and Iwate Medical School. Pop. (1955) 142,875.

MORISCO, any of the Moors who remained in Spain after the conquest of Granada by Ferdinand of Castile in 1492. Those Moors who had previously submitted to Christian sovereigns in Spain were known as Mudjares, and their condition from the eleventh to the fourteenth century was at least tolerable. From the fourteenth century on, political and religious persecution of the Moors became common.They were practically offered the alternatives of expulsion or Christian baptism. Those who chose baptism were the objects of continual suspicion on the part of both the church and the state; and the oppression that they endured resulted in several revolts, which were cruelly suppressed. The total and final expulsion, 1609–10, when they numbered 500,000, lost to Spain an army of efficient artisans and farmers. See MOOR.

MORISON, SAMUEL ELIOT, 1887– , Pulitzer prize-winning U.S. historian, was born in Boston, was educated at Harvard, Oxford, and the École des Sciences Politiques, Paris, and taught at Harvard, 1915–55. He wrote numerous studies on the development of the New England colonies and on the life of Christopher Columbus, on whom he became the foremost authority. During World War II he served as historian of naval operations. His works include *Maritime History of Massachusetts* (1921); *Builders of Bay Colony* (1930); *Tercentennial History of Harvard University* (5 vols. 1930–36); with Henry Steele Commager, *Growth of the American Republic* (1942); *Admiral of the Ocean Sea* (1942), a biography of Columbus that won the 1943 Pulitzer prize; nine volumes in the series *History of the United States Naval Operations in World War II; By Land and by Sea* (1954); and *John Paul Jones: A Sailor's Biography* (1959), which won the 1960 Pulitzer prize for biography.

MORLAND, GEORGE, 1763–1804, English painter, was born in London, the son of a painter. At the age of 10 he exhibited in the Royal Academy and gained a reputation copying Dutch and Flemish masters. In 1782 he left home, began a life of dissipation, and painted his pictures to discharge his debts. He worked with great rapidity, relying on his memory for his subjects. He is chiefly celebrated for his animal paintings and scenes of country life, such as *Inside of a Stable* and *Dogs Fighting;* but he also executed graceful and unaffected domestic scenes, such as *The Tea Garden.*

MORLEY, CHRISTOPHER, 1890–1957, U.S. writer, was born in Haverford, Pa., and was educated at Haverford College and at Oxford (Rhodes scholar, 1910–13). He was on the editorial staffs of Doubleday, Page and Company, the *Ladies Home Journal*, the Philadelphia *Evening Public Ledger*, and the New York *Evening Post*, and was a contributing editor of the *Saturday Review of Literature*, 1924–41. Literary whimsey marked his early novels, *Parnassus on Wheels* (1917) and *The Haunted Bookshop* (1919), and fantasies, *Where the Blue Begins* (1922) and *Thunder on the Left* (1925). The same flavor was found in the essays *Shandygaff* (1918) and in the poems *The Rocking Horse* (1919) and *Chimney Smoke* (1921). In his later novels, including *Human Being* (1932), *Kitty Foyle* (1939), and *Thorofare* (1942), he turned to realistic themes, but continued his reflective, witty style in such books as *The Old Mandarin* (1947), *The Ironing Board* (1949), *The Man Who Made Friends with Himself* (1949), and a collection of verse, *Gentlemen's Relish* (1955).

MORLEY, EDWARD WILLIAMS, 1838–1923, U.S. scientist, was born in Newark, N.J., and studied at Williams College. He was professor of natural history and chemistry at Western Reserve University, 1869–1906. He studied variations in atmospheric oxygen content; determined the exact ratio in which oxygen and hydrogen unite by weight to form water; and invented a new kind of manometer to measure the pressure and thermal expansion of air. With Albert A. Michelson he developed the interferometer.

MORLEY, JOHN, 1st Viscount Morley of Blackburn, 1838–1923, English government official, was born in Blackburn and was educated at Cheltenham and at Lincoln College, Oxford. He first became known as a writer and journalist, editing the *Fortnightly Review*, 1867–82, the *Pall Mall Gazette*, 1880–83, and *Macmillan's Magazine*, 1883–85, and publishing the biographies *Edmund Burke* (1867), *Voltaire* (1872), and *Diderot and the Encyclopaedists* (1878). He was a member of parliament, 1883–95, 1896–1908, and served as chief secretary for Ireland, 1886 and 1892–95. He was chief secretary for India, 1905–10, and lord president of the council of state, 1910–14, a position he resigned (because of his pacifist convictions) when Great Britain entered World War II. His other writings include the critical *Studies in Literature* (1891) and *Recollections* (1917).

MORLEY, municipal borough, N central England, Yorkshire County, West Riding; 4 miles SSW of Leeds, with which it is connected by a railroad. Morley has manufactures of woolen and leather goods, glass, and textile machinery. Coal mines and stone quarries are nearby. The borough was incorporated in 1885. Pop. (1951) 39,783.

MORMON, a member of a religious body comprising two main groups—the Church of Jesus Christ of Latter-day Saints and the Reorganized Church of Jesus Christ of Latter-day Saints—and five smaller sects. The founder was Joseph Smith, a farmer's son born in 1805 in Sharon, Vt. Taken to Palmyra, N.Y., as a young lad, he became deeply interested in religion. According to Mormon doctrine, in 1820 he had a vision of the Father and the Son (the First Vision) and later he was visited by an angel (an ancient resurrected American prophet, Moroni) who revealed to him the whereabouts of an ancient record that he later obtained and translated into English as the Book of Mormon. See SMITH, JOSEPH.

Book of Mormon. Smith claimed that this record, engraved on plates of gold, contained the history of the ancient peoples of America. As a means of translating the record, the angel also gave him the Urim and Thummin (Lev. 8:8; Neh. 7:65), described as two transparent stones set in the rim of a bow and attached to a breastplate similar to that worn by Aaron. The compilers of this record are said to have

UNION PACIFIC R.R.

Los Angeles is the site of the largest Mormon temple ever built. The temple, much influenced by the architecture of the Mayas, is surmounted by a statue of the angel Moroni.

been Mormon and his son, Moroni; the latter hid the record in the Hill Cumorah, near Manchester, N.Y., where its presence was revealed to Joseph Smith in 1823; it was translated into English between 1827 and 1829 and published in 1830. Of several theories advanced as to the origin of the book by those who opposed Joseph Smith, none has been generally accepted.

Early Trials. In 1829, together with Oliver Cowdery, Smith received the priesthood, or divine authority, under the hands of John the Baptist, Peter, James, and John; by that authority he founded the Church of Jesus Christ of Latter-day Saints at Fayette, N.Y., in 1830. He soon moved to Kirtland, Ohio, where he was joined by Sidney Rigdon (1830) and Brigham Young (1832). The presidency was established in 1833, the apostolate of 12 in 1835, and the foreign mission in 1837. In Kirtland a temple was built and a bank was founded, but the latter failed. Rigdon and Smith were forced to flee to Missouri where a colony had been founded in 1831. Feeling against the Mormons became so intense that Gov. Lilburn W. Boggs of Missouri issued an order for their expulsion or extermination; 12,000 persons, driven from Missouri during the winter of 1839, took refuge in Illinois. The town of Commerce, Ill., was bought, its name changed to Nauvoo (1840), and a charter obtained. Smith was mayor of the town and commander in chief of the Nauvoo Legion, and the city council was controlled by the Mormons. Religious propaganda brought large numbers to the town; 1,614 persons came from Great Britain alone in 1842. Nauvoo was soon the largest settlement in the state.

The Mormon church organization aroused anxiety and widespread antagonism among those who recognized its strength. A revelation on "celestial marriage" is said to have been received by Smith about this time, although it was not published until 1852. In 1844 the Nauvoo *Expositor* was started by former Mormons for the purpose of "exposing" Mormonism and its founder, and after one number was issued its office and equipment were destroyed by order of the city council. This act brought opposition to a head; Joseph Smith and his brother, Hyrum, were arrested and placed in jail in Carthage. There they were shot by a mob while awaiting trial, June 27, 1844.

Leadership of Brigham Young. At a special conference of the church held in August, 1844, Brigham Young was sustained as leader by the united vote of the members; this action was repeated at the regular conference in October, 1844 (See YOUNG, BRIGHAM). In 1860 Joseph Smith III, a son of the founder, became president of the Reorganized church, which had been formed in 1852.

The Nauvoo charter was repealed in 1845, and during the next year the Mormons were driven from the city. They journeyed across the plains and settled near the Great Salt Lake. While crossing the plains they furnished the U.S. government a battalion of 500 men for the war with Mexico. Salt Lake City was founded in 1847. After the treaty with Mexico the Mormons tried to enter the Union as the State of Deseret. Their commonwealth was admitted in 1850 as the Territory of Utah, and Young was appointed governor. From 1852, when the revelation on "celestial marriage" (including a vision of Joseph Smith in 1843 which permitted plural marriage) was made public, to 1890 when the church forbade the practice, Utah was in conflict with the federal authorities. In 1862 a congressional enactment made polygamy punishable by fine and imprisonment; and when the laws against plural marriage were declared constitutional the Mormon church forbade the practice by proclamation of Pres. Wilford Woodruff in 1890.

Church tenets and Organization. The theoretical foundation for most of the Mormon sects is the same. The Bible, Book of Mormon, and Doctrine and Covenants form the basis for a belief that looks for a continuation of revelation and miracles, an American Zion, a millennium, and the palingenesis or rebirth of the earth under Christ's rule. Universal tolerance of other faiths, the literal resurrection of the body, baptism by immersion and (by proxy) for the dead, are Mormon tenets. Industry and payment of debts are insisted on, and the social instinct and co-operative spirit are well developed.

Two orders of priesthood exist—the higher is that of Melchizedek; the lower, that of Aaron. To the former belong apostles, high priests, patriarchs, seventies, elders, and bishops; to the latter, priests, teachers, and deacons. The first presidency—the president and two counselors—forms the highest authority, followed by the 12 apostles and the seventies. These bodies are divided into stakes, which are subdivided into wards. Each stake has a president and two counselors; each ward, a bishop and two counselors, priests, teachers, and deacons.

In 1951 David O. McKay was elected ninth president of the Church of Jesus Christ of Latter-day Saints; headquarters are in Salt Lake City. The Reorganized church since 1904 has had its headquarters in Independence, Missouri. Its presidents have been Joseph Smith III (1860–1914), son of the Mormon founder, and his descendants: Frederick Smith (1914–46), Israel Smith (1946–58), and presently William Wallace Smith (1958–).

The Mormon Tabernacle Choir since 1932 has broadcast regularly a Sunday morning worship service over a national radio network. Mormon temples have been erected in Utah, Idaho, Arizona, California, Hawaii, Canada, Switzerland, New Zealand, and England. More than 5,000 missionaries are assigned to missions in North America, South America, Europe, the Far East, and the islands of the Pacific Ocean. They serve for two years or more at their own expense as proselytes and teachers of the Mormon faith. The Salt Lake City headquarters reported a membership of over 2,000,000 (1965). The Reorganized church had a membership of about 165,000 (1963). About 70 per cent of Utah's population is Mormon. JOSEPH ANDERSON

BIBLIOG.–P. Nibley, *Brigham Young: The Man and His Work* (1936); J. F. Smith, *Teachings of the Prophet Joseph Smith* (1938); A. Jensen, *Encyclopedic History of the Church of Latter-day Saints* (1941); M. Harmer, *Story of the Mormon Pioneers* (1943); G. H. Durham, *Joseph Smith, Prophet Statesman* (1944); J. Smith, Jr., trans., *Book of Mormon* (ed. 1944); F. Brodie, *No Man Knows My History* (1945); T. F. O'Dea, *Mormons*, (1957); R. B. West, *Kingdom of the Saints* (1957); W. Mulder, ed., *Homeward to Zion* (1957), *Among the Mormons* (1958).

MORMON TRAIL, the route followed by the Mormons in 1847 from the Missouri River to Great Salt Lake. The Mormon Trail started from the site of modern Omaha, Neb., on the west bank of the Missouri. It followed the Oregon Trail along the north bank of the Platte River to Fort Laramie and across modern Wyoming to Fort Bridger. There it left the Oregon Trail to continue southwestward to the valley of the Great Salt Lake in present Utah. The route was used until about 1859.

MORNAY, PHILIPPE DE, seigneur du Plessis-Marly, known as Duplessis-Mornay, 1549–1623, French Huguenot leader, was born in Buhy, Normandy, and studied at Heidelberg and Pavia. Escaping the St. Bartholomew Massacre, 1572, he spent a year in England and returned to France to join the army of Henry of Navarre. De Mornay was Henry's diplomatic agent in England and the Low Countries, 1577–82, and later became governor of Saumur, where he founded a Protestant university in 1593. About 1588 De Mornay became the Protestant leader of France and earned the sobriquet "the Huguenot pope." He retired from court life when Henry renounced Protestantism, 1593, and was removed from Saumur by Louis XIII, 1621. He wrote theological works and *Memoires* (2 vols. 1624–25).

MORNING-GLORY, an annual or perennial twining herb of the morning-glory family, *Convolvu-*

laceae. Approximately 400 species of morning-glory are included in the genus *Ipomoea*, and a few are found in the genus *Argyreia.* These cultivated plants have heart-shaped leaves and a profusion of trumpet-shaped flowers that usually close by noon. Morning-glories are easily trained to trellises and fences and often are used to cover unsightly objects. Some of the most beautiful morning-glories were developed in Japan and were called imperials or emperors. By 1830 the cultivation of this plant was a popular hobby there, and a single rare seed often commanded a high price. Packaged Japanese morning-glory seeds usually consist of numerous strains with a wide variation in color. *Ipomoea*, adaptable to a wide variety of surroundings, is distributed throughout the world. The common morning-glory, *I. purpurea*, is an annual vine found so profuse in fields and along roadsides as to be considered a weed. See IPOMOEA.

MORNY, DUC CHARLES AUGUSTE LOUIS JOSEPH DE, 1811–65, French political leader, was the natural son of Hortense Beauharnais and Auguste Charles Joseph, comte de Flahaut, and was a half-brother of Napoleon III. He fought in Algeria, 1834–35, and returned to France to speculate in several commercial undertakings. He became a deputy, 1842, and managed the coup d'état of Louis Napoleon in 1851. He was minister of interior, 1851–52, president of the *corps législatif* (as the lower house of the legislature was then called), 1854–65, and ambassador to Russia, 1856–57.

MORO, ANTONIO, also known as Anthonis Mor and Sir Anthony More, 1512?–?76, Dutch portrait painter, was born in Utrecht, and studied with Jan van Scorel. About 1550 Charles V summoned him to Madrid to do portraits of the royal family. In England Moro executed several paintings of Mary Tudor, queen of England. He was commissioned by Philip II of Spain to paint the portraits of members of his court. Moro was a naturalist, but his ability to portray personality gave each portrait an individuality. Others of his portraits are of Alvarez de Toledo, duke of Alva, Archduchess Margaret of Parma, and Alessandro Farnese.

MORO, member of a Malayan people of the Philippines, living mostly in the coastal areas of S and W Mindanao, S Palawan, and the Sulu Archipelago. The Moros are similar to the other Malayan peoples of the Philippines, both racially and culturally, but they were converted to Islam by Moslem traders and teachers who came to the islands in the fourteenth century and after. One group of Moros, variously known as Samal Moros and as sea gypsies, is not indigenous to the Philippines, having come from the Malay Peninsula in outrigger canoes.

The Moros established powerful kingdoms, notably Sulu and Magindanao, which became wealthy from their trade with far-flung places. When the Spaniards invaded the Philippines in the sixteenth century, they met with fierce resistance from the Moros, who were never effectively subdued during more than three centuries of Spanish occupation.

The Moros are essentially an agricultural people, but they are also skillful fishermen and pearl divers. They once had a reputation as smugglers and pirates. Moro metalworkers have long been famous for their bronze and brass casts and for their steel blades—krises, campilans, barongs, and "beheading knives."

Although the culture of the Moros remained largely similar to that of the other Malayan peoples of the Philippines, original customs were abandoned whenever they came into conflict with Islam. Polygyny and slavery, probably introduced from India, flourished under Muslim influence. Social differentiation also was accentuated after the conversion of the Moros to Islam. The military and political power of the sultans of Sulu and Magindanao vanished before the arrival of the Americans in the Philippines.

MORO, city, N Oregon, seat of Sherman County; on the Union Pacific Railroad and U.S. highway 97; 93 miles E of Portland. Moro is situated in the Oregon wheat country. A cereal grains experiment station is maintained there. Pop. (1960) 327.

MOROCCO, a constitutional monarchy in NW Africa; bounded by the Mediterranean Sea on the N, Algeria on the E and SE, Spanish Sahara on the SW, and the Atlantic Ocean on the W; area 171,305 sq. mi.; pop. (1961 census) 11,598,070. Rabat is the official capital and the principal residence of the king, who occasionally resides also in the other traditional capitals—Fez (Fès), Marrakech, and Meknès. See map in Atlas, Vol. 20.

PHYSICAL FACTORS

Morocco may be divided into five natural regions; the Rif and Atlas Mountain ranges, the coastal lowlands, the alluvial plains of the Haouz and Sous in the southwest, the central plateaus, and the arid tablelands in the south and east. The Rif parallels the Mediterranean coast and is separated from the Atlas by the Taza Gap. The Atlas is made up of three parallel ranges running generally southwest-northeast—the Middle Atlas, the High Atlas (Grand Atlas), and the Anti-Atlas. The Djebel Toubkal, or Toubka (13,665 ft.), in the High Atlas is the highest peak in North Africa. The coastal lowlands, along the Atlantic, include a series of three fertile plains—the Rharb, with Port Lyautey as its principal center; the Chaouia, around Casablanca; and the Doukkala, around Mazagan and Safi. The irrigated alluvial plains of the Haouz, with Marrakech as main center, and the Sous Depression, near Agadir, are in a semiarid region. The central plateaus occupy the area between the Atlas and the coastal lowlands; and the tablelands mark the transition from the Atlas to the Sahara.

The short Oum er Rbia, Sebou, Bou Regreg, Tensift, Lucus, Moulouya, and Sous rivers, rising in the Atlas and the Rif, drain northern and western Morocco. The streams rising in the south and southeast Atlas end their courses in Sahara Desert basins and are dry in most seasons. The major agricultural areas are along the lower river courses of the north and west. Extensive drainage and irrigation projects affect more than 2 million acres. The rivers of Morocco are not navigable for large vessels.

Morocco north of the Atlas has a Mediterranean climate—subtropical with dry summers. The summers of the coastal areas, influenced by the ocean, are cooler than those of the interior. A semiarid subtropical steppe climate prevails south of the Atlas near the Sahara. Average rainfall ranges from 35 inches in the western Rif and Middle Atlas to less than 10 inches near the Sahara.

Location Map of Morocco

Morocco

Mediterranean broadleaf scrub woodland, including cork oaks, and junipers, is the dominant vegetation in the north. Green oaks and cedars are found on the wet northern slopes of the mountains, and esparto grass characterizes the eastern plateau region. The area bordering the Sahara has mainly desert shrubs and wasteland.

Social and Economic Factors

Culture. The majority of the population is concentrated along the Atlantic and Mediterranean coasts. The native population is basically Berber and belongs to many different tribes, but the Arab invasions in the seventh and eleventh centuries resulted in the adoption of the Arabic language and the Islamic religion. The 180,000 Jews and 400,000 French and other Europeans live chiefly in the urban areas.

PRINCIPAL CITIES

City	Population 1951-1952 Census	1961 Census
Casablanca	682,388	961,000
Marrakech	215,312	242,000
Rabat (capital)	156,209	225,000
Fez	179,372	216,000
Meknès	140,380	177,000
Tangier	180,000 *	142,000
Oujda	80,546	129,000
Tetuán	100,000 *	101,000

*1956 est.

Although illiteracy is high, educational reforms begun by French and Moroccan authorities after World War I resulted in a high annual increase in school enrollment. In 1961 there were 796,000 students enrolled in elementary schools, 59,000 in secondary schools, and 4,700 in institutions of higher education. Of this total about 80,000 were European students—chiefly French. Postgraduate institutions include the Center of Advanced Scientific Studies, founded in 1940, and the Institute of Advanced Moroccan Studies, founded in 1920 by Marshal Louis Hubert Lyautey—both in Rabat. In addition to schools of the Western type, there are many Moslem schools, attached to mosques, in which education of the traditional type is offered; in these more than half the Moroccan students are enrolled. The most famous Moslem institution is the Kairouine University in Fez, which was one of the leading centers of learning in the world during the Middle Ages.

Economy. Agriculture is the chief industry of Morocco, engaging about 70 per cent of the population and supplying about 45 per cent of the exports. The dominant crops are wheat, barley, maize, and other cereals, citrus fruit, vegetables, olives and other oleaginous plants, almonds, dates, and grapes. The cultivation of rice, flax, sisal, cotton, tobacco, and sugar beets was developed after World War II. Morocco's crop production is variable because of the cyclical occurrence of dry years and locust plagues. The important livestock industry is largely native owned. In 1962 there were about 11 million sheep, 5 million goats, and 2 million cattle.

Forests of cork oak and wild palmetto are exploited on a large scale. In 1961 Morocco exported 32,359 tons of canned sardines—18 per cent of the total fish catch. Safi, on the Atlantic coast, is the leading fishing port of North Africa and one of the world's largest sardine fishing ports.

Mining is Morocco's second largest industry and most of its production is exported. Phosphate is the principal mineral mined and the leading export of the country; production amounted to about 8 million tons in 1961 and was surpassed only by that of the United States. The phosphate mining centers of Khouribga and Louis Gentil are connected by railroad with the ports of Safi and Casablanca. The

EWING GALLOWAY

Tractor-drawn wagon is loaded with sacks of grain during harvest time in Morocco. Wheat, barley, and other cereals are dominant crops in this largely agricultural country.

1961 production of other important minerals included 1,462,000 tons of iron ore, mined near Aït Amar; 410,000 tons of anthracite coal from Djérada; 457,000 tons of manganese from Ouanizarhte and Bou Arfa; 128,000 tons of lead, chiefly from the Oujda area; 70,000 tons of zinc; 82,000 tons of barite; 12,900 tons of cobalt; and 80,000 tons of crude petroleum from the Rharb Plain near Petitjean.

The principal manufactures of Morocco are handicrafts and processed fish and agricultural products, flour, vegetable oil, and leather. Other manufactured products are cement, brick, tile, textiles, and footwear. The production of superphosphates for fertilizer is the only important industry based on the country's mineral resources. Although the handicraft industry dates from the Middle Ages, modern industries were not developed in Morocco until the establishment of the French protectorate.

Casablanca, the principal seaport of Morocco, handles approximately 70 per cent of the total port traffic, which amounted to 13,718,000 tons in 1960. Other major ports are Tangier, Safi, Port Lyautey, Fédala, Agadir, Mogador, and Mazagan. Morocco in 1962 had 1,130 miles of railways, 40 per cent electrified. The main line extends from Marrakech north to Casablanca, Rabat, and Port Lyautey, then east to Fez, Taza, Oujda, and the Algerian border. Other important lines operate from Tangier to Meknès and from Oujda to Colomb-Béchar in Algeria. Many short lines connect inland mining and agricultural centers with coastal cities. The well developed highway system of Morocco totaled 8,250 miles in 1962, of which approximately 4,250 miles were primary paved roads. Most of the airlines serving Morocco are French owned. The principal airports are at Casablanca, Tangier, Tetuán, Meknès, Oujda, Marrakech, Rabat, and Agadir.

Administration and History

Government. Morocco is a constitutional monarchy headed by a king who holds supreme civil and religious authority. A new constitution in 1962 authorized a bicameral legislature with a house of representatives elected by direct popular vote, and a house of councilors elected by political authorities and special interest groups. The king appoints the prime minister and the cabinet ministers and has the right to dissolve parliament and approve legislation. The judicial system was organized in the early 1960's on the basis of the French and Islamic legal codes and French legal procedure. The country is divided into the five urban prefectures of Casablanca, Fez, Marrakech, Meknès, and Rabat and the 19 provinces of Agadir, Beni Mellal, Casablanca, Fez, Larache, Marrakech, Mazagan, Meknès, Nador, Ouanizarhte, Oujda, Rabat, Rif, Safi, Tafilalet, Tangier, Taza, Tetuán, and Xauen.

Pre-Islamic Period. Prehistoric remains found in Morocco include megalithic monuments of considerable interest, but little is known of the people who left them. The Berbers, a pastoral and agricultural people of Hamitic speech, settled in Morocco in early antiquity. Although they later mingled with

EWING GALLOWAY

Containers woven in Morocco are employed by these freight handlers at a Casablanca dock. Dar el Beida is the Arab name for Casablanca, northwest Africa's leading seaport.

Arab, Negro, Andalusian, and other elements, they continue to form the basis of the population and largely retain their identity in the mountainous areas of the Rif and the Atlas.

The Phoenicians established trading posts along the coast of northern Morocco where they were succeeded by the Carthaginians. About the sixth century B.C. Hanno led an expedition from Carthage to the west coast of Africa to modern Sierra Leone, and new trading posts were founded. The Carthaginians, however, effectively controlled only the ports, such as Rusaddir (Melilla), Tingis (Tangier), Lixus (Larache), and Shella (Salé), from which they traded with the tribes in the interior. The Berbers continued to live much as before the arrival of the Phoenicians and Carthaginians.

After the destruction of Carthage by the Romans in 146 B.C., Morocco was temporarily free of foreign influence, but under Emperor Claudius I, A.D. 42, the Romans extended their power to Morocco. Suetonius Paulinus organized the province of Mauretania Tingitana in northern Morocco, with Tingis as its capital. Later the Romans founded Volubilis as the capital of the interior, while Tingis remained the capital of the coastal area. Mauretania Tingitana produced wheat and its mines yielded iron, copper, and other metals. The Berbers, however, refused to submit and the Romans were unable to extend their control to southern Morocco. The towns did not prosper greatly and the introduction of Christianity increased internal unrest.

The Vandals, a Germanic tribe, overran northern Africa, taking Carthage in 439, and King Genseric founded a Vandal kingdom which included Morocco, Algeria, Tunisia, Tripolitania, Sardinia, and Corsica. The Berbers, however, were not significantly influenced by the Vandals, who paid little attention to Morocco. Belisarius, under the Byzantine Emperor Justinian I, captured Tangier and Ceuta in 533, but the Byzantines occupied only a few ports in Morocco. Their commercial and cultural influence, however, penetrated into the interior.

Islamic Period. After conquering Tunisia and founding Kairouan, the Arab leader Okba overran Algeria and entered Ceuta in 682. The conquest of Morocco was completed by Mussa ibn-Noceir and the country was annexed to the Ommiad caliphate of Baghdad in 709.

In spite of their initial resistance to the invaders, the Berbers mixed freely with the Arabs, who were but few in number. They readily accepted Islam, although they retained much of their original religion and culture. In 711 Tariq, a Berber, led the Saracens —largely Berbers—across the Strait of Gibraltar to invade Spain and France to Poitiers, where they were turned back by Charles Martel in 732.

The accession of the Abbasside dynasty in Baghdad marked the beginning of the dislocation of the Arab empire. Abd-er-Rahman I established the Ommiad Caliphate of Córdoba, which controlled most of Spain from 756 to 1031.

The Idrisids. In Morocco the separatist movement first took the form of the Kharijite heresy, but orthodoxy prevailed with the establishment of the Idrisid dynasty by Idris in 788. Idris, a descendant of the Prophet through his son Ali, had fled to Morocco after the defeat of the descendants of Ali by the Abbassides. He made Oulili (Volubilis) his capital and ruled until 793 when he was poisoned by agents of the Abbasside caliph of Baghdad, Haroun al-Rashid. He was buried in Moulay Idris, which became a holy city.

After a regency, Idris was succeeded in 804 by Idris II, his son by a Berber woman. Idris II organized the first central government of Morocco. In 808 he founded Fez, which soon rivaled Córdoba and Kairouine as one of the great cultural centers of Islam, its universities attracting scholars from the whole Moslem world.

The sons of Idris II divided the country and quarreled with the Fatimid dynasty of Egypt and the Ommiad dynasty of Spain. The Idrisids were defeated and replaced by short-lived Berber dynasties—the Meknassas, the Maghraouas, and the Berghouatas.

The Almoravides. In the eleventh century Morocco was invaded first by the Hilalians, nomadic Arabs from upper Egypt, and then by the Sanhajas, nomadic Berbers from the Adrar (in modern Mauritania). The Sanhajas adhered to a very rigorous religious movement that eventually gave rise to the Almoravide dynasty. Led by Yusuf ibn-Tashfin, they conquered southern Morocco, making Marrakech their capital. Ibn-Tashfin then undertook the conquest of northern Morocco. In Spain the Moslem emirs who ruled the country after the division of the Ommiad caliphate of Córdoba were hard pressed by Alfonso VI, king of León and Castile, and asked the Almoravides for help. Ibn-Tashfin landed in Spain, routed the Christians at the Battle of Zellaca in 1086, and annexed the emirates to his empire. Returning to Morocco, he made Fez the capital of an empire that extended from Spain to Senegal.

The Almoravide Dynasty marked the beginning of a great civilization. Under Ali ibn-Yusuf, who succeeded ibn-Tashfin in 1106, the arts flourished and found their expression in architectural masterpieces such as the Great Mosque in Tlemcen and the Karoubine Mosque in Fez. Economic prosperity followed the construction of important irrigation works in Spain and Morocco.

The Almohades. While the Almoravides became decadent, the Almohade movement, based on an ascetic unitarian religion, developed among the Masmudas, a Berber tribe from the Atlas. Their leader ibn-Tumart, a scholar who had studied in the most famous universities of the time—in Córdoba, Cairo, and Damascus—laid the foundations of a new dynasty.

He was succeeded by Abd-al-Mumin, who gained control of Morocco and Spain and then extended his power to Algeria, Tunisia, Tripolitania, and the Sudan. The Almohades, controlling the gold route of the Sudan, became wealthy and Moroccan civilization flourished.

The Almohade period was the most brilliant in Moroccan history. Although it lasted little more than a century, 1147–1269, it saw great developments in art and architecture, in philosophy and medicine. It was one of the major factors in the shaping of Spanish civilization and the chief agent for the transmission of Greek philosophy and science to western Europe. The geographer al-Idrisi and the philosophers ibn-Tufail and Averroës lived during this period.

Abd-al-Mumin's successors, abu-Yusuf Yaqub and al-Mansur, continued his work. The reign of al-Mansur is generally considered the apogee of Moorish civilization. During that period agriculture, industry, and commerce prospered and the Almohade fleet, one of the largest in the world, was mistress of the

Mediterranean. The achievements of Hispano-Mauresque art were notable; among them were the Giralda in Seville and the Koutoubia in Marrakech. The city of Rabat was founded.

The later Almohades were faced with difficulties in the Sudan and in Spain. They were defeated at the Battle of Navas de Tolosa, 1212, and Córdoba was taken by Ferdinand III of Castile, 1236.

The Merinides. Faced with widespread rebellion, the Almohades asked assistance from the Merinides, who represented a small group of Zenata Berber tribes in eastern Morocco. The Merinides took advantage of the situation to oust the Almohades. Abu-Yusuf-Yaqub acceded to the throne in 1258 and gained control of southern Spain and the Tlemcen area (in modern Algeria) in addition to Morocco.

The Merinide period was comparatively prosperous in spite of warring with neighboring countries. New universities and architectural treasures appeared in Fez, Marrakech, and Meknès, the Merinide capitals. Among the famous men of this period were the explorer ibn-Batuta and the historian ibn-Khaldun. By the end of the fifteenth century, however, the Merinides were losing their last possessions in Spain. Granada, the last Moorish stronghold there, fell in 1492. Most Muslims were expelled from Spain, those who remained becoming known as Moriscos.

In the sixteenth century the decadent Merinide dynasty was displaced by the Beni Outta Dynasty, also of Berber origin, which allowed the Portuguese and the Spaniards to acquire bases on Moroccan soil. At the same time the independence of the country was endangered by Turkish conquest of Algeria and Tunisia.

The Saadians. The nomadic tribes soon reacted against the encroachments on Moroccan independence permitted by the sedentary tribes under the Merinides. Nomads from the Sous, in southern Morocco, established the Saadian Dynasty after taking Marrakech in 1520 and Fez in 1548. The Portuguese were expelled from Agadir in 1541, retaining only Mazagan, and the Saadians won a decisive victory over King Sebastian of Portugal at Alcazarquivir in 1578. Sultan Ahmed al-Mansur, who reigned from 1578 to 1603, extended his power to the Sudan, obtaining control of Timbuktu.

The Alaouites. The Saadians were displaced by the Alaouites, an Arab dynasty from Sijilmassa in the Tafilalet, which is still the ruling dynasty. Ismail, who reigned from 1672 to 1727, enlarged Meknès, one of the three capitals, which was said to rival Versailles. An authoritarian ruler, he subdued the pirates who had founded an independent republic in Salé and forced the English and the Spaniards from their bases in Morocco. He was careful, however, to maintain good relations with France.

After Ismail's death Morocco reverted to anarchy. In the following century Sultan Abd-er-Rahman restored order among the tribes, but attacked the French in Algeria. His defeat at the Battle of Isly in 1844 opened Morocco to European influence. Spain took Tetuán in 1860 and England began economic penetration of the country.

Sultan Hasan attempted to reorganize the country and reached an agreement with France, but after his death in 1894 the excesses of his successor, Abd-al-Aziz IV, led to widespread rebellion. France, Spain, England, Germany, Italy, and the United States competed for favorable treatment of their trade in the area. In 1905 Kaiser William II of Germany attempted a military intervention in Morocco, but an international conference held at Algeciras, Spain, in 1906 recognized French and Spanish zones of influence. The French intervened in Morocco in 1907 after a massacre of Europeans in Casablanca, and Gen. Albert d'Amade occupied the Chaouïa. Abd-al-Aziz, accused of having sold Morocco to the French, was forced to abdicate, 1908, in favor of his brother Abd-al-Hafiz. In 1911 Germany sent a gunboat to Agadir in violation of the Algeciras Conference, but was forced to withdraw.

On Mar. 30, 1912, the sultan of Morocco signed the Treaty of Fez, placing Morocco under a French protectorate. The Franco-Spanish Convention of Nov. 27, 1912, established a Spanish protectorate over part of the country. On Dec. 18, 1923, an international zone was set up in Tangier by France, Spain, and Great Britain.

Louis Hubert Gonzalve Lyautey, who had already distinguished himself under Joseph Simon Gallieni, was nominated resident-general in charge of the French administration. Avoiding military force, he preferred to use political action. An admirer of Moroccan civilization, he respected local customs and was able to restore order rapidly by concluding agreements with the tribal chiefs. By the beginning of World War I the situation had become stable enough to permit recruitment of Moroccan troops to fight in France. In 1921 Abd-el-Krim led a rebellion in the Rif Mountains; he surrendered in 1926 after stubborn resistance. Having achieved the complete unification of the country for the first time in history, Marshal Lyautey left Morocco in 1926.

After World War I, Europeans—mainly French, Spanish, and Italian—settled in Morocco, where they lived apart from the native Berbers and Jews. The French developed roads, railroads, airlines, mines, industries, and ports such as Casablanca.

During World War II, Adm. François Darlan took over the French administration of Morocco in the name of the puppet Vichy regime but was assassinated a few days later, and Morocco rallied the Free French led by Gen. Charles de Gaulle. Moroccan troops distinguished themselves in the campaigns of Tunisia, Sicily, Italy, and France.

After the war an independence movement developed among the European-educated upper class. Full independence was gained through successive steps and was accompanied by internal troubles involving Arabs, Berbers, Jews, and French alike. Finally El Glaoui, the pasha of Marrakech and leader of the Berber tribes, made his submission to the Arab leader Sultan Mohammed V. In 1955 the traditional sherifian government was replaced by a cabinet system. In 1956 France terminated the Treaty of Fez; Spain also ended its protectorate; and an agreement among France, Spain, Great Britain, Italy, the United States, Belgium, the Netherlands, Sweden, and Portugal abolished the international status of Tangier. On November 12 of that year the national consultative assembly of 76 members, selected by the sultan, was inaugurated. The months following independence were marked by new disorders during which many followers of El Glaoui were killed. The title of the sultan was changed to king in 1957. Shortly thereafter, Morocco sought evacuation of U.S. and French air bases. Withdrawal of French forces was completed in 1961. The same year, after the death of Mohammed V, the new king, Hassan II, urged the enactment of a constitution which was ratified in 1962, making Morocco a constitutional monarchy. Morocco accepted Soviet military aid and also signed agreements with France on economic and technical co-operation. In 1963 Moroccan and Algerian forces clashed in border disputes.

Bibliography

History and Culture: B. Meakin, *Moorish Empire* (1889); C. E. Andrews, *Old Morocco* (1923); E. Westermark, *Ritual and Belief in Morocco* (1926); D. E. Ashford, *Political Change in Morocco* (1961).

Description and Travel: E. de Amicis, *Morocco: Its People and Places* (2 vols. 1908); F. Ossendowski, *Fire of Desert Folk* (1926); R. B. Cunningham-Graham, *Mogreb-el-Acksa* (1930); P. Loti, *Morocco* (ed. 1930); P. Turnbull, *Black Barbary* (1935); S. Sitwell, *Mauretania: Warrior, Man, and Woman* (1940); P. Mayne, *Alleys of Marrakesh* (1953); J. L. Miege, *Morocco* (1953); O. H. Warne, comp., *Morocco* (1953); Ahmed Sefrioui, *Morocco* (1958).

MORON. See Mental Deficiency.

MORONE, GIOVANNI DI, 1509–80, Italian Roman Catholic prelate, was born in Milan, was appointed bishop of Modena by Clement VII, 1529, and named cardinal by Paul III, 1542. Noted for his liberal views (he counseled charity in dealing with the Lutherans and believed the Protestants were justified in many of their complaints about the Roman Catholic clergy), Morone was accused of heresy by Paul IV and imprisoned, 1557–60. Pius IV reopened the case, 1560, and found the cardinal innocent of all charges.

MORONI, GAETANO, 1802–83, Italian author of the *Dizionario di erudizione storico-ecclesiastica* (1840–61), was born in Rome. He served as secretary to Pope Gregory XVI and Pope Pius IX. The *Dizionario* is a rich source of information on the pontifical court, the administration of the papal states, and kindred subjects. As Gregory XVI's private secretary, Moroni is said to have written at least 100,000 letters.

MORONI, GIOVANNI BATTISTA, or Giambattista Moroni, 1525?–78, Italian artist of the Brescian school, was born in Albino and received his training from Moretto da Brescia. He became one of the finest Renaissance portrait painters, and his work won the praise of Titian and influenced the work of Sir Anthony Van Dyck. Among Moroni's portraits are *Titian's Schoolmaster*, *Portrait of a Man*, *Portrait of a Lady*, *Man in Black*, *Pope Pius IV*, and *Scholar*.

MORONOBU, HISHIKAWA, 1625?–?95, Japanese artist who originated ukiyoye (floating world) print making, a genre tradition that depicted people at their everyday chores, military scenes, actors, and beautiful women. An embroidery worker and pattern designer of dresses, Moronobu began to design single-sheet black and white prints, albums of engravings, and picture books, opening up a new artistic field—the application of the painting technique to printing. Moronobu was a painter as well as an engraver; among his best known paintings are the screens *House in Yoshiwara* and *Scene at the Nakamura Theatre*, both in the Boston Museum of Art.

MORPHEUS, in Greek and Roman mythology, the god of dreams and the son of Hypnos (Somnus), god of sleep.

MORPHINE, an alkaloid of opium and its chief active ingredient (see Opium). Morphine is a bitter-tasting white powder that is soluble in water. It is used medically to relieve pain, and may be injected or taken orally. When morphine is administered, reactions to pain such as anxiety and fear fail to appear and the person often acquires a sense of well-being out of proportion to his general health. Because it acts to allay anxiety and fear, morphine is sometimes given before surgery (see Anesthesia). Tolerance for the drug is rapidly acquired, however, and addiction is the gravest danger from its use. Sale of morphine in the United States is under control of the U.S. Bureau of Narcotics. (See Drug Addiction; Narcotic.) Morphine poisoning can result from an overdose of the drug. Coma, slow respiration, and constricted pupils are symptoms of this toxic state, and death results from respiratory failure. Nalorphine has been found highly useful in combating acute morphine poisoning. See Codeine; Drug; Meperidine; Methadone; Nalorphine.

MORPHOLOGY, a subdivision of biology that deals with plant and animal structure as a whole. Other subdivisions such as anatomy, histology, and cytology often require dissection and technical equipment to ascertain differences in structure whereas morphology requires only shrewd observation and description.

One of the aims of the morphologist is the investigation of the relationships that exist in the plant and animal kingdoms, and the discrimination between adapted characters and those inherited from a supposed common ancestor. Morphologists, along with many other scientists, seek a means of accurately classifying living things. They use their science as one of the simplest and most obvious methods of placing organisms in their respective phylogenetic groups. Such work is sometimes termed comparative morphology. Both plant and animal morphological data are helpful in other fields—as in cross-pollination for the production of successful hybrids, and in the production of effective insecticides. See Botany; Plant; Zoology.

MORPHY, PAUL CHARLES, 1837–84, U.S. chess player, was born in New Orleans, La., and at the age of 12 was considered the amateur chess champion of that city. He was graduated from the University of Louisiana's law school, 1857, and attended the first American Chess Conference in the same year, defeating the assembled players. In Europe, 1858–59, he defeated the foremost chess experts, including the German champion, Adolph Anderssen, and established himself as the world's chess champion. He returned to New Orleans to practice law, but he was unsuccessful. He played his last recorded game of chess in 1869, and during his last years was mentally deranged. Morphy was famed for his ability at blindfold chess.

MORRILL, JUSTIN SMITH, 1810–98, U.S. legislator, was born in Strafford, Vt., and was educated in the public schools. He was a Republican member of the House of Representatives, 1855–67, and of the Senate, 1867–98. In 1857 he introduced a bill for the establishment of state colleges for the teaching of agriculture and the mechanic arts; the bill became law in 1862. This act and the second Morrill Act, 1890, gave $25,000 annually to all land-grant colleges. He wrote the Morrill Tariff Act of 1861, and introduced and was a principal champion of the tariff acts of 1862 and 1864. See Tariff, *Free Trade After* 1860.

MORRILL, LOT MYRICK, 1812–83, U.S. cabinet officer, was born in Belgrade, Me. Originally a Democrat, he joined the Republican party in 1856. He was governor of Maine, 1858–60, U.S. senator, 1861–76, and secretary of the treasury in Pres. Ulysses S. Grant's cabinet, 1876–77.

MORRILL ACTS. See Agricultural Education, *The Morrill Act;* Land-Grant College.

MORRILTON, city, central Arkansas, seat of Conway County; on the Arkansas River, the Missouri Pacific Railroad, and U.S. highway 64; 40 miles NW of Little Rock. Morrilton's industries include meat processing, cotton raising, lumber and cottonseed oil milling, and dairying. Petit Jean State Park is close at hand. The city was settled during the 1870's. Pop. (1960) 5,997.

MORRIS, CLARA, 1848–1925, U.S. actress, was born in Toronto, Canada, the daughter of Charles La Montagne and Sarah Jane Proctor, who took the name Morrison when she found her marriage to be bigamous. Clara was raised in Cleveland, Ohio, where she received her early stage training. She was star of Augustin Daly's 5th Avenue Company in New York, 1870–73, then of Palmer's Union Square Theater from 1873 to her retirement in the mid-1890's. Popular in emotional roles, she played in *Man and Wife*, *L'Article 47*, *Miss Multon*, *Camille*, and *The New Magdalen*.

MORRIS, GOUVERNEUR, 1752–1816, U.S. patriot, was born in Morrisania, N.Y., was graduated from King's College (Columbia University), 1768, studied law, and was admitted to the bar when he was 19. He was opposed to the revolutionary party but in May, 1775, became a member of the New York provincial congress and took a prominent part in its activities, continuing to oppose a rupture with Great Britain. After reconciliation became clearly impossible, he worked zealously for the patriot cause even though some members of his family were loyalists.

Morris was a member of the convention that drafted the New York state constitution, 1776, and served in the Continental Congress, 1778–79. Early in 1778 he was appointed to a committee to visit the Continental Army at Valley Forge; he spent most of the winter in the camp, where he formed a warm attachment for George Washington. In the Continental Congress Morris headed the committee appointed to confer with the British commissioners regarding Lord Frederick North's plan of reconciliation, 1778. Morris' *Observations on the American Revolution* (1779) gives his view of the causes of the war and an account of the discussion and correspondence with the British commissioners. He drafted the Congress' instructions to Benjamin Franklin when the latter was appointed minister to France and, as chairman of the committee to correspond with the American ministers abroad, drew up the report and instructions that formed the basis for the Peace Treaty of 1783.

Morris refused to promote in the Congress his state's claims to Vermont and was defeated in the election for Congress in 1779. He moved to Philadelphia, where he built up a large law practice. In 1780 he published in the *Pennsylvania Packet*, a series of "Essays on the Finance, Currency, and Internal Trade of the United States," which attracted the attention of Robert Morris (no relation of Gouverneur Morris). When Robert Morris became superintendent of finance, under the new government, 1781, he made the younger Morris his assistant, a position that the latter held until 1785. In 1783 Gouverneur Morris prepared for Congress a report on the value of foreign coins and a plan for an American coinage, in which the decimal system was employed.

In the Constitutional Convention of 1787 Morris took a Federalist position against the states' rights faction but, when outvoted, gave loyal support to the resulting document, and it was to him that the preparation of the final draft of the Constitution was entrusted. He spent several years in Europe on business matters after 1789 and served as minister to France, 1792–94. His diaries constitute an important record of the French Revolution. He then traveled in Europe, 1794–98, and on his return to the United States served in the U.S. Senate, 1800–03. Because of his extreme Federalist views he was not re-elected to the Senate. Disillusioned with the increasingly liberal trend of national politics, Morris spent the rest of his years in retirement. During the War of 1812 his hatred for the Republican regime then in power led him to support the Northern secession disunion movement. His last years were an unhappy end to a brilliant career. A. C. Morris edited *The Diary and Letters of Gouverneur Morris* (2 vols. 1888). His *Diary of the French Revolution* (1939) was edited by B. C. Davenport.

MORRIS, LEWIS, 1726–98, half brother of Gouverneur Morris, colonial American patriot, a signer of the Declaration of Independence, was born in Morrisania, N.Y., succeeded his father as lord of the manor, 1762, and became a leading opponent of British policy in the colonies. He served in the Continental Congress, 1775, became brigadier general in command of the militia of Westchester County, 1776, and returned to Congress to sign the Declaration. After the war he held several public offices in New York state.

MORRIS, ROBERT, 1734–1806, U.S. patriot and financier of the Revolutionary War, was born in or near Liverpool, England, came to America in 1748, became a partner in the Philadelphia shipping firm of [Thomas] Willing, Morris and Company in 1754, and acquired considerable wealth. In September, 1775, a contract was arranged between a secret committee of the Continental Congress and the firm of Willing and Morris for the importation of arms and ammunition. Shortly thereafter Morris became a member of the Congress; he was placed on the secret committee through whose hands much of the principal congressional business passed, and he later served on many other committees, including that to establish a navy. Yet he was long opposed to a complete break with England; in July, 1776, he voted against the Declaration of Independence, regarding it as premature. A month later he changed his mind and signed the document.

When, late in 1776, the approach of the British forced Congress to flee from Philadelphia to Baltimore, Morris remained behind and became the leading member of the committee upon whom the conduct of affairs there devolved. His operations included borrowing and advancing money, buying specie, and negotiating with the creditors of the government. There can be no doubt that he made large profits on these transactions, and although his conduct was honest and public-spirited throughout, the unfortunate mixture of public need and private opportunity exposed him to bitter criticism. But even after a limitation in the Pennsylvania Constitution forced his retirement from Congress in 1778 his financial relations with that body continued.

Morris was a member of the Pennsylvania assembly, 1778–79, 1780–81, and in 1781 was chosen by Congress to be superintendent of finance of the government. With the treasury empty, he borrowed money on his own credit to finance the continuation of the war. Through his efforts the war was brought to a successful conclusion, but he could not secure the revenue necessary to pay the public debt; his proposal for taxes on imports, land, and spirits met no response. He retired late in 1784 after carrying through the payment of the troops. He served again in the Pennsylvania assembly, 1785–86, and as a member of the Constitutional Convention, 1787, favored a strong central government. While a member of the U.S. Senate, 1789–95, his private business ventures came to disaster because of his extensive speculation in land. In December, 1797, he was arrested for debt and imprisoned, 1798–1801, being finally released under the federal bankruptcy law. He spent the rest of his life in retirement.

MORRIS, ROGER, 1727–94, British soldier and loyalist, was born in Yorkshire, England, and came to America with Edward Braddock's army in 1755, serving in the French and Indian War. He resigned from the army in 1764, married Mary Philipse, 1758, and about 1765 built the famous Morris (later Jumel) Mansion in New York City, used by George Washington as his headquarters for a time during the Revolution. Morris returned to England, 1775–77, reluctant to take arms on either side. He came back to America in 1777, and served as British inspector of claims of refugees. Mary Philipse Morris, 1730–1825, his wife and a famous New York heiress and beauty, was born in Philipse Manor House on the Hudson River. In 1776 she and her husband were attainted by the New York State legislature and their property confiscated. In 1783 the Morris family moved permanently to York, England. The Morris children, not included in the act of attainder that confiscated the estate, sold their rights to John Jacob Astor in 1809.

MORRIS, WILLIAM, 1834–96, English poet and artist, was born in Walthamstow, Essex. He was educated privately, and at Exeter College, Oxford, where he formed a lifelong friendship with Edward Burne-Jones. Influenced by the works of John Ruskin and Thomas Carlyle and by visits to France, 1854–55, Morris developed a deep enthusiasm for medieval architecture and craftsmanship and began the study of architecture. Under the influence of Dante Gabriel Rossetti he abandoned architecture for painting, and in 1857 with Burne-Jones set up a studio in London. Meanwhile he had written much imaginative and romantic poetry, published in the *Oxford and Cambridge* magazine (which he had founded in 1856). In 1858 his first major work, *The Defence of Guenevere*, appeared. In 1861 with Rossetti, Burne-Jones, and others he established a decorating firm in London. The company designed and built furniture and manufactured stained glass, wallpaper, and tapestries.

Morris was the moving spirit, and divided his energies between designing and the study of dyeing and other technical processes. Through his efforts to destroy ugliness in home decoration, considerable reform was effected in Victorian taste.

Morris continued his literary work, publishing *Life and Death of Jason* (1867) and *The Earthly Paradise* (3 vols. 1868–70). In 1872 he took up his residence at the ancient manor house of Kelmscott, Oxford, jointly with Rossetti; and in the year following published *Love Is Enough. Three Northern Love Stories*, translations of the Norse sagas, appeared in 1875, and in the same year he took over the entire business of the firm. He continued his writing, publishing an individualized translation of the *Aeneid* (1875) and an epic poem, *Sigurd the Volsung* (1876). In 1883 Morris joined the Socialist Democratic Federation, and in 1885 was among those who formed the Socialist League. He was active as a reformer and frequently lectured to workingmen.

He published a translation of *The Odyssey* in 1887 and *Poems by the Way* in 1891. His publications in prose include *The Aims of Art* (1887), *Signs of Change* (1888), *A Dream of John Ball* (1888), *The House of the Wolfings* (1889), *The Roots of the Mountains* (1890), *The Story of the Glittering Plain* (1890), *News from Nowhere* (1891), *The Wood Beyond the World* (1894), *Child Christopher* (1895), *The Well at the World's End* (1896), *Old French Romances* (trans. 1896), *The Water of the Wondrous Isles* (1897), and *The Story of the Sundering Flood* (1898). Among the chief occupations of his later years were the writing of prose romances in an exquisite if rather artificial English and an attempt to revive the forgotten typographic arts of the fifteenth century and to awaken interest in artistic printing and bookmaking. At the Kelmscott Press in Hammersmith he designed type, ornamental borders, and binding for fine books. He issued a series of beautiful books, notably a volume of the works of Geoffrey Chaucer illustrated by Burne-Jones (1896).

BIBLIOG.–R. P. Arnot, *William Morris: The Man and the Myth* (1964); Peter Faulkner, *William Morris and W. B. Yeats* (1962); J. B. Glasier, *William Morris and the Early Days of the Socialist Movement* (1921); H. H. Sparling, *The Kelmscott Press and William Morris* (1924).

MORRIS, WILLIAM RICHARD, 1st Viscount Nuffield, 1877–1963, British automobile manufacturer and philanthropist, born at Worcester. At the age of sixteen he was apprenticed in a bicycle shop; nine months later, with a borrowed capital of $20, he opened his own shop. He soon moved on to the manufacture of motorcycles, and in 1912 produced his first automobile. During World War I he turned his works over to war production, but in 1919 went back to making automobiles. His two models, the "Morris Cowley" and the slightly more expensive "Morris Oxford," were phenominally successful, and by 1925 annual sales had risen to 60,000. During World War II Morris again turned to war production, and also served as director general of maintenance at the British Air Ministry. He made generous grants to hospitals, charitable foundations, and universities, particularly to Oxford University where he founded and endowed a new college, Nuffield College. He was made a baronet in 1929, a baron in 1934, and a viscount in 1938.

MORRIS, city, NE Illinois, seat of Grundy County; on the Illinois River; 55 miles SW of Chicago. An industrial and shipping center for an area rich in bituminous coal, clay, and agricultural potential, the city manufactures vending machines and paper, limestone, leather, food, and rubber products. Gebhard Woods State Park is nearby. Morris was settled in 1834, platted in 1842, and incorporated in 1857. (For population, see Illinois map in Atlas.)

MORRIS DANCE, an English dance derived from the Morisco, an ancient Moorish dance introduced into Europe by the Moors of Spain. The morris dance was introduced into England in the reign of Edward III. It became a rustic dance, adapted to village festivals and May games; later, characters in costume —Robin Hood, Friar Tuck, Maid Marian, Little John, and a hobbyhorse—were added. The dance was suppressed by the Puritans, but a modified form survived in the north of England.

MORRISON, BARON HERBERT STANLEY, 1888–1965, British Labour party leader, was born in Brixton, a suburb of London. He was London Labour party secretary, 1915–47; national chairman of the Labour party, 1928–29; and a member of parliament, 1923–24, 1929–31, and after 1935. During World War II he was minister of supply in Winston Churchill's coalition cabinet, 1940; home secretary and minister of home security, 1940–45; and a member of the war cabinet, 1942–45. After the Labour party's rise to power, 1945, Morrison was lord president of the council, deputy prime minister, and leader of the house, 1945–51. He encouraged moderation in the nationalization of industry. He became foreign secretary, 1951, but his party was voted out of office that year. Morrison then served as deputy leader of parliament, 1951–55. He wrote *Socialization and Transport* (1933), *The Peaceful Revolution* (1949), and other books. He became Baron Morrison of Lambeth, 1959.

MORRISON, ROBERT, 1782–1834, British missionary, born at Buller's Green, Northumberland. He was apprenticed as a last maker, but in 1798 gave up his trade to enter the church. In 1807 he was sent by the London Missionary Society to Canton. There he worked on a Chinese grammar and a translation of the New Testament. After 1809 he served as an interpreter for the East India Company. In 1818 he established an Anglo-Chinese college at Malacca to train missionaries for the Far East. Morrison wrote numerous books, the most notable being his *Dictionary of the Chinese Language* (1815–23).

MORRISTOWN, town, N New Jersey, seat of Morris County; on the Whippany River; 15 miles W of Newark. Morristown has manufactures of clothing, umbrellas, paving materials, and electrical and metal products. Points of interest include Morristown National Historical Park; the granite and marble municipal building; and Campfield House, scene of the courtship of Alexander Hamilton and Betsy Schuyler in the winter of 1779–80. Morristown was founded by Puritans in 1710 as West Hanover. In 1739 the town's name was changed to honor Lewis Morris, then governor of New Jersey. It played a key role in America's early struggle for independence. The natural fortress of the Watchung Mountains south of the town, the roads leading to the Hudson and Delaware rivers, the proximity of both the Speedwell ironworks and Jacob Ford's gunpowder mill, and the patriotism of the local citizenry, influenced Gen. George Washington in selecting the town as the camp site for his Continental Army during the winters of 1776–77 and 1779–80. Morristown was later the home of Thomas Nast, Bret Harte, Frank R. Stockton, and Alfred Vail, who assisted Samuel F. B. Morse in developing the electric telegraph there in 1838. The town was incorporated in 1865. (For population, see New Jersey map in Atlas.)

MORRISTOWN, city, NE Tennessee, seat of Hamblen County; 40 miles ENE of Knoxville. Morristown is in the heart of the light Burley tobacco region. In addition to tobacco, principal farm products of the area are hay, corn, wheat, livestock, and poultry. Industries in the city produce tires, furniture, hosiery, textiles, dairy products, and canned goods. Morristown is the site of the Morristown Normal and Industrial College. The most famous local personage was Davy Crockett, who once lived in Morristown and married there. The city was incorporated in 1855. (For population, see Tennessee map in Atlas.)

MORRISTOWN NATIONAL HISTORICAL PARK, N New Jersey, Morris County; area 958 acres. It consists of three units: George Washington's headquarters and historical museum (Ford Mansion),

Fort Nonsense, and Jockey Hollow. The first two are in Morristown; the third 3 miles southwest. There are sites of important Continental Army encampments during the Revolutionary War. The Ford Mansion, at the rear of which is a museum, was Washington's headquarters during the winter of 1779–80. The museum ranks second to Mount Vernon as a storehouse of Washington relics. Fort Nonsense is a reconstructed earthwork built at Washington's order in 1777 as a defense for supplies stored in Morristown; its name derives from a rumor that it was built only for the pleasure of the soldiers. Jockey Hollow, the site of most of the Continental Army's encampments in 1779–80, is a wildlife sanctuary. Morristown National Historical Park was established in 1933.

MORRISVILLE, borough, SE Pennsylvania, Bucks County; on the Delaware River, the Pennsylvania Railroad, and U.S. highway 1; 1 mile SW of Trenton, N.J. Morrisville is the site of one of the largest steel plants in the United States. Other industries in the borough produce hard rubber and plastic products, tile, and firebrick. Morrisville, originally known as the Falls of Delaware, was renamed in honor of Robert Morris, a signer of the Declaration of Independence. It was settled in 1624 and incorporated in 1804. Pop. (1960) 7,790.

DELTA—C&S AIR LINES

A modern lighthouse rises above the walls of Castillo del Morro, which stands at the harbor mouth in Havana, Cuba.

MORRO, CASTILLO DEL, any one of several forts built by the Spaniards in the West Indies. The most famous is that located near the entrance to the harbor of Havana, Cuba. It was built in 1589 to protect the city from sea attacks, and was captured by the British in 1726 during the Seven Years' War. Another fort of the same name stands on a promontory commanding the entrance to the harbor of Santiago de Cuba; it was taken by the Americans in 1898 during the Spanish-American War. Morro Castle is also a picturesque fort defending the entrance to the harbor of San Juan, Puerto Rico.

MORROW, DWIGHT WHITNEY, 1873–1931, U.S. public official, was born in Huntington, W. Va., became a partner in a New York law firm, 1905, and was a member of the banking firm of J. P. Morgan and Company, 1914–27. As U.S. ambassador to Mexico, 1927–30, Morrow greatly improved U.S. relations with that country. His daughter, Anne, was married in 1929 to Charles A. Lindbergh, the aviator.

MORSE, JEDIDIAH, 1761–1826, U.S. geographer and Congregational clergyman, was born in Woodstock, Conn. In 1786, three years after he was graduated from Yale, he was ordained a minister. As minister at Charlestown, Mass., 1789–1819, he became noted for defending orthodoxy and opposing Unitarianism. He is chiefly remembered, however, as author of the first American geographies and gazetteers: his *Geography Made Easy* (1784), *The American Geography* (1789), and *Elements of Geography* (1795) were long the best known geography textbooks in American schools. Jedidiah was the father of Samuel F. B. and Sidney E. Morse.

MORSE, SAMUEL FINLEY BREESE, 1791–1872, U.S. painter and inventor of the electric telegraph and of Morse code, was born in Charlestown, Mass., a son of Jedidiah Morse. After being graduated from Yale College, 1810, he studied painting in London under Washington Allston and Benjamin West. Upon his return to the United States, 1815, he tried to establish himself as a painter. By the twentieth century much of Morse's work was highly regarded, but it was met with indifference during his lifetime. Perhaps the best known of his paintings are two portraits of the Marquis de Lafayette and *The Old House of Representatives,* in the Corcoran Gallery, Washington, D.C. Morse was a founder of the National Academy of Design and was its first president, 1826–42. In 1832 he became professor of painting and sculpture at the University of the City of New York (later New York University) and later became professor of the literature of the arts of design. He and John William Draper introduced the Daguerre process of photography into the United States, and the commercial studio they opened eased the poverty of the years when Morse was experimenting with the telegraph.

LIB. OF CONGRESS

Samuel F. B. Morse

It was on a return voyage from a European trip, 1829–32, that Morse conceived the idea of an electromagnetic recording telegraph. In discussing recent electrical discoveries with Charles T. Jackson, pioneer in etherization, Morse became convinced of the feasibility of his idea. In his artist's sketchbook he drew diagrams of a sending and a receiving apparatus and of the system of dots and dashes that was later developed into the Morse code. Lack of means kept Morse from devoting much time to his invention, but finally he secured financial assistance from Alfred Vail at whose house and ironworks near Morristown, N.J., he carried out the experiments that made his telegraph a practical success. He was also indebted to Joseph Henry for improvements on his electromagnet. Perhaps Morse's most brilliant achievement in developing the telegraph was devising a system of relays that made it possible to transmit messages unlimited distances. In 1843 Congress voted $30,000 for the experimental copper-wire line that Ezra Cornell strung between Washington and Baltimore. Over this line Morse sent from the Supreme Court chamber on May 24, 1844, the message, "What hath God wrought!"

Morse filed a caveat on his invention in 1837, but after its practicality had been proved and the Washington-Baltimore line had been extended to New York he was involved in a series of lawsuits, in all of which Morse's claims were upheld. When the U.S. Congress refused to buy the invention, Amos Kendall, former U.S. postmaster general, became the inventor's financial agent and both men became wealthy through the private development of the telegraph.

MORSE, SIDNEY EDWARDS, 1794–1871, U.S. journalist, geographer, and inventor, was born in Charlestown, Mass., was graduated from Yale in 1811, and studied theology at the Andover Theological Seminary, 1817–20. With his brother Richard

Cary Morse he established the New York *Observer*, a religious newspaper, in New York City, 1823, and edited it until 1858. He was associated with another brother, Samuel F. B. Morse, in inventing improvements in pumps; and with Henry A. Munson in introducing improvements in processes for printing maps. He wrote *An Atlas of the United States* (1823), *North American Atlas* (1842), *A System of Geography for the Use of Schools* (1844), *Memorabilia in the Life of Jedidiah Morse* (1867), and other works.

MORSE CODE. See TELEGRAPHY.

MORTAR, a smoothbore, muzzle-loading weapon designed for high-angle fire. Mortars were first developed in the sixteenth century, and since the Napoleonic period artillery weapons have been classified as field guns and mortars. During the American Civil War heavy-caliber, short-barreled mortars were used for siege purposes, but they were superseded by the more versatile howitzer as heavy artillery.

The need for a short-range, high-trajectory weapon for use in the trenches caused lightweight mortars to be developed during World War I, and, although hazardous to operate and lacking in accuracy, they had been so improved by the beginning of World War II as to be considered one of the more effective antipersonnel weapons. The modern mortar is essentially used by infantry and armored units. It has the tactical advantage of forcing a defending enemy to cover during an attack.

MORTAR, a building material similar to concrete, containing a grout of cement and water to which are added aggregates of sand or fine gravel. Mortar may contain lime or gypsum products in place of or added to the cement to aid the setting or hardening process. All mortars are fluid or plastic as mixed but hydrate into a solid mass. The aggregates, or coarse material, in mortar are much finer than in concrete, and it is usually specified that they must be able to pass through a screen with openings of ¼ inch. By varying the proportions of the constituents of mortar, one can obtain mortars of different grades.

In the building industry mortar has many applications. One of the most important is to fill the spaces between bricks and stone in masonry construction, wherein the mortar also acts as a binder to hold the structure together. Mortar is also used as a plaster, applied with a trowel to a backing of wood or metal lath; in the form of a semiliquid mixture for applying stucco to a building; and in concrete construction to form the binding layer between batches of concrete poured at different times, as in the construction of dams and other large masonry structures. Mineral coloring materials are sometimes added. See CEMENT; BRICKLAYING; MASONRY; STUCCO.

MORTAR AND PESTLE, the two parts of an appliance for grinding, pounding, or mixing substances. Both the mortar, or bowl, and the pestle, a club-shaped bar rounded at one end, may be of iron, porcelain, glass, agate, or stainless steel. The earliest application of mortars and pestles seems to have been made by Roman slaves, who used them for grinding grain. They are still used by pharmacists and industrial, research, and educational laboratories for producing test batches of chemical and organic compounds.

MORTE D'ARTHUR, a prose epic by the English writer, Sir Thomas Malory, translated from French and English romances, is a selection and reworking of the Arthurian stories. It was finished about 1470 and first published in 1485 by William Caxton, who divided it into 21 books and gave the title of the last part to the entire work. A fuller contemporary manuscript than the Caxton text was discovered in 1933. Around the figure of Arthur, Malory weaves the adventures of Lancelot and Guinevere, Merlin, the wizard, Galahad, Tristan, the quest for the Holy Grail, the dissolution of the Round Table, and many more stories that incorporate the traditions of chivalry. See ARTHURIAN LEGEND; HOLY GRAIL.

MORTGAGE, a transfer of some interest or estate in real or personal property as security for a debt or obligation. There are two main documents in a mortgage transaction. The first is a bond or note, also called a principal note or mortgage note, which the borrower, or mortgagor, signs as evidence of the debt. The other is the mortgage, also signed by the borrower, which describes and transfers the interest in the specific property that is being pledged as security for the debt. Mortgages are also called deeds of trust, deeds to secure debt, or security deeds.

Historically, mortgage law is a phase of the development of money and credit; as borrowers sought money from lenders, the lenders demanded specific assurances, the most important of which were security and prompt payment. The modern mortgage is the resulting legal device, showing the influence of the mortgagee who sought to claim the mortgaged property completely and immediately upon default of payment by the borrower, and the influence of the courts and legislatures that declared against harsh and undue forfeitures by granting the borrower a right to redeem the property after default of payment.

The civil law of Rome was the earliest legal system in which the rights connected with mortgages were fully defined. It is not known whether mortgages existed in Anglo-Saxon law; the laws of feud and tenure would probably have opposed such pledges of real property. In early English common law a mortgage was a conditional sale of land and a transfer of title. (See BILL OF SALE; DEED.) The transfer of title to the creditor became permanent if the debtor defaulted, and there was no redress for the debtor, even if he was only one day late in paying.

Equity courts ultimately permitted debtors to redeem the property after a default upon payment of the entire debt and all accumulated interest. As this right to redeem became recognized, creditors were forced to appeal to equity to obtain a decree directing the debtor to redeem within a designated time or forever be barred and foreclosed. Thus a real estate mortgage in the English law came to be regarded as a lien on the property rather than a transfer of title. See EQUITY; LIEN: REDEMPTION.

United States. The common law doctrine or fiction that the legal title passed to the mortgagee persisted in the United States, despite the jurisdiction assumed by English courts of equity and the resulting lien theory. All of the 50 states follow either the lien or the common law doctrines, but the practical differences are minor; the debtor retains the use and the enjoyment of the property and the creditor is assured that the property is available as security for the debt if the debtor does not pay.

During the term of a mortgage the creditor is entitled to demand that his security be unimpaired, and hence the mortgagor cannot remove buildings, cut timber, mine ore, or otherwise diminish the security without the permission of the mortgagee. All states, including those that use the common law rule that the mortgage is a conditional sale of the land, hold that the mortgagor retains the legal title against all the world except the mortgagee. Thus the mortgagee has no rights or liabilities of ownership; he cannot sue a trespasser for damages, nor is he liable for damages sustained on the premises. The mortgagor has the right to sell or lease the property subject to the rights of the mortgagee.

Failure to pay interest or installments when due is usually stipulated to make the entire debt payable immediately; such acceleration of payment is generally held to be legal. If the debtor defaults and the property is not sold for a sum sufficient to pay the debt, interest, and expenses of the foreclosure sale, the mortgagor is still liable for the deficiency.

The mortgagor's right to redeem his property, even after foreclosure, exists as an equitable right and is also guaranteed in most states by statutes that define the length of time permitted to redeem, requirements for the debtor to give notice of his intent to redeem, the bond and security required from the debtor to permit his continued possession of the property during the redemption period, and other requirements and restrictions.

Types. Mortgages are classified as real or chattel mortgages, depending upon the class of security conveyed. A second mortgage is one that conveys an interest in property already subject to a mortgage as security for another debt or obligation; there is no limit to the number of mortgages that may be made upon a single piece of property. Foreclosure under a first mortgage eliminates the rights of the mortgagees under the second and succeeding mortgages. Conversely, a purchaser at a foreclosure sale under a second mortgage acquires the title to the property subject to the first mortgage.

Mortgages are also closed or open; a closed mortgage is security for a debt that is fixed as to amount and an open mortgage permits the debt to be increased under the same mortgage document. Purchase-money mortgages, the most common type, are given to sellers in whole or partial payment of the purchase price; such mortgages take priority over all rights in, claims to, and liens against the property that come into existence when the purchaser takes title and executes the mortgage. Equitable mortgages, also called defective mortgages, are those in which the defect can be eliminated by decree of a court in equity. Equity will also enforce a written agreement to give a creditor a mortgage on land if the agreement identifies the land with reasonable certainty.

Mortgage Finance

Mortgage finance, or mortgage banking, is that part of the credit system that deals with real estate financing by mortgage loans. Mortgage finance used more new investment capital during the first half of the twentieth century than any other form of finance. Mortgage loans can be made on any type of real property, but are used most frequently to finance single family homes. Mortgage loans are used in many other ways; a corporation, for example, can issue mortgage bonds, pledging all or specific assets of the corporation as security. See Bond; Commercial Finance; Corporation.

The conventional mortgage, the kind that evolved through several centuries and was a simple transfer from the borrower to the lender, underwent several changes in the twentieth century. The creation of the Federal Housing Administration (FHA) as an anti-depression measure in 1934 made it possible to secure FHA mortgage insurance. (See Federal Housing Authority.) The Servicemen's Readjustment Act after World War II brought another new type of mortgage into being, the Veterans Administration (VA) home mortgage loan. See Veterans Administration.

A prospective mortgagor has a choice among several types of financial institutions that deal in mortgage loans including federal savings and loan associations, mortgage banking companies, insurance companies, commercial banks, savings banks, and trust companies. Savings and loan companies usually make conventional loans; banks and savings banks make conventional as well as FHA and VA loans; mortgage bankers make all three kinds of loans, but generally sell the loans to institutional investors such as savings banks and insurance companies instead of retaining them for their own account. See Banks and Banking, Commercial Bank Operations, *Loans and Credit;* Savings and Loan Association, *Method of Operation.*

Prior to 1930 most mortgage loans were made for terms of three to five years and interest payments were due annually or semiannually; the principal sum was usually repayable in a single payment at the end of the term. The 1930's popularized the amortized loan, one in which the borrower pays the interest, the sum borrowed, taxes, insurance premiums, and any other charges in monthly installments spread over a long period. Thus the borrower is aware of how much he has to pay each month and each payment increases the net value of his interest in the property. The amortized mortgage is generally credited as the major factor in making the United States a nation of homeowners, because it enabled purchases of real estate on the installment plan.

Mortgage finance practices vary as to the amount of down payment, interest rate, and length of term of the mortgage. Usually a down payment is required, although it may be as low as 3 per cent of the purchase price. Interest rates of private lenders vary; FHA and VA interest rates are regulated by Congress and have been changed from time to time. Since the amortized loan became popular, the terms of mortgages have increased to periods of from 15 to 30 years contrasted to the previous terms of from 3 to 5 years. See Amortization.

MORTIMER, one of the great families of the medieval English aristocracy. The Mortimers were of Norman origin. Ralph Mortimer went to England with William the Conqueror, and received extensive lands on the Welsh frontier. His descendants played a prominent part in English politics and in the Welsh wars. It was not, however, until the late thirteenth century that the Mortimers, thanks to lucky marriages bringing them vast estates, were able to play the role of great magnates.

The most famous of the family was undoubtedly Roger Mortimer (1287?–1330). After spending many years fighting in Wales and Ireland, Mortimer rebelled against King Edward II, 1321. The following year he was forced to submit to the king and was imprisoned. Escaping in 1324, Mortimer fled to the French court where he found Isabella, Edward II's wife, and became her lover. In September, 1326, Mortimer and Isabella returned to England to lead the rebellious barons. Edward II was captured, deposed by the parliament, and (September, 1327) murdered. For the next three years, in the name of the young Edward III, Mortimer ruled England. In 1328 he was created earl of March. He made many enemies, however, among them the young king himself. On Oct. 18, 1330, his enemies suddenly overcame him in his apartments, and on November 29 they hanged him as a traitor to the crown.

His grandson and heir, Roger (1328–60), fought for Edward III in France and was eventually allowed to recover the family lands as well as the title, earl of March. His son, Edmund (1351–81), married Philippa, daughter of Lionel of Clarence, third son of Edward III. Thus the blood of the Mortimers was transmitted to the later Yorkist kings of England. This marriage also made them earls of Ulster.

The son of Edmund and Philippa, Roger (1374–98), married the niece of King Richard II, who in 1385 designated him heir presumptive to the throne. Roger was killed fighting in Ireland, 1398, but after the death of Richard II, 1400, many Englishmen regarded Roger's son Edmund (1391–1425) as legitimate king rather than the Lancastrian Henry IV. Yet Edmund himself loyally served the Lancastrians. He died childless on Jan. 18, 1425. With this 5th earl of March the direct line of the Mortimers ended. Edmund's lands and titles passed to his nephew, Richard, the father of the Yorkist King Edward IV.

John R. Williams

MORTMAIN, the condition or status of land that is held by ecclesiastical, charitable, or other corporations whereby the land is in perpetual tenure or cannot be transferred. Mortmain is derived from the French words *morte main* meaning dead hand, and was applied in the sense of a death grip on property. The supposition was that the corporation was incapable of rendering the feudal services of tenure and that the title could not be conveyed. It was of great historical importance in England, where extensive grants of land were made to the church, thereby avoiding tenure to the lords of the manor and to the king. At one time more than half of the kingdom was in mortmain. Laws were enacted at various times after the Magna Charta to restrain mortmain, but means were found to avoid the laws, such as transfer by trust. Several states in the United States have enacted laws limiting the right of religious corporations to take or hold title to land, and a few states have laws restricting the gift of lands to charities.

MORTON, FERDINAND, real name Ferdinand Josephe la Menthe, known as "Jelly Roll" Morton, 1885?–1941, U.S. Creole jazz pianist and singer, band leader, and composer, considered by most critics to have been one of the two or three most creative and influential figures in the history of jazz, was born in Gulfport, Miss., but spent most of his youth in New Orleans. He began playing the guitar at the age of 7, the piano at 10, absorbing a wide variety of musical influences—Spanish American, French, American Negro. He made his first of several hundred phonograph records in Richmond, Ind., 1922–23. His most important records were those of "Jelly Roll Morton's Red Hot Peppers," some of whose performances are considered perhaps the most important, durable jazz music recorded before 1930, and in which were prefigured virtually every important music characteristic developed by the large bands of the 1930's—a period during which Morton sank into obscurity and poor health. In 1938 he recorded an "oral autobiography" for the Library of Congress, producing more than 120 records of talking, singing, and piano playing, most of them not issued to the public until the late 1940's, and then at the wrong speed; some of the spoken material on these records was expanded into the book *Mr. Jelly Roll* (1950) by Alan Lomax. Morton was a prolific composer, and many of his hundreds of compositions possess unique qualities that were evidently originated by him rather than derived from traditional ragtime and blues sources.

MORTON, JAMES DOUGLAS, 4th **EARL OF,** 1525?–81, Scottish regent, was born in Dalkeith, and succeeded his father-in-law as earl of Morton in 1553. When Mary, Queen of Scots, assumed her throne, 1561, Morton became a privy councilor, and two years later lord high chancellor. He supported the marriage of Mary and Henry Stewart, Lord Darnley, 1565. Subsequently Morton escaped to England after leading the armed band that murdered the queen's minister, David Rizzio, 1566, but was pardoned the following year. Returning to Scotland, he helped James Stewart, 1st earl of Murray (Moray), to defeat Mary at Langside, 1568, and was Murray's confidant during the latter's regency. Morton became regent, 1572, and maintained peace for six years; but eventually he lost the favor of nobility and church, and in 1578 yielded the regency on the decision of a convention at Stirling Castle. In 1580 Morton's enemies accused him of complicity in Darnley's murder; he was tried, convicted, and beheaded at Edinburgh.

MORTON, JULIUS STERLING, 1832–1902, U.S. cabinet officer, was born in Adams, N.Y., was educated at the University of Michigan and at Union College, and settled in Nebraska, 1854, where he founded and edited the Nebraska City *News.* A Democrat, he was a member of the territorial legislature, 1855–56, 1856–57; secretary of the territory, 1858–61; and secretary of agriculture in Pres. Grover Cleveland's cabinet, 1893–97. Morton originated the practice, later adopted by a number of states, of setting aside an annual Arbor Day to be observed by the planting of trees.

MORTON, LEVI PARSONS, 1824–1920, U.S. banker and Republican political figure, was born in Shoreham, Vt. After a few years as a shopkeeper in Hanover, N.H., he lived in Boston and then in New York, where he built up a successful banking business. He was minister to France, 1881–85, vice-president of the United States during the presidency of Benjamin Harrison, 1889–93, and governor of New York, 1895–97.

MORTON, NATHANIEL, 1613–85, colonial American historian, was born in Leiden, Holland, and was brought to Plymouth, Mass., in 1623. He was secretary of Plymouth Colony after 1647. In 1669 he published *New Englands Memoriall*, a history of the colony.

MORTON, OLIVER PERRY, in full Oliver Hazard Perry Throck Morton, 1823–77, U.S. political figure, was born in Salisbury, Ind., studied at Miami University, and became a successful lawyer at Centerville, Ind. Joining the People's (later Republican) party, he was elected lieutenant governor of Indiana, 1860, and succeeded Henry S. Lane as governor, 1861. A strong supporter of Abraham Lincoln, Morton raised troops for the Union cause despite pro-South pressure groups and a Democratic state legislature (elected in 1862) that held back appropriations. He was re-elected governor in 1864. In 1867 he was elected to the U.S. Senate and, though partly paralyzed after 1865, was active in carrying through severe Reconstruction measures and the 15th (Negro suffrage) Amendment to the Constitution.

MORTON, PAUL, 1857–1911, U.S. cabinet officer, was born in Detroit, Mich., the son of Julius Sterling Morton. He was associated with the Burlington Railway System, 1872–90, and became third vice-president of the Santa Fe System, 1896, and second vice-president, 1898. He was secretary of the navy in the cabinet of Pres. Theodore Roosevelt, 1904–05, and later headed the Equitable Life Assurance Society.

MORTON, THOMAS, 1575?–?1647, English adventurer, visited New England with Thomas Weston, 1622, and in 1626 acquired control of a settlement at Mount Wollaston (later Quincy, Mass.) and renamed it Ma-re-Mount or Merry Mount. Morton encouraged a hedonistic life typified by an 80-foot Maypole, and further outraged the Pilgrims by trading guns and alcohol to the Indians. In 1628 a Pilgrim expedition under Myles Standish broke up Merry Mount and captured Morton. He was deported to England, but returned in 1629; was captured and tried by the Puritans of Massachusetts Bay and sent back to England again, 1630, serving a short term in Exeter prison. In 1637 he published in Amsterdam his *New English Canaan*, a lampoon on the Pilgrims in which Myles Standish figured as Captain Shrimp. Morton was jailed on his next visit to Plymouth, 1644–45, and upon release went to Maine. His life provided material for Nathaniel Hawthorne's allegorical tale *The Maypole of Merry Mount* (1837) and for John Lothrop Motley's novels *Morton's Hope* (1839) and *Merry Mount* (1849).

MORTON, THOMAS, 1764?–1838, English dramatist, was born at Whickham, Durham. From 1792 he produced many successful plays, the best known being *Speed the Plough* (1798), which introduced the proverbial Mrs. Grundy. His most popular plays were *The Way to Get Married* (1796) and *Town and Country* (1807).

MORTON, WILLIAM THOMAS GREEN, 1819–68, U.S. dentist who gave the first public demonstration of the use of ether as general anesthesia, was born in Charlton, Mass., studied dentistry in Baltimore, and in 1842 started practice in Boston. In 1844 he matriculated at Harvard Medical School, but lack of funds prevented his completing his studies for a medical degree. He studied chemistry under Charles T Jackson, who demonstrated to his students the anesthetic properties of sulfuric ether. Morton conducted a series of experiments with ether and on Oct. 16, 1846, at the Massachusetts General Hospital gave a public demonstration of its use. He then applied for the U.S. and European patents for the application of ether in surgical operations, and published the results of his experiments. His claims were opposed by Jackson, Horace Wells, and Crawford W. Long, and there is no doubt that these men contributed to the discovery. Morton's decisive contribution was his willingness to accept responsibility for the results of his experiments. Morton obtained U.S. patents in his and Jackson's names and offered use of his rights without remuneration to all charitable institutions.

MORTON, town, NW Texas, seat of Cochran County; on the Llano Estacado, or Staked Plain; 55 miles W of Lubbock. It is surrounded by a ranching, farming, and oil area and is a market and shipping point for cattle, cotton, and petroleum products. An oil refinery is located in the town. Morton was incorporated in 1934. Pop. (1960) 2,731.

MORTON GROVE, village, NE Illinois, Cook County; on the Milwaukee Railroad and U.S. highway 41; a residential suburb 15 miles NNW of Chicago. Main products are pharmaceuticals. The population of the village more than quadrupled between 1950 and 1958. Morton Grove was incorporated in 1895. Pop. (1960) 20,533.

MOSAIC, a virus disease of plants that characteristically produces a mottled effect on the foliage and sometimes on other parts of the plant. Infected plants may be dwarfed, bear few flowers, lack vigor, and show other signs of abnormality. Mosaics constitute the largest group of plant diseases caused by viruses. Nucleic acid and protein are always present in a virus that produces a mosaic.

Little can be done once a plant becomes infected; therefore efforts at control are centered in prevention. Most mosaics are transmitted by insects; aphids are frequently carriers. Spraying with insecticides has some beneficial effect, but infected plants must sometimes be destroyed to prevent spread of the mosaic.

Severe losses of sugar cane and tobacco plants from mosaic infection have led to the development of resistant varieties of these plants. Among other plants susceptible to the disease are the potato, bean, tomato, and tulip. Fruits of plants do not contract mosaics as readily as does the plant itself. See PLANT DISEASE; STANLEY, WENDELL MEREDITH; TOBACCO.

MOSAIC, an ornamental art in which pieces of marble, enamel, or glass are arranged in groups or patterns to decorate the surface of walls, floors, furniture, and jewelry. To construct a mosaic the artisan plasters the surface to be decorated, applies his design to the surface with a stencil, and finally fits bits of marble, enamel, or colored glass to the surface. After the colored pieces are in their proper places, the entire surface is flattened, washed, and burnished. This process may be varied; mosaic artisans may apply the mosaic to the paper design, placing whole sheets on the wall or floor at one time. When the mosaic has set, the paper is washed away. The best mosaic artisans avoid excessive precision in fitting the pieces together; slight variations in the surface of the mosaic and in the width between mosaic pieces give depth to the finished product.

Early History. Mosaic was used in Egypt and Assyria for the decoration of jewelry and pottery. The first mosaics were bits of marble or colored stone set in ivory according to simple geometrical designs. The art spread through the Middle East and was advanced in Greece, where mosaics were used to decorate columns on homes, public buildings, and temples. The pictorial mosaic had not yet developed.

The geometric floor mosaic was largely a Roman innovation, and many of the great public buildings of ancient Rome were so ornamented. The Romans were the first to do pictorial mosaics—portraits, landscapes, and historical scenes. The finest examples are the landscapes on the floors in Hadrian's Villa and in the famous gladiator pavement of the Baths of Caracalla. The buildings erected in Roman colonies carried the art of mosaic to France, Spain, Germany, and North Africa.

CITY ART MUS., ST. LOUIS

Fifth Century Mosaic from Antioch, Syria

Christian Era. Early Christians, although denying the value of most pagan art forms, took mosaic as their own and the first Christian basilicas were decorated with crude pictorial representations of Christ. Before 600 the best mosaic work was done in Constantinople. The Byzantine artisans used gold to make their wall and ceiling mosaics impressively sumptuous. The gold mosaic cube was fabricated from a sheet of gold leaf made to adhere to a glass or enamel cube, then covered by a thin sheet of glass to prevent tarnishing. In the fifth and sixth centuries the city of Ravenna became the center of mosaic art in the Western world. In the early Middle Ages mosaic was the typical artistic expression, and elaborate designs were created by the medieval artisans; series of panels describing the main events in the lives of saints were made. The art declined in the eighth century, but in the eleventh century had a revival that resulted in the beautiful mosaics of St. Mark's Church in Venice and those in the churches of Palermo, Monreale, and Rome. During the Renaissance several great artists, including Titian, Raphael, and Tintoretto, contributed the designs (cartoons) for mosaics, but the art gradually lost favor.

Moslem Mosaics, although not equaling the Christian in variety, reflect painstaking artistry. Typical examples, purely geometrical in design, can be seen in the mosques of Cairo. The art of mosaic was also practiced in the Western Hemisphere by the Aztec, Indian, and Mexican civilizations.

In the Nineteenth Century mosaic had a brief revival, but it never regained its earlier popularity. In the United States the finest samples of nineteenth century mosaic work were perhaps those in the Cathedral of St. John the Divine, New York, which were designed and executed by Louis Tiffany. In the mid-twentieth century there was another renaissance, especially in the decoration of furniture, and the art had a considerable vogue among hobbyists.

BIBLIOG.–C. H. Sherrill, *Mosaics in Italy, Palestine, Syria, Turkey and Greece* (1933); E. W. Anthony, *History of Mosaics* (1935); D. Levi, *Antioch Mosaic Pavements* (2 vols. 1947); O. Demus, *Byzantine Mosaic Decoration* (1948), *Mosaics of Norman Sicily* (1950); A. Grabar, *Byzantine Painting* (1953); G. Bovini, *Ravenna Mosaics* (1957); E. A. Hendrickson, *Mosaics: Hobby and Art* (1957); J. L. Young, *Course in Making Mosaics* (1958).

MOSBY, JOHN SINGLETON, 1833–1916, Confederate soldier in the U.S. Civil War, was born in Edgemont, Va., and began the practice of law in 1855. At the outbreak of the Civil War he joined the Confederate Army, and participated in the Battle of Bull Run. In June, 1862, as a scout, he guided James (Jeb) Stuart's cavalry regiment (of which Mosby was also adjutant) in a raid on Gen. George McClellan's army. In 1863 he organized an independent body of cavalry (rangers) which he commanded until the end of the war. He captured Gen. E. H. Stoughton at Fairfax Courthouse, inside the Union lines, 1863, and in 1864 captured Philip Sheridan's supply train at Berryville and destroyed a portion of the Baltimore

NOVOSTI FROM SOVFOTO

Public housing projects, newly built on the outskirts of Moscow, have abandoned the ornate style of Stalin's day.

and Ohio Railroad. After each raid his force would scatter, to meet again at a designated time and place. Mosby became a colonel, 1865, disbanded his men in April, and surrendered himself in June. After the war he returned to the practice of law, in Warrenton, Va.; became a Republican; was U.S. consul at Hong Kong, 1878–85; and after 1885 practiced law in San Francisco. He was assistant attorney in the U.S. Department of Justice, 1904–10. Mosby published *Mosby's War Reminiscences* (1887) and *Stuart's Cavalry in the Gettysburg Campaign* (1911).

MOSCHUS, a mid-second century B.C. Greek bucolic poet, was a native of Syracuse, and called himself a pupil of the poet Bion. Moschus' was a spirited style, but overly elegant. His extant idyls are usually published with the works of Bion and Theocritus.

MOSCOW, city, NW Idaho, seat of Latah County; located on U.S. highway 95, 64 miles SSE of Spokane, Wash. Moscow is in the heart of Idaho's Palouse River country, with its rich soil of black volcanic ash and its unusually heavy yields of grains and peas. The city has lumber, agricultural machinery, brick, and clay industries. The University of Idaho and a large experimental forestry station are located there. Moscow was founded in 1871. (For population, see Idaho map in Atlas.)

MOSCOW, Russian *Moskva*, region, U.S.S.R., a subdivision of the Russian Soviet Federated Socialist Republic; bounded by the regions of Kalinin on the N, Yaroslavl on the NE, Vladimir on the E, Ryazan on the SE, Tula and Kaluga on the SW, and Smolensk on the W; area 18,688 sq. mi. The region is situated in the heart of European Russia; it includes portions of the Klin-Dmitrov and Smolensk-Moscow Hills, with a terrain gradually sloping from an average elevation of 525 feet in the northwest to 323 feet in the lowland drained by the Moskva, Klyazma, and Oka rivers in the southeast. Natural resources include lignite, peat, phosphorites, and ceramic clay. Up to 40 per cent of the area is forested. The region is one of the most industrialized areas in the U.S.S.R., accounting for one fifth of the value of Soviet industrial output. Major industries are metalworking, printing, and the manufacture of heavy machinery, precision instruments and tools, textiles, chemicals, pharmaceuticals, clothing, footwear, and food products. Farms in the city's outskirts supply vegetables for the capital and for other industrial cities of the region; dairying and poultry farming are also extensive. The city of Moscow, though governed independently of the region, is its capital. In 1957 the southernmost portion of Moscow Region, the Stalinogorsk coal, power, and chemical industry basin, with a population of more than 250,000, was transferred to Tula Region.

MOSCOW, Russian *Moskva*, city; capital of the U.S.S.R., the Russian Soviet Federated Socialist Republic, and Moscow Region; on the Moskva River; 395 miles SE of Leningrad; area 129 sq. mi.; population (1967 est.) 6,464,000. The buildings of the city stand on predominantly level ground except in the southwest, where the Lenin Hills exceed 600 feet. Moscow has a continental climate with mean temperatures of 12°F in January and 66° in July; the lowest temperature on record is 44° below zero, and the highest 99°. The average annual precipitation is 23 inches.

SETTING

City Plan. Moscow developed on a radial-circular pattern with three concentric belts of fortifications surrounding the city's nucleus, the Kremlin and Red Square. The inner ring consisted of the Kremlin's brick walls, built between 1485 and 1516, and the adjacent Kitaigorod Wall (1535–38), which enclosed the city's bazaar section until its remnants were torn down after the 1917 Revolution. The second fortified belt, about a mile from the center, enclosed White City, built in the late sixteenth century and demolished by the mid-eighteenth century to allow for boulevards. In the seventeenth century the third ring of fortifications was built in the form of an earthen rampart around the city's suburbs. Leveled at the end of the eighteenth century, it became the Sadovoye Koltso, the outer belt avenue circling Moscow at about a 2-mile radius. Country roads that radiated from the Kremlin in all directions became streets and were intersected by lanes, many of which retained a provincial appearance at the turn of the twentieth century.

The Kremlin, or citadel, was built in the twelfth century. It was at first only a wooden stockade on slightly elevated ground between the Neglinnaya and Moskva rivers enclosing about one twentieth of its present 65.5 acres. Between 1485 and 1516, under Ivan III and Basil III, a formidable fortress was constructed on the site. Major engineering feats were performed in draining swampy ground, partially diverting the Neglinnaya River, and erecting upon deep stone foundations crenelated Renaissance brick walls topped by 19 fortress towers—a triangular structure flanked on two sides by the Moskva and Neglinnaya rivers and on the third by a deep artificial moat. Within the walls the Granovitaya and Naberezhnaya palaces were built and Uspenski Cathedral was reconstructed. In 1625, during the reign of Michael, the first Romanov czar, when the Kremlin had become obsolete as a fortress, the Spasskaya Tower was covered with a lofty roofed superstructure. By 1686 all the other Kremlin towers were thus roofed, and the citadel took on its present-day appearance.

Within the Kremlin, next to the Uspenski Cathedral, where Ivan IV (the Terrible) in 1547 and all succeeding czars were crowned, is the city's tallest bell and watch tower (275 ft.), begun in 1505 under Ivan III and completed in 1600 under Boris Godunov. Nearby on a low platform stand the Czar Pushka, a famous 32-ton decorative cannon of the sixteenth century, and the Czar Kolokol, the world's largest bell (198 tons) cast in the eighteenth century, damaged in the great fire of 1737, and never used. The sixteenth century Archangel cathedral contains the tombs of all the Moscow princes and czars from Ivan I to Ivan V except Boris Godunov. Sacred paintings of great value are preserved in the fifteenth century Cathedral of the Annunciation.

Red Square, adjoining the Kremlin on the east, is the second oldest part of Moscow. In earliest times it was used as a meeting and market place, and along its eastern side clustered trading booths and stores of the Kitaigorod. At the square's southern end, abutting on the Moskva River, is the Cathedral of St. Basil the Blessed, erected in mid-sixteenth century under Ivan IV; its Byzantine-Middle Eastern style marked the beginning of the so-called Moscow school of architecture which lasted until the early eighteenth century. St. Basil, now a museum of religious art, consists of a cluster of eight pillar-like churches with onion-shaped domes, symmetrically placed around the tallest ninth pillar with its pointed dome; each of the eight lower domes, all richly ornamented, is of a different height, shape, and size. In front of St. Basil is a stone platform from which decrees of the czars were read and on which the condemned were beheaded.

At the northern end of Red Square is the state historical museum built in the nineteenth century. Near the Spasskaya Gate, against the background of the Kremlin wall, is the mausoleum of Nikolai Lenin. The body of Joseph Stalin was buried there, but was removed in 1961 after a general Soviet rejection and downgrading of his regime. The upper story of the mausoleum is used as a reviewing stand for parades. Along the wall are the graves of Soviet leaders and several hundred Bolshevik fighters who fell during the 1917 Revolution. The opposite, long side of Red Square is flanked by the central department store. In the 1920's a number of smaller structures, including churches, were demolished to permit a spacious approach to and an unobstructed view of the impressive square, which is 1,065 yards long and 140 yards wide.

Pre-Revolutionary Architecture. After the transfer of Russia's capital to St. Petersburg, 1712, Peter I issued a decree, 1714, limiting the erection of stone buildings to the new capital, but in 1728 the decree was broadened to include Moscow. After the great Moscow fire of 1737 there was a revival of construction in the city, and during the second half of the eighteenth century an architectural style known as Moscow classicism emerged. Buildings of that period include the Pashkov House, later converted into the Rumiantsev Museum and after the 1917 Revolution made part of the Lenin Library; the Kremlin senate (now the supreme soviet) building; and the old Moscow University. Many important buildings were damaged or destroyed in another fire in 1812, but during the next 30 years the Moscow reconstruction commission rebuilt most of them, erected the Bolshoi Theater and other structures surrounding the square in front of it, and laid out several parks. The late nineteenth and early twentieth centuries saw important additions to the city's structures: a number of monumental railway terminals, all placed beyond the outer ring of boulevards, the Sadovoye Koltso. Large blocks of apartment houses began rising in increasing numbers among the mostly wooden, low homes of the widespread city.

Post-Revolutionary Construction. The transfer of the capital from St. Petersburg to Moscow following the 1917 Revolution opened a new chapter in its architectural development. During the 1920's most building consisted of adding new stories to the existing tenements, but during the 1930's a program of extensive construction of industrial and public buildings was begun. The general plan approved for Moscow in 1935 emphasized development of the city's radial-circular pattern. The main thoroughfares—Gorkiy, Bolshaya Kaluzhskaya, Bolshaya Ordynka, Pokrovka, and Mozhayskoye Shosse streets, the inner ring of Gogolevsky, Tverskaya, and Petrovsky boulevards, and the Sadovoye Koltso—were widened up to 300 feet, and many squares were expanded.

After World War II the building of industrial structures in the city was prohibited and, in addition to public structures of all kinds, large-scale housing developments began rising in all parts of Moscow. A completely new residential section emerged in the southwestern outskirts among the Lenin Hills. The city's skyline was also radically changed. In 1947 the Soviet government decreed the construction of eight skyscrapers 16 to 34 stories high. Seven were completed in the early 1950's, but the construction of the last, scheduled to accommodate central government offices, was halted in 1954. At that time growing official dissatisfaction with the style of the buildings, conceived as magnified versions of the Kremlin towers, caused the government to order a change to a simpler architectural style. The tallest structure is the 32-story Moscow University (1948–53) on the Lenin Hills, visible from most of the city and providing a splendid panorama of Moscow from the upper stories.

Cultural Factors

Science and Learning. The number of educational and scientific institutions and of people engaged in scientific research work in Moscow is impressive. During the 1956–57 academic year 187,000 full-time students were enrolled in Moscow schools of higher education. The largest of these were Moscow M. V. Lomonosov State University (the oldest Russian university, founded in 1755 on the initiative of the noted naturalist), the Power Engineering Institute, the N.E. Bauman Institute of Technology, Institute of Railway Transport Engineers, G. V. Plekhanov Economics Institute, and two schools of medicine. There were also institutes of chemical engineering, pedagogy, economics, automotive engineering, architecture, mining engineering, electrical engineering, textile industry, and agriculture. About 675 primary and secondary schools had 630,000 pupils and 30,400 teachers.

The Academy of Sciences, created by Peter I in 1724 and moved from Leningrad to Moscow in 1934, has some 15,000 professional employees, eight departments, more than 50 specialized scientific and research institutes, various committees and commissions, and 16 branches, dispersed throughout the U.S.S.R., that co-operate with the academies of other Soviet republics. The library of the academy contained more than 5 million books and magazines; other institutions with large science collections are Moscow University, the ministry of higher education,

Moscow State University is situated on Lenin Hills at the city's outskirts. The university was founded in 1755 and has become the Soviet Union's leading educational center.
SOVFOTO

SOVFOTO

One of Moscow's major attractions is the impressive Central stadium. Many national and international athletic events are held in the huge sports bowl.

the All-Union Foreign Book Library, and the Central Polytechnical Library. The major book collection in the U.S.S.R. is housed in the Lenin Library and contained some 15 million items including about 9 million books and pamphlets.

Theater, Music, and Art. Moscow has more than two dozen theaters—excluding movie theaters—seating 27,000 persons. The largest are the Bolshoi, dating from 1825, the Great Kremlin theater (1961), and the Central theater of the Soviet army (1929). The Bolshoi, leading theater for ballet and opera, features works of the great Russian composers performed by renowned artists. Moscow's oldest theater, the Maly, which opened in 1824, established realism on the Russian stage. Other outstanding theaters are the Moscow Art, founded in 1898 by the producers Stanislavski and Vasili Ivanovich Nemirovich-Danchenko and notable for its association with the playwrights Anton Chekhov and Maksim Gorkiy, and the Vakhtangov, for whose productions Aram Ilich Khachaturian and Dimitri Shostakovich have written music. Moscow has several children's theaters. One of the U.S.S.R.'s leading music centers is the state Tshaikovsky Conservatory, which numbered among its students Sergei Rachmaninoff, Alexander Scriabin, and Khachaturian. Foremost among the city's orchestras is the state symphony.

There are about 50 art galleries and museums in Moscow. The state Tretyakov Gallery contains one of the world's great collections of art. The Tolstoy, Dostoevsky, Pushkin, Gogol, Gorkiy, Mayakovsky, and Ostrovsky museums show exhibits connected with life in Moscow and with the work of these writers. The three Lenin museums and those of the Revolution and of the Soviet army contain Soviet historical objects.

Economic Factors

Manufacturing. Moscow is the focal point for all Soviet industry. There new models of all kinds of equipment are designed and prototypes are built and tested, to be later assigned for production to industrial enterprises throughout the country. This incubator role of the Moscow industries is largely aided by the co-operation of the various institutes and committees of the Academy of Sciences.

Moscow and its immediate vicinity constitute one of the most industrialized areas in the Soviet Union. The city produces more than 15 per cent of the U.S.S.R.'s entire output. The machine, machine tool, tool, and instrument industries were expanded after World War I. Nearly half of the industrial labor force was employed in metalworking and machine industries in the late 1950's. About one-quarter of the labor force worked in consumer goods industries. Other workers were in food, chemical, rubber, printing, woodworking, and building material industries. The leading postrevoluntionary plants in Moscow manufacture automobiles, aircraft, bearings, machine tools, electrical engineering products, electric bulbs and radio tubes, timepieces, and precision machinery such as calculating and computing machines, measuring and scientific instruments, and gauges. Alloys and special steels for these industries are supplied by a large Moscow steelworks. The chemical industry produces dyes, colors and varnishes, technical and consumer rubber goods, cosmetics, and pharmaceuticals. Printing and publishing is also a first-rank industry.

Moscow has maintained its prerevolutionary role as the center of the country's textile industry, especially in the production of high-grade cottons, silks, and woolens. Garment, knit goods, and footwear production is also important. The largest meat processing plant in the U.S.S.R., flour mills, mechanized bakeries, dairies, confectionery plants, distilleries, and breweries cater to the food needs of the Muscovites, who are better provided with consumer goods than those living elsewhere in the Soviet Union.

Moscow's electricity is supplied by local power stations and hydroelectric installations at Kuibyshev and Volgograd. The city receives its natural gas from two long-distance pipelines, one from the Saratov area, and the other from Dashava in the Ukraine.

Transportation. Moscow is served by all forms of transportation. It has 9 passenger terminals, 11 major railroad trunk lines (connected inside the city by a circular line), and more than 20 freight stations. Three airports, Central, Vnukovo, and Bykovo, serve the Moscow metropolitan area. The magnitude of the Moscow railway junction can be judged by comparing the area of its tracks and installations (more than 6,500 acres) with the area of the city's streets and squares (more than 8,600 acres). Major suburban railways serving Moscow are electrified.

The capital is connected through the Moscow Canal with the upper Volga system and thus with the Baltic, White, Caspian, and Black seas. The 79-mile canal, built between 1932 and 1937, extends from the Volga at Ivankovo, Kalinin Region, to the Moskva River near the edge of Moscow. It is carried across the Klin-Dmitrov Hills by powerful pumping installations and is accessible to ships of 8.5 feet draft. It forms numerous reservoirs along its route and discharges into the Moskva River 47 cubic yards of water per second, replenishing the city water supply.

There are three river ports—the northern, southern, and northwestern. Passenger service is offered from the river ports to Gorki, Ufa, and Rostov-on-Don via the Moskva and Oka rivers or the Moscow-Volga Canal. Moscow handles about 40 million tons of rail freight and about 11 million tons of waterborne cargo each year.

A number of motor highways radiate from the city, the major roads being those to Minsk, Kharkov, Leningrad, and Gorkiy. Moscow is the hub of the Soviet airline system; including air force bases, it has

Workers assemble engines at an automobile plant in Moscow. Most of the Soviet Union's heavy industry is concentrated in the Moscow area.

SOVFOTO

SOVFOTO

Moscow's Kremlin, surrounded by a medieval style wall that is 45–50 feet high, nearly 1½ miles long, and fortified by 19 ornately structured seventeenth century towers, dominates the Soviet capital, of which it is the central point.

a denser concentration of airfields than does any other area of comparable size in the Soviet Union.

City transportation is furnished mainly by the Moscow subway. Begun in 1932, by the late 1950's it had four basic radial lines and one complete belt line with 60 stations in service. It carries nearly 2.5 million passengers each day and is well known for its lavish underground stations. During World War II it served as an effective network of air-raid shelters. Modern trolley buses and buses have largely replaced streetcars in the city.

History

The city was founded in the twelfth century on an elevated site at the junction of the Moskva and Neglinnaya rivers, now the southwest portion of the Kremlin. In 1156 Yuri Dolgoruki, prince of Suzdal, built there a wooden stockade, the future Kremlin. At first a town in the Suzdal-Vladimir principality, during the thirteenth century the settlement and the countryside around it developed as a separate principality. In the winter of 1237–38 it was devastated and burned by the Mongols.

Eastern Influences. In the fourteenth century two Moscow princes, Yuri Danilovich and Ivan Kalita, vassals of the Mongol khans, were appointed great princes to rule the Muscovites on behalf of the khans; they exacted taxes from the population and accumulated wealth and influence. Under Ivan Kalita, in 1326, the metropolitan see of the Russian Byzantine church was moved from Vladimir to Moscow. By the second half of the fourteenth century the great princes of Moscow assumed an increasingly important role in organizing resistance of Russian principalities and cities against their Mongol overlords. The combination of military leadership in the fight against the Mongols, ecclesiastical ascendancy over other Russian cities, and central location led to the rise of Moscow as the nucleus of the future centralized Russian state and empire. In 1380 Dmitri Donskoi, great prince of Vladimir and Moscow, defeated the Mongol forces at the Battle of Kulikovo Pole, and although in 1382 the Mongols again sacked the city, their superiority rapidly declined.

The centuries of contacts with the Mongols, however, gave the Russian culture centered in Moscow the orientation to the East that has endured to modern times—an influence strengthened by Moscow's association with the Byzantine Orthodox church, especially after the marriage, 1472, of Ivan III and Princess Sophia, niece of the last Byzantine emperor, Constantine XI. The arrival in Moscow of Sophia's court opened a new epoch in the cultural life of the city, which became the capital of the country, Ivan III having proclaimed himself "Lord of all Russia" to whom other princes were subject.

Rise to Pre-eminence. The position of Moscow as Russia's undisputed capital was finally established under Ivan IV (the Terrible), who crushed the Mongols, capturing their strongholds of Kazan (1552) and Astrakhan (1554) on the Volga, and sacked the city of Novgorod (1570), actually subordinated to Moscow in 1578. From the sixteenth century on, Moscow, as a seat of autocratic rulers holding absolute power, set the cultural and political standards for all Russia. The city was occupied from 1610 to 1612 by the Polish King Sigismund III, who vainly attempted to include Russia in the Polish-Lithuanian union.

After the accession of the Romanov dynasty, 1613, western Europeans began to come to Moscow. Because their ideas were alien to the city's Oriental traditions, they were obliged to live in the so-called German or foreign suburb. Thus developed a center of Western learning, culture, and influence that attracted progressive Russians, including Peter I, who as a young czar, in 1699, founded in the city the school of mathematics and navigation. Even after Peter moved the capital to St. Petersburg, 1712, Moscow retained its importance as Russia's foremost cultural and spiritual center.

1812. The army of Napoleon I captured Moscow in September, 1812, but abandoned it the next month. They were forced to withdraw when nearly three-fourths of the buildings in the city were destroyed in a great conflagration caused by Russian incendiary groups in order to destroy supplies and housing, thus rendering the wintering of French troops in the city impossible.

FABER FROVA—PHOTOREPORTERS

Lenin's tomb (at left) on Moscow's Red Square is visited by many thousands of Soviet citizens every year.

After the Bolshevik Revolution. In 1917 the capital of the country was once again moved to Moscow, which became the residence of the Soviet leaders Lenin and Stalin.

During World War II Moscow was a prime objective of the German army and its fall seemed imminent until, in mid-October, 1941, the winter checked the German offensive. All the members of the Soviet government, with the exception of Stalin, were evacuated to Kuibyshev together with the diplomatic corps, and returned to the capital in 1943 when the German troops withdrew.

A number of extensive urban redevelopment plans were undertaken in the 1960's in Moscow and its suburbs as part of a project to make Moscow the model city for other U.S.S.R. urban centers.

BIBLIOG.–Vladimir Chernov and Marcel Girard, *Splendors of Moscow and Its Surroundings* (1967); David D. Duncan, *Great Treasures of the Kremlin* (1968 ed.); John Fennell, *The Emergence of Moscow, 1304–1359* (1968); Sigmund Von Herberstein, *Description of Moscow* (1968); *Nagel Travel Guide to Moscow and Leningrad* (1958); Karel Neubert and A. R. Mills, *Portrait of Moscow* (1965); Daria Olivier, *The Burning of Moscow, 1812* (1966); Stephen and Barbara Rosenfeld, *Return from Red Square* (1967); E. Swick, *Vacation in Moscow* (1966); Arthur Voyce, *Moscow and the Roots of Russian Culture* (1964).

MOSELEY, HENRY GWYN-JEFFREYS, 1887–1915, British physicist, was born in Weymouth. He was graduated from Trinity College, Oxford, 1910. He became a lecturer in physics at the University of Manchester, and was associated with Lord Ernest Rutherford in investigating radioactivity. Moseley studied the X-ray spectra of elements and discovered the principles known as law of atomic numbers, according to which the square root of the frequency of the X rays produced when an element is bombarded with cathode rays is directly proportional to the atomic number of this element. Since Moseley's experiments had shown that elements of higher atomic weight produce X rays of shorter wave length, he was able to draw up a new periodic table for the 92 known elements based on the numerical position of each element according to its X-ray wave length. Moseley was killed in World War I.

MOSELLE, department, NE France, Lorraine; bounded by Luxembourg on the N, the German states of Rhineland-Palatinate and Saarland on the NE, and the departments of Bas-Rhin on the E and Meurthe-et-Moselle on the S and W. The department's area is 2,403 sq. mi. Central Moselle is situated on the Lorraine Plateau and the southeastern part is traversed by the north Vosges Mountains; the department is drained by the Saar and Moselle rivers and their tributaries and is extensively canalized. Large areas of Moselle are forested, and there are many shallow lakes on the plateau. Principal crops include cereals, tobacco, and fruits. Wine is made from grapes grown along the west bank of the Moselle River. The well-known Lorraine iron ore is mined in the Thionville Basin and in the Orne Valley; coal is mined in the Forbach-St. Avold district, a south extension of the Saar field; sodium and potassium deposits are also exploited. Metallurgy, concentrated in the Metz-Thionville region, is the chief industry. Other products include glass, leather, shoes, porcelain, wood, and preserved foods. Moselle has a large German-speaking population and was part of Germany during 1871–1918 and 1940–44. Principal cities include Metz (the capital), Thionville, and Forbach. (For population, see table in France article.)

MOSELLE RIVER, or Mosel River, NE France and W Germany; rises in the central Vosges Mountains of France, flows generally N and NE past the cities of Remiremont, Epinal, Toul, Metz, Thionville, and Trier, forming part of the border between Luxembourg and the West German Republic, and enters the Rhine at Koblenz; length 320 miles. The Moselle is confined to a narrow valley for most of its course. Vineyards along its banks are the source of the famous Moselle wines. There are numerous historic ruins in the area traversed by the river. Chief tributaries are the Meurthe, Saar, and Sauer rivers. Canals connect the Moselle with the Rhine, Meuse, and the Seine. The Moselle canal connecting France and Germany was opened in 1964.

MOSES, the deliverer, lawgiver, leader, and prophet of Israel. He was born of slave parents in Egypt between 1500 and 1200 B.C.; most reliable evidence points to the later date. His father, Amram, and mother, Jochebed, belonged to the tribe of Levi; they probably lived in Goshen and endured all the hardships of slave life. One brother, Aaron, and a sister, Miriam, are other family members. Both mother and sister figured prominently in the events that saved the infant's life and brought him into the Egyptian court as the adopted son of Pharaoh's daughter. In the Book of Exodus we learn that

Michelangelo's *Moses*

METROPOLITAN MUSEUM OF ART

three months after Moses' birth, Jochebed thwarted Pharoah's decree that all male infants be drowned by placing her son in a pitch-sealed ark among the bulrushes at the bathing place used by Pharaoh's daughter. Miriam, stationed nearby to watch over her baby brother, saw the Egyptian princess draw him from the water and suggested a Hebrew nurse; the child's own mother, Jochebed, thus became the mentor of his earliest years. The name Moses, given him by Pharaoh's daughter, in the Egyptian is *ms* (child or son); in the Hebrew, *mosheh* (drawn out), descriptive of his rescue from the river. After receiving in Egyptian libraries and universities the best education available in his day, Moses was prepared for a life of public service. The course of plans made for him, however, at this point took a sudden turn. Interfering when he saw a Hebrew slave mistreated by an Egyptian taskmaster, Moses killed the Egyptian and was obliged to flee to escape the wrath of Egyptian authorities. In the hill country of Midian, through an act of courtesy to a group of shepherdesses, he was introduced to their father, Jethro (Reuel), priest of Midian. In this home Moses found not only a wife—one of Jethro's daughters, Zipporah—but contentment in his task of tending his father-in-law's flocks and in the opportunity for meditation and study.

The Burning Bush. This second phase of Moses' life spanned 40 years and ended almost as suddenly as did the first. One day, when his duties as shepherd took him through the wilderness to Mt. Horeb, he saw a bush burning but not consumed. As he approached it, God spoke from the burning bush and commissioned Moses to lead His people out of their bondage in Egypt. When God answered Moses' last excuse by agreeing that his brother Aaron should be spokesman, the newly appointed leader entered upon his duties with characteristic vigor (Ex. 3:2–4:28).

After accomplishing their first task of convincing the elders of the children of Israel that Moses had been called to deliver their people from Egyptian bondage, Moses and Aaron set about the more difficult assignment of obtaining Israel's release from Pharaoh. First refusing outright, then weakening under the impact of a plague, but afterwards breaking his repeated promises to let the Israelites go, Pharaoh finally yielded unconditionally as a result of a still more terrible plague. This final evidence of God's power brought death to the first-born throughout Egypt—excepting only those of the Israelites, whose blood-sprinkled doorposts the death angel passed over. A Passover feast was instituted in observance of their deliverance. (See PASSOVER.) Preparing for departure, the children of Israel "borrowed" from their Egyptian neighbors what they needed for the long journey to the Promised Land (Ex. 4:29–12:36).

Exodus. When Pharaoh again broke his promise and pursued the Israelites to the edge of the Red Sea, there was murmuring against Moses until God intervened and gave him the power miraculously to lead the children of Israel through the Red Sea on dry land while Pharaoh's hosts were drowning in an attempt to follow (Ex. 12:37–14:31). From the Red Sea Moses led the children of Israel through Marah, where the bitter waters were made sweet; Elim, the site of 12 wells and 70 palm trees; the wilderness of Sin, where manna and quail were provided daily as food for the people; Rephidim, where Horeb's smitten rock gave water, Moses' uplifted hands gave strength to the Israelities in defeating the Amalekites, Jethro brought Moses' wife and children to him, and Moses paid heed to Jethro's advice about appointment of judges and others to assist him in carrying out his administrative duties (Ex. 15:1–18:27).

The Commandments. The Israelites next proceeded to Sinai where Moses went up into the Mount of God and, by divine instruction, three days later led the people to the nether part of the mount where they received the Ten Commandments in oral form (Ex. 19:1–20:17). Moses led them in ratifying the covenant and in reciting all the words and judgments of God, then spent 40 days on the mount and was given detailed instruction in building and furnishing the tabernacle as well as a description of the worship ceremonies (Ex. 20:18–31:17). God then gave Moses the two tables of stone on which was written the Decalogue; these Moses smashed in indignation as he returned to the foot of the mount to find that, during his absence, the people had made a golden calf and were worshiping it without protest from Aaron. He returned to the mount, praying for the people, and after 40 days came back with two new tables of the Law. Moses then supervised construction of the tabernacle and articles for Israel's worship, such as the ark of the covenant (Ex. 31:18–40:38).

In the Book of Leviticus we are told that when all preparations had been completed, Moses received from God the rules of worship for the congregation. He then proceeded to consecrate Aaron and his sons as priests, the serious nature of this office being shown in the death of two sons for violating a rule of sacrifice. Various other laws and observances were announced. The last days at Sinai were occupied with a census, which showed the total of the 11 tribes as 603,550. The Levites, numbered separately, were set apart as the priestly tribe. Each family was assigned duties.

The Wilderness. The Book of Numbers relates how, when Moses gave the order to march, almost 14 months after the children of Israel had left Egypt, they moved forward from Sinai. En route, 12 spies went ahead to scout the territory to be conquered; all except Joshua and Caleb gave an unfavorable report. The people believed the majority and so were condemned to wander in the wilderness 40 years because of their lack of faith. God fed them with quail and manna and, after all who were more than 20 years old at the time of the spies' report had died, Israel again moved toward the Promised Land. At Kadesh Miriam died. Because the people murmured so strongly about lack of water, Moses smote the rock at Meribah (instead of speaking to it, as God had commanded) and provided drink. For this act he and Aaron were deprived of the right to enter the Promised Land; Aaron died a short time later, after his son Eleazar had been invested with the priesthood. A plague of fiery serpents was sent among the rebellious Israelites en route from Mt. Hor to Moab; Moses held aloft a brass serpent and those who looked at it in faith were healed. Defeating the Amorites and Og, king of Bashan, the victorious Israelites pushed on to the Plains of Moab; across the Jordan River lay Palestine. Moses ordered a second census and found that the 11 tribes had 601,730 members, a net loss of less than 2,000 during the wilderness wanderings.

The Promised Land. As recorded in Deuteronomy, Moses drew all the tribes about him at Moab and delivered his farewell addresses to them. Sometimes his messages were fired with evangelistic fervor. He named Joshua as his successor and gave his blessing to the various tribes. From Mt. Pisgah's lofty heights on Nebo, he viewed the Promised Land. Then, at the moment of Moses' death, God took him to his secret grave in a valley in the land of Moab.

As liberator of his people, Moses ranks high with students of history and politics. As lawgiver, he is in a class to himself; the "Ten Words" formed the basis of an elaborate system of laws covering every area of life. As the responsible author of the Pentateuch, the first five books in the Bible, Moses has written his name indelibly among the immortals. As prophet, he holds a pre-eminent place among those chosen to receive Jehovah's message and deliver it to His people. In intercessory prayer, Moses ranks among the great saints of all ages. KYLE M. YATES

BIBLIOG.-E. Fleg, *Life of Moses* (ed. 1933); L. Golding, *In the Steps of Moses* (1943); M. Buber, *Moses* (1948); F. B. Meyer, *Moses: Servant of God* (ed. 1953); S. Freud, *Moses and Monotheism* (ed. 1955); H. H. Hobbs, *Moses' Mighty Men* (1958).

PHILLIPS GALLERY, WASHINGTON © GRANDMA MOSES PROPERTIES, INC.
***McDonell Farm,* by Grandma Moses**

MOSES, ANNA MARY ROBERTSON, known as Grandma Moses, 1860–1961, U.S. painter, was born in Washington County, New York. At the age of 12 she began work as a hired girl and at 25 married a farmer. When too old for farm chores, she took up needlework, 1936, but was forced to abandon her "yarn pictures" because of failing eyesight and began to paint with oils. Essentially a folk artist (a "modern primitive"), she painted gay scenes of country life. In 1940 she had her first exhibit in New York City and her work received popular, if not always critical, acclaim and became widely known through reproduction on Christmas cards. Among her paintings are *From My Window*, *The First Skating*, and *The Old Checkered House*.

MOSES, ROBERT, 1888–   , U.S. administrator, was born in New Haven, Conn., and was graduated from Yale, 1909, and Columbia (Ph.D. degree), 1914. He became chairman of the New York State Council of Parks, 1924, and was secretary of the state of New York, 1927–28. In 1934 he was Republican candidate for governor of New York and was appointed New York City park commissioner. As park commissioner he carried out a vast and widely emulated program of improvements in the city park and highway systems.

MOSLEM. See Islam.

MOSLEM ART AND ARCHITECTURE. When, in the second quarter of the seventh century, the Arabs with their new faith, Islam, and an embryonic state organization, began the conquest of the ancient areas of human civilization from North Africa and Spain to India, they brought practically no architectural or artistic techniques with them. But the new religion which was theirs, embodied certain principles and ideas that were to affect their art profoundly. For example, the idea of the total sovereignty of God as the only Creator led to a curtailment, but never the abandonment, of the representation of living beings, especially in religious art, and in consequence to a greater emphasis on purely decorative values. Another aspect of the faith was the necessity for a place where the believers could gather and pray. Thus was created the mosque and its main component parts: an area for the community to gather, a minaret from which the people were called to prayer, a mihrab (niche indicating the direction of Mecca), a mimbar (pulpit for the imam, or leader of the community). For the implementation of these and a few other ideas of the same order, the Moslems (or Muslems) had to rely at the beginning on the artists and architects of the conquered areas: Christians steeped in the Roman and Byzantine traditions in the lands west of the Euphrates, Persians in the eastern part of the empire. The cross between the artistic traditions of the conquered areas and the new Moslem ideas created Islamic or Moslem art. Later, other outside sources, such as Turkish and Indian traditions, also helped to shape this art.

Moslem Art and Architecture

From Spain to India the art of the Moslems varied a great deal but, in spite of such variations, certain general principles were common to the whole Islamic world.

Architecture. The main architectural problem of the mosque was the organization of a large space for great numbers of the faithful. Several solutions to this problem are found in the tenth century mosque of Córdoba with its wonderful play of arches and columns giving the impression of a forest, in the eighth century mosque of Damascus with its quiet arcaded court and majestic façade, in the fourteenth century mosque of Isfahan with its powerful rhythm of two tiers of keel arches on each side of a large central archway, or in the sixteenth century mosque of Suleiman I, the Magnificent, in Istanbul. Private piety in the Islamic world also had its architectural expression in, for instance, the large number of mausoleums found in cities and in the country from Morocco to India. At times these monuments to private piety reached monumental proportions, as in the Taj Mahal in India, built as a memorial to the favorite wife of a Mogul prince. Another type of building for which the Moslems were much praised in the Middle Ages was the palace. Little has remained of their palaces, except several ruins from the earliest period in Syria and the magnificent Alhambra of Granada, where the succession of splendidly decorated rooms gives a faint idea of what the ideals expressed in the "Arabian Nights" must have been. Most of these architectural developments were remarkable for the brilliant surface decoration of colored tiles, paintings, stucco sculpture, stone carvings, or mosaics which gave an added element of depth and color to the constructions of the Moslems.

The Decorative Arts, either simply the various techniques of wall covering or the making of precious objects in gold, silver, brass, glass, silk, and ceramics were developed by the Moslems from the very beginning of their history and served to give a general climate of luxury to their surroundings. In most elaborate ways use was made of geometric and vegetal motives, to which was added a characteristically Moslem feature—the letters of the Arabic alphabet, either singly or in pious or well-wishing sentences. At times animal and even human elements were welded in, as in the most curious development of "animated" writing—letters with human or animal shapes. All these elements combined to create the arabesque, which covered a whole surface with an endless, complicated pattern, generally involving one or more vegetal stems with leaves and fruits or flowers winding around each other. In later times animal and human figures also appear, especially in metalwork, where scenes of hunting and merry-making characteristic of princely life occur, and in ceramics, where quieter and more contemplative figures are seen in a simplified landscape. In these objects of the minor arts the human figure rarely acquires full three-dimensional form, but is merely suggested by a few lines, for the Moslem artist was often more interested in decorative form and in symbols than in the depiction of visual reality. Another major Islamic decorative art is carpet-making. Persian and Turkish rugs are famous throughout the world. This is an art that started later than the others and embodied most of their principles of decoration, but which survived as a major form past mid-twentieth century.

Painting. The best known and most remarkable Moslem paintings do not appear before the twelfth century and after 1300 the best examples arise in Persia more often than elsewhere in the Moslem world. They consist essentially in the illumination and illustration of manuscripts. Before 1300 the illustrations were quite simple and served as a running commentary on the text. But in Persia, where the texts illustrated were either the great epic poems celebrating the glorious history of Persia or half-mystical,

MOSLEM ART AND ARCHITECTURE

CITY ART MUS., ST. LOUIS

This seventeenth century arabesque rug from Usak, Turkey, is bordered with Kufic writing.

MUS. OF FINE ARTS, BOSTON — ART INST. OF CHICAGO

The glass lamp at left is fourteenth century Syrian and the faïence jug at right is fifteenth century Spanish.

SPANISH TOURIST OFFICE

The halls of the Alhambra in Granada are noted for their intricate and delicate ornamentation.

Typical of Turkish mosques, with domes and minarets, is the sixteenth century Mosque of Suleiman I in Istanbul.

***Two Apothecaries* illuminates a Mesopotamian edition, 1222, of writings of Dioscorides.**

MUS. OF FINE ARTS, BOSTON

half-worldly lyrical poems, new and more complex images appear. The characteristic Persian illustration consists of an idealized landscape with blossoming trees and flowers, or the audience hall of a palace. Within this setting are seen, in a profusion of colors, representations of courtly life, with receptions, hunting, or moonlit love scenes. The artists were not interested in giving an actual representation of such events. Rather, they tried to create a mood—the mood of an ideal world where, amidst an eternal spring, handsome princes and fair ladies lead a life of merriment and happiness. In later times portraiture was also developed by Persian, Turkish, and Indian artists. It shows us a wonderfully expressive gallery of princes, noblemen, sometimes even peasants or shepherds, while a series of historical paintings depict the great events of the day. In this way Moslem painting reflected the actual life of the times, but its greatest quality is in suggesting the more idealized dream of one of the world's great civilizations. After the seventeenth century, painting, like all other Moslem artistic activities except rugmaking, declined considerably. See BYZANTINE ART; BYZANTINE ARCHITECTURE; INDIAN ART AND ARCHITECTURE; PERSIAN ART AND ARCHITECTURE. OLEG GRABAR

BIBLIOGRAPHY

ART: T. W. Arnold, *Painting in Islam* (1928), (with A. Guillaume) *Legacy of Islam* (1931); M. S. Dimand, *Handbook of Muhammadan Art* (ed. 1947); L. Ashton, ed., *Art of India and Pakistan* (1951); Freer Gallery, *Ars Orientalis: Arts of Islam and the East* (2 vols. 1954–57); R. P. Wilson, *Islamic Art* (1957).

ARCHITECTURE: A. F. Calvert, *Alhambra* (1904); M. S. Briggs, *Muhammadan Architecture in Egypt and Palestine* (1924); P. Brown, *Indian Architecture* (1942); J. Terry, *Charm of Indo-Islamic Architecture* (1955); D. N. Wilber, *Architecture of Islamic Iran* (1955).

MOSMAN, municipality, SE Australia, New South Wales; on Port Jackson Bay; 4 miles NNE of Sydney, of which it is a suburb. Candy and leather goods are produced in Mosman. Pop. (1954) 25,901.

MOSQUERA, TOMÁS CIPRIANO DE, 1798–1878, Colombian public official, was born in Popayán. For his service in the war of independence, Simón Bolívar made him a general, 1829. He was president of New Granada, 1845–49, and instituted many reforms. In 1861 he led a revolt against the conservatives; a new constitution changed the name New Granada to the United States of Colombia and gave Mosquera dictatorial powers. Elected president, 1863, he instituted anticlerical measures. He left office, 1864, was re-elected, 1866, but was deposed by a revolution, 1867, and was banished for three years. On his return he became governor of Cauca and a congressman. He wrote a biography of Bolívar (1853).

MOSQUERO, village, NE New Mexico, Harding and San Miguel counties, seat of Harding County; on the Southern Pacific Railroad; 41 miles NNW of Tucumcari. It is the shipping point for a nearby dry-ice industry. Pop. (1960) 310.

MOSQUITO, a small, winged insect pest with plumelike or feathery antennae, belonging to the mosquito family, *Culicidae*, of the order Diptera, or two-winged flies (see FLY). Two large groups, or tribes, of the mosquito family are of primary importance: the anophelines, or *Anophelini*, and the culicines, or *Culicini*. The genus *Anopheles* and three other genera constitute the tribe *Anophelini*, which contains more than 400 species distributed throughout the world. Only *Anopheles* mosquitoes are able to transmit malaria and although 14 species are found in the United States, only two are serious vectors—*A. quadrimaculatus* and *A. freeborni* (see MALARIA). Among the genera that make up the culicine tribe are *Culex*, which includes *C. pipiens*, the house mosquito, and *Aedes*, which includes *A. aegypti*, the yellow fever mosquito (see YELLOW FEVER). More than 400 species of *Aedes* and more than 450 species of *Culex* occur throughout the world.

Structure. The body of the mosquito, like that of other insects, is composed of three essential parts—head, segmented body, and flexible abdomen. Members of the mosquito family have sphere-shaped heads with compound eyes, a pair of antennae, and elongated mouth parts. The antennae, which arise high on the face and between the eyes, are large and bushy in the male but thin and sparse in the female. The mouth parts arise on the lower part of the face and extend forward and downward to form a proboscis. The proboscis consists of six thin stylets enclosed in a sheath which is drawn back during feeding. Four of the stylets are concerned with penetration: two maxillae with sawlike tips and two mandibles with needle-like tips. When penetration of the feeding ground has been accomplished, the remaining two stylets are inserted. Secretion from the mosquito's salivary gland is forced through the narrow channel of one of the stylets into the pierced area. This stylet then functions as the floor of a canal, the other stylet as the roof, and the liquid feeding is withdrawn. On either side of the proboscis is a palpus, or feeler. The palpi are almost as long as the proboscis in all mosquitoes except females of the culicine tribe, in which they are very short.

The mosquito's thorax is compact and arched. It is composed of three segments but the first and third are obscured by the second, which is greatly enlarged to allow room for the wing muscle. The mosquito's long, narrow wings, unlike those of any other insect of the fly group, have rows of scales along the posterior margin and on the veins. The abdomen is cylindrical and tapers slightly. The mosquito has three pairs of legs. They are long and extremely slender, and end in claws that in some species have many minute tooth-like projections.

Habits. The normal range of flight for adults varies within a radius of ½ to 1 mile from the breeding area, although some species can migrate 10 or 12 miles. Adult mosquitoes are most active when light is subdued, such as at twilight, at night, or in dense shade. Like various other insects, many female

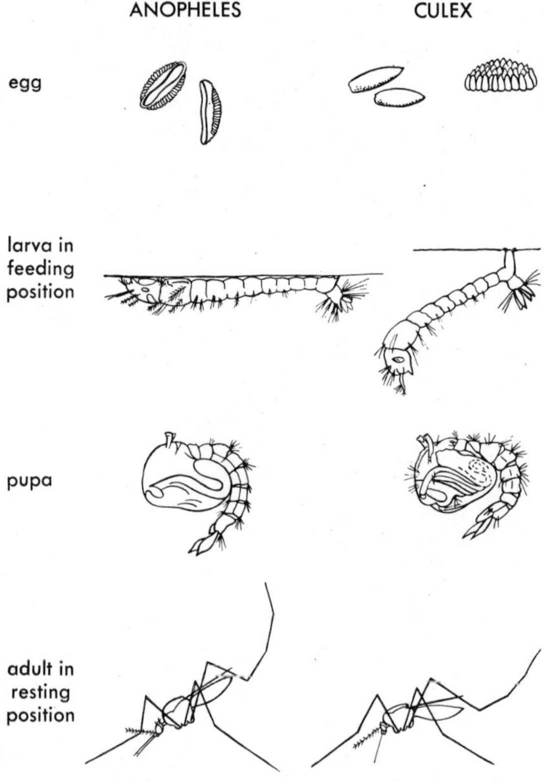

Life Cycles of Anopheline and Culicine Mosquitoes

mosquitoes buzz or sing (see BUZZING). Some mosquitoes hibernate in dark, moist, protected places.

Mosquitoes mate almost immediately after they emerge from their pupal shells. The males gather in great swarms, often over some conspicuous object such as a bush or tree, where they hover while individual females dart in to choose their mate. Swarming is not a universal habit of the mosquito family, however, for in some species—*Aedes aegypti*, for example—the males seek out the females while in flight. The males usually live only a short time after mating. The females seek a blood meal immediately after fertilization, for blood seems to be necessary for development of the eggs. Only the females seek blood, although they occasionally feed upon plant juices and nectar just as the males do.

Eggs and Larvae. The females lay large numbers of minute elongated eggs, usually in rafts, on the surface of water or near watercourses. Those of the genus *Anopheles*, however, lay their eggs singly or in loose clusters that are provided with special air floats. The eggs hatch into wigglers, or larvae. All mosquito larvae are aquatic and may inhabit fresh, brackish, or salt water. Anopheline larvae rest horizontally just beneath the surface film while feeding. They maintain themselves in position by means of peculiar float hairs that appear on some or all of the abdominal segments. Surface organisms constitute their principal food. Culex larvae suspend themselves head downward at an angle of about 45° to the surface. A long siphon or breathing tube covered by five flaps is attached to a segment of the body near the tail. The larvae maintain themselves on the surface by pushing the tip of the siphon through the surface film and extending the flaps to catch the film for support. These larvae are not surface feeders but feed while hanging to the surface film or roaming over the bottom debris. Mosquito larvae obtain their food by sweeping into their mouth parts any organisms that can be gathered by rapidly moving mouth brushes, which consist of masses of curving hairs located just above the chewing mouth parts. The duration of the larval stage varies with species and climate; it may last only a few days or be prolonged throughout an entire winter.

Pupae. The larvae transform into pupae that look like question marks with the curl of the mark greatly thickened. Thorax, head, and appendages are compressed into a large oval mass; the abdomen is slender and hangs downward. The pupae are equipped with air sacks and are buoyant. They rest at the surface and breathe through two horns or breathing tubes that arise from the thorax. All are active, but they take no food. They swim by flicking their abdomen from side to side. The pupal period is short, rarely exceeding six days. A mature mosquito emerges from and rests on the pupal case until its wings and body harden, when it is ready for flight and mating.

Disease Carriers. Mosquitoes are the carriers of many diseases to which human beings and animals are susceptible. It is necessary for some disease organisms to spend part of their life cycle within the body of these insects and another part within the body of man or animals. When a disease-carrying mosquito injects its saliva in preparation for feeding, it also injects the disease organisms into the blood stream of the host. If disease organisms are present in the blood of the host, the mosquito will ingest them during its feeding.

Mosquitoes are carriers not only of malaria and yellow fever but also of many other diseases. Dengue, or breakbone fever, is transmitted by several species of *Aedes*. Filariasis and elephantiasis are transmitted by at least 50 different species belonging to the genera *Anopheles*, *Aedes*, *Culex*, and *Mansonia*. Several species of *Culex* are carriers of encephalitis. See ENCEPHALITIS; DENGUE FEVER; FILARIASIS; SLEEPING SICKNESS.

Control. Mosquito control is concerned chiefly with the proper handling and control of water. The methods used depend upon the area to be treated. Land may be drained to remove small pools of standing and stagnant water; or water may be impounded in large dams to reduce rapid and excessive runoff. Breeding places around large ponds, lakes, or reservoirs may be eliminated by filling and grading or by keeping the margins of such bodies of water clean. Top-feeding fishes, particularly minnows of the *Gambusia* species, have been introduced in lakes and ponds to destroy mosquito larvae. Insecticides such as petroleum oils, Paris green, and DDT in oil emulsions, water suspension, and dusts are another means of control. The interiors and exteriors of homes and buildings can be treated with a DDT solution so as to leave a residue (about 200 mg per sq. ft. of surface) that normally will kill all mosquitoes and flies resting on the surfaces. Aerosol bombs containing DDT and pyrethrins with Freon gas have also proved valuable. ROBERT MATHESON

BIBLIOG.–S. J. Carpenter and W. J. La Casse, *Mosquitoes of North America* (1955); A. N. Clements, *Physiology of Mosquitoes* (1963); W. R. Horsfall, *Mosquitoes* (1955); E. Pampana, *Textbook of Malaria Eradication* (1963); F. Russell and others, *Practical Malariology* (1963).

MOSQUITO COAST, Spanish Mosquitia, region, Central America; extends along the Caribbean Sea from the Aguán River in Honduras to the San Juan River in Nicaragua. It is a large, undeveloped, and sparsely settled region of tropical forest lowlands with many marshy lagoons along the coast. The region is inhabited mainly by Mosquito Indians. Principal products include hardwoods, coconuts, bananas, manioc, and beef. The region was a British protectorate from 1655 to 1860 when it was ceded to Honduras and Nicaragua.

MOSS, plants of the phylum Bryophyta, class Musci, characterized by a conspicuous, independent gametophyte (haploid, gamete-producing) generation of a stemlike aerial structure with leaflike scales and rootlike absorptive structures called rhizoids. All of these mosses lack the vascular tissues characteristic of higher plants. The gametophyte may be monoecious (both sex organs on the same plant) or dioecious (male and female organs on separate plants), the sex organs being produced at the tips of the aerial structures. The zygote undergoes its initial development within the archegonium (female receptacle) and eventually gives rise to the small, almost parasitic sporophyte which produces and releases spores. The spores undergo meiosis and generate new gametophytes.

There are about 14,000 species in the four orders of mosses: *Bryales*, or true moss, is the largest order; *Andreaeales* include only two genera, whose capsules split lengthwise when spores are released; *Sphagnales*, or peat mosses, live in bogs and have dark spherical capsules; and a small group, *Phascales*, whose capsules do not open but eventually decay. The haircap moss, *Polytrichum*, is a representative moss plant. The leaves, unlike those of higher plants, are usually only one or two cells thick.

Mosses thrive in moist habitats throughout the world. Some grow on trees, some in bogs; others are aquatic. Still others may form dense mats that cover forested areas. See ALTERNATION OF GENERATIONS; BRYOPHYTES; LIVERWORTS.

Use. Dried moss plants are soft and may be used as packing material for fragile goods and as stuffing for upholstery. Moss absorbs water readily and thus helps to prevent soil erosion. Compressed peat moss is burned for fuel in some parts of the world.

BIBLIOG.–Ruth S. Breen, *Mosses of Florida* (1963); A. J. Grout, *Mosses with Hand Lens and Microscope* (1965).

MOSSADEGH, MOHAMMED, 1880–1967, Iranian government official, was born in Tehran. He became premier in 1951 and immediately got into conflict with Britain over the nationalization of the British-owned Anglo-Iranian Oil Company. Mossadegh succeeded in driving the company from Iran, but his precipitate actions brought the country to bankruptcy.

Forced to resign, July, 1952, he returned as premier a week later. In 1953 he tried to force the shah from the throne, but was himself dismissed from power, arrested, and sentenced to three years' imprisonment. He was released in 1956.

MOSSBAUER, RUDOLF LUDWIG, 1929– , German Nobel laureate in physics, 1961; born in Munich. He took his doctorate at Heidelberg in 1958. He was named senior research fellow at the California Institute of Technology in 1960, where he was appointed professor in 1961.

MOSSBAUER EFFECT, or recoil-free gamma-ray resonance absorption, a method for producing a continual train of γ rays whose frequency is very high and almost constant. The effect provides physicists with the most accurate of atomic clocks.

Many radioactive nuclei, when excited, emit high-frequency γ rays, but after each emission they recoil, much as a rifle kicks back after firing a bullet. The quantity of recoil is variable and, therefore, by the Doppler effect, the frequency of the radiation emitted is also variable. But in certain crystals, the recoil—instead of being restricted to the emitting nucleus—is evenly distributed throughout the large number of nuclei which compose the entire crystal and is therefore negligible. As a result the frequency at which radiation is emitted is almost constant.

These regular emissions are the tick-tock of the atomic clock. But clocks also require devices to record the ticking—hands by which we can read the time. The ticks of the Mössbauer clock are much too frequent to permit direct reading. Instead, a more roundabout means is employed. If the rays resulting from recoil-free emission are made to strike a nucleus of the same type as the emitter—a recoil-free absorber—the absorber will send out rays of the same frequency as it has received. This phenomenon is called nuclear resonance. Struck by sympathetic pulses pitched at its natural frequency, the receiver nucleus—like a violin string—is set vibrating. Now if the frequency of the emitter is but slightly altered—by as little as one hundredth of a tick in every million million ticks, the receiver will not re-emit the radiation. This makes it possible to detect alterations in frequency (and, therefore, time) as tiny as 10^{-14} second. This, in turn, has permitted physicists to investigate phenomena—such as those predicted by the theories of relativity—that alter time and frequency by infinitesimal quantities. Special relativity predicts that if a fast runner carries a watch, it will lose time at the rate of one hundredth of a tick in a million million ticks. It predicts, as well, that a watch will slow by about the same quantity if it is placed atop a skyscraper, rather than on its ground floor, because up there the gravitational potential is greater. General relativity declares that gravitational fields very subtly change the frequency of light: they tint it very slightly redder. All these forecasts, which could not be tested because the quantities involved were so tiny, have now been verified by Mössbauer clocks.

MOSSEL BAY, in Afrikaans Mosselbaai, town, Republic of South Africa, S Cape Province; seaport on Mossel Bay of the Indian Ocean; 225 miles E of Cape Town. The town is a fishing, agricultural, and tourist center; ochre and quartzite mines are nearby. Seal Island, with large seal herds, is immediately north of the town. Mossel Bay was visited by Bartholomeu Diaz in 1487 and Vasco da Gama in 1497. A Catholic mission, the first Christian place of worship in South Africa, was built there in 1501. (For population, see southern Africa map in Atlas.)

MOST, city, Czechoslovakia, NW Bohemia; in the foothills of the Erzgebirge; 45 miles NW of Prague. The city is a railway junction, a lignite mining center, and the starting point of a gas pipeline to Prague; it also has food processing and metallurgic industries, porcelain works, and a large electric power plant supplying Prague. (For population, see Czechoslovakia map in Atlas.)

MOSTAGANEM, city, NW Algeria, Oran Department; on the E shore of the Gulf of Arzew of the Mediterranean; 180 miles WSW of Algiers. Mostaganem is a trading center for the products of the surrounding coastal lowland and the nearby high plateau and coastal Tell Mountains. Exports include wine, vegetables, cereals, sheep, wool, and esparto grass for fibers. Silver and lead are mined nearby. (For population, see northern Africa map in Atlas.)

MOSTAR, city, Yugoslavia, Bosnia and Hercegovina People's Republic, central Hercegovina; in the mountainous Karst Region, on the Neretva River, 26 miles from the Adriatic. Bauxite and lignite are mined and grapes and cherries are grown in the area. The city is the seat of a Roman Catholic and an Orthodox bishop. Half of the population is Muslim and several mosques give the city an Oriental appearance. Mostar was a Roman stronghold captured in the fifteenth century by the Turks, who made it an administrative center. It passed to Austria in 1878 and became part of Yugoslavia after World War I. (For population, see Balkan States map in Atlas.)

MOST-FAVORED-NATION CLAUSE, in international treaties, grants to signatory state commercial rights equal to those enjoyed by any other state (specifically, by the "most favored" state). The term does not imply special privileges—merely equality of opportunity. Today, such agreements are normally bilateral: the states involved are of equal international status, and the most-favored-nation agreement is reciprocal. Unilateral agreements, binding only one party not to discriminate against the other, imply the former's inferior status. The commercial advantages of most-favored-nation status are twofold: it guarantees non-discriminatory practice by the other party, and it ensures that any future concessions made to a third state must be granted to the state possessing most-favored-nation status.

Most-favored-nation agreements were originally concerned solely with tariffs; later they came to include other matters, such as literary copyrights, patents, or airspace.

The Anglo-French agreement of 1860 to lower tariffs marks the beginning of the spread of most-favored-nation agreements in modern times. The United States, however, retained a conditional form of such agreements which denied automatic extension of privileges except under certain conditions. Other countries also on occasions evaded the unconditional form, usually by elaborate classification of articles in tariffs. A notorious example occurs in the German tariff of 1902, which selected for special consideration "large dappled mountain cattle, reared at least 300 meters above sea level . . ."

When, after World War I, U.S. exports changed from predominantly agricultural to predominantly industrial, the country met high tariffs in Europe, and the advantages of equal treatment caused a decisive reversal of policy in favor of an unconditional form of most-favored-nation agreements. In the negotiations that led to the General Agreement on Tariffs and Trade in 1945 the United States led the successful campaign for unconditional most-favored-nation agreements. See COMMERCIAL TREATY; GATT; TARIFF.

MOSUL, province, N Iraq. Drained by the Tigris River, the province supports some agriculture and nomadic herding; it also has large oil deposits. The Assyrian Empire had its beginnings in the area. (For population, see table in Iraq article.)

MOSUL, city, N Iraq, capital of Mosul Province; on the Tigris River; 225 miles NNW of Baghdad. Mosul, in the center of a rich oil and agricultural region, is Iraq's second largest city and the chief market town of north Iraq. Roads and railroads connect Mosul with Baghdad, Turkey, and Syria; and the city is a scheduled airline stop. Pipelines carry oil, the most important export, to the Mediterranean, to Haifa in Israel, and to Tripoli in Syria.

EWING GALLOWAY

Mosul is located in the old Kurdistan region of northern Iraq. It is the second largest city in the country and is of great importance both economically and strategically.

There is trade in grain, fruit, livestock, cotton, wool, gallnuts, metalware, and hides. The city is inhabited chiefly by Arabs; the surrounding area has a large Kurd population. Mosul contains many mosques and several Assyrian (Nestorian) churches. It is near the ruins of the ancient Assyrian capital of Nineveh, and the sites of other ancient towns that are important archaeologically. At various times Mosul was under the domination of Arabs, Mongols, Persians, and Turks. It was at one period a prosperous trading center known for its manufacture of muslin cotton. Joined to Turkey in 1638, the city became part of Iraq in 1925–26. Pop. (1956 est.) 140,245.

MOTEL, a roadside establishment designed specifically to provide motorists with overnight accommodations. Lodgings may be separate small buildings, known as cabins, or individual bedroom and bath units, more or less identical, aligned under a common roof. Automobile parking space is provided, commonly adjacent to the sleeping unit. Motels are usually located most favorably with respect to highway traffic on the outskirts of cities; some that approach hotel style of layout and service are in metropolitan business or resort areas.

Rental rates are generally more economical than hotel rates; the guest performs many services for himself; informality of proprietor-guest relationship as well as of dress is typical; the traveler's car is always at hand. Luxurious accommodations increased with the spread of the motel business, until many establishments provided cooking and laundry facilities, television, air conditioning, central lounges, restaurants, shops, swimming pools, gas station service, and outdoor theaters. The average motel of 1960 was a single-story building of 20 units.

The U.S. motel industry began in 1913 when some miners' cabins were renovated for transient occupancy in Douglas, Ariz. Automobile travel, especially after World War II, caused motels to flourish into a $7 billion business by 1958, with 57,000 motels lodging some 1.5 million guests nightly and grossing $2 billion in yearly receipts. Most U.S. motels are individually owned but some chain operation exists. Several motel associations set standards for maintenance, facilities, and services, and publish lists of approved lodgings for the benefit of the motoring public.

MOTET, generally a sacred polyphonic choral composition of moderate length, similar in form to the secular madrigal. Widely divergent conceptions of the motet have existed since the thirteenth century. During the sixteenth century a motet was a polyphonic vocal work based on a Latin scriptural or ecclesiastical prose text, in one or (at most) two divisions or movements without instrumental accompaniment. The motet was commonly sung in the Roman Catholic service during High Mass, between the Credo and the Sanctus, either taking the place of or following the Offertory. Even during this period, however, there were motets on metrical, on secular, and on non-Latin texts. In the seventeenth century, motets with instrumental accompaniments appeared. In England the motet became indistinguishable from the anthem. Johann Sebastian Bach and other German composers produced choral works called motets without written accompaniment, though in performance probably accompanied on the organ. Georg Händel wrote a variety of motets on Latin texts, some elaborate enough to be classifiable as cantatas (a short type of oratorio). In the nineteenth century the general conception of the motet was that of a short sacred cantata.
IRWIN FISCHER

MOTH. See BUTTERFLY AND MOTH.

MOTHER CAREY'S CHICKEN. See PETREL.

MOTHER GOOSE, an imaginary figure associated in the English-speaking world with a wide and varied collection of nursery rhymes, most of which were in existence long before they were attributed to Mother Goose. Originally Mother Goose was associated with a collection of tales that appeared in France in 1650. It was not until 1697, however, that her name was definitively attached to children's literature, when a minor French poet and architect, Charles Perrault, brought out a collection called *Histoires ou contes du temps passé*. On the frontispiece of that work appeared an illustration of children listening to a storytelling goose, and above them was worked in the legend *Contes de ma mère l'oye* (Tales of Mother Goose). The original collection of eight stories included such perennial favorites as "Sleeping Beauty," "Little Red Riding Hood," "Hop O'My Thumb," and "Cinderella." An English translation of this collection had appeared by 1729, and reprints and new editions, attesting to the growing popularity of the stories and their web-footed teller, followed with great frequency and regularity. It was almost inevitable, therefore, that the other staple of children's fare, nursery rhymes, should also be attributed to her. And perhaps by 1765, but certainly by 1781, a collection of such rhymes, without the prose tales, had appeared under the title of *Mother Goose's Melodies*. The second edition of this famous work (long thought to be the original edition) was brought out in Worcester, Mass., about 1785. The twentieth century canon of nursery rhymes (and only nursery rhymes) associated with Mother Goose was extensive and varied, although not all may appear in any one compilation.

Many of the rhymes enshrine obscure and forgotten relics of cultural history. The provenance and the occasions for the composition of a large number of these songs would seem to have little to relate them to the nursery. This is not true of such relative late-comers as alphabet rhymes, tongue twisters, and some rhymes about animals. But some, like "London Bridge Is Falling Down," record venerable folk rituals entailing the sacrificial murder of children. Some are old nature spells and incantations, like "Rain, Rain, Go Away." Some chronicle cryptically a long-forgotten murder or scandal, like "Who Killed Cock Robin?" Others were once lampoons and satirical squibs on prominent political and social figures. The most famous of all lullabies, "Rock-a-bye Baby," is said to have originated in the time of James II, or at least to have served to lampoon the British royal line at that time. There is good evidence that "Little Jack Horner" immortalizes a notorious bit of double dealing connected with the confiscation of monastic lands by Henry VIII. "Bobby Shafto" was sung by the supporters of Robert Shafto, who stood for parliament in the election of 1761. In the English wool trade the tradition remained current that the division of bags in "Baa, Baa, Black Sheep" refers to the export tax on wool imposed in 1275. Whatever their origin, appropriate nursery rhymes have always been used to point a domestic or public moral, and modern advertising has exploited their familiarity with clever adaptations.

The Mother Goose rhymes, to most who have grown up with them, are inseparable from their illustrations, and a long line of illustrators, including Edward Lear, Sir John Tenniel, and Walt Disney, devoted their skill to them. A mid-twentieth century collection by Walt Disney, however, deviated from the tradition, representing almost every figure of the rhymes by Mickey or Minnie Mouse, Donald Duck and a few of the other standard Disney creations; the history of the rhymes themselves shows that children's imaginations are not so limited.

MOTHER HUBBARD, English nursery rhyme character who went to the cupboard to fetch her dog a bone but found the cupboard bare. She then went to various merchants on errands for the dog, and each time she returned she found him doing something ridiculous. The poem was written by Sarah Catherine Martin and first published in 1805 as *The Comic Adventures of Old Mother Hubbard and Her Dog*. The character Mother Hubbard was known as early as the sixteenth century.

MOTHER LODE, the major lode or mineral vein in a particular area and the one from which smaller deposits subsequently may have been formed. (See LODE.) In the United States the great quartz vein of California is generally known as the Mother Lode. This deposit is about a mile wide and extends for 120 miles in a southwest-northeast direction along the foothills of the Sierra Nevada, between the towns of Mariposa (where highway 49 begins) and Auburn. Some of the gold mined in the region during the California gold rush of 1849 and later existed as part of the major vein; other gold was found in alluvial deposits. These deposits were formed when the gold-bearing quartz veins suffered water erosion and were decomposed into the gold-bearing gravel.

MOTHER-OF-PEARL, the hard, iridescent lining of pearl-bearing mollusks, notably oysters from the Indian Ocean. It is used in the production of buttons, inlaid furniture and musical instruments, knife handles, combs, and similar objects. The waste part of the shell is crushed and used for fertilizer, poultry feed, and stucco. Mother-of-pearl is also known as nacre.

MOTHER'S DAY, the second Sunday in May, dates from May, 1907, as a day for honoring the home and motherhood. Miss Anna Jarvis of Philadelphia is credited with originating the idea of having sons and daughters pay tribute to their mothers on a special day. The day was celebrated by a number of cities in the United States by 1910. In May, 1913, a resolution passed both houses of Congress recommending the observance of the day by Congress and the executive departments. In 1914 Congress authorized the President to designate by annual proclamation the second Sunday in May as Mother's Day. The first proclamation of Mother's Day was issued by Pres. Woodrow Wilson on May 9, 1914. Similar proclamations have been issued annually by his successors. It is customary on Mother's Day to wear a red carnation if one's mother is alive, and a white carnation if she is dead. Children often present gifts to their mothers on this day. Mother's Day is similarly celebrated in Canada

MOTHERWELL AND WISHAW, burgh, central Scotland in N Lanark County, near the Clyde River; 12 miles ESE of Glasgow, with which it is connected by railroad and highway. Both Motherwell and Wishaw owe their importance to coal and iron deposits nearby. Ironworks, steelworks, and plants for the manufacture of railway equipment, boilers, electrical equipment, cement, and hosiery are among the industries. The two towns were united in 1920. Pop. (1956 est.) 70,300.

MOTHERWORT, any weedy herb of the genus *Leonurus*, belonging to the mint family, *Labiatae*. The leaves are opposite and divided or toothed; the small pink or white flowers grow in clusters in the axils. The perennial *L. cardiaca*, often called motherwort or lion's-tail, bears small, woolly white flowers. It grows to a height of 5 feet and is a weed throughout North America. Motherwort is native to Eurasia.

MOTION, the change of position of a body during a period of time. The idea of motion is associated with concepts of mass and velocity and therefore is closely allied to momentum, the dynamic quantity that is the product of the mass of a body and its velocity. See MOMENTUM.

Like velocity, motion must always be related to some kind of co-ordinate system. Thus the phrase "a body is at rest" ordinarily means that the body is at rest with respect to earth, and a car said to be traveling at a speed of 60 mph is moving at that speed with respect to some point on the earth's surface that is at rest with respect to the earth. Bodies may move in many ways, at many speeds, and in many directions. The speed of a body may be constant; it may be changing continuously; or it may change in an irregular manner. The direction of motion may remain the same; it may change according to a pattern; or it may change erratically.

Galileo's discovery of various fundamental laws permitted the first fruitful exploration of the relationships between force and motion. For example Galileo showed that, neglecting air resistance, the speed of falling bodies is independent of their mass; and that bodies always change speed in the same manner if dropped from a height or rolled down a smooth (frictionless) plane.

Discoveries in astronomy made during this period led Johann Kepler, with the aid of Tycho Brahe's measurements, to establish laws of planetary motions. (See KEPLER'S LAWS.) In the seventeenth century Sir Isaac Newton proposed his three laws of motion that helped to clarify the concepts of force, acceleration, mass, and momentum.

NEWTON'S LAWS OF MOTION

I. Every body at rest tends to remain at rest and every body in motion tends to continue in motion in a straight line unless acted upon by an outside force.

II. If a body is acted upon by some outside force, the change in velocity of the body is in the direction of the applied force, is proportional to that force, and is inversely proportional to the mass of the body.

III. To every action there is an equal and opposite reaction.

The First Law. Newton's first and second laws are based on inertia, that property of matter that causes a body to resist a change in motion. (See INERTIA; MASS.) The first law states that all bodies have inertia and the conditions under which one can determine whether an outside force is acting on a system. For example, the fall of a book from a table on which it has been resting indicates either that some force must have acted on the book that had not previously acted on it, or that one of a combination of forces that had held the book at rest has been removed or has changed direction or magnitude. Finally, the first law states that a force or forces are acting on bodies that are not moving at a uniform speed and in a straight line. For example, a stone twirled at the end of a string tends to fly off in a straight line tangent to the circle the stone is describing if the string breaks. The fact that the earth and the other planets do not fly off in a straight line tangent to their paths and that electrons continue to orbit around a nucleus can be explained by assuming that one or more forces affect such motion, which therefore is neither uniform nor rectilinear.

The Second Law is an extension of the first or, more properly, the first law is a corollary of the second. It enables calculation of changes in motion resulting from forces of known magnitude, and of the magnitude of a force by observing the motions of bodies affected. Actually this law provides a definition of force. Stated in terms of momentum, it says that the rate at which momentum of a body changes with respect to time is proportional to the force applied and is in the direction of that force. As an equation it is stated $F=\frac{k(m_2v_2-m_1v_1)}{t}$, where F is force,

k is a constant denoting the unit of force employed, m_1 and v_1 are the initial mass and velocity of the body, m_2 and v_2 are the final mass and velocity of the body, and t is the time during which the force was applied and the change took place. If the mass of the body remains constant, the expression may be rewritten as $F=\frac{km(v_2-v_1)}{t}$. Since $\frac{v_1-v_2}{t}$, or the change in velocity with respect to time, is acceleration (a), the equation may be reduced to $F=kma$. If the units are so chosen that $k=1$, this expression may further be reduced to $F=ma$, or force equals mass times acceleration. Units that make $k=1$ include the dyne in the centimeter-gram-second system, the newton in the meter-kilogram-second system, the poundal in the foot-pound-second system, and the pound of force in the British engineering system.

Using the second law one can calculate, for example, the force necessary to increase to a rate of 60 mph in 5 seconds the speed of a 4,000-pound car traveling at a rate of 15 mph along a level road. In feet per second the initial and final velocities are 22 and 88, respectively. Then $F=\frac{m(v_1-v_2)}{t}=(4{,}000\text{ lb.})\frac{(88\text{ ft./sec.}-22\text{ ft./sec.})}{5\text{ sec.}}=\frac{4{,}000\text{ lb.}\times 66\text{ ft./sec.}}{5\text{ sec.}}=52{,}800\text{ foot-pounds/sec.}^2$

Recognition of Newton's second law of motion has been important in astronomical calculations and discoveries. The planet Neptune was discovered because observed motions of the planet Uranus could not be accounted for by known forces acting on Uranus.

The Third Law implies that it is impossible for a single action to exist and that if a force is exerted on a body an equal and opposite force will be exerted by the body. The third law may be illustrated by two marbles that collide and then rebound. The forces exerted by the two marbles on each other must be equal but opposite in direction. This is expressed in the form of an equation as

$$\frac{(m_1v_2-m_1v_1)}{t}=-\frac{(m_2u_2-m_2u_1)}{t}.$$

The minus sign indicates that the two forces are acting in opposite directions; m_1 is the weight of the first marble and v_1 and v_2 its initial and final velocities. Similarly m_2 is the weight of the second marble; u_1 and u_2 are its initial and final velocities. The time during which the marbles were in contact and the change in velocity occurred is represented by *t;* it is the same for both marbles. Multiplying both sides by t and expanding, the expression becomes $m_1v_2-m_1v_1=-m_2u_2+m_2u_1$, or $m_1v_2+m_2u_2=m_1v_1+m_2u_1$. The left side of this equation represents the total momentum of the marbles after impact, and the right side their momentum before impact. There has been no change in total momentum, that is, the momentum of the system as a whole has been conserved. Newton's third law therefore is known as the law of conservation of momentum. See FORCE; GRAVITATION; MECHANICS.

MOTION. See PROCEDURE, *Appellate Procedure;* TRIAL, *Motions and Objections.*

MOTION PICTURE

Art, technology, and business have made the "movies" a part of the modern way of life.

MOTION PICTURE, a series of still pictures which, when projected in rapid succession upon a screen or other reflecting surface, produces in onlookers the illusion of continuous movement. Each picture depicts a successive stage in a movement as photographed by a motion picture camera on strips of film 35 mm, 16 mm, or 8 mm in width. Because of the physiological effect known as persistence of vision, by which visual stimuli in rapid succession seem to be blended together, the successive pictures (known as frames) when projected at the same speed at which they were originally photographed (usually 24 frames per second) give the viewer the illusion of seeing the motion reproduced on the screen. A "slow motion" effect can be created by increasing the number of frames photographed per second, while projecting them at the normal rate. "Fast motion" is obtained by decreasing the number of frames photographed per second while projecting them at the normal rate.

EARLY HISTORY

Motion pictures in the modern sense first appeared late in the nineteenth century, but the phenomenon of visual persistence was known to the ancient Greeks; by 1825 Sir John Herschel demonstrated that when a coin is spun in the air at a certain speed it is possible to see both sides at once. In 1833 a device called the zoetrope (or wheel of life) was patented by W. G. Horner. It consisted of a hollow cylinder slotted at regular intervals; inside were hand-drawn pictures of successive stages in a motion; as the cylinder was revolved rapidly these pictures, when observed through the slots one after the other, seemed to re-create the motion depicted in the drawings. Later devices of this type were Coleman Sellers' kinematoscope, 1861, with the pictures mounted on a wheel; and Henry Renno Heyl's phasmatrope, first exhibited in 1870.

In the 1870's, an eccentric English photographer named Eadweard James Muybridge, assisted by John D. Isaacs, used 24 cameras to make serial photographs of horses and other animals and human beings in motion, and subsequently designed the zoopraxiscope (a modification of the zoetrope), 1879, for projecting the photographic plates one after the other on a screen; this device marks the first appearance of the shutter for cutting off light between pictures in sequence. Muybridge was perhaps the first to project serial photographs, using the magic-lantern principle dating from the seventeenth century. During the same period the French physiologist, Etienne Jules Marey, was conducting similar experiments, but these were incidental to his real interest—the influence of bodily movements on the circulation of the blood; nevertheless, he improved upon Muybridge's methods, 1882. In 1888 Muybridge suggested to Thomas Alva Edison that the zoopraxiscope might be combined with Edison's phonograph, but Edison, in co-operation with William K. L. Dickson, had already begun experiments of his own.

In a sense the kinetoscope, devised in 1889 by Edison and Dickson, was a backward step in that the principle of the magic lantern (that is, projection) was ignored; the kinetoscope was a peep-show device in which one person might view sequential still pictures in motion. The kinetoscope, however, made use of the nitrocellulose film developed in 1888–89 by George Eastman and the Rev. Hannibal Goodwin. Dickson, not Edison, is credited with devising the sprocket system of moving the film through the camera, and he also demonstrated to Edison (Oct. 6, 1889) that the kinetoscope could effectively be used in conjunction with the phonograph. At about the same time William Friese-Greene, in England, was experimenting with film in strips, first of paper and later of celluloid.

Edison, at first little interested in the kinetoscope, did not bother to patent it until 1891. In 1894 the kinetoscope made its first public appearance in a New York amusement parlor and was soon popular. In the meantime Thomas Armat of Washington, D.C. (working for a time with F. Charles Jenkins), the brothers Lumière (Louis and Auguste) in France, and many others worked with varying degrees of success at combining the principles of peep show and magic lantern. The first projector marketed by Edison, after 1896, was called the Armat vitascope, since it was essentially identical with the Armat-Jenkins phantoscope of the year before.

Dickson meanwhile had broken with Edison and allied himself with a group (E. B. Koopman, Herman Casler, and H. N. Marvin) that developed a peep show, the mutoscope, and later a motion picture projector, the American biograph, using a film wider than Edison's so as to avoid charges of patent infringement. Such charges, however, were not long in coming. In 1897 began Edison's protracted legal wars, principally against American Mutoscope and the Biograph Company. As motion pictures became a more profitable business, the situation was a complex of suit and countersuit. An armistice was declared in 1908–09 with the formation of the "co-operative" Motion Picture Patents Company, but the patent wars soon broke out again and continued until 1915. Actually the question of who invented motion pictures is so complex that no simple answer is possible. It is certain that, contrary to popular misconceptions, motion pictures were not invented by Edison, and that in fact he contributed little to their development. The basic principles involved antedated the work of all claimants; and dozens of men in the United States, in England, in France, and elsewhere made important contributions and freely borrowed and modified each other's ideas and equipment.

Motion Pictures as an Artistic Medium

For many years motion pictures were considered too trivial and vulgar to be called art. The astounding commercial success of the motion picture industry was one of the reasons why many years passed before more than a few eccentrics regarded the motion picture as anything but popular entertainment, and as such on a lower level than vaudeville. The transition took place much earlier and much more rapidly in Europe than in the United States and for this reason the general run of films made in Europe before 1927 (when the "silent era" is said to have ended) was on a higher artistic level than the general run in the United States—this despite the fact that the United States produced a number of film masterpieces (several of the films of David Wark Griffith, for example) that greatly influenced European production. Formal recognition in the United States of motion pictures as an artistic medium did not come until the establishment in 1935 of the film archive at the Museum of Modern Art in New York City.

Because of the diverse (largely commercial) uses made of the motion picture and its aesthetic ambiguity in consequence, historians of the motion picture have found their task difficult. In a sense there is no single history of the motion picture, but instead a number of histories—of the documentary film, the American film, the German (and French, and Italian, and English) film, the experimental film, the educational (or public information, or propaganda) film, the animated film, and others (see Animated Film; Audio-Visual Education; Communication; Documentary Film). Although these separate histories are not mutually exclusive, there are various significant and sometimes conflicting approaches to the medium reflected in them.

Form and Content. The various criteria employed by historians and critics of the motion picture can be grouped generally on the basis of their adherence to either one of two schools of thought, based on the traditional distinction between form and content in arts. (See Form.) One group maintains that motion pictures should be evaluated in terms of their contribution to the technical (that is, formal) advancement of film art as such, and that the question of content is secondary. According to the contrary view, the medium (that is, by implication, the form) is secondary to the use to which it is put: one may admit the technical excellence of a film, yet repudiate the film by reason of its foolish, immoral, subversive, or criminal content. Thus *The Triumph of the Will* (1934–37), a Nazi propaganda film, has been highly praised for its superb utilization of the unique qualities of the film medium. To one school of critics the fact that the film expresses distasteful ideas and concepts is irrelevant; critics of the other school may condemn the film, despite its technical excellence, because of its ideological or moral content. By the same token, many believe that D. W. Griffith's *Birth of a Nation* (1915), generally recognized as a milestone in the artistic development of the motion picture, is marred by reason of its apparent social implications.

Considerations such as these have been of great significance in matters of film censorship, and also bear upon a distinction fundamental to all discussion of the subject: that between films as art and films as entertainment. A film may make a notable contribution to motion picture art, yet be suspect as entertainment by reason of its content; similarly, a film may make no contribution to film art, yet may be excellent as entertainment, as propaganda, or as an instrument of education.

Highlights in Silent Motion Picture History, 1893–1927

The first motion picture studio was Edison's famous "Black Maria," in Orange, N.J., a small tar-paper-covered building with a hinged roof that could be folded back to let in the sunlight. The Black Maria, with W. K. L. Dickson supervising, began production in February, 1893. One of the first films produced there was a re-enactment of *The Execution of Mary, Queen of Scots* (1893–94), made initially for the kinetoscope but later adapted for projection. The famous (and in its day, notorious) *May Irwin–John C. Rice Kiss* (1896), featuring two celebrated stage performers re-enacting for the camera a notable moment from their stage vehicle, *The Widow Jones*, also came from the Edison studio. In France, Georges Méliés delighted early film audiences with the surrealistic trick photography (including double exposure) of *A Trip to the Moon* (1902) and *The Doctor's Secret* (1908). Méliés was a pioneer in using stage make-up, lighting, and sets in films, and in these respects American producers followed his lead. Some historians credit Méliés with being first to use the close-up, the flash back, the fade-out, and the dissolve.

Many films of this period were topical views of contemporary scenes, entirely without plot or incident. Sometimes, prefiguring later film comedy, a simple comic (usually slapstick) incident, without plot, would be filmed, such as *Wash Day Troubles* (1895), made at the Black Maria. An 11,000-foot film (perhaps the longest up to that time) by Enoch Rector of the Corbett-Fitzsimmons prize fight in 1897 foreshadowed newsreels and documentaries, and proved that people were willing to look at motion pictures of long duration. In Pittsburgh, Pa., John P. Harris and Harry Davis opened the world's first nickelodeon to show this film.

Motion an End in Itself. *The Great Train Robbery* (1903), directed by Edwin S. Porter for the Edison Company and featuring "Bronco Billy" Anderson, was perhaps the first film to tell a connected story. It includes, in crude form, techniques that were to be highly influential later—there is a close-up, its outdoor sequences are untheatrical, the camera is made to move to follow the action. The film also ushered in the most perennially successful of film genres—the western with its ritualistic good-*vs.*-evil moral tone, its stereotyped "chase" scenes, and the like; western heroes such as Bronco Billy, William S. Hart, Tom Mix, Hoot Gibson, Gene Autry, and Roy Rogers (the latter two with guitars) became famous throughout the world. If *The Great Train Robbery* demonstrated that the motion picture could be used for telling stories, other films of the same period showed that a film might also be a real-life incident, photographed while it happened, or an incident from history as re-enacted; a skit out of vaudeville or burlesque; a bit of fantasy or whimsey with emphasis on trick camera effects; a famous stage play, or scenes from a play, in which famous stage personalities would appear (such as the *films d'art* produced after 1908 in France, featuring actors from the Comédie Française). But whatever the ostensible subject matter of a film, for many the real subject matter of any motion picture was the motion itself—the one essential quality of the new medium. Later historians and critics were to view all films with this idea in mind, and were to condemn all attempts to make the motion picture the vehicle for stage plays and other "uncinematic" material.

Hollywood. The first complete motion picture made in the Los Angeles area was William N. Selig's *In the Sultan's Power* (1908), but there was motion picture activity in the region by 1904. In 1909 the Bison Company began making westerns in Edendale, Calif. Biograph (which in 1907 had obtained the services of D. W. Griffith) and the Essanay and Kalem companies moved to California to take advantage of the sunshine. Griffith in 1910 inaugurated a policy of regular production during the winter months in the Los Angeles area. The first company to locate in the area that was to become Hollywood was the Nestor Film Company.

The period before World War I was one of feverish and sometimes contradictory activity in the motion picture industry. On the one hand, in 1912 New York theater operator Adolph Zukor imported from France a *film d'art*, *Queen Elizabeth*, in which Sarah Bernhardt played the title role. This film was notable for having Bernhardt but contributed nothing to motion picture art as such; moreover, it gave impetus to the star system then beginning to develop. On the other hand D. W. Griffith was at work—*A Corner in Wheat* (1909), *The New York Hat* (with Mary Pickford and Lionel Barrymore, 1912), among others. Hardly less important, in 1913 Charlie Chaplin, probably the greatest of the screen comedians, went to work for $150 a week at Mack Sennett's slapstick comedy factory in Hollywood. As the public's enthusiasm for one- and two-reel short films of the "Keystone Kops," the Sennett bathing beauties, Fatty Arbuckle, Mabel Normand, and the rest of the slapstick pantheon continued unabated, Sennett produced the first full-length comedy, *Tillie's Punctured Romance* (1914), with Marie Dressler and Chaplin. This, more than any other film up to that time, convinced movie exhibitors that the public not only would accept, but wanted, feature-length films.

Griffith. In his epic of the Civil War and the Reconstruction, *The Birth of a Nation* (1915), Griffith summed up and expanded upon virtually everything then known about making motion pictures and, in addition, pointed the way that motion picture technique was to take (see BIRTH OF A NATION). Rapid cross cutting, the split screen, fadeouts, dissolves, and other devices that later became commonplace were used in this film with a daring and a facility never before approached. Griffith's most brilliant film, however, was yet to come: *Intolerance* (1916).

D. W. Griffith's *Intolerance*, 1916, portrays the painful consequences of men's prejudices by the use of parallel stories set in four historical epochs, ancient to modern.
MUS. OF MODERN ART

It has been said of *Intolerance* that "it is the end and justification of that whole school of American cinematography based on the terse cutting and disjunctive assembly of film" that began with *The Great Train Robbery* (Iris Barry in the *Bulletin of The Museum of Modern Art*, Vol. XVI). The film consists of four separate but analogous stories showing intolerance wreaking havoc in ancient Babylonia, in biblical times, in France during the reign of Charles IX, and in modern times. The four stories are interwoven in a complex, suspense-building manner until, in the last two reels (of a 130-minute film that includes almost 1,400 separate shots) "the climax of all four stories approaches and history itself seems to pour like a cataract across the screen." Further, "in his direction of the immense crowd scenes, Griffith achieves the impossible for . . . the eye is irresistibly drawn to the one significant detail." This film, highly influential the world over, was the greatest single influence upon Russian film making after the 1917 Revolution. Many critics believe that in its use of the technique of montage *Intolerance* defined once and for all time the proper course for future development of the medium. See GRIFFITH, DAVID LEWELYN WARK.

Big Business. Apart from his many important contributions to film technique, Griffith brought massive spectacle to the screen, and with it higher production costs. The burgeoning star system compounded the matter. For example, in 1916, after Charles Chaplin left Keystone Comedies to join Mutual Film Corporation, his yearly salary as a star was $670,000. Other high-salaried stars of the period were the "vamp" Theda Bara; Douglas Fairbanks (Sr.), who combined adventurous acrobatics with a flair for comedy; William S. Hart, dour western hero; and Mary Pickford, the very opposite of the vamp. Motion pictures were by then big business, controlled by bankers in New York City, although most U.S. films were made in California. Griffith was one of the first to suffer from this situation, and spent more and more of his time in New York on financial matters. The Edison Company, unable to compete in the new atmosphere, expired in 1916.

As big business, movies were expected first of all to make money; the comparatively free and easy days that had made *Intolerance* possible were fast disappearing. From the artistic standpoint the result was that in the post-World War I period, as more and more art critics began to take motion pictures seriously (in large measure as the result of Griffith's work) aesthetic leadership in motion pictures was assumed by European producers. A great many of the truly significant U.S. films during the 1920's were made by producers and directors imported from Europe, such as F. W. Murnau, whose *Sunrise* (1927) appeared toward the end of the silent era, and Josef von Sternberg, remembered for *Underworld* (1927) and others. Griffith's later films, such as *Broken Blossoms* (1919) and *Way Down East* (1920), produced for United Artists (a joint distribution company that Griffith formed with Mary Pickford, Charles Chaplin, and Douglas Fairbanks, Sr.), were important and influential, but were exceptional for their time.

The fate of *Greed* (1923–24), written and directed by Erich von Stroheim, illustrates the conflict between commercial and artistic factors that influenced American production during the last decade of the silent film. The film's producers, Metro-Goldwyn-Mayer, ordered Von Stroheim to stop with the 30 reels (more than six hours' running time) that he had already filmed, and finally had someone else cut it to 10 reels (126 minutes). See GREED.

CULVER SERVICE

Greed, produced in 1924 for Metro-Goldwyn-Mayer by Erich von Stroheim, develops the theme of man's lust for money and the self-destruction that it inevitably causes.

Serious films such as *Greed* were not popular enough to justify huge expenditures of money unless, like King Vidor's *The Big Parade* (1925), they had a "sure-fire" subject such as the Great War. Comedies, comparatively inexpensive to produce, invariably made money. The costume extravaganzas of Cecil B. De Mille cost a great deal to produce, but they were highly profitable, however negligible artistically they might seem to the critics (see DE MILLE, CECIL BLOUNT). The attitude then developing in Hollywood was favorable toward large expenditures, but only if the money was spent on a "sure thing"; eventually the process of determining "what the public wants" was to become as important a part of the motion picture business as writing, directing, acting, and the other operations directly connected with production.

Comedy. Not all popular pictures were insignificant artistically. Comedies were popular and Hollywood had several comedians of genius besides Chaplin. Among the high spots of film comedy in this period were Buster Keaton in *The Navigator* (1924), *The General* (1927), and others; Stan Laurel and Oliver Hardy in *Two Tars* (1928) and many others; Harold Lloyd in *The Freshman* (1925) and others; and the films of Harry Langdon. Chaplin appeared in dozens of comedies as well as the important melodrama (in which he appeared only briefly) *A Woman of Paris* (1923), which he wrote and directed with great skill. See CHAPLIN, CHARLES SPENCER.

The forgotten, behind-the-scenes genius of American film comedy was Mack Sennett, who from its beginnings helped develop and bring out the individual comic styles of Lloyd, Langdon, Keaton, and most of the silent era's other great comedians not even excepting Chaplin. Much of the film comedy of the 1930's and after, owed a great debt to Sennett and his disciples. In the development of the motion picture as an artistic medium most historians agree that the work of the great Hollywood comedians was of much more importance than the majority of the films that in the 1920's were considered superb—the flamboyant vehicles for the matinee idol Rudolph Valentino, for example; and the films of "the man with a thousand faces," Lon Chaney, a major star of the period, whose films such as *The Hunchback of Notre Dame* (1923) were interesting primarily for Chaney's ingenious use of theatrical make-up. The films of Douglas Fairbanks, Sr., however, continued to be highly regarded, perhaps because he infused his costume dramas—such as *The Mark of Zorro* (1920), *Robin Hood* (1922), and *The Thief of Bagdad* (1924)—with light-hearted touches of comic bravura. His *Wild and Wooly* (1919), among others, was definitely satirical in tone. His films communicated a sense of movement, as did the better comedies.

With the coming of the sound film, first in *Don Juan* (1926), with John Barrymore, significant changes were to take place in Hollywood. In the meantime, however, European producers and directors after World War I had done at least as much artistically with the silent film as had American producers. During the silent era, when there was no language barrier, the films of several European countries were popular and influential in the United States.

Germany. The golden era of film making in Germany began with the bizarre *Cabinet of Dr. Caligari* (1919), one of the most enigmatic films ever made, and for several reasons one of the more important (see CABINET OF DR. CALIGARI, THE). To it can be attributed the appearance of the "horror movie" genre, both in Europe and, after 1921, in the United States. Although its principal immediate effect was to give film critics a new standard by which to condemn more conventional films, it had considerable direct influence upon film making (particularly in matters of theme and atmosphere and in encouraging experimentation). Other German film masterpieces of the 1920's were Arthur Robison's *Warning Shadows* (1922); Fritz Lang's *Destiny* (1921), *Siegfried* (1923), and *Metropolis* (1926); F. W. Murnau's revolutionary *The Last Laugh* (1924), starring Emil Jannings, in which the moving camera technique was developed and employed as never before; E. A. Dupont's *Variety* (1925), also with Jannings; and George Wilhelm Pabst's unrealistic but brilliant *The Treasure* (1924) and his brutally realistic *The Joyless Street* (1925), and *The Love of Jeanne Ney* (1927), starring Greta Garbo.

U.S.S.R. The brilliant Russian director Sergei M. Eisenstein, under the influence of Griffith's *Intolerance*, brought to new perfection the technique of montage in such films as *Battleship Potemkin* (1925)—whose Odessa Steps massacre sequence has been called the most influential six minutes in the history of the motion picture. The Russian theorists worked out mathematically the complex rhythms and other effects, particularly those relating to montage, that Griffith had improvised intuitively. Among other notable Russian films of the silent period were Eisenstein's *Strike* (1924) and *Ten Days That Shook the World* (1928); and the films of Vsevolod Pudovkin, including *Mother* (1925), *The End of St. Petersburg* (1927), and *Storm over Asia* (1928). The analytical writings of Dziga Vertov, Eisenstein, Pudovkin, and other Russian directors influenced film making and film criticism throughout the world.

France. As the silent era drew to a close, France's greatest period in motion picture history was yet to come, but the importance of French films during the 1930's was foreshadowed by the brilliant works of René Clair, such as the comedy *The Italian Straw Hat* (1928), and by the many experimental movements of the 1920's, paralleling those in painting, literature, and the other arts. Among motion picture experimentalists in France were Germaine Dulac, Fernand

Buster Keaton, seen here in *The Cameraman*, grew famous as lovable deadpan whose knowing innocence won out in its hilarious struggles with an unco-operative universe.

GEORGE EASTMAN HOUSE, INC.

MUS. OF MODERN ART

The production of Sergei Eisenstein's *Potemkin* in 1925 was one of the milestones of film history. This dramatic shot is from the very influential Odessa Steps sequence.

Léger, René Clair, Marcel Duchamp, Cavalcanti, and Man Ray. One of the greatest masterpieces of the silent film era was *The Passion of Joan of Arc* (1928), produced in France by the Danish director Carl Theodor Dreyer. The film has been strongly criticized by some as "uncinematic" and static, but has been given the highest praise by other film historians for its almost miraculous expressiveness and depth. So excellent are the directing, acting, and photography that the viewer seems to hear dialogue although the film is silent; for this reason this picture is frequently cited in connection with the transition from silent to talking pictures. See DREYER, CARL THEODOR.

COLOR AND SOUND

Almost from the outset attempts were made to develop motion pictures with sound and in color. After many false starts both in the United States and abroad, Warner Brothers and the Vitaphone Corporation released in 1926 the first successful talking film (using disks): *Don Juan*, starring John Barrymore. The first successful color process had its first triumph in the same year. Although the Technicolor Motion Picture Corporation had demonstrated its successful process in 1922, Douglas Fairbanks' *The Black Pirate* (1926) was the first Technicolor feature film. Both sound and color were novelties, however, and the great bulk of pictures produced continued silent and in black and white. William Fox's demonstration of sound photographed on film, 1927, and the Al Jolson vehicle *The Jazz Singer* (1927), in which the popular vocalist sang a song and delivered a few lines of dialogue in sound photographed on film, convinced the industry that sound was no mere novelty: the public wanted it. The Warner Brothers' gangster film *The Lights of New York* (1928) was the first picture to employ sound throughout. Many important stars of the silent era were ruined when it was found that they had poor speaking voices.

These mechanical innovations (as distinct from technical innovations in the aesthetic realm) were not unmixed blessings, and many critics date the decline of the motion picture as an art form from the introduction of them. Apart from this possibility, it is certain that in the early years of sound films there occurred something of an aesthetic regression to pre-Griffith days. Many, perhaps most, of the films in the late 1920's and early 1930's talked but did little else; much that had been learned in the silent era about the motion in motion pictures was neglected by an industry bemused with sound and its special problems. Dreyer's *The Passion of Joan of Arc* without sound, and Charles Chaplin's *City Lights* (1931) and *Modern Times* (1936), both without spoken dialogue and using sound sparingly, seemed to be more expressive than most films of the period in which performers imported from Broadway talked fluently.

Fairly early in the 1930's the industry began to adjust to the situation and the motion picture became not merely a visual medium of artistic expression but an audio-visual one. King Vidor's *Hallelujah* (1929) was a major turning point in the transition. Despite the advances made in the use of sound, however, it was the opinion of some critics that the audio and visual aspects of films are so fundamentally opposed that full integration of the two is impossible. The efforts of the French director René Clair to make creative use of asynchronous sound (sound against image) contributed to several great films but had little real influence; and the attempts in the same direction by Soviet film makers were stifled by the "socialist realism" of Joseph Stalin.

Color, the use of which became common in the 1930's, was an even more difficult aesthetic problem and its use up to *Gone with the Wind* (1939) was merely incidental: the film would have been essentially the same in black and white. Apart from various experimental films, integral use of color in the motion picture continued to be rare. Such use was demonstrated in portions of John Huston's film about Toulouse-Lautrec, *Moulin Rouge* (1953), in which color was effectively used in the manner of Toulouse-Lautrec; and in the magnificent Japanese film *Gate of Hell* (1954), thought by many to be one of the finest films ever made. Also notable were the experiments in color music (abstract moving images integrated with music) of the Canadian film artist Norman McLaren and others.

Effects of Color and Sound on Motion Picture Production. In the silent days the essential elements of the production were already defined. The producer was overseer of all aspects (including financial) of the production of a picture or of a number of pictures at once. The director, aided by various assistants and in conjunction with the cinematographer, translated the scenario from words on a page to images on film, and later supervised (in one degree or another) the editing of masses of film into the finished motion picture; some directors, like Griffith, Von Stroheim, Eisenstein, and Dreyer, supervised editing closely or did it themselves, recognizing that all earlier work on a film might be undone by poor editing. Then there were the actors, ranging from the stars down through featured players, bit players, and extras—the latter comprising most of the "cast of thousands" mentioned in the advertisements. Finally there were people who designed sets, applied make-up to the actors' faces, selected costumes, obtained properties, and performed other work essential to production.

With the introduction of sound and color all these functions became more difficult. These changes meant that motion pictures became much more expensive to produce—a fact that tightened the control of the business office in the major companies and drove many independent motion picture producers out of business. It became even more difficult for the single creative individual such as Griffith to operate. Nevertheless important and creative pictures still emerged from Hollywood and other centers of activity in France and elsewhere.

ARTISTIC DEVELOPMENT OF THE SOUND FILM

France. In the 1930's the French motion picture came into its own. Apart from their intrinsic merits, the French films of this period are particularly significant because many French directors were imported by Hollywood in the late 1930's (and had influenced Hollywood production even before this).

Avant-garde experimentation for which the French and Germans were noted in the 1920's disappeared in

Germany with the rise of Hitlerism but continued apace in France; the value of such experimentation lay not so much in the experimental films themselves (although many were excellent) as in the influence they exerted on motion pictures made for a wider audience.

René Clair's outstanding films *Sous les toits de Paris* (1929), *Le Million* (1931), and *A nous la Liberté* (1932) are particularly notable for the fact that in both, sound was used as a tool and not as a self-justifying device; the last named anticipated Chaplin's *Modern Times* (1936) in both its use of sound and its indictment of industrialism. Clair's idea of the proper use of sound in films (which he regarded as fundamentally visual) is called the principle of asynchronous sound, or (in critic Arthur Knight's words) "sound used against rather than with the images . . . [giving] a new freedom and fluidity" to the use of sound. Thus, "he worked with a minimum of dialogue, using music, choruses and sound effects to counterpoint and comment upon his visuals." (See CLAIR, RENÉ.) Jean Vigo produced two almost surrealistic, thoroughly delightful films, *L'Atalante* (1934) and *Zéro de conduite* (1932), both making creative use of the audio element by carefully subordinating it to the visual, and making use of Clair's principles.

Marcel Pagnol, a playwright, thought of the screen as a way of preserving theatrical drama; his films have been criticized as "uncinematic" and lacking in film sense. Nevertheless several of them, notably the 1932–33 trilogy *Marius*, *Fanny*, and *César* (six hours over-all in length) and the superb *Angèle*, are masterpieces. Filmed plays they may be, but they are full of charming atmosphere and effective dialogue and are excellently performed by such actors as the immortal Raimu, Pierre Fresnay, Charpin, and (in *Angèle*) Fernandel. It is true, however, that these excellent films are more notable as contributions to the theater than as *motion* pictures.

Jean Renoir directed such notable films as *The Lower Depths* (1936), with Jean Gabin and Louis Jouvet, and *La Grande Illusion* (1937), with Gabin, Fresnay, and Erich von Stroheim. These films, like many others of the French in the 1930's, such as Jacques Feyder's *Carnival in Flanders* (1936), Julien Duvivier's *Pépé le Moko* (1938), Marcel Carné's *Quai des brumes* (1938), *Le jour se lève* (1939), and *Les enfants du paradis* (1943), were criticized by film purists as theatrical but were notable for their excellent acting and superior content (see CARNÉ, MARCEL). Also important are the films of Jean Cocteau, *Sang d'un poète* (1930), *Orpheus* (1950), and others; and those of Henri-Georges Clouzot, *Le Corbeau* (1943), *Salaire de la peur* (1953), and *Les Diaboliques* (1955) among others, all of them critical and popluar successes in Europe and in the United States (see COCTEAU, JEAN; CLOUZOT, HENRI-GEORGES). Among the important French directors who made films in Hollywood were Clair, Renoir, Duvivier, and Carné. Developments in the French cinema in the late 1950's and 1960's resulted in what was called the New Wave. The direction of François Truffaut in *The 400 Blows* (1959), *Jules and Jim* (1962), and *Shoot the Piano Player* (1962); and of Alain Resnais in *Hiroshima, Mon Amour* (1959) and *Last Year at Marienbad* (1961) showed great complexity of thought and technical virtuosity.

La Grande Illusion, 1937, starring Erich von Stroheim and directed by Jean Renoir, makes an impassioned plea for the end of war. The film was long banned in Germany.
MUS. OF MODERN ART

England. England produced no significant film art until the advent, in the late 1920's, of Alfred Hitchcock, who soon became famous as a master of the crime-suspense film (with large doses of the comic and grotesque thrown in) such as *Blackmail* (1929), *The 39 Steps* (1935), *The Secret Agent* (1935), *The Woman Alone* (1936), and *The Lady Vanishes* (1938). After 1928, under the aegis of John Grierson, the British directors Paul Rotha, Len Lye, Ralph Bond, Grierson himself, and others made notable contributions to the documentary film, developing this genre in a manner quite different from that of the American school of Robert Flaherty. After World War II British art cinema flourished, especially in Sir Laurence Olivier's Shakespearean films such as *Henry V* (1945), notable also for its effective use of color; in the crime-suspense film (although without the aid of Hitchcock, who had long since gone to Hollywood); and in frothy comedies in which British "types" are depicted responding with utmost gravity to wildly improbable situations. Performers such as Ralph Richardson, Margaret Rutherford, Alec Guinness, Peter Sellers, and many others attained considerable popularity in the United States, as did such directors as Carol Reed. Another serious director, David Lean, made *The Bridge on the River Kwai* (1957) and *Lawrence of Arabia* (1962). By the 1960's, British cinema was emphasizing social protest movies depicting the squalor of life in the industrial north of England. In this vein, Tony Richardson directed *Look Back in Anger* (1958), *A Taste of Honey* (1961), and *The Loneliness of the Long Distance Runner* (1962), as well as such films as *Tom Jones* (1963).

Germany produced a number of important films in the early 1930's, including Pabst's *Westfront 1918* (1930), *Die Dreigroschenoper* (1930), and *Kameradschaft* (1931); and *M* (1931), whose director Fritz Lang and star Peter Lorre both went to Hollywood. The rise of Hitlerism drove most of the best talent out of Germany as the technically superb German picture industry was turned to propaganda uses, exemplified in Leni Riefenstahl's *Olympia* (1939). Pabst remained in Germany but his work declined somewhat in quality; after World War II he directed a notable film about *The Last Ten Days* (1955) of Adolf Hitler.

U.S.S.R. Russian film making, too, declined in the 1930's, especially after 1935 when officialdom decreed that the films must abandon montage, which Eisenstein and others had so skillfully developed, in favor of "socialist realism." Attempts on the part of some Soviet theorists (Dziga Vertov, *Three Songs About Lenin*, 1934, and others) to develop a montage of sound to complement visual montage were also discouraged and ultimately stifled. The later films of Eisenstein such as *Alexander Nevsky* (1938) and the brilliant, moody, slow-moving *Ivan the Terrible* (part I, 1944) appear to be attempts at a compromise between his own principles and the official Soviet program; later portions of the Ivan trilogy were suppressed by the Stalin regime. *Ivan the Terrible* (part II, about 1945) was not released until 1959, when non-Soviet critics acclaimed it as even better than part I. Part III was never completed. Certain of the films of social realism, such as Grigori Kosintzev's *Youth of Maxim Gorky*, are not without merit as motion pictures apart from their lapses into propagandistic unrealism. The post-Stalin thaw in the arts resulted in such sensitive films as *The Cranes Are Flying* (1959), *Ballad of a*

MUS. OF MODERN ART

Open City, 1946, was the first film directed by Roberto Rossellini. It is an extraordinarily realistic, superbly handled film depicting Rome during the German occupation.

Soldier (1961), and *A Summer to Remember* (1961), emphasizing the individual and personal quality of human experience.

Poland. The 1960's witnessed the production of several exciting Polish films, notably *Ashes and Diamonds* (1958) and *Knife in the Water* (1962).

Sweden. No sound film made in Sweden prior to World War II equaled the silent *Story of Gösta Berling* (1924), starring Greta Garbo and directed by Mauritz Stiller. After World War II, however, the Swedish film industry entered a period of greatness, principally through the work of Ingmar Bergman, who produced a number of film masterpieces, notably *The Seventh Seal* (1956), *Wild Strawberries* (1957). Both films were compared to those of the Danish director, Carl Theodor Dreyer, in that they deal with ideas and feelings much more abstract than those usually treated in films.

Denmark made its greatest contribution to film art in Carl Theodor Dreyer, whose films were unpopular in Denmark but recognized elsewhere as works of genius; notable among his later works are *Day of Wrath* (1944), which some critics include among the few truly great films, and *Ordet* (1956).

Italy produced little of importance to film history until after World War II when Italian neorealism, beginning with Roberto Rosselini's *Open City* (1945), attracted much attention. Other significant films of this school are Rosselini's *Paisan* (1946) and *Germany Year Zero* (1947), Luigi Zampa's *To Live in Peace* (1947), and Vittorio de Sica's *Shoeshine* (1945) and

Howard Hughes's 1932 production *Scarface*, starring Paul Muni, remains among the best of the "gangster" films. It was written by Ben Hecht and directed by Howard Hawks.

MUS. OF MODERN ART

The Bicycle Thief (1948). In the following decade three major directorial talents were revealed. Luchino Visconti continued the realism of the 1940's in *Rocco and His Brothers* (1961). More unconventional and inventive, Federico Fellini directed *La Strada* (1954), *La Dolce Vita* (1960), and *8½* (1963), revealing remarkable technical skill as well as a vision of modern degeneracy. Michelangelo Antonioni's films are generally more somber, though perhaps more brilliant. *L'Avventura* (1960), *La Notte* (1961), and *L'Eclisse* (1961) depict characters searching for any meaning in life.

Japan and India. Certain Japanese films, such as Akira Kurosawa's *Rashomon* (1951), blended the technique of the German, French, and Russian masters with realism and Japanese theatrical artificiality, with excellent results. India, like Japan one of the major production centers in terms of quantity, produced little or no work of artistic significance until the later 1950's, when the young director Satyjit Ray made the prize-winning Aputrilogy (1956–1960).

Latin America. Serious films of high quality have also come from Mexico, Argentina, and Brazil. The unflinching examination of human nature in the brilliant direction of Luis Buñuel won particular acclaim. Buñuel's rare gifts shine brightly in *The Young and the Damned* (1950) and *Viridiana* (1961).

United States. *The Broadway Melody* (1929) is an important early example of the many musical films

MUS. OF MODERN ART

Dashiell Hammett's detective story *The Maltese Falcon* was made into a film in 1941 by John Huston, who gained recognition as one of Hollywood's most capable directors.

that followed the advent of sound. Also notable in this genre are *42nd Street* (1932), starring Ruby Keeler; the many films of Fred Astaire, with Ginger Rogers and other dancing partners, beginning with *Flying Down to Rio* (1933); and much later the *Road to Rio* and other "Road" pictures of Bing Crosby-Bob Hope-Dorothy Lamour. Later, successful Broadway musicals were made into equally successful films, such as *Oklahoma* (1955) and *West Side Story* (1961).

Another perennial film style, so saturated with clichés (like the western and the musical) as to be almost ritualistic, was the gangster film, exemplified by *Little Caesar* (1930), with Edward G. Robinson; Howard Hughes's violent *Scarface* (1932), with Paul

MUS. OF MODERN ART

The zany Marx brothers—Harpo, Chico, and Groucho—made a generation of viewers laugh at their hilarious antics. The scene is from *A Night at the Opera,* filmed in 1935.

Muni and George Raft (the latter casually flipping a silver dollar while mowing down his enemies); and *The Public Enemy* (1931), in which James Cagney became famous by mashing half a grapefruit in Mae Clarke's face. Also popular were horror films such as *Frankenstein* (1930), with Boris Karloff, and its successors; the Dracula series featuring the great (until typed by Hollywood) Hungarian actor Bela Lugosi; and the horror-adventure film *King Kong* (1933). Other favorites were romantic adventure films deriving from the Douglas Fairbanks tradition, such as *The Prisoner of Zenda* (1937), starring Ronald Colman and Douglas Fairbanks, Jr.; and war adventure films such as *Hell's Angels* (1930), with Jean Harlow.

Detective films of high quality ranged from those in the humorous style inaugurated by Myrna Loy and William Powell in *The Thin Man* (1934) to those emphasizing violence such as John Huston's *The Maltese Falcon* (1941), starring Humphrey Bogart. The first type was related to the light domestic comedy such as *Nothing Sacred* (1937), with Carole Lombard, and to films exemplifying the celebrated Ernst Lubitsch "touch" such as *Design for Living* (1933), with Gary Cooper, Miriam Hopkins, and Fredric March. That the western thriller could be put to significant artistic use was first demonstrated by John Ford in *Stagecoach* (1939); later examples were *High Noon* (1952), *The Fastest Gun Alive* (1956), and *The Magnificent Seven* (1960).

Outstanding Broadway plays were made into motion pictures, such as Eugene O'Neill's *The Long Voyage Home* (1940), directed by John Ford, and Tennessee Williams's *A Streetcar Named Desire* (1952), directed by Elia Kazan. Many important novels became important films, for example, *All Quiet on the Western Front* (1930), with Lew Ayres; *The Grapes of Wrath* (1940), directed by John Ford; and *East of Eden* (1955), from a novel by John Steinbeck and directed by Elia Kazan. A brilliant and influential film not adopted from another medium was Orson Welles's *Citizen Kane* (1940). Welles's *The Magnificent Ambersons* (1942), adapted from the Booth Tarkington novel, suffered a fate similar to that of Von Stroheim's *Greed*, but was most impressive.

Film Comedy continued to flourish in Hollywood after the introduction of sound. Laurel and Hardy in *Brats* (1932) and dozens more, Chaplin, and many other comedians of the silent days, made an easy transition to the new medium. Chaplin largely ignored sound until *The Great Dictator* (1940). Even in his later films, however, such as *Monsieur Verdoux* (1947) and *Limelight* (1952), he made conservative use of the new tool. Buster Keaton, however, considered by some authorities a greater silent comedian than Chaplin, was relatively unsuccessful in sound films. The Marx brothers (Groucho, Harpo, Chico, and for a time Zeppo), in *The Coconuts* (1929), *Animal Crackers* (1930), *Duck Soup* (1933), *A Night at the Opera*

(1935), *A Day at the Races* (1937), and others; and W. C. Fields, in *You're Telling Me* (1934), *It's a Gift* (1934), *The Bank Dick* (1940), and many others; were notable for their ability to take advantage of the humorous possibilities of both motion and sound. The Marx brothers, Fields, and other comedians probably made better use of the insight of René Clair into asynchronous sound than did many more pretentious, dramatic directors. Popular comedy duos were Abbott and Costello in the '40s and, in the '50s, Dean Martin and Jerry Lewis. The best comic combinations of script, acting, and direction were creations of Billy Wilder, such as *Some Like it Hot* (1959) and *The Apartment* (1960).

A genre of movie particularly associated with Hollywood and persisting since the early days of the industry is the spectacular. Cecil B. de Mille, whose name is practically synonomous with the spectacular, produced a silent version of *The Ten Commandments* in 1923 and redid the movie on a far more lavish scale in 1955. Other films of this type include *Sparticus* (1960) and *Cleopatra* (1963), the most expensive movie ever made, with a cost of $40,000,000.

In a more sober and serious vein, American movies began to deal with the subject of race relations. In the early '60s *I Passed for White* was such a film and the experimental *Shadows*, directed by John Cassavetes. The Broadway play *A Raisin in the Sun* was made into a movie in (1961).

The star system, based on financial rather than artistic considerations, was more firmly entrenched in Hollywood than elsewhere in the world, but this did not always work to the disadvantage of the film art. Stars such as Greta Garbo and Marlene Dietrich in the '30s and '40s, or Marilyn Monroe and Elizabeth Taylor in the '50s and '60s, could draw an audience to any movie, but their personal lives suffered from the merciless glare of publicity.

An emphasis on mechanical innovations began early in the 1960s with 3-D (stereoscopic) movies, requiring members of the audience to wear polarizing spectacles. This was soon abandoned as too cumbersome and emphasis was shifted to wider screens to enhance the illusion of depth, stereophonic sound systems, and renewed emphasis on realistic color. Among the many new systems were Cinerama, Filmorama, Vista-Vision, Cinemiracle, and Circarama.

BILL DOLL AND CO.

Michael Todd's *Around the World in 80 Days,* featuring David Niven and the Latin American comedian Cantinflas, was an extravagant adaptation of the Jules Verne classic.

Censorship. Historians of the American film have often charged that its artistic progress was impeded by censorship. During most of the 1920's Hollywood was ostensibly regulating itself through the Motion Picture Producers and Distributors of America, the trade organization known popularly as the Hays office (after the film "czar" Will Hays); but many groups concerned with the morals of the movies were not satisfied. A Catholic Legion of Decency (not an official agency of the Roman Catholic church) was formed in 1933; its members were pledged to exert pressure on Hollywood by not attending motion pictures condemned as immoral by the organization's officers. In response to this development and to various threats of federal and local governmental regulation, the MPPDA in 1934 set up the Production Code Administration, whose function was to apply the so-called production code (a list of prohibitions) in such a way as to anticipate what might be objected to by the Legion of Decency and other groups, and to remove such elements from pictures before release so as to avert boycotts by private groups and possible censorship by state and local governments. The production code was much criticized—as too strict by some, as too lax by others—but in general served its stated purpose. The most telling criticism of the code was that it governed only details and exerted little influence on the over-all tone of a film. Another criticism, particularly after World War II, was that the code had not kept up with changing times. The code was revised late in 1956, but only in matters of detail, not in its basic principles and approach. Various U.S. Supreme Court decisions in 1957–59 all but eliminated state and local censorship laws and enforcement agencies, but unofficial censorship continued. See CENSORSHIP.

A significant development in American movies by the sixties was the growth in the number of independent producers. Many stars, such as Marlon Brando and Burt Lancaster, created their own companies to produce movies in which they would often act and direct, thereby competing with the large Hollywood organizations. New techniques in moviemaking, such as lightweight cameras and extremely sensitive film, were used to good effect.

Internationalism, by the 1960's, had become a fact of the movie-industry life. Not only were foreign movies shown increasingly in the United States, but U.S. companies were making movies abroad, taking advantage of cheap labor, attractive location sites, tax loopholes, and subsidies from foreign governments. Moreover, more and more films were coming to be written, produced, directed, and acted by individuals from different nations, so that no one country could fully claim the film.

BIBLIOGRAPHY

Rudolph Arnheim, *Film as Art* (1958); Daniel Blum, *Pictorial History of the Talkies* (1958); Jean Cocteau, *Diary of a Film* (1950); Sergei Eisenstein, *Film Form* (1949); Museum of Modern Art, *Silent Film* (1949); Hortense Powdermaker, *Hollywood: The Dream Factory* (1950); V. I. Pudovkin, *Film Technique and Acting;* Lillian Ross, *Picture* (1962); Gilbert Seldes, *Seven Lively Arts* (1957).

MOTION SICKNESS, a condition characterized by dizziness, perspiration, and nausea, resulting from motions peculiar to riding in vehicles such as automobiles, trains, airplanes, and conveyances in amusement parks. Symptoms in order of increasing severity and occurrence are a feeling of uneasiness, cold sweating and ashen color, salivation, nausea, vomiting, and prostration. In time many individuals develop a tolerance to the motions that are involved, but some others are never able to make an adjustment sufficient to prevent illness.

Causes. Motion sickness may be produced by stimulation of the organ of balance in the inner ear (see EQUILIBRIUM). It may also be produced by disorientation, as has been done experimentally by revolving a room around an individual so that floor and ceiling may be reversed. Thus it appears that sensations from the eyes and sensations from the organ of balance in the inner ear play a part in causing motion sickness. Infants have relatively undeveloped organs of balance and are relatively resistant; blind and deaf persons also are relatively resistant. Psychological and gastrointestinal sensations are believed to play a role in motion sickness, too.

Treatment. Motion sickness may be reduced in severity or prevented by remaining near the center of gravity of a vehicle so that motion is reduced to a minimum. Simple measures such as lying down, holding the head as still as possible, and fixing the eyes on a stationary object sometimes are helpful. Various sedative drugs often are of value; one of the most effective of such drugs is dimenhydrinate (Dramamine). Scopolamine may also be used. See DIMENHYDRINATE; SCOPOLAMINE.

HERMAN S. WIGODSKY, M.D.

MOTIVATION, that predisposition (itself the subject of much controversy) within the individual which arouses, sustains and directs his behavior. Motivation involves such factors as biological and emotional needs that can only be inferred from observed behavior. In experimenting with mice, psychologists distinguish physiological needs such as those for food, water and sexual satisfaction. These needs are common to most animals but mice appear to have innate patterns of behavior in their fulfillment which are referred to as instincts. Human beings, however, are motivated to satisfy these needs through learned patterns of behavior that vary from one culture to another. See INSTINCT.

It has been held that the desire to fulfill needs, as motivation of an organism, can be accounted for in terms of tension reduction. According to this theory, the organism which has been deprived seeks food, water, and sex because of its tissue needs, which through an intricate chemical process create a feeling of tension. The organism seeks to restore the equilibrium and thus reduce the tension; therefore it is motivated to act. This theory may account for the behavior of lower animals; however, it does not explain human behavior.

Numerous theories have sought to account for the motivations of human beings. Some postulate a stimulus-response principle in which people are impelled to act in response to certain stimuli. Others adhere to the pleasure-pain theory in which humans are motivated to maximize their pleasure and minimize their pain. Some account for behavior in terms of a reward-punishment principle of motivation. Although these theories may account for some behavior, they err in being oversimplifications.

All human beings have emotional needs for love, security, self-respect, and self-assertion. These needs are social because they derive from man's existence within society, and they are common to all cultures. Expression of them differs because prestige in one group may go to hunters and fishermen, while in another it may be conferred upon doctors and scientists.

Even though human beings have both physiological and emotional needs that have been defined, their motivations are complex and difficult to analyze. The craving for food may be motivated by a need for love; sexual activity may be motivated simultaneously by the need for love, security, and self-assertion. Many of the real motives and their order of significance for an individual can sometimes only be determined psychologically.

Emotional needs are generally more significant in determining human motivation than the physiological ones, although under extreme conditions of deprivation or peril the need for food, water, and self-preservation will become the prime motivating factors.

MOTIVE, in law, the inducement, cause, or reason for an action. Motive differs from intent in that it is the force that impels the action to a definite result, whereas intent is identified with the particular means used to effect such a result. (See INTENT.) The motive of a murder is not important except as it aids in completing proof of a crime that might otherwise remain in doubt. An act that is legal in itself and violates no right does not become actionable because the motive prompting it was wrong. See MURDER.

MOTLEY, JOHN LOTHROP, 1814–77, U.S. historian, was born in Dorchester, Mass., was graduated from Harvard University, 1831, and studied at the universities of Göttingen and Berlin in Germany, where he became a friend of Otto von Bismarck. Back in America, he studied law and was admitted to the bar, 1837. He wrote two novels about Merry Mount, *Morton's Hope* (1839) and *Merry Mount* (1849), neither of which was well received (see MERRY MOUNT). Motley served in the U.S. legation at St. Petersburg, 1841, and in the Massachusetts legislature, 1849; and was U.S. minister to Austria, 1861–67, and to Great Britain, 1869–70. He died in Dorchester, England.

As Historian. In 1847 Motley began collecting material for a detailed history of the Netherlands. Dissatisfied with his first draft (based on sources in the Boston library), he went to Europe, 1851, and made an exhaustive survey of materials in the archives at The Hague, Brussels, and Dresden. The first part of his history, *Rise of the Dutch Republic*, covering the period from the abdication of Charles V to the assassination of William the Silent, appeared in 1856. *History of the United Netherlands* (4 vols. 1860–67) and *The Life and Death of John Barneveld* (2 vols. 1874) covered the later course of Dutch history up to the Thirty Years' War. A fourth work, on the Thirty Years' War, was never completed. In his history of the Netherlands Motley sought to correlate the progress of Protestantism and the development of democratic civilization. He tended to oversimplify the conflict between absolutism and liberalism and to exaggerate the personal contrasts between such protagonists as William of Orange and Philip II. However, the dramatic sweep of the work and the skillful integration of colorful detail made it one of the masterpieces of historical literature, and it increased the prestige of U.S. scholarship throughout the world. G. E. Woodberry edited Motley's correspondence for *Literary Memoirs of the Nineteenth Century* (1921).

MOTON, ROBERT RUSSA, 1867–1940, U.S. educator, was born in Amelia County, Virginia, and was graduated from Hampton Institute, 1890, which he headed, 1890–1916. He succeeded Booker T. Washington as principal of Tuskeegee Institute, 1915–35. Moton wrote *Racial Good Will* (1916); an autobiography, *Finding a Way Out* (1920); and *What the Negro Thinks* (1929).

MOTOR, a machine in which electrical energy input is converted into mechanical energy output. In some countries a motor is considered to be a dynamo, but a generator is not. In the United States this distinction is not customarily made; either a generator or a motor may be called a dynamo. (See GENERATOR.) The same physical machine may operate as either a motor or a generator, depending upon the type of controls installed. Furthermore, in some applications a machine may sometimes provide motor action and at other times generator action without any change in electrical connections on the machine itself. The essential difference between a motor and a generator lies in the power source. A motor depends on an external source of electrical current, which it uses for rotational mechanical energy. A generator must be supplied with some form of mechanical energy, such as that provided by a steam engine or hydraulic turbine, which it converts to electrical energy.

The experimental laws of Michael Faraday (1831) and André Marie Ampère (1820) are the basis of all generator and motor action. The first dynamo, developed by H. Pixii in 1832, produced alternating current, and, in order to change the current flow to one of constant direction of voltage, Pixii constructed the first commutator, which effectively reversed the current every half cycle. For many years all efforts in the development of electrical machinery were directed to the use of direct-current motors and generators because the application of alternating-current voltages to external circuits presented problems not solvable until about 1885. The development of the alternating-current motor can be said to date from 1888 with the invention of the induction motor.

DIRECT-CURRENT MOTORS

Direct-current motors provide easy control of speed and torque and have wide use in cranes, elevators, steel-mill roll drives, auxiliary equipment in aircraft, and traction equipment. In physical construction direct-current motors and direct-current generators are similar. (See GENERATOR, Direct-Current Machines.) Action is also similar, for when voltage is applied to the dynamo terminals of any direct-current machine, torque develops, motion ensues, and motor action results.

The starting current of a direct-current motor is excessively high, sometimes reaching 2,000 per cent of the rated motor value. However, a starting rheostat, which consists of a resistance placed across the armature circuit, materially reduces the starting current. As the motor gains speed and the counter-electromotive force increases correspondingly, the resistance is removed step by step.

Types. Direct-current motors, like generators, are classified according to the type of excitation. The shunt motor is the counterpart of the shunt-wound generator, with the field coils connected in parallel with the armature. Its speed can be varied over a wide range by adding resistance in either field or armature circuit. If the magnetic flux remains constant, the developed torque is directly proportional to the armature current. Under these conditions the speed-torque characteristic is a straight line with a negative slope (Fig. 1a). Armature reaction causes the speed-torque characteristic to droop as shown in Fig. 1b. The starting torque of a shunt motor depends on starting resistance and in a typical case may be 150 per cent of the rated torque.

In series direct-current motors, the field coils are connected in series with the armature. As all flux is produced by the armature current, the developed torque is approximately proportional to the square of the armature current. As a result the starting torque of a series motor is higher than that of a shunt motor of the same full-load rating. Because of the high no-

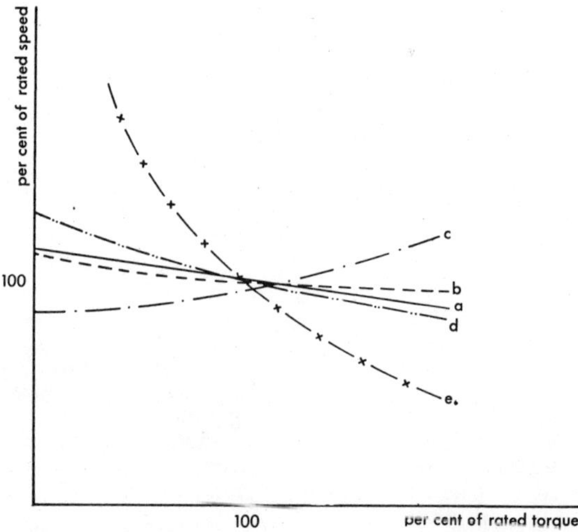

Fig. 1. Speed-Torque Characteristics for Various Direct-Current-Motors. Lines *a* and *b* are for shunt-wound motors, *c* and *d* for compound-wound, and *e* for series-wound motors.

load speed, it is never safe to remove all of the load while rated voltage is applied.

Compound motors have both a shunt-type and a series-type winding on their field poles. When the motive force of the field windings is additive, a cumulatively compounded series field results; conversely, when the effect is subtractive, a differentially compounded series field motor results. The differentially compounded motor is essentially the same as a shunt motor, with a severe armature reaction and a rising speed-torque characteristic (Fig. 1c). The speed of a cumulatively compounded motor falls more rapidly than that of a shunt motor, but becomes stable at higher values of torque (Fig. 1d). Excessive speed and current may occur in a shunt motor or in a differentially compounded motor. All direct-current motors should have overload protection in the form of a fuse or a circuit breaker.

Alternating-Current Motors

Alternating-current motors are generally divided into three classes: induction, synchronous, and commutator. Many of the motors used to drive household electric appliances are of the induction type, usually single-phase induction motors that range from a very small fraction of 1 horsepower to 5 horsepower. Three-phase induction motors, the only polyphase type in common commercial use in the United States, range in size from 3 to more than 20,000 horsepower.

In principle, all polyphase motors are the same. The rotating magnetic field is of the utmost importance in the production of torque in either the polyphase synchronous or the polyphase induction motor. If balanced three-phase currents are supplied to a symmetrically wound three-phase stator, the imposed currents will produce a uniformly rotating magnetic field. This rotating field revolves at uniform speed, with the shaft of the motor as the axis of rotation, and tends to drag the rotor of the motor around with it.

The rotor of a polyphase induction motor is massive and rugged, and is frequently called a squirrel-cage rotor because of an obvious resemblance. In modern construction the rotor may consist of a steel shaft upon which are pressed circular steel laminations whose peripheries are slotted. The laminations are stacked on the shaft in such a way that the slots usually form a somewhat skewed raceway. A shaft thus assembled is frequently used as a die-cast mold for the longitudinal conductors. When aluminum is poured into this mold the metal fills the raceways to form the longitudinal conductors of the rotor. At both ends of the rotor, aluminum rings are cast integral with the longitudinal rotor bars just described. The rings together with the bars form what in appearance is similar to a squirrel cage. In this construction no electrical connections to the rotor are necessary, the only connections being to the stator. Induction motors are frequently made completely sealed for use in locations where there is an explosion hazard.

Induction motors operate slightly below synchronous speed so that no voltages or currents will be induced in the rotor thereby causing forces or torque on the conductors. By changing the resistance of the rotor bars in an induction motor, maximum torque can be made to occur at any speed. For a low-resistance rotor the maximum torque occurs at a higher speed than for a high-resistance rotor (Fig. 2).

Multispeed induction motors are made by arranging the stator so that it can be connected for more than one pair of poles. For fixed frequencies, speeds will vary in indirect ratio to the number of poles connected, following the equation: $f=\frac{P}{2}\times\frac{rpm}{60}$ where f is the frequency and P is the number of poles in the stator. Thus, with fixed frequency, if an induction motor has a speed of 3,600 rpm when connected for 2 poles, it will have a speed of 1,800 rpm if connected for 4 poles, 1,200 rpm for 6 poles, and so on. Having

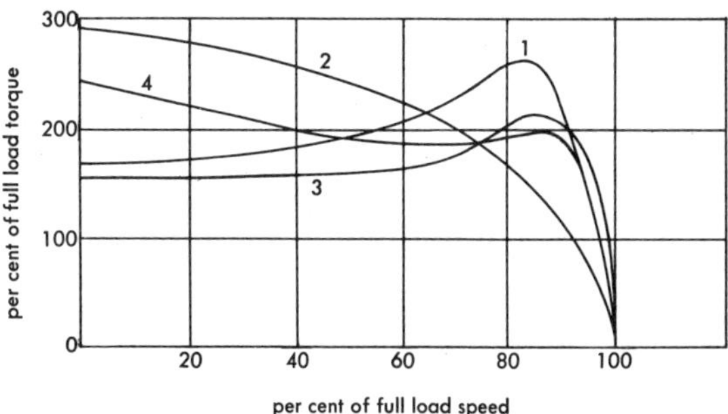

Fig. 2. Torque Characteristics of a Squirrel-Cage Motor. Curves 1, 3, and 4 have low rotor resistance with maximum torque at high speed. In curve 2 rotor resistance is high.

but one change of speed, a motor of this type costs little more than a single-speed motor; the cost rises sharply for three- and four-speed motors.

Adjustable, or variable, speed induction motors, commonly called slip-ring motors, are constructed by using a rotor that is wire-wound with connections to collector, or slip, rings. By inserting various amounts of resistance between the slip rings, different speeds may be obtained at any given torque load (Fig. 3).

Single-phase induction motors operate on the same general principle as polyphase induction motors, with two modifications: first, for starting, an auxiliary winding is necessary to create an additional phase artificially within the motor itself; second, it may have a mechanically operated switching mechanism to cut out the special provisions for starting after the motor has come up to speed. Single-phase motors are generally of fractional or small horsepower, and are designed to operate when connected to a two-wire

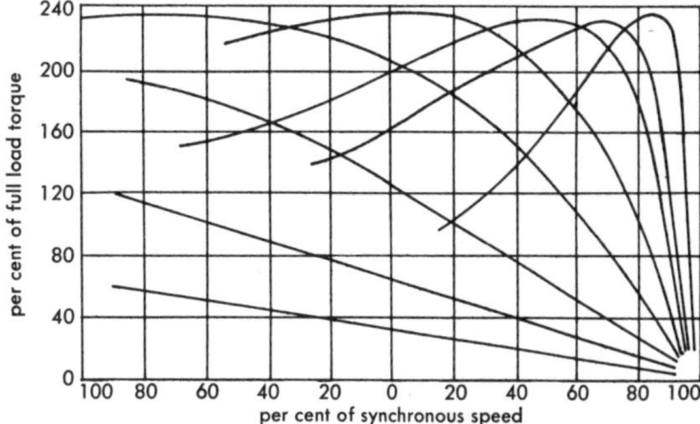

Fig. 3. Speed-Torque Curves of Slip-Ring Induction Motor. Different speeds may be obtained at any given torque load by varying the amounts of resistance between slip rings.

alternating current source. Single-phase induction motors are usually classified according to the auxiliary means used to provide the necessary starting torque, namely: split-phase, resistance-start, capacitor-start, capacitor, or shaded-pole. With the exception of shaded-pole motors, all of these are split-phase types. The true split-phase motor has main and auxiliary windings, with a provision made for opening the auxiliary or starting winding by means of a centrifugal switch similar to a governor, or by a relay, after the motor has started. The resistance-start motor has a resistor connected in series with the auxiliary winding and has a greater starting torque than the split-phase motor. In the capacitor-start motors, stored electrical energy between conductors of different potential is connected in series with the auxiliary winding, and makes possible a higher starting torque than in either the split-phase or the resistance-start motor. The capacitor motor is similar to the capacitor-start motor except that the auxiliary winding remains in the circuit after starting, resulting in a higher power factor and a higher pull-out torque than for any of the other split-phase types. By means of a switch or relay, capacitance is decreased after the motor approaches full speed (Fig. 4).

Some very small single-phase induction motors, known as shaded-pole motors, are especially designed to drive small fans and similar types of loads and need no auxiliary switching. The phase splitting is accomplished by a heavy copper loop, which encircles part of each pole face and retards the changing of flux through the loop. As a result, the flux of a pole tends to sweep across the face of the shaded portion of the pole instead of merely having a time variation of field strength more or less uniform over the whole pole face. This sweeping of the flux can be considered to be a crude rotating magnetic field sufficient in strength to produce a small starting torque adequate for the very light starting load of the devices for which this type of motor is designed.

Polyphase synchronous motors are characterized by a rotating field that locks in with the direct-current field poles of the rotor. This means that the rotor turns at exactly the same speed as does the rotating magnetic field. The relationship for the speed of the rotating magnetic field is the same as for that of the synchronous generator. (See GENERATOR, Alternating-Current Machines, *Alternating-Current Generators.*) This rotational speed is made possible by the alternating currents induced in the pole faces of the rotor. This effect may be enhanced if an amortisseur, or squirrel-cage, type of winding is placed in the pole faces of the rotor. Synchronous motor action occurs only at synchronous speed. In starting, a synchronous motor is brought near synchronous speed by induction motor action, and then the rotor is pulled into step by the induced pull-in torque. The motor then runs by synchronous motor action. Some external prime mover may also be used in starting. It is used first to drive the motor as a synchronous generator. Then, with the switch to the stator supply open, the rotor field current is adjusted until the voltage of the generator is equal to that of the supply. The stator switch is closed the instant the voltages are in step and thus synchronized. At that moment the prime mover is disconnected, while the machine continues to operate as a synchronous motor.

The direct-current series motor can be operated on alternating current since the current direction changes simultaneously in both field and armature. This type of motor, known as a universal motor, performs well in the smaller sizes, from 1/500 to about ½ horsepower, but in the larger sizes inductive effects of the field and armature tend to create serious commutation difficulties. The field structure of universal motors is a stack of laminations bolted together, fitted with field windings. The armature also consists of a stack of laminations, which are pressed onto a shaft with the slots skewed. Universal motors are widely used where the current source may be either direct or alternating current, where high speeds and light weight are advantageous, and where it is desirable to use a motor whose speed adjusts automatically to the size of the load. A portable electric drill is a typical, ideal application for a universal motor.

Another commutator-type motor is the repulsion alternating-current commutator motor, having essentially the same operating characteristics as the alternating-current series motor. It differs in three important respects: the rotor is inductively fed; the brushes are connected together to form a short circuit; and the field winding is distributed. Both the alternating-current series motor and the repulsion motor have a speed torque characteristic resembling the direct-current series motor.

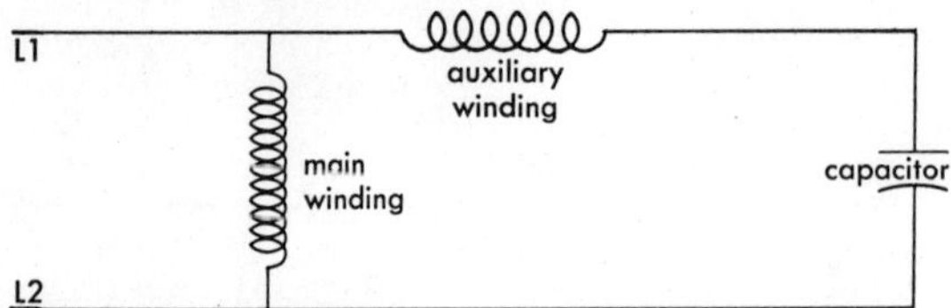

Fig. 4. Connection Diagram of a Capacitor-Type Motor. Capacitors, connected in series with auxiliary winding, increase starting torque and improve the power factor.

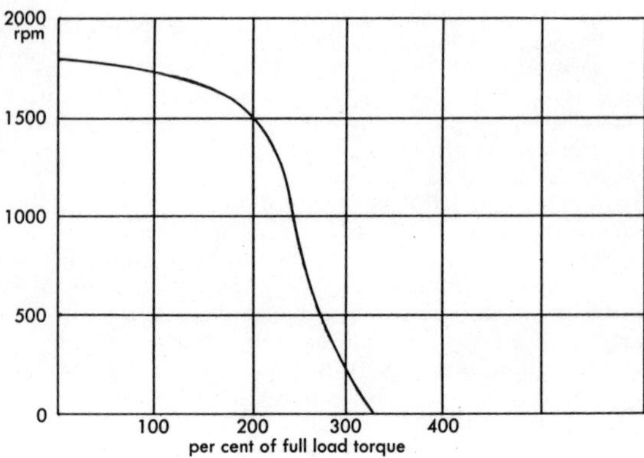

Fig. 5. Speed-Torque of an 1800-rpm Normal-Speed, Single-Phase, Repulsion-Induction Motor. Curve combines repulsion effect with the effect of the induction motor.

The repulsion-induction motor is another type of single-phase motor. Before the capacitor-start motor came into common use for applications requiring high starting torque, the repulsion-inductor motor was the accepted type. Its rotor has two windings, one with a commutator and the other with a bar winding. This motor also utilizes shorted brushes. Its operation combines the repulsion effect with the induction effect. As a result the speed-torque curve is a cross between that of the repulsion motor and the induction motor (Fig. 5).

Synchronous Condensers. It is often desirable to improve the effects of lagging current in an electrical system caused by induction motors, lightly loaded transformers, and other magnetic devices in the circuit. Such a lag is not economical, because the current delivered must exceed the amount of current realized by at least the ratio of the power factor to unity. Synchronous condensers are used to improve the power factor of an electrical system, as they are similar to synchronous motors; if their purpose is only to correct the power factor, they need not be designed to carry a load. Increased current is applied to the rotor field windings to cause overexcitation, which results in a leading power factor. A desirable condition exists when the leading power factor, thus created, balances the lagging power factor.

If the machine is used to drive a load, the synchronous condenser reverts to a synchronous motor, which still has the ability of power factor correction by overexcitation of the fields, but the amount of power factor correction is limited by the rating of the stator winding. Therefore, as the load increases, the synchronous motor becomes increasingly less able to correct a power factor.

Synchronous Converter. A direct-current generator may also generate alternating currents by the addition of slip rings. (See GENERATOR.) Such a double-current generator may be run as a synchronous motor, by taking energy from a proper alternating-current circuit and delivering direct current from the commutator. In this application the machine is called a synchronous converter. See MAGNETISM.

Applications. The type of motor best suited to any purpose depends upon such factors as starting torque requirements; starting and stopping speeds required; whether speed is constant or variable; whether the load is steady or intermittent; dampness, dirt, and explosion hazard; and whether the load is directly connected or driven by belts, chains, or gear reductions.

Because of their speed-change characteristics, series-wound direct-current motors are well adapted for driving cranes and hoists, whereas shunt-wound direct-current motors are used to drive line shafts and uniform-speed machine tools and reciprocating pumps. Differentially compounded motors have limited use because of their instability when starting and carrying overloads, but cumulatively compounded motors have wide application where the starting torque is heavy, as in elevators.

Since the polyphase squirrel-cage motor can be built to perform well at constant speeds over long periods of time, it finds wide use where such endurance is required. Because of its lack of sparking, the squirrel-cage induction motor is much to be preferred for installations in flour mills, powder plants, sawmills, and textile factories. Woodworking equipment, including planers, band saws, and circular saws, are usually powered by squirrel-cage induction motors, although synchronous motors are often used for the benefit of power factor correction.

Many household appliances are driven by universal motors, which operate on either direct or alternating current. Portable drills, saws, sanders, and routers are familiar tools that use the universal motor. Other applications include the vacuum cleaner, sewing machine, food mixer, and desk fan.

J. A. M. LYON; ENDRIK NOGES

BIBLIOG.–P. L. Alger, *Nature of Polyphase Induction Machines* (1951); P. B. Harwood, *Control of Electric Motors* (1953); H. Vickers, *Induction Motor* (ed. 1953); G. W. Heumann, *Magnetic Control of Industrial Motors* (ed. 1954); R. Rosenberg, *Electric Motor Repair* (ed. 1954); P. Kemp and W. H. Date, *A. C. Generators and Motors* (1956); E. Molloy, *Data Book on Electric Motors* (1957); B. Adkins, *General Theory of Electrical Machines* (1958).

MOTORBOAT, a watercraft powered by one or more internal combustion engines. The first motor-driven boat is believed to have been used in England in 1885, and a small launch powered by a Daimler automobile type of engine was shown at the Paris Exhibition in 1889. The use of spacesaving and weight-saving internal combustion engines represented a great step forward from bulky steam launches, the only mechanically powered boats available before the advent of the motorboat.

Motorboats range in size from the smallest outboard motor-powered canoe or rowboat to the luxurious twin-engined cruiser with living and sleeping accommodations for eight or more people. Motorboats may be classified in two general groups, those powered by inboard motors and those powered by outboard motors (see OUTBOARD MOTOR).

Inboard motorboats may be classed as runabouts or speedboats, utility boats or sportsmen, and cruisers of either the express or the luxury type. Boats of each of the several classes are designed and in most cases used to satisfy the whims or requirements of owners.

Runabouts or Speedboats are the least expensive inboard motorboats; nevertheless racing speedboats and hydroplanes which belong in this general class may cost many thousands of dollars. Most runabouts range from 15 to 30 feet over-all and are designed primarily for speed and appearance. The power plant usually is mounted just aft of amidships. In smaller runabouts there are two cockpits forward of the engine compartment, and larger boats have an extra cockpit in the stern of the boat. Engines in runabouts generally are direct drive, power being transmitted to the propeller without the use of reduction gears. This is done because most runabouts are comparatively light and designed for speeds of 30 to 55 mph depending on the horsepower of the motor. Racing speedboats and hydroplanes of necessity have more complicated engine-to-propeller transmissions. Hydroplanes are racing craft with a step built into the hull which permits the forward part of the boat to rise out of the water at high speeds thereby reducing water friction.

Utility Boats, also called sportsmen, are among the most popular craft in the history of motorboating.

WIDE WORLD

With jet engines, speedboats have attained speeds of more than 200 mph. One of the modern racers, Donald Campbell's *Bluebird*, is pictured above at its launching in 1955.

They range from 16 to about 25 feet over-all; the part forward of the windshield is decked over and the remainder of the boat is left open with a variety of possible seating arrangements. As the pseudonym implies, they are used mostly for sports and are especially suitable for fishing, for towing aquaplanes and water skis, and for other aquatic sports. Although at top speed they are not quite as fast as boats of the runabout class, they are more practical. For this reason they have gained wide favor among motorboating enthusiasts.

Cruisers. The true cruiser ranges in over-all length from about 24 to 75 feet for luxury vessels. The primary purpose of a cruiser is to provide complete living accommodations afloat for 4 to 10 persons. Many people use their cruisers as floating summer homes, living aboard during leisure hours and moving anchorage to suit their pleasure. A typical small cruiser has a large open cockpit aft for fishing or sun-bathing. Forward in the enclosed cabin of the small cruiser is a dining area with lower and upper berths that convert to a lounge for daytime use. Further forward is the ship's galley and toilet facilities are just beyond.

In addition to open cockpit model cruisers there are several other stock types including the small trunk cabin cruiser with a below-deck cabin extending above the deck in a built-up structure to provide headroom. Another type is the raised deck cruiser, providing below-deck headroom without the superstructure. The sedan cabin cruiser has a glass enclosed deckhouse just forward of the open rear cockpit. Variations of these models are double cabin cruisers with an open bridge separating forward and aft cabin areas, and many flying bridge types that have the boat's controls all together in a specially built section above the deckhouse.

Just before World War II boat manufacturers featured a new line of express cruisers engineered to combine the speed of a runabout with the comfort of a cruiser. Then wartime use of patrol torpedo (PT) boats, aircraft rescue cruisers, and many other fast and highly maneuverable craft did much to promote acceptance of the express cruiser class. These boats vary from 23 feet to more than 40 feet in length, and generally are powered by one or two engines that provide speeds up to 40 mph. Small express cruisers sleep only two persons and have small galley and toilet facilities whereas larger boats of this class provide accommodations for six to eight persons.

Hulls. The oldest type of hull used for motorboats has a rounded bilge with a sharp bow that spreads the water apart as the boat moves forward. Since it takes more power to push through the water than to ride over it, the rounded bilge hull was found to be slower than a V bottom hull. V bottoms, thin at the keel but with broad running surfaces at and above the water line, tend to make the boat rise out of the water as it attains speed and cause the boat to run over rather than through the water. A still later development is a combination of rounded bilge forward and a modified V aft, which combines advantages of each type.

High-speed racing boats or hydroplanes usually have modified V bottoms with a lateral step or steps located somewhat aft of amidships. This breaks suction caused by high speeds and minimizes wetted surfaces thus reducing friction and resulting in higher speeds. The design of a hydroplane hull depends upon such factors as type of craft and weight distribution. A boat generally is considered a hydroplane if there is a step in the hull.

Power Plants. The most common type of motor used in motorboats is a gasoline-fueled, internal combustion engine which differs only slightly from an automobile engine. The principal difference is that because of an unlimited water supply the boat motor need not recirculate water for cooling. Boat engines are mounted in reverse of conventional automobile engines, with the flywheel forward, the drive coming from the rear through a reverse gear. Cruisers and heavy work boats usually have reduction gears that enable a boat to carry a larger propeller turning at a lower rpm; this reduces slippage and increases efficiency.

Because boat engines operate nearer their peak horsepower output than do motorcars, they must be more rugged and capable of operating at sustained high speeds. The average boat engine is driven 90 per cent of the time at 75 to 100 per cent of its peak horsepower output, which corresponds to driving an automobile at speeds ranging from 70 to 90 mph continuously.

Boat engines generally are mounted in single, twin, or even triple installations aft of amidships and power is transmitted either directly or through a reduction gear to the propeller. The drive is accomplished by coupling a shaft along the bottom of the boat through a shaft log, a watertight connection mounted inside the bottom planking. On the aft end of the shaft is a propeller, which may have two, three, or four blades depending upon the type of boat and the purpose for which it is designed. Two-blade propellers are used almost exclusively for racing, while the three-blade is more commonly used for pleasure boats. The four-blade wheel is usually used on larger ships and commercial craft.

Motorboat Racing. Approximately 500 official motorboat races in the United States each year draw more than 4,000 participants and hundreds of thousands of spectators. Rules for inboard racing are formulated by the American Power Boat Association and those for outboard racing by the National Outboard Association. In each category amateur and professional races are held. Craft range in size from great unlimited hydroplanes to midget outboards, powered by supercharged or stock motors.

Motorboat racing developed greatly during the 1920's. In 1939 Sir Malcolm Campbell set a record speed of 141.74 mph with his unlimited hydroplane *Bluebird II*. That mark stood until 1950 when Stanley S. Sayres' *Slo'Mo-Shun* set a mark of 160.32 mph on Lake Washington, Seattle. He increased the speed record to 178.50 mph with the same boat on the same lake in 1952. By the late 1950's jet-powered boats were traveling more than 225 mph.

In the United States major races are the Gold Cup, in Detroit; British International (Harmsworth) Trophy, Detroit; President's Cup, Washington, D.C.; Silver Cup, Detroit; Sahara Cup, Lake Mead, Nev.; and the Memorial Regatta, Detroit.

MOTORCYCLE, a two-wheeled vehicle propelled by an internal combustion engine, sometimes having a third wheel for the support of a sidecar or luggage carrier. In the earliest practical motorcycles, built in the 1890's, the attempt was made to retain as nearly as possible the frame and appearance of the bicycle. Like the automobile, however, the motorcycle, with the passing of the years, developed a more or less distinctive type and form of its own. The one exception to this is the motorbike, a comparatively inexpensive adaptation of a gasoline engine to a bicycle frame.

Engine Characteristics. The earlier motorcycle engines were all one-cylindered, but two-cylinder and four-cylinder motors soon became more in demand. Although motorcycle engines usually develop 10 to 12 brake horsepower, it is customary to describe them in terms of their piston displacement—from 30 to 74 cubic inches. Motorcycle engines designed for great speed or unusually heavy service may develop 50 or more brake horsepower. See HORSEPOWER.

For several years all American motorcycles have used air-cooled engines. Although a few European makes continued to use water-cooled engines into the late 1950's, they were not particularly favored by motorcyclists on account of the extra weight and added complication of the cooling system. Jump-spark ignition, battery operated as with automobiles, is used on all stock models, the magneto system being used only for special requirements. Three types of engine lubrication are in use: splash, dry sump, and pressure. In the splash system oil from a tank is fed to the crankcase by means of a mechanical pump supplemented by a hand-operated pump. The flywheel and connecting rods splash the oil to the working parts of the motor. In the dry sump system, oil is pumped from a tank to the crankcase, where it is forced and splashed to the working parts, then returned to the tank for continual recirculation. During this process the oil is filtered and cooled. In the pressure system the oil is placed in the crankcase, as in the automobile engine, and pumped and splashed to the working parts.

Gasoline and oil tanks rest on the longitudinal frame members. They are usually built in one unit, with partitions separating the main fuel tank, the reserve fuel tank, and the lubricating oil tank. One type of four-cylinder engine, however, that uses an oil-gasoline mixture and depends on the pressure lubrication system, uses no separate oil tank.

Starting. Motorcycle engines of the earliest types were started by pushing the machine, the engine being permanently connected to the rear wheel by means of a belt or chain. Later a clutch was added and the engine was started by pedaling. This pedaling turned the rear wheel, which was jacked up by a stand, and the wheel turned the engine until it started. A coaster-brake mechanism then disconnected the pedals from the wheel and the rider pushed the machine down from the stand, straddled the seat, and eased in the friction clutch.

The next important improvements in the development of the motorcycle were the variable-speed transmission and the kick starter. The transmission with two or three speeds made it possible to negotiate steep hills and rough roads more easily. The kick starter eliminated the necessity of putting the machine on a stand to start the motor. The engine crankshaft could be spun three or four revolutions by one downward thrust of the foot on the starter pedal.

Transmission. Footboards are provided for the rider's feet. Close to one of them is the clutch control pedal; near the other is the brake pedal, which actuates an internal expanding brake on the rear wheel. A hand lever near one of the handle bar grips actuates a front-wheel brake. The transmission control is a lever extending upward along the gasoline tank and the transmission itself is located at the rear of the motor and on the same shaft as one of the members of the clutch. The other clutch member is chain-driven from the crankshaft, and a second chain drives the rear wheel. Speed is governed by adjusting the flow of fuel from the carburetor to the engine, and by advancing or retarding the spark by turning the handle bar grips. Motorcycle wheel bases range from 52½ to 60 inches; tires generally are 5 inches in cross section, mounted on 18- or 19-inch wheels.

Sidecars and Three-wheeled Vehicles. About 1905 the sidecar made its appearance, providing space for an extra passenger in a basketlike car mounted on an axle extending to a third wheel from the motorcycle's rear wheel. Some later sidecars had enclosed boxlike carriers and were used extensively for metropolitan small-package deliveries.

During World War I the American Expeditionary Forces made extensive use of motorcycles and sidecars for message carrying and for scouting. These military uses were extended by Adolf Hitler in World War II when the German army used armored motorcycles for break-through troops behind tank attacks. The early success of the motorcycle in warfare led to its adoption as a police vehicle. Police departments use three-wheelers with rear enclosures containing two-way radio equipment and other police equipment. In many cities motorcycle units have replaced mounted police.

Motorcycle Racing is a popular sport in the United States and western Europe. In the United States it is under the auspices of the American Motorcycle Association. Although ½-mile and 1-mile dirt tracks are numerous throughout North America, the outstanding motorcycle racing centers are at Daytona Beach, Fla.; Bonneville, Utah; Langhorne, Pa.; and Springfield, Ill. Standard events for both direct-drive (racing) motors and stock motors include dirt track and cross-country racing, straightaway, and hill climbing. In straightaway racing, speeds greater than 150 mph have been attained, whereas good performances on ½-mile dirt tracks are timed at 65 to 70 mph, increasing to an average of 85 mph on 1-mile dirt tracks.

Motor Scooters are small two-wheeled or three-wheeled vehicles powered by an air-cooled motor driving the rear wheel or wheels. They are usually identified by a running board that extends between the front and rear wheels, and a box or covering over the motor that serves as a seat or that may provide space for parcels when the scooter is used for delivery purposes. Usually powered by motors ranging from ½ to 5 horsepower, motor scooters attain speeds of only 17 mph for the smaller motors, and up to 40 mph for those more highly powered. In noncongested areas motor scooters are frequently used by children younger than the legal age for driving automobiles.

MOTORSHIP, a nautical vessel driven by diesel engine power. Although diesel engines had been used to propel vessels on inland or coastal waterways since about 1904, not until just before World War I did diesel-powered motorships begin to replace reciprocating steam engines in deep-sea transportation. By that time diesel engines of more than 1,000 horsepower had been built, with assured performance and reliability equal to that of the long-established steam engine. Diesel engines had the advantage of requiring less space than did coal-burning steam plants, and used only 0.36 pounds of fuel per horsepower-hour, compared with fuel consumption of 0.6 pounds per horsepower-hour which was the best performance of steam-powered ships. In addition to more economical propulsive power, diesels permitted a substantially greater pay load through savings in fuel storage space.

Gripsholm, transocean motorship of 23,500 gross tonnage, is powered by twin diesel engines totaling 22,600 hp to drive the ship through the water at a speed of 19 knots.

SWEDISH-AMERICAN LINE AGENCY, INC.

In this field the pioneer ocean-going cargo vessel was the Danish ship *Selandia*, a vessel of 5,000 gross tons powered with 1,800 diesel hp. The *Gripsholm* was the first diesel passenger ship to cross the Atlantic. Built in 1925, she had a displacement of 18,000 gross tons and was powered with two diesels totaling 12,500 hp. After serving for more than 30 years the *Gripsholm* was replaced in 1957 by a new and larger ship of the same name, having 23,500 gross tonnage and powered with 22,600 hp to drive the vessel through the water at 19 knots.

By the middle 1950's motorships had almost completely replaced steam-propelled ships in new construction of vessels up to 35,000 tons displacement. Larger vessels were powered by high-temperature, high-pressure steam turbines; highly efficient gas turbines were being used on the largest ocean-going ships. Diesel power for submarines started to give way to atomic power and the future of the diesel for this exacting service became questionable.

Motorships may be propelled through a reduction gear from the engine shaft, or the transmission may be a conventional diesel-electric drive. See DIESEL POWER; INTERNAL COMBUSTION ENGINE, Diesel Engines.

MOTOR TRANSPORT. See TRANSPORTATION, *Trucks;* TRUCKING; MOTOR TRUCK.

MOTOR TRUCK, a self-powered wheeled vehicle used chiefly to transport goods. The first recorded sale of a motor truck was in 1896 to Shepard and Company, merchants in Providence, R.I. The vehicle was steam powered and side-chain driven. Also in 1896 a gasoline-powered delivery wagon was entered in a Memorial Day race in New York City. The first truck trailer was built in 1898, and a crude, oil-burning tractor was built in the same year. The initial U.S. Army purchase of trucks was made by the signal corps in 1899, but just too late to be used in the Spanish-American War.

The U.S. Army's purchase of trucks for use in World War I provided the major impetus for expansion of the industry. Because the war ended before any large number of trucks could be shipped overseas, the army was forced to sell a great many vehicles as surplus. It was this move that led to the eventual nationwide adoption of trucks as vehicles for delivery. As pneumatic tires replaced solid rubber ones, and as better roads were built, truck speeds increased from 15 to 45 mph or more and long-haul truck operations became common. By 1941 trucks were traveling 34½ billion miles yearly over rural roads and 21 billion miles a year on urban streets.

Private operators own approximately 85 per cent of all trucks. The rest, in the for-hire class, are divided among contract carriers, who haul freight under contracts with specific firms; and common carriers, such as household furniture movers, whose services are available to the general public. For-hire trucks are licensed under state and national regulating agencies, which have certain powers over rates and which set up operating and safety rules.

Types of Carriers. The period between World War I and World War II was marked by the development of numerous types of special-purpose trucks. Several manufacturers offer more than 100 different truck models; therefore it is impossible to class any of them as standard. Special types exist for agriculture, lumbering, mining, military use, construction, public utilities, local retail delivery, long-distance hauling, and other services. The capacities of the trucks vary from 250 pounds to 75 or more tons; their engine horsepowers range from 60 to 350 or more, with up to 15 forward and three reverse speeds.

The most popular type of truck is that having a body of less than 1-ton capacity, with an enclosed driver's cab and engine in front and the open boxlike body in back. Second in popularity is the stake or

WILLYS SALES CORP.

Versatile forward control 1½-ton capacity Jeep truck is power driven in all four wheels. The cab is situated directly above the engine, increasing the load capacity.

platform truck of 1½-ton capacity, and third is the light panel delivery truck with an enclosed body. These three types, which make up approximately 70 per cent of all trucks made, are used primarily for local hauling. Other chief types include the large covered van that handles dry freight of all kinds, such as almost all household goods moved in the United States; the dump truck, such as that used for coal delivery in cities; tank trucks for hauling gasoline, milk, and other liquid cargoes; the rack type; and the express or screened-side type.

Although a truck seldom carries more than a 20-ton load, the truck trailer often handles 30 tons or more in regular operation and has won increasing favor for heavy or bulky loads. Models of truck trailers range through all the usual heavy-duty body types. The trailer is pulled by a tractor unit that has an engine and driver's cab mounted on a short chassis. A coupling device connects the tractor with the load-carrying trailer. The semitrailer, the most popular of the truck-trailer units, has wheels only at the rear; its front is supported by the tractor's rear wheels or, when not coupled to the tractor, rests on a special support. The tractor unit can be kept in constant use, pulling one trailer while another is being loaded or unloaded. Furthermore, because it can distribute the total weight of vehicle and load over more wheels, the truck trailer can carry larger and bulkier loads and still keep within the 18,000-pound axle-load limit commonly imposed for transport over state highways.

A typically large tractor-trailer combination has a maximum total loaded weight of 40 tons, a 200-horsepower motor (usually of the diesel type), and a trailer body 7 feet high, 8 feet wide, and 35 feet long; the trailer weighs 5 tons, the tractor 6 tons. In West Coast states, where higher gross loads are permitted, 34-ton gross truck-trailer weights are common. The largest truck trailer ever built was an off-the-road model with a gross load of 500 tons; it was used during World War II to transport equipment to New Mexico for the building of the first atomic bomb.

Weight Classes. Unlike passenger cars, most gasoline-driven trucks must give heavy service at lower speeds; therefore their power plants and running gear have a relatively heavy build and large cooling system. Because trucks are capable of carrying widely varying tonnages, manufacturers adopted the gross vehicle weight (GVW) classification—the maximum total weight of both the vehicle and the load that the vehicle is designed to handle satisfactorily. There are four GVW classes. The light class, usually speedy local delivery units, includes vehicles of less than 9,000 pounds loaded weight. The medium class, made up of trucks used to carry up to 2 tons in local or long-distance freight, has a GVW of 9,000 to 16,000 pounds. Light-heavy is the class including vehicles with a GVW of 16,000 to 24,000 pounds, and is generally suited for carrying loads of up to 6 tons; the heavy-heavy class includes vehicles with a GVW of more than 24,000 pounds. In addition, there is the off-the-road truck, designed to carry heavy loads through regions that have no roads.

Chassis. The chassis arrangement of a gasoline-powered truck is similar to that of a passenger car; in fact, passenger car chassis are sometimes used for light trucks. The truck engine is mounted at the front end of the frame and is connected through a clutch with the transmission gearing, which is usually located close to the engine. Such a system is unit power plant construction. Light and medium trucks can be operated effectively with an automatic transmission.

A sliding gear transmission with three forward speeds and one reverse speed is common in light trucks; four or more forward speeds are common in medium trucks; heavy-duty trucks sometimes have 15 forward and three reverse speeds. The propeller shaft, which usually has two or more universal joints, transmits power from the transmission to the rear axle through bevel, internal, or worm gears. (See GEAR.) Many light trucks use the bevel drive employed in passenger cars, but heavier trucks use internal or worm drives.

Although the four-cylinder truck engine was in general replaced by six- or eight-cylinder models (including the V-8 engine), the jeep, employed in World War II, was adapted to civilian use in special cases. Some trucks employ the pancake engine, which requires less vertical space because of its horizontally opposed cylinders. In some cases all of it can be put under the floor of the driver's cab; in other cases part of it is put under the floor and part in a section that protrudes forward. Both the pancake and standard engines are used in cab-over-engine trucks, which are popular for heavy-duty operations, particularly where the power unit is used to pull a semitrailer. With the cab forward over the engine, the pay-load weight can be better distributed over the front and back wheels and the driver can have better vision. A cab-over-engine arrangement of the tractor-truck also permits the load-carrying unit such as a semitrailer to utilize its maximum capacity.

The rims of each rear wheel on trucks of more than 2½-ton capacity are usually double width and carry two tires—called dual tires—side by side. The tread of the rear wheels is usually 3 to 6 inches wider than the tread of the tires on the front wheels, which have single rims. Six-wheel trucks, with two driving axles and four driving wheels—called a tandem type—at the rear are common for heavy duty. Tandem wheels also are used in trailers and semitrailers. The six-wheel truck with six-wheel trailer is popular on the Pacific Coast, as is the six-wheel semitrailer. Four-wheel-drive trucks also are available; they distribute the load so that all wheels have about equal tractive power. On some four-wheel trucks all wheels are con-

Tractor-semitrailer dump truck, used to move dirt in super-highway and toll road building, has 18 heavy-duty tires. The truck is equipped with a telescoping hydraulic lift.

INTERNATIONAL HARVESTER CORP.

trolled by the steering mechanism; some eight-wheel trucks have four-wheel steering also.

Farm trucks frequently have a power take-off, which permits them to drive rotary saws, corn shellers, and other farm machinery. Wheels with special rims and treads enable these trucks to run over fields and haul harrows, hayrakes, and other agricultural implements.

Some trailers are made of aluminum, which reduces weight, and the driver's cab and other parts of the chassis of some heavy-duty models are made of aluminum and magnesium. In certain parts of the country, notably on the West Coast, straight trucks pull four- or six-wheel trailers; and where state laws permit, a tractor-truck with semitrailer is frequently coupled to a four- or six-wheel full trailer. Wire threads are sometimes used in the manufacture of truck tires to add strength.

Power. Although gasoline engines power most trucks and have no rival for general service, the diesel truck has found increasing use for heavy service. The diesel, operating on fuel oil, achieves up to 50 per cent more power, but because of state taxes on fuel oil, the economy that would ordinarily result is negligible. Maintenance costs are comparable to those for gasoline engines. In the early post–World War II period, diesels continued to be preferred for extra-heavy-duty hauling. Later, gasoline engines with 200 to 300 horsepower were developed in competition with these diesels.

Steam trucks continue in use in Europe because of high fuel costs but are almost unknown in the United States. The electric truck, popular in the United States before 1920, became an oddity on roads and streets. A special type of electric truck, however, is widely used in manufacturing plants, warehouses, and railroad stations. Many have small gasoline engines that generate electricity for motive power, and others, which operate on batteries, can go up to 40 miles on a single charging. Their load capacity ranges from 1½ to 20 tons, although smaller units are more popular. For inside work, solid rubber tires 8 to 28 inches in diameter are used. The wheel base may vary from 34 inches to 7 feet. Special adaptations of this vehicle include hoisting platforms or forks for heavy loads.

John Denler

MOTRIL, town, Spain, Granada province, 2 miles from the Mediterranean Sea. Located in a temperate region, Motril is a trading center for the surrounding agricultural region, whose products include sugar cane, fruits, and grains. (For population, see Spain map in Atlas.)

MOTT, FRANK LUTHER, 1886–1964, U.S. educator and journalist, was born in Keokuk County, Iowa, and attended the University of Chicago and Columbia University. He edited several small Iowa newspapers, then taught writing and journalism at Simpson College and at the University of Iowa, where he was director of the school of journalism, 1927–42. He was dean of the school of journalism at the University of Missouri, 1942–51. Mott wrote *American Journalism, a History . . . 1690–1940* (1941); *Golden Multitudes* (1947); and *A History of American Magazines* (4 vols., 1930–57), complete only through the first part of the twentieth century. He was awarded a 1939 Pulitzer prize.

MOTT, JOHN RALEIGH, 1865–1955, U.S. Nobel prize-winning social worker, was born in Livingston Manor, N.Y. He served as student secretary, 1888–1915, foreign secretary, 1898–1915, and general secretary, 1915–31, of the International Committee of the Young Men's Christian Associations in the United States and Canada, and was chairman of the World's Alliance of Young Men's Christian Associations, 1926–47. He also served as general secretary, 1895–1920, and chairman, 1920–28, of the World's Student Christian Federation and as chairman of the International Missionary Council, 1921–42. For his efforts to promote world brotherhood he shared the 1946 Nobel peace prize with Emily Greene Balch. In 1948 he was made honorary president of the World Council of Churches. His publications include *The Decisive Hour of Christian Missions* (1910), *The Present Day Summons to the World Mission of Christianity* (1931), and *The Larger Evangelism* (1944).

MOTT, LUCRETIA COFFIN, 1793–1880, U.S. reformer, was born in Nantucket, Mass., and was educated in the Friends' Boarding School at Nine Partners, near Poughkeepsie, N.Y., where she met James Mott (1788–1868) whom she married, 1811. After teaching for a time, she became a preacher in the Society of Friends. In the schism which arose in that sect over the slavery question she championed the cause of the abolitionist Elias Hicks. Both she and her husband took an active part in the abolition campaign and were delegates to the World's Anti-slavery Convention in London, 1840; but all women were excluded from active participation in the convention proceedings and this led Mrs. Mott to become a stanch advocate of women's rights. She and Elizabeth Cady Stanton were the leaders in organizing the Seneca Falls Convention of 1848, at which the women's rights movement was launched, and where Mrs. Mott helped draw up a Declaration of Sentiments. She was also an advocate of temperance and the universal peace movement.

MOTT, VALENTINE, 1785–1865, U.S. surgeon, was born in Glen Cove, N.Y., and studied at Columbia College where he became professor of surgery, 1810. He continued in the position after the medical department was merged with the New York College of Physicians and Surgeons, 1813, but resigned in 1826 to help found the short-lived Rutgers Medical College. He was again on the faculty of the College of Physicians and Surgeons, 1830–35, and held the chair of surgery and surgical anatomy in the newly founded medical department of the University of the City of New York, 1841–50. He was one of the better surgeons of his time, being especially successful in the removal of tumors and stones in the bladder, in ligating large arteries, and in amputations.

MOUFLON, a heavy-horned wild sheep, one of the few native species remaining in Europe. The mouflon, *Ovis musimon*, measures only about 27 inches at the shoulder. In summer its coat is bright reddish brown, its underparts are light colored and there is a whitish saddle marking on its back. In winter the saddle becomes broader and the coat darker, and the fur becomes quite woolly. The heavy, spiraled horns of the rams form an almost complete circle. These animals graze in mountain pastures and dwell among rocks. They are found mainly in dense heather forests on the islands of Sardinia and Corsica. Modern domestic sheep are believed to be descendants of mouflon. See Sheep.

MOULINS, town, central France, capital of Allier Department; on the E bank of the Allier River; 90 miles NW of Lyons. Moulins is a rail and commercial center; it has ironworks and tanneries and manufactures of perfume, furniture, tools, hosiery, furs, and shoes. Features of interest include the fifteenth-century cathedral, which contains a fine triptych; the ruined castle of the dukes of Bourbon, who made Moulins their residence and capital of the duchy in the fifteenth century; and, in a former convent founded by Ste. Chantal in 1616, the tomb of Henri de Montmorency (1595–1632), marshal of France and grandson of Duc Anne de Montmorency. At Moulins in 1566 Charles IX held an assembly that adopted important administrative reforms propounded by Michel de L'Hôpital. (For population, see France map in Atlas.)

MOULMEIN, or Maulmein, town, S Burma, capital of Tenasserim Division and of Amherst District; at the mouths of the Salween and Ataran rivers; a port on the Gulf of Martaban of the Andaman Sea, from which it is separated by Bilagyun Island; 103 miles ESE of Rangoon and opposite Martaban. Moulmein is connected by railroad and highway with

Rangoon. There is air service to Rangoon, and Salween River steamers depart from Moulmein's harbor. The city's industries are based on rice, lumber, and rubber produced in the area; rice and teak are exported. Nearby are several interesting pagodas and limestone caves. Pop. (1953) 101,720.

MOULTON, FOREST RAY, 1872–1952, U.S. astronomer, was born near Reed City (later Le Roy), Mich., the eldest of six brothers including Harold G. Moulton. He studied at Albion College and at the University of Chicago, where he received his Ph.D. degree, 1899, and taught astronomy, 1900–26. He was an associate editor of the *Transactions of the American Mathematical Society*, 1907–12. During World War I he served in the ordnance department of the U.S. Army. In 1936 he became permanent secretary of the American Association for the Advancement of Science. He collaborated with Thomas C. Chamberlin in the development of the planetesimal hypothesis of the origin of the solar system. His books include *Descriptive Astronomy* (1911), *Consider the Heavens* (1935), and *Autobiography of Science* (1945).

MOULTON, HAROLD GLENN, 1883– , U.S. economist, was born in Le Roy, Mich., studied at Albion College and then at the University of Chicago, where he received his Ph.D. degree, 1914. He taught economics at the University of Chicago until 1922, when he became president of the Institute of Economics, Washington, D.C. When the latter merged with two other institutes, 1927, to form the Brookings Institution, Moulton became president of the new organization; from 1952 he was president emeritus. He wrote *Japan: An Economic and Financial Appraisal* (1931), *Income and Economic Progress* (1935), *The Recovery Problem in the United States* (1937), *Capital Expansion, Employment and Economic Stability* (1940), *Regulation of the Securities Market* (1946), *Controlling Factors in Economic Development* (1949), and *The Dynamic Economy* (1950).

MOULTON, town, NW Alabama, seat of Lawrence County; 75 miles NNW of Birmingham. Cotton ginning and lumber milling are main industries in Moulton, one of the oldest established towns in the state. It was incorporated in 1818. Pop. (1960) 1,716.

MOULTRIE, WILLIAM, 1730–1805, American Revolutionary soldier, was born in Charleston, S.C. He served in the South Carolina house of commons and was a captain in the war with the Cherokee Indians, 1761. He was a member of the provincial congress, 1775, and was commissioned colonel of the 2nd South Carolina regiment. Moultrie distinguished himself, 1776, by his successful defense of the fort on Sullivan's Island, Charleston Harbor, against a British fleet. Commissioned a brigadier general in 1779, he held Charleston against a British advance until superseded by Gen. Benjamin Lincoln. On the surrender of Charleston, 1780, Moultrie became a prisoner, but was exchanged, 1782, and made a major general. He was governor of South Carolina, 1785–86 and 1794–96, and wrote *Memoirs of the American Revolution* (1802).

MOULTRIE, city, SW Georgia, seat of Colquitt County; on the Ochlockonee River, the Atlantic Coast Line, the Georgia Northern, and the Georgia and Florida railroads, and U.S. highway 319; 113 miles S of Macon. Moultrie is the tobacco market and commercial center for the local farm area. Its industries include meat processing, food canning, aluminum die-casting, peanut processing, and cotton milling. Moultrie was incorporated in 1859. Pop. (1960) 15,764.

MOUND BUILDERS, prehistoric inhabitants of North America who constructed various kinds of earthworks. Early investigators considered the mounds the work of a vanished people and offered theories to account for them. Modern archaeology showed that they were built by various groups of American Indians. The mounds can be roughly classified as burial mounds (including effigy mounds) produced primarily by woodland tribes, and truncated pyramidal structures used mainly as platforms for ceremonial buildings. The most notable burial mounds belong to the Hopewell culture that had spread from Ohio across central Illinois. Some of the burial mounds contained pottery and other articles. Effigy mounds in the form of snakes, birds, and other animals were numerous in Wisconsin. They are thought to represent the totems of the individuals buried in them. The pyramidal mounds were erected primarily by tribes of the middle and lower Mississippi Valley and show Mexican influence. See ARCHAEOLOGY, American Archaeology, *Mound Builders;* TOTEMISM. FAY-COOPER COLE

MOUND CITY, city, S Illinois, seat of Pulaski County; on the Ohio River, the Illinois Central and the New York Central railroads, and U.S. highway 51; 5 miles N of Cairo. Shipbuilding has been an important industry in the city since the Civil War. Its other manufactures include wood products, canned goods, and flour. Mound City was incorporated in 1857. Pop. (1960) 1,669.

MOUND CITY, city, E Kansas, seat of Linn County; 78 miles SE of Topeka. The city is situated in a fruit and livestock region. There are coal mines and oil and gas wells nearby. Pop. (1960) 661.

MOUND CITY, town, N South Dakota, seat of Campbell County; on U.S. highway 83; 80 miles WNW of Aberdeen. The town is situated in wheat and dairy country, near the Oahe Reservoir of the Missouri River Basin Project. Mound City was settled in 1884, was incorporated as a village in 1885 and as a town in 1927. Pop. (1960) 144.

MOUND CITY GROUP NATIONAL MONUMENT, a 57-acre tract, S Ohio, Ross County, 4 miles N of Chillicothe. The monument contains a group of 24 burial mounds enclosed within a low earth embankment that embraces 13 acres. The mounds, first explored in 1846, have yielded human bones, sacrificial altars, ornaments, and utensils of pre-Columbian culture. A number of the mounds have been restored. Mound City Group National Monument was established in 1923.

MOUNDSVILLE, city, N West Virginia, seat of Marshall County; on the Ohio River at the mouth of Little Grave Creek, on the Baltimore and Ohio Railroad and U.S. highway 250; 11 miles S of Wheeling. Principal manufactures include chemicals, table glassware, brooms, toys, and clothing. There are zinc refineries, oil and gas wells, and coal mines in the immediate area. Moundsville is the site of the state penitentiary and contains one of the country's largest Indian burial mounds, from which the city takes its name. Moundsville was settled in 1774. In 1865 it was consolidated with Elizabethtown to the north and incorporated as a city. Pop. (1960) 15,163.

MOUNT, WILLIAM SIDNEY, 1807–68, U.S. portrait and genre painter, was born in Setauket, N.Y. At first a sign painter, he studied at the National Academy of Design, 1826–27, and won success with portraiture and such delineations of farm life and Negro character as *Dance of the Haymakers, Music Hath Charms* and *Raffling for the Goose.*

MOUNT, meaning mountain when placed before a proper name. Place names beginning with *Mount,* including U.S. mountains that are within national parks, appear in THE AMERICAN PEOPLES ENCYCLOPEDIA under MOUNT. For all other mountains see articles under the principal word, as EVEREST, MOUNT.

MOUNTAIN, a land form of comparatively steep slopes and relatively small summit area rising well above its surroundings. The highest elevation of a mountain is a peak if the slopes culminate in a single point, a ridge if slopes culminate in a line of more or less constant elevation. Normally the over-all slope of a mountain consists of a series of diverging and converging slopes of a multitude of valleys and gullies in its surface. These slopes average between 20° and 25° from horizontal although near the summits they may exceed 35°. In some instances there may be sheer or even overhanging cliffs. The relative relief (that is,

THE CHANGING SURFACE OF THE EARTH

Erosion

Vulcanism

Diastrophism

Just as a sculptor works both by adding material and by cutting or chipping material away, so do the *forces* of nature. Many forces in nature are always at work shaping and changing surface features of the earth. Some of the basic forces which act as the tools for the constantly changing earth's surface are: running water, glaciers, wind and waves (***erosion***), volcanic action (***vulcanism***), and the lifting of solid parts of the earth from within (***diastrophism***) in building mountains and in raising plains.

The following *Trans-Vision* will demonstrate some of the changes brought about by these forces of *erosion, diastrophism,* and *vulcanism.* Turn the *Trans-Vision* pages one by one and carefully read the corresponding explanation of each type of activity. By close observation of the features of each new picture, you will notice the effects these forces could have on an imaginary portion of the earth's crust. The area shown is quite large; at the far horizon it is perhaps two hundred miles wide. The period of time the story covers is about thirty million years, which emphasizes the fact that although changes are continuous, they occur quite slowly. A fairly accurate impression of time might be obtained if you understand that each page you turn accounts for a passage of several millions of years.

(There are five numbered color plates to the *Trans-Vision* and a corresponding column of text material, also numbered, that calls your attention to the important features of the changing earth's surface. The last page of the *Trans-Vision* contains a glossary of some terms that will assist you in understanding the effects of *erosion, vulcanism,* and *diastrophism.*)

Plate 1 The land shown in the picture contains two mountainous areas: a ***range of complex mountains*** in the upper left is high, rugged, and capped with snow; to the right there is a ***range*** of ***folded mountains*** (*green*) in a stage of late maturity. Between the two, and in the center, are the smooth rounded remnants of very old mountains cut on each side by two ***water gaps.***

Rivers running through these water gaps connect the vast area of a rising ***plateau*** in the upper right-hand part of the scene (*tan color*) and the great *valley* in the center which extends to the lower left of the picture. The rivers join at the head of the valley to form the main stem of a large river which flows on the right-hand side of the valley. The floor of the valley is taken up with *foothills* which gradually rise into the range of complex mountains. These foothills or ***piedmont*** may consist partly of material which was raised at the same time the mountains were, and partly of material *eroded* and washed down from the higher mountains.

A large *piedmont glacier* resulting from the merger of smaller *valley glaciers* is shown moving down from the complex ranges. As it flows, this glacier carries mountain debris which usually appears as stripes on the glacier surface. These stripes are called *lateral moraines.* In the lower end of the glacier large cracks or *crevasses* open. As the glacier melts, it forms streams and rivers which find their way to the main river. Where the smooth surface of the foothills does not provide natural river beds, the streams break up and run together in an aimless way producing ***braided streams.*** Notice that in the complex mountains the rivers are many and small because large valleys have not yet been formed. In the folded mountains, well-developed valleys feed rivers of substantial size.

Plate 2 Several million years later, we note that ***EROSION*** has: (1) *cut* down the height of the complex mountain chain on the left; (2) *enlarged* the depressions in this chain into distinct *ridges;* (3) *carved* the foothills into more rugged forms; (4) *smoothed* and *rounded* the folded mountains and *widened* the valleys between them; (5) *deepened* the water gaps; (6) started to *cut* into the rising plateau; and (7) *built* a ***delta*** at the mouth of the large river and *deposited* material along the underwater ***continental shelf*** bordering the shoreline.

Less snow now is fed into the glacier and its rate of melting causes its lower edge to retreat. This glacial retreat has exposed large heaps of rock and other debris called a ***terminal moraine*** which serves as a dam for a lake formed from the melted snow.

Movements of the solid parts of the earth or ***DIASTROPHISM*** have: (1) through one great fracture or *fault* in the rock, caused the far area of the folded mountains to rise and form a low chain of ***block mountains*** (on the exposed surface of the fault a cross-section of the folded mountain is still clearly visible, providing an excellent sample of up-and-down segments of the compressed, wavelike ***crust***); (2) altered the shoreline, particularly of the folded mountain chain. The offshore area is "weighed down" by the accumulation of eroded materials. The shoreline in the bay once close to the edge of the foothills, is marked by a rise of ground known as the ***fall line.***

Finally, the *movements of molten rock* beneath the earth's surface called ***VOLCANISM*** have: (1) forced a horizontal sheet of molten rock or ***magma*** beneath the low hills to the left of the folded mountains, thus causing them to rise; (2) produced an eruption on the coastal plain at the lower left, building a steep volcanic *cone of cinder.*

Plate 3 During another long period of time, perhaps several millions of years, the complex mountains on the left have been eroded bit by bit until, reduced in height, they carry a much smaller mantle of snow. This feeds less snow to the glacier which continues to recede, exposing the valley which it cut.

Glacial melt now descends this valley as a river, carving a new *V-shaped* valley within it. On the right-hand wall is another valley intersecting the main one quite high above its floor. This is called a ***hanging valley*** and occurs where a branch of the glacier fed in.

Overflow from the lake (Plate 2) originally formed a river which dropped over the fall line. In the intervening years this waterfall has slowly cut a narrow valley or ***gorge*** through the foothills and, more rapidly, through the less resistant terminal moraine, thus draining the lake.

Other valleys have appeared in the old complex mountains (left)—the result of many small valleys and gorges growing together. Note, too, that the old folded mountains (center) are dwindling in size, their valleys are widening and their rivers are running more slowly.

As some mountains are worn down by the process of erosion, others are raised, very probably by the enormous force brought about by contraction of the earth's crust. Thus, the block mountains on the right have risen still higher, acquiring a covering of snow and are beginning to develop glaciers. Behind them the rising plateau is showing definite signs of being divided by *canyons* and sharp steplike *basins.*

The eroded materials carried to the sea form deltas at the protected mouths of rivers. Spread out by wave action, these materials form a smooth, gently sloping continental shelf.

In the meantime, volcanism has not been idle. The sheet of magma which forced itself beneath the old mountains between the water gaps raised them higher and extended this movement into the side of the folded mountains. This had a curious result. The river which ran through the water gap on the right could not cut through as rapidly as the ground rose; therefore, it cut a new course behind and around the old mountains. What was a water gap has now become an abandoned stream valley or ***wind gap.*** Traces of the old mountains above the *magma sill* have largely disappeared and the valley bottom has been worn lower so that the face of the sill has been exposed. (A sill is solidified magma in horizontal rock formations.)

A volcanic eruption has buried what remained of the cinder cone. The sides of the new lava volcano slope gradually to a much broader base and are intersected by *dikes.* (A ***dike*** is solidified magma in vertical cracks or fissures.) This volcano has become inactive and its crater is largely filled by a lake.

Waves, wind, rain, and frost have cut down the elevation and area of the offshore island. The material which composed the island tended to form beaches and a shelf around it comparable, on a small scale, to the continental shelf. This material has been widely distributed by wave and ocean current.

Plate 4 We are now taking another look at the same section of the earth's crust after another period of several million years has passed.

During this interval, volcanism has played an important role in the further lifting and shifting of the block mountains on the right. These have now reached full maturity and support a vast glacier whose edges reach the shoreline. This is called a *tidewater glacier* and it flows slowly to the sea through old valleys of the folded mountains. The foot of the glacier has a clifflike appearance, because large masses of ice, ***icebergs,*** break off and float away as a result of the rise and fall of the tide.

The plateau in the back of these new mountains is beginning to break up into large canyons and, in its farther and dryer reaches, to show early forms of *mesa* development.

The *palisaded* magma sill has lost much of its character through erosion; and the old complex mountains (left) have reduced into a system of weathered rounded shapes, separating well-developed valleys, each constituting a ***watershed.*** Each watershed supplies a rather large stream which flows into the main river. The main river and its tributaries *drain* a vast basin which includes all the area visible except that of the old folded mountains and the glacier.

The foothills have been worn low and almost smooth. The rivers have become slow, broad, and *meandering.* Occasional lakes, probably old sections of rivers, have appeared in the valley floor.

Enormous amounts of ***silt*** (small soil particles between clay particles and sand grains in size), brought down over the millions of years by the rivers, have built deltas and added a great weight to the continental shelf. This, in turn, may cause a *sinking of the shoreline.*

At the lower left, much of the lava cone has worn away and the intersecting dikes, which are weathering more slowly, begin to show through the layers of lava and earth that once concealed them.

Plate 5 The horizon line has become quite smooth with the disappearance of the complex mountain chain (left). Only remnants of the old folded mountains (center) remain as gentle hills. The lava cone has weathered away, exposing the magma backbone of the dikes. Even the fairly recent block mountains on the right have lessened in bulk.

As a consequence, the tidewater glacier has retracted, exposing a deeply indented coastline. This coastline was gradually carved by the former glacier as was the *submarine valley* noticeable offshore. Here again we find characteristic hanging valleys.

Sheer weight of material, massed in a continental shelf, has depressed the coastline, flooding the seaward end of the river valleys to form large bays. ***Sand bars*** have been built up by wave and current action in the shallow offshore waters, but note that the deltas have either disappeared under water or been washed away after the disappearance of the island.

Areas at the top of the scene which were once occupied by the plateau are now carved into vast valleys and gorges. Sheer walls alternate with sloping terraces of debris. Here and there, where an area of strata has proven resistant to erosion, it has protected the material under it. This has formed high, straight-walled, flat-top remnants of the early plateau, called *mesas.*

Even the volcanic sill or the old palisades (center), have lost their identity by being worn away or buried.

In this way, nature carves and molds her subject—a never ending, always changing process. Perhaps, let us say almost certainly, future *diastrophic* and *volcanic processes* will raise, or *rejuvenate,* new areas only to have them, in turn, attacked by the wearing forces of erosion.

TRANS-VISION® MILPRINT, INC.
MILWAUKEE, WISCONSIN

5

Glossary

block mountains Mountains that result from faulting.

braided stream A stream whose channel is filled with deposits that split it into many small channels.

complex mountains Mountains that result from a combination of faulting, folding, and volcanic action.

continental shelf Relatively shallow ocean floor bordering a continental land mass.

crust The outer layer of the solid earth.

delta A triangular deposit at the mouth of a stream.

diastrophism Movement of the solid parts of the earth.

dike Solidified magma in vertical cracks or fissures.

erosion The removal or wearing away of soil and rock fragments by natural agents.

fall line Region where a coastal plain adjoins the old land, characterized by numerous waterfalls.

folded mountains Mountains that result from the folding of rocks.

gorge Narrow ravine between steep rocky mountains or hills.

hanging valley The valley of a tributary which enters the main valley from a considerable height above the main stream bed.

magma Molten rock materials below the earth's surface.

meanders Wide curves typical of well-developed streams.

mountain range A group of mountains having a common origin.

piedmont Hills at the foot of mountains.

plateau A broad, elevated tract of flat land.

sand bar A ridge of sand formed in a river bed, at the mouth of a harbor or along the shoreline.

silt Soil particles intermediate in size between clay particles and sand grains.

terminal moraine Heaps of rock and gravel deposited by a glacier at its base or edge.

volcanism A general term including all types of activity due to movement of magma.

volcano The opening from which molten rock reaches the surface of the earth together with the accumulations of volcanic materials deposited around the opening.

water gap A valley that cuts across a mountain ridge and through which a stream runs.

watershed An area drained by a river or lake system.

wind gap An abandoned stream valley cutting across a ridge.

The design, story, and art work for the "Trans-Vision" was under the direction of F. R. Gruger, Jr. The original art was done by D. G. Summers. The consultant for the project was Andrew McIntyre of the Department of Geology, Columbia University.

the difference in relief within a limited area) of mountains has been generally fixed by geographers as between 1,000 and 3,000 feet to distinguish them from hills, which they resemble in many ways.

In matters of name, deference is made to local usage. The area of southern Assam in India with elevations of more than 6,000 feet is called the Khasi Hills; in eastern United States the Blue Ridge Mountains rise to elevations of only 4,000 feet. Perhaps the Khasi Hills, high as they are, are only hills in contrast to the nearby Himalayas with many peaks above 20,000 feet. Another type of mountain is the dissected edge of a plateau, as for example the Western Ghats of India, the Great Khingan Mountains of China, and the Drakensburg Mountains of South Africa. Except for isolated erosional remnants, these areas generally lack small summit areas and strictly speaking are not mountains at all.

Hierarchy of Mountain Areas. Starting with single peaks and ridges there is a hierarchy of size and arrangement among mountain areas. An essentially linear arrangement of peaks and ridges of similar origin is called a mountain range. If the arrangement is essentially circular, it is a mountain group. Several associated ranges or groups are a mountain system. A number of systems in the same region, but of different origins, form a mountain chain; several chains that together constitute the mountain axis of a continent are called a cordillera. Thus the western cordillera of North America includes a number of chains, one of which is the Rocky Mountains. The Rockies in turn consist of a number of systems such as the southern Rockies. In turn this system is divided into a number of ranges and groups, as the San Juan Mountains and the Sangre de Cristo Range.

Distribution of Mountain Areas. The great mountain cordilleras of the world are distributed in a well defined pattern which corresponds to the pattern of major earth crustal instability. This distribution emphasizes the youthful character of mountains in the history of the earth's surface.

One of the major zones of mountain building activity borders the Pacific Ocean. Starting in Antarctica, this ring of mountains continues as the Andes of South America, runs through western North America, curves through the Aleutians and the great island arcs off the Asiatic coast, and includes the mountains of eastern Australia. A second major zone of great mountains centers in the Pamir knot of northern Pakistan, eastern Afghanistan, and the Tadzhik Soviet Socialist Republic. From this central knot adjoining series extend to the northeast to meet the Pacific ring of mountains at Bering Strait; a second series runs to the east and southeast as the mighty Himalayas with extensions reaching the Pacific border zone in the East Indies. A third series extends westward including en route such mountains as the Elburz, the Caucasus, the Carpathians, the Alps, the Pyrenees, and the Great Atlas Mountains. Only in Africa are there really high peaks and major mountain masses that are not part of these major cordilleras.

McGowan Peak in the rugged Sawtooth Range of Idaho rises above Stanley Lake near the source of the Salmon River.
IDAHO DEPT. OF COMMERCE AND DEVELOPMENT

Most mountains that lie outside of these major cordilleras are older, and the predominant molders of the present surface have been agents of erosion rather than forces of uplift; examples are the Appalachians, the mountains of Scandinavia, and the Urals. They are ancient residual forms whose highest points rise scarcely more than a mile above sea level.

Submarine Mountains bear the same relationship to the ocean floor as surface mountains do to the earth's surface. Most notable of submarine mountain systems is the mid-Atlantic Ridge which rises 5,000 to 10,000 feet above the floor of the Atlantic Ocean and extends from Iceland to Antarctica. Projecting above the ridge are a number of peaks, some of which protrude above sea level to form small islands in mid-Atlantic such as the Azores. Similar ridges occur in the southeast Pacific and Indian oceans. In addition to these extensive systems there are isolated peaks and short ridges dotting the ocean floors, particularly in the Pacific Basin. Many of these are volcanic peaks. The Hawaiian Islands are examples of such volcanic peaks, built up on an extensive ridge and sufficiently high relative to the level of the ocean to constitute an island chain.

Origin of Mountains

Four major earth shaping forces are responsible for the development of mountains: crustal folding, faulting, intrusive vulcanism, and extrusive vulcanism. On the basis of origin four types of mountains may be recognized: folded, fault-block, dome, and conical, each type essentially (though not necessarily exclusively) a result of one of the four processes.

Folded Mountains are generally found in a pattern of roughly parallel ranges resulting from arching or folding of the earth's crust by lateral compression. In some instances ridges are the tops of the folds, and intervening valleys are the bottoms. More commonly the parallel arrangement is a result of differential erosion of tilted rock layers; the more erosion-resistant rocks stand in relief as the ranges, and areas of less resistant rock are eroded to form valleys. This condition is well illustrated by the folded Appalachians of eastern United States.

Lateral compression may also involve faulting and give rise to parallel ranges separated by deep trenches as is the case in the northern Rockies. Most of the earth's mightiest mountains—the Himalayas, the Alps, and the Andes—are folded mountains on a grand scale.

Fault-Block Mountains have been formed not so much by compression and folding as by vertical movement of blocks of the earth's crust bounded by fault slippage zones. Some blocks may be elevated while others remain at the same level or become depressed as a result of lateral tension. Block mountains usually are isolated or widely spaced; some are small, others extremely large. Some are tilted by a succession of movements along a single fault line to produce an asymmetric range, such as the Sierra Nevadas, with a gradual slope on one side and a very steep slope, the fault scarp, on the other side. In other instances movement may have been along parallel faults, producing blocklike horsts, basinlike grabens, or long rift valleys such as those in east Africa.

Intrusive Vulcanism, in which molten material moves toward the surface of the earth, often results in doming of the earth's crust; erosion later removes the top of the dome to expose igneous rock underneath. Mountains produced in this fashion generally will have a radial pattern of ridges and valleys. The eroded remnants of the original overlaying rock may be in the form of a series of ridges encircling the

IMPORTANT MOUNTAINS OF THE WORLD*

Name	Location	Height in Feet
North America		
McKinley	Rocky Mtns.—Alaska	20,320
Logan	Rocky Mtns.—Canada	19,850
Orizaba(Citlaltepetl)	Sierra Madre—Mexico	18,700
Saint Elias	Rocky Mtns.—Alaska, Canada	18,008
Popocatepetl	Sierra Madre—Mexico	17,887
Foraker	Rocky Mtns.—Alaska	17,395
Ixtaccihuatl	Sierra Madre—Mexico	17,342
Lucania	Rocky Mtns.—Canada	17,150
King	Rocky Mtns.—Canada	17,130
Blackburn	Rocky Mtns.—Alaska	16,523
Steele	Rocky Mtns.—Canada	16,439
Bona	Rocky Mtns.—Alaska	16,421
Sanford	Rocky Mtns.—Alaska	16,208
Wood	Rocky Mtns.—Canada	15,880
Vancouver	Rocky Mtns.—Canada, Alaska	15,700
Fairweather	Rocky Mtns.—Canada, Alaska	15,300
Toluca	Sierra Madre—Mexico	15,020
Whitney	Sierra Nevada—California	14,495
Elbert	Rocky Mtns.—Colorado	14,431
Rainier	Cascade Range—Washington	14,410
Evans	Rocky Mtns.—Colorado	14,260
Longs Peak	Rocky Mtns.—Colorado	14,255
Wilson	Rocky Mtns.—Colorado	14,246
Shasta	Cascade Range—California	14,162
Pikes Peak	Rocky Mtns.—Colorado	14,110
Kennedy	Rocky Mtns.—Canada	13,900
Tajumulco	Sierra Madre—Guatemala	13,816
Gannett Peak	Rocky Mtns.—Wyoming	13,785
Grand Teton	Rocky Mtns.—Wyoming	13,766
Hayes	Rocky Mtns.—Alaska	13,740
Kings Peak	Rocky Mtns.—Utah	13,498
Waddington	Rocky Mtns.—Canada	13,260
Robson	Rocky Mtns.—Canada	12,972
Gerdine	Rocky Mtns.—Alaska	12,600
Chirripó Grande	Cordillera de Talamanca—Costa Rica	12,533
Witherspoon	Rocky Mtns.—Alaska	12,023
Hood	Cascade Range—Oregon	11,245
Duarte	Cordillera Central—Dominican Republic	10,115
Harney Peak	Black Hills—South Dakota	7,242
Mitchell	Blue Ridge Mtns.—North Carolina	6,684
Clingmans Dome	Great Smoky Mtns.—Tennessee	6,642
Washington	White Mtns.—New Hampshire	6,288
Marcy	Adirondack Mtns.—New York	5,344
Katahdin	White Mtns.—Maine	5,268
South America		
Aconcagua	Andes—Argentina	22,834
Ojos del Salado	Andes—Chile, Argentina	22,590
Tupungato	Andes—Chile, Argentina	22,310
Falso Azufre	Andes—Chile, Argentina	22,271
Pissis	Andes—Argentina	22,240
Huascarán	Andes—Peru	22,205
Tocorpuri	Andes—Bolivia, Chile	22,162
Llullaillaco	Andes—Chile, Argentina	22,015
Mercedario	Andes—Argentina	21,885
Yerupaja	Andes—Peru	21,758
Incahuasi	Andes—Chile, Argentina	21,720
Coropuna	Andes—Peru	21,696
Ancohuma	Andes—Bolivia	21,492
Sajama	Andes—Bolivia	21,390
Cachi	Andes—Argentina	21,325
Nacimiento	Andes—Argentina	21,300
Illampu	Andes—Bolivia	21,275
Illimani	Andes—Bolivia	21,185
Antofalla	Andes—Argentina	21,100
Bonete	Andes—Argentina	21,030
Ausangate	Andes—Peru	20,945
Acay	Andes—Argentina	20,800
Parinacota	Andes—Chile, Bolivia	20,767
Chimborazo	Andes—Ecuador	20,577
Pomarepe	Andes—Chile, Bolivia	20,472
Pular	Andes—Chile	20,375
Aucanquilcha	Andes—Chile	20,275
Chachani	Andes—Peru	19,960
Copiapó	Andes—Chile	19,950
Plomo	Andes—Chile, Argentina	19,850
Sillajhuay	Andes—Chile, Bolivia	19,695
Tacora	Andes—Peru, Chile	19,520
Quimsacruz	Andes—Bolivia	19,357
Cotopaxi	Andes—Ecuador	19,344
Misti	Andes—Peru	19,166
Cayambe	Andes—Ecuador	19,014
Cristóbal Colón	Andes—Colombia	18,950
Huila	Andes—Colombia	18,865
Huagaruancha	Andes—Peru	18,858
Antisana	Andes—Ecuador	18,714
Tolima	Andes—Colombia	18,438
Chorolque	Andes—Bolivia	18,422
Vilcanota	Andes—Peru	17,988
Morococala	Andes—Bolivia	17,644
Sangay	Andes—Ecuador	17,454
Tunari	Andes—Bolivia	17,046
Bolívar	Andes—Venezuela	16,411
Cotacachi	Andes—Ecuador	16,292
Pichincha	Andes—Ecuador	15,423
Puracé	Andes—Colombia	15,420
Galán	Andes—Argentina	15,400
Bandeira	Brazilian Plateau—Brazil	9,462
Africa		
Kilimanjaro (Kibo)	Kilimanjaro Highlands—Tanzania	19,565
Kenya	East African Plateau—Kenya	17,040
Stanley	Ruwenzori Mtns.—The Congo, Uganda	16,795
Ras Dashan	Simen Mtns.—Ethiopia	15,157
Karisimbi	Virunga Range—The Congo, Rwanda	14,780
Elgon	East African Plateau—Uganda-Kenya	14,178
Toubkal	Atlas—Morocco	13,665
Cameroun	Cameroun	13,350
Thabantshonyana	Drakensberg—Lesotho	11,425
Emi Koussi	Tibesti Mountains—Chad	11,204
Tahat	Ahaggar Mtns.—Algeria	9,850
Asia and Europe		
Everest (Chomolungma)	Himalayas—China, Nepal	29,028
Godwin Austen (K2)	Himalayas—Kashmir	28,250
Kanchenjunga	Himalayas—Nepal, Sikkim	28,166
Lhotse (El)	Himalayas—China, Nepal	27,890
Makalu	Himalayas—Nepal, China	27,790
Cho Oyu	Himalayas—Nepal, China	26,867
Dhaulagiri	Himalayas—Nepal	26,810
Nanga Parbat	Himalayas—Kashmir and Jammu	26,660
Manaslu	Himalayas—Nepal	26,658
Annapurna	Himalayas—Nepal	26,502
Gasherbrum	Himalayas—Kashmir	26,470
Gosainthan	Himalayas—China	26,291
Distaghil	Himalayas—Kashmir	25,868
Nanda Devi	Himalayas—India	25,645
Rakaposhi	Himalayas—Kashmir	25,550
Kamet	Himalayas—India	25,447
Namcha Barwa	Himalayas—China	25,445
Gurla Mandhata	Himalayas—China	25,355
Ulugh Muztagh	Kunlun—China	25,340
Tirich Mir	Hindu Kush—Pakistan	25,263
Kungur	Kunlun—China	25,146
Amne Machin	Kunlun—China	25,000
Minya Konka	Tahsüeh—China	24,900
Communism	Pamirs—U.S.S.R.	24,590
Teram Kangri	Himalayas—Mongolia	24,511
Pobeda	Tien Shan—U.S.S.R., China	24,406
Muztagh Ata	Kunlun—China	24,388
Aling Kangri	Trans-Himalayas—China	24,000
Chomo Lhari	Himalayas—China, Bhutan	23,997
Muztagh	Kunlun—China	23,890
Gauri Sankar	Himalayas—China, Nepal	23,440
Nunkun	Himalayas—Kashmir	23,410
Api	Himalayas—Nepal	23,399
Lenin	Trans-Altai—U.S.S.R.	23,382
Trisul	Himalayas—India	23,360
Kangto	Himalayas—China, India	23,260
Nyenchen Tanglha	Trans-Himalayas—China	23,255
Lombo Kangra	Trans-Himalayas—China	23,165
Shilla	Himalayas—India	23,050
Chomo Gangar	Trans-Himalayas—China	22,968
Khan Tengri	Tien Shan—China, U.S.S.R.	22,949
Kedarnath	Himalayas—India	22,770

IMPORTANT MOUNTAINS OF THE WORLD*

Name	Location	Height in Feet	Name	Location	Height in Feet
Chung Muztagh	Kunlun—China	22,700	Stalin (Musala)	East Rila Mtns.—Bulgaria	9,596
Kailas	Trans-Himalayas—China	22,028	Olympus	Greece	9,570
Grosvenor	Tahsüeh—China	21,190	Triglav	Julian Alps—Yugoslavia	9,395
Sumpa Kangri	Kunlun—China	20,670	Cinto	Corsica	8,891
Demavend	Elburz—Iran	18,600	Stalin (Gerlach)	Carpathians—Czechoslovakia	8,737
Elbrus	Caucasus—U.S.S.R.	18,481	Dodabetta	Nilgiri Hills—South India	8,640
Dykh-Tau	Caucasus—U.S.S.R.	17,054	Negoivl	Transylvanian Alps—Rumania	8,361
Ararat	Lesser Caucasus—Turkey	16,945	Galdhopiggen	Jotunheim Mtns.—Norway	8,097
Kazbek	Caucasus—U.S.S.R.	16,541	Hekla	Iceland	4,747
Klyuchevskaya Sopka	Sredinny Mtns.—U.S.S.R.	15,912	Ben Nevis	Scotland	4,406
Mont Blanc	Alps—France, Italy	15,781	Vesuvius	Italy	3,891
Dufourspitze	Alps—Italy, Switzerland	15,203	OCEANIA		
Matterhorn	Alps—Switzerland, Italy	14,701	Carstensz	Nassau—New Guinea	16,400
Jungfrau	Alps—Switzerland	13,653	Idenburg	Nassau—New Guinea	15,750
Sinkao (Morrison)	Formosa	13,599	Wilhelmina	Orange—New Guinea	15,585
Grossglockner	Alps—Austria	12,460	Markham	Antarctica	15,100
Fujiyama	Japan	12,389	Mauna Kea	Hawaii	13,796
Mulhacén	Sierra Nevada—Spain	11,411	Mauna Loa	Hawaii	13,675
Aneto	Pyrenees—Spain	11,168	Kinabalu	South Crocker Mtns.—Borneo	13,455
Etna	Sicily	10,741	Kerinchi	Barisan Mtns.—Sumatra	12,467
Qurnet es Sauda	Lebanon	10,131	Cook	New Zealand	12,349
Zugspitze	Alps—Germany	9,721	Mahameru	Java	12,060
Apo	Mindanao	9,690	Kosciusko	Australia	7,305

*Not all-inclusive; listed are better known peaks but not all the highest in any given range or country.

central dome. The Black Hills of South Dakota illustrate this condition.

Extrusive Vulcanism produces true mountains of accumulation by piling up lavas, fragments of volcanic rock, and volcanic ash around the craters of volcanoes. Well known examples are Shasta, Hood, and Rainier in the United States; Popocatepetl in Mexico; Etna and Vesuvius in Italy; Fuji in Japan; and Kilimanjaro in Africa. Most volcanoes are approximately conical but in those which have been long extinct this form may have been greatly modified by weathering and erosion. Some ancient volcanic mountains have worn away so that all that remains are stumps of the hard crystalline rocks that once plugged the vents through which igneous materials were emitted.

Residual Mountains and Dunes. In addition to mountains caused by the four major earth-shaking forces, there are residual mountains, those that result from a combination of wind and water erosion of relatively flat upland areas. They generally have steep slopes and flat tops; those with larger summit areas are known as mesas, those with small summit areas, as buttes. They are typical of arid and semiarid areas such as the Great Plains and the Colorado Plateau of western United States. Monadnocks are steep-sloped residual mountains in humid areas such as the eastern United States. They result from the fact that their component rocks have greater resistance to water erosion than do the rocks of the surrounding area.

Dunes are hills or ridges that result from the deposition of sand by strong winds. They are generally located along lake and ocean coasts and in desert areas.

MOUNTAIN TOPOGRAPHY

Characteristics of minor relief features of mountains depend not only upon the tectonic forces—diastrophism and vulcanism—that originally produced them but also upon the kind and arrangement of rocks of which they are composed and the kind, intensity, and extent of weathering and erosion to which they have been subjected. Running water, wind, ice, and snow all play a part of molding surface detail.

Life Cycle of a Mountain. In the beginning, mountain streams are youthful and their valleys are normally steep sided and deep. In turn, steep slopes encourage rapid runoff and further denudation. Thus angularity and starkness are characteristic of youthful stream-eroded mountains. As the cycle continues, valleys broaden, slopes become less steep, and intervening ridges become more rounded. Unless more uplift occurs the mountains eventually degenerate into hills.

Where snow and ice fields abound the process of erosion takes another aspect and when the glaciers and snow fields diminish a terrain more conspicuously open and rounded is exposed. Main valleys are U shaped, straight, and of almost equal width from mouth to head. Minor ridges are removed and major ridges reduced to knife-edged divides surmounted by angular pyramidal peaks or horns. In major ranges such as the Alps, the Himalayas, the Andes, and the Rockies, practically all types of topographic detail—from ice and snow fields at the highest elevations to rounded topography in the foothills—may be presented.

Importance of Mountains. Steep slopes, thin soils, and danger of erosion make widespread agriculture in mountain areas virtually impossible. Since agriculture is difficult, grassland and forests are permitted to dominate, thus establishing the basis for grazing and lumbering industries. Forces that shaped the mountains also produced concentrations of mineral ores, and mining is another economic potential of mountain areas. The combination of steep slopes and precipitation heavier than that of adjacent flatter areas gives mountains a greater potential for developing water power than exists in other land form regions. Finally, mountains are attractive recreation areas and especially those located near great concentrations of population have become tourist centers.

Mountains have long been noted as refuge areas for men and animals. Small independent and semi-independent mountain countries such as Switzerland, Andorra, Liechtenstein, and Nepal are political vestiges of this role of mountains. Mountain people, because of isolation and enforced self-sufficiency, tend to be clannish and conservative. Since mountains may be great barriers to trade and transportation, so that passes through them are of great strategic importance, political boundaries are often drawn along mountain divides because of their defensive and separative character.

Mountains are also significant as climatic controls. The Himalayas, for example, are barriers to cold air from the north, and as a result almost the entire Indian subcontinent has a tropical climate in spite of its latitudinal position. Many western mountains of the United States, lying as they do at right angles to prevailing winds, have wet western slopes and arid lands on the leeward sides. Rapid local changes in climate and weather are also a feature of mountain lands. These changes are the result of differences in exposure to winds, in receipts of solar energy, and particularly in altitude which affects temperatures. Because of these variables it is possible for a mountain in a tropical area to have almost all types of climate within a relatively short distance, from tropical rain forest at its base to icecap at its summit. This vertical zoning of environment adds to the self-sufficient character of many mountain economies.

ALFRED W. BOOTH

MOUNTAIN ASH, a deciduous tree or shrub with handsome foliage and ornamental red pomes, belonging to the genus *Sorbus* of the rose family, *Rosaceae*. The leaves grow alternately and are either simple or compound with pinnate leaflets. Showy white flowers appear in thick flat-topped clusters, or corymbs, in late spring. The fruit is a bright red pome resembling a berry. The 80 to 100 species are native in the north temperate zone and require little moisture. Usually they are propagated by seeds, or by layering, which is the rooting of shoots still attached to the mother plant. *S. americana* is the American mountain ash; it has bright green foliage and grows to 30 feet. *S. aucuparia*, or rowan tree, is the European mountain ash; it has long been cultivated and may grow 50 feet high. The leaves are a dull green. Fruit of *S. aucuparia* var. *edulis* sometimes is used in preserves.

MOUNTAIN BROOK, city, N central Alabama, Jefferson County; on Shades Creek and U.S. highway 280; 3 miles SE of Birmingham, of which it is a residential suburb. The city was incorporated in 1942. Pop. (1960) 12,680.

MOUNTAIN CITY, town, extreme NE Tennessee, seat of Johnson County; on U.S. highway 421; 90 miles WSW of Winston-Salem, N.C. The town is situated in a high valley between the Stone Mountains to the east and the Iron Mountains to the west. It is a trade center for the local farm area. Mountain City was incorporated in 1905. Pop. (1960) 1,379.

MOUNTAIN CLIMBING, a sport that is usually concerned with attempting to reach mountain heights that present difficulties, as distinguished from following upland trails or ascending easy slopes. Mountain climbing differs from many other sports in requiring no opponents or quarry, no standard area, and no formulated rules. There is no clear-cut distinction between winning and losing. Many famous climbs have been frustrated short of their summit goal. During a reconnaissance expedition, on the other hand, normally no attempt is made on the peak itself.

Mountains offer opportunities for rock climbing and snow and ice climbing; sometimes a single ascent requires both. Difficulties of terrain commonly encountered include extremely steep and narrow slopes; minimal hand and foot holds, on the surface or in cracks; vertical pitches; overhangs; faces that must be traversed; chimneys; and couloirs, or gorges, so wide that the climber cannot touch both walls at once. Surfaces may be wet or rotten, covered with moss or glare ice; climbers are often exposed to high winds and extreme cold while in precarious places. Ice climbing may necessitate the cutting of each step. Standard mountain climbing equipment includes heavy clothing, spiked or hobnailed boots, ropes, ice axes, and sometimes pitons and snap rings for securing ropes over areas that offer no supports or belaying points. Climbers frequently rope themselves together at intervals of 20 to 40 feet, with the most experienced member leading the ascent and the weakest in the middle of the group. Thus a person who loses his footing can usually be checked before the fall becomes disastrous. External dangers, most of which are avoided or minimized by an experienced guide or

UPI

Sports-minded amateur mountain climbers look on as one of their group makes a difficult ascent up the sheer wall of a mountain. Another climber pulls in the rope from above.

leader, include sudden storms, falling rocks, concealed crevasses, avalanches, and unsuspected snow cornices.

The continuous history of mountaineering did not begin until about 1760, when Horace Bénédict de Saussure began a long series of geological explorations throughout the Alps. He concentrated on Mont Blanc (15,781 ft.), which he climbed in 1787. His *Voyages dans les Alpes* (1779–96) was even more influential than his ascents. Interest in the Alps, especially among Englishmen, grew steadily; the Alpine Club was founded in 1858. In 1863 the club's publication, *The Alpine Journal*, "a record of mountain adventure and scientific observation," was instituted. Between 1850 and 1870 all the principal summits of the Alps were reached by pioneers such as Alfred Wills, Leslie Stephen, John Ball, F. F. Tuckett, A. W. Moore, and John Tyndall. In 1865 the Matterhorn (14,701 ft.), one of the most difficult and celebrated Alpine peaks, was climbed by Edward Whymper and a party of six, four of whom were killed on the descent. After 1870 emphasis was placed on finding more difficult routes up mountains already climbed.

Other mountainous areas also attracted climbers. In 1868 a party climbed several peaks in the Caucasus. Peaks in Alaska, East Africa, and South America were successfully attempted before 1900. Since the turn of the century, these and other areas have been popular, but the most eagerly accepted challenges have been provided by the Himalayas.

The highest summit in the world, Mt. Everest (29,028 ft.), was reached on May 29, 1953, by a British expedition led by Sir John Hunt. The final assault was made by Edmund Hillary of New Zealand and Tensing Norkey, a Sherpa tribesman of Nepal. At least 11 previous attempts had failed. Many other Himalayan peaks have been sought. In 1883 W. W. Graham climbed Kabru (24,002 ft.) to establish a record not broken until Prince Luigi Amadeo, duke of the Abruzzi, reached a height of 24,600 feet on Godwin-Austen (K2) in 1909. In 1931 Frank Smythe and Eric Shipton ascended Kamet (25,447 ft.), and this record was surpassed in 1936 when an Anglo-American group climbed Nanda Devi (25,645 ft.). In

1950 a French team climbed Annapurna I (26,502 ft.); 1953 saw the ascent of Nanga Parbat (26,660 ft.) by a German-Austrian party. Italian climbers scaled Godwin-Austen (28,250 ft.), the second highest peak of the world, in 1954; in 1955 Kanchenjunga (28,166 ft.), the third highest, and Makalu (27,790 ft.) yielded respectively to British and French parties. Swiss mountaineers climbed Lhotse or E1 (27,890 ft.), sister peak of Mt. Everest, in 1956, and a Japanese party ascended Manaslu (26,658 ft.).

Mt. McKinley (20,320 ft.), the highest in North America, was first climbed in 1910, and Mount Logan (19,850 ft.), Canada's highest, in 1925. Aconcagua (22,834 ft.), the highest peak in the Western Hemisphere, was first ascended in 1897.

In addition to prodigious physical feats, mountaineering has stimulated a long history of excellent descriptive and scientific literature. See MOUNTAIN.

W. R. IRWIN

BIBLIOG.–L. Stephen, *Playground of Europe* (1871); C. King, *Mountaineering in the Sierra Nevada* (1872); R. L. G. Irving, *Romance of Mountaineering* (1935); H. W. Tilman, *Mount Everest* (1948); G. W. Young, *Mountain Craft* (1949); C.-E. Engel, *History of Mountaineering in the Alps* (1950); F. S. Smythe, *Climbs in the Canadian Rockies* (1951); M. Herzog, *Annapurna* (1952); J. Hunt, *Conquest of Everest* (1954); E. Hillary, *High Adventure* (1955); P. Bauer, *Siege of Nanga Parbat, 1856–1953* (1956); A. Desio, *Victory over K2* (1956); C. Evans, *On Climbing* (1957); G. A. Smith, *Introduction to Mountaineering* (1957).

MOUNTAIN HOME, town, N Arkansas, seat of Baxter County; on U.S. highway 62; 115 miles N of Little Rock. The town is situated in the Ozarks on a high plateau between the White and North Fork rivers. Mountain Home is predominantly an agricultural and resort town. Pop. (1960) 2,105.

MOUNTAIN HOME, city, SW Idaho, seat of Elmore County; on the Union Pacific Railroad and U.S. highways 20, 26, and 30; 30 miles SE of Boise. Mountain Home is situated in the irrigated Snake River area, where fruit and hay are produced. It is a shipping point for cattle and sheep, and lumbering is the principal industry. Copper, silver, and gold mines are located nearby. Mountain Home was incorporated as a village in 1896 and as a city in 1946. Pop. (1960) 9,344.

MOUNTAIN LAUREL. See KALMIA.

MOUNTAIN MEADOWS MASSACRE took place in Mountain Meadows, a small valley in SW Utah, 300 miles SSW of Salt Lake City, on Sept. 11, 1857. A group of Mormons and Paiute Indians battled a party of some 137 emigrants, mainly from Arkansas, on their way to California. All the emigrants with the exception of the youngest children were killed. Since relations were strained between the Mormons and the federal government, which had sent troops to subdue them, the Mormons were blamed for the massacre and it was reported that the Mormon leader Brigham Young had made threats against emigrants who came to settle in Utah. Actually Young had given instructions to his people to give all possible assistance and protection to emigrants passing through Utah. The massacre seems to have been caused by the arrogant and lawless behavior of the emigrants, particularly the group known as the "Missouri wild-cats." John D. Lee, leader of those Mormons who had participated in the battle, was nevertheless executed in 1877.

MOUNTAIN MEN, early pioneers in the Rocky Mountains area. They came originally as fur trappers soon after Pierre de La Vérendrye and others had explored the territory which was then part of French Louisiana and later became modern Montana, Wyoming, and Colorado. The first mountain men were French, but later many were Spanish or American. The mountain men sold the skins of the beavers they caught in steel traps to fur companies established in St. Louis, Mo. Some were hired trappers who were paid annual wages by fur companies; others were skin trappers who sold their beaver skins to a single fur company; and others were free trappers who dealt with any company they wished. The mountain men, mingling with the Indians, whose way of life they adopted to some extent, wore buckskins and moccasins and lived in buffalo skin lodges. Some of the most famous were Jim Beckwourth, Jim Bridger, Kit Carson, Thomas Fitzpatrick, Jedediah Smith, and Bill Williams. The mountain men gathered annually at Green River, Wyo., and other traditional meeting places for their major social and economic undertakings of the year. Their earnings immediately went back to the fur companies, which sold them liquor, supplies, and trade goods. The Hudson's Bay Company sent fur trappers up the Columbia River into the territory of modern Idaho, Nevada, and Utah.

Changes in fashion caused a slump in the beaver skin business and the mountain men turned to trade with the Indians to make their living. When troops came to the Rocky Mountain area to subdue the Indians, the mountain men became scouts and guides. By 1850 the lands obtained from the Indians had been settled by immigrants and the mountain men were no longer met in the area.

MOUNTAINS OF THE MOON. See RUWENZORI.

MOUNTAIN STATE, nickname given to West Virginia because of its mountainous terrain. See PANHANDLE STATE.

MOUNTAIN VIEW, village, S Alaska; 3 miles E of Anchorage. Nearby is Fort Richardson, Alaskan headquarters of the U.S. Army during World War II. Pop. about 2,900.

MOUNTAIN VIEW, town, N Arkansas, seat of Stone County; 80 miles N of Little Rock. Mountain View is a popular summer resort in the Ozarks. Agriculture, woodworking, and cotton ginning are its major industries. Pop. (1960) 983.

MOUNTAIN VIEW, city, W central California, Santa Clara County; on the Southern Pacific Railroad and U.S. highway 101; 6 miles SE of Palo Alto. Mountain View is in a fruit growing region and the city is a fruit and vegetable canning center. Manufactures include electronic equipment and wood products. The city was incorporated in 1902. Pop. (1960) 30,889.

MOUNT AIRY, town, NW North Carolina, Surrey County; on the Southern Railway, and U.S. highways 52 and 601; 35 miles NW of Winston-Salem. It is surrounded by the Blue Ridge foothills. Industries in the town include granite quarrying, textiles, and furniture making. Mount Airy was incorporated in 1885. Pop. (1960) 7,055.

MOUNT AYR, town, S Iowa, seat of Ringgold County; on the Burlington Railroad and U.S. highway 169; 73 miles SSW of Des Moines. The town is situated on a high, rolling prairie in a grain and livestock area. Mount Ayr was founded about 1855 and incorporated in 1875. Pop. (1960) 1,738.

MOUNTBATTEN LOUIS, 1st **EARL MOUNTBATTEN OF BURMA,** 1900– , English naval officer and government official, was born Louis Francis Albert Victor Nicholas of Battenberg, at Frogmore House, Windsor, and entered the royal navy in 1913. During World War II he was chief of British combined operations, 1942–43 (see COMMANDO), and Allied supreme commander in southeast Asia, 1943–46. As the last British viceroy and the first governor general of India, 1947–48, he did much to improve British-Indian relations. He was commander in chief of Allied forces in the Mediterranean, 1953–54, and became first sea lord and chief of the naval staff, 1955, and chairman of the chiefs of staff committee, 1959.

MOUNT CARMEL, city, SE Illinois, seat of Wabash County; on the Wabash River and the New York Central and the Southern railroads; 34 miles NNW of Evansville, Ind. The city is in a rich agricultural region producing corn, wheat, and soybeans. There are bituminous coal mines, oil wells, and railroad shops; and clothing, paper products, flour, and electrical and sports equipment are manufactured. Mount Carmel was incorporated in 1825. Pop. (1960) 8,594.

MOUNT CARMEL, borough, E central Pennsylvania, Northumberland County; on the Lehigh Valley, the Pennsylvania, and the Reading railroads and U.S. highway 122; 51 miles WNW of Allentown. The borough has 12 anthracite coal mines operating within a 5-mile radius. Manufactures include chemicals, clothing, cigars, and beer. Mount Carmel was incorporated in 1864. Pop. (1960) 10,760.

MOUNT CARMEL CAVES, two excavations on Mount Carmel in Palestine (Israel) made in 1931–32 by a British-American expedition. The two caves, Mugharet es-Skhul (Cave of the Kids) and et-Tabun (the Oven), yielded implements from early and middle Mousterian, a period of paleolithic culture that marked the culmination of Neanderthal man. (See ANTHROPOLOGY, *Neanderthal Man.*) Skeletal remains indicated a heterogeneous people. A number of Skhul skeletons were tall and straight-limbed, indicating men who were like Neanderthal man in some respects but otherwise like modern man. In the Tabun Cave a skeleton of a woman was found that was primarily Neanderthal, but had primitive features of modern man. The find was important as evidence of *Homo sapiens* in the Lower Paleolithic period, which ranged from about 100,000 to 50,000 B.C.

MOUNT CARROLL, city, NW Illinois, seat of Carroll County; on the Milwaukee Railroad and U.S. highway 52; 48 miles WSW of Rockford. The city is in an agricultural area. Dairy products, livestock, and grain are grown. Mount Carroll was incorporated in 1867. Pop. (1960) 2,056.

MOUNT CLEMENS, city, SE Michigan, seat of Macomb County; on the Clinton River, the Grand Trunk Railroad, and U.S. highway 25; 20 miles NNE of Detroit. Mineral waters pumped from deep wells have made Mount Clemens a popular health resort. The city's manufactures include farm implements, pottery, dinnerware, metal products, beet sugar, power boats, and house trailers. The growing of roses is an important industry. The city was platted in 1818 by Christian Clemens, and was incorporated as a village in 1837 and as a city in 1879. Pop. (1960) 21,016.

MOUNT DESERT ISLAND, off the E coast of Maine, Hancock County; 40 miles SE of Bangor. It is the largest island in the archipelago extending from Frenchman Bay to Penobscot Bay. A drawbridge connects the island with the mainland. Mount Desert Island is 15 miles long and 8 miles wide, with an area of more than 100 square miles. Its rocky, wooded surface is dotted with 18 hills and 26 lakes and ponds. Samuel de Champlain, who explored the area in 1604, gave the island its name in honor of his patron, Pierre du Guast, sieur de Monts. In 1612 a French missionary settlement there was destroyed by the English, who coveted the island; 101 years later the French reluctantly ceded it to them. Following the American Revolution it was governed by Massachusetts until 1819 when it became a part of Maine. Since the middle of the nineteenth century Mount Desert Island has become a fashionable resort. Forest fires in 1947 destroyed many estates and much of the village of Bar Harbor. Part of Acadia National Park is situated on the island.

MOUNT EDEN, borough, New Zealand, N Island, at the base of Mount Eden (644 ft.); adjoining Auckland, of which it is a residential suburb. Pop. (1955 est.) 19,550.

MOUNT EPHRAIM, borough, SW New Jersey, Camden County; on the Pennsylvania-Reading Seashore Railroad; 5 miles S of Camden. Mount Ephraim is situated in a fruit and vegetable growing region. It was settled before 1800 and incorporated in 1926. Pop. (1960) 5,447.

MOUNT GILEAD, village, central Ohio, seat of Morrow County; on the New York Central Railroad and U.S. highway 42; 16 miles ESE of Marion. The village's manufactures include hydraulic presses, electrical apparatus, pottery, and chemicals. Mount Gilead State Reserve is nearby. Mount Gilead was founded about 1824 and incorporated in 1848. Pop. (1960) 2,788.

MOUNT HEALTHY, city, SW Ohio, Hamilton County; on U.S. highway 127; 8 miles N of Cincinnati of which it is a suburb. Manufactures include machine tools, bricks, flour, and clothing. The city, formerly named Mount Pleasant, was founded in 1817. Pop. (1960) 6,553.

MOUNT HOLLY, unincorporated village, SW central New Jersey, seat of Burlington County; on Rancocas Creek and the Pennsylvania Railroad; 18 miles ENE of Camden. It is a trade center for the local agricultural region. The village's manufactures include clothing, dyes, textiles, and leather goods. Mount Holly was settled by Quakers in 1676. John Woolman, famous American Quaker, lived there. During the American Revolution it was occupied by the British. Many eighteenth century buildings survive. Pop. (1960) 13,271.

MOUNT HOLYOKE COLLEGE, a nonsectarian, private institution of higher learning for women in South Hadley, Mass. The school was chartered in 1836 as Mount Holyoke Female Seminary, with instruction first being offered in 1837. The name of the college was changed to Mount Holyoke Seminary and College in 1888. The shorter name was adopted in 1893. Mount Holyoke offers a general liberal arts program. Distinctive educational programs include an honors program in the junior and senior years, a student-operated campus radio station, and a cooperative program with Hartford Hospital School of Nursing. Special library collections include first editions of books by Charles Lamb (1775–1834). The college offers the bachelor's and master's degrees. See COLLEGES AND UNIVERSITIES.

MOUNT IDA, city, W Arkansas, seat of Montgomery County; on U.S. highway 270; 78 miles WSW of Little Rock. Beef cattle raised in the vicinity are shipped from Mount Ida to Kansas City. Other industries include dairying and sawmilling. Mount Ida was settled in 1836. Pop. (1960) 564.

MOUNT KISCO, village, SE New York, Westchester County; on the New York Central Railroad; 21 miles NNE of Yonkers. The village has a radium extracting plant and manufactures of furniture, copper tubing, wood products, and machinery. Mount Kisco was incorporated in 1874. Pop. (1960) 6,805.

MOUNT McKINLEY NATIONAL PARK, S central Alaska, in the Alaska Range, a spectacular mountain area of 3,030 sq. mi. whose principal scenic

Mount McKinley, situated in south central Alaska, is the highest peak in North America. It is the main feature of rugged Mount McKinley National Park, established in 1917.

PHOTO BY CANNS, FAIRBANKS, ALASKA

feature is Mount McKinley (20,320 ft.), the highest peak in North America. The park, established in 1917 and enlarged in 1922 and 1932 includes other high peaks, among them Mount Foraker (17,395 ft.), Mount Hunter (14,573 ft.), Mount Brooks (11,939 ft.), and Mount Russell (11,670 ft.), and vast glacier fields. Mount McKinley rises abruptly from a plain at an elevation of 2,500 to 3,000 feet to soar 17,000 feet above the timber line. There are two peaks: south peak (20,320 ft.) and north peak (19,470 ft.). Two-thirds of the mountain is snow covered throughout the year.

All of the great northward-flowing glaciers of the Alaska Range rise on Mount McKinley and Mount Foraker. The largest are the Herron on Mount Foraker and the Peters and the Muldrow on Mount McKinley. The glacier fronts are covered by rock debris which is carried off by glacial streams as fast as it accumulates. Geologists are of the opinion that glaciers of the Alaska Range are gradually receding.

Mount McKinley National Park is notable for its wildlife. More than 35 kinds of mammals live in the park including Alaska moose, Alaska mountain sheep, Toklet grizzly bear, and caribou. Among 112 kinds of birds in the park are the ptarmigan, surfbird, sea gull, and wandering tattler. Mackinaw trout and arctic grayling are found in the mountain streams. White spruce is the commonest kind of tree in the park; others are white birch, cottonwood, quaking aspen, and willow; there are also a variety of shrubs.

Within park boundaries are more than 100 miles of graveled roadway and many foot trails. The Alaskan Railroad connects the park with Seward, Anchorage, and Fairbanks.

Mount McKinley was discovered by William A. Dickey in 1896, and the north peak was first ascended by William Taylor and Peter Anderson in 1910. In 1913 Archdeacon Hudson Stuck and Harry P. Karstens scaled the south peak. Alfred D. Lindley, Harry J. Liek, Erling Strom, and Grant Pearson were first to ascend both peaks (1932).

MOUNT OF OLIVES, or Olivet, a hill east of Jerusalem, separated from the city by the Valley of Jehoshaphat through which the Brook Kidron runs. According to the Bible, David fled from Absalom by way of this mount (II Sam. 15:30), and it was probably the site of altars dedicated by Solomon to Chemosh (I Kings 11:7). During His ministry Jesus often went to this mount; the garden of Gethsemane was on its western slope (Luke 21:37, 22:39; John 8:1). The Bible reports that it was from its summit, a Sabbath day's journey from Jerusalem, that Jesus ascended into heaven after His resurrection (Acts 1:12). Zechariah prophesied that this mount would be the scene of Christ's return to earth (Zech. 14:4). It is the highest (2,700 ft.) of four peaks in the range that are called Olivet.

MOUNT OLIVER, borough, SW Pennsylvania, Allegheny County; on the Monongahela River. Although completely surrounded by the southern part of Pittsburgh, Mount Oliver is an independent municipality. The borough was incorporated in 1892. Pop. (1960) 5,980.

MOUNT OLIVET, city, NE Kentucky, seat of Robertson County; on U.S. highway 62; 42 miles NE of Lexington. The town is built on seven hills in the bluegrass agricultural region. Tobacco, livestock, and dairying are the principal industries. Mount Olivet was incorporated in 1871. Pop. (1960) 386.

MOUNT PLEASANT, city, SE Iowa, seat of Henry County; on the Burlington Railroad and U.S. highways 34 and 218; 28 miles NW of Burlington. Pens, seeds, canned goods, pennants, and badges are produced in the city. Limestone quarries are situated nearby. Mount Pleasant is the site of Iowa Wesleyan College, a soldiers' and sailors' hospital, and a state mental hospital. The city was settled in 1834 and incorporated in 1842. Pop. (1960) 7,339.

MOUNT PLEASANT, city, central Michigan, seat of Isabella County; on the Chippewa River, the Ann Arbor and the Chesapeake and Ohio railroads, and U.S. highway 27; 60 miles N of Lansing. Its manufactures include automotive parts, plumbing fixtures, condensed milk, and inedible fats and tallows. There are also oil and sugar refineries. The city is the seat of Central Michigan College. Mount Pleasant, settled in 1859, was incorporated as a village in 1875 and as a city in 1889. Pop. (1960) 14,875.

MOUNT PLEASANT, borough, SW Pennsylvania, Westmoreland County; on the Baltimore and Ohio Railroad; 32 miles SE of Pittsburgh. The borough is situated in an agricultural and bituminous coal-mining district. Coke, glassware, cigars, iron castings, and cement products are manufactured. Mount Pleasant was settled in 1755, laid out in 1797, and incorporated in 1828. Pop. (1960) 6,107.

MOUNT PLEASANT, city, NE Texas, seat of Titus County; on the St. Louis Southwestern Railway and U.S. highways 67 and 271; 110 miles ENE of Dallas. Industries in Mount Pleasant, formerly an important lumbering center, include cottonseed oil milling, oil refining, milk processing, and pottery manufacturing. The city was settled in 1846 and incorporated in 1900. Pop. (1960) 8,027.

MOUNT RAINIER, city, S central Maryland, Prince George County; 30 miles SW of Baltimore. Mount Rainier is a northeast suburb of Washington, D.C. It was incorporated as a town in 1910 and as a city in 1945. Pop. (1960) 9,855.

MOUNT RAINIER NATIONAL PARK, SW Washington, in the Cascade Range; an area of 377 square miles dominated by Mount Rainier (14,410 ft.). Twenty-six glaciers, which form one of the world's largest single-peak glacier systems, extend down Mt. Rainier's sides to the rivers below. The ice-coated peak rises 11,000 feet above a forested base that spreads over 100 square miles. Mount Rainier's last volcanic eruption occurred in 1870, the same year the mountain was first scaled by man. Other mountains in the park include Mount Fremont (7,300 ft.); Pinnacle Peak (6,562 ft.); Crystal Peak (6,515 ft.); and Lane Peak (6,000 ft.). In contrast to the park's gaunt peaks and masses of ice are its forested valleys, alpine meadows, and fields of wild flowers. Dozens of tourist trails wind amidst spectacular scenery. Mount Rainier National Park was established in 1899 and enlarged in 1931.

MOUNT REVELSTOKE NATIONAL PARK, Canada, SE British Columbia, bordering the Columbia River valley; area 100 sq. mi. The park is situated on the western slope of the Selkirk Mountains; its most dominant feature is Mount Revelstoke (7,390 ft.). Virgin timberlands, mountain ranges, alpine meadows, and blue lakes extend in every direction.

Majestic Mount Rainier towers above the rugged landscape of the national park bearing its name. The peak, covered with perennial glaciers, is the nation's eleventh highest.
RAINIER NATL. PARK CO.

The park is reached by an 18-mile highway that ascends gradually from the town of Revelstoke. Fishing, camping, and hiking in summer and skiing in winter make the park a popular vacation spot. Mount Revelstoke National Park was established in 1914.

MOUNT ROBSON PROVINCIAL PARK, Canada, E British Columbia; 65 miles long, 10 to 20 miles wide; crossed by the Canadian National Railway over Yellowhead Pass on the E boundary; in the Canadian Rockies adjoining Jasper National Park to the E and Hamber Provincial Park to the SW. The park is a picturesque area of high peaks and glaciers and includes Mount Robson (12,972 ft.), highest peak in the Canadian Rockies. At the foot of Mount Robson is Berg Lake, a resort center. The park was established in 1913.

MOUNT ROYAL, town, Canada, S Québec; on Montreal Island; on the Canadian Pacific and the Canadian National railways; a suburb, 4 miles W of Montreal; pop. (1956) 15,940.

MOUNT RUSHMORE NATIONAL MEMORIAL, in the Black Hills of SW South Dakota, Pennington County; 25 miles SW of Rapid City. The memorial, established in 1929, comprises 1,278 acres of wooded mountains. On Mount Rushmore's face are carved the features of George Washington, Thomas Jefferson, Abraham Lincoln, and Theodore Roosevelt in heroic proportions. The memorial site was dedicated in 1925, and in 1927 Gutzon Borglum began work on the first head, that of Washington. Each of the heads is about 60 feet in height.

CATERPILLAR TRACTOR CO.

A popular U.S. tourist attraction is Mount Rushmore in the Black Hills of South Dakota, where, carved in stone, are the likenesses of four former American Presidents.

MOUNT STERLING, city, W Illinois, seat of Brown County; on the Wabash Railroad and U.S. highway 24; 34 miles E of Quincy. The city is in an agricultural and bituminous coal region. Dairying is its principal industry. Mount Sterling was settled in 1830 and incorporated in 1837. Pop. (1960) 2,262.

MOUNT STERLING, city, NE central Kentucky, seat of Montgomery County; on the Chesapeake and Ohio Railroad, and U.S. highways 460 and 60; 30 miles E of Lexington. It is situated in the outer bluegrass agricultural area. Manufactures of the city include clothing, soft drinks, concrete and cotton products, crushed lime, feed, flour, and lumber. Mount Sterling was platted in 1793. It was sacked by Confederate troops in 1863. Pop. (1960) 5,370.

MOUNT UNION COLLEGE. See COLLEGES AND UNIVERSITIES.

MOUNT VERNON, city, E central Georgia, seat of Montgomery County; on U.S. highway 280; 76 miles SE of Macon. Mount Vernon is situated near the Oconee River in an agricultural and timber area. Brewton-Parker Junior College is in the city. Pop. (1960) 1,166.

MOUNT VERNON, city, S Illinois, seat of Jefferson County; on the Chicago and Eastern Illinois, the Louisville and Nashville, the Missouri Pacific, and the Southern railroads and U.S. highway 460; 73 miles ESE of East St. Louis. Mount Vernon is a trade, shipping, and processing center for the surrounding oil and agricultural region. Manufactures include heavy machinery, clothing, shoes, food products, and stoves. The city was founded in 1819 by colonists from the Carolinas and Virginia. Pop. (1960) 15,566.

MOUNT VERNON, city, extreme SW Indiana, seat of Posey County; on the Ohio River near its confluence with the Wabash, on the Chicago and Eastern Illinois and the Louisville and Nashville railroads; 18 miles SW of Evansville. It is a trading center for the surrounding farm area. Oil is refined, and farm machinery and food products are manufactured. The city was incorporated in 1865. Pop. (1960) 5,970.

MOUNT VERNON, town, central Kentucky, seat of Rockcastle County; on the old Wilderness Road, the Louisville and Nashville Railroad, and U.S. highways 150 and 25; 48 miles S of Lexington. It is in a coal mining and agricultural area, and there are limestone and sandstone quarries. Nearby are the Great Saltpeter Caves and Cumberland National Forest. Mount Vernon was incorporated in 1818. Pop. (1960) 1,177.

MOUNT VERNON, city, SW Missouri, seat of Lawrence County; on the Frisco Railway; 30 miles WSW of Springfield. It is in the Ozarks in a farm and dairy region. A large milk condensing plant is operated there. Mount Vernon is the site of the state tuberculosis sanatorium. The city was laid out in 1845. Pop. (1960) 2,381.

MOUNT VERNON, city, SE New York, Westchester County; on the Bronx River and the New York Central and the New York, New Haven and Hartford railroads; adjacent to New York City on the NE. Mount Vernon is in the New York City metropolitan area, immediately north of the Bronx. A great variety of products are manufactured in the city, which also is an oil distribution point and a printing and publishing center. St. Paul's church (?1761), occupied by Hessian troops during the American Revolution, was established as a national historic site in 1943. The first settlement was made in 1664 by a group of 10 families who claimed the area for Connecticut. An election held in Mount Vernon in 1733 brought to a successful conclusion the efforts of the New York newspaperman John Peter Zenger to establish freedom of the press. Mount Vernon was incorporated in 1892. Pop. (1960) 76,010.

MOUNT VERNON, city, central Ohio, seat of Knox County; on the Kokosing River, the Baltimore and Ohio and the Pennsylvania railroads, and U.S. highway 36; 70 miles SW of Akron. The city is an agricultural trading center for the area. Manufactures include diesel and steam engines, gasoline, paperboard and glass products, and machine tools. Mount Vernon was laid out in 1805. Pop. (1960) 13,284.

MOUNT VERNON, town, NE Texas, seat of Franklin County; near White Oak Bayou, on the St. Louis Southwestern Railway and U.S. highway 67; 95 miles ENE of Dallas. Mount Vernon is a trade and processing center in an agricultural, oil, and timber region. It was incorporated in 1910. Pop. (1960) 1,338.

MOUNT VERNON, city, NW Washington, seat of Skagit County; on the Skagit River, the Great Northern Railway, and U.S. highway 99; 31 miles N of Everett. The city is in the heart of the northwest fishing and resort area and has manufactures of frozen food and dairy products. It was settled in 1877. Pop. (1960) 7,921.

VIRGINIA DEPT. OF CONSERVATION AND DEVELOPMENT

Mount Vernon, overlooking the beautiful Potomac River in Virginia near Washington, D.C., was at one time the home and is now the final resting place of George Washington.

MOUNT VERNON, national shrine and former estate of George Washington, N Virginia, Fairfax County; on the W bank of the Potomac River and on the Mount Vernon Memorial Highway; 15 miles SSW of Washington, D.C. The estate originally was known as Little Hunting Creek Plantation, and later was renamed in honor of a British admiral, Edward Vernon. The Georgian-style mansion is situated on a plateau 200 feet above the Potomac and commands an impressive view of the countryside. It houses a valuable collection of Washingtonian relics, and there are two marble sarcophagi containing the remains of Washington and his wife, Martha. The mansion is supposed to have been built either in 1735 by Washington's father, Augustine, or in 1743 by his elder brother, Lawrence. George Washington began living in Mount Vernon in 1747, and came into possession of the estate in 1752 after his brother's death. He enlarged and improved the property, and in 1759 brought his bride there. It was his residence until 1775 when he left to take his seat in the Continental Congress. He lived there from 1783 until his death in 1799, except during his years as President. In 1860 the mansion and 6 acres were purchased by the Mount Vernon Ladies' Association to secure the property as a lasting memorial to the first President of the United States.

MOUNT WILSON AND PALOMAR OBSERVATORIES, two astronomical observatories on two southern California mountaintops administered jointly by Carnegie Institution of Washington and California Institute of Technology.

Mount Wilson Observatory was established in 1904 by George Ellery Hale for the purpose of investigating the sun as a typical star in connection with a larger program of study of stellar evolution. Early results were so promising that Carnegie Institution of Washington, which had helped to finance the original project, undertook support of the observatory as a major research department. By 1918 Mount Wilson had two tower telescopes 60 feet and 150 feet high for observing the sun, two reflecting telescopes with mirrors 60 inches and 100 inches in diameter for stellar observations, and a number of smaller instruments, a powerhouse, and living quarters for the staff. In 1924 Hale erected in Pasadena a solar observatory that later became the property of Mount Wilson. Astronomers live at the observatory on the mountain while making observations; their other work is carried on in Pasadena at the offices of the observatory and its library, physical laboratory, and machine and optical shops.

Mount Wilson Observatory is in Los Angeles County, California, on a peak of the Sierra Madre Range 5,700 feet above sea level. The site was selected because of favorable atmospheric conditions, adequate water supply, and accessibility to Pasadena and Los Angeles. Mount Wilson is high enough so that fog and haze seldom interfere seriously with astronomical observations, but not so high as to experience the severe storms that sometimes do occur at greater elevations.

Publications of the Mount Wilson Observatory have been continuous since 1905. They include major papers covering measures of distances and motions of stars individually and collectively; determinations of the brightness of stars; investigations of magnetic polarities of sunspot groups; forms and motions of solar prominences; constitution of the atmospheres of the sun, stars, and planets, obscuring effects of interstellar matter; source of luminosity in gaseous nebulae; and form, structure, and apparent velocities of extragalactic stellar systems. Astronomical results from the observatory have been supplemented and advanced by laboratory analysis of the behavior of matter under known conditions.

Palomar Mountain Observatory. In 1946 a change was made in the organization of the Mount Wilson and Palomar Mountain observatories by agreement between the California Institute of Technology in Pasadena and the Carnegie Institution of Washington. The two observatories became a single operating unit, with the equipment of both available as needed for research.

Palomar Mountain Observatory is 5,500 feet above sea level in San Diego County, California, about 100 miles southeast of Mount Wilson. It is easily accessible but far from the lights of Pasadena and Los Angeles. Atmospheric conditions are about the same as at Mount Wilson. In 1948 a 200-inch reflector telescope —the largest in the world up to that time—was installed at Palomar Mountain. This instrument was built with funds granted by the International Education board to the California Institute of Technology in 1928. Other instruments at Palomar Mountain include the 18-inch and 48-inch Schmidt telescopes, the latter completed in 1948. The usable aperture of its correcting plate actually measures 49.5 inches and the mirror has a 72-inch diameter. See ASTRONOMY; OBSERVATORY. ROBERT S. RICHARDSON

MOURNING CLOAK, a rare tortoise-shell butterfly, *Nymphalis antiopa*, belonging to the family *Oecophoridae*. The upper surface of the adult is velvety brown with purplish spots that are attractive in the sunlight; the undersurface is brown and the wings have yellow marginal bands. The adult mourning cloak lays black eggs, which it prefers to deposit on willow branches. The black, velvety larvae have many protruding black spines and are peppered with red and white dots. Adults hibernate in winter in hollow trees and other old wood, but often emerge before the snow is gone. The mourning cloak is found throughout most of the Northern Hemisphere. See BUTTERFLY AND MOTH.

MOURNING DOVE, a small pigeon-like bird that is about one foot in length, with a tail that is characteristically longer than the wings (see DOVE; PIGEON). Like certain other members of the family *Columbidae*, it has a gray-blue back and a reddish-fawn undersurface. This species, *Zenaidura macroura*, which is commonly seen over most of North America and much of the West Indies, has a distinctive call, a melodic cooing with the first syllable accented and followed by a "ha" sound. The mourning dove builds its nest in a careless manner. It consists of a flat pile of twigs, loosely put together, in which the bird lays one or two white eggs twice, or three times, annually. This bird is often confused with other members of the suborder Columbae which consists of the pigeons and doves. It is sometimes erroneously referred to as a turtle dove, but this name is more appropriately used as the common name of a few birds classified within the genus *Streptopelia*, of the European species. *S. turtur*, for example.

MOUSE, a small rodent usually of the families *Muridae* and *Cricetidae*. Rats and mice are alike in having long, scaly tails, comparatively large ears, and pointed, bare muzzles. They differ mainly in

GEORGE MCCLELLAN BRADT

Pocket Mouse

size, the smaller being the mouse. They have invaded nearly all parts of the world. The house mouse, *Mus musculus*, belonging to the family *Muridae*, is now cosmopolitan but originally was a native of Asia. It is about 6 inches long from nose to tip of tail, has relatively large ears, and is uniformly brown. Its chief natural food is grain. Its movements are active and graceful. It is extremely prolific. White mice used in scientific research have been produced from brown house mice.

Native mice of America are members of the family *Cricetidae*. Among the species are the white-footed mouse or field mouse of the genus *Peromyscus;* the short-tailed meadow mouse, *Microtus;* grasshopper mouse, *Onychomys;* harvest mouse, *Reithrodontomys;* and lemming mouse, *Synaptomys*. The jumping mouse of the family *Zapodidae*, a small mouse with very long tail and hind legs, is more closely allied to jerboas, desert rodents of Asia, Africa, and eastern Europe, than to true mice.

Almost all species of mice are destructive to such plants as young fruit trees and rose bushes because they gnaw bark from the stems near the root. They also destroy grass and grain. Mice store large quantities of grain, beechnuts, chestnuts, and the like in their winter burrows. Some natural enemies of mice are hawks, owls, cranes, butcherbirds, skunks, weasels, snakes, and lizards. See RAT; RODENTIA.

MOUSE DEER. See CHEVROTAIN.

MOUSE TOWER, a tower on the Rhine River near Bingen, Germany; and, more generally, any tower or building associated popularly with a European legend in which a heartless miser is devoured by mice. The story is told in several European countries. The best known version is that concerning the archbishop Hatto of Mainz, first told about 1290 by a priest, Siegfried von Meissen. Hatto fled to the tower in the Rhine to escape from mice sent to devour him as punishment for his burning of starving people in a granary during a famine, but the mice crossed the river and ate him alive. Among victims in other versions of the mouse-miser legend were Adolf, a bishop of Cologne; the Swiss Freiherr von Güttingen; and the German bishop Widerolf. The tower near Bingen dates from the thirteenth century, and was rebuilt in 1855. It was a toll station for the nearby city of Ehrenfels, and later was made a signal station for the Rhine River traffic passing through the Bingen Locks. *Mäuseturm* (mouse tower) may be a popular corruption of *Mautturm* (toll tower). See HATTO II.

MOUSSORGSKY, MODEST PETROVICH, also Musorgski or Mussorgsky, 1839–81, Russian composer, was born in Karevo in the government of Pskov. Both his parents were musical, and his mother was his first piano teacher. Even after he entered the army, 1856, Moussorgsky continued his musical pursuits as an amateur. In 1857 he met Mili Balakirev, Aleksandr Dargomyzhski, and other earnest young Russian composers, and became so absorbed in music that he quit the army, 1858, and took employment as a government clerk. Recognition came slowly, and he became nervous and morbid and took to dissipation and reckless living—which helped neither his financial situation nor his health. By 1869, however, his operatic masterpiece, *Boris Godunov*, was completed, although it was not produced in St. Petersburg until 1874. Moussorgsky continued to live and work in St. Petersburg until 1881, sharing rooms with Nikolai Rimski-Korsakov until the latter's marriage. After this, poverty and ill health again brought depression, which Moussorgsky fought with drugs and alcohol. He died at 42 in the military hospital in St. Petersburg. His second opera, *Khovanshchina*, was complete at his death, except for the instrumentation, which he entrusted to Rimski-Korsakov. The latter musician also revised *Boris Godunov*, which was performed in the revised form until the original version was published in 1928.

Moussorgsky had no formal theoretical education, and his technique was at times deficient; yet his striking originality and intense dramatic feeling carried him through. His creative genius was probably the purest of all Russian composers of his time and for a long time after. It shines not only in his operas but in his songs and in his *Pictures at an Exhibition* for piano, later orchestrated by Maurice Ravel. His *Night on Bald Mountain*, an orchestral fantasia, although often performed, is more superficial. It is primarily upon *Boris Godunov*, the opera of the mad czar, dying in fear and remorse for his crimes, that Moussorgsky's reputation rests secure.

IRWIN FISCHER

MOUTH, or buccal or oral cavity, the first part of the digestive system and the opening through which food is ingested. In human beings the floor, roof, and anterior and posterior boundaries of the mouth are formed by the tongue, palate, lips, and glossopalatine arch, respectively. The lateral walls of the mouth are formed by the cheeks. (See HEAD.) The teeth are housed in the mouth, embedded in the upper and lower jaws (see TEETH). The mouth and the pharynx are continuous. The human mouth consists of two major divisions: the vestibule, the outer and smaller of the two; and the mouth cavity, the inner and larger division.

The vestibule is bounded anteriorly by the inner portions of the lips, laterally by the cheeks, and posteriorly by the teeth and gums of the upper and lower jaws. When the jaws are closed this division is continuous with the cavity proper through openings behind the wisdom teeth on each side and through narrow slits between opposing teeth.

The mouth cavity extends from the glossopalatine arch forward to the teeth. Epithelium from this cavity forms a blind pouch known as Rathke's pouch, which fuses with the brain wall to form the anterior lobe of the pituitary gland. Substances secreted into the mouth cavity by submaxillary and sublingual glands and by the parotid glands form part of the saliva.

In human beings and in some animals numerous small mucus-secreting glands keep the inner surfaces of the lips moist. A few animals—for example turtles, beaked monotremes, and birds—have dry, cornified mouths almost without mucous glands.

The angle to which the mouth of an animal may be opened is limited by the fleshy cheeks. Because they lack cheeks, an alligator or a bird can open its mouth to great extent. See DIGESTION; SALIVARY GLAND.

MOWRER, EDGAR ANSEL, 1892– , U.S. journalist, was born in Bloomington, Ill., and was graduated from the University of Michigan, 1913. He joined the staff of the Chicago *Daily News* and was connected with the European bureaus of the *News* until 1940. On his return to the United States he was deputy director of the Office of Facts and Figures and Office of War Information until 1943. After 1943 Mowrer was active as a broadcaster and columnist on foreign affairs. His *Germany Puts the Clock Back* (1932, Pulitzer prize) was prophetic in its warning of the threat of nazism. Other works include *The Future of Politics* (1930), *The Dragon Wakes* (1938), *Global War* (with Marthe Rajchman, 1942), *The Nightmare of American Foreign Policy* (1948), and *Challenge and Decision* (1950).

MOZAMBIQUE (Moçambique), overseas province of Portugal, SE Africa, one of the few remaining dependent territories in Africa; bounded by Tanzania and Malawi on the N; the Mozambique Channel on the E; Swaziland and South Africa on the S; and Rhodesia on the W; about 302,250 square miles in area; population (1966) about 7,000,000, mainly African, with over 135,000 Europeans, 3,000 Chinese, and several thousand persons of Arab and Indian ancestry. The capital is Lourenço Marques. See southern Africa map in Atlas.

Physical Features

Mozambique is a low-lying, tropical territory with a coastline over 1,600 miles in length, broken by inlets and bordered by islands. Major rivers from north to south are the Ruvuma (Rovuma), Zambezi, Pungwe, Save, Limpopo, and Incomati. Except for small highland areas in the north and central sections, most of the land is less than 2,000 feet above sea level. Tropical conditions prevail except in the southern quarter of the country. The Mozambique Current raises temperature and humidity in coastal areas. Mozambique is well-endowed with water power (the Zambezi River) and harbors (Lourenço Marques and Nacala are two of the best natural ports on the coast of East Africa).

Most of the soil is rather poor. There are stretches of littoral savanna in the northeast, around Beira, and in the south, and generally more fertile savanna in plateau areas in the west and northwest. Rainfall is low for the tropics, averaging about 40 inches a year along the coast. North of the Save River an extensive tsetse fly belt precludes the development of large-scale mixed farming and human settlement. In the twentieth century, however, the government has tried to open more of Mozambique to human settlement and cattle raising. Methods include medical campaigns, bush clearance, drainage, and the settlement of farming families from abroad. Recent medical advances enable inhabitants to live more safely and comfortably than before. Still, tropical diseases are enduring scourges for man and animal.

Social Features

The great majority of people speak languages formerly known as "Bantu" (now classified in the Benue-Congo branch of the Niger-Kordofanian linguistic family). Tribal groups include the Makonde, Ndau, Tonga, Chope, Ronga, Swazi, and Makua. Educated Africans speak Portuguese as well as their own tribal languages. In response to a growing missionary and Church effort, many Africans have attended schools either in the bush or in towns.

The traditional way of life centered on the small village or homestead, made up of kinship groups. In the fifteenth century, the central section of Mozambique was part of a centralized Bantu state, the Karanga kingdom of Monomotapa, but many of the Africans lived apart in small, fragmented kinship groups. Today African traditions in social and religious affairs persist. Often the chief focus of allegiance for the rural African is the family, clan, or tribe. Africans worship the spirits of their ancestors very often in conjunction with Christian and Islamic beliefs and practice. Even in urban areas, where tribal influences are weaker, many Africans retain some traditional animist belief. See AFRICA.

In contrast to traditional Bantu society, the European minority is concentrated in larger towns and cities and rarely amalgamates elements of non-European belief. Nearly 60 per cent of the European population resides in the two largest cities, Lourenço Marques and Beira. Moreover, Europeans in Mozambique enjoy a standard of living which is generally higher than that of metropolitan Portugal. Cultural

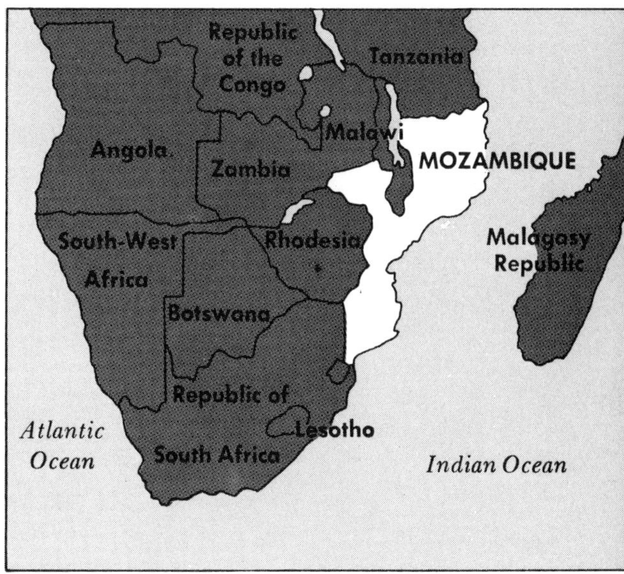

Location Map of Mozambique

life resembles life in Portugal (one tenth the size of Mozambique), but with a freer, more "outdoor" character. Popular sports are European soccer (*futebol*), bull-fighting, hunting, and deep-sea fishing. Portuguese entertainers and journalists tour the country, but indigenous news media and entertainment have developed. Mozambique's newspapers and European political associations have gained a reputation for being outspoken and sometimes critical of Portugal.

Although some racial segregation was practiced in various public places in urban Mozambique until the early 1960's, today society is multiracial in character, and integration in schools is becoming more the rule than the exception. (Increasing white immigration from Portugal is a complicating factor.) The pace of social integration is slow but steady.

Each year nearly 500,000 men live and work outside Mozambique in Tanzania, Malawi, Rhodesia, and South Africa. (Included in this number are some 100,000 Africans in Tanzania who are refugees in the political sense.) This labor migration profoundly affects Mozambican society. As many men are away from the villages, family life suffers and population growth is hampered. The system of labor migration developed after 1870 and was formalized by international agreements in the twentieth century. By agreement most labor recruitment for the South African mines takes place south of 22° S latitude, so that southern Mozambique is more affected than northern. Taxes in the south are higher, and Africans there have more money and resources for successful farming; northern Mozambique is less economically developed, therefore, than the south.

The migrant labor system has long been criticized because, although it provides the government with revenue needed for development and raises the standard of living, a high price is paid, in social and political discontent among returning African laborers, disintegration of families, and local labor shortages. There are signs that this migration is diminishing slightly with the improvement of agricultural and commercial opportunities in Mozambique and developments in neighboring countries that discourage immigration. A Mozambican nationalist leader, Dr. Eduardo Mondelane, suggested another probable result of this migration by many different Mozambique peoples: political unity across tribal lines in the modern nationalist movements.

Until recently nearly all education was the responsibility of the Church and missions. Illiteracy is estimated at between 90 and 95 per cent of the

African population. Few Africans reach higher educational levels as a stringent testing system regulates entrance into high schools. Among signs of progress in the 1960's was the establishment (1963) of a university faculty at Lourenço Marques.

Mozambique is short of hospitals and doctors and lacks an adequate supply of anit-tsetse vaccines.

Economic Features

Unlike most other territories in southern Africa, Mozambique is not well-endowed with mineral resources. A weak transportation network, the deadly tsetse fly, and conservative traditions among Portuguese businessmen have slowed economic development. Since 1960, however, an increased awareness of the advantages of foreign investment has aided the essentially artificial economy. Mozambique has long played the role of the colonial dependent in economics; in classic mercantilist practice, Portugal, as the dominant customer, controlled Mozambique with a strict tariff and exchange system. Hence, Mozambique's raw materials were exchanged for finished goods manufactured almost exclusively in Portugal. Recent developments have weakened this system which was seldom beneficial to Mozambique's economy. In the 1960's the country came to depend less upon goods and services produced outside for major revenue earnings.

Mining. Mozambique possesses major mineral reserves in coal and beryl (a metal used in aircraft construction) but has only small amounts of gold, bauxite, and iron. Discovery in 1966 of a reserve of oil near Beira brightened the economic picture. Despite extensive geologic surveys since 1910, the government has located few significant mineral finds which can compare with the copper of Zambia or the gold of South Africa.

Agriculture. The leaching of mineral content from the soils in the tropical conditions restricts really productive farming to limited regions, such as the alluvial soil of river valleys. Many African farmers grow their own food and are entering only gradually the cash crop economy. Cotton is the major African farm crop while maize is favored by Europeans. Other important cash crops are cashews, sisal (for rope), tea, coffee, beans, sugar, and rice. Although it is the largest world exporter of cashew nuts, Mozambique still lacks a processing plant for its own crop. Pastoralism is important especially in the southern districts of Tete and Gaza. There, Africans own most of the cattle, but meat production is limited by the tsetse fly, and the control campaign is expensive and slow.

Since 1961, the government has encouraged foreign capital investment and has attempted to eliminate the annual trade deficit. Improved road and railroad communications and new manufacturing installations have quickened the pace of economic development.

History and Government

Archaeology reveals stone ruins in western Mozambique, the sites of pre-1400 Bantu states. The Portuguese invaded at the end of the fifteenth century and soon dominated the Arab-Swahili coastal trade system. After several centuries of disjointed trade effort on the coast, Portugal participated in the so-called "scramble" for Africa in the late nineteenth century and established new forts in the interior. Defeating the Shangana (Nguni) kingdom of Chief Gungunhana in 1895–98, the Portuguese struggled to consolidate their weak sovereignty. They understood the economic and strategic importance of the port of Lourenço Marques, and between 1890 and 1919 they signed agreements with Britain, South Africa, and Germany to demarcate the territory's frontiers.

Mozambique became dependent upon alien factors: revenue from South Africa for the use of the capital's port and railroad; migrant labor earnings;

CAMERA PRESS-PIX

In a factory at Lourenço Marques, cashew nuts are split, cleaned, graded, and roasted before being exported.

and the administration and capital of four major chartered colonial companies which virtually controlled most of Mozambique until their charters expired in the 1940's. After the rise to power of Premier António de Oliveira Salazar in 1928–30, Portugal increased control in the form of centralized administration, civil legislation, economic plans, and increased European immigration. In 1951, Portugal changed the designation of Mozambique from that of "colony" to "overseas province," in the face of increasing criticism of its policies in the UN.

The governor-general is the major Portuguese official and representative of the Lisbon overseas ministry. Although more power is now delegated to a legislative council of elected and appointed members, the Lisbon government retains essential control of Mozambique. The province is divided for administration into nine districts.

Historically in Portuguese administration, an overseas crisis tends to encourage reform. Warfare in Angola in 1961 had this effect for Mozambique, and in September, 1961, Portugal abolished the old system of citizenship classification, the *regime do indigenato*, increased Mozambique's direct representation in the national assembly in Lisbon, and liberalized the economic structure. In theory, all Mozambican persons are citizens now; but voting qualifications of literacy or income tax payments remain in force. Violence in Angola and the threat of it in Mozambique also encouraged efforts to settle more Portuguese in the province. The Limpopo Valley settlement and irrigation scheme was stepped up, and an army of over 25,000 troops was dispatched to live in Mozambique. Demobilized soldiers, the government hoped, might be settled in selected river valleys.

In an atmosphere of rising tension and pressure from independent African states to the north, the Portuguese prepared to meet African nationalist opposition in Mozambique. The first guerrilla attack came in late September, 1964. It was organized by the major African nationalist party in exile, FRELIMO (Front for the Liberation of Mozambique), led by Dr. Eduardo Mondelane, a U.S.-educated anthropologist born in Gaza district. At first the guerrilla war appeared to affect only the northernmost provinces; African units operated chiefly from FRELIMO headquarters in Dar es Salaam, Tanzania. In 1966 the war widened as the nationalists tried to inspire the rural masses to oust the Portuguese.

The growing war in the north and similar wars in Angola and Guinea laid heavy financial burdens on Portugal and encouraged speculation that Mozambique might soon become an independent African-led state like her neighbors Malawi and Tanzania. The outcome depended on the actions of four distinct political forces: the Lisbon Government, the European settlers, the African masses, and the small but growing African nationlist parties. Conservative pressures from European-led Rhodesia and South Africa also influenced the situation. DOUGLAS L. WHEELER

BIBLIOG.-James Duffy, *Portugal in Africa* (1962); Antonio de Figueiredo, *Portugal and Its Empire: The Truth* (1961); C. F. Spence, *Moçambique* (1963).

MOZAMBIQUE, Portuguese *Moçambique*, seaport, Portuguese overseas province of Mozambique, located on a coral island, 3 miles from the shores of Mossuril Bay in the Mozambique Channel of the Indian Ocean. Oil seed and tobacco are processed, and soap is manufactured. The city is the site of three forts, the most famous of which is St. Sebastian (1508–11). The inhabitants are mostly Muslims. (For population, see southern Africa map in Atlas.)

MOZARABS, Christians under Moorish rule in Spain who retained their own government, liturgy, and hierarchy. Their ecclesiastical head was the archbishop of Toledo. They elected their own ruler, who was responsible to the Muslim caliph. They adopted Arabic speech and writing, and their culture was greatly influenced by Muslim civilization.

MOZART, WOLFGANG AMADEUS, 1756–91, Austrian composer, born in Salzburg. His father, Leopold, was court composer and later chapel master of the Archbishop of Salzburg. Wolfgang, when only three, showed a phenomenal gift for music, and his father began giving him harpsichord lessons along with his sister. At six, Wolfgang began composing little pieces. By seven, he was also learning to play the violin and the organ.

Leopold, aware that he had sired a *Wunderkind*, determined to devote his life to his son's education and career. Between 1762 and 1766 the family visited numerous European capitals, where Wolfgang's performances invariably won acclaim. During this period his first published compositions—four sonatas for violin and pianoforte (Köchel Catalog Nos. 2-5)—appeared; he also wrote his first symphonies and six more violin sonatas. His early teachers included Johann Christian Bach, Michael Haydn, and Adlgasser (the Salzburg cathedral organist).

In Vienna in 1768, Mozart wrote his first Italian *opera buffa*, *La finta semplice*. Unfortunately, intrigues against him prevented its production. However, his German operetta *Bastien und Bastienne* was successfully produced.

In 1769, father and son departed for Italy, where Wolfgang's gifts as performer and composer were everywhere acclaimed. His first *opera seria*, *Mitridate*, was successfully performed in Milan. After returning to Salzburg briefly in 1771, they set out again for Milan where Wolfgang's opera *Ascanio in Alba*, written for the wedding of the Archduke Ferdinand to the Princess Beatrice of Modena, was received with thunderous approval. This early climax in the 15-year-old's career was followed by a change of fortune. His opera *Lucio Silla* was cooly received in Milan, and he never returned to Italy. In Salzburg Mozart's protector, the archbishop, died, and his unmusical successor took no interest in the young composer. Ironically, for the remaining two decades of his life, Mozart, recognized by many—especially jealous colleagues—as a genius, could not find an appropriate permanent post.

From age fifteen to seventeen, Mozart remained under the influence of Italian models, composing numerous symphonies, divertimenti, and sacred pieces. In 1773 an unsuccessful journey to Vienna to seek a job brought Mozart once more into contact with German music, especially the quartets of Haydn, which had an enormous impact on his music. Upon his return to Salzburg, Mozart plunged into creative activity that culminated in a series of symphonies (K. 183, 200, 201, 202) and marked the beginning of his mastery of the *stil galant*, a courtly style that subordinates depth and intensity of expression to elegance and brilliance of effect.

La finta giardiniera, composed for the Carnival of 1775 in Munich, proved to be another high point in the young man's career. It was followed closely by *Il Re pastore*, performed in Salzburg during a visit of the Archduke Maximilian. The works of this period were typical of Mozart's courtly style. His command of the violin shows plainly in the virtuoso writing of the five concertos for that instrument, though Mozart himself disliked playing the instrument in public. The two years that followed were extremely fertile. He wrote many works in a suave *galant* style refined of all crudities, and for a time concentrated on religious music exclusively.

At the age of 21 Mozart was skilled on three instruments and experienced in all manners of composition. He set out with his mother to try to obtain employment suited to his talents and commensurate with his stature. His journey took him through Munich, Augsburg, and Mannheim. On arriving in Paris he received little attention. But through the influence of his benefactor, Baron Grimm, Mozart received a few commissions and several lady pupils. At the request of Le Gros, director of the famed Concert Spirituel, he composed his *Sinfonie concertante* for four wind instruments and orchestra and the Paris symphony, composed *à la française*, in three movements, which greatly pleased Parisian audiences. In 1778 Mozart's mother died, and shortly thereafter Mozart left Paris, defeated, his expectations unrealized. He had been too naive to succeed on so rough a career battleground. Out of ruffled pride perhaps, he had refused the one good job offer that had been made to him, that of organist at Versailles. He reluctantly returned to Salzburg, where he succeeded Adlgasser as Konzertmeister and court organist in 1779.

It was not until the opera *Idomeneo*, first performed for the Grand Carnival of Munich in 1781, established Mozart's position as a major dramatic composer that he was able to leave the service of the archbishop for good.

For the remaining decade of his life Mozart had to make his way on his own. He settled in Vienna to seek pupils, publishers, and position. A commission to write an opera resulted in the delicious German singspiel, *Die Entführung aus dem Serail*, successfully produced in 1782, despite the malicious machinations with which Mozart was almost constantly surrounded. Very shortly thereafter, he married Constanze Weber, the third daughter of the family with whom he had been living in Vienna. His wife, who undoubtedly cared for him, was frivolous, immature, and inept in the management of the house-

In a 1781 painting by Johann Nepomuk della Croce, Wolfgang Mozart sits beside his sister, under a portrait of their mother. Their father, Leopold, holds a violin.

AUSTRIAN INSTITUTE

hold, and the Mozarts were never thereafter out of financial difficulties. During this period he made the acquaintance of the Baron van Swieten, who introduced him to the oratorios of Handel and the *Forty-eight preludes and fugues* of Johann Sebastian Bach. These works opened a new world to Mozart and, inevitably, his own writing became richer and more contrapuntal in texture. Without a permanent post, Mozart had to depend on lessons and concerts, the meager receipts of which disappeared rapidly. For each concert, in order to stimulate subscriptions, Mozart usually composed a new piano concerto; this incomparable body of works represents a new dimension in concerto literature and a high point of his own instrumental output.

In 1786 a musical comedy, *Der Schauspieldirektor*, was produced at a Shönbrunn fête. Gratified to be writing for the stage once more, Mozart also completed his immortal *Le Nozze di Figaro* (The Marriage of Figaro) with libretto, after Beaumarchais, by Lorenzo da Ponte; it was an apparent initial success, but received relatively few performances in Vienna and led neither to a job nor to new commissions. In Prague, however, it was a brilliant success. During these years he also produced a steady stream of instrumental masterworks: profound, limpid, and moving, which contemporary Viennese critics managed to find artificial, heavy, and incomprehensible. It was for his appreciative Czech public that he composed on commission what is perhaps his greatest work, the opera *Don Giovanni* (1787). In the same year Mozart lost his father, met the young Beethoven, and, following the death of Gluck, who had been official court composer at an annual stipend of 2,000 florins, was at last appointed by the emperor as chamber composer, with a reduced salary of 800 florins. The salary was too little, and Mozart's financial situation continued to be desperate. *Don Giovanni* had little success in its Viennese production, the number of his pupils dwindled, and his subscription concerts had to be abandoned for want of paying audiences. Despite everything, Mozart remained optimistic and confident, and his creative powers were in no way diminished. In the summer of 1788 he wrote his monumental trio of symphonies—Nos. 39, 40, 41 (the Jupiter) in E*b*, G minor, and C (K. 543, 550, 551)—among the greatest of the century. They were never performed during his lifetime.

In the following year, he again set out on tour, to Berlin via Prague, Dresden, and Leipzig. Receipts and results were meager; the hoped-for job as kapellmeister to the king of Prussia was not forthcoming. In 1790 his *opera buffa*, *Così fan tutte*, was successfully produced in Vienna. Joseph II had commissioned it, and the talented court poet, Da Ponte, provided the libretto. However, any effect the opera might have had on Mozart's career was nullified by the emperor's illness and subsequent death. His successor, Leopold II, rejected Mozart's application for the post of second chapel master. He was dealt another blow when he had to say good-bye to his best friend and mentor, Haydn, who was leaving Vienna (1791) to give a series of concerts in London. They were never to meet again.

Mozart's debts continued to accumulate, and his hitherto robust constitution began to deteriorate. Toward the end of 1789 the strain began to show, and there was a slowdown in his productivity. The year 1790 was critical and tragic. Aside from *Così*, finished in January, the great string quintet in D (K. 593), completed in December, represents the only important work written during the twelve-month period. In October he went to Frankfort for the coronation of Leopold II; it was his last concert tour and no more successful than the rest.

In 1791, although no real change occurred in his situation, he entered one of the most prolific periods of his career. A number of works from this final year, such as the quintet in E*b* (K. 614) and his last piano concerto (K. 595 in B*b*) possess a unique serenity of mood and an ineffable perfection of classical structure and style. For the coronation in Prague of Leopold II as king of Bohemia, he wrote the *opera seria*, *La Clemenza di Tito*, which was performed on Sept. 6, 1791. Suffering from overwork and fatigue, he returned to Vienna to complete work on *Die Zauberflöte* (The Magic Flute), a wondrous singspiel written at the request and to the libretto of Emanuel Schikaneder, manager of a little theater and an old Salzburg acquaintance.

His last work, the *Requiem*, was commissioned by a mysterious and anonymous stranger, who was later revealed as Count Walsegg, an amateur posing as a composer by performing other men's works under his own name. Mozart's work on the *Requiem* was delayed by the need to complete his last two operas. After *Die Zauberflöte*, it was interrupted by severe fainting fits and deep depressions. Mozart was obsessed with the idea that the *Requiem* would be his own death song; he was destined never to complete it. Eventually the work had to be finished by his pupil and disciple, Süssmayr. He died on Dec. 5, 1791, just short of the age of 36, of what was diagnosed as malignant typhus fever.

There was no sphere of musical composition in which Mozart did not excel. His output of over 600 works encompassed virtually every genre current in his day. It included operas, dozens of solo arias for individual singers and other composers' operas, sacred music of all kinds, *lieder* with piano accompaniment, symphonies, some two hundred other orchestral works, some fifty concertos for piano, violin, and various wind instruments, a vast quantity of chamber music, and a great body of works of all kinds for piano. BARRY S. BROOK

BIBLIOG.–Emily Anderson, ed., *Letters of Mozart and His Family* (2nd ed. 1966, 2 vols.); O. E. Deutsch, *Mozart, A Documentary Biography* (1965); Alfred Einstein, *Mozart, His Character and His Work* (1945); W. J. Turner, *Mozart: The Man and His Works* (rev. ed., 1966).

MU'ALLAQAT, the name given to an Arabic anthology of seven pre-Islamic odes. The anthology is considered to contain the finest early Arabic poetry. Its compilation is attributed to Hammad al Rawiyah (d. 772?). The Mu'allaqat presents a full picture of pre-Islamic Bedouin life. The origins of the anthology's title are obscure.

MUCILAGE, an extract of plant cells that is insoluble in alcohol and when dispersed in water forms a somewhat viscous, slippery, sticky liquid. Chemically mucilages are carbohydrate polymers, related to starches and sugars but with a high molecular weight. Mucilages are used as adhesives, especially paper adhesives; to improve the strength of starch paste; to stabilize dairy products such as ice cream; and to increase the strength of papers.

MUCKRAKERS, a school of writers whose works exposed abuses in U.S. economic, social, and political life, and focused attention on such evils as slums, prostitution, and juvenile delinquency in the early 1900's. In 1906 Pres. Theodore Roosevelt called these writers muckrakers, claiming that they gloried in the filth they raked up. Among the early works of this school, published between 1902 and 1904, were *Frenzied Finance*, by Thomas W. Lawson; *History of the Standard Oil Company*, by Ida M. Tarbell; and *The Shame of the Cities*, by Lincoln Steffens. The most famous book produced by writers of this school was Upton Sinclair's *The Jungle*, a novel about conditions in the Chicago stockyards and meat-packing plants.

MUCOUS MEMBRANE, a fibrous tissue lubricated by mucus that lines many hollow organs and some body passages that communicate with the exterior, such as the alimentary, respiratory, and genitourinary tracts. It also lines the eyelid and covers the eye. Healthy mucous membrane is pinkish red. Its structure is the same wherever it is found: the outside layer, or surface epithelium, the middle layer, or basement epithelium, and the deepest layer, which consists of connective tissue (see CONNECTIVE TISSUE). The membrane is usually kept moist by glands that secrete a viscid, slippery substance called mucus, which is produced by mechanical or chemical stimuli. Mucous glands are numerous in nearly all mucous membrane except that which lines the genitourinary tract.

MUCUS, a clear, thick secretion produced by special cells in mucous membrane and in certain other tissue such as that in the salivary glands (see MUCOUS MEMBRANE; SALIVARY GLAND). The main constituent of mucus is mucin, a fundamental protein also called glycoprotein (see PROTEIN). Mucin is slippery, sticky, and ropy; it resembles and is a constituent of egg white. Mucus lubricates the surface it covers, such as the lining of the mouth. Some protection against bacteria is afforded by mucus, since it traps such foreign substances and keeps them from moving deeper into the body. In the windpipe, masses of mucus and bacteria are moved toward the mouth and removed as sputum. Special cells, sometimes called goblet cells, produce droplets of mucus.

MUD, a mixture of finely divided earth or rock particles, or both, with water. Any such soggy or sticky mass sometimes is considered mud, but clays (see CLAY) often are classed separately. Muds may be distinguished physically from clays by their behavior when baked: clays harden and retain shape but muds crumble. Mud tends to be less easily shaped than clay, which contains aluminum silicate.

Mud deposits are formed in sheltered estuaries, freshwater lakes, bends in slow-moving streams, and oceans, especially along continental shelves. Oceanic muds include coral muds, which result from the wearing away of the calcareous skeleton of coral; volcanic muds, which are caused by deposition of wind-blown volcanic ash; and blue, green, and red muds contributed by rivers. Green muds owe their color to a mineral, glauconite. Blue muds are deposited near land, and red muds are laid down near mouths of large rivers such as the Amazon and the Orinoco.

MUD PUPPY, an amphibian found in the streams and ponds of the central and eastern United States. The body of the mud puppy, *Necturus maculosus*, is slender and about 12 inches long. The skin, which secretes mucus, is dark brown with indistinct black markings. The broad head has permanent, red, bushy gills; the limbs are short; and the flattened tail occupies about one third of the total body length. The animal is permanently aquatic, spending much of its time in the mud, and feeds on snails, crayfish, insects, and small fish. Mating occurs in the fall, and 18 to 180 eggs are laid the following spring.

MUENCH, ALOISIUS JOSEPH CARDINAL, 1889–1962, U.S. Roman Catholic prelate, was born in Milwaukee, Wis., ordained a priest, 1913, and did graduate work at the University of Louvain, the Sorbonne, and Oxford and Cambridge universities. He was consecrated bishop of Fargo, N.D., 1935; was liaison official between the Roman Catholic Church and the U.S. military government in Germany, 1946–49; was elevated to archbishop, 1950; and became papal nuncio to Germany, 1951. Pope John XXIII created him a cardinal in 1959. At the time of his death he was the only American ever to have served on the Roman Curia, the governing body of the Roman Catholic Church.

MUFFLER, a device used to quiet the noise of an internal combustion engine's exhaust. Following combustion, exhaust gases in an automobile engine are forced from the cylinder into an exhaust manifold that gives the gases a chance for quick expansion. From the manifold the gases go through an exhaust pipe into the muffler. In the muffler the gases enter an enlarged chamber and usually pass through a series of baffles, steel wool, or some other porous material that serves the dual purpose of permitting

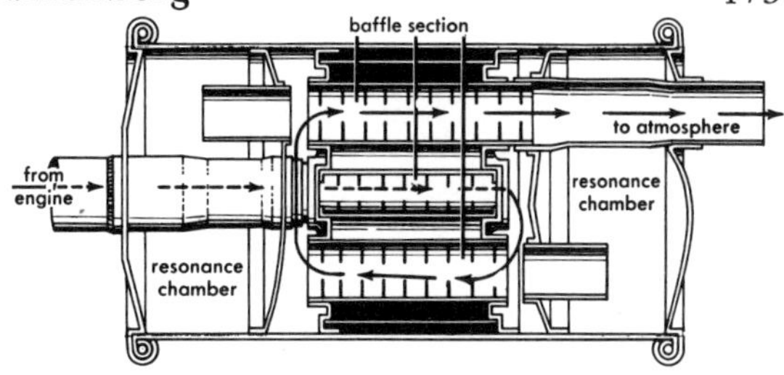

Cutaway Diagram of an Automobile Muffler

further expansion of the gases and creating the desired sound-deadening effect. This must be accomplished without causing a back pressure, which would result in loss of power and in increased fuel consumption. From the muffler the exhaust gases pass to the tail pipe and on out into the atmosphere.

In 1928 the President's Highway Safety Conference prescribed, in a set of automobile traffic codes that have been adopted almost in their entirety by every state in the United States, the mandatory use of mufflers or some other device for noise reduction. In the early history of motoring, mufflers were known as silencers, probably because they employed principles of the Maxim silencer. See AUTOMOBILE.

MUGGLETON, LODOWICKE, 1609–98, English sectarian, was born in London. A journeyman tailor who claimed to have a divine commission to declare a new faith, he founded (with his cousin John Reeve, 1608–58) the sect of the Muggletonians, 1652. Formalized in *The Transcendent Spirituall Treatise* (1652), his system is a curious medley of rationalism and literal adherence to Scripture. Muggleton was imprisoned for blasphemy, 1653, and his authority was disputed twice, 1660 and 1670; nevertheless he won a number of followers.

MUGLA, province, SW Turkey; bounded on the E by the Elmali Mountains, on the S by the Mediterranean Sea and on the W by the Aegean Sea; area of the province 4,925 square miles. Muğla is drained by the Dalaman and Koca rivers. Chief centers besides Muğla, the capital, are Fethiye and Milâs. The province produces sesame, millet, tobacco, olives, and wheat. There are deposits of chromium, manganese, antimony, silver, asbestos, salt, lignite, and emery. Muğla was formerly known as Mentese. (For population, see table in Turkey article.)

The capital city, Muğla, is primarily an agricultural community producing millet, wheat, tobacco, olives, and onions. Deposits of chromium and emery are nearby. Formerly known as Mentese, Muğla was capital of an independent duchy in the thirteenth century. (For population, see Turkey map in Atlas.)

MUGWUMP (from the Algonquian *mugquump*, a chief), in the early nineteenth century denoted strength or power in Masonic organizations. Specifically, a mugwump was one of the Republicans who seceded from the party and voted for Grover Cleveland, the Democratic candidate in the U.S. presidential election of 1884, because of his devotion to civil service reform. The mugwump vote was a decisive factor in the election of Cleveland as the first Democratic president since the American Civil War. Later, any independent voter was sometimes called a mugwump.

MUHLBERG, BATTLE OF, a battle fought on Apr. 24, 1547, at Mühlberg on the Elbe River (now in East Germany, state of Kottbus, district of Bad Liebenwerda, 36 miles E of Leipzig). It opposed the forces of Emperor Charles V to those of the Schmalkaldic League, which grouped the Protestant principalities and the free cities. Charles V won the battle and Elector John Frederick I of Saxony, one of the leaders of the Protestant forces, was made prisoner.

MUHLENBERG, FREDERICK AUGUSTUS CONRAD, 1750–1801, U.S. clergyman and first speaker of the House of Representatives, the son of Heinrich Melchior Mühlenberg, was born in New

Providence (later Trappe), Pa. He studied in Halle, Germany, returned to the United States, 1770, and was ordained in the Lutheran ministry. He served several congregations in Pennsylvania, and was pastor of the Christ German Lutheran Church in New York City, 1773–76. In 1779 he was elected to the Continental Congress, and became active in political affairs. He served in the general assembly, the convention to ratify the federal Constitution, and the federal house of representatives, 1789–97, and was speaker during the first and third U.S. Congresses.

MÜHLENBERG, HEINRICH MELCHIOR, Americanized as Henry Melchior Muhlenberg, 1711–87, German-American Lutheran clergyman, considered the founder of the Lutheran church in the United States, was born in Einbeck, Hanover, Germany. He entered the University of Göttingen, 1735, and in 1738 went to Halle to continue his theological studies. After ordination, he was pastor of a church in Grosshennersdorf, Lusatia, 1739–41, and in 1742 accepted a call to serve three Lutheran congregations in Pennsylvania. With the aid of other ministers sent from Germany, Mühlenberg supervised the expanding Lutheran organizations from Maryland to New York. In 1748 he organized the first Lutheran synod in America. While in Philadelphia, 1762, he introduced for the congregation there a constitution that was the model for other Lutheran congregations.

MUHLENBERG, JOHN PETER GABRIEL, 1746–1807, colonial American Lutheran minister and military and political figure, son of Heinrich Mühlenberg, was born in Trappe, Pa., studied for the ministry, and in 1769 became his father's assistant in two New Jersey parishes; he was called to Woodstock, Va., 1772. In 1775, at the outbreak of the Revolutionary War, he accepted a colonel's commission in the Continental Army and raised a regiment, the 8th Virginia or German regiment which took part in many of the principal southern battles of the war. Muhlenberg was promoted to the rank of brigadier general, 1777, and brevetted major general, 1783. Moving to Pennsylvania, he was elected to the U.S. Congress, 1789–91, 1793–95, and 1799–1801. After 1802 he was customs collector of Philadelphia.

MUHLENBERG, WILLIAM AUGUSTUS, 1796–1877, U.S. Episcopalian clergyman, great-grandson of Heinrich Mühlenberg, was born in Philadelphia, and was ordained a priest in 1820. He was rector of the Church of the Holy Communion in New York City, 1846–58, and was associated with St. Luke's Hospital, which he founded, after 1858. He also established an Episcopalian sisterhood and worked to improve the church hymnody.

MUHLENBERG COLLEGE, a private, Lutheran-affiliated institution of higher learning for men at Allentown, Pa. The school was established as Allentown Seminary in 1848. The name was changed to Allentown Collegiate Institute and Military Academy in 1864. The shorter name was adopted in 1867. Muhlenberg offers a general liberal arts program. Distinctive educational programs include co-operative arrangements with Columbia University and the University of Pennsylvania in engineering and with Duke University in forestry. The college library contains a special collection on Pennsylvania German. See COLLEGES AND UNIVERSITIES.

MÜHLHAUSEN, or Mühlhausen In Thüringen, city, SW Germany, in the East German state of Erfurt; on the Unstrut River; 28 miles NW of Erfurt. The city is an important railway junction. It has metalworking, machine building, locomotive repair, electrical equipment, radio tube, and food processing plants and it is an important textile center. Bicycles, shoes, and cigars also are produced. Mühlhausen is an old city (there is mention of it in documents dating from 775) and many of its tenth century fortifications are preserved. There are thirteenth and fourteenth century churches, the city hall dating from 1605, and numerous houses of comparable venerability. Mühlhausen received city rights about 1200 and became a Reichstadt (free imperial city) in 1256. It was a center of the order of Teutonic Knights in the thirteenth century and an Anabaptist center after the Reformation. During the Peasants' War in 1525, Thomas Münzer was executed there. Mühlhausen became Prussian in 1815 and lost all free city rights. After World War II it was included in the Soviet occupation zone of Germany. Pop. (1956) 47,122.

MUIR, EDWIN, 1887–1959, Scottish writer, was born in Deerness, Orkney, and worked as a clerk for a number of years before he was able to support himself as a journalist and writer. He was warden of Newbattle Abbey College, Dalkeith, 1950–55. Muir wrote three novels, *The Marionette* (1927), *The Three Brothers* (1931), and *Poor Tom* (1932); several volumes of criticism, including *Latitudes* (1924), *The Structure of the Novel* (1928), and *The Present Age, from 1914* (1939); and verse—*Collected Poems* (1953) and *One Foot in Eden* (1956)—noted for its directness and metaphysical quality.

MUIR, JOHN, 1838–1914, U.S. naturalist, was born in Dunbar, Scotland, came to Wisconsin with his parents in 1849, grew up on a farm near Portage, and studied at the University of Wisconsin, 1860–63. In 1867 he set out on a walking trip to the Gulf of Mexico, recording his observations of people, flora, and fauna in a diary posthumously published as *A Thousand-Mile Walk to the Gulf* (1916). In 1868 he went to the Yosemite Valley where he spent six years making botanical and geological studies and developing a theory of glacial formations. Later he explored in the northwest and in Alaska, where he discovered the glacier that bears his name. In 1881–91 Muir earned enough as a California fruit farmer to devote himself entirely to nature study and to the cause of conservation, particularly of western forests. Through his and Robert Underwood Johnson's efforts the Yosemite National Park Bill was passed, 1890. In 1897, when political and commercial interests tried to nullify the forest reserves created by Pres. Grover Cleveland, Muir wrote impassioned articles that aroused public interest in a national conservation policy. He was partly responsible for the conservation program initiated by Pres. Theodore Roosevelt.

MUIR WOODS NATIONAL MONUMENT, W California, Marin County, 12 miles N of San Fran-

DEPT. OF THE INTERIOR

Coast redwoods, the tallest trees in the world, stand like giants in Muir Woods National Monument. The oldest tree in the monument is believed to be more than 2,000 years of age.

cisco; an area of 425 acres lying at the base of Mount Tamalpais. In the area is a virgin stand of coast redwoods, one of which is 17 feet in diameter, 246 feet high, and more than 2,000 years old. The woods were given to the U.S. government by former Congressman William Kent and his wife, Elizabeth Thatcher Kent. At their request the area was named for the naturalist John Muir. The park was established in 1908.

MUKDEN, officially Shenyang, NE China, capital of Liaoning Province: on the Hun River, a tributary of the Liao; on the Dairen-Mukden-Changchuñ Railroad; 220 miles NNE of Dairen and 380 miles ENE of Peking. Mukden is China's fourth largest city and the industrial and political center of Manchuria. Covering an area of 1,200 square miles, it consists of the old Chinese city in the east and the new city in the west—the former Japanese railway concession district developed after 1905. The Chinese section is bounded by a 10-mile earthwall and includes an inner city which is the site of the former Manchu imperial palace. East of the city is an arsenal district with a large airfield. The extreme western part of Mukden was built up by the Japanese after 1937 with office and apartment buildings, workers' homes, and factories. At the north edge of the city are tombs of early Manchu emperors. Mukden produces about one fourth of the total Chinese output of machinery. It also has chemical and ordnance plants and factories that manufacture machine tools, electrical equipment, pneumatic tools, railroad cars, cables, matches, paper, cotton and silk textiles, soybean products, seed oil, and flour. The city is the seat of several universities and of an eminent medical college.

The city was originally called Mukden, a Manchu name. As the Manchu capital in the seventeenth century, it was known as Shengking. In 1658, after the capital had been moved to Peking, the city's name was changed to Fengtien. With the reinstatement of Manchus in the city after the Chinese Revolution, 1912, it again was known as Mukden until 1928, when it became Shenyang. The modern development of Mukden started in 1900 when the Russians built the Manchurian railroad. The city was the seat of the Manchurian war lord Chang Tso-lin until the 1930's, when the Japanese created the puppet state of Manchukuo under a Manchu ruler. In 1949 Mukden became the seat of the Manchurian regional government. Pop. (1953) 2,213,000.

MULATTO, the first-generation offspring of parents, one of whom is white and the other Negro. In popular usage in the United States, any person whose physical appearance indicates intermixture of white and Negro blood is also called a mulatto. In the latter sense a quadroon, octoroon, or quintroon is considered a mulatto even though he has only a quarter, eighth, or sixteenth Negro blood respectively. Shades of hybridism are distinguished by special names, which, however, are differently applied in various areas of the world. For example, in the United States a Creole is a white person descended from early French or Spanish settlers in certain sections of the South, whereas in Brazil a Creole is generally a Negro and in Peru a white and mestizo cross; sambo, generally a Negro and mulatto cross, is a Carib half-breed on Saint Vincent Island in the West Indies; and pardo, a mulatto in Brazil, is any half-breed in Argentina.

MULBERRY, any small tree, shrub, or herb of a group of plants belonging to the mulberry family, *Moraceae*, and more specifically to the genus *Morus*, which includes about 10 species of trees. Mulberry trees of the genus *Morus* grow in deep, moist soil throughout temperate and tropical climates. They are usually about 30 to 50 feet high although the white mulberry, *M. alba*, may grow to 80 feet. Mulberry trees have short trunks 1 to 1½ feet thick that divide into many branches to form rounded, compact silhouettes. These plants have broad, rounded leaves and small yellow flowers arranged in catkins. The fruit resembles a blackberry in appearance and color. The best known species is the white mulberry, *M. alba*, named for the color of its berry. Originally the tree was grown in China and Formosa and was introduced to eastern United States as an ornamental. A Russian variety of *M. alba* is particularly hardy and has been adapted as a shrubbery windbreak in the plains states. *M. australis* is a shrubby tree that bears small, sweet, dark-red berries; it is native to Japan and China. *M. nigra*, the black mulberry, originated in Persia. It is cultivated in Europe and Asia for its black berries; in southern United States it grows wild along roadsides and in protected gullies. *M. rubra*, the red mulberry, is native to the eastern United States and is also called the American mulberry. In China the species best known for the culture of the silkworm is *M. multicaulis*, which was the plant used in the unsuccessful attempts to establish the silk industry in North America. The sweet fruit of this plant is black and its dull green leaves are larger than those of *M. alba*, a species of which it is often considered a variety. An ornamental variety of the white mulberry, known as the weeping mulberry, *M. alba* var. *pendula*, is widely cultivated for its long and drooping branches. Because of the hardiness of the Russian mulberry, *M. alba* var. *tatarica*, the weeping mulberry is frequently grafted onto its stem. The mulberry family has economic value. Fig, mulberry, and breadfruit trees produce edible fruits. From species of the genus *Cannalus* come hemp and marijuana; from *Castilla* and *Ficus*, a rubber latex; and from *Humulus*, hops used in brewing. In countries that produce raw silk, foliage of mulberry trees is used as food for the silkworms (see SILK, *The Silkworm*).

MULCHING is the process of applying to the surface of soil a layer of some material to protect the soil and the roots of plants. Substances commonly used for this purpose—known as mulches—include leaves, straw, hay, ground corn cobs, sawdust, peat moss, shredded corn stover, and a special plastic film and processed paper. Usually the mulch is placed between and around plants growing in the soil. Mulching checks evaporation of water from the soil, reduces the temperature of the surface soil, checks soil erosion caused by water or wind, keeps the surface soil loose, checks weed growth, and prevents injury to the roots of plants during the winter.

When organic materials—notably straw, ground corn cobs, and sawdust—are used for mulching, they are decomposed by soil microorganisms. Under favorable conditions these microorganisms multiply rapidly and deplete the soil of nitrogen, often at the expense of growing plants. This detrimental effect may be prevented by adding to the soil before the mulch is applied a commercial fertilizer of a high nitrogen content.

MULE, the hybrid offspring of a male ass and a female horse. The animal's muzzle is usually whitish; the rest of the short, velvety coat usually is dark brown and shows a tendency to revert to the striping that probably prevailed among primitive horses. The mule has small feet and a thin mane and tail, but its most notable feature is the long, erect, close-set ears. These animals vary in size. Draft mules are about 16 hands, or 64 inches, high at the withers; farm mules, 15 hands, or 60 inches; and mules commonly used in the mountains, or mining mules, 12 to 16 hands, or 48 to 64 inches. The weight ranges between 600 and 1,300 pounds.

The economic value of the mule is based entirely on ability to work. The animal reaches full strength at eight years and is able to do hard work until it is 14 or 15 years old. If carefully handled a mule ordinarily may be broken in about 10 days and trained in approximately three months. In southern United States mules are used primarily as pack animals in mountainous regions and for drayage such as plowing. A mule has a stronger constitution than does a horse and is remarkably resistant to disease. Bulkier than an ass, the mule is also superior in muscular strength. Although unfamiliar noises and sights easily frighten a mule, it ordinarily has a patient disposition. A mule seems to possess a capacity for avoiding injury; it is sure-footed and tolerates heat well. The animal feeds best on timothy hay or oats. Unlike most animals, a mule will not overfeed nor will it touch water when overheated.

Various ancient civilizations bred mules, and each strain is named for the region in which it was developed. The Catalonian and Andalusian strains are most popular; other breeds are Majorca, Poitou, and Maltese. In modern times most breeding of mules has been done in Spain. In the United States the majority of mules are bred in Missouri.

Although there are two authenticated cases of living offspring of mule mares, the mule is almost always sterile among its own kind. The offspring of a stallion and a female ass is a hinny.

HARRY ENGLES-NATIONAL AUDUBON SOCIETY

Adult Buck Mule Deer

MULE DEER, a species of North American deer ranging west of the Rocky Mountains to the Pacific Ocean, from central Mexico to northern Manitoba. The mule deer, *Odocoileus hemionus*, is so named because of its large ears. It is similar to other black-tailed deer, but is largest of the group. The adult buck measures about 42 inches in height at the shoulder and 60 inches in length, and weighs approximately 400 pounds. Antlers rise vertically and divide evenly twice to produce four or more spikes on each antler. The coat varies from yellow- or brown-red in summer to gray-brown in winter. A large white rump patch is partially covered by a slender white tail with a black tip. Unlike other deer the mule deer does not erect its tail when it is alarmed. It has a characteristic jumping gait. Its hind legs have large scent glands. Gregarious in nature, the mule deer follows regular migration trails from forests and bushy lowlands to uplands each summer. Its diet consists of grasses, low woody plants, and mosses. Mating occurs in November and the doe gives birth to one to three fawns the following June. See DEER.

MULHEIM AN DER RUHR, city, W Germany, in the West German state of North Rhine-Westphalia; on the Ruhr River and at a junction point for several railways; adjoining Duisburg on the W, Oberhausen on the N, and Essen on the E. Coal is mined nearby, and electrical machines, motors, machine parts, cement, textiles, shoes, processed foods, beer, and leather are produced. The city has existed since the eleventh century. It belonged to the landgraves of Hesse-Darmstadt from 1766 to 1806. In the period 1878–1929 Mülheim annexed a number of nearby towns. (For population, see Germany map in Atlas.)

MULHOUSE, city, E France, Haut-Rhin Department; in the Alsatian lowland, on the Ill River and the Rhône-Rhine Canal; 240 miles ESE of Paris. Mulhouse, an important textile-manufacturing center, had become world famous for its dyeing and printing techniques by the end of the eighteenth century. Plants producing dyes, explosives, and other chemicals utilize large potash deposits nearby. Other industries in Mulhouse include paper and flour milling, printing, tanning, and brewing. The city is the seat of several chemical and textile institutes. Mulhouse became a free imperial city in the thirteenth century and was a member of the Swiss Confederation from 1515 until 1798, when it voted to join France. In 1953 a workmen's residential district was laid out on the northeastern outskirts of the city. As a city of Alsace, Mulhouse belonged to Germany from 1871 until the end of World War I. (For population, see France map in Atlas.)

MULLEIN, any one of a group of biennial herbs belonging to the figwort family, Scrophulariaceae, and comprising the genus *Verbascum*. Plants of this group grow 3 to 6 feet high and usually have alternate, simple, oblong leaves that are gray-green. The flowers appear as clusters along the tip of the shoot and are usually pale yellow or cream colored. The plant originated in Eurasia and has become a weed in North America, although it is sometimes used as a border plant. The common mullein, *V. Thapsus*, is a familiar roadside weed whose first-year rosette makes an attractive planting.

MULLER, GEORG ELIAS, 1850–1934, German psychophysicist, was born in Grimma, studied at the universities of Leipzig and Göttingen, and was associated with the University of Göttingen, 1873–1921, except for a year at the University of Chernovtsy, 1880–81. He rephrased and elaborated upon methods first formulated by Gustav Theodor Fechner, and conducted research into the psychophysics of vision and memory. In his *Zur Psychophysik der Gesichtsempfindungen* (1896–97) he formulated a theory of color vision. His *Zur Grundlegung der Psychophysik* (1878) and *Geischtspunkte und Tatsachen der psychophysichen Methodik* (1913) came to be considered as classics.

MULLER, HERMANN JOSEPH, 1890–1967, Nobel prize-winning U.S. biologist, was born in New York, N.Y., and studied at Columbia University. He taught at the University of Texas, 1920–36, was senior geneticist at the Institute of Genetics, Moscow, 1933–37, and research associate and lecturer at the Institute of Animal Genetics at the University of Edinburgh, 1937–40. Muller taught at Amherst College, 1940–45, and in 1945 became professor of zoology at Indiana University. He was awarded the 1946 Nobel prize in physiology and medicine for his discovery in 1926 that X rays can change genetic patterns of species and thus produce different physical characteristics in later generations. He was the first to provide evidence that the gene is an indivisible unit and estimated the number and size of genes in a chromosome. He wrote *The Mechanism of Mendelian Heredity* (with others, 1915; ed. 1922), *Out of the Night* (1935), and *Genetics, Medicine and Man* (with others, 1947). In the post-World War II controversy over the hazards of atomic weapons testing, he maintained that such testing could result in "tens of thousands" of injurious mutations in the succeeding generation. See GENE.

MULLER, JOHANNES PETER, 1801–58, German physiologist, was born in Koblenz, studied at Bonn and Berlin universities, and taught physiology at Bonn, 1824–33, and Berlin, 1833–58. Müller formulated the specific energy theory of the nervous system, which states that each nerve has its own special sensory or motor function. He wrote *Handbuch der Physiologie des Menschen* (1833–40).

MÜLLER, PAUL HERMAN, 1899–1965, Nobel prize-winning Swiss chemist, was born in Olten. At 17 he began working for a chemical company, but continued his studies and received his doctorate from Basel University, 1925. He developed new tanning substances and in 1935 began research on new synthetic contact disinfectants and insecticides. In 1939 he discovered the insecticidal properties of DDT, for which he received the 1949 Nobel prize in medicine.

MÜLLER, WILHELM, 1794–1827, German lyric poet, was born in Dessau and studied at the University of Berlin. He fought in the War of Liberation against Napoleon, 1813–14, and became a teacher, 1819, and ducal librarian in Dessau. His principal works are *Lieder der Griechen* (1821–24), *Neugriechische Volkslieder* (1825), and *Lyrische Reisen* (1827). Many of his poems, including *Die schöne Müllerin* and *Winterreise*, were set to music by Franz Schubert.

MÜLLER, WILLIAM JOHN, 1812–45, English painter, was born in Bristol. His early work consisted chiefly of scenes of Wales and Gloucestershire. After traveling in Egypt, Greece, and Asia Minor, 1838–41, he executed many oils and water colors depicting Oriental life and scenery, among them *The Slave Market*, *The Tent Scene*, and *Head of a Cingari*.

MULLET, a commercially important marine fish found abundantly in tropic and temperate coastal waters. Mullets comprise the family *Mugilidae* although occasionally some species of the sucker family, *Catostomidae*, are called mullets. The common striped mullet, *Mugil cephalus*, is about 24 inches long with silver sides and a broad, rounded, dark blue-green back. The fish is a bottom feeder, taking in a mouthful of mud and straining microscopic plant and animal life through gill rakers while expelling the mud. The young have teeth that disappear when adult feeding habits are established. The mullet of the east coast of North America usually reproduces in Florida waters from November to February, but sometimes it breeds in fresh-water inlets. The mullet swims in schools. It is an abundant source of food, some 37 million pounds being caught by net each year in the Gulf of Mexico. Two other species are the blueback or white mullet, *M. curema*, found from Cape Cod to Brazil and from Lower California to Chile; and *M. trichodon*, the fantail, found from Key West to Brazil. The Australian mullet, *M. dobula*, is also important commercially.

MULLIGAN LETTERS, a series of letters written by James G. Blaine, speaker of the House of Representatives, to Warren Fisher, Jr., a Boston businessman, about bonds of the Little Rock and Fort Smith Railroad. It was claimed that they indicated Blaine had used his position for private gain. James Mulligan, an employee of Fisher, had the letters, but Blaine obtained and read them on the floor of the House, June 5, 1876. He and his friends claimed complete vindication, but the letters were published and helped defeat Blaine when he was a candidate in the presidential election of 1884.

MULLINS, town, E South Carolina, Marion County; on the Atlantic Coast Line and the Seaboard Air Line railroads; 74 miles W of Wilmington, N.C. Tobacco grown in the area is marketed in Mullins. Cotton, lumber, and furniture are also produced. Pop. (1960) 6,229.

MULREADY, WILLIAM, 1786–1863, Irish painter, was born in Ennis, county Clare, and was brought up in London where he became a pupil in the Royal Academy schools. His early pictures such as *Old Kaspar* (1807) and *The Rattle* (1808) showed the influence of Dutch art. He was elected Associate Royal Academician, 1815; and became a full member in 1816, the year in which his *Fight Interrupted* was exhibited. After 1827 his work showed masterly execution, splendid coloring, delicate technique, and perfection of drawing. Examples of this later period are *The Seven Ages* (1838), *The Sonnet* (1839), and *Choosing the Wedding Gown* (1846).

MULTAN, city, Pakistan, E central West Pakistan Province, capital of Multan Division; near the Chenab River; a highway and railroad junction 195 miles SW of Lahore. Multan produces cotton, silk, carpets, food products, pottery, tile and enameled ware, ivory and silver ornaments, and leather goods. The city is at the site of an ancient Hindu temple. There are ruins of the temple, tombs of two Moslem saints, and a large military fort. From about 300 B.C. Multan suffered repeated conquests. It was captured by Mahmud of Ghazni in 1005 and by Tamerlane in 1398. It was under Afghan control when seized by the Sikhs under Ranjit Singh, 1818. A Sikh revolt in 1848 started the second Sikh War. The city fell to British control in 1849. Pop. (1951) 190,122.

MULTIPLE BIRTH, the birth of two or more individuals born of the same parent and at the same time. Most mammals normally bear several young at one time, and these offspring are referred to as litter mates. However, larger mammals, like cattle, horses, and human beings usually give birth to only one offspring at a time.

The occurrence of multiple births in human beings seems to be hereditary but the exact mechanism involved is not known. However, two kinds of twins are recognized: identical twins, produced from a single fertilized egg and also called one-egg, monozygotic or uni-ovular twins; and fraternal twins produced from two separate fertilized eggs and also called two-egg, dizygotic or bi-ovular twins. Fraternal twins are no more closely related than are other siblings. Identical twins, on the other hand, are genetically equivalent. Fraternal and identical twins can usually be differentiated readily in that identical twins look remarkably alike, are always of the same sex, and have a similarity of blood types, finger-print patterns, hair whorls, eye and hair coloration, left or right handedness, and many other characteristics.

The production of more than two children at one time is sometimes called supertwinning. Three born at one time, triplets, may be all identical, identical and fraternal, or all fraternal. If they are all identical, such triplets resulted from the development of a single fertilized egg or zygote. The zygote in this case had divided once to produce two identical cells, one of which then separated again to produce two more identical cells. Each of these three cells were capable of developing into a new individual. Mixed identical and fraternal triplets may arise from two separately fertilized eggs. One of the zygotes develops normally to produce one child, while the other cleaves early to form two identical cells, which subsequently separate and form new individuals. Fraternal triplets may be produced from three separate fertilized eggs. In the same manner quadruplets may be produced from 2, 3, or 4 eggs; likewise, quintuplets may be produced from 2, 3, 4, or 5 eggs; and the individuals constituting these multiple births, may be all fraternal, all identical, or mixed.

In man, multiple births occur in relatively constant ratios. In the United States, twins occur in about 1.15 per cent of total births, or about one twin birth to 86 single births. For triplets the ratio is about $1:86^2$, and for quadruplets it is about $1:86^3$. The incidence for quintuplets is one set for every 57 million births.

The chances of twins surviving are probably about one-fifth as good as the survival chances of babies of single births. Prenatal and postnatal deaths and premature birth are the special hazards of all multiple births, and such dangers increase progressively for triplets, quadruplets, and quintuplets. Surviving human quintuplets include the Dionnes of Canada, all of whom reached the age of 20 and the Diligentis of Argentina.

Twins are rarely born joined together. These conjoined, or Siamese, twins may be superficially united and therefore separable through surgical means, or more deeply united and not subject to separation. Rarely children are born with parts of the body duplicated, for example with two heads for a single body, or one head and all or portions of the body repeated. It has been suggested that such children arise as a result of incompleteness of the twinning division of an original single fertilized egg. These children seldom survive for more than a few weeks at best, however.

MULTIPLE PERSONALITY, a condition in which the main stream of thought has divided so that two or more personalities exist within the same individual. (See DISSOCIATION.) Each personality seems to be well integrated of itself. The primary personality, the original representative of mental function, is usually unaware of secondary personalities that develop. The reverse is usually true of the secondary personalities: they command the entire memory and acknowledge the existence of other personalities. Primary and secondary personalities may alternate frequently or only a few times in a lifetime. See AMNESIA.

The phenomenon of multiple personality may appear in the absence of organic disease and is therefore a disturbance in function, not structure, of the mind. It often is associated with hysteria. (See HYSTERIA.) When multiple personalities form, thoughts, desires, and ambitions that are unacceptable to the primary personality for moral or other reasons are repressed from consciousness. This repressed material is gradually integrated into one or more secondary personalities, each with its own preferences, mannerisms, and ideals. If the primary personality then is subjected to a jarring emotional experience, a secondary personality may emerge and control behavior for a time.

General maladjustment and unfortunate, memorable childhood experiences seem to play a part in the development of this condition. Hypnosis and psychotherapy have been used in its treatment. See HYPNOSIS; PSYCHIATRY; PSYCHOTHERAPY.

MULTIPLE PROPORTIONS, LAW OF. See ATOMIC THEORY.

MULTIPLE SCLEROSIS, a chronic or acute disease of the central nervous system, characterized by disturbances of vision, speech, and muscular coordination. The cause is unknown but the disease is believed to result from a nutritional disease or disturbance. Spastic paraplegia or weakness and rigidity of the legs is the most common symptom of multiple sclerosis. Intensification of symptoms followed by prolonged remission that may last for weeks or years is typical; thus only one or two attacks may occur over a period of several years. In advanced stages of the disease the individual develops scanning speech—deliberate pronunciation with prolonged pauses between each syllable. A coarse tremor becomes evident when body movements are made, and nystagmus, or rapid involuntary movements of the eyeballs, develops. There is no specific treatment for multiple sclerosis, but it is important to maintain general health and to avoid fatigue, particularly in the acute phases of the disease. A nutritious diet is required. Physical therapy sometimes helps to overcome spastic weakness of legs or arms and enables maximum function.

DAVID CLEVELAND, M.D.

MULTIPLE STAR, a system of three or more stars that constitute a single gravitational group, moving together through space. Among ternary systems in which all three members are visible is α Centauri. In this system a bright pair with apparent magnitudes of 0.3 to 1.7 revolve about their common center of gravity in an 80-year period; a 10th magnitude companion, too remote to permit an estimate of its period about them, is the third star. It is Proxima Centauri, which is nearer to the sun than is any other known star. The star Castor (α Geminorum) has three visual components, each of which is a double star of the type called spectroscopic binary. The system is therefore sextuplet. See DOUBLE STAR.

ξ Ursae Majoris, whose two visual components were discovered by William Herschel in 1780, was the first system for which an orbit was computed, the period being 60 years. The brighter star, A, is a spectroscopic binary. The period of this A is 1.8 years. The fainter star of the visual pair, B, is also a spectroscopic binary; thus the system is quadruplet. Another quadruplet system is ζ Cancri. It consists of a pair of stars more than five seconds of arc (5″) apart. The brighter one is itself a close visual double whose separation is nearly 1″, with a period of 60 years. Regular variations in the position of a third star indicate that it and an unseen companion revolve about their common center of gravity in about 17.6 years. The ϵ Lyrae system apparently is quadruplet, having a visual pair 207″ apart, each a visual double. Since one of the four is a spectroscopic binary, the system actually is quintuplet. The periods of the close pairs are estimated to be hundreds of years.

It has been estimated that 4 or 5 per cent of all binary stars are connected gravitationally to one or more additional members. These constitute multiple star systems, the most common arrangement being a close pair and a more distant single star.

MULTIPLICATION, a mathematical process by which a large number of identical figures or symbols may be added together in a relatively short time.

Method. Multiplication involves a simple form that is a kind of addition. For example, to multiply 324 by 29 the following is used:

```
  324
   29
 ----
 2916
 648
 ----
 9396
```

The top number is the multiplicand, or the number that is to be multiplied; the second number is the multiplier, or the number that shows how many times the multiplicand is to be added. The first line below the two numbers indicates that those numbers are to be multiplied. The first number below the line is a partial product, the second number below the line also is a partial product, and the partial products added together as indicated yield the final product.

The first partial product is obtained by multiplying 324 by 9. Actually three separate steps are involved in performing this operation. First 4 is multiplied by 9, yielding 36; then 20 is multiplied by 9, yielding 180; and finally 300 is multiplied by 9, yielding 2700. The sums of 2700, 180, and 36 is 2916. In practice these three steps are combined into a single step. Nine times 4 ones is 36 ones, or 3 tens and 6 ones; the 6 is written down, the 3 is temporarily remembered. Nine times 2 tens is 18 tens; however, there are 3 tens left over from the previous multiplication that now must be added to the 18 tens, making 21 tens. The 1 is put down to the left of the 6, and the 2 is temporarily remembered. Nine times 3 hundreds is 27 hundreds; there are 2 hundreds left over from the previous multiplication that must be added now, making 29 hundreds, so 29 is put down to the left of the 1. In every case units are placed to the right, tens one space toward the left, and hundreds two spaces toward the left. The second partial product is obtained in the same manner as the first. In obtaining the second partial product one is multiplying by units of 10 (20 is 2 times 10), all numbers are shifted one space toward the left of those in the first partial product.

Principles. Multiplication as used in arithmetic and ordinary algebra is based on certain principles and laws. The commutative principle states that the product of two numbers is independent of the order in which they are multiplied. That is, $ab = ba$, or 324 times 29 equals 29 times 324. The associative law is merely an extension of the commutative law, and states that when three numbers are multiplied, the result will be the same whether the product of the first two numbers is multiplied by the third number, the product of the last two numbers is multiplied by the first number, or the product of the first and third number is multiplied by the second number. The distributive law states that the sum of two numbers can be multiplied by a third number either by first adding the two numbers and multiplying their sum by the multiplier, or by multiplying each term separately and then adding the products. In other words, $(a+b)m = am + bm$, or the sum of 4 plus 3, multiplied by 5, is equal to the sum of the product of 4 multiplied by 5, plus the product of 3 multiplied by 5.

Conventions. In mathematics the use of symbols and notations is essential, both as a short cut and as a way to clarify problems. In multiplication, common symbols are × and ( ). Thus 4×5 and (4) (5) both mean 4 multiplied by 5. If letters rather than numbers are used a lack of any sign also indicates multiplication. Thus *ab* means *a* multiplied by *b*. Unless otherwise indicated multiplication is performed before addition or subtraction; thus 5×6+4 means that first 5 is to be multiplied by 6, and then 4 is to be added to the product; however, in such cases the use of parentheses to prevent confusion is desirable. See MATHEMATICAL NOTATION.

A positive number times a negative number yields a negative product: (3) (−5) = −15. Two negative numbers multiplied together, however, yield a positive product: (−3) (−5) = 15.

Short Cuts. The most efficient short cuts are electronic devices such as computers, mechanical devices such as slide rules, and devices that use tables such as those of logarithms. There are, however, some short cuts suitable for multiplication done on paper or in the head. For example, to multiply by 25 one can multiply first by 100 and then divide by 4.

Various methods are used to check accuracy of multiplication, the most reliable being division of the product by multiplicand or multiplier.

Dimensions. Only like quantities can be added, but it is possible to multiply certain unlike quantities. Thus one cannot add 3 feet to 8 pounds, but one can multiply 3 feet by 8 pounds, the product being 24 foot-pounds. See ALGEBRA; ARITHMETIC; FACTOR; MATHEMATICS; NUMBER.

MUMFORD, LEWIS, 1895– , U.S. social philosopher, was born in Flushing, Long Island, and grew up in New York City. He studied at City College, New York and Columbia universities, and the New School for Social Research, but did not take an academic degree. He was associate editor of *The Dial*, 1919; acting editor of the (London) *Sociological Review*, 1920; lecturer on the development of American culture at the School of International Studies, Geneva, 1925, and on sociology, 1929; secretary of the Regional Planning Association of America, 1932–38; member of the board of higher education, New York, 1935–37; member of the commission on teacher education, American Council of Education, 1938–44; professor of humanities, Stanford University, 1942–44; visiting professor in architecture, North Carolina State College, 1948–52; and visiting professor of land and city planning, University of Pennsylvania, from 1951. From about 1915 the principal influence on his intellectual development was the British biologist and educator Sir Patrick Geddes, the force of whose ideas can be felt in Mumford's most important writings, especially his four-volume "Renewal of Life" series consisting of *Technics and Civilization* (1934), *The Culture of Cities* (1938), *The Condition of Man* (1944), and *The Conduct of Life* (1951). This work constitutes the central effort of Mumford's life, and most of his earlier works may be regarded as preparatory to it, his later works as amplifications. His other works include *The Story of Utopias* (1922), *Sticks and Stones* (1924; rev. ed. 1955), *The Golden Day* (1926, ed. 1934), *Herman Melville* (1929), *The Brown Decades: A Study of the Arts in America, 1865–1895* (1931, ed. 1955), *Men Must Act* (1939), *City Development, Studies in Disintegration and Renewal* (1945), *Values for Survival* (1946), *Green Memories* (1947), *Art and Technics* (1952), *In the Name of Sanity* (1954), *The Human Prospect* (1955), *The Roots of Contemporary Architecture* (1956), *The Transformation of Man* (1956), *From the Ground Up* (1956), and *The City in History* (1961).

MUMPS, or epidemic parotitis, an acute virus disease usually characterized by swelling of the salivary glands, especially the parotids. Mumps is not highly contagious; most infections probably result from direct contact with an infected person or with air contaminated with the virus by coughing or sneezing. See SALIVARY GLAND.

Symptoms. Mumps usually appears 17 to 21 days after exposure to the disease. (See COMMUNICABLE DISEASE.) The commonest symptom is swelling of one or both parotid glands, which lie at the angle of the jaw just beneath the ear. Swelling of these glands may be great enough to distort facial features slightly. The involved gland may be sore and jaw movement painful. Swelling begins to subside about the third day and usually disappears in about one week. Headache, fever, and general malaise in varying degrees accompany the disease. Complications resulting from mumps may include orchitis, or inflammation of the testes; and meningoencephalitis, or inflammation of the brain and its membranes. Recovery from mumps is usually rapid and complete.

Treatment. Rest in bed while fever and swelling persist is important. Heat applied to swollen areas sometimes makes the patient more comfortable, and salicylates often are given to relieve pain. Contraction of mumps usually affords lifelong immunity to the disease. Artificial immunization has not been completely successful, but injections of immune serum and gamma globulin are thought to be helpful in preventing severe forms of the disease. See GLOBULIN; VACCINE.

Occurrence. Mumps occurs throughout the world. In the United States it is most prevalent during late winter and in spring. Both sexes are equally susceptible, usually contracting the disease between the ages of 5 and 15. About 75 per cent of all cases of mumps reported in children run their courses without complication.

MUNCH, ANDREAS, 1811–84, Norwegian poet and dramatist, was born in Christiania (later Oslo). Among his works are *Poems Old and New* (1848), *Grief and Consolation* (1852), and the plays *King Sverre's Youth* (1837), *An Evening at Giske* (1855), and *Lord William Russell* (1857). He was also the author of translations from Sir Walter Scott and Alfred Lord Tennyson.

MUNCH, CHARLES, 1891– , French conductor, was born in Strasbourg, and studied at the Strasbourg Conservatory and in Paris and Berlin, where he specialized in the violin. In the 1930's he conducted various orchestras in Paris, in 1938 becoming director of the famous Orchestre du Conservatoire. In 1947 Münch came to the United States as a guest conductor of the New York Philharmonic Orchestra, and in 1949 succeeded Serge Koussevitzky as conductor of the Boston Symphony Orchestra. He retired in the fall of 1962.

MUNCHHAUSEN, BARON KARL FRIEDRICH HIERONYMUS, VON 1720–97, German soldier and raconteur, was born in Bodenwerder, Hanover. After serving with the Russian army in the campaigns against the Turks, he retired to his estates in Hanover and became celebrated for the tall stories, usually based on his military and hunting exploits, with which he entertained his guests. Rudolph Erich Raspe (1737–94), a German adventurer and man of letters who had known Münchhausen, fled to England in 1775 to escape a charge of swindling and published there a satirical fantasy, *Baron Munchausen's Narrative of His Marvellous Travels and Campaigns in Russia* (1785), which immediately became popular. In later editions, others enlarged the work by adding stories from such sources as Lucian's *Vera historia*, eighteenth-century chapbooks, and the Scottish traveler James Bruce's report on his travels in Africa. In the course of this expansion the baron was transformed from a genial satirist trifling with human credulity to a fabulous liar whose inventions burlesqued the extravagant travelers' tales then current.

MUNCIE, city, E Indiana, seat of Delaware County; on the White River, the Chesapeake and Ohio, the Muncie and Western, the New York Central, the Nickel Plate, and the Pennsylvania railroads, and U.S. highway 35; a scheduled airline stop; 52 miles NE of Indianapolis. Muncie is a thriving railroad and industrial city and a trade center for the surrounding agricultural region. Principal manufactures include glassware, automobile parts, electrical equipment, metal parts, cutlery, and silverware. Muncie derived its name from Chief Muncie, leader of a Delaware Indian tribe who lived along the White River. The city is the site of Ball State Teachers College. Nationwide attention was focused upon Muncie with publication of *Middletown* (1929) and *Middletown in Transition* (1937), sociological studies of the city written by Robert S. and Helen Merrell Lynd. Muncie was founded in 1827, and was incorporated as a town in 1847 and as a city in 1885. Pop. (1960) 68,603.

MUNDAY, ANTHONY, 1553–1633, English dramatist, was born in London, was employed as a journalist to spy upon the activities of English Catholics in France and Italy, and reported his observations in *The English Romayne Lyfe* (1582). He was afterward a player in the Earl of Oxford's company, 1579–84, and collaborated in several plays including *John a Kent and John a Cumber* (1595), the first part of *Sir John Oldcastle* (1600), and two plays based on the Robin Hood legend, *The Downfall of Robert, Earle of Huntington* (1599) and *The Death of Robert, Earle of Huntington* (1601). He also composed ballads, translated chivalric romances such as *Palladino of England* (1588) and *Amadis de Gaule* (1590), and wrote many pageants for the city of London, becoming chief pageant writer, 1605–16. He was a rival of Ben Jonson and Thomas Middleton.

MUNDELEIN, GEORGE WILLIAM CARDINAL, 1872–1939, U.S. Roman Catholic churchman, was born in New York, N.Y., and was educated at Manhattan College, St. Vincent Seminary, and at Rome, where he was ordained, 1895. He became chancellor of the Brooklyn diocese, 1897, and auxiliary bishop, 1909. In 1915 he became archbishop of Chicago, where he established uniform methods in the parochial schools, helped to found the Catholic Youth Organization and the Associated Catholic Charities, and developed St. Mary's of the Lake Seminary. In 1924 he was elevated to the cardinalate, becoming the first cardinal from a middle western bishopric. Mundelein College was named for him.

MUNFORDVILLE, city, central Kentucky, seat of Hart County; on the Green River, the Louisville and Nashville Railroad, and U.S. highway 31W; 67 miles S of Louisville and 13 miles NE of Mammoth Cave. Retail trade and flour milling are the main occupations. The city was the site of a Civil War battle in September, 1863. Pop. (1960) 1,157.

MUNHALL, borough, SW Pennsylvania, in Allegheny County; on the Monongahela River and the Baltimore and Ohio, the Bessemer and Lake Erie, the Pennsylvania, the Pittsburgh and Lake Erie, and the Union railroads; adjoining Homestead, at the ESE limits of Pittsburgh. In 1886 the first open-hearth furnace in the United States was put into operation in Munhall. The borough was the site of the Homestead Strike in 1892. Munhall was incorporated in 1900. Pop. (1960) 17,312.

MUNI, PAUL, 1895– , U.S. actor, was born Muni Weisenfreund in Lemberg, Austria, was brought to the United States in 1902, and became a U.S. citizen in 1923. He appeared on the stage in *We Americans*, *Key Largo*, *Death of a Salesman*, *Inherit the Wind*, and in a number of other plays; in motion pictures including *The Life of Louis Pasteur* (for which he won a Motion Picture Academy award, 1936), *The Good Earth*, and *We Are Not Alone;* and in a number of television productions.

MUNICH, German München, city, SE Germany, capital of the West German state of Bavaria and of the administrative district of Upper Bavaria; on the Isar River; 310 miles SW of Berlin; pop. (1958) 1,033,694. Munich is an important junction of European railroads, highways, and airlines, and a commercial and cultural center.

Industry. The leading industries are brewing and the manufacture of motors, auto bodies, railway equipment, precision and optical instruments, machines, pharmaceuticals, paper goods, gloves, and malt. Most of Munich's heavy industry was destroyed during World War II, but much was restored in postwar years. Munich is noted as an arts and crafts center. There is an important trade in art products and books, and the city has numerous publishing houses.

Cultural Features. Before World War II Munich was one of the handsomest cities of Europe, with many parks, monuments, museums, and fine examples of rococo and Renaissance architecture. Among the buildings destroyed or heavily damaged during the war was the former residence of the dukes of Bavaria. The fifteenth century Church of Our Lady and much of the old town also were damaged or destroyed. Munich's museum and art collections were removed for safekeeping during the war and returned after 1947. The collection of Flemish, Dutch, German, and French masters was placed after the war in the Museum of Art. In the Schack Gallery are more modern works chiefly by Bavarian artists; and in the Bavarian National Museum are examples of medieval and Renaissance art. The Glyptothek Museum houses ancient and modern sculpture, and in the German museum are collections illustrating achievements in natural sciences and technical arts. The Bavarian State Library in Munich has more than 2 million books and manuscripts.

Munich is the seat of many institutions of higher learning, including the university, founded in 1472 in Ingolstadt and established in Munich in 1826. The Academy of Music, the Bavarian Academy of Arts and Sciences, and an institute of technology are also in Munich. In the last part of the nineteenth century the city was a German music and drama center, greatly influenced by Wagnerian tradition.

Munich was founded in 1158 by Duke Henry the Lion, who established a market place and mint; in the thirteenth century it became a city and the residence of Wittelsbach princes. In the sixteenth century Munich's great art collections were begun by Duke Albert V of Bavaria. Munich became the capital of the kingdom of Bavaria during the Napoleonic era, and under Ludwig I the city was enriched by construction of numerous buildings, transfer of the university from Ingolstadt, and royal encouragement of the arts. Munich's cultural growth continued during the reigns of Maximilian II and Ludwig II.

Nazi Regime. After the fall of the monarchy in 1918, Munich became a focal point for National Socialist agitation and in February, 1920, the German National Socialist Workers (Nazi) party was organized in Munich. Three years later the abortive beer-hall Putsch took place in Munich. In 1933 the Nazis made Munich the center of the Nazi movement, using its cultural reputation to add prestige to the

Tri-arched Hall of the Generals was the scene of Hitler's unsuccessful first attempt to seize power, Nov. 9, 1923. To the right is the Roman Baroque Church of the Theatines.

GERMAN TOURIST INFORMATION OFFICE

party's political propaganda. The Munich Pact of 1938 was signed in the official Munich residence of Adolf Hitler. During World War II the city was heavily bombed by the Allied air forces, and fell to the U.S. 7th Army on Apr. 29, 1945.

MUNICH CONFERENCE, a conference held at Munich, Germany, Sept. 29–30, 1938, to settle German demands for Czechoslovakian territory inhabited by Sudeten Germans. The principals attending the conference were Premier Benito Mussolini of Italy, Chancellor Adolf Hitler of Germany, Prime Minister Arthur Neville Chamberlain of Great Britain, and Premier Edouard Daladier of France. It was agreed that Germany should occupy the Sudetenland in western Czechoslovakia, including vital border defenses that were not to be destroyed by Czechoslovakia before German occupation. Certain adjacent areas were to be taken over according to the results of plebiscites conducted by an international commission composed of representatives of Italy, Germany, France, Great Britain, and Czechoslovakia. The commission also had authority to set permanent boundaries between Germany and Czechoslovakia on an ethnographic basis. The agreement marked the culmination of appeasement policies by Great Britain and France in their efforts to prevent the outbreak of World War II. See CZECHOSLOVAKIA, Administration and History, *The Republic;* GERMANY, The Empire and The Republic; SUDETENLAND.

MUNICH, UNIVERSITY OF, or Ludwig-Maximilians-Universität München, an institution of higher learning at Munich, Germany, founded in 1472. The university has faculties of theology, law, political economy, medicine, veterinary science, philosophy, and natural sciences. In the mid-1960's the school had more than 700 teachers and approximately 18,000 students. The university library contained about 800,000 volumes.

MUNICIPALITY, a legally incorporated or otherwise duly authorized association of inhabitants of a limited area for local government or other public purposes. Municipalities have no relation to size; they encompass all cities, boroughs, and villages in the United States. Towns are also included as municipalities in all but eight states—New York, Wisconsin, and six New England states—where "town" is a local term for the government unit which the other states call a "township" government.

There are between 17,000 and 18,000 municipalities in the United States and more than 4,000 in Canada. Approximately 1,000 new municipalities were created in the United States from 1940 to 1960 and about twice that many town and township governments were abandoned as a result of new incorporations. See CITY; CITY GOVERNMENT; LOCAL GOVERNMENT.

Municipalities, like cities, villages, or incorporated towns, have both governmental and proprietary functions. Governmental duties include maintenance of order and protection of the public health and safety. Proprietary functions include maintenance of water works and other municipal utilities.

History. Ancient city-states of Athens, Syracuse, and Rome had jurisdiction over areas beyond the official municipal areas, and at first were politically independent. Alexander the Great (356–323 B.C.) organized the cities of his time into a system to which they were subordinated. Rome followed that example, the very word *municipium* implying a relationship of the local community to the state. The later Roman system carefully tied the municipality into a federated system and took into consideration the protection of the empire without destroying local government. This principle persisted after Rome fell, with Mediterranean cities maintaining their unity as political entities. When the Middle Ages ended, many free cities in western Europe federated, as in the Hanseatic League. (See HANSEATIC LEAGUE.) The communes of France and the boroughs of England were set up to end the rule of feudal barons. Municipalities were thus pioneers in modern representative government since they were generally governed by some semblance of popular will. When modern nations began to develop in the fifteenth and sixteenth centuries, however, municipal areas had to yield some of their autonomy.

Municipal Home Rule. In the United States the municipality is legally under charter from the state government through which local autonomy is granted. Home rule was the result of reaction against legislative control over municipalities. Between 1870 and 1900 the principle that cities should be permitted to frame their own charters became widely accepted. The basic philosophy was that the people of each municipality—those primarily interested in and directly affected by their government and administration—should have the right to draft their own charters and embody in them whatever plan of government they preferred, and to exercise such corporate powers as were not inconsistent with the constitution and the laws of the state. The Missouri Constitution of 1875 was the first to grant this authority. Many other states have expanded municipal and county home rule, especially in the areas of urban renewal, annexation, and incorporation. In Canada the British North America Act of 1867 gave the provincial legislatures the exclusive power to make laws relating to municipalities. Municipalities in Canada have no assurance of autonomy since a provincial legislature can abolish or modify the structure or powers of local governmental units.

MUNICIPAL OWNERSHIP is the ownership and operation of enterprises by a municipal government. In the United States these enterprises have largely been concerned with utilities such as water, electricity, and gas supply. These and other utilities, such as transportation facilities and communication media, have usually involved an issue of public policy as to whether they should be publicly owned and operated, or privately owned and publicly regulated.

A public utility provides an indispensable service, is universally available to all, and is a so-called natural monopoly, but primarily it is subject to special public regulation with respect to its prices, profits, and standards of service. (See PUBLIC UTILITY.) Municipal functions that are closely related to public utilities are sometimes called near utilities. These are numerous and include such services as airports, abbatoirs, sewers, markets, bridges, tunnels, toll roads, and municipal auditoriums. There are also freight and bus terminal facilities, wharves, piers, ferries, fuel yards, ice plants, laundries, central heating systems, and municipal opera companies, libraries, and other cultural institutions. The largest single expenditure of municipal governments in the United States is for education, and yet this is never considered within the category of municipal ownership.

Policy Issue. Since about 1920 the main difference of opinion in the United States concerning public versus private ownership of municipal services has been in the area of electrical utilities and local transportation. At mid-twentieth century public housing, too, though not considered a public utility, had become a subject of controversy because it impinged on many private interests in the economy. Little public debate was aroused, on the other hand, in the area of municipal water supply; about 1850 this field was almost entirely a private matter, but a century later it was more than 85 per cent a public responsibility. Also with respect to airport ownership and operation, there was little opposition to increasing municipal government control.

Except in the areas of power, transportation, and housing, municipal ownership has not caused deep political divisions. It is largely regarded as a practical issue revolving around specific proposals. Frequently even the most conservative suburban communities own their own electricity supply systems as well as other services, and the issue of public versus private ownership seldom arises. The increase in the number of municipal services has kept pace with the steady growth of cities, their populations, and their technologies.

Areas of Operation. The issue of the municipal electric plant became prominent in the United States soon after 1933 when the federal government began to offer financial help to cities in building or acquiring power plants and in building transmission lines into rural areas. The Rural Electrification Administration was authorized to make loans up to 45 per cent of the cost of the plant, and if the debt limit was a factor it sometimes made outright grants for this purpose. The principal growth of municipal power plants has been in cities and towns with less than 10,000 population. In 1962 only 18 per cent of all cities of more than 5,000 population owned or operated generating or distribution stations, and only 41 cities with populations of more than 50,000 had public plants. As early as 1937 one-third of the 6,000 plants serving 18,778 cities were publicly owned. The rate of growth slowed down somewhat thereafter, especially in the less populous cities where the uneconomic factor of small size is a consideration.

The depression of the 1930's also saw the rise of the public housing movement and the entry of the U.S. government into this field with the Housing Act of 1937. To participate in the federal program, the various states authorized local governments to establish housing authorities (similar to public corporations) for the purpose of clearing slums and building and operating low-cost housing units. After World War II the housing program was expanded at both federal and municipal levels to alleviate the population problem created in cities that had experienced a wartime boom, to promote urban redevelopment, and to prevent the growth of slums.

In contrast to the controversial areas of electricity supply and housing, city responsibility for airport construction and operation caused scarcely any public comment. Eight of America's 10 largest cities and two-thirds of those with populations of 100,000 and more entrust the development of airport facilities to municipal authorities, who in turn often lease the facilities to private operators.

Despite these trends in municipal ownership in the United States, generalizations about the character of such ownership are not reliable. There are important regional differences. In West Virginia, for example, 43 per cent of the urban population is served by municipal water systems, while in Minnesota and Michigan the corresponding figure is 98.9 per cent. When there were 57 municipal electric plants in New York State, Tennessee had 376 and Nebraska 324. It is almost, but not quite, correct to say that the farther west one goes, the more one finds municipalities undertaking public services. Los Angeles, for example, is outstanding as a municipal supplier of water and electric power. Six large U.S. cities—New York, Philadelphia, Detroit, Cleveland, San Francisco, and Seattle—operate their own transportation systems; yet only the last two are on the West Coast. And although about 100 gas plants are municipally owned, compared with 1,700 under private management, the public plants are located in such diversified cities as Knoxville, Houston, Philadelphia, and Richmond. Milwaukee, a city which long had a Socialist administration, owned only its water supply system and its sewage treatment plant as major utilities.

Historical Development. With few exceptions, municipal ownership in the United States has never been a live political issue as it was in Great Britain and in most of western Europe during the late nineteenth and early twentieth centuries. There has been no Social Democratic party in the United States and, indeed, no strong Socialist movement of any kind. In England and Germany, by contrast, and under such differing political leaders as Joseph Chamberlain and Otto von Bismarck, municipal ownership of water, gas, and electricity supply and of local transportation became nearly universal. After the 1930's if less was heard of municipal ownership in Europe and England, it was because municipal ownership was gradually superseded by national ownership in one field after another.

Legal Requirements. Before a municipality in the United States may undertake a new function it must obtain authority from the state which created and empowered it. Such new authority may require a statutory enactment or, in the case of cities with the home-rule type of charter, the authority should be deducible from the charter. In general the courts have interpreted broadly the legal authority of American municipalities to undertake so-called proprietary functions. Hence few legal difficulties are encountered by the proponents of municipal ownership.

Sometimes a more serious difficulty is the tax limitation that may be imposed on a city by either constitutional or charter provisions, restricting the city's freedom to incur debts for long-term improvements. Once the city decides to extend its activities to buy an existing facility or to construct a new one, two courses of action are possible outside of general taxation: the issuance of bonds and special assessment. The usual course is to sell bonds. If these are revenue bonds and not general obligations of the city government, they fall outside the possible debt limits. Revenue bonds are secured by the new property and are repayable out of revenue from it. Special assessment, a financial charge levied on property owners who stand to benefit from the proposed improvement, is frequently not as equitable or efficient as issuing bonds; therefore it is more often used for the extension and improvement of existing services than for the creation of new ones.

U.S. MUNICIPAL OWNERSHIP AND OPERATION OF UTILITIES*

UTILITY	All Cities Over 5,000 No.	All Cities Over 5,000 Per Cent	Over 500,000	250,000 to 500,000	100,000 to 250,000	50,000 to 100,000	25,000 to 50,000	10,000 to 25,000	5,000 to 10,000
Airport	641	—	38	39	59	82	145	278	—
Water supply and distribution	1,894	68.3	17	25	62	113	251	570	856
Sewage treatment plant	1,727	62.3	14	23	54	90	218	552	776
Electric generation and distribution	281	10.1	5	2	10	11	35	85	133
Electric distribution only	245	8.7	0	0	5	8	19	72	141
Water distribution only	196	6.9	1	1	6	19	24	73	72
Gas distribution only	134	4.7	0	1	3	5	12	28	85
Transportation systems	60	2.1	7	1	7	8	20	9	8
Gas manufacturing and distribution	48	1.7	3	2	2	2	3	15	21
No municipal ownership	392	14.2	0	0	4	16	42	151	179
Cities not reporting	278	—	2	0	1	16	46	143	70

*1961

The Municipal Yearbook, 1962

In comparison with most European nations, including Great Britain, the United States has legal difficulties as well as political and property attitudes that predispose it toward a more moderate growth of municipal ownership and operation. See GOVERNMENT OWNERSHIP. MARSHALL E. DIMOCK

MUNISING, city, N central part of the Upper Peninsula of Michigan, seat of Alger County; on Munising Bay of Lake Superior facing Grand Island; on the Lake Superior and Ishpeming Railroad; 35 miles ESE of Marquette. Lumbering and the manufacture of paper and wood products are the principal industries. Munising was incorporated as a city in 1916. Pop. (1960) 4,228.

MUNITIONS are weapons, machines, and materials used in warfare. Munitions used on land include numerous types, and in general may be classified according to the arm of service in which they are used. The principal function of nearly all weapons used in warfare is to discharge projectiles against the enemy. The most common projectiles are the bullet, the shell, the rocket, and the aerial bomb. They are launched by the rifle, the machine gun, the howitzer, the mortar, various kinds of antitank and antiaircraft guns and rocket launchers, and the airplane. Other equipment considered as munitions are vehicles used for transportation and apparatus for communication, construction, and supply.

Munitions of naval warfare include all types of ships and their auxiliaries. Naval ammunition includes the shell, the torpedo, the depth charge, and the aerial bomb. The shell constitutes the chief offensive power of the heavier class of warships. Torpedoes may be carried by surface vessels, submarines, or airplanes. The depth charge, an antisubmarine weapon, is chiefly carried by destroyers. Naval airplanes usually operate from aircraft carriers, and may be armed with machine guns and light cannon. See AERONAUTICS; AMMUNITION; ARMY, U.S.; ARTILLERY; BOMB; BULLET; CARTRIDGE; FIELD ARTILLERY; GUN; HOWITZER; MORTAR; NAVY, U.S.; RIFLE; SUBMARINE; TANK; TORPEDO.

MUNKÁCSY, MIHÁLY, original surname Lieb, 1844–1900, Hungarian painter of religious, narrative, and historical subjects, was born in Munkács (Mukachevo), studied painting in Munich and Düsseldorf, and settled in Paris, 1872. His first important picture, *Last Day of a Condemned Prisoner* (1868–69), won the gold medal at the Salon of 1872 and established his reputation. Among his best known paintings are *Milton Dictating "Paradise Lost" to His Daughters* (1878), *Christ Before Pilate* (1881), *Golgotha* (1883), and *Death of Mozart* (1884).

MUNN v. ILLINOIS. See SUPREME COURT OF THE UNITED STATES, Historic Decisions of the Supreme Court, *The Period of Transition in Commerce;* PUBLIC UTILITY, *Historical Background.*

MUNRO, DANA CARLETON, 1866–1933, U.S. historian, was born in Bristol, R.I. He taught medieval history at the University of Pennsylvania, 1893, European history at the University of Wisconsin, 1902–15, and medieval history at Princeton University, 1915–33. An authority on the Crusades, he wrote *The Middle Ages* (1902) and *A Guide to the Study of Medieval History* (1931).

MUNRO, HECTOR HUGH. See SAKI.

MUNSEE, a North American Indian tribe of the Algonquian linguistic stock, generally considered as a division of the Delaware. When they first came into contact with the Dutch in 1607, the Munsees were mostly settled around the headwaters of the Delaware River in a region that later became parts of New Jersey, New York, and Pennsylvania. In 1720 they came under the domination of the Iroquois from whom they freed themselves with French backing. In 1751 they began to settle in Ohio, but the majority of them were massacred by white settlers in 1782. The Munsees were sent to Kansas in 1835, but most of them later moved to Oklahoma, Wisconsin, or Ontario.

MUNSEY, FRANK ANDREW, 1854–1925, U.S. publisher, was born in Mercer, Me., worked as a telegraph operator in Maine, and in 1882 went to New York City where he began the publication of a juvenile weekly, *The Golden Argosy*. In 1889 appeared *Munsey's Weekly*, changed in 1891 to *Munsey's Magazine*, a monthly publication, profusely illustrated, and the first of the 10-cent magazines to attain a large circulation. Munsey subsequently launched many other magazines, including the *Scrap Book*, *Quaker*, *Railroad Man's Magazine*, and *All-Story Magazine;* and acquired various newspapers, including the New York *Mail*, *Herald*, *Press*, *Sun*, *Globe*, and *Evening Telegram*, and the Baltimore *Star* and Philadelphia *Times*. When a magazine was not profitable Munsey would kill it and start another, and he merged and killed newspapers with such frequency he became known as the executioner of newspapers. He wrote a number of books, including *Afloat in a Large City* (1887), *The Boy Broker* (1888), *A Tragedy of Errors* (1889), *Under Fire* (1890), and *Derringforth* (1894).

MUNSTER, town, extreme NW Indiana, Lake County; on the Monon Railroad and U.S. highway 6; 4 miles S of Hammond. Bricks and bedding are manufactured. Pop. (1960) 10,313.

MÜNSTER, city, W Germany, in the West German state of North Rhine-Westphalia (formerly the capital of the Prussian province of Westphalia); on the Dortmond-Ems Canal; 80 miles NE of Cologne. It is the marketing center of a rich agricultural region. Industries include flour milling, distilling, and brewing and the manufacture of agricultural and mining machinery, textiles, and furniture. Before World War II Münster had arcaded market places, gabled houses, and medieval squares and churches; among them were a much-decorated thirteenth century cathedral; the Church of St. Lambert and the Church of Our Lady, Gothic buildings dating from the fourteenth century; the Romanesque Church of St. Ludger built about 1170; the Church of St. Maurice founded about 1070; and the fourteenth century Gothic *Rathaus*, where the Peace of Westphalia was signed in 1648. All were destroyed or severely damaged by heavy bombing and artillery fire during the war. All of the buildings of the University of Münster, except those of the medical college also were lost.

Münster was founded about 800 and was created a bishopric by Charlemagne. Its original name, Mimegardevoord, was changed to Münster about the tenth century; it became a town after 1180. Münster was a member of the Hanseatic League in the thirteenth century, and became an important trading center. During the Reformation the city was the scene of struggles between the Roman Catholic bishop and Anabaptists led by John of Leiden, and for a short time was dominated by Anabaptists. Münster was ruled by prince-bishops until 1803 when the bishopric was secularized and citizens gained control of local administration. Münster passed to Prussia in 1814. After 1945 it became a city in North Rhine-Westphalia. Pop. (1957) 164,228.

MUNSTER, largest province of Ireland, occupying SW coastal sections of the island; bounded on the N by Connacht, E by Leinster, S by the St. George

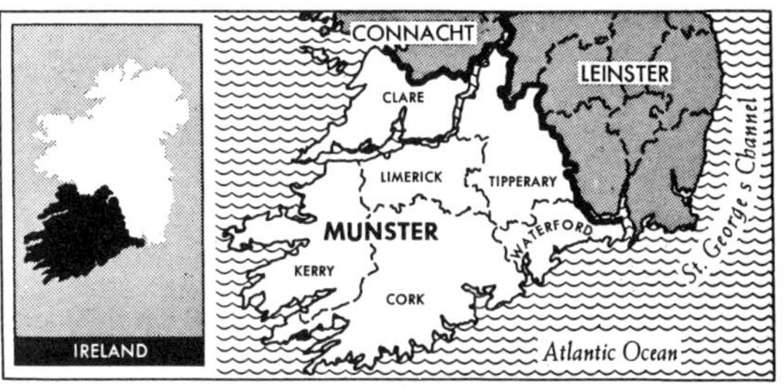

Location Map of Munster

Channel, and W by the Atlantic Ocean; area 9,316.5 sq. mi.; pop. (1956) 876,620. The province includes six counties: Clare, Cork, Kerry, Waterford, Limerick, and Tipperary; the latter two are inland. Munster has hundreds of miles of seacoast and dozens of good harbors. The terrain generally is mountainous with peaks 2,000 to 3,000 feet high. Coal is mined, and there are stone and marble quarries. The principal rivers are the Shannon, Lee, Blackwater, and Suir, in whose fertile valleys there are dairy farms and fields of barley, corn, and potatoes. The principal cities are Limerick, Waterford, Cork, and Cóbh. The Rock of Cashel is in Tipperary; Blarney Castle with its "stone" is in Cork; and the beautiful town of Killarney is in Kerry. Other leading towns are Mallow, Tralee, Kenmare, and Bantry.

MÜNSTERBERG, HUGO, 1863–1916, German experimental psychologist, was born in Danzig, studied medicine at the University of Leipzig, and became interested in experimental psychology. After a period at Heidelberg, he became an instructor in philosophy at Freiburg, 1887, where he instituted a laboratory for experimental psychology. At the instigation of William James, Münsterberg took charge of the Harvard psychology laboratory, 1892, and remained there for the rest of his life, except for intervals at Freiburg, 1895–97, and Berlin, 1911–12. Münsterberg was precursor of the behaviorists, and one of the first workers in the field of applied psychology, especially in crime detection and industrial psychology. He wrote *Grundzüge der Psychologie* (1900), *On the Witness Stand* (1908, ed. 1927), *Psychology and Industrial Efficiency* (1913), and *Psychology, General and Applied* (1915).

MUNTHE, AXEL MARTIN FREDRIK, 1857–1949, Swedish writer and physician, was educated at the University of Uppsala and in Paris, where he studied under the psychiatrist Jean Martin Charcot. He practiced in France and Italy, acquiring a reputation as a consulting psychiatrist, and was for many years the personal physician of Sweden's royal family. His anecdotal and somewhat fictionized memoirs, *The Story of San Michele* (1929), headed the list of U.S. best sellers in 1930.

MUNTJAC, a small, primitive deer found predominantly in the jungles of southern India and ranging through Burma, China, and parts of Indonesia. The muntjac, *Muntiacus muntjac*, has a large mahogany-red body, a thick neck, short legs, and a long tail with a white tip. The animal stands about 20 inches high and weighs about 30 pounds. The ears are large and round and there is a buff-colored V on the face. Only the male has antlers, which are 5 to 6 inches long with two points. The upper canine teeth of the male overhang the lower jaw; they are used to slash an opponent during combat. Mating occurs in January or February, usually producing one fawn the following June. Difficult to track, the solitary muntjac provides great sport for hunters, who call it the barking deer because of its alarm and mating calls. See DEER.

MUNTZ METAL, a metallic alloy containing approximately 60 per cent copper and 40 per cent zinc, permissible impurities of lead and iron not to exceed a total of 0.35 per cent. Invented by G. F. Muntz of Birmingham, England, in 1832, the alloy is characterized by its yellow color; sometimes it is called yellow brass. Muntz metal is well adapted for hot-rolling as well as cold-rolling methods. In the annealed state its tensile strength is more than 54,000 pounds psi; this is increased to 70,000 pounds in the half-hard condition. The alloy is used for architectural trim, sheathing, nuts and bolts, heat exchanger and condenser parts, and tubing.

MÜNZER, THOMAS, 1490?–1525, German Anabaptist leader, was born in Stolberg in the Harz Mountains, studied at Leipzig and Frankfurt, and became a Protestant preacher at Zwickau, 1520. At first a follower of Martin Luther, Münzer was expelled from Zwickau, 1521, because of his increasingly radical views. While preaching in Bohemia and several German cities he organized the Anabaptist sect. Claiming direct inspiration by the Holy Ghost, Münzer attacked Luther and urged his followers to revolt against any suppressors. He began to preach in Mülhausen, 1524, gained control of the city administration, and instituted a communal form of organization. At the outbreak of the Peasants' Revolt, 1525, he headed an army of 8,000 peasants (Luther strongly opposed the revolt). Defeated at the Battle of Frankenhausen, Münzer was captured and put to death. See ANABAPTISTS.

MURAD I, also Amurath, 1319–89, Ottoman sultan, succeeded his father, Orkhan, in 1359. The chief events of his reign center around his invasions of the Balkan Peninsula. He captured Adrianople, 1365; conquered most of Bulgaria, 1369–72; and took Macedonia, 1371, and Sofia, 1385. In 1389 Murad was victorious over a coalition of Serbs, Bosnians, Bulgars, Albanians, and Wallachians at Kossovo. He was assassinated just by a Serb, after the battle and was succeeded by his son Bajazet I.

MURAD II, also Amurath, 1403?–51, Ottoman sultan, succeeded his father Mohammed I in 1421, and in 1422 suppressed a rebellion headed by the pretender Mustapha and unsuccessfully besieged Constantinople. He conducted wars with Venice, 1425–30, taking Salonika, Albania, and Epirus; and after several battles, 1443–48, defeated the Hungarian hero János Hunyadi at Kossovo, 1448. Murad was succeeded by his son Mohammed II.

MURAD III, also Amurath, 1546–95, Ottoman sultan, succeeded his father, Selim II, in 1574. Murad's reign, dominated by his viziers and his harem, began the deterioration of the Ottoman power. Financial troubles caused frequent rebellions within Turkey; but a war with Persia, 1577–90, ended with Ottoman annexation of Georgia, Luristan, Shirvan, and part of Azerbaijan.

MURAD IV, also Amurath, 1609?–40, Ottoman sultan, succeeded his uncle Mustapha I in 1623. Anarchy existed in Turkey during the first years of his reign, with the Janizary guard dominating the government; but in 1632 Murad gained the power to suppress the Janizaries, and began a reign of terror that restored the authority of the sultan. In a war with Persia he recaptured Baghdad, 1638.

MURAD V, also Amurath, 1840–1904, Ottoman sultan, son of Sultan Abdul Medjid, was kept prisoner during the reign of his uncle, Abdul Aziz, 1861–76, but on the latter's deposition was proclaimed sultan, 1876; in the same year he was judged insane, deposed, and succeeded by his brother, Abdul Hamid II.

MURAL, the painted decoration of the ceilings, structural members, and walls of buildings. Probably as old as architecture (which it complements), mural painting was practiced among the early Egyptians at least 4,000 years before the Christian Era. These early murals were bountiful in concept, and spread over columns, moldings, and other available space in brilliantly colored patterns; figures in horizontal bands embellished walls, and ceilings were commonly studded with stars and sacred symbols reflecting the sky world so central to Egyptian religion. Murals were usually executed upon a thin skin of fine lime laid over the actual construction; this skin served as a smooth absorbent for the (frequently) brilliant pigments. Since the Egyptians did not employ the fresco technique, they were not restricted to the narrow range of earth colors and could use hues that would have been destroyed by the fresh lime of fresco. Combinations of tints that would be harsh in themselves were avoided by the use of thin separating lines of white or yellow. The paintings of animals and birds tended toward realism, whereas the human figure was stylized and its colors were arbitrarily conventional (white for female flesh, red for male). Heads were painted in profile, without shading. There was no

METROPOLITAN MUS. OF ART

These crop-harvesting sequences were painted on the wall of a tomb in Thebes, Egypt, in the fifteenth century B.C.

MURAL

***The Death of St. Francis,* one of a series of murals by Giotto di Bondone, illustrates a tendency, seen in thirteenth century Italian art, toward naturalism in form and setting.**

UNIVERSITY PRINTS

This detail from Michelangelo's murals on the ceiling of the Sistine Chapel depicts *The Creation of the Sun and the Moon.* The nine ceiling panels were finished in 1512.

FRATELLI ALINARI

Typical of dramatic, symbolical murals by twentieth century Mexican muralists is *The Departure of Quetzalcoatl,* from a fresco series by José Clemente Orozco.

DARTMOUTH COLLEGE

attempt at perspective. A pool, for example, would be depicted as seen from above, the fish in the pool shown in profile. Although such conventions may have limited the artist, they gave his work the sense of architectural propriety that never violates the structural character of the wall as a perpendicular plane—one of the prime requisites of mural painting. It is likely, but not certain, that Egyptian buildings were elaborately painted outside as well as inside.

Classical Murals. The Greeks used color as freely as did the Egyptians, applying paint to their marble statues and reliefs and to the inside and outside of their buildings. Greek murals, however, are known only through written descriptions. Apparently the Greeks used mural painting chiefly to decorate temples and public buildings, and only rarely for tombs, differing in this respect from the Etruscan custom. The Romans are thought to have decorated their interior walls with marble or painted imitation of marble up to the time of the empire, when they developed an architectural style in which painted columns formed a frame for landscape and figure painting. Thus, in the decorations of the Villa of the Mysteries in Pompeii are elaborate figure compositions, as also in the famous *Nozze aldobrandini* in the Vatican Library, which is presumed to be a representation of ritual marriage in ancient Rome. Oftener, however, Roman murals consist of a single figure isolated in the center of a painted panel, and in general the emphasis seems to have been on decorating a room in which painting was often combined with elaborately modeled stucco, rather than on figure and landscape composition. The painted work excavated in the baths of Titus and elsewhere in Rome during the sixteenth century aroused great admiration among the Italian painters of the time and influenced the later art of the Renaissance. The Roman paintings, particularly the grotesques, patterns of scrollwork, and realistic foliage and animal figures were admired by Raphael and his pupils for their freedom of technique and their inventiveness. Sixteenth century reproductions of these highly decorative paintings were numerous and detailed. See MOSAIC.

Italian Murals. The catacombs of Rome and Naples have yielded fourth century murals which are interesting principally as a late manifestation of classical painting imbued with a Christian purpose. By the fifth and sixth centuries the degenerated Roman art of these murals was replaced by a stronger (if stiffer) style—the Byzantine. The stylized type figures of this art remained unchanged for many centuries, and it is impossible to assign dates on the basis of style variations. It was not until the thirteenth century that the traditional Byzantine forms and coloring were superseded by the Italian art developed at Florence, Pisa, and Siena. Most renowned of the earlier mural painters was Giotto di Bondone (1266?–1367), who attempted more natural subjects in naturalistic setting and perspective.

In the early centuries the church had been divided on the question of representing Christ or any other member of the Trinity in painting. The councils of the church had repeatedly upheld the biblical injunction against graven images, and iconoclastic bishops had even defaced pictures of Christ painted on the walls of churches. In the earliest catacomb paintings Christ had appeared in pagan guise—as Hermes Criophoros, or Hermes Psychopompos. But gradually the propaganda value of mural paintings as lessons in sacred history for the illiterate masses had become evident, and by the late Middle Ages in Italy the way was clear for the humanistic revival of classicism that led to the Renaissance. Giotto's murals at Assisi and Florence, although worn by time, could at mid-twentieth century still be seen in the churches where they were painted. The fourteenth century school of Siena developed an imaginative type of mural painting, but failed to follow the road to naturalism taken by Giotto. It remained for the fifteenth century Florentine school to develop the style of mural decoration that later art historians were to associate with the Renaissance. The frescoes by Tommaso Guidi Masaccio (1401–28) in Santa Maria del Carmine were studied by the leading figures of the high Renaissance. Fra Angelico's (1387–1455) frescoes in St. Mark's are among the masterpieces of world painting; they are marked by a mystic insight and coloration. Benozzo Gozzoli (1420–98) is famous for his frescoes at San Gimignano and Pisa; Luca Signorelli (1441–1523) and his master Piero della Francesca (1417–92) produced powerful frescoes at Arezzo. All these muralists initiated a period of inspired church decoration that culminated in masterpieces by Leonardo da Vinci (*The Last Supper*), Raphael (*The School of Athens*), and Michelangelo (*The Last Judgment*), where the naturalist school flowered in a framework of monumental design. Almost all the great artistic figures of the Renaissance were muralists, working in fresco and tempera. It was not until the triumph of Venetian painting in the sixteenth century that mural painting was displaced in importance by easel painting and its oil technique. A late Venetian, Giovanni Battista Tiepolo (1693–1770), revived mural decoration in the grand manner of secular baroque. His early frescoes were done in Venice, and his later work in Madrid, where he created frescoes for palaces after 1763. Also working in Madrid, about a half century later, Francisco Goya y Lucientes decorated the entire Chapel of San Antonio de la Florida with painting that presaged the dynamic possibilities of twentieth century modern art.

French Murals. In the eighteenth century a rather reduced and intimate type of mural work was carried out by Jean Fragonard and François Boucher, of whose art fine examples can be seen in the Frick Museum, New York. Eugène Delacroix, one of the great nineteenth century colorists, executed murals for the chamber of deputies, the library of the senate, and the Church of Saint-Sulpice, all in Paris.

Murals in the Americas. The outstanding new world muralists were Mexicans, trained in European painting but looking to native Indian culture for themes. The Mexican school came into being in close connection with the Mexican Revolution, and by 1920 the Mexican government had turned over acres of wall space in government buildings and schools to the revolutionary painters, and had become the patron of one of the greatest enterprises in the history of mural painting. Matched only by the religious frescoes of the Florentine Renaissance, the antireligious frescoes of Mexico influenced an entire generation and helped set the tone of the country for decades. Muralists became governors of provinces, military advisers, leaders of parties, men of affairs—much as they had in Florence and the other Italian city-states. The leaders of the Mexican movement were Diego Rivera, trained in Paris during the heroic period of modern painting, José Clemente Orozco, Bernardo O'Higgins, Juan O'Gorman, and David Alfaro Siqueiros. The first practitioner of the new popular art seems to have been the ubiquitous "Dr. Atl" (Gerardo Murillo), volcanologist, inventor, and revolutionary painter. Fresco was the leading technique used until Siqueiros introduced such innovations as pyroxylin paint. ANTHONY KERRIGAN

BIBLIOG.-F. Crowninshield, *Mural Painting* (1887); F. H. Jackson, *Mural Painting* (1904); J. Ward, *Fresco Painting* (1909); W. Bayes, *Art of Decorative Painting* (1927); G. Hale, *Fresco Painting* (1933); H. Feibusch, *Mural Painting* (1946); E. W. Anthony, *Romanesque Frescoes* (1951); A. Maiuri, *Roman Painting* (1953); A. Grabar, *Byzantine Painting* (1953); M. P. Merrifield, *Art of Fresco Painting* (ed. 1953); G. Yazdani, *Ajanta* (4 vols. 1955); UNESCO, *Yugoslavia: Mediaeval Frescoes* (1955), *Masaccio* (1957).

MURANO, town, N Italy, Venezia Province, Veneto Region; on five islets in Venice Lagoon; 1 mile N of Venice. Murano is an important center for the production of fine Venetian glass, and there is an interesting collection of ancient and modern glass in the town museum. The Basilica of Santi Maria e Donato in Murano dates from the seventh century. The Church of St. Peter the Martyr contains important paintings. Pop. (1951) 7,576.

MURA RIVER. See MUR RIVER.

MURAT, JOACHIM, 1767–1815, French military leader and king of Naples, was born in La Bastide, near Cahors, and entered the French army in 1791. In 1796 he accompanied Napoleon I to Italy and then to Egypt, and on their return aided the coup d'état of 1799. Napoleon rewarded him with the command of the consular guard and the hand of his youngest sister, Caroline, 1800. Murat commanded the French cavalry at Marengo, at Austerlitz, through the Prussian campaign, and again in Spain; and his dash and daring contributed greatly to the French victories. In 1808 he was made king of Naples as Joachim I Napoleon. During the campaign against Russia he commanded the cavalry, but after the disastrous battle at Leipzig he deserted Napoleon and concluded a treaty with Austria in an attempt to save his own throne. After Napoleon's escape from Elba, Murat declared war on Austria, and was defeated at Tolentino. After Napoleon's overthrow at Waterloo, Murat escaped to Corsica, where he raised some troops, invaded Italy, was taken prisoner, court-martialed, and shot.

MURATORI, LODOVICO ANTONIO, 1672–1750, Italian antiquary, was born near Vignola, ordained a priest, 1694, and appointed a librarian at the Ambrosiana Library in Milan. After 1700 he was keeper of the archives at Modena. Muratori produced a 28-volume *Rerum italicarum scriptores* (1723–51) containing the works of medieval (500–1500) writers of Italian history. In the third volume of another compilation of historical sources, *Antiquitates Italicae medii aevi* (6 vols. 1738–42), he published the "Muratorian Canon," the surviving portion of a Roman document, written probably about 190, which contains an almost complete list of the New Testament writings regarded by the unknown author as canonical. This is the earliest such list known.

MURAT RIVER. See EUPHRATES RIVER.

MURCHISON, SIR RODERICK IMPEY, 1792–1871, British geologist, was born in Tarradale, Scotland. He entered the army, 1807, and served with Arthur Wellesley (later the duke of Wellington) in the Peninsular War. He left the army, 1814, and became active in the London Geological Society, before which he read his first scientific paper in 1825. In the 1830's his investigations of the fossiliferous strata of England and Wales resulted in the establishment of a new system which he named Silurian, 1835. Researches with Adam Sedgwick in Devonshire and Germany led to their jointly founding the Devonian system, 1839. Murchison then did a survey of Russian geological formations, established the Permian system, 1841, and published *The Geology of Russia and the Ural Mountains* (1845). He was a founder, 1830, and frequent president, of the Royal Geographical Society; and became director general of the geological survey and the Royal School of Mines, 1855.

MURCIA, province, SE Spain; bounded by the Mediterranean on the S and by the provinces of Almeria and Granada on the W, Albacete on the N, and Alicante on the E; area 4,069 sq. mi.; pop. (1958) 797,369. The province is generally mountainous with some fertile valleys and an alluvial plain along the coast. Murcia is drained by the Segura River and its tributaries. Chief cities are Murcia, the capital, and Lorca, Yecla, and the port of Cartagena. Agricultural products include truck produce, cereals, olive oil, wine, pepper, rice, hemp, and sheep. Fishing is a major activity. Lead-silver ore, iron, zinc, and sulfur are mined. There is some manufacturing of textiles and furniture. Originally under Carthaginian rule and later under the control of Romans and Visigoths, Murcia was part of an independent Moorish kingdom of Murcia created in the eleventh century.

MURCIA, city, SE Spain, capital of Murcia Province; on the Segúra River; 18 miles NNW of Cartagena. A highway and railroad junction, Murcia is an agricultural trade center dealing in truck produce, almonds, cereals, olive oil, and pepper. Its industries include silkworm culture, fruit and vegetable canning, silk and cotton spinning, tanning, and the making of hats and soap. The city is the site of a university (1915) and a conservatory of music and drama (1916), a fourteenth century Gothic cathedral, an eighteenth century episcopal palace, and an archaeological museum. Settled by the Romans, Murcia rose to importance under the Moors who made it the capital of the independent duchy of Murcia in the eleventh century. It was sacked and severely damaged during the Civil War, 1936–39. Pop. (1958 est.) 240,931.

MURDER is the wrongful killing of a person with the premeditated intent to cause death. (See INTENT; MALICE.) Since one is conclusively presumed to intend the probable consequences of his act, he who intentionally inflicts a wound likely to cause the victim's death is said to have intended such death and is guilty of murder. Where A intends to kill B but by accident kills C instead, A is said to have intended C's death by virtue of the doctrine of transferred intent. Premeditated intent is a necessary element of murder; where the intent arises on the spur of the moment the offense is common law manslaughter and in some states statutory second degree murder. See HOMICIDE; MANSLAUGHTER.

Attributes of Murder. The act of killing is not criminal unless the doer possesses that degree of mentality which is necessary to form the required intent. An insane person thus cannot be guilty of murder unless the act was committed during a lucid interval. At common law, a child under 7 years of age could not be guilty of a felony, and children between the ages of 7 and 13, although presumed prima facie incapable of the requisite intent, might be convicted on a showing to the contrary and suffer death. Although intoxication will not excuse the act of killing, such circumstance will reduce the offense to manslaughter where the degree of intoxication is sufficient to negate premeditation. The killing of an unborn child was not murder at common law, but it was murder if the child were later born and died of injuries suffered in the womb. Most states have provided that the killing of an unborn child is manslaughter. The inducing of abortion was not murder at common law, but it is manslaughter by various American statutes.

If an accidental killing occurs while the wrongdoer is engaged in the commission of a felony (rape, larceny, burglary, robbery, or arson), the killing is murder notwithstanding the complete absence of intent, premeditated or otherwise, to cause death. If accidental death occurs while the wrongdoer is engaged in committing a misdemeanor or other unlawful act (such as a trespass) the unintended killing is mere manslaughter. If the wrongdoer commits a battery (see BATTERY) on the victim and intends grievous bodily harm, the victim's unintended resultant death is murder, but if only slight harm is intended the killing is manslaughter.

To constitute murder at common law, the death must occur within one year and a day inclusive of the day on which the injury was inflicted. The victim's death must result from an act of the accused, a requirement that is sometimes complicated by causal contribution from plural sources. Where A and B simultaneously inflict wounds on C each of which in itself would be fatal, both are guilty of the murder of C. Where A's and B's causal contributions are consecutive in time, only one of them can be guilty of murder. Suppose that A inflicts a mortal wound on C, and that while C is in the hospital B unlawfully sets fire to the hospital and C is burned to death. B is guilty of felony-murder and A is guilty only of attempted murder. This result is explained by saying that B is the last wrongdoer, or that A's causal contribution (placing C in the hospital) is a mere condition upon which the real cause of death, the heat from the burning of the building, operated.

An accidental killing carries no criminal penalty (and the doer is liable civilly only in case of negligence) unless the accident happens while the doer is engaged in an unlawful act. A justifiable killing is one committed for the prevention of any forcible and atrocious crime, the execution by the proper official of a person sentenced to death in a regular proceeding, or a killing to prevent the escape of a prisoner or a person charged with a felony. The killing by military personnel of other enemy military personnel in the furtherance of war is not murder.

A killing in self-defense carries neither civil nor criminal liability, although the law at an earlier date subjected one who killed in self-defense to confiscation of property on the ground that both aggressor and victim were at fault. To be considered an act of self-defense, the killing must be reasonably necessary to prevent a like harm to the one attacked. The common law required the accused to retreat to avoid the violence of the assault. Modern law does not impose upon the accused the burden of determining whether retreat would be dangerous, and thus failure to retreat is no longer conclusive of guilt.

Those who assist the wrongdoer in the act of killing are guilty of murder as principals. It is not necessary that one so assisting actually participate in the act. It is enough that he is present and lending his encouragement. One who advises or procures another to kill the victim is guilty of murder as an accessory before the fact. One who after the killing and with guilty knowledge assists in concealing the crime or helps the perpetrator to escape is guilty of murder as an accessory after the fact. See ACCESSORY.

Degrees. There are no degrees of murder at common law. By statute, however, murder in the first and second degrees is recognized by most U.S. jurisdictions, and third degree murder by a few. These statutes confine murder in the first degree to homicide committed by poison, lying in wait, and other deliberate and premeditated killings, and those accompanying burglary, arson, rape, and robbery. Murder in the second degree occurs when there is no deliberately formed plan to take life and the wrongdoer is not engaged in committing one of the latter felonies, but where nevertheless there is an intent to kill formed instantaneously and the killing is without such provocation as would reduce the crime to manslaughter. Murder in the third degree is defined as reckless homicide or felony-murder committed while engaged in a felony other than those specified for first degree murder.

Trial. The accused is tried in the state where the act causing death was committed, because one state will not enforce the criminal law of another state. In most states the accused may be tried in either the county where the act was committed or the county where death ensued if each occurred in a different county; and he is entitled to a change of venue and may be tried in a different county on a showing that the state of public opinion prevents a fair trial. A person who is charged with a crime in one state and flees to another state need not be extradited by the second state. The obligation to deliver up the fugitive is thought to be moral only and based on comity among the states, although the literal wording of the Constitution (Article IV, Section 2) is to the contrary.

In a criminal trial the prosecution has the burden of proving guilt "beyond a reasonable doubt" in the sense that it must persuade the jury with evidence that the accused is in fact guilty. If it fails to do this, the prisoner is released, and in the usual case the prohibition in the state constitutions against double jeopardy attaches and the accused cannot be retried for the same capital offense. There is no statute of limitations for murder, that is, no time limit within which a person must be prosecuted.

Punishment. One who intentionally causes another's death is liable civilly for damages to the deceased's dependents under the wrongful death statute, as well as being liable for criminal punishment. The punishment for first degree murder varies among the states. In many states life imprisonment may be imposed instead of death, the jury deciding or recommending the particular sentence. The death penalty has been abolished in Alaska, Hawaii, Maine, Michigan, Minnesota, North Dakota, Rhode Island, and Wisconsin. In several states a verdict of manslaughter may be returned by the jury when the accused is charged with murder. Electrocution is the method of execution in Alabama, Arkansas, Connecticut, Florida, Georgia, Illinois, Indiana, Kentucky, Louisiana, Massachusetts, Nebraska, New Jersey, New York, Ohio, Oklahoma, Pennsylvania, South Carolina, South Dakota, Tennessee, Texas, Vermont, Virginia, and West Virginia. Lethal gas is the means used in Arizona, California, Colorado, Maryland, Mississippi, Missouri, Nevada, New Mexico, North Carolina, Oregon, and Wyoming. Hanging is prescribed in Delaware, Idaho, Iowa, Kansas, Montana, New Hampshire, and Washington. In Utah the accused may choose between a firing squad and hanging. Under federal legislation first and second degrees of murder are recognized, and within the special maritime and territorial jurisdiction of the federal government, whoever is guilty of murder in the first degree shall suffer death unless the jury specifies "without capital punishment." See CAPITAL PUNISHMENT. NEVILLE ROSS

MURDO, city, S central South Dakota, seat of Jones County; on the Milwaukee Railroad and U.S. highways 16 and 83; 38 miles SSW of Pierre. Livestock, poultry, and grain are produced in the area. Pop. (1960) 783.

MURFREESBORO, town, SW Arkansas, seat of Pike County; 95 miles SW of Little Rock. Lumber mills and wood products manufacture are the principal industries. Nearby is the only diamond mine in the United States. Pop. (1960) 1,096.

MURFREESBORO, city, central Tennessee, seat of Rutherford County; on the Louisville and Nashville Railroad and U.S. highways 41, 70S, and 231; 32 miles SE of Nashville. Murfreesboro is an important red cedar market and a shipping point for livestock, dairy products, and cotton. Principal manufactures include hosiery, silk and rayon goods, textile machinery, and lumber. Murfreesboro is the site of Middle Tennessee State College. The city was incorporated in 1817, and was the state capital from 1819 until 1825. It was named for Col. Hardy Murfree, a Revolutionary War soldier. Nearby is Stones River National Military Park, at the site of the Civil War Battle of Murfreesboro (Stones River). Pop. (1960) 18,991.

MURFREESBORO, BATTLE OF, or Battle of Stones River, a battle of the American Civil War, fought at Murfreesboro, Tenn., Dec. 31, 1862–Jan. 2, 1863, between a Confederate Army under Gen. Braxton Bragg and a Union force, the Army of the Cumberland, led by Gen. William Starke Rosecrans. The battle started early on the morning of December 31. Bragg attacked the Union flank, which was driven back in disorder, but the center of the Union Army held and the line was re-formed. During the next day Rosecrans occupied positions above the Stones River which came under heavy Confederate attack, but the fire of Gen. Thomas Leonidas Crittenden's guns and a charge by an Indiana unit made without orders on January 2 stopped the Confederate advance. Bragg retreated toward Chattanooga. Casualties were heavy on both sides, the North leaving 1,677 dead and the South 1,294.

MURGER, HENRI, 1822–61, French novelist and poet, was a native of Paris. He studied painting for several years and later served as secretary to Count Aleksei K. Tolstoi. His first and best known book, *Scènes de la vie de bohème*, which appeared serially in *Le Corsair* (1847–49), was a series of romantic, florid tales of artist and student life. Episodes in this work inspired Giacomo Puccini's opera *La Bohème* (1896).

MURGHAB RIVER, or Murgub River, rises in the N slopes of the Paropamisus Range, NW Afghanistan, and flows W and then NW into SE Turkmen Soviet Socialist Republic and N to Mary where it dries up in the Kara-Kum Desert. It is 529 miles long, and receives the Kaman and Kushk rivers.

MURIATIC ACID. See HYDROCHLORIC ACID.

MURILLO, BARTOLOMÉ ESTÉBAN, 1617–82, Spanish painter, was born in Seville into humble circumstances. His people recognized the boy's talent and he was apprenticed to the painter Juan del Castillo, an unimaginative but serious artist. The artist's materials in Castillo's studio included (it is said) only a few plaster casts and some stray fragments of sculpture; models were unavailable, and the apprentices would pose in turn. From Castillo, Murillo learned to paint "correctly," and he was soon earning his living by turning out *pinturas de feria* (pictures for the fair), religious images sold to the throngs at fair time and shipped overseas for Christian converts among the Indians in the Americas. Except in isolated pictures, Murillo never entirely overcame the pleasing style he developed in manufacturing prettified Madonnas for the market place. An unabashed appeal to the sentimental instincts of the mass was forever afterward his hallmark.

Travel and Influences. By 1642 Murillo was eager to visit the world centers of painting, especially in Italy. Not yet able to afford the trip to Rome, he went to Madrid and there was received by his fellow Sevillan, Diego Velázquez, court painter, who set Murillo to studying the Italian and Flemish masters in the Royal Gallery. For two years Murillo worked at copying, particularly the works of Jusepe (José) Ribera, the Italianized Spaniard, and Anthony Van Dyck, two painters who (together with Peter Paul Rubens, Michelangelo da Caravaggio, Titian, and Velázquez himself) remained the chief influences on Murillo's art. After two years of study Murillo earned the recommendation of the court painter, who presented his paintings to the king. The way was then open for the desired trip to Rome, but Murillo unexpectedly chose to return home to Seville.

Successive Styles. The Franciscan monks of the Convent of San Francisco were at that time seeking an inexpensive painter to adorn the walls of their cloister. Murillo contracted for the work, and covered the walls with 11 paintings, which variously revealed the strong color of Ribera, the chiaroscuro of Caravaggio, the powerful realism of Velázquez, and the suggestiveness of Van Dyck. In total effect, however, these early paintings came to be known as examples of Murillo's so-called *estilo frío* (cold style), for they showed a formal concern with line and color as opposed to his later emphasis on atmosphere. A canvas from this period titled *The Blessed Giles Before Pope Gregory IX* (purchased in 1957 by the North Carolina Museum of Art) is one of his great works. The inscription refers to the saint's ecstasy at the time of his appearance before the pope in Perugia, and the mystic portrait of Giles, as well as the studies of the other figures—a gamut of religious archetypes—is among the finest portraiture by any artist of the period. A style perhaps more characteristic, the *estilo cálido* (warm style), made its appearance about 1652. In the interval between his cold and warm periods, Murillo married a wealthy lady of Seville, thus enhancing his position in society, already fairly secure by reason of the popularity of his art. The *estilo cálido* was marked by luminous skin tones and vibrant colors. His outlines became softer, his figures rounder, and his colors warmer. Some of the best examples of this period are *The Nativity of the Virgin*, a *San Leandro*, and a *San Isidro* (the latter two in the Seville cathedral). In 1660 he opened an academy of art, and directed it actively for a time. His final style, the *estilo vaporoso* (misty style), in which the outlines tend to be lost in the light and shade, was developed about the time he was commissioned to paint 11 panels for the renovated Hospital de la Caridad, Seville. Begun in 1661, they occupied the artist for four years; the best of these paintings were later removed from the hospital and eventually came into the possession of various European museums. Generally considered his masterpieces, they include *Moses Striking the Rock*, *The Prodigal's Return*, and *St. Elizabeth of Hungary*. These paintings are not all in any one of his styles, and in some he combined all three styles.

In 1682, at the Capuchin Chapel of Saint Catherine, Cádiz, where he was painting *The Mystic Marriage of Saint Catherine*, Murillo fell from the scaffolding and suffered injuries from which he never recovered.

ANTHONY KERRIGAN

Murillo's *Flight into Egypt*

THE HERMITAGE, LENINGRAD, U.S.S.R.

MURMANSK, region, U.S.S.R., subdivision of the Russian Soviet Federated Socialist Republic; bounded on the N by the Barents Sea, E and S by the White Sea, S by the Karelian Autonomous Soviet Socialist Republic, W by Finland, and NW by Norway; area 53,100 sq. mi.; pop. (1956 official est.) 474,000, composed of Russians with Karelian and Lapp minorities. The Kola Peninsula comprises more than two thirds of the region's territory, composed of granite and gneiss formations with heavy glaciation effects. The region lies beyond the Arctic Circle, but the influence of the Gulf Stream keeps its shores ice-free the year around. Its northeast half is covered with tundra; the southwest is forested. The elevation reaches 3,963 feet in the Khibiny Mountains. The region abounds in marshes, lakes, and swift rivers with many rapids. As a result of the discovery in the 1930's of mineral deposits, including iron, copper, nephelite, columbium, platinum, nickel, apatites, phosphorites, and mica, large-scale power and mining industries developed. The most important of these are the Niva, Kandalaksha, and Tuloma hydroelectric stations and the mines and concentrating plants at Kirovsk, Monchegorsk, Yena, Nikel, and Pechenga. Murmansk Sea fisheries account for one fifth of the total Soviet catch. Lumbering and sawmilling are also major activities.

MURMANSK, city, U.S.S.R., Russian Soviet Federated Socialist Republic, capital of Murmansk Region, on the E coast of Kola Gulf of the Barents Sea; terminal point of the Kirov Railway; 635 miles NNE of Leningrad. Murmansk is the Soviet Union's northernmost ice-free port and its gateway to the North Atlantic. It has a large fish-processing combine, cold storage and cooperage plants, ship repair yards, and food products factories, and is a supply center for the merchant marine and for large fishing flotillas. It exports apatites, lumber, and food products and imports fish and coal from Spitsbergen and miscel-

SOVFOTO

Murmansk, founded in 1915, is located within the Arctic Circle in the Russian S.F.S.R. The city is on one of the Soviet Union's most important outlets to the Atlantic.

laneous industrial equipment. It is the seat of a teachers college, a merchant marine school, the Polar Research Institute of Fisheries and Oceanography, and administrative offices of the Soviet Arctic Sea route. During World War II Murmansk played an important role as the only Soviet European seaport accessible to American and British lend-lease convoys with military supplies, and it was about 50 per cent destroyed by German bombing. The city was largely rebuilt by the late 1940's, but declined in importance after the war as a result of Soviet annexation of several ice-free ports in the Baltic countries. Pop. (1956 official est.) 168,000.

MURNER, THOMAS, 1457–1537, German priest and satirist, an opponent of the Reformation, was born in Oberehnheim, studied at the Franciscan school in Strasbourg, and became a wandering scholar and preacher in Germany, France, and Poland. His religious poems gained him the position of poet laureate, 1505, under Emperor Maximilian I, and about 1509 he was made a doctor of theology at Verona. His most celebrated satirical works were *Narrenbeschwörung* (Exorcism of Fools), 1512, and *Von dem grossen Lutherischen Narren, wie ihn Doctor Murner beschworen hat* (On the Great Lutheran Fool: How Doctor Murner Has Exorcised Him), 1522.

MURORAN, city, Japan, SW Hokkaidō; on the NE coast of Uchiura Bay; 55 miles SSW of Sapporo. Muroran is an industrial center as well as one of the principal ports of Hokkaidō. Manufactures include pig iron, steel, machinery, electrical equipment, and synthetics derived from petroleum; the city's industries utilize coal from the nearby Yubari field. Coal, lumber, and paper are exported from Muroran's port. The city is the seat of the seaweed research laboratory of Hokkaidō Imperial University. The surrounding area has numerous hot springs. Pop. (1956) 135,571.

MURPHY, CHARLES FRANCIS, 1858–1924, U.S. political boss, was born in New York, N.Y., was elected leader of the 18th assembly district, 1892, and appointed commissioner of docks and ferries, 1897. On the retirement of Richard Croker, boss of Tammany Hall (the city Democratic political machine), Murphy was chosen his successor, 1902. As boss of Tammany, 1902–24, Murphy was probably largely responsible for the election of three mayors (George B. McClellan, William J. Gaynor, and John F. Hylan) and two New York governors (John A. Dix and William Sulzer) and exercised considerable influence in national politics as well.

MURPHY, FRANK, 1890–1949, U.S. jurist, was born in Harbor Beach, Mich., studied law at the University of Michigan, taught law at the University of Detroit, 1922–27, and was judge in the recorder's court in Detroit, 1923–30. He was mayor of Detroit, 1930–33, the governor general and high commissioner of the Philippines 1933–36, the governor of Michigan, 1936–38, and U.S. attorney general, 1939–40. In 1940 Pres. Franklin D. Roosevelt appointed him associate justice of the U.S. Supreme Court.

MURPHY, JOHN BENJAMIN, 1857–1916, U.S. surgeon, was born near Appleton, Wis., and practiced medicine in Chicago. After 1895 he was chief of the surgical staff of Mercy Hospital. He invented the Murphy button, a device that improves gastrointestinal surgery by helping to approximate the ends of severed intestines, and popularized artificial pneumothorax (collapsing a diseased lung so as to arrest the progress of tuberculosis).

MURPHY, WALTER PATTON, 1873–1942, U.S. industrialist and philanthropist, was born in Pittsburgh, Pa., and became president of the Standard Railway Equipment Manufacturing Company in 1919. He erected manufacturing plants in the United States and Canada for the production of his patented railroad supplies. Among his many philanthropies was a donation that established the Northwestern University Technological Institute.

WALTER DILL SCOTT

MURPHY, WILLIAM PARRY, 1892– , U.S. Nobel prize-winning physician, was born in Stoughton, Wis. He practiced medicine in Boston after 1923 and became an associate in medicine at the Peter Bent Brigham Hospital, 1928, and at the Harvard Medical School, 1935. His research in diseases of the blood led to his discovery of liver therapy in treating pernicious anemia, for which he shared the 1934 Nobel prize in medicine with George R. Minot (co-discoverer of the treatment) and George H. Whipple. Murphy also was noted for his research on diabetes. See ANEMIA.

MURPHY, city, SW Idaho, seat of Owyhee County; 33 miles SW of Boise. The city is located in farming and cattle country. It is on the path of the old Oregon Trail. Pop. (1957) 54.

MURPHY, town, extreme SW North Carolina, seat of Cherokee County; on the Hiwassee River, the Louisville and Nashville and the Southern railroads, and U.S. highways 19, 64, and 129; 89 miles SW of Asheville. Murphy is primarily a resort town, and produces lumber, hosiery, and yarn. The town was founded about 1830. Pop. (1960) 2,235.

MURPHYSBORO, city, SW Illinois, Jackson County; on the Big Muddy River and the Gulf, Mobile and Ohio, the Missouri Pacific, and the Illinois Central railroads; 76 miles SE of East St. Louis. The city is the trade and shipping center of the surrounding dairy country. Principal manufactures include shoes, flour, dairy products, clothing, and beverages. There are coal and silica deposits in the vicinity. Murphysboro was founded in 1843 and incorporated in 1867. Pop. (1960) 8,673.

MURRAY, ALEXANDER STUART, 1841–1904, Scottish archaeologist, was born near Arbroath. He was assistant keeper, 1867–86, and keeper, 1886–1904, of the Greek and Roman antiquities of the British Museum, and conducted excavations in Cyprus, 1894–96. His writings include *A Manual of Mythology* (1873 and numerous later editions), *Handbook of Greek Archaeology* (1892), and *The Sculptures of the Parthenon* (1903).

MURRAY, GEORGE GILBERT AIMÉ, 1866–1957, British classicist, was born in Sydney, Australia, studied at St. John's College, Oxford, and was professor of Greek at Glasgow University, 1889–99, and regius professor of Greek at Oxford, 1908–36. He was widely known for his translations of the plays of Euripides, Sophocles, Aristophanes, and Menander; for many books, including *History of Ancient Greek Literature* (1897), *The Classical Tradition in Poetry* (1927), *From the League to the U.N.* (1947), and *Hellenism and the Modern World* (1953); and for his advocacy of the movement for international union.

MURRAY, JAMES, 1719?–94, British governor of Canada, was born in Scotland. He entered the army at an early age and served in the West Indies and Europe. Taking his regiment to America, 1757, he commanded a brigade at the Siege of Louisburg, 1758, and was one of Gen. James Wolfe's three brigade commanders in the Battle of the Heights of Abraham, 1759. He was left in command of Québec after its surrender and defended it against the French; was appointed governor of Québec, 1760; and was governor of Canada, 1763–66. His attempt to conciliate the French Canadians brought him the enmity of English residents; he was recalled in 1766, faced an inquiry at the house of lords, and was exonerated. In 1774 he was appointed governor of Minorca, and defended it against the French and Spanish troops led by Louis des Balbes de Berton de Crillon, 1781–82, capitulating only after a defense of nearly a year. He returned to England, was tried by a court-martial, acquitted, and made a general, 1783.

MURRAY, SIR JAMES AUGUSTUS HENRY, 1837–1915, British lexicographer, was born in Roxburghshire, Scotland. He taught school, 1855–85, chiefly at Hawick and Mill Hill, near London. In 1879 he assumed the editorship of the *New English Dictionary on Historical Principles*, the purpose of which was "to furnish an adequate account of the meaning, origin, and history of English words now in general use, or known to have been in use at any time during the last 700 years." The 10-volume work (1884–1928) was almost complete at his death. He also wrote *The Dialect of the Southern Counties of Scotland* (1873).

MURRAY, JAMES STEWART, 1st **EARL OF,** 1531?–70, Scottish regent, natural son of James V and half brother of Mary, Queen of Scots. His surname is sometimes spelled Stuart Murray (or Moray). He studied at St. Andrews, 1541–44, and accompanied Mary to France, 1548. He was a Protestant sympathizer, and from 1556 he was the leader of the Reformers. After the return of Mary, 1561, he tried to dissuade her from "Romanizing" Scotland. He attempted to reconcile Elizabeth I and Mary until Mary married Henry Stewart, earl of Darnley, 1565. Murray then broke with his sister and was compelled to take refuge in England. He returned to Scotland, 1566, after the murder of David Rizzio, was implicated in the murder of Darnley, and left for France, 1567. He returned on Mary's abdication the same year, and was chosen regent. He defeated Mary's forces at Langside, 1568.

MURRAY, JOHN, 1741–1815, U.S. clergyman, called the father of American Universalism, was born in Alton, England, and while still a boy was taken to Cork, Ireland. Returning to England, he was a member of George Whitefield's Tabernacle, London, but in 1760 came under the influence of Universalism as preached by James Relly and was excommunicated by the Methodists. He came to America, 1770, preached the doctrine of universal salvation in New Jersey, New York, and New England; and in 1774 he made his home in Gloucester, Mass. In 1775 he became chaplain to the Rhode Island regiments, but ill health forced him to leave the army, and in 1779 he became minister of the Independent Church of Christ, Gloucester. In 1793 he was installed as minister of a society of Universalists in Boston.

MURRAY, LINDLEY, 1745–1826, Anglo-American grammarian, was born in Swatara, Pa., the son of a Quaker. He made a fortune as a merchant in New York City and in 1784 moved to York, England, where he devoted himself to writing educational and religious works. He is best known as author of *A Grammar of the English Language* (1795).

MURRAY, PHILIP, 1886–1952, U.S. labor leader, was born of Irish parents in Blantyre, Scotland, and at the age of 10 began to work in the coal mines, work that he resumed when his family emigrated to Pennsylvania, 1902. In 1911 he became a U.S. citizen. In 1912 he was elected to the United Mine Workers international board. He was elected UMW vice-president in 1920 (an office he held until 1942), and worked with UMW President John L. Lewis in miners' negotiations and in setting up the Congress of Industrial Organizations. He organized the Steel Workers Organizing Committee (later United Steelworkers of America), 1936, and became its chairman. In 1940, when he succeeded Lewis as president of the CIO, he continued to serve as president of the steelworkers. In 1950 he proposed that all U.S. trade unions be united, a proposal partially realized by the American Federation of Labor–CIO merger, 1956.

MURRAY, THOMAS RANDOLPH, 1st **EARL OF,** died 1332, Scottish regent, was the nephew of King Robert I, the Bruce of Scotland. Fighting for the Bruce in 1306, Murray (or Moray) was captured at Methven and in order to save himself from execution swore allegiance to Edward I. In 1308 he was recaptured by Sir James Douglas, and from that time was a faithful follower of Bruce, who made him earl of Murray. He captured Edinburgh, 1314, went on the expedition into England, 1316, was sent to England as a diplomat, 1328, and became regent when Bruce died, 1329.

MURRAY, city, SW Kentucky, seat of Calloway County; on the East Fork Clarks River and the Louisville and Nashville Railroad; 36 miles SE of Paducah. Murray is in a tobacco and livestock area, and has an annual purebred Jersey cattle exhibition. The city is the site of Murray State Teachers College. Pop. (1960) 9,303.

MURRAY, city, N Utah, Salt Lake County; on the Jordan River, the Denver and Rio Grande Western and the Union Pacific railroads, and U.S. highways 50, 89, and 91; 7 miles S of Salt Lake City. The city is a farm goods trade center. Its industries include smelting, food processing, and canning. Murray was founded in 1869 and is named for Eli H. Murray, governor of Utah, 1880–86. The city was incorporated in 1902. Pop. (1960) 16,806.

MURRAY RIVER, Australia's longest river, rises in the Muniong Range of the Australian Alps near Mount Kosciusko in SE New South Wales and flows in a westerly direction through Albury, Echuca, Swan Hill, Mildura, and Renmark, south into Lake Alexandria, and then into Encounter Bay and the Indian Ocean; length about 1,520 miles. For 1,200 miles the Murray constitutes the boundary between New South Wales and Victoria. With its tributaries the river drains an area of 414,253 square miles—about one-seventh of the continent. Among the Murray's tributaries are the Murrumbidgee–Lachlan River system and the Goulburn and Loddon rivers. The Hume Dam at Albury forms Australia's largest reservoir, with a capacity of 2 million acre-feet.

MUR RIVER, or Mura River, Austria, Hungary, and Yugoslavia; rises in the Hohe Tauern Mountains in Austria near the border between the provinces of Salzburg and Carinthia and flows first E, then generally S, past Graz in Austria, to Legrad, Yugoslavia, where it enters the Drava River; length about 300 miles. The Mur forms parts of the Austria-Yugoslavia and Hungary-Yugoslavia borders. There are hydroelectric stations in Austria at Mixnitz, Peggau, and Graz. The Mur is navigable from Graz to Legrad, a distance of about 125 miles.

MURRUMBIDGEE RIVER, Australia, rises in the Muniong Range of the Australian Alps near Cooma in SE New South Wales, flows N through the Australian Capital Territory and then W through Wagga Wagga and Narrandera to the Victoria border where it joins the Murray River; length about 1,050 miles. Its major tributary is the Lachlan.

MURRY, JOHN MIDDLETON, 1889–1957, English writer and editor, was born in London and studied at Brasenose College, Oxford. He edited the *Athenaeum*, 1919–21; founded and edited the *Adelphi*, 1923–48; and edited a pacifist journal, *Peace News*, 1940–46. Murry, who once described himself as "part snob, part coward, part sentimentalist," was noted for turning savagely upon those who were, at one time or another, his closest friends. D. H. Lawrence and Aldous Huxley, who were among those accorded this treatment, drew extremely unflattering fictionalized portraits of Murry—Lawrence in *Women in Love*

(1920) and *Aaron's Rod* (1922) and Huxley in *Point Counter Point* (1928). Among Murry's many books are *The Evolution of an Intellectual* (1920); the novels *Still Life* (1916) and *The Voyage* (1924); *Studies in Keats* (1930); the autobiography *Between Two Worlds* (1930); an uncomplimentary biography of Lawrence, *Son of Woman* (1931); and *Unprofessional Essays* (1956).

MURSHIDABAD, town, E India, E West Bengal State, Murshidabad District; on the Bhagirathi River; immediately N of Berhampore. Traditional industries still carried on in Murshidabad include ivory carving, embroidering, and silk weaving. Agricultural products of the area are rice, oilseed, jute, wheat, and barley. The town was the capital of Bengal, 1704–90, and is still the residence of the titular nawabs of Bengal.

MUS, or Mush, also Moush, province, SE Turkey, in Armenia; bounded by the provinces of Erzurum on the N, Bingöl and Diyarbakir on the W, Bitlis and Siirt on the S, and Agri on the E; area totals 2,946 square miles. Elevations reach 10,000 feet in the south. Mus is drained by the Marat River, a headstream of the Euphrates. Main centers besides Muş, the capital, are Manzikert and Bulanik. The economy hinges on wheat and sheep. Muş was part of the Armenian Empire (2400–612 B.C.) and of the medieval Armenian Ardzrunian kingdom. In World War I the Turks massacred many Armenian inhabitants. The population consists of Turkicized Armenians and Kurds. (For population, see table in Turkey article.)

Muş, the capital town, lies near Lake Van, 100 miles W of Van. There are important mineral springs and wheat fields. In Muş are ruins of a tenth century Armenian castle built by King Moushegh Daronian and the ancient Armenian pilgrimage monastery of Sourp Garabed. A famous war dance is named for Muş. The citizens are Turkicized Armenians. (For population, see Turkey map in Atlas.)

MUSACEAE, the banana family, a group of tropical perennial herbs, some of which resemble trees in their size and wood. The family consists of six genera and approximately 60 species. The genus *Heliconia*, to which 30 of the species belong, is composed of stout tropical American herbs with large, oblong leaves. The genus *Musa*, made up of 20 species, includes the common banana, *M. sapientum*. It is the most important member of the family economically (see BANANA.) Members of the Musaceae family bear flowers that are irregular and grow in spikes with subtending spathes. The immense convoluted leaves have parallel veins. The Musaceae are monocotyledons.

MUSA DAG, or Musa Dogh, mountain, S Turkey, in Cilicia, Hatay Province; on the Mediterranean Sea; elevation 4,446 feet; 15 miles W of Antioch. In World War I a group of Armenian mountaineers from nearby Zeitun, called *Kaj* (braves), paralyzed the entire Turkish East army by holding strategic Musa Dag, an act which facilitated the Allied war victory. The heroic defense by these Armenians inspired Franz Werfel to write the book *The Forty Days of Musa Dagh.*

MUSASHINO, city, Japan, central Honshu, Tokyo Prefecture, immediately east of Tokyo. Musashino is a largely residential community. It is a trading center for raw silk, wheat, and sweet potatoes; and it has a precision instrument plant, metalworks, and an electrical machinery factory.

MUSCA, the Fly, a southern constellation that lies just south of Crux, the Southern Cross, and therefore is too close to the south celestial pole to be seen from Canada or most of the United States. In places from which it can be observed it appears on the meridian at about 10 P.M. on May 9. Musca contains a few stars that are brighter than the fourth magnitude, as well as some star clusters and variable stars. One of these variables, R Muscae, a star close to α Muscae on the star map, changes from magnitude 6.5 to magnitude 7.6 and back to magnitude 6.5 in less than a day. The brightest star in the constellation is α Muscae; the second brightest is β Muscae, which is really a double star whose components are little more than one second of arc apart.

MUSCARINE, a crystalline alkaloid found naturally in the fly fungus mushroom, *Amanita muscaria*, and produced synthetically as a nitrogen ester derived from choline. (See ALKALOID; ESTER.) The compound, $C_8H_{19}NO_3$, is a white, moisture-absorbing crystal or sirupy liquid. It is soluble in water and in alcohol and slightly soluble in chloroform or ether. When ingested by the body, it increases the flow of saliva, tears, and perspiration. Vomiting and diarrhea are induced along with increased and labored breathing. The heart slows and the pupils of the eyes contract. Mental confusion and dizziness also occur. If untreated, patients suffering muscarine poisoning may have convulsions, a few hours after which coma and death usually follow. General antidotes for mushroom poisoning are not appropriate in muscarine poisoning, since they usually increase vomiting and diarrhea. Atropine is the specific antidote for muscarine poisoning.

DAVID HOLDEN—CAMERA PRESS-PIX

Spectators squat on Muscat's battlements to watch a hockey match. Hockey is the favorite local sport.

MUSCAT, or Mascat, also Masqat, town, E Arabian Peninsula, capital of Muscat and Oman independent sultanate; on the Gulf of Oman of the Arabian Sea; 527 miles WSW of Karachi, Pakistan. Shut off from the interior by rugged mountains, Muscat is connected by highway with Matrah to the northwest, the chief commercial center of the state and the starting point for caravan routes. Muscat is a port of call on the steamer route between Bombay, India, and Basra, Iraq. Trade is carried on chiefly with India, Pakistan, and the Persian Gulf states. Rice, wheat, flour, coffee, sugar, and cotton piece goods are principal imports, and dates, limes, pomegranates, mother-of-pearl, and fish are exported. The city is the residence of the sultan and a British consul. It has a British-operated post office and telephone and telegraph system. The Portuguese captured Muscat in 1508. After losing Hormuz in 1622, they made Muscat their Arabian headquarters until they were expelled in 1648 by the Persians. (For population, see Near East map in Atlas.)

MUSCAT AND OMAN, also Oman, sultanate, SW Asia, extending along the Arabian Sea and the Gulf of Oman for almost 1,000 miles, and inland about 100 miles to an ill-defined border on the edge of the Arabian Desert; bounded by Trucial Oman on the NW, Saudi Arabia on the W, and Aden (Qishn and Socotra sultanates) on the SW; area about 82,000 sq. mi.; pop. (1965 est.) 700,000. Muscat and Oman includes the detached areas of Ruus al jibal (to the north on the Masandam Peninsula) and Gwadar, an enclave on the West Pakistan coast. Muscat is the capital. See map in Atlas, Vol. 20.

Physical Features. Three physical regions may be distinguished: the rugged Akhdar Mountains (highest point Jebal Sham, 9,900 ft.), the narrow coastal plains, and the interior plateau, which borders on the great desert Rub'al Khali ("Empty Quarter"). The climate is dry and hot, although in winter temperatures range between 60° and 70°F. Average annual rainfall in Muscat is only between 3 and 4 inches. Sporadic rainfall in the higher hills, mostly in winter and averaging more than 10 inches annually, results in torrential flows through deep gorges that drain either to the sea or to interior salt basins. There are fertile soils on the coastal plains, in the lower valleys, and in the scattered oases. Natural vegetation in the more humid areas includes oleander, tamarisk, euphorbia, buckthorn, acacia, and milkbush; thin, sandy soil and desert shrubs characterize the interior tableland.

Social Features. The population is mainly Arab, particularly in the interior, but there are also Persians, Baluchi, Indians, and Negroes in the northeastern coastal towns and Qaras in the southwest. Most of the country's inhabitants live on the northeast coast. The cities include Muscat, Matrah, Sohar, Nizwa, 'Ibri, and Salala; all except Matrah and Salala have fewer than 10,000 inhabitants.

Economic Features. Agriculture is the leading occupation but is limited by a severe water shortage. Dates, cereals, sugarcane, vegetables, grapes, limes, pomegranates, and mangoes are the chief products. Camels bred in Oman are prized in Arabia. Fishing and pearl harvesting are important in the Gulf of Oman; some manufacturing of copper and brass utensils, leather and woven goods, and mother-of-pearl items is carried on in the towns. Commercial production of crude oil was begun in 1964, and export was begun in 1967. In 1968 production was more than 11 million tons a year. There are no railroads, but there is an auto road that connects Muscat with other towns on the northern coast.

Government. Muscat and Oman is a monarchy that is ruled by a dynasty dating from 1741. There are strong trading ties with Great Britain. There is a semi-independent state in the Akhdar Mountains. The sultan of Muscat and Oman is assisted in legislative and administrative duties by a semiofficial council of leading chiefs.

History. Muscat and Oman was an early link between the Mediterranean and the Far East, and its sailors were widely known. In the seventh century it became part of the Islamic world but remained largely independent of the caliphates and the Turks. Before the twelfth century it elected chieftains who ruled from Nizwa, and thereafter it was loosely governed by nomadic chieftains. In 1508 Muscat and its hinterland passed to the Portuguese, who held it until 1648 when it passed into Persian control. In mid-eighteenth century the Persians were expelled, and a vast sultanate, which soon came to rule over much of southwest Asia and northeast Africa, was established. After the death of Said bin Sultan in 1856 the sultanate began to decline and came under British influence. A treaty of friendship and commerce in 1951 reaffirmed British connections with Muscat. In 1967 Britain returned the Kuria Muria Islands to the sultanate. See ARABIAN PENINSULA.

GEORGE J. JENNINGS

BIBLIOG.–W. Phillips, *Unknown Oman* (1966); *Oman: A History* (1968); W. Thesiger, *Arabian Sands* (1959).

MUSCATEL, a sweet, full-bodied, fortified wine made from several varieties of muscat grapes and produced in France, Spain, Portugal, Italy, and the United States. If made from such grapes as Muscat Frontignan and Muscat Canelli, muscatel is a white wine; if made from a dark-skinned variety such as Muscat St. Laurent or Muscat Hamburg, it is a red wine. The California variety primarily uses Muscat of Alexandria grapes. It is the practice in France and Spain to expose the grapes to the warm sun until they have almost shriveled to raisins. The dense must, or juice, obtained by pressing the grapes is fermented, but before all the sugar has been converted into alcohol the must is fortified by the addition of brandy; as a result the alcoholic content of the wine may be increased to 21 per cent.

MUSCATINE, city, SE Iowa, seat of Muscatine county; on the high bluffs of the Mississippi River; 27 miles SW of Davenport. A bridge on the Mississippi connects Iowa and Illinois at Muscatine. The city is predominantly a manufacturing center; its industries include millworking, food processing, and the manufacture of pearl buttons and office equipment. Melons are grown on nearby Muscatine Island. Muscatine is a trading center for the surrounding rural area. Founded in 1833 as a trading post, the settlement originally was named Bloomington. Later it was renamed for Mascoutin Indians living in the area. (For population, see Iowa map in Atlas.)

MUSCLE, animal tissue composed of fibers, either in cells or syncytia (many cells fused together), specialized for the process of contraction through its characteristic proteins, actin, myosin, and tropomyosin. See ANATOMY, HUMAN.

Movement is the simple, common sign by which we distinguish whether or not an animal is alive; and in all save the most primitive organisms, movement is produced by muscle cells. In mammals like ourselves, cells of this type make up about 40 per cent of the body mass—all the meaty part in fact—and a large fraction of the central nervous system is devoted to controlling their movements. Clearly it is upon the strength, swiftness, and endurance of their muscles that most animals have depended for survival, so we may assume that the contractile machinery has been refined within its limits as far as the forces of natural selection can ensure.

Despite the wide apparent differences found among animals, it seems that the essential biochemical mechanism for contraction is everywhere the same: the machinery consists of protein (usually actomyosin) and the fuel is always provided by adenosine triphosphate (ATP), which yields energy when it is hydrolyzed to adenosine diphosphate (ADP). See ADENOSINE DIPHOSPHATE AND ADENOSINE TRIPHOSPHATE; EVOLUTION; HYDROLYSIS; PROTEIN.

In examining different types of muscle, therefore, we are merely looking at variations on a theme and trying to understand how the basic mechanism is adapted to suit the particular job that the muscle must perform. One essential fact about the contractile mechanism is that chemical energy must be expended continuously all the time a force is being exerted, even though no external work is being performed. In this important respect muscle differs from a rubber band, which can, of course, exert tension continuously without cost. Although it is possible for muscles to be specialized so that they can maintain tension economically, they thereby are unable to shorten rapidly and produce large amounts of mechanical power. Both properties cannot, it seems, be combined in a given muscle type probably because the actomyosin is specialized for either a high or a low rate of ATP splitting. For this reason it is quite common to find "slow" and "fast" muscles within a single limb—each muscle doing the job for which it is best suited.

Another important source of difference is the way in which contraction is controlled. In the case of skeletal muscles, whose function is to produce coordinated movements, the muscle must not contract until it receives orders from the central nervous system to do so. At the other extreme is cardiac (heart) muscle, which must keep on contracting rhythmically throughout life. This rhythmic activity is generated within the muscle cells; the nervous connections of the heart serve merely to modify the beat, not to initiate it. Intermediate properties are found in smooth muscles in the walls of the gut and other viscera, such as blood vessel walls and the ducts of glands, in which the nerves serve to initiate contractions as well as to modify the self-generated contractile rhythm. See HEART; INTESTINE; STOMACH.

Chemical Composition. As with most tissues, muscle consists largely of water (about 80 per cent) and cannot function without it. Replacement even by the closely related substance D_2O (heavy water) stops the muscle from functioning. The remaining 20 per cent consists largely of protein; this is, incidentally, the reason why meat is such a valuable food. About one fifth of this protein is inert and insoluble. Much of it is in the form of collagen fibers, which serve to bind the muscle fibers together and to transmit their force to the tendons. Similar protein within the cells performs a similar structural function. Another fifth of the protein is similar to what might be found in any other metabolically active tissue and consists largely of the very many enzymes that are responsible for catalyzing and guiding the intense chemical processes necessary for the maintenance of the contractile machinery. The remainder is made up of the special contractile proteins that are the distinguishing feature of muscle. Two types of protein, myosin and actin, are known to be absolutely essential for contraction; they constitute roughly 35 per cent and 15 per cent of the total protein respectively. A third type of protein, tropomyosin, is also fairly abundant (10 per cent of total), and it is probably involved in the mechanism by which contraction is switched on and off by the active control of the calcium ion concentration within the cell.

Myosin consists of molecules with a weight of 500,000, which are visible with the electron microscope. They sre shaped like spermatozoa though they are very much smaller, having a compact "head" region about 40 A wide by 300 A long and a long "tail" about 20 A wide and 1,000 A long (1 A, or angstrom unit = 10^{-8} cm). The head of the myosin molecule seems to be the very kernel of the contractile machinery for it possesses two distinct chemically active sites, one for binding it to actin and the other for catalyzing the hydrolysis of ATP. Thus, within this small volume there are the means both for producing breakdown of the chemical fuel and also for producing a mechanical effect. The function of the tail seems to be purely mechanical; myosin molecules, both in solution and in muscle fibers, tend to aggregate and form filaments whose tails run parallel to one another along the axis of the filament and whose heads protrude as knobs from its surface in a regular helical arrangement.

The actin molecules are smaller (molecular weight 60,000) and approximately spherical, with a diameter of 55 A. They also have a tendency to polymerize, that is, link together to form long chains, Characteristically, two such chains form simultaneously, winding around each other to form a two-stranded rope. Actin has no enzymatic properties, but it does bind ATP. This bound ATP is split to ADP but remains bound when the molecules polymerize.

When solutions of actin and myosin are mixed, they combine to form actomyosin, and the solution becomes very viscous. If ATP is added along with the cofactors calcium and magnesium, active splitting of ATP occurs and at the same time the protein not only precipitates, but it shrinks down actively to form a dense plug. The significance of this "superprecipitation" was appreciated in the early 1940's by Albert Szent-Györgyi, who correctly predicted that if, instead of their random arrangement in solution, the actomyosin molecules could be properly oriented, as they are in living muscle, they would actively shorten and develop tension. If the ATP is added under conditions where no splitting can occur—for example, if there is insufficient calcium ion to activate the ATPase (the ATP-splitting site on the myosin head)—then actomyosin dissociates again into its two constituent proteins and the viscosity of the solution falls. This is the counterpart of relaxation in living muscle.

In addition to the proteins, other substances of interest are those involved in supplying the contractile machine with energy. ATP is the only fuel that the contractile proteins can react with directly, but not much of it is present—only about 3 mM/kg (millimoles per kilogram), which is enough for eight brief contractions. Since a living muscle can perform many more contractions than that, it is evident that the broken down ATP must be rapidly regenerated from other energy stores. The one closest to hand is phosphorylcreatine (PC), which is held in equilibrium with ATP by a special enzyme, creatine phosphotransferase (CPT).

Electron micrographs of the three types of muscle: cardiac (x 13,725); skeletal (x 13,050); and smooth (x 17,325).

PORTER AND BONNEVILLE, FINE STRUCTURE OF CELLS AND TISSUES (1968), LEA AND FEBIGER

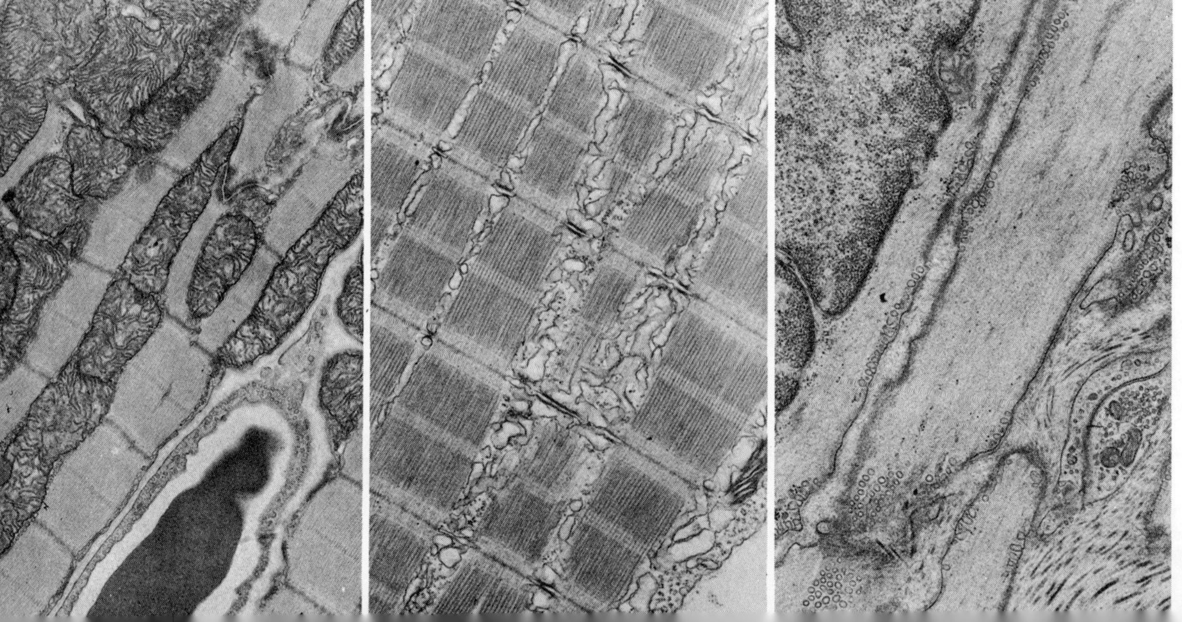

(a = during activity)

$$\mathrm{ADP} + \mathrm{PC} \underset{b}{\overset{a}{\rightleftharpoons}} \mathrm{ATP} + \mathrm{Creatine}$$

(b = during recovery)

This reaction proceeds rapidly even during activity, so that the only net reaction is the breakdown of PC, and the level of ATP remains unaltered. Moreover, there is a much larger quantity of PC present—about 20 mM/kg, or enough for nearly 100 contractions. Even so, the store of PC must finally be regenerated; the energy for this is derived from the much slower process of oxidative phosphorylation in which the energy obtained from oxidizing glycogen, the carbohydrate store of muscle, is partly used to rephosphorylate ADP. When this happens, the equilibrium shown above is displaced so that the reaction then runs from right to left and PC is rebuilt. If the supply of oxygen is insufficient (oxygen debt), as may occur during even moderate exercise, additional energy may be obtained from glycogen by hydrolyzing it to lactic acid (which later must be oxidized). Glycogen is such a concentrated store of energy that it suffices for 600 to 20,000 contractions, depending on the state of nutrition of the muscle and the availability of oxygen.

A third group of important substances is the inorganic ions. The vital roles of calcium and magnesium as cofactors to enzymes have already been described. Inorganic ions are also important in determining the ionic strength (roughly speaking, the charge density) of the interior of the cell, which has a vital effect on the properties of proteins. Indeed, the reactions of actin and myosin described above are found only within quite narrow limits of ionic strength. Finally, the potassium ions in the cells (and the sodium ions outside) are instrumental in setting up the differences of electrical potential across the cell membrane upon which the system of signaling instructions from the brain and spinal cord depends. See BIOCHEMISTRY; METABOLISM.

Structure and Ultrastructure. One of the greatest achievements of molecular biology has been the correlation of the chemical events with the observable ultrastructure of the muscle and with the changes that occur during contraction. The structure of muscles visible through the light microscope (maximum resolution about 0.5 μ, or 0.5×10^{-4} cm, set by the wavelength of visible light) has been studied for more than a century. These studies form the basis for the present classification of muscles into striated (with a regularly repeated pattern of cross-banding) and smooth types (lacking such cross-banding). All types of muscle are composed of elongated fibers, which may be either single cells or syncytia. In vertebrates both the cardiac and the skeletal muscles are striated, and smooth muscles are used only for internal control of gut, blood vessels, and other viscera. In other phyla, striated muscles are usually found in situations where fast action is required, e.g., in the wing muscles of insects. However, the functional distinction is not clear-cut, and unstriated muscles are found with a wide variety of functional characteristics and, indeed, of internal structures.

The small, spindle-shaped smooth muscle cells of vertebrates, though they contain actin and myosin of the usual type, have not so far yielded clear evidence of unique internal ultrastructure. For this reason the remainder of this section will deal with the ultrastructure of striated muscles, where advances have been made recently in correlating ultrastructure, chemistry, and molecular configuration.

The internal structure of a typical striated muscle fiber is indicated diagrammatically in Fig. 1. The whole fiber, a syncytium formed by the fusion of many cells, is a cylinder 50 to 100 μ in diameter, with a tough outer skin called the sarcolemma. The fiber, which may be many centimeters long, is subdivided at regular intervals by transverse Z discs into sarcomeres. The contractile protein forms solid cords, or fibrils, about 1 μ in diameter, which run continuously from one end of the fiber to the other. In between the fibrils is the sarcoplasm, which contains many of the enzymes involved in energy supply, glycogen granules, and at least three types of important organelles.

Figure 1

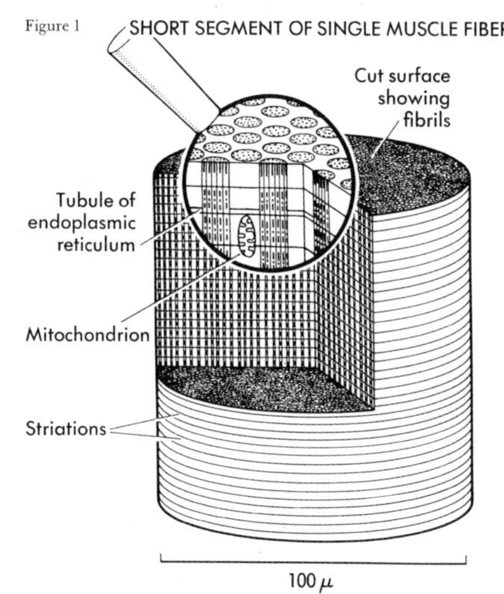

D. R. WILKIE, MUSCLE (1968), EDWARD ARNOLD LTD., LONDON

Nuclei lie just beneath the sarcolemma and seem to be essentially similar to the nuclei in other cells. Mitochondria, where oxidative phosphorylation occurs, also resemble those from other active tissues. They are most numerous in types of muscle that have a high rate of oxidative metabolism, such as the heart muscle of small mammals. The location of a mitochondrion is indicated in Fig. 1.

Sarcoplasmic reticulum is seen in a characteristic form, though the precise details differ from one type of muscle to another. The arrangement in frog muscle is shown in Fig. 2. Fine transverse tubules

FROM PEACHEY, 1965, IN D. R. WILKIE, MUSCLE (1968), EDWARD ARNOLD LTD., LONDON

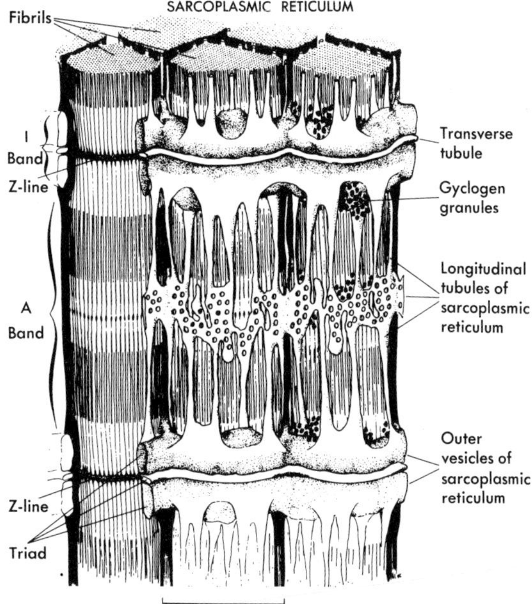

Figure 2

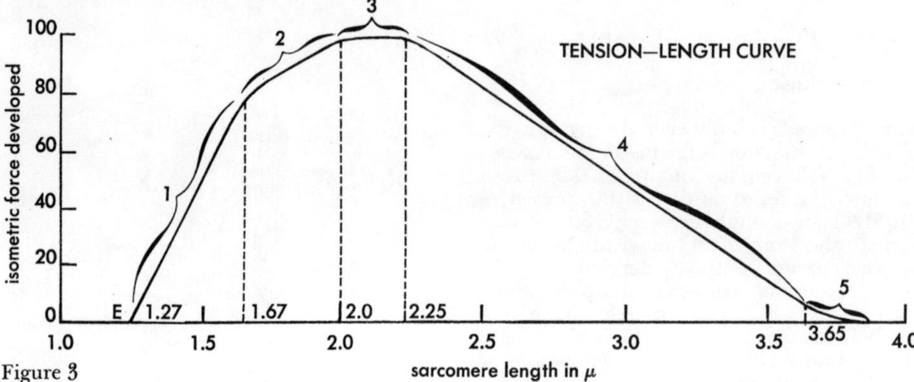

Figure 3

extend in from the surface (where they are open) along the plane of the Z discs. Extending longitudinally between the fibrils are other ramifying tubules. At intervals the two systems come into close contact, forming structures called triads. In resting muscle it appears that the ionized calcium is actively accumulated by the outer vesicles of the triads, to such a degree that its concentration in the sarcoplasm is reduced below the level (about 10^{-8} molar) at which the actomyosin ATPase can operate. When the surface of the fiber becomes depolarized, a message, presumably electrical in nature, passes in along the transverse tubules and triggers off the release of calcium. This then activates the biochemical mechanism of contraction.

The fibrils themselves are solid cords of protein with the banded structure that gives rise to the striation of the fiber as a whole. The central part of the sarcomere is occupied by the A band, a region of high order and protein density. The banded structure becomes far more intelligible when examined at high magnification, for the protein is then seen to be arranged in fine filaments (as in the left-hand part of Fig. 2). The filaments characteristic of the A band are about 100 A in diameter. They are arranged in a very regular hexagonal pattern and consist of myosin. The central zone of the myosin filaments is thinner than the rest because it contains no heads and thus no ATPase; and at the very center is a denser region where the myosin filaments appear to be held in register by transverse struts.

Attached to the Z discs, and extending between the myosin filaments, are thinner filaments (about 50 A in diameter) that consist largely of actin. The two sets of filaments can slide freely past each other and this is what happens when the muscle changes in length. ATP can diffuse into the fibril from the sarcoplasm. Thus there are present in the region of overlap all the constituents that have been shown biochemically to be necessary for contraction, and there is good evidence that this is where contractile force is actually developed. The exact details of how the conversion of chemical into mechanical energy occurs are still not known. The enzymatically active myosin heads thst stick out around the myosin filaments may act as cross-bridges in forming attachments to the actin. If so, they might have to undergo quite a complicated motion; for the observed shortening of muscle is so great that each cross-bridge would be obliged to attach, shorten, and detach several times, rather like a person pulling in a rope hand over hand. On the other hand, there is evidence to support a scheme whereby during contraction there is an active change in the effective angle of a rigid attachment of the myosin globular part of the cross-bridge to the actin filament. It proposes that the head is attached to the myosin backbone by two flexible couplings separated by a linear region 400 A long that allows, over a considerable range of interfilament spacings, attachment with the same orientation. See CELL.

The mechanical properties of muscle are important both for the light that they shed on the fundamental contractile mechanism and also because the usefulness of muscle to the organism resides in its capacity to exert force and perform work. If a muscle is held at fixed length (isometric) and stimulated, it develops a force. The amount of force depends on the length (Fig. 3) because of the way in which the overlap of the filaments varies with length. Presumably the double overlap of actin filaments at short lengths reduces tension development because it interferes with the regular pattern of attachments to the myosin filaments. Skeletal muscles are arranged in the body so that they operate close to their optimal length.

Under isometric conditions no external work is done, though a certain amount of internal work is performed in stretching tendons and other internal elastic structures. External work is done if the active muscle is allowed to shorten and lift a load. The simplest case to consider is the one where the force remains constant (isotonic contraction). As might be anticipated from Fig. 3, the larger the load, the smaller is the distance that it can be lifted. The relation between force and speed is also quite characteristic (Fig. 4). Even when completely unloaded the muscle has a fixed maximum speed of shortening, V_0, just as under isometric conditions it has a maximum tension, F_0. In between, the points fall on a smooth curve of the shape shown. This curve can be fitted accurately by several equations. The best known of these was devised by A. V. Hill in 1938; it treats the curve as part of a rectangular hyperbola

$$(F + a)(V + b) = (F_0 + a)b$$

where a and b are constants.

The explanation at molecular level for the shape of the force-velocity curve is still not known; in-

Figure 4 FORCE—VELOCITY CURVE

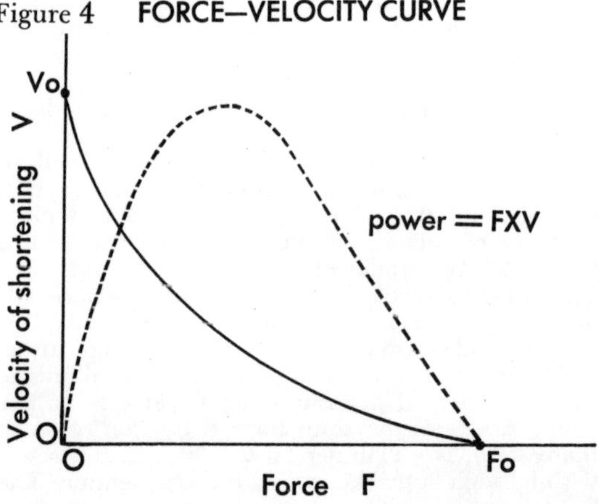

deed, it is one of the aims of theories about the action of the cross-bridges to produce such an explanation. The practical consequences of the shape of the curve are, however, quite plain. The mechanical power production ($F \times V$, indicated by the interrupted line) is zero at both ends of the curve and rises to a maximum at a point where F and V are at about one third of their maximal values. In order to perform a given task most effectively, therefore, it must be matched to the force and speed of the muscles. This matching is seen in very clear form in the choice of gear ratio for a bicycle; it is also involved in setting the size for hand tools such as spades, which must be neither too big nor too small. Smooth and cardiac muscles also have force-length and force-velocity curves similar to Figs. 3 and 4. The main differernces are that whole muscles, as distinct from isolated single fibers, have connective tissue between fibers, so that an appreciable force may be required to stretch the resting muscle. If so, the total tension in the active muscle will be the sum of two components that depend on length, the resting tension curve plus a bell-shaped curve (similar to Fig. 3) denoting the extra tension developed on activation.

The force-velocity curves from different muscles are similar to each other, save that some are more curved than others. The value of F_0 does not vary widely—from about 1 to 4 kg/cm^2; but V_0 varies over a much wider range—from 0.1 muscle lengths/sec (tortoise at 0°C) to 24 muscle lengths/sec (mouse at 35°C). The maximum power output likewise varies; for human muscle it is approximately 0.3 hp/kg muscle in a single movement.

The only muscles that seem to differ markedly from this pattern are the wing muscles of certain insects. These are very regularly cross-striated but their myosin filaments extend the full length of the sarcomere and appear in electron micrographs to be permanently bonded to the actin filaments. Such muscles operate over only a very short range of lengths, so they do not give curves similar to Figs. 3 and 4. Their characteristic property is to exhibit negative mechanical resistance. If they are connected to a system that can oscillate mechanically (during life the wings and thorax provide such a system) it will be thrown into vibrations that are maintained all the time that the muscle is active. Despite the smallness of the length changes, the frequency is so high that a considerable quantity of power may be generated.

Energetics and Thermodynamics. Muscle is essentially a machine for converting chemical energy into mechanical energy, but, unlike a heat engine, it operates at uniform temperature. It has already been explained how the ATP that is broken down by the contracting proteins is rapidly regenerated, so that the only net reaction during a brief contraction is the hydrolysis of PC. During recovery, however (or during the late stages of a contraction of long duration), energy is made available from the recovery processes—oxidation or hydrolysis of glycogen—to rephosphorylate ADP and thus finally rebuild the store of PC. Just what it is that switches the recovery processes on is a matter of considerable interest. Oxidative phosphorylation in the mitochondria is certainly provoked by even the small traces of ADP resulting from contraction; and the enzymes at the beginning (i.e., the glycogen end) of the glycolytic chain are also rapidly changed from an inactive to an active form, though what product of the contractile activity is responsible is still not clear. See GLYCOLYSIS; KREBS CYCLE.

Even though during normal exercise both initial and recovery processes may run concurrently, the distinction between them remains important. In the initial process an actual transformation of energy from one form to another takes place, while the recovery process is a purely chemical sequence. Moreover, the two can be separated experimentally, since the recovery process can be prevented by withholding oxygen and poisoning the glycolytic enzymes.

The distinction between the two was first clearly demonstrated by A. V. Hill in 1913 as a result of his studies on the heat production of muscles. It had been known for some time that muscles produced heat during activity—indeed, shivering is an important mechanism of heat production that homeothermic animals like ourselves use to maintain body temperature. Hill noticed that an approximately equal quantity of heat was produced for about 20 minutes after contraction had ceased, and he attributed it to the recovery processes. This explanation was supported by the demonstration that the recovery heat was very much reduced if oxygen was withheld from the muscle. See BODY TEMPERATURE; HILL, ARCHIBALD VIVIAN.

The heat production of muscles has continued to be studied as the outward sign of the chemical changes within. The rise of temperature is small (e.g., a few thousandths of a degree in the brief contraction of a frog's muscle), but sensitive techniques have been developed for measuring the change accurately and even for following its time course. These have revealed that very little heat is produced during relaxation and that the rate of heat production is greater when a muscle is shortening than when it is not.

The relation between energy production and chemical change is set by the First Law of Thermodynamics, which states that over any chosen interval of time:

$$\text{heat produced} + \text{work produced} = n_1\,(-\Delta H_1) + n_2\,(-\Delta H_2), \text{ etc.}$$

where n is the number of moles of each reaction and ΔH is the corresponding enthalpy change in kcal/mole. The enthalpy change is, of course, the ordinary heat of reaction as measured in an open calorimeter at atmospheric pressure, taken with a negative sign, so that $-\Delta H$ is a positive quantity in an exothermic reaction. In experiments in which the recovery processes sre suppressed, so that the only net reaction is the breakdown of PC, it is indeed found that under a wide variety of conditions of contraction, (work + heat) is proportional to ΔPC and the corresponding ΔH is -11.0 kcal/mole. See ENTHALPY; THERMODYNAMICS.

A more difficult problem is to determine the efficiency of muscular contraction, E. $E = \dfrac{\text{work obtained}}{W_{max}}$, where W_{max} is the maximum work that could theoretically be obtained from the same chemical reactions; that is, it is equal to the total change of free energy. Thus, $W_{max} = n_1(-\Delta F_1) + n_2(-\Delta F_2)$, etc.

For the whole process of contraction followed by oxidative recovery, ΔF is known to be about —700 kcal/mole glycogen; and it can be calculated that the efficiency is never greater than 20 to 25 per cent in the muscles of either frogs or human beings. Thus more than three quarters of the free energy available is wasted by irreversible degradation into heat. Now there would certainly be great advantages for an animal that was able to evolve muscles of higher efficiency without sacrificing mechanical performance. There must be a good reason why such muscles have not evolved, and if we knew the reason it would teach us something important about the design of the contractile machine. When an engineer is confronted by an inefficient machine, his first concern is to find out in what parts most of the energy wastage is occurring. When we ask the same question about the contractile machine the answer is most unsatisfactory. Since we do not know what value to assign to ΔF for the splitting of PC *in vivo*, we still do not know whether most of the energy wastage occurs during the conversion of chemical energy into mechanical work in the initial process, or during the much slower and purely chemical sequence of the recovery process. See WORK.

In considering the factors that limit exercise in a whole animal, the important distinction is not so much between initial and recovery processes as between hydrolytic energy sources (PC splitting, formation of lactate from glycogen) and oxidative ones, since the two have quite different characteristics as energy sources. Everything necessary for the hydrolytic reactions is already present in the muscle. They can therefore proceed at very high rates although the total amount of energy is limited. For oxidation, on the other hand, oxygen must be brought in from the atmosphere via lungs and bloodstream. This severely limits the rate at which energy can be produced, although the total amount of energy available is virtually unlimited because of the very large amounts of foodstuffs stored in the body: enough for one month of life for normal people, one year for the obese (a gallon of fat provides enough energy to bicycle 2,000 miles).

The consequences of this dual mechanism is that we are able to work very hard for short periods of time, up to 4 hp for a single impulsive movement such as that of a sprinter accelerating at the start of a race. However, as tasks of longer and longer duration are attempted, the relative contribution of the hydrolytic stores diminishes and the power output falls toward the level available from oxidation. Oxygen consumed at 1L/min yields about 0.1 hp. Even the best athletes cannot consume much more than 5L/min, so their steady-state power output cannot exceed 0.5 hp. Most ordinary people do well to achieve 0.3 hp. Among other animals it is interesting to note that some of them have muscles specialized in one or the other type of energy source. Thus the rabbit, with its white muscles, depends almost exclusively on hydrolytic energy to enable it to sprint to its burrow. The hare, on the other hand, which has no burrow, has red muscles and depends on oxidation for the endurance that it needs to escape from its enemies.

The Control of Contraction. The initiation of contraction at the biochemical level by the release of calcium from the endoplasmic reticulum has already been described, and it was mentioned that this process was set going by the depolarization of the membrane of the muscle fiber. This will now be explained. Muscle cells, like nerve cells and axons, normally have a potential difference of 50 to 100 mV between the negatively charged inside and the outside, and it is maintained because the resting cell membrane is impermeable to sodium. It is when this potential difference becomes smaller that contraction is initiated. Moreover, if the change of potential is rapid enough the permeability of the membrane itself is altered so that it becomes briefly very permeable to sodium. The result is an action potential, or explosive depolarization that is propagated along the muscle fiber. The strength of contraction is, over a certain range at least, graded according to the degree of depolarization. However, the explosive nature of the action potential ensures that during life the membrane is either fully depolarized or not depolarized at all; this is the basis of the so-called "all-or-none" law.

The normal sequence of events *in vivo* is that such an action potential originates in the spinal cord and is transmitted down a motor nerve fiber to the muscle. Within the muscle the nerve fiber branches, each branch passing to a muscle fiber. The recipient group of muscle fibers, which are obliged by this arrangement to contract all together, is called a motor unit. Its size varies from 5 to 2,000 fibers, depending on the accuracy of control required.

The terminal branches of the nerve axon are very fine, and the electrical energy in their action potential is too small to depolarize the much larger muscle fiber directly. However, there is a special junctional region, the end-plate, that acts as a power amplifier. The arrival of an impulse down the nerve fiber triggers off the release of a small quantity of acetyl choline, which acts directly on the membrane of the muscle fiber and initiates an action potential in it.

In response to a single action potential, most skeletal muscles respond by giving a twitch—a brief contraction followed by relaxation. Since the electrical response is very brief compared with the twitch, it is possible to generate a second action potential long before the response to the first has died away. If this is repeated at a high enough frequency the result is a maintained contraction, or tetanus. In cardiac muscle the action potential lasts about as long as the mechanical response, so this type of muscle cannot be tetanized, which is just as well from the functional point of view.

Coordination of Movement. Muscles in the body relax completely when they are not called on to exert a force. By voluntary control it is possible to contract even single motor units at will, and the strength of contraction is smoothly controllable up to a maximal value by controlling the number of motor units activated and the frequency of the action potentials stimulating them.

Muscles can only pull, they cannot push; and the elaborate movements of the body result from the way that the muscles are attached to the system of levers provided by the skeleton. These attachments are far subtler than may at first sight appear, for most muscles run over not one pivoting joint, but over two or even more. This means that the muscle can produce a variety of movements; the biceps, for instance, since it extends from the outer tip of the shoulder blade to the ulna in the forearm, can raise the arm from the trunk, flex the elbow, and rotate the forearm into a palm-upward position. Which of these movements actually occurs depends on which other muscles contract at the same time, thus neutralizing the unwanted actions. When driving in a screw with the forearm horizontal, for example, the elbow is prevented from flexing by an appropriate contraction of the triceps, which can easily be felt.

Even the simplest movements thus involve the cooperative action of several muscles, and quite a large fraction of brain and spinal cord is employed in ensuring this cooperation and checking on its success by means of sensory receptors in the muscles, tendons, and joints. The result, perhaps the skilled movement of a dancer or athlete, is easy to admire but very difficult to analyze. D. R. WILKIE

BIBLIOG.–R. D. Adams, D. Denny-Brown, and C. M. Pearson, *Diseases of Muscle* (1962 ed.); Hugh Davson, *A Textbook of General Physiology* (1964 ed.); Peter Karpovich, *Physiology of Muscular Activity* (1965 ed.); D. R. Wilkie, *Muscle* (1968).

MUSCLE, DISEASES OF, disorders affecting striated muscle. The diseases are of diverse and, in many cases, unknown origins. Undoubtedly, the intricate structure of the muscle fiber must play a large part in its various susceptibilities to malfunction. Only one portion of the fiber may be affected, the remainder left to degenerate, atrophy, or regenerate according to the disease and its severity. See ANATOMY, HUMAN; DISEASE; MUSCLE.

Attempts at classifying these disorders have been mostly on the basis of the following factors or combinations thereof: the primary chemical anatomic site affected; causative agents; clinical syndrome presented. However, no one system of classification so far has been satisfactory or complete in all respects.

The diagnostic attributes of a muscular disease are reflected in altered quantity and quality of contraction, and in the topography, or distribution, of muscular involvement. There is no single disease in which all of the muscles of the body are affected. Each disorder has its own unique topography and reflects the unique structural qualities of the musculature, its characteristics stemming from such factors as fiber size and number, vascular supply, and/or subtle metabolic differences. Many diseases that initially affect other tissues (such as collagen, nerve, and vascular disorders and systemic neoplasms) may ultimately affect voluntary muscles, but they are not considered to be true muscle diseases. One disease, myasthenia gravis, is due to a defect at the myoneural junction and is manifested by a characteristic syndrome of episodic, progressive muscular weakness. See CONNECTIVE TISSUE, DISEASES OF; PARALYSIS; POLIOMYELITIS.

Trauma, infection, disuse, and senility are the most common causes of muscular malfunction. The rarer myopathies, all with genetic components to a greater or lesser degree, include: the muscular dystrophies; congenital disorders such as amyotonia congenita (marked by gross weakness and flaccidity in infants) and several types of myotonias (inability of the muscle to relax after contraction); abnormal hormone control by the thyroid, adrenal, parathyroid, or pituitary glands; periodic flaccid paralyses (commonly associated with a cation imbalance, usually potassium); and malfunctions due to developmental, structural, or enzymic defects of the muscle cell. See CELL; ENDOCRINOLOGY; HEREDITY; HORMONE; ION; METABOLISM; METABOLISM, DISEASES OF; MUSCULAR DYSTROPHY.

BIBLIOG.–R. D. Adams, D. Denny-Brown, and C. M. Pearson, *Diseases of Muscle* (1962 ed.); P. B. Beeson and W. McDermott, eds., *Textbook of Medicine* (1967 ed.); G. H. Bourne, ed., *The Structure and Function of Muscle*, Vol. III (1960); T. R. Harrison and others, *Principles of Internal Medicine* (1966 ed.).

MUSCLE SCHOALS, a series of rapids on the Tennessee River in Alabama, formerly about 36 miles long with a drop of 132 feet. Congress first acted in 1828 to improve the shoals, then navigable only seasonally. Army engineers dug a channel that by 1890 made the river navigable in all seasons. The National Defense Act of 1916 led to the construction of a hydroelectric dam and two nitrate plants for the manufacture of munitions during World War I. Although the Muscle Shoals projects were later neglected because of political controversy over public ownership of utilities, they formed the nucleus of the Tennessee Valley Authority development project in 1933. See TENNESSEE VALLEY AUTHORITY.

MUSCOVITE, a mineral of the mica group, formula $KAl_2Si_3AlO_{10}(OH)_2$. Muscovite occurs as thin, transparent sheets, and as pale green, pale red, or pale brown monoclinic crystals with specific gravity 2.77-2.88 and hardness 2.5-3.0. The mineral is birefringent; i.e., it exhibits double refraction. It is the commonest of the mica minerals, and it is found as a principal constituent of fine-grained sediments, many metamorphic rocks, some classes of igneous rocks, and particularly in granite. Large crystals of muscovite occur in veins. In the form of thin, transparent sheets, it was once used for window panes in Russia, where it was commonly known as Muscovy glass; hence the origin of the name. Both natural and synthetic muscovite are used in the electrical and electronic industries, chiefly for insulation; in paper and paint manufacturing; as a lubricant, dusting powder, and filler; and for producing special artistic effects, as in decorative inlay work.

MUSCOVY COMPANY, an early joint-stock trading company initiated by Sebastian Cabot and chartered in England in 1555. Having reached an agreement with Tsar Ivan IV, the Terrible, the company engaged in trading and exploring in Russia and Asia and participated in the search for a northwest passage. After Tsar Alexei rescinded its privileges in 1649, it declined in importance, surviving as one among many companies trading with Russia.

MUSCOVY DUCK, a perching bird, *Cairina moschata*, of the duck family, Anatidae, ranging from Mexico to Argentina. It has a long, broad body and usually weighs 8 to 10 pounds. The plumage of the Muscovy duck has white wing patches on a lustrous blue-black background. Although this hardy breed has been domesticated in Brazil and Germany, the Muscovy duck's varying size, egg production, and quality of meat have not made it marketable on a large scale in the United States.

MUSCULAR DYSTROPHY, a group of diseases of genetic origin that occur usually before the age of thirty and that are characterized by muscular weakness that progresses to final atrophy or wasting. There are no lesions in the nervous system. These diseases are classified into three main groups: the Duchenne variety, predominantly affecting young males, with involvement first of the pelvic and leg muscles; the fascio-scapulo-humeral form, in which the face and pectoral girdle are affected first; and the other limb-girdle dystrophies, of varying patterns of weakness and wasting. Pain is seldom a factor in muscular dystrophy. Symptoms depend upon changes in the muscles and loss of strength. The person whose facial muscles are affected looks drawn and haggard and loses expressiveness. When shoulder muscles are affected the whole shoulder area droops and the scapulae stand out in a wing form. When the disease occurs in children, it usually affects the muscles of the buttocks and of the calves of the legs. In the first and last types the muscles increase in bulk but also become weak because the muscle tissue is replaced by fat. There is no known cure for muscular dystrophy. See METABOLISM, DISEASES OF; MUSCLE; MUSCLE, DISEASES OF.

MUSES, in Greek mythology, nine goddesses who became the patronesses of the liberal arts and sciences. The daughters of Zeus and Mnemosyne, the personification of memory, these nine goddesses were Clio, the muse of history, represented with a papyrus roll or books; Euterpe, of lyric poetry, who carried a flute; Thalia, of comedy and pastoral poetry, whose attributes were a comic mask and a shepherd's staff; Melpomene, of tragedy, usually distinguished by a tragic mask; Terpsichore, of choral song and dance, represented with a lyre; Erato, of love poetry, who also usually bore a lyre; Polyhymnia, of sacred song, represented in an attitude of reflection; Urania, of astronomy, shown holding compasses and a globe; and Calliope, of epic poetry, usually distinguished by a tablet and stylus. The Muses were frequently associated in legend with Apollo, who as their leader was called Musagetes. They were first worshiped among the Thracians, and a large cult existed at Pieria; hence the Muses were sometimes called Pierides.

MUSEUM, an institution for research, teaching, exhibition, and conservation in one or more fields of human activity, such as art, science, history, or industry. It often occupies a single building, such as the great national museums or famous art museums like the Louvre in Paris and the Metropolitan Museum in New York. It may, however, consist of a number of buildings, each housing a separate department or otherwise situated to display its contents to best advantage. Outdoor museums may display actual examples of objects or eras in their chosen field, such as the history of house architecture or geological development and plant life of a certain region.

Museums may be classified in several ways. According to fields of specialization, for example, there are museums of art, history, archaeology, ethnology, technology, and natural science. Classified by the type of effective control, there are, for example, school, college and university, company, private, and public museums. Others might be considered in special categories—as, for example, children's museums, which do not usually restrict themselves to one field but present numerous subjects in a manner that is meaningful to children, such as by emphasizing three-dimensional objects to heighten the reality of the children's experience and providing opportunities to handle many of the specimens.

Purpose. The purpose of a museum has varied in time and in place. Before the early nineteenth century only private collections were known as museums; they contained whatever objects were of interest to their owners. As museums became public institutions, their purpose was simply to house and display whatever collections came into their possession. Many European museums owe their existence to the assembling of various private collections—of kings, nobles, merchants, religious groups, and others. The British Museum, founded in 1753, originated with the collection of a physician, Sir Hans Sloane (1660–1753). (See BRITISH MUSEUM.) The Louvre, opened to the general public in 1793, exhibited the royal collections. The Prado in Madrid also began with the royal collections. (See PRADO.) It was founded in 1819, but was used in its early years mainly by art students, professors, foreigners, and well-to-do persons. In Europe it was often difficult for the general public to gain admittance to museums. Without adequate preparation the visitor, even if he complied with the various procedures required, could learn little from museum exhibits, for they were not arranged in a selective, coherent, and informative manner; to him they were just collections of curiosities. As museums began to recognize their wider public responsibility they began to make exhibits more informative to the nonspecialist.

In the United States museums have largely evolved as public institutions, and so there has been much emphasis upon their educational function. Although the essence of a museum is the preservation and exhibition of objects and a museum must devote a large portion of its efforts to this end, the purpose of the museum is significant in the selection of objects and the manner of their exhibition. If an exhibit is to inform and educate, it will be selected and arranged to provide the greatest opportunity to understand man's development or achievement in art or science. Objects may be grouped together to depict, for example, the life of an American Indian tribe or the interior of a colonial home. Paintings may be arranged according to a particular school or period of time. As museums have become more educational in purpose, their activities have been enlarged by providing lectures and specialized tours; classes in art, music, dance, and theater to encourage participation in the arts; loan collections to schools or other museums; and the publication of informative material. Research is confined

The British Museum, famous for its National Library and its vast collections of printed matter and art objects, contains the Elgin Marbles from the Parthenon at Athens.
BRITISH MUS.

generally to specialists who use museum collections as their primary source material, as in the fields of archaeology and paleontology. Art museums, which may have the additional purpose of increasing man's aesthetic appreciation and enjoyment, need to pay particular attention to the arrangement and lighting facilities for its objects.

History. The museum in Western culture precedes ancient history. The emergence of the museum as a concrete thing cannot be fixed in time by historians. Archaeologists frequently unearth unusual assemblages of objects that represent prehistoric private collections. The word *museum* itself is derived from the ancient Greek temple of the Muses, which was a place for study or meditation. The museum of Alexandria contained a wide collection of specimens, and this encyclopedic approach to learning has been characteristic of museums since then.

During the Renaissance private collections of curiosities or objects of art were variously known as museums, galleries, closets, or cabinets. They were assembled by wealthy noblemen who became interested in antiquities during the revival of classical influence. Throughout succeeding centuries it became the hobby of the rich to collect objects during their travels to serve as symbols of their wealth and leisure.

The eighteenth century collector usually restricted his accumulation to related objects, and it is from this type of individual museum that the art gallery, natural history museum, and other specific types of museums had their beginning. In the transference of the private picture gallery to the public art museum the contemporary conception of paintings as decoration was carried over into exhibition. Works of art were hung in tiers according to size, shape, and color in large, high-walled rooms, and it was not until the individual painting became more important than the decorative ensemble that modern installation practices were instituted. See ASHMOLEAN MUSEUM; ESCORIAL; HAGUE, THE.

In the United States two of the earliest private collections that became public museums were the Peale Museum in Philadelphia and the old Boston Museum of the early nineteenth century. These were private ventures; admission was charged and the museums not only contained collections of art, minerals, and zoological phenomena, but had a tendency to include side shows, convention halls, and even legitimate theaters. The history of vaudeville in the United States, for example, owes something to the museums of the past—the "professor" in the museum of the 1850's bore a striking resemblance to the barker in the carnival of 1910.

The conception of a museum as a public institution with responsibilities to all the people rather than merely to those who would or could pay admission was greatly encouraged by the founding of the Smithsonian Institution in Washington, D.C., in 1846. James Smithson (1765–1829) had two ideas of far-reaching significance in the museum field: that the United States should have a competent museum of science, and that such a museum should be free to the public. Smithson's concept included not only the preservation and presentation of objects but also the conducting of scientific research and the dissemination of the knowledge so gained through the publication of reports. (See SMITHSONIAN INSTITUTION.) Not long after Smithson, Louis Agassiz (1807–73), a European immigrant, established at Harvard University the plan that eventually resulted in the extensive system of scientific museums in Cambridge, Mass. To a considerable degree Agassiz' scheme provided the prototype for the university museum. See ACADEMY OF NATURAL SCIENCES OF PHILADELPHIA; AMERICAN MUSEUM OF NATURAL HISTORY; BROOKLYN INSTITUTE OF ARTS AND SCIENCES.

The fine arts museum in the United States evolved from collections of paintings and sculptures held by private individuals, libraries, and gentlemen's clubs and the miscellany that accumulated in local, state, and federal buildings. At first large art museums were to be found in only a few of the major population centers, but after World War I they spread to smaller cities, enabling most people to visit a museum of fine art with little trouble or expense. See HUNTINGTON LIBRARY AND ART GALLERY; METROPOLITAN MUSEUM OF ART; NATIONAL GALLERY OF ART.

Philanthropy. Much of the development of museums, especially those founded by philanthropists, is closely associated with prominent individuals. Desiring to see their wealth devoted to useful purposes, leaders in industry and finance in the United States and abroad contributed increasingly to museums after the mid-nineteenth century. In most instances such men aided already existing museums by granting them funds for special purposes or by presenting them with valuable pictures or collections purchased for that purpose. Some, however, established museums. The first of the major philanthropists in the United States was George Peabody (1795–1869), who attained great stature as an international financier. In his native New England he founded three museums—the Peabody Museum at Salem, Mass., the Peabody Museum of Natural History at Yale University, and the Peabody Museum of Archaeology and Ethnology at Harvard University. See PEABODY, GEORGE.

World's Fairs express the progress of their times and contain relatively extensive museum exhibits. A great impetus to the expansion of museums in the United States was the Centennial Exposition in 1876 at Philadelphia, which gave the American public the opportunity to see many outstanding European and Oriental works of art. A world's fair itself sometimes serves as the basis for the founding of a museum. At its conclusion the local promoters may find themselves in the possession of museum material from all parts of the world. The actual owners—individuals, corporations, or foreign countries—would often prefer to be relieved of the expense of transporting the material back home. A local philanthropist may provide a suitable building for the permanent housing of these carefully selected exhibits. This was the case in the founding of the Field Museum of Natural History in Chicago. Originally known as the Columbian Museum, its collection began with materials from the World's Columbian Exposition of 1893. Marshall Field was the philanthropist who provided the funds to construct a permanent building.

UPI

The Solomon R. Guggenheim Museum in New York City was designed by Frank Lloyd Wright. Paintings are displayed along single spiral ramp within the windowless cylinder.

Specialized Museums. In modern times there has been a development of small specialized museums. These vary considerably in subject matter and are widely scattered geographically. There are museums specializing in such subjects as early automobiles, cowboy life, clocks and watches, fox hunting, medals, and electric streetcars. There are also museums of historic houses that have been preserved and restored. Regional or site museums are of the type found at Mesa Verde National Park in Colorado or at Paestum, Italy, where excavations unearthed ancient ruins.

The United Nations Educational, Scientific, and Cultural Organization has a museums and monuments division to assist in the growing worldwide interest in museums, particularly in underdeveloped countries. This division offers consultation services to member nations of UNESCO; initiates various educational and protective programs, such as a manual for the protection of cultural materials in times of armed conflict; and publishes materials pertaining to museums.

J. O. BREW

BIBLIOG.–S. Lane Faison, Jr., *Guide to the Art Museums of New England* (1958); Herbert and Marjorie Katz, *Museums, U.S.A.* (1965); Eric Larrabee, ed., *Museums and Education* (1968); Jane and Theodore Norman, *Traveler's Guide to Europe's Art* (1959); Walter Pach, *The Art Museum in America* (1948); Smithsonian Institution, *Museums Directory of the U.S. and Canada* (1965 ed.); Eloise Spaeth, *American Art Museums and Galleries* (1960); Francis H. Taylor, *The Taste of Angels* (1948); UNESCO, *Organization of Museums* (1967).

IMPORTANT MUSEUMS OF THE WORLD

COUNTRY AND CITY	MUSEUM	YEAR FOUNDED	COLLECTIONS
ARGENTINA			
Buenos Aires	Museo Argentino de Ciencias Naturales (Argentine Museum of Natural Sciences)	1823	Two million botanical, geological, and zoological exhibits
	Museo Etnográfico (Ethnographical Museum)	1904	Archaeology of Central and South America; anthropology; ethnography of the Americas, Asia, Oceania, and Africa
	Museo Nacional de Bellas Artes (National Museum of Fine Arts)	1895	Classical art; modern European, American, and Argentinian art
AUSTRALIA			
Adelaide	South Australian Museum	1856	Zoology of central and southern Australia, ethnology of Australia
Melbourne	National Gallery of Victoria	1859	Paintings—old masters and modern; sculpture and minor arts
Sydney	Australian Museum	1827	Natural history, mineralogy, paleontology, ethnology
AUSTRIA			
Vienna	Graphische Sammlung Albertina (Albertina Graphic Art Collection)	1776	About 1 million prints; 32,000 drawings; miniatures; sketchbooks
	Kunsthistorisches Museum (Museum of Fine Arts)	1891	One of the finest general art collections—European paintings, antiquities, armor, musical instruments, costumes and carriages
	Naturhistorisches Museum (Natural History Museum)	1748	Zoology, anthropology, geology, mineralogy, paleontology, botany
	Osterreichische Galerie (Austrian Gallery)		Controls three museums which contain Austrian medieval painting and sculpture, baroque art, and nineteenth and twentieth century painting and sculpture

IMPORTANT MUSEUMS OF THE WORLD (Continued)

COUNTRY AND CITY	MUSEUM	YEAR FOUNDED	COLLECTIONS
BELGIUM			
Antwerp	Koninklijk Museum voor Schone Kunsten (Royal Museum for Fine Arts)	1810	Paintings by Dutch masters, nineteenth and twentieth century Belgian art
Brussels	Musées Royaux d'Art et d'Histoire (Royal Museums of Art and History)	1835	Prehistoric, Egyptian, Greek, Roman, Oriental, and American Indian antiquities; tapestries; lace; embroidery; stained glass; gold and silver work
BRAZIL			
Rio de Janeiro	Museu Nacional (National Museum)	1818	Anthropology, geology, ethnography, mineralogy, zoology, botany
São Paulo	Museu de Arte de São Paulo (São Paulo Art Museum)	1947	Classical and contemporary European and Brazilian art
CANADA			
Montreal	Montreal Museum of Fine Arts	1860	European and Canadian paintings; decorative arts; primitive, Chinese, Middle Eastern, and Peruvian art
Ottawa	Canadian Museum of Human History	1957	Canadian anthropology, ethnology, archaeology, history
	Canadian Museum of Natural History	1842	Mineralogy, zoology, geology, botany, paleontology
	National Gallery of Canada	1880	General collection of European paintings, sculpture, prints, and drawings; extensive collection of Canadian sculpture and paintings
Toronto	Art Gallery of Toronto	1900	Fifteenth–eighteenth century European paintings; French impressionist paintings; contemporary sculpture, drawings, prints
	Royal Ontario Museum	1912	Division of art and archaeology—general art collection, including extensive Chinese art and archaeology collection and the Sigmund Samuel Canadiana collection; division of geology and mineralogy; division of zoology and paleontology
Québec	Museum of Laval University	1852	Natural history, astronomical and mathematical instruments, numismatics, European and Canadian paintings
DENMARK			
Copenhagen	Nationalmuseet (National Museum)	1807	Danish prehistory, history, and folk collections; royal medals and coins; ethnography; classical antiquities
	Statens Museum for Kunst (Royal Museum of Fine Arts)	1760	Danish sculpture and paintings, old masters, contemporary French art, nineteenth and twentieth century Scandinavian art
EGYPT			
Alexandria	Greco-Roman Museum	1892	Greek, Roman, and Coptic antiquities
Cairo	Egyptian Museum	1900	Egyptian antiquities, prehistoric period to sixteenth century A.D.
FRANCE			
Paris	Musée de l'Armée (Museum of the Army)	1670	Arms, armor, banners, and other military souvenirs; tomb of Napoleon Bonaparte
	Musée de l'Homme (Museum of Man)	1878	Anthropology and ethnography
	Musée de Cluny (Cluny Museum)	1844	Medieval sculpture, clothing, tapestries, household articles, embroidery, ecclesiastical articles
	Musée Guimet (Guimet Museum)	1889	Far Eastern art and religion
	Musée de Jeu de Paume ("Tennis" Museum)	1920	Impressionist and postimpressionist paintings; part of the Louvre collection
	Musée du Louvre	1793	Vast collection of art of all periods, from all over the world
	Musée National d'Art Moderne (National Museum of Modern Art)	1937	Modern sculpture and paintings
	Musée National d'Histoire Naturelle (National Museum of Natural History)	1635	In the Jardin des Plantes; indoor and outdoor botanical, mineralogical, zoological, paleontological, and anatomical exhibits
	Musée Rodin (Rodin Museum)	1916	Sculpture and drawings of François Rodin
Versailles	Musée National de Versailles et des Trianons (National Museum of Versailles and the Trianons)	1837	Sculpture and paintings of the sixteenth–twentieth centuries and household furnishings of the seventeeth–nineteenth centuries; in the Château de Versailles
GERMANY (West)			
Berlin (West)	Dahlem Museum	1951	Collections formerly housed in the Kaiser Friedrich Museum in East Berlin—paintings of the fourteenth–nineteenth centuries, woodcuts, handicrafts—and modern art
Frankfurt am Main	Städelsches Kunstinstitut (Städel Art Institute)	1817	Paintings of the fourteenth–twentieth centuries
Hanover	Kestner-Museum	1889	Egyptian, Etruscan, Greek, and Roman objects; medieval art and MSS; drawings and prints; handicrafts
Munich	Alte Pinakothek (Old Picture Gallery)	1836	Old masters
	Deutsches Museum (German Museum)	1903	One of the world's largest technical museums; exhibits concerned with textile manufacture, chemical laboratories, mining, musical instruments, and so forth

IMPORTANT MUSEUMS OF THE WORLD (Continued)

COUNTRY AND CITY	MUSEUM	YEAR FOUNDED	COLLECTIONS
	Schack-Galerie und Neue Pinakothek (Schack Gallery and New Picture Gallery)	1874	Nineteenth century art
GREAT BRITAIN			
London	British Museum	1753	Vast general art collection—prehistoric, ancient, medieval, and Oriental art collections; coins; ceramics; drawings; prints; MSS, and books; includes the National Library and two natural history museums, one in London and one in Tring, Hertfordshire
	National Gallery	1824	Vast collection of European paintings of all periods, with the exception of contemporary works
	National Portrait Gallery	1857	More than 3,000 portraits of distinguished British men and women
	Royal College of Surgeons Museum	1813	Approximately 26,000 medical specimens
	Science Museum (National Museum of Science and Industry)	1857	Exhibits concerned with atomic physics, radio communication, mining, land and water transport, and a wide variety of other industrial and scientific subjects
	Tate Gallery	1897	Modern foreign paintings, national collections of British paintings, modern sculpture
	Victoria and Albert Museum	1852	Probably the world's finest collection of applied arts of all periods and countries; the Wellington Museum is a branch of the Victoria and Albert
Oxford	Ashmolean Museum	1683	Oxford University's archaeology and art collections—paintings, engravings, miniatures, etchings; Egyptian, Mesopotamian, Syrian, and British antiquities; medieval art; ceramics; silver
Edinburgh	National Gallery of Scotland	1859	European paintings, early Middle Ages to the present
	Royal Scottish Museum	1854	Ethnography, natural history, art, archaeology
Cardiff	National Museum of Wales	1907	Art, archaeology, zoology, geology, botany
GREECE			
Athens	Byzantine Museum	1914	Early Christian mosaics
	National Archaeological Museum	1866	Prehistoric, archaic, and classical Greek art and architecture
	Stoa of Attalos	1956	Ancient stoa, or market hall, reconstructed 1953–56, contains art objects and marble inscriptions excavated from the ancient market place
INDIA			
Baroda	Baroda Museum and Picture Gallery	1894	Ancient, medieval, and modern Indian art and architecture; Egyptian, Greek, Roman, and general European art collections; geology; ethnology; zoology; botany, industrial art; numismatics
New Delhi	National Museum of India	1948	Indian antiquities, bronzes, terra-cotta figurines, illustrated MSS, sculpture, miniature paintings, fabrics
IRELAND (Republic of Ireland)			
Dublin	National Gallery of Ireland	1864	Portraits of eminent Irishmen; Irish paintings of the nineteenth–twentieth centuries; English, Flemish, and Italian masters
	National Museum	1731	Irish antiquities, minor arts, history, natural history
ITALY			
Bologna	Museo Civico (Civic Museum)	1881	Egyptian, Greek, Roman, Etruscan antiquities; Italian medieval and Renaissance sculpture and minor arts
Florence	Galleria dell'Accademia (Gallery of the Academy)	1784	Extensive collection of Michelangelo's sculpture; Italian paintings of the thirteenth–sixteenth centuries
	Galleria degli Uffizi (Uffizi Gallery)	16th cent.	In the Uffizi Palace; renowned collection of Italian art of all schools and periods, especially Florentine Renaissance paintings; also Flemish, French, and German paintings
	Galleria Palatina (Palatine Gallery)	16th cent.	In the Pitti Palace; paintings, chiefly Italian masterpieces of the sixteenth–seventeenth centuries
	Museo Nazionale (National Museum) or Bargello	1865	Italian sculpture, especially Renaissance; minor arts including armor, glass, tapestries, ivories, ecclesiastical articles
	Museo di S. Marco o dell'Angelico (Museum of St. Mark or of the Angelico)	1869	Most complete collection of Fra Angelico's paintings
Milan	Pinacoteca di Brera (Brera Gallery of Paintings)	1809	Italian paintings of various schools, especially the Venetian and Lombard schools

IMPORTANT MUSEUMS OF THE WORLD (Continued)

COUNTRY AND CITY	MUSEUM	YEAR FOUNDED	COLLECTIONS
Naples	Museo Nazionale (National Museum)	18th cent.	Farnese collection of sculpture, precious stones, and coins; Borgia collection of Egyptian antiquities; bronzes, mosaics, and paintings discovered at Pompeii, Herculaneum, and Stabia
Rome and Vatican City	Museo Capitolino (Capitoline Museum)	1471	Vast collection of antique sculpture
	Museo e Galleria Borghese (Borghese Gallery and Museum)	about 1616	Classical and baroque sculpture, paintings by Italian masters
	Musei e Gallerie del Vaticano (Vatican Museums and Galleries)	16th cent.	Six museums and galleries containing the world's largest collection of ancient art; also Renaissance paintings
	Museo del Laterano (Lateran Museum)	1843	In the Lateran Palace; three museums containing a Vatican City collection of ancient Greek and Roman art, early Christian art (especially sarcophagi and inscriptions), and ethnological material
	Museo Nazionale Romano (National Roman Museum)	1889	Greek, Hellenistic, and Roman mosaics, paintings, bronzes, and sculpture
Venice	Galleria dell'Accademia (Gallery of the Academy)	1755	Most important collection of Venetian paintings, early Middle Ages to eighteenth century
JAPAN			
Kyoto	Kyoto Daigaku Bungakubu Chinretsukan (Museum of Faculty of Letters, Kyoto University)	1911	Archaeology, geography, and history of the Orient
Tokyo	Kokuritsu Hakubutsukan (National Museum)	1872	Oriental fine and decorative arts, including sculpture, paintings, textiles, calligraphy
	Kokuritsu Kagaku Hakubutsukan (National Science Museum)	1931	Almost a half million physics, engineering, chemistry, astronomy, geology, botany, and zoology exhibits
MEXICO			
Mexico City	Museo Nacional de Antropología (National Museum of Anthropology)	1825	Archaeology, anthropology, ethnology, and popular arts of the Americas, especially Mexico
	Museo Nacional de Historia (National Museum of History)	1822	European and Mexican fine and minor arts, postconquest history of Mexico
THE NETHERLANDS			
Amsterdam	Rijksmuseum (State Museum)	1808	Rich collection of European paintings, especially northern Dutch, fifteenth century to present; medieval and Renaissance decorative arts; drawings and etchings; Dutch history; ceramics
The Hague	Mauritshuis, or Koninklijk Kabinet van Schilderijen (Royal Museum of Painting)	1821	Dutch paintings, fifteenth–eighteenth centuries
Rotterdam	Museum Boymans	1847	Paintings—old masters and contemporary; excellent collection of prints and drawings; sculpture; minor arts
NORTHERN IRELAND			
Belfast	Belfast Museum and Art Gallery	1888	Irish antiquities, natural history, and ethnography; paintings; sculpture
NORWAY			
Bygdöy	Norsk Folkemuseum (Norwegian Folk Museum)	1894	Indoor exhibits—Norwegian weaving, rural culture, Henrik Ibsen's study; outdoor museum—farms typical of various parts of Norway, almost 150 old buildings
Oslo	Nasjonalgalleriet (National Gallery)	1837	Norwegian sculpture and paintings, European masters, modern Scandinavian and French art
PORTUGAL			
Lisbon	Museu Nacional de Arte Antiga (National Museum of Ancient Art)	1883	Flemish, Dutch, and sixteenth century Portuguese paintings; Persian and Portuguese carpets; Portuguese, Spanish, and Italian tapestries and embroidery; silver; ceramics
SPAIN			
Barcelona	Museo de Bellas Artes de Cataluña, or Museo de Arte Antiguo (Museum of Fine Arts of Catalonia, or Museum of Ancient Art)	1934	Spanish Romanesque and Gothic sculpture and paintings, including reconstructions of church interiors
Madrid	Museo del Prado (Prado Museum)	1819	Most important collection of Spanish paintings; also many paintings by Flemish, French, and Italian masters
	Museo Etnológico (Ethnological Museum)	1875	Anthropology and ethnology, notable collections from the Philippines and Spanish Guinea
	Museo Nacional de Arte Moderno (National Museum of Modern Art)	1895	Nineteenth and twentieth century Spanish sculpture and paintings
SWEDEN			
Stockholm	Nationalmuseum (National Museum)	1792	General art collection, especially eighteenth century paintings, engravings, and drawings and modern Swedish arts and crafts
	Nordiska Museet (Northern Museum)	1873	Swedish arts and crafts, Middle Ages to present; arms and armor; a branch, the Skansen Open-air Museum, contains many old buildings and a zoo

IMPORTANT MUSEUMS OF THE WORLD (Continued)

COUNTRY AND CITY	MUSEUM	YEAR FOUNDED	COLLECTIONS
SWITZERLAND			
Basel	Offentliche Kunstsammlung (Public Art Collection)	1662	Paintings by Swiss and German masters; Swiss paintings, eighteenth–twentieth centuries; modern French and German sculpture and paintings
Bern	Kunstmuseum (Art Museum)	1879	Renaissance Italian paintings; Swiss paintings, fifteenth–nineteenth centuries; modern Swiss, German, and French paintings
Geneva	Musée d'Art et d'Histoire (Museum of Art and History)	1910	General European painting collection, especially primitives; Middle Eastern, Egyptian, classical, and Swiss archaeology and history; coins; decorative and plastic arts
Zürich	Kunsthaus (Art Museum)	1787	Swiss and other European paintings, twelfth century to present; modern German and French sculpture
TURKEY			
Istanbul	Istanbul Arkeoloji Müzeleri (Archaeological Museums of Istanbul)	1869	Comprises four museums—one of them a Byzantine castle—containing prehistoric, Oriental, Greek, Roman, and Byzantine antiquities
UNION OF SOVIET SOCIALIST REPUBLICS			
Leningrad	State Hermitage Museum	1764	Outstanding collection of western European paintings; also ancient Greek and Middle and Far Eastern art
	State Russian Museum	1898	200,000 Russian art exhibits
Moscow	Museum of the Revolution	1923	History of Moscow revolutions, seventeenth–twentieth centuries
	State Historical Museum	1873	Russian history, earliest times to mid-nineteenth century
	State Museum of Modern Western Art	1917	Western European (especially French) and North and South American art, mid-nineteenth century to present
	State Tretyakov Gallery	1856	Most extensive collection of Russian art, eleventh century to present
UNITED STATES			
Baltimore, Md.	Baltimore Museum of Art	1914	Extensive general art collections, Oceanic and African sculpture, prints of the fifteenth–twentieth centuries, early Christian mosaics
Boston, Mass.	Boston Museum of Fine Arts	1870	Oriental art, European and American paintings and decorative arts, large textiles and prints and drawings departments
Brooklyn, N.Y.	Brooklyn Museum (a department of the Brooklyn Institute of Arts and Sciences)	1889	Aboriginal and colonial American art, African and Far and Middle Eastern objects, medieval and Renaissance art, European and American paintings
Buffalo, N.Y.	Buffalo Museum of Science	1861	Exhibits relating the development of science, South Pacific and African art, Marchand wax flowers, Malvina Hoffman bronzes, Transparent Man, Bermuda coral reef
Cambridge, Mass.	Peabody Museum of Archaeology and Ethnology	1866	Harvard University's comprehensive collections in archaeology, ethnology, and physical anthropology
Chicago, Ill.	Adler Planetarium and Astronomical Museum	1930	First U.S. planetarium; large collection of astronomical instruments
	Art Institute of Chicago	1879	European and American paintings and sculpture, Oriental arts, medieval and Renaissance art, prints and drawings, decorative arts, Thorne miniature rooms
	Chicago Historical Society	1856	Outstanding collection of Lincolniana
	Field Museum of Natural History	1893	Botany, anthropology, zoology, geology
	John G. Shedd Aquarium	1930	About 10,000 fresh- and salt-water specimens
	Museum of Science and Industry	1926	Exhibits relating applications of scientific discoveries to industry
	Oriental Institute of the University of Chicago	1919	Assyrian-Hittite-Syrian, Sumerian-Babylonian, Iranian, and Palestinian objects
Cincinnati, Ohio	Cincinnati Art Museum	1880	General painting, sculpture, and prints and drawings collections; decorative arts
Cleveland, Ohio	Cleveland Museum of Art	1913	General collection including classical and Oriental art, Italian and other primitives, arms and armor
	Cleveland Museum of Natural History	1920	Botanical and ethnological material; shells, minerals, insects, precious and semiprecious stones; Spitz Planetarium; operates city aquarium
Cooperstown, N.Y.	National Baseball Hall of Fame and Museum	1939	Hall of fame plaques, equipment, pictures
Corning, N.Y.	Corning Museum of Glass	1951	Glassmaking techniques, 1500 B.C. to present
Dearborn, Mich.	Greenfield Village and Henry Ford Museum	1929	Museums and historic structures, covering 200 acres, which trace the development of transportation, communication, power, lighting, and the decorative arts in the United States

IMPORTANT MUSEUMS OF THE WORLD (Continued)

COUNTRY AND CITY	MUSEUM	YEAR FOUNDED	COLLECTIONS
Detroit, Mich.	Detroit Institute of Arts	1885	General art collections, extensive collections of Italian sculpture and seventeenth century Dutch paintings
Los Angeles, Calif.	Griffith Observatory and Planetarium	1935	Observatory, science hall, planetarium and space travel projectors
Newport News, Va.	Mariners' Museum	1930	Native canoes and boats, ship models, prints and paintings
New York, N.Y.	American Museum of Natural History	1869	Anthropology, natural history, ecology; operates Hayden Planetarium
	Cooper Union's Museum for the Arts of Decoration	1896	Applied and decorative arts, 1500 B.C. to present, including furniture, textiles, woodwork, metalwork, thousands of original designs
	Frick Collection	1935	Sculpture, fifteenth–eighteenth centuries; paintings, fourteenth–nineteenth centuries; drawings and prints; furniture; porcelains, enamels
	Metropolitan Museum of Art	1870	Largest general art collection in the United States; a branch, The Cloisters, at Fort Tryon Park, contains medieval art
	Museum of Modern Art	1929	Paintings, sculpture, drawings, and prints, from about 1875 to present; departments of photography and architecture and design
	Solomon R. Guggenheim Museum	1937	Twentieth century paintings and sculpture
	Whitney Museum of American Art	1930	Twentieth century American paintings, sculpture, prints, and drawings
Philadelphia, Pa.	Pennsylvania Academy of the Fine Arts	1805	American paintings and sculpture, eighteenth century to present
	Philadelphia Museum of Art	1875	Far Eastern and European art, first century A.D. to present; American art, colonial period to present
San Francisco, Calif.	California Academy of Sciences	1853	Natural History Museum, Morrison Planetarium, Steinhart Aquarium, African Hall
	San Francisco Museum of Art	1916	Contemporary paintings, sculpture, prints, drawings
San Marino, Calif.	Henry E. Huntington Library and Art Gallery	1919	Eighteenth century English portraits and landscapes, French and English decorative arts, rare books and MSS, botanic gardens
Santa Fe, N.M.	Museum of New Mexico	1909	Southwestern history, ethnology, art, archaeology
Washington, D.C.	Corcoran Gallery of Art	1869	American art, European paintings and drawings, Greek and Etruscan antiquities, tapestries, laces, furniture, rugs, majolica
	Dumbarton Oaks Research Library and Collection	1940	Harvard University's center for studies in Byzantine and medieval humanities; Byzantine and early Christian art collections
	Smithsonian Institution	1846	National Foundation for Scientific Research; administers 10 bureaus, including:
	Freer Gallery of Art	1906	Middle and Far Eastern art, large James McNeill Whistler collection, biblical MSS
	National Air Museum	1946	Collections illustrating development of aviation in the United States
	National Collection of Fine Arts	1906	Oriental, European, and American paintings; sculpture, miniature paintings; textiles, jewelry, glass, ceramics
	National Gallery of Art	1937	One of the outstanding general art collections of the world—paintings, sculpture, decorative arts, drawings, prints
	United States National Museum	1850	Natural science, history, and engineering and industry exhibits
Williamsburg, Va.	Colonial Williamsburg	1926	Restored homes, public buildings, gardens, taverns, and shops of the colonial capital of Virginia

MUSEUM OF MODERN ART, at 11 West 53rd Street, New York, N.Y., was founded in 1929 by Mrs. John D. Rockefeller, A. Conger Goodyear (who served as the museum's first president), Lillie P. Bliss, Paul J. Sachs, Frank Crowninshield, and Mrs. W. Murray Crane. Its first director was Alfred H. Barr, Jr. The museum's six-story permanent building, designed by Edward Stone and Philip Goodwin, was erected in 1939; an annex (21 West 53rd Street), designed by Philip C. Johnson, was added in 1951. After a disastrous fire (April, 1958) in which several valuable paintings were destroyed and a number of others seriously damaged, extensive remodeling of all galleries was undertaken to make the museum building more fire resistant.

Operations. The museum's function is one of collecting and exhibiting and fostering public awareness of the artistic endeavors of mankind from about 1875 to "the present." Under the direction of René d'Harnoncourt after 1949, the museum's activities have included a continuing exhibition of its extensive permanent collection; about 25 temporary exhibitions in the visual arts each year; daily showings of historically important motion pictures in the museum's 500-seat auditorium, where numerous lectures, symposia, and special events are also presented; the circulation of educational exhibitions throughout the United States, Canada, Europe, Asia, and Latin America; and the publication of hundreds of books, pamphlets, and catalogues related to art movements, individual artists, and exhibitions. The museum's annual budget is in excess of $2 million, 70 per cent of which is met by a worldwide membership of more than 25,000, by admission fees, by the sale of books and reproductions, and by other services; the remaining 30 per cent is met through contributions by private donors and charitable foundations.

The Permanent Collections of the museum include about 650 paintings, more than 250 sculptures, and more than 5,000 prints, as well as illustrated books and portfolios by modern artists. The department of architecture and design, directed by Arthur Drexler, includes an extensive collection of architectural models, plans, photographs, and color slides; about 200 examples of furniture from 1860 to "the present"; and a huge industrial and graphic design collection. The department of photography, under the direction of Edward Steichen, was founded in 1940, and includes hundreds of examples of twentieth century photography by Alfred Stieglitz, Henri Cartier-Bresson, Man Ray, Edward Weston, Ansel Adams, and Paul Strand, as well as Steichen himself. The film library, founded in 1935 as a pioneering step toward the serious study of the motion picture in its artistic, psychosociological, and historical aspects, contains many historically significant films and constitutes the world's most important archive of the motion picture. Films are shown daily to the museum public and are circulated to educational institutions and film societies throughout the country.

Educational Services. The museum's library, including more than 15,000 books, periodicals, and catalogues, 10,000 clippings on art, film, and dance, and 25,000 lantern slides in color and black and white, is a world center for research in the visual arts. Under certain limitations most of these and other library resources are available for use by the public. The department of art education provides art instruction for all age levels (from the age of three). The curriculum includes courses in puppet making, clay work, painting, drawing, and lecture courses in photography, architecture, art history, and design. The department circulates about 120 exhibitions to local schools each year.

MUSEUM OF PRIMITIVE ART, at 15 West 54th Street, New York, N.Y., was founded in February, 1957, by Nelson A. Rockefeller, who was its first president. The museum is devoted to the arts of the indigenous peoples of the Americas, Africa, and Oceania, and of the early phases of the civilizations of Asia and Europe. After its first year of operation the museum had a collection consisting of more than 750 sculptures, masks, ceramics, textiles, gold objects, and pieces of jewelry—all selected for their exceptional beauty and rarity. Several informational services were maintained, among them an archive of photographs of objects in other collections and a library of works on primitive art, culture, and society.

MUSHROOM, the spore-bearing fruit body, or basidiocarp, of any fleshy fungus included in the order Agaricales, containing seven families, about 180 genera, and some 7,000 species, more than 500 of which occur in eastern United States. Like other fungi, mushrooms lack chlorophyll and related pigments and are thus incapable of manufacturing their own food from inorganic substances (see FUNGI, *True Fungi*). They are heterotrophic, deriving nourishment from organic matter, and live as parasites upon plant or animal hosts or as saprophytes on decomposing organic remains. Mushrooms often occur in close association with mosses or ferns and have a symbiotic association with the roots of conifers and flowering plants but never with algae (see SYMBIOSIS). They are found on all continents, in all climatic zones, and at all altitudes, but they are never truly aquatic. Mushrooms are highly seasonal because development of the fruit depends on suitable environmental conditions.

Most mushrooms are richly colored. It has been claimed that their colors are richer and more varied than those found in flowering plants. Pigments are found within the mushroom cells, in the cell walls, or between the cells. Often several chemically and physically different kinds of pigments are combined.

Classification. The seven families included in the order Agaricales may be characterized as follows:

Exobasidiaceae consist of three genera with about 15 species of parasites, forming galls covered by hymenium, the sporing layer of the fruit body. They are parasitic to members of the heath family, *Ericaceae*.

Thelephoraceae are made up of 35 genera with about 900 species, most of which are saprophytic on wood; the hymenium is smooth, and the cap, or pileus, is never club shaped.

Clavariaceae, the club or coral fungi, include nine genera with 300 species, mostly saprophytic on ground or wood. The hymenium is smooth and the pileus is clavate, or club shaped. The fruit body is upright, simple or branched, dendroid or coralloid, and edible.

Hydnaceae include 21 genera with 300 species of saprophytes living on wood or on the ground. The hymenium is found on toothlike spines that project downward.

Polyporaceae are composed of 19 genera with 1,000 species growing mostly on wood, either as parasites or more often by attacking the heartwood. The hymenium occurs in tubes and the pileus is not fleshy. The fruit bodies are sometimes quite large, often shelflike and woody, and are perennial in some genera. Some are edible.

Boletaceae are pore fungi like the *Polyporaceae* and include seven genera with 220 species. The fruit body is almost always found on the ground. The pileus is fleshy and the hymenium occurs in tubes. Some members of this family are poisonous, others may be used for food.

Agaricaceae are the gill fungi, mushrooms, and toadstools, and comprise 88 genera and about 4,000 species. Hymenium lines the gills on both sides. The mycelium, or main body of the mushroom, may be perennial. The pileus is fleshy and usually borne on a stipe, or stem. Most *Agaricaceae* are saprophytes. Many forms are poisonous.

Reproduction and Growth. The common gilled mushroom sheds a single-celled spore, or basidiospore, that is either male or female determined. The cells germinate and grow into filaments, or hyphae, which eventually meet to establish binucleate cells, each of which contains a male and a female determined nucleus. Characteristic clamp connections are formed laterally between adjacent cells, a structural condition that then allows pairs of newly formed nuclei to enter new cells (see CONJUGATION). The binuclear hyphae form a dense, feltlike underground mass called the mycelium, which is the main body of the fungus from which the fruit bodies, or basidiocarps, arise. The young, round fruit bodies are called buttons, which open to form a mature mushroom. On the lower side of the cap are the radially arranged gills, or lamellae. Each gill is lined with fertile tissue, the hymenium. Spores are formed in the terminal cells of the hyphae that form the gills. Each mushroom may produce hundreds of thousands of spores. Spore prints may be obtained by placing the pileus on a white or black piece of paper allowing time for the spores to fall on it in characteristic pattern. The color of the spores is used to classify mushrooms as white, light green, light red, rosy or salmon, yellow or brown, purplish or black. Among the black-spored mushrooms are many species of the genus *Coprinus*, known as inky cap mushrooms because their gills liquefy into an inky black fluid when the cap deteriorates.

The growth of certain plants depends upon the presence of mushrooms in symbiotic association with their roots. The association is known as mycorrhiza and usually is not harmful. Sometimes the fungus is found outside the roots as in many trees, but it also occurs in well marked layers inside the roots, as in orchids and in members of the heath family, *Ericaceae*.

Fairy rings, or fungus rings, are formed by mushrooms that belong to any one of about 60 species.

The fairy rings are often seen in grassland or in lawns, less commonly in woods. See FAIRY RING.

Edibility. Of the several hundred species of mushrooms found in the eastern United States, less than 25 are poisonous. Most poisonous species belong to the genus *Amanita*, one of the best known being the fly agaric, *A. muscaria*. Poisoning by *Amanita* species is caused by the muscarine present in these mushrooms and is almost always fatal (see MUSCARINE; POISON). Species of *Agaricus*, *Cantharellus*, *Coprinus*, *Lepiota*, *Marasmius*, and *Tricholoma* (gill fungi), and *Boletus* (pore fungus) are most commonly eaten. Edible fungi have long been a favorite food, as for example the fungi suilli, *Boletus edulis*, of the Romans. In Europe up to about 60 species of edible mushrooms are commonly marketed.

Cultivation. In the United States the common or field mushroom, *Agaricus campestris*, and a few related species are cultivated for sale. Mushrooms grow best in humid places where temperatures range between 50° and 60°F. Light is not harmful to their growth, but it is not necessary. Mushroom farmers may use special sheds, tunnels, caves, or old mines to grow the fungus. Suitably moist beds of carefully prepared compost and soil are seeded to a depth of 1 inch with pieces of mycelium from a pure culture. Most beds may be harvested several times. In the tropics *Volvaria volvacea* and *V. diplasia*, the edible species of straw mushrooms, are widely cultivated. In Burma *V. diplasia* is grown on wet rice straw. This species requires a minimum temperature of 70°F. In Japan and China millions of pounds of the *shii-take* mushroom, *Cortinellus berkelyanus*, are raised annually on wet wood of oaks and related trees. The *matsu-take* mushroom, *Armillaria matsutake*, is another important edible fungus widely used and cultivated in Japan.

Mushrooms were once commonly used as medicine. The female, white, or purging agaric, *Fomes officinalis*, was at one time regarded as a universal remedy. Various antibiotics have been produced from mushrooms—for example, biformin and biformic acid from *Polyporus biformis*, clitocybin from *Clitocybe candida*, polyporin from *Polyporus sanguineus*, and pleurotin from *Pleurotus griseus*. Various mushrooms, including the fly agaric, *Agaricus muscaria*, are stimulants capable of producing visions. In southern Mexico knowledge of certain sacred mushrooms and their properties dates from Aztec times. Various species of *Psilocybe* are eaten during secret ceremonies performed by healers.

Mushrooms can cause tree diseases and the decay of timber. Because most mushrooms are saprophytes, they predispose trees to mechanical injury by making them more susceptible to windfall and rendering their wood useless for lumber. Mushrooms usually grow in the dead heartwood of living trees where they break down the original composition of cell walls.

Armillaria root rot, caused by *Armillaria mellea*, attacks forest and orchard trees as well as potato tubers. It is most destructive to stone fruits and citrus trees in the Pacific states. The edible beefsteak (or liver) fungus, *Fistulina hepatica*, causes brown oak. A striking phenomenon is seen when old tree stumps become luminous because of the presence of certain mushrooms in the decaying wood. THEODOR JUST

BIBLIOG.–H. T. Güsson and W. S. Odell, *Mushrooms and Toadstools* (1927); M. McKenney, *Mushrooms of Field and Wood* (1929); W. S. Thomas, *Field Book of Common Gilled Mushrooms* (ed. 1935); L. C. C. Krieger, *Mushroom Handbook* (1936); V. O. Graham, *Mushrooms of the Great Lakes Region* (1944); C. M. Christensen, *Common Edible Mushrooms* (1943); *Common Fleshy Fungi* (1946); F. A. and F. T. Wolf, *Fungi* (2 vols. 1947); G. C. Ainsworth and G. R. Bisby, *Dictionary of the Fungi* (ed. 1950); E. A. Bessey, *Morphology and Taxonomy of Fungi* (1950); A. P. Kelley, *Mycotrophy in Plants* (1950); H. C. I. Gwynne-Vaughan and B. Barnes, *Structure and Development of Fungi* (ed. 1951); E. A. Gäumann, *Fungi* (1952); L. O. Overholts, *Polyporaceae of the United States, Alaska and Canada* (1953); V. P. and G. Wasson, *Mushrooms, Russia and History* (1957); A. H. Smith, *Mushroom Hunter's Field Guide* (1958).

MUSIC, a rhythmic arrangement of clearly differentiated sounds that seems orderly and meaningful to a listener, a community, or (in the largest sense) to all of human society. A musical progression (that is, a melody) may be meaningful to one group of listeners and meaningless to another, since appreciation of beauty varies from one locality to another, and from one century to another. There are many different kinds of music, each meeting the aesthetic needs of a certain society at a given time. Both the Orient and Negro Africa produced unique musical traditions. The most magnificent flowering of music as an art, however, had its center in Europe, and European music has come to dominate all parallel musical developments. Differences among national types of European music are profound, but are largely outweighed by the many more qualities they have in common. See CHINESE MUSIC; NEGRO, In Africa, *African Negro Art and Music;* ORIENTAL MUSIC.

Origins of Music derive from the physiology of the human being—in his possession of vocal cords capable of producing differentiated sounds. A primitive rhythmic element is present in the measured walk and in communal marching. Rhythmic precision also has utilitarian value in labor. Asymmetrical rhythms of great complexity, however, are found in primitive societies; a deliberate nervous disruption of the steady flow of rhythmic beat may have been the means of self-expression in early social groups. Melody may be said to exist with as few as two different consecutive sounds, and considerable effect can be achieved by varying the rhythm in melodies containing but a few notes. When melodic variety is considerable, rhythm need not be variegated; when the rhythmic pattern changes constantly, a very few notes will suffice as a melodic element.

THEORY OF MUSIC

By the sixth century B.C., Pythagoras had established ratios for the principal musical pitch intervals. Thus the ancients knew that one string twice as long as another—thickness and tension being equal— produced a sound an octave deeper; that the ratio of 3:2 corresponded to the perfect fifth, and the ratio 4:3 to the perfect fourth. On this basis other intervals were mathematically derived. The Pythagoreans originated the mystical concept of a harmony of the spheres, in which the distances between celestial bodies were thought to have been governed by musical intervals (see INTERVAL).

What might be defined as a cosmic harmony does exist independently of man's artistic efforts. It is formed by the natural subdivisions of a single vibrating string into sections (½, ⅓, ¼, ⅕, ⅙, and so forth). This so-called series of overtones (partials) is the foundation of the modern major mode (see MODE). Musical composition followed the natural formation of the overtones empirically before the complete formulation of its theory. Thus the major

MUSHROOMS
Conventional Forms

Vermilion Hygrophorus

Violet Cortenarius

Russula

Meadow Mushroom

Indigo Lactarius

Fly Mushroom

Caesar's Mushroom

Blushing Amanita

RUTHERFORD PLATT

MUSHROOMS
Odd Forms

Pale Yellow Clavaria

Bracket Fungus (Drawing Pad)

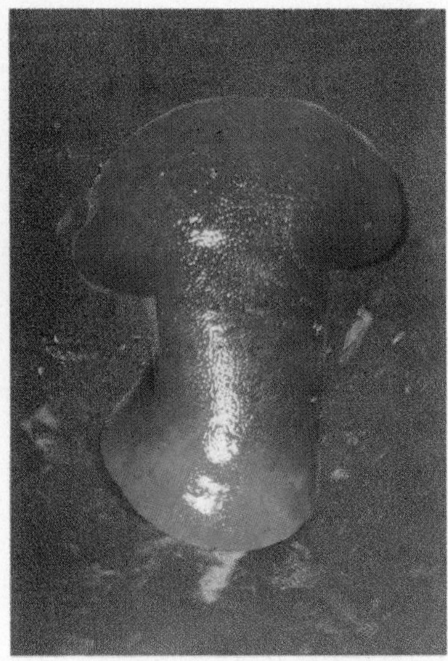

Beefsteak Mushroom

Bracket Fungus (Zoned)

Bracket Fungus (Mahogany)

Club Clavaria

Stinkhorn

Coral Clavaria

RUTHERFORD PLATT

mode actually has a natural advantage over the minor mode. The entire history of music seems to follow the expansion of man's awareness of musical intervals, from unisons and octaves in the earliest period to the intervals of fifths and fourths (called perfect because of their simple ratios), major and minor thirds, and finally the dissonant intervals of seconds and sevenths, augmented and diminished intervals.

Scales and Intervals. A scale of five notes (pentatonic) was developed in many parts of the world in antiquity. That this scale was the product of a natural selection is demonstrated by the fact that similar forms of it were generated in the Orient, among American Indians, and in Scotland, Ireland, and Brittany. The enduring quality of the pentatonic scale may reflect the instinctive desire of early man to sing melodies in clearly differentiated spacious intervals. However, Greece, the cradle of music, generated scales of much narrower intervals, including steps smaller than a semitone (half-step).

The established scale in Western music is the diatonic scale, having seven degrees and encompassing an octave. It is represented by the white keys of the piano keyboard. A diatonic scale can start on any one of the seven notes and thus provide seven different modes. With the addition of the five notes of the pentatonic scale (the black keys on the piano keyboard), a 12-note chromatic scale is formed. But the semitones composing this full scale were acoustically different from one another, so that modulation from one tonality (key) to another was not feasible because the intervals were distorted. The problem was that of tuning: if the perfect fifth had to be really perfect, major thirds and minor thirds could not be accurately fitted into the intervallic scheme. This incommensurability was finally resolved by a drastic decision: the octave was divided into 12 equal intervals. As a result, the perfect fifth became somewhat less perfect, but modulation and transposition into other keys became possible without interval distortion. Johann Sebastian Bach (1685–1750) codified this change in

Notation by means of neumes drawn above the words, as on this eleventh century sheet, indicates the melodic curve, basic accents, and phrasing, but not the level of pitch.

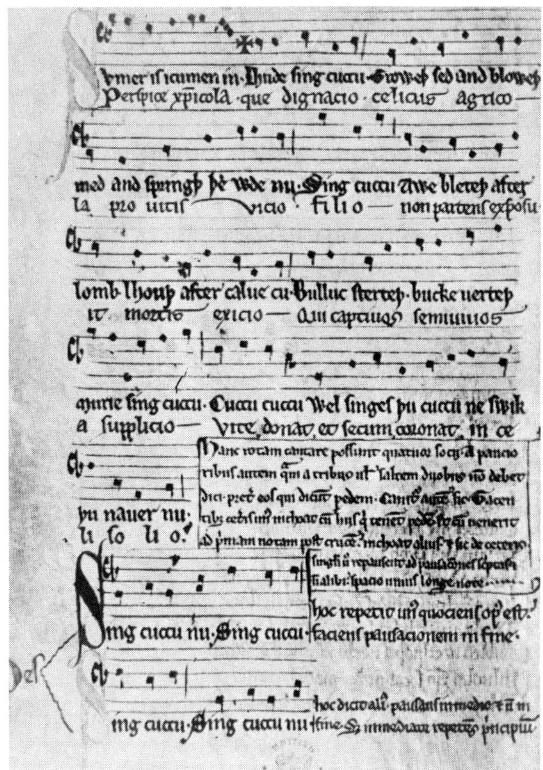

BRITISH MUS.

Reading Rota, "Sumer is icumen in," about 1225

his *Well Tempered Clavier*, containing preludes and fugues in every major and minor key. The scale was tempered; the semitones were made equal.

Rhythm and Meter. Rhythm is musical motion; its variety is determined by the relative duration of successive melodic notes. Meter indicates the number of units or beats in a given measure or bar. Thus each bar of a waltz has three beats, but not necessarily three notes; a simple alternation of two notes, the first twice as long as the second, is the formula for an elementary waltz rhythm. Each measure of a march has four beats; but it may be formed by a rhythmic figure of only three notes, the first twice as long as each of the remaining two. Meter is a framework within which a rhythmic melody performs its motion. Sometimes the rhythmic accent of the musical phrase falls on an offbeat; such a noncoincidence of accent and principal beat is syncopation.

Tempo. The speed of performance materially affects a composition. A stately saraband can be converted into a waltz by increasing the tempo, or speed. A lively polka can be made into a funeral march by slowing down the movement. Correctness of tempo, therefore, is essential to proper interpretation of a musical work. Tempo is usually indicated by Italian terms such as andante (at a walk), allegro (lively), and largo (very slow) and their diminutives—andantino, allegretto, larghetto; or, for the fast, tempi, vivace and presto and their superlatives—vivacissimo, prestissimo. Invention of the metronome enabled composers to indicate tempo by marking the number of beats per minute. Thus a quarter note equaling 60 shows that each quarter note lasts one second. The metronome mark of 120 indicates that each beat lasts half a second.

Notation. St. Isidore of Seville (seventh century) said that musical sounds could not be written down (*scribi non possunt*) and therefore could be preserved only by oral transmission from one generation to the next. But the necessities of religious musical instruction promoted the invention of a musical notation indicating, with some degree of precision, the pitch

PARKE-BERNET GALLERIES

An illuminated leaf from a fifteenth century French folio of antiphony illustrates music notation with notes placed on a four-line staff. The fifth line was added much later.

and relative duration of individual notes. In Christian monasteries scribes drew a yellow line to indicate the position of C and underneath, a red line, indicating F, a fifth below; this arrangement provided a rudimentary guide for singers. Guido d'Arezzo (990–1050) added two black lines, one above the yellow line and the other below, corresponding to the notes E and A. Pitch could then be indicated within the margin of a third, intermediate notes being placed between the lines. Guido established the system of solmization; the scale thus formed was ut, re, mi, fa, sol, la. Later, ut was replaced by the more euphonious do. Still later, the syllable si was added to the scale.

To indicate the position of notes on the staff, movable clefs were invented, perhaps by Guido. Of these, the most common in medieval music was the C clef. By placing it on the lowest line, room was provided for high notes; by placing it on the fourth line, lower notes were accommodated. The F clef indicated the position of F a fifth below C. Some centuries later the G clef, indicating the position of G a fifth above C, came into use. Thus the clefs were selected at intervals of a fifth (F-C-G).

The notes of modern notation evolved from the medieval neumes (Greek equivalent of Latin *nota*, or note), which were derived from accent signs in cursive writing. The acute sign gave rise to an upward vocal inflection; the grave accent, to a downward inflection. Gradually a complex system of melodic writing was developed, indicating a melodic turn by various undulating lines and detached notes by a series of dots. Rules were established as to relative duration of individual musical sounds in such neumes. In the earlier medieval manuscripts neumatic signs were used interlinearly, but after staff notation was introduced the notes assumed a squared shape. Sounds of longer duration were represented by oblongs; diamond-shaped neumes appeared in the fourteenth century, and it was not until the seventeenth century that the familiar round notes of modern notation came into general use. By the year 1200 a fifth line was added to the staff, thus completing the form of modern notation, although the uses to which the fifth line were put varied throughout several centuries and were not fully standardized until sometime in the seventeenth century.

Another type of notation, developed simultaneously with the staff, was the tablature, in which numbers and letters were used to indicate graphically the production of sound upon an instrument. Tablature notation is still used in popular editions of guitar music. In the twentieth century a new representational type of tablature, *Klavarskribo*, was introduced in Holland. In this method the notes are placed on a diagram of a piano keyboard (or of the strings of a stringed instrument, the valves of a trumpet, and so forth) and the music is read downward rather than from left to right. It has the advantage of immediate visual association.

Instruments. The most ancient instruments were drums; the sound was produced by percussion—simple beating on the surface. A hollowed log of wood may still serve as a percussion instrument in Africa and in South America; in old Mexico, human skulls were used. Primitive wind instruments were fashioned out of animal horns and from reeds; stringed instruments were made by stretching dried catgut between two fixed points. The basic musical tools—the stringed instruments, wind instruments, and percussion instruments—were used in the most remote times and places of human history. The prototypes of modern musical instruments were developed in ancient Greece, and poetic legends surround their origins.

In the playing of stringed instruments the sound was produced by plucking, a method that persisted for many centuries before the invention of the bow. The group of plucked instruments comprised the harp, the guitar, and a variety of lutes; the bowed instruments emerged during the Renaissance. The family of viols of different sizes became the principal concert instruments in Elizabethan England, but

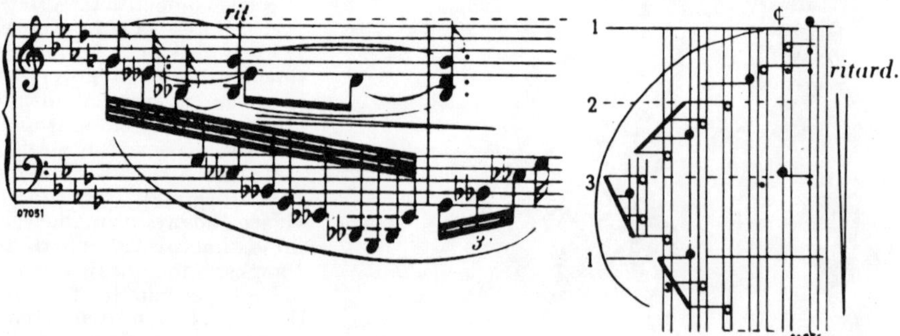

Two methods of notating the same fragment of an intermezzo by Brahms are shown. The European method of notation uses a staff of two clefs of five horizontal lines each and a key signature of five flats. The double-flat marks next to some notes are called accidentals and are exceptions to the key signature. Flags and lines attached to stems of notes indicate their relative duration. In Klavarskribo notation, right, the keyboard is represented literally: vertical lines are black keys and the spaces between the lines are white keys. Middle C is indicated at the top (¢), and the numbers 1, 2, and 3 at the left indicate time (3/4). Standard European notation reads from left to right; however Klavarskribo notation is read from top to bottom.

soon were supplanted by the more brilliant violin family, which included also the viola, the violoncello, and the double bass. The victory of the violins over other forms of stringed instruments was made possible by the genius of Italian violinmakers, of whom the greatest was probably Antonius Stradivarius (1644–1737).

Of the wind instruments, the recorder (a vertical flute) enjoyed great popularity during the Renaissance, but soon fell into disuse until its revival in the twentieth century. Wind instruments that have established themselves permanently are flutes, oboes, English horns, clarinets, and bassoons (woodwinds); French horns, trumpets, trombones and tubas (brasses); and a relative newcomer, the saxophone, named after its inventor, Aldophe Sax (1814–94).

The organ is the most ancient keyboard instrument, and the Roman Emperor Nero (A.D. 37–68) is said to have played a hydraulus (water organ) in which air compressed by the pressure of water was blown into pipes; the water mechanism later gave way to the more practical bellows. In the twentieth century there were electric organs capable of producing enormous sonorities. The harpsichord, a keyboard instrument that produces sound by the plucking of strings through an ingenious mechanism, flourished during the Renaissance and through the eighteenth century, as did a number of similar instruments. The clavichord was invented in the twelfth century and, greatly modified, outlived the harpsichord in popularity among composers. Its strings were not plucked when the keys were depressed, but were "stroked." Both harpsichord and clavichord were superseded by the pianoforte, a true percussion instrument (using hammers) invented in 1709 by the Italian instrument maker Bartolomeo Cristofori (1655–1731). As the name indicates, it could play both softly (piano) and loudly (forte); thus its dynamic range is more varied than that of the harpsichord. But the harpsichord refused to die; in the twentieth century a renascence of old instruments brought the harpsichord back to favor, mainly through the efforts of Wanda Landowska (1879–1959) in France and Arnold Dolmetsch (1858–1940) in England.

Scientific methods of sound production through electromagnetism were developed in the twentieth century. The inventor of the first electronic instrument, 1921, was Leo Theremin (1896–) of Moscow.

Techniques of Composition

Counterpoint. When melodies were combined in simultaneous singing, rules had to be established regarding the euphony of such combinations. If two identical melodies were made to move together at the distance of a fourth or a fifth, the result was called organum. This was the simplest type of counterpoint, one point (that is, a note) moving against another. Soon the upper voice of the organum acquired greater freedom of movement; there might be several consecutive notes against one. As counterpoint continued to develop, a terminology was elaborated: the basic melody was *cantus firmus* (the fixed chant), the moving upper voice, *duplum*. The logical step was the addition of another voice above, the *triplum*, and still another, the *quadruplum*. Five species of counterpoint were thus established: (1) note against note; (2) two consecutive notes against one note; (3) three, four, six, or more consecutive notes against a note; (4) syncopated counterpoint produced by noncoincident notes; (5) free, or florid, counterpoint. In actual composition, the advanced fifth species, florid counterpoint, acquired greatest practical value; the great masters of the fifteenth century Netherlands school, and after them Pierluigi da Palestrina in the sixteenth century and Johann Sebastian Bach in the eighteenth, elevated contrapuntal writing to a sublime art.

Canon and Fugue. One of the most important contrapuntal forms is canon. In canonic singing a single voice begins a musical phrase; after it has sung a few notes, another voice enters with the same musical phrase, while the first continues to sing a new melodic fragment in perfect euphony with the entry of the second voice. The second voice then imitates the musical fragment used by the first, and so on *ad infinitum*, or until an arbitrary ending. Masters of canonic art exercised their ingenuity by writing canons in inversion—that is, imitating the melody upside down so that the high notes become low notes and vice versa. Bach, in his last work, *The Art of the Fugue*, included several instances of such canons by inversion. The impulse to sing in canon revealed itself for the first time perhaps in the English song *Sumer is Icumen In*, composed by some unknown genius between 1250 and 1300. The work is remarkable for the perfect harmonic agreement of the successive entries, four voices in all, with two static basses.

With all its ingenuities, canonic imitation was still a purely mechanical process. But it gave rise to one of the most artistic musical forms, the fugue. Whereas canon was principally a vocal form, fugues were written for instruments. A well developed fugue must have at least three voices; four, five, and six are common. After a purely canonic section of the fugue is completed, there is a free development using the thematic fragments of the main subject and modulating freely into related keys. In the concluding section of the fugue, the subject re-enters, often accompanied by full chords. Bach's great collection of 48 preludes and fugues, *The Well Tempered Clavier*, provides superlative instruction in fugal writing. See Fugue.

Harmony. In harmony, as in counterpoint, several notes are sung or played simultaneously. But there is a great difference between counterpoint and harmony. Ideally, all contrapuntal voices are independent, each voice pursuing a distinctive melodic line; counterpoint is a free intermingling of different voices, calculated to produce both euphony and interdependent motion. Harmony is a compact tonal conglomerate, serving to enhance a melody.

Three different notes, arranged in intervals of major and minor thirds, form a triad, major or minor. These three notes can be arranged in three different positions through the process of inversion, so that each of the three notes appears in the bass. When a fourth different note is placed a third above a triad, seventh chords are obtained; more notes of the diatonic scale may be added, forming the chords of the ninth, the eleventh, and the thirteenth, much used in modern music. Triads are concords, or consonances; chords with more than three different notes (seventh chords, ninths, and so forth) are discords, or dissonances.

In the early stages of harmonic development the principal key was firmly maintained throughout a short musical composition; modulations were made briefly into the closely related keys. With the evolution of harmonic writing, transitions were made from the central tonality to remote keys through the use of chromatic notes. Modern harmony, formulated in the second half of the nineteenth century, established a total freedom of widely ranging modulations, but the law of supremacy of consonances remained in force. Virtually every piece written before 1900 ended on a chord having not more than three different notes—that is, a triad; all dissonant chords used by classical and romantic composers were resolved into concords. Beginning in the last decade of the nineteenth century, however, a harmonic revolution took place. Unresolved chords were left unattended, or were strung out in a series of consecutive progressions without coming to rest on a concord. The key signature all but disappeared from musical scores, partly because dissonant chords belonged to no tonality, partly because modulations were so frequent that tonality became too fluid to be anchored to a single tonal center. Many chords once regarded as dissonances came to be considered consonances—major triads with the added sixth, the added seventh, the added ninth, and the added thirteenth. See HARMONY.

MUSICAL FORMS

Form in music is an arrangement of successive sounds that possesses an element of recognizable symmetry. Such an arrangement may be nothing more complex than an upward run of a few notes followed by a downward run along the same notes. On the highest level, form is a complex edifice of rhythms and harmonies in which formal relationship is revealed by subtle similarities and contrasts almost beyond the grasp of an unprepared listener. Paradoxically, a free association of musical thoughts, which may appear to some as formless, may be the acme of a philosophically conceived and expertly executed musical formal design.

When a musical composition consists of two contrasting sections, the form is binary; when there are three such phrases or sections, the form is ternary. The third section is usually a more or less precise copy of the first. Art songs are constructed in this manner, and ternary form is often called song form.

Court Dances in old Europe were the most symmetrical of all musical compositions. The classical suite contains several court dances (saraband, minuet, gavotte, pavane, and others). The most popular court dances are in ternary form—minuet, gavotte; there seems to be a particular satisfaction in returning to the original section after the contrasting middle section. For an ending, a coda (Italian for tail) is often appended.

Rondo and Sonata are classical expansions of ternary form. In a rondo the main part is alternated with different new sections in a variety of ways. The sonata has two contrasting themes, each clearly stated in the exposition, then subjected to free variations in the development; the two themes are restated in the recapitulation. The first movement of a classical sonata is the only one cast in sonata form; the second, slow movement may be an air with variations; the third, a minuet or its elaboration, known as scherzo; and the last, finale, is usually in rondo form.

Chamber Music. For centuries wealthy patrons of art—the aristocracy and royalty—maintained musical performances in their palaces and mansions. Chamber music, which literally is music performed in a chamber, originated from this practice. In modern usage compositions for no more than nine instruments are classified as chamber music; those for a larger ensemble, approaching the dimension of an orchestra, as chamber orchestra. The most common types of chamber music are sonatas for a stringed instrument with piano—violin sonatas, cello sonatas; piano trios, scored for violin, cello, and piano; string quartets, for two violins, viola, and cello; and piano quintets, for piano with string quartet. Compositions for wind instruments, in combination with stringed instruments and piano in small ensembles, also fall within the category of chamber music. The twentieth century composer Paul Hindemith wrote chamber music for every instrument of the orchestra including the rare bass oboe, the heckelphone.

Symphony means nothing more than "together sounding"; this sense prevailed for many centuries, so that contrapuntal pieces for a keyboard instrument, choral works with an instrumental accompaniment, or the overtures to operas were called symphonies. In the middle of the eighteenth century *symphony* acquired the familiar meaning of a highly developed orchestral composition, in sonata form, containing several movements. The standard form of a symphony was firmly established by Franz Joseph Haydn and Wolfgang Amadeus Mozart and further developed by Ludwig van Beethoven, Franz Schubert, Felix Mendelssohn, and Robert Schumann. Like an instrumental sonata, a full-fledged symphony contains four movements. The last movement is usually the most brilliant; often the entire range of orchestral sonority is used, for the practical purpose of providing a rousing finale and eliciting applause. In the nineteenth century Peter Ilich Tschaikovsky, however, concluded his last symphony, the *Pathétique*, on the softest pianissimo: the work seemed too mournful for any display of brilliance.

Beethoven broke with the symphonic tradition by writing the famous choral ending in his ninth symphony. In the twentieth century many composers used the chorus in their symphonies; of these, Igor Stravinsky's *Symphony of the Psalms* is the most famous.

Concerto. The instrumental concerto follows the structure of the sonata and serves to display a particular instrument and its performer to best advantage. Violin concertos were the earliest display pieces; but for sheer sonority, concertos for piano and orchestra take the lead in musical literature. There are some remarkable concertos for the cello; the conductor Serge Koussevitzky (1874–1951) wrote a concerto for a double bass and orchestra. Richard Strauss (1864–1949) wrote concertos for the French horn with orchestra. The modern French composer Darius Milhaud (1892–) wrote a concerto for mouth organ with orchestra. The U.S. composer Morton Gould (1913–) composed a concerto for a tap dancer with orchestra.

Symphonic Poem is the freest orchestral form, governed solely by an association of ideas. Franz Liszt (1811–86) originated the form, and Richard Strauss elaborated it to the point of literal storytelling. All of Strauss's famous symphonic poems were written before he was 35; he lived another 50 years but never produced works as emotionally moving as his *Don Juan*, which he wrote at the age of 24, or as enchanting and witty as his *Till Eulenspiegel*, written when he was 30.

The Variation Form is the most fruitful exercise in musical composition. A given theme is adorned by musical frills and ornaments in many and various ways, so that each variation acquires a distinct character. A fine eighteenth century classical set of variations is the so-called *Harmonious Blacksmith* of Georg Friedrich Handel (1685–1757); the English composer Sir Edward Elgar (1857–1934) wrote an orchestral set which he entitled *Enigma Variations*, declaring that the theme itself was a contrapuntal counterpart of a hidden real theme.

Absolute Music and Program Music. Whereas painting and sculpture have objects in the outside world as models, music is nurtured by its own peculiar processes, follows its own inner logic, and induces emotional responses according to some unanalyzable psychological principle of communication. The purest music is appreciated for its intrinsic value alone; such music is said to be absolute, or abstract. Bach's instrumental compositions are excellent examples.

In contradistinction, there is much music that endeavors to describe, to illustrate, to evoke a memory. Such music is called program music, for it announces its message in advance. The most suitable subjects for program music are geographical places; through the use of folk songs and dances of some picturesque land, an impression of a musical visit is created, as in Maurice Ravel's *Bolero*, Nikolai Rimski-Korsakov's *Spanish Caprice*, Richard Strauss's *Alpine Symphony*, Claude Debussy's *La Mer* (The Sea), and George Gershwin's *An American in Paris*. Mood pictures are represented in such compositions as Schumann's *Träumerei* and Tschaikovsky's *Chanson Triste*. Many works of program music are taken from literary masterpieces: for example The *Faust Symphony* of Liszt, the philosophical symphonic poem *Thus Spake Zarathustra* of Richard Strauss. Modest Moussorgsky's piano suite *Pictures at an Exhibition* is one of the most vivid examples of program music, representing a variety of images—melancholy ("The Old Castle"), majestic ("The Great Gate of Kiev"), and comical ("Ballet of Unhatched Chickens in their Eggshells"). Hector

Berlioz in his *Fantastic Symphony* described his romantic passion for an English actress. Scientific subjects are treated by Edgar Varese (1885–) in his extraordinary scores *Ionization* and *Hyperprism*. Imitation of natural sounds is sometimes attempted; the most famous instance is the imitation of the nightingale, the quail, and the cuckoo in Beethoven's *Pastoral* Symphony; Ottorino Respighi's *Pines of Rome* uses a recording of a nightingale's song. See FORM.

HISTORICAL EVOLUTION OF MUSIC

From earliest times, music served as an accompaniment of national events, popular festivals, court ceremonies, and religious worship. There are many references in the Bible to ritual singing and to playing upon various instruments. The unit of the musical scale, the tetrachord, was established in ancient Greece, whose philosophers attached ethical values to their modes: thus the Dorian mode possessed the qualities of strength and manliness; the Lydian, gentleness and femininity; the Phrygian, passion. The Greek name for scales was *harmoniai*, from which the modern term *harmony* came; but Greek music was entirely monophonic, having a single melodic line.

Church Modes. The Christian church adopted the Greek names of modes. In church modes, however, intervals were counted upward instead of downward as in the Greek method; as a result, a difference in terminology arose. St. Ambrose of Milan (333–97) established the first system of church modes; Pope St. Gregory the Great (540?–604) ordered the final codification of church music with eight principal modes. An adequate notation was developed; beautiful parchment manuscripts were prepared by experienced and imaginative monks; copies were made to satisfy the needs of churches throughout Christendom, and Gregorian chant (the system of singing according to Gregory the Great) became the prime medium of artistic composition.

Ars Antiqua. With the development of counterpoint, great schools of composition emerged. Two master composers, Leoninus and Perotinus, who worked at the Cathedral of Notre Dame in Paris in the last half of the twelfth century, founded the so-called *ars antiqua;* Leoninus wrote beautiful examples of organum, a polyphonic art of limited means but great variety; Perotinus built more complex polyphonic forms, containing several parts moving in considerable freedom.

Ars Nova. So rapidly did the art of composition develop after Leoninus and Perotinus that medieval theorists of the fourteenth century proudly referred to their works as *ars nova* (new art) in contradistinction to *ars antiqua*. A remarkable flowering of *ars nova* was achieved in France by Guillaume de Machaut (1300–77), a poet as well as a composer and one of the earliest masters of secular song. In Italy Francesco Landini (1325–97) carried on the tradition of *ars nova*.

Minnesinger, Meistersinger, Troubadour, and Trouvère. Parallel with the growth of polyphonic music under the aegis of the church, secular music of chivalrous love was developed during the Middle Ages in France and Germany. The composers of this music were troubadours in southern France and trouvères in northern France. These poet-musicians belonged to the aristocracy of their respective societies; one of them, the trouvère Thibaut IV, was a king. Among the minnesingers was Tannhäuser, immortalized by Richard Wagner in a famous opera. Wagner also wrote of the guild of craftsmen, Meistersinger, who practiced singing as an avocation, but were bound by strict rules of poetry and music. The most famous of the Meistersinger was Hans Sachs (1494–1576).

Medieval Songs and Anthems. One of the most fruitful developments of sacred music was the motet, a choral work without accompaniment to a text in Latin. Motets were originally part of the church service, but soon acquired a secular character, with texts in the vernacular. A church hymn often served as a *cantus firmus*, the foundation for a contrapuntal part that carried a love song in French or German. Motets flourished for six centuries, 1200–1800, before being replaced by the anthem.

Great Age of Polyphony. The theory of medieval counterpoint was fully formulated by the fourteenth century, and the way was open to the artistic exploitation of this new technique. There arose an illustrious Flemish school of contrapuntists founded by Guillaume Dufay (1400–74), who wrote songs to French texts and sacred motets; his successors were Johannes Ockeghem (1420–95) and Jacob Obrecht (1452–1505). This phase of the Netherlands school is often called Burgundian because Dufay, Ockeghem, and Obrecht worked within the kingdom of Burgundy. The new generation of the Netherlands school was represented by the great Josquin Deprès (1450–1521). The third and final phase was illuminated by the genius of Orlando di Lasso (1524–94), one of whose contemporaries—the Italian master Palestrina (1526–94)—perfected the art of sacred choral music. In Spain, Tomás Luis de Victoria (1548–1611) wrote church music comparable to Palestrina's.

Madrigal, Opera, Oratorio. Of late medieval and early Renaissance secular songs, the most attractive was the madrigal, a lyric poem of amorous content but allowing for a great variety of expression from sentimental to comical. Gesualdo of Venosa (1560–1613) wrote madrigals in a bold chromatic style well in advance of his contemporaries. The art of madrigal flourished in Elizabethan England, where its greatest representatives were William Byrd (1542–1623) and Orlando Gibbons (1583–1625). When Orazio Vecchi (1550–1605), an Italian composer at the court of Modena, connected a number of madrigals into a series that had a certain dramatic continuity—he called the result a harmonic comedy—he had made the decisive step towards the creation of a new form of theatrical music, the opera (see MADRIGAL; OPERA). During the same period there arose in Italy a type of choral composition on a sacred subject, called oratorio. The greatest composers of early oratorios in Italy were Emilio de'Cavalieri (1550–1602), Giacomo Carissimi (1605–74), and Alessandro Scarlatti (1660–1725). In Germany the first great composer of oratorios was Heinrich Schütz (1585–1672). Händel and Mendelssohn wrote oratorios that are standard works in the choral repertory. Handel's greatest are *Israel in Egypt* and *Messiah.* Mendelssohn's best are *St. Paul* and *Elijah.* Among modern oratorios, Arthur Honegger's *King David* has achieved telling effect. Another type of dramatic choral work is the cantata. It may be written to a secular text, and may even be of a frivolous nature, as in Bach's *Coffee Cantata*. See ORATORIO.

Ballet. Dance is a natural bodily expression of joy and contentment; folk dances are universal, and are accompanied by singing and playing upon instruments. Ballet is an art form in which the succession of dances is arranged with careful regard to their variety, and the music is selected with the same purpose in view. Ballet as a spectacle was established by the Florentine master Jean Baptiste Lully (1632–87). In the following century Lully's disciple Jean Philippe Rameau (1683–1764), the great French musician who laid the foundation of modern harmonic theory, created stage music of exquisite grace and the style of French theater music was by then firmly set. In the nineteenth century, ballet in France became a sumptuous spectacle; it was almost like a concerto for a ballerina as soloist, accompanied by the *corps de ballet*. French ballet set the tone for choreographic art in all Europe. The Russians were entranced with it, and soon began cultivating a ballet of their own. Tschaikovsky wrote the ballet scores *Swan Lake* and *The Nutcracker*, which became perennial favorites. The Russian ballet impresario Serge Diaghilev (1872–1929) indirectly influenced the entire course of modern music, for it was for him that Stravinsky composed his revolutionary scores *Petrouchka* and *The Rite of Spring*, which influenced the style of composition everywhere. See BALLET; DANCE.

Keyboard Music. The organ was the mainstay of instrumental music in the church. The history of organ music in the great cathedrals of Europe shines with names of master musicians. In the Cathedral of San Marco in Venice, Andrea Gabrieli (1510–86) and his nephew Giovanni Gabrieli (1557–1612) were among the most illustrious organists and composers of the Renaissance; European musicians flocked to Venice to study with them. At St. Peter's in Rome, the concerts given by Girolamo Frescobaldi (1583–1643), an outstanding composer and organist, attracted masses of people. Johann Sebastian Bach served as organist in several Protestant churches in Germany. César Franck (1822–90) was for many years organist of the Church of St. Clotilde in Paris. Max Reger (1873–1916) was greatly esteemed in Germany both as organist and as composer.

What the organ was to church, the harpsichord (in England the virginal and spinet, in France the clavecin) was to home and concert hall. A vast musical literature exists for the harpsichord, for it was capable of producing the sharp-edged sound eminently suitable for rapid digital execution. In France the greatest clavecinistes were François Couperin (1668–1733), and Rameau, both of whom wrote charming harpsichord pieces for the ladies of Paris society, thus creating the type of composition characteristic of *style galant*. Their contemporary Domenico Scarlatti (1685–1757) wrote remarkable sonatas and other pieces for the harpsichord. See KEYBOARD MUSIC.

Styles: Gothic, Baroque, Rococo. In medieval universities music was a part of the scientific quadrivium—along with arithmetic, geometry, and astronomy. Medieval theorists treated music as a scientific study concerned with intervals and time divisions. Theological considerations played an important part; thus triple time was designated as "perfect" because of the theological perfection of the Trinity. Later music historians could no longer place music among exact sciences, and devised a chronology approximating the stylistic evolution of the fine arts. Musical periods were designated as gothic, 1200–1450, Renaissance, 1450–1600, baroque, 1600–1750, and rococo, 1750–1800. The eighteenth century was also designated as the classical age, the nineteenth century as the romantic age, the twentieth century as the modern age. The division of music history into periods bearing designations peculiar to the fine arts is justified by a certain parallelism between prevailing trends in art and in music. Gothic art was a utilitarian and intricate Nordic elaboration upon Grecian classicism; correspondingly, *ars nova* in music was marked by a practical application of involved contrapuntal designs. Renaissance art was a return to classicism in a new guise; the music of the Renaissance emphasized logic in formal construction. Baroque art represented a decorative palace culture; and the instrumental music of the baroque period was splendidly ornate. Rococo architecture was florid and richly ornamented; music of the rococo period was distinguished by great artistry of detail and lapidary precision of workmanship.

WORCESTER ART MUS.
This sixteenth century oil, *Woman Playing a Clavichord*, is attributed to the Flemish painter Jan van Hemessen.

Classical Age. The essence of classicism in music is formality of design combined with dignity of content and mastery of craft. But classicism at its best does not imply rigidity of style or pedantry of treatment; lyric expressiveness and vivacity of musical motion are the finest ingredients of great classical music. Such composers as Johann Sebastian Bach, Händel, Haydn, and Mozart were not pompous; within the strict conventions of their time they created music of individual charm as well as of artistic grandeur. Bach and Händel possessed all the characteristics of dignity and craftsmanship that are essential in classical music. Bach remained in Germany as an organist and cantor; Händel went to England and was buried in Westminster Abbey. Händel's music was more worldly than Bach's, but Bach prevailed over Händel as a pure musician. The name of Antonio Vivaldi (1678–1741) would perhaps have been as glorious as those of Bach and Händel, had the scope of his musical production been wider. His greatness lies in his instrumental music, particularly his orchestral concertos of the type of the *concerto grosso*, in which a group of solo instruments alternates with the playing of the full orchestra, thus creating a succession of vivid contrasts. Haydn (1732–1809) and Mozart (1756–91) gave color and definition to the second half of the eighteenth century, as Bach and Händel gave to the first. Haydn, the reputed father of the symphony, was also the creator of the string quartet. Mozart was an all-embracing genius; he wrote operas, symphonies, chamber music, and piano works with equal brilliance, mastery, and communicative power.

Age of Romance. The transition from the classical serenity and simplicity of the eighteenth century to the romantic upsurge and complexity of the nineteenth was symbolized in Beethoven (1770–1827); he began his career as an eighteenth century composer, in spirit as well as in chronology, but as his interest shifted from form to self-expression he created a new code of musical aesthetics. Eighteenth century composers wrote music in great quantities; Haydn composed more than 100 symphonies. This productivity was natural; there existed a classical formula according to which these works were written, and it is sometimes difficult for scholars to distinguish between genuine and spurious works of composers of that period. Beethoven, however, entered upon a course of highly individualistic composition. Each work was to him a separate experience. Such emphasis on diversity for its own sake is one of the main characteristics of romanticism, and is found in Schubert, Schumann, Chopin, and others, many of whom did much of this work in Vienna.

Franz Schubert (1797–1828) imparted new distinction to the German song, creating a genre of artistic lied which became a model for German song composers through the nineteenth century. The romantic spirit of Robert Schumann (1810–56) was shown in his life as well as in his works, which were subjective

ALBRIGHT ART GALLERY

Raoul Dufy's *Homage to Mozart*

to the core. He composed music as one would write a diary, confiding to it his intimate secrets; his *Carnival* contains allusions that were intelligible only to friends. Schumann conjured up imaginary characters whom he endowed with traits pertaining to the different aspects of his own nature. That he died insane was an ironic finale to his romantic life. Frédéric Chopin (1810–49) expressed the romantic ideals without the aid of a literary program, merely by writing exquisite music for the piano. But the titles of his compositions —nocturnes, ballades—illustrate his devotion to romantic imagery.

Felix Mendelssohn (1809–47) was a classicist among his romantic contemporaries. In his music the formal design is paramount, but the melodic flow is typically romantic. His *Songs Without Words* are an epitome of romantic expression, wordless but eloquent. Johannes Brahms (1833–97) was a romantic in classical garments whose symphonies, piano works, and songs embody the finest qualities of German craftsmanship and the poetic spirit of the Viennese classics.

The names of Anton Bruckner (1824–96) and Gustav Mahler (1860–1911) are often coupled together as the last great romanticists of Vienna. They wrote symphonic music and shunned the musical theater as a popular and therefore inferior genre. Both stood aloof from the public, and both had to wait a long time for recognition.

Hector Berlioz (1803–69) carried the spirit of French romanticism to the utmost degree of subjectivism. In his works he attempted to create new forms, carried by a free association and centered upon a fixed idea; that he succeeded in imposing his will upon musical matter demonstrates not only his capacity but the readiness of the world to accept such revolutionary ideas.

Franz Liszt (1811–86) was the creator of the symphonic poem, a romantic form par excellence. Literary inspiration guided him in his composition; program music was his aesthetic credo.

Romantic Nationalism. Romantic idealism was closely associated with nationalism. Romanticism strives to attain the utmost freedom of artistic expression; nationalism endeavors to accomplish a similar liberation of the national ideal. Witness, for instance, the strong element of romantic nationalism in the music dramas of the German Richard Wagner (1813–83). In the nineteenth century, national aspirations revealed themselves in the domain of music in lands theretofore musically dormant. In Russia the national spirit became manifest in the operas of Mikhail Glinka (1803–57) and in the formation of the National School of Music represented by the names of Rimski-Korsakov (1844–1908), Modest Moussorgsky (1839–81), and Aleksandr Borodin (1833–87). Tschaikovsky (1840–93) stood aloof from conscious nationalism, but in his romantic symphonies and songs he expressed the Russian soul perhaps even more intimately than did his nationalist colleagues. The romantic spirit also animated the great Russian pianist Anton Rubinstein (1829–94), who was the composer of now forgotten symphonies and operas and of still remembered romantic piano pieces. The last great Russian romanticist was Sergei Rachmaninoff (1873–1943). Anton Arensky (1861–1906) possessed a similar talent for romantic and melancholic music in a characteristic Russian style, but his works failed to attract music lovers. Sergei Taneyev (1856–1915) was Russia's mightiest contrapuntist; but his music is unknown outside Russia. Nikolai Medtner (1880–1951) was a Russian romanticist whose piano compositions possess great merit but somehow lack the intimate quality that appeals to music lovers at large. Aleksandr Scriabin (1872–1915) was a solitary figure in Russian music. His overriding ambition was to elevate music to the point of pantheistic philosophy; the titles of his symphonic works express this preoccupation: *Divine Poem*, *Poem of Ecstasy*, *Poem of Fire.* He based his harmony on a six-note chord, which he called the mystic chord, derived from the upper overtone that cannot be heard by an ordinary ear.

In Bohemia, Antonín Dvořák (1841–1908) and Bedřich Smetana (1824–84) wrote music redolent of national folkways. Dvořák's most famous work is a symphony composed during his visit in America and entitled *From the New World.* Smetana's best score is *My Fatherland*, a cycle of symphonic pictures of his native country.

Scandinavian romantic nationalism was musically expressed by Edvard Grieg (1843–1908), a Norwegian who gave expression to native elements in lyric compositions of great charm. Carl Nielsen (1865–1931) was the most important Danish romantic nationalist. In Finland Jean Sibelius (1865–1957) created impressive works and transformed the Finnish epic *Kalevala* into a series of symphonic poems.

Béla Bartók (1881–1945), the Hungarian master, was nationalist, romantic, modernist, and a scholar whose work in collecting folk songs in his native Transylvania was of great importance to musical ethnography. In his own music he ingeniously and effectively applied modern devices to the authentic folk songs. His compatriot Zoltán Kodály (1882–), Bartók's fellow folk song collector, wrote symphonic and vocal music of great distinction, sparkling with Hungarian rhythms. The Rumanian Georges Enesco (1881–1955) wrote a group of symphonic works based on Rumanian melorhythms (melodies and rhythms). In Italy romantic nationalism in modern times was cultivated by Alfredo Casella (1883–1947), Ottorino Respighi (1879–1936), Francesco Malipiero (1882–), and Ildebrando Pizzetti (1880–). In their individually diverse manners they applied modernist techniques to subjects intimately connected with Italian melodic resources.

England and America. After the golden age of Elizabethan madrigals, there appeared on the English horizon only one musical star of the first magnitude: Henry Purcell (1659–95), composer of melodious songs and dramatic music for the theater. Though English to the core, Purcell emulated Italian models, and so declared himself. In the eighteenth century

England imported Händel, and for a century after him English music was in thrall of Händel's art. In the nineteenth century Mendelssohn captivated the minds of musical England. Romantic nationalism in England did not come into its own until the advent of Sir Edward Elgar (1857–1934); his most striking composition is the first military march from *Pomp and Circumstance*, which breathes the spirit of England at its proudest moment. Among other English composers, Frederick Delius (1862–1934) wrote programmatic music somewhat tinged with impressionism, as did Gustav Holst (1874–1934). The most remarkable composer of symphonic music in twentieth century England was Ralph Vaughan Williams (1872–1958), whose *London Symphony* gives a musical picture of the city. Other modern English romantics are Arthur Bliss (1891–), Edmund Rubbra (1901–), and William Walton (1902–). Benjamin Britten (1913–), composer of remarkably effective operas, has also written symphonic and chamber music of great originality and ingratiating simplicity.

America received its musical culture from Germany. Edward MacDowell (1861–1908), for example, was educated in Germany, acquiring a mastery of technique rare among American musicians of his time. Animated by the spirit of national romanticism, he wrote pieces characteristic of the native scene, including Indian folkways. His album of piano pieces, *New England Idyls*, gives a vivid panorama of rural America. Other significant American composers were New Englanders: Arthur Foote (1853–1937), George Chadwick (1854–1931), Horatio Parker (1863–1919), Frederick Converse (1871–1940), Henry Hadley (1871–1937), Daniel Gregory Mason (1873–1953)—most of them under the influence of German music. An exception was Henry Franklin Gilbert (1868–1928), who used native themes in a truly American, non-Germanic manner. Several American composers followed French trends and created pieces of singular exotic charm: Charles Martin Loeffler (1861–1935), a native of Alsace, who made his home in Boston; Charles T. Griffes (1884–1920); and Edward Burlingame Hill (1872–1960).

The greatest American musical innovator was Charles Ives (1874–1954), a Connecticut Yankee, who, although trained academically, wrote music unlike anything in Europe or America, completely free from restraints. Despite the radical idiom of his music, it is unmistakably American: the very titles reflect the American scene—*Concord Sonata; Three Places in New England; Lincoln, The Great Commoner*.

The new generation of American composers was oriented toward musical Paris rather than Germany; several of them won international fame: Walter Piston (1894–), the American classicist; Howard Hanson (1896–), the romanticist; Roger Sessions (1896–), the radical; Henry Cowell (1897–), the brilliant experimentalist; Roy Harris (1898–), the Westerner; George Antheil (1900–59), the ultramodernist; Aaron Copland (1900–), the astute limner of the American scene. Among those born in the twentieth century are Paul Creston (1906–), William Schuman (1910–), Samuel Barber (1910–), Norman Dello Joio (1913–), David Diamond (1916–), and Peter Mennin (1923–). Leonard Bernstein (1918–), the most famous U.S.-born symphony conductor, has a talent for composing symphonic music in a vigorous modern manner as well as for writing popular musical comedies.

In the wake of wars and revolutions, many illustrious European composers emigrated to America: Sergei Rachmaninoff; Igor Stravinsky (1882–); Arnold Schönberg (1874–1951); Ernest Bloch (1880–1959), the Swiss-born composer of impassioned music of Jewish inspiration; the Vienna-born Ernst Krenek (1900–); the brilliant German composer of theater music, Kurt Weill (1900–50).

If North America was at first a musical colony of Germany, South America paid its allegiance to Italy. Melodious song rather than hard counterpoint is of the essence in Latin American music. The first significant composer in South America was the Brazilian Carlos Gomes (1839–96), whose Italian operas on Indian subjects were widely performed. In later times Heitor Villa-Lobos (1887–1959) of Brazil revealed a veritable genius for imaginative and original music in the native vein. His *Bachianas Brasileiras*, uniting Brazilian melorhythms with Bachian counterpoint, are unique. In Mexico Carlos Chávez (1899–) composed fine symphonies and chamber music. Silvestre Revueltas (1900–40) was a Mexican composer of singular native force.

Impressionism. The link between painting and music was intimately established by French composers of the last decade of the nineteenth century in a movement that became known as impressionism. The term was first applied, derisively, to the style of the painter Claude Monet, who exhibited a painting entitled *Impressions*. When Claude Debussy (1862–1918) wrote his exquisite symphonic tableau *Prélude à l'après-midi d'un faune* (Prelude to the Afternoon of a Faun) 1894, the label impressionism was attached to him and his disciples, although Debussy himself pointedly rejected it. The musical style of impressionism is characterized by extreme dispersal of sonorous matter and virtual abandonment of formal development. Where the romanticists painted in large strokes of tone color, Debussy reduced products of his palette to fine daubs, minutely distributed with the care of an expert miniaturist. His musical triptych *La Mer* portrays the moods of the sea, from serene calm to ominous turbulence, in the spirit of subtle adumbration rather than realistic representation; his piano piece *Clair de Lune* is a gem of tone painting, depicting the elusive moonbeams with an ethereal delicacy.

Impressionism was not born with Debussy, but was anticipated by several composers in France. Harmonies characteristic of impressionist music were cultivated by Gabriel Fauré (1845–1924), the first to adopt a style of subdued colors, whose songs set the tone for much French vocal music. Vincent d'Indy (1851–1931) was, with Fauré and Debussy, a builder of the modern French style of composition; his music was inspired by an eternal France of old, but the harmonic dress of his instrumental works sparkles with more modern colors. Florent Schmitt (1870–1958), a prolific French composer, combined a strong classical sense with a free impressionist development; the complexity of his contrapuntal texture is unusual among French musicians. Paul Dukas (1865–1935) was a master of program music in an impressionist vein; his celebrated orchestral piece *Sorcerer's Apprentice* recreates Goethe's ironic ballad with superlative skill and humor. Albert Roussel (1869–1937) cultivated an evocative art in the impressionistic manner; but he was also a classicist in the formal logic of his symphonic music.

Maurice Ravel (1875–1937) was, after Debussy, the most illustrious composer of the impressionist era. So precise and so perfect was his craftsmanship that he was once described as the Swiss watchmaker of modern music. His power of tone painting was unequaled. In his choreographic poem *La Valse* he evoked the splendor and excitement of the Second Empire. In his ballet *Bolero* he conjured up a coruscating Spanish dance; the score is all the more remarkable because it sustains the motion of the music by using a single rhythmic figure throughout, with the theme presented in an infinite variety of tone colors.

Postimpressionism. Impressionism lost its lustre after the brutalizing experience of World War I. Young French musicians found a prophet in the person of Erik Satie (1866–1925), a composer who preached complete freedom from social and artistic conventions. The so-called Group of Six formed in Paris in 1920 was much under Satie's influence; but at least three of its members became famous in their own right—Arthur Honegger (1892–1955), Darius

Milhaud (1892–), and François Poulenc (1899–1963). Among younger French composers who developed in the atmosphere of postimpressionism the most significant is Olivier Messiaen (1908–), whose resources embraced many fields; his immense symphonic work *Turangalila* is inspired by Hindu philosophy but incorporates modernistic devices, including an electronic keyboard instrument.

Expressionism. Impressionism received its artistic impulse from the outside world, viewed through a subjective prism and colored by the musician's perceptive eye and ear. Expressionism projected an inner idea onto the outside world, coloring reality with subjective philosophy. Impressionism, with its subtilized rainbow hues, was basically optimistic and typically French; expressionism was created in central Europe—in Austria and Germany—and revealed the darksome recesses of morbid psychology. Impressionism adopted the method of swiftly changing opalescent and iridescent harmonies; expressionism found a congenial idiom in a complete negation of tonal relationship—atonality.

Despite its extremely subjective and unworldly character, expressionism found a powerful echo in a world in turmoil. The man who had sufficient genius to create expressionist works of compelling power was Arnold Schönberg; he tore tradition into shreds, but the elusive poetry of his music haunted even those who thought it was not music at all. Schönberg's disciple Alban Berg (1885–1935) created a masterpiece of expressionist drama in his atonal opera *Wozzeck*, in which the singers on the stage and the instruments in the orchestra are agonized by the tremendous impact of the dreamlike yet brutal story. Another Schönberg disciple, Anton von Webern (1883–1945), wrote few works, and even these few were very short (one lasts but 19 seconds and contains only six bars, with an upbeat), yet exercised a profound influence on musicians in the second half of the twentieth century.

Neoclassicism. As a reaction to romanticism, impressionism, and expressionism, in the 1920's emerged a powerful movement that brought back classicism in a new guise. The slogan "Back to Bach" was sounded, and modern musicians abandoned programmatic designs in favor of classical forms. Ferruccio Busoni (1866–1924) was the first to urge a return to classicism, but the musician who actually turned the tide was the modernist Stravinsky. Abandoning his Russian-inspired ballet music, he began to write works in a purely classical form, enriched with neoclassical dissonances. In the subject matter of his new ballets, Stravinsky returned to Greek mythology in such works as *Persephone* and *Apollo Musagète* and the oratorio *Oedipus Rex*.

In Germany Paul Hindemith (1895–), a master of modern counterpoint, wrote music in classical forms, but with a distinct aura of late romanticism. He was a firm believer in the virtue of classical music that can be performed at home by amateurs, and was a leader in the musical utilitarianism known as *Gebrauchsmusik;* under his influence many composers adopted a more "practical" method of composition. The art of stylization became a major consideration among neoclassicists, because it opens for modern use the entire field of old music. Thus Carl Orff (1895–) achieved great success with his scenic oratorio *Carmina Burana* (1938), using medieval student songs in a modern setting. In this and other neoclassical works, old music and new are brought together with fruitful results.

Neoprimitivism. Whereas neoclassical music goes back to Bach, modern musicians in search of more forceful effects found inspiration in primitive songs and rhythms of populations as yet largely untouched by modern civilization. Such primitive tunes rarely go beyond the range of four or five notes; musical phrases are extremely short and the rhythm is repetitive. Because of these very limitations, the effect is sometimes fascinating. There is an element of primitivism in impressionist melodies, which are often abrupt; but the richness of harmony compensates for this reduction in melodic extension. Composers attracted by primitive subjects dispense with such perfumed harmonies and adopt stark and bleak sonorities. Stravinsky's *Rite of Spring* builds harmonic blocks to invoke the primitive landscape of pagan Russia. Sergei Prokofiev's (1891–1953), *Scythian Suite* produces a similar effect. Surfeited with over-refined musical culture, composers are eager to use primitivistic designs to produce a strong impact upon jaded senses.

Modern Techniques

Polytonality. New techniques were needed for the new music of the twentieth century. As an experiment, unrelated triads were combined into a single chord. Amazingly, the most remotely related keys, whose tonics stood at the distance of a tritone (as for instance C major and F-sharp major), made a most euphonious combination. The tritone had been the *diabolus in musica* of medieval theorists, diabolical in both melodic and contrapuntal practice. Simultaneous use of different keys acquired the learned name of polytonality. In actual practice only two different keys are superimposed, and the more logical term would be bitonality. Theoretically it is possible to put together four different triads without duplication of notes, but such quadritonality has never been systematically explored. See Key; Atonal Music.

Atonality. In classical music, melody serves the purpose of establishing a definite feeling of key. Twentieth century composers adopted the opposite principle, namely, the avoidance of melodic turns that suggest tonality (see Melody). The diabolical tritone has taken the place of the old-fashioned fifth in atonal writing. The octave was avoided, and the major seventh was enthroned in its place. Intervals formerly regarded as unwieldy became privileged members of the melody.

Twelve-Tone Method. With traditional rules abolished and dissonance emancipated, a new code of musical laws was imperatively needed. Such a code was provided in the method of composing with 12 tones formulated by Schönberg. In this system a musical composition is built on a series of 12 different notes, a tone row. The theme may be inverted so that high notes become low notes and ascending intervals become descending intervals. It may be played backwards, forming a retrograde series. This retrograde form may again be inverted. These metamorphoses result in the formation of four serial forms. Since each of these can be transposed so as to start on any of the 12 chromatic notes, 48 different forms are generated by a tone row. The basic series can be used melodically, contrapuntally, and harmonically, so that a series of 12 notes is distributed in two or more parts. Although in theory no component tone is to be repeated until all 12 have been used, in practical composition considerable freedom exists. The fund of possible melodies in the 12-tone method was known as dodecaphonic music (dodeka is Greek for twelve).

Quarter-Tone Music. Systematic attempts have been made to promote a scale of microtones—divisions smaller than semitones—particularly that of 24 intervals to an octave, resulting in quarter tones. Alois Hába (1893–) wrote music in quarter tones and established a school of quarter-tone music (and also sixth-tone music) at the Prague Conservatory. Rimski-Korsakov's grandson, George, founded a quarter-tone ensemble in Leningrad. By 1900 Julian Carrillo (1875–) of Mexico had experimented with quarter tones and published a textbook, *The Thirteenth Sound* (that is, the sound beyond the 12 chromatic notes).

Jazz. One of the most powerful phenomenons of modern music was jazz, a type of vigorous, lyrical, syncopated, largely improvised music that originated in the United States (see Jazz). Jazz spread throughout the world, and many European composers such as Ravel and Milhaud introduced elements of it into their works. Some composers, such as George Gershwin (1898–1937), produced works that aimed at raising jazz to the level of serious concert music; one of these, *Rhapsody in Blue*, became one of the most popular of twentieth century compositions. See Folk Music.

Musique Concrète. With the invention of electronic instruments capable of producing tones of any frequency and tone color, interest was stimulated in the use of such resources in actual composition. In 1948 a Paris radio engineer began experimenting with recording various sounds around him—noises, conversation, whistling. He then treated the result by scientific means such as speeding up the sound (thus raising the pitch) and playing the recordings backward. He named the product *musique concrète* to emphasize its concrete origin without the aid of immaterial inspiration. In America John Cage (1912–) experimented along similar lines with his "prepared piano," changing the tone of each individual key by putting small coins, nails, and other objects on the strings. This technique was the outgrowth of early experiments of Henry Cowell (1897–), who developed the art of playing directly on the piano strings and introduced the so-called tone clusters (played on the keyboard by the forearms)—actually used by the jazz pianist "Jelly Roll" Morton (1885–1941) long before they were discovered independently by Cowell.

Before World War I a group of Italian futurists, spiritually led by the poet Emilio Marinetti (1876–1944), gave concerts of "noise orchestras" containing all sorts of sounds—except melodious ones. But the louder noise of battle soon engulfed them; the future of the Italian futurists was lamentable in its inconsequence. A remnant of the futurist spirit was caught by the American composer George Antheil, who wrote *Ballet mécanique*, scored for a noisy ensemble including several airplane propellers.

Soviet Music. After the Revolution of 1917 Russian composers experimented with new sonorities and new musical ideas suitable for the socialist society. The Soviet composer Dmitri Shostakovitch (1906–) wrote a symphony in which he imitated the factory whistle; Aleksandr Mossolov (1900–) produced a score called the *Iron Foundry*. But such methods were soon declared unworthy, and Soviet composers were urged by the Soviet government to write music according to the ideal of "socialist realism," functional in purpose and pleasing to the senses. Shostakovitch and other Soviet composers such as Aram Khatchaturian (1903–) changed their methods.

Among composers of the older generation who accepted the Soviet principle of nationally colored, realistic music were Nikolai Miaskovsky (1881–1950), who wrote 27 symphonies, and Sergei Prokofiev author of a *Classical Symphony*, the opera *Love for Three Oranges*, and the fairy tale *Peter and the Wolf*.

Musical Education is as old as music itself, but the first scientific method of musical instruction in historical times was the Guidonian hand, the visual method of indicating the position of scale notes upon the joints of the finger introduced by Guido d'Arezzo about the year 1000. Practical and theoretical teaching was part of the program of the Meistersinger in the Renaissance period. Methods of teaching have varied widely, each teacher believing his system to be the best. The first conservatories of music originated in Italy in the sixteenth century, but were connected with charity institutions and bore such names as Hospital for Incurables or Hospital of Mendicants. The great Conservatoire de Paris was established in 1795. In Germany the most famous music school was the Leipzig Conservatory, founded by Mendelssohn in 1843. In Russia the St. Petersburg Conservatory was founded by Anton Rubinstein in 1862, the Moscow Conservatory by his brother Nikolai Rubenstein (1835–81) in 1866. Higher musical learning was provided in England by Royal Colleges of Music. In the United States the New England Conservatory of Music was founded in 1867. Among dozens of fine conservatories in the United States, three have achieved great renown: the Eastman School of Music, founded by George Eastman (1854–1932) as part of the University of Rochester, N.Y., in 1919; the Juilliard School of Music in New York, N.Y., established with the funds of Augustus D. Juilliard (1836–1919) after his death; and the Curtis Institute of Music in Philadelphia, founded in 1924.

Problems of Musical Aesthetics and Criticism. What is beautiful in music, and what is not, cannot be settled in absolute terms. Environment and tradition establish the norms of musical aesthetics for any period. Music history, viewed from the standpoint of aesthetics, presents a curious spectacle of successive denunciations of new works followed by reluctant acceptance and eventual establishment of the novelty as a standard, until a bolder innovator breaks the latest tradition and is denounced in his turn. Claudio Monteverdi (1567–1643) was attacked for his use of unprepared dissonance; Beethoven was denounced as a cultivator of barbaric discords; Wagner was described as a madman. Debussy's *La Mer* (The Sea) was characterized as "Mal de Mer" (Sea Sickness), and Stravinsky's *Sacre du Printemps* (Rite of Spring) as "Massacre du Printemps" (Massacre of Spring). When Tschaikovsky's famous piano concerto in B-flat minor received its world première (not in Russia, but in Boston, Mass.), a critic opined that the work was as difficult for general comprehension as the name of the composer himself. Such violent attacks on Beethoven, Wagner, Tschaikovsky, and Debussy—all within a single century—convincingly demonstrate the relativity of tastes in art. The most talented, and the most vicious, music critic in modern times was Eduard Hanslick (1825–1904), who attacked Wagner and Liszt with ferocity. But he was also the pioneer of musical aesthetics; his book *On the Beautiful in Music* exercised profound influence. In England, Ernest Newman (1868–1959) was a perceptive commentator on music, and continued to write into his 90th year. In America, James Huneker (1860–1921) and Philip Hale (1854–1934) were fine stylists. The most famous Russian critic was Vladimir Stasov (1824–1906), who launched the national Russian movement.

The Future of Music. Richard Wagner proudly called his art the music of the future. Indeed, the Wagnerian creed almost became a dogma among musicians of succeeding generations. But the vanguard of twentieth century composers rebelled against Wagner and embraced the variegated methods of impressionism, expressionism, and neoclassicism. A state of musical eclecticism existed at the mid-twentieth century—perhaps an eclecticism of confusion, or perhaps the augury of a new strong musical style, incorporating the best elements among the great musical achievements of the past.

Nicolas Slonimsky

Bibliography

Theory: Paul Hindemith, *Elementary Training for Musicians* (1946); E. Toch, *Shaping Forces in Music* (1948); H. Leichentritt, *Musical Form* (1951); H. A. Murphy and E. J. Stringham, *Creative Harmony and Musicianship* (1951); C. Sachs, *Rhythm and Tempo* (1952); F. Rothschild, *Lost Tradition in Music* (1953); G. Haydon, *Introduction to Musicology* (1954); Arnold Schönberg, *Structural Functions of Harmony* (1954); C. H. Kitson, *Art of Counterpoint* (ed. 1950), *Evolution of Harmony* (1953), *Elementary Harmony* (3 vols. 1955); H. L. Boatwright, *Introduction to the Theory of Music* (1956); R. O. Morris, *Structure of Music* (1956); R. O. Morris and H. K. Andrews, *Oxford Harmony* (2 vols. 1956); Walter Piston, *Harmony* (ed. 1949), *Orchestration* (1955), *Counterpoint* (1956); A. Hutchings, *Invention and Composition of Music* (1958); R. Reti, *Tonality, Atonality, Pantonality* (1958).

History, General: P. H. Lang, *Music in Western Civilization* (1941); D. N. Ferguson, *History of Musical Thought* (ed. 1948); A. T. Davison and W. Apel, *Historical Anthology of Music* (2 vols. 1946–49); C. Sachs, *History of Musical Instru-*

ments (1940), *Our Musical Heritage* (1948); W. O. Strunk, ed., *Source Readings in Musical History* (1950); H. Leichentritt, *Music of the Western Nations* (1956); G. E. H. Abraham, ed., *History of Music in Sound* (7 vols. 1953–57); C. Burney, *History of Music* (1789, 2 vols. ed. 1957); P. Garvie, ed., *Music and Western Man* (1958).

HISTORY, ANCIENT, EASTERN, AND MEDIEVAL: C. Engel, *Music of the Most Ancient Nations, Particularly of the Assyrians, Egyptians and Hebrews* (1929); G. Reese, *Music in the Middle Ages* (1940); C. Sachs, *Rise of Music in the Ancient World* (1943); A. Hughes, ed., *Early Medieval Music up to 1300* (1954); T. Georgiades, *Greek Music, Verse and Dance* (1956); J. Kyagambiddwa, *African Music from the Source of the Nile* (1956); E. J. Wellesz, *History of Byzantine Music and Hymnography* (1949), *Ancient and Oriental Music* (1957); A. Harman, *Mediaeval and Early Renaissance Music up to 1525* (1958).

HISTORY, RENAISSANCE: A. Einstein, *Italian Madrigal* (3 vols. 1949); M. F. Bukofzer, *Studies in Medieval and Renaissance Music* (1951); E. H. Fellows, *English Madrigal* (1952); Thomas Morley, *Plain and Easy Introduction to Practical Music* (1597, ed. 1952); G. Reese, *Music in the Renaissance* (1954); A. Hughes, ed., *Ars Nova and the Renaissance* (1953–57); A. Harman, *Late Renaissance and Baroque Music (1525–1750)* (1958).

HISTORY, BAROQUE AND CLASSICAL: A. Dolmetsch, *Interpretation of the Music of the 17th and 18th Centuries* (ed. 1946); A. L. Bacharach, ed., *From the 16th Century to the Time of Beethoven* (1948); C. P. E. Bach, *Essay on the True Art of Playing Keyboard Instruments* (1762, ed. 1951); A. A. Carse, *18th Century Symphonies* (1951); D. F. Tovey, *Companion to the Art of the Fugue* (1951); F. Rothschild, *Lost Tradition in Music* (1953); Albert Schweitzer, *Johann Sebastian Bach* (2 vols. ed. 1955); R. M. Stevenson, *Music Before the Classic Era* (1955); A. Einstein, *Mozart: His Character, His Work* (ed. 1957); A. Harman, *Late Renaissance and Baroque Music (1525–1750)* (1958).

HISTORY, ROMANTIC: A. Einstein, *Music in the Romantic Era* (1947); E. Hanslick, *Vienna's Golden Years of Music, 1850–1900* (1951); A. L. Bacharach, ed., *Romantic Age* (1952); B. V. Asaf'ev, *Russian Music from the Beginning of the Nineteenth Century* (1953); W. H. Mellers, *Romanticism and the 20th Century* (1957).

HISTORY, MODERN: R. Leibowitz, *Schoenberg and His School* (1949); N. Slonimsky, *Music Since 1900* (ed. 1949); G. E. H. Abraham, *Eight Soviet Composers* (1946), *This Modern Music* (1952); J. Culshaw, *Century of Music* (1952); N. Demuth, *Musical Trends in the 20th Century* (1952); A. L. Bacharach, ed., *Twentieth Century* (1954); A. V. Ol'khovskii, *Music under the Soviets* (1954); H. Hartog, ed., *European Music in the Twentieth Century* (1957).

ANALYSIS AND CRITICISM: E. Blom, *Limitations of Music* (1928); A. Einstein, *Greatness in Music* (1941); Robert Schumann, *On Music and Musicians* (ed. 1947); Igor Stravinsky, *Poetics of Music* (1947); R. Rolland, *Essays on Music* (1948); C. T. Smith, *Music and Reason* (1948); D. F. Tovey, *Essays in Musical Analysis* (6 vols. ed. 1944), *Main Stream of Music* (1950); M. Bernstein, *Introduction to Music* (ed. 1951); W. H. Mellers, *Music and Society* (ed. 1951); V. Thompson, *Art of Judging Music* (1948), *Music Right and Left* (1951); Paul Hindemith, *Composer's World* (1952); Darius Milhaud, *Notes Without Music* (1952); W. B. Barlow, *Foundations of Music* (1953); H. Weinstock, *Music as an Art* (1953); T. Dart, *Interpretation of Music* (1954); S. Morgenstern, ed., *Composers on Music* (1955); George Bernard Shaw, *On Music* (ed. 1955); V. Zuckerkandl, *Sound and Symbol* (1955); Hector Berlioz, *Evenings with the Orchestra* (1853, ed. 1956); A. Einstein, *Essays on Music* (1956); L. B. Meyer, *Emotion and Meaning in Music* (1956); F. B. Busoni, *Essence of Music* (1957); Aaron Copland, *What to Listen for in Music* (ed. 1957); E. Newman, *From the World of Music* (1957).

HISTORY, AMERICAN: G. Chase, *America's Music* (1954); J. T. Howard, *Our American Music: 300 Years of It* (ed. 1954); J. T. Howard and G. K. Bellows, *Short History of Music in America* (1957).

MUSICAL COMEDY, a combination of music, drama, and dancing, constituting a light theatrical entertainment closely related to operetta and comic opera. Musical comedy in the United States was strongly influenced by vaudeville and burlesque. Among the first musical comedies were *In Town* (England, 1892) and *Belle of New York* (United States, 1898). Plot was subservient to music and dancing in most musical comedies. The musical revue differs from the musical comedy in that it is a series of unrelated skits or episodes and characteristically has elements of topical and social satire. Among widely known writers and composers of musical comedy were

VANDAMM

One of the sprightliest musical comedies, *Oklahoma!*, by Rodgers and Hammerstein, won a 1944 Pulitzer prize. "The Surrey with the Fringe on Top" was among its hit tunes.

Oscar Hammerstein II, Richard Rodgers, Lorenz Hart, Jerome Kern, Kurt Weill, George and Ira Gershwin, Cole Porter, Rudolf Friml, George S. Kaufman, Morrie Ryskind, Moss Hart, Victor Herbert, Sigmund Romberg, Alan Jay Lerner, and Frederick Loewe. Among the most popular U.S. musical comedies were *Rose-Marie* (1925), *Showboat* (1928), *Of Thee I Sing* (1932), *Oklahoma!* (1943), *Carousel* (1945), *My Fair Lady* (1956), *West Side Story* (1957), *Fiorello!* (1959), and *The Sound of Music* (1959). The motion picture musical comedy was almost wholly derived from stage tradition.

MUSICAL GLASSES, a musical instrument consisting of a set of glasses of equal size containing varying amounts of water, the pitch of the note produced by each glass being proportional to the quantity of water in it. The instrument in its original form was played by rubbing the glasses with wet fingers. See HARMONICA.

MUSIC BOX, a mechanical musical instrument developed from the musical snuffbox of the eighteenth century. The musical sounds are generated by the vibrating teeth of a steel comb. The teeth are tuned to produce the notes of the musical scale, and their points are in juxtaposition to a revolving brass cylinder, which is set in motion by the winding of a spring. The surface of the cylinder is studded with small projecting pins, so arranged that as the cylinder turns they pluck and set in vibration those teeth that will produce the desired combination or succession of sounds. A single cylinder may be noted to play up to 36 tunes, the change from one to another being produced by moving the cylinder to bring a different group of pins into play. Like other mechanical instruments, such as the player piano, music boxes have often inspired craftsmen to elaborate feats of decoration; and some music boxes, varying in size from those that are easily portable to those so large as to dominate the *decor* of a room, are prized by fanciers of decorative arts.

HENRY FORD MUS. AND GREENFIELD VILLAGE

This eighteenth century music box, of the "parlor barrel" type, has three cylinders, each with 10 tunes.

MUSIC HALL, a British public hall for musical entertainment or variety performances (comic skits, songs and dances, juggling acts, and the like). From the time of Queen Elizabeth I the variety element struggled for entrance into the regular theater. After the passage of the Theatre Act, 1843, more clearly defining the line between legitimate theater and variety, music halls flourished. In most of them smoking, drinking, and eating were permitted in the audience, and performers who failed to please were often peppered with garbage. In America the music hall (such as that of Weber and Fields, New York City) was soon superseded by the continuous-show vaudeville house, and later by houses offering a mixed program of moving pictures and vaudeville. Both English music hall and American vaudeville theater were eventually largely displaced by movies, radio, and television.

MUSIC LIBRARY ASSOCIATION, an organization founded in 1931 to promote the development of music libraries and to encourage studies in the organization and administration of music libraries and the use of music in libraries. Its official publication is *Notes* and its headquarters are in the music division of the Library of Congress at Washington, D.C.

MILDRED OTHMER PETERSON

MUSIC THERAPY, the use of music in the treatment of disease. Music has a physiological as well as a psychological effect on most people. It is used to treat the symptoms rather than the underlying causes of disease, however, and cannot be considered therapeutic except in the sense that recreation and diversion in general are therapeutic, unless applied by one who understands the possible effects its individual uses may have.

Music was used in the treatment of disease, especially of mental disease, by many primitive tribes. Witch doctors and medicine men have used it not only to heal their patients but to lift themselves into a state of ecstasy in which they might exert unusual powers over their tribes.

Some of the ways in which music may be utilized are through passive listening, active or directed listening, performing, and creating—such as composing pieces and constructing instruments.

Effects. The principal therapeutic value of music lies in its influence upon the emotions. Music justifies itself as a psychological tool through its ability to create and change moods; to provide socially acceptable emotional outlets; and to influence the ego by developing self-assurance, pride of achievement, and other facets of the personality. It can be used to hold attention as well as to stimulate association and the power of imagination. Music plays an important role in taking the patient's attention away from himself and his problems.

Music is invaluable in bringing about feelings of unity, even in the most heterogeneous groups. This factor is vitally important in the treatment of mental disease where patients may be asocial and need to be resocialized. Participation in musical activities fosters co-operation and improvement in general attitude and may aid the process of rebuilding a disintegrated personality.

In Hospitals. During World War I music was prescribed for use in the treatment of war neuroses. As an accompaniment to exercise, it was used extensively in government hospitals during World War II. Finger and arm exercise in playing keyboard instruments, and mouth and jaw development from blowing wind instruments have been valuable in treating orthopedic patients and persons with paralysis. Increased emphasis has been placed on the functional uses of music. It has been used in general therapy in government hospitals and in veterans hospitals.

Uses. Passive listening may act as an aid to digestion and as a sedative at bedtime. In many mental hospitals, fighting, pushing, and quarreling cease, and table manners improve, when soft waltzes and light semiclassical compositions are played at mealtime. In the operating room favorite compositions reduce fear and tension and seem to lessen pain when local anesthetics are employed. Dentists have found that many patients are less annoyed by the buzz of the drill if earphones transmit music. Psychiatrists have found that music can sometimes soothe persons in the manic phase of manic-depressive psychosis as well as arouse those in the depressive state. See MANIC-DEPRESSIVE PSYCHOSIS.

In active listening the individual's attention is directed to various phases of the selections to be performed so as to arouse the person's interest and develop his imagination; thus his pleasure is increased and his powers of concentration are strengthened. Most authorities agree that participation has great possibilities. Exercising to music, dancing, singing, or playing an instrument brings emotional release, develops group feeling, and increases self-confidence. Music therapy can be recreational, vocational, and occupational. Music participation is a means to an end, the perfection of the musical performance remaining secondary to its effect on the patient.

Creativity, where creative talent is present, can be of great therapeutic value. Building an instrument, no matter how crude, often helps to bolster the ego and is an incentive to learn to play. Writing a tune and harmonizing it can provide a great source of satisfaction. Rhythm elicits both muscular and sensory responses. Some muscular responses result without involving the higher centers of the brain, making music a means for treating patients who have regressed to primitive or childish levels. Persons with schizophrenia who have lost all contact with reality may be aroused by exposure to music that has a strong, pronounced rhythm. (See SCHIZOPHRENIA.) Participation in rhythm bands provides an opportunity for muscular response and emotional release of instinctual drives in socially acceptable ways. Hearing and singing familiar melodies stimulate sensory responses that require little or no thought. As the individual's interest and enjoyment increase and his thought processes are challenged, a desire to master the other elements of music will often follow. E. G. GILLILAND

BIBLIOG.-W. Van de Wall, *Music in Hospitals* (1946); D. Soibelman, *Therapeutic and Industrial Uses of Music* (1948); Music Research Foundation, *Music and Your Emotions* (1952); E. Podolsky, ed., *Music Therapy* (1954); National Association for Music Therapy, *Music Therapy, 1954* (1956).

MUSIL, ROBERT, 1880–1942, Austrian novelist, dramatist, an essayist, born in Klagenfurt. He is best known for his novel *Der Mann ohne Eigenschaften* (1930–33; Eng. tr. *The Man Without Qualities*, 1953), an encyclopedic account of prewar Austria. The experimental and rather disintegrated form of his novels has led critics to compare him to Joyce and Proust. Among his works are a novel, *Die Verwirrungen des Zöglings Törless* (1906, Eng. tr. *Young Törless*), two plays, *Der Schwärmer* (1921) and *Vinzenz* (1923), and a collection of essays, *Nachlass zu Lebzeiten* (1936).

MUSK, a strongly odorous substance secreted by glands found in many kinds of animals. The heavy odor usually is strongest during mating season. Most members of the weasel family, *Mustelidae*, possess such glands; the musky odor given off by the skunk being the most memorable. Some reptiles, the crocodile among them, have musk glands. The male musk deer, *Moschus moschiferus*, of Tibet secretes musk that is highly valued in perfumery where it is used to delay evaporation, or as a fixative. The strong-smelling, yellow fluid secreted by the glands of the civet cat of tropical Asia is also used in the perfume industry (see PERFUME, *Ingredients*).

MUSK DEER, a deer of the subfamily *Moschinae* found throughout eastern and central Asia north to Siberia, and in the Himalayas up to an elevation of 12,000 feet. The musk deer, *Moschus moschiferus*, stands about 1½ feet high and has a dull, gray-brown coat that is coarse-haired and pitted in appearance. The ears are long. The upper canine teeth of the male protrude, forming tusks; neither sex has antlers or tail. A saclike musk gland in the abdomen of the male is one of the sources of the musk used in the manufacture of perfumes. Musk deer are adapted to cold, and they feed on the lichens, grass, and foliage of the steppes and mountains. The deer live in pairs and are extremely active and sure-footed, relying on flight from their enemies as a means of self-protection. The doe usually gives birth to a single fawn annually.

MUSKEGON, city and port of entry, W lower Michigan, seat of Muskegon County; near the E shore of Lake Michigan, at the mouth of the Muskegon River; on the Grand Trunk, the Chesapeake and Ohio, and the Pennsylvania railroads and U.S. highways 16 and 31; a scheduled airline stop; 34 miles NW of Grand Rapids. Muskegon, near the dunes resort region, is an important industrial center and a lake port with a natural land-locked harbor. Its manufactures include automobile engines, parts, and equipment; foundry products; store, office, and bowling equipment; and paper. About 1810 a fur trading post was established on the site, but not until about 1834 was a permanent settlement founded; Muskegon was incorporated as a village in 1861 and as a city in 1869. During the last half of the nineteenth century it was a major lumber center. Pop. (1960) 46,485.

MUSKEGON HEIGHTS, city, W lower Michigan, Muskegon County; on the Chesapeake and Ohio, the Grand Trunk, and the Pennsylvania railroads and U.S. highways 16 and 31; 3 miles S of Muskegon. The city is a residential and industrial suburb of Muskegon; machinery is manufactured. The city was incorporated in 1903. Pop. (1960) 19,552.

MUSKELLUNGE, a prize game and food fish of the pike family, *Esocidae,* ranging sparsely in the cool, deep water of the Great Lakes and the St. Lawrence River regions. The muskellunge, *Esox masquinongy,* is a long, slim fish weighing about 75 pounds and averaging 6 feet in length. Its back is dark gray, and its sides and belly are a lighter gray with small, dark spots. The muskellunge has no scales on its cheeks nor gill covers below its eyes. Its smaller relative the pike lacks scales only on its gill covers and has light spots on its sides. The muskellunge has large, square dorsal and anal fins near the tail, and a pair of both pectoral and pelvic fins. During the last part of April and the first part of May the female spawns 100,000 to 300,000 eggs. The young grow rapidly and in two weeks are voracious feeders on their adult diet of small fish. Muskellunge may be caught on light tackle with live bait or spoon trolling. See PIKE.

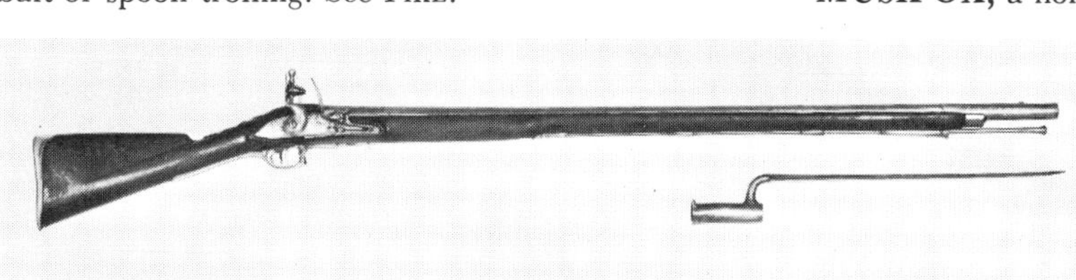
NEW YORK HIST. SOC.
Seventeenth Century English Flintlock Musket and Bayonet

MUSKET, an early form of smoothbore, hand firearm, usually discharging a single ball or pellet. The Spaniards are credited with introducing a type of musket, the harquebus, about the middle of the sixteenth century. A cumbersome weapon whose matchlock firing mechanism was not sufficiently reliable, it was superseded by the snaphance and the wheel lock mechanisms. The flintlock musket was developed in the late sixteenth century and the percussion musket in the early nineteenth. Although the best muskets were inferior to the rifle in range and accuracy, some were still in use during the American Civil War. See FIREARMS; RIFLE.

MUSKINGUM COLLEGE. See COLLEGES AND UNIVERSITIES.

MUSKINGUM RIVER, central and SE Ohio; formed by the junction of the Walhonding and Tuscarawas rivers near Coshocton; flows S through Zanesville, where it is joined by the Licking River, and then to Marietta, where it joins the Ohio River; length about 110 miles. The Muskingum has been improved for commercial navigation by a series of locks and dams and is used primarily for cargoes of coal, gravel, and sand.

MUSKOGEE, one of a North American Indian tribe of the Muskhogean linguistic stock. The Muskogee were relatively advanced maize growers; they settled mainly in the areas of present Georgia and Alabama. They were probably met by the Spanish explorer Hernando de Soto in 1540. The Muskogee formed one of the major elements in the Creek confederacy, which played an important part in the history of the region, because of its strategic location near the meeting point of the English, French, and Spanish colonies. After the Creek-American War of 1813–14, many of them joined the Seminole in Florida. Although they showed capacity to adapt their way of life to the economy of the whites, the Muskogee were forcibly removed to Indian Territory —modern Oklahoma—after 1836. See CREEK.

MUSKOGEE, city, E Oklahoma, seat of Muskogee County; near the junction of the Arkansas, Neosho, and Verdigris rivers; on the Frisco, the Kansas, Oklahoma and Gulf, the Midland Valley, and the Missouri-Kansas-Texas railroads and U.S. highways 62, 64, and 69; a scheduled airline stop; 45 miles SE of Tulsa. Muskogee, the third largest city in Oklahoma, is a railroad and trade center. Industries include oil refining, meat processing, and the manufacture of leather, iron, steel, glass, paper, cotton, and oil field equipment. Muskogee is the headquarters of the Indian agency for the Five Civilized Tribes; the site of Bacone University, world's only accredited Indian college; and the home of Muskogee Municipal Junior College. The city was settled in 1872 and incorporated in 1898. Pop. (1960) 38,059.

MUSKOKA LAKES, E Canada, Ontario; E of Georgian Bay of Lake Huron. The Muskoka Lakes form part of an area of about 10,000 square miles, famed also for its rivers, waterfalls, and forests and popular with hunters and fishermen. Notable lakes in the district are Muskoka, Joseph, Rosseau, and Lake of Bays. The Muskoka Lakes region is drained by the Muskoka River flowing into Georgian Bay. During the summer months excursion steamers ply the lake routes.

MUSK OX, a horned animal found in the American arctic and on the coasts of Greenland. The musk ox, *Ovibos moschatus,* has a strong musky odor and resembles a small, chunky ox with humped shoulders and short tail. Its dark brown or blackish hair sometimes sweeps the ground. Bulls weigh 500 to 900 pounds and stand about 5 feet high at the shoulder; cows are approximately a third smaller.

Musk Ox
U.S. FISH AND WILDLIFE SERV.

Both bulls and cows have sharp horns, those of the adult males being flattened at the base and almost meeting over the forehead to form a protecting boss. During the mating season, from July to September, the bulls fight for possession of the cows. Usually only one musk ox calf is born to each cow the following April or May. Musk oxen eat lichens, the buds and tender twigs of dwarf birch, alder, and willows, and herbs such as saxifrage and horsetail.

To defend themselves, musk oxen rush into a compact circular group with tails together in the center and brandishing their horns on all sides. Since the species is of vital importance to the Eskimos for food, bedding, and implements, the Canadian government has decreed total protection for the surviving animals. The heavy wool of the musk ox reputedly does not shrink when woven, but because it cannot be separated from the coarse guard hairs easily, it is not in commercial demand. VICTOR H. CAHALANE

CHICAGO NATURAL HIST. MUS.

Muskrat Atop Its House

MUSKRAT, an aquatic rodent ranging widely throughout the wooded areas of the colder temperate regions of North America. The muskrat, *Ondatra zibethicus*, has a rounded body about 25 inches long, including a hairless, scaly, and laterally flattened tail about 10 inches long. The body is covered with short, dense, red-brown underfur and a longer dark brown or black, sparse outer fur. The legs are short and the feet small, and although only the hind feet are webbed, the animal is an excellent swimmer. The muskrat, or musquash, is omnivorous, eating mussels, crayfish, and vegetation. It builds two types of shelter. In fresh-water and occasionally salt-water swamps the muskrat builds a characteristically mounded house of sticks and vegetation that is sometimes eaten during winter. Such a house is usually 5 to 6 feet in diameter at the surface of the water and 3 to 4 feet high. The other type is built along rivers and lakes having steep banks, where the muskrat burrows an underwater entrance about 10 feet into the bank and then upward to a dry chamber above the water level.

The fur of the muskrat is durable and waterproof, and more than 10 million animals are trapped in the United States each year. Muskrat has been retailed under a variety of names besides its own, including Hudson seal, Russian otter, marsh rabbit, red seal, and river mink. According to the U.S. Fur Products Labeling Act of 1952, however, this fur must always be labeled as muskrat, regardless of other names by which it is known. The female produces three litters of 4 to 11 young annually.

MUSSEL, a marine or fresh-water mollusk belonging to the class *Pelecypoda*. The mussel attaches itself to wharfing and rocks, and even to other mussels, by means of a tuft of long, tough, fibrous threads known collectively as the byssus. The mussel has an equivalve, elongate shell with pearly white lining. Although ordinarily stationary in habit, this mollusk is able to move about by means of its footlike byssus.

Marine mussels comprise the family *Mytilidae*. The common mussel, *Mytilus edulis*, is abundant in the tidelands of temperate North America and Europe. Many are found at low tide on the mud flats of river deltas. In France, and to a lesser degree in Great Britain, the mussel is cultivated for food, but in America it is seldom eaten. The horse mussel, *Modiolus modiolus*, is found in deep water along the rocky coasts of Europe and North America; it may grow to 9 inches in length, but does not ordinarily exceed 4 to 5 inches. The thick shell is glossy brown.

Fresh-water mussels, or clams, are grouped in the family *Unionidae*, which includes more than 1,000 species. The fresh-water mussel may be found in most river and lake systems of Europe and North America. Except for the genus *Stophitus*, the larva is parasitic on the gills of fish, and the adult mussel is valued as food. The shell of the thick-shelled species is used for making buttons, and pearls of considerable value are sometimes obtained from the mussel. See BUTTON; MOLLUSCA.

MUSSELBURGH, burgh, E Scotland, Midlothian County; on the Firth of Forth, at the mouth of the Esk River; 5 miles E of Edinburgh, of which it is a suburb. Paper, fishing nets, wire, and beer are produced. Musselburgh was the birthplace of David M. Moir, nineteenth century physician and author, and is the site of a seaweed research station. Pop. (1951) 17,012.

MUSSET, ALFRED DE, in full Louis Charles Alfred de Musset, 1810–57, French writer, was born in Paris and was educated at the Collège Henri IV. At the age of 17 he began to write poetry, and while still a schoolboy was introduced to the group of writers and artists known as the *cénacle*. Musset's first published work, *Contes d'Espagne et d'Italie* (1829), written with the exuberance of youth, was a great success; these poems show the influence of Victor Hugo and Lord Byron, but Musset also proved himself an able parodist of romantic verse as in "Ballade à la lune." His first play, *La Nuit Vénitienne* (1830), was a failure in production and, disgusted with the theater, Musset determined to write plays to be read only. *Le Spectacle dans un fauteuil* (1832) included the drama *La Coupe et les lèvres*, the delicate comedy *A quoi rêvent les jeunes filles*, and the Byronic poem *Namouna*. In 1833 appeared the tragicomedies *Les Caprices de Marianne* and *André del Sarto* and the cynical poem *Rolla*.

In 1833 Musset formed a liaison with George Sand. After a short time in Paris they went to Italy, where their relationship ended bitterly. Back in Paris, Musset poured out his melancholy and suffering in the love poems *La Nuit de mai* (1835), *La Nuit de décembre* (1835), *La Nuit d'août* (1836), *La Nuit d'octobre* (1837), and *Souvenir* (1841). *La Confession d'un enfant du siècle* (1836), an account of his relations with George Sand, is a curious mixture of intense earnestness and cynicism. Meanwhile he continued to write romantic comedies: *Fantasio* (1833), *On ne badine pas avec l'amour* (1834), *Lorenzaccio* (1834), and *Il ne faut jurer de rien* (1836). Although most of Musset's plays were not written to be produced, they are probably the only plays of the romantic period that are successfully staged in the twentieth century.

His brother, Paul de Musset (1804–80), novelist, wrote *Lui et elle* (1860) in reply to George Sand's story of her relationship with Musset, *Elle et lui;* and a eulogistic life of Alfred, *Biographie d'Alfred de Musset* (1877).

MUSSOLINI, BENITO, 1883–1945, Italian dictator and founder of fascism, was born in Predappio, the son of a blacksmith and a schoolteacher, took a degree at Forli, and taught school briefly in 1901–02. He went to Switzerland and engaged in socialistic agitation there until expelled from the country. Back in Italy, he devoted his energies to journalism, editing radical journals such as *La Lotta di classe* (The Class Struggle), *Avanti!*, and later *Il popolo d'Italia*. His publications bitterly attacked the Italian monarchy, but when World War I broke out in 1914, Mussolini became an ardent nationalist; later he enlisted in the army, serving until he was badly wounded in 1917.

Rise to Power. Postwar Italy was torn by depression and disillusionment. Discarding his leftist radicalism, Mussolini in 1919 created the Fascist party (*Fasci di combattimento*), made up largely of young hooligans and old-line reactionaries, ostensibly and ostentatiously dedicated to the destruction of communism by any means (see FASCISM). In 1921 Mussolini and 35 of his party were elected to the chamber of deputies. Sensing that the Socialists were losing popular favor, Mussolini waited for an opportunity to seize power. When, amid chaos, the feeble middle-of-the-road government of Giovanni Giolitti resigned, Mussolini ordered 30,000 of his blackshirted Fascisti to march on Rome (Oct. 30, 1922). Cowed by this show of force, the moderates allowed Mussolini (Il Duce) to become dictator of Italy.

Benito Mussolini

Italian fascism organized labor and capital into national confederations under close government supervision. Workers were unionized and given certain social benefits; employers profited from integration and the elimination of destructive competition. A program of public works was developed and there was a slight improvement in the standard of living. The price of these gains was the loss of personal freedom for all. Those who disagreed with Mussolini were ruthlessly suppressed.

Not content with dominating Italy, Mussolini dreamed (and talked incessantly) of creating a new Roman Empire. Defying the League of Nations, he attacked Ethiopia and reduced that peaceful African nation to a state of vassalage, 1935–36. In 1936, when the Spanish Civil War broke out, Mussolini poured 100,000 troops into Spain on the side of the rebels. In October, 1936, he allied himself formally with Nazi Germany, forging what he himself called the Rome-Berlin Axis.

World War II. In 1940 Mussolini entered World War II, delivering to France what U.S. Pres. Franklin D. Roosevelt called "a stab in the back" at a time when the French were already reeling before the German panzer divisions. War for Italy, however, was an almost unbroken series of defeats for Mussolini's armies. His efforts to sweep the Balkans were a miserable failure until helped by German reinforcements. His soldiers in North Africa were no match for British troops. Later, in Sicily, Anglo-American forces swept his men aside almost without resistance.

The invasion of Sicily in July, 1943, resulted in Mussolini's downfall. He was imprisoned, but the Germans rescued him and installed him as a puppet ruler in northern Italy. In April, 1945, as Allied armies closed in from all sides, Mussolini attempted an escape to Switzerland, but was captured by Italian partisans and put to death. For days his corpse was left hanging by the heels in the piazza of Milan beside that of his mistress, Clara Petacci. Neither his widow nor their six children were seriously molested.

Mussolini the Man. During Mussolini's lifetime anti-Fascists outside Italy portrayed him as something of a comic figure, with jutting jaw, absurdly belligerent mannerisms, oratorical gestures, and love of grandiose display. He was no joke, however, to those Italians who resisted his tyrannical rule for more than 20 years. There was an element of tragedy in his career, for Mussolini was a man of intelligence, learning, and some culture, who began life with the real interests of his people at heart. He was, however, corrupted by power and by his childish dreams of military glory for Italy. He seems to have seen twentieth century Italy as imperial Rome with himself playing the part of Julius Caesar. But the empire Mussolini dreamed of never materialized and he himself ended as a mere "sawdust Caesar," dangling ignominiously from the end of a rope. See ITALY, Modern Italy, *Rise of Fascism*, *World War II*.

JOHN A. GARRATY

BIBLIOG.–M. G. Sarfatti, *Life of Benito Mussolini* (1925); W. Bolitho, *Italy Under Mussolini* (1926); V. J. Bordeaux, *Benito Mussolini, the Man* (1927); A. Robertson, *Mussolini and the New Italy* (1928); L. Kemechey, *Il Duce* (1930); C. A. Petrie, *Mussolini* (1931); E. Ludwig, *Talks with Mussolini* (1933); D. H. Darrah, *Hail Caesar!* (1936); G. Megaro, *Mussolini in the Making* (1938); G. Pini, *Official Life of Benito Mussolini* (1939); T. B. Morgan, *Spurs on the Boot* (1941); G. Seldes, *Sawdust Caesar* (ed. 1941); M. Foot, *Trial of Mussolini* (1943); E. Wiskemann, *Rome-Berlin Axis* (1949); P. Monelli, *Mussolini* (1954); R. Dabrowski, *Mussolini: Twilight and Fall* (1956).

MUSTANG, a wild horse that flourished on the western plains of North America until the end of the nineteenth century. They were the progeny of Arabian horses brought to North America by Spanish explorers; by the early eighteenth century there were numerous wild herds containing, it has been estimated, millions of mustangs. The Plains Indians used mustangs in hunting buffalo and their whole way of life was transformed and enriched thereby. White men moving westward found the mustang (or cayuse, Indian pony, or bronco) to be a versatile, dependable mount; mustangers trapped, broke, and trained the animals. Herds of mustangs were greatly reduced by the end of the nineteenth century, and most of the remaining herds were killed for hides and for making dog food.

MUSTARD, an annual herb with loose, upright basal leaves, belonging to the mustard family, *Cruciferae*. The mustard plant belongs to the genus *Brassica*, which has about 40 species including broccoli, Brussels sprouts, cabbage, cauliflower, collard, kale, kohlrabi, rutabaga, and turnip (see BRASSICA). The mustard plant was used by the ancient Greeks and Romans as a condiment. The plants are grown throughout Asia, Europe, and North America and are regarded as weeds in many areas. There are three prominent species: Chinese, or leaf, mustard, *B. juncea;* black mustard, *B. nigra;* and white mustard, *B. hirta*. See CHARLOCK.

Leaf mustard is a species grown mainly in China and India for use as greens; the leaves resemble those of lettuce in shape. In India the plant is used as cooking spice. Oil pressed from the seeds is used as a food flavoring and as an ointment.

Black mustard is cultivated in southern California, where it sometimes grows 16 feet high during seasons of heavy rainfall. Black mustard is planted in early autumn to make the seeds develop quickly. Its small seed pods rise vertically, close to the main stem and near the tip of the plant. The dark brown seeds are ground for commercial mustard seasoning or pressed for an oil used in making soaps and medicines.

White mustard, which is cultivated in the United States and Europe, grows 3 to 4 feet high and has oval leaves and yellow flowers one-half inch long. Its seed pods are larger than those of black mustard. When the seeds are ripe they are ground and treated with water. An enzymatic action produces a mixture that is the base of commercial mustards. Commercially ground mustards are mixtures of black and white mustards and are used as spices. Mustard is used medically as an emetic, a gastric stimulant, and a counter-irritant.

MUSTARD GAS. See CHEMICAL WARFARE.

MUT, an ancient Egyptian goddess, "the mother." She was the wife of Ammon (Amen, Amon) and the mother of Khonsu (Khensu), and with them was worshiped as a member of the divine triad at Thebes. Her special emblem was the vulture, and she was also represented by the lion.

MUTATION. See GENE; HEREDITY; EVOLUTION.

MUTH, KARL, 1867–1944, German writer and editor who effectively encouraged the reawakening of

Roman Catholic interest in German cultural research and contemporary affairs, was born in Worms. He founded and edited, 1903–41, the journal *Hochland*, and wrote *Steht die katholische Belletristik auf der Höhe der Zeit?* (1898), *Die literarischen Aufgaben der deutschen Katholiken* (1899), *Religion, Kunst und Poesie* (1914), and other works.

MUTINY, an open revolt by two or more persons against constituted authority, applied generally to the armed forces of a country or to a rebellion on a ship at sea. Mutinies may take the form of collective passive resistance or physical assault and result usually from one or more dissatisfactions—as with food, housing, or working conditions—or from revolutionary propaganda. Armed forces may mutiny because of low morale following a long war, serious defeat, or heavy losses, as did the Russian and Austro-Hungarian armies and the German navy during World War I. There have been attempts to distinguish between mutiny and the right to strike of civilian seamen who are members of a labor union. It is generally conceded that a strike that occurs when a ship is in port is not mutiny. See MARITIME LAW, *Rights of Seamen.*

United States. During the Revolutionary War there were several mutinies that took place among the Continental troops, the most extensive being the mutiny of six regiments at Morristown, Pa., in 1781. Gen. Robert Howe quelled a rebellion of three regiments in New Jersey in 1781 and a mutiny of Pennsylvania recruits in 1783. During the War of 1812 soldiers mutinied in New York at Manlius, Utica, and Buffalo. A sergeant and five privates of a regiment of Tennessee militia were hanged for mutiny in 1814, a case that was made a campaign issue when Gen. Andrew Jackson became a candidate for the presidency. A mutiny took place aboard the brig *Somers* in 1842 that resulted in the hanging of three persons.

Until 1950 punishment for mutiny by members of the U.S. Armed Forces was provided for in the articles of war. In that year a uniform code of military justice for the Army, Navy, and Air Force was adopted. The death penalty is not mandatory for mutinous members of the armed forces; the decision on the amount and kind of punishment remains with a general court-martial. See COURTS, MILITARY; MILITARY LAW.

Other Countries. One of the most widely known sea mutinies was the mutiny on the British ship *Bounty* in 1789. (See BOUNTY, MUTINY ON THE; BLIGH, WILLIAM; PITCAIRN ISLAND.) The most famous British mutiny was the Sepoy Mutiny, a revolt of native Indian troops in 1857–58. (See SEPOY MUTINY.) Other examples of mutinous uprisings include those of the crew of the Russian cruiser *Potemkin* in 1905, of the Brazilian navy in 1893, and of the Chilean navy in 1932. During World War II many Ukrainians in the Soviet forces mutinied and fought with the German army. Mutinies occurred among the armies and navies of various Latin American countries after World War II.

MUTISM, the condition or state of being mute, or without power of speech. A mute is one who does not speak whether from physical inability, disinclination, or other causes—which may be physical or psychological. The mechanism of speech is complex and involves certain areas of the brain. In general, one side of the brain, usually the left, is more amenable to speech education than the other. See BRAIN, Cerebral Hemispheres, or Cerebrum, *Gray Matter;* LANGUAGE DEVELOPMENT; SPEECH.

Congenital, or Deaf and Dumb, Mutism. Mutism is most frequently the result of early acquired or congenital deafness, a defect which is present at birth. Certain diseases such as meningitis and, rarely, mumps, can cause deafness in infancy and early childhood. If a child is totally deaf, either because of some congenital condition or as a result of illness or trauma, shock, or injury, during his first year of life, he probably will not learn to speak without corrective training. Most cases of muteness are thus the result of deafness instead of defective speech apparatus. The child learns to speak by imitating others. He listens to conversation and learns that certain sounds made by one individual produce specific results in another individual, and gradually he becomes aware of the meaning of words. It is necessary, therefore, for the child to hear accurately so that the complicated process of speech may be learned. Deaf mutes can and should be trained in special schools and classes to acquire education commensurate with their age and intelligence. They should be taught to read lips and to speak, or articulate, thus avoiding the need for a complex sign language that is usually only understood by other deaf mutes. To be able to speak to and understand others in as normal a fashion as possible will help the deaf mute immeasurably in finally being able to make a good vocational and social adjustment. See DEAFNESS.

Traumatic Mutism. An injury or defect of the speech areas of the brain will produce speech defects or even mutism. Injury to the speech center may occur before birth, during the birth process, or later in life from some external source such as a blow on the head. It is probable that many of the speech defects in mentally deficient individuals are of traumatic origin. Those speech defects that occur as a result of various types of cerebral injuries are known as aphasias. See APHASIA.

Other structures such as the larynx, pharynx, tongue, and respiratory organs must be intact and capable of functioning correctly for the proper development of speech. Injury to any one of them might result in mutism. Mutism may be on occasion an unavoidable result of necessary surgery, such as removal of the larynx. See LARYNX.

Hysterical Mutism. Psychological trauma can sometimes be intense enough to produce a hysterical reaction of speechlessness. Some examples of hysterical mutism have been found among soldiers who have been subjected to extremely frightening battle conditions, and others, particularly children, who have witnessed terrifying scenes. See HYSTERIA; PSYCHIATRY.

Psychotic Mutism. One of the characteristic findings of mental disease is an alteration of the stream of talk. True mutism, in which there are no utterances, may be associated with such phenomena as extreme depression, expression of complete indifference to the environment, negativism, and hallucinations (see PSYCHOSIS). In the catatonic stupor of schizophrenia, voluntary activity decreases. In some cases the patient may even lie motionless and remain mute. See SCHIZOPHRENIA.

Treatment. Teaching a mute person to speak is a long, difficult process that requires considerable patience and perseverance by both teacher and pupil. The capabilities of the pupil determine the teaching methods used and the degree of normality in speech that is ultimately reached. Where intelligence is normal or only slightly impaired, a well trained therapist can teach a willing pupil to speak quite intelligibly. Some of the teaching methods employed include the use of a mirror to help the pupil mimic the facial movements of the therapist, and the use of the sense of touch in demonstrating the muscular movement involved in speech.

Drugs such as amobarbital, pentobarbital, and thiopental are used in the treatment of mutism of a psychological nature. The drug is usually administered intravenously, and its effect is to reduce the consciousness and inhibitions of the patient thereby making him more receptive to suggestion. While under the effects of such a drug, the mute will often speak and reveal some of his emotional problems. Effective psychotherapy may be given simultaneously because of the patient's increased susceptibility to advice. See PSYCHOTHERAPY.

MUTTRA. See MATHURA.

MUTUAL BENEFIT SOCIETY, a fraternal organization existing primarily for purposes of insurance, with ritual and social functions being of secondary importance. Among the oldest mutual benefit societies in the United States are the Supreme Council of the Royal Arcanum founded in 1877, with headquarters at Boston, Mass., and 40,000 members in 425 local groups in the mid-1950's; The Maccabees (1878), Detroit, Mich., 200,000 members in 930 local groups; Modern Woodmen of America (1883), Rock Island, Ill., 460,000 members in 6,000 local groups; and Woodmen of the World Life Insurance Society (1890), Omaha, Neb., 437,500 members in 4,000 local groups. The mutual benefit society was originally set up under a system of assessment for death benefits, but after 1910 it operated under an established code of minimum actuarial standards. In addition to death benefits many of the organizations pay old age relief and sickness and accident benefits. See FRATERNAL INSURANCE.

MUTUAL SECURITY PROGRAM, an instrument of U.S. foreign policy that attempts by economic and military aid to strengthen and develop the countries of the free world as security against aggression. The program includes treaties, reciprocal trade legislation, making capital available to international banks, exchange programs, and foreign aid of various kinds.

Marshall Plan. After World War II a plan for European recovery was presented by Sec. of State George C. Marshall. In June, 1947, he proposed that the United States help improve economic conditions in Europe. Marshall called upon European nations to draft a report stating their economic status and outlining a program for their economic needs. Although the Marshall Plan was presented after a failure of crops and a severe winter, it was not an emergency relief measure but a self-help plan for Europe and other areas.

In response to Marshall's proposal, 16 nations of western Europe met at Paris to formulate an economic recovery plan based upon American financial assistance and European co-operation. The plan was originally offered to all European nations. The Soviet Union opposed the plan and with its satellites refused to attend the Paris conference.

The conference provided for a Committee for European Economic Co-operation. A permanent organization was subsequently established, the Organization for European Economic Co-operation (OEEC). In April, 1948, the U.S. Congress created the Economic Co-operation Administration (ECA) and provided for more than $6 billion in aid.

Development. In 1951 the ECA became the Mutual Security Administration as the emphasis shifted from economic recovery to military defense. The MSA furnished military and technical assistance as well as economic aid. The MSA in turn was superseded in 1953 by the Foreign Operations Administration in order to centralize control and direction of the various assistance programs. For fiscal 1954 Congress appropriated more than $5.1 billion. Aid was granted to countries in Asia, Africa, and other areas as well as to European countries.

International Co-operation Administration. In 1955 the FOA was abolished and its functions and offices were transferred to the International Co-operation Administration, a semiautonomous unit within the Department of State. For fiscal 1958 Congress appropriated $3.5 billion for the mutual security program, which included both military and nonmilitary aid. Military assistance included weapons, air bases, supply lines, and communication and transportation in many areas. Defense support or economic assistance enabled countries to have a larger defense than they normally would have been able to have, and also to undertake measures for economic development. The United States maintained technical assistance programs in more than 50 countries. American specialists were sent to help in such fields as agriculture, health, education, industry, transportation, housing, and community development. Funds were also available for special assistance programs, such as aid for refugees. Military aid was administered by the Department of Defense, but the ICA was responsible for over-all co-ordination of both military and nonmilitary aid.

Development Loan Fund. The Development Loan Fund was established in 1957 to help finance worthwhile economic projects in underdeveloped countries. The fund made loans to nations, organizations, and individuals on the basis of the feasibility of projects proposed, their estimated contribution to the economic growth of the country receiving the aid, the availability of other financial resources, and the possibility of adverse effects on the U.S. economy. Loans were made only when repayment was reasonably certain. Since the date of its inception, the fund received loan applications totalling many times the amount of money available. By 1961, Congress had appropriated $1.9 million for the fund.

MUYBRIDGE, EADWEARD, originally Edward James Muggeridge, 1830–1904, U.S. motion picture pioneer, was born in Kingston-on-Thames, England. Coming to the United States about 1850, he did photographic work on the Pacific coast for the U.S. Coast and Geodetic Survey. In 1872 Leland Stanford asked him to find whether all four feet of a running horse are ever off the ground at once. Muybridge obtained a series of photographs in silhouette which proved that there is a moment when all the feet are off the ground. He then photographed dogs, birds, and other animals in motion and invented the zoopraxiscope, 1879, by which he produced the illusion of motion on a screen. He wrote *Descriptive Zoopraxography* (1893) and *The Human Figure in Motion* (1901). See MOTION PICTURE, Early History.

MUZAFFARGARH, a town, district and tehsil, West Pakistan, Bahawalpur state; area of district about 5,600 square miles. Dates and mangoes are grown, and camels are raised. The town is a trading center and is the location of four colleges.

MUZAFFARPUR, city, NE India, Bihar State, capital of Muzaffarpur District and of Tirhut Division; on a branch of the Gandak River; 42 miles NNE of Patna. Muzaffarpur is a railroad and highway junction on the direct trade route from Patna to Katmandu, Nepal. Rice, wheat, barley, corn, tobacco, sugar cane, oilseed, and cutlery are produced in the area. (For population, see India map in Atlas.)

MUZIANO, GIROLAMO, known as Girolamo Bressano, 1528?–92, Italian artist, the founder of St. Luke's Academy in Rome, was born in Aquafredda. He painted landscapes and historical scenes, and contributed much to the development of mosaic art. His paintings include *The Resurrection of Lazarus*, *Circumcision*, *Ascension*, and *Christ Giving the Keys to St. Peter*.

MUZO, village, NW central Colombia, Boyacá Department; near the Carare River; 62 miles N of Bogotá. Muzo is famous for its government-owned emerald mines, said to be the world's largest; other products are coffee and cattle. The village was founded by the Spanish in 1558. (For population, see Colombia map in Atlas.)

MUZTAGH ATA, mountain range, W China, Sinkiang Province, forms a part of the Kunlun System and extends for 196 miles in a NNW-SSE direction along the western China border opposite the Pamirs. The highest peak in the range is the Kungur Massif (25,146 ft.), 69 miles southwest of Kashgar. Muztagh Ata Peak, 93 miles southwest of Kashgar, is 24,388 feet high.

MUZZEY, DAVID SAVILLE, 1870– , U.S. historian and author, born in Lexington, Mass. He was graduate professor of American history at Columbia University (1923–38). He was a frequent public lecturer and published extensively.

MWERU, LAKE, also Moero or Meru, central Africa, in the western branch of the Great Rift Valley, at an altitude of 3,025 feet; lies between Northern Rhodesia on the E and the Congo on the W. Lake Mweru is about 70 miles long and 25 miles wide. The Luapula River enters its southern end and the Luvua River emerges from the northern end to join the Congo River. David Livingstone explored the eastern shore of the lake in 1867, and Alfred Sharpe circumnavigated it in 1892.

MYCENAE, ancient city, S Greece, Peloponnesus, province of Argolis, 7 miles N of Argos. Benefiting from its strategic location within a short distance of the Gulf of Argolis, the Gulf of Corinth, and the Saronic Gulf, where several trade routes converged, the city became the main center of the so-called Mycenaean civilization. See Aegean Civilization.

Mycenae was first settled by a non-Hellenic people, who may have been related to the Cretans, during the early Bronze Age, 3000?–?2800 B.C. It was occupied by the Achaeans, probably one of the first Hellenic groups to reach Greece, during the middle Bronze Age, 2100?–?1600 B.C.

Mycenaean civilization probably started to develop under Cretan influence, but retained its distinctive character and may, in its turn, have influenced the Minoan culture of Cnossus. Unlike the Cretans, the Mycenaeans may never have invented a system of writing, but evidence on this point is ambiguous, since the Minoan Linear B script, developed probably on Crete but perhaps by a Greek-born ruler of part of that island, was a medium for writing in the Greek language. Early in the late Bronze Age, the so-called Shaft Grave Dynasty had risen to power. The shaft graves in which rulers of this dynasty were buried were first excavated, 1876, by Heinrich Schliemann, who found them rich in gold and other treasures (see Troy). The Shaft Grave Dynasty was succeeded by the so-called Beehive Tomb Dynasty, whose rulers were buried in tombs shaped like beehives. The tombs were architectural masterpieces, but had been robbed of their treasure long before being excavated by archaeologists. The Beehive Tomb Dynasty endured through the later phases of the late Bronze Age, during which Mycenaean civilization reached its zenith. Decline began after ?1300 B.C., and the city was destroyed altogether in ?1100 B.C.

Mycenae influenced the early culture and history of most of the Greek peninsula and archipelago. The most famous Mycenaean site (other than Mycenae itself) was Tiryns. Among other important Mycenaean cities were Pílos, Orchomenus, Thebes, and Athens. Mycenae maintained close relations with Crete, Cyprus, Sicily, Macedonia, Palestine, and Egypt.

Mycenae was rebuilt during the early Iron Age and appears to have been of some importance in the sixth and fifth centuries B.C., but it never regained its former power. The modern village of Mikinai (pop. 626) is located southwest of the ruins.

Bibliog:–H. Schliemann, *Mycenae: Narrative of Research at Mycenae and Tiryns* (1878); C. Tsountas and J. I. Manatt, *Mycenaean Age* (1897); D. G. Hogarth, *Essays in Aegean Archaeology* (1927); A. J. Evans, *Shaft Graves and Beehive Tombs* (1929); M. P. Nilsson, *Mycenaean Origin of Greek Mythology* (1932), *Homer and Mycenae* (1933); A. J. B. Wace, *Chamber Tombs at Mycenae* (1932), *Mycenae: Archaeological History and Guide* (1949); L. Cottrell, *Bull of Minos* (1953); G. E. Mylonas, *Ancient Mycenae* (1957); N.G.L. Hammond, A History of Greece to 322 B.C. (1959).

MYELITIS, inflammation of the spinal cord. Myelitis may be acute or chronic, and its symptoms vary according to the part of the spinal cord affected. The condition is rare compared with other diseases that attack the nervous system. It may follow trauma, various infective diseases, and, rarely, vaccination; and any marked loss of muscular power or of sensation may be caused by it. Infantile paralysis, shingles, and rabies are forms of myelitis. Several types of myelitis are associated with syphilis.

MYCORRHIZA, or "fungus root," an association of a fungus with the root of a green plant. There are two main types: (1) ectotrophic, in which filaments of the fungus web around the plant rootlets, and (2) endotrophic, in which the fungus actually infiltrates root cells. The mycorrhizae of oak, beech, and most conifers are ectotrophic; those of orchids, heather, and most fruit trees, endotrophic. Most mycorrhizae are symbiotic. In these, fungi obtain food partly from the plants, while the plants in turn receive from the fungi nitrogen and minerals.

MYMENSINGH, city, Pakistan, N East Pakistan Province, Dacca Division, capital of Mymensingh District; on the Brahmaputra River; 70 miles N of Dacca, with which it is connected by highway and railroad. Mymensingh is the center of an area producing rice, jute, oilseed, sugar cane, and tobacco; electrical supplies are manufactured. It was formerly known as Nasirabad. (For population, see Pakistan map in Atlas.)

MYNAH, or myna, a name applied to several birds of the starling family. Hill mynahs (*Graculae religiosae*) fly through the forests of India and Ceylon in huge flocks, living on wild fruit and emitting hoarse, basso chuckles and loud, ringing cries. Their glossy coats are violet-black, and flashy yellow wattles frame their heads. Caught and caged, they readily learn to mimic their captors' speech, though they are apter pupils to previously trained mynahs than to men. The Indian house mynah (*Acridotheres tristis*) can also be trained to say words. Its body plumage is dark brown and its wing and tail are flecked with white. Naked patches of orange skin surround its eyes.

MYRDAL, KARL GUNNAR, 1898– , Swedish economist, was born in Gustaf, Dalecarlia, and was graduated from the University of Stockholm, 1927, where he taught after 1933. He was executive secretary of the UN Economic Commission for Europe, 1947–57. Myrdal wrote *An American Dilemma: The Negro Problem and Modern Democracy* (1944), *An International Economy, Problems and Prospects* (1956), and *Rich Lands and Poor* (1958).

MYRICA, a genus of woody shrubs native to the Northern Hemisphere, bearing simple ornamental leaves and pulpy fruit and belonging to the sweet gale family, *Myricaceae*. The flowers are unisexual and are borne in catkins; the alternate leaves are usually oblong and evergreen. Both the drupelike fruit and the leaves are often waxy. *Myrica cerifera*, the wax myrtle, sometimes grows 40 feet high as a slender tree. The bayberry, *M. pensylvanica*, bears gray-white fruit and is a hardy plant growing in southeastern United States. *M. californica*, the California bayberry, is a species similar to *M. pensylvanica* but growing from Washington to California. *M. Gale*, sweet gale, grows as a hardy shrub 1 to 5 feet high in North America and Europe. The wax myrtle and sweet gale prefer a moist, peaty soil; the bayberry and the California bayberry prefer sandy and sterile soil.

MYRMIDON, one of an ancient people of Greece who, according to Homer, lived in Phthiotis, in Thessaly, and were led by Achilles in the Trojan War. Traditionally the Myrmidons were descended from ants transformed into men by Zeus at the request of Aeacus, son of Zeus by Aegina. They are said to have come to Thessaly from the island of Aegina.

MYRON, fifth century B.C. Greek sculptor, was born in Eleutherae, Boeotia, was a pupil of Ageladas, and worked largely in Athens. Myron was most celebrated for his bronze statues of athletes in motion, the best known being the *Discobolus* or *The Discus Thrower*. None of his works are extant, but copies of the *Discobolus* are in the Vatican and the British Museum, and a copy of his *Marsyas* is in the Lateran Museum, Rome.

MYRRH, a yellow or red-brown aromatic gum resin obtained from any one of a group of trees of the genus *Commiphora*, belonging to the bursera family, *Burseraceae*. The most common source of myrrh is the myrrh tree, *C. abyssinica*, of eastern Africa and Arabia.

Because of its aromatic properties, myrrh has been used since ancient times as an ingredient of incense and perfume. It has a bitter, pungent taste. It acts as a mild, local irritant and is sometimes used in mouthwashes. To collect myrrh, slashes are made in the bark of the tree and the resin is allowed to flow into the cuts and harden. It is then chipped from the bark, dried, and packaged for export. A European perennial herb, sweet cicely, *Myrrhis odorata*, of the *Umbelliferae* or parsley family, is sometimes called myrrh. It grows 3 feet high and bears small white flowers.

MYRTLE, a group of shrubs and trees within the myrtle family, *Myrtaceae*, and belonging specifically to the genus *Myrtus*, which includes about 70 species. The myrtle is native to subtropical South America and Australia and southern Europe and western Asia. The common myrtle, *M. communis*, bears ovate leaves about 2 inches long and white or reddish flowers about 3 inches long; the fruit is a blue-black berry about one-half inch in diameter. It is commonly found in the Mediterranean area, and the leaves were fashioned into head wreaths by the ancient Greeks and Romans and worn as tokens of honor.

The Chilean guava, *M. Ugni*, is native to Chile, and can range in size from a shrub to a huge tree. Its ovate leaves are downy when young, but later become leathery with a shiny upper surface and a whitish lower surface. The edible fruit is a shiny purple berry that has a pleasant odor and taste. The wood is hard and heavy and is used in Chile for press screws.

Myrtles are grown as ornamental shrubs out-of-doors in California and southern United States and in greenhouses in the north. The plants are propagated from seed or from partially ripe cuttings.

MYSIA, a historical region of ancient Asia Minor, bordered by the Sea of Marmara and Bithynia on the N, Phrygia on the E, Lydia on the S, and the Aegean Sea on the W. Mysia was conquered by Croesus, king of Lydia, in the sixth century B.C. and annexed to the Persian Empire after the victory of Cyrus the Great over Croesus. In the fourth century B.C., Mysia was subjugated by Alexander the Great. The area passed later to Syria, which ruled it until 190 B.C., and then to Pergamum which held it from 190 B.C. to 130 B.C. when it became part of the Roman province of Asia.

MYSORE, state, SW India; bounded by the states of Bombay on the N, Andhra Pradesh on the E, and Madras and Kerala on the S, the Arabian Sea and the Goa District of Portuguese India on the W; area of the state, 74,326 square miles. Mysore consists of the Western Ghats in the west with an elevation of more than 6,000 feet, hill country in the south (about 4,000 ft.), and plains in the east and north (about 2,000 ft.). Drainage is generally to the east. The Cauvery and Penner rivers are in the south; the Kistna and its tributaries, the Tungabhadra and the Bhima, in the north central section of the state; and the Godayari in the north. Chief centers are Bangalore, the administrative capital; Mysore, the dynastic capital; and Kolar. Mysore is crossed by two railroads and more than 11,000 miles of highway. Air service is supplied to Bangalore. Most of the people of Mysore are Hindus. Kannada (or Karanese) is the most common language. The University of Mysore, with 24 colleges, is in the city.

Receiving ample rainfall and being well irrigated, Mysore has fertile soil and is practically famine free. Coffee, tea, rubber, cardamom, pepper, rice, sugar cane, and cotton are grown; silk, cotton, and wool textiles, sandalwood oil, iron and steel, chemicals, paper, and aircraft are manufactured. The gold mined in the Kolar gold fields comprises nearly all of that mineral produced in India. Handicrafts—such as silk and cotton weaving, goldsmithing, and the making of pottery and wicker articles—are encouraged by the government. Mysore is recognized as a pioneer in India's hydroelectric development.

Mysore has been under Hindu rule for most of its history. Its administration was handled by the British from 1831 to 1881. In 1947 it joined the Indian Dominion, and in 1950 it became a state in the Indian Republic. In 1956 its boundaries were enlarged to include the former Coorg State and parts of the former states of Madras, Bombay, and Hyderabad. For administrative purposes, Mysore is divided into 20 districts.

(For population, see India map in Atlas.)

MYSORE, or Maisur, city, SW India, dynastic capital of Mysore State and capital of Mysore District; a railroad and a highway junction 80 miles SW of Bangalore. Mysore is noted for its silks, sandalwood, perfumes, and ivory, metal, and wood handicrafts. The city also produces cotton textiles, paints and varnishes, bricks and tiles, plastics, and vegetable oils. Mysore is the site of the colleges of commerce, engineering, education, and law divisions of the University of Mysore. A major point of interest is the maharaja's palace, built in 1897 within an ancient fort, which contains a famous throne of gold and silver carved with Hindu mythological figures. Founded in the sixteenth century, Mysore was the capital of the state from 1799 until 1831, when the British removed the administration to Bangalore. (For population, see India map in Atlas.)

MYSTERIES, rites or services performed in secret. The word should not be confused with the religious doctrine known as mysticism, nor with the mystery plays of the Middle Ages (the name of which is accurately "mistery," or trade guild, after the groups who performed them).

The participants in the rites called mysteries must undergo some sort of initiation and must abjure from revealing any part of the mysteries to the uninitiated. The most famous mystery cults were pre-Christian; but because of their removal in time and their grounding in secrecy, they are only partly understood by modern scholars. The ancient mysteries performed at Eleusis, 14 miles from Athens, probably had to do with the theme of death and revival—specifically with the Persephone myth of the seasons, more profoundly with human death and a blessed state beyond. Another famous Greek mystery cult was on the island of Samothrace. Still others are known to have existed in Egypt and the Roman world. The mysteries involved in the Eucharist in the Christian religion present, perhaps, a partial parallel to the rites of ancient mystery cults, by the nature of their solemnity and the intensive initial indoctrination of the communicants.

MYSTERY STORY, any piece of popular fiction, long or short, involving dramatically and predominantly a mystery and its solution, and primarily depending on suspense for its effect. Thus detective stories, riddle stories, spy stories, secret service stories, stories of buried treasure in which a cipher is involved, some crime stories, and many stories of supernatural terror and pseudo science—in short, puzzle stories of almost every kind—are mystery stories. In the mid-twentieth century the most fashionable of the mystery categories was the suspense story, usually an account of evil intentions frustrated in the nick of time (a nameless menace, a threat of impending murder, or some comparable danger to innocence), although it might be almost any horror story or tale of terror in which mounting suspense was the principal element. The mystery novel more and more nearly approached the "serious" novel of character analysis—a development reflected particularly in the pure suspense story.

Historically, all mystery fictions have much in common. Although the mystery story as a literary genre is not old, its origins are lost in antiquity. Its seeds are to be found in ancient myths, legends, anecdotes, superstitions. Primitive examples exist in the ancient literatures of Egypt, China, India, and the Semitic nations. There are admirable mystery stories in the Bible and in certain of the Greek and Roman classics. The modern mystery story probably began with the eighteenth century Gothic novel, in which medieval magic and occultism are a background for romantic love and melodramatic violence. When a soluble puzzle and a measure of rational solution were added to supernatural mystery, the detective story was in sight. The Gothic tale persisted as an influence well into the nineteenth century in the work of such writers as J. Sheridan LeFanu and Wilkie Collins.

The greatest name in the modern mystery field is that of Edgar Allan Poe (1809–49), who raised the tale of mystery and terror to the level of literature and invented the modern short-story form. Among his numerous successors were such outstanding novelists and storytellers as Robert Louis Stevenson, Rudyard Kipling, Arthur Conan Doyle, Ambrose Bierce, Algernon Blackwood, Arthur Machen, John Buchan, Edgar Wallace, E. W. Hornung, and E. Phillips Oppenheim. Excluding straight detective story writers (see DETECTIVE STORY), important mid-twentieth century masters of mystery were Graham Greene, Michael Innes, Eric Ambler, Georges Simenon, Stanley Ellin, John Dickson Carr, and Charlotte Armstrong. VINCENT STARRETT

MYSTICISM, the body of doctrine or teaching that deals with an immediate and intuitive form of knowledge that is, or appears to be, beyond the world of normal sense perception and human reasoning. The mystical experience may be brief or relatively permanent. It may be accompanied by above-normal phenomena such as levitations, locutions, and mystical wounds—all of which, however, are understood to be accessory and accidental; the essential and ever-present element in the experience is the beyond-normal intuition of a transcendent object. All mystical experiences are not essentially the same. Rather, there appear to exist three types of such experience: the mysticism of nature, monistic mysticism, and theistic mysticism.

In the mysticism of nature, the person undergoing the experience is intensely aware of nature or the physical world as a transcendent unity or "allness," while at the same time equally aware that this allness is in him and he in it. This type of experience is not religious in the ordinary use of the word, but it can properly be called mystical because in it nature serves as a substitute for divinity. This appears to be the type of mystical experience that Aldous Huxley induced in himself by use of the narcotic mescaline and that he described in *Doors of Perception* (1954).

In monistic mysticism the mystic perceives himself as identical with the Absolute while at the same time perceiving that nothing except the Absolute exists. This type of mysticism is prevalent in India, especially among Indian mystics who base their experiences on the doctrine of Sankara Acharya, the ninth century teacher (see VEDANTA). From India monistic mysticism penetrated a great part of Moslem mysticism.

Theistic mysticism neither makes an "all" of the physical world, as does the mysticism of nature, nor denies the existence of the physical world, as does monistic mysticism. In theistic mysticism there exists a transcendent and supreme reality; it is with this reality that the theistic mystic seeks an intimate union, but without losing his own identity.

Within theistic mysticism can be detected two further distinct types of mystical experience. One of these, seen in the experience of men like Plotinus, may be called philosophical mysticism; the other, exemplified in the great Spanish mystics St. John of the Cross and St. Teresa of Ávila, can be described as Christian mysticism (see PLOTINUS; CRUZ, SAN JUAN DE LA; TERESA, SAINT). The first is based on a doctrine of the Supreme Being as He is philosophically conceived; the mystical experience is open only to those highly endowed with metaphysical abilities and, when achieved, the experience is regarded as the fruit of the percipient's own efforts. Christian mysticism, however, is based on the Christian conception of the God who is love; moreover, Christian mystical experience is open to the simple as well as to the highly gifted and, when it is attained, the experience is perceived not as the natural result of the mystic's efforts but as a gift bestowed by the God whom the mystic seeks.

The comparative study of religious psychology describes and classifies the various types of mystical experience; it cannot judge their respective value and validity. Such a judgment is properly the work of philosophical and theological reflection on the data assembled by the psychologist of religion. Thus scrutinized, to the reflective Christian both the mysticism of nature and monistic mysticism appear illusory; and theistic mysticism of the philosophical kind, while acknowledged as a valid experience, has been classified as only a dim shadow of Christian mystical experience.

Mystical experiences of one type or another are to be found in all religions with the sole exception of Zoroastrianism; there the mystical element either was not present or was not permanently recorded. A complete study of mysticism in all its varying manifestations would include an investigation of the Neoplatonic mysticism of Plotinus and Philo; of Judaic prophetism and Hasidism; of Moslem Sufism; of Yoga and other Indian mysticism; and of the varying manifestations of mystical experience throughout Christian history. See PHILO JUDAEUS; NEOPLATONISM; PROPHET; HASIDIM; SUFISM; YOGA. R. F. SMITH, S.J.

BIBLIOG.–E. Gall, *Mysticism Through the Ages* (1934); J. de Marquette, *Introduction to Comparative Mysticism* (1949); G. W. Bullett, *English Mystics* (1950); E. C. Butler, *Western Mysticism* (ed. 1951); E. A. Peers, ed., *Mystics of Spain* (1952); F. Gaynor, ed., *Dictionary of Mysticism* (1953); G. G. Scholem, *Major Trends in Jewish Mysticism* (ed. 1954); W. R. Inge, *Christian Mysticism* (ed. 1956); E. Underhill, *Mysticism* (ed. 1956); R. Otto, *Mysticism, East and West* (1957); R. C. Petry, ed., *Late Medieval Mysticism* (1957); D. T. Suzuki, *Mysticism: Christian and Buddhist* (1957).

MYTHOLOGY, a collective body of myths—stories about gods or other supermundane or superhuman beings. Such stories are found in all known cultures and probably were designed originally to serve two main purposes. First, in a world unconscious of (or uninterested in) organic processes, myths accounted for natural phenomena by representing such phenomena as being the results of the willful actions and adventures of external powers. Second, myths provided the necessary authority and validation for various traditional practices and institutions. For these reasons, myths were frequently recited at public rituals and embodied in magical spells. See MAGIC.

Beliefs Versus Folk Tales. In their primary form, myths belong more to the sphere of religion than to literature and art, for what they relate are traditional beliefs in common rather than mere individual fancies (see RELIGION). In course of time, however, these beliefs fade or are superseded, and the time-honored myths then survive only as folk tales—a quarry of inherited popular lore which poets and artists may proceed to mine at will (see FOLKLORE). It is in this secondary form that the majority of myths have come down to us. Accordingly, myths cannot always be taken as evidence of living faith, and in assessing their significance within a given culture due allowance must be made for the fact that myths may still be told even though they are no longer believed literally, and for the possibility that under such circumstances the myths may have undergone artistic manipulation and embellishment.

Types of Myths. Myths may be divided into certain broad categories, determined by their themes. Thus they may deal with (1) the origin and organization of the world; (2) the creation and nature of man; (3) the genesis and characteristics of natural phenomena—animal and vegetable, astral and meteorological; (4) the rhythms of nature and the alternation of the seasons; (5) the inherent antitheses of the natural order, both physical and "moral," such as light and darkness, good and evil; (6) the primordial history of the world and its ultimate fate; (7) the nature of other worlds such as realms of bliss or torment, abodes of the gods and of the dead; and (8) primeval relations between gods and traditional heroes. Moreover, in the hands of poets and imaginative writers, myths often degenerate into biographical anecdotes.

Myths told to account for traditional usages and institutions, or to account for personal or local names (see NAME), are termed etiological, from the Greek *aitia* (cause) and *logos* (lore, story). Such myths are not always invented on the spur of the moment; often they represent mere secondary exploitations of tales long current in their own right. Thus, the familiar biblical legend of Jacob's struggle with the angel (Gen. 32:24–32) is basically a form of a well known myth dealing with an encounter between a traveler and the spirit of a river; but because the patriarch was said to have been smitten on the hip, the Hebrew writer added the secondary, etiological detail that "therefore to this day the Israelites do not eat the sinew of the hip which is upon the thigh." See BIBLE; EDDA; EPIC; LEGEND; SAGA; VEDAS.

COMPARATIVE MYTHOLOGY

Within each of the aforementioned categories, the many stories told in different cultures often show remarkable similarities. Some of these similarities are discussed below.

Origin and Organization of the World. Alike in the Bible, in the Babylonian cosmologies, and among the Egyptians, the present world is said to have been preceded by chaotic waters, and this idea recurs not only in the Indic Rig-Veda, in the *Iliad* of Homer, and in the Scandinavian Eddas, but also in the myths of such diverse and historically unrelated peoples as the Yoruba of the Sudan, the pygmies of Gabon, the Iroquois, Crow, and Creek Indians of North America, the ancient Mexicans, and the Quiché of Guatemala. The basic notion probably arose not so much out of natural history as out of the fact that water, because it is shapeless and seemingly ungenerated, might readily be imagined by the primitive mind to have preceded all that has shape and substance. An alternative concept, that the world was hatched out of an egg, is attested not only among the ancient Egyptians, Phoenicians, Hindus, Iranians (Persians), and Greeks, but also in Polynesia. See COSMOLOGY AND COSMOGONY; CALENDAR.

Creation and Nature of Man. The statement in the Bible (Gen. 2:7 and Job 33:6) and in Babylonian texts to the effect that man was molded out of clay finds parallels in the Egyptian tale that he was shaped by the potter-god Khnemu, or Khnum (and by Ptah or Ptah and Khnemu), and in the legends of Australian primitives that man was fashioned from loam by the divine Pund-jel. Widespread, too, is the story that woman was formed from the flesh of man. Although most familiar to Occidentals through the Bible, this tale occurs also in the quite unrelated myths of the Tahitians, the Maoris of New Zealand, the Karens of Burma, and the Bedel Tatars of Siberia. See CREATION.

Natural Phenomena have likewise inspired similar myths in different parts of the globe. Quite common, for instance, is the notion that thunder is caused by the flapping wings of a giant stormbird. Such a creature appears not only in the Imgig of the Sumerians, the Garuda (or Garduda) of Indic (Vedic) mythology and the Hraesveglur of the Eddas, but also among such diverse peoples as the Finns, the Shetland Islanders, the Aztecs of Mexico, and the Tlingit and Athabascas of North America. So, too, the Indic Rahu, whose swallowing of the sun causes eclipses, finds his direct counterpart not only in the wolf named Skoll among the Scandinavians and in the Tiknis (or Tiklis) of the Lithuanians, but equally in ancient Greece and China and among the Negritos of Borneo, and in Burma and Iraq. See ANIMAL WORSHIP; ANIMISM.

The same parallelism obtains also in the case of many astral myths. Orion is a giant huntsman not only to the Greeks but equally to the Hottentots, the Buriats of eastern Mongolia, the Zuñi of New Mexico, and the Loango and Bakongo of Africa; and the Milky Way is almost everywhere regarded as the highway of souls. See CONSTELLATION.

The Rhythms of Nature and the Alternation of the Seasons are represented throughout the world as the death and resurrection, or withdrawal and return, of a personified spirit (god) of fertility. Among representatives of this being in ancient myths are the Tammuz of the Babylonians, the Osiris of the Egyptians, the Attis of the Phrygians, and the "Baal Puissant" of the Canaanites; also, a Hittite text (second millennium B.C.) describes the disappearance and subsequent restoration of the analogous deity, Telipinu. And there are modern parallels. In Rumania, for example, it is (or was) customary to perform annually a mock burial and resurrection of a clay puppet called Scalojan (Drought); and in parts of Russia similar popular ceremonies were associated with a comparable figure named Kostrobonko. See NATURE WORSHIP; PHALLIC WORSHIP.

Antitheses of the Physical and Moral Order. Dualistic myths, portraying the antitheses of nature as the conflicts of opposing gods, are likewise almost universal. The standard instances from antiquity are those of the evil Set (or Sut) and the good and noble Horus in Egypt, and of the benign Ormazd (or Hormazu or Ahura Mazda) and the evil Ahriman among the Zoroastrian Persians. The latter antithesis appears in turn to have been one of the primary sources of the familiar Judaeo-Christian concept of the struggle between God and Satan (or Belial). This, too, is not without its counterparts among more modern peoples. The Incas of Peru accounted for the alternation of day and night as the perpetual battle of the god Pigunao against the god Apocatequil; the Pentecost Islanders tell of the constant rivalry between Tagar, representing good, and Suque, representing bad; and the Hottentots of that between the analogous Tsui-Goab and Gaunab. See DUALISM.

Primordial History of the World, and Its Fate. A fancy shared by many peoples is that the present world is the successor of a previous one which was destroyed by flood either through the machinations of a satanic marplot or in retribution for human misdeeds. More than 90 parallels to the biblical story of a primeval deluge have been recorded, several of them (those of the Babylonians, the Macusis of British Guiana, the Island Caribs, and the Yaguas of South America) including the familiar motif of the rescue of favored individuals in an ark, and others (those of the Babylonians and the Algonquins) that of the successive dispatch of birds in search of dry land. Moreover, the biblical Ararat, on which the ark rested, finds analogies in American myth in Mt. Colhuacan on the Pacific coast, Mt. Apoala in Upper Mixteca, and Mt. Neba in the province of the Guaymies. Further, the notion that a new race of men was created out of stones thrown by the survivors occurs not only in the well known classical myth of Deucalion and Pyrrha, but also—to cite but a few of many examples—among the Macusis and the Tamanaks of the Orinoco, and in the Norse tale of Bergelmir and Ymir. See DELUGE, THE.

Other Worlds. Myths about divine and infernal other worlds also run on parallel lines. To the biblical Eden, for instance, corresponds more or less the Greek Garden of the Hesperides, and standard features of this blissful abode in the most diverse cultures are the tree and fountain of life and the magical rivers, often portrayed as flowing with honey. Moreover, the *four* streams of the Hebrew version (Gen. 2:10) find their equivalents in those which flow from the Hindu paradise on Mt. Meru, from the cave of Circe in Homer's *Odyssey*, and from the gardens of delight in American and Polynesian myths. Conversely, the idea that the land of the dead lies across a perilous river was entertained alike by the Babylonians (the river Hubur) and the Greeks (Lethe, the river of oblivion), and is a feature of the Celtic *imramas* (tales of journeys to the faërie realm). It is present also in myths related by the Huron, Iroquois, and Athabascan Indians of North America, and by the Araucanians of Chile. In German folklore it is sometimes identified with the Rhine.

A constant motif, too, is the belief that he who eats of the food of the other world can never return to the world of men. In Greek myth, Persephone is trapped in Hades through eating seeds of a pomegranate handed to her by Pluto; in Japanese myth, Izanagi cannot retrieve his wife Izanami from the ghostly Land of Yomi because she has eaten food there; and in the Finnish *Kalevala*, the hero Wainamoinen eschews such fare in the land of Manala in order to insure his ability to return. See HADES; HEAVEN; HELL.

Ancestral Heroes throughout the world are often endowed with the same or similar mythical traits. The Hebrew Moses, the Babylonian Sargon of Agade, the Greek Jason, the Roman Romulus, the British King Arthur (see ARTHURIAN LEGEND), and the Welsh Llew Llangaeffes, among many others, are exposed in childhood but found and nurtured by strangers or animals, and eventually return to lead their peoples. In many cases (Arthur, Nero, Frederick I Barbarossa, for example), it is said of them that they have not really died but are sleeping on a distant hill and will reappear in the hour of their country's need. See ANCESTOR WORSHIP; APOTHEOSIS; HERO.

ORIGINS AND IMPLICATIONS OF MYTHS

Why Such Similarities? It was formerly believed that similarities among the myths of diverse cultures might be explained on the hypothesis that all of them had been diffused in the remote past from a common center, variously located by scholars in Egypt, Mesopotamia, and India. This hypothesis lacks adequate historical backing, and has been generally discarded in favor of the alternate view that peoples living at the same general level of civilization, or confronted by the same natural phenomena, are likely to evolve the same basic ideas and concepts. This view, too, is admittedly precarious, for there is no proof that the various cultures involved were (or are) actually on the same level, or that the myths which appear in them are in all cases primitive. Nevertheless, some measure of support for it is perhaps afforded by comparative semantics. It is a fact, for example, that in languages which are philologically quite distinct and whose speakers are historically unrelated, objects are frequently designated and concepts expressed by means of the same images. To give but one illustration, in both Semitic and Indo-European speech the source of a river is described as its head, the outflow as its mouth, and the banks as its hands. In addition to such philological evidence, this view receives support in the fact that parallelism in myths often reflects an analogous parallelism in ritual procedures and seasonal situations. See RITUAL; DANCE, The Essence of Dance, *Tribal Dance*, Development of Dance Around the World, *Oriental Dance*, *Antiquity*.

Functions and Techniques. If the function of myth is to explain natural phenomena or to validate traditional usages, then the technique by which this is accomplished is that of translating present and punctual events into terms of ideal and atemporal situations. So regarded, the "truth" of a myth lies not in its factual veracity but in its affective value—that is, in the extent to which it is able to convey the continuing and durative import of that which happens at a particular moment of time.

When, however, primitive faith breaks down and myths degenerate into mere literary monuments or oral traditions, the need is often felt to validate them on other grounds. This is done in two principal ways: by transference and by rationalization. Transference consists in boldly transplanting the contents and traits (motifs) of the traditional myths to the sagas dealing with historical personalities—such as Alexander the Great, King Arthur, and Charlemagne. There is little doubt that something like this has occurred in the evolution of certain myths, but even if this is the case in particular instances, it presupposes the existence of the myths that are so transplanted, and reveals next to nothing about the origins or meanings of the myths themselves. Rationalization is a still more complex problem for the mythologist.

Rationalization consists in interpreting the traditional stories on historical, symbolic, or allegorical lines. Thus, according to one view, that known as euhemerism after the Greek thinker Euhemerus who first advanced it in the fourth century B.C., myths are simply exaggerated and transmogrified accounts of events involving important individuals or groups in the remote past. Osiris, Tammuz, and Zeus, for instance, would originally have been kings or heroes of Egypt, Babylonia, and Greece respectively; and the biblical tale of the relations between Jacob and Esau would reflect the relations that existed between the Israelites and the Edomites. Another view identifies the central characters of traditional myths, such as Apollo, Artemis, and the Indic Maruts, with such natural phenomena as sun, moon, stars, rain, and winds; *or* (in the theory of Sir James Frazer) with the spirit of fertility that dies and revives from year to year; *or* with abstract qualities such as love, hate, war, death—personified for the purpose of conveying moral truths in dramatic form. Yet another theory, associated especially with the nineteenth century philologist Friedrich Max Müller, maintains that myths are, at bottom, a "disease of language," and that their significance may best be apprehended by simply etymologizing the names of their leading figures. The biblical Samson (Hebrew, *Shimshon*), for example, would personify the sun, because that is the meaning of the Hebrew word *shemesh;* and the shearing of his locks by Delilah would represent the curtailment of the sun's rays by the shades of night. Similarly, the pursuit of Daphne by Apollo would represent the pursuit of the *dawn* (related to *Daphne* etymologically) by the rising sun.

None of these theories is really satisfactory, for none will stand up against the results of comparative research. It is obvious, for instance, that when essentially the same myth turns up among peoples of utterly diverse culture and language, it cannot be derived from historical events or linguistic peculiarities unique to one of them.

Myth and Ritual. It has become increasingly clear that in many cases myths are projected out of seasonal events and recurrent rituals. Deluge stories, for example, are often inspired by the phenomenon of annual inundation (as by the Nile River in Egypt), upon the subsidence of which the world is, so to speak, reborn. Similarly, stories of holy unions between gods and goddesses, such as those of Zeus and Hera or Ishtar (Astarte) and Tammuz, reflect the widespread rite of mating king and sacred bride at the New Year festival as a means of promoting the fertility of the realm; and tales of successive dynasties in heaven, each overthrowing its predecessor and ruling for a limited period—for example, the Greek Uranus (Ouranos), Cronus (Kronos), and Zeus, or the Hittite myth of Alalu, Anu, and Kumarbi—are seemingly based on the common custom of appointing kings for fixed terms (see CHRONOLOGY, *Historical Chronology*). So, too, the virtually universal myth recounting the victory of the sky god over a dragon of the waters (Yahweh or Jahveh over Leviathan, the Indic Indra over Vritra, Zeus over Typhon, the Canaanite Baal over the Babylonian sea god Yamm, to name a few examples) reflects the widespread popular custom—

one still observed in several parts of the world—of mimetically (through imitative or sympathetic rituals) "subduing" the spirit of the swollen rivers at the onset of the rainy season. See JEHOVAH; YAHWEH.

The fact that such underlying rituals and situations are common to the most diverse cultures in large measure explains the otherwise puzzling similarity of myths in different and unrelated parts of the globe.

In more absolute terms, too, the relation of myth to ritual has become increasingly clear. Previously, this relation was held to be necessarily genealogical, myth being a later explanation of ritual, or ritual a subsequent enactment of myth. Scholars at mid-twentieth century, however, more and more regarded them as correlatives—the "long shot" and "close-up" views of the same thing—myth being but an expression in lasting, quasi-historical terms of that which ritual at the given moment represents as being concrete and actual.

Myth and Literature. Myths that are projected out of seasonal situations and rituals are in their most primitive stage little more than the accompanying librettos of religious performances or pantomimes. Later, however, when those performances (rituals) are themselves discarded, the myths often survive in their own right and in turn set the model for certain types of literary composition. In view of this, considerable attention has been given by scholars to the problem of recognizing the ritualistic elements behind conventional literary styles. The underlying assumption of such investigations is that seasonal rituals fall everywhere into a more or less standard pattern, involving the death and resurrection of a fertility spirit or a combat between principals or teams representing life and death, summer and winter, old and new, and the like, followed by the installation of the victorious leader as king, the mating of him with a sacred bride, and so forth. Such patterns, albeit considerably modified and attentuated, have been detected in several branches of literature commonly considered as vehicles of myth—in classical Greek drama, in ancient Near Eastern epic poems, in some of the hymns of the Indic Rig-Veda, in the Scandinavian Eddas, in legends of the Holy Grail (see HOLY GRAIL), and in the view of some scholars even in some of the biblical Psalms. Although the theory has sometimes been carried to extremes, such excesses scarcely invalidate its basic proposition, for what is at stake is not the undisputable origin of this or that particular composition, but the origin(s) of certain literary genres as a whole.

The Psychology of Myth. Some twentieth century psychologists, and especially the psychoanalysts, have found several apparent points of similarity between the themes and images employed in traditional myths and those characteristic of dreams and other subconscious states. On the basis of such observations, attempts have been made (notably by Carl G. Jung) to interpret myths in terms of subliminal symbols and subconscious drives. The story of Zeus' mutilation of his father, Cronus (Kronos), for example, has been taken to articulate the inherent hostility of the younger toward the older generation, and myths of creation by fire to be motivated by sexual considerations. Conversely, certain familiar psychotic states have come, in conventional parlance, to be named after myths in which they are held to be expressed. The most common example of this is the so-called Oedipus complex. See PSYCHOANALYSIS.

Such interpretations, despite their popularity, invite the utmost caution, for the plain fact is that all too many of them are marked by a blithe disregard of the documented literary evolution of the stories involved, and by a consequent failure to distinguish primary from secondary elements, or basic motifs from later embellishments. Such interpretations also reflect a tendency to generalize grandly on the basis of exceedingly limited clinical observation, and to posit as universal human traits certain psychotic states and experiences that may reflect at best only the conditions of particular, sophisticated social environments, and at worst only the conditions of certain individuals.

Apart from psychoanalytical interpretations, the study of myth has in the twentieth century shifted perceptibly away from a merely literary to a more psychological frame of reference. Accordingly, more attention is given to the nature of the mythmaking process (*mythopoeia*) itself than to questions concerning the origins and affiliations of particular myths. The work of the philosopher Ernst Cassirer (1874–1945) has been especially germinal in this respect. Cassirer was perhaps the first to point out clearly the fact that (contrary to earlier suppositions) myth is not a mere literary artifact, but issues out of a distinct and autonomous activity of the human mind—an activity parallel with, but independent of, that mental activity which produces logical thought and intellectual discourse. So regarded, myth is interpreted as the outgrowth of mental activity similar to that involved in the creation of poetry.

This acute perception has led to a growing rejection of the older view (associated especially with the French sociologist Lucien Lévy-Bruhl) that the element of apparent irrationality that is so prominent in myths is simply a relic of the primitive "prelogical thinking" which created them—that is, of a stage of civilization when the mind was innocent of all logical categories. The Lévy-Bruhl position (which was already suspect by reason of the fact that no such prelogical stage is anywhere historically or anthropologically attested, and the fact that myths are by no means always primitive) was rendered utterly unnecessary when it was realized that the human mind, at any level of culture, in fact operates affectively as well as intellectually—by impression as well as synthesis. This insight, set against the positivistic approach of nineteenth century investigators, enables mythologists to recognize that in a very real sense myth is not merely a functional technique of ancient and allegedly primitive cultures, but a perennial aspect of all human mental activity—a faculty parallel with and distinct from that of logical thought, and as such a mainspring of poetry and art. So regarded, it would seem that myth may do for any present time what memory does for the past and hope does for the future.

See articles on religious systems having important mythological aspects, especially BABYLONIAN RELIGION; BUDDHISM; HINDUISM; ISLAM; JAINISM; JUDAISM; LAMAISM; TAOISM; WITCHCRAFT; ZOROASTRIANISM. See also ASSYRIA; BABYLONIA, *Pioneers of Civilization;* BRETON LANGUAGE AND LITERATURE; CELTIC LANGUAGE AND LITERATURE; CHINA, Social Factors, *Religion;* CHINESE LANGUAGE AND LITERATURE; CUNEIFORM, *Types of Cuneiform Literature;* EGYPT, History, *The Character of Ancient Egypt;* EGYPTIAN ART AND ARCHITECTURE, *Symbolism*, *Egyptian Literature;* GERMAN LANGUAGE AND LITERATURE, Literature, *Middle High German;* GREECE, History, map: Historical and Mythological Map of Ancient Greece; GREEK LANGUAGE AND LITERATURE, Literature, *Tragedy;* INDIA, Early History, *The Vedic Age;* INDIAN, AMERICAN, Social Conditions, *Social Organization and Religion;* JAPAN, Social Factors, *Religion;* PERSIAN LANGUAGE AND LITERATURE; SANSKRIT LANGUAGE AND LITERATURE; and entries on the religious and mythological books, persons, deities, animals, prophets, creatures, and concepts mentioned in this article and in those listed above.

THEODOR H. GASTER

BIBLIOGRAPHY

GENERAL: M. D. Conway, *Demonology and Devil-Lore* (2 vols. 1879); J. Harrison, *Ancient Art and Ritual* (1913); Andrew Lang, *Myth, Ritual and Religion* (2 vols. 1913); L. Spence, *Introduction to Mythology* (1921); B. Malinowski, *Myth in Primitive Psychology* (1926); J. A. Macculloch, ed., *Mythology of All Races* (12 vols. 1918–31); F. C. Bray, *World of Myths* (1935); S. Thompson, *Motif-Index of Folk-Literature* (6 vols. 1932–36); A. S. Murray, *Manual of Mythology* (1946); E.

Rosenstock-Huessy, *Out of Revolution* (1938), *Christian Future* (1946); E. M. Butler, *Myth of the Magus* (1948); P. Lum, *Stars in Our Heaven* (1948); H. R. Zimmer, *King and the Corpse* (1948); R. V. Chase, *Quest for Myth* (1949); C. G. Jung and C. Kerényi, *Essays on a Science of Mythology* (1949); E. Fromm, *Forgotten Language* (1951); L. S. de Camp and W. Lev, *Lands Beyond* (1952); P. G. Woodcock, *Short Dictionary of Mythology* (1953); G. H. Mees, *Revelation in the Wilderness* (3 vols. 1954); A. W. Watts, *Myth and Ritual in Christianity* (1954); P. Wheelwright, *Burning Fountain* (1954); G. E. Daniel and others, *Myth or Legend* (1955); E. Neumann, *Great Mother* (1955); T. A. Sebeok, ed., *Myth: A Symposium* (1955); Lord Raglan (F. R. Somerset), *Hero* (ed. 1956); E. Cassirer, *Language and Myth* (1953), *Philosophy of Symbolic Forms* (3 vols. 1953–57); T. Reik, *Myth and Guilt* (1957); R. Graves, *White Goddess* (ed. 1958); J. Campbell, *Hero with a Thousand Faces* (1949), *Masks of God* (1959); J. G. Frazer, *Fear of Death in Primitive Religions* (3 vols. 1933–36), *Golden Bough* (13 vols. ed. 1952; 2 vols. abr. ed. 1957), *New Golden Bough* (newly abr., rev., and annot. by T. H. Gaster, 1959); E. O. James, *Cult of the Mother Goddess* (1959); *Larousse Encyclopedia of Mythology* (Eng. trans. by R. Aldington and D. Ames, 1959).

PRE-HELLENIC: W. M. Flinders Petrie, *Religion of Ancient Egypt* (1908); D. A. Mackenzie, *Egyptian Myth and Legend* (1913), *Myths of Babylonia and Assyria* (1921); B. Brown, ed., *Wisdom of the Egyptians* (1923); S. H. Langdon, *Semitic Mythology* (1931); H. Frankfort and others, *Intellectual Adventure of Ancient Man* (1947), *Ancient Egyptian Religion* (1948); J. J. Obermann, *Ugaritic Mythology* (1948); E. A. T. W. Budge, *Egyptian Magic* (1899), *Gods of the Egyptians* (1904), *Osiris and the Egyptian Resurrection* (1911), *Book of the Dead* (ed. 1949); L. Spence, *Myths and Legends of Ancient Egypt* (1949); J. B. Pritchard, ed., *Ancient Near Eastern Texts Relating to the Old Testament* (1950); H. I. Bell, *Cults and Creeds in Graeco-Roman Egypt* (1953); A. Piankoff and N. Rambova, eds., *Mythological Papyri* (1957); T. H. Gaster, *Thespis* (1950), *Oldest Stories in the World* (ed. 1958).

CLASSICAL: John Ruskin, *Queen of the Air* (1872); A. Fairbanks, *Mythology of Greece and Rome* (1907); Hesiod, *Theogony* (ed. 1914); J. G. Frazer, trans., *Apollodorus, The Library* (2 vols. 1921); W. S. Fox, *Greek and Roman Mythology* (1928); A. R. H. Moncrieff, *Classic Myth and Legend* (1934); C. Valerius Flaccus, *Argonautica* (ed. 1934); Nonnus, *Dionysiaca* (3 vols. ed. 1940); Ovid, *Metamorphoses* (2 vols. ed. 1933–46); M. P. Nillson, *History of Greek Religion* (ed. 1949); K. Kérenyi, *Gods of the Greeks* (1951); D. S. Norton and P. Rushton, *Classical Myths in English Literature* (1952); J. J. Seznec, *Survival of the Pagan Gods* (1952); W. F. Otto, *Homeric Gods* (1954); R. Graves, *Greek Myths* (2 vols. 1955); J. E. Harrison, *Prolegomena to the Study of Greek Religion* (ed. 1955); R. Warner, *Men and Gods* (1951), *Vengeance of the Gods* (1955); C. Kingsley, *Heroes* (ed. 1956); H. J. Rose, *Handbook of Greek Mythology* (ed. 1958).

NORSE: J. L. K. Grimm, *Teutonic Mythology* (4 vols. 1880–88); W. A. Craigie, *Religion of Ancient Scandinavia* (1908); D. A. Mackenzie, *Teutonic Myth and Legend* (1917); P. A. Munch, *Norse Mythology, Legends of Gods and Heroes* (ed. 1942); Snorri Sturluson, *Prose Edda* (ed. 1946); D. G. Hosford, *Sons of the Volsungs* (1949); B. Branston, *Gods of the North* (1955), *Lost Gods of England* (1958).

CELTIC: T. F. O'Rahilly, *Early Irish History and Mythology* (1946); M. L. Sjoestedt-Jonval, *Gods and Heroes of the Celts*

Xochipilli, Aztec Deity of Flowers, Love, and Music

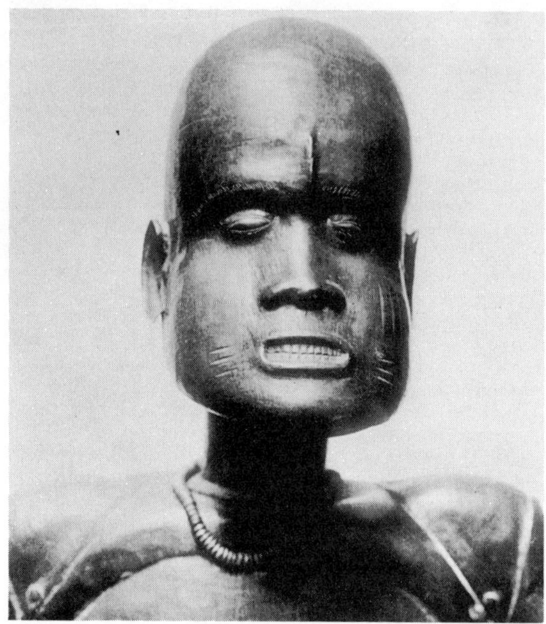

Gu, Dahoman Divinity of Iron, War, Weapons, and Tools

(1949); T. W. Rolleston, *Myths and Legends of the Celtic Race* (1950); P. Kavanagh, *Irish Mythology* (3 vols., 1959).

EASTERN: D. A. Mackenzie, *Indian Myth and Legend* (1913); P. Thomas, *Epics, Myths and Legends of India* (ed. 1949); P. Wheeler, ed., *Sacred Scriptures of the Japanese* (1952); V. Elwin, ed. and trans., *Tribal Myths of Orissa* (1954); H. R. Zimmer, *Art of Indian Asia* (2 vols. 1954); E. T. C. Werner, *Myths and Legends of China* (ed. 1957).

AMERICAN: L. Spence, *Magic and Mysteries of Mexico* (1930); *Black Elk, Sacred Pipe* (1953); C. Clark and T. B. Williams, *Pomo Indian Myths* (1954); P. Radin, *Trickster* (1956); L. Séjourné, *Burning Water* (1957); K. Spencer *Mythology and Values* (1957).

THE PRINCIPAL PANTHEONS

The accompanying table indicates only a few of the principal figures in some of the more important mythologies of antiquity. Greek mythology had more than 30,000 deities and other mythical beings; various other systems were even more prolific. Just as only a few of many beings are included here, so too only a few of many possible analogues among mythical beings and myths can be indicated—but enough to illustrate the fact that similar myths often developed in widely separated cultures. Such resemblances, however, are often only superficial. There was, for example, a Roman analogue for each of the 12 principal gods of Greece, but these analogies, made by the Romans themselves, were often strained almost to the breaking point and reflected no more than the Roman desire to make the gods of all peoples their own; most of the principal Roman gods (even including Jupiter) existed in their own right long before certain of the attributes of Greek gods were ascribed to them. Moreover, parallels that seem exact at first glance are often found on closer examination to be nonexistent. Thus, the Greek Apollo is a sun-god, and so is the Egyptian Ra, or Re, but they cannot properly be equated with each other since their functions within their respective systems were wholly different. A similarity in name can also be misleading. Thus the Persian Mithra (or Mithras) was originally a god of light and wisdom. The Mithraistic cult spread over much of the ancient world, but was radically different from place to place; and by the second millennium A.D. had been transformed from one of the more elevated cults in antiquity to the Satanism of the Middle Ages and the Renaissance. For clarification of many of these relationships, see the separate articles on the mythological figures mentioned.

IMPORTANT CHARACTERS IN THE WORLD'S MAJOR MYTHOLOGIES

Major Figures	General Characteristics and Myths	Likely Analogues in Other Mythologies
	GREEK	
OLYMPIAN DEITIES		
Zeus	Chief of the 12 gods and goddesses dwelling on Mt. Olympus; most powerful of the gods, yet not omnipotent (subject to the workings of the Fates, or Moirai)	Roman *Jupiter* (or Father Jove) originally *Diespater* (Father of the Sky), protector and genius of men; possibly the Vedic *Dyaus;* the Teutonic *Tiu* (or *Tyr*, or *Ziu*, or *Saxnot*) in part; the Norse *Odin* and, in some details, *Thor;* Egyptian *Amun-Ra*
Hera	Zeus' spouse, not his equal or the queen of heaven, yet with a large cult of her own; Roman Juno more powerful	Roman *Juno*, Jupiter's consort, queen of heaven, genius of womankind; possibly the Norse *Frigga* (not Freyja), wife of Odin
Athena	Goddess of wisdom; patroness of city life, urban arts and crafts, victory (Nikē); goddess of Athens in particular; not as powerful as the Roman Minerva	*Minerva*, goddess of war, arts and crafts, wisdom, and valor, and third member of the great Roman triad; Babylonian *Ishtar* (*Astarte*, *Ashtoreth*, and so forth) in part
Aphrodite and **Adonis**	Aphrodite is goddess of love and beauty, born from the foam of the sea; mother of Eros (Roman Cupid); a lover of the mortal youth Adonis (from the Semitic *adon* "lord," or Hebrew *adonai*, "my Lord")	Roman *Venus*, the spirit of desire; the Babylonian *Ishtar* in part; Adonis related to Babylonian *Tammuz* among others (see Persephone below)
Demeter	Goddess of the tilled earth, fertility; the "Great Mother"; specifically a goddess of corn	Roman *Ceres* (English word *cereal*), protectress of agriculture; Babylonian *Ishtar* in part; also all fertility deities
Poseidon	Lord of the sea; also god of horses and earthquakes	*Neptune*, old Roman god of water; in Norse mythology the agonized writhings of *Loki*, chained to a rock so that painful adder poison drops on his face, caused earthquakes
Apollo or **Phoebus** ("light" or "inspired")	Sun-god; god of light, music, medicine, prophecy, archery and other manual activities	Roman *Apollo*, at first god of healing, then of medicine and prophecies; Persian *Mithra* in part; the Norse *Odin* as "light-god," and the Norse *Balder* or *Baldr* in part
Ares	Savage and bloodthirsty god of war hated by other deities. Roman analogue was at first god of agriculture, then of war	Roman *Mars*, father of the founder of Rome (Romulus); also Roman *Quirinus;* possibly the Teutonic *Tiu* (the Romans made this identification)
Hephaestus	God of fire—the lame smith who forged Zeus' thunderbolts and whose assistants made the hero Achilles' armor	Roman *Vulcan* (*Mulciber*, the hammer god), an early Italian earth deity; Egyptian *Ptah*, the "potter"; the zwerge (black elves) of the Norse forged Thor's hammer
Hermes	The "inventor," patron of merchants and thieves, commerce in general, athletics, roads, fertility, luck, and wealth	Roman *Mercury*, messenger of the gods who guides dead souls; possibly the Egyptian *Thoth* in part
Artemis	The virgin huntress, embodying purity and inaccessibility; probably derived from an Oriental fertility deity	Roman *Diana*, goddess of the moon, the chase, the woods, women and childbirth; Artemis sometimes identified by Greeks with their own *Selene* and *Hecate*, both moon (or earth) goddesses
Hestia	Goddess of the hearth and of the fire in it	*Vesta*, a household deity who was fed part of each meal; others were the *lares*, the *penates*, and *Janus*
LESSER DEITIES		
Hades, also called **Pluto** (giver of abundance) by the Greeks	Ruler of the underworld (Hades) and of the shades therein	Roman *Pluto;* Babylonian *Nergal;* Hindu *Yama;* Egyptian *Osiris*, *Anubis*, and others; the Norse goddess *Freyja* (not Frigga) in part
Persephone	Wife of Hades, and co-ruler with him of the underworld and the shades; a daughter of Demeter. Story of her being kidnaped by Hades may be related to those of Isis and Osiris (Egypt), Ishtar and Tammuz (Babylonia), Astarte and Adonis (Syria), Cybele and Attis (Phrygia)	Primitive Italian *Libitina;* Roman *Proserpina;* Babylonian *Ninmug* (*Ereshkigal*) or *Laz;* Egyptian *Nephtys* in part; also thematically, but not functionally, *Isis*, *Ishtar*, *Astarte*, *Cybele* as noted to the left
Cronus or **Kronos**	Son of Uranus or Ouranos (heaven) and Gaea (earth); father by Ops (Rhea) of Hestia, Demeter, Hera, Hades, Poseidon, and Zeus who overthrew him as he had overthrown Uranus	*Saturn*, identified by Romans with Cronus, was almost wholly different in his attributes, which resemble those of *Demeter;* Cronus identified by Cretans with Egyptian *Khonsu* (or *Khensu*); the Norse *Ymir* was overthrown by Odin as was Cronus by Zeus; a Phoenician *Cronos* was also identified with Saturn by the Romans
Ops	Wife of Cronus	Identified with the Roman *Rhea*, wife of Saturn, and also by name with the Roman *Ops*, goddess of wealth
Helios	The sun-god, who sees and hears everything; an informer	Roman *Sol*

IMPORTANT CHARACTERS IN THE WORLD'S MAJOR MYTHOLOGIES (Continued)

Major Figures	General Characteristics and Myths	Likely Analogues in Other Mythologies
Heracles	A semidivine son of Zeus; performed 12 noteworthy labors; his cult especially powerful among the Dorians	Roman *Hercules*, god of joy and wine, represented by the lyre; related vaguely to the culture heroes of various mythologies
Priapus	God of the fertility of gardens, bees, flocks, herds, and people; a son of Aphrodite and Dionysus; so horribly deformed that statues of him were used as scarecrows	Roman *Priapus;* related in his fertility significance to many other fertility deities of antiquity
Pan	God of flocks and shepherds, whose cult was especially prominent in Arcadia. He wandered through forests playing his syrinx (pipes of Pan) and dancing with the nymphs, occasionally appearing to frighten a traveler	Roman *Faunus*
	EGYPTIAN	
Ra or **Re**	The sun-god, whose cult center was the city of Heliopolis, which became the political center of Egypt under a dynasty of pharaohs coming from the "Hawk" tribe on the Nile Delta—this tribe having won out over various other totemic tribes (crocodile, jackal, ibis, and the like). The political victory of this tribe largely accounted for the importance of that tribe's chief god, Horus	Related analogically to many solar deities but cannot plausibly be identified with any of them, although the Romans (who fitted the gods of all peoples into their pantheon) identified him with *Jupiter*
Horus	In an early form, a god of life and goodness, the sun, day, and so forth. His eyes are the sun and the moon. Set steals one of Horus' eyes (the sun) and is attacked in return. Thoth makes peace and allots the night to Set, the day to Horus. In a later form, Horus is the son of Osiris, and the latter's avenger. Horus had many forms and names	
Osiris and **Isis,** his wife; **Thoth,** a moon-god who invented numbers and arithmetic, astronomy and geometry; **Nephtys,** a protectress of the dead, and (like her sister Isis) a mother goddess; **Anubis,** god of embalming, and an attendant of Isis	The Egyptian god of the dead and the central figure of Egyptian mythology in its fullest development. He was the son of Ra and Nut, or of Nut and Geb, and taught the Egyptians the arts of agriculture (barley, wheat in particular) and how to make bread, wine, and beer; moreover he taught all of the arts and crafts, invented writing, and produced a code of law—aided by his wife Isis and the chief scribe Thoth. Osiris' brother, Set (a solar deity, the pig), hating him, seals Osiris in a chest which floats out to sea and eventually to Syria, where a sycamore tree grows up around it; later the king of Byblos has this tree made into a pillar for his palace. Eventually Osiris' wife Isis recovers the chest and takes Osiris' body back to Egypt in a coffin. Set finds the body and has it dismembered and the parts scattered. Helped by her sister Nephtys and by Thoth and Anubis, Isis gathers all the parts but one and reassembles them, whereupon Osiris is restored to eternal life. Horus, Osiris' son, avenges his father and is declared Osiris' heir by the other gods. This myth is interpreted by historians as a reflection of the unification of Upper and Lower Egypt—Set representing Upper Egypt, Osiris Lower Egypt, Horus the unifier of the two. The death and resurrection of Osiris represented the sinking and flooding of the Nile River—a cycle upon which Egypt's economy depended; the myth was also related to mummification rituals	Babylonian *Tammuz;* Greek *Hadès* *Isis* resembles *Ishtar* *Thoth*, the scribe, comparable in various respects to the "culture heroes" of all mythologies, and has been identified specifically with aspects of the Norse *Odin* and *Mimir*, and with the Greek *Hermes*, among others
Hathor and **Sekhmet**	A daughter of Ra (Re), the sun-god. Old and no longer respected in the degree he feels his due, Ra entrusts Hathor with the task of destroying mankind—this despite the fact that Hathor was revered as the goddess of love and beauty. She was to be assisted in her work of destruction by Sekhmet, the fire-goddess, who was sometimes identified with Hathor. The two proceed to carry out their task. Seeing them slaughtering wildly, wading in blood, Ra relents and asks them to stop, but they continue killing. Ra then floods the world with 7,000 vessels of beer mixed with narcotic mandrake; Hathor and Sekhmet drink so much of this beverage (which soon includes the blood of those they have killed) that they become too drunk to continue the slaughter	Hathor resembles the Babylonian *Ishtar* to a great extent, especially in her character as goddess of love and beauty *and* a cause of human misery and death; can also be likened to such figures as *Venus*, *Aphrodite*, *Demeter*, but no explicit identification is possible
Ammon or **Amon** or **Amun** or **Amen** and **Amun-Ra** or **Amon-Re**	A predynastic deity, probably of agriculture, later associated with several dynastic deities, notably with Ra or Re, the sun-god. As Amun-Ra he was the supreme deity of Egypt during and after the eighteenth dynasty, being regarded as chief of the gods, the creator of the universe. The pharaohs claimed descent from him. He was specifically associated with the city of Thebes, whose theophany centered in the triad of Amun-Ra, his wife Mut, the vulture regarded as mother of the gods and of the world; and Khonsu, their son, the traveler (sometimes Khensu)	No clear-cut identification is possible, but Amun-Ra obviously was regarded in somewhat the same light as such figures as *Zeus*, *Jupiter*, and other "kings" of the gods in various mythologies. *Khonsu* was identified with *Cronus* by the Cretans
Aton or **Aten**	The "sun disk," or "solar disk," whose quasi-monotheistic cult was fostered during the reign of Pharaoh Ikhnaton (Akhenaten), centering in Heliopolis, in opposition to the cult of Amun-Ra and its priesthood. The degree to which the cult reflected merely political rivalries is disputed by scholars. During his reign Ikhnaton systematically destroyed the images of Amun-Ra, replacing them with the symbols of Aton; the symbols of Aton were later systematically destroyed and images of Amun-Ra restored	The apparent monotheism embodied in the cult of Aton has led some to see in it the beginnings of higher religion (Islam, Judaism, Christianity); others reject this notion

IMPORTANT CHARACTERS IN THE WORLD'S MAJOR MYTHOLOGIES (Continued)

Major Figures	General Characteristics and Myths	Likely Analogues in Other Mythologies
	MESOPOTAMIAN *The region to the east of the Mediterranean Sea, including the cities and regions of Eridu, Ur, Larsa, Lagash, Nippur, Akkad, Babylon, Erech or Uruk, Sumer, and others. The pantheons of these places differed relatively little since at various times deities and myths that had originated in one locality were transplanted to others.*	
The Great Babylonian Triad	*Anu*, heaven (consort *Anatu*); *Ea*, the waters (consort *Damkina*) and *Bel*, the earth, "Lord of the Mountain" (consort *Belit*)	
Secondary Triad	*Sin*, god of the moon (consort *Ningal*); *Shamash*, god of the sun (consort *Aja*); *Adad* or *Ramman*, god of the atmosphere (storm—thunder, lightning, flood, famine)	
Ishtar or **Ashtart** or **Astarte** along the Mediterranean coast; **Astar** or **Istar** among the Semites; called **Ashtoreth** by Hebrews; identified with **Ninlil** in Nippur, **Nanai** in Erech, and **Zarpanit** in the city of Babylon	The most omnipresent deity of antiquity, and the only goddess not known primarily as consort to a god. As Ishtar she was specifically the Sumerian-Babylonian goddess of fertility. The likely and possible analogues given here are only a few of the many proposed by mythologists, and by the ancients themselves, and some authorities postulate an earlier common worship of an earth goddess or "great mother." Ishtar's consorts were legion, but the most famous was Tammuz. The story of her rescue of Tammuz from the world of the dead closely parallels the Greek-Syrian story of Aphrodite and Adonis; another likely parallel is the Egyptian Isis-Osiris myth. In the Gilgamesh epic Ishtar is accused of having destroyed her "husband" Tammuz and this has led mythologists to suppose that before resurrecting Tammuz, she had herself caused his demise. She appears to have represented bountiful life overflowing into death—the giver and destroyer of life—and was often considered the goddess of war and storms	Among several Greek analogues, the most important are *Demeter* and *Aphrodite* (consonantal shift); called *Syria Dea* by Lucian; worshiped in Egypt after 1800 B.C. as the war-goddess *Qodshu;* likely analogue to Egyptian *Hathor* and *Isis;* Syrian *Balthi* and *Qedeshet;* equated with various other Babylonian deities such as *Damkina*, as whom she was the mother of *Tammuz;* likened by some philologists to the biblical *Esther;* her cult may have been related to the Greek idea that the beginning of love is the beginning of death
Tammuz, called **Dumuzi** (the anointed) in the Sumerian tongue	A god of vegetation whose death and resurrection represented the seasonal cycles of growth and decay. He was especially honored by women. In the Adapa myth Tammuz and a deity named Gishzida are guards at the gate of heaven who intercede with Anu in behalf of Adapa. In the Ishtar-Tammuz myth (the Sumerians called him her brother, the Babylonians her son or her lover), Tammuz is gored to death by a wild boar and descends to Aralu (Hades), which is ruled by Ishtar's sister, Ereshkigal. Ishtar descends to Aralu to rescue Tammuz, but is detained, humiliated, and tortured by the jealous Ereshkigal. Deprived of the fruitful influence of Ishtar, the earth languishes; and Ereshkigal is ordered by the gods to release her. She refuses to leave Aralu without Tammuz, and thus Tammuz is resurrected. The whole sequence was thought to recur annually	Incontestably analogous to the Syrian-Greek hero *Adonis*, and very likely to the Egyptian deity *Osiris;* appears in various Mesopotamian myths as *Urukagina*, *Gudea*, and *Siniddina*, sometimes identified with a Babylonian god of the powers of darkness, *Kingu*, as whom Tammuz was the second consort of *Tiamat*, she-dragon by whose defeat *Marduk* becomes chief of the gods, whereupon he used Kingu's blood mixed with clay to fashion the first man; Tammuz is mentioned in the Bible in Ezek. 8:14
Adapa	The first man, and a sage, son of the god Ea, Adapa was given all wisdom and all such qualities as to make him a god, except immortality. As a priest of the temple at Eridu his principal duty was, as "that mortal with clean hands," to keep the table of the gods supplied with food, especially fish of which the gods were particularly fond. As Adapa is fishing one day, his boat is overturned and in his fury Adapa breaks the wings of the south wind. Angry that the south wind can no longer blow, Anu summons Adapa to explain himself. Ea warns Adapa not to accept anything Anu may offer to eat and drink. Tammuz and Gishzida intercede with Anu in Adapa's behalf, and, no longer angry, Anu offers Adapa food and drink—actually the bread and water of eternal life. Recalling Ea's warning, Adapa refuses the food, thus forfeiting immortality for himself and for all mankind	Has been identified by Hebrew scholars with the biblical *Adam*, principally on the philological ground that linguistically *m* and *p* are interchangeable. Moreover, Adam, meaning "man," was perhaps derived from the word *adamah*, earth
Gilgamesh or **Izdubar** or **Gishdubar** and **Utnapishtim** or **Ziudsudra**	Principal hero of Babylonian mythology, whose epic story is told in 12 cuneiform tablets discovered in 1872. He was a ruler of Uruk, one-third human and two-thirds divine, who defeats Engidu and wins his friendship; the two then share many wonderful adventures until Engidu is killed and descends to the underworld. Alone, Gilgamesh sets out in search of eternal life, and specifically in search of his ancestor Utnapishtim (the far away), who had won immortality through his exemplary conduct during the flood. Gigamesh finds this ancestor, who tells him of the flood. Enlil, hating mankind, had persuaded Anu to bring the flood; but Ea warned Utnapishtim of the coming deluge, telling him to build a gufa (boat) and to have on it animals of every kind. Later the boat was grounded on Mt. Niser and Utnapishtim sent out a dove, then a swallow, then a raven; when the raven failed to return, Utnapishtim knew there was land. Enlil, enraged that anyone survived the deluge, was pacified by Ea; and later Utnapishtim was made a god. Gilgamesh then undergoes a rigorous test wherein he must conquer sleep; but he fails and does not become a god. He visits Engidu in the underworld and from him receives an edifying description of that place. Then he himself dies	Can be related to many mythological heroes, but plausibly to very few, notably to the "mighty hunter" *Nimrod* (Gen. 10:8–10); but Nimrod is also identified by some scholars with the Babylonian *Marduk* and with a number of other mythological and historical persons, including *Orion*. *Utnapishtim* is related analogically, if not historically, to the biblical *Noah;* the two names are related linguistically

IMPORTANT CHARACTERS IN THE WORLD'S MAJOR MYTHOLOGIES (Continued)

Major Figures	General Characteristics and Myths	Likely Analogues in Other Mythologies
Marduk or **Bel-Marduk**	Babylonian god of the spring sun, and the chief figure in the Babylonian pantheon after his victory over the she-dragon Tiamat. Marduk was the offspring of Damkina and El ("god," the supreme being) or of Ea. Marduk grows to great strength and when the gods are threatened by Tiamat and the brood of ogres to which she has given birth, and all other methods for fighting her have failed, Marduk is promised that he will be made supreme among them if he will but defeat Tiamat. This he does (in one of the most gruesome battles of any mythology). Now supreme, he splits open Tiamat's body, drains it of blood, and makes one half the dome of heaven, the other into the earth. He then makes the first man. By one account he has Tiamat's consort Kingu sacrificed, and with his blood and some clay makes man. By another account Marduk decapitates himself and forms man of his own blood. Through his victory over Tiamat, Marduk displaced Bel in the great triad and assumed a position higher than that of the other figures in it, and thereafter was accorded a respect and obedience on the part of the Babylonians far exceeding that granted gods before	Possibly related to the biblical *Nimrod;* appears in the Bible as *Bel* or *Merodach* (Isa. 46: 1, Jer. 50: 2); related to the very early Sumerian culture hero *Tagtug*, and possibly to the secondary hero of the Gilgamesh epic, *Utnapishtim*
	PERSIAN AND ZOROASTRIAN	
Mithra or **Mithras**	God of the invincible sun in the Vedic hymns, later elevated by the Persians to the position of chief of the heavenly beings, the ahuras. In a subsequent reform of Persian religion by Zarathustra, Mithra was downgraded, as were the other two principal pre-Zoroastrian deities, Anahita (goddess of fertility and the earth) and Haoma (a bull god, who dies and is reborn). In the meantime, however, Mithraism was introduced into the Roman empire and had reached Rome itself by the first century B.C.; thereafter it competed with Christianity	
Ahura-Mazda or **Ormazd** or **Ormuzd** or **Hormazu**	The lord of light, the supreme god who appeared to Zarathustra and gave him the Avesta (Book of Wisdom). The seven aspects or qualities of Ahura-Mazda were Light, Good Mind, Right, Dominion, Piety, Well-Being, and Immortality. Later followers of Zoroastrianism interpreted these qualities as anthropomorphic beings constantly at war with the forces of evil under the command of Ahriman	
Ahriman or **Angro-Mainyus**	Ruler of the dark world, with the devas, a host of demons and devils, at his command	
	SCANDINAVIAN AND TEUTONIC	
Ymir and the **Jotunns** **Asgard** and **Midgard** **Heimdall**	Ymir was ancestor and ruler of the Reimthursen (frost giants) or Jotunns. He was created by the toppling of the northern ice of Niflheim into the void of the Ginnungagap. In this "old world" he feeds on the milk of the cow (or Mother Earth) Audhumla, who, in turn, lives by licking ice blocks. This process gives rise to Buri, or Bur, who becomes father of Bori or Bor, who becomes father of Odin, Vili, and Ve, who slay Ymir and transmute him into a "new world" wherein Ymir's flesh is the earth, his bones the mountains, his teeth the cliffs and crags, his blood the seas and oceans, his skull the heavens, and his brains the clouds. This new world is Asgard, an elaborate land of the gods wherein live Odin and the 12 Aesir, and a variety of dwarfs, elves, and the like. Asgard is above and in the midst of Midgard, home of men. Yggdrasill, the world tree, stretches up to heaven, overshadowing Valhalla, the hall of heroes; while its three roots reach into Hel, into Midgard, and into the land of giants, Utgarthar, the latter connected to Asgard by the rainbow bridge (Bifrost) guarded by Heimdall, the watchman who can hear the grass grow and who will warn the gods of the approach of the attacking frost giants. Around the sea spanned by the rainbow bridge is curled a huge snake, Jormungand. Within Asgard are 12 palaces and many other dwellings and halls	Ymir is analogous to the Greek *Cronus* in one respect at least—he was overthrown by Odin as Cronus was overthrown by Zeus, just as Cronus earlier had overthrown Uranus. Asgard as the abode of the principal deities is analogous to the Greek *Mt. Olympus* but is infinitely more complex geographically. Hel is analogous to many places of the dead, such as the Greek *Hades*. The frost giants are vaguely reminiscent in their functional relationships to various beasts and creatures in other theologies such as the Greek *centaur*, the Arthurian *dragon*, and so forth
Odin or **Woden** or **Wotan**	Father of the gods and of men, and as such known as the all-father. Essentially he is the life-giving breath of the heavens, and all of the Aesir are aspects of him; apart from this, he appears as himself in the *Eddas* under no less than 53 different names. He is a solar deity and also god of the dead, of cunning (he invented military tactics), poetry, and wisdom—, among other things. He is a son of Bori and also appears as both the son and the father of Thor. He created the first man, Ash, and woman, Alder, when he stumbled upon their lifeless bodies one day and forthwith endowed them with life—without inquiring into whence the bodies had come. *Odin* is related to the English *Wednesday*	Clearest analogue is to the Hindu *Brahma;* as a culture hero (poetry, writing, etc.) Odin is analogous to Egyptian *Thoth*, among others; he is related to all the Greek Olympians, but especially to *Zeus* and *Apollo;* Odin has also been linked, on philological grounds, to the Vedic storm-god, *Vata* (wind)

IMPORTANT CHARACTERS IN THE WORLD'S MAJOR MYTHOLOGIES (Continued)

Major Figures	General Characteristics and Myths	Likely Analogues in Other Mythologies
Frigga and **Freyja**	The wife of Odin, Frigga is of all the goddesses the best loved by him with whom she sits, enthroned, and surveys all the world, knowing all and exercising great control over all the forces of nature. Very late Teutonic myths confused Frigga with Freyja, an entirely different goddess into whose charge passed exactly one-half of the dead fallen in battle, and who presided over beneficent nature—sunshine, rain, harvest. Probably because of this mistaken identification, Freyja has erroneously been called the wife of Odin. *Frigga* survives in the word *Friday*	Greek *Hera*, Roman *Juno* Freyja is possibly in slight degree analogous to the Greek *Hades* and other deities in charge of the dead; but if this is true, Odin is also analogous to Hades, for he had charge of the rest of the dead heroes
Thor or **Donar** or **Thunar**	Thor, son of Odin by Mother Earth, is the god of thunder—a cosmic commotion caused by Thor's energetic use of his hammer, Miolnir (the Crusher), for whose proper use Thor has to wear iron gloves and a special belt. Thor's cult is thought to have antedated the Aesir, and after the appearance of the cult of Odin the two appear to have been in competition—with the aristocratic Odin the favorite of kings and chieftains, the churlish Thor the better liked among common folk. Brave, strong, stupidly blustering, and brutal, Thor and his hammer sanctified marriages and burials until the advent of Christianity. He lived in the grandest (540 stories) of Asgard's mansions, Bilskirnir. His name survives in the English *Thursday*	*Donar* was the Teutonic name for the god of thunder—mythologists disagree as to whether the two were the same god; analogous to the Greek *Zeus* as god of thunder and lightning; Thor's dwarfs (*zwerge*), or black elves, served him as *Hephaestus* and his assistants served Zeus
Balder or **Baldr** or **Baldur**	The shining god, whose palace is Breidablik. Son of Odin and Frigga, Balder was the most beautiful of the Aesir, and the embodiment of the euphoria inspired by the sunlight. The dour myth of the death of Balder, the sun, may have expressed the gloom of the northern winters. Loki, learning that of all creatures in nature only the mistletoe had not promised to spare Balder any hurt, induces the blind Hoth or Höthr, god of winter, to shoot mistletoe at the sun to kill it. The wrath of the gods at Balder's death is great, their vengeance swift—though Loki tries to escape by changing into a salmon. Balder's return to life becomes dependent upon the condition that all things, alive and not, shall weep for him (spring rains). Things are never quite the same again, however, and it is clear that Loki's jealousy of Balder is the beginning of the end—the Götterdämmerung celebrated by Richard Wagner	In function Balder would seem partially analogous to the Greek-Syrian *Adonis*, the Babylonian *Tammuz*, and other deities whose death and resurrection represented the cycles of the seasons; but in most other respects Balder differs from these deities. His relation to other solar deities is equally obvious, but even more misleading since he was not the central figure that the sun-gods in other pantheons were—Amun-Ra, Apollo, and others who seem more like Odin than like Balder. But it is also true that Balder, as all the Aesir, was really a manifestation of Odin
Tiu or **Ziu** or **Tyr**	Primarily the god of athletics and of war, who permits one of his hands to be bitten off by the wolf Fenrir so that the animal can be bound in a net. Tiu's name survives in the English *Tuesday*	Thought by philologists to be one of the "shining gods" by reason of the etymological relation of his name to the Sanskrit *Dyaus*, the Greek *Zeùs*, and the Latin *Deus* (Roman *Jupiter*)
Bragi, **Iduna** and **Mimir**	Bragi, one of the Aesir, is a god of poetry and eloquence, famous also for his wit and cunning. His wife, Iduna, is a giantess and as such dwells in Utgarthar, the underworld whence all the Jotunns had been driven. She is, for reasons that are obscure, guardian of the apples upon which the Aesir depend for sustenance. Through treachery, Loki delivers Iduna into the hands of the giant Thiasi. The Aesir, near death for lack of apples, order Loki to rescue her, and this he manages to do. The strange fact that the Aesir should allow the apples to be in the custody of a giantess—presumably their enemy—is possibly explained by the fact that Iduna is sometimes identified as one of the Asynjor, the attendants to Frigga. Equally inconsistent is the role of Mimir, a deity of wisdom and knowledge, who is simultaneously one of the giants and an uncle of Odin, frequently consulted by the latter in matters of import. He dwells by the Yggdrasill, from beneath whose roots bubbles Mimir's well of wisdom. Such inconsistencies are explained by some in terms of the possibility that the rivalry of the gods of the Aesir and the frost giants was the mythical representation of actual tribal rivalries, since in the human realm it would not be unlikely for there to be inconsistent loyalties	As a culture hero, Bragi may be related analogically to the Egyptian *Thoth*, among others. Iduna has sometimes been likened to the Greek hero *Hercules*, whose theft of the apples of the Hesperides is the reverse of Iduna's connection with apples. Mimir, like Bragi, is related analogically to other culture heroes, such as the Greek *Hermes*
Loki	One of the most enigmatic of Nordic deities. He is a dwarf, yet beautiful; though of the Aesir, he is the son of a giant, Farbauti. Often he appears as the embodiment of mischief, frequently tinged with demonic maliciousness. His name means—or is supposed to mean—"the closer," which only adds to the confusion. It is clear, though the reasons are highly obscure, that he more than any other figure in Nordic mythology brings about the Ragnarok—the "doom" of the gods—and in his Nibelungen tetralogy Richard Wagner depicted Loki as the demonic personification of fire. Loki eats the heart of a courtesan and thereby becomes pregnant, whence there come into being three horrible monsters: the wolf Fenrir; the serpent Jormungand; and the goddess of death, Hel or Hela, whose food is the bone marrow and brains of men. Loki brings about the death of Balder, bringing upon himself	Numerous analogues have been suggested, all with a certain plausibility: *Merlin* of Arthurian legend; the Vedic *Vritra;* the Greek *Prometheus;* Roman *Vulcan* (but not necessarily his Greek analogue, *Hephaestus*); *Lucifer* (that is, Mephistopheles, the devil); and others. As both a friend and enemy of the Aesir (and therefore of mankind), Loki would seem functionally analogous to *Ishtar* and similar deities. The identification with *Lucifer* depends largely upon etymological similarities of the names. *Hel* has been identified with the Hindu *Kali*

IMPORTANT CHARACTERS IN THE WORLD'S MAJOR MYTHOLOGIES (Continued)

Major Figures	General Characteristics and Myths	Likely Analogues in Other Mythologies
	the wrath of the Aesir. He hides in the guise of a salmon but is caught in a net and bound to a rock in a dank cave, with an adder suspended over his head so that the poison will drop upon it. His consort Signe catches the drops of poison in a bowl as they fall, but from time to time she must empty the bowl, and then drops of poison strike Loki's face, causing him great pain; earthquakes were thought to consist of his writhings at such moments	
Surt or **Surtur** or **Surtr**	He, among the giants, who brings the Ragnarok to its fiery conclusion. Through Loki's treachery, Balder is dead—that he apparently can be resurrected for brief periods is small comfort. There comes a terrible winter of three years, during which plants, trees, and animals die; mankind starves, suffers from the pitiless cold, engages in brutal murder and incest; there are many floods, and the world tree Yggdrasill sways to its very roots. The giants and evil demons united come against the Aesir, and Heimdall the watchman sounds the horn of warning—a cock crows. Loki is set free and joins the demons. Fenrir the wolf slays Odin. Thor manages to slay the earth serpent, Jormungand, but that creature's last poisonous breaths cause Thor to suffocate. Soon all the gods and monsters have perished except Surt—who is now perhaps Loki as well. As Surt grows more and more gigantic, the sun turns black, the earth sinks into the sea, the stars fall from the heavens and land no one knows where. Finally Surt plunges everything into a sea of fire that consumes even Surt himself. Yet two human beings have miraculously survived—the youth Lif and the maiden Lifthrasir—to begin the new world. Again flowers bloom and the grain ripens as the Aesir return in new forms. By some accounts Heimdall also survives and founds the new order	There are no plausible analogues to Surt. The Ragnarok is possibly related functionally to the deluge myths in other systems, in that all that was before is swept away and the world begins anew. *Ragnarok* means "judgment of the gods" (that is, *upon* them); later stories confused this word with *ragnarökr*, "twilight of the gods," a confusion perpetuated in the Götterdämmerung in Richard Wagner's music drama *Der Ring des Nibelungen*

Relief Depicting King Ptolemy II Before the Goddess Isis, Ancient Egyptian Deity of the Earth and Sky

MYTILENE, city, Greece, capital of the Aegean Islands Division and Lesbos Nome; on the SE coast of Lesbos Island; 12 miles W of the Turkish mainland. Situated on the Mytilene Channel of the Aegean Sea, the city is an active port, carrying on trade in olive oil, grains, fruits, and hides. Soap manufacturing and sponge fishing are important industries. With the exception of two revolts in 428 and 412 B.C. Mytilene remained substantially loyal to Athens until made a part of the Roman Empire. The city was held by the Genoese from 1355 until taken by the Turks in 1462; it was neutral from 1920 until again becoming a part of Greece in 1923. In ancient times the city was famous for its wines, and was the birthplace of the famous pirate brothers Arouj and Khair-ed-Din Barbarossa. Pop. (1951) 27,161.

MYTISHCHI, city, U.S.S.R., Russian Soviet Federated Socialist Republic, Moscow Region, 12 miles NNE of Moscow. Mytishchi is an industrial center on a railroad, the center of Mytishchi District. Its manufactures include railroad cars for the Moscow subway, tools, silica bricks, and decorative castings. It is the seat of industrial colleges and of a forestry institute. Pop. (1956 official est.) 91,000.

MYXEDEMA. See ENDOCRINE GLAND, *The Thyroid Gland*.

N

The form of the letter N has changed little throughout the history of scripts derived from the North Semitic. In many languages there has been frequent alternation between M and N. Some of the historical forms of N are shown in the top row. They are hieroglyph 1, Phoenician 2, Greek 3, Roman (Trajan) 4, Irish uncial 5, Caroline 6, and Gutenberg black-letter 7. Common forms of the letter N as it appears today are illustrated in the bottom row. They are handwritten cursive capital 8, handwritten lowercase 9, roman capital 10, roman lowercase 11, roman small capital 12, italic capital 13, italic lowercase 14, sans serif capital 15, and sans serif lowercase 16.

N, the fourteenth letter of the Roman alphabet, has varied little in form since its earliest appearance. Its ancestor in the North Semitic languages was a letter called *nun* which signified fish. *N* is a nasal consonant, the sound of which is produced by closing the mouth passage with the point of the tongue and opening the nasal passage by lowering the soft palate. The breath passes through the nostrils. *N* corresponds to the point stop *t*, and there are as many different *n*'s as there are *t*'s. Depending on the point at which the oral closure occurs, *n* may be dental, alveolar, palatal, velar, or cacuminal. No single language makes use of all these sounds. In English the voiced alveolar *n* (*not*, *win*) is the most frequent sound of the letter. A common phonetic change of *n* is into *ng*, the back nasal. This sound corresponds to the back stops *k* and *g*, and the change frequently takes place before these letters (as in *bank*, *finger*, *uncle*, and *anxious*). When the *g* following the *n* becomes silent, as it often does, *ng* then symbolizes the back nasal sound (as in *long*).

NABLUS, town, NW Jordan, in valley between Mt. Gerizim and Mt. Ebal, 32 miles N of Jerusalem. Built A.D. 72 under Emperor Vespasian, it is a market town with a predominantly Arab population. It is located on the site of the ancient Samaritan religious center of Shechem, destroyed in 128 B.C. (For population, see Jordan map in Atlas.)

NABOKOV, VLADIMIR VLADIMIROVICH, 1899–   , U.S. author, born in St. Petersburg, Russia, and educated at St. Petersburg and at Trinity College, Cambridge. An émigré after the Russian Revolution, he lived in Germany and France, 1922–40, went to the United States, 1940, and became a U.S. citizen, 1945. He taught at Wellesley College, 1941–48, and at Cornell University, 1948–59. His works include *Laughter in the Dark* (1936), *Despair* (1937), *The Real Life of Sebastian Knight* (1941), *Bend Sinister* (1947), *Lolita* (1956), *Invitation to a Beheading* (Eng. tr. 1959), *Nine Stories* (1947), *Conclusive Evidence: A Memoir* (1951), *Pnin* (1957), *Nabokov's Dozen* (1958), *Pale Fire* (1962), *The Gift* (1963), *The Defense* (1964), *The Eye* (1965), and *Speak, Memory* (an autobiography, 1966). In 1964 he published his monumental translation with commentary of Pushkin's verse novel *Eugene Onegin*.

NACOGDOCHES, city, E central Texas, seat of Nacogdoches County; 149 miles SE of Dallas. The city is a railroad and industrial center located in a rich timber area; its manufactures include lumber and clay and petroleum products. Stephen F. Austin State College is located there. (For population, see Texas map in Atlas.)

NADELMAN, ELIE, 1885–1946, U.S. sculptor, born in Warsaw, Poland. He studied there and in Munich. In 1905 he went to Paris, where he had his first one-man show, 1909, and was associated with Pablo Picasso. He went to the United States, 1917, and became a U.S. citizen, 1927. His works include *La Mystérieuse*, *Woman Seated*, *Tango*, and *Acrobat*.

NADIR, in astronomy, a point on the celestial sphere directly beneath the observer and hence opposite his zenith, which is the point in the sky directly over his head.

NADIR SHAH, dynastic name Tahmasp Kuli Khan, 1688–1747, shah of Persia, born of Turkish parents in Khurasan. In 1726 he took up arms for Tahmasp II of Persia, whom he aided in ousting the Ghalzai Afghan leader, Mahmud, who had usurped the Persian throne in 1722. As a reward Nadir received four Persian provinces. He then won several victories against the Turks, but meanwhile Tahmasp was defeated at Hamadan and forced to sign a disgraceful peace. Nadir thereupon deposed Tahmasp, 1732, set up the latter's year-old son Abbas III as puppet king, and became regent. Four years later he deposed the child and succeeded as shah himself. Nadir's conquests extended the borders of the Persian empire from the Indus and Oxus rivers to the Euphrates River and the Caspian Sea. He conquered Bokhara and Khiva, 1740, and took Kars from the Turks, 1745. He was assassinated by one of his guards.

NAEVIUS, GNAEUS, 270?–201? B.C., Roman epic and dramatic poet, born probably in Campania. His career as a dramatist began about 235 B.C. and lasted 30 years. His attacks on the Roman nobility led to his imprisonment and later his banishment to Utica. He wrote an epic on the First Punic War and many comedies and tragedies adapted from the Greek Stage. Only fragments of his work are extant.

NAGA HILLS, an undeveloped area on the N India-Burma border between the Brahmaputra and Chindwin rivers. It is densely wooded and drained by several small streams. The average elevation is 6,000 feet. Most of the inhabitants of the Naga Hills are Nagas, a Tibeto-Burman group.

NAGALAND, State, E India, comprising the former Naga Hills district of Assam and the former Tuensang Frontier division of the North-East Frontier; area 6,236 square miles. Under the Nagaland Regulations of 1961, the area became known as Nagaland, with the status of a separate state of the Indian

Union. Previously it had been administered by the president of India through the governor of Assam. Since 1961 it has had greater local autonomy.

Naga tribes have been waging guerrilla warfare since the 1950's, in an effort to obtain independence from the Indian government. According to a 1960 official estimate, there were an estimated 1,500 active rebels.

NAGANO, OSAMI, 1880–1947, Japanese admiral, was born in Kochi. He was minister of the Imperial navy, 1936–37, commander in chief of the Japanese fleet, 1937, and chief of the naval general staff, 1941. He planned and supervised the Japanese attack on Pearl Harbor, Dec. 7, 1941, was subsequently indicted as a war criminal, and died during the trial.

NAGANO, city, central Japan, central Honshu; capital of Nagano Prefecture; on a branch of the Shinano River; 110 miles NW of Tokyo. Nagano's industries include printing, woodworking, production of raw silk, and the manufacture of earthenware and foodstuffs—including sun-dried persimmons. The city is noted for the seventh century Buddhist Temple of Zenkoji, a typical example of the *gongen-zukuri* style of temple architecture. There is an underground prayer gallery around the base of the structure to which worshipers throng from all parts of Japan. Nagano University is situated in the city. (For population, see Japan map in Atlas.)

NAGAOKA, city, central Japan, N central Honshu, Niigata Prefecture; on the Shinano River; 35 miles SSW of Niigata. Nagaoka lies in a rich farm region and because of its rail and highway connections with coastal towns is also an important industrial center. The nearby Echigo oilfield adds to Nagaoka's economic importance. Many of the inhabitants are engaged in oil refining and engineering work; others are employed by the chemical plant and textile mills. Sake, electrical machinery, paper, and metalwork are among the city's manufactures. (For population, see Japan map in Atlas.)

NAGASAKI, city, Japan, W Kyushū, capital of Nagasaki Prefecture; on S Hizen Peninsula between Sonogi and Nomo peninsulas; 600 miles WSW of Tokyo. Nagasaki is a city at the head of an inlet 2.5 miles long and less than a mile wide, lying on the Nagasaki Bay harbor, in the valley between the Urakami and the Nakashima rivers. Shipbuilding always has been the main industry of the city; Nagasaki ranks first in the output of ships in Japan. Since World War II it has not regained its former place as a leading commercial city; however, it exports coal, cotton, yarn, cement, dried fish, and rice. The raising of rice and cotton, and fishing and mining, are major occupations.

Nagasaki was the first Japanese port to be opened for commerce with the West. It was visited by the Portuguese in 1545; in 1560 it was opened by the Dutch, in 1854 to United States, and in 1858 to other Occidental countries. As the first port of entry for ships coming into Japan from the south and the west, Nagasaki was a chief refueling point; later when the port of Moji was opened, Nagasaki lost its monopoly as a coaling station. Nagasaki became a Christian center when St. Francis Xavier introduced the faith to Japan in 1549. The church suffered severe persecution by the shoguns, but the devout kept faith secretly, and when the Urakami Church was opened in 1865, Nagasaki was considered the Rome of the Orient. On Aug. 9, 1945, an atomic bomb was exploded that demolished one third of the city and killed or wounded about 75,000 persons.

Terraced hillsides that had been the site of Nagasaki's residential district were left in a black ruin after the atom bomb was dropped on the city in August, 1945.

U.S. AIR FORCE

At mid-century Nagasaki sought to restore itself by reconstruction plans that included projects supported by popular subscription, secular rebuilding programs, and municipal efforts to develop foreign trade, agriculture, and industry. (For population, see Japan map in Atlas.) PAUL YUNG

NAGEL, CHARLES, 1849–1940, U.S. lawyer, was born in Colorado County, Texas. He served in the Missouri legislature, 1881–83, was a member of the St. Louis Law School faculty, 1885–1909, and was president of the St. Louis city council, 1893–97. During 1909–13, as secretary of commerce and labor in Pres. William Howard Taft's cabinet, he organized the Chamber of Commerce of the United States.

NAGELI, KARL WILHELM VON, 1817–91, Swiss botanist, was born in Kilchberg. Nägeli (or Naegeli) was professor of botany at the University of Freiburg, 1852–55, at the University of Zürich, 1855–58, and at the University of Munich, 1858–91. He studied the nuclei and the mode of growth of cells, and formulated the micellar theory of growth. He also discovered the antheridia and spermatozoids of ferns.

NAGERCOIL, or Nagarcoil, city, S India, Madras State, capital of Kanniyakumari District; 43 miles SE of Trivandrum, with which it is connected by a highway. Nagercoil has manufactures of rope, mats, electrical supplies, and sugar. It is the site of the ruins of a ninth-century Jain temple. (For population, see India map in Atlas.)

NAGORNO-KARABAKH AUTONOMOUS REGION, U.S.S.R., W Azerbaijan Soviet Socialist Republic (area 1,738 sq. mi.). Elevations range from 1,970 to 12,200 feet. Main products are apricots, silk, tobacco, cotton, wine, cheese, horses, cattle, carpets, and wood and leather goods. Principal centers are Stepanakert, the capital, and Martuni. While Karabakh was part of the Armenian Empire (2400–612 B.C.) and the medieval Armenian Bagradunian kingdom, its mountaineers were famed as *Kaj* (braves) because of their warlike traits and became the subject of several Armenian epics. Nagorno-Karabakh Autonomous Region was formed in 1923. (For population, see U.S.S.R. map in Atlas.)

NAGOYA, city, central Japan, Honshu, capital of Aichi Prefecture; on Ise Bay, at the mouth of the Shonai River; 90 miles ENE of Osaka. Nagoya is the third largest city and the fourth most important seaport in Japan. Many of the goods produced in the city's textile mills, wood processing shops, dyeing and chemical plants, and engineering metalworks are exported. Porcelain made in Nagoya according to a process dating from the early thirteenth century is world famous. Cloisonné enamel originated in Nagoya and is still made there. Other manufactures include sake, flour, pottery, woolen goods, lacquer ware, glass, cement, railroad equipment, and machinery for textile mills. Before and during World War II Nagoya was well known for construction of airplanes and airplane engines; for this reason the city was bombed (1944–45) and 40 per cent destroyed.

The city's educational institutions include Nagoya University, seven colleges, and some 400 lower and intermediate schools. Nagoya contains some of the oldest and most sacred shrines in Japan. Nagoya Castle is a fine example of medieval architecture, with granite walls 15 to 18 feet thick, a 5-story tower 144 feet high, and a copper roof on which stand 8-foot gold dolphins. Adjoining the castle is a palace housing many art treasures. The second century *Atsuta Jingu* Shinto shrine guards the *Kusanagi-no-Tsurugi* (grass cutting sword), one of the three imperial treasures (the other two are a sacred mirror at the Ise Shrines and a jewel kept at the Tokyo Palace). Among the chief Buddhist temples are the *Kwannon;* the *Higashi Hongwanji*, which houses paintings of celebrated Japanese artists including Sesshu, Tannyu, and others; and the *Kakuozan* Temple, that contains Buddhist relics presented to Japan in 1890 by the king of Siam. (For population, see Japan map in Atlas.) PAUL YUNG

NAGPUR, city, central India, capital of Nagpur District, in the state of Maharashtra; a railroad and highway junction; 265 miles N of Hyderabad and 380 miles NE of Bombay. Nagpur is a leading trade center for cereals, vegetables, and fruit; it is especially well known for its Nagpur oranges. There are sawmills, rubber processing plants, and iron foundries. Manufactures include cotton textiles and textile machinery, explosives, paper, furniture, and pottery. Manganese is mined nearby. The city is the site of the University of Nagpur and of Anglican and Roman Catholic cathedrals. Nagpur was the capital of the Mahratta kingdom of Nagpur from 1743 to 1861. In 1817 the British successfully defended the fortified Sitabaldi Hill in the center of the city from a Mahratta attack, and in 1853 gained complete control of the city. In 1861 Nagpur became the capital of the newly formed Madhya Pradesh. In 1960, Nagpur became a part of the new state of Maharashtra. (For population, see India map in Atlas.)

NAGUIB, MOHAMMED, 1901– , Egyptian army officer and political leader, was born in Khartoum. He played a major role in the 1952 coup d'état that deposed Farouk I from the Egyptian throne. Naguib became premier and in 1953 was granted absolute power for a three-year period, becoming president as well as premier. He was "retired" in 1954—apparently in a bloodless coup d'état engineered by his successor, Gamal Nasser.

NAGURSKI, BRONISLAW, known as Bronko, 1908– , U.S. football player, was born in International Falls, Minn. A graduate of the University of Minnesota, he was an All-America selection at both tackle and fullback in 1929. He played professionally with the Chicago Bears, 1930–37 and 1943. and was named All-League fullback three years, 1932–34. He was elected to the football hall of fame in 1951. Nagurski was also a professional wrestler.

NAGY, FERENC, 1903– , Hungarian political leader, was born in Blisse and in 1930 became secretary general of the newly founded Independent Smallholders party. He was elected to the legislature, 1939; joined the anti-Nazi resistance movement during World War II; and became president of the national assembly and minister of reconstruction, 1945, and prime minister, 1946. Nagy fled to the United States when the Communists took over the government, 1947, and in 1951 became president of the Central Eastern European Committee, an organization of exiles from several Communist-dominated countries.

NAGYKANIZSA, city, SW Hungary, Zala County; 65 miles WNW of Pécs, near the Yugoslav border. Nagykanizsa is a railroad junction and agricultural market, and has manufactures of shoes, machines, bricks, and food products. There are important oil deposits in the vicinity. (For population, see Hungary map in Atlas.)

NAGYKOROS, town, central Hungary, in the agricultural plain between the Danube and Tisza rivers, 44 miles SE of Budapest. The town is a rail and market center for fruits, grains, onions, livestock, melons, cucumbers, and wine produced in the surrounding area, and it has flour mills and distilleries. (For population, see Hungary map in Atlas.)

NAHA, formerly Nawa or Nafa, city, in the Ryūkyū Islands, on the SW coast of Okinawa Island, on an inlet of East China Sea. It is the largest city on Okinawa, and has excellent port facilities. The city produces textiles, lacquer ware, Panama hats, pottery, sugar and dried fish, some of which are exported. Naha is the site of Ryūkyū University, founded in 1950. The city was capital of the Ryūkyū Prefecture until August, 1945. After World War II the United States was given jurisdictional rights over the Ryūkyūs and Naha became administrative capital and headquarters of the U.S. military governor. (For population, see Japan map in Atlas.)

NAHANT, town, NE Massachusetts, Essex County, on a narrow peninsula extending southward from Lynn into Massachusetts Bay; 9 miles NE of Boston. It is a popular vacation spot. The area was first settled in 1630, when the land was purchased from the Indians. Originally a part of Lynn, Nahant was incorporated separately in 1853. Pop. (1960) 3,960.

NAHUATL, or Nahua, any one of a group of tribes speaking Nahuatl, a language of Uto-Aztecan linguistic stock, spoken by more than a million Indians in Mexico and Central America. In the pre-Columbian era Nahuatl peoples lived west and northwest of the Maya (see MAYA). After the decline of the classic Maya civilization in the eleventh century, the Toltec—a Nahuatl tribe—dominated the area between Lake Nicaragua and the Rio Grande. The Toltec developed government and adopted from the Maya many cultural patterns which they spread among subordinate Nahuatl groups. Other Nahuatl tribes settled in regions that correspond to modern Nicaragua and Costa Rica, where they later were influenced by circum-Caribbean tribes. The administrative and agricultural heritage of the Toltec passed to the Aztec, the dominant Nahuatl tribe at the time of the Spanish Conquest (1519). See AZTEC; MEXICO; TOLTEC; UTO-AZTECAN FAMILY.

NAHUEL HUAPI NATIONAL PARK, W Argentina, Neuquén and Río Negro provinces, in the Andes Mountains along the Chile border. The area embraces more than 19.5 million acres of forest, snow-capped mountains, rushing rivers and waterfalls, and glacial lakes. The largest lake is Nahuel Huapí, 40 miles long and 6 miles wide at an altitude of 2,516 feet. Nahuel Huapí (Tiger Island) National Park was established in 1922. The park is accessible by highway, railroad, and air from cities in Argentina and Chile and the various sections of the park are connected by more than 250 miles of highway. Resort towns in the region are the park headquarters, San Carlos de Bariloche, and Nahuel Huapí. The park's year-round sports include mountain climbing, skiing, sailing, riding, fishing, golfing, and hunting.

NAHUM, prophet of the seventh century B.C. (seventh of the minor prophets) and author of the Old Testament book called by his name. Little is known of his life, even the location of his native city Elkosh (1:1) being uncertain; St. Jerome placed it in Galilee, whereas others have claimed Judah as its site. Nahum's prophecy is a dramatic, vivid poem foretelling the destruction of Nineveh (3:1 ff.), that took place in 612 B.C. Since he mentions the conquest of Thebes (No-Amon) by Ashurbanipal (about 661 B.C.) as a past event (3:8), his prophetic ministry is placed between the two dates. Prophets contemporary with Nahum were Zephaniah, Habakkuk, and Jeremiah.

NAIL, a thin, rodlike piece of metal used to fasten materials (usually wood) together, and consisting of a shank with a point at one end and ordinarily a head at the other. The nail is driven into the material by impact, breaking the fibers of the material and forcing them inward. The broken fibers become forces against the shank and thus oppose the removal or loosening of the nail. The most important utilitarian characteristics of nails are their resistance to driving and to withdrawal, both of which may be accomplished by selection of nails with the proper size and shape of shank, the correct type of head, and the desired design of barbs or indentations around the upper shank. Nails must also have a desirable lateral load carrying capacity to withstand the possible side thrust of the pieces being joined; and they must have favorable wood splitting characteristics to resist grain-wise splitting as the nail enters the wood.

Types. Metal nails may be either cut or made from wire. The cut nail, usually sheared or punched from a flat steel sheet, has a tapered shank, is rectangular in cross section, and has a head formed automatically by a hammer-blow operation. There are many types of wire nails, each used for some specific purpose, but four types—common, finishing, casing, and lath—are best known and most widely used. The common nail has a flat head and a diamond-shaped point, and is used principally in framing, sheathing, and other rough carpentry in which the work is hidden or appearance is unimportant. The finishing nail has a thinner shank than that of a common nail of the same length and a head with a diameter only slightly greater than the diameter of the shank; thus the head can be sunk into the material and be less conspicuous. Casing nails are used for cabinet work, interior trim, and similar applications not so fine as to require

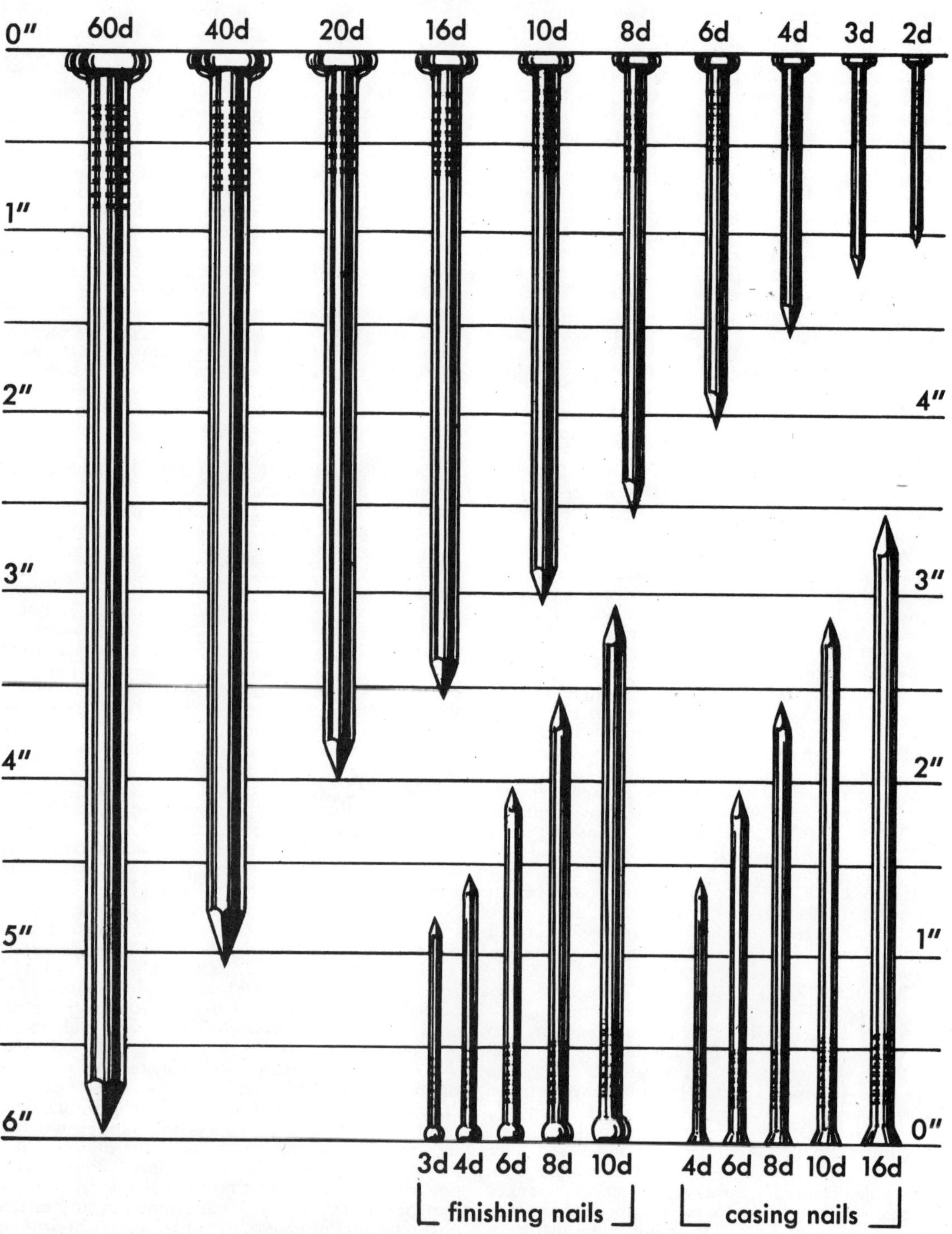

Nails Most Commonly Used—Actual Size

finishing nails. Lath nails are blue and have heads of exceptionally large diameter.

Less common types include scaffold nails, masonry nails, and boat nails. The scaffold nail has two heads (the nail is driven in as far as the lower head, leaving the top head exposed for easy withdrawal), and is used principally in temporary construction work. Masonry nails are designed mainly to support light loads, and have spiral flutings on the shank to improve holding power in masonry. Boat nails, either round or square, are made to resist the corrosive action of sea water, and may have a shank up to 15 inches long. They are made of steel or copper.

Aluminum and copper nails are used where exposure to the elements occurs, and where no discoloration of the surrounding surface is permissible.

Although cast nails have been produced from several metals, they are generally brittle and their use is limited to special applications.

History and Development. Early metal nails, made of wrought iron, were commonly produced by driving hot iron through a graded series of successively smaller holes that forced the metal into the required shape. The ancient Greeks and Romans used metal nails to attach terra-cotta facings to timber and stone structures, often embellishing any exposed heads. Medieval carpenters used wooden nails when working with large pieces of timber, and the coffer makers of the Middle Ages used brass nails to keep leather taut while stretching it over wooden frames.

Cut nails, which were made originally by shearing the shank of the nail from a piece of iron plate and then forming the head and the point, were in use in the eighteenth century. The development in France of nails made from steel wire resulted in a decrease in the demand for—and consequently in the production of—cut nails.

The first nail-making machine was developed in 1759, but mass production of nails was not achieved until the 1860's when the Bessemer converter for making steel and the wire-nail machine were perfected.

Production. In the modern method of producing wire nails the first step is to feed steel wire into machines that automatically cut it into uniform lengths. Cutters then form the heads and points of the nails.

The formation of annular or spiral shallow threads in the upper shank constitutes the second step of the manufacturing process. Formerly the shanks of wire nails often had little barbs or indentations that supposedly increased the nails' holding power; later, tests disclosed that in many cases the barbs actually decreased the holding power. The threads on modern nails—either the annular type (parallel rings around the shank) or the helical type (spiraling around the shank)—accomplish what the former indentations and barbs were supposed to do.

In cases where special properties are required, one or more additional processes, such as hardening, galvanizing, plating, coating, or dipping, are often necessary.

Production of wire nails in the United States in 1965 amounted to 310,000 short tons.

Sizes: The English originally classified nails according to the price of 100 nails of a given size. Thus, small nails sold for 2 pennies per hundred and were called 2-penny (2d) nails; nails of a larger size were priced at 10 pennies per hundred and became known as 10d nails. Later the penny size of the nail came to indicate its length. For example, a 2d nail has a 1-inch shank, a 10d nail a 3-inch shank, and a 60d nail a 6-inch shank. Nails larger than 60d are called spikes and are designated by their dimensions; nails smaller than 2d are called brads.

The rule most commonly used to determine the proper length of a nail for a particular purpose is that it should be approximately three times the thickness of the piece of material being attached or joined.

NAIL, a structural modification of the skin that is borne near the end of the finger and toe of many mammals. The claws and hoofs of certain mammals are naillike structures. The nail is horny and consists mostly of a visible body. Growth occurs as a result of cells multiplying in the nail root, which is concealed beneath the fold of skin at the base of the nail. The pale crescent-shaped area at the base of the nail is called the lunula and has less color than does the rest of the nail because there are fewer blood vessels beneath it. In human beings nail growth is fastest on the middle finger and slowest on the little finger. The average rate of growth is about ⅛ inch per month. Nail growth is more rapid in males than in females.

NAIRNSHIRE, or Nairn, county, NE Scotland; bounded by Moray Firth on the N and by the counties of Moray on the E and Inverness on the S and W;

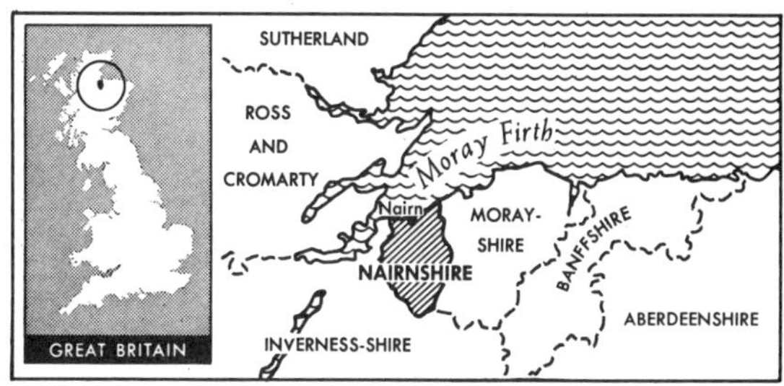

Location Map of Nairnshire

area of the county is 163 sq. mi. Nairn is drained by the Findhorn and Nairn rivers. The region rises from lowlands along the firth to moorlands between the rivers, and climbs in the south to highlands of more than 2,000 feet elevation. Nairn, at the mouth of the Nairn River on Moray Firth, is the capital and chief city. Chief occupations are farming, cattle and sheep raising, and fishing. Granite quarries are scattered throughout the county.

NAIROBI, city, capital of Kenya; located at the foot of the Kikuyu Hills, about 300 miles NW of Mombasa. The city, elevation 5,542 feet, is in view of Mount Kilimanjaro to the southeast and Mount Kenya to the north. It is the headquarters of the East African Common Services Organization. Nairobi's industries include meat processing, canning, flour milling, and manufacture of pottery, furniture, chemicals, and leather goods. Nairobi is a starting point and outfitting center for safaris. Among many public and private buildings of note are the

The most important city in eastern Africa, Nairobi is the region's center of finance, commerce, and industry.

MARC AND EVELYNE BERNHEIM

Coryndon Memorial Museum, the McMillan Library, and an Anglican cathedral. Nairobi National Park, a game reserve for lions, giraffes, antelopes, and hippopotamuses, is nearby. The site of present-day Nairobi was selected in 1899 as headquarters for the Uganda Railway. The city thus established grew rapidly, since the altitude and climate of the area was found to be ideal for European residents. The capital was moved there from Mombasa in 1907. Nairobi was proclaimed a city by Royal Charter in 1950. (For population, see southern Africa map in Atlas.)

NAJIN, also Haji, city, North Korea, N Hamgyong Province, seat of Najin-gun (county); on the Sea of Japan; 40 miles NE of Chongjin. Najin is an ice-free fishing port and a military base, well sheltered by two islands. The commercial port (2/3 sq. mi. in area) can handle ten 8,000-ton ships, twenty 7,000-ton ships, and ten 4,000-ton ships. The port is connected by a 9½-mile tunnel with the nearby port of Unggi. (For population, see Japan map in Atlas.)

NAKHICHEVAN, city, Caucasian U.S.S.R., Azerbaijan Soviet Socialist Republic, capital of Nakhichevan Autonomous Soviet Socialist Republic; near the Aras River; 83 miles SE of Yerevan, Armenia. It has a cannery, a winery, a distillery, brickyards, lime kilns, farm implement repair shops, and a leather goods factory. A branch of the Azerbaijan Academy of Sciences is in the city. According to Armenian legend Noah founded Nakhichevan, which in Armenian means first descent. It was famed in antiquity for its rare Armenian wines and was the residence of Armenian princes of the second millennium B.C. Nakhichevan remained an important city of medieval Armenia under the Bagradunian dynasty until it fell to the Moslems in the eleventh century. Ptolemy called it Naxuana. (For population, see U.S.S.R. map in Atlas.)

NAKHICHEVAN AUTONOMOUS SOVIET SOCIALIST REPUBLIC, U.S.S.R., a detached part and SW of the Azerbaijan Soviet Socialist Republic; bounded on the N and E by the Armenian Soviet Socialist Republic; on the S and W by Iran, and on the NW by Turkey; area 2,100 sq. mi.; pop. (1959 official est.) 142,000. The region is highly mountainous in the north and east, reaching elevations of 13,100 feet, and is drained in the south and west by the Aras River whose valley lies at an average elevation of 2,650 feet. A branch of the Transcaucasian Railroad connects the region with Yerevan and Baku and another line runs to Tabriz. Winters are severe and summers hot. Principal products are cereals, apricots, grapes, tobacco, cotton, rice, sheep, salt, arsenic, and pyrites. Food processing, wine making, and silk and carpet weaving are leading industries. Main centers besides Nakhichevan, the capital, are Norashen and Dzhulfa.

Nakhichevan's history dates from the third millennium B.C. when its Armenian inhabitants allied themselves with the Armenian Empire (2400–612 B.C.). In the latter year the population became vassals of the Medes. The region was regained by the Armenian Emperor Tigranes II the Great in the first century B.C. and became important for its mineral wealth. During the Middle Ages, as part of the Armenian kingdom of the Bagradunians, Nakhichevan was famed for its Oriental rug centers and its numerous red stone cathedrals, many of which were ravaged by the Mongols in 1235 and later by the Turks. Nearly 85 per cent of the Armenian population was forcibly converted to Islam and Turkified during the Ottoman period. In 1826 czarist Russia took the area from Persia. It was temporarily lost during the 1917 Bolshevik Revolution, reconquered by Armenian Communists in 1920, and formed into the Nakhichevan Autonomous Soviet Socialist Republic in 1924.

NAKHON RATCHASIMA, town, SE central Thailand, capital of Nakhon Ratchasima Province; on the Mun River; 135 miles NE of Bangkok. A railroad, highway, and airline junction, Nakhon Ratchasima is the chief trade and communications center for eastern Thailand. Silkworm culture is a major occupation, and copper is mined nearby. Founded in the seventeenth century, the city formerly was referred to as Khorat or Korat. (For population, see southeast Asia map in Atlas.)

NALORPHINE, a rapid-acting drug that occurs as a colorless solid, soluble in water. It is derived from morphine by making a substitution in the chemical framework of morphine. Nalorphine is used chiefly to counteract morphine poisoning; it is injected to relieve circulatory or respiratory depression caused by morphine and other narcotics such as meperidine and methadone (see MORPHINE). Drug addicts respond to nalorphine by exhibiting many of the symptoms of narcotics withdrawal (see DRUG ADDICTION).

NAMALAND, or Namaqualand, region, SW Africa, along the Atlantic Ocean. It includes the southern part of South-West Africa and the northern part of Cape of Good Hope Province, Republic of South Africa. It is divided by the Orange River into Great Namaland to the north and Little Namaland to the south. There are copper deposits and diamond and tungsten mines in the region. Natives of Namaland are the Hottentot tribe of Namaquas or Nama.

NAMANGAN, region, U.S.S.R., Soviet central Asia, Uzbek Soviet Socialist Republic; bounded on the N and NE by Kirgiz Soviet Socialist Republic, on the E and SE by Andizhan Region, on the SW by Tadzhik Soviet Socialist Republic, and on the NW by Tashkent Region; area 2,700 sq. mi.; pop. (1959 est.) 594,000. Namangan is drained by the Namangan and Syr Darya rivers and their tributaries flowing from the Kirgiz Mountains in the north. The region has a high water-power potential and there is extensive cotton farming on irrigated land, mainly along the North Fergana Canal. Grapes and other fruits are grown, and the sericulture of the region accounts for 10 per cent of Uzbek silk cocoon output. Industries process local agricultural raw materials. The chief cities are Namangan (the capital), Chust, and Kassansay.

NAMANGAN, city, U.S.S.R., Uzbek Soviet Socialist Republic, capital of Namangan Region; in the N Fergana Valley; on the Namangansay River, the North Fergana Canal, and a branch of the Tashkent Railroad; 50 miles NE of Kokand. Namangan's industries include cotton cleaning, oil, and cotton textile mills, meat processing and cold storage plants, a winery, a cannery, a brewery, and two hydroelectric power stations. The city has several technical and vocational schools. (For population, see U.S.S.R. map in Atlas.)

NAME, a characteristic word or combination of words applied to an entity or class of entities to distinguish it from all others. A branch of linguistics known as onomastics is concerned with the study of names. Every object has a class name which it shares with all specimens of the species to which it belongs; thus all buildings are buildings, all books are books. Many objects and practically all persons also have individual names, usually called proper names, or simply names. Proper names of greatest significance and interest are personal names; of slightly less interest are the names of places (Washington, Moscow, or Trafalgar Square) and of those "things" deemed of sufficient individuality and distinction to be properly named (Parthenon, THE AMERICAN PEOPLES ENCYCLOPEDIA, Sistine Chapel, or the *Mona Lisa*).

In Law, a name consists of the given names and surnames; the middle name or initial of a person is not generally recognized by the courts as a part of his legal name. Name prefixes (Mr., Mrs., and the like) and suffixes (Jr. and Sr.) are not part of a person's legal name. Abbreviations of Christian names are commonly recognized by the courts, but such recognition has not generally been extended to abbreviations of surnames. Under the common law a person may adopt both a different surname and a different Christian name; if the new name is confirmed by usage and is generally known, and if the change was not motivated by fraud, it becomes his legal name. While this is the rule in the United States except where changed by statute, most states have statutes providing a method for changing a person's name with the sanction of the courts, usually requiring the applicant to state some reason for the step. In some jurisdictions a change of name will be permitted only upon a showing of a resulting pecuniary benefit. A woman upon marriage legally assumes her husband's surname and retains it even after an absolute divorce, unless the decree provides for the resumption of her maiden name. Under the doctrine of *idem sonans*, a document designating an individual by a name that corresponds in sound with the individual's true name is generally held legally sufficient notwithstanding an incorrect spelling of the name in the document. The common law right to do business under an assumed or fictitious name is largely subject to regulation by statutes designed to protect the public from fraudulent practices. The law generally protects persons and corporations in the use of trade names that have become generally known by usage as against persons who may fraudulently assume them for the purpose of benefiting by the business reputation and good faith that trade names may carry with them. The name of a corporation is said to be the very essence of its being, and in general a corporation must contract, sue, and be sued in its corporate name.

Personal Names. In modern civilized societies there are at least two elements in virtually every personal name: the given name or names (known among Christians as the baptismal or Christian name) and the family name, or surname. The latter, although seemingly the more fundamental, appeared relatively late (perhaps in the ninth century in Europe), and was not in common use (with a few exceptions) until the classical Renaissance when, in the sixteenth century, civil and ecclesiastical ordinances required the registration of surnames. After that time their use became standard, although with some national variations. In Spain and Latin America, and to a certain extent in Switzerland and elsewhere, it was customary to add the wife's maiden surname to that of the husband, using the word for *and* (Ortega *y* Gassett) or a hyphen (Blasco-Ibañez); elsewhere the surname of the husband (and father) was deemed paramount, the wife sometimes keeping her maiden surname as her own middle name (that is, as part of her given name). In some languages surnames have both a masculine and a feminine form; hence, in Russian, Petrov (masc.) and Petrova (fem.). The Jews in Europe and the Americas were late in adopting surnames (Austria 1782–83, France 1803, Prussia 1812, Bavaria 1813), and even at mid-twentieth century many orthodox Jews regarded the surname as a mere legal convenience.

First Names generally expressed, originally, circumstances of the child's birth or appearance, or the religion or position of the parents; or were given later in life in accordance with the appearance, character, or history of the individual. In early times plant and animal names, descriptive epithets, the names of qualities and deities, were commonly given to human beings as names. As Europe became Christianized, first names were more and more chosen in terms of their association with Christianity, and those relatively few Greek, Roman, and Hebrew names that came into common use among European (and later American) Christians were largely those associated specifically with the history of Christianity. In addition, Christianity absorbed and invested with Christian significance the many names deriving from the hundreds of pagan tribes that were gradually won over to the Christian persuasion.

Depending upon a host of factors, most of them matters of chance, there were many fashions in names involving both the revival of earlier names and the appearance of new ones. The unusual prominence of the bearer of a certain name has ever meant a vogue for that name; thus such names as Augustine, Benedict, Martin (popes) and Charles, William, Elizabeth, Mary, George, John (prominent rulers) have been popular. In later times the names of U.S. Presidents and other national figures have initiated vogues, even to the extent of transforming surnames such as Washington, Lincoln, Roosevelt, Dewey, and Wilson into given names. Historical events have influenced personal names. For example, the Norman Conquest of England (1066) brought German, and to a lesser extent French, names to the British Isles, displacing Old English names; the humanistic revival of Latin studies led to a revival of many Roman names and to the Latinizing of non-Roman ones (Descartes—Cartesius); the Reformation led to a vogue in Hebrew names from the Bible and to such new contributions as Faith, Hope, Charity, Prudence, Mercy.

A name such as Mercy, in having a meaning apart from its use as a name, does not differ in this respect from other names; all personal names, both given names and surnames, meant something originally. Francis, of Germanic origin, meant free. Anne, the Germanic version of Ann, from the Hebrew Hannah, meant grace. From the Greek, Theodore, the name given by St. Augustine of Hippo to his son, means gift of God. Rachel derives from the Hebrew word for ewe, Ruth from the Hebrew word meaning the compassionate one. Jonathan, from Hebrew, means God has given, and the Hebrew Nathaniel means gift of God (Nathan, a diminutive, means the given). The Gaelic Donald means prince of the universe, the Celtic Donald means the dark (closely related, the Celtic Douglas means from the black stream).

Surnames. In ancient Greece a patronymic was used as a surname of sorts; this use of the father's name as surname for the son (. . . the son of . . .) was later a common source of surnames. In Rome three or four names were employed, in this order: *praenomen* (first name, distinguishing the individual); *nomen gentile* (the name indicating *gens*, clan—actually closer to the modern first name than to the modern family name); *cognomen* (roughly the equivalent of the modern surname, or family name, and often also the name of a place); and finally, only sometimes used, the *cognomen secundum* or agnomen (a special surname given to a man for some service). Hence, in the full name of Publius' Cornelius Scipio Africanus major, Publius was a common Roman *praenomen;* Cornelius was a clan name, *nomen gentile;* Scipio (literally staff or wand) was a family name or *cognomen* of the *gens* Cornelia; and the Africanus (literally belonging to Africa) was an *agnomen* commemorating the elder (major) Scipio's victory in Africa over Hannibal. Such usages, however, were distinctly the exception in antiquity; they reflect the fact that Greece and Rome were culturally more complex than the rest of Europe. The surnames of modern times derive from a host of sources. All surnames originally had meaning, but in the course of time many of these meanings have been lost; relatively few people in the twentieth century are aware of them. Harkening back to Greek and Roman practice, many modern surnames derive from the first (and only) name of a father (patronymic); from the name of a place with which the person or his ancestors were associated (roughly equivalent to the Roman *cognomen*); and from his deeds or those of his ancestors (roughly, the Roman *agnomen*), analogous in the most general sense to his occupation, whether notable or not.

The name David Ben-Gurion means David son of Gurion, Gurion having been the given name of

David's father; even in modern usage Gurion is not regarded among Jews as a surname in the ordinary sense. More typical are these examples: *Fitz* (a form of the French *fils*), *p* or *b* in names of Welsh derivation (the equivalent of *ap*, son), *Mac*, *O'*, and final *s*, the Scandinavian *son* or *sen*, and the Russian *vich*, all of which convey the notion "son of" in such surnames as Fitzgerald, Ivanovich, Jones, Price, Pedersen, O'Connell, MacQuarrie, and McSorley. Surnames expressing local origin are usually (but not always) characterized by *de*, *di*, *du*, *von*, *van*, *atte*, *at*, or *a* before the name of the place: Devries, Dupont, Vanderwalker, Atwell, and the like. Continental place names are reflected in such family names as Fleming, Picard, St. Clair, Gascoigne, Berlin; such English names as London, Townsend, Welsh, and Scott derive from the names of districts, towns, estates, countries, and counties in England. Topographic peculiarities of the land of origin or association are expressed in such names as Field, Ford, Hill, Rivers, Bridges, Burroughs. Occupations are reflected in such names as Archer, Fisher, Porter, Shepherd, Smith, Taylor (Russian Portnoy, German Schneider), Baker (French Boulanger), Clark, Knight, Fuller, Spicer, Barker, and (presumably jocose) Pope and King; and outstanding personal or physical qualities and accomplishments gave rise to such names as Barbarossa (red beard), Dogood, Lovejoy, Lightfoot, Truman, Young, Black, Bold, Rich, Short, Whitehead, White (German Weiss, Italian Bianco, French Le Blanc). Animal names—some jocose, some alluding to emblems—include Fox, Bird, Lamb. Some names, such as Smithson, are patronymical expressions of occupation.

In the United States many new names came into existence through the tendency of immigrants to translate their names into English or to assume English equivalents. The Jews have shown the greatest willingness to change their names, partly because they did not assume surnames until forced to do so by legal decrees in the late eighteenth and early nineteenth centuries and are thus less bound to their surnames by tradition than are Christians. Americans of Spanish origin have preserved their names perhaps more insistently than any other group of immigrants. Negroes inherited no surnames from Africa, but assumed them, slaves taking the name of the master.

Place Names. As is the case with surnames, the origins of place names (studied by that branch of onomastics known as toponymy) are so plentiful as to be virtually limitless; although many place names are seemingly meaningless, all presumably had meaning at one time, and the quest for original meaning in place names often provides important clues for historians and philologists. There are some especially common sources from which names of natural features are drawn. The name may describe a distinctive quality of a place (Yellow River, Rocky Mountains) or indicate a particular incident associated with it (Death Valley). It may indicate possession (Zululand), or it may honor a person (Lake Victoria). Similarly, among the common sources for names of cities are the physical characteristics of the area (Long Beach, Marblehead), personal names of families or heroes (Washington, Lawrenceburg, Leningrad), the religious beliefs of the inhabitants (San Francisco, Trinidad), and miscellaneous events, experiences, emotions and aspirations associated with the place (Sunset, Hard Times Landing, Sweet Home, Independence).

Western European place names frequently can be traced back to periods of domination by various peoples. Thus many names were left by the Celts (Rhine river, Vienna, Kent); by the Romans (Aix, Cologne, and, indirectly, many British names, such as Lancaster—from *castra*, camp); and by the Germanic tribes (Lombardy, Wessex).

In the United States, explorers and settlers adopted many Indian names, sometimes transferring these names to new sites. Much more commonly, however, they chose names from their own languages, at times naming places after European cities, rivers, etc. Because settlement went ahead at such a rapid pace and the pressure to establish names was therefore great, there was a substantial amount of repetition and of transfer of names.

Occult, Magical Significance has often been ascribed to names in general or to particular names. In the earliest days of human speech all language was inherently of a sacred character; to a degree, even in modern times, any word may be invested with a certain magic by poets or orators, and personal and national names retain a power long absent from mere words. In antiquity words did not *represent* objects or persons; they *were* the objects or persons, and thus could be employed in magic spells and incantations to the betterment or detriment of the objects or persons involved. Hence the real name of the city of Rome, for example, was a state secret (since lost entirely); it was believed that if this real name were known to Rome's enemies, it could be used to control, even to destroy, the city and its people. In the practice of "sympathetic magic" through the ages, even into the twentieth century, a person's name was thought to *be* the person; commonly so in antiquity, although considerably less so at mid-twentieth century, many people kept their real names secret or allowed them to be known only with the greatest of circumspection. Names were involved in many of the activities of astrologers, numerologists, and other practitioners of magical divination. Even at mid-twentieth century there were many people who associated names with certain movements and configurations of the stars and the planets, or who attached a numerical value to each letter of the alphabet and found significant meaning in the fact, for example, that the numerical total formed by the first name equaled the numerical total of the surname.

In the area of theology, varying concepts of names have played significant roles throughout history. For example, among Hebrew tribes the name of God (the so-called Tetragrammaton, variously spelled IHVH, JHVH, JHWH, YHVH, YHWH, and variously transliterated by modern scholars as Yahweh, Yahve, Jehovah, and the like) could not be uttered or written except at Yom Kippur by the high priest, who pronounced it so softly that no one could hear the pronunciation (those in the congregation substituted the words Adonai or Elohim). In the Middle Ages, Jewish "wonder workers" were thought to be wonder workers precisely because they knew the pronunciation of this sacred name, and such a mystic was called a Baal Shem (Master of the Name). Among many Christians, the head is bowed at the mention of the name of Jesus. In addition, children of several Christian sects are baptized with a Christian name, particularly that of a saint; frequently, too, the name is drawn from the Old Testament.

NAMPA, city, SW Idaho, Canyon County; on the Union Pacific Railroad and U.S. highway 30; 18 miles W of Boise. It is in the Boise River irrigation area between the Boise and Snake rivers. Nampa is the shipping center for a rich agricultural area; principal products include livestock, hybrid sweet corn seed, fruits, beet sugar, dairy products, feed, potatoes, flour, and beverages. Just outside the city are gold and silver mines. Nampa is the site of Northwest Nazarene College. The city was first settled in 1885 and was named for the leader of an Indian tribe residing there. (For population, see Idaho map in Atlas.)

NAMPO, or Chinnampo, city, NW Korea, in the province of South Pyŏngan, at the mouth of the Taedong River and on an inlet leading to Korea Bay; 40 miles SW of Pyŏngyang. Nampo has a deep water port, which is open to ocean vessels except during an occasional ice block in winter. The leading industries include the production of vegetable oil, flour, chemicals, and iron products. Gold is refined. Rice, coal, iron, and paper are exported.

NAMUR, province, S Belgium; bounded by the provinces of Brabant on the N, Liège on the NE, and Luxembourg on the E, by France on the S, and by Hainaut Province on the W; area 1,413 sq. mi.; pop. (1956) 365,709. Namur is a hilly region drained by the Meuse and Sambre rivers, and the soil is generally fertile. Part of the Ardennes forest lies in the south. The majority of the population are Walloons (French speaking). There are important quarries (marble, chalk, white sand) and some coal and iron mines in the province. Dairying and fruit growing are major occupations. The province is subdivided into the arrondissements of Namur, Dinant, and Philippeville; the city of Namur is the capital. Namur was part of the second kingdom of Burgundy in the fifteenth century, and was under Spanish and, later, Dutch domination until Belgium's independence in 1831. The province was formed by the merging of the former county of Namur with parts of Liège bishopric and Hainaut Province. Pop. (1960) 371,489.

NAMUR, city, SE Belgium, capital of Namur Province; at the confluence of the Sambre and Meuse rivers; 35 miles SE of Brussels. Namur is an industrial center with cutlery, leather goods, and glass factories and brass and iron foundries. It has the seventeenth century Church of St. Loup, the eighteenth century Cathedral of St. Aubain, and an archaeological museum that houses Roman and Flemish antiquities. The site of the old citadel on the promontory at the fork between the two rivers, identified with a fortified camp in Roman times, has been converted into a park. Namur is believed to have been the headquarters of the Spanish general Don John of Austria in the sixteenth century. It was captured by Louis XIV, 1692, and by William III of Orange, 1695. Captured by French revolutionary forces, 1792, it remained a French possession until 1814. It became Belgian following the revolution against Dutch rule, 1830. In World War I Namur was captured by the Germans in 1914 after strong resistance, and the city was heavily damaged in World War II. Pop. (1956) 32,307.

NANAIMO, city, Canada, SW British Columbia Province; on Vancouver Island; on the Strait of Georgia, on the Canadian Pacific and the Esquimalt and Nanaimo railways; 41 miles W of Vancouver. Nanaimo is in a farming, lumbering, and coal mining district. It has a good harbor and extensive herring fisheries. The major tourist attraction is a fort built by the Hudson's Bay Company in 1852. Nanaimo was settled in 1851 and incorporated in 1874. Pop. (1956) 12,705.

NANCHANG, city, central China, capital of Kiangsi Province; on the Kan River at head of the Poyang Lake delta; 160 miles SE of Hankow. Nanchang is a river port, railroad junction, and an air transportation center. It is in a fertile alluvial plain whose chief products are tea and rice. Cotton textiles, matches, soap, glass, motorcycles, pottery, oils and fats, paper, automobile parts, farm implements, and chemicals are manufactured in the city. Nanchang is the site of a university and a medical school. The city was built in the twelfth century, during the Sung period, and became an independent municipality in 1935. Pop. (1956 est.) 300,000.

NANCHENG, also Hanchung, town, N China, SW Shensi Province, seat of Nancheng County; S of Tsinling Divide, on the S bank of the Han River; 135 miles SW of Sian. Nancheng has an airport and is on rail and highway transportation routes, but it depends chiefly on its Han River trade. Silk, cotton textiles, matches, lacquer and tung oil are the principal products of the town. Pop. (1957 est.) 60,000.

NANCY, city, NE France, capital of Meurthe-et-Moselle Department; on the Meurthe River immediately above its junction with the Moselle River, on the Marne-Rhine Canal and the Orient-Express Railway; 179 miles E of Paris. The city is the cultural, industrial, and commercial capital of Lorraine and an important railroad center. Nancy is located near the Lorraine iron basin, the Saar coal basin, and the Lorraine salt deposits. It has steel mills, railroad yards and repair shops, printing plants, and breweries. Among the city's manufactures are building materials, automobiles and spare parts, farm implements, cast-iron pipes, bronze objects, furniture, glassware, pottery, wool, cotton, clothes, shoes, hats, transmission belts, tobacco, brandy, canned food, flour, biscuits, chocolate, and candies.

The old town is built around the Renaissance ducal palace, which now houses an archaeological and historical museum. The old town is the site of the thirteenth century Saint-Epvre Church and the Church of the Cordeliers (1842). The Porte de la Craffe (1463), one of the city's old gates, is an example of medieval fortification. The Place Stanislas, one of the largest public squares in Europe, is enclosed by wrought-iron railings covered with gold leaves, for which Nancy has been nicknamed the City of the Golden Gates. Other points of interest are the Place Carrière with its triumphal arch, the palace of justice, the government palace, and the Church of Bon-Secours. In the city parks are race tracks and botanic and zoological gardens.

Educational institutions include the University of Nancy, the École Professionelle de l'Est, the École des Beaux-Arts, the Conservatoire de Musique, the Institut Coloniale, the École Nationale des Eaux et Forêts, the École des Mines, the Institut Chimique, the École de Brasserie, the Institut Agronomique, and the École d'Agriculture Mathieu-de-Dombasle.

Nancy was built by the dukes of Lorraine in the ninth century and became their capital in the twelfth century. Duke René II of Lorraine defeated Charles the Bold of Burgundy at the Battle of Nancy in 1477. Nancy fell to the kings of France, 1633, but was restored to the dukes of Lorraine by the Treaty of Ryswick, 1697. In 1776, at the death of Stanislas, king of Poland and duke of Lorraine, the city passed to France. Nancy was occupied by the Prussians during the Franco-Prussian War (1870–71), and after the war its population was almost doubled by the influx of refugees from the portions of Alsace and Lorraine occupied by the Prussians. In World War I a major battle was fought and won by the French near Nancy. In World War II the city was occupied by the Germans. Pop. (1954) 124,797.

NANDA DEVI, mountain of the Himalayas, N India, Uttar Pradesh State, Garhwal District, 209 miles NE of Delhi. There are two peaks, the higher 25,645 feet. Nanda Devi is in an area difficult of access because of surrounding mountains. Some Indians believe that the mountain is the home of Nanda, a wife of the Hindu deity Siva. Nanda Devi was first conquered in 1936 by a party of English and American mountaineers.

NANGA PARBAT, mountain of the Himalayas, N India, Kashmir and Jammu State; 49 miles SSE of Gilgit; elevation 26,660 feet. Eighth-highest mountain in the world, since 1895 it has claimed the lives of more than 25 persons trying to climb the summit. It was first scaled in 1953 by an Austrian, Herman Buhl. The name Nanga Parbat means naked mountain.

NANKING, or Nan-Ching, city, E central China, Kiangsu Province; on the S bank of the Yangtze River; 150 miles from the East China Sea; 170 miles WNW of Shanghai. One of the five great cities of China, Nanking is easily accessible by water and has railway connections with Shanghai and Tientsin. It is connected with the water-front city of Siakwan by a city rail line. There are several picturesque lakes near the city. The largest is Hsuanwu-hu; and a smaller one, Motsou-hu, is famous for its romantic history. Pop. (1957 est.) 1,400,000.

Cultural Center. For centuries Nanking has upheld Chinese traditions and culture. Nanking University, Chengchih University, Ginling College, several scientific research organizations, and a number of

EWING GALLOWAY

This gold-domed building in Nanking housed the offices of the Nationalist ministry of justice during the years when the Kuomintang government of Chiang Kai-shek ruled China.

Taoist and Buddhist temples are there. One of the Buddhist temples, towering majestically on the Chihsia Mountain, dates from the fifth century. In the eastern hills are tombs of emperors of the Ming and Sung dynasties, and there are unusual mortuary statues of men and animals. The most famous of these tombs is that of the first Ming emperor and his consort. The mausoleum of Sun Yat-sen, leader of the revolution that overthrew the Manchu Dynasty in 1911, is on the slope of Purple Mountain outside Nanking.

Massive walls, 40 feet high and 26 miles long, with 13 gates, surround Nanking. The architecture of the city generally is traditional but some newer public buildings embody Western styles. One of the most remarkable of Nanking's public buildings was destroyed in 1853, during the Taiping Rebellion. It was an octagonal tower designed by the Emperor Yung-lo and built in the fifteenth century as a memorial to his mother. It was 260 feet high with outer walls of white porcelain tile. Each of its nine stories was marked by projections of green glazed porcelain tile; five large pearls (to insure the city's safety from flood, fire, storm, and civil disturbance) were attached to chains hanging from the apex of the building to the eaves of the roof.

Economic Factors. Nanking is famous for manufactures of fine porcelains, fans, and silk damasks and tapestries. A yellow cloth called nankeen was first woven in the city and is named for it. Other products include textiles, paper, India ink, pottery, and artificial flowers. Across the river, suburban Pukow has a chemical plant that manufactures fertilizer. In the area around Nanking large quantities of rice, tea, beans, peanuts, and hemp are grown. Nanking is an important trade center. To the city from outlying districts come cotton goods and yarn, metals, petroleum products, cigarettes, and sugar; shipments of skins, frozen meats, and dairy products pass through the city en route to other parts of China. The city was opened to foreign trade in 1899.

Near Nanking marble figures line the avenue to the tombs of the Ming Dynasty emperors. Nanking was the capital of China during the first years of the Ming Dynasty's rule.

NORTHWEST ORIENT AIRLINES

History. The city was first known as Yehtsen, then as Kinling. During the Han Dynasty, 206 B.C.–A.D. 25, the name became Tanyang. The city, which was the capital of Wu State in the third century, became the capital of China during the Eastern Chin (Tsin) Dynasty, 316–420. During the Tang period, 618–906, it was called Kiangnan and Shengchow. In 1368 the first emperor of the Ming Dynasty renamed the city Yingtien, also calling it Nanking (southern capital). A later Ming emperor moved the capital to Peking (northern capital) in 1403. When the Manchus took over Nanking in 1644 they built a wall around it and called it Kiangning. In 1853 Taiping revolutionaries who conquered the Manchus made Nanking the seat of government; although they were suppressed by the Manchus 11 years later, Nanking remained the capital city of China until 1912. In that year Sun Yat-sen formed the Nationalist government and moved the capital to Peking. In 1927 at Nanking occurred the notorious Sacony Hill incident, in which U.S. nationals were outraged by the soldiery of Chinese war lords, and U.S. Marines and gunboats in the Yangtze were forced to fire into the mob to prevent a massacre. When Chiang Kai-shek gained control of the government in 1928, the ancient city of Nanking again became the capital. Nine years later, during the Sino-Japanese War, the city fell to Japanese invaders, but escaped serious damage. A puppet government established in 1940 ruled Japanese-held territory from Nanking. The city remained the center of government under the Nationalists (1946) but when Communists won control of China three years later, the capital was once again moved to Peking. Nanking was made the capital of Kiangsu in 1952. PAUL YUNG

NAN LING, or Nan Shan, mountain system, S China, on the borders of Kwantung, Hunan, and Kwangsi provinces; 450 miles from E to W. The system marks the division between north China and Canton cultures and languages. It forms the watershed between tributaries of the Yangtze River and rivers flowing to the South China Sea, and constitutes the northern boundary of the Si River basin and Kwantung Province. A climatic divide reaching 6,000 feet in elevation, the mountains shelter the region to the south (Kwantung and Kwangsi) from cold air masses of Hunan Province to the north. The range is not related to the Nan Shan in central China.

NANNA, in Nordic mythology, the goddess of flowers and vegetables, the wife of the god Balder. She died of grief at her husband's death and, from the underworld, sent blossoms to beautify the earth.

NANNING, formerly Yungning, city, S China, capital of Kwangsi Chuang Autonomous Region; on the N bank of the Yü, a tributary of the West River; on the Litang-Munankwan Railroad 115 miles SW of Liuchow. Because of its railroad, highway, and river connections with Lungtsin and with cities of Yunnan Province and of neighboring Vietnam, Nanning is an important commercial center. Trade in the city deals in sugar cane, fruit, processed meats, machinery, cotton and silk textiles, processed tung oil and rice produced in the immediate vicinity, as well as antimony, hides, and beans produced in western Kwangsi Province. The city was opened to foreign trade in 1907. It was capital of Kwangsi Province, 1913–36. Pop. (1958 est.) 260,000.

NANPING, formerly Yenping, city, SE China, N central Fukien Province; on the Min River and the Yinctan-Amoy Railroad; 85 miles WNW of Foochow. Nanping is on the highway from Hangchow and at the confluence of the Futun, Kien, and Sha rivers which form the Min. It is an important shipping center for chemicals, machinery, bamboo paper, processed tea, and timber produced in the vicinity. (For population, see China map in Atlas.)

NANSEN, FRIDTJOF, 1861–1930, Nobel prize-winning Norwegian explorer, was born in Store Fröen and educated at the University of Christiania. He made his first trip into the arctic seas in 1883 to obtain zoological specimens, and the same year became curator of the Natural History Museum, Bergen. In 1888 he crossed the icefields of Greenland on skis and described his achievement in *The First Crossing of Greenland* (1890). Heading a North Polar Expedition, he sailed on the *Fram* to the New Siberian Islands, 1893, and from there the ship drifted north in an ice floe for 2 years. In 1895 Nansen and F. H. Johansen left the ship and set out by sledge for the pole; they proceeded to the latitude of 86°14′N, 220 miles farther north than any previous explorer had reached. Then, after spending a winter in Franz Josef Land, they returned to Norway, 1896. The results of the trip were published in *The Norwegian North Polar Expedition 1893–96: Scientific Results* (6 vols., 1900–06).

Prominent in the movement for the peaceful separation of Norway from Sweden, Nansen was the first Norwegian minister to England, 1906–08. He resigned to become professor of oceanography at Christiania University. He made several scientific voyages in the North Atlantic, 1910–14. Requested by the first council of the League of Nations to investigate the prisoner-of-war problem, 1920, he returned 450,000 prisoners to their homes, supervised relief work among Russian, Greek, and Armenian refugees, and helped establish, 1921, the Nansen Passport Bureau to provide identity papers for displaced persons. For his efforts to repatriate prisoners of war and for directing Red Cross famine relief work in the Volga Valley and southern Ukraine region, 1921–23, Nansen received the 1922 Nobel peace prize. His death canceled his plans for a dirigible trip to the North Pole. Nansen wrote *Norway and the Union with Sweden* (1905), *Russia and Peace* (1924), and *Armenia and the Near East* (1928).

NAN SHAN, or Southern Mountains, N central China, a system of parallel ranges on Tsinghai-Kansu border, running from NW to SE for about 600 miles through the neck of Kansu Province S of the Silk Road. It reaches an elevation of more than 20,000 feet and includes the Humboldt, Richthofen, and Tatung mountains. The Nan Shan system is one of the most important in central Asia. The Tsaidam swamps stretch from the southwest slopes of the Nan Shan, and the Ala Shan Desert extends to the northeast. In the Humboldt Mountains is the Amnermurgil, one of several large glaciers in the western Nan Mountains. Many rivers rise in the snow-capped peaks, creating numerous high plateaus and valleys. Koko Nor (Tsing Hai), a salt lake, lies in the southeast.

NANTERRE, city, N France, Hauts-de-Seine Department; at the foot of Mt. Valérien; 7 miles NW of Paris, of which it is a suburb. Nanterre has a port on the Seine River. Products of the city include chemicals, electrical equipment, paints, perfumes, hosiery, pharmaceuticals, bronze, and aluminum. Nanterre was founded as a shrine of St. Geneviève (422?–512), the patron saint of Paris. (For population, see France map in Atlas.)

NANTES, city, W France, capital of the department of Loire-Atlantique, on the Loire River 35 miles from the Atlantic Ocean. A major seaport, it is connected by canal with St. Nazaire at the mouth of the Loire. Nantes is a city of bridges, as it extends along the banks of numerous branches of the Loire and occupies several islands. Leading industries are shipbuilding and food processing; manufactures and chief exports include machines, locomotives, chemicals, sugar, tobacco, textiles, and wine. The city has a museum of fine arts; botanic gardens; the Cathedral of St. Pierre, unfinished until the nineteenth century; and a ninth or tenth century ducal palace rebuilt in the fifteenth century, where Henry IV issued the Edict of Nantes, Apr. 13, 1598.

FRENCH CULTURAL SERVICES

The Porte St.-Pierre, a late Gothic town gate in Nantes, adjoins the cathedral, at left. The ancient Gallic town is now a busy industrial city and a commercial seaport.

In antiquity, Nantes was the capital of the Namnetes, a Gallic tribe. It was occupied by the Normans, 843–936, and became the capital of Brittany in the tenth century. Nantes passed to France in the fifteenth century. During the French Revolution it was the scene of mass execution by drowning, 1793–94. (For population, see France map in Atlas.)

NANTES, EDICT OF, a law issued by Henry IV of France, Apr. 13, 1598, giving legal status to the Huguenots, or Protestants, in France. The edict provided for liberty of conscience and for freedom of worship in places where churches were already established and on the estates of Huguenot nobles. It granted full civil rights to Protestants, including the right to hold office; to determine issues under the edict, special courts were created on which some judges were to be Protestants. The Huguenots were given control of about 200 fortified towns for eight years. The edict was intended to end the religious wars that had divided France. Louis XIV made it a policy to interpret the provisions of the edict strictly. This policy led to his formal revocation of the edict, Oct. 18, 1685. The restrictions imposed and the attempts at conversion by force drove thousands of Huguenots from France.

NANTEUIL, ROBERT, 1623–78, French engraver, was born in Reims, and probably studied engraving with Nicolas Regnesson. About 1647 he went to Paris, where he was commissioned to engrave the portraits of several members of the Paris parliament; he reproduced these portraits in copper. In 1658 he was named designer and engraver to Louis XIV. In 1660 the king raised the status of engraving from a mechanical art to that of a fine art, and this decision was attributed mainly to the influence of Nanteuil. Nanteuil's portraits are noted for their individual characteristics and precision of draftsmanship; the color, executed with only three crayons, is tasteful and simple. He executed more than 200 portraits; the best are those of Louis XIV; Jules Cardinal Mazarin; Henri de La Tour d'Auvergne, vicomte de Turenne; and Jean Loret.

NANTICOKE, a North American Indian tribe of the Algonquian linguistic stock, closely related to the

Conoy and Unalachtigo Delaware, formerly living in eastern Maryland and southern Delaware. The Nanticoke were subdued by Maryland colonists in 1678 after 40 years of sporadic warfare. In the early eighteenth century part of the tribe migrated northward, and by 1748 had settled with Iroquois in southern New York. Others of the Nanticoke migrated westward with groups of the Mahican and Wappinger, and by 1784 had merged with the Delaware in the Ohio Valley. The tribal name is that of a river and town in Delaware, and of towns in New York and Pennsylvania. The Nanticoke population is estimated to have been 2,700 in 1600 and about 500 in 1722. Descendants of the Nanticoke and related tribes (known in the nineteenth century as Choptank, Wicocomoco, and Wiwash) who remained at their old site are largely of mixed Indian-Negro blood, and are known to number more than 700.

NANTICOKE, city, NE central Pennsylvania; on the Susquehanna River, and the Jersey Central and the Pennsylvania railroads; 7 miles WSW of Wilkes-Barre. It is an anthracite coal mining center and has manufactures of textiles, cigars, and farm machinery. It occupies the former site of a Nanticoke Indian village and owes its beginning to the availability of water power from Nanticoke Falls. It was incorporated as a borough in 1874 and as a city in 1926. Pop. (1960) 15,601.

NANTUCKET, village, SE Massachusetts, seat of Nantucket County; on the N shore of Nantucket Island; 50 miles ESE of New Bedford. Ferry steamers connect Nantucket with Hyannis and New Bedford. Settled in 1659, it became an important whaling port and later developed as a summer resort. Pop. (1960) 2,804.

NANTUCKET ISLAND, off the SE coast of Massachusetts in the Atlantic Ocean; comprising, with nearby Tuckernuck and Muskeget Islands, the Massachusetts County of Nantucket; 11 miles S of Cape Cod from which it is separated by Nantucket Sound, and 12 miles ESE of Martha's Vineyard from which it is separated by Muskeget Channel; area 46 sq. mi., including Tuckernuck and Muskeget Islands; pop. (1960) 3,559. Somewhat triangular in shape, Nantucket Island has maximum east-west and north-south distances of 15 and 11 miles respectively. The surface of the island is level, for the most part, with a few trees and fine beaches. The village of Nantucket on the northern coast is the county seat and the largest community; pop. (1960) 2,804. It is served by ferry steamers and an airline. The village has many quaint homes and old cobblestone streets which maintain the atmosphere of the past. The island is traversed by a highway that connects the village of Nantucket with the smaller resort villages of Maddaket, Surfside, Siasconset, Polpis, Quidnet, and Wauwinet.

Discovered by Bartholomew Gosnold in 1602, Nantucket Island was included in the royal grant to the Plymouth Company in 1621, became part of the province of New York in 1660, and was ceded to Massachusetts in 1692. The first settlement was Maddaket, 1659; Nantucket village was founded in 1673. During the first half of the nineteenth century Nantucket was an important whaling port. As the whaling industry declined, shipyards, woolen mills, and nail factories were developed. In the twentieth century the summer tourist industry became the mainstay of the island's economy.

NANTY GLO, borough, SW central Pennsylvania, Cambria County; near Lick Creek and on the Cambria and Indiana and the Pennsylvania railroads; 12 miles NNE of Johnstown in bituminous coal country. Nanty Glo was founded in 1888. Pop. (1960) 4,608.

NAOGEORGUS, 1511–63, German writer of Latin plays and supporter of Martin Luther, was born Thomas Kirchmair, Kirchmeyer, or Kirchmaier, in Hubelschmeiss, near Straubing. His plays, written to be performed by and to educate schoolboys, were influential, bitter attacks on Roman Catholicism. Among them are *Pammachius* (1538), which depicted the pope as the Antichrist; *Incendia* (1541); *Hieremias* (1551); and *Judas Iscariotes* (1552). Naogeorgus also wrote the satirical poem *Regnum papisticum* (1553).

NAPA, city, W central California, seat of Napa County; at the head of barge navigation on the Napa River; on the Southern Pacific Railroad; 40 miles N of Oakland. Napa is a shipping point for agricultural products, mostly fruit, of the Napa Valley. The main industries are fruit processing, dairying, and the manufacture of leather goods. It has a junior college and nearby is a state mental hospital. Napa was settled in 1840 and incorporated in 1872. Pop. (1960) 22,170.

NAPALM, an agent used primarily to thicken gasoline. During World War II a gasoline mixture containing 4 to 6 per cent napalm was used for flame throwers, and one containing about 12 per cent for incendiary bombs. Napalm consists of aluminum sulfate combined with several acids, such as naphthenic acid, oleic acid, and coconut acid. Napalm has also been used as a germicide and as a liquid soap.

NAPANEE, town, Canada, S Ontario, seat of Lennox and Addington County; on the N shore of Lake Ontario, the Napanee River, the Bay of Quinte, and the Canadian National Railway; 25 miles W of Kingston. The town has lumber and grist mills and canneries. Pop. (1956) 4,273.

NAPERVILLE, city, NE Illinois; on the W branch of the Du Page River, on the Burlington Railroad and U.S. highway 34; 7 miles E of Aurora and 30 miles W of Chicago. North Central College and Evangelical Theological Seminary are in Naperville. Boilers, burlap bags, and cheese are among the city's varied manufactures. Naperville was settled in 1831 and incorporated in 1857. Pop. (1960) 12,933.

NAPHTHA, a group of highly flammable and volatile hydrocarbons in liquid form obtained by the distillation of carbonaceous substances, such as petroleum, wood, and coal. Most naphtha is the distillation of paraffin-base or mixed crude oils. The boiling point of naphtha is 40° to 150°C (100° to 300°F). Most naphtha is used for dry-cleaning clothes—as a solvent for grease, resins, and gums. Naphtha with a lower volatility is used as a solvent and thinner for quick-drying paints and varnishes.

NAPHTHALENE, an aromatic hydrocarbon having the formula $C_{10}H_8$, is obtained from the heavy oil fractions distilled from coal tar. It crystallizes from this oil on cooling and is filtered off and washed with water to remove the adhering creosote oils. This process yields the crude naphthalene of commerce, which may be further purified by distillation, washing with acid and alkali, and finally sublimed to yield flake naphthalene—colorless, leafy, rhombic crystals with a peculiar penetrating odor. Naphthalene has a specific gravity of 1.15, melts at 80°C (176°F), boils at 218°C (424°F), and burns with a luminous, smoky flame. It is slightly soluble in hot water but highly so in organic solvents. Manufactured as moth balls, it is widely used to protect fabrics against moths and to disguise disagreeable odors.

When oxidized in the presence of vanadium pentoxide, naphthalene yields phthalic anhydride, the starting point in the synthesis of anthraquinone, which is largely used as an intermediate in the manufacture of vat dyes. On reduction in the presence of nascent hydrogen or gaseous hydrogen and a catalyst, naphthalene yields tetrahydronaphthalene, manufactured and sold as a solvent under the name tetralin.

The constitution of naphthalene is represented by this structural formula:

```
       CH      CH
     //   \   /   \\
   CH       C       CH
   |        ||      |
   CH       C       CH
     \\   /   \   //
       CH      CH
```

It is seen to consist of two condensed six-carbon member rings joined by two mutually shared, or coordinate covalent carbon atoms (see VALENCE, *Coordinate Covalence*). Naphthalene may be chlorinated, nitrated, or sulfonated in a manner similar to that for benzene, yielding substitution products. Of these products, the sulfonic acids and nitro derivatives may be used in the preparation of azo dyes. Exhaustive chlorination results in the halowaxes, nonflammable substances that have high dielectric constants.

NAPHTHOL, a chemical substance, $C_{10}H_7OH$. It occurs naturally in coal tar, but it is usually prepared artificially as either of two white crystalline hydroxyl derivatives of naphthalene. One of these derivatives is known as α-naphthol, or 1-naphthol; the other is β-naphthol, or 2-naphthol. Both have the properties of the phenols. Both are volatile, and α-naphthol has a specific gravity of 1.224, melts at 96°C (205°F), and boils at 279°C (534°F); β-naphthol has a specific gravity of 1.217, melts at 122°C (252°F), and boils at 285°C (545°F). The naphthols are most extensively used as synthesizers in the preparation of azo dyes. They are also used as starting materials in the preparation of rubber oxidants, pharmaceuticals, and perfumes. β-naphthol is also a disinfectant. See DYEING.

NAPIER, JOHN, 1550–1617, Scottish mathematician, was born in Merchiston Castle, near Edinburgh. Napier (or Neper) was educated at St. Andrews and probably studied on the Continent. He was a pioneer in the decimal system of mathematical notation, and invented logarithms, which eliminated many laborious arithmetical operations that the solution of the simplest trigonometrical problems up to that time had exacted. His logarithmical tables were published, 1614, as *Mirifici Logarithmorum canonis descriptio*, and were followed in 1619 by an explanatory work, *Mirifici Logarithmorum canonis constructio*. He also wrote a theological treatise, *Plaine Discovery of the Whole Revelation of Saint John* (1593) and *Rabdologioe seu numerationis per virgulas libri duo* (1615); the latter set forth methods for simplifying the processes of multiplication and division by the use of "Napier's rods" or "bones," a mechanical calculating device.

NAPIER, SIR WILLIAM FRANCIS PATRICK, 1785–1860, British soldier and historian, was born in Celbridge, county Kildare, Ireland. He entered the army in 1800, became captain, 1804, and served in the expedition against Copenhagen, 1807, and in the Peninsular Campaign, 1808. He retired, 1819, became colonel, 1830, and general, 1859. Besides an authoritative *History of the Peninsular War* (6 vols. 1828–40), he published a history of *Sir Charles Napier's Administration of Scinde* (1851) and *Life and Opinions of General Sir C. J. Napier* (1857).

His brother Sir Charles James Napier (1782–1853), British general, served in the Peninsular War, and was largely responsible for the conquest of Sind, 1842–43, and its annexation to British India.

NAPIER, borough, New Zealand; on Hawke Bay, E coast of North Island; 170 miles NE of Wellington. It is the capital of Hawke's Bay provincial district and is in but independent of Hawke's Bay County. Napier is a seaport in a grazing, dairying, and fruit growing area. It is a popular winter resort with a pleasant climate and fine beaches. Napier's industries produce meat, dairy goods, tobacco, and woolens. (For population, see New Zealand map in Atlas.)

NAPLES, or Napoli, province, S Italy, Campania Division; bounded by Latium Division on the NW, Abruzzi e Molise Division on the N, the Campanian provinces of Benevento on the NE and Avellino on the E, and the Tyrrhenian Sea on the S and SW; area 1,206 sq. mi. The province includes the islands of Procida, Ischia, Capri, and Ventotene. Chief rivers are the Volturno and the Liri. In the south and along the western border the province is mountainous, with volcanic formations in the south (Vesuvius); north of heights around the Bay of Naples is a fertile alluvial plain. Olive oil, wine, hemp, cotton, and chestnuts are produced, and macaroni, chemicals, machinery, motors, hardware, musical instruments, and textiles are manufactured. The capital is Naples. Pop. (1958 est.) 2,341,055.

NAPLES, or Napoli, city, S Italy; capital of Campania Division and of Naples Province; at the foot of the Phlegraean Fields, on the N shore of the Bay of Naples; 120 miles SE of Rome. Vesuvius Volcano, with the ruined cities of Pompeii and Herculaneum at its foot, lies to the southeast; south of the city and across the bay is the island of Capri; to the west are the islands of Procida and Ischia. Pop. (1961) 1,179,608.

Commerce and Industry. Naples has one of the most important ports in Italy, especially for passenger service; tourist trade is a major source of revenue for the city. Principal exports are macaroni, olive oil, textiles, gloves, and canned goods, and imports are largely raw materials and foodstuffs. Major industries of Naples include food preservation, steel and iron production, shipbuilding, and the manufacture of gloves, shoes, chemicals, and cotton and silk goods.

Buildings and Streets. Naples is built on the slopes of the rocky uplands above the bay; it is divided by a ridge into the old section to the east and the new section to the north and west.

As a cultural and artistic center Naples is especially famous for the National Museum, which houses the Farnese collection and many objects excavated from the ruins of Pompeii and Herculaneum. The Filangeri Civic Museum has sculpture and paintings, and the Capodimonte Museum houses eighteenth century Neapolitan porcelain. The San Carlo Opera, one of Italy's largest opera houses, was built in 1737. The university, founded in 1224, is one of the most important in Italy. There are several art academies and a conservatory. The institute of marine zoology at Naples has a fine aquarium.

In the old section of Naples near the port are the Castel Nuovo (1279–82), built as a royal residence, and the royal palace (1600–02), housing the Victor Emmanuel III National Library. The thirteenth century Church of Santa Maria del Carmine and the fourteenth century Santa Chiara Church in this section were badly damaged in World War II. A fourteenth century cathedral contains relics of St. Januarius (San Gennaro), patron saint of Naples.

The Castel dell'Ovo stands at the entrance to the harbor, and on Capodimonte overlooking the city are the Castel Sant'Elmo, the Floridiana gardens, and the monastery of San Martino. The tomb of Virgil is west of the city.

Perhaps the best known street in Naples is the historic Via Roma (or Via Toledo), which runs north through the city. Following the curving western shore of the bay are the Riviera di Chiaia and the Via

The Villa Comunale, a public garden next to the sea, is the site of the Neopolitan Aquarium, a zoological station, and numerous statues of literary and historic personages.
ITALIAN STATE TOURIST OFFICE

Carracciola, with Villa Nazionale Park between them. The Corso Vittorio Emanuele winds through hills behind the city and affords fine views of Naples and its harbor.

History. Naples was founded about 600 B.C. as a Greek colony, known first as Parthenope. Later colonists from Athens built a new town, or Neapolis, for themselves, and called the old town Palaeopolis. The two settlements fell to Rome in 328 B.C., and Palaeopolis disappeared while Neapolis became a center of Roman culture and the residence of Roman notables. After the fall of the Roman Empire, Naples was ruled by Goths, then by Lombards, and in 536 was taken by Byzantine forces under Belisarius. Naples was an independent duchy from 763 to 1139, when it was seized by Normans and became part of the kingdom of Sicily. Naples and Sicily became Spanish dependencies in 1504, were taken by Austria in 1707, and were reconquered by Spain in 1734. In 1799 Naples fell to France and became the capital of the short-lived French Parthenopean republic. It was under Napoleonic rule until 1815, when it returned to Bourbon control under Ferdinand IV. After a period of relative calm the city fell to the forces of Giuseppe Garibaldi in 1860 and was incorporated in the newly established kingdom of Italy in 1861. In 1884 Naples was devastated by a cholera epidemic. During World War II the Naples harbor and numerous notable buildings were damaged by Allied bombing and by the depredations of retreating Germans. See TWO SICILIES.

BIBLIOG.–Edward Hutton, *Naples and Campania Revisited* (1958); Arno Wrubel, *Gulf of Naples* (1962).

NAPOLEON I, original name Napoleone Buonaparte (after 1796 Napoléon Bonaparte), called *le petit caporal* (the Little Corporal), 1769–1821, emperor of the French, born of Italian parents in Ajaccio, Corsica, on Aug. 15, 1769. He was the fourth child and second son of Carlo Buonaparte, a lawyer reputedly of noble Corsican birth, and his beautiful wife Letizia Ramolino. Napoleon received a military education in France, at Brienne and Paris, and when the Revolution broke out he held a commission as first lieutenant in the French army. At first his sympathies lay with the Corsican patriots who fought for independence, but he soon cast his lot with the Revolution. As captain of artillery he helped recapture the Mediterranean seaport of Toulon from the French Royalists and the English in 1793. For the next 2 years his fortunes varied, but after October, 1795 (*Vendémiaire* according to the revolutionary calendar), when he suppressed the Parisian insurrectionists, thus saving the Convention, his rise was rapid. In reward for his services, although not without the helpful intervention of widowed Joséphine de Beauharnais, whom he had married on Mar. 9, 1796, he was named commander of the army of Italy. Prepared by his earlier study of mountain fighting, he made brilliant use of the new principles of warfare to win spectacular victories over the opposing Sardinians and Austrians (Lodi, where his soldiers dubbed him "little corporal"; Castiglione; Arcole; and Rivoli). These he followed up by negotiating the Treaty of Campoformio (1797) with the Austrians; this treaty confirmed the existing French annexation of the Netherlands and guaranteed to France possession of the west bank of the Rhine. Meantime, while fruitless negotiations were being held with Great Britain, Bonaparte undertook the reorganization of northern Italy under French auspices. In 1798 he was placed in command of a carefully prepared expedition to conquer Egypt, which was to be part of a larger plan to cut the British off from India. Bonaparte's victories over the Turkish armies were nullified by Horatio Nelson's destruction of his fleet at Abu Qir Bay (Aug. 1, 1798), which doomed the venture to failure. Turning over command of his troops to a subordinate, Bonaparte succeeded in reaching France in October, 1799. His reverses notwithstanding (partly because he had withheld the news), he found himself on his return the man of the hour—welcomed by compatriots who had had more than enough of the discredited government of the Directory. Bonaparte joined with Emmanuel Joseph Siéyès and other plotters in the coup d'état of *Brumaire*, or November, 1799. Quickly "revising" the constitution, the plotters set up the decennial consulate in which Bonaparte was nominally first consul but actually the effective head.

Reorganization of Revolutionary France, 1800–04. *Brumaire* gave Bonaparte not power, but an opportunity to fulfill the destiny in which he was acquiring an almost mystic faith. He used that opportunity with astonishing vigor and rapidity to crush the Austrians (who had joined the second coalition) at Marengo in northern Italy, and to impose upon them the Peace Treaty of Lunéville in 1801. Again only Great Britain remained as a threat to France and, war-weary and isolated, it also made peace in the following year (Peace of Amiens). Thus the triumphant first consul pacified the Continent and ended 10 years of revolutionary wars. Surrounding himself with dedicated and technically competent associates and acting with unflagging energy and boundless confidence in himself, Bonaparte utilized his victories and the interval of peace to make himself virtual dictator of France. In the eyes of the overwhelming majority of French his absolute power seemed merited. By the time he became emperor in 1804—a position, like his earlier one, formally ratified by plebiscites—he had already dazzled all France and Europe by a remarkable reorganization of the institutions of his country. He suppressed brigandage and disorder, secured life and property, founded the Bank of France, regularized the collection of taxes, and gave encouragement and financial aid to France's disrupted

Napoleon I by François Gérard
FRENCH CULTURAL SERVICES

industries. The coronation ceremony itself (in Paris, Dec. 2, 1804— following senate "ratification" the previous May 18) was a splendid affair, marked by the greatest of pomp and circumstance. Just as Pope Pius VII was about to place the crown upon his head, Napoleon took the crown in his hands, turned his back upon the pope, and crowned himself while facing the "people"; he then crowned Josephine. Nominally ruler by the will of the people, the dynamic, decisive, and resolute leader actually governed France in the manner of the enlightened despots of the eighteenth century, setting up central and local administrative systems characterized by honesty, efficiency, and stability. In the new civil code (*Code Napoléon*, 1804–10) he systematized the mass of revolutionary legislation with the principles of Roman and customary law derived from France's historic past. To overcome the opposition of the papacy and win the good will of Roman Catholics within France he negotiated a compromise settlement with Pius VII, the Concordat of 1801, which satisfied the moderates on both sides and regulated church-state relations for more than a century. By restoring health to a sick organism and by strengthening France's foundations without repudiating the essential achievements of 1789, he most fully merited the appellation that he gave himself, "the child of the Revolution." Only one thing was lacking—liberty.

Napoleonic Europe, 1803–15. Napoleon was not content merely with governing regenerated France. A combination of personal ambition and civilizing, missionary zeal impelled him to extend his sway over Europe. The peace was broken in 1803, and for 12 years Europe was rent by war. Napoleon's intention to invade England across the channel was thwarted in 1805 by the defeat of Adm. Pierre de Villeneuve, culminating in Admiral Nelson's destruction of the French and Spanish naval squadrons at Trafalgar (Oct. 21, 1805). Henceforth Napoleon waged economic war on Britain under his "Continental system," organizing his tremendous land power in a vast effort to overcome Britain's naval superiority and bring that country to terms by sealing the European continent to British manufactured and colonial goods. He fought and defeated Austria, Prussia, and Russia on the fields of battle (Ulm, Austerlitz, Jena, Auerstedt, and Friedland), and with each victory he extended French military and civilian control. His own military genius and the superb Grand Army that he commanded account in large part for the victories that astonished and terrified the world; also important were the mutual mistrust and traditional expansionist rivalries of the powers, who were as ready to ally themselves with Napoleon as against him. By the treaties of Tilsit (1807), when the defeated Alexander I of Russia allied himself with Napoleon in support of the economic boycott of Britain, Napoleon's effective control over France and Europe reached its height (though not its greatest territorial extent). Within France the constructive reforms of the Consulate had been continued after the founding of the empire. The *Code Napoléon* was completed and the entire system of public instruction was organized and coordinated under central control. Although the emperor established the Legion of Honor and created a new landed nobility, he retained equality and kept careers open to talent. Judged in the light of the "liberty" that the Revolution had won for the individual, Napoleonic France had reverted to a despotism that stifled thought and crushed political freedom. More and more the empire became a police state. But there was no alternative to his rule. Until the final years of military disaster, appalling loss of life, and economic depression, Frenchmen were grateful for the blessings of order, efficiency, and prosperity, and resigned themselves to enduring the costs of triumph and glory.

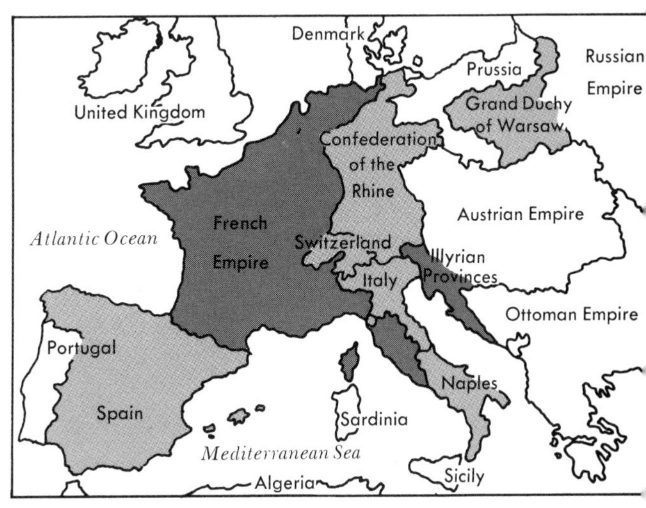

Europe in 1812, at the height of Napoleon's power: dark gray areas represent the French empire; light gray areas, states under Napoleonic control.

From Tilsit on, the tide turned against Napoleon. The attempt to conquer Portugal involved him in a Spanish venture that bled him of thousands of his best troops. In 1809 he again crushed Austria (battles of Aspern and Wagram), but in the following year Russia cut itself loose from the alliance of Tilsit. Napoleon now decided to contract a "dynastic marriage" and simultaneously opened negotiations with Alexander I for the hand of his sister (knowing the tsar would refuse) and with the emperor of Austria, Francis I, for the hand of Francis' daughter, Marie Louise. Alexander refused as expected, and Napoleon married Marie on April 1, 1810—having divorced Joséphine the preceding December. The union only seemed to cement the Austrian alliance, since Austria abandoned Napoleon when it became politically desirable to do so. Napoleon made grandiose plans to humble Alexander, but his invasion of Russia in 1812 turned out a disaster so nightmarish that it became almost legendary. Humbled and partitioned Prussia rose against him in the following year, joining Russia in a military alliance to which Austria soon adhered. Napoleon's shattering defeat at Leipzig on Oct. 16–19, 1813, was the beginning of the end. In 1814 the allies, financed largely by Britain, invaded France and captured Paris. On April 11 Napoleon was forced to abdicate. The Treaty of Fontainebleau allowed him to retain the title "emperor"—but only of the tiny island of Elba, where alone he was to be sovereign, and which he was not to leave. But the agreements reached in the Congress of Vienna tried to ignore the social forces to which the French Revolution had given expression. Knowing of the increasing dissatisfaction of the French people with their new ruler, Louis XVIII, Napoleon in 1815 escaped from Elba. During his last desperate effort (the Hundred Days) Napoleon had the support of the peasants and the old soldiers (it is said that shortly after his return soldiers sent to stop him blocked his advance near Grenoble, whereupon Napoleon bared his chest to their fire—and they threw down their weapons and cried "*Vive l' Empereur*") and of many of the French middle class as well. But to retain this support Napoleon had to make liberal concessions—the people wanted neither empire nor Bourbon monarchy. His efforts to conciliate the French middle class met with some success; his efforts to conciliate the Allies by saying that he was for peace, failed: he was branded "an Enemy and Disturber of the tranquillity of the World." War was the result and the end came on the field of Waterloo (June 18, 1815). Napoleon abdicated again in favor of his son (in vain, for Louis XVIII regained his throne) and, failing to escape to America, threw himself upon the mercy of the British who confined him to the island of St. Helena, a place described by Napoleon as of "salubrious climate," where he lived a few more years in restricted circumstances and at odds with his British captors. He died of cancer on May 5, 1821. Much later, in 1840, his remains were removed (by order of Louis Philippe) to the Hôtel des Invalides, Paris. See FRANCE; FRANCIS II; WATERLOO, BATTLE OF.

At St. Helena he became the first of the contributors to the Napoleonic legend, and in the memoirs that he dictated there he protested that the reactionary powers had defeated his ideal of establishing a European federation. The reality was otherwise. In a sense the Napoleonic Wars were an irrepressible conflict. On the one side were the monarchs and the privileged aristocracies that abhorred and feared the revolution that Napoleon had disciplined but nevertheless consolidated; on the other, the *grande nation*, a moving menace to their power and security, their ideals, values, and institutions. In its emperor France had a soldier of genius whose vast ambition and crusading sense of mission fused with the *élan* of the nation. Behind him was the pressure of business interests to oust and supplant England as the great exporter of manufactured goods. And in Napoleon's mind, little by little, a vision rooted itself of a unified European world centered in France and governed according to French institutions. Distance, time, nationalistic feelings, and hatred of the foreign "liberators" joined to defeat Napoleon's premature and oppressive conception of the new Europe. But on the forces of history that defeated him he left a permanent mark. The Europe he conquered and lost was never the same again. LEO GERSHOY

BIBLIOG.–Geoffrey Bruun, *Europe and the French Imperium: 1799–1814* (1938); Philippe Paul de Ségur, *Napoleon's Russian Campaign* (1958); R. F. Delderfield, *Retreat from Moscow* (1967); H. C. Deutsch, *Genesis of Napoleonic Imperialism* (1938); H. A. L. Fisher, *Napoleon* (1945); Leo Gershoy, *The French Revolution and Napoleon* (1933); Pieter Geyl, *Napoleon: For and Against* (1949); Albert Guérard, *Napoleon I* (1956); J. Christopher Herold, *Age of Napoleon* (1963); Maurice Hutt, *Napoleon* (1965); Henry Lachouque, *Napoleon's Battles: A History of his Campaigns*, tr. Roy Monkcom (1966); Emil Ludwig, *Napoleon* (1950 ed.); Felix M. Markham, *Napoleon and the Awakening of Europe* (1954); André Maurois, *Napoleon*, tr. D. J. S. Thomson (1964); Frances Mossiker, *Napoleon and Josephine* (1964); J. M. Thompson, *Napoleon Bonaparte, His Rise and Fall* (1952); U.S. Military Academy, Department of Military Art and Engineering, *Military History and Atlas of the Napoleonic Wars*, ed. V. J. Esposito and J. R. Elting (1964).

NAPOLEON II, in full François Charles Joseph Bonaparte, duc de Reichstadt, called L'Aiglon (the Eaglet), 1811–32, born in Paris, the son of Napoleon I and Marie Louise. At his birth he received the title "king of Rome" and on his father's abdication in 1814 he became Napoleon II of France, but the Allies refused to accept him. He spent the rest of his life at the Austrian court with his grandfather, Francis II, and in 1818 became duc de Reichstadt. Edmond Rostand based his play *l'Aiglon* on the life of Napoleon II.

Napoleon II

CULVER PICTURES

NAPOLEON III, Charles Louis Napoleon Bonaparte, 1808–73, emperor of the French, son of Louis Bonaparte, king of Holland, and Hortense de Beauharnais, and nephew of Napoleon I. He became Bonapartist pretender on the death of Napoleon's son in 1832. He spent the early part of his life in exile in Germany, Italy, Switzerland, and England, and visited the United States briefly in 1837. He took part in an insurrection in central Italy in 1831 and twice, in 1836 and in 1840, attempted to lead a Bonapartist coup against the July Monarchy in France. After the last attempt he was imprisoned in the fortress of Ham, from which he made a spectacular escape in 1846. In these years he wrote various pamphlets, notably *Napoleonic Ideas* (1839) and *The Extinction of Pauperism* (1844), which showed the influence of the vague, idealistic socialism of the time.

The strength of Bonapartist sentiment in France and the consequent prestige of his name ensured his election by an overwhelming vote as president of the Second French Republic in December, 1848.

Rather than surrender this office at the end of the 4-year term, he carried out a coup d'etat with the help of the army in December, 1851, and revived the empire in France in the following year. A repressive authoritarian regime was established, which severely restricted freedom of the press and of association and effectively stifled political opposition and discussion. It was based, however, on popular vote in the form of the plebiscite, and, after the disturbances of 1848, enjoyed a large measure of support.

After 1860 the regime became progressively more liberal in an attempt to forestall or placate growing opposition. In January, 1870, a short-lived, semi-parliamentary system was set up with a former Republican, Emile Ollivier, as prime minister.

Character. Napoleon III was an enigmatic figure who retained the conspiratorial style of his early years. He liked to govern through a small number of ministers whom he knew well, men like Morny, Fould, Persigny, and Rouher; they were responsible individually to him and never formed a coherent cabinet. He often kept ministers in the dark about his policy and liked to spring surprises on them and on the country. It was typical of him that he was influenced both by his Roman Catholic and conservative Spanish wife, the Empress Eugénie, and by his anticlerical and liberal cousin, Prince Napoleon.

Economic Policy. In contrast to the laissez-faire theory of earlier governments, Napoleon III believed that the state should play an active part in the economy. During his reign France underwent intense economic development, particularly in banking, railways, heavy industry and textiles, land reclamation, and urbanization. Paris was replanned and provided with a new street system, public parks, and modern drainage and water supply. Napoleon also took steps to foster the expansion of French and international trade, reversing the prevailing protectionism. He negotiated a series of commercial treaties, incorporating a measure of tariff reduction, with nearly all the countries of Europe, starting with England in 1860. This policy was not popular with the unadventurous industrial and agricultural interests in France and did much to turn them against the regime.

THE BETTMANN ARCHIVE

Napoleon III

Foreign Policy. Napoleon made France an active colonial power. He was the first French sovereign to visit Algeria, where he showed special concern for the interests of the native inhabitants. French protectorates were established in Cambodia in 1863 and by 1867 Cochin China (South Vietnam) was annexed.

Napoleon's foreign policy was often farsighted. He actively supported the claims of such repressed nations as Rumania and Italy to self-determination. France's participation with England in the Crimean War (1854–56) against Russia preserved the Ottoman empire and restored France to the rank of a great power. In 1859 France again went to war, to champion Italian independence against Austria. After Austria had been defeated and France had gained Nice and Savoy in reward, the progress of Italian unification became a source of embarrassment to Napoleon as it threatened the temporal power of the pope and thus stirred up Roman Catholic opposition at home. The unsuccessful Mexican expedition (1862–67) and France's helpless neutrality in the Austro-Prussian War of 1866 further discredited the regime. The mishandling of the question of the Hohenzollern candidacy to the Spanish throne and the consequent impetuous declaration of war on Prussia in July, 1870, finally destroyed it. The French army, badly equipped, badly organized, and badly led, was forced to surrender at Sedan. Napoleon III was taken prisoner and the empire was overthrown in Paris (September). After a long illness, Napoleon died in England in January, 1873. STEPHEN WILSON

BIBLIOG.–M. Blanchard, *Le Second Empire* (1950); J. P. T. Bury, *Napoleon III and the Second Empire* (1964); J. M. Thompson, *Louis Napoleon and the Second Empire* (1954); R. L. Williams, *The World of Napoleon III, 1851–1870* (1957).

NAPOLEON, EUGENE LOUIS JEAN JOSEPH, 1856–79, known as the prince imperial, the only son of Napoleon III and the empress Eugénie, born in Paris. He was with his father at Saarbrück at the outbreak of the Franco-Prussian War, but when the war went against France he was sent to England. He attended the Royal Academy at Woolwich (1872–75) and volunteered his services at the outbreak of the Zulu War, during which he was killed in an ambush.

NAPO RIVER, rises near Cotopaxi Volcano in the Andes Mountains, N central Ecuador, and flows generally E into Peru and SE to Francisco de Orellana where it joins the Amazon River. It is about 550 miles long. The Coca and Aguarico rivers are northern tributaries and the Curaray River merges with the Napo on the south.

NARA, city, Japan, W central Honshu, capital of Nara Prefecture, 20 miles E of Osaka. Nara is one of the chief cultural and religious centers of Japan, and is an industrial city as well, with factories that produce writing brushes, ink, lacquer ware, and diverse novelties. It is also the seat of several universities. Nara was the capital of Japan from 710 to 784, and several museums in the city (grouped around a large deer park) contain valuable collections of historical and cultural objects dating from that period.

NARASINHA, in Hindu mythology, the fourth incarnation of Vishnu, in the form of a man-lion. Vishnu assumed the half-man, half-lion incarnation in order to slay the demon Hiranyakasipu.

NARAYANGANJ, city, E Pakistan, Dacca District; on a tributary of the Meghna River; 12 miles SSE of Dacca. Narayanganj is the river port for Dacca and the two cities are connected by a highway and a railroad. Narayanganj is a trade center for jute, rice, fish, and oilseeds. Industries include milling of jute, rice, sugar, cotton, and the manufacture of leather goods and footwear. (For population, see Pakistan map in Atlas.)

NARBADA RIVER, also Narmada, central India; rises 108 miles ESE of Jabalpur in Madhya Pradesh State and flows generally W past Mandla, Jabalpur, and Hoshangabad and WSW to Broach in Gujarat State, where it forms a long estuary of the Gulf of Cambay of the Arabian Sea; length 750 miles. Much of its course is in the valley between the Vindhya and Satpura mountain ranges. The river is navigable for seagoing vessels for some 60 miles during part of the year. The Narbada is the traditional boundary between Hindustan and the Deccan region. It is a sacred Hindu stream with many pilgrimage sites and bathing ghats along its banks. Called Namados in ancient times, it was also known as the Nerbudda.

NARBONNE, city, S France, Aude Department; 5 miles from the Gulf of Lions, 120 miles W of Marseille. Narbonne lies in the rich plain of the Aude River. It is a center for trade in wine, liquors, honey, and leather. Industries include brick and tile making, uranium and sulfur refining, distilling, and milling grain. The Robine Canal divides Narbonne into old and new sections. Landmarks are the archbishops' palace, which houses a collection of paintings, ceramics, and pottery; the unfinished thirteenth-century Cathedral of St. Just; and the churches of St. Paul Serge and St. Sebastian. The town antedates Roman occupation. It was the site of Narbo Martius, the first Roman colony established in Gaul (118 B.C.), and was occupied successively by Visigoths, Saracens, and Franks. Narbonne became part of France in 1507. (For population, see France map in Atlas.)

NARCISSUS, died A.D. 54, freedman secretary of the Roman emperor Claudius I. A trusted figure at court, he acquired a fortune and considerable influence over the emperor. He was at least indirectly responsible for the death of Claudius's third wife, Messalina, and for this service was made a quaestor by the emperor in A.D. 48. After Claudius's death **in** A.D. 54, however, Narcissus was imprisoned by Claudius's successor, Nero, and either died by his

AGRACI-ART REFERENCE BUREAU

Detail of *Echo and Narcissus* by Poussin (Louvre)

own hand or was murdered at the instigation of Agrippina the Younger, Claudius's fourth wife.

NARCISSUS, in Greek mythology, an extremely beautiful young man, the son of the river god Cephissus and the nymph Leiriope. Proud of his own beauty, Narcissus rejected all his lovers, among them the nymph Echo, who lived the rest of her life in the woods, her form fading from grief until all that remained was her voice—an echo. Nemesis, holding Narcissus responsible for Echo's fate, punished him: while he drank at a certain fountain, Narcissus was made to see his own image and to fall in love with its beauty. So intense was his self-love that he pined away and was transformed into the flower that bears his name.

NARCISSUS, a genus of spring-blooming bulb plants of the amaryllis family, Amaryllidaceae. *Narcissus* is native to central Europe, the Mediterranean region, and eastward to China and Japan.

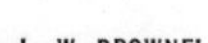

Narcissus poeticus

L. W. BROWNELL

The plants rise from truncated bulbs to a height of 1 to 2 feet. Long, narrow leaves grow to almost the full height of the plant. The flower is the most distinctive feature of the plant, since the axis is at a right angle to the stem. *Narcissus* blossoms vary from white to yellow, and some varieties range to pink. Six petals comprise a saucerlike perianth, from which arises a corona, or crown, that is cup- or trumpet-shaped. The shape of the corona determines the three groups of cultivated *Narcissus*. The first is the true daffodil and has a trumpetlike crown; the English daffodil, *N. pseudo-narcissus*, has a large, single, yellow flower at the tip of the stem. The second group comprises the chalice flowers. *N. incomparabilis*, a plant typical of this group, is considered by many botanists to be a hybrid of *N. pseudo-narcissus* and *N. poeticus*. It often produces flowers with a light-yellow or white perianth and a yellow or orange corona. The true narcissus is in the third group and has a characteristic short crown. The poet's narcissus, *N. poeticus*, is typical. Flowers of this group are sometimes called jonquils. *Narcissus* plants grow in turfy loam out of doors, and have grown well in the Pacific Northwest and in Virginia where bulbs are raised commercially. The plants may be grown indoors in bowls containing water and gravel. See DAFFODIL.

NARCOLEPSY, a fairly uncommon, chronic disorder of the sleep mechanism in both males and females, characterized by a sudden and uncontrollable desire for sleep during the daytime. The disorder ranges in severity from mild, almost normal drowsiness during boring or soporific situations to incapacitation; episodes last from a few seconds to about 20 minutes, and the victim is easily rousable. Narcolepsy may be caused by lesions in the hypothalamus (a part of the brain concerned with control and coordination of some fundamental physiologic processes and emotions) due to infection, tumor, or injury, but in some cases there is no apparent cause (idiopathic narcolepsy). About 75 per cent of narcoleptics are also afflicted with cataplexy, a sudden, brief, complete muscular relaxation associated with emotion. Narcolepsy usually occurs insidiously during adolescence, and the symptoms persist if not treated. Stimulants are used—coffee or tea with meals plus doses of methyl phenidate or dextroamphetamine. See BRAIN; HYPOTHALAMUS; SLEEP.

NARCOTIC, any of a class of habit-forming drugs that relieve pain and in sufficient dosage produce sleep. Unlike general anesthetics, narcotics relieve pain before, and often without, producing sleep. (See ANESTHESIA.) Their sleep-producing effects differentiate them from analgesics, which also relieve pain. (See ANALGESIC.) Barbiturates sometimes are considered narcotics because they depress the central nervous system in much the same way as do narcotics, but they do not have the pain-relieving properties of narcotics. (See BARBITURATE.) Federal narcotics legislation is directed chiefly against marijuana and misuse of opium, cocaine, and synthetic opiates.

Narcotics of the opium group (see OPIUM; HEROIN; CODEINE; MORPHINE) depress the central nervous system by acting upon sensory nerve cells in the cerebrum of the brain to relieve sensations of pain without affecting the motor nerves. (See BRAIN.) They also act on the medulla of the brain, depressing the respiratory centers. (See RESPIRATION.) Like opiates, marijuana, a derivative of the hemp plant, also depresses the central nervous system. See MARIJUANA.

Cocaine, a derivative of the coca plant (see ERYTHROXYLUM), stimulates the central nervous system instead of depressing it. This drug blocks nerve conduction when it is applied locally; it is therefore used as a local anesthetic. Initial stimulation of the central nervous system is followed by depression, first of the cerebrum and, with increasing dosages, of vital medullary centers, until death from respiratory failure may result. See DRUG ADDICTION.

TRAFFIC AND CONTROL

The importing of opium for smoking was prohibited in the United States by a federal law passed in 1909, but basic federal legislation upon which the U.S. system of narcotics control rests is the Harrison Act of 1914. That act imposed a federal tax on products of opium (heroin and morphine) and of coca leaves (cocaine), and required all persons handling these drugs to be registered and to keep appropriate records. The use of narcotics was limited by the act to authorized medical persons "in good faith" and "in the course of professional practice only," but these phrases were not defined in the law. The Harrison Act is a revenue measure, and is enforced by the U.S. Treasury Department. It has been progressively amended to cover new synthetic drugs that are habit forming in the same sense as is opium, and federal legislative acts since 1914 have been designed to strengthen, extend, or supplement its provisions. The Narcotic Drug Import and Export Act of 1922 tightened controls over imports and exports, and specified that possession of drugs by unauthorized persons was a criminal offense. The Narcotic Hospital Law of 1929 established U.S. public health service hospitals for research and for retention and treatment of addicts at Fort Worth, Tex., and at Lexington, Ky.; and the Marijuana Tax Act of 1937 brought marijuana under the same federal control that the Harrison Act had imposed on opiates and cocaine. In addition the federal government sponsored the Uniform Narcotic Drug Act, drafted in 1932 by the National Conference of Commissioners on Uniform State Laws, that places state police power behind adequate uniform control measures.

Enforcement of the Harrison Act was challenged by some members of the medical profession when the Treasury Department's interpretation denied doctors the right to prescribe narcotics for treatment of drug addicts, and between 1919 and 1924 the U.S. Supreme Court handed down a number of inconsistent decisions. In the Linder Case in 1924 the court affirmed that medical prescription of narcotics for addicts was not in itself a crime and that treatment of addicts was a medical matter. In 1962, the court ruled that a California statute making addiction per se a crime was unconstitutional.

Illicit Drug Traffic. Addicts not undergoing treatment are prevented by enforcement of the Harrison Act from obtaining supplies through drugstores and doctors, and many turn to the illicit drug traffic, which developed on a national scale shortly after World War I. This traffic is a dominant factor in the spread of drug addiction. The operators of illicit drug traffic, usually nonaddicts, cannot easily be apprehended or convicted on narcotics charges, and the impact of law enforcement usually falls upon the addict or the small distributor. No legal distinction is made between peddlers who are addicts and those who are not, although addicts are declared to be sick persons.

Available figures indicate that there are more drug addicts in the United States than in all other Western nations combined, and rising rates of addiction after World War II, notably among young persons, aroused public indignation and concern. Resulting federal legislation in 1951 more than doubled the average prison sentence of federal offenders; it also authorized substantial increase in the number of federal narcotics agents. Most states and many large cities enacted similar laws, but the tendency of local legislation after 1951 was to treat addiction as a crime, disregarding the problem of curbing the illicit traffic which promotes addiction. After 1951 the number of narcotics cases at the federal level declined but sharp increases at the local level brought the national total to record heights. Following a series of congressional hearings and investigations in 1956 further increases in federal penalties were authorized, including the death penalty in some cases.

Minority opinion has attributed high and rising rates of drug addiction in the United States to failure of the punitive approach, and has argued in favor of control that legalizes medical prescription of drugs for addicts. Such plans have long been used in European countries.

International Control of narcotics includes limitation of narcotics production to legitimate medical and scientific needs, control of production and distribution of such drugs, and suppression of illicit drug traffic. Basic international agreements were drawn up at The Hague in 1912 and Geneva in 1925 and 1931; these were implemented by the League of Nations and later by the United Nations Organization. Four bodies of the UN were established to regulate and supervise legitimate narcotic drug industry: the Commission on Narcotic Drugs; the Permanent Central Opium Board; the Drug Supervisory Body; and the Expert Committee on Drugs Liable to Produce Addiction, a branch of the World Health Organization. See CRIME; JUVENILE DELINQUENCY; PRISON.

ALFRED R. LINDESMITH

BIBLIOG.–Harry J. Anslinger and William F. Tompkins, *Traffic in Narcotics* (1953); David P. Ausubel, *Drug Addiction: Physiological, Psychological and Sociological Aspects* (1958); Jacob A. Buckwalter, *Merchants of Misery* (1961); Robert S. De Ropp, *Drugs and the Mind* (1957); Dorothy L. C. C. Tompkins, comp., *Drug Addiction: A Bibliography* (1960).

NARINO, department, SW Colombia; bounded by the states of Cauca on the N and Putumayo on the E, by Ecuador on the S, and the Pacific Ocean on the W; area 12,571 sq. mi.; pop. (1962 est.) 620,670. Nariño is bisected by the Andes Mountains; a coastal plain lies to the west, and part of the Amazon Basin to the east. The population is concentrated in the intermontane valleys, where Pasto, the capital, is located. The chief products are bananas and coffee.

NARRAGANSET, a North American Indian tribe of the Algonquian linguistic family formerly living in Rhode Island. The early alliance of the Narraganset with the English and their neutrality during the Pequot War in 1637 are in part attributed to the influence of Roger Williams. The Narraganset, who numbered about 4,000 in 1600, were nearly exterminated by the white settlers during King Philip's War in 1675–76. Some of the survivors joined various distant tribes, while others were allowed to settle among the eastern Niantic. That tribe, enlarged by Narraganset refugees, took the name Narraganset. In 1788 many members of the new Narraganset tribe united with the Brothertons in New York. The tribe later intermarried with whites and Negroes and lost its identity.

Essentially forest hunters, the Narraganset also cultivated the soil, raising corn, squash, and beans. Their dwellings were mostly bark huts, and their clothing included skin trousers, leggings, and soft-soled moccasins for men, skin skirts and robes for women. Each village had its own chief, responsible to a supreme chief.

NARRAGANSETT, town, S Rhode Island, Washington County; on Rhode Island Sound and U.S. highway 1; 28 miles S of Providence. Narragansett is primarily a summer resort, although there is some farming and fishing. The town includes the village of Narragansett Pier. It is named for the former Indian tribe of the area. Settled in 1675, Narragansett was separated from South Kingstown in 1888 and incorporated as a municipality in 1901. Pop. (1960) 3,444.

NARRAGANSETT BAY, inlet of the Atlantic Ocean, in Rhode Island immediately N of Providence. Maximum north-south and east-west distances are 29 and 16 miles respectively. Narragansett Bay has several islands, the largest being Rhode, Conanicut, and Prudence. Newport is at the entrance to the bay.

NARROWS, THE, a strait connecting upper and lower New York bays, separating Staten Island and Long Island. Maximum north-south and east-west distances are 3 and 2 miles respectively.

NARSES, 478?–?573, general of the Byzantine Empire under Emperor Justinian I, was of Armenian descent, born in that part of Armenia ruled by Persia. A eunuch, he entered service in the emperor's household and became chamberlain and then treasurer. He helped to put down the Nika Riots in Constantinople, 532, thereby saving the emperor his throne, and in 538 was sent to Italy as joint commander, with Belisarius, of the imperial army. The two generals quarreled and Narses was recalled to Constantinople, 539; but after Belisarius fell from official favor, 549, Narses was appointed sole commander in Italy. He defeated the Gothic King Totila, 552, and his successor, Teja, 553; retook Rome; and completed the imperial reconquest of Italy by driving off an invasion of Alamanni and Franks, 553–55. Narses was appointed prefect of Italy, 554, and took up residence at Ravenna. Charged with avarice by his subjects, he was recalled by Emperor Justin II, 567.

NARTHEX, in architecture, a vestibule or porch extending across the main entrance of a basilica or church, either immediately inside or outside the façade. Usually it is only in early Christian churches that such vestibules are known as narthexes; later they were called porches or porticoes. Penitents and catechumens were not admitted beyond the inner narthex.

NARVA, city, U.S.S.R., NE Estonian Soviet Socialist Republic; on the Narva River; 7 miles from the Gulf of Finland and 85 miles SW of Leningrad. The Kreenholm Cotton Mill (1857), once one of the largest in Europe, is at Narva; the city also has food processing plants and sawmills. Most of the buildings in the old city were destroyed during World War II; a new town was constructed on the west bank of the river. The Ivangorod Fortress (1492), built by Ivan III, is on the east bank of the river in the Russian Soviet Federated Socialist Republic. A hydroelectric station completed in 1955 immediately south of Narva has formed a large reservoir on the Narva River. Narva was founded in 1223 and for a time belonged to Denmark. In 1346 the town fell to the Teutonic Knights. The fortress built by the Danes in the thirteenth century was destroyed in World War II. Narva was won for Russia by Peter the Great in 1704. Pop. (1956 est.) 30,000. THEODORE SHABAD

NARVIK, city, N Norway, Nordland County; on the Ofotfjord; 95 miles SSW of Tromsö, with which it is connected by highway. Narvik is the terminus of an electric railroad from Sweden. With a harbor ice-free the year round, Narvik is a shipping center for iron ore mined in the Kiruna and Gällivare fields in Sweden. Pop. (1950) 10,944.

NARWHAL, a small arctic whale belonging to the family *Monodontidae*. The narwhal, *Monodon monoceros*, is about 16 feet long. It has a stubby body, mottled gray above and white below; a laterally flattened tail; and a pair of small pectoral fins that provide locomotion. The narwhal's head is blunt and its eyes and mouth are small. The only teeth in the upper jaw are a pair of canines; in the male the left tooth usually develops into a clockwise-twisted tusk that may reach a length of 9 feet. During mating season this tusk may be used as a weapon for fighting, but seems to serve no other purpose as the animal's usual disposition is playful. The cow bears one or two calves a year. Narwhals swim in small schools, bulls apart from cows. These whales occur primarily in and near Lancaster Sound, north of Baffin Island. Narwhals feed on fish, shrimp, and cuttlefish.

NARYN RIVER, U.S.S.R., in the Kirghiz and Uzbek Soviet Socialist republics; length about 450 miles. The Naryn rises from glacial formations on northern slopes of the Tien Mountains and flows in a westerly direction until it merges near Balykchi with the Kara River to form the Syr River.

THEODORE SHABAD

NASEBY, parish, England, in Northamptonshire, 12 miles NE of Rugby. The decisive battle of the civil war of 1642–46 was fought nearby on June 14, 1645, when the newly organized New Model army under Oliver Cromwell and Lord Thomas Fairfax inflicted a crushing defeat on the forces of Charles I. The Royalist army never fully recovered, but the New Model army set a pattern of discipline and training that formed the basis of the British regular army. Pop. (1951) 400. See ENGLAND, History, *The Civil War*.

NASH, JOHN, 1752–1835, English architect and civic planner, was born in London. Among his outstanding achievements were the designing of Regent Street, the Regent Park District, and the Haymarket Theater and the redesigning of Buckingham House (later Buckingham Palace). An adherent of the neoclassic Regency style, Nash pioneered in using stucco for the façades of civic structures.

NASH, OGDEN, 1902– , U.S. writer noted for satirical verse characterized by odd rhymes and peculiar inversions, was born Frederic Ogden Nash in Rye, N.Y. After a year at Harvard, 1920–21, he was successively a teacher at St. George's School, Newport, R.I., a bond salesman, an advertising writer, a manuscript reader, and a member of *The New Yorker* editorial staff. His books include *Hard Lines* (1931), *The Primrose Path* (1935), *I'm a Stranger Here Myself* (1938), *The Face Is Familiar* (1940), *Many Long Years Ago* (1945), *Versus* (1949), *Parents Keep Out* (1951), and *The Private Dining Room* (1953). He was coauthor with S. J. Perelman and Kurt Weill of the musical comedy *One Touch of Venus* (1943).

NASH, RICHARD, known as Beau Nash, 1674–1762, English gambler, was born in Swansea, Wales, studied law, and became master of ceremonies at Bath, 1705, where he abolished dueling, organized the amusements, and established himself as social arbiter. After gambling was abolished by Parliament, 1745, the resort pensioned him. He was noted for his excellent manners and taste and for his extravagance.

NASH, THOMAS, 1567–1601, English writer, was born in Lowestoft, England. Nash (or Nashe) was educated at St. John's College, Cambridge, but how long he stayed or whether he received a degree is unknown. By 1588 he had settled down in London to the precarious existence of the literary hack. A formidable controversialist, his talent for invective and abuse brought him few friends. Nash devoted his *The Anatomie of Absurditie* (1589) to attacking writers of lesser ability than his own. In a scurrilous exchange of abuse between Puritan pamphleteers and the apologists of the established church, which was known as the Martin Marprelate Controversy, Nash vigorously defended the church; his shots were wide enough to involve side issues and personalities and eventually Nash's share of the controversy became a private feud with the learned Gabriel Harvey, whom Nash demolished effectively in *Have With You to Saffron Walden* (1596).

As a poet Nash is less memorable, and his major claim to distinction in playwriting was his share in the composition of *The Isle of Dogs* (1597), a play that caused him much trouble with the authorities. His most successful work was *The Unfortunate Traveller* (1594), an energetic picaresque novel which in excellency and manner anticipates the work of Daniel Defoe. Among his other works are *Pierce Penilesse His Supplication to the Divell* (1592) and *Christs Teares over Jerusalem* (1593).

NASHUA, city, SE New Hampshire, one of the two seats of Hillsboro County, at the confluence of the Merrimack and Nashua rivers; on the Boston and Maine Railroad and U.S. highway 3; 31 miles S of Concord. It is the second-largest city in New Hampshire. Manufactures of the city include textiles, wood and paper products, woolen blankets, shoes and boots, and hardware. Nashua is the seat of Rivier College. The first permanent settlement was made in 1656 and in 1673 the town was incorporated as Dunstable, but in 1803 was named Nashua for an Indian tribe residing there. A charter granted by George II, 1747, is in the Nashua Public Library. Elias Howe perfected his sewing machine in Nashua, and the first waxed paper wrapper for bread was made there. Pop. (1960) 39,096.

NASHVILLE, city, SW Arkansas, seat of Howard County; on the Graysonia, Nashville and Ashdown and the Missouri Pacific railroads; 40 miles NNE of Texarkana and 70 miles SW of Hot Springs National Park. It is a shipping point for the surrounding agricultural area. Pop. (1960) 3,579.

NASHVILLE, city, S central Georgia, seat of Berrien County; on the Georgia and Florida Railroad and U.S. highway 129; 30 miles N of Valdosta. It is most important as a tobacco market but also has canneries and light manufacturing. Nashville was incorporated in 1892. Pop. (1960) 4,070.

NASHVILLE, city, S Illinois, seat of Washington County; on the Louisville and Nashville and Missouri-Illinois railroads and U.S. highway 460; 50 miles ESE of East St. Louis. Nashville is in an agricultural region. There are bituminous coal mines nearby. The city was incorporated in 1853. Pop. (1960) 2,606.

NASHVILLE, town, S central Indiana, seat of Brown County; 19 miles E of Bloomington. Nashville serves tourists visiting the scenic region (the most notable feature of which is Brown County State Park) in which the town is located. The town has an art museum. Pop. (1960) 489.

NASHVILLE, town, E central North Carolina, seat of Nash County; on the Atlantic Coast Line Railroad and U.S. highway 64; 10 miles W of Rocky Mount. It is located in a tobacco and timber region. Nashville was named for the Revolutionary War patriot Francis Nash. Pop. (1960) 1,423.

NASHVILLE, city, N central Tennessee, capital of the state and seat of Davidson County; on the Cumberland River, the Louisville and Nashville and the Tennessee Central railroads, and U.S. highways 31, 41, 70, and 431; a scheduled airline stop; 113 miles NW of Chattanooga. As the state's second-largest city (after Memphis) and a port of entry, Nashville is the commercial, communications, and educational center of central Tennessee. The city has railroad repair shops, printing and publishing houses, meat plants, flour and feed mills, stoneworks, and foundries. The principal manufactures are rayon, shoes, hosiery, cellophane, tobacco products, clothing, stoves, fertilizer, bricks, cement, cotton goods, lumber, chemicals, barges, heaters, and surgical instruments. Nashville is the site of six major institutions of higher learning: Fisk University, founded 1865; Vanderbilt University, 1872; David Lipscomb College, 1891; George Peabody College for Teachers, 1875; Scarritt College for Christian Workers, 1924; and The Tennessee Agricultural and Industrial State University, 1909. All but the last named are under private control.

TENN. CONSERVATION DEPT.

Tennessee's capitol, in Nashville, located on Cedar Knob, faces beautifully landscaped Memorial Square. Statues of Sam Davis and Andrew Jackson are located on the grounds.

The state capitol, situated on Nashville's highest hill, was built in 1855 in the Greek Revival style of architecture. Within the capitol grounds are the tombs of Pres. James K. Polk and his wife. Other buildings of interest within the capitol area are those housing the Tennessee supreme court, the state library and archives, and offices of the various state departments. One of these buildings, containing an auditorium and several museums, was built as a World War I memorial. A reproduction of the Parthenon, built in 1897, stands in Centennial Park. Also in the city is a replica (constructed 1930) of Fort Nashborough, the original settlement of Nashville; and a few miles east of the city is the Hermitage, Pres. Andrew Jackson's home and burial place. Rebuilt several times by Jackson, the mansion's present version dates from 1835.

Nashville was founded in 1779 as Fort Nashborough, the central one of seven forts built along the Cumberland River. In 1784 the settlement was renamed Nashville and incorporated as a town; it became a city in 1806. In 1843 it was made capital of the state. As the northern terminus of the Natchez Trace, and with the coming of the steamboats, Nashville prospered as a trade center. The city was captured by Union forces in 1862 and was used as a Union base until the end of the Civil War. On Dec. 15 and 16, 1864, in the Battle of Nashville, Confederate troops under Gen. John B. Hood were defeated by Union forces led by Gen. George H. Thomas. The post-Civil War depression in Nashville was followed by improvements in transportation, the establishment of numerous new industries, and the growth of the city as an educational center. Pop. (1960) 170,874.

NASHVILLE CONVENTION, a meeting of delegates from nine southern states held in June and November of 1850, at Nashville, Tenn., to oppose legislation restricting slavery in the territories. The convention considered resolutions stating that the territories belonged to the people of the United

States, who had the right to migrate to them accompanied by their slaves, and that the U.S. Congress "must" protect them from doing so. The resolutions had no effect in law and so changed nothing. See COMPROMISE OF 1850; WILMOT PROVISO.

NASIK, city, W India, Maharashtra state; capital of Nasik district; on the Godavari River; about 100 miles NE of Bombay. Nasik is a Hindu pilgrimage site, and temples and shrines line the riverbanks. The city is the location of a college affiliated with Poona University. Brassware and copperware are manufactured. Outside the city are Buddhist caves dating from the first century B.C. to the sixth century A.D. (For population, see India map in Atlas.)

NASMYTH, ALEXANDER, 1758–1840, Scottish portrait and landscape painter and architect, was born in Edinburgh. He studied under Allan Ramsay and was for a time his assistant in London. In Edinburgh, after 1778, Nasmyth won renown as a landscapist, but he is most famous for his portrait, now in Scotland's National Gallery, of Scotland's famous poet Robert Burns, who was his close friend. Nasmyth's son Patrick (1787–1831), also a landscapist, surpassed his father in this genre. Another son, James (1808–90), invented the steam hammer (patented 1842) and other machine tools.

NASSAU, historical region in W Germany, since 1949 a part of the German Federal Republic. The county of Nassau was established in 1160 with the town of Nassau as its capital. The Nassau Dynasty divided into two branches in 1255 when Otto, younger brother of the ruling Walram II, founded the Ottonian branch that later became the Dutch branch of the House of Orange. Nassau became a principality in 1688, and was enlarged and made a duchy and a member of the Confederation of the Rhine in 1806. Following the Congress of Vienna in 1815, the Duchy of Nassau became a part of the German Confederation and participated in the *Zollverein*, a customs union organized in 1833 among the German states. In 1866, Nassau sided with Austria in the war between Austria and Prussia for control of the German states. After the Prussian victory, it was annexed to Prussia and became part of the province of Hesse-Nassau. After World War II, the region was under U. S. military administration until 1949, when it became part of Hesse, a state in the German Federal Republic.

NASSAU, city, West Indies, NE New Providence Island; capital of the Bahama Islands; 185 miles ESE of Miami. It is the principal city and commercial center of the Bahamas, and is a winter resort famous for its beaches and semitropical climate. The city's harbor can accommodate ships of up to 24 feet draft. It is a shipping center for sponges, tomatoes, sisal, and citrus fruit. Founded by the British late in the seventeenth century, Nassau frequently was attacked and plundered both by pirates and the French and Spanish navies. (For population, see Bahama Islands map in Atlas.)

NASSER, GAMAL ABDEL, 1918–70, first president of the United Arab Republic (Egypt), was born in Beni Mor, Asyût province, Upper Egypt. He was educated at the Royal Military Academy in Cairo and was commissioned in the army. During the 1940's, Nasser was the leader of a group of officers known as the Free Officers movement, dedicated to the cause of Egyptian nationalism. He fought in the Palestine War of 1948–49, and was severely wounded. In 1952, Nasser helped to organize the coup that overthrew King Farouk I and that replaced him with a military junta in which Maj. Gen. Mohammed Naguib was premier and Nasser was deputy premier. The following year a republic was established. Naguib was considered too authoritarian a leader, however, and in 1954, Nasser arranged his ouster, assuming the premiership himself. In the same year he secured the withdrawal of British forces from the Suez Canal Zone.

In 1956 Nasser was elected president of Egypt.

UPI

Gamal Abdel Nasser

Shortly afterward the United States withdrew the offer of a loan to build a huge Nile River dam. Nasser in turn nationalized the Suez Canal Company; in retaliation, British and French troops landed in the Canal area and Israeli forces advanced into the Sinai Peninsula. A halt in the fighting and the withdrawal of foreign troops were effected under United Nations auspices. Eventually an Egyptian canal authority was established, which operated the canal and collected its revenues. Nasser emerged from the incident as the foremost champion of the Arab peoples. To the Arab world, he had defied the Western powers, and won. Long an advocate of Arab unity, in 1958 he created the United Arab Republic, uniting Syria and Egypt. A month later, Yemen joined the union. With Nasser as president, the union lasted until 1961, when Syria seceded.

Throughout his rule, Nasser opposed Israel, charging that it was an aggressive state occupying Arab lands. Arab-Israeli tension again erupted in the Six-Day War of June, 1967, in which Egypt was swiftly defeated. Israeli forces overran the Sinai Peninsula as far as the east bank of the Suez Canal. The Soviet Union later replaced most of the arms that the Egyptians lost in the war.

In his domestic policies, which he called Arab Socialism, Nasser instituted important land reforms and nationalized most of Egypt's industry. The construction of the Aswan High Dam, with Soviet aid, begun in 1960 and completed 10 years later, was a major accomplishment.

BIBLIOG.–Peter Mansfield, *Nasser's Egypt* (1965); Keith Wheelock, *Nasser's New Egypt* (1960).

NAST, THOMAS, 1840–1902, U.S. cartoonist and illustrator, was born in Landau, Bavaria, but was taken to the United States at the age of six. He studied art in New York City with Theodore Kaufmann, and at the National Academy of Design. After 1857 he contributed cartoons and drawings to *Frank Leslie's Illustrated Newspaper*, *Harper's Weekly*, *New York Illustrated News*, *Illustrated London News*, and other periodicals. He became a staff artist for *Harper's* in 1862. During the Civil War his drawings stimulated patriotism in the North; Pres. Abraham Lincoln called him "our best recruiting sergeant." After the war Nast devoted himself to political cartooning, and crusaded against the corrupt Tweed political machine in New York City; his cartoons played a large part in the eventual overthrow of Tweed. He created a ferocious cartoon tiger to symbolize Tammany Hall (the New York Democratic political machine), an elephant to represent the Republican party, and a donkey to represent the Democratic party. In 1886, he ended his connection with *Harper's* but continued to contribute to other periodicals, and in 1892–93 published *Nast's Weekly*. In 1902, he was appointed U.S. consul general at Guayaquil, Ecuador, and died there of yellow fever. In addition to contributing to periodicals, Nast illustrated a number of books, among them Petroleum V. Nasby's (David Ross Locke) *Swingin' Round the Cirkle* (1867) and *Ekkoes from Kentucky* (1868); Mary Dodge's *Hans Brinker* (1867); and Mark Vale's *Humpty Dumpty* (1868).

F. J. MEINE

Self-Caricature by Thomas Nast

NASTURTIUM, a climbing herbaceous plant belonging to *Tropaeolum*, the only genus of the nasturtium family, *Tropaeolaceae;* also a hardy aquatic cress, *Nasturtium officinale*, a member of the mustard family, *Cruciferae*. The garden nasturtium, *T. majus*, is an annual, with oval- or kidney-shaped leaves about 2 inches across and yellow-to-orange or red flowers. Nasturtiums grow in warm, sunny climates and are native from Mexico to Chile. A dwarf variety, *T. minus*, is not a climber and is used as ground cover. The watercress, *N. officinale*, is a floating or creeping, many-branched biennial (see CRESS).

NATAL, city, NE Brazil, capital of Rio Grande do Norte state; on the Atlantic Ocean, at the mouth of the Potengi River; 161 miles N of Recife. It is a highway, railroad, and international airline junction, and the chief port of the state. It sends cotton, sugar, salt, and hides to other coastal cities. Natal's industries include cotton mills and salt refineries. The city was founded in the 1590's by the Portuguese. It was occupied by the Dutch in 1633–54. During World War II, the United States enlarged nearby Parnamirim Airfield, where planes were ferried to Freetown and Dakar in Africa. Pop. (1960) 196,370.

NATAL, smallest but most densely populated province of the Republic of South Africa; bounded on the N by Transvaal Province, Swaziland, and Mozambique, on the E by the Indian Ocean, on the S by Cape Province, and on the W by Basutoland and Orange Free State; area 33,578 sq. mi.; pop. (1960) 2,933,447. The province extends about 350 miles along the ocean and about 160 miles inland.

Physical Factors. From the Drakensberg Mountains Natal descends toward the coast in three natural divisions: heights, plateau area, and coastal plain. The coastal plain, narrow in the south, widens into the Makatini Flats of Zululand in the north. Of

In Zululand, situated within Natal Province, women and children gather straw for their thatched huts, while a Zulu native painstakingly stretches hides for a shield.

INFORMATION SERVICE OF SOUTH AFRICA

UNION OF SOUTH AFRICA GOVT. INFORMATION OFFICE

Durban's sea front has an imposing array of modern flats and hotels. The city, also known as Port Natal, is one of the most important South African commercial centers.

several lakes in that section, St. Lucia is the largest. There are many rivers in Natal, but not even the largest, the Tugela, is navigable. The warm Mozambique Current gives the coastal area a moderate subtropical climate, with average monthly temperatures ranging between 43.7° and 88.7°F (at Durban); in the central plateau region the extremes are 34.5° and 98.4° (at Pietermaritzburg). Average annual rainfall in Natal is generally between 35 and 40 inches. The coolest and driest weather is usually in June and July.

Social Factors. The native Africans in Natal are Bantus, of whom there were 2,155,824 in 1960. In the same year there were 394,237 "Asians," mostly Indians; 340,293 "Europeans," many of them of English descent; and 43,093 "Coloreds" of racially-mixed descent. Natal's "Asian" population is larger than that in any of the other provinces.

The capital of Natal is Pietermaritzburg, but the chief city in other respects is Durban. All of Natal's other urban centers are very much smaller. Among these are Ladysmith, Newcastle, Vryheid, Dundee, Glencoe, and Estcourt.

Most of the Natalese people adhere to one or another of the "animistic" religions of the Hottentots, Bushmen, and Bantus. The "Asiatics," for the most part, are of the Hindu faith. The Dutch Reformed, Methodist, and (principally) Anglican churches are well represented among Natalese of European descent.

There are technical colleges and branches of Natal University at Durban and Pietermaritzburg, Sultan College at Durban, and a college of agriculture at Cedara—all under federal control. Statistically, the vast majority of schools in Natal are for non-European children, but most of these provide only the most rudimentary of primary instruction and social indoctrination. For European children there were about 230 primary and secondary schools in 1960.

Economic Factors. The principal occupation in Natal is farming, and the chief product is sugar cane, most of which is grown along the narrow coastal strip; annual production amounts to about one million short tons. Citrus fruits, pineapples, and cotton are grown; corn is the chief cereal crop. Wattle bark, used in tanning, is produced in the interior. Both meat and dairy cattle are raised, as are sheep. Whaling is a major source of employment and income.

The principal mineral product is coal, but chromium, tin, gold, and tungsten are also mined.

Manufacturing is relatively unimportant except for sugar mills at Durban. There are also small iron foundries and plants manufacturing farm machinery, utensils, and leather in Durban and Pietermaritzburg.

Natal's railways, harbors, and air services are operated by the South African Railways and Harbor Administration. The chief rail lines extend northwest from Durban through Pietermaritzburg over the

Drakensberg Mountains to Bloemfontein. Coastal lines run northeast into Zululand. Air service from Durban and the capital connects with the main central and east African airlines.

History. The coast at Durban was sighted by the Portuguese navigator Vasco da Gama in 1497. Natal was visited by the English in 1684, but no European settlement was made until the founding of Durban in 1824. It was reached by the Boers during their great trek, 1835–37. Natal was at war with the Zulus, 1838–40 and with the English, 1840–43; it was made a British colony, 1843, and annexed to the Cape Colony, 1844. Natal was given a separate government in 1845 and was made a separate colony in 1856. It annexed Zululand in 1897 and other districts in the north in 1903; it was the scene of battles during the Boer War, 1899–1902. Natal became an original province of the Union of South Africa in 1910. Since 1896, restrictive measures against the large Indian population have caused recurrent unrest. See UNION OF SOUTH AFRICA; SOUTH AFRICA, REPUBLIC OF.

NATANYA, town, NW Israel; on the Plain of Sharon and the Mediterranean Sea; 18 miles N of Tel Aviv. The town is a seaside resort and an industrial center with diamond-polishing workshops, a tin factory, and a brewery. Natanya, founded in 1929, was named for the U.S. philanthropist Nathan Straus. Pop. (1961 est.) 40,907.

NATCHEZ, a North American Indian tribe, of Muskhogean linguistic stock, which lived near the site of Natchez, Miss. The first record of the Natchez was made by Robert Cavelier, Sieur de La Salle, in 1682; at that time their population was probably 6,000, of which about 1,200 were warriors. The Natchez engaged in agriculture and had a monarchial government that embodied a rigid caste system. They practiced sun worship. Following negotiations by Pierre Lemoyne, Sieur d'Iberville, a mission was established among the Natchez in 1700, and in 1716 his brother Jean Baptiste Lemoyne, Sieur de Bienville, built Fort Rosalie on the site of the present city of Natchez. Except for two minor conflicts, relations between the Natchez and French were friendly until 1729, when the French commandant of Fort Rosalie provoked an uprising in which the Natchez killed 200 whites and destroyed the fort. In 1731, however, the Natchez were overcome by the French and their Indian allies. About 400 Natchez were captured and sold into slavery, and the remainder dispersed. Of these, some merged with the Creek, who later settled at Eufaula, Okla.; most of the others joined the Cherokee nation.

NATCHEZ, city, SW Mississippi, seat of Adams County; on the Mississippi River; on the Illinois Central, the Mississippi Central, the Missouri Pacific, and the Natchez and Southern railroads and U.S. highways 61, 65, 84, and 98; a scheduled airline stop; 89 miles SW of Jackson. Natchez, one of the earliest settlements in Mississippi, and once the center of ante-bellum culture, became a trading and shipping center for cotton and other products of the surrounding agricultural area. Food processing, rubber tires, textiles, and lumber are the most important industries. Rich in traditional Southern atmosphere, Natchez attracts many tourists who visit such places as The Briars, built in 1812, where Varina Howell was married to Jefferson Davis in 1845; the parish house of San Salvador, constructed at the order of the king of Spain in 1786; Mercer House, in which Andrew Jackson once lodged; and King's Tavern, the oldest house in Natchez. These and many ante-bellum homes are open to view each spring during the pilgrimage season.

The city, situated on bluffs high above the Mississippi, was named for the Natchez Indians who once inhabited the region. Land grants were issued as early as 1702, but not until 1716 was a permanent settlement established; in that year Jean Baptiste Lemoyne, Sieur de Bienville, built a fort which he named Rosalie. By the Treaty of Paris, 1763, Natchez passed into the hands of the British, who held

MISS. AGRICULTURAL & INDUSTRIAL BOARD

Dunleith, a stately ante-bellum mansion in Natchez, is one of the many points of interest in the city that is opened to the public during the annually held Natchez Pilgrimage.

the town until 1779. Then the Spanish came into control, but in 1798 American settlers dispossessed the Spaniards and made Natchez the capital of the Territory of Mississippi; it remained the capital until 1802 and was incorporated in 1803. From 1817, when the steamboat was introduced, until the start of the Civil War, Natchez was one of the world's leading cotton ports. In 1863, during the Civil War, the city was captured by Union troops. Pop. (1960) 23,791.

BIBLIOG.–H. T. Kane, *Natchez on the Mississippi* (1947); W. Johnson, *Natchez* (1951); E. L. Bailey, *Look at Natchez* (1953); N. N. Oliver, *This Too Is Natchez* (1953); R. G. Pishel, *Natchez, Museum City of the Old South* (1959).

NATCHEZ TRACE, a migration and trade route connecting the site of Nashville, Tenn., and Natchez, Miss. The route was widened from a narrow Indian trail after the U.S. government obtained land rights from the Chickasaw and Choctaw Indians in 1801. Although Natchez Trace was frequently used by traders and mail carriers traveling north from New Orleans, its primary importance lay in encouraging the settlement and political and economic development of the lower Mississippi Valley. The importance of the Natchez Trace declined with the development of steamship transportation in the 1830's.

NATCHITOCHES, a confederacy of North American Indians, part of the Caddo division, of the Caddoan linguistic stock, who lived near the site of the city of Natchitoches in NW Louisiana. The confederacy included the Doustioni, Ouachita, Yatasi, and Natchitoches Indians. Followers of Robert Cavelier, Sieur de La Salle, described them as a "powerful nation." Although visited by Henry de Tonti, 1690, and by Jean Baptiste Lemoyne, Sieur de Bienville, 1700, a close alliance between Natchitoches and the French did not begin until 1702 when the Natchitoches sought aid after a crop failure. Louis Juchereau de St. Denis, commandant of a French fort at the mouth of the Mississippi, first settled the Natchitoches with the Acolapissa on Lake Pontchartrain, then in 1713–14 relocated them at their old home on the Red River. Fort St. Jean Baptiste was built at this site, and the community developed as a trade center. In 1731 the tribe assisted St. Denis in putting down the Natchez uprising. Disease reduced the population of the Natchitoches until by the late eighteenth century they had lost their identity as a tribe. A count in 1825 revealed that there were only 61 left.

NATCHITOCHES, city, NW Louisiana, seat of Natchitoches Parish; on the Cane River; on the Texas and Pacific Railway; 70 miles SE of Shreveport. Bricks, lumber, tile, and cottonseed products are manufactured, and the city is a commercial center for the surrounding cotton country. Northwestern State College is in Natchitoches. The American cemetery in the city marks the site of Fort St. Jean Baptiste, established in 1714 as a trading and military post, making Natchitoches the oldest settlement in Louisiana. Natchitoches was incorporated as a city in 1819. (For population, see Louisiana map in Atlas.)

NATHAN, a famous prophet during the reigns of David and Solomon. Through him God told David that the house of the Lord, which the king wanted to build, would be built by his son, Solomon (II Sam. 7:1–17). Nathan also pointed out to David his sin in taking Bath-sheba, wife of Uriah the Hittite, and causing her husband to be killed in the front lines of a battle (II Sam. 12:1–15).

The name Nathan is also given to several other persons in the Bible: a son of Attai (I Chron. 2:36), a son of David (II Sam. 5:14), the father of Igal (II Sam. 23:36), a messenger of Ezra (Ezra 8:16), and a son of Bani (Ezra 10:39).

NATHAN, GEORGE JEAN, 1882–1958, U.S. dramatic critic, editor, and author, was born in Fort Wayne, Ind., and studied at Cornell University and the University of Bologna, Italy. He joined with H. L. Mencken in editing *The Smart Set*, 1914–23; in founding *The American Mercury*, 1924 (of which Nathan was contributing editor, 1925–30, and drama critic, 1924–30 and 1940–51); and in writing *Heliogabalus* (1920), a play, and *The American Credo* (1920), a broadside against then-current prejudices. Nathan's other books, most of which deal with the theater, include *Since Ibsen* (1933), *Encyclopedia of the Theatre* (1940), *The Bachelor Life* (1941), and an annual compilation, *The Theater Book of the Year* (1943–51). He was drama critic of several magazines besides *The American Mercury*, including *Vanity Fair*, *The Saturday Review of Literature*, and *Esquire*. Wit and cynicism, Nathan's trademarks, were accompanied by a thorough knowledge of the theater and a keen interest in its improvement. He was an early champion of such playwrights as Eugene O'Neill and William Saroyan.

NATHANAEL, a disciple of Jesus Christ, mentioned by this name only in John 1:45–51. Circumstantial evidence seems to favor the view that Nathanael is the first name of Bartholomew "son of Tolmai" who is mentioned in all three of the Synoptic Gospels (Matt. 10:3; Mark 3:18; Luke 6:14), where Nathanael is omitted. In these lists of the disciples Bartholomew's name always appears after that of Philip, who found Nathanael and brought him to Jesus (John 1:45–47). When Jesus said that He had known Nathanael earlier, "under the fig tree," Nathanael accepted Him immediately as the Son of God (John 1:47–49). See BARTHOLOMEW.

NATICK, town, E Massachusetts; on the Charles River, at the head of Lake Cochituate, about 16 miles WSW of Boston. Shoes, organs, metal and electronic equipment are manufactured. Natick was established by John Eliot in 1651 as a "praying town" for converting the Indians to Christianity. It was incorporated in 1781. (For population, see Massachusetts map in Atlas.)

NATION, CARRY, 1846–1911, U.S. agitator for temperance, was born Carry Amelia Moore, in Gerrand County, Kentucky. Her schooling was brief and sporadic. In 1867, she married Dr. Charles Gloyd, an alcoholic and a Mason, and their brief and unhappy life together incited in her a violent hatred of both liquor and fraternal orders. She left her second husband, David Nation (who divorced her for desertion in 1901) to campaign for the enforcement of the Kansas Temperance Law. In 1900, she wrecked the saloon of Wichita's Hotel Carey with a hatchet and served seven weeks in jail; she was arrested more than 30 times in her subsequent travels and "hatchetations," which she considered her divinely inspired mission.

NATIONAL ACADEMY OF DESIGN, an organization of U.S. artists established in 1825, and incorporated in 1828, to further the cultivation of the fine arts. Its members number 250 and are either academicians or associates. Membership is divided among painters, sculptors, architects, graphic artists, and aquarellists. First president and a founder of the academy was Samuel F. B. Morse. Affiliated with the Metropolitan Museum of Art, the academy maintains an art school and holds annual exhibitions.

NATIONAL ACADEMY OF SCIENCES—NATIONAL ACADEMY OF ENGINEERING—NATIONAL RESEARCH COUNCIL, a U.S. private nonprofit organization which operates under a Congressional charter signed by Abraham Lincoln in 1863 creating the National Academy of Sciences for the purpose of advancing science and engineering and their use for the general welfare, and to advise the federal government.

The National Academy of Sciences has fifteen sections: mathematics, astronomy, physics, engineering, chemistry, geology, botany, zoology and anatomy, physiology, pathology and microbiology, anthropology, psychology, geophysics, biochemistry, and applied biology. Members are elected to the academy in recognition of distinguished contributions to research; as of July 1, 1966, there were 740 members.

In December, 1964, the National Academy of Engineering was organized under the original NAS charter in order to recognize outstanding achievements in the field of engineering and to serve as a mechanism for enabling engineers to participate at the highest level in the consideration of national problems. As of May 1, 1966, there were 95 members.

Serving as the principal operating agency of both academies is the National Research Council, organized by the NAS in 1916 at the request of President Woodrow Wilson to mobilize the research resources of the nation. Almost all the activities undertaken by either academy are performed within one of the eight divisions of the Research Council: behavioral sciences, biology and agriculture, chemistry and chemical technology, earth sciences, engineering, mathematical sciences, medical sciences, and physical sciences. The general work of the council is done through a wide variety of committees, boards, and institutes whose membership, now numbering 5,000, is drawn from the national community of scientists and engineers.

The operating expenses of the overall organization are derived from contracts with and grants from both public and private organizations and from private gifts. Headquarters are in Washington, D.C.

HOWARD J. LEWIS

NATIONAL AERONAUTICS AND SPACE ADMINISTRATION (NASA), the U.S. government agency for the exploration and utilization of space, was established in October, 1958. Its purposes, and those of the U.S. space research programs, are: (1) to preserve the role of the United States as a leader in aeronautical and space technology and its peaceful applications; (2) to expand human knowledge; (3) to improve the technology of aeronautical and space vehicles; (4) to develop and operate vehicles for manned space flight; (5) to utilize the nation's scientific and engineering resources as effectively as possible; (6) to maintain interchange of information and discoveries between the civilian space administration and national defense agencies; (7) to cooperate with other nations in aeronautical and space activities and in their peaceful application; and (8) to study the benefits, opportunities, and problems involved in aeronautical and space activities for peaceful and scientific purposes.

To these ends, NASA plans, directs, and conducts aeronautical and space activities, arranges for the participation of the scientific community in planning measurements and observations, and seeks to provide for the widest practicable dissemination of information about its activities and their results.

Initial Organization. The nucleus of NASA was the National Advisory Committee for Aeronautics (NACA), which had been responsible for U.S. research since 1915. Within the first months of its existence, NASA absorbed the small Project Vanguard group of the Naval Research Laboratory, and the Jet Propulsion Laboratory (JPL) which had been under army jurisdiction. JPL continued to be operated under contract by the California Institute of Technology, Pasadena, its responsibility being the development of spacecraft for unmanned lunar and planetary exploration. A few weeks after the formation of NASA, a Space Task Group was established at Langley Research Center, Hampton, Va., to conduct Project Mercury, the first U.S. manned space flight program. In 1962, this Group was enlarged and moved to the Manned Spacecraft Center, Houston, Tex.

The Devélopment Operation Division of the Army Ballistic Missile Agency, Huntsville, Ala., became part of NASA late in 1959. This organization, headed by Wernher von Braun, included many of the rocket specialists who had developed V-1 and V-2 missiles for the German Army during World War II. Under NASA, these and other specialists became the staff of the George C. Marshall Space Flight Center, with responsibility for developing major launch vehicles.

From the National Advisory Committee for Aeronautics, NASA acquired Ames Research Center, Moffett Field, Calif.; the Flight Research Center, Edwards, Calif.; Langley Research Center, Langley, Va.; Lewis Research Center, Cleveland, Ohio; and a small rocket-launching station at Wallops Island, Va. NASA established new launching centers at Cape Canaveral, Fla., and Lompoc, Calif. Goddard Space Flight Center was established by NASA at Greenbelt, Md., to develop sounding rockets and unmanned earth-orbiting spacecraft experiments. Other stations were the Nuclear Rocket Development Station, Jackass Flats, Nev.; Plum Brook Research Station, Sandusky, Ohio; Michoud Operations, a rocket assembly plant in New Orlenas, La.; Mississippi Test Facility for ground testing large rockets in southwest Mississippi, 50 miles east of New Orleans; Goddard Institute of Space Studies, New York City; and two small operations offices in Santa Monica, Calif., and Cambridge, Mass.

Reorganization. In May, 1961, Pres. John F. Kennedy called for a speedier development of booster rockets and manned spacecraft, and for more extensive unmanned space exploration preparatory to landing a man on the moon before 1970. He also called for accelerated programs to develop nuclear rockets and satellite systems for world-wide communications and weather observation. Congress overwhelmingly endorsed his proposals.

These enlarged responsibilities led to the administrative reorganization of NASA, Nov. 1, 1961, and the establishment of four major headquarters program offices (Space Sciences, Applications, Manned Space Flight, and Advanced Research and Technology) and a supporting activity, Tracking and Data Acquisition. NASA and the U.S. Department of Defense established a close liaison, at both policy and program management levels, to assure adequate exchange of knowledge and capabilities.

Major Accomplishments of NASA

The Space Sciences Program. Energy distribution and the time variation of radiation in the Great Radiation Belt (the Van Allen Belt) werè measured, and it was demonstrated for the first time that the radiation belt and auroras are manifestations of the same phenomenon.

Through analysis of a satellite orbit, it was discovered that the earth's geoid (the surface along which gravitational force is equal) is slightly pear-shaped, with the stem at the North Pole.

Radiation and magnetic fields in interplanetary space, as many as 22.5 million miles from the earth, were measured, and it was demonstrated that a single solar storm gave rise to phenomena in interplanetary space, near the earth, and on the earth's surface.

The density and temperature of electrons and ions in the earth's upper atmosphere were measured, and it was demonstrated that they are disturbed by the activity of the sun.

Atmospheric density at high altitudes was measured and correlated with the activity of the sun.

The so-called "steady state" theory of the origin of the universe was partially discredited as a result of NASA research. This theory holds that matter and antimatter are continuously being created in space, slowly giving rise to new stars and galaxies in the voids between older stars and galaxies which are, it would seem, rushing away from each other at great speed. But if matter and antimatter were being created continuously, there would be a steady production of gamma rays in space. Satellite observations of gamma radiation indicate, however, that it is 1,000 times less intense than would be expected under the steady state theory.

It was discovered that a diffuse layer of helium surrounds the earth between altitudes of 600 and 1,500 miles.

It was found that the earth's magnetic field merges with the interplanetary magnetic field at a distance of about 40,000 miles from earth, and that the interplanetary magnetic field undergoes sudden variations in intensity and direction.

An unmanned spacecraft, Mariner II, was launched Aug. 27, 1962, on a trajectory that was to take it close to the planet Venus. Its initial trajectory would have taken it 233,000 miles from Venus, but on Sept. 4, 1962, when Mariner II was almost 1.5 million miles from earth, a radio signal commanded the firing of an on-board rocket that changed the direction of flight so as to bring the heavily instrumented vehicle within data-gathering range of Venus.

The Applications Program. The feasibility was demonstrated of intercontinental communication by means of earth satellites used as both passive reflectors and active relay stations.

Satellites were developed that obtain and transmit to earth photographs of the earth's cloud cover as seen from above its atmosphere, and measurements were made of visible and infrared radiation emitted and reflected by the earth and the atmosphere. The experimental meteorological satellites made it possible for the U.S. Weather Bureau to report the existence of hurricanes two days earlier than before. Experiments indicated that radiation data can be used in measuring the extent of cloud cover at night and the temperatures of the earth's surface and cloud tops.

Manned Space Flight Program. Spacecraft, launch vehicles, and ground communication facilities to support a man in orbital flight were demonstrated by the Project Mercury astronauts. The astronauts made scientific observations and tested flight equipment and operational methods.

Development of the first stage of the Saturn C-I launch vehicle, generating thrust of 1 million pounds, and with the ability to increase thrust to 1.15 million pounds, was well under way in 1962. This vehicle was designed to put loads of up to 20,000 pounds into orbit and to provide boost power for three-man Apollo spacecraft.

The Advanced Research and Technology Program. The feasibility of a rocket engine burning liquid hydrogen and liquid oxygen was demonstrated. The combination promised to be about 40 per cent more effective than the commonly used kerosene-liquid oxygen combination.

Considerable progress was made in the development of a single kerosene-liquid oxygen engine generating 1.5 million pounds of thrust.

Materials were developed to withstand the heat of re-entering the earth's atmosphere at speeds of about 25,000 miles per hour.

A four-stage rocket was developed, the Scout, by which a small spacecraft can be launched into orbit at a total cost of only about $1 million.

In co-operation with the U.S. Air Force and the U.S. Navy, NASA conducted research in the operation of an aircraft at six times the speed of sound and at altitudes of more than 50 miles.

Research on vertical-takeoff-and-landing (VTOL), and short-takeoff-and-landing (STOL) aircraft was advanced to the point that most flying and handling qualifications and criteria could be documented.

Tracking and Data Acquisition. Three systems of radio and radar stations were established around the world to track and receive data from satellites and to control satellites and spacecraft on missions to deep space.

International Co-operation. NASA's co-operative activities with more than 55 countries involved satellite, sounding rocket, and ground-based meteorology, communications, and ionosphere-sounding programs; a worldwide network of tracking and data acquisition stations; and exchange of personnel.

James E. Webb

NATIONAL ANTHEM, a musical composition chosen by a nation as representative of the spirit of the country and to be sung or played on official occasions. National anthems were a manifestation of the rise of nationalism, and were not so named until early in the nineteenth century. Some are patriotic verses sung to indigenous folk tunes, drinking songs, and the like (see Marseillaise, La; Star Spangled Banner, The), but most of them were composed expressly as national anthems. A short list of representative examples follows:

Austria—*Austrian National Anthem;* music, *Bundeslied* from *Eine kleine Maurerkantate,* Wolfgang Amadeus Mozart; words by Paula Preradovic; 1946.

Canada—*God Save the King.* National song, *O Canada;* words in French by Adolphe Routhier, 1880, English translation by R. S. Weir, 1908; music by Calixa Lavallée.

China—*San min chu I* (The Three Principles of the People); music by Ch'eng Mao-Yün; words by Sun Yat-sen; adopted 1928 by the Kuomintang.

Germany—*Deutschland über Alles* (Germany Above All); music by Franz Joseph Haydn; words by H. A. Hoffmann von Fallersleben; 1922. The music of *Deutschland über Alles* became the national anthem of the German Federal Republic, 1952. The Democratic Republic adopted as its anthem *Auferstanden aus Ruinen* (Resurrected from Ruins), written in 1949, music by Hans Eisler, words by J. R. Becher.

Great Britain—*God Save the King* (officially *God Save the Queen* during the reigns of Victoria and Elizabeth II); origin obscure; sometimes attributed to Henry Carey. *God Save the King* is also the national anthem of all British colonies and possessions.

India—*Jana gana mana Adhinayak* (Lord of the People, of Society, and of the Mind); music and words by Rabindranath Tagore; 1950.

Indonesia—*Indonesia Raya;* music by Wage Rudolf Supratman, written 1927; 1949.

Israel—*Hatikvah* (The Hope); music from a Hebrew folk melody; words by N. H. Imber; 1948.

Poland—*Jeszcze Polska nie zginela* (Poland Is Not Yet Forsaken); music attributed to M. K. Ogínski; words by Józef Wybicki; first sung 1797.

Union of Soviet Socialist Republics—*Gimn sovyetskovo soyuza* (Hymn of the Soviet Union); music by A. V. Aleksandrov; words by Sergei Mikhalkov and El-Registan; 1944.

NATIONAL ASSOCIATION FOR MENTAL HEALTH, INC., a voluntary U.S. organization that attempts to improve methods and services in research, prevention, detection, diagnosis, and treatment of the mentally ill and retarded. Activities include hospital inspection and rating and aid to state and local governments in setting up psychiatric services. The NAMH was formed in 1950 as a merger of the National Committee for Mental Hygiene (1909), the National Mental Health Foundation (1946), and the Psychiatric Foundation (1946). In 1961, the association had approximately 750 state and local affiliates. Membership of the organization is primarily nonprofessional, but professional people on committees and staff guide and carry out the technical and scientific work. The NAMH cosponsors Mental Health Week and annually conducts the Mental Health Fund Campaign. Headquarters are in New York, N.Y.

NATIONAL ASSOCIATION FOR THE ADVANCEMENT OF COLORED PEOPLE, an interracial organization founded in 1909 "for the purpose of establishing equal citizenship rights for all Americans." Goals of the association include the end of segregation in public facilities, free exercise of the right to vote, employment on the basis of individual merit, and freedom of residence. The NAACP attempts to promote racial equality by legal, legislative, and educational means. In the mid-1960's the association had about 400,000 members throughout the United States. Both the membership and the national staff are multiracial, with an estimated 10 to 15 per cent of whites among the members. There are more than 1,600 local branches, youth councils, and college chapters, which in turn form 35 state conferences and several regional conferences. Field workers are sent where they are needed. The NAACP in the 1960's began promoting civil rights through such measures as sit-in and pray-in demonstrations, and picketing. The organization was one of the leading sponsors of the "March on Washington" by 200,000 civil rights' supporters in August, 1963. The demonstration was the largest of its kind ever held. Publications include the monthly magazine *Crisis* and pamphlets. Headquarters are in New York City.

NATIONAL ASSOCIATION OF BROADCASTERS, an organization of U.S. radio (and later television) station and network executives, founded in 1922, with the object of fostering and promoting the development of the art of radio (and television) broadcasting. The membership includes both active and associate members, with only the former allowed to vote. National headquarters are in Washington, D.C. Membership is about 2,900.

NATIONAL ASSOCIATION OF EVANGELICALS, a voluntary U.S. organization of more than 40 denominations, as well as individual churches, Bible schools, colleges, seminaries, ministerial fellowships, evangelistic groups, and individual Christians. The association was organized at St. Louis, Mo., in 1942, to provide a representative voice for conservative Protestantism; affiliation is dependent upon acceptance of a statement of faith. This statement emphasizes the authority of the written Word of God, the Trinity, the nature and work of Christ, the need for spiritual regeneration, the ministry of the Holy Spirit, future rewards and punishments, and Christian spiritual unity. Membership, through affiliated denominations and churches, exceeds 2 million, and it represents more than 10 million. NAE commissions provide service in chaplaincy, education, and evangelical and social action, and maintain relations with evangelical organizations in other nations through the World Evangelical Fellowship. The Evangelical Foreign Missions Association, the National Religious Broadcasters, the National Association of Christian Schools, and the National Sunday School Association are autonomous agencies affiliated with NAE and are its service arms in their fields. Headquarters are in Wheaton, Ill.; an office of public affairs is maintained in Washington, D.C., and there are seven regional offices. *United Evangelical Action,* the official journal, is published bimonthly in Cincinnati, Ohio.

George L. Ford

NATIONAL ASSOCIATION OF MANUFACTURERS (NAM), a voluntary organization of more than 20,000 U. S. business firms, was founded in 1895 for the purpose of protecting traditional principles of individual freedom and equality of opportunity in America. NAM participated in establishing the department of commerce in 1903, and helped to strengthen the Interstate Commerce Act and to organize the Chamber of Commerce of the United States and the National Industrial Conference Board. The association advocated establishment of the parcel post system and construction of the Panama Canal.

The association's programs cover many phases of industrial and economic activity, but NAM's major objectives are the improvement of employer-employee relations, economy and efficiency in government, and sound and equitable taxation. NAM maintains a program of supporting legislation to further its principles.

Approximately 83 per cent of NAM member companies have fewer than 500 employees; more than 25 per cent have fewer than 50. NAM policies are instituted through committees of more than 3,000 businessmen who serve without pay, and must be approved by at least 120 of the 180 members of the association's board of directors. There are 13 branch offices of NAM and headquarters are in New York, N.Y. Its law department and government relations division are located in Washington, D.C. The weekly *NAM News* is the association's principal publication.

NATIONAL AUDUBON SOCIETY, a publicly endowed U.S. association established in 1905 to conduct a program of public education in protection of wildlife. Efforts of the society have led to establishment of bird sanctuaries and to passage of laws protecting birds. Its membership, which is open to anyone, was 33,000 in 1961. It consists of persons interested in the conservation of natural resources and places special emphasis on the preservation of wildlife, wildlife habitats, plants, soil, and water. The organization also fosters the intelligent and wise use of the nation's resources in the interest of human progress. The Society publishes the bimonthly *Audubon Magazine*. It also sponsors the Junior Audubon Society which has a membership of about 250,000 school children. The organization maintains headquarters in New York, N.Y.

NATIONAL BASKETBALL ASSOCIATION. See BASKETBALL.

NATIONAL BOXING ASSOCIATION. See BOXING.

NATIONAL BROADCASTING COMPANY. See BROADCASTING, *Development of Networks;* RADIO CORPORATION OF AMERICA.

NATIONAL BUREAU OF STANDARDS, an agency of the U.S. Department of Commerce, created by act of Congress in 1901 in accordance with the constitutional power of Congress to fix the standards of weights and measures. Research and development work in the physical sciences comprise the greater part of the bureau's program. This work grows out of its primary function: the custody, maintenance, and development of national standards of measurement for physical quantities such as length, mass, time, volume, temperature, light, color, electrical energy, radioactivity, X-ray intensity, viscosity, sound, and radio frequency. The testing, calibration, and certification of standards and standard measuring apparatus is a service that the bureau renders not only to the federal, state, and municipal governments but also to scientific societies, educational institutions, and firms or individuals engaged in pursuits requiring the use of standards. In addition to the extensive laboratories in Washington, D.C., involving many branches of science and engineering, the Bureau operates radio and cryogenic laboratories in Boulder, Colo.

NATIONAL CATHOLIC EDUCATIONAL ASSOCIATION, founded in 1904, is a voluntary U.S. organization of individuals and institutions interested in the welfare of Roman Catholic education. The association acts as a clearinghouse for Catholic educational information by providing for the study, discussion, and publication of matters pertaining to religious instruction and training as well as to the entire program of arts and sciences. Departments of the NCEA are concerned with college and university, secondary school, elementary school, school superintendents, major seminary, minor seminary, and special education. The official organ of the NCEA is the quarterly *National Catholic Educational Association Bulletin*. Membership in 1958 exceeded 11,000. Headquarters are in Washington, D.C. The association carries on its program of activities in co-operation with the Catholic school system.

NATIONAL CATHOLIC WELFARE CONFERENCE, an organization of the Roman Catholic bishops in the United States which has as its purpose the unification and co-ordination of Catholic efforts in education, social welfare, and other activities. The NCWC is primarily a liaison agency facilitating the exchange of information and services among Catholic organizations and co-ordinating the activities of these organizations. A board of 10 bishops, elected annually, administers the conference. Members of the board serve as chairmen of the eight regularly constituted departments: executive, education, press, social action, legal, lay organizations, Catholic Action study, and youth. In addition to these departmental activities, the conference works for the solution of specific problems through special episcopal committees, which include the committee on the Confraternity of Christian Doctrine, episcopal committee on the motion pictures and Legion of Decency, committee on the National Organization for Decent Literature, committee on the American Board of Catholic Missions, Bishops' War Emergency and Relief Committee, committee on the Propagation of the Faith, and committee for the North American College in Rome. JEX MARTIN

NATIONAL CEMETERIES, U.S., the cemeteries maintained by the federal government for the burial of persons honorably separated from the U.S. Armed Services, and of U.S. citizens who, in time of war, served with honor in the armed forces of an allied nation. National cemeteries, proper, are administered by two separate jurisdictions: the Quartermaster Corps of the Department of the Army and the National Park Service of the Department of the Interior. In addition there are U.S. overseas military cemeteries under the jurisdiction of the American Battle Monuments Commission, an independent agency established by Congress in 1923 to commemorate the overseas theaters of operations of the American Expeditionary Force during World War I.

Although Congress authorized a military cemetery in Mexico City in 1850, the "National Cemetery System" dates to 1862, when Congress appropriated funds to purchase land for military cemeteries. Cemetery administration was placed under the Quartermaster General's Department (after 1912 the Quartermaster Corps) of the War Department. By 1870, 73 national cemeteries had been established.

Eight permanent U.S. cemeteries were established in France, Belgium, and Great Britain during World War I for the interment of U.S. overseas dead (unless the next of kin requested reburial in the United States). In 1934 the overseas cemeteries were transferred from the War Department to the American Battle Monuments Commission. After 1949 the 14 permanent overseas cemeteries established in 1947 for the interment of the U.S. dead of World War II, were placed under jurisdiction of the commission.

Beginning in 1933 certain national cemeteries, deemed to be national shrines, were transferred from the War Department to the Department of the Interior. See NATIONAL PARKS.

Provided space is available, a widow or widower, and dependent child or children of a service-eligible person may be buried free of charge in the same grave as is his kin or in a grave adjoining that of his kin. Similarly, a pre-deceased spouse and dependent child or children may be buried in a national cemetery provided the service-eligible person agrees to be buried in the same grave or an adjoining one.

U.S. NATIONAL CEMETERIES*

National Cemeteries	Year Established	Total Acreage	Total Interments
Alexandria (Pineville, La.)	1867	8.23	5,853
Alexandria (Va.)	1862	5.50	3,669
Alton (Ill.)	1948	0.48	438
Andersonville (Ga.)	1865	117.06	14,194
Andersonville Prison Park (Ga.)	—	84.20	—
Annapolis (Md.)	1862	4.12	2,780
Arlington (Fort Myer, Va.)	1864	420.23	102,101
Balls Bluff (Leesburg, Va.)	1865	0.057	54
Baltimore (Md.)	1936	72.23	13,204
Barrancas (Warrington, Fla.)	1868	29.91	4,439
Baton Rouge (La.)	1867	7.69	4,959
Beaufort (S.C.)	1863	28.92	9,725
Beverly (N.J.)	1864	64.55	15,403
Black Hills (Sturgis, S.D.)	1948*	105.90	1,042
Camp Butler (Springfield, Ill.)	1862	39.25	3,569
Camp Nelson (Nicholasville, Ky.)	1866	9.75	4,462
Cave Hill (Louisville, Ky.)	1863	4.11	5,673
Chattanooga (Tenn.)	1867	120.80	17,839
City Point (Hopewell, Va.)	1866	6.66	5,515
Cold Harbor (Richmond, Va.)	1866	1.43	1,987
Corinth (Miss.)	1866	20.00	5,923
Crown Hill (Indianapolis, Ind.)	1866	1.37	794
Culpeper (Va.)	1867	6.47	1,470
Cypress Hills (Brooklyn, N.Y.)	1862	18.20	19,681
Danville (Ky.)	1862	0.31	392
Danville (Va.)	1867	3.50	1,760
Fayetteville (Ark.)	1867	6.11	2,043
Finn's Point (Salem, N.J.)	1875	4.59	2,702
Florence (S.C.)	1865	5.87	3,331
Ft. Bliss (Tex.)	1939	59.85	4,633
Ft. Gibson (Okla.)	1868	32.21	3,967
Ft. Harrison (Va.)	1866	1.55	844
Ft. Leavenworth (Kan.)	1862	35.95	7,936
Fort Logan (Colo.)	1950	136.80	2,378
Fort McPherson (Maxwell, Neb.)	1873	20.00	2,362
Fort Rosecrans (San Diego, Calif.)	1934	70.43	17,259
Fort Sam Houston (San Antonio, Tex.)	1931	60.11	12,268
Fort Scott (Kan.)	1862	10.51	1,911
Fort Smith (Ark.)	1867	14.59	3,634
Fort Snelling (Minneapolis, Minn.)	1939	178.56	19,103
Glendale (Va.)	1866	2.08	1,208
Golden Gate (San Bruno, Calif.)	1938	161.50	46,473
Grafton (W.Va.)	1867	3.21	2,005
Hampton (Va.)	1866	26.53	17,489
Jefferson Barracks (St. Louis, Mo.)	1863	306.98	33,188
Jefferson City (Mo.)	1867	2.01	1,300
Keokuk (Iowa)	1862	20.20	1,819
Knoxville (Tenn.)	1863	9.83	5,472
Lebanon (Ky.)	1867	2.83	995
Lexington (Ky.)	1863	0.75	1,383
Little Rock (Ark.)	1868	24.95	9,916
Long Island (Farmingdale, L.I., N.Y.)	1936	364.00	68,290
Loudon Park (Baltimore, Md.)	1862	5.60	6,412
Marietta (Ga.)	1866	23.26	12,841
Memphis (Tenn.)	1867	44.15	19,350
Mill Springs (West Somerset, Ky.)	1862	3.50	998
Mobile (Ala.)	1865	5.24	4,379
Mound City (Ill.)	1864	10.50	6,055
Nashville (Madison, Tenn.)	1867	65.00	18,991
Natchez (Miss.)	1866	10.72	4,134
National Memorial Cemetery of the Pacific (Hawaii)	1948	112.00	16,995
New Albany (Ind.)	1862	6.31	4,828
New Bern (N.C.)	1867	7.68	3,870
Perryville (Ky.)	1931	4.39	
Philadelphia (Pa.)	1862	13.32	10,788
Port Hudson (La.)	1866	8.04	3,899
Puerto Rico (San Juan)	1948	108.24	2,162
Quincy (Ill.)	1899	0.45	410
Raleigh (N.C.)	1865	6.95	1,726
Richmond (Va.)	1866	9.74	8,129
Rock Island (Ill.)	1863	27.50	3,797
St. Augustine (Fla.)	1881	1.36	2,563
Salisbury (N.C.)	1865	5.97	12,806
San Antonio (Tex.)	1867	3.66	3,076
San Francisco (Calif.)	1884	53.34	23,095
Santa Fe (N.M.)	1875	34.59	3,406
Seven Pines (Va.)	1866	1.90	1,423
Sitka (Alaska)	1924	1.19	360
Soldiers' Home (D.C.)	1862	15.80	11,563
Springfield (Mo.)	1867	13.82	5,012
Staunton (Va.)	1867	1.15	806
Willamette (Ore.)	1950	201.45	6,412
Wilmington (N.C.)	1867	5.06	2,918
Winchester (Va.)	1866	4.89	4,817
Woodlawn (Elmira, N.Y.)	1874	7.62	4,831
Zachary Taylor (Louisville, Ky.)	1928	16.43	7,804
Total Cemeteries Under the Department of the Army		3,588.32	741,491

*As of September 30, 1959. Includes only those in the 50 states and in Puerto Rico; excludes all cemeteries under the U.S. Department of the Interior

NATIONAL CITY, city, S California, on San Diego Bay, the San Diego and Arizona Eastern and the Santa Fe railroads, and U.S. highway 101; 4 miles SSE of San Diego, of which it is a residential suburb. Pop. (1960) 32,771.

NATIONAL CIVIC FEDERATION, a U.S. labor-management organization established in 1900, for the purpose of bringing together employer, employee, and the general public to solve national industrial disputes. The leaders of the federation were Samuel Gompers and Marcus Alonzo Hanna. The federation encouraged the principle of collective bargaining and promoted the enactment of minimum wage and workmen's compensation laws and other legislation. The organization was particularly influential from 1900 to 1905, a period during which it helped to settle such industrial disputes as the Coal Strike of 1902.

NATIONAL COLLEGE OF EDUCATION, a coeducational, privately controlled, nonsectarian teachers college at Evanston, Ill. The school's single objective is the preparation of elementary school personnel. The college was established as the Chicago Kindergarten College in 1886 and became the National Kindergarten College in 1912. In 1917 the name was changed to National Kindergarten and Elementary College and the present name was adopted in 1930. The bachelor's degree is offered, with a master's degree being offered in elementary education. The college library has a special collection of books and periodicals on child psychology. See COLLEGES AND UNIVERSITIES.

NATIONAL COLLEGIATE ATHLETIC ASSOCIATION, an organization of U.S. colleges, universities, and athletic conferences originally formed in 1905 for the purpose of instituting needed changes in the game of football. The functions of NCAA were later broadened to include the stimulation of intercollegiate and intramural sports, the publishing of rules of play, maintenance of athletic records, regulation of college athletic contests and eligibility rules, co-operation with similar amateur athletic organizations, and legislation and regulation of any phase of intercollegiate athletics of general concern to the more than 400 member institutions. The NCAA conducts championship meets and tournaments in baseball, basketball, boxing, cross-country, fencing, golf, gymnastics, ice hockey, skiing, swimming, tennis, track and field, and wrestling. NCAA maintains national headquarters in Kansas City, Mo.

NATIONAL CONFERENCE OF CHRISTIANS AND JEWS, INC., a U.S. organization to promote justice, amity, understanding, and co-operation among Protestants, Catholics, and Jews. The organization was founded in 1928 to analyze, moderate, and finally eliminate intergroup prejudices that hamper religious, business, social, and political relations. The conference has a membership of 225,000; there are 64 regional offices, with a Canadian office in Toronto and a European office in Geneva, Switzerland. In 1951 the Ford Foundation contributed $1 million for construction of permanent conference headquarters at 43 West 57th Street, New York, N.Y.

A quarterly, *Conference, The Magazine of Human Relations*, and pamphlets and bulletins are published by the organization. The conference program, arranged in co-operation with educational, religious, and community organizations, keynotes education; news releases and feature material are provided for use by newspapers, radio and television, and motion pictures. NCCJ sponsors the Religious News Service, which gathers and distributes general religious news from all parts of the world. WILLARD JOHNSON

NATIONAL CONFERENCE ON SOCIAL WELFARE, established in 1874, is an organization interested in all aspects of health and welfare in the United States. Its major function is an annual forum that attempts to effect an exchange of techniques and ideas between laymen and professionals, to improve standards of performance, and to develop the public's support of and participation in social welfare activities. Topics discussed include protection of children, unemployment, and family breakdown. In the early 1960's the organization had more than 6,500 members, including both individuals and agencies. Although state conferences of social work have no administrative relationship with the NCSW, the national staff is available for guidance. The national office serves as the secretariat for the Association of State Conferences, for which it conducts regional and national meetings. Publications of the NCSW include the quarterly *Conference Bulletin* and the annual *Social Welfare Forum*. Headquarters are in Columbus, Ohio.

NATIONAL CONGRESS OF PARENTS AND TEACHERS, founded in Washington, D.C., in 1897, is a nonsectarian and nonpartisan volunteer organization of parents, teachers, and other citizens interested in the promotion of closer relationships between home and school, and of laws for the care and protection of young people. As the national parent-teacher association, the NCPT is a service information center for the entire membership. The congress develops its program through conferences, committees, and projects. Activities include cosponsorship of American Education Week, encouragement of classes and workshops devoted to parent and family-life education, a nationwide civil defense program, and the combating of juvenile delinquency. The organization favors federal legislation to protect child labor, federal funds for the construction of public schools (after approved surveys), adequate appropriations for the U.S. Office of Education, welfare agencies, the school lunch program, and support of the United Nations.

In 1959 the NCPT had more than 11,500,000 members in 45,336 Parent-Teacher Associations. It had 52 branches in each of the states, the District of Columbia, and Europe (American military installations schools). State branches have authority to organize local units, or PTA's, within the state and are responsible for supervising and directing them. A field staff is employed by the national organization to give professional assistance to state branches in all areas of parent-teacher work. Each state sends voting delegates to an annual national convention, which is the governing body of the NCPT. The delegates elect national officers and transact other business. Publications of the NCPT include the official magazine *The National Parent-Teacher: The P.T.A. Magazine*. Headquarters are maintained in Chicago.

NATIONAL CONVENTION. See FRENCH REVOLUTION, *The Convention*.

NATIONAL COUNCIL OF CATHOLIC MEN. See ROMAN CATHOLIC ORGANIZATIONS.

NATIONAL COUNCIL OF CATHOLIC WOMEN. See ROMAN CATHOLIC ORGANIZATIONS.

NATIONAL COUNCIL OF FARMER CO-OPERATIVES. See CO-OPERATIVE, Co-operatives in the United States, *National Federations*.

NATIONAL COUNCIL OF GEOGRAPHY TEACHERS. See GEOGRAPHIC SOCIETY.

NATIONAL COUNCIL OF JEWISH WOMEN. See JEWISH ORGANIZATIONS, *Social Welfare Agencies*.

NATIONAL COUNCIL OF THE CHURCHES OF CHRIST IN THE UNITED STATES OF AMERICA is constituted by, responsible to, and under the direction of 34 Protestant and Orthodox religious bodies numbering more than 38 million members. Membership is open to communions that are constituted as autonomous church bodies, possess a history that demonstrates permanence and stability, have an established order of government and ministry, and acknowledge Jesus Christ as Divine Lord and Saviour. These religious bodies, in association with more than 900 state and local councils of churches and 2,000 ministerial associations, co-ordinate many varied programs.

Organization. The national council, constituted in 1950 at Cleveland, Ohio, is an outgrowth of years of common church endeavor. It was formed by the union of 13 church organizations, including the International Council of Religious Education, successor to the American Sunday School Union (1824); the Foreign Missions Conference of North America (1893); the Missionary Education Movement, organized in 1902 by home and foreign mission boards for the joint production of missionary literature; the Federal Council of Churches (1908); the Home Missions Council (1908); the National Protestant Council on Higher Education, successor to the Council of Church Boards on Education (1911); and the United Stewardship Council (1920).

The services of the national council go beyond its Protestant and Orthodox member communions. Representatives of 33 additional U.S. bodies or agencies, plus four Canadian bodies, co-operate with one or more council services. The council is governed by a general assembly of 700 delegated representatives—475 clergy and 225 laymen—named directly or approved by the member communions. Between sessions of the triennial assembly the supervisory body is the general board of 256 members, which meets several times a year. Headquarters of the council are in New York, N.Y.

Program. Through its division of Christian education the council develops objectives, general guidance materials, curriculum outlines, and leadership training opportunities for the Christian education of children, youth, adults, and families. It administers the United Christian Youth Movement, the co-operative agency of Protestant youth; the United Student Christian Council, the Student Volunteer Movement, the Interseminary Committee, and the Faculty Christian Fellowship, representing aspects of religious life on college campuses. Church-related colleges in the

United States work through the division to co-ordinate their efforts; programs are also developed to provide a Christian ministry on nonchurch campuses. Textbooks, filmstrips, maps, and plays for missionary education are published through Friendship Press. The division authorized and fostered the Bible translation efforts that resulted in the Revised Standard Version of the Bible.

The division of Christian life and work endeavors to relate religion to the spiritual, moral, and social conditions of the nation. Its departments of international affairs, economic life, racial and cultural relations, religious liberty, and social welfare seek to sharpen the concern of individual Christians and of the churches in these crucial areas. Through its department of pastoral services, program assistance and counsel are given to the religious ministry in hospitals, prisons, and other institutions. The department of worship and the arts seeks to relate religion to music, drama, architecture, literature, and the graphic arts. Still another department seeks to stimulate and co-ordinate the fund raising activities of the churches and their stewardship education.

Division of Home Missions. The member denominations, through the division of home missions, study new approaches, co-ordinate resources, and initiate work related to church life in the United States. Special departments are concerned with the needs of urban and rural churches. A church building consultation service is provided. The migrant ministry serves 150,000 seasonal farm workers in 34 states with Sunday schools, adult education, vacation church schools, recreational activities, child care, and community centers. This department also works to provide migrants with legal, social, and economic protection. The denominations co-operate through the division in providing varied services for American Indians, Spanish-speaking Americans, and other groups that have special needs.

Division of Foreign Missions is responsible for the co-ordination, interpretation, and strengthening of the 79 member foreign mission boards and agencies. It provides counseling and training enterprises for missionaries and maintains a medical office to safeguard the health of missionaries and their families. Special missionary needs are met through such means as a rural mission program, focusing attention on agriculture and village problems; a world literacy program in 200 languages by which millions of illiterates have been taught to read; an audio-visual agency which employs modern techniques for the mass proclamation of the Christian gospel. Assistance is also given to overseas union churches that seek to provide religious fellowship for Americans living abroad.

Other Agencies. Church World Service is the agency through which American churches provide a worldwide program of emergency relief and reconstruction that includes the distribution of clothing, food, medicines, and seeds. Other important services are the resettlement of refugees and temporary provision in refugee camps for housing, medical care, and rehabilitation of the physically disabled.

Other activities of the national council include a united program of evangelism; the co-ordination of lay activities through United Church Men and United Church Women; religious programing on radio and TV by the broadcasting and film commission; the supervision, co-ordination, and interpretation of religious research by the bureau of research and survey; the Washington office, an information and service agency for both government and church organizations; and a clearinghouse and consultation service for state and local councils of churches.

HELEN F. SPAULDING

BIBLIOG.–R. W. Barstow, ed., *Christian Faith in Action* (1951); National Council of Churches of Christ in America, *Cooperative Christianity in the United States* (ed. 1952), *The National Council of Churches* (1957).

NATIONAL DAIRY PRODUCTS CORPORATION is a U.S. business engaged primarily in the manufacture, processing, and distribution of dairy and other food products. Among the important divisions of this worldwide organization are Kraft Foods, producing cheeses and other food products; Sealtest, producing ice cream, milk, and milk specialties; Breakstone Foods, producing sour cream, butter, and cheeses; Sugar Creek Creamery, producing butter; Humko, manufacturing oils and shortening; and Metro Glass Company, manufacturing jars and bottles. Because of the nature of its products and business, the company maintains many widely distributed plants, most of which are relatively small. National Dairy Products Corporation was incorporated in 1923 in Delaware and maintains its general offices in New York, N.Y. In 1959 the company had 48,809 employees.

NATIONAL DEBT. See PUBLIC FINANCE, *Public Debt.*

NATIONAL EDITORIAL ASSOCIATION, a nonprofit organization of some 6,000 newspaper editors and publishers in the United States, founded in 1885 to promote the interests of the newspaper business, to improve standards of journalism, to serve as an exchange for information on newspaper management, and to provide various community services. It serves primarily nonmetropolitan daily, semiweekly, and weekly newspapers. The association is noted for its annual Better Newspapers contest, which offers awards in all major categories of newspaper publishing, and for its opposition to federal legislation to increase the cost of newspaper publishing by raising postage and minimum wage rates. It publishes a monthly magazine, *The National Publisher.* National headquarters are in Chicago.

NATIONAL EDUCATION ASSOCIATION. See EDUCATION, Educational Associations; TEACHERS' ORGANIZATIONS.

NATIONAL EXCHANGE CLUB, a federation of U.S. business and professional men's civic service clubs founded in 1917 to promote the mutual education and improvement of its members and of the community in which its chapters are located. In 1959 the club had 1,500 local groups with a total membership of about 85,000. Material for its educational program is provided by the club's monthly magazine, the *Exchangite.* Headquarters of the organization are in Toledo, Ohio.

NATIONAL FARMERS UNION, officially the Farmers Educational and Cooperative Union of America, is a farm organization whose purpose is the preservation and improvement of the U.S. family-farm system of agriculture. It was founded in 1902 at Point, Tex., by Newton Gresham and other small farmers who had been active in the Farmers' Alliance (see FARMERS' ALLIANCE). In 1959, with headquarters in Denver, Colo., it had a membership of about 300,000 farm families with approximately 700,000 voting members. The Farmers Union is the third largest and traditionally the most radical of the national farm organizations, having its roots in the agrarian populist movements of the nineteenth century. It has waged a continuous fight for equality and justice—and against rural poverty—by means of educational, political, and economic practices, and particularly by sponsoring and participating in marketing and consumer co-operatives. Its strength is centralized in Wisconsin and the wheat-growing states of the Great Plains. See AGRICULTURE IN THE UNITED STATES, Agricultural Activities, *Farmers' Organizations;* CO-OPERATIVE, Co-operatives in the United States.

NATIONAL FEDERATION OF MUSIC CLUBS, a U.S. organization founded in 1898 for the purpose of bringing into working relation with one another music clubs and individuals directly or indirectly associated with musical activity, with a view to aiding and encouraging musical standards throughout the United States. Every two years four prizes of $1,000 each are offered to young musical artists, and annual prizes for composition are offered to members. The federation publishes *Music Clubs Magazine* and *Junior Keynotes* and distributes monthly lists reviewing new U.S. compositions. Headquarters are in Chicago, Ill.

NATIONAL FIRE PROTECTION ASSOCIATION, organized in 1896 and incorporated in 1930, is a U.S. nonprofit engineering and educational organization devoted to limiting loss of life and property by fire. The association acts as a clearinghouse for information on fire prevention, fire fighting procedures, and fire protection methods and for analyses of fire experience. The NFPA has more than 100 technical committees developing and revising standards. These standards are widely adopted by cities and states and by insurance companies. Publications of the association include the *Quarterly*, the organization's technical journal. The NFPA sponsors Fire Prevention Week as part of its public education program. Members come principally from the United States, Canada, England, and Australia, although 45 other countries are represented. In 1959 the NFPA's membership was composed of more than 17,000 individuals. Headquarters are in Boston, Mass.

NATIONAL FORESTS of the United States, more than 185 million acres of public lands managed by the Forest Service of the U.S. Department of Agriculture to protect watersheds and insure sustained production of forests and forest products. As distinguished from national parks and monuments, which are established essentially to preserve areas of scenic, historic, or scientific importance, the national forests are administered under a conservation program that emphasizes wise, multiple-purpose use of all available resources including domestic, agricultural, and industrial water supply, timber stands, range land, recreational facilities, and fish and game wildlife.

Administration. Since the national forests were established in 1891, the conservation provisions of the Weeks Act of 1911 and later laws have allowed the purchase by the federal government of land for the purpose of protecting streams and timbered areas. Most of the area acquired has been in mountainous or hilly regions and includes 22 million acres east of the Great Plains, southern stands of cypress and sand pine, desert scrubs, mountain spruce and firs, mixed eastern hardwoods, and west coast redwood forests.

Gifford Pinchot, first chief of the forest service, set the precedent of decentralization with different regulations for each region. The forest service directs the maintenance of the forests, conducts research, helps control some of the 80,000 forest fires that usually occur each year, combats diseases affecting forest trees, and promotes co-operation between state and private timber management. The national forests contain one-sixth of the nation's commercial forest land and furnish one-tenth of its timber. Sale of forest products brings an income of about $75 million per year; one-fourth of this reverts to the states and counties within which the forests are located, and one-tenth is used to maintain the 178,000 miles of road and 108,000 miles of trails in the forests. Mining activities are regulated by the Bureau of Land Management although simple rock collecting may be carried on without a permit. Four million head of livestock graze on the national forest ranges each year, and nearly a million people make their living at least in part from the national forests.

Recreation. No admission fee is required of the 35 million people who annually visit the forests although fees may be charged by caretakers and concessionaires. There are about 5,300 camp and picnic sites with accommodations for 300,000 people, 183 ski areas with ski lifts or tows, and 83 wilderness areas in the most primitive regions. The Forest Service Program includes the construction of a well marked 2,265-mile Pacific Crest Trail crossing 19 national forests in the West to match the existing Appalachian Trail in the East, which extends 2,050 miles from Maine to Georgia and passes through 800 miles of national forests. In many national forests it is possible to lease land as sites for summer homes. ALBERT W. BROWN

AREAS UNDER FOREST SERVICE ADMINISTRATION*

States and Possessions	Acres
Alabama	632,034
Alaska	20,741,994
Arizona	11,400,868
Arkansas	2,408,807
California	19,979,589
Colorado	14,347,876
Connecticut	———
Delaware	———
Florida	1,075,035
Georgia	786,929
Hawaii	———
Idaho	20,349,803
Illinois	211,855
Indiana	124,769
Iowa	5,196
Kansas	107,114
Kentucky	460,031
Louisiana	591,409
Maine	50,021
Maryland	———
Massachusetts	1,651
Michigan	2,581,218
Minnesota	2,808,306
Mississippi	1,134,098
Missouri	1,374,348
Montana	16,635,568
Nebraska	339,716
Nevada	5,058,028
New Hampshire	678,220
New Jersey	———
New Mexico	9,090,308
New York	13,747
North Carolina	1,124,168
North Dakota	1,104,850
Ohio	109,493
Oklahoma	270,885
Oregon	15,466,517
Pennsylvania	471,154
Puerto Rico	34,265
South Carolina	587,260
South Dakota	2,004,482
Tennessee	595,982
Texas	775,265
Utah	7,918,431
Vermont	232,208
Virginia	1,453,409
Virgin Islands	———
Washington	9,730,114
West Virginia	904,092
Wisconsin	1,469,359
Wyoming	9,144,438

*1961

BIBLIOG.–W. B. Greely, *Forest Policy* (1953); K. P. Davis, *American Forest Management* (1954); S. T. Dana, *Forest and Range Policy* (1956); M. S. B. Bruère, *Your Forests* (1957); C. F. Brockman, *Recreational Use of Wild Lands* (1959); A. H. Carhart, *National Forests* (1959); H. A. Meyer and others, *Forest Management* (1961).

NATIONAL FORMULARY, usually abbreviated N.F., is an official standard of drugs and drug mixtures not listed in the *United States Pharmacopeia* (see PHARMACOPOEIA). Although originally copyrighted and published every 10 years by the American Pharmaceutical Association, it acquired legal status by an act of Congress (Pure Food and Drug Act, June 30, 1906). This law provides that all official preparations contained in the *National Formulary* must be made or manufactured according to the requirements of the standards set up by the *National Formulary*. Revisions and new editions of this work, published at intervals, describe requirements as to identity, quality, purity, strength, and storage for preparations listed. The authority of this reference book is unquestioned in all federal and most state courts. THEODORE KOPPANYI

NATIONAL FOUNDATION, formerly the National Foundation for Infantile Paralysis, a private, nonprofit organization, the activities of which include giving support to medical research, professional education, and disease prevention, and giving direct aid to patients. The research program includes the study of poliomyelitis, viruses in general, the nature of cells, diseases of the nervous system, arthritis, and birth defects, but is flexible enough to be directed opportunely toward other health problems of major importance. The efforts of this organization, which was founded in 1938 under the leadership of Pres. Franklin D. Roosevelt, were concentrated originally on the problems of poliomyelitis. In 1958, following the development, widespread use, and encouraging results of the Salk vaccine, the goals of the organization were broadened and the new name was adopted. The foundation has 3,100 local groups and conducts an annual fund-raising campaign, the New March of Dimes, during January. Its headquarters are in New York, N.Y.

NATIONAL GALLERY, on Trafalgar Square, London, the principal depository of paintings owned by the British government. The present building was completed in 1838 and later was enlarged several times. The nucleus of the museum was the John Angerstein collection of 38 paintings, purchased in 1824 for $285,000. Numerous bequests and purchases resulted in an outstanding collection noted especially for its works by English, Dutch, and Italian painters. The National Portrait Gallery adjoins the National Gallery.

NATIONAL GALLERY OF ART, at Constitution Avenue and Sixth Street, Washington, D.C., was established by act of Congress in 1937 as a bureau of the Smithsonian Institution and was opened to the public in 1941. It is supported by public funds and belongs to the citizens of the United States, but building construction was financed by a $15 million donation from Andrew Mellon. The Mellon collection of paintings (by Raphael, Botticelli, Rembrandt, Vermeer, and many others) and thirteenth to nineteenth century sculptures forms the nucleus of the museum's exhibits—more than 16,000 paintings, sculptures, drawings and prints, and examples of decorative arts.

Other gifts rapidly added to the National Gallery's collection. The Samuel H. Kress collection of Italian paintings and sculptures dating from the fourteenth to eighteenth centuries includes works by Giotto, Giovanni Bellini, Fra Filippo Lippi, and Giorgione; and the Kress collection of French paintings has works by Chardin, Watteau, Boucher, and Ingres. The National Gallery has Joseph E. Widener's collection of sculptures and paintings (among them 14 Rembrandts); the Lessing J. Rosenwald collection of drawings and prints by Albrecht Dürer, Rembrandt, William Blake, and others; and the Richter archives of photographs of paintings, a gift of Solomon R. Guggenheim. Chester Dale donated masterpieces by Tintoretto, El Greco, Rubens, and Zurbarán, and made an indefinite loan of his collection of nineteenth and twentieth century French paintings.

Mounted on a fountain in the National Gallery of Art in Washington, D.C., is a bronze statue of Mercury by the late Renaissance Flemish sculptor Giovanni da Bologna.

NATL. GALLERY OF ART, WASHINGTON, D.C.

The Index of American Design, placed in the gallery by the U.S. government, is a collection of some 22,000 water colors and photographs of American folk arts and crafts. The gallery has a library of more than 13,000 volumes.

NATIONAL GEOGRAPHIC SOCIETY. See GEOGRAPHIC SOCIETY.

NATIONAL GUARD, in the United States, is the organized land and air militia of the separate states, under the direction of state governors except in time of war or emergency when all or part of any state force may be integrated with federal armed forces.

Origin. The theory that militia should be the nation's chief source of military power was established in colonial America. Federal use of state militia is authorized in Section 8 of the first article of the federal Constitution. A New York regiment of state militia was designated a National Guard in 1824 as a compliment to Marie du Motier, marquis de Lafayette (then head of the National Guard of France), and by 1900 most states designated their militia as such, but it did not become the official name until the Dick Act of 1903. That act and its amendments (1906 and 1908), designed to reorganize state militias so that they might serve the national government more effectively, created two classes of militia—the National Guard and an inactive reserve—and increased the annual federal allotment to the National Guard. It provided for federal inspection, and for armament and discipline uniform with that of the Regular Army; lengthened the period for which the guard could be used by the federal government; and authorized federal use of militia beyond the continental boundaries of the United States.

Organization. Inadequacies in effectiveness and structure of the National Guard that became apparent during the expedition to Mexico against Pancho Villa in 1916 led to enactment of the National Defense Act of 1916. This act provided for greater uniformity between the National Guard and the Regular Army by making the guard on active duty part of the U.S. Army, and authorized the President to draft the entire guard into active service in time of war or national emergency as declared by the U.S. Congress. The National Guard was accordingly drafted into the Army by the Conscription Act of 1917. In 1920 an amendment recognized the National Guard along with the Regular Army as the nation's first line of defense; divided it for administrative purposes into nine corps areas; and authorized its strength according to a ratio of 800 members to one congressional representative.

The National Guard Act of 1933 further integrated the guard with the Regular Army by creating the dual status of the guard—the National Guard under state control, and the National Guard of the United States when on active duty in service of the United States. Since it was a part of the U.S. Army, the entire guard was activated in World War II in accordance with the Selective Training and Service Act of 1940. During the war structural changes were made within the National Guard so that organization of its units conformed to the units of the Regular Army.

After the war mass discharge of service personnel left the nation without a National Guard, but steps were taken in 1945 to reactivate and reorganize it. The Armed Forces Reserve Act of 1952 provided that in the event of war or emergency declared by Congress the guard may be ordered into active federal service for the duration and six months; if the guard is ordered into service in time of emergency proclaimed by the President, the period of service is 24 months. During the Korean conflict one-third of the National Guard's ground forces and 85 per cent of the Air National Guard were in active federal service. See MILITIA; ARMY, U.S.

NATIONAL HEALTH COUNCIL, founded in 1921, is an organization of national voluntary agencies. It co-operates with federal, state, and local health authorities and with related health agencies and community groups to promote better health, and to broaden their scope of usefulness. Councils are established to help advance effectiveness of health agencies. In 1961 the National Health Council consisted of 71 member organizations. An annual convention-meeting is held either in February or March. Headquarters are in New York City.

NATIONAL HIGHWAY USERS CONFERENCE, a nonprofit organization composed of U.S. associations interested in the safe, economic, and efficient development of highway transportation. Member groups include associations of motorbus, trucking, and petroleum industries; agricultural, shipper, and rural letter-carrier organizations; motor vehicle and tire manufacturers; and automobile dealers. Through its engineering service and departments of legislative reporting, public information, research, and safety the NHUC serves more than 1,900 national and state organizations of highway users. Headquarters are in Washington, D.C.

NATIONAL HOCKEY LEAGUE. See ICE HOCKEY, *Development*.

NATIONAL HOLY NAME SOCIETY. See ROMAN CATHOLIC ORGANIZATIONS.

NATIONAL INCOME is the total amount of money received by the individuals and business enterprises of a nation for productive effort, calculated on an annual basis. See INCOME.

Significance. In modern economics, national income is significant primarily for four reasons. First, there is an increasing demand for a measurement of economic welfare. Such measurement has been a historic objective of national income statisticians in many countries, and after the inception of the United Nations national income comparisons became a matter of increasing international political and economic interest.

Second, national income computations are used to estimate a country's capacity to produce because production is reflected in the income figure and it is much easier statistically to measure income than to measure production directly. During World War II the ability to estimate potential U.S. national income gave the United States a perspective of its war production potential that was impossible to gain by examining the capacity of individual industries.

Third, national income has come to play a predominant role in economic analysis. As a result of political and economic events since the early 1930's, government has been charged with the responsibility for mass unemployment. In almost all democratic countries it has therefore become a matter of national policy to maintain a high national income as a means of insuring a satisfactory level of employment. In line with this political trend, twentieth century economists led by John Maynard Keynes (1883–1946) built a theory of national income determination on a short-term basis to meet the needs of the policy makers—an approach that is in sharp contrast to the ideas of the classical economists who set their sights on distant economic horizons and largely ignored short-run economic fluctuations.

Fourth, in the post-World War II period virtually all countries became preoccupied with the classical problems of long-run rates of growth of their national economies; the relative rates of growth of national incomes became important strategic factors in international relations. Throughout underdeveloped countries, especially in the Middle and Far East, the question of whether national income can increase faster than population became a crucial one.

Factors Included in National Income. National income can be considered as the total earnings of the factors of production—land, labor, and capital. Statistical difficulties arise, however, when an attempt is made to determine what constitutes productive effort so that income payments outside this classification can be eliminated from computations. See PRODUCTION.

When a person receives dividends or interest, no new productive effort takes place. The amount of interest and dividends are included in the income of the stockholders and consequently a like amount should be deducted from the income of the corporation; likewise, a gift from one person to another must not be included twice.

Government relief payments or benefits to veterans are excluded from national income. Interest on the national debt is generally excluded since it is considered to be paid to discharge a past contract rather than to compensate for a service currently performed.

If the products sold by a business include raw materials purchased from another business, the computation includes the value of raw materials only once. Similarly, it is necessary to deduct depreciation of fixed capital equipment to avoid double counting. It has been suggested that some of the services performed by government for businesses should not be considered as intermediate products—that such wages as those of the policemen who protect business property should not be included in the national income. Statisticians, however, have found no satisfactory way to give effect to this view, and incomes arising from all services rendered by government are included in the figures.

There has been considerable debate on how taxes should be treated. For example, there is no single answer to the question as to whether taxes that are passed on to the consumer should be included as income. If it is desired that total incomes add up to the total value of current production, all taxes must be included as income. On the other hand, if it is desired

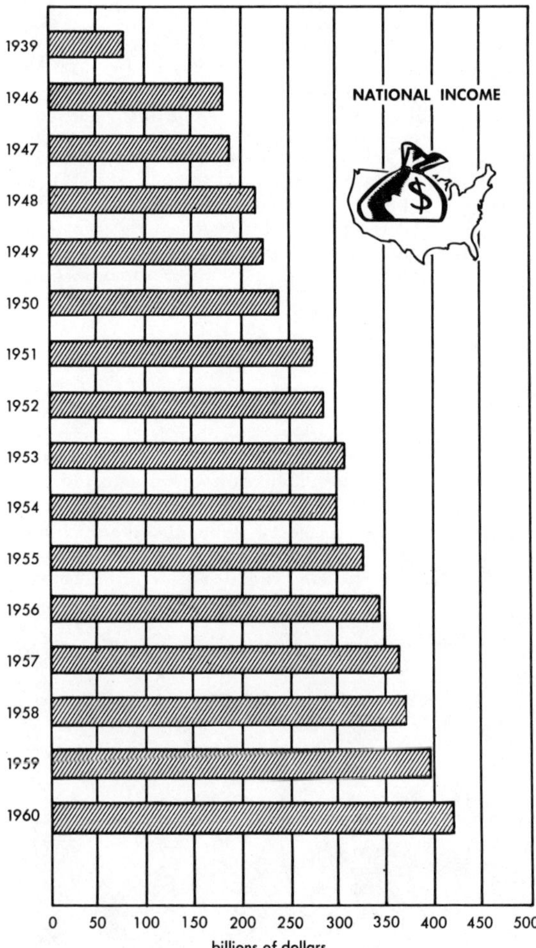

that the relative earnings of the factors of production be correctly reflected, taxes that are shifted should not be included as income. Official statistics usually include two figures: "net national income at market prices," from which no tax deductions are made; and "net national income at factor prices," which does not include indirect taxes. It is thus assumed, with doubtful justification, that indirect taxes are shifted but that all direct taxes are paid out of income. See TAXATION.

A concept that has acquired wide popularity is that of the "gross national product," which is net national income at market prices before allowance is made for depreciation of fixed plant and equipment. For some analytic purposes this gross figure is preferable to a net figure. Also, from the short-period point of view, gross national product gives a better indication of productive potential because it is possible to defer replacement of fixed equipment for a limited period and thus free resources for current production.

All these concepts relate to the income of residents of a country, and so include income earned by them from investments and services rendered abroad. Incomes earned by foreigners in the country concerned are excluded.

Most of the uses of the national income concept require comparisons from year to year or from country to country, and in most cases interest centers not on money income, but rather on real income—the amount of goods and services that money income can buy. Thus it is necessary to devise some way to express the national income in dollars of constant purchasing power. For instance, if comparisons with the pre-World War II period are desired, current national income is estimated in terms of, say, 1939 prices. The process of deflating current dollars to some base year gives rise to some of the most difficult statistical and theoretical questions in the national income field. Unless real-income measurements are handled properly, they are open to grave misuse.

Measurement of Economic Welfare. It would be preferable to measure economic welfare from the aspect of production rather than from an income approach. Were a record available of the quantities and prices of all goods and services produced during two or more years (or in two or more countries), it would be simple to express the figures in terms of index numbers that would help reveal whether welfare had increased or diminished. (See INDEX NUMBER.) Because, however, the statistical data necessary for the construction of such indexes are usually not available, persons interested in making this investigation must fall back on a method in which the national income figure is adjusted by some general price index—such as the cost-of-living index, which is used most frequently. The results of such computations are necessarily only approximations. See COST OF LIVING.

Since price indexes are based on records of market prices, the correct national income figure to adjust is clearly national income at market prices. If national income at factor prices were used for this purpose, the measurement of real income would be affected by changes in indirect tax rates.

At the very best, these indexes can only reveal the direction of change and cannot correctly be used to estimate how much change in welfare has occurred. Such a comparison could lead ultimately to the absurd conclusion that, if real national income has doubled, the country is twice as happy or satisfied.

The fact that tastes do not remain unchanged generally invalidates welfare comparisons except for those based on short periods. The essence of economic growth is that tastes change under the impetus of changing technology. Without such changes of taste a country could not progress. Attempts to compare the welfare of people of various nations cause similar difficulties; moreover, the usefulness of such comparisons is equally questionable.

Measurement of Quantity of Production. National income has appreciable validity when used as the basis for an index of capacity to produce, but for this purpose, too, the figures must be used with caution. For example, the real income of the United States in the late 1950's was three times what it was in 1929 and real income per capita in the United States was about 30 times that in China. This comparison, however, does not mean that the United States had the capacity to provide its citizens with three times the amount of goods they had in 1929—thrice as many houses, thrice as much clothing, or thrice as much food. More emphatically, the comparison does not mean that the United States could have supported 5 billion Chinese at the existing Chinese standard of living. Even so, the estimates are often useful and valid. It is by no means absurd to say that the combined incomes of 1,000 Americans could have supported 30,000 Chinese, for such a comparison could be made without defying the law of diminishing returns (see DIMINISHING RETURNS). Similarly, if real national income increased by, say, 10 per cent from one year to the next, it would be permissible to say that the country's capacity to satisfy human wants had increased.

The Price Index is used as an adjustment factor, or deflator, to evaluate the cost of a given amount of goods and services. When applied to national income figures, price indexes purport to express the capacity of the country to buy, either at home or abroad, comparable amounts of like goods and services represented by the price index. Since, however, patterns of national production often vary widely, the validity of the real-income measurement depends on the extent to which the goods produced actually could be exchanged for the goods represented in the price index. For example, the usefulness of wartime national income figures deflated by the cost-of-living index has serious limitations. More than 50 per cent of the U.S. national income during World War II was earned by the manufacture of war-purpose goods for the government. How accurately this portion of national income can be related to the civilian cost-of-living goods is open to question. Similar difficulties arise, in less acute form, in dealing with peacetime government production.

National Income as a Concept for Economic Analysis. Keynes brought about a revolution in economic thought with his theory of determining national income on a short-run basis. The essence of Keynes' theory is the rejection of Say's law (which maintains that supply creates its own demand) with his introduction of the concept of effective demand.

The classical economists hold that in the long run the recipients of the national income, regardless of its size, spend it entirely on either consumption goods or investment goods. The Keynesian position holds that there is no such identity between income and spending but, rather, that at low levels of income the public spends proportionally more money on consumption goods and at high levels proportionally less.

To carry out adequately the Keynesian type of analysis, it is necessary to determine the expenditure behavior of many economic groups—government, businesses, consumers, and so forth. It is also necessary to study their behavior relative to different classes of goods, such as durable and nondurable goods. Finally, it is necessary to know the laws of the distribution of national income among groups with different expenditure behavior. In short, a complete statement of the "social accounts" is required for national income, not merely a single figure.

National Income and Economic Growth. Modern theories of economic growth are concerned (as were those of the classical economists) largely with the effect that the accumulation of capital has on total output, and it is generally held that countries adhere to an output-capital ratio that changes little, if at all, when considered in terms of long periods of time. If, in addition, a country saves a given proportion of its income, its potential rate of economic growth is determined by multiplying its output-capital ratio by its savings-capital ratio. The potential indicated as a result of this computation, however, will be realized only if total demand, as determined by Keynesian analysis, is sufficient to insure full use of productive capacity; otherwise growth will be impeded either by depressions or by chronic tendencies toward excess productive capacity. A logically satisfactory theory of growth of the national income involves a combination of the Keynesian and the classical analysis.

Compilation of National Income Statistics was pioneered during the first half of the twentieth century in the United States and in England—preeminently by Colin Clark of England and Simon Kuznets of the United States. Examples set by these two countries have been followed throughout the British Commonwealth and most of Europe.

J. R. N. Stone of Cambridge University is credited with transforming national income computation into a more comprehensive process of social accounting. The same approach has been followed in the national income division of the U.S. Department of Commerce. Although the United Nations made the improvement of national income statistics throughout the world one of the major aspects of its statistical work, estimates in many countries come from unreliable sources. See BUSINESS CYCLE; CAPITAL; FINANCE, Public Finance.

ARTHUR SMITHIES

BIBLIOG.–Robert M. Biggs, *National Income Analysis and Forecasting* (1956); Phyllis Deane, ed., *Bibliography on Income and Wealth* (vol. 1–7) (1946–1956) (1960); Melvin L. Greenhut and Frank H. Jackson, *Intermediate Income and Growth Theory* (1961); *Income and Wealth Series* (8 vols.) (1951–1960); Simon Kuznets, ed., *Income and Wealth in the United States: Trends and Structures* (1952); Paul F. Studenski, *Income of Nations* (*With Corrections and Emendations*) (2 pts.) (1961).

NATIONAL INDUSTRIAL CONFERENCE BOARD, an independent, nonprofit U.S. organization founded in 1916 to advance education and research in business economics and management, and to promote development of free enterprise by assembling, analyzing, and disseminating information about economic conditions. Membership of the board consists of leading industrialists; it maintains a research department of economists whose services are available to subscribing industrial and commercial firms, labor unions, trade associations, government agencies, and educational institutions. Publications include two monthlies, *Conference Board Business Record* and the *Conference Board Management Record*, and also individual studies. Headquarters are in New York, N.Y.

NATIONAL INSTITUTE OF ARTS AND LETTERS, for the protection and advancement of literature, sculpture, painting, music, and architecture, was organized in 1898 by the American Social Science Association and incorporated by an act of Congress, 1912. Qualification for membership, which is limited to 250, is notable achievement in art, music, or literature. The institute awards an annual gold medal to a U.S. citizen for distinguished achievement in arts or letters. In 1904 the institute organized the American Academy of Arts and Letters. Headquarters of the institute are in New York, N.Y.

NATIONALISM is a political doctrine that regards the good of a nation or national group as paramount and of overriding value. Nationalism depends upon a sense of unity shared by people with a common background of religion, language, political tradition, race, or any combination of such elements in varying degrees of importance. For example, religion was important in the development of nationalism in Pakistan and India, but less so in the development of German nationalism. Common political traditions established Switzerland and the United States as nations, although a common language was not present in Switzerland and common race was not a factor in the United States. Not all nationality groups, however, have political autonomy. The Jews for centuries had no common political entity, and between 1453 and 1821 the Greeks had no state of their own.

Within the American colonies, nationalist sentiments developed in the eighteenth century which led to the Declaration of Independence and the Revolutionary War. The colonists developed a sense of unity through shared economic interests, territorial expansion, and establishment of political and social institutions. This sense of unity was strengthened even further by uniform resentment of England's taxation of the colonies coupled with its failure to grant sufficient political autonomy.

In nineteenth century Europe, nationalism found expression in a general movement toward political emancipation and autonomy of nationality groups—a movement recognized in the theory of national self-determination that was propounded by Pres. Woodrow Wilson in the early part of the twentieth century. This theory was applied to the Austro-Hungarian Empire after World War I; many of the nationality groups that had composed the empire either became nation-states (a national group having political autonomy) as did the Yugoslavs and Czechs, or elected to become part of an already independent state, as did the Italians. The U.S.S.R., established during the same period is, however, a union of many nationality groups, all of which owe allegiance to the same state. See NATIONALITY; STATE.

In the twentieth century, despite heightened international co-operation and the development of international bodies such as the League of Nations and the United Nations, nationalism has remained a potent and frequently disruptive force. The doctrine of nationalism influenced the development of self-government in many colonies and brought about their political emancipation.

Early Manifestations. The appearance of nationalism and of nation-states is a modern European phenomenon. Political groups in antiquity such as ancient Egypt, Phoenicia, and Assyria had not developed the state of collective consciousness associated with nationalism. The city-state of ancient Greece was a political community claiming the absolute loyalty of its citizens and constantly warring with other city-states; national feelings among the Greeks of that time can be traced to the distinction they made between themselves and barbarians rather than to feelings of allegiance toward a city-state other than their own. (See CITY-STATE.) The Roman Empire, based upon the strength of Roman legions and Roman law, included almost all the peoples of its time, yet there was no Roman nation. With the fall of the Roman Empire and the barbarian invasions, all except personal ties disappeared and in the feudal period the most important bond was personal, between lord and vassal.

In the Renaissance, social, economic, political, and intellectual factors together formed the matrix for nationalism in Europe. The printing press undermined any class monopoly on learning, and adoption of vernaculars for literary expression brought national languages into existence. The Protestant Reformation eventually led to national churches. In several countries monarchs allied themselves with towns against feudal lords and set up centralized, sovereign kingdoms. As trade and commerce developed, the commercial middle classes of towns, unfettered by traditions and loyalties, demanded the protection of strong central authority and the economic advantages of larger territorial units. In eighteenth century Europe replacement of religious training by secular instruction led to national educational systems, and as education brought cultural and political awakening, the rights of the people rather than authority of the king demanded attention. Poets, writers, and scholars emphasized the cultural traditions of their people and developed national literatures that stressed unique national contributions. The king was no longer the state—the state became the possession of the whole people; land no longer belonged to the monarch but to those who lived upon it. A country became a fatherland, and nation and state began to have the same meaning.

Europe. In England political centralization advanced further than elsewhere in Europe, and a lively sense of national unity developed in the seventeenth and eighteenth centuries. Agricultural upper classes and commercial middle classes exercised political power through Parliament, and gradually came to feel that they were the nation—a sentiment popularized by John Locke (1632–1704) and Edmund Burke (1729–97). The popular sovereignty theory of Jean Jacques Rousseau (1712–78) developed in eighteenth century France and helped to bring about the French Revolution—which in turn became a powerful activating force toward nationalism. Other European peoples crystallized their national feelings as they fought to free themselves from the imperialism of Napoleon Bonaparte (1769–1821), and even though extranational forces triumphed at the Congress of Vienna (1814–15), the movement toward national independence continued. See VIENNA, CONGRESS OF.

Nationalism developed most spectacularly in Germany and Italy. In Germany, a land divided into numerous principalities, it began as a cultural movement. After 1820, however, it became political nationalism—at first democratic and liberal but eventually directed by Prince Otto von Bismarck (1815–98) to bring about German unification (1870) and Prussian autocracy. (See BISMARCK, PRINCE OTTO EDUARD LEOPOLD VON.) In Italy, then only a geographical expression, a similar development took place. Through the efforts of nineteenth century leaders—Giuseppe Mazzini (1805–72), an idealistic nationalist; Giuseppe Garibaldi (1808–82), popular guerrilla leader; Camillo Cavour (1810–61), liberal statesman; and Victor Emmanuel II (1820–78), statesman king—modern Italy became a reality in 1861. See MAZZINI, GIUSEPPE; GARIBALDI, GIUSEPPE; CAVOUR, CAMILLO BENSO, CONTE DI; VICTOR EMMANUEL II; IRREDENTISM.

Elsewhere in western Europe nationalism had become dominant by mid-nineteenth century. In Southeastern Europe the nationalism of the Balkan peoples brought about numerous conflicts until all Balkan nations were free of Turkish rule. (See BALKAN WARS.) At the end of World War I, a number of national states—Austria, Hungary, Poland, Yugoslavia, and Czechoslovakia—were established through the breakup of the Austro-Hungarian Empire. National independence was gained by Finns, Lithuanians, Latvians, and Estonians; in several areas plebiscites expressed the wishes of the population as to which nation-state the majority preferred.

Asia. The first people in Asia to develop a strong national consciousness were the Japanese. Their nationalism developed out of religion, monarchy, and militarism, and centered around worship of the emperor; it was militaristic and imperialistic, and led to World War II. In China strong nationalistic sentiment developed after 1900, but did not overcome the influence of family ties nor regional loyalties until political power was won by the Communists. In India rising nationalism led to termination of political control by the British in 1947; religious differences between Hindus and Moslems in India brought about the establishment of Pakistan as a separate nation-state. Elsewhere—especially in Burma, Ceylon, Indonesia, former French Indochina, and the Philippines—nationalism and anti-imperialism developed together, leading to independence movements with varying degrees of success.

Turkey under Mustapha Kemal Pasha (see ATATÜRK, MUSTAPHA KEMAL) displayed strong nationalistic attitudes after World War I. The movement spread throughout the Middle East to Iran, Egypt, and other Arab states. Zionism is a manifestation of nationalism of a dispersed and often persecuted religious group (see ZIONISM). It resulted in the establishment of Israel in 1948.

Africa. In Africa, especially after World War II, colonial powers granted national independence to natives trained in self-government—either as a matter of policy or because they were forced to do so by native uprisings. Morocco, Tunisia, Libya, the Sudan, and Ghana became independent states. In other areas of Africa, dependent territories acquired increasing degrees of self-government.

Extreme Nationalism. Nationalism tends to be an inherently conservative force, and places collective interest above the interests of the individual. In the nineteenth century, however, manifestations of national independence stemmed from doctrines of equality, liberty, and fraternity of the French Revolution, and stood for liberalism and political democracy in opposition to autocratic monarchs and the aspirations of feudal lords. Some twentieth century manifestations of nationalism, on the other hand, had a pronounced antiliberal and antidemocratic character; the most extreme and virulent form was fascism. Italian fascism insisted that the nation-state had a life and purpose of its own, superior to the lives of individuals. German national socialism was similar, but even more extreme. Both movements were totalitarian in domestic policy and imperialistic in international policy (see IMPERIALISM). Although defeat in World War II ended Fascist government in Italy, Germany, and Japan, Fascist nationalistic theories continued to dominate in Spain, and to find adherents in other countries. See FASCISM; NATIONAL SOCIALISM.

Communism. Originally communism opposed nationalism. Inspired by Karl Marx (1818–83) and Friedrich Engels (1820–95), Communists were more interested in economic class than in a nation, and most modern Communists give primary loyalty to the Soviet Union rather than to their own nations. The Soviet Union, however, fostered nationalism during World War II in an effort to win the fullest support of its people, and has been charged with preaching nationalism to bring about revolutionary movements in the colonies of other countries. Although the U.S.S.R. often has affirmed its allegiance to the principle of national self-determination, Yugoslavia broke away from Soviet domination because that principle had been violated.

Authorities in the field of history have observed that historical development need not necessarily end at nationalism. Some state that, just as tribalism, feudalism, and other systems of loyalty gave way to nationalism in the eighteenth and nineteenth centuries, so may nationalism be another intermediate form in the progression of political organization. See INTERNATIONALISM. ROY C. MACRIDIS

BIBLIOG.–American Academy of Political and Social Science, *Latin America's Nationalistic Revolutions* (1961); Walter Bagehot, *Physics and Politics* (1959); Frederick C. Barghoorn, *Soviet Russian Nationalism* (1956); Karl W. Deutsch, *Interdisciplinary Bibliography on Nationalism, 1935–1953* (1956); Abba S. Eban, *Tide of Nationalism* (1959); Rupert Emerson, *From Empire to Nation* (1960); Carlton J. H. Hayes, *Historical Evolution of Modern Nationalism* (1931), *Nationalism: A Religion* (1960); Élie Kedourie, *Nationalism* (1961); Hans Kohn, *American Nationalism* (1957), *Mind of Germany* (1960); John T. Marcus, *Neutralism and Nationalism in France* (1959); Hazem Z. Nuseibeh, *Ideas of Arab Nationalism* (1957); Bernard Semmel, *Imperialism and Social Reform: English Social-Imperial Thought, 1895–1914* (1960); Boyd C. Shafer, *Nationalism: Myth and Reality* (1955); Ndabaningi Sithole, *African Nationalism* (1959); Roman Smal-Stocki, *Captive Nations* (1960); Benjamin T. Spencer, *Quest for Nationality* (1957); Eric B. Strauss, *Irish Nationalism and British Democracy* (1951); Philip W. Thayer, ed., *Nationalism and Progress in Free Asia* (1956).

NATIONALITY in international law is the relationship between an individual and a sovereign state in accordance with which he owes allegiance to the state and is entitled to its protection; or the status of material things as property of the state, subject to its jurisdiction. Nationality does not necessarily imply the right to exercise civic or political functions that go with citizenship, but frequently no distinction is made between nationality and citizenship. (See CITIZENSHIP.) The question of nationality is important when an individual appeals to a government for protection and another government contests his claim. Persons who have no nationality are stateless persons, who remain to some degree outside the protection of the law. The Hague Convention of 1930 provided that a sovereign state should determine by its own law who are its nationals. The Universal Declaration of Human Rights, approved by the General Assembly of the United Nations in 1948, stated that everyone had the right to a nationality and that no one could be deprived of nationality, or denied the right to change it. The declaration, however, contained no sanctions by which its principles might be enforced.

Nationality is acquired by birth or by naturalization. (See NATURALIZATION.) Nationality through birth on the soil (*jus soli*) frequently conflicts with nationality based on parentage (*jus sanguinis*), and dual nationality results when one state follows the rule of birth on the soil and another the rule of parentage. Nationality acquired by naturalization may conflict with that acquired by birth. For example, in the mid-nineteenth century the United States claimed that nationality acquired by naturalization took priority over nationality by birth, but certain European states affirmed the principle of indelible allegiance because of nationality acquired at birth. (See ALLEGIANCE.) In cases where colonies declare their independence, a general change of nationality takes place; this is true also in cases of cession of territory.

In another sense, particular racial or religious groups, such as Polish, Irish, Armenian, or Arab nationals, during periods of political subjection are frequently considered to be nationalities distinct from the state to which the group owes allegiance. See ALIEN; INTERNATIONAL LAW, *Persons in International Law.* CHARLES G. FENWICK

NATIONALIZATION. See SOCIALISM; COMMUNISM; GOVERNMENT OWNERSHIP; GREAT BRITAIN, Economic Factors; MUNICIPAL OWNERSHIP.

NATIONAL JEWISH WELFARE BOARD. See JEWISH ORGANIZATIONS, *Social Welfare Agencies.*

NATIONAL LABOR RELATIONS BOARD, an independent federal agency created by the National Labor Relations Act of 1935 and continued by the Taft-Hartley Labor Management Relations Act of 1947. (See LABOR RELATIONS, *Taft-Hartley Act.*) The NLRA affirms the right of employees to organize and to bargain collectively. See COLLECTIVE BARGAINING.

During the depression of the 1930's the aims of labor organization and collective bargaining became increasingly acceptable, and the Norris-La Guardia Act of 1932 practically eliminated the use of injunctions in labor disputes. The National Industrial Recovery Act (1933) required guarantees of employees' rights to organize and bargain collectively without coercion. (See INJUNCTION, Injunctions in Labor Disputes, *Controlling Legislation;* NATIONAL RECOVERY ADMINISTRATION.) The NLRA was drafted with more precision and more detailed provisions for enforcement than these earlier acts, but not until 1937 when its constitutionality was sustained by the Supreme Court did it become an effective instrument in labor-management relations.

The board originally had three members appointed by the President and confirmed by the Senate. Its main offices are in Washington, D.C., and 22 regional offices and 7 subregional offices are in the larger cities of the United States. There is also a regional office in Puerto Rico. Before amendment by the Taft-Hartley Act the board issued cease-and-desist orders to prevent interference with employees' rights to organize and bargain collectively, and to prevent domination of a union by an employer. It settled disputes concerning discrimination against or discharge of an employee because of union activity. The board also decided appropriate collective bargaining units; certified names of employee representatives or ascertained them by secret ballot; and ordered and conducted hearings on violations of the act. To implement enforcement the board had power to issue subpoenas, administer oaths, conduct investigations, and petition circuit courts of appeals to enforce cease-and-desist orders.

Labor organization developed rapidly after the passage of NLRA, and by the end of World War II the managements of industries were demanding government curbs of some labor practices. As a result, in 1947 the Taft-Hartley Act was passed, amending some of the provisions of NLRA; new provisions banned the closed shop, withdrew foremen and supervisors from employee status, guaranteed the right of free speech in employers' communications to employees, defined some union activities as unfair labor practices subject to cease-and-desist orders, outlawed secondary boycotts and jurisdictional strikes, and revised rules covering certification of unions as representatives of employees. The board was increased to five members, although it may delegate its powers to any three or more members, and the act provided for appointment of a general counsel by the President, to have authority in determining whether complaints should be issued or prosecuted. The NLRA and the Taft-Hartley amendments were further amended by the Labor-Management Reporting and Disclosure Act of 1959 (Landrum-Griffin Act), which added a "bill of rights" for union members. The act also included guarantees of fair election of union officers and against corruption in the handling of union finances. State labor agencies and courts were authorized to handle "no man's land" cases that were formerly outside the jurisdiction of the states and the NLRB. Regulations against organizational and recognition picketing were strengthened, and airline, railroad, farm, and government workers were brought under the restrictions against secondary boycotts and recognition and organizational picketing. Agreements by an employer not to do business with firms designated unfair—by the union, so-called hot cargo contracts—were prohibited. See LABOR MOVEMENT, Labor Legislation.

NATIONAL LEAD COMPANY, an operating and holding company with worldwide subsidiaries, manufactures paints and paint materials; pigments and chemicals; oils; lead and lead alloys; zinc, aluminum, brass, and magnesium die castings; acid-handling equipment; oil-well drilling materials; and titanium alloys and pigments. The National Lead Company was incorporated in New Jersey in 1891. It is affiliated with the R-N Corporation, a company jointly owned with Republic Steel Corporation and organized for the development of a new, direct reduction process for iron ores; and with the Metals Corporation of America, jointly owned with Allegheny Ludlum Steel Corporation and organized to produce and distribute titanium metal and products. National Lead also operates a jointly owned plastics research and development project with the Celanese Corporation. In 1954 the company became the contract operator of the Atomic Energy Commission's raw material development laboratory in Winchester, Mass., to develop uranium ore concentrating processes, and in 1956 received the contract for operation of a uranium plant in Monticello, Utah. The company had 21,326 employees in 1959. General offices are in New York, N.Y.

NATIONAL LEAGUE, the first organized of present major baseball leagues, came into existence in 1876 after professional baseball had fallen into disrepute under supervision of the National Association of Professional Baseball Players. Charter members of the National League were the teams of Chicago, Boston, New York, Philadelphia, Hartford, St. Louis, Cincinnati, and Louisville. William A. Hulbert of Chicago was the main force behind the organization of the National League and became its president in

1877. Changes were frequently made in teams comprising the National League until 1900. Membership thereafter remained unchanged until 1953 when Milwaukee replaced Boston. In 1957 Los Angeles and San Francisco replaced Brooklyn and New York. In 1959 the National League was composed of eight members: the Milwaukee Braves, Los Angeles Dodgers, San Francisco Giants, Chicago Cubs, Cincinnati Reds, Philadelphia Phillies, Pittsburgh Pirates, and St. Louis Cardinals. The membership was increased to 10 in 1962 with the addition of the Houston Colts and the New York Mets. National League headquarters are in Cincinnati, Ohio. WARREN C. GILES

NATIONAL LEGAL AID AND DEFENDER ASSOCIATION, formerly National Legal Aid Association, a central clearinghouse for U.S. organizations that provide legal aid and defender services to persons who cannot afford to pay lawyers' fees. The association, founded in 1923 as an affiliate of the American Bar Association (ABA), represents its member organizations nationally. Services to its members include establishing minimum standards of practice, providing research on legal problems facing member organizations, and distributing publications, such as the *Legal Aid Brief Case*, about the legal aid field. The first Legal Aid Society was established in 1876, but the development of other officers was slow. In the late 1940's, the National Legal Aid and Defender Association and the ABA inaugurated a nationwide campaign to strengthen existing offices and establish new facilities. By the 1960's there were about 350 legal offices handling civil cases and about 100 defender services. Legal aid and defender offices serve more than a half-million clients. Headquarters of the organization are at the American Bar center in Chicago. See AMERICAN BAR ASSOCIATION.

NATIONAL MUNICIPAL LEAGUE, founded in 1894, is a nonprofit, nonpartisan educational association of U.S. individuals and organizations that acts as a clearinghouse for information on better state and local government. In co-operation with local civic organizations the league prepares model laws and systems of administration on such subjects as civil service and budgets. Special books, pamphlets, and reports are published throughout the year, such as the monthly *National Civic Review*. The league is cosponsor of the annual All-America Cities award competition, based on outstanding action taken by citizens in civic improvement and in solving major community problems. Membership in the National Municipal League totals about 5,000. Headquarters are in New York City.

NATIONAL MUSIC COUNCIL, an organization of U.S. music associations, founded in 1940 to foster co-operation among representatives of all phases of musical activity, from composers and performers to music publishers and instrument manufacturers. The association provides for interchange of information and discussion among the member groups, encourages the co-ordination of the efforts of the various organizations, organizes fact-finding commissions for the solution of important problems, encourages the development and appreciation of the art of music, and fosters high professional and industrial standards. *The National Music Council Bulletin* is published three times a year. Headquarters are in New York City.

NATIONAL PARKS, in the United States, are tracts of public land reserved from sale or other disposition by special act of Congress for the enjoyment, recreation, and education of all the people. National parks are like national museums in that the major purpose of their establishment is generally to preserve that part of the nation's outstanding natural and historical heritage peculiar to each of them, for the benefit and enjoyment of present and future generations. Natural conditions are maintained as much as possible in the national parks. Fallen trees, for example, are allowed to decay where they fall. No hunting, mining, or grazing is allowed. The attractiveness of the parks cannot be exploited commercially for profit, and activities detracting from natural conditions are not encouraged.

W. RAY SCOTT, NATL. PARK CONCESSIONS, INC.

The perpendicular walls of Santa Elena Canyon rise 1,500 feet over the waters of the Rio Grande, which separates Big Bend National Park, Texas, from Mexico.

Yellowstone, the earliest U.S. national park, was created in 1872 as "a public park or pleasuring-ground for the benefit and enjoyment of the people." The first national park east of the Rocky Mountains was Wind Cave, established in 1903 in the scenic Black Hills region of South Dakota. Almost all of the extremes of natural conditions existing in the United States can be found in our national parks. In climate, the parks vary from subtropical Everglades to subarctic Mount McKinley National Park. The dryness of Big Bend contrasts with the humidity of Olympic National Park. The volcanic activity of historical times in Lassen Volcanic National Park is quite different from the stable timelessness with which the Colorado River makes its way through Grand Canyon National Park. The alpine peaks of Grand Teton are matched in natural splendor by the depths of Mammoth Cave, Wind Cave, and Carlsbad Caverns National Parks. The thermal activity of Yellowstone, the tremendous trees of Sequoia, the frozen grandeur of Glacier, the alpine meadows of Rocky Mountain, the surf-pounded ocean shores of Acadia, and the peaceful rolling haze of Great Smoky Mountains National Parks can refresh and bring enjoyment to people of all tastes.

Opportunities for Recreation. The parks offer opportunities for the naturalist to observe plants and animals in native habitats. To preserve the natural conditions, considerable effort is made to prevent visitors from starting destructive fires, from molesting the plants and animals, and from littering the park grounds. Special groups may obtain permits from the park superintendent to collect geological, botanical, or zoological specimens for scientific study. The national parks and monuments are game sanctuaries, and therefore beneficial to hunters because the wildlife multiplies under park protection and eventually overflows into adjoining territory. Fishing is permitted in the national parks under regulations that insure against depletion of the fish supply. Any person fishing in the waters of Yosemite, Sequoia, Lassen Volcanic, Kings Canyon, Grand Canyon, Rocky Mountain, Grand Teton, Acadia, Olympic, Wind Cave, Great Smoky Mountains, Mammoth Cave, Shenandoah, or Zion National Park, Lake Mead National Recreation Area, or any monument under the jurisdiction of the National Park Service must secure a sporting fishing license as required by the laws of the state or states in which the park or monument is located. Streams and lakes in many national parks are stocked.

All permanent ranger positions for the parks are filled by civil service appointment. Ranger duties include checking travel, directing traffic, enforcing rules and regulations for the protection of parks, giving information to tourists, fire fighting, improving trails, repairing telephone lines, protecting wild animals, planting fish, and supervising campgrounds. A number of seasonal park rangers work during the summer months. Many of these temporary rangers are schoolteachers who work as park naturalists during the summer to interpret the park and its geology, flora, and fauna to visitors.

Administration. National parks are under the control of the secretary of the interior, who administers them through the director of the National Park Service. A superintendent is in charge of each national park. Hotel, lodge, and transportation service are provided within some parks by private enterprise on franchise or concession from the Department of the Interior. All public utilities are under supervision of the National Park Service. Public automobile camps, equipped with sanitary conveniences, are provided by the government for the benefit of motoring visitors who carry their own equipment. In many of the parks naturalist services, consisting of conducted hikes, lectures, and campfire programs, are provided free.

Legal Status. The public land within the boundaries of a national park is reserved as the permanent property of the government from all forms of appropriation. All public land laws for the passage of title from public to private ownership are suspended within the national parks. Many of the parks, however, include within their boundaries tracts of private land that were sold or granted by the government before the reservation for park purposes was made. The legal status of such privately owned tracts is not affected by the reservation of the surrounding government land. Because some grazing and mineral leases were privately held when the areas were set aside as parks or monuments, limited activities of these kinds have gone on, but such leases are not renewed. The federal government, as owner of all the parks, may pass laws to protect its ownership from trespass and enforce them in the federal courts. But in some parks federal jurisdiction extends to the protection not only of federal property, but of all private and public rights whatsoever, to the complete exclusion of state authority. This exclusive federal jurisdiction may exist because the reserved lands have never been a part, or subjected to the jurisdiction, of any state. Thus Yellowstone was created before Montana, Wyoming, and Idaho became states, as was Sulphur Springs Reservation, subsequently known as Platt National Park, before Oklahoma became a state. At the time these states were formed, exclusive jurisdiction over the parks was reserved by Congress. Such reservation was not made for Hot Springs National Park when Arkansas was admitted into the Union, but the state later ceded exclusive jurisdiction of the park area to the federal government. The state of Washington, by act of Mar. 16, 1901, tendered a like cession of exclusive jurisdiction over Mount Rainier National Park. Montana, by act of Feb. 17, 1914, followed suit in regard to Glacier National Park. Jurisdiction over other national parks was ceded by the states in which they are located and accepted by Congress.

National Monuments are another form of public reservation administered by the National Park Service. They differ from the national parks in that they may be set aside by the President without a special act of Congress and may be established for specific historical, scientific, or educational reasons rather than for the more general reasons that apply in the establishment of national parks. Under the Antiquities Act of June 8, 1906, the President is authorized to reserve by proclamation as national monuments public lands containing "historic landmarks, historic and prehistoric structures, and other objects of historic and prehistoric and scientific interest." National monuments also may be established by specific acts of Congress. Every monument is administered by a superintendent or custodian. National monuments are of four general types—prehistoric, historic, geologic, and biologic. Prehistoric national monuments include ruins of the homes of prehistoric inhabitants of the United States, such as the Aztec Ruins National Monument, in New Mexico. Historic monuments include structures built by white settlers, such as Big Hole Battlefield National Monument, in Montana. Geologic monuments include areas of special geological interest, such as Arches National Monument, in Utah. Biologic monuments include areas particularly interesting for their flora and fauna, such as the Channel Islands National Monument in California. The establishment of national cemeteries was authorized in 1862; they were transferred from the War Department to the National Park Service in 1933.

National Recreation Areas. The National Park Service develops and administers, under agreement with the Bureau of Reclamation and the Bureau of Indian Affairs, several recreational areas. These are Coulee Dam in Washington (98,500 acres); Lake Mead in Arizona and Utah (1,899,729 acres), containing the largest artificial lake in the United States; Glen Canyon in Arizona and Utah (1,429,006 acres); and Shadow Mountain in Colorado (15,540 acres), adjacent to Rocky Mountain National Park.

Other National Reservations. In addition to the national parks, monuments, and recreation areas, other areas supervised by the National Park Service are national memorials, memorial parks, cemeteries, historical parks, historical sites, military parks, battlefield parks, battlefield sites, parkways, the national capital parks in the Washington, D.C., area, and national seashore recreational areas.

History. Credit for initiating the national park system is given to Cornelius Hedges, a Montana judge and member of the Washburn-Langford-Doane Expedition of 1870, who persuaded others of the party around a campfire at what is now Madison Junction, Wyo., to stand behind the project. An act of Congress in 1872 provided for the permanent reservation of Yellowstone National Park and marked the beginning of a federal system of parks. Under Pres. Abraham Lincoln, however, the Yosemite Valley and the Mariposa Grove became a public park under the custody of the state of California. The National Park Service was established Aug. 25, 1916, with Stephen T. Mather as its first director. Until the 1933 Reorganization Act brought them all together under the National Park Service, some of the military parks and areas and some historical monuments were under the direction of the War Department and the national monuments lying within the national forests under the direction of the forest service of the Department of Agriculture. The act of 1933 transferred these, as well as the park system of Washington, D.C., to the jurisdiction of the National Park Service. Little work was done to improve facilities during World War II but in 1956, in view of the large increase in the number of visitors, the Department of Interior instituted a 10-year program to improve and modernize facilities in the national parks. Long-range plans were also made, so that at least 66 million visitors could be accommodated in the parks and monuments by 1966. Appropriations of more than $60 million were planned for an inclusive program of road and bridge construction, removal and relocation of old facilities, new and improved camp facilities, and better self-guiding tours. ALBERT W. BROWN

BIBLIOG.–R. Steel, *Let's Visit Our National Parks* (1947); I. R. Melbo, *Our Country's National Parks* (2 vols. ed. 1950); D. Butcher, *Exploring Our National Parks and Monuments* (ed. 1954); F. Tilden, *Interpreting Our Heritage* (1957); P. Thomson, *Wonders of Our National Parks* (1961).

NATIONAL PARKS, MONUMENTS, AND SITES

NATIONAL PARKS

Name	Estab.	Acreage	Location	Outstanding Features
Acadia	1919	41,634	Maine	Scenic Mount Desert Island
Big Bend	1944	708,221	Texas	Scenery in the great bend of the Rio Grande
Bryce Canyon	1928	36,010	Utah	Colorful rock pinnacles
Carlsbad Caverns	1930	49,447	Mew Mexico	Connected caverns of curious formations
Crater Lake	1902	160,290	Oregon	Scenic heart of a once active volcano
Everglades	1947	1,400,533	Florida	Great swamplands of Florida
Glacier	1910	1,013,129	Montana	Mountains and lakes sculptured by many glaciers
Grand Canyon	1919	673,575	Arizona	Scenic gorge of colorful rock masses
Grand Teton	1929	310,350	Wyoming	Jackson Hole and the scenic peaks of the Teton Range
Great Smoky Mountains	1930	511,714	North Carolina-Tennessee	Beautiful mountains and luxuriant plant life
Haleakala	1961	26,402	Hawaii	Dormant Haleakala Volcano
Hawaii Volcanoes	1916	220,344	Hawaii	Volcanic area and tropical vegetation
Hot Springs	1921	1,001	Arkansas	47 mineral hot springs
Isle Royale	1940	539,341	Michigan	Forested island with moose herds and old copper mines
Kings Canyon	1940	454,650	California	Scenic canyons of the Kings River
Lassen Volcanic	1916	106,933	California	Volcanic area
Mammoth Cave	1936	51,354	Kentucky	Scenic underground passages of limestone formations
Mesa Verde	1906	51,333	Colorado	Prehistoric cliff dwellings
Mount McKinley	1917	1,939,493	Alaska	Large glaciers of the Alaska Range
Mount Rainier	1899	241,782	Washington	Many glaciers on one magnificent peak
Olympic	1938	896,599	Washington	Scenic remnant of ancient forests
Petrified Forest	1906	94,189	Arizona	Natural exhibit of petrified wood
Platt	1906	912	Oklahoma	Cold mineral springs
Rocky Mountain	1915	260,018	Colorado	Many mountains over 10,000 feet
Sequoia	1890	386,550	California	Oldest and largest trees in the world
Shenandoah	1935	212,303	Virginia	The heart of the Blue Ridge Mountains
Virgin Islands	1956	15,150	Virgin Islands	Tropical climate and sandy beaches
Wind Cave	1903	28,059	South Dakota	Scenic caverns in the Black Hills
Yellowstone	1872	2,221,772	Wyoming-Montana-Idaho	Greatest geyser area in the world
Yosemite	1890	760,951	California	Scenic mountain area of granite cliffs and waterfalls
Zion	1919	147,034	Utah	Colorful gorge in the desert

NATIONAL MONUMENTS

Name	Estab.	Acreage	Location	Outstanding Features
Andrew Johnson	1942	16	Tennessee	Andrew Johnson's home and grave
Arches	1929	34,009	Utah	Extraordinary sandstone formations and fossils
Aztec Ruins	1923	27	New Mexico	Ruins of an American Indian town
Badlands	1939	111,529	South Dakota	Badlands containing animal fossils
Bandelier	1916	30,703	New Mexico	Ruins of pueblo homes built in canyon-slashed slopes of the Pajarito Plateau
Big Hole Battlefield	1910	200	Montana	Site of a battle during the retreat of Chief Joseph and his Nez Percés in 1877
Black Canyon of the Gunnison	1933	13,682	Colorado	Sheer-walled canyon
Booker T. Washington	1957	199	Virginia	Birthplace of famous Negro leader
Buck Island Reef	1961	850	Virgin Islands	Extensive marine gardens
Cabrillo	1913	80	California	Memorial to Juan Rodriguez Cabrillo discoverer of San Diego Bay, 1542
Canyon de Chelly	1931	83,840	Arizona	Indian ruins built at the base of red cliffs and in caves of the canyon walls

NATIONAL MONUMENTS (continued)

Name	Estab.	Acres	Location	Outstanding Features
Capitol Reef	1937	39,172	Utah	Colorful buttressed sandstone dissected by narrow gorges
Capulin Mountain	1916	775	New Mexico	A recently extinct volcano
Casa Grande	1918	472	Arizona	Ruined adobe tower built by Indians of the Gila Valley in the fourteenth century
Castillo de San Marcos	1924	21	Florida	Oldest masonry fort in the United States (1672)
Castle Clinton	1950	1	New York	Part of the early defenses of New York Harbor
Cedar Breaks	1933	6,154	Utah	Amphitheater eroded into the Pink Cliffs
Chaco Canyon	1907	21,509	New Mexico	Major pueblo ruins representing the height of pueblo civilization
Channel Islands	1938	18,166	California	Large rookery of sea lions and unique plants and animals
Chesapeake and Ohio Canal	1961	4,474	West Virginia–Maryland	One of the least-altered of the older U.S. canals
Chiricahua	1924	10,645	Arizona	Unusual rock formations
Colorado	1911	17,692	Colorado	Monoliths and formations formed by erosion and sandstone
Craters of the Moon	1924	53,545	Idaho	Volcanic phenomena
Custer Battlefield	1946	765	Montana	Site of the Battle of Little Bighorn River, 1876
Death Valley	1933	1,907,760	California-Nevada	Desert, natural phenomena, extensive salt beds, and borax formations
Devils Postpile	1911	798	California	A remnant of a basaltic lava flow
Devils Tower	1906	1,346	Wyoming	An 865-foot tower of columnar volcanic rocks
Dinosaur	1915	205,136	Utah-Colorado	Dinosaur fossil remains
Effigy Mounds	1949	1,467	Iowa	Prehistoric earth mounds shaped like animals
El Morro	1906	1,278	New Mexico	Inscription rock, records of early explorers
Fort Frederica	1945	250	Georgia	Built 1736–54 by Gen. James E. Oglethorpe
Fort Jefferson	1935	47,125	Florida	Large all-masonry fortification and an outstanding bird refuge
Fort Matanzas	1924	228	Florida	Spanish fort built in 1737
Fort McHenry	1939	43	Maryland	The fort whose defense in 1814 inspired the writing of the U.S. national anthem
Fort Pulaski	1924	5,516	Georgia	Early nineteenth century fort
Fort Sumter	1948	2	South Carolina	Opening engagement of the Civil War
Fort Union	1956	720	New Mexico	Guarded southwestern frontier in the nineteenth century
George Washington Birthplace	1930	393	Virginia	Birthplace of George Washington
George Washington Carver	1951	210	Missouri	George W. Carver's birthplace
Gila Cliff Dwellings	1907	533	New Mexico	Well preserved cliff dwellings
Glacier Bay	1925	2,274,595	Alaska	Tidewater glaciers
Grand Canyon	1932	198,280	Arizona	View of the inner gorge of Grand Canyon
Grand Portage	1960	770	Minnesota	Nine-mile portage on a principal route of Indians and traders into the Northwest
Gran Quivira	1909	610	New Mexico	Ruins of Spanish missions and of pueblos
Great Sand Dunes	1932	36,740	Colorado	Among the largest and highest sand dunes in the United States
Harpers Ferry	1944	1,500	West Virginia–Maryland	Site of the John Brown Raid
Homestead National Monument of America	1939	163	Nebraska	Site of first claim under the Homestead Act of 1862
Hovenweep	1923	505	Utah-Colorado	Groups of prehistoric towers, pueblos, and cliff dwellings
Jewel Cave	1908	1,275	South Dakota	Chambers of limestone formation connected by narrow passages
Joshua Tree	1936	557,992	California	Stand of Joshua trees
Katmai	1918	2,697,590	Alaska	A dying volcanic area, including the Valley of Ten Thousand Smokes
Lava Beds	1925	46,239	California	Volcanic area, theater of the Modoc Indian War, 1873
Lehman Caves	1922	640	Nevada	Limestone caverns containing numerous stalactite and stalagmite formations
Montezuma Castle	1906	783	Arizona	One of the most interesting cliff dwellings in the United States
Mound City Group	1923	68	Ohio	Prehistoric Indian mounds
Muir Woods	1908	502	California	Virgin stand of coast redwoods
Natural Bridges	1908	7,600	Utah	Three natural bridges
Navajo	1909	360	Arizona	Three large and elaborate cliff dwellings
Ocmulgee	1936	683	Georgia	Remains of mounds and prehistoric towns
Oregon Caves	1909	480	Oregon	Limestone cave formation
Organ Pipe Cactus	1937	330,874	Arizona	Traces of historic Spanish route and desert plants found nowhere else in the United States
Perry's Victory and International Peace Memorial	1936	14	Ohio	Monument commemorating a century of peace between the United States and Canada

NATIONAL MONUMENTS (continued)

Name	Estab.	Acres	Location	Outstanding Features
Pinnacles	1908	14,497	California	Rock formations 500 to 1,200 feet high with numerous caves and volcanic features
Pipe Spring	1923	40	Arizona	Historic Mormon fort
Pipestone	1937	283	Minnesota	Contains material used in the making of ceremonial peace pipes
Rainbow Bridge	1910	160	Utah	Greatest of the world's known natural bridges
Russell Cave	1961	310	Alabama	Cave containing record of human habitation from about 6000 B.C. to about A.D. 1650
Saguaro	1933	78,644	Arizona	Cactus forest
Scotts Bluff	1919	3,451	Nebraska	Landmark on the Oregon Trail
Sitka	1910	54	Alaska	Exhibits of totem poles
Statue of Liberty	1924	10	New York	Commemorates alliance between France and the United States during the Revolutionary War, 1775–81
Sunset Crater	1930	3,040	Arizona	Colorful volcanic cone
Timpanogos Cave	1922	250	Utah	Limestone cavern with passageways
Tonto	1907	1,120	Arizona	Large Pueblo cliff dwellings of the fourteenth century
Tumacacori	1908	10	Arizona	Site of Spanish Catholic mission
Tuzigoot	1939	43	Arizona	Excavated ruins of a prehistoric pueblo
Walnut Canyon	1915	1,879	Arizona	Cliff dwellings under ledges of limestone
White Sands	1933	146,535	New Mexico	White gypsum sand dunes
Wupatki	1924	35,554	Arizona	Red sandstone prehistoric pueblos
Yucca House	1919	10	Colorado	Ruins of pueblos

NATIONAL HISTORICAL PARKS

Name	Estab.	Acres	Location	Outstanding Features
Appomattox Court House	1954	972	Virginia	Site of Gen. Robert E. Lee's surrender
Chalmette	1939	135	Louisiana	Site of part of the Battle of New Orleans, 1814–15
City of Refuge	1961	182	Hawaii	Prehistoric house sites and spectacular shore scenery
Colonial	1936	9,430	Virginia	First permanent English settlement in America, and scene of the Battle of Yorktown, 1781
Cumberland Gap	1955	20,193	Kentucky-Tennessee-Virginia	Crossing of Wilderness Road used by settlers to reach Mississippi River
Independence	1948	21	Pennsylvania	Scene of the adoption of the Declaration of Independence
Minute Man	1959	750	Massachusetts	Revolutionary battle site
Morristown	1933	958	New Jersey	Military encampments during the Revolutionary War
Saratoga	1948	5,500	New York	Site of decisive Revolutionary battle

NATIONAL PARKWAYS

Name	Estab.	Acres	Location	Outstanding Features
Blue Ridge	1933	65,110	Virginia-North Carolina	Highway in the Blue Ridge Mountains
George Washington Memorial	1930	6,569	Virginia-Maryland	Highway connecting landmarks associated with George Washington
Natchez Trace	1934	45,297	Mississippi-Tennessee-Alabama	Highway generally following the old Natchez Trace

NATIONAL MEMORIALS

Name	Estab.	Acres	Location	Outstanding Features
Coronado	1952	2,834	Arizona	Route of sixteenth century Spanish explorers
Custis-Lee Mansion	1925	3	Virginia	Ante-bellum home of Robert E. Lee
De Soto	1949	30	Florida	Site of the landing of Hernando de Soto's expedition
Federal Hall	1939	0.45	New York	First seat of the U.S. government
Fort Caroline	1950	119	Florida	Site of old French settlement in Florida
Fort Clatsop	1958	125	Oregon	Site of Lewis and Clark encampment
General Grant	1959	0.76	New York	Ulysses S. Grant tomb and memorial
House Where Lincoln Died	1896	0.05	District of Columbia	Refurnished in 1860's style
Lincoln Memorial	1922	0.61	District of Columbia	Statue of Abraham Lincoln
Lincoln Museum	1932	0.18	District of Columbia	Site of Lincoln's assassination
Mount Rushmore	1929	1,278	South Dakota	Carved features of presidents George Washington, Thomas Jefferson, Abraham Lincoln, and Theodore Roosevelt on the face of Mt. Rushmore
Thomas Jefferson	1943	1.2	District of Columbia	Colonnaded structure with inscriptions based upon writings of Jefferson
Washington Monument	1885	0.37	District of Columbia	Obelisk commemorating George Washington
Wright Brothers	1927	314	North Carolina	Site of pioneer airplane flight

NATIONAL HISTORIC SITES

Name	Estab.	Acres	Location	Outstanding Features
Abraham Lincoln Birthplace	1916	116	Kentucky	Lincoln's birthplace cabin
Adams	1946	5	Massachusetts	House of historic Adams family
Christiansted	1952	8	Virgin Islands	Buildings commemorate colonial development of the Virgin Islands
Edison	1955	18	New Jersey	Laboratory and home of the inventor
Fort Laramie	1938	564	Wyoming	Military post on wagon trails west
Fort Raleigh	1941	143	North Carolina	Site of the first attempted English settlement in America
Fort Vancouver	1954	90	Washington	Site of military and trading post for the Pacific Northwest in the 1800's
Hampton	1948	45	Maryland	Eighteenth century Georgian mansion
Home of Franklin D. Roosevelt	1944	94	New York	Birthplace of Franklin D. Roosevelt
Hopewell Village	1938	848	Pennsylvania	Old iron-making village
Jefferson National Expansion Memorial	1935	85	Missouri	Commemorates territorial expansion of the United States
Saint Thomas	1961	2	Virgin Islands	Oldest structure in Virgin Islands
Salem Maritime	1938	11	Massachusetts	Relics of early New England history
San Juan	1949	40	Puerto Rico	Old masonry fortifications
Vanderbilt Mansion	1940	212	New York	Frederick W. Vanderbilt mansion
Whitman Mission	1940	98	Washington	Oregon trail landmark where Dr. Whitman ministered to the Indians

NATIONAL BATTLEFIELD PARKS

Name	Estab.	Acres	Location	Outstanding Features
Kennesaw Mountain	1947	3,682	Georgia	Site of Civil War battle
Manassas	1940	3,108	Virginia	Site of the Battles of Bull Run
Richmond	1944	744	Virginia	Site of Civil War battles

NATIONAL CAPITAL PARKS

Name	Estab.	Acres	Location	Outstanding Features
National Capital	1790	36,195	District of Columbia–Virginia–Maryland	The parks system of Washington, D.C.

NATIONAL MILITARY PARKS

Name	Estab.	Acres	Location	Outstanding Features
Chickamauga and Chattanooga	1890	8,190	Georgia-Tennessee	Civil War battlefields of Chickamauga, Orchard Knob, Lookout Mountain, and Missionary Ridge
Fort Donelson	1928	600	Tennessee	Civil War fortification
Fredericksburg and Spotsylvania	1927	3,672	Virginia	Site of major battles of the Civil War
Gettysburg	1895	3,409	Pennsylvania	Site of an important battle during the Civil War and of the delivery of the famous address
Guilford Courthouse	1917	224	North Carolina	Site of an important battle of the Revolutionary War in 1781
Horseshoe Bend	1959	2,040	Alabama	Site of 1814 battle which resulted in white settlement in Alabama
Kings Mountain	1931	3,950	South Carolina	Site of a 1780 Revolutionary War battle
Moores Creek	1926	49	North Carolina	Site of a battle between North Carolina Patriots and Loyalists in 1776
Pea Ridge	1960	4,283	Arkansas	Scene of famous Civil War engagement
Shiloh	1894	3,564	Tennessee	Site of the Battle of Shiloh, 1862
Vicksburg	1899	1,648	Mississippi	Civil War fortifications

NATIONAL MEMORIAL PARK

Name	Estab.	Acres	Location	Outstanding Features
Theodore Roosevelt	1949	70,374	North Dakota	Badlands; part of Elkhorn Ranch

NATIONAL BATTLEFIELD SITES

Name	Estab.	Acres	Location	Outstanding Features
Antietam	1890	784	Maryland	Civil War
Brices Cross Roads	1929	1	Mississippi	Civil War
Cowpens	1929	1	South Carolina	Revolutionary War

NATIONAL RECREATION AREAS

Name	Estab.	Acres	Location	Outstanding Features
Coulee Dam	1946	98,500	Washington	Franklin D. Roosevelt Lake
Glen Canyon	1958	1,429,006	Arizona-Utah	World's third highest dam
Lake Mead	1936	1,951,928	Arizona, Nevada	Lake Mead
Shadow Mountain	1952	18,240	Colorado	Shadow Mountain Lake and Lake Granby

NATIONAL SEASHORE RECREATIONAL AREA

Name	Estab.	Acres	Location	Outstanding Features
Cape Cod	1962	—	Massachusetts	Scenic beach areas, fishing
Cape Hatteras	1936	28,500	North Carolina	Fishing, wildlife, beaches
Padre Island	1962	—	Texas	Beaches, fishing
Point Reyes	1962	—	California	Fishing, scenic beaches

NATIONAL BATTLEFIELDS

Name	Estab.	Acres	Location	Outstanding Features
Fort Necessity	1931	500	Pennsylvania	Opening battle of French-Indian War
Petersburg	1926	2,731	Virginia	Scene of 1864–65 "Battle of the Crater"
Stones River	1927	331	Tennessee	Site of battle beginning Union's offensive to trisect the Confederacy
Tupelo	1929	1.5	Mississippi	Commemorates Civil War Battle

NATIONAL CEMETERIES

Name	Acres	Location	Name	Acres	Location
Antietam	11.4	Maryland	Poplar Grove	8.7	Virginia
Battleground	1.0	District of Columbia	Shiloh	10.3	Tennessee
Fort Donelson	15.3	Tennessee	Stones River	20.1	Tennessee
Fredericksburg	12.0	Virginia	Vicksburg	117.9	Mississippi
Gettysburg	20.6	Pennsylvania	Yorktown	2.9	Virginia

NATIONAL RECOVERY ADMINISTRATION, an independent U.S. federal agency created by presidential order in 1933 to promote and enforce codes of fair competition in industry as provided by the National Industrial Recovery Act of 1933. The NIRA, a New Deal measure designed to help combat the depression of the 1930's, authorized the President to formulate or approve such codes in the interests of economic recovery. With the President's approval, the NRA permitted trade associations to draw up codes intended to end cutthroat competition, stabilize the price structure, and fix prices. The codes were expressly exempted from the provisions of the antitrust laws. Labor's gains included minimum wage and maximum hour guarantees, the abolition of child labor, and the right to bargain collectively. The act also set up a $3.3 billion program under the Public Works Administration. (See PUBLIC WORKS.)

The uncertain legal basis of the act led Pres. Franklin Delano Roosevelt's administration to rely on psychological pressure in persuading all elements of the economy to co-operate. For example, the Blue Eagle, symbol of the NRA, served as an award of merit for display by employers who had signed a code of fair competition. The National Industrial Recovery Act, however, was declared unconstitutional by the Supreme Court in *Schechter Poultry Corp.* v. *United States*, 295 U.S. 495 (1935). The court held unanimously that the act invaded the reserved powers of the state to regulate intrastate commerce and that the code-making authority given to the President was an unconstitutional delegation of legislative powers. Essential provisions of the NIRA, except price-fixing powers, were restored in later legislation.

NATIONAL RECREATION ASSOCIATION, founded in 1906, is a nonprofit, nonsectarian civic organization whose goal is to help Americans of all ages make the most satisfying use of their leisure time. Aid is given local public and private recreation groups and individual recreation leaders by a nationwide information program on the use and values of leisure and by the association's staff. The NRA has a membership of about 6,000 individuals and 1,800 public and private recreational agencies. Headquarters of the NRA are in New York City.

NATIONAL REPUBLICAN PARTY, a short-lived political party which took part in the presidential election of 1832. The election of 1824 was a wide-open affair with many candidates although the Republican party of Jefferson was the only political organization in the United States. When the election was thrown into the House of Representatives the principal candidates were Andrew Jackson and John Quincy Adams, the latter finally being chosen. Incensed at this result, the Jackson men then withdrew, so that two political groups appeared. The Clay-Adams group eventually took the name of National Republicans, whereas their opponents called themselves Democratic Republicans. For the election of 1832 the National Republicans nominated Henry Clay, but he was defeated by Jackson. In 1834 the National Republican party was absorbed by the new Whig party and the Democratic Republicans were the Democratic party.

NATIONAL RESEARCH COUNCIL OF CANADA, the agency of the Canadian government concerned with stimulating, correlating, and assisting with scientific and technological research. The council was organized in 1917 and one of its first accomplishments was to provide for financial aid for research and postgraduate training. In subsequent years the correlation of industrial and scientific research was undertaken by the council.

The division of administration and awards is the administrative body of the National Research Council of Canada. The honorary advisory council is the organization's governing body; it has five standing committees: two deal with scholarships and grants in aid to research, and three are concerned with membership of the council staff, research journals, and a review of laboratory work.

Included among the scientific services provided by the council are a large scientific library and a service that furnishes industry with technical information. The council sponsors associate committees in research and operates several large laboratories comprising nine divisions: applied biology, pure chemistry, applied chemistry, pure physics, applied physics, building research, mechanical engineering, radio and electrical engineering, and medical research.

NATIONAL RESOURCES PLANNING BOARD, a former U.S. agency whose primary function was to collect and prepare information and recommendations for the President to be used in planning the development and use of national resources, especially in an effort to offset the hardships of economic depressions and unemployment. The board was established July 1, 1939, as a part of Pres. Franklin D. Roosevelt's governmental reorganization plan, an outgrowth of New Deal emphasis on national planning. It was in effect a combination of the national resources committee and the federal employment stabilization office, and was made a part of the Executive Office of the President. In 1940 the board was instructed to develop a six-year program in conjunction with the Bureau of the Budget for the construction of federal public works projects. Congress abolished the board Aug. 31, 1943.

NATIONAL RIFLE ASSOCIATION OF AMERICA, a nonprofit organization concerned with educating and training Americans in safe and efficient handling of firearms, fostering knowledge of small arms and ability to use them, and promoting public safety, law and order, and national defense. Headquarters of NRA are in Washington, D.C. The association is supported by fees from more than 270,000 members. *The American Rifleman* is the official publication. See TARGET SHOOTING.

PAUL B. CARDINAL

NATIONAL ROAD, or Great National Pike, the great emigrant highway into the midwest constructed by the U.S. government in the early nineteenth century from Cumberland, Md., to Vandalia, Ill. The project was initiated in 1806 by Henry Clay, but construction did not begin until 1811. The section from Cumberland to Wheeling, W.Va., was completed in 1818. Further construction was delayed for several years by difficulties over states' rights. In addition a bill providing tollgates to pay for repairs

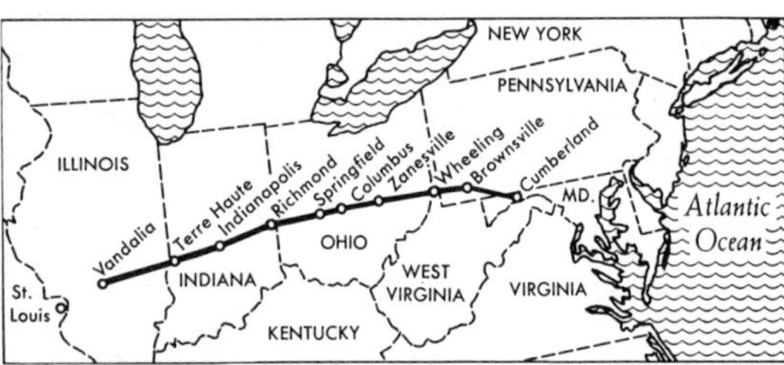

The National Road, 1811–40

was vetoed in 1822. Construction was authorized in 1825 to Zanesville, Ohio, over Zane's Trace (see ZANE'S TRACE). The road was continued through Ohio, reaching Columbus in 1833, but no further progress was made during the Jackson administration. Work was resumed under Pres. Martin Van Buren. By 1840 the road stretched 800 miles to Vandalia, but it never reached St. Louis as originally proposed. The road, which cost nearly $7 million, was well constructed with a macadamized surface and stone bridges. It was turned over to the states, which erected tollgates to finance repairs. Until the coming of the railroads the National Road was well traveled, especially between Baltimore and Wheeling. It later became U.S. highway 40. See OVERLAND TRAILS; INTERNAL IMPROVEMENTS.

BIBLIOG.–T. B. Searight, *Old Pike* (1894); A. B. Hulbert, *Old National Road* (1901), *Cumberland Road* (1904); J. S. Young, *Political and Constitutional Study of the Cumberland Road* (1904); J. M. Lowe, *National Old Trails Road* (1925); P. D. Jordan, *National Road* (1948).

NATIONAL SAFETY COUNCIL, a noncommercial, nonprofit association founded in 1913 for the purpose of reducing the number and severity of all kinds of accidents. The council is interested in safety in industry, traffic and transportation, school and home, and on the farm, and gathers and distributes information on the causes and prevention of accidents. Information is obtained from members, from the council's staff of statistical, educational, and engineering technicians, and from government sources. NSC members include individuals and organizations interested in safety. In 1959 there were approximately 9,600 members in the council. There were about 250 autonomous local and state safety organizations as well as volunteer groups in small communities; as affiliates of NSC they adhered to the general operating policies of the parent organization. NSC publications include a monthly magazine, *National Safety News*. Headquarters are in Chicago, and regional offices are in New York City and San Francisco. See ACCIDENTS.

NATIONAL SCIENCE FOUNDATION, an agency of the federal government, established by Congress in 1950 for the purpose of promoting the progress of science and advancing the national health, prosperity, and welfare. The foundation supports basic research in the sciences and engineering, programs for improving science education, studies of science manpower supply and demand, programs for making scientific information more readily available, and compilation of data on the national effort in scientific research and development. The foundation awards grants for basic research in the sciences and engineering; supervises research facilities, such as the National Radio Astronomy Observatory at Green Bank, W.Va.; and sponsors conferences and symposia on specific aspects of science.

Fellowships are available for study and advanced training in the sciences and engineering at the graduate and postdoctoral level. Institutes that provide supplementary subject-matter training for high school and college teachers of science and mathematics are also supported.

The foundation maintains the national register of scientific and technical personnel and supports other programs designed to provide the federal government with knowledge of the nation's resources of scientific manpower—supply, demand, utilization, and characteristics.

This agency supports translation of Russian abstracts of scientific papers; publication of English editions of Russian scientific journals; and collections of chemical and biological serial publications. In the area of scientific documentation the foundation seeks to strengthen and improve means of publishing and disseminating results of scientific research, as well as organizing and searching scientific literature. Studies of language structure are made to determine the feasibility of using machines in translating or in indexing and searching scientific information.

The foundation makes a number of regular and special studies of the United States' over-all effort in scientific research, development, and education.

ALAN T. WATERMAN

NATIONAL SECURITY COUNCIL, the top civilian planning and policy agency concerned with the defense of the United States. Created by the National Security Act of 1947, the council include the President, vice-president, secretaries of state and defense departments, and the director of the office of emergency planning. The council recommends to the President measures that concern the integration of domestic, foreign, and military policies that relate to national security; and assesses and appraises objectives, commitments, and risks of the United States in relation to actual and potential military power. The President does not ordinarily meet with the group but makes decisions on the basis of its reports and may request its assistance at any time.

The Central Intelligence Agency, under the direction of the National Security Council, is a major source of information on overseas affairs for the council. The CIA is headed by a director and a deputy director. It advises the council on intelligence matters related to national security; makes recommendations for the co-ordination of such intelligence activities of other government agencies and departments; correlates and evaluates such intelligence and provides for its proper dissemination within the government; performs other intelligence duties that the council assigns it. See CENTRAL INTELLIGENCE AGENCY.

NATIONAL SECURITY RESOURCES BOARD, originally established as an independent agency by the National Security Act of 1947 to advise the President in matters concerning the co-ordination of military, industrial, and civilian mobilization in the event of war. In 1949 the board was transferred to the executive office of the President. Membership consisted of a chairman and a vice-chairman—both of whom were civilians appointed by the President with senate approval—and those heads and representatives of the various executive departments and independent agencies appointed by the President. The chairman of the board was also a member of the National Security Council. In 1953 the National Security Resources Board was abolished and all its functions were transferred to the director of the Office of Defense Mobilization.

NATIONAL SOCIALISM, an authoritarian, totalitarian, imperialistic political movement or system of government based upon the ideology of the National Socialist German Workers' (Nazi) party. In the name of this party, Adolf Hitler (see HITLER, ADOLF) assumed political power in Germany in 1933, abolished the democratic institutions of the German Weimar Republic (1918–33), and established a new form of government—the Nazi system.

Origins. Significant among reasons for the rise of national socialism in Germany were the relative newness of German national unity—proclaimed in 1870—and the youthful virulence of German nationalism, which emphasized the supremacy of the German nation over its citizens and of the German peoples in the world. Strong militaristic, paternalistic, and authoritarian traditions of German monarchy and aristocracy and Germany's situation in the heart of Europe, which seemed to justify expansionist aspirations in the name of needed vital space, provided the background for German national socialism (see GEOPOLITICS). Other factors in its development were German industrialization, to which colonial outlets were denied by British and French imperialism, and the failure of Germany to establish political and military hegemony in Europe in World War I.

Immediate Causes. After World War I Germany was sharply divided; the left was represented by the Communist and the Social Democratic parties, the right by conservative groups that were eventually absorbed into the National Socialist movement. As the groups were equally strong, particularly in the last years of the republic, government by any group for a reasonable period of time was impossible (see CABINET, Continental Europe). Then the depression of 1929 brought widespread unemployment, and many Germans—chiefly industrialists, the army, and the middle classes—became increasingly alarmed at the growing strength of left-wing parties. In despair over their economic situation and deeply aggrieved by loss of political status, many Germans willingly embraced the new ideology that promised to restore Germany's greatness and their personal economic security. They were taught to associate their predicament with democratic institutions, with the prosperity of the Jewish population (of less than a quarter million), and with the Treaty of Versailles which had underscored Germany's defeat by limiting the fatherland militarily and economically. See VERSAILLES, TREATY OF.

History of the Party. The Nazi party was founded in 1918 by Gottfried Feder; its members primarily were disheartened veterans and frustrated intellectuals until Adolf Hitler, Rudolf Hess, Hermann Wilhelm Goering, Alfred Rosenberg, and Paul Joseph Goebbels obtained control. The main platform of the party was anti-Semitism, anticommunism, abrogation of the Treaty of Versailles, and revival of German national and military strength.

The party attracted little attention at first, and that mostly from veterans, the lower middle classes, and some militarists and industrialists. Gen. Erich Friedrich Wilhelm Ludendorff became a member, lending the prestige of his name and rank to the movement. Then in 1923 the party staged an unsuccessful coup in Munich (the beer hall *Putsch*) that led to Hitler's arrest and brief imprisonment. Until 1929 the party was unsuccessful, but by 1930 the situation had changed. Middle classes, industrialists, and the army were frightened by the growing strength of the Communists. At the same time friction between the two labor parties—the Communists and the Social Democrats—weakened the labor front that had been solidly against Hitler, and in the 1932 elections the Nazi party received the highest number of votes, 37.3 per cent of the total. Hitler won the support of most industrialists by promising to curb anticapitalist party policies. Then, with the cabinet unable to govern and the Reichstag frequently unable to agree on a cabinet, Hitler was asked in January 1933 by Paul von Hindenburg, president of the republic, to become chancellor, and in the election of Mar. 5, 1933, the party received 43.9 per cent of the popular vote. The Communist party subsequently was dissolved, and Hitler won sweeping emergency powers to govern by decree. He then proceeded to tighten his control of the party; in 1934 left-wing, anticapitalistic elements of the party were eliminated in a blood purge.

Ideology. German national socialism reflected a number of nineteenth century myths; most significant was belief in the supremacy of national goals, to which individual values and rights were subordinate. Sources of this Nazi doctrine were Rosenberg's *Myth of the 20th Century*, written in 1920, and Hitler's *Mein Kampf*, written in 1923 while he was imprisoned. These writings declared that the proper role and function of the state encompassed social, educational, economic, religious, and personal manifestations of individual and group life, and insisted on active participation of the people in political life—apathy or indifference was not to be tolerated. Further, the Aryan race, whose purest embodiment was taken to be the German nation, was destined to govern the world. The goals of the state and the policies made in pursuance of these goals were to be determined by the leader (*Führer*), supposedly endowed with uncanny perception of historical trends.

Implementation of the Ideology. All political groups and parties in Germany were soon dissolved, with the exception of the Nazi party and its affiliates; trade unions were dissolved and a single labor front under control of Nazi leaders was established. Churches were subjected to severe restrictions, and the German Evangelical Church union was promoted and then taken over by the Nazis to spread their ideology. The extremists, or "German Christians," tried to eradicate all Jewish influences from Christianity and to rewrite the Bible according to Nazi race theories. The Nazis encouraged the German Faith movement, which sought to revive the Teutonic gods and the celebration of pagan festivals. Press and radio were controlled by the state; schools became instruments of National Socialist ideology, and athletic and youth associations were reorganized to foster National Socialist ideas. A secret police group was organized as an instrument of supervision and repression. See GESTAPO.

In 1936 economic activity, including that of industrial magnates who had supported the Nazi party, was regulated by establishment of a four-year plan. At the same time Germans were encouraged to assert their supposed racial supremacy. The Nürnberg Laws of 1936 prohibited marriages between Aryans and Jews and disqualified Jews from public office; eventually Jews were also removed from the liberal professions. Finally the official policy became one of physical extermination; more than 7 million Jews were put to death under hideous conditions, first in Germany and later, during World War II, wherever German armies gained a foothold. Slavs were similarly treated.

Political institutions of the German state were refashioned to give to the leader unfettered power. The federal system was abolished in effect, states becoming simply administrative units for implementation of Nazi party policy. The upper federal chamber was dissolved, and the Reichstag existed only to assent to decisions made by the Führer. The Nazi party was the sole vehicle of political expression; top party members controlled the state, lower echelons held important administrative positions throughout the country, and military-like organizations such as the SA (*Sturmabteilung*) and the SS (*Schutzstaffel*), recruited from party members, represented the hard core of the Nazis.

Territorial arrangements of the Treaty of Versailles were challenged, and two of the most pervasive German attitudes—militarism and armed expansion—were proclaimed by Nazi leaders. In 1933 Germany withdrew from the League of Nations; in 1935 military conscription was reintroduced; in 1936 the Rhineland was reoccupied; in 1938 Austria was annexed; in the same year the Sudeten region of Czechoslovakia was incorporated into Germany. None of these aggrandizements, in defiance of the Treaty of Paris and numerous subsequent agreements, was seriously opposed by Western powers. Finally in March, 1939, Czechoslovakia was occupied and on September 1 Germany attacked Poland and occupied the western half of the country; the eastern half was taken over by the Soviet Union under the terms of a German-Soviet nonaggression pact (1939). Germany's outright military aggression at last provoked a declaration of war by Britain and France on Sept. 3, 1939, and World War II began. See WORLD WAR II.

Postwar Period. After Germany's defeat an Allied tribunal tried and sentenced to death the most important Nazis and sent others to prison for terms up to life (see WAR CRIMES). Prosperity in West Germany and ensuing political stability under a German democratic constitution adopted after World War II, coupled with a Communist regime in East Germany, accounted for the virtual disappearance of national socialism in Germany. See GERMANY, The Empire and the Republic, *The Rise of Hitler*. ROY C. MACRIDIS

BIBLIOG.-H. Lichtenberger, *Third Reich* (1937); J. K. Pollock, *Government of Greater Germany* (1938); H. Rauschning, *Revolution of Nihilism* (1939); Adolf Hitler, *Mein Kampf* (ed. 1943); J. Goebbels, *Diaries, 1942–1943* (1948); A. François-Poncet, *Fateful Years* (1949); E. G. Reichmann, *Hostages of Civilization* (1951); L. B. Namier, *In the Nazi Era* (1952); A. L. C. Bullock, *Hitler: A Study in Tyranny* (1953); M. S. Mayer, *They Thought They Were Free* (1955); T. L. Jarman, *Rise and Fall of Nazi Germany* (1956), J. L. Tenenbaum, *Race and Reich* (1956); G. R. Reitlinger, *S.S.: Alibi of a Nation, 1922–1945* (1957).

NATIONAL TRAVELERS AID ASSOCIATION, a service organization for assisting people who are traveling away from home. Travelers Aid desks usually are located in railroad, bus, and air terminals. The national association was founded in 1917 by local Travelers Aid societies as a central, unifying agency. Activities of the national organization are directed toward establishing and maintaining standards among member groups, conducting research, and developing and distributing literature and information about the work of Travelers Aid Societies. In 1959 there were more than 100 Travelers Aid Societies in the United States and 2 in Canada. There also were 1,000 co-operating representatives, who provided professional service in more than 3,000 communities. In many cities Travelers Aid societies have paid staff workers and unpaid volunteers; the paid staff are professional social workers; volunteers usually work at information desks and handle simple inquiries and do other routine jobs under professional supervision. Each Travelers Aid Society is an autonomous organization whose funds come from local sources. Headquarters of the national association are in New York.

NATIONAL TUBERCULOSIS ASSOCIATION, a federation of state and local associations of physicians, nurses, and laymen interested in the control of tuberculosis. The association is a private, nonprofit organization founded in Atlantic City, N.J., on June 6, 1904. Headquarters are in New York City.

The major activities of the association include guidance and co-ordination of all forms of tuberculosis research; health education based on research; recruiting, training, and placement of personnel; bringing new tuberculosis patients under treatment; and providing educational material and other supplies for the use of affiliated state and local associations. The association co-operates with community agencies, such as schools and colleges, public health departments, and welfare organizations and with the medical and nursing professions. In 1961 the association had approximately 2,700 local affiliates (most of them on a countywide basis) located in each of the 50 states and in Guam, the Virgin Islands, Puerto Rico and the Panama Canal Zone.

Publications include the *Monthly Bulletin*, a scientific magazine; *The American Review of Respiratory Diseases*, a technical journal; *Tuberculosis Abstracts*, pamphlets issued monthly that may be adapted for local distribution; and *Transactions*, a volume composed of papers read at the annual meetings. The organization is financed by the annual sale of its Christmas seals, identified by a double-barred cross adapted from the Cross of Lorraine that has been the association's emblem since its founding.

NATIONAL UNIVERSITY OF IRELAND, an institution of higher learning founded under the Universities Act of 1908, which dissolved the Royal University of Ireland. The national university began full operations in 1909. It is composed of constituent colleges at Maynooth, Galway, Cork, and Dublin. St. Patrick's College, Maynooth, founded in 1795, has faculties of arts, canon law, philosophy, science, and theology. The college at Galway, founded in 1845, has faculties of arts, Celtic studies, commerce, engineering, law, medicine, and science. The college at Cork (1849) has faculties of arts, Celtic studies, commerce, dairy science, engineering, law, medicine, and science. The college at Dublin (1909) has faculties of arts, Celtic studies, commerce, engineering and architecture, general agriculture, law, medicine, philosophy, science, and veterinary science. Each of the schools has separate library facilities, total volumes numbering more than 800,000. Combined student enrollment in the early 1960's was approximately 6,500.

NATIONAL URBAN LEAGUE, an interracial social service organization founded in 1913 to help improve economic and social conditions of Negroes in U.S. cities. Its studies to determine living conditions of Negroes have grown to include information on other nonwhite groups. The league provides consultant services of specialists to communities throughout the United States, co-ordinates the work of local Urban leagues, and undertakes public education programs in health, juvenile delinquency, and fair employment practices. It is supported by contributions from foundations, corporations, labor unions, and individuals, and annual dues from local leagues. In 1960, 63 local Urban leagues were active in 31 states. Headquarters are in New York, and there are regional offices at Atlanta, Ga., and Hollywood, Calif. See NEGRO, American Negro Organizations.

NATIONAL WAR COLLEGE was established in Washington, D.C., in 1943 as the Army and Navy Staff College. After World War II the scope of instruction was enlarged to include integration of U.S. foreign policy and military policy, whereupon the Department of State entered the program. After July 1, 1946, the institution was known as the National War College. The purpose of the college is to prepare selected military officers for command and joint staff duties in the highest echelons of the armed forces, and to promote understanding between the armed forces and other agencies of government that might be essential to national war effort.

The 10-month course is in two semesters; the first is devoted to study of foreign policy and international relations, the second to military matters. The program consists of lectures, committee study, and seminars. A class usually is composed of 30 officers each from the Army, Navy, and Air Force, and 15 to 20 officers from the Department of State. The course is given in Washington, D.C., in buildings formerly occupied by the Army War College. The Industrial College of the Armed Forces occupies adjacent buildings, and courses of the two colleges are integrated. See ARMED FORCES STAFF COLLEGE, THE; INDUSTRIAL COLLEGE OF THE ARMED FORCES; MILITARY AND NAVAL EDUCATION.

NATIONAL WOMAN'S CHRISTIAN TEMPERANCE UNION is a nonsectarian organization whose chief purpose is to educate the general public concerning what it regards as the harmful nature of intoxicating beverages. Commonly referred to as the WCTU, it was organized in 1874 by a convention of church women in Cleveland. It has been a leading supporter of state laws requiring temperance instruction in the schools and has been active in the temperance movement. (See PROHIBITION; TEMPERANCE MOVEMENT.) Frances Elizabeth Willard (see WILLARD, FRANCES ELIZABETH CAROLINE) was president of the organization from 1879 until 1898, and under her direction the WCTU developed its temperance program and became active in other fields, including world peace, prison reform, woman suffrage, child labor, and moral education.

The program of the WCTU is under the direction of five national officers; standing committees; a bureau of legislation with a representative in Washington, D.C., to evaluate legislative trends and direct organization action; a bureau of narcotic education; and a publicity bureau.

The WCTU was the first woman's society built on the framework of local, county, district, and state affiliation under national direction. It functions in all of the states and in Puerto Rico. The World WCTU, founded in 1883, has groups in 70 countries and holds an international convention every three years. In the early 1960's the national organization had about 10,000 local groups with a membership of approximately 225,000. Honorary membership is open to men. Young people are enrolled in two branches—the Loyal Temperance Legion for children and the Youth Temperance Council for older youths. The Iota Sigma WCTU, designed for business and professional women, has evening meetings.

WCTU activities are financed through membership dues, special gifts, annuities, bequests, and other sources. Publications of the National WCTU Publishing House include *The Union Signal* for adults and *The Young Crusader* for children. A library containing temperance literature is maintained at national headquarters in Evanston, Ill. See ANTI-SALOON LEAGUE OF AMERICA.

NATIVE AMERICAN PARTY. See KNOW-NOTHING PARTY.

NATIVITY, the birth of Christ or the annual commemoration of that event, now synonymous with Christmas, is both a legal holiday and a church festival in most Christian communities. Earliest mention of December 25 as the date of special religious services held in memory of Christ's coming into the world is found in the Philocalian calendar, which indicated observance of that date by the church in Rome in 336. There was no clear distinction made between the Nativity and Epiphany until then, and some churches, notably the Armenian, still celebrate them together on January 6. Although there have been various reasons advanced for the choice of December 25 as the anniversary of Christ's birth, there is no indication in ecclesiastical or secular documents to support any of them. See CHRISTMAS; EPIPHANY.

The birth of Christ has been one of the most popular subjects of Christian art from earliest times. Among the famous painters and sculptors who have depicted the Nativity are Giotto, Duccio, Fra Angelico, Fra Filippo Lippi, Bellini, Botticelli, Mantegna, Tintoretto, Correggio, Van der Goes, Dürer, and El Greco.

METROPOLITAN MUS. OF ART

***Nativity*, by Dutch Renaissance Painter Gerard David**

NATO. See NORTH ATLANTIC TREATY ORGANIZATION.

NATROLITE, a mineral of the zeolite family, has a hardness of 5 to 5½ and a specific gravity of 2.25. It is recognized mainly by its radiating transparent to translucent crystals, generally colorless or white but sometimes tinted yellow to red. The mineral is a hydrous sodium aluminum silicate with a formula of $Na_2Al_2Si_3O_{10}$ $2H_2O$. Natrolite is of secondary origin, found lining cavities in basalt and associated with other zeolites and calcite. It is found in Czechoslovakia, France, Italy, and Nova Scotia, and New Jersey.

NATTIER, JEAN MARC, 1685–1766, French portrait painter, was born in Paris and studied under his father, Marc Nattier. At 15 he won first prize at the academy. In 1715 he went to Amsterdam where he met Peter the Great of Russia and painted the members of the Russian royal family. In 1718, following his *Petrification of Phineus and His Companions*, he was accepted into the academy as a historical painter, but soon turned to portrait work. As the leading court portraitist of Louis XV he made portraits of the royal household, including Marie Leszczynska and Madame de Pompadour. He often painted his sitters in mythological or historical guise. His paintings have great charm and purity of line and in color favor a bright blue.

TOLEDO MUS. OF ART

***Portrait of the Princesse de Rohan*, a painting by Jean Marc Nattier**

NATURAL BRIDGE, W central Virginia, Rockbridge County, one of the natural wonders of the United States. The structure supports U.S. highway 11 as it crosses Cedar Creek. Natural Bridge probably was carved out of limestone by a subterranean river. The arch is 215 feet high and 50 to 150 feet wide, and has a maximum span of 90 feet. It is all that remains of a huge prehistoric limestone bed. A federal juvenile correctional institution is operated there.

VIRGINIA CONSERVATION COMM.
Natural Bridge near Lexington, Va., is a mammoth arch of limestone, over 200 feet in height.

NATURAL BRIDGES NATIONAL MONUMENT, SE Utah, San Juan County, a park area of 2,650 acres with three natural sandstone arches—Owachomo, Kachina, and Sipapu—formed by water erosion. The largest arch rises 222 feet above the stream bed and has a span of 261 feet. Included in the park are caves and ruins of ancient cave dwellings. The monument was established in 1908. Ute, Paiute, and Hopi Indians have claimed the area.

NATURAL GAS, a mixture of gases, economically important as fuels, produced naturally from organic matter below the surface of the earth. It consists mainly of paraffins, chiefly methane, Ch_4 (80 to 95 per cent), with the remainder made up of other hydrocarbons (ethane, C_2H_6, propane, C_3H_8, and butane, C_4H_{10}); carbon dioxide, CO_2; carbon monoxide, CO; nitrogen, N; hydrogen, H; helium, He; and sometimes hydrogen sulfide, H_2S; traces of other gases; and water vapor. See FUEL, Gaseous Fuels; HYDROCARBON; METHANE.

Natural gas has a specific gravity of 0.60 to 0.65 as compared with air (sp. gr. = 1), and weighs 47 to 49 pounds per 1,000 cubic feet. There are two types generally recognized: dry gas, which usually comes from gas wells whose natural gasoline vapors are recoverable as liquid to an extent not to exceed 0.75 gallon per cubic foot; and wet, or casinghead, gas whose natural gasoline vapors are recoverable to an extent exceeding 0.75 gallon per cubic foot. In general, wet gases come from wells that may also produce petroleum, whereas dry gases issue in the form of vapor from wells that do not produce petroleum.

Natural gas has been known to man for many centuries. About 1000 B.C. the seepage of gas from a crevice in the side of Mount Parnassus caused the Greeks to attribute mystic properties to the spot, upon which they erected a temple and established the Oracle of Delphi (see ORACLE). The Chinese, at about the same time, piped natural gas through lengths of hollow bamboo, and burned the gas to evaporate brine in the production of salt.

The first commercial production of natural gas in the United States was, in 1820, from a well in Fredonia, N.Y. By the end of the nineteenth century substantial quantities of natural gas were being used in industry and for home and commercial lighting, but it was not until means of transporting large quantities of gas long distances through pipelines, and procedures for metering gas in quantity were developed, that natural gas as a fuel became of great economic importance to the nation.

Occurrence. Natural gas is found in many countries throughout the world, mostly in rocks of sedimentary origin, such as limestone, sandstone, and shale. It is found in the dry state in gaseous form or, when associated with liquid petroleum, as wet gas. The occurrence of natural gas seems to belong to the entire geologic series, with some predominance of appearance in the rocks of the Paleozoic and Cenozoic eras.

In the United States natural gas deposits are found in 29 states, by far the greatest concentration being in the southwestern states. In the interests of conservation of natural resources, careful estimates are made of the geologically proved recoverable reserves of natural gas in the United States and Canada. On Jan. 1, 1959, there were more than 254.1 trillion cubic feet in proved reserves in the United States and 22 trillion cubic feet of reserves in Canada. Proved reserve figures vary from year to year because new discoveries are made, old fields become depleted, and technological advances may result in higher yields than previously estimated. Natural gas is usually discovered as a result of a search for petroleum, and similar methods are used in the exploration and extraction of both of these substances. See NATURAL RESOURCES.

Production. To produce natural gas of commercial value as fuel, involves several basic operations such as drilling the well; extracting the gas; transporting it to a refinery where liquid hydrocarbons and other undesirable constituents can be removed; transporting it to points of consumption or storage; and storing.

Various substances are removed from the natural gas by means of compression, refrigeration, and absorption. These substances include the commercially valuable light hydrocarbons (ethane and propane) as well as the heavier hydrocarbons (butane and the heavier paraffins) and constituents such as water vapor, nitrogen, and sulfur that adversely affect the combustible qualities of the gas. Procedures and production volume have benefited greatly from technological progress, particularly since the 1940's. See GAS MANUFACTURE.

In 1958 the United States produced slightly more than 11 trillion cubic feet of natural gas, a yield that amounted to 87 per cent of the world's total production. In that year Canada produced in excess of 170 billion cubic feet, or 1.7 per cent of the world's supply; more than 80 per cent of it came from the province of Alberta. Large reserves of natural gas were discovered in British Columbia in the 1950's, and the country became a major producer shortly thereafter. Other countries that produce natural gas include China, Italy, Indonesia, Mexico, Rumania, the U.S.S.R., and Venezuela. Of these the U.S.S.R. is the largest producer—supplying more than 4 per cent of the world's supply in 1956.

Transportation and Storage. Because of its tendency to escape, the only practical way to transport natural gas is by pipeline; in fact, the principal factor that led to the tremendous growth of the industry was the successful development of the welded steel pipeline. Before that time most of the natural gas was wasted by escaping to the atmosphere, or by burning at the wellhead.

A casinghead flare is sometimes used to burn off the gas encountered in oil drilling operations where it is deemed unsound to build a gathering system and conserve the gas.
UNIV. OF ILLINOIS

In the producing fields, pipelines known as gathering lines bring the gas from the individual wells to a central point for delivery into a main. Pressures in the main line range from 300 to 1,000 pounds per square inch (psi). Dry gas usually emerges from the well at sufficient pressure to deliver it to the main line, but if wet gas is produced at the well it is necessary first to remove the moisture and the other undesirable elements and then deliver the gas to the main after the pressure has been boosted by the use of pumps. The main transmission pipelines extend from the producing fields and natural gasoline refineries to every section of the United States through the means of booster stations, located approximately 100 miles apart.

The first long-distance natural-gas pipeline, an 8-inch pipe of white pine 25 miles long, was laid in New York in 1870. The first iron pipeline was laid in 1872 to carry gas 5½ miles into Titusville, Pa. Early gasline pressures were 80 pounds psi. In 1957 the United States had 524,800 miles of natural gas pipelines including distribution and gathering mains and cross-country transmission lines. Pipe up to 30 inches in diameter carried the gas at pressures up to 1,000 pounds psi.

From the main transmission lines the gas must be delivered to some form of storage tank such as the immense gas holders seen in urban centers. From these the gas is channeled to the consumer. In many localities the demand for gas during the winter months reaches a peak that exceeds the capacity of the pipelines. Consequently a system of huge underground storage reservoirs has been developed, located when possible, near major consuming centers. These underground storage chambers may be depleted gas fields, abandoned mines, or cavernous rock formations. In the United States in 1959 there were 205 such underground pools with a capacity of approximately 2.7 trillion cubic feet.

Uses. Natural gas, with a fuel value that averages 1,050 British thermal units (Btu) per cubic foot, supplied more than 29 per cent of the energy derived from mineral fuels and water power in the United States in 1957. In that year there were in excess of 30 million residential and commercial customers for natural gas and 132,000 industrial customers. The residential and commercial customers consumed more than 30 billion therms (1 therm = 100,000 Btu) of natural gas, for which they paid $2.3 billion, whereas the industrial customers consumed 40 billion therms for which they paid $1.1 billion. The discrepancy reflects the wide spread between the two classes of rates.

Principal residential uses of natural gas are home heating, hot water heating, refrigeration, cooking, and clothes drying. Industrially, natural gas is used in the oil and gas fields for processing; for the production of carbon black, and for many other chemical processes; and as a fuel in the glass, cement, ceramic, and metallurgical fields. See GAS APPLIANCE; CARBON BLACK.

Organization and Regulation. A single company rarely engages in all phases of the natural gas industry from extraction to production and distribution. Since natural gas so frequently is found with petroleum, the extraction and production of natural gas by-products is usually carried on by oil companies. The transmission and distribution of the natural gas is essentially a part of a nation's public utility system.

Regulation of the natural gas industry in the United States is based on the Public Utility Holding Company Act of 1935 and the Natural Gas Act of 1938. The former places certain restrictions on holding companies originally formed as a means of financing the tremendous expense of laying natural gas pipelines. The Natural Gas Act of 1938 provided for the regulation of natural gas in interstate commerce under the jurisdiction of the Federal Power Commission. This commission is composed of five commissioners, appointed by the President, subject to Senate approval. The commission regulates the transportation and sale of natural gas in interstate commerce; investigates the need and, when necessary, directs the natural gas companies to establish additional physical connections; rules on the abandonment of existing facilities; fosters a uniform accounting system; evaluates applications for new facilities; and generally keeps the public and Congress advised as to the state of the natural gas industry. The industry is further controlled by state and local regulations. See FEDERAL POWER COMMISSION.

NATURAL HISTORY, the general, collective study of the past and present world of nature—animal, vegetable, and mineral. The first thorough study of natural history was made by Aristotle, who recorded accounts of travels and added his own observations of various forms of animal life, all preserved in his work, *De Anima.* Although his ideas did influence medieval thought, it was not until the eighteenth century that the over-all concept of the study of natural forces was developed. The Swiss educator Johann Pestalozzi incorporated a course of nature study to popularize some of his educational theories. (See PESTALOZZI, JOHANN HEINRICH.) The energetic Swiss-American naturalist Jean Louis Agassiz, professor of natural history at the University of Neuchâtel, did research on fossil fishes and echinoderms during the 1830's, and on Alpine glacier phenomena in the Bernese Oberland area (1840–44). (See AGASSIZ, JEAN LOUIS RODOLPHE.) This work, together with his lectures in America, "On the Plan of the Creation," (1846–48) and his expeditions—to Lake Superior, 1848, and to the Florida Reefs, 1850–51—awakened a new and co-ordinated concept of the study of natural events. The Marine Biological Laboratory at Woods Hole, Mass., is the site of Agassiz' outdoor laboratory, established in 1873. In France, naturalist Jean Fabre was the first to record the habits and life history of living insects, and his poetic descriptions were studied in schools in France, England, and the United States. (See FABRE, JEAN HENRI.) The museum movement of modern times, co-ordinating various sciences, has perpetuated the natural history concept, and twentieth century authors have popularized the interrelationships of these fields of science.

BIBLIOG.–William D. Burden, *Look to the Wilderness* (1960); Thomas R. Henry, *Strangest Things in the World* (1958); Paul G. Howes, *This World of Living Things* (1959); Joseph W. Krutch, *Desert Year* (1960); *Forgotten Peninsula: A Naturalist in Baja California* (1961); Meriwether Lewis and William Clark, *Natural History of the Lewis and Clark Expedition* (1961); Gavin Maxwell, *Ring of Bright Water* (1961).

NATURALISM is that philosophical viewpoint which finds final facts to be all alike—facts of nature. The source of all truth, beauty, and goodness, the ground of all meaning and value, is held to be the material universe investigated by science and disclosed in sense experience. The reason of things, the causes of phenomena, the purposes of life, are to be found by examination of the physical facts which conjointly constitute nature. There is no going behind these facts to anything more ultimate. Apart from the actualities of nature there is nothing—mere nonentity. See EMPIRICISM; MATERIALISM; POSITIVISM; SCIENTIFIC METHOD.

The origins of naturalism are the origins of philosophy itself, inasmuch as philosophy in the Western world had its beginnings in the attempt by the members of the Greek school of Miletus (624–524 B.C.) to explain all things as arising out of a single, basic natural stuff. Thus Thales (624–550 B.C.) found the substance of the world to be water, and Anaximenes (588–524 B.C.), taking cognizance of the phenomena of condensation and rarefaction, thought it to be air. In the cosmology of Democritus (460–370 B.C.) naturalism emerged as materialism—the universe consisting of material particles, atoms, combining and separating, in motion in empty space. With the Sophists (fifth century B.C.) naturalism became humanism (man is the measure of all things) and empiricism (knowledge is perception). According to Strato (about 288–268 B.C.) nature itself is God, and all phenomena are to be explained in terms of the forces of heat and cold. Lucretius (96–55 B.C.), following Democritus, taught the formation of the universe as the falling of material atoms through the void of space, and held the soul to be material also.

Superseded during the Middle Ages by Christian supernaturalism, naturalism was reborn in the Renaissance as the humanism of Petrarch (1304–74) and Boccaccio (1313–75), the pantheism (the world is God) of Marsilio Ficino (1433–99) and Giordano Bruno (1548–1600). In the experimental science of Galileo (1564–1642) naturalism came of age.

Thomas Hobbes (1588–1679), adopting the conclusions of sixteenth century science, maintained the universe to be simply matter in motion and, by nearly three centuries, anticipated the notions of behavioristic psychology with his theory of mind as the physical energy of the brain. Extending his mechanistic materialism to social and political philosophy, Hobbes argued in *Leviathan* (1650) his conviction that all law and government have their origin in purely naturalistic principles. For good or ill his influence on the subsequent development of English thought was decisive. Applying Hobbesian theories to the problem of knowledge, John Locke (1632–1704) concluded that there is nothing in the mind which was not first in the senses; George Berkeley (1685–1753) insisted that to be is to be perceived; and David Hume (1711–76) demolished the traditional structures of philosophy by showing all truth to be merely custom or habit, and mind to be nothing more than the succession of its physical states. A naturalism of a rather different stripe was preached by Jean Jacques Rousseau (1712–78). Bidding man abjure the artificialities of convention and society, Rousseau advised a return to nature and to nature's law.

But nature's law was soon to change. Charles Darwin's *Origin of Species* (1859) and Albert Einstein's *Special Theory of Relativity* (1905) engendered a scientific revolution which, in the first half of the twentieth century, was to find philosophical expression as the revival of naturalism in various forms of realism, in vitalism, energism, and physicalism. In the broad area of sociology and education, naturalism, as expounded by John Dewey (1859–1952), continued past mid-century to be the dominant attitude of the American culture. ROBERT C. WHITTEMORE

NATURALIZATION, the process by which aliens are admitted to citizenship. (See ALIEN.) Essentially it consists of renouncing all allegiance and fidelity to one state or monarch and taking oath of allegiance and fidelity to another state or monarch. Ordinarily naturalization is an individual action, in which a person takes the initiative in changing his citizenship. It may, however, take place without action on the part of the individual, as when citizenship of the wife is changed by naturalization of the husband (as in the United States before 1922) or when naturalization of a parent confers the same change on minor children. Naturalization also may be collective, as in the transfer of territory from one state to another. In such an instance the persons affected may usually choose to retain their former nationality although often under onerous conditions. The treaties ceding Louisiana, Florida, Mexican Territory, and Alaska to the United States provided for naturalization of inhabitants. The people of Texas acquired U.S. citizenship through a joint resolution of Congress, and laws passed by Congress bestowed citizenship upon Hawaiians (1900), Puerto Ricans (1917), and Indians (1924).

In the United States naturalization has been regarded as a right of every individual. At first this practice was contrary to the policies of most other countries where the prevailing doctrine held that a subject could not change his allegiance without the consent of his sovereign. See ALLEGIANCE; NATIONALITY.

Naturalization in the United States is a function of the federal government. The Constitution gives Congress the power "To establish an uniform rule of naturalization." At one time the Supreme Court held that both federal and state governments might exercise this power, but in 1817 the court ruled that Congress had exclusive power.

The McCarran-Walter Immigration and Nationality Act of 1952 codified existing immigration, naturalization, and deportation statutes, and removed race as a barrier to naturalization. Citizenship was denied to those unable to read, write, and speak words in ordinary usage in the English language, except for persons who on the effective date of the act had at least 20 years residence in the United States and were either physically unable to comply with the rule or were more than 50 years old. Citizenship also was withheld from persons convicted of deserting U.S. military or naval forces during wartime or of evading a draft by leaving the country in wartime. Advocates of totalitarian forms of government or of overthrow of the U.S. government by force or violence are barred from naturalization; so also are individuals guilty of unlawful assault or killing any U.S. governmental officer, of sabotage, or of unlawful damage or destruction of property. Citizenship is denied by the act to persons who cannot demonstrate knowledge and understanding of the U.S. form of government and the history of the United States.

U.S. Regulations. No declaration of intention, previously demanded of applicants for naturalization, was required under the McCarran-Walter Act, but the applicant must have been lawfully admitted to the United States for permanent residence. He must have lived in the United States for five years immediately preceding the date of his petition; he must have been physically present in the United States at least half that time and a resident within the state in which the petition was filed for at least six months. Continuous absence from the United States of more than six months but less than one year during the five-year period is permissible if the petitioner is able to satisfy the court that he did not abandon U.S. residence during that time, but absence of a year or more breaks continuity of residence unless application to preserve residence is made in advance. Such application may be made by individuals who are to be employed or engaged abroad by the U.S. government, an American research institution, an American firm or corporation engaged in the development of the foreign trade and commerce of the United States, or a public international organization of which the United States is a member by treaty or statute.

First citizenship papers, or declarations of intention, although not required by the act, are issued on request. Such a request may be made by an alien doctor, for example, who desires a medical license, since most states forbid the issuance of licenses for the practice of medicine and certain other occupations to aliens who have not applied for naturalization papers.

Following an individual's application for naturalization, the immigration and naturalization service conducts preliminary hearings to determine his eligibility. Burden of proof of lawful entry into the United States rests with the petitioner. He must appear for a final hearing in open court not sooner than 30 days after he files his application, but he may not be heard less than 60 days before a general election within the jurisdiction of the court. Before being admitted to citizenship the petitioner must renounce all allegiance to foreign state or potentate, and take an oath of loyalty to the United States.

If an alien is married to, and has lived in marital union with, a citizen of the United States for at least three years, he can be naturalized after complying with all naturalization conditions except the residence

U.S. DEPT. OF JUSTICE

These applicants, having met the necessary residence and other requirements, become citizens of the United States by swearing allegiance and fidelity to their new homeland.

requirement; this is reduced to three years. Spouses of U.S. citizens living abroad in the employ of the U.S. government, an American research institution recognized by the attorney general, an American firm or corporation engaged in foreign trade and commerce, or an international organization in which the United States participates, may be exempted from residence requirements.

Naturalization of a husband does not make his alien wife a U.S. citizen; she must acquire her own citizenship. Legitimate alien children under age 16, however, derive citizenship upon naturalization of both parents, a surviving parent, or the parent to whom sole legal custody has been awarded, if the child then resides or begins to reside in the United States. This rule does not apply to adopted children.

The Immigration and Naturalization Service has been a bureau of the Department of Justice since 1940. All activities relating to immigration and deportation of aliens are its province; the commissioner has charge of registration and fingerprinting of aliens within the United States, its territories, and its possessions. He is authorized to make rules and regulations necessary to administer the law; to prescribe the nature and scope of examination of petitioners for naturalization; to promote instruction in citizenship among applicants; and to keep records of each alien arriving in the United States. Duplicates of certificates of naturalization granted since September, 1906, are filed in the archives of the service. See CITIZENSHIP, United States, British Commonwealth, *Canada*, Other Countries.

BIBLIOG.–Margaret E. Hall, *How To Become a Citizen of the United States* (Legal Almanac Ser. 8) (1956); Edith Lowenstein, *Alien and the Immigration Law* (1958); Ann M. O'Conke, *Short-Cut to Citizenship* (1960).

NATURAL LAW, or law of nature, is a sum of fundamental moral and legal rules for man's social life that directly arise out of the essential nature of man as a rational and social physical person, and recognizable by natural reason. These rules subdivided into (a) *first principles:* do good and avoid evil, the Golden Rule, help to realize the common good, and respect the dignity of the human person and its rights; (b) *immediate conclusions*, corresponding to the Ten Commandments—that is, honor one's parents and obey lawful authority, do not commit murder, theft, perjury, or adultery; and (c) *remote conclusions* that forbid such things as embezzlement, purposive lying, and sedition, are claimed by various moral and legal philosophies to be universally valid, observed almost everywhere and through the ages. Although occasionally the laws and customs of a civilization have resulted in habitual violation of these rules, such violations are said to be exceptions that do not invalidate the universal character of the rules. They are thought to be at once foundation and critical norm for positive—that is, man-made—law which ought to be derived from it and if in contradiction to natural law is not obliging as being against the higher law. Natural law is the basis of man-made law, civil, penal, administrative, and international law.

Natural-law rules must be made concrete in the interests of the security of the positive legal order of society. Natural law forbids injuring life, and charges public authority to impose remedy and punishment, but it is left to positive law to determine the kind and amount of punishment, the criminal or civil procedures by which crime or tort and their punishment are to be established, and the particular courts of law to accomplish this function. In these matters there is great diversity in positive law because of differences in national character, economic systems, and cultural progress.

Besides the meaning of *natural* in referring to man's nature as of proximate origin—the ultimate origin being the Creator of man—and the meaning of natural reason as the principle of cognition, *natural* also distinguishes these rules from divine revealed law, as for example the sacraments of Christianity. There is nothing contradictory between natural and divine law, because the rules of natural law may be expressly revealed in the Scriptures as the will of God. Opposed to natural law is moral and legal positivism which contends that all laws are merely the product of God's or man's arbitrary will.

Greece. Natural law is so human that the earliest cultures knew and obeyed it. Distinguished from the concept "all men are natural law jurists," is the philosophical and scholarly effort to elaborate a theory of natural law. For Western civilization this theory began in Greek philosophy. Some Sophists, such as Hippias (fifth century B.C.) and Alcidamas (fourth century B.C.), spoke of unwritten laws, eternal and unchangeable, which were higher than the laws of the Greek city-state and before which men were equal and free, brethren and fellow citizens. (See SOPHISM.) These Sophists distinguished between what is just by nature and what is just by the will of public authority—as did also Plato (about 427–347 B.C.) and Aristotle (384–322 B.C.). Plato conceived of absolute ideas: the good, the true, the just; these ideas were for man, to be grasped and realized. They become ideals of action: thus the true, good, and just law considers only the common good, not a partial good of party or a special group (*The Laws*, IV, 715). Aristotle distinguished between the particular laws of Greeks and other nations and of various Greek city-states. These he contrasted with certain basic rules immediately evident, which are valid in themselves as just, independent of any human authority.

Rome. Of greatest impact on the doctrine of natural law were the late Roman Stoics, who influenced Roman jurists and Roman law. (See STOICISM.) Earlier, however, the jurists had, in advising the judges of the court for foreigners, already developed a set of rules based on reason and the common elements of the law of all nations, according to which they judged suits between foreigners or between foreigners and Roman citizens. As a basis for this commonness they took the Stoic doctrine of a natural law. The rules were to worship God, to acknowledge man to be a sacred being, the right of self-defense, to live morally and honestly, to injure no one, and to give each his own—the latter as a perpetual and constant will was defined as justice. These rules they called *jus gentium*, rules that all nations recognized in their national legal codes and in their relations with each other. (See JUS GENTIUM.) They were valid everywhere, at all times, and for all men. Without this universalism the Roman law could never have survived the nation that created it.

The Fathers of the Church, contemporaries of some of the great Roman jurists, amalgamated into their social ethics the natural law that they found also in Christian revelation. With Christian tradition thus preserving natural law during the barbarian invasions, and with the revival of learning in general and of Roman law studies specifically in connection with the development of canon law, Scholastic philosophy gave the theory of natural law particular attention. Scholastic philosophy held that the universe with man as its noblest part was ordered by God as the Creator and Providence by the eternal law, the product of divine wisdom and reason. Man as a rational and free creature participated in this law, which was recognized by his reason and grasped as a moral order to be realized in man's personal and social life. This natural law was thought to be the foundation of all man-made law and its critical norm. Ruler and ruled were equally subject to it; a man-made law in contradiction to it was not equity but iniquity, and to refuse obedience was not sedition but lawful resistance. Since in its classic period the English common law was formed by clerics trained in this philosophy, the natural law exerted a tremendous influence on it.

Reaction Against Absolutism. Natural law and the doctrine of natural rights, liberties, and immunities based upon it and developed during the Middle Ages served as a rejection of the theory of the divine right of kings which accompanied the rise of absolutism. Natural law stated that public authority issued originally from the people, who had only transferred it to the ruler for the realization of the common good. Natural law also served as a basis for the establishment of international law by Francisco Vittoria (1480–1546) and Francisco Suárez (1548–1617), on whom Hugo Grotius (1583–1645) then built up the first systematic treatise in 1625. (See INTERNATIONAL LAW, *History of International Law.*) By reason of the prevailing individualism and rationalism in the seventeenth and eighteenth centuries, natural rights developed in contrast to natural law as objective rules and were supported by the religious individualism of Protestant groups. The groups formed the basis for the liberal revolutions in England, France, and subsequently in other countries.

Secularization. At the same time, starting with Grotius, a secularization of natural law took place by which the divine origin of natural law and rights was neglected. Instead, natural law was increasingly interpreted in the sense of the physical sciences, as by Thomas Hobbes (1588–1679) and Baruch Spinoza (1632–77). It also underwent the criticism of David Hume (1711–76). This critical process, together with glorification of customary folk law by such romanticists as Joseph de Maistre (1754–1821), Georg Wilhelm Friedrich Hegel (1770–1831), and Friedrich Carl von Savigny (1779–1861) and the philosophy of positivism and utilitarianism developed by Jeremy Bentham (1748–1832), James Mill (1773–1836), Auguste Comte (1798–1857), John Austin (1790–1859), and John Stuart Mill (1806–73) undermined natural law by stating that all law is the product of the historical, national will of the sovereign nation. (See POSITIVISM; UTILITARIANISM.) These doctrines, and Marxist materialism (See COMMUNISM, *Marxian Communism*), could have no relation to the supra-historical and ideal rules of natural law and natural rights.

Revival of Natural Law. Great upheavals such as world wars and totalitarianism with its contempt for rights and law suggested to many that the positivistic approach to matters of individual ethics and national and international politics is basically inadequate, and consequently there was a progressive revival of natural law in ethics, jurisprudence, and political theory. See ETHICS; LAW, The Maturity of Law, *Law of Nature;* METAPHYSICS. HEINRICH A. ROMMEN

BIBLIOG.-H. A. Rommen, *Natural Law* (1947); A. P. D'Entrèves, *Natural Law* (1951); E. C. Gerhart, *American Liberty and Natural Law* (1953); L. Strauss, *Natural Right and History* (1953); A. L. Harding, *Origins of the Natural Law Tradition* (1954); Saint Thomas Aquinas, *Nature and Grace* (ed. 1954); R. M. Craig, *Natural Order for Human Existence* (1957); O. F. von Gierke, *Natural Law and the Theory of Society, 1500 to 1800* (1957); P. J. Stanlis, *Edmund Burke and the Natural Law* (1958).

NATURAL RESOURCES are those things in nature that man uses. Although from the beginning man has depended on the things he finds in his natural environment, it has been only recently that he stopped taking them for granted and began to think about them collectively.

RESOURCES AND THEIR CLASSIFICATIONS

Resource Bases. The simplest classification of natural resources is according to where they are found, or by the resource base—sunlight, air, water, and land.

Sunlight is the primary source of all energy on earth (except for the as yet tiny artificial production of nuclear power). From sunlight man receives immediate heat and light as well as the energy stored in plant life and in precipitation.

Air, the earth's atmosphere, is the protective blanket in which all life on earth is immersed. It is the source of carbon dioxide for plant life, and oxygen vital to man.

Water of the rivers, lakes, and oceans is a natural resource from which food and minerals are taken, upon which ships travel, by which hydroelectric power is generated, and which is used for recreation purposes. Water itself—from precipitation, ground water, or surface water—is used directly by man for drinking, and for industry and irrigation.

Land is the setting for almost all human life—for homes, factories, and roads; for activities such as agriculture, lumbering, and hunting; and for political areas and natural barriers. From land itself most mineral resources are taken.

All these resource bases interact to produce and modify climatic and weather conditions.

Resource Products. Another method of classifying natural resources is by their products. These products are all the things obtained from the resource base, and include even raw materials that have been subjected to an initial step in the production process. The rate of output of resource products depends mainly on the amounts of mechanization, manpower, and technical skill applied to the resource base, and thus varies from time to time and from place to place. Even those natural resources that are readily available to man with little or no effort on his part, such as the air he breathes and the heat of the sun, have become subject to alteration as in air conditioning and refrigeration.

Renewable or Nonrenewable Resources. Another common method of classifying natural resources is to divide them into renewable and nonrenewable categories. Timber, wildlife, farm crops and animals, and fresh water are renewable resources. Nonrenewable resources include metallic ores and nonmetallic minerals such as the fossil fuels—coal, petroleum, and natural gas. Although the total supply of nonrenewable resources cannot be known, it is obviously reduced by consumption.

The practical distinction between renewables and nonrenewables is not clear-cut. Renewal of crops and forests, for example, is not automatic, but must be furthered by adequate care of the soil and good management. Likewise, usable supplies of surface and ground water may be impaired because their renewal is affected by neglect or overuse of watersheds. Nonrenewable resources can be conserved by greater investment in exploration and development, improved extraction and utilization, re-use of scrap metals, and through substitution of materials derived from the more plentiful resources for those that come from scarcer resources. In a literal sense, the so-called nonrenewable mineral resources are renewable, but only over periods of millions of years. For all practical purposes these resources are not replaced. See CONSERVATION.

Potential or Usable Resources. Potentially, natural resources include every physical substance and energy force in the world. The usability of natural resources is determined by man's ability to utilize them under the prevailing economic, technological, and social conditions of a given time and place. For example: coal was generally considered to be valueless black rock until the sixteenth and seventeenth centuries; the oil wells of Burma in the eighteenth century were a mere curiosity to westerners (who later based national policies on petroleum); bauxite did not become important as a source of aluminum until the twentieth century when cheap electric power became available for refining processes; and uranium was little more than a scientific curiosity until the dawn of atomic power in the 1940's. Better resource products and substitutes are continually sought to replace resources that have, or might, become scarce. Owing to technological development, the number of usable resources steadily increases.

Most changes in usable resources have added to their number, but many natural resources that were once important have become less so or even eclipsed. For example, the substitution of tractors for horses and other draft animals has increased the importance of iron ore in relation to soil used for raising fodder crops. Similarly, flint gave way to bronze, and bronze to iron; bayberries for candles and whale oil and kerosene for lamps lost their old significance with the development of electric power; and leather, natural rubber, and silk lost much of their earlier dominance with the development of chemical industries and artificial plastics and fibers.

Thus, changes in resource products, or advancing technology, cause changes in use of the resource bases.

BRITISH COLUMBIA GOVT. TRAVEL BUR.

Natural resources are the useful or potentially useful properties found in nature, including air and sunlight, lakes and streams, soil and minerals, forests and game.

Resources and People

History. Man's conversion of the resource base into resource products originated in prehistoric times with the manufacture of stone tools and weapons for hunting and fighting, crude attempts at agriculture, and the primitive mining and forging of metals. Some of those operations required appreciable skill and organization. Elaborate terraces and irrigation systems made possible the large-scale food production that supported the ancient empires of the Middle East. By the time of the Roman Empire many of the minerals known to modern man were in common use, textbooks on agriculture were being written, and engineers were building great highways, aqueducts, and sewers, and designing mills to be run by water power.

Until modern times, except for local or temporary situations, man was not primarily concerned with the supply of natural resources, but rather focused his attention on finding new or better ways of using the resource base—especially in the case of minerals. Even in agriculture, most of the pressures on food supply resulted primarily from social and economic disorganization rather than from lack of productive land. Most of the modern major problems in the field of natural resources involve the question of supply: Are there enough basic resources to meet the need for resource products at reasonable cost? Will there be enough in the future? The great and continually increasing demand for resource products and services results from the increasing numbers of people in the world, each of whom demands more of the products derived from the resource base. The population of the world A.D. 1 was approximately 200 million and it was not until 1600 that it reached 500 million. Since then population growth has accelerated. There were about 906 million people on earth in 1800, approximately 1.6 billion in 1900, and about 2.8 billion in 1957.

With the beginning of the Industrial Revolution in England at the start of the nineteenth century the rate of use of natural resources began to rise rapidly throughout most of the world. Coal, hydroelectric power, petroleum, and natural gas came into large-scale use. Metals, formerly used mainly for weapons, small tools, and ornaments, went into the fabrication of power-driven machinery, ships, and rails. The new manufacturing processes and transportation facilities produced and distributed a steadily increasing amount of goods, thus further accelerating the demand for raw materials. Simultaneously, power-driven farm equipment created a commercial agriculture of a magnitude that multiplied the drain on soil fertility.

Thus the combination of two main factors, increased population and greater consumption of all kinds of goods per person, helped to create the modern set of resource problems. Previously there was relatively little long-term destruction of soil. Although wood was the only important fuel and provided the only shipbuilding material, the countries of Europe did not worry about their timber supplies until the seventeenth and eighteenth centuries. In 1800 world production of pig iron was about 500,000 short tons; by World War II the total was 125 million tons. In 1850 more than three-fourths of the world's power supply came from work animals, about one-sixth from human labor, and only one-twentieth from mineral fuels and water power. By 1950 mineral fuels and water power supplied all but about 6 per cent of the world's power.

Trends in Requirements and Supplies. The sharpest increase in use of natural resources has occurred in connection with the principal raw materials of modern industry: energy fuels, metals, and other minerals.

For example, in 1921 five minerals—copper, lead, zinc, tin, and nickel—constituted more than 80 per cent of the nonferrous metals and plastics production of the United States. By 1950 the use of aluminum, magnesium, and plastics had replaced the five traditional metals to such a degree that they had declined to only 30 per cent of the total.

Demands upon natural resources have increased steadily and undoubtedly will continue to do so, but the adequacy of remaining supplies of nonrenewable mineral resources can only be roughly estimated. New methods of extraction from known mineral reserves may be found, or advances in technology may make possible the use of much lower grades. In the eighteenth century, for example, ore containing 13 per cent copper was considered the poorest commercial grade. By 1900 the average grade of copper ore mined in the United States was 5 per cent, and by 1950 it was less than 1 per cent. Similar progress made it possible to use iron ores of lower grade than the 1950 average of more than 50 per cent iron content. The immense taconite deposits in the Lake Superior region, which contain only 25 to 35 per cent iron and were once considered unprofitable to mine, began to be exploited following World War II.

New deposits of minerals may be discovered. In 1952, for example, a vast natural gas field with proved reserves of 2,280 billion cubic feet was discovered in West Pakistan. New coal reserves estimated at 900 billion tons were discovered in Siberia after World War II. In the Sahara Desert a new oil field began producing in 1956, and in the 1950's an immense oil deposit was located in Alberta, Canada. Because of frequent discoveries of new mineral resources by geologic expeditions it is believed that known reserves can keep well ahead of increasing consumption.

The limits of the earth's surface also would seem to set a limit on future production of renewable farm, forest, and aquatic products. New techniques in genetics and soil management, however, continually result in increases in yields. Success of experiments in growing algae for food or in hydroponics (growing plants in soilless chemical solutions) also could expand the limits of usable resources. In addition, large areas of the earth's land surface still lie unused for food and fiber production. They include semidesert lands that need irrigation, marshlands that need drainage, and savanna lands in tropical regions where better control of plant and livestock diseases is needed. The vast untapped resources of the three-fourths of the earth's surface that is covered by ocean could also further extend the future of both renewable and nonrenewable resources. As yet there is no evidence that economic growth in advanced countries has been checked by shortages of raw materials.

Natural Resources and Economic Power. A strong national economy has its basis in a high level of technology and social organization supported by ample supplies of raw materials, particularly metal ores and mineral fuels. The combination of materials and technology is important even in agricultural countries. There these factors determine whether the economy is one in which much of a nation's manpower must be used solely to feed, clothe, and house

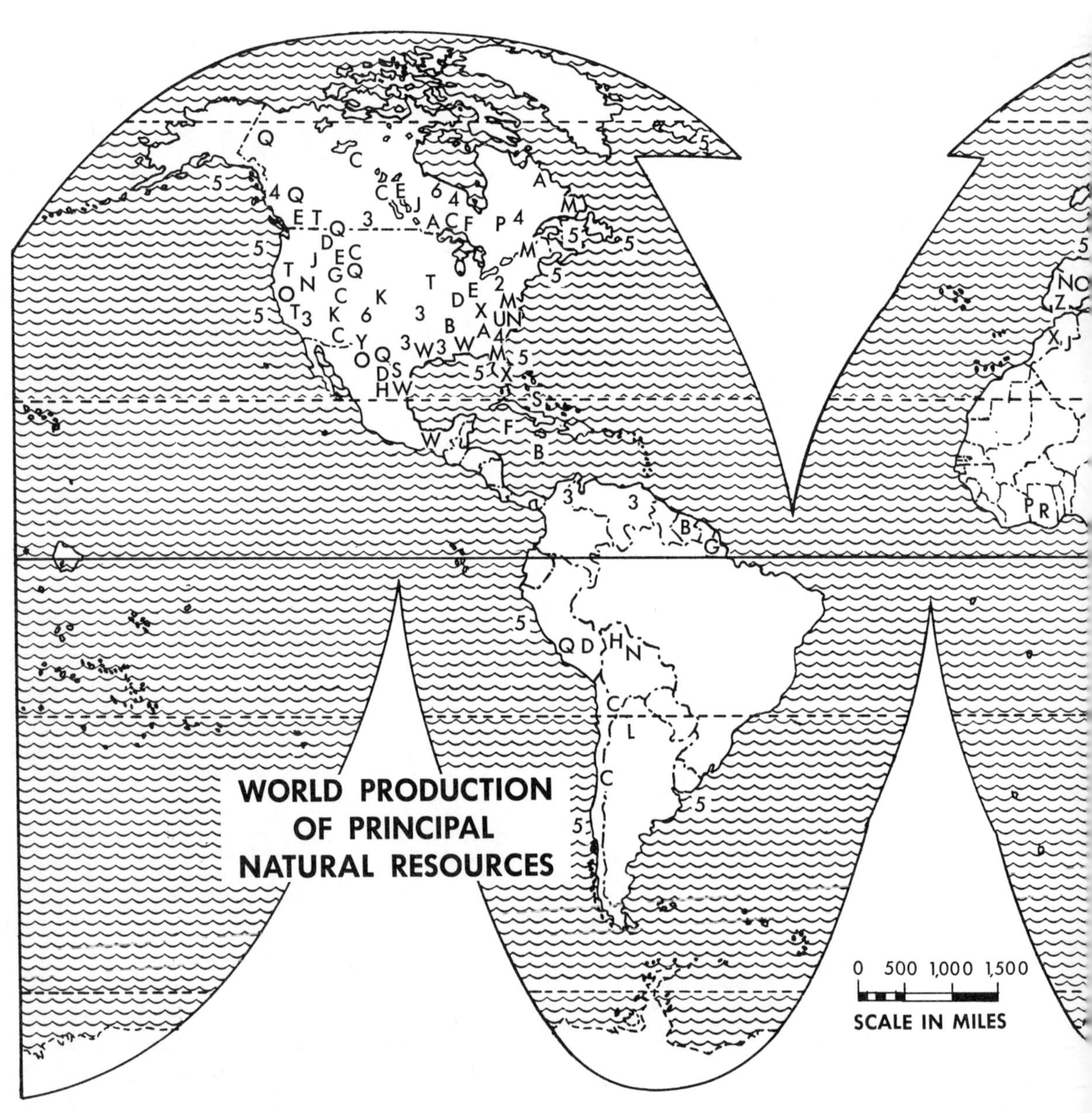

the population, or one in which productive large-scale mechanized farming and forestry free most of the working force for other kinds of production. Military strength, which is closely allied to economic strength, depends directly on plentiful raw materials.

It is unsafe, however, to generalize about natural resources and economic power although possession of important resources has often been the major factor in starting a nation on the road to economic strength. For large or integrated groups of countries, possession of a variety of natural resources appears to be a distinct advantage. But this is not invariably true, and in the case of smaller countries there have been many exceptions. Outstanding examples are Great Britain and Italy, both of which, through imports, were able to supply their industries with raw materials and become world powers despite their small size and the insufficient domestic supplies of petroleum in Great Britain and of coal, iron ore, and petroleum in Italy.

No country is completely self-sufficient. The United States, with its wealth of raw materials, has never depended entirely on its own resources, and after the 1940's changed from a net exporter to a net importer of raw materials that include petroleum, iron and other metals, and forest products. Magnesium and molybdenum are the only metals in which the United States still is relatively self-sufficient. Because even the largest countries are not self-sufficient in all the raw materials of industry, many resource problems and policies are concerned with tariffs, import quotas, investment in underdeveloped countries, currency arrangements, political boycotts, and other man-made aids or hindrances to world trade.

HENRY JARRETT

SUNLIGHT

Sunlight or insolation is a natural resource that varies from place to place on the earth's surface largely because of latitude. The Equator receives about two and one-half times as much sunlight annually as does either pole. During the year, however, the distribution of sunlight over the earth varies greatly, depending mainly on seasonal changes in the angle of the sun's rays and in the length of the day.

For example, in June, when the sun is directly overhead at the Tropic of Cancer and is below the

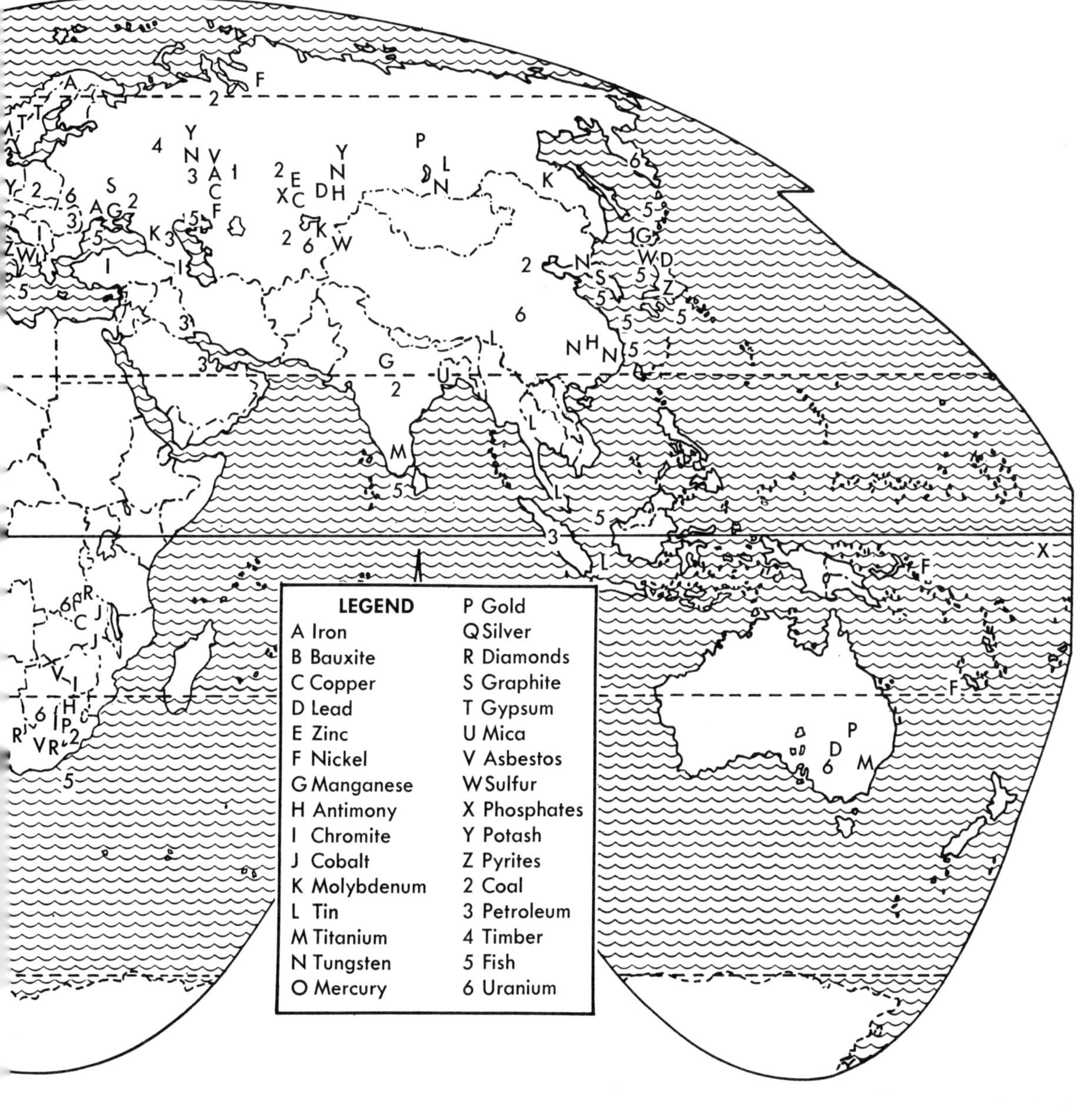

horizon south of the Antarctic Circle, points along the Tropic of Cancer receive more sunlight than do those along the Equator, and points in the antarctic receive none. Similarly, in December, when the sun is directly overhead at the Tropic of Capricorn and is below the horizon north of the Arctic Circle, points along the Tropic of Capricorn receive more sunlight than do those along the Equator, and points in the arctic receive none. In March and September, when the sun is overhead at the Equator and is at the horizon at the Arctic and Antarctic circles, points along the Equator receive the most sunlight. Thus, the arctic and antarctic summers are short but intense, and plants sprout and mature rapidly. In the tropics, sunlight varies so little throughout the year that there are no winter and summer seasons.

Altitude also affects the amount of sunlight reaching a given point on the earth's surface. Upland areas receive more sunlight than do lowlands of the same latitude because there is a thinner air layer over them to absorb, diffuse, and reflect the sunlight. Other minor factors that affect distribution of sunlight include the slightly closer proximity of the earth to the sun during the Southern Hemisphere summer, and variations in cloud and dust cover. Climate and weather conditions in a given locality, particularly in the middle latitudes, are greatly affected by factors other than sunlight. These include the relationship of the area to large land and water masses, precipitation, prevailing winds, and topography. See CLIMATE; SUN.

AIR

The atmosphere that encloses the earth is used primarily for its oxygen—for breathing, for heating (fire), and for industrial processes. Air is also a source of nitrogen and rare gases for industry, and of carbon dioxide for plant growth. The atmosphere is the medium for weather processes and for air transport. Rapid air movements, or winds, have been used for many centuries to turn windmills, and in modern times they have become increasingly useful for electric power generation. See AERODYNAMICS; ATMOSPHERE; ATMOSPHERIC CIRCULATION; ATMOSPHERIC PRESSURE; MASS.

WATER

Distribution of precipitation depends on many factors, most important of which are atmospheric heating and accessibility of an area to moist winds. Precipitation is affected by an area's latitude and by its location on the eastern or western side of a land mass and on the windward or leeward side of an upland. Precipitation tends to be greatest along the Equator and least at the poles. In the intermediate latitudes it tends to be greater in the 40's and 50's than in the 20's and 30's. The western and central parts of the continents tend to be the driest. The windward sides of mountain ranges are much wetter than the leeward sides. Precipitation also varies from season to season, particularly over the larger land masses, where it generally is greatest in the summer.

The world's surface waters have historically facilitated the movement of people and goods, particularly in areas of mountains or thick forests. The Amazon, Ohio, and Rhine rivers, for example, have provided such easy passages. Surface waters have also been a means for cheap transport, particularly of bulk cargoes, such as on the Great Lakes and the oceans. (See WATERWAYS, INLAND.) Water bodies also serve as barriers to movement, and often are convenient political boundaries. Rivers are widely used for the generation of electric power, particularly where large, steady volumes of water descend through moderately deep valleys. Africa, because of its relatively high average elevation and the great drop of its rivers, is the continent with the largest potential for hydroelectric power. The greatest development, however, has occurred in the most industrialized countries such as the United States, Canada, Japan, Italy, the Soviet Union, and France. Other major water-power countries are Sweden, Norway, Germany, Switzerland, and Spain. See WATER POWER.

The oceans, lakes, and streams of the world are a particularly rich source of renewable food resources. These include fish, crustaceans, sea mammals, and seaweed. Although the oceans cover three-fourths of the earth's surface, only a relatively small number of the vast numbers of aquatic-life species they contain are commercially exploited. (See FISHERIES.) The seas and lakes are also becoming increasingly important sources of minerals, such as salt and other metallic compounds.

Another use of the world's water surfaces is for recreation. Examples of recreational use can be found in diverse spots such as Niagara Falls, the many lakes of the Laurentian Upland, the bathing beaches of the Great Lakes, and the scenic gorge of the Rhine River.

Perhaps the most important uses of water itself, whether on the surface, from the ground, or directly from precipitation, are for drinking, washing, and irrigation. These uses depend more or less on methods of securing and storing the water—by reservoirs, wells, snow banks, or rain barrels. Some areas of the world are so arid that drinking water has to be shipped in. There are extensive fertile regions that are prevented from becoming productive farm land primarily by lack of water. The Central Valley of California was once that kind of region until irrigation helped develop it into a major producer of farm wealth within the United States. See WATER SUPPLY; RESERVOIR; IRRIGATION.

One of the principal factors in choosing the site for a modern industrial plant is the availability of large quantities of fresh water—for cooling, for washing, for steam, and as a chemical solvent. This consideration is especially vital to the steel, chemical, paper, and textile industries. See WATER.

LAND

Land Forms. The features of the earth's surface, and the materials that compose its crust, form the land resource base. Geologic forces are responsible for the distribution and location of various minerals and types of rock, and gradational forces such as weathering, erosion, and deposition of materials by water, wind, ice, and plants and animals have further sculptured the earth's surface. The land forms of the earth's surface, although dynamic in relation to the millions of years of geologic time, are relatively static in relation to man's use of them as a natural resource. See GEOLOGY, Minerals and Rocks, Surface of the Earth; LAND; PHYSIOGRAPHY.

The flat lands or plains have been the principal locations for human settlement, largely because it is easy to move across them and to erect structures upon them, while mountain areas have served as barriers and as more difficult building sites. The flat lands include coastal plains such as in northeast China, northwest Europe, and northeast United States, and extensive river plains such as the Ganges in India, the Yellow and Yangtze in China, and the Mississippi in the United States. In rugged land, settlement is mainly restricted to the flat plateaus or narrow river valleys such as in Nepal, south China, and the upper Ohio Valley. Flat lands are generally the most suitable areas for agriculture, although in hilly areas, such as in Java and Ceylon, terracing has permitted intensive agricultural development. Flat lands also are virtually a necessity for industrial plants and principal land transportation routes. In mountainous regions, uplift and erosion have frequently made mineral deposits easily exploitable, and large volumes of rapidly descending water in those regions furnish the natural base for hydroelectric power. See GEOPOLITICS.

Soils are a natural resource of the land upon which agriculture is chiefly based. Soil is the topmost layer of the earth's crust, and is formed by weathering processes and the natural addition of animal and plant matter. It is an exhaustible resource, but with good land management and replenishment of nutrients lost through cropping it can be a renewable resource. Poor agricultural practices, such as destruction of plant cover and improper plowing, may result in erosion that causes permanent destruction of fertile soils. See SOIL CONSERVATION; AGRICULTURAL ENGINEERING.

The world distribution of the principal soil groups demonstrates their close relationship to geologic formations, topography, climate, and vegetation. Fundamental differences exist between soils of humid lands and those of dry lands. The mature soils of humid lands are largely developed under forest vegetation. They are leached of both organic and mineral plant foods, and tend to be acidic and only moderately fertile. The effects of chemical processes on these soils are influenced by temperature variations. In high latitudes, where low temperatures retard decay of organic matter, evaporation of surface water, and the essential mixing action of earthworms, dominant soils are the podsols. They are characteristic of the Canadian and Eurasian subarctic regions and are generally suited only to acid-tolerant grains such as rye and to root crops such as potatoes and beets.

Soils that develop in the humid low latitudes where heat and moisture cause more rapid decay of organic matter are called latosols. Despite their ability to support dense natural vegetation, most of these soils are relatively infertile, and exposure to the drying sun and to torrential precipitation hastens erosion. The latosols occupy the tropical rainy regions of South America, Africa, and southeast Asia. In mid-latitude regions where mixed forests of broadleaf deciduous and coniferous evergreen trees form the climax vegetation, soils exhibit characteristics of both latosols and podsols, and are moderately fertile. They support dense populations and cover much of eastern United States, northwest and north central Europe, and parts of China.

Subhumid regions, where grasses form the natural vegetation, have soils of high humus content, resulting from the decay of roots to depths of several feet. These soils closely reflect the amount of effective precipitation, grading from the deep, rich prairie and chernozem (black earth) soils on the humid margins to the chestnut brown and desertic soils of steppe and semidesert. These soils tend to be unleached, but capillary action of soil water during dry periods causes a layer of lime and other soluble alkaline minerals to accumulate, especially in the more arid regions. Where precipitation is adequate and dependable, these soils are highly prized for grain production. The prairie and chernozem soils lie in a broad swath across the interior plains of North America, west of the 90th meridian from the Gulf of Mexico into Canada. In Europe and Asia they extend in a broad east-west belt from the Danube Basin into central Asia, pinched to a narrow strip by the cold from the north and the Asian highlands to the south. They are also found in north China, the uplands of central India, and the Argentine pampa. On the drier margins of these regions the chestnut brown and desertic soils receive only enough moisture to support sparse grasses and livestock grazing. They are generally located in the Great Plains and Rocky Mountains of North America, Patagonia in Argentina, border areas of the Australian desert, the steppes of central Asia, areas bordering the Mediterranean Sea, and the extensive savannas of east and south central Africa. In true desert areas, soils are thin, salty, alkaline, and lacking in humus, unfit for agriculture or grazing but frequently valuable for salt mining.

Some of the richest soils in the world are the alluvial soils deposited by floodwaters in river basins. In parts of China, southeast Asia, India, Japan, and the Middle East, deep alluvial soils are the basis of dense agricultural populations. In parts of the western Mississippi Valley, north China, western Asia, and eastern Europe there are deep deposits of loess soils, which are fine, wind-deposited silts of high fertility. Infertile waterlogged tundra soils are characteristic of the permafrost areas of the Canadian and Soviet arctic.

FREEPORT SULPHUR CO.

Liquid and gaseous minerals, such as sulfur, natural gas, and oil, are obtained by drilling. Solid minerals, such as iron ore, and limestone, are either mined or quarried.

Soil types vary not only horizontally but also, in mountain areas, according to their elevation. Thus, in a generally arid area there may be desertic soils at the mountain bases, chestnut brown soils and forest-floor podsols on the mountainsides, and tundra soils on the highest mountain peaks and ridges—all within a relatively small area. See SOIL.

Natural Vegetation. In preagricultural cultures the gathering of wild plants, fruits, and nuts provided much of the food and other necessities of life. In modern times, however, except among a few surviving, primitive peoples, natural vegetation serves as a source of man's food only indirectly—through the consumption of animals and cultivated plants. The natural climax vegetation of the inhabited parts of the world has long been replaced by cultivated crops, economically valuable trees, or seminatural vegetation, often consisting of introduced or preclimax species. Forests, both mature and planted, are the source of fuel, construction materials, and pulp. Cultivated trees yield food and industrial crops such as fruits, spices, vegetable oils, and rubber. Of increasing significance is the aesthetic and recreational value of forests. Watershed forests are essential to the conservation of water and soils, and the use of trees as shelter belts is important in the reduction of wind erosion on open plains. See FOREST.

Natural grasses provide pasture for livestock, and as green fertilizer and soil cover they help to create and maintain the productivity of soil and to reduce erosion. The tough grasses of tropical savannas are used for fuel, construction material, and, after burning, for fertilizing-ash. Desert shrubs and grass and the sparse mosses, lichens, and sedges of the arctic tundra provide food and moisture for wildlife. The distribution of natural vegetation types is closely related to the distribution of major soil and climate types. See PLANT GEOGRAPHY, *Ecology*; ECOLOGY.

Animal Wildlife is another natural resource of the land that is of less importance than in earlier times. Wild animals served prehistoric peoples as a major source of food, skins, and bone implements, and some of them were the forebears of present domestic animals. Hunting and trapping is still of major importance to a few present-day primitive civilizations. In modern industrialized civilizations many fur-bearing animals are raised on special farms, although others are hunted in their native wild state. Hunting of wildlife is also a popular sport. See FUR; HUNTING; WILDLIFE CONSERVATION; ZOOGEOGRAPHY.

Minerals are the natural resources most commonly recognized. Exploitation of the world's mineral wealth, however, is difficult to measure, mainly because of incomplete data and because of different and uncorrelated methods of measurement. Another complication in evaluating worldwide distributions is that the production of each mineral may vary considerably from year to year. The variation may be a result of depletion, changing market prices, exploitation of previously undeveloped resources, or the application of more efficient production techniques. See MINING.

Iron Ore is by far the most exploited of mineral resources. It is the basic raw material for steel, and thus is the foundation of modern industry. Hematite (Fe_2O_3) is the most commonly mined iron ore in the United States, amounting to about 70 per cent of the total; magnetite ore (Fe_3O_4) comprises most of the remainder. An increasing percentage of U.S. ore is lower-grade taconite, which needs to be concentrated before being smelted.

World production of iron ore increased from an annual average of 128 million long tons during the period 1948–53 to 274 million long tons in 1961. Principal mining areas in the United States are in the Mesabi Range in northeast Minnesota (with about two-thirds of U.S. production), the Upper Peninsula of Michigan, and northern Alabama. Other sizable ore fields are in upstate New York and southeast Pennsylvania. A development along the Québec-Labrador border has become the principal source of Canadian iron ore, while large amounts continue to be mined in the older Steep Rock and Michipicoten areas around Lake Superior. Other Canadian mining areas are at Bell Island (Newfoundland) and in British Columbia. About two-thirds of all U.S. and Canadian iron ore is shipped through Great Lakes ports—mainly Superior, Duluth, and Two Harbors.

Principal iron-mining areas of the Soviet Union are at Krivoy Rog in Ukraine, at Kerch in Crimea, and at Magnitogorsk in the Ural Mountains. The huge Lorraine iron ore field is mainly in France but extends into Luxembourg and Belgium. Northern Sweden is a leading source of high-quality iron ore. Other principal suppliers of iron ore are mines in England, Germany, and Spain. Vast deposits are being developed in Venezuela, North Africa, India, Peru, and Chile. Total world reserves are about 58 billion long tons, of which more than 10 billion are in the United States, 8 billion in France, and 7 billion in Brazil.

Bauxite (hydrated aluminum oxide ore) is the major source of aluminum. Of the 1961 world production of 25 million long tons, the United States mined only 1.5 million, almost entirely from Arkansas. The world's principal bauxite mines are in Jamaica (first developed in 1952), Surinam (Dutch Guiana), and British Guiana. Other large producers are France and the Soviet Union. Total world reserves are estimated at about 1.2 billion short tons, of which China and Hungary each have 150 million and Cameroun, Guinea, and Mali have at least 100 million.

Copper Ore mined in the United States accounts for more than one-fourth of world production. About half of U.S. production comes from a number of areas in Arizona, most important of which are at Morenci, Globe-Miami, Bisbee, Ajo, Old Hat, and Ray. Utah's production comes mainly from one mine at Bingham, the largest in the United States. Other major copper districts are at Butte, Mont., Central, N.M., Ely, Nev., and in Michigan's Upper Peninsula. Almost half of Canada's copper is mined in the Sudbury district of Ontario, and about one-third comes from Québec, whose principal mining district is at Noranda in the northwest. Another major Canadian copper-mining district is at Flin Flon on the Manitoba-Saskatchewan border. Chile's copper mines are in the northern desert provinces of Atacama and Terapacá. African production comes primarily from the copper belt of Northern Rhodesia and The Congo. Soviet copper is mined largely in Kazakhstan. World reserves are estimated conservatively at 111 million short tons, of which 26 per cent is in the United States, 26 per cent in Africa, and 23 per cent in Chile.

Lead. More than one-third of U.S. lead mining is done in St. Francois and Washington counties in southeast Missouri, and about one-fifth in the Coeur d'Alene region of northern Idaho. Other major U.S. lead mining areas are at Bingham and Park City, Utah, and Metaline, Wash.; around Joplin in Missouri, Kansas, and Oklahoma; at Butte, Mont.; and in Colorado and Arizona. Most of Australia's lead is mined at Broken Hill in New South Wales, other major lead districts being at Cloncurry in Queensland, Captain's Flat in New South Wales, and Read-Roseberry in Tasmania. Principal Soviet lead mines are at Ust-Kamenogorsk and Tekeli in Kazakhstan. Mexico's principal lead districts are in Chihuahua and Zacatecas. Three-fourths of Canada's lead is mined in British Columbia, and other sizable mining districts are in Newfoundland and Yukon. Other major lead-mining nations are Peru, Morocco, Yugoslavia, Germany, and Spain.

Zinc mining in the United States is widely scattered. New York, the leading zinc state in 1962, accounted for only one-eighth of total U.S. production —mainly from mines in St. Lawrence County. Other leading mining areas are in east Tennessee, Shoshone County in Idaho, the Butte area in Montana, and in Colorado, Utah, Arizona, and New Mexico. Half of Canada's zinc is mined near Trail in British Columbia. Other principal Canadian zinc-mining districts are at Flin Flon in Manitoba and Saskatchewan, and in Quebec and Newfoundland. Soviet zinc is mined principally in the Altai Mountains of Kazakhstan and in Novosibirsk Region. Other major zinc-mining countries are Australia, Mexico, Peru, Japan, Italy, Poland, The Congo, and Germany.

Nickel. About 3 per cent of the world's nickel comes from the United States, mainly from mines at Riddle, Ore., Fredericktown, Mo., and Cobalt, Idaho. Mines in Canada supply more than three-fifths of the world's nickel, mainly from the Sudbury district of Ontario, the Lynn Lake area of Manitoba, and the Rankin Inlet area of the Northwest Territories. Soviet nickel is mined in the Ural Mountains, on the Kola Peninsula, and at Norilsk in northern Siberia. New Caledonia and Cuba are also major nickel producers.

Manganese Ore output in the United States was 21,500 short tons in 1961, 0.7 per cent that of the Soviet Union. Nevada, Arizona, and Montana were the principal sources in the United States. Soviet manganese ore is mined mainly from a vast reserve at Nikopol in south Ukraine. Most of India's manganese ore comes from Madhya Pradesh State, most of Brazil's from Amapá State, and Japan's largely from Hokkaido.

Antimony mining in the United States is confined to Shoshone County in Idaho, and the total is only 1 per cent of world production. Almost one-third of world antimony-ore mining is in China, mainly from the Sikwangshan area of central Hunan. Mines in the Union of South Africa are mainly in the Pietersburg district of Transvaal, and Soviet production is mainly from the Altai Mountains of Kazakhstan. Bolivia and Mexico are also major producers. China's antimony reserves more than equal those of the rest of the world, and Bolivia has considerable reserves.

Barite produced in the United States comes largely from Arkansas and Missouri. Nova Scotia is the source of almost all Canada's barite. Germany's Thuringian Forest and Mexico are leading producers, and considerable barite is mined in Peru, Italy, and Sweden.

Chromite mined in the United States accounts for only 3 per cent of world production, mostly from Stillwater County in Montana. Mines in the Philippines (mainly in Zambales and Pangasinan provinces) produce about one-sixth of the world's total, as do mines in western and southeastern Turkey and in western Transvaal in the Union of South Africa. The Great Dike area in Southern Rhodesia, the Ural Mountains and Armenia in the Soviet Union, and

Albania are also major chromite producers.

Cobalt mined in the United States comes almost entirely from Lemhi County in central Idaho. Canada's cobalt mines are in northern and central Ontario and in Manitoba. About three-fifths of the world's cobalt ore is mined in The Congo, mainly in Katanga Province. Northern Rhodesia and Morocco are also major cobalt-mining countries.

Molybdenum. The United States is the source of four-fifths of world production, mainly from Colorado, Utah, Arizona, and other western states. Mines in the Caucasus, Kazakhstan, and the far east of the Soviet Union produce about half of the remainder, and other major molybdenum mines are in Yugoslavia, northern Chile, Canada, Japan, and Norway.

Tin. The only major source of tin in the Western Hemisphere is the highlands of Bolivia, from which is mined about one-seventh of world production. The world's major tin-mine area is in Malaya and accounts for two-fifths of total world production. Other major sources of tin are the Indonesian islands of Bangka, Billiton, and Singkep, offshore operations in Thailand, Yunnan in China, and Transbaikalia, Yakutia, and Kazakhstan in the U.S.S.R.

Titanium. More than one-third of world production comes from the United States, mostly from mines in Virginia, Florida, South Carolina, and New York. Canadian titanium comes from Québec. Titanium-mining areas in south India supply about one-sixth of world production. Other major producing countries are Norway, Australia, Finland, and Malaya.

Tungsten. The United States produces about one-tenth of the world supply, mainly from mines in Vance County in North Carolina, Pershing County in Nevada, and Inyo County in California. Canadian tungsten comes from mines in British Columbia. Mines in Kiangsi, Hunan, and Kwangtung in China produce almost one-third of the world supply. Soviet mines are mainly in the Urals, Kazakhstan, and Transbaikalia. Other major tungsten producers are Korea, Bolivia, and Portugal.

Mercury production in the United States is about one-eighth of the world total. About half of U.S. production is from California; Nevada and Alaska are also major producers. Principal world mercury producers are Italy and Spain. Mexico, the Soviet Union, and Yugoslavia are also major producers. Almost half the world's measured mercury reserves are in the Soviet Union, and other large reserves are in Italy, the United States, Canada, Yugoslavia, and Spain.

Gold. The United States mines only 4 per cent of world production, mostly from South Dakota, Utah, Alaska, California, and Arizona. Canadian gold is mined in Ontario and Québec. More than two-fifths of world gold production comes from mines in the Witwatersrand and Odendaalsrus fields in the Union of South Africa. Siberian gold fields in the U.S.S.R. produce about one-fourth of the world's supply, and other leading areas are in Australia, Ghana, and Southern Rhodesia.

Silver mines in the United States, mainly in Idaho, Utah, California, and Colorado, account for about one-sixth of world production. Canadian silver, about one-eighth of world production, is mined in British Columbia, Ontario, and Yukon. Mexican silver, about one-fifth of world production, comes largely from Chihuahua. Peru and the Soviet Union are also major silver producers.

Uranium. The United States is a leading producer of uranium ore (measured by uranium oxide content). Utah produces about one-third, New Mexico about one-fourth, and Colorado about one-fifth of total U.S. production. Canadian production is mainly from the Blind River area in northern Ontario, the Beaverlodge area in northern Saskatchewan, the Bancroft area in southeastern Ontario, and the Northwest Territories. Soviet uranium mines are mainly in the Fergana area of central Asia, the Angara Shield in northern Siberia, at Lake Baykal, and on Kamchatka Peninsula. Other principal uranium-mining areas are in Eastern Europe, Australia, China, The Congo, and the Union of South Africa.

Salts are produced from brine, rock-salt mines and dry lake beds. These include the halides, nitrates, and sulfides of sodium, magnesium, and calcium. Most U.S. production of common salt (sodium chloride), which amounts to almost one-third of the world total, is from brine and comes largely from Michigan, Texas, New York, Louisiana, and Ohio. Other major salt-producing areas in the world are Szechwan and the coastal areas of east China, and Lake Bashkunchak near the Caspian Sea, Artemorsk in Ukraine, and the Solikamsk-Berezniki area near the Urals in the Soviet Union. Great Britain, Germany, and India are also leading salt-producing countries.

Coal has been the world's principal mineral fuel for many decades and remains, together with iron ore and petroleum, one of man's most important mineral resources. Total world production of coal reached almost 2.2 billion short tons in 1961. Coal mines in the United States produced 422 million, or about one-fifth, of which 94 per cent was bituminous coal. Most U.S. coal is mined in the Appalachian region, mainly from West Virginia and Pennsylvania; the Illinois–Indiana–western Kentucky region is also a major source of coal. Virtually all U.S. anthracite coal mines are in the Schuylkill, Wyoming, and Lehigh valleys of Pennsylvania; they produce almost one-fifth of world production. Mines in the Soviet Union produce almost half of the world's anthracite, and Germany and France are also leading producers.

Soviet coal is mined chiefly in the Donets Basin of eastern Ukraine and Rostov Region, the Kuznetsk Basin of western Siberia, and the Karaganda area of central Kazakhstan. Smaller supplies of coal come from the Moscow-Tula area, the Pechora Basin in the far north, and the Kizel Basin in the Urals. The bulk of Germany's anthracite and bituminous coal is mined in the Ruhr Valley, and there is considerable production in the Saar. Lignite is mined mainly in east central Germany. Great Britain's coal mines are chiefly in south Wales, around Newcastle in northeast England, and in the midlands. There are large coal fields in the Silesian areas of Czechoslovakia and Poland, in north France and Belgium, and in Liaoning, Hopei, Shansi, and Anhwei provinces in northeast and east China. Considerable coal is also mined in India, Japan, and the Union of South Africa. Principal world coal reserves are in China, the United States, and the Soviet Union.

Petroleum. World production of crude petroleum reached a total of 1.1 billion metric tons in 1961, compared with .47 billion in 1948. Oil wells in the United States in 1952 produced more than one-half of the total. With the rapid development of oil fields elsewhere in the world, however, U.S. production dropped to about one third of the total by 1961. Major oil fields in the United States are along the Louisiana and Texas Gulf Coast, in west Texas, in east Texas, and in California's San Joaquin Valley and Los Angeles Basin. Other principal oil-producing areas are in Oklahoma, north Texas, Kansas, and Wyoming.

About one-fifth of world oil output comes from the Middle East, almost entirely from fields in the Persian Gulf areas of Iran, Iraq, Kuwait, Saudi Arabia, Bahrein, and Qatar. Soviet oil production comes mainly from the Caucasus—at Baku, Grozny, and Maikop—although an increasing proportion comes from oil fields between the Volga River and the Urals and from the Emba Region in Kazakhstan. Venezuela's oil is pumped from fields mainly grouped around Lake Maracaibo in Zulia State and in the eastern state of Anzoátegui. Other major petroleum fields are in Mexico, Indonesia (Sumatra), and Rumania. Total proved world petroleum reserves are estimated at 276 billion barrels. More than three-fifths lies in the

Middle East, and most of the rest lies in the United States, the Soviet Union, and Venezuela.

Natural gas. Exploitation of natural gas resources is largely confined to the United States. About half of U.S. natural gas production comes from wells in Texas, and much of the rest is from Louisiana. Other major producing states are Oklahoma, New Mexico, Kansas, and California. Oil wells furnish about one-third of the total supply. Outside the United States the leading natural gas producers are the Soviet Union, Rumania, Canada, Italy, and Mexico. A rare by-product of natural gas production is helium, whose main sources are in Texas and New Mexico.

Peat. Most of the world's production is in the central and northwestern forest areas of European U.S.S.R. The only other sizable developed peat resources are in Ireland and Germany.

Diamonds and Corundum are produced mostly in Africa. Almost three-fourths of the world total is mined in the Lubilash District of The Congo, and mines in Southern Rhodesia produce almost half of the corundum. The Union of South Africa, Ghana, and the Soviet Union are also major producers.

Fluorspar production in the United States comes mainly from Illinois and Kentucky near the Ohio River, from Ravalli County in Montana, and from Colorado. Canadian fluorspar is mined in Newfoundland, and Mexico's chief mines are in Coahuila. Other principal fluorspar-mining countries are Germany, the Soviet Union, and Italy.

Graphite. About half the world's graphite production comes from Sihung in southern Korea. Other major sources of graphite are in Ukraine and near Krasnoyarsk in the Soviet Union, in Mexico, in central Europe, and in Madagascar.

Gypsum production in the United States is about one-fourth of the world total; Michigan, California, Iowa, and Texas are the leading states. Principal Canadian mines are at East Kootenay in British Columbia. Other principal mining areas are France, the United Kingdom, and the Soviet Union.

Mica. North Carolina is the source of most U.S. mica production; other chief areas are in New Hampshire, South Dakota, Arizona, and New Mexico. India's mica mines are mainly in the Hazaribagh District of Bihar. Soviet production is largely concentrated at the southwest tip of Lake Baikal and in the upper Lena Basin.

Pumice production in the United States is mainly in California, Arizona, New Mexico, and Hawaii. About two-fifths of world production is in West Germany, and Italy mines about one-third.

Asbestos. About half of the world's production is mined in a long narrow belt that runs from south Quebec into Vermont. Soviet asbestos mines are chiefly in the central Urals, and other large mines are in the Shabani-Belingwe and Mashaba areas of Southern Rhodesia and in Transvaal in the Union of South Africa.

Feldspar. Much of the world's production is mined in the United States, largely in North Carolina and California. Other principal mining areas are in Germany and elsewhere in western Europe.

Sulfur. More than two-thirds of the world's native sulfur comes from the United States, mainly from the Texas and Louisiana Gulf coasts. Mexico, whose production was almost negligible before 1954, mines about one-seventh of the world's sulfur from the Coatzacoalcos Valley. The only other sizable sulfur-producing countries are Japan, Italy, and Uzbekistan in the U.S.S.R.

Pyrite mining in the United States is largely in Tennessee, but the principal world source is Okayama Prefecture in Japan. Spain, Italy, and Canada are also major producers.

Phosphate Rock (mainly apatite) mining in the United States, which produces about two-fifths of the world's total, is confined mostly to Florida. Other leading phosphate-mining states are Tennessee and Idaho. Soviet mines are largely in the Dzhambul area at the Kazakh-Kirgiz border, on the Kola Peninsula, and at Kandagach in west Kazakhstan. Moroccan phosphate rock is mined mainly near Khouribga, and Tunisian mines are near Gafsa. Nauru Island in the southwest Pacific Ocean is also a major source of phosphate.

Potash. The United States mines about one-fourth of the world's potash, almost entirely from the Carlsbad region of New Mexico. The world's major concentration of potash mining is in central Germany. Mines in Alsace of France and at Solikamsk in the Soviet Urals are also principal sources.

Stone Minerals such as limestone, sandstone, slate, granite, marble, and quartzite, and construction materials such as clays, sand, and gravel are produced from a great many localities scattered over the world. See MINERALOGY.

World Production of Important Natural Resources

Hydroelectric Power: Installed Capacity 1961	in millions of kilowatts
United States	33,092
Canada	18,643
U.S.S.R.	14,781
Japan	12,678
Italy	12,612
France	10,231

Roundwood 1961	in millions of cubic meters
U.S.S.R.	351.0
United States	293.2
Canada	92.8
Indonesia	82.4
Japan	74.8

Iron ore 1961	1,000 metric tons
U.S.S.R.	68,440
China (mainland)	45,000
United States	39,174
France	21,638
Sweden	14,131
Canada	10,003
Venezuela	9,322

Copper ore 1961	1,000 metric tons
United States	1057.0
Northern Rhodesia	568.9
Chile	543.4
Canada	398.3
Congo	295.2

Bauxite 1961	1,000 metric tons
Jamaica	6,615
U.S.S.R.	4,000
Surinam	3,405
British Guiana	2,412
France	2,190

Lead ore 1961	1,000 metric tons
Australia	274.1
United States	237.6
Canada	209.0
Mexico	181.3

Zinc ore 1961	1,000 metric tons
United States	421.3
Canada	377.4
Australia	292.8
Mexico	269.0

Nickel ore 1961	metric tons
Canada	211,366
U.S.S.R.	60,000
New Caledonia	54,000

Antimony 1961	metric tons
China (mainland)	17,000
South Africa	10,708
Bolivia	6,740

Chrome ore 1961	1,000 metric tons
South Africa	396.7
Rhodesia and Nyasaland	257.3
Philippines	241.0
Turkey	211.5

Manganese ore 1961	1,000 metric tons
U.S.S.R.	2,700.0
South Africa	548.8
India	498.0
Brazil	439.8
Morocco	261.3

Cobalt ore 1961	metric tons
Congo (Léopoldville)	8,328
Rhodesia and Nyasaland	1,708
Canada	1,444
Morocco	1,293

Molybdenum ore 1961	metric tons
United States	30,192
U.S.S.R.	5,400
Chile	1,831

Tin concentrates 1961	In metric tons
Malaya	56,927
China (mainland)	24,400
Bolivia	20,996
Indonesia	18,872
Thailand	13,484

Salt 1961	1,000 metric tons
United States	23,325
China (mainland)	14,000
U.S.S.R.	7,500
United Kingdom	5,760
West Germany	4,680

Tungsten ore 1960	metric tons
Chain (mainland)	12,200
U.S.S.R.	5,700
United States	3,814
South Korea	3,195
North Korea	3,000

Mercury 1960	metric tons
Italy	1,913
Spain	1,593
Japan	1,158
United States	1,145

Gold 1961	kilograms
South Africa	713,558
Canada	138,167
United States	48,733

Silver 1961	metric tons
Mexico	1,255.0
United States	1,085.5
Peru	1,044.5
Canada	969.4

Coal 1960	1,000 metric tons
China (mainland)	420,000
United States	391,526
U.S.S.R.	374,925
United Kingdom	196,712
West Germany	143,205
Poland	104,438
France	55,960
India	52,593
Japan	51,067
South Africa	38,173

Lignite 1961	1,000 metric tons
East Germany	236,926
U.S.S.R.	133,516
West Germany	97,267

Crude petroleum 1961	1,000 metric tons
United States	354,303
U.S.S.R.	166,068
Venezuela	155,888
Kuwait	82,675
Saudi Arabia	69,232

Diamonds 1961	1,000 metric carats
Congo (Léopoldville)	18,143
South Africa	3,788
Ghana	3,214

Asbestos 1961	1,000 metric tons
Canada	1,062.5
South Africa	176.8

Native sulfur 1960	1,000 metric tons
United States	5,118
Mexico	1,336

Pyrites 1961	1,000 metric tons
Japan	3,931
Spain	2,076
Italy	1,579

Phosphate 1961	1,000 metric tons
United States	18,857
Morocco	7,950
Tunisia	1,982

Potash 1961	1,000 metric tons
United States	2,478
West Germany	2,400
France	1,938

United Nations Statistical Yearbook—1962

Bibliog.–L. M. Fanning, ed., *Our Oil Resources* (1945); R. W. Brooker, *World's Wealth* (1949); E. W. Zimmermann, *World Resources and Industries* (ed. 1951); E. Ayres and C. A. Scarlott, *Energy Sources, the Wealth of the World* (1952); P. E. McNall, *Our Natural Resources* (1954); S. W. Allen, *Conserving Natural Resources* (1955); B. Lyons, *Tomorrow's Birthright* (1955); Political and Economic Planning, *World Population and Resources* (1955); A. Scott, *Natural Resources* (1955); L. D. Stamp, *Man and the Land* (1955); M. W. Straus, *Why Not Survive?* (1955); W. L. Thomas and others, *Man's Role in Changing the Face of the Earth* (1956); H. S. Brown and others, *Next Hundred Years* (1957); C. H. Callison, ed., *America's Natural Resources* (1957); R. R. Doane, *World Balance Sheet* (1957); V. C. Finch and others, *Elements of Geography* (ed. 1957); U.S. Department of the Interior, Bureau of Mines, *Minerals Yearbook* (1963); U.S. Department of Agriculture Yearbooks (1957–1963).

NATURAL SELECTION, a theory proposed in 1859 by Charles Darwin as an explanation of the causes of organic development and change in animals and plants. Three groups of observable facts led Darwin to his theory, which he published in his book *The Origin of Species by Means of Natural Selection.* The first observation was that organisms multiply greatly in numbers and that this increase in numbers is not merely additive but multiplicative, since the total number of offspring is always greater than the total number of parents. Second, the numbers of individuals of a given species remain reasonably constant. Despite the excess offspring, proportionately few individuals reach reproductive status because of competition with others for the available necessities of life, primarily food and shelter. The elimination of many individuals that have not reached reproductive status has become known as the struggle for existence and favors the survival of the fittest. Third, all organisms display wide variation in many of their characteristics. Darwin regarded most of these minor variations as heritable. An example is seen in the work of breeders who carefully select from among their stock, individuals conspicuous for certain characteristics. In view of the fact that artificial selection can attain such distinct breeds of farm animals and varieties of crop plants, Darwin suspected that natural (nonhuman) selection could be similarly operative and lead to the origin of new species through the cumulative effects of minor heritable variations. A fundamental assumption of the theory is that in the struggle for existence, differential survival occurs, as different types of offspring survive in each generation. The obvious result of this is differential transmission of heritable variations, which is considered to be the really important feature of natural selection.

The process of natural selection has also been described as the "sum total of life's hazards" that selects individuals on the basis of competence to reproduce and thus may be regarded as nonrandom reproduction. In the past these hazards have been taken as an indication of the negative or noncreative impact of natural selection. Since Darwin's time, however, the modes of inheritance have become known, and heritable variation, called mutation, is generally attributed to separate, individual changes in the genetical constitution of one organism. (See HEREDITY.) Natural selection in turn is considered an active and creative force that affects the hereditary apparatus of the individual and ultimately the genetic structure of the entire population. This interpretation of natural selection is the core of Neo-Darwinism.

As an essentially historical process natural selection molds the separate hereditary units into a co-ordinated whole in the face of an ever-changing environment. It affects primarily mutations, that is, heritable changes appearing constantly and spontaneously in every natural population. For successful operation natural selection requires three conditions: (1) organisms must be physically able to reach new environments; (2) they must be constitutionally fit to live in new environments; and (3) they must be able to find suitable habitats in new environments.

THEODOR JUST

NATURE WORSHIP, or naturism, the worship of one or more powers of nature as gods. The anthropomorphic tendency in these natural religions frequently has led to personification of obvious natural forces such as the sun, thunder, rain, or the moon. Rivers, springs, trees, mountains, animals, and especially the reproductive energy of plants and animals have all been symbolized and worshiped. The sun, as the source of heat and light, has been personified and deified under many names; worship of fire is allied to sun worship. The intense cold of the north, on the other hand, led early Scandinavians to include in their mythology powerful frost giants. Thunder and rain have been deified as Jupiter Tonans and Jupiter Pluvius. The moon and the "hosts of heaven" (a figure of speech which itself denotes personification) likewise have had devotees. See MYTHOLOGY.

NAUCRATIS, a Greek trading settlement of ancient Egypt, near the west (Canopic) mouth of the Nile. Naucratis was founded by Milesians during the reign of Psamtik I (663–609 B.C.), who encouraged Greek traders to settle there. Amasis II (569?–520? B.C.) granted trade concessions at Naucratis to cities such as Aegina, Chios, Miletus, Mytilene, Phocaeae, and Samos, and for some time it was the only Greek trading center permitted in Egypt. After Alexandria was founded in 332 B.C., Naucratis declined in importance, although coins were made at its site after the conquest of Egypt by Rome. The site was excavated in 1884 by the British egyptologist Sir Flinders Petrie.

NAUGATUCK, borough, SW Connecticut, New Haven County; on the Naugatuck River; about 15 miles NW of New Haven; 27 miles SW of Hartford. The city has been a rubber-goods manufacturing center since 1843. At that time Henry and Charles Goodyear established a plant that pioneered Charles Goodyear's vulcanizing process. Castings, chemicals, candy, and plastics also are made in Naugatuck. The borough was settled in 1702 as the Society of Salem Bridge; its present name derives from an Indian word meaning one tree. It was incorporated as a town in 1844, as a borough in 1893. (For population, see Connecticut map in Atlas.)

NAUHEIM, or Bad Nauheim, town, W central Germany in the West German state of Hesse; in the Taunus Mountains; 17 miles NE of Frankfurt. Its saline springs, impregnated with carbon dioxide and iron, make it a popular health resort. (For population, see Germany map in Atlas.)

NAUMBURG, E central Germany, in the East German state of Saxony-Anhalt; on the Saale River near its junction with the Unstrut; 30 miles SW of Leipzig. Industries include manufacture of textiles, toys, soap, combs, and machinery. The thirteenth-century cathedral of Sts. Peter and Paul has notable sculpture. Naumburg was founded in the eleventh century by the margraves of Meissen and was annexed to Prussia in 1815. (For population, see Germany map in Atlas.)

NAURU ISLAND, formerly Pleasant Island, SW Pacific Ocean, 0°32′S lat. and 166°55′E long.; 450 miles W of the Gilbert Islands; 3.5 miles long, 2.5 miles wide, and 12 miles in circumference; area 5,263 acres (8.2 square miles). The island is a raised atoll, oval in shape. A central plateau attains an elevation of 213 feet above sea level, and a sandy beach 100 to 300 yards wide encircles the island. Nauru has no anchorage; a coral reef that is exposed at low tide surrounds the island. Important phosphate deposits in the central plateau are mined for export by the British Phosphate Commission—an agency of Australia, the United Kingdom, and New Zealand. Royalties are paid to Nauruan landowners and to a trust fund to benefit the natives when the island's phosphate deposits are exhausted. Nauruans, a Micronesian people, accounted for approximately half the 1965 population; more than one quarter of the population were other Pacific Islanders; about one sixth were Chinese; the remainder were Europeans. Most of the Chinese residents are employed in mining operations. Nauru was discovered by the British in 1798, annexed by Germany in 1888, and after 1920 was held by Australia under a League of Nations mandate. After World War II the island became a UN trusteeship assigned in 1947 to Australia, New Zealand, and the United Kingdom. Australia appointed the administrative authority. On Jan. 31, 1968, Nauru was granted independence and became the Republic of Nauru, one of the world's smallest independent countries. It did not choose to apply for United Nations membership. (For population, see Pacific Ocean map in Atlas.) OTIS W. FREEMAN

NAUSICAA, in Homer's *Odyssey*, the daughter of Alcinoüs, king of the Phaeacians. Odysseus, when he was shipwrecked on the coast of Phaeacia, found Nausicaä playing ball on the shore. She took him to her father's court where he was kindly received.

NAUTCH, a ritual dance performed in India by dancing girls (called nautch girls) attached to the temples. The dance is characterized by slow, rhythmic movements of the body and little use of the feet.

NAUTILUS, a marine animal of the order Cephalopoda related to the cuttlefish, and the only direct descendant of numerous fossil forms that flourished during Devonian times. Best known of four remaining species is the pearly, or chambered, nautilus, *Nautilus pompilius*. The mollusk lives in the largest, outermost chamber of a many-chambered, coiled shell that is enlarged spirally in one plane; a hood protects the exposed portion of the animal. Tentacles from the head protrude from under the hood to sweep in food, and a siphon and an eye also are evident externally. The internal structure of the nautilus includes four gills and four kidneys. Unlike some other cephalopods, the nautilus has no ink sac. The immature nautilus lives in a small shell bent like a horn; as the animal grows it secretes calcareous material to enlarge the shell spirally. Periodically the animal withdraws outward and secretes material to form a doorlike partition that seals off the previously occupied compartment. All chambers of the shell, however, are connected by a calcareous organic tube

JOSEPH SMITH HISTORIC PROPERTIES

The Joseph Smith homestead in Nauvoo was the home of the founder of the Mormons from 1839 to 1843. The structure is maintained by his followers and is open to tourists.

and are filled with oxygen and nitrogen. The nautilus ranges at the bottom of the Indian and eastern Pacific oceans, usually in shallow areas but sometimes to depths of 18,000 feet, where it breeds.

NAUVOO, city, W Illinois, Hancock County; on the Mississippi River; 40 miles N of Quincy. Nauvoo is in a fruit and grain producing area. In 1839 the Mormons purchased the newly settled village of Commerce and in 1840 renamed it Nauvoo; it was incorporated in 1841. They abandoned the village, 1846, and it was occupied next by a French communal group, the Icarians, from 1849 to 1856. In the 1850's and 1860's it was settled by German immigrants. A number of Mormon and Icarian buildings are preserved. Pop. (1960) 1,039.

NAVAHO, or Navajo, a North American Indian tribe of Athapascan linguistic stock, living on reservation lands in NE Arizona, NW New Mexico, and SE Utah. The Navaho have assimilated a number of other peoples (Shoshoni, Pueblo, Yuma, and others), and there are more than 50 Navaho clans.

The earliest European accounts of the Navaho are those of Franciscan missionaries, dating from about 1630, but anthropological data indicate that a closely related people existed in what is now southwestern United States as early as 1000. The Navaho were hostile toward white settlers from the beginning of Spanish colonization, although they were not warlike in principle as were some Indian tribes. Navaho acts of aggression against other Indians and against whites were made usually in search of food, livestock, and slaves, but the savagery of their predatory expeditions was second to none.

USDA

A Navaho woman, using the simple hand method followed by the Navaho Indians for the past 150 years, weaves one of the colorful rugs that are hallmarks of Navaho culture.

After 1846 the U.S. government tried to subdue the Navaho and an expedition led by Col. John W. Washington forced some Navaho bands to agree to the Treaty of Canyon de Chelly in 1849; but this and later treaties proved ineffective because Navaho chiefs could not control their clans. During the Civil War Navaho hostilities increased in frequency and violence. In 1863 an expedition led by Col. Christopher (Kit) Carson destroyed most of their sheep, and forced the Navaho to surrender. They were confined to a small reservation near Fort Sumner, N.M., until a treaty concluded there in June, 1868, provided for their resettlement on a reservation of 3.5 million acres in their old territory. By 1950 the reservation area had been enlarged to more than 15.7 million acres.

SANTA FE RY.

Traditional jewelry is made by a skilled silversmith of the Navaho tribe in Arizona. The silver jewelry of the Navahos, often inset with turquoise, is world famous.

The Navaho lived by hunting and primitive agriculture until sheep were introduced by the Spanish in the seventeenth century. Subsequently the Navaho were sheep raisers, and their almost complete dependence upon a wool-and-mutton economy led to serious economic difficulties in the twentieth century. The Indians maintained excessively large flocks of sheep that overgrazed the land; and they resisted efforts of the U.S. government to introduce modern methods of animal husbandry and farming. At mid-twentieth century Navaho industry, though limited, included manufacturing of cement products, sawmilling and arts and crafts. Leases of mineral rights on the reservation supplemented tribal income.

The modern Navaho dress reflects both tribal and Spanish influence. Men generally affect more colorful attire than women. Most Navaho live in hogans, traditional structures made of logs and earth, preferred because the cylindrical design has religious significance to the Indians. Although exposed to Christianity since the seventeenth century, the Navaho for the most part have clung to their own complex religion with its song rites, ceremonial dances, elaborate legends, and forms of "witchcraft."

Reservation Navaho are permitted limited self-government; adaptation to such government has been delayed by the family and small-clan structure of Navaho society and the absence of tribal unity. A representative body called the tribal council may initiate laws but these are subject to the approval of the federal commissioner of Indian affairs.

The Navaho population was estimated at 8,000 in 1860; and it increased slightly by 1869. During the twentieth century, Navaho population grew remarkably, and was about 100,000 in 1970—larger than that of any other U.S. Indian tribe.

BIBLIOG.–L. A. Armer, *In Navaho Land* (1962); J. D. Forbes, *Apache, Navaho, and Spaniard* (1960); Laura Gilpin, *Enduring Navaho* (1968); F. J. Newcomb, *Navaho Neighbors* (1966); R. M. Underhill, *Navajos* (1967 ed.).

NAVAL ACADEMY, U.S., the undergraduate college of the U.S. Navy, located at Annapolis, Md. Its head and superintendent is a rear admiral. The Naval Academy's mission is to prepare young men for careers as officers in the naval service. The academy is accredited by the Middle States Association of Colleges and Secondary Schools. Midshipmen graduates of its 4-year course are awarded the bachelor of science degree and are commissioned ensigns in the U.S. Navy or second lieutenants in the U.S. Marine Corps.

History. The academy was founded as the Naval School in 1845. Its site in Annapolis, Fort Severn, was an army post located at the mouth of the Severn River on the Chesapeake Bay. A faculty of four officers and three civilians offered courses in naval tactics, gunnery, engineering, chemistry, mathematics, astronomy, French, and English. Sixty midshipmen, formed in two classes, attended the first convocation.

Although the course of instruction was 5 years, only the first and last years were spent at the new Naval School in Annapolis. The intervening three were spent at sea. In 1850–51 the Naval School was reorganized as the U.S. Naval Academy and the course of study became 4 consecutive years. Summer training cruises with the fleet replaced the omitted sea service, a practice still followed today. At the outbreak of the Civil War the academy was moved temporarily to Newport, R.I. In 1865 it returned permanently to Annapolis.

The physical facilities at Annapolis have improved greatly through the years. Old Fort Severn's original 10 acres have been expanded to 302 acres, largely through a series of landfills in the Severn River. Construction of the majority of buildings, in French Renaissance style, was begun in 1899 with a congressional appropriation of $10 million. Other improvements have followed. Recently a construction and rehabilitation program was begun, to provide completely modern, fully air-conditioned facilities throughout the academy by 1974. New science and mathematics buildings, completed in 1968, were the first of several buildings scheduled to be completed under this program. The science building, Michelson Hall, is named for Albert Michelson, a graduate of the class of 1873 and the first U.S. scientist to be awarded a Nobel prize.

Students walk to classes past the U.S. Naval Academy's science buildings, Michelson and Chauvenet halls.
JOHN CARL WARNECKE AND ASSOCIATES

Curriculum. Changes in the academy's traditional curriculum began with the 1959–60 academic year when provision was made for incoming midshipmen to validate previous college-level work and to substitute elective courses for equivalent courses in the basic curriculum. Concurrently, capable midshipmen were encouraged to carry more than the minimum number of courses. The academy's first academic dean was appointed in 1963, the first civilian academic dean at a service academy. Under the Trident Scholar Program, also initiated in 1963, a limited number of exceptional students are selected to engage in independent study and research under a faculty advisor during their senior year.

The academy's curriculum provides broad liberal education in mathematics, science, social science, and the humanities as well as a background in seamenship, navigation, engineering, and weaponry. Over 300 electives and 24 majors are offered. Capable students may undertake graduate work at the academy and enroll immediately after graduation for completion of their M.A. programs at participating universities or at the Naval Postgraduate School, Monterey, Calif.

The Naval Academy faculty of more than 600 is comprised of approximately equal numbers of officers and civilians. While the officers provide a continuing input of new ideas and experience from the fleet, the civilians provide a core of professional scholarship and teaching experience as well as continuity in the academy's educational program.

Entrance Requirements. Young men are appointed to the Naval Academy without regard to race, creed, or national origin. To be considered for appointment candidates must obtain a nomination from one of the several sources authorized by law. Most candidates are nominated by members of Congress. Each congressman may have five midshipmen attending the academy at any one time and may nominate up to 10 candidates for each vacancy. Other nominations are available to armed forces personnel and their dependents.

Candidates must be unmarried male citizens of the United States between the ages of 17 to 22 (on July 1, year of entry) and of good moral character. College Entrance Examination Board tests and secondary school records must be acceptable. A secondary school program showing at least 3 years of mathematics, including advanced algebra, geometry, and trigonometry; 4 years of English, 2 years of a foreign language; and 1 year each of chemistry and physics is recommended. Candidates must pass medical and physical aptitude examinations. Recommendations and evidence of leadership potential are important.

About 1,350 candidates enter the academy each year. The authorized enrollment is 4,500 students. Room, board, tuition, medical and dental care, and a monthly salary are provided. See MILITARY AND NAVAL EDUCATION. WILLIAM S. SHIELDS

NAVAL ARCHITECTS AND MARINE ENGINEERS, SOCIETY OF, an organization incorporated in 1893 to promote the art and science of shipbuilding, both governmental and commercial, in the United States. The society's membership of approximately 9,000 consists of naval architects, marine engineers, engineers in fields allied with the marine industry, and professors of naval architecture or marine engineering. The society maintains an endowment fund that is used for such purposes as scholarship awards, special research, sponsorship and publication of books and reports, and a research fund to carry out its research program. The organization is divided into 10 sections; the principal office is in New York City and other offices are maintained in the major shipbuilding areas of the United States. The society publishes *Transactions*, which has appeared annually since the founding of the organization; *Society Bulletin*, issued three times each year; and the annual *Year Book*.

NAVAL ARCHITECTURE, one of the oldest of the engineering professions, is concerned primarily with the design of nautical vessels. The naval architect is essentially a designer of ships; his work is an art that is also an exacting science since he must reconcile, in an economical and efficient manner, factors of propulsion to factors of resistance, load carrying capacity, and general seaworthiness. The fundamental axiom with which the naval architect is concerned is Archimedes' principle—the total weight of a vessel equals the weight of the water displaced.

Guided by seven requisites of ship design—buoyancy, stability, propulsion, steering, strength, endurance, and utility—the architect determines the proper form, proportions, and dimensions necessary to satisfy the service requirements for a particular vessel. It is a rare event, however, when a naval architect experiments with designs, and it is far rarer that his experiments are successful. He is ordinarily limited to designs that are based on proved theories and that are already incorporated in ships. Therefore it is important that the architect have a working knowledge of plans used in ships in operation.

When the type of ship and its proposed use have been established, the architectural work is usually divided into six steps. The first step is to make a preliminary determination of the size and displacement of the ship and the principal dimensions and coefficients to be used. The second is to draw the lines of the ship and to estimate and distribute throughout the ship the predetermined weight groups—hull and fittings; boilers, engines, and auxiliaries; fuel and water; and officers and crew. The third step involves the drawing of principal plans—including detailed location and weight of component members, parts, fittings, and subdivisions—and the calculation of the total exact weight. The fourth step is the making of detailed and final calculations, including the determination of the precise center of gravity in each component part. In the fifth step detailed plans are drawn of all the minor components. The sixth and last step is the drawing of detailed blueprints for construction. See Ship, Ship Construction.

NAVAL BASE, a place used to harbor, supply, and repair warships and auxiliary vessels. Many ports and harbors have been designated naval bases. After World War II the U.S. Navy standardized the designation of facilities that service its ships; a naval base was defined as a land site for heavy maintenance and berthing of active and reserve fleets, with facilities of supply and naval construction. See Harbor, *Naval Harbors;* Navy, U.S.

NAVAL CONFERENCE, an international meeting for the joint limitation of naval armaments and the discussion of rules of naval warfare. Such conferences were held frequently after 1900. Naval disarmament was first officially proposed by Czar Nicholas II of Russia when he issued invitations for the first Hague Conference in 1899. (See Hague Conference.) This conference, however, merely passed a resolution declaring the need for a reduction in military expenditures. At the London Naval Conference of 1908–09 a convention was drawn up that stated rules of naval warfare. Although it remained unratified, it influenced international law. See Declaration of London.

The Washington Conference of 1921–22 was called by Pres. Warren G. Harding and was attended by the United States, Great Britain, Japan, Italy, France, and some smaller countries. Among the several treaties negotiated was the Naval Limitation Treaty of 1922 that imposed limitations on capital ships. Until 1931 no capital ships were to be built except for replacement of vessels 20 or more years old. The replacement vessels were not to exceed 35,000 tons each nor to carry guns of more than 16 inches. The total capital ship replacements were not to exceed 525,000 tons for the United States and Great Britain, 315,000 tons for Japan, and 175,000 tons each for Italy and France. A ratio of 5-5-3-1.67-1.67 was thus set. The treaty also limited aircraft carriers to 135,000 tons each for the United States and Great Britain, 81,000 for Japan, and 60,000 each for Italy and France. No agreement could be reached on other types of vessels. As a result of the agreement 68 ships built or in the process of being built were scrapped by the five powers.

The Geneva Conference of 1927 was called by Pres. Calvin Coolidge in an attempt to extend the quota system to destroyers, cruisers, and submarines. The conference failed since Italy and France refused to attend and the United States, Great Britain, and Japan failed to agree on ratios for smaller naval craft.

The London Naval Treaty of 1930 was the result of the London Naval Conference of that year. The suspension of capital ship construction, originally scheduled for 10 years after the Washington Conference, was extended until 1936 and another conference was planned for 1935. The United States, Great Britain, and Japan reached an agreement concerning limitations on cruisers, giving the first two virtual parity. The ratio for destroyers was set at 10-10-7 and each nation was allotted 52,700 tons for submarines. It was also agreed to retain the aircraft carrier tonnage at approximately the same ratio as under the Naval Limitation Treaty of 1922. Italy and France opposed the ratios and refused to enter the agreement.

The United States, Great Britain, Japan, Italy and France attended the second London Naval Conference held in 1935. Japan demanded naval parity with the United States and Great Britain and when this demand was rejected the Japanese delegates withdrew from the conference. The second London Naval Treaty had so many escape clauses that it accomplished little. The outbreak of World War II ended treaty limitations on all armaments, and postwar attempts at naval as well as general disarmament made little or no headway. See Disarmament, *Disarmament Movement*.

NAVAL EDUCATION. See Military and Naval Education.

NAVAL HISTORICAL FOUNDATION, an institution whose purpose is to disseminate information about the maritime history of the United States so that the American people may better understand the relation of sea power to national defense. The foundation was incorporated in 1926. It maintains the Truxton-Decatur Naval Museum in Washington, D.C., and issues literature and copies of paintings and prints bearing upon the history and technical development of the Navy, the Marine Corps, the Coast Guard, and the Merchant Marine.

John B. Heffernan

NAVAL OBSERVATORY, the division of the U.S. government that is primarily concerned with the making and publishing of astronomical observations for sea and air navigation. The observatory is in northwest Washington, D.C.; there master clocks for the United States are kept and their accuracy is checked against the transit of stars. Radio signals transmitted from the observatory are used to check chronometers at sea, to define standard time in the United States, to serve as a basis for longitude determinations by the U.S. Coast and Geodetic Survey, and to fix the standard-frequencies broadcast by the National Bureau of Standards.

The observatory originally was established as a Depot of Charts and Instruments, 1830. In 1844 it was re-established as the Naval Observatory, on a site north of the present Lincoln Memorial, and in 1893 was moved to its present location. In 1894 the Nautical Almanac Office, founded in 1849 in Cambridge, Mass., and moved to Washington, D.C., in 1866, was combined with the Naval Observatory. Three volumes are published annually by the observatory for use by navigators and astronomers, giving predicted locations of principal celestial objects. These publications are the *American Nautical Almanac*, the *American Ephemeris and Nautical Almanac*, and the *American Air Almanac*.

NAVAL RESERVE, U.S., a force composed of militarily inactive, qualified naval officers and enlisted personnel that is available for immediate active service in time of war or national emergency. The Naval Reserve was created in 1916 as the U.S. Navy Reserve Force, and was reorganized by acts of Congress in 1925 and in 1938; the Naval Reserve Act of 1938 made the reserve a part of the U.S. Navy.

The four principal components of the Naval Reserve are the fleet reserve, the organized reserve, the volunteer reserve, and the merchant marine reserve. The fleet reserve is composed of former officers and enlisted personnel of the regular Navy. In initial stages of mobilization this group may be utilized with no further training to fill positions that require experienced personnel. The organized reserve is composed of officers and enlisted personnel who are required to qualify for and maintain efficiency in their naval duties by periodic drills and training cruises. To meet early requirements of mobilization organized reserve personnel, submarine, surface, and air branches may be utilized immediately. The volunteer reserve is composed of officers and enlisted personnel who are qualified or partly qualified for naval duty and are not assigned to one of the other three reserve components. Mobilization of these volunteers is intended to meet the needs of an expanding naval service until new personnel are trained. The merchant marine reserve is composed of experienced personnel who follow or are in training for careers at sea. In all components, personnel are classified for general line duty or special professional, technical, or scientific duties.

JOHN B. HEFFERNAN

NAVAL STORES, originally tars and pitches used to treat the rigging of sailing ships and for calking the seams of wooden vessels; in modern times, the products of turpentine and resin as derived from pine and fir trees.

Naval stores are obtained by chipping a bare face beneath the bark of the tree, from which the gum runs into a collecting cup; by steam distillation, which makes possible the reclamation of naval stores from stumps; and by skimming off the rosin that coagulates when turpentine volatilizes and subsequently condenses in the pulp manufacturing process. Gum naval stores are those derived from trees; lightwood, those from stumps; and wood naval stores, those from pulp.

Naval stores were produced in lands of the Mediterranean before the Christian Era. Naval stores constitute one of the oldest industries in North America, originating in Nova Scotia in 1606. Two years later naval stores were produced in Virginia. They later became a valuable export of the colonies. Although the industry at first was centered in New England, by 1850 most of the U.S. production was supplied by North Carolina and South Carolina, where better yielding trees grew. As the supply of trees became exhausted, the industry moved farther south and by 1950 most of the naval stores of the United States were produced in Alabama, Florida, Georgia, Louisiana, Mississippi, and South Carolina. Georgia and Florida for many years have produced more than 90 per cent of the total U.S. production, which is half of total world production.

Since the 1920's naval stores have grown to a $100 million industry in the United States. By the late 1950's the naval stores of turpentine and rosin, with by-products such as pine oil and tall oil, had assumed a vital role in the production of paint, varnish, lacquer, linoleum, rubber tires, soaps, greases, detergents, printing inks, and paper. See TURPENTINE; RESIN.

NAVAL STRATEGY AND TACTICS. Naval strategy is the planned use of sea power and related facilities to control the sea and to deny or limit its use to any adversary. Naval tactics is the employment of naval forces in contact with the enemy. Strategy is based on a body of concepts relating to national policies and governing the over-all disposition of naval strength; tactics is concerned with the conduct of more localized hostilities in which two opposing forces are in actual contact. See MILITARY STRATEGY AND TACTICS.

STRATEGY

The tools of naval strategy depend on two basic factors: the tasks that a nation anticipates it will originate in support of its own positive national policies; and the tasks that will be imposed by the aims of an enemy or potential enemy. Although it is difficult to estimate the plans of a potential enemy, a knowledge of his military strength will provide a rough estimate of his capabilities.

World War I. In World War I Great Britain, whose strength was based on sea power, fought Germany, whose strength lay in the control of the land mass of central Europe. Britain's resources lay overseas on the British Empire, and its ability to carry on a war in Europe depended on keeping the sea lanes open to its resources. Germany's problem was to deny Britain access to these resources. After the Battle of Jutland (1916), when the British navy turned back the German fleet in a surface action, the only naval weapon left to Germany was the submarine. (See JUTLAND, BATTLE OF.) Although German submarine warfare inflicted heavy losses on British merchant and naval shipping, it never succeeded in blockading the British Isles. Britain had the problem of blockading Europe and at the same time keeping open its own sea communications. It succeeded in both with the effect that Germany, which although a land power had never been self-sufficient in Europe, was unable to carry on the war. See SEA POWER.

World War II. During World War II the Allied forces, through mobility conferred by command of the seas, were able to pool resources of men and matériel and concentrate them at nearly any place in the several areas of operation. Germany and Japan, on the other hand, lacking control of the sea, were unable to co-ordinate their military efforts. In Europe the Allies, through control of the Atlantic coastal waters, immobilized many German military units from the Pyrenees to the Norwegian-Finnish border by the threat of the potential ability to invade Europe. In the Pacific the United States was able through control of the seas to concentrate overwhelming force against selected Japanese positions, whereas Japan, after losses at the battles of Midway and the Philippine Sea, was forced into a defensive war from fixed island positions. See LEYTE GULF, BATTLE FOR; MIDWAY, BATTLE OF; WORLD WAR II, *Turn of the Tide in the Pacific*, *The Pacific Offensive*.

The scope of naval strategy is far greater than the mere destruction of the enemy's forces. Unless correlated with a nation's war policy, a too limited strategy, although tactically successful, may lead to defeat. An example may be taken of the war aims of Japan in the Pacific. They included the occupation of certain strategic areas, the building of strong perimeters of defense throughout the western and southern Pacific, and defense of these positions against attack by the United States. As Japan never thought the United States' sea power could be destroyed permanently, there was never a plan for total defeat of the United States. Rather, Japan's strategy was to defend the ocean areas it controlled. Its assumption was that the effort to seize such positions would be so costly that the United States would consent to a compromise peace, as the Russians had done in the Russo-Japanese War of 1904–05 (see RUSSO-JAPANESE WAR). Consequently Japanese naval strategy called for the temporary neutralization of the U.S. Pacific Fleet. This was effectively accomplished at Pearl Harbor (Dec. 7, 1941), and although the operation was strategically and tactically successful it served only to delay the U.S. counteroffensive.

Peacetime Strategy and the Limited War. With the end of World War II and the advent of the nuclear age, the Western wartime policy of total war in military and naval matters underwent modification. Postwar planning, treaties, and trade pacts were concerned with potential control of the sea. The North Atlantic Treaty Organization, for example, would not have been practicable without the potential capability of its members to control the Atlantic Ocean areas. Greece and Turkey could not have joined the Atlantic community except for the assurance that the Mediterranean could be effectively controlled by friendly maritime forces. (See NORTH ATLANTIC TREATY ORGANIZATION.) Complete domination of all sea areas at all times, however, is not essential.

With the development of atomic weapons, naval strategy after World War II was more and more concerned with the problem of deterring thermonuclear warfare. In the broadest context, the determination of naval strategy has always involved careful consideration of the weapons available to the adversaries, geographical factors, the ultimate aims of the nations in conflict, and the ethical and psychological character of the peoples concerned. A few H-bombs could destroy the industrial complex of any nation. Obviously a prime objective of a nation's military strategy must be to prevent this from happening. See ATOMIC BOMB; GUIDED MISSILE; HYDROGEN BOMB; ROCKET.

To deter nuclear aggression, a defending nation must have adequate reprisal forces. These forces should be designed to give the defending nation maximum mobility, concealability, and immunity to surprise attack. Moreover, their use should involve minimum hazard to the civilian population they are designed to protect. In line with these requirements, U.S. naval defense strategy envisions full utilization of the oceans adjacent to the United States and those sea areas washing the shore lines of the adversary. Mobile ocean-launching sites are regarded as relatively invulnerable to long-range ballistic missiles. In the late 1950's existing weapons systems such as aircraft carriers and guided-missile-launching submarines were believed capable of making a substantial contribution to the total U.S. retaliatory effort. Other reprisal systems (such as ballistic-missile-launching ships, submarines, and seaplanes with low-level attack capability) were regarded as promising weapons of deterrence. (See ANTIAIRCRAFT DEFENSES.) The nuclear-powered, ballistic-missile-launching submarine had emerged as a prime factor in U.S. strategy for the deterrence of general nuclear war.

If there is no premium on striking the first nuclear blow; if disaster appears to be inevitable to the nuclear aggressor; if reprisal forces maintain a guaranteed delivery capability (as well as precious time to deliberate, even after the decision has been made to retaliate)—then the chance for a nuclear stalemate seems very good. But such a stalemate would not eliminate the possibility of armed conflict between nations or groups of nations; rather it would likely mean that such wars as did occur would be fought on a limited basis—that is, without the use of the full potential of thermonuclear weapons. "Limited war" is one in which the major combatants do not choose to risk their very existence. If it is waged with sufficient restraint so that neither side is driven by the other to an act of desperation, it follows that neither side can hope to gain the unconditional surrender of the other. The Korean conflict is a classic example. It was fought in a limited area. Both Communist and UN forces had the capability to expand the conflict; both sides considered such a venture but rejected it as not worth the risk. Nuclear and toxic weapons were available to both sides, yet neither side used them. Neither side committed its full potential of manpower and conventional weapons. Future limited wars, of course, may not follow the Korean pattern. In particular, they may or may not include the limited use of thermo-

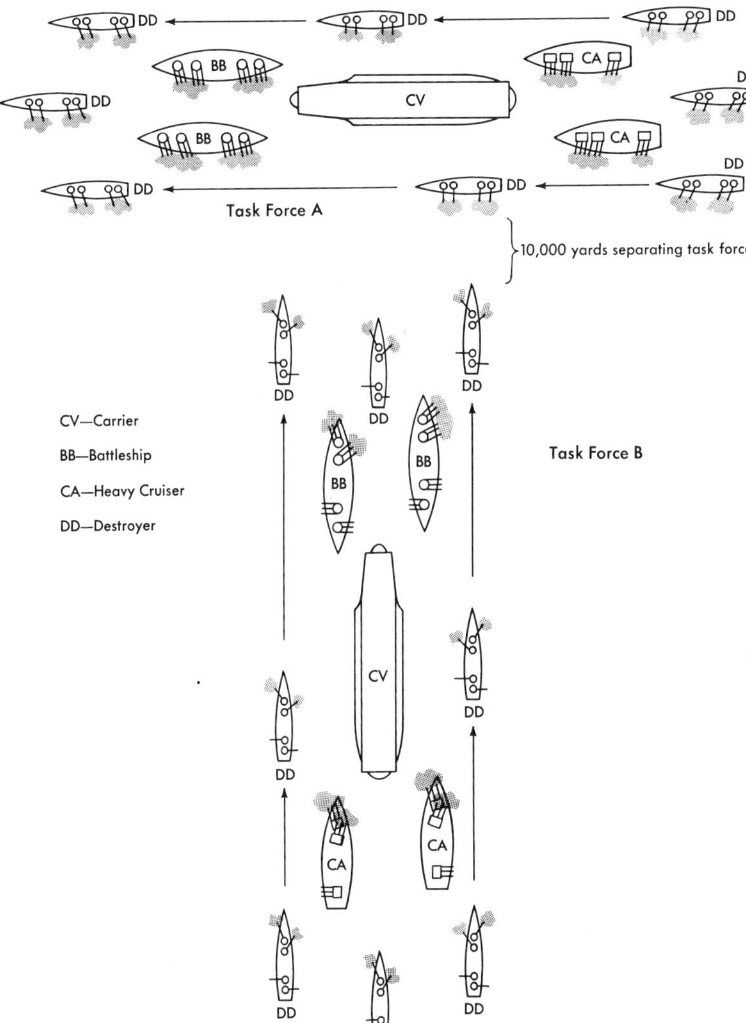

Task Force A is in the advantageous position of "crossing the T" and can bring all the main batteries of its capital ships, in this case 42 rifles, to bear on Task Force B. Task Force B can utilize only the forward batteries of its capital ships, 24 rifles, because its aft batteries are blocked by superstructure. The ratio of advantage in the fire power of the escort vessels similarly favors Task Force A in this maneuver.

nuclear weapons of some type. See AIR WARFARE, *Naval Aviation, Limited War Concepts;* KOREAN CONFLICT.

Taking into account considerations such as these, the U.S. Navy has developed limited war strategy so that it will be flexible and versatile, making use of the weapons that can be readily moved from place to place, and that can be used under many diverse circumstances. Carrier task forces are a proved and potent weapon of limited war as well as of general nuclear war, and amphibious forces such as those which landed U.S. military units at Lebanon in July, 1958, are effective in limited situations.

TACTICS

Throughout the centuries of naval combat, tactics have depended on ship design, weapons, size of opposing fleets, and the geography of the sea areas. In the Battle of Salamis (480 B.C.) the Greek navies led by Themistocles were able to lure the Persians into a narrow channel and through use of battering-rams were able to win a decisive victory. See THEMISTOCLES.

Crossing the T. The ideal deployment of surface craft is achieved when two columns of ships converge at a sufficiently wide angle, approximating 90 degrees, so that one column in effect forms the horizontal bar and the other the vertical bar of the letter T. The column forming the crossbar then has the advantage as it can fire all of its batteries at the other column, which is restricted to the use of its forward batteries only and so deprived of a substantial proportion of its firepower.

In 1805, off Cape Trafalgar, Spain, British Adm. Horatio Nelson triumphed over French Adm. Pierre de Villeneuve in perhaps one of the greatest tactical victories of history. The French fleet was under blockade of a smaller British fleet when Napoleon Bonaparte ordered Villeneuve to attack. Although a skilled naval officer, Villeneuve lacked self-confidence when, with a Spanish-French fleet of 33 vessels, he met Nelson, who commanded 26 English ships of the line manned by superbly trained crews. So well did the English commanders know their job that Cuthbert Collingwood, Nelson's second in command, was heard to say that he wished Nelson would make no more signals—they all knew what they had to do. Nelson's tactics were varied. Nelson split up the enemy's battle line, causing confusion, and obtained local superiority. He threatened to cross the T, but instead sailed between ships of the enemy line, firing broadsides at ships on either side. (See TRAFALGAR, BATTLE OF.) The T was crossed by the Japanese in Tsushima Straits (1905) with the result that the Russians were overwhelmingly defeated. Admiral Sir John Jellicoe again crossed the T in the Battle of Jutland (1916), but the results were not as decisive as the Japanese victory. A notable example of crossing the T during World War II occurred at Surigao Strait during the Battle for Leyte Gulf, Oct. 25, 1944. By executing the T maneuver, U.S. surface forces sank five of seven Japanese ships.

The Submarine. Although the submarine was employed extensively in World War I, more tactical uses were developed during World War II. Once more Germany depended heavily on its U-boats to cut the supply lines of the Allies. During the first year of war Allied losses exceeded new construction. The effort of the few air and surface craft available to oppose the U-boats was futile in deterring the attacks on merchant vessels. German U-boat commanders brazenly surfaced and sank ships by shellfire even within sight of the U.S. coast.

To oppose this threat the U.S. Navy sent every available patrol vessel, including converted yachts and civilian craft, into convoy work. All types of heavier-than-air and lighter-than-air craft, both Army and Navy, were assigned to antisubmarine patrol. This effort, effective as it was within its limitations, did not supply the answer. Although the enemy was driven off U.S. coastal waters, he was not forced off the seas. Operating in wolf packs in the mid-Atlantic sea lanes, safely out of range of land-based aircraft, U-boats continued to take a heavy toll of merchant shipping. The answer to this was the escort carrier, a small aircraft carrier converted from former merchant hulls. These carriers, with a support force of destroyer escorts, were formed into "killer" teams, which greatly lessened the effectiveness of the German submarines.

In the Pacific immediately after the attack on Pearl Harbor the only offensive weapon that remained in the U.S. Navy was the submarine. Submarines were engaged in many tactical operations in addition to the sinking of enemy ships; they were engaged in rescue work, reconnaissance, and even bombardment missions in support of amphibious operations. During 1944, which was the year of the heaviest sinkings, U.S. submarines destroyed approximately 600 Japanese ships. See SUBMARINE.

Carrier Task Forces. With the many island objectives in the Pacific, U.S. Navy tactics centered around carrier task forces and amphibious forces, each serving a separate function. The carrier was a product of peacetime planning, but the tactics and effective use of the carrier were not fully understood until Dec. 7, 1941, when the Japanese navy taught the U.S. Navy in one day what could be accomplished with a carrier task force.

For all practical purposes the aircraft carrier was a completely new weapon in 1941. Except for occasional forays under disadvantageous conditions, some ferrying work, and one brilliant operation at Taranto, Italy (November, 1940), where heavy units of the Italian Navy were torpedoed by carrier-based planes, the British Navy had not been given an opportunity to use carriers to their full advantage. Nor did the geography of the North Sea and Mediterranean encourage their use against land-based planes.

The first Pacific raids in 1942 were unpretentious in scale but important in effect, for it was during this period that the U.S. Navy discovered the potentialities and limitations of ship-borne aircraft, particularly in regard to their greater striking range. The added range factor was dramatically demonstrated on Apr. 18, 1942, when carrier-based Army Air Force bombers under the command of Brig. Gen. James H. Doolittle bombed Tokyo.

It was in this early phase of fighting in the Pacific that U.S. fleet carrier tactics were developed. Because the U.S. Navy lacked battleships, it could take no reckless chance of encountering a superior Japanese fleet. The special characteristics of the carrier task force were a range that would permit it to roam over the great distances of the Pacific and a tactical speed approaching 30 knots. This extreme range and speed enabled the carriers to send planes over Guadalcanal one week and Tarawa the next.

In the early days of the Pacific war the U.S. fleet was inferior to the Japanese fleet in firepower; tactics had to replace weight of salvo. Thus forces under Adm. William F. Halsey learned to use the weather fronts defensively and offensively, steaming under a protective overcast and launching aircraft where they could break into clear skies for lightning thrusts at the enemy's fleet and island bases.

After the Battle of the Coral Sea, May 4–8, 1942, a naval tactic was developed that proved as revolutionary as the change from sail to steam. Tactically it was the first decisive engagement in history where carriers played the dominant role and where surface ships did not exchange a shot. This battle taught the lesson that carriers could operate together for mutual protection and at the same time co-ordinate air strikes against the enemy. See CORAL SEA, BATTLE OF THE.

Fast Carriers. In the Battle of Midway June 3–6, 1942, it was determined that carrier aircraft had become the decisive factor in control of the sea. And it was apparent that victories could not be won until control of the air had been achieved.

The Gilbert Islands became the first battleground of the modern fast carrier force, and established the carrier as an essential component of amphibious operations. A force was generally composed of three to five task groups, which included carriers, battleships, cruisers, and destroyers, and each task group was sent on a separate mission or was utilized with other groups in attacking a priority target. The forces were arranged so that the destroyers offered protection against enemy submarines and surface raiders, and all ships furnished antiaircraft protection to the more valuable carriers. The carrier force also served as a strategic screen for the more vulnerable craft—transports, supply ships, landing craft, escort carriers, command ships, and fire support ships of the amphibious forces. That is, it interposed itself between the landing forces and the areas of greatest mobile enemy power. The job of a carrier force may be to destroy the enemy's combat air strength in the area to be occupied; it may be to bomb his air facilities, destroy his shipping, burn his parked planes, and in general destroy his will to resist. Again it may be the function of such a force to make a diversionary sweep over territory that is remote from the real objective in order to deceive the enemy. In effect a fast carrier force is a floating air base, with sometimes as many as 1,500 aircraft available for action, that can be moved at high speed to any position on the ocean. This new kind of base enabled the U.S. Navy during World War II to concentrate enormous fighter and bomber power at any given place at any chosen time, making it possible to focus more air power in a critical area than could the enemy. Concentration remained a basic principle in the air as well as on the sea. See Naval Base; Task Force.

The modern aircraft carrier is a valuable contribution to deterrence of nuclear war. Its mobility makes it essentially invulnerable to enemy surface-to-surface missiles. Defended by a defensive fight cover, air-to-air and surface-to-air missiles, and antisubmarine weapons, including nuclear depth bombs, its destruction is a costly project for any adversary. See Aircraft Carrier.

Amphibious Warfare. During World War II the tactics of the amphibious forces became as complex as the operation of the fast carriers. New weapons and old weapons were merged to form tactical units. The escort carrier and destroyer escort, designed originally to fight German U-boats and land-based planes, were adapted to the need of the amphibians for close air support on beachheads. Old battleships were raised from their graves at Pearl Harbor to provide the heaviest kind of floating artillery during invasion and to serve also as protection against enemy surface forces that might threaten the landing forces. The old battleships, escort carriers, cruisers, and destroyers made up a support force new in warfare and amazingly helpful in speeding up advances across the Pacific. After World War II, however, battleships became obsolete. See Amphibious Warfare; Navy, U.S.; World War II, *The Invasion of Normandy*.

Frank Albert Manson

Bibliog.–J. P. Cranwell, *Destiny of Sea Power and Its Influence on Land Power and Air Power* (1941); B. Brodie, *Guide to Naval Strategy* (ed. 1944); L. J. Levert, *Fundamentals of Naval Warfare* (1947); G. S. Graham, *Empire of the North Atlantic* (1950); R. C. Anderson, *Naval Wars in the Levant, 1559–1853* (1952); H. W. Baldwin, *Sea Fights and Shipwrecks* (1955); E. B. Potter and J. R. Fredland, eds., *United States and World Sea Power* (1955); E. J. Kingston-McCloughry, *Global Strategy* (1957); A. T. Mahan, *Interest of America in Sea Power, Present and Future* (1897), *Sea Power in Its Relations to the War of 1812* (1905), *Naval Administration and Warfare* (1908), *Major Operations of the Navies in the War of American Independence* (1913), *Naval Strategy Compared and Contrasted with the Principles and Practice of Military Operations on Land* (1915), *Influence of Sea Power upon the French Revolution and Empire, 1793–1812* (ed. 1918), *Influence of Sea Power upon History* (ed. 1957).

NAVAL WAR COLLEGE, a postgraduate school of the U.S. Navy administered by the Bureau of Naval Personnel to train officers of the Navy and other branches of the armed forces for higher command. The Naval War College, first of its kind in the world, was established in 1884 near the present college on Coaster's Harbor Island, Newport, R.I. Its curriculum includes logistics, strategy, tactics, and international affairs, and is periodically revised. The students are officers of all ranks, although special courses are reserved for the higher ranks. An atmosphere of informality and scholarship prevails at the college, and students usually wear civilian dress. See Navy, U.S.

NAVARINO. See Pílos.

NAVARRE, province, NE Spain; bounded by France and Guipúzcoa Province on the N, by the provinces of Huesca and Zaragoza on the E and Zaragoza and Logroño on the S, and by Álava Province and the Ebro River on the W; area 4,023.6 sq. mi.; pop. (1958) 395,961. Much of the province is mountainous; the lower slopes are heavily forested, providing rich grounds for the lumber industry. Other areas yield grains, fruit, and sugar beets. Navarre is one of Spain's richest livestock and game areas. The processing of agricultural products is important, and there is some manufacturing centered in Pamplona, the capital. Tudela and Estella are also principal cities. Navarre is drained by the Ebro River, which flows to the Mediterranean; other important rivers include the Aragón, the Arga, and the Ega.

The first king of Navarre was Sancho García in the early eleventh century. Navarre was a dependency of France from the thirteenth to the early sixteenth century, when it became integrated with Spain. During the Carlist Wars in the nineteenth century, French troops held Navarre for a time. The province was the scene of much fighting in the Spanish Civil War. See Basques.

NAVARRETE, MARTÍN FERNÁNDEZ DE, 1765–1844, Spanish historian, was born in Avalos. He entered the Spanish navy, 1780, was commissioned to collect documents about Spanish naval history, 1789, and became director of the Royal Academy of History, 1824. His chief work was the *Colección de las viajes y descubrimientos que hicieron por mar los españoles desde fines del siglo XV* (7 vols. 1825–65).

NAVAS DE TOLOSA, BATTLE OF, fought in July, 1212, at that village in Andalusia, S Spain. An army composed of Spanish, Portuguese, and Crusaders led by Alfonso VIII of Castile (1155–1214) decisively defeated the Moorish forces of Mohammed I of Granada (1203–1273). The battle ended the power of the Almohades dynasty in Spain. See Almohades; Morocco, Administration and History, *The Almohades*.

NAVASOTA, city, SE central Texas, Grimes County; near the confluence of the Brazos and Navasota rivers; on the Missouri Pacific, the Santa Fe, and the Southern Pacific railroads; 65 miles NW of Houston. Navasota manufactures cottonseed oil, and ships cattle, lumber, and cotton. The city was incorporated in 1866. Pop. (1960) 4,937.

NAVE, the central and principal part of a church, extending from the front to or beyond the transept, or (where there is no transept) to the chancel. Ecclesiastically, the nave is that part of the church assigned to the laity, the chancel being reserved for the clergy. It was formerly the general custom, and has remained so in many Roman Catholic and Protestant Episcopal churches, to separate the chancel from the nave by a screen. In the case of churches which are oriented, the nave is that part of the church west of the transept. Frequently the architectural nave is flanked by side aisles, the nave separated from them by columns, and the church lighted by clerestory windows. See Cathedral; Church Architecture.

NAVICERT, a certificate issued during times of war to prevent the search, seizure, or detention of noncontraband goods by forces of the belligerent nation issuing the document. The navicert is usually drawn up in the belligerent's consular office in a neutral country and commonly is used to certify the noncontraband status of goods bound for a neutral port. First used in World War I, the document facilitated the shipment of goods through blockaded waters.

NAVIGATION, the art of determining the position of a ship or aircraft at any time and of directing its movement from one place to another. Navigation falls into two broad classifications: geonavigation, in which position is determined by means of fixed objects on sea or land; and celestial navigation, in which position is computed from observations of certain celestial bodies.

History. The art of navigation developed slowly through the centuries with little advance until the Middle Ages when the compass, probably borrowed from the Chinese, came into use by Arabian navigators. The Crusaders brought the compass to Europe; but scientific principles of navigation were not applied until after 1418, when they were used for voyages made under the direction of Prince Henry (often called the Navigator) of Portugal.

One of the early inventions used to determine longitude (first described in 1496) was the cross-staff, which measures the distance between two heavenly bodies; from this came the forestaff and backstaff.

The astrolabe, developed in the early sixteenth century (see ASTROLABE), was part of the equipment of Bartholomeu Diaz, Vasco da Gama, and Christopher Columbus. The log line, a device for measuring speed, was invented in 1577 (see LOG). Because of a lack of reliable methods for determining longitude, early voyages generally were made by sailing north or south ("running the latitude down") to the desired latitude and then proceeding east or west until landfall was reached. From this practice various methods were slowly developed for computing the difference in longitude made good from the course and distance sailed; finally, about 1620, tables of logarithms and trigonometric solutions were devised for computing distances made good. Thus arithmetic, trigonometry, and logarithms gradually supplanted instrumental calculation. About that time the English mathematician, Edmund Gunter (1581–1626), introduced the crossbow for determining altitude, but it was a crude instrument. The modern science of navigation began with the invention of the sextant in 1731 and the chronometer in 1738.

Position, Direction, and Distance. Position is indicated in latitude and longitude (see LATITUDE AND LONGITUDE). Latitude (L or lat.) gives the position north or south of the Equator, and longitude (λ or long.) the position east or west of the prime meridian of Greenwich, England. Both latitude and longitude are measured in degrees, minutes, and tenths of arc. For example, the position of the Chicago Range Station is indicated as 41°49′N lat. and 87°47′W long.

In the United States the measure of distance is the U.S. nautical sea mile, or 6,080.27 feet, chosen because it is almost the length of a minute of arc on either the Equator or a meridian of longitude, and the unit of speed is the knot (kt.), which is nautical miles per hour. For navigation purposes distance between two places not too far apart is measured along the rhumb, or straight, line between them. (See MAP, *Map Projections.*) Such a measurement, however, does not represent the shortest distance between the two places. Since the earth is round, the shortest distance between two places is the lesser arc of a great circle passing through them, and in traveling greater distances a ship sails a course determined by a series of rhumb lines that are changed at convenient intervals to approximate the great circle course. (See GREAT CIRCLE.) Such a course is plotted on a Mercator's chart of the area involved. On this type of chart the parallels of latitudes and the meridians of longitude are represented as straight lines, and any rhumb line drawn cuts all meridians at the same angle. Although directions or bearings on a Mercator's chart are not exactly true, they can be used as true for the range of visibility. Since radio direction bearings follow great circles, they cannot be plotted as rhumb lines on a Mercator's chart.

Either a gyrocompass or a magnetic compass (see COMPASS) can be used to determine the direction to steer by or to take the bearings of other objects. The gyrocompass gives true direction within small, computable limits; the magnetic compass readings must be corrected for both the earth's magnetic variation and local variation (called deviation) caused by the iron in the ship.

Various types of instruments are used for plotting bearing lines, courses, and distances on charts and include protractors, parallel motion arms, or arms pivoted on the center of a protractor. The dead-reckoning tracer is a mechanical instrument that records continuously the dead-reckoning latitude and longitude of the ship.

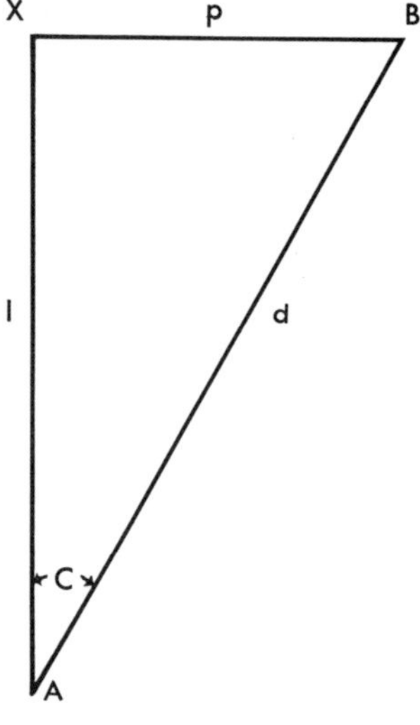

Figure 1

The Sailings. When out of sight of land, one plots position as the coordinates of longitude and latitude. (See COORDINATES, *Latitude and Longitude.*) Since sailing various courses and distances brings the ship into different latitudes and longitudes and since these must be known for proper plotting, some means must be at hand for determining the changes in these lines of reference. These changes can be determined by observation of at least two celestial bodies, by radio bearings, or by dead reckoning. Dead reckoning consists of determining position by applying to the last known position the true courses steered and the distance run without allowing for current. If allowances are made for the effect that current had on the course, the position is called an estimated position. Dead reckoning may be plotted on charts or computed by means of various standard formulas.

If the sailing is for a short distance only, a method of navigation called plane sailing is often used. Small areas of the earth's surface may be assumed to be plane surfaces. To sail a short distance by this method, a triangle such as is shown in Fig. 1 is devised and solved for one of its angles. In this figure, point A is the original position of the ship and point B is the position to which the ship is to be sailed. AX, or l, is the meridian of position A; and AB, or d, is the straight line course that must be followed by the ship. XB, or p, is the departure (east or west) of the ship sailing from A to B. The angle C determines the course the ship must sail to reach point B in the given distance AB.

To solve the triangle for the angle of C, trigonometry may be used. (See TRIGONOMETRY.) Any of the following equations will give the angle C:

$$\sin C=\frac{p}{d}$$

$$\cos C=\frac{l}{d}$$

$$\tan C=\frac{p}{l}$$

Thus, if any two of the factors involved are known, it is a simple matter to solve the problem for the angle.

For example, if the distance from A and B, or d, is known to be 30 miles, and that from X to B, or p, is known to be 15 miles, then the formula $\sin C=\frac{p}{d}$ may be used and, therefore, $\sin C=\frac{15}{30}=0.5$. From trigonometric tables, one ascertains that the angle whose sin is 0.5 equals 30°. This means that a course should be set 30° northeasterly of A if the ship is to reach point B after sailing 30 miles.

If the sailing involves a significant change in latitude a similar method may be used to chart the course. For such sailing, the middle latitude, or that latitude that is approximately midway between the two points, is used to measure departure, p. The difference in longitude is then calculated by means of the formula $DLO=p \sec L_m$, where DLO is the difference in longitude, p is the departure, and L_m is the middle latitude. The error introduced by this method is immaterial in a day's sailing, providing the latitude does not exceed 50°. Furthermore, the Equator cannot be used as a middle latitude since its latitude is 0°; hence the method is not applicable to courses whose middle latitude would be the Equator. For greater distances, Mercator sailing must be employed.

When the track of a ship involves successive courses, several right triangles must be solved—the solutions of which are greatly facilitated by the traverse tables. These tables, which derive their name from the fact that such tracks are called traverse tracks, tabulate for any course and for any distance up to 600 miles the value of L (change in latitude) and the value of p (departure).

Piloting is the process of conducting a ship in harbors, channels, and along coasts where known objects, beacons, or other aids are available for fixing position and where the depth of water or obstructions require constant attention and changes in course. Generally the bearings, distance, and courses are plotted on a chart. The course is the direction prescribed for the vessel to follow from the last known position, but because of steering irregularities, current, and wind, it is rarely the exact path of the ship. The dead-reckoning positions are plotted along this course. An accurate position of a ship is assured when two or more of the plotted lines of position cross. The lines are obtained by plotting various data, such as the ship's bearings or the position of a celestial body.

The lines of position may be obtained by sighting, over a compass, objects on shore marked on the chart, or from radio direction finder bearings from a shore station. If there is a difference in time in observing two objects, the run of the ship must be allowed for by advancing the first line of position on the chart along the course line equal to the distance run. This is known as a running fix and is reliable if a steady course was maintained and there was no current. One special case of a running fix is the bow and beam bearing. To obtain a bearing by this means, the time it takes for a given object to appear first 45° off the bow and again 90° off the bow is noted. The first bearing is then advanced along the plotted course line for the distance that was run during the time that elapsed between the two bearings. The position of the ship off the object at the time of the second bearing is equal to the distance run between bearings.

Piloting also involves the use of soundings and tide tables, which give the time of high and low tides, the height of rise at certain points or ports, and other pertinent data. The various light lists are also essential tools of the navigator—providing data on navigational aids such as buoys, lights, distance-finding stations, and fog signals.

Celestial Navigation involves determination of position by means of data on celestial bodies. The earth's spherical coordinates of position are latitude and longitude. Nautical astronomy employs similar celestial coordinates so that the relative positions of places on the earth and of observed celestial bodies may be compared. See COORDINATES, CELESTIAL.

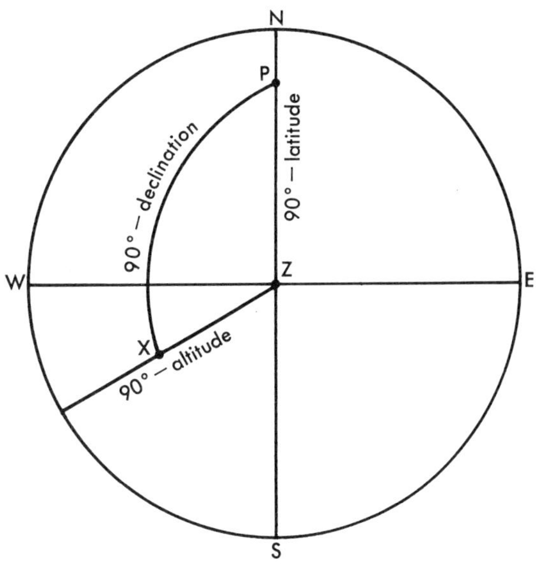

Figure 2

Celestial navigation makes use of such configurations as Fig. 2, in which PZX is a spherical, or astronomical, triangle; arc PX is the polar distance of the body (90° − declination); ZX is its zenith distance (90° − altitude); and PZ is the colatitude (90° − latitude) of the observer. The navigator measures the altitude with a sextant and computes the other coordinates. The sextant, an instrument that is similar to a protractor, measures the angle of a celestial body from the horizon. A navigator knowing the geographical position of the sun at an assumed latitude and longitude can then consult a navigation table to ascertain what his sextant reading would be if he were at exactly that position. If his sextant reading is less, he is further away from the celestial body and his assumed position; if his sextant reading is identical with that given by the tables, he is at the exact assumed position; and if his sextant reading is greater he is closer to the celestial body than his assumed position. Each minute of latitude is equal to 1 nautical mile in his position. See SEXTANT; ASTRONOMY, *Celestial Sphere: Circle and Coordinates.*

The navigational stars, about 55 of them in all, are so distant that they appear to remain in fixed relative positions. Their apparent motion is caused by the earth's rotation. The navigational bodies belonging to the solar system include four planets—Venus, Mars, Jupiter, and Saturn—and the sun and the moon. They are near enough to have their real motion in space observed; also they appear to move because of the earth's motion. The predicted positions of these bodies are tabulated for any required instant in the *Nautical or Air Almanac.* The exact time of the observation must therefore be known. The advent of the chronometer, and later, radio time signals, was a boon to navigation. The periods of morning and evening twilight—during which stars, planets, and horizon can best be seen through a sextant—are approximately 20 minutes each.

The three kinds of time used in navigation are mean time, apparent time, and sidereal time, depending on whether the mean sun, the true sun, or a star is selected as the point of reference. (See TIME, *Solar and Sidereal Times.*) Civil time, standard time, and zone time are derived from mean time as measured by the motion of the mean sun. For navigational purposes the hours of civil time are numbered from 0^h at lower transit to 24^h at the next lower transit.

The data in the almanacs are tabulated for Greenwich civil time (GCT).

Observations for Latitude. Latitude may be found by observing the altitude of a celestial body as it crosses the observer's meridian, computing its zenith distance, and combining that distance with the declination obtained from the almanac. How it is combined depends on the relationship of the latitude and the declination. Its meridian or highest altitude is determined from successive readings with the sextant as it nears the meridian. Corrections to the observed altitude of the sun to obtain the true altitude are taken from the almanac and other tables.

The latitude of a place is equal to the altitude of the elevated pole; therefore the north star when in the Northern Hemisphere can be used to obtain latitude because its polar distance is approximately only one degree as it moves around the pole. Appropriate corrections to be applied to its observed altitude are contained in the almanacs.

Modern tables of computed altitudes and azimuths (bearings) of celestial bodies simplify navigation. The observer selects the computed values corresponding to his assumed or dead-reckoning position and compares them with his observed altitude and azimuth. If the altitude at the instant of observation is greater than the computed altitude, his true position is nearer the body (that is, to the subsolar point in the case of the sun). If the observed altitude is less, he is farther away. The line of position is drawn at right angles to the computed azimuth or bearing line of the body, and the distance toward or away along this azimuth is 1 nautical mile for each minute of difference in altitude. By crossing two or more lines of position, he establishes a "fix" or position; therefore, observations and computations for longitude alone are seldom employed. T. G. RICHARDS

BIBLIOG.–C. D. Lane and J. H. Montgomery, *Navigation the Easy Way* (1949); H. A. Calahan, *Sky and the Sailor* (1952); P. A. Collinder, *History of Marine Navigation* (1955); G. J. Sonnenberg, *Radar and Electronic Navigation* (ed. 1955); S. B. Luce, *Textbook of Seamanship* (ed. 1956); L. B. Olson, *Small Boat Seamanship* (1956); B. Dutton, *Navigation and Nautical Astronomy* (2 vols. ed. 1957); J. H. H. Grover, *Radio Aids to Air Navigation* (1957); E. G. R. Taylor, *Haven-finding Art* (1957).

NAVIGATION ACTS, laws designed to give the shipping interests of a nation a monopoly, or a decided advantage over foreign shipping interests, in carrying merchandise to and from ports in the nation or its possessions. See MERCANTILISM.

In Great Britain these laws were known collectively as acts of trade, although some were specifically called acts of navigation. The first English navigation act was passed in 1381 during the reign of Richard II, but such legislation did not become national policy until the latter part of the seventeenth century. In 1651 such an act was passed to cripple Dutch shipping which threatened British interests. This act was reaffirmed by the acts of 1660–61, which were designed to strengthen the British navy and merchant marine, to make the colonies a source of raw materials and products that were not made in England, and to provide a colonial market for British manufactured goods. The Staple Act of 1663 required that before European merchandise could be sent to American colonies, it had to be unloaded in England. Legislation passed in 1670, 1673, and 1696 gave English ships a monopoly on trade between colonial ports, between the colonies and England, and between the colonies and foreign countries. The navigation acts also specified which products could be exported from a colony to another colony or to England.

The navigation acts, as well as the British trade acts that prohibited the colonies from trading directly with one another, and the restrictions that were later placed on colonial manufactures, have been included among the factors leading to the American Revolution; but it is unlikely that they played a significant role in this respect. The purpose of both navigation and trade acts was to build a commercial empire that would benefit all participants by eliminating foreign competition. Although some laws favored one colony over another, the acts were not designed to favor England over the colonies. As English nationals, colonists benefited from the acts in many ways. The colonists' products were given preferential treatment on the British market; under an elaborate system of bounties British goods were less expensive to import than foreign goods; and the restrictions on colonial manufactured products meant little since manufacturing in America generally was not profitable. American resentment did not become serious until after 1765, when taxes were levied against the colonies; the first Continental congress met in 1774 to protest abuses, but it specifically approved the navigation acts.

British restrictions on foreign shipping were removed in 1854, but the Customs Act of 1853 enabled Britain to place restrictions on the ships of a foreign country trading with British possessions if that foreign country had first restricted British shipping.

United States. In 1789 the first Congress passed several acts to encourage American shipping. The first provided for a 10 per cent discount of duties levied on foreign goods if the goods were imported in American vessels; duty on tea imported by foreign vessels was twice as much as the levy on tea brought by U.S. carriers. Following English precedent, the U.S. Congress defined American vessels as American built, wholly American owned, and manned by crews at least three-fourths of whom were U.S. citizens. The act of July 20, 1789, discouraged foreign vessels from engaging in U.S. coastal trade by levying exorbitant tonnage taxes. These preferential duties and tonnage taxes later were abolished by reciprocity treaties that had been made possible by acts of Congress in 1817 and 1828; the provision defining American ships as vessels built in the United States was greatly modified by the Panama Canal Act of 1912 and the Shipping Act of 1914. See MERCHANT MARINE; TRADE ROUTES, OCEAN; TARIFF.

NAVIGATORS' ISLANDS. See SAMOA.

NAVOJOA, town, NW Mexico, Sonora State; in a mountainous region along the Mayo River; on federal highway 15; 170 miles S of Hermosillo. A trade and agricultural center, Navojoa is a rail junction and has an airport. Most of the inhabitants are Mayo Indians, noted for their fine hand-woven baskets and serapes. Pop. (1950) 17,342.

NÁVPAKTOS, or Lepanto, town, W Greece; on the Strait of Lepanto at the entrance to the Gulf of Corinth; 85 miles WNW of Athens. Ancient Návpaktos was settled with Athenian help by Messenians who had been expelled from their country by the Spartans in 459 B.C. The city was a major Athenian naval base but was taken by the Achaeans in 399 B.C. Philip of Macedon captured it in 338 B.C. and gave it to Aetolia. It lost importance thereafter. It was held by Venice in the fifteenth century and then by the Ottoman Empire until it was returned to Greece in 1832. In the Strait, Oct. 7, 1571, Don John of Austria, commanding the fleet of the Holy League, which included Spain, Venice, and the Papal States, defeated a larger Turkish fleet under Ali Pasha. The Turks lost more than 100 vessels, and about 15,000 Christian slaves were released from the Turkish galleys. The victory, the last great sea battle fought with galleys, marked the decline of Turkish power and prestige in the Mediterranean.

NÁVPLION, or Nauplia, city, S Greece, E Peloponnesus Region, capital of Argolís and Corinthia Province; at the northern end of the Gulf of Argólis, 60 miles SW of Athens. Návplion is a trading center and fishing port. Industries include tobacco processing and vegetable canning. Before the Roman conquest of Greece in the second century B.C., Návplion was a major seaport. Variously held by the Venetians, Turks, and French, the city was captured by the Greeks in 1822 during the Greek war for independence. It was capital of Greece, 1830–1834. Pop. (1951) 8,446.

NAVSARI, or Nosari, town, W India, N central Bombay State, Surat District; on the Purna River; 140 miles N of Bombay, with which it is connected by a railroad and a highway. Navsari is a trade center for cotton, millet, and timber. Manufactures include cotton and silk textiles, wood carvings, copper and brass products, leather goods, soap, and perfume. The city is a headquarters of the Parsi religious sect. It was a part of Baroda State until 1949. Pop. (1951) 44,663.

NAVY, the aggregate of a nation's warships including surface craft, submarines, naval aircraft, and auxiliary vessels; the personnel required to man them; and the organization concerned with their administration and maintenance. Originally a navy was thought of as including all the ships of a nation—warships, merchant ships, and fishing craft. In the ancient Greek states naval vessels were sometimes partially or completely outfitted and commanded by private citizens. This system persisted in the British navy for a time. All modern navies are administered by governmental departments. See NAVY, U.S. DEPARTMENT OF THE.

Naval Vessels were originally driven by oars or sails and differed little from other ships. Gradually there evolved specialized types of warships: ships of the line with 70 to 140 guns on upper, or weather, deck and on two or three gun decks, analogous to modern battleships; frigates having 24 to 60 guns on the weather deck and on one gun deck, corresponding to modern cruisers; and sloops of war with 4 to 30 guns on the weather deck, performing functions similar to those of the modern destroyers, destroyer escorts, and patrol craft. Ships of the line and frigates were ship-rigged with square sails. A ship-rigged sloop of war was called a corvette. Steam propulsion was applied to some warships before 1850. Later, when warships were protected by iron and steel armor, the maximum number of guns was reduced and the caliber, range, and accuracy of those remaining were increased. New types of warships developed after 1860 included the torpedo boat, the destroyer, the submarine, and the aircraft carrier. A number of largely noncombat ships are essential to the modern navy. Among them are mine layers, mine sweepers, seaplane tenders, submarine tenders, repair ships, store ships, oilers (tankers with equipment for refueling at sea), ammunition vessels, transports, ocean-going tugs, and hospital ships. Hospital ships, in accordance with international law, are completely unarmed.

World War II brought many special types of vessels for particular purposes. In the U.S. Navy the old name "frigate" was given to a class of ships smaller than a cruiser but larger than a destroyer. Other new classes of vessels that became regular parts of the fleet were command ships; antiaircraft cruisers; escort carriers; destroyer escorts; attack transports; landing ships—large, medium, and small—for tanks, infantry, and boats; rocket gunboats; and various types of specialized repair ships.

In 1958 the types of vessels in commission in the U.S. Navy included aircraft carriers; cruisers—large, heavy, light, and antiaircraft; frigates; submarines; destroyer, submarine, and seaplane tenders; mine sweepers; mine layers; submarine chasers; motor torpedo boats; ammunition ships; repair ships; oilers; attack transports; store and cargo ships; transports (ships of the military sea transportation service); seagoing tugs; hospital ships; and various types of landing ships—vehicle (LSV), dock (LSD), tank (LST), medium (rocket) (LSM,R), utility (LSU), and support (LSS,L). Although in 1958 the United States had a total of 15 battleships and Great Britain had a total of 5, these ships were not in commission. See BATTLESHIP.

HISTORY

Phoenicia, Athens, Carthage, and Rome were the first nations to maintain fleets of fighting ships that were used to protect their maritime commerce, to harass the commerce of rival peoples, and to control distant colonies. During the Middle Ages the Byzantine Empire maintained a navy for many centuries, and later the Italian republics and other Mediterranean countries possessed large fleets of warships. In the north, Vikings used fleets of small, fast, seaworthy craft in raiding expeditions. King Alfred the Great (845–901) founded the British navy. Later, France, Spain, and Russia built navies. Under Henry VIII and Elizabeth I the British navy was reorganized and expanded and in 1588 smashed the Spanish naval power. From that time the British navy remained supreme although it was occasionally challenged by the Dutch or French. In the nineteenth century Italy, Austria, and Japan developed strong navies, and in the early twentieth century Germany became a major naval power.

The U.S. Navy was enlarged during the Civil War but was soon reduced. It was expanded again near the end of the nineteenth century. After World War I, Great Britain and the United States emerged as the greatest naval powers, almost equal in strength. Next in size was the fleet of Japan; Italy, France, and the U.S.S.R. had smaller fleets. With the addition (after 1930) of Germany to the latter group this relative power relationship existed at the outbreak of war in 1939. See NAVAL CONFERENCE.

World War II. Beginning in 1939, naval building programs were immediately enlarged so that despite losses, which fell heaviest on France and Italy, the ratio of naval strength remained essentially the same until the end of 1941 when Japan and the United States entered the war. The United States thereafter became the greatest naval power the world had ever seen, while Japan's naval strength was steadily reduced until by the end of the war it had few craft fit for service. The British, Canadian, and Australian navies suffered heavy losses, but through increased building and U.S. lend-lease aid had gained in strength by the end of the war. Much of France's naval strength had been destroyed or immobilized by Great Britain to prevent its falling to the Germans; Free French naval activity in support of the Allies was gradually increased as the European war proceeded but remained a negligible factor.

Although Germany had an efficient navy in 1939 it was small and lacked naval aircraft and aircraft carriers. World War II occupation of Norway was costly to the German navy, which was further reduced when German attempts to stop convoys to the U.S.S.R. placed small groups of German vessels in conflict with superior British forces. German submarine warfare inflicted severe losses on U.S. and British shipping in the Atlantic, but the submarine campaign was ultimately defeated by the convoy system and more particularly by the use of aircraft carriers and destroyers in hunting groups near convoys and in areas that the submarines tried to use for refueling and maintenance. German naval plans for offensive mining were revealed by premature use of the magnetic mine by the German air force; the British thus had advance warning and ample time to prepare countermeasures. The Italian navy was of little help to the Germans. Although the Italian fleet appeared formidable on paper, Italian ship designers had sacrificed gun power and hull protection to speed; and the Italians suffered from a severe shortage of fuel oil during the war. At the end of the war, when Italy still had much of its fleet, a large part was given to the U.S.S.R.

As in World War I, the navies of the Allied Powers brought the margin of victory. Great Britain was hard pressed by the submarine campaign against shipping; by the mining of harbors, entrance channels, and coastal waters; by the bombing of factories, shipyards, port areas, and cities; and by the presence of German troops and air forces in Norway, Denmark, the Netherlands, Belgium, and France. Yet, despite these difficulties, food, raw materials, and munitions were brought to Great Britain by sea. A powerful Allied fleet in the Mediterranean was supported and supplied, while considerable bodies of troops and large air forces were sent there with their equipment. Naval power as exercised through the convoy system kept the sea lanes open and brought in the U.S. forces that landed in Normandy in June, 1944.

Naval War in the Pacific. After the crippling blow at Pearl Harbor, followed by the destruction of two large British ships off Malaya, the Japanese navy destroyed the small U.S. squadron in the Far East and Dutch naval vessels in the East Indies. Thus freed from naval interference, the Japanese proceeded to occupy the Philippines, Indonesia, Malaya, other portions of the mainland, and various Pacific islands. Later they pushed out to Alaskan islands, New Guinea, and the eastern Solomons. Both the United States and Japan had integrated naval aviation in their fleets, and the Japanese had developed effective night-fighting tactics while possessing superior torpedoes and skill in using them. Japanese strategy, however, was poor. Faulty planning, including inadequate use of fleet carriers and carrier planes, was partly responsible for Japanese losses in the battles of the Coral Sea, Guadalcanal, and Midway and for the sacrifice of carrier pilots in the air above Rabaul. As the U.S. submarine campaign progressed, serious losses were inflicted on Japanese shipping, and the burden of supplying bypassed islands led to the diversion of Japanese submarines from their earlier rather successful uses. The climax came with the invasion of Saipan and the Battle of the Philippine Sea: the Japanese high command knew then that the war was lost. The success of the Allies was in large measure the result of the effective integration of aviation in the fleet, and the careful co-ordination of submarine and fleet operations. See NAVAL STRATEGY AND TACTICS.

Trends. In the late 1950's public discussions of naval problems indicated that the U.S. Navy was building a fleet carrier with nuclear power, and that this form of propulsion had been used successfully in submarines for several years and would be adapted to future carriers, cruisers, and destroyers. Guided missiles were replacing guns in cruisers and destroyers.

JOHN B. HEFFERNAN

BIBLIOG.–W. Hovgaard, *Modern History of Warships* (1920); H. C. Bywater, *Navies and Nations* (1927); W. L. Rogers, *Greek and Roman Naval Warfare* (1937), *Naval Warfare Under Oars* (1939); R. Kafka and R. L. Pepperburg, eds., *Warships of the World* (1947); M. A. Lewis, *Navy of Britain* (1948); H. W. Richmond, *Navy as an Instrument of Policy, 1558–1727* (1953); J. B. Lewellen, *Atomic Submarine* (1954); G. C. Manning, *Basic Design of Ships* (1946), *Theory and Technique of Ship Design* (1956); M. H. Albert, *Broadsides and Boarders* (1957); R. V. B. Blackman, ed. and comp., *World's Warships* (1956), *Jane's Fighting Ships* (annual).

NAVY, ROYAL CANADIAN, was established by the Naval Service Act of May 4, 1910, for the defense of Canada in event of war with Germany. It is independent of the British navy, although nominally the English monarch is its commander in chief. In its early years the Royal Canadian Navy was administered by the Department of Naval Service under the Ministry of Marine and Fisheries. Its first vessels were purchased from Great Britain and the United States, and during World War I its activities were confined to convoy duty and patrol of the coast of Canada. The Royal Canadian (naval) Air Service was formed in September, 1918.

After that war three reserve groups were formed: the Royal Canadian Naval Reserve, composed of trained naval personnel; the Royal Canadian Naval Volunteer Reserve, open to persons with no previous naval experience; and a Seamen's Service, composed

CANADIAN CONSULATE GENERAL

H.M.C.S. *Bonaventure*, a light aircraft carrier, was built in Northern Ireland and joined the Royal Canadian Navy in 1957. The ship has a complement of 1,263 officers and men.

of career merchant seamen. The National Defence Act of 1922 combined the defense services under the Department of National Defence and was patterned after similar acts in Australia and South Africa. Technical services of the navy included radio telegraph service, hydrographic survey, tidal and current survey, fisheries protection service, and patrol of northern waters. The threat of war with Germany led to the expansion of the fleet in 1936 and the creation of the Canadian Fleet Reserve in 1938. In 1938 the Fishermen's Reserve was established to meet Japanese encroachment in the Pacific.

At the beginning of World War II the Royal Canadian Navy had 13 ships in active service. By 1945 the fleet included more than 900 vessels, about 400 of them equipped for offensive action. Most were built in Canadian yards; others were obtained from the United Kingdom or converted from peacetime service. Early in the war most Canadian-built ships were escort and patrol vessels; after 1943 the construction of landing craft was emphasized. Aircraft carriers in service were the *Nabob* and the *Puncher*, both obtained from the royal British navy and manned by Canadian and British crews. The carriers *Warrior* and *Magnificent*, wholly Canadian, were not put into service until after the war.

The Naval Service Act of 1910 provided for the Royal Naval College of Canada, which opened that year at Halifax. It was discontinued in 1922 and during the interim between wars a small number of cadets were sent to the Royal Naval College, Dartmouth, England. The Royal Naval College of Canada was reopened in 1942. Sea cadets for the regular and reserve services receive three years of academic training at 35 colleges and universities plus two years of summer training, including cruises.

Under the North Atlantic Treaty Organization several Canadian ships joined the Atlantic command. Some vessels participated in the Korean conflict. In 1954 the arctic patrol vessel *Labrador* became the first warship ever to circle North America.

NAVY, U.S. Although the United States had not yet formally come into existence, the beginning of an American Navy appeared early in the Revolution. Captains Jeremiah O'Brien and Benjamin Foster of Machias, Me., with a force of volunteers (including four brothers of O'Brien), captured the armed schooner *Margaretta* from her Royal Navy crew on June 12, 1775. O'Brien used the captured guns to fit out a privateer which took several prizes. On June 15, 1775, Rhode Island commissioned two sloops under Capt. Abraham Whipple, who destroyed a tender belonging to a British frigate. Subsequent privateering, authorized by the Continental Congress and the individual states, inflicted heavy losses on British merchants. It was, however, wasteful of men; at the peak, 1781, about 450 American privateers were operating, employing 15,000 men. See PRIVATEER.

Revolutionary Period

Beginning of U.S. Naval Tradition. As commander of the Continental Army, George Washington created a small naval force to capture or destroy supplies intended for the British army in Boston. He employed seafaring men who belonged to regiments from Salem, Beverly, Marblehead, and other seacoast communities. Captain Nicholson Broughton sailed in the schooner *Hannah* from Beverly, Sept. 5, 1775, and entered Gloucester with a prize two days later. John Manley, the most successful of Washington's naval officers, was the commodore of Washington's squadron. On November 29, in the *Lee*, Manley and a crew of 50 Marblehead men took the brigantine *Nancy*, loaded with munitions sorely needed by the Continental Army.

After the Rhode Island delegates had presented a resolution from their state assembly, the Congress debated the question of a navy. Some members considered it madness to send out ships against the overwhelmingly powerful British royal navy, then numbering 270 vessels, 80 of which were in North American waters. Under the leadership of John Adams, however, the Congress resolved, Oct. 13, 1775, to fit out two vessels; two more were provided for on October 30; and on November 5 the naval committee chose Esek Hopkins of Rhode Island as commander in chief of the fleet. On December 13 the Congress resolved to build 13 men-of-war. With eight hastily converted war vessels Hopkins sailed from Delaware Bay, Feb. 17, 1776. On March 4 he captured Nassau in the West Indies; the booty included 88 cannon, 15 mortars, valuable ordnance stores, and 24 barrels of gunpowder; but the British were able to save 8 guns and 162 barrels of gunpowder. Hopkins' squadron fought an indecisive battle with the 20-gun British frigate *Glasgow* on Apr. 6, 1776, near Block Island. A few days later Hopkins landed his captured guns at New London, Conn., but after an inquiry and considerable acrimonious debate (with John Adams taking Hopkins' side) the Continental Congress censured him on August 16. On Mar. 26, 1777, the Congress resolved to suspend Commodore Hopkins from his command; no other officer was given the title he had held.

Naval Achievements During the Revolution. The Continental Navy attained a maximum size of 34 ships and fewer than 5,000 men in 1777, but dwindled afterward until at the time of the surrender at Yorktown there were only two ships in commission and two under construction. Yet the Navy accomplished much during the war and established imperishable traditions. Captain Nicholas Biddle served under Hopkins; took a number of valuable prizes on independent cruises; and was lost in action against a British ship of the line, Mar. 7, 1778. Captain Samuel Chew was also killed in action, and Capts. Lambert Wickes and John Young were lost at sea with their vessels after making excellent records. John Paul Jones, who had begun his naval career as the first lieutenant of the Hopkins squadron, became especially well known for his famous reply to a British demand for surrender; with the old *Bon Homme Richard* sinking under him, he answered, "I have not yet begun to fight." John Barry commanded the *Lexington* in early 1776 with marked success around the Delaware Capes. Later, in the frigate *Alliance*, he captured two of the king's ships and fought the last naval action of the war. Gustavus Conyngham, John Manley, John P. Rathbun, Samuel Tucker, and Abraham Whipple also made names for themselves.

The victories at Saratoga and Yorktown came in large measure through the assistance given the Continental Army by naval forces. The foresight of Gens. George Washington and Philip Schuyler had provided some gunboats at the northern end of Lake Champlain. When Gen. Benedict Arnold and his troops retreating from Canada arrived there in June, 1776, they began to build additional small vessels. This small squadron prevented the British Army from advancing southward on the lake during the summer. The British Fleet in the St. Lawrence River sent shipwrights, carpenters, and seamen up the Richelieu River to the lake and they outbuilt the Americans. Although Arnold and his men were defeated, Oct. 11–13, 1776, they had succeeded in delaying the British advance for a year. In 1777 Gen. John Burgoyne's army was captured at Saratoga, and this event brought about the French alliance; Washington asked for and was promised a fleet of French vessels. (See Saratoga, Battles of.) Basing his plans on this promise, Washington initiated the campaign that was to end the war. The French army, under Jean de Vimeur, comte de Rochambeau, left Newport, R.I., in June, 1781, and marched to the Hudson River. On August 14 American and French troops started their march into Virginia from the vicinity of New York City. Comte François de Grasse, admiral of the French fleet, reached the Chesapeake August 30, and on September 5 fought the British in the Battle on the Virginia Capes. The French and British remained in sight of each other for three days; on the fourth day De Grasse headed for the Chesapeake again and placed his fleet between the British army under Gen. Charles Cornwallis and the British fleet under Adm. Thomas Graves. If the French ships had been defeated, the royal navy could have rescued Cornwallis' forces. Thus the victory of the French fleet insured the surrender of the British at Yorktown. See Yorktown, Siege of.

Expansion. After the Revolution the Continental Navy was dissolved. The new ship of the line, *America*, was presented to France, and all other vessels were sold. Complete naval disarmament was accomplished in 1785. Foreign commerce increased steadily after the war, and considerable quantities of wheat were shipped to the Mediterranean. Taking advantage of the fact that the United States had no navy, the Barbary powers began capturing U.S. ships. By 1793 Algeria alone had seized 13 vessels, and 119 Americans were being held for ransom and 7 had died in prison. Protests were ignored. Congress finally authorized the building of six frigates.

In 1797 the *United States* (44 guns) was launched at Philadelphia (Capt. John Barry), the *Constitution* (44 guns) at Boston (Capt. Samuel Nicholson), and the *Constellation* (36 guns) at Baltimore (Capt. Thomas Truxtun). The ships were designed by Joshua Humphreys and were among the finest frigates ever built; they were heavily armed and built to protect themselves. The 44-gun ships had a length of 175 feet, beam of 43.5 feet, depth of hold 14.5 feet, and a tonnage of 1,607, old measurement. The 36-gun ship was 161 feet long with a 40-foot beam, 13.5-foot hold, and weight of 1,278 tons. The *Constitution* is preserved at Boston, the *Constellation* at Baltimore.

The U.S. frigate *Philadelphia* fell into enemy hands during the war with Tripoli but was boarded and burned by a U.S. Navy raiding party headed by Lt. Stephen Decatur.

U.S. MARINE CORPS

In April, 1798, Congress authorized the President to build, purchase, or hire 12 vessels not to exceed 22 guns and in the same month created the Department of the Navy. On June 18 Benjamin Stoddert became the first secretary, and within the month 12 more ships were ordered.

During the brief naval war with revolutionary France, 1798–1800, the Navy did creditable work; the record of Captain Truxtun on the *Constellation* was especially brilliant. General insurance rates on U.S. ships decreased 50 per cent, exports increased, and the Navy gained prestige, self-confidence, and experience. Trained leaders of this war later helped subdue the Barbary powers and upheld U.S. rights in the War of 1812. While hostilities with France were still in progress, Congress on Feb. 25, 1799, authorized the building of six ships of the line, but the war ended before construction had proceeded beyond collecting materials, and Congress ordered the Navy reduced to a peacetime footing. Vessels retained were the 44-gun *Constitution*, *President*, and *United States*, the 36-gun *Constellation*, *Congress*, and *Chesapeake*, and six smaller frigates.

Nineteenth Century

Tripolitan War. In 1801 the piratical Barbary state of Tripoli, to which the maritime Christian nations had been paying tribute, declared war on the United States. The ensuing naval war was at first feebly prosecuted but eventually concluded in 1805 when the U.S. Navy forced the bey of Tripoli to abolish by formal treaty all annual payments from the United States. See Tripoli War.

Prelude to War with England. In 1805 Congress endorsed Pres. Thomas Jefferson's "gunboat policy" by authorizing the construction of 25 gunboats; in the next two years 213 more were added. These boats were intended for "the defense of our harbors," but were so small that their guns were all but useless in rough weather; a single heavy frigate with room and wind for maneuvering was a match for all of them. Because of this fundamental weakness the United States could do nothing but protest against the British practice of impressing seamen from U.S. ships for service on their own. The Jefferson administration sought to protect U.S. vessels by means of an embargo; in 1809, this policy having failed, Congress ordered into commission the frigates *United States*, *President*, *Essex*, and *John Adams*, and during the next two years the Navy was greatly strengthened.

War of 1812. The government at first proposed to lay up the Navy in ports because of the overwhelming superiority of the British, but this policy was soon abandoned. There followed a series of brilliant single-ship victories, the most notable being that of the *Constitution* (Capt. Isaac Hull) over the *Guerrière*. (See Constitution.) Later, however, U.S. ships were driven from the sea and blockaded in ports; in 1814 the Washington Navy Yard, and the ships there, were burned to prevent their capture. Offsetting such defeats were the naval victories of Com. Oliver H. Perry on Lake Erie, and of Com. Thomas Macdonough on Lake Champlain. These two naval victories were important factors behind British willingness to make peace on terms that the Americans could accept. See War of 1812, *Military and Naval Events*.

U.S.S. *Constitution*, nicknamed "Old Ironsides," struck a major blow for U.S. Navy prestige when it unexpectedly defeated the British frigate *Guerrière*, on Aug. 19, 1812.

Defeat of the Barbary States. Immediately after the War of 1812 squadrons under Commodores William Bainbridge and Stephen Decatur were sent into the Mediterranean to chastise Algiers, which had reverted to its piratical depredations on U.S. ships while the Navy was preoccupied with hostilities against the British. Decatur quickly defeated the Algerian navy and forced the bey to sign a treaty by which he agreed to give up all tribute and to treat all Americans with respect and consideration. Decatur exacted similar terms from Tunis and Tripoli. Bainbridge arrived too late to participate in the short campaign. See Barbary States.

A Sea Power. For 15 years after the War of 1812 the Navy was engaged chiefly in the suppression of piracy in the West Indies. The first steam-powered man-of-war, the *Demologos*, was launched in 1815. In 1832 a naval expedition punished the natives of Qualloo Battoo, Sumatra, for the murder of U.S. sailors. In 1838 Lt. Charles Wilkes began his famous four-year expedition of exploration into Antarctica and the islands of the Pacific; he is noted as the discoverer of the south polar continent. The U.S.S. *Princeton*, launched in 1843, was the first screw-propelled warship. On Oct. 1, 1844, the Naval Observatory was established at Washington, and on Aug. 15, 1845, the Naval Academy was founded at Annapolis. See Naval Academy, U.S.; Naval Observatory.

During the Mexican War the Navy established a blockade and operated chiefly as support to the Army. The Pacific squadron, however—first under the command of Com. John D. Sloat, later under Com. Robert F. Stockton—took possession of California with aid from John C. Frémont and Gen. Stephen W. Kearny. In 1854 Com. Matthew C. Perry brought about the opening of Japan to foreign trade. In the same year the Navy made the first survey of the Isthmus of Panama; the next year it made many surveys in the North Pacific. In 1859 a large squadron forced Paraguay to recognize U.S. rights.

Civil War. When war came in 1861, the Navy was hampered by the neglect of the preceding years. Moreover, in the "bloodless surrender" of the Norfolk yard, 11 ships (more than one-fourth of the number in commission) were destroyed and more than 1,200 naval guns were lost to the Confederates. Although the role of the Navy was indispensable, most of its operations in the Civil War were unspectacular since the South had few seagoing ships. A tight blockade enforced by the Navy prevented the Confederacy from sending its cotton abroad in exchange for war supplies. Command of the sea enabled the North to select its points of attack. The most notable operations were the opening of the Mississippi by Commodores David G. Farragut and Andrew H. Foote; the Battle of Mobile Bay; the actions between the *Monitor* and *Merrimac*, and the *Kearsarge* and *Alabama;* the destruction of the *Albemarle* by Lt. William B. Cushing; and Confederate torpedo work. Confederate raiders, the most important of which were the *Alabama*, *Florida*, *Georgia*, and *Shenandoah*, destroyed many millions of dollars worth of U.S. shipping and practically drove the U.S. Merchant Marine from the seas. See Mobile Bay; Monitor and Merrimac.

Beginning of the Modern Navy. The Civil War was followed by a period of financial retrenchment on the part of the government. A few already obsolete wooden cruisers were constructed, little else; by 1881 the United States had a relative position as a naval power not much better than at the beginning of the century. In 1883, however, Congress provided for three small cruisers "to be constructed of steel of domestic manufacture," which resulted in the building of the first U.S. steel mills.

The Spanish-American War brought about many improvements in U.S. naval policy. The rapid destruction of the Spanish vessels at Manila and Santiago, showing dramatically how ineffective weak ships could be, induced a more liberal support for the Navy. In the next seven years 20 battleships and 13 large cruisers were ordered. There was much controversy as to the value of the armored cruisers, but they were widely supported by popular opinion even though they cost almost as much as battleships. Wireless telegraphy was first installed on warships in 1899; the name *radio* was devised by the Navy soon afterward.

The coming of Theodore Roosevelt to the presidency (1901–09) gave the Navy a prestige and morale it had never before enjoyed in time of peace. Author of a history of the naval War of 1812 and a former assistant secretary of the navy, Roosevelt had an understanding of and an interest in the navy. As President he fostered the development of naval gunnery; sponsored a cruise around the world, 1907–08, which brought the fleet to a high pitch of efficiency; and by his influence founded the modern naval power of the United States. During the same period the writings of Rear Adm. Alfred Thayer Mahan on the influence of sea power in history were becoming more widely known, especially abroad. See MAHAN, ALFRED THAYER.

WORLD WAR I

When hostilities broke out in 1914 Pres. Woodrow Wilson at first opposed agitation for naval preparedness. Nevertheless the Naval Appropriation Act of 1915 provided for the construction of two battleships, six destroyers, two fleet submarines, and one fuel ship. A naval reserve was established and $1 million was allotted for the development of naval aviation. Prompted by popular demand for a navy second only to that of Great Britain, Congress authorized in 1916 the expenditure of about $315 million for ship construction and better equipment in navy yards. The Naval Act of 1917, passed when war was imminent, provided for the construction of 3 battleships, 1 battle cruiser, 3 escort cruisers, 15 destroyers, 1 destroyer tender, 1 submarine tender, and 38 coast submarines of about 800 tons each. All vessels provided for in the act were laid down in 1917, as were 4 battle cruisers and 3 scout cruisers provided for in 1916.

U.S. Entry into the War brought the Navy an unusual problem in the use of sea power. The natural objective of naval power in war is control of the seas to enable friendly commerce to move freely and to drive enemy ships from the ocean lanes. From the start of the war the British navy had exercised such control, except over the Baltic. Germany had countered with the submarine, which was employed to destroy British commerce; the German objective was to deprive the British of essential foodstuffs and war matériels. By early 1917 the rate of ship losses was so high that Britain's existence was in jeopardy. After U.S. entry into the war, Rear Adm. William S. Sims was sent to London as naval representative; later he became commander of all U.S. naval forces in European waters. Sims was instrumental in securing the adoption of the convoy system for the protection of merchantmen. In this convoy system all U.S. destroyers were employed, as well as gunboats, old cruisers, coast guard vessels, and converted yachts. One division of five battleships joined the British grand fleet in the North Sea, another was stationed off the west coast of Ireland; U.S. submarines stationed off the Irish coast assisted in the dangerous submarine counterpatrol; submarine chasers equipped with listening devices were sent into the English Channel; mine squadrons laid the immense North Sea mine barrage; and naval planes operated over the Belgian ports held by the enemy.

U.S. merchantmen were armed with guns and gun crews provided by the Navy. The home fleet, augmented by old recommissioned ships, became a great training squadron. Interned German merchant vessels were seized, repaired and reconditioned, and manned by naval personnel. Dutch ships were requisitioned and similarly manned. The Navy expanded from 7,911 officers and 81,613 enlisted men on Apr. 6, 1917 (including regulars and reserves, and also Coast Guard, which came under naval jurisdiction on the declaration of war), to 34,292 officers and 503,742 enlisted men, including both regulars and reserves, on Nov. 11, 1918. Some officers of the Public Health Service and of the Coast and Geodetic Survey served also under naval control.

Naval Losses, comparatively small, included the destroyer *Chauncey*, rammed and sunk in the Mediterranean; the destroyer *Jacob Jones*, torpedoed and sunk in the English Channel; the armored cruiser *San Diego*, torpedoed and sunk off Long Island; two transports (both former German liners), *President Lincoln* and *Covington*, torpedoed and sunk; the Coast Guard ship *Tampa*, lost with all hands (118 officers and men), probably torpedoed; and various converted craft.

Postwar Naval Limitation. The Washington Conference on the Limitation of Armaments, 1921–22, called by invitation of the United States and with nine nations in attendance, established a 5:5:3:1.67:1.67 ratio of capital ships for the United States, Great Britain, Japan, France, and Italy respectively. The United States, which then had nine battleships and six battle cruisers under construction, made the proposal, which included the scrapping of the ships already laid down and of the older obsolete battleships. The United States and Great Britain were to have naval equality with a limitation of 525,000 tons for capital ships and 135,000 tons for aircraft carriers. There was to be a 10-year "holiday" in the construction of capital ships; the holiday was later extended to 1936. See NAVAL CONFERENCE.

With the end of naval limitation in the mid-1930's new types of vessels were developed—most of them larger and faster than older ships. The first eight of the new U.S. battleships were of 35,000 tons, each with main batteries of nine 16-inch guns and speeds of 30 knots; later ships were designed to displace 45,000 tons. New cruisers were generally larger, faster, and more heavily gunned and armored, as were the destroyers.

WORLD WAR II

Before U.S. entry into the war the Navy engaged in the escort of convoy operations in the North Atlantic, developed bases, and speeded up its shipbuilding program. On Dec. 7, 1941, at 7:50 on a Sunday morning, there came from planes launched from six carriers the Japanese attack on the U.S. Fleet in Pearl Harbor, in what was still at that time the Territory of Hawaii. U.S. losses were staggering: the battleships *Arizona* and *Oklahoma* were damaged beyond repair; the *West Virginia* and *California* were sunk in the shallow water of their berths; the *Nevada* was run aground to prevent sinking; the *Pennsylvania* (in dry dock) was damaged comparatively little; the *Maryland* and *Tennessee* were little damaged directly but were set afire by oil burning on the surface of the water; the mine layer *Oglala* and the target ship *Utah* were sunk; three cruisers, three destroyers, and other ships badly damaged. The Navy and Marine Corps lost 2,119 men (killed or missing), and there were 785 wounded. See PEARL HARBOR.

Japanese Successes. Within a short time Guam fell to the Japanese; Wake Island was captured; the Philippines were overwhelmed; British Malaya and Singapore were conquered with astonishing rapidity; the Netherlands Indies (Indonesia) were overrun. Such successful operations were possible because the Japanese had naval control of the Pacific. (See NAVAL STRATEGY AND TACTICS, Strategy, *World War II.*) In January and February, 1942, the small U.S. Asiatic Fleet and the Dutch Navy attempted to impede the Japanese advance toward Indonesia; U.S. losses included the cruiser *Houston*, three destroyers, two auxiliaries, and damage to several other ships. About the same time Adm. William F. Halsey was conducting hit-and-run raids on Japanese positions in the Marshall and Gilbert islands, using small task forces built around aircraft carriers and cruisers.

Coral Sea and Midway. With bases in the New Guinea–New Britain–Solomon Islands area, the Japanese were in position to threaten all Melanesia and even Australia. The Japanese advance was halted, however, May 7–8, 1942, by the Battle of the Coral Sea, the first naval engagement in which surface vessels did not exchange a single shot (all the fighting was done by carrier-based aircraft). Japanese losses included one carrier, some auxiliaries, and many planes; U.S. losses included the carrier *Lexington*, a destroyer, and a tanker. (See CORAL SEA, BATTLE OF THE.) On June 6, 1942, Adm. Raymond A. Spruance inflicted a decisive defeat on the Japanese at Midway, destroying four carriers and a heavy cruiser, and severely damaging other ships; the United States lost the carrier *Yorktown* and one destroyer. This was the turning point of the war and one of the most decisive naval battles in history. Besides their loss of four aircraft carriers the Japanese lost a large proportion of their best carrier pilots. See MIDWAY, BATTLE OF; AIRCRAFT CARRIER.

On Aug. 7, 1942, the 1st Marine Division landed on Guadalcanal to open the U.S. offensive. After a series of naval engagements and land battles in the Solomon Islands area the Guadalcanal campaign ended on Feb. 8, 1943, with a U.S. victory. The Navy lost 2 carriers, the *Wasp* and *Hornet;* 5 heavy cruisers, *Vincennes*, *Quincy*, *Astoria*, *Northampton*, and *Chicago;* 2 light cruisers, *Atlanta* and *Juneau;* 1 transport; and 16 destroyers. The Japanese lost 2 battleships, 1 aircraft carrier, 2 heavy cruisers, 2 light cruisers, 12 destroyers, and several transports. In the Battle of Savo Island, Aug. 9, 1942, the U.S. Navy was surprised and suffered heavy losses; the Battle of Santa Cruz Archipelago, Oct. 26, 1942, however, was a brilliant American victory.

Advance Westward. During 1943 the westward advance began under Admiral Halsey. In battles at Kula Gulf, July 6; Kolombangara, July 13; and Vella Gulf, August 6; the Japanese lost heavily, while the U.S. Navy lost only the cruiser *Helena* and the destroyer *Guin*. The Russell Islands, New Georgia, and Bougainville were taken; the strong Japanese base at Rabaul on New Britain Island was neutralized and bypassed by the seizure of the Admiralty Islands. Manus in the Admiralty Islands was converted into an advance naval base. The U.S. Army made notable progress in recovering New Guinea from the enemy. In this period the Japanese lost many efficient carrier pilots and failed to produce equally skilled replacements.

Amphibious Assaults. In November, 1943, Admiral Spruance led an offensive against the Gilbert Islands; Makin Atoll was taken quickly by Army units, but at Tarawa the Marines, before finally overcoming Japanese resistance in a bitter four-day struggle, suffered the heaviest losses in their history. In January, 1944, the offensive struck the Marshall Islands: Roi, Namur, Kwajalein, Majuro, and Eniwetok atolls were captured in amphibious assaults. The Japanese naval fortress at Truk was bombarded, bombed, and bypassed.

CANADIAN NATL. HARBOURS BOARD

The 45,000-ton battleship U.S.S. *Iowa* was laid down at the New York Navy Yard, June 1940; launched, August 1942; and completed, February 1943, at a cost of $100 million.

Atlantic and European Theaters. During 1942 and early 1943 German submarines off the North American coast inflicted severe shipping losses and forced the United States to embark on a heavy program of escort vessels. In the European theater the Navy co-operated with the Army in amphibious assaults on the coast of French Morocco in North Africa, Nov. 8, 1942; on Sicily, July 10, 1943; at Salerno, Sept. 9, 1943; at Anzio, Jan. 22, 1944; in Normandy, June 6, 1944; and in southern France, Aug. 15, 1944. Naval gunfire played an important role (perhaps decisive in some instances) in the success of all the European landings. German Field Marshal Karl von Rundstedt reported to his headquarters that naval gunfire in support of the Allies' Normandy landings was reaching so far inland as to prevent effective German counterattacks; after the war he confirmed the statement. See WORLD WAR II, *Sicily and Italy*, *The Invasion of Normandy*.

Philippine Sea. In June, 1944, successful landings were made on Saipan, Guam, and Tinian; and in the Battle of the Philippine Sea, June 19–20, the Japanese lost 2 carriers, 2 destroyers, and 1 tanker and sustained severe damage to 11 other ships. The Japanese also lost 395 carrier-based aircraft and 31 float planes (92 and 72 per cent, respectively, of these types in the fleet), besides approximately 50 planes based on Guam. American losses included 130 planes and 76 pilots and crewmen.

Leyte Gulf. In September, 1944, landings were made on Peleliu and Angaur in the western Carolines. On October 20, U.S. troops landed on Leyte Island in the Philippines. The Japanese marshaled most of their remaining naval force to repulse this attack; the three resulting naval actions were known collectively as the Battle for Leyte Gulf. The U.S. Navy lost 1 carrier, 2 escort carriers, 2 destroyers, and 1 destroyer escort; the Japanese navy lost 3 battleships, 4 carriers, 10 cruisers, and 9 destroyers. (See LEYTE GULF, BATTLE FOR.) On Jan. 9, 1945, the U.S. Navy assisted the Army in landings in Lingayan Gulf on Luzon. Further U.S. naval losses were suffered in this and other landings and in attacks launched by kamikaze (suicide) planes; but U.S. carrier planes more than compensated. During 1944, U.S. submarines sank 492 large cargo vessels totaling more than 2 million tons, and destroyed one-third of all major enemy combatant ships sent to the bottom.

Iwo Jima and Okinawa. In February, 1945, Iwo Jima was captured by U.S. Marines despite a determined Japanese defense; marine and naval casualties included 5,617 dead and 17,000 wounded, and naval vessels suffered severe damage through kamikaze attacks. On Apr. 1, 1945, the assault on Okinawa began; not until June 23 was resistance completely overcome. Again the greatest threat came from kamikaze planes; 30 U.S. ships were sunk, more than 200 were damaged—including 10 battleships, 13 carriers, 5 cruisers, and 67 destroyers. No navy had ever suffered so heavily in a single operation. Casualties included 4,907 naval personnel killed and 4,824 injured. (See OKINAWA.) Meanwhile Admiral Halsey's fleet bombarded Japanese home islands. The Japa-

U.S. NAVY

After an operating period at sea, the crew of the U.S.S. *Forrestal* prepares to take shore leave in Naples, Italy.

U.S. NAVY

Navy amphibian vehicle has propellers for water travel, special rubber tracks for land travel.

U.S. NAVY

U.S. NAVY

Radarmen in the central intelligence command of the U.S.S. *Saratoga* plot the ship's position.

U.S. NAVY

Navy divers prepare to submerge beneath arctic ice pack to test underwater breathing apparatus.

Massive electronic brain simulates naval battles so that battle plans may be studied and their strategy evaluated.

U.S. NAVY

Nuclear-powered U.S.S. *Nautilus* (SSN 571) made first transpolar journey beneath arctic icecap.

U.S. NAVY

nese high command had known that the war was all but lost after the Battle of the Philippine Sea; their later losses practically wiped out the Japanese navy. The United States and Japan ended hostilities Aug. 15, 1945. Germany had been out of the war since May 7, 1945. Sea power had recaptured or isolated all of the early Japanese conquests in the Pacific area and almost completely destroyed the Japanese merchant fleet as well as the imperial Japanese navy. Ship losses included 12 battleships and 21 aircraft carriers. This had been the greatest maritime struggle in history. The U.S. Navy, despite its losses during the war, was larger in August, 1945, than it had ever been before, both actually and relatively. See NAVY, History, *World War II, Naval War in the Pacific.*

KOREAN CONFLICT

Navy participation in the Korean conflict began on June 25, 1950, and continued until the armistice, July 27, 1953. Naval vessels bombarded shore positions in support of Marines and troops; carrier planes furnished air support for ground operations; the peninsula was effectively blockaded; a naval amphibious force landed 10,029 troops and 2,025 vehicles at Pohang in defense of the Pusan perimeter; U.S. Marines joined the troops on shore. General Douglas MacArthur assumed the offensive at Inchon, Sept. 15, 1950, when the Navy landed the 1st Marine Division and the 7th Army Division in one of the best planned and most skillfully executed amphibious operations ever performed. Other amphibious operations of various types followed. In December, 1950, an amphibious force of nearly 200 vessels under Rear Adm. James H. Doyle evacuated nearly 105,000 troops and about 100,000 Korean civilians from Hungnam, as well as nearly 18,000 vehicles and more than 300,000 tons of supplies. Dangerous and carefully planted mine fields were discovered in October, 1950, and mine problems continued thereafter. At one time or another 16 aircraft carriers were employed—13 American, 2 British, and 1 Australian. Gunfire support was given at various times by 4 battleships, 8 cruisers, and about 80 destroyers. Ten other countries were represented by one or more naval vessels. The U.S. military sea transportation carried a total of nearly 5 million passengers, 52 million tons of cargo, and nearly 22 million tons of fuel oil into or out of, or moved within, the Far East. Five naval and Marine Corps planes were destroyed in aerial combat, and 559 planes were lost to enemy antiaircraft fire. More than 4 million rounds of ammunition were fired by naval vessels. Enemy mines sank 4 minesweepers and 1 tug. Fire from enemy shore batteries damaged 81 ships, machine gun fire 1, and mines 5. Naval casualties included 458 killed or missing and presumed dead, 1,576 injured, and 9 not accounted for; U.S. Marine Corps casualties included 3,300 killed in action, 541 who died of wounds, 21 who died after being captured, 6 captured and presumed dead, and 394 missing and presumed dead. Deaths totaled 4,262; wounded in action, 26,038.

Nuclear-powered U.S.S. *George Washington*, launched in June 1959, is equipped with 16 firing tubes designed to launch the Polaris, a ballistic missile with a 1,200-mile range.
U.S. NAVY

THE FORCES AFLOAT

Early Fleet Organization. From time to time different policies have been followed in the disposition of U.S. men-of-war in commission. Until the Civil War nearly all ships in full commission were employed on foreign cruises, "showing the flag" and protecting U.S. rights and citizens in distant places. Substantially the same practice was followed between 1866 and 1898, although there was an effort to keep the ships in squadrons rather than have them act singly. There were a European squadron, a South American squadron, and an Asiatic squadron. After 1899 there were an Atlantic Fleet and a Pacific Fleet (much smaller), and both operated chiefly in home waters; there was also an Asiatic Fleet, besides small European and South American squadrons. In 1919 the principal combatant strength of the Navy was divided almost equally between an Atlantic and a Pacific Fleet, with a small Asiatic Fleet which included the Yangtze patrol of river gunboats; a small European squadron; and a special service squadron in the Caribbean. In the years immediately after World War I the Navy evolved a new fleet organization which replaced the Atlantic and Pacific fleets. Under the new system the principal naval force was concentrated in home waters and was organized into the U.S. Fleet, commanded by an admiral. There were four principal divisions of the U.S. Fleet: the battle force, the scouting force, the submarine force, and the fleet base force.

After World War II the majority of U.S. warships were placed out of commission but preserved for future use by being "moth-balled." This process consisted of coating (with a corrosion-proofing material) all gun mounts, electrical mounts, and machinery exposed to the weather; ship hulls were sealed and the interior air was dehydrated.

By the late 1950's there were a Pacific Fleet with headquarters on shore at Pearl Harbor and two subsidiary fleets in the Pacific Ocean: the 1st Fleet in the eastern Pacific and the 7th Fleet in the Far East. The submarine *Nautilus* (the world's first atomic ship), commissioned in 1954, was followed by several other nuclear-powered submarines. By 1964 nuclear-powered craft included an aircraft carrier (*Enterprise*), a guided-missile frigate (*Bainbridge*), and a guided-missile cruiser (*Long Beach*). See AIRCRAFT CARRIER; BATTLESHIP; CRUISER; DESTROYER; SUBMARINE.

Naval Shore Activities. Beginning with six navy yards in 1799, the Navy was compelled to develop numerous shore facilities. By the 1960's the huge network of naval land and shore installations included numerous training installations, many of them highly specialized, for officers and enlisted men; many observational and research facilities (engineering, hydrographical, ordnance, medical, astronomical, meteorological, and others); and bases for supply and maintenance of ships and personnel, hospitals, shipyards, air stations, and the like, both within continental United States and abroad. JOHN B. HEFFERNAN

BIBLIOG.–Theodore Roosevelt, *Naval War of 1812* (ed. 1897); A. T. Mahan, *Admiral Farragut* (ed. 1904), *From Sail to Steam* (1907); F. E. Chadwick, *Spanish-American War* (2 vols. 1911); G. R. Clark and others, *Short History of the United States Navy* (ed. 1939); K. Banning, *Fleet Today* (1942); C. S. Alden, *United States Navy: A History* (1943); Aviation History Unit, *Navy's Air War* (1946); H. H. and M. Sprout, *Rise of American Naval Power, 1776–1918* (1946); A. D. Turnbull and C. L. Lord, *History of United States Naval Aviation* (1949); T. Roscoe, *This Is Your Navy* (1950); R. H. Connery, *Navy and Industrial Mobilization in World War II* (1951); S. E. Morison, *History of United States Naval Operations in World War II* (11 vols. 1947–57); Raymond Blackman, *Jane's Fighting Ships* (1962–63).

NAVY, U.S. DEPARTMENT OF THE, one of the three military divisions of the executive Department of Defense, the others being the Department of the Army and the Department of the Air Force. During the Revolutionary War, naval affairs were administered by various committees and boards. In 1781 the post of secretary of marine was created and later it was called agent of marine. Under the federal Constitution an act was passed in 1789 that gave the administration of naval affairs to the secretary of war. In 1798 a law created a department of navy headed by a secretary of navy who held cabinet rank. The National Security Act of 1947 placed the department under the national military establishment, which two years later became the department of defense.

The secretary of the navy is a civilian. He is assisted by several civilian administrators, including the undersecretary of the navy, assistant secretary of the navy, and assistant secretary of the navy for air. The principal naval adviser and the ranking navy officer is the chief of naval operations. He is also the naval member of the joint chiefs of staff. Within the department are the bureaus of aeronautics, medicine and surgery, naval personnel, ordnance, ships, supplies and accounts, and yards and docks, and the offices of the judge advocate general, naval research, information, comptroller, general counsel, naval petroleum and oil shale reserves, and legislative liaison. The Marine Corps is part of the Department of the Navy but is a complete operating unit in itself; the Marine Corps commandant is directly responsible to the secretary of the navy for the administration, discipline, and internal organization of the corps. In wartime the coast guard operates under navy jurisdiction. The Department of the Navy also administers the government of several mid-Pacific island possessions. See DEFENSE, U.S. DEPARTMENT OF.

NAVY LEAGUE OF THE UNITED STATES, an association whose purpose is to stimulate public interest in the Navy. The league has endeavored to do this through its magazine *Sea Power*, through newspaper and magazine publicity, and by sponsoring and participating in the annual observance of Navy Day. The organization was incorporated in New York State in 1902. Membership numbers about 15,000 and headquarters are in Washington, D.C.

NÁXOS, island, Greece, largest and most fertile of the Cyclades, in the Aegean Sea; about 20 miles long and 12 miles wide; area 174 sq. mi.; pop. (1951 est.) 18,600. There are 30 villages and small towns on the island, whose capital is the city of Náxos (1951 pop. 2,547) on the northwest coast of the island. Náxos has been famous for its wines since ancient times, when it was a center for Dionysian revels, and for olive oil, nuts, fruits, cotton, corn, and emery. The granite and marble quarries on Náxos have been worked since the seventh century B.C. and Naxian marble was used in the Apollo at Delos and the Sphinx at Delphi. The island was colonized by Ionians about 1000 B.C., was subdued by Persians in 490 B.C., and was later controlled by Athenians. Náxos was made a duchy by the Venetians, 1207; a Turkish possession, 1579; and a section of Greece, 1830.

NAXOS, an ancient Greek colony on the E coast of Sicily near Mount Etna. Founded by Chalcis in 735 B.C., it was the first Greek settlement in Sicily and firmly supported Athens in the west. It was destroyed by the tyrant Dionysius of Syracuse, 403 B.C.; and in 358 B.C. its scattered inhabitants were resettled at Tauromenium nearby. There is a belief that some of them settled the Aegean island now known as Naxos, which they named after their extinct city.

NAYARIT, state, W Mexico; bounded by the Pacific on the W and by the states of Sinaloa and Durango on the N and Jalisco on the E and S; area 10,547 sq. mi.; pop. (1957) 354,741. Important rivers within the state include the Rio Grande de Santiago, the Acaponeta, the San Pedro, and the Huaynamota. Nayarit has a subtropical climate with wild and mountainous sections in the east and hot, humid coastal plains along the ocean. These fertile plains yield sugar cane, cotton, and corn. Gold, silver, lead, and copper are mined in the state. Nayarit was formed in 1917 from the territory of Tepic; it includes the islands of Tres Marías and San Juanito. The capital is Tepic, and Tuxpan is the next most important city.

NAYAR RIVER, N India, N Uttar Pradesh State; formed by the junction of two streams near Lansdowne; flows generally W about 50 miles and merges with the Ganges River near Davaprayag. The Narva is the site of a major power and irrigation project consisting of a dam and hydroelectric plant near Lansdowne and another hydroelectric installation at the mouth of the river.

NAZARETH, borough, E Pennsylvania, Northampton County; on the Delaware, Lackawanna, and Western and the Lehigh and New England railroads; 13 miles NE of Allentown. Nazareth has manufactures of clothing and cement, and coal is mined nearby. Nazareth was settled, 1740, by a group of Moravians and incorporated in 1863. Pop. (1960) 6,209.

NAZARETH, town, N Israel, Lower Galilee; 60 miles N of Jerusalem. The town lies on the slope of a 1,600-foot hill in the midst of a fertile district about halfway between the southern end of the Lake of Galilee and the Mediterranean Sea. Nazareth is noted primarily for the scriptural account of it as the boyhood home of Jesus (Matt. 2:23; Luke 4:16). Joseph and Mary resided in Nazareth before and after the birth of Jesus, and the village was Jesus' home until His baptism by St. John the Baptist. Little is known of the early history of Nazareth. There is no mention of it in the Old Testament. Early Christians paid little or no attention to Nazareth until the sixth century when pilgrimages were made to the shrine of the Virgin. The village was especially revered by the medieval Crusaders; members of the First Crusade, led by Tancred, occupied the area. The town was taken by Saladin in about 1100 but returned to the Christians in 1197. In 1291 the Crusaders lost Nazareth and the town was destroyed. The Franciscans returned in 1468 but were driven out in 1517 during the Turkish conquest of Palestine. Not until 1620 were Christians again permitted to return to Nazareth. The Franciscans established themselves in Nazareth despite Moslem persecution; in 1730 they reconstructed the Church and Convent of the Annunciation (earlier buildings were said to have been completed in 1300), which are still in existence. Later Christian churches were built by Greeks and

Nazareth, the town where Jesus spent His childhood, has been twice destroyed and rebuilt since biblical times. Its religious places draw thousands of visitors yearly.
EWING GALLOWAY

Protestants. Among traditional places of interest to travelers in Nazareth are the Convent of the Ladies of Nazareth, the Church of St. Joseph, and the Church of St. Gabriel (each said by some to be constructed on the site of the house of St. Joseph, where Jesus was raised); the Chapel of the Table of Christ; and the Virgin's Well, just outside the town. The present town, under Israeli control since 1948, is thought to be in about the same location as the original. (For population, see Israel map in Atlas.)

NAZARITE, or Nazirite, one of the group of ancient Israelites who were consecrated by special vow to the Lord. The name, from the Hebrew verb meaning to separate, took on added significance as the Nazarites separated themselves for special service to God by a vow included in the legislation given at Sinai (Num. 6:1–21). Provisions of the vow were threefold: abstinence from eating or drinking the fruit of the vine, from cutting one's hair (because it was a product of the body devoted to God), and from coming into contact with the dead (which would result in ceremonial defilement). The Mosaic law provided means for purification and for renewal of the vow if someone died suddenly in the presence of a Nazarite; the manner of ending the vow, when the period for which it was taken had concluded, was also detailed (Num. 6:13–21). Some Nazarite vows, as in the case of Samson, were made from birth (Judges 13:5). The angel's commands to Zacharias concerning the birth of John the Baptist, though probably not a Nazarite, included a part of the Nazarite vow (Luke 1:15), which John kept (Luke 7:33). See John the Baptist, Saint; Samson.

NAZILLI, town, W Turkey; near the Menderes River; 282 miles SW of Ankara. Located on a highway and the railroad, Nazilli is a market center for the surrounding agricultural area, which produces cotton, grains, and olives. Textiles are manufactured, and antimony, emery, and lignite are mined. (For population, see Turkey map in Atlas.)

NAZIMOVA, ALLA, 1879–1945, Russian actress, was born at Yalta in the Crimea, studied dramatic art with Stanislavski in Moscow, and by 1904 was a leading actress in St. Petersburg. She first appeared in New York in 1905 and made her English-speaking debut in *Hedda Gabler*, 1906. She became especially noted as an interpreter of Henrik Ibsen and appeared in *A Doll's House*, 1907, *The Master Builder*, 1908, and *Ghosts*, 1935–36. She also starred in *The Cherry Orchard*, 1929, *Katerina*, 1930, and *Mourning Becomes Electra*, 1931, and acted in motion pictures.

NAZISM. See National Socialism.

NDOLA, city, N central Zambia, 170 miles N of Lusaka, the capital, and about 10 miles E of the border with the Democratic Republic of the Congo. Ndola is in a rich copper belt which straddles the Zambian-Congo border. It is an important commercial and industrial center and is on the main Lusaka-Lubumbashi railroad, with spurs to nearby mining centers. Industries include copper, iron, and chemical works, as well as sawmilling and the manufacture of soap and piping. Ndola, a slave-trading center until the late nineteenth century, became an administrative center in 1904 and a municipality in 1932. (For population, see southern Africa map in Atlas.)

NEAGH, LOUGH, lake, E central Northern Ireland; between the counties of Antrim on the N and E, Armagh on the S, and Tyrone and Londonderry on the W; area 153 sq. mi.; maximum N-S and E-W distances 17 and 12 miles respectively; maximum depth 102 feet. Lough Neagh is the largest lake in the British Isles. It is fed by the Upper Bann, Blackwater, Ballinderry, and Main rivers, and drains north into the Lower Bann.

NEA IONIA, formerly Podarades, town, SE Greece, Attica Province; 4 miles from the center of Athens, of which it is a residential suburb. A rapid growth in population came with an influx of refugees from Asia Minor at the end of World War I, and the town soon became a center for textile and clothing manufacturing.

NEALE, SIR JOHN ERNEST, 1890– , English historian and biographer, was born in Liverpool, studied at Liverpool University and University College, London, and became Astor Professor of English history at the University of London, 1927. Neale, a fellow of the British Academy and a trustee of the British Museum, was renowned for his scholarship on the political and parliamentary events of the sixteenth century. His *Queen Elizabeth* (1934), which attained great popularity, was hailed by many critics as a masterpiece of biography. Among his other works are *The Age of Catherine de Medici* (1943), *The Elizabethan House of Commons* (1949), and *Essays in Elizabethan History* (1958). He was knighted in 1955.

NEALE, JOHN MASON, 1818–66, English clergyman and hymnologist, was born in London and was graduated from Trinity College, Cambridge, 1840. He strongly supported High Church views. He became warden of Sackville College, East Grinstead, 1846, where he founded the nursing Sisterhood of St. Margaret. His *Mediaeval Hymns and Sequences* (1851; enlarged 1863) included the translation of "De contemptu mundi," by Bernard of Cluny, parts of which became well known as the hymns "To Thee, O Dear, Dear Country," "Jerusalem the Golden," and "Brief Life Is Here Our Portion." Neale also wrote church histories, readings for children, theological discussions, and sermons. He was author of *An Introduction to the History of the Holy Eastern Church* (2 vols., 1850).

NEAPOLIS, a town of ancient Greece that served as the seaport of nearby Philippi. At Neapolis, St. Paul preached what was probably the first Christian sermon delivered in Europe (Acts 16:9–11). The modern port of Kaválla in Macedonia, Greece, is perhaps on or near the former site of Neapolis. Many ancient Greek and Roman cities (including present-day Naples) were named Neapolis, which in Greek meant "new city." See Philippi.

NEARCHUS, fourth century B.C. Macedonian officer of Alexander the Great, was born in Crete. He commanded a fleet that sailed down the Indus, along the southern coast of Baluchistan and Persia, and up the Persian Gulf and the Euphrates to Babylon, 325–324 B.C. His account of the voyage is preserved in Arrianus's *Indica*. After Alexander's death he joined Antigonus and was given the government of the provinces of Lycia and Pamphylia.

NEATH, municipal borough, S Wales, Glamorganshire; on the Neath River; 6 miles NE of Swansea. Neath is a railroad and highway junction with tinplate, iron, copper, and chemical works. It has the remains of an abbey founded in the twelfth century and of an ancient castle which was burned in 1231. The port of Briton Ferry, 2 miles to the south, was added to the borough in 1922. (For population, see England map in Atlas.)

NEBEL, OTTO, 1892– , German painter, was born in Berlin, studied architecture for a time, and traveled widely throughout Europe before settling in Bern, Switzerland. Nebel's paintings are characteristically whimsical geometrical studies, in which simple, seemingly careless shapes, reminiscent of those found in Joan Miró's paintings, are arranged in an almost haphazard fashion against an unvariegated white or colored background. The influence of Wassily Kandinsky, under whom Nebel once studied, may be seen in the visual movement of many of the designs by the artist.

NEBO, or Nabu, the Babylonian god of wisdom and patron of priests and scribes. He was regarded as the interpreter and son of Marduk and had a temple at Borsippa. As god of wisdom, Nebo was credited with the introduction of writing on stone and tablets and all learning was traced to him. He was associated with Ea as a cultural deity. Pilgrimages were made to Borsippa at the New Year.

NEBRASKA

LINCOLN C. OF C.

Great herds of cattle and an expansive sea of grain thrive on the vast plain of this state.

NEBRASKA, state, N central United States; bounded by South Dakota on the N, Iowa and Missouri on the E, Kansas and Colorado on the S, and Colorado and Wyoming on the W; area 77,237 sq. mi., including 584 sq. mi. of inland water; pop. (1960) 1,411,330. The Missouri River marks the northeast and east borders of the state. In area Nebraska is the 15th largest state; its maximum measurements are 430 miles east to west and 210 miles north to south. In population it ranks 34th among the states. The state motto is "Equality Before the Law." Nebraska was the 37th state to enter the Union. The goldenrod is the state flower, and the western meadow lark is the state bird. In 1945 Nebraska's popular name was changed from Tree Planters' state to Cornhusker state. Omaha is the largest city, Lincoln the capital. See map in Atlas, Vol. 20. For the state flag in color, see FLAG.

PHYSICAL FACTORS

Topography. Nebraska consists of an undulating plain with a gradual slope from west to southeast. In the northern and western parts the surface is broken by hills, some of them more than 5,000 feet high. The valleys are shallow, varying in width from one-fourth of a mile along the smaller streams to 23 miles along the Missouri and the Platte. The highest point (5,340 ft.) is in Banner County near the Colorado border; the lowest point (840 ft.) is in Richardson County in the southeast corner of the state. More than half of Nebraska lies in a loess region covering 42,000 square miles in the southern, eastern, and central sections. This area contains well drained, fertile farmland. In the west central section there are 20,000 square miles of grass-covered sand hills. Along the western border there are 15,000 square miles of high plains having little vegetation. The area is broken by canyons and marked with rugged buttes. There are two wooded mountain ranges: Wildcat Range, lying in Banner and Scotts Bluff counties; and Pine Ridge Range in Sioux, Dawes, and Sheridan counties. The three latter counties contain part of the rough terrain once known as the Badlands, a part of the Pierre shale formation. The land is excellent for grazing, but slightly rough and dry for farming.

Rivers and Lakes. The most important river is the Missouri along the eastern border of the state. The Platte, formed by the North Platte and the South Platte, flows across the state from west to east and empties into the Missouri. The northern part of the state is drained by the Niobrara; the southern and southwestern by the Republican; and the central part by the Loup and the Elkhorn.

Nebraska's lake region is situated mostly in the sand-hill area at the headwaters of the Elkhorn and the Loup. There are several hundred small lakes in the region.

Climate. Nebraska's climate is continental, with hot summers and cold winters. The weather is variable. Warm moist air from the Gulf of Mexico, hot dry air from the southwest, cool dry air from the North Pacific, and cold dry air from Canada meet in mid-continent Nebraska. Average mean annual temperature is 49.6°F; extremes of 118°F and −47°F have been recorded. Precipitation decreases from east to west. The state's average rainfall per year is 22.65 inches; snowfall averages 29.7 inches. Two- to three-week dry spells are common during June, July, and August. Prevailing winds are from the northwest. The chinook that comes down the east slope of the Rockies considerably raises the temperature of northwest Nebraska. Cloud-free days average 185. The growing season varies from 164 days in the southeast to 122 days in the northwest.

Soils and Natural Vegetation. In general, Nebraska's soil is fertile and easily tilled. There are deposits of glacial drift along the Missouri. Throughout the rest of the state the soil is a fine sand mixed with clay and humus.

More than 200 species of native forage grasses grow in Nebraska. Because of scanty rainfall only short grasses grow in the western section; there are taller species in eastern Nebraska. Cactus and other desert plants grow in the west, soapwood and yucca on the plains and high ridges. On the prairies there are violet, phlox, spiderwort, poppy, lady's-slipper, goldenrod, and several varieties of the wild rose.

Coniferous trees are found on the Wildcat and Pine Ridge ranges. Common varieties on the ridges include yellow pine, red cedar, white Norway pine, and white spruce. Birches grow in the canyons of the Pine Ridge country. Trees in the eastern section include oak, basswood, hickory, and sycamore. Thriving in the valley bottoms are cottonwood, ash, box elder, walnut, and hackberry. Nebraska has a number of native shrubs and small trees, such as wild plum and chokecherry. The Osage orange has been introduced in the east. Sagebrush and greasewood grow on the plains. Covering only 3 per cent of Nebraska's land area, however, trees are of little commercial importance.

Animals. Varieties of animals in Nebraska include the coyote, fox, jack rabbit, badger, striped ground squirrel, and prairie dog. The porcupine, wood rat, and red squirrel live in the wooded sections. Many varieties of ducks and geese feed in Nebraska during migratory flights. The lakes and ponds of the sand-hill country are a breeding ground for many water birds. Common birds are the blackbird, mourning dove, pigeon, brown thrush, catbird, woodpecker, crow, jay, and western meadow lark.

Trout are found in the streams of western Nebraska; bass in the lakes. Other native fish are perch, sucker, walleyed pike, buffalo, and pickerel. Carp, catfish, crappie, bullhead, and sunfish are found in prairie streams.

SOCIAL FACTORS

Population. In 1960 the population of Nebraska was 1,411,330, having increased by 85,820 or 6.5 per cent, since 1950 (compared with an increase of 0.7

PRINCIPAL CITIES

City	Population 1950 Census	1960 Census
Omaha	251,117	301,598
Lincoln	98,884	128,521
Grand Island	22,682	25,742
Hastings	20,211	21,412
Fremont	14,762	19,698
North Platte	15,443	17,184
Kearney	12,115	14,210
Scottsbluff	12,858	13,377
Norfolk	11,335	13,111
Beatrice	11,813	12,132

per cent during 1940–50). Nebraska ranked 34th among the states in population in 1960. Approximately 54 per cent of the state's population lived in urban areas.

Education. General supervision of schools is vested in the state superintendent of public instruction. Attendance of children between the ages of 7 and 16 in rural and village schools is compulsory for at least 120 days annually; and, in cities of 1,000 or more inhabitants, for the complete school session. Few states in the nation have less illiteracy. State normal schools for teachers are located at Kearney, Peru, Chadron, and Wayne. Other institutions of higher learning are the University of Nebraska, Lincoln; Creighton University, Omaha; York College, York; Dana College, Blair; Doane College, Crete; Hastings College, Hastings; Midland College, Fremont; the Municipal University of Omaha, Omaha; Nebraska Wesleyan College, Lincoln; Nebraska Central College, Central City; and Union College, Lincoln.

Public Welfare. State charitable and correctional institutions are under the jurisdiction of the department of public welfare and the state board of control. State institutions include hospitals for the insane at Lincoln, Norfolk, and Ingleside; tuberculosis hospital, Kearney; home for dependent children, Lincoln; soldiers' and sailors' homes, Grand Island and Milford; school for the blind, Nebraska City; school for the deaf, Omaha; institute for the feeble-minded, Beatrice; girls' industrial school, Geneva; boys' industrial school, Kearney; industrial home for women, Milford; reformatory for women, York; reformatory for men, Lincoln; state farm, Genoa; and state penitentiary, Lincoln. West of Omaha is Father Flanagan's Boys' home—an unusual welfare institution, founded in 1917, for neglected and homeless boys.

PRINCIPAL CROPS

	Unit (in thousands)	1957-61 Average	1963 Estimate
Beans, dry	bag	1,160	1,520
Corn	bushel	284,489	287,392
Hay	ton	6,786	6,307
Oats	bushel	41,536	26,847
Sorghum	bushel	73,178	102,406
Soybeans	bushel	5,042	9,291
Sugar beets	ton	1,057	1,590
Wheat	bushel	84,990	63,490

ECONOMIC FACTORS

Agriculture. Chief source of the state's wealth is its agricultural resources. Nebraska is one of the nation's leading states in corn and grain production and cattle raising. Its average corn yield for the years 1957–61 of 284,489 bushels placed it fifth among the states. In 1963 it was fifth in the production of wheat and dry beans.

The chief irrigated areas are along the Platte and North Platte rivers in Scotts Bluff, Morrill, Lincoln, Dawson, and Buffalo counties. A soil erosion control program includes contour farming, strip cropping, gully control, terracing, systematic crop rotation, construction of ponds and reservoirs, and protection against prairie and forest fires.

Nebraska is an important livestock state. Large hay and corn crops and the vast pasture lands of the western section provide abundant feed. Beef cattle, hogs, horses, mules, sheep, and goats are bred and raised. Dairying is important, as are poultry raising and egg production. In 1962 Nebraska had 88,000 farms, which averaged 581 acres in size. In 1962 crops were valued at $434,487,000, livestock at $934,034,000.

Other Industries. Nebraska's manufacturing interests were considerably expanded in the 1940's and 1950's. Its meat processing industry ranks high among the states, and Omaha is one of the top three livestock-receiving centers in the country. Next in value are dairy products—butter, cheese, and condensed and evaporated milk—followed by flour and gristmill products. Railroad shop construction and repair, centered at Omaha and Lincoln, is a substantial industry. Other industries and products include printing and publishing; coffee and spice roasting and grinding; foundry and machine-shop products; structural and ornamental iron and steelwork; planing-mill products; copper, tin, and sheet-iron work; furniture; animal feeds; canning and preserving; saddlery and harnesses; drugs and medicines; paints and varnishes; and ice cream, ices, and confectioneries. In 1962 there were 2,301 manufacturing establishments employing 68,800 wage earners. Value added by manufacture was $658,836,000.

The mineral resources of Nebraska are relatively small. In 1962 Nebraska ranked 28th among the states in the value of its mineral production, with an output valued at $108,249,000; crude petroleum accounted for more than 60 per cent of the total.

MINERAL PRODUCTION

Mineral	1954	1962
Clay	$ 163,831	$ 142,000
Natural gas	796,000	2,708,000
Crude petroleum	21,400,000	70,326,000
Sand and gravel	6,992,314	9,797,000
Stone	3,511,494	6,626,000
Others	10,529,361	18,650,000
Total	$42,393,000	$108,249,000

Transportation. The eastern and southeastern sections of Nebraska are well covered with a network of railroads, centering around Omaha. The western sections of the state have a small number of major trunk lines. Principal lines are the Union Pacific, the North Western, the Burlington, the Rock Island, the Missouri Pacific, the Milwaukee, the Wabash, and the Great Western. Railroad construction in Nebraska began in 1865 when the Union Pacific line was laid west from Omaha. A good system of bus lines also serves the state. Adequate state highways traverse most sections. The principal U.S. highways, from east to west, are 6, 34, 30, 26, 275, and 20; from north to south, 73, 75, 77, 81, 281, 83, 383, 283, and 183. Nebraska's highway system was built after 1917, when increased traffic promoted the need for transcontinental highways. Airlines serve Omaha, North Platte, Scottsbluff, and Alliance.

Tourist Attractions. Nebraska has many landmarks associated with covered-wagon days. Scotts Bluff National Monument, near the Colorado border, preserves a well known landmark on the Oregon Trail. Near Beatrice is Homestead National Monument, marking the first claim filed under the Homestead Act of 1862. The state has marked the sites of many forts important in the settling of Nebraska. Fort Robinson, Fort Cook, and Fort Omaha are still in

NEBRASKA

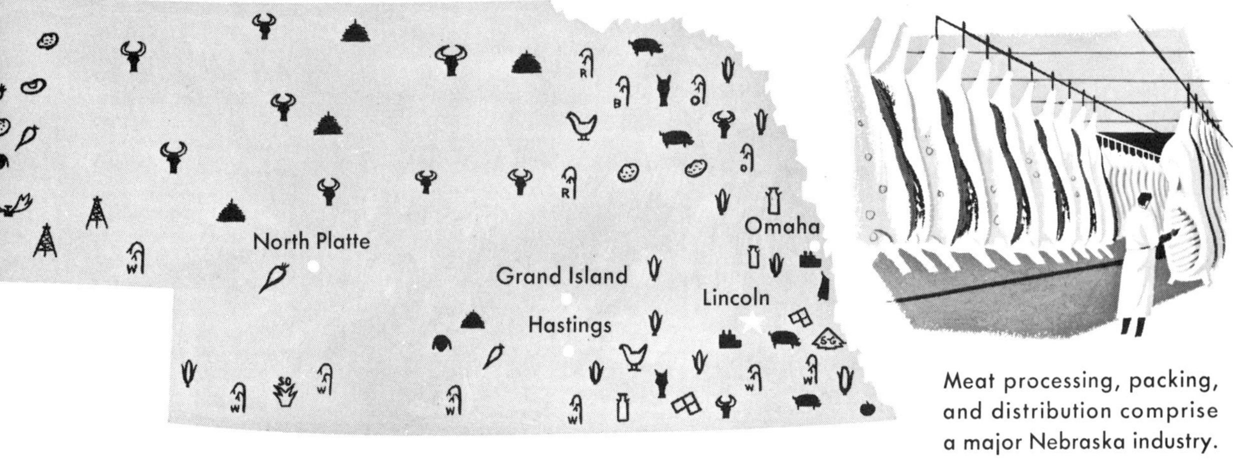

Meat processing, packing, and distribution comprise a major Nebraska industry.

PRINCIPAL RESOURCES, INDUSTRIES, AND PRODUCTS

Apples	Natural gas		
Barley	Oats		
Beans	Petroleum		
Cattle	Potatoes		
Corn	Poultry		
Dairy products	Rye		
Diversified manufacturing	Sand and gravel		
Hay	Sheep		
Hogs	Sorghum		
Horses and mules	Stone		
Meat processing	Sugar beets		
	Wheat		

State Bird—Western Meadow Lark

State Seal

State Flower—Goldenrod

The Sandhills region of the state provides much of the pasture land needed for Nebraska's great cattle herds.

The production of corn, one of the most important crops grown in Nebraska, is concentrated in the Missouri Valley.

Closed-circuit television plays an important role at Strategic Air Command (SAC) headquarters in Nebraska.

BOYS TOWN

Located 10 miles west of Omaha is world-famed Boys Town, an unusual welfare institution for homeless boys founded by Father Flanagan. There are facilities for 1,000 youths.

active use. At Fort McPherson is the McPherson National Cemetery, containing the graves of soldiers and scouts who explored and established much of the Old West. A former home of Buffalo Bill is located near North Platte.

Fossil quarries are found near Agate Springs and Ainsworth. Several other sites have been excavated and the prehistoric remains removed to museums within the state. Chimney Rock, near Bayard, consists of a reddish sandstone plateau from which rises a jagged spire that can be seen for miles.

The state maintains 10 parks, including Fort Kearney Park, built on the site of the historic frontier post; Niobrara Island, a game reservation; Ponca, a woodland area overlooking the Missouri; Victoria Springs, containing several mineral springs; Chadron, a wooded region in the upland country; Stolley Park, containing historic frontier buildings; and Arbor Lodge Park, containing a memorial arboretum and museum.

Government

The constitution of Nebraska was adopted in 1875. In order to amend it, three-fifths of the legislature must approve of the proposal, which is then submitted to the people for referendum. A one-house, or unicameral, legislature was adopted in 1934; it has 43 members, who are elected for four-year terms, with half of the membership elected every two years. Regular sessions are held in odd-numbered years. An amendment regulating legislative apportionment of the state was passed in 1962. It provided that a weight of 20 to 30 per cent be given to area, and the remainder to population.

Administrative officers of the state are the governor, lieutenant governor, secretary of state, auditor, treasurer, attorney general, a three-member railroad commission, and university regents and board of public instruction, both six-member groups. An amendment in 1962 increased the term of the governor and the lieutenant-governor from two to four years. The governor has the normal veto powers, but his veto can be overridden by a three-fifths vote of the elected legislature. His appointments are subject to legislative approval, but he may remove any officer that he appointed for incompetence, neglect of duty, or malfeasance. The judicial authority is vested in a supreme court of seven judges.

About two-thirds of the counties have commissions with administrative and quasi-judicial functions. The other counties have the supervisor-township plan. Municipal home rule permits any city to frame its own charter, subject to constitutional and statutory limitations; and city government may be of the mayor-council, the commission, or the city manager form. Nebraska is represented in Congress by two senators and three representatives.

History

The region that comprises modern Nebraska was claimed for France by Robert Cavelier de La Salle in 1682, but early French explorers and traders left few accounts of the region. In 1720 a Spanish expedition from Santa Fe under Pedro de Villasur explored the territory along the North Platte River, but returned to New Mexico when attacked by Indians. All territory west of the Mississippi was transferred to Spain by the Treaty of Paris in 1759. In 1800 Napoleon Bonaparte forced Spain to re-cede the territory to France, and in 1803 he sold it to the United States (see LOUISIANA PURCHASE). Early U.S. exploration of the Nebraska region was made by the Lewis and Clark Expedition in 1805 and by Lt. Zebulon M. Pike in 1806.

The early U.S. settlements were trading posts; the first of these, Bellevue, was established about 1810. The Missouri River towns of Fort Atkinson, Omaha, and Nebraska City were founded by 1826; however, settlement west of the Missouri River was slow. Major Stephen H. Long explored the region between the Missouri River and the Rocky Mountains in 1820 and declared it unfit for cultivation. Much of the western migration before 1850 was to the Pacific Coast and Utah, and although many emigrants passed through the plains region few remained. Theoretically the land belonged to the Indians; after the Missouri Compromise of 1820, however, it became a pawn in the slavery controversy. In 1844 Rep. Stephen A. Douglas of Illinois advocated that Kansas and Nebraska territories be created and that the slavery question be decided by each territory. The plan of Douglas was enacted in 1854 as the Kansas-Nebraska Act that abrogated the Missouri Compromise (see MISSOURI COMPROMISE). The bill provided that all of the territory between 37° and 40°N lat. as Kansas Territory, and all north of 40°N lat. as Nebraska Territory. It further provided that the territories should be admitted to statehood with or without slavery as their constitutions prescribed. Subsequent changes transferred the region north of the 43rd parallel to Dakota Territory and a small tract in the southwest to Colorado. A tract between 104° and 110°W long. was incorporated in Idaho Territory. In 1866 Congress approved admission of Nebraska to the Union, but Pres. Andrew Johnson did not sign the bill. Nebraska became a state on Mar. 1, 1867, by a bill that was passed over the President's veto. In 1882 Congress added about 600 square miles to the state by extending its northern boundary eastward along the 43rd parallel to the main channel of the Missouri River.

In the early twentieth century the state legislature provided for the initiative and referendum; a board of

Strategic air command (SAC) war room at Offutt Air Force Base is situated 45 feet underground. In case of surprise attack, emergency war plans would be directed from here.

USAF

NEBRASKA

DIV. OF NEBRASKA RESOURCES
Nebraska's wheat production is concentrated in the south-central counties of the state. The acreage is devoted predominantly to the hardy winter strains.

USDA
The North Platte Valley, one of world's largest irrigated valleys, has a high average yield of sugar beets per acre.

CUDAHY PACKING CO.
Luncheon meat is processed, canned, and weighed in a packing plant at Omaha. The city is one of the world's most important centers of meat packing and processing.

ALLIED CHEMICAL
Apparatus of a large nitrogen ammonia plant is part of heavy industry situated in Omaha, Nebraska, industrial and distribution hub.

At the Valentine National Wildlife Refuge, birds are trapped and banded for migration studies. The refuge is a haven for the American bison and Texas longhorn.
VALENTINE NATL. WILDLIFE REFUGE

NEBRASKA
Highlights of History

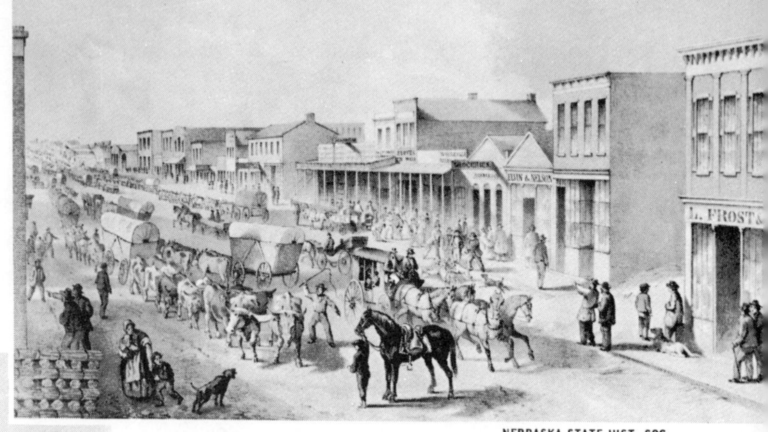

NEBRASKA STATE HIST. SOC.

Nebraska City began as a trading post in the 1850's and by 1865 had evolved into a bustling river town.

NEBRASKA STATE HIST. SOC.

Cheese Creek Ranch, situated on the Oregon Trail, sold provisions to settlers moving West during the 1860's.

WIDE WORLD

Omaha City, later Omaha, is seen here in 1867, the year in which Nebraska became the 37th state of the Union.

NEBRASKA STATE HIST. SOC.

Fort Kearney, built in 1848 on the Platte River, was for more than 20 years a stronghold against the Sioux.

NEBRASKA STATE HIST. SOC

Houses of sod were built for lack of other material on the nearly treeless plain. Spring rains brought the dormant sod to life with weeds, morning-glories, and prairie roses.

Material for use in the construction of the Union Pacific Railroad was brought by river boat to Omaha, where first ground was broken on the east-west route Dec. 2, 1863.

UNION PACIFIC R.R.

commissioners for state institutions; mothers' pensions; workmen's compensation; statewide prohibition; nonpartisan ballots for election of judiciary; and the consolidation of various agencies under the governor in order to unify the state's business. A law also permits cities of more than 5,000 population to frame their own charters.

The entry of the United States into World War I caused great controversy in Nebraska because of the large foreign-born population and midwest isolationism. Czech and Polish groups that favored U.S. participation in the war were opposed by 230,000 persons who were German-born or of German extraction, and a significant number of Irish traditionally hostile to England. In 1915 the distinguished Nebraskan William Jennings Bryan resigned as U.S. secretary of state in protest against Pres. Wilson's pro-Allied policies. After U.S. entry into the war, 57,526 Nebraskan men and women served in the nation's armed forces; of these, 1,655 were casualties.

The depression of 1929 made farm tenancy a serious problem, and in 1933 the legislature passed a mortgage and moratorium bill. Although Nebraska was traditionally conservative in politics, the twentieth century brought a more progressive trend, particularly in the area of administrative reform. The early leader was Bryan, and later George W. Norris, an outstanding liberal, served Nebraska in the U.S. Senate as a Democrat, a Republican, and an Independent. Since 1900 Nebraska has cast its electoral votes for the Republican candidates for president and vice-president in a majority of the elections.

Opposition to U.S. involvement in World War II was not as bitter as that before World War I, although isolationist sentiment remained strong. The state was not suited for war industries, but its large area and scattered population made Nebraska a practical site for Air Force training. A prisoner-of-war camp was located at Atlanta. About 120,000 men and women served in the armed forces, of whom 3,839 lost their lives. After the war, Nebraska shared in the nationwide prosperity. In 1944 a flood control act provided for projects to utilize the power of the Missouri River and permit better irrigation. Shortly after the war the headquarters of the newly created Strategic Air Command of the U.S. Air Force was located at Offutt Field, Omaha. In 1949 the U.S. Supreme Court upheld the 1946 amendment of the Nebraska constitution that banned the closed union shop. Nebraska's agricultural production continued to expand in the 1960's, in part owing to the increased use of irrigated water. The second highest yield of corn per acre in the state's history was recorded in 1962.

Bibliog.–American Guide Series, *Nebraska: A Guide to the Cornhusker State* (1939); Adam C. Breckenridge, *One House for Two: Nebraska's Unicameral Legislature* (1957); Harry F. Cunningham, *Capitol* (1954); Virginia Faulkner, *Roundup: A Nebraska Reader* (1957); Lilian L. Fitzpatrick, *Nebraska Place-Names* (1960); John R. Johnson, *Representative Nebraskans* (1954); J. Sterling Morton and Albert Watkins, *Illustrated History of Nebraska* (3 vols.) (1905–1913); *Nebraska History* (periodical); Bruce H. Nicoll and Ken R. Keller, *Know Nebraska* (1961); James C. Olson, *History of Nebraska* (1954).

NEBRASKA, UNIVERSITY OF, founded 1869, is a land-grant, state-controlled, coeducational institution of higher learning located at Lincoln. Instruction was first offered in 1871. Divisions of the university include colleges of arts and sciences (1872), agriculture (1872), law (1892), medicine (1902), engineering and architecture (1909), pharmacy (1915), dentistry (1919), and business administration (1919); schools of nursing (1917), journalism (1923), music (1933), and fine arts (1939); agricultural experiment station (1887); farmers' institute (1897); university extension division (1908); graduate college (1909); teachers college (1909); teachers college high school (1911); Nebraska conservation and survey division (1913); Nebraska school of agriculture at Curtis (1914); agricultural extension service (1915); department of military science and tactics (1917); engineering experiment station (1923); graduate school of social work (1937); and university junior division (1940). The college of medicine and the school of nursing are at Omaha. The University of Nebraska Press was founded in 1942.

UNIV. OF NEBRASKA

At commencement exercises graduating students march down the main mall of the University of Nebraska. In the center of the mall is the Ralph Mueller carillon tower.

The bachelor's degree is offered, the master's degree by most departments, and the doctor's degree in major fields. Distinctive educational programs include summer field trips conducted by the geology department, inspection trips by students in agriculture, engineering, and pharmacy, and summer workshops in education. Army, Navy, and Air Force ROTC units are maintained on the campus. Special library collections include works on the French Revolution, Woodrow Wilson, communism and the Industrial Workers of the World, and the Middle West. See Colleges and Universities.

NEBRASKA CITY, city, SE Nebraska, seat of Otoe County; on the Missouri River, the Burlington and the Missouri Pacific railroads, and U.S. highways 73 and 75; 45 miles S of Omaha. Nebraska City is in a diversified agricultural area and has manufactures of feed, clothing, bricks, canned goods, and dairy products. Arbor Lodge State Park at Nebraska City was formerly the home of Julius Sterling Morton. Settled early in the 1850's, the city was incorporated in 1855. (For population, see Nebraska map in Atlas.)

NEBUCHADNEZZAR, Nebuchadrezzar or Nebuchadnezzar II, more correctly Nabu-kuduri-uçur, king of Babylonia, died 562 B.C. As crown prince he led the army of his father, King Nabopolassar, against the Egyptians and defeated the Egyptian King Necho II at Carchemish, 605 B.C., thereby ending Necho's scheme to control Syria and the Jewish kingdoms of Israel and Judah. On the death of Nabopolassar, Nebuchadnezzar became king, 605 or 604. In 597 he invaded Judah and placed a puppet king, Zedekiah, on the throne at Jerusalem. When Zedekiah revolted, Nebuchadnezzar again took Jerusalem, 586, destroyed the city, and exiled thousands of Jews into what was later known as Babylonian Captivity. In 572 he plundered Egypt. Nebuchadnezzar was a brilliant administrator and builder as well as military leader, and under him the Babylonian Empire reached its last great peak. In Babylon, the capital city, he restored temples and built the Hanging Gardens (for one of his wives) and the great walls and canals surrounding the city. According to the Book of Daniel, Nebuchadnezzar suffered for several years with a peculiar type of insanity; during this period he ate grass.

NEBULA, any object of perceptible size in the sky that lies outside the solar system and cannot be classed as a star. Nebulae are divided into two almost unrelated main classes: galactic and extragalactic (or anagalactic). The first class consists of the diffuse,

YERKES OBSERVATORY

Spiral Nebula in Ursa Major

hazy areas in the sky that are situated in or near the Milky Way and that are believed to belong to the galactic system. The galactic nebulae are included in a system only a few hundred or a few thousand light-years in extent. They are further designated as dark, reflection, emission, and planetary nebulae. The second class, the extragalactic nebulae, are in every section of the sky except the Milky Way and consist of hundreds of millions of stars so distant as to appear as faint patches of light under the most powerful telescopes. One, the great nebula in Andromeda, is visible to the naked eye. See GALAXY; MILKY WAY.

Dark Nebulae are condensations in the interstellar matter in the earth's galaxy. These enormous clouds of dust and gas, which may contain matter equivalent to 100 suns, are often found in the Milky Way, where they reach diameters up to 100 light-years. They absorb the light of the more distant stars, and therefore appear as dark patches against a bright background of stars. See INTERSTELLAR MATTER.

Reflection Nebulae. The light of a bright star inside or close to one of the black clouds is scattered and reflected by the dust particles, and parts of the cloud appear as a faint glow, or a reflection nebula. The association between a star and the interstellar matter may be so close that the nebula varies in brightness if the star is a variable star. A reflection nebula is bluish and has an absorption spectrum that is the same as that of the illuminating star. The flood of radiation from the star can blow the nebular material away; the combination of this repulsion and the opposing gravitational pull of the star contributes to the odd shapes of nebulae. In most cases the stars are only passing through the nebulae so that in perhaps a million years most of these objects will have new shapes or even will have disappeared.

Dark S-shaped Nebula in Constellation Ophiuchus

MOUNT WILSON OBS.

Emission Nebulae. The intense ultraviolet radiation from a very hot star near interstellar matter makes the gases of the nebula fluorescent, usually with a greenish color. Such nebulae are associated with B-type stars that have surface temperatures higher than 25,000°F. The spectrum of such a nebula, unlike that of the associated star, has bright emission lines. The ultraviolet light from the hot star ionizes the nebular gases (removes one or more of the outer orbital electrons from the atoms); then, as the atoms and electrons recombine, the emission lines of the chemical elements in the gas appear. Among the strongest lines are those of hydrogen, helium, oxygen, nitrogen, neon, and sulfur. The great nebula in Orion, which can be seen with the naked eye, is of the emission type. Dark as well as reflection and emission nebulae, some of which are of enormous size, have been detected in extragalactic systems, especially in those of the spiral type and in the Magellanic Clouds.

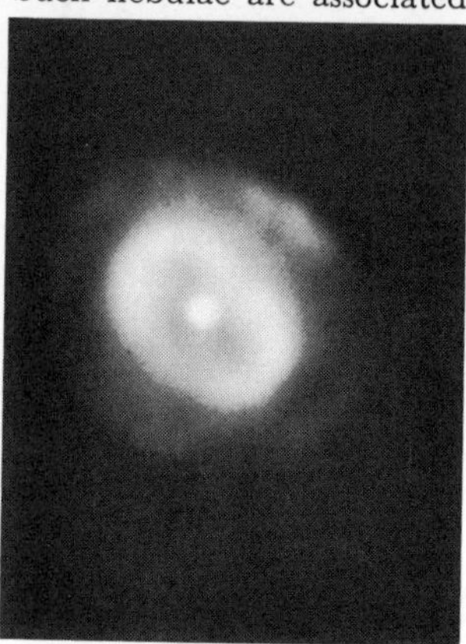

MOUNT WILSON OBS.

Planetary Nebula lying within the Constellation Andromeda

Planetary Nebulae. In about 100 small planetary or ring nebulae, the nebula and star form a more permanent unit. In the telescope they appear as small doughnut-like shapes brightest at the edges. They are less than a light-year in diameter. Their center stars are the hottest known, with surface temperatures up to 200,000°F. Because of the high-energy radiation from the star, which causes the fluorescence, the spectrum of the nebula is of the emission type whose lines come from highly ionized elements. The ring of gas is probably the still-expanding remnant of an explosion that occurred many thousands of years ago when the star threw off its outer atmosphere. Near some novae are small nebulae, probably of similar type (see NEBULIUM; NOVA). See ASTRONOMY; CYGNUS; LYRA; ORION.

JESSE L. GREENSTEIN

BIBLIOG.–L. Goldberg and L. H. Aller, *Atoms, Stars, and Nebulae* (1943); J. C. Duncan, *Astronomy* (1955); L. H. Aller, *Gaseous Nebulae* (1956); J. Dufay, *Galactic Nebulae and Interstellar Matter* (1957); A. S. Eddington, *Expanding Universe* (1958); R. H. Baker, *Astronomy* (1959).

NEBULAR HYPOTHESIS. See SOLAR SYSTEM, Origin of the Solar System, *The Nebular Hypothesis.*

NEBULIUM, a hypothetical chemical element once thought to cause certain bright emission lines in the spectra of gaseous nebulae. (See SPECTRUM; NEBULA.) In 1927 nebulium was identified as atoms of oxygen, hydrogen, and neon that are singly or doubly ionized, that is, have lost one or two orbital electrons, respectively. (See ION.) The nebulium lines have been termed forbidden because they occur only in a system of rarefied gases and not, therefore, in the atmosphere of the earth.

NECHAKO RIVER, W Canada, central British Columbia; rises in the Coast Mountain lakes of Eutsuk, Ootsa, Tahtsa, Tetachuk, and Whitesail and flows E and N to Fort Fraser, then E to the Fraser River at Prince George; length about 250 miles. Kenny Dam, one of the largest earth-filled dams, is on the upper Tahtsa tributary.

U.S. GEOLOGICAL SURVEY

A spectacular example of a geological neck is the Devils Tower in the Black Hills of Wyoming. The massive columns of igneous rock rise 865 feet above the top of the ridge.

NECHES RIVER, E Texas; rises in Van Zandt County, flows SE through a fertile farming and oil-producing region, and empties into Sabine Lake; length about 250 miles. The section of the river between Beaumont and Sabine Lake has a deepwater channel.

NECK, or plug, a nearly circular mass of igneous rock resulting from the hardening of lava in the throat of a volcano and its subsequent exposure as the result of the erosion of the surrounding cone. Necks are found in old volcanic regions. Devils Tower, a neck in northeastern Wyoming, is 600 feet high. Other examples are found in Texas and California in the United States, and in Scotland, France, and South Africa.

NECKAM, ALEXANDER, also Necham, 1157–1217, English scholar and the first European to write about the use of the magnetic needle in navigation, was born in St. Albans, Hertfordshire. He studied at Oxford and in Paris, became an Augustinian canon, and in 1213 was chosen abbot of Cirencester. His writings include theological, grammatical, and scientific treatises and Latin poems.

NECKAR RIVER, S Germany; rises near Schwenningen in SW Württemberg and flows NE past Rottenburg and Tübingen, NNW past Plochingen and Cannstatt (a suburb of Stuttgart), and W past Eberbach and Heidelberg to Mannheim where it enters the Rhine; length 228 miles. The Neckar is navigable for about 115 miles, from its mouth to Cannstatt.

NECKER, JACQUES, 1732–1804, French banker and finance minister of Louis XVI, was born in Geneva. He went to Paris, 1747, and served his apprenticeship in a banking house. He established the Bank of Thellusson and Necker soon afterward and amassed a fortune during the Seven Years' War. In 1764 he married Suzanne Curehod (1739–94), who presided over one of the leading salons of Paris and encouraged her husband to enter public life. Their daughter was the writer, Madame de Staël (Anne Louise Germaine Necker). In 1776 Louis XVI made Necker director general of finances (because of his Protestantism he was unable to hold the title of minister). He attempted to correct the abuses of the French financial system and emphasized the need for retrenchment. In 1781 Necker appealed to public opinion in the *Compte rendu*, a statement of the financial position of France. It was too optimistic in many particulars and concealed the real bankruptcy of the country, but was important in that for the first time the citizens of France learned on official authority the immensity of the financial burdens of the state. Necker's dismissal in 1781 made him a popular hero. He was recalled in 1788 and again made director general of finance. He recommended the calling of the states-general as a means of obtaining a grant of money, but when the meeting got out of hand he was again dismissed. His second dismissal, July 11, 1789, was one of the direct causes of the attack on the Bastille. In consequence of the popular victory, he was recalled on July 20 but was unable to cope with the situation and resigned in September, 1790, thereafter living in Switzerland. His *Oeuvres complètes* (1820–21) appeared in 15 volumes.

LIB. OF CONGRESS

Jacques Necker

NECTAR, in Greek mythology, the winelike drink of the gods of Mount Olympus, their food being ambrosia. Drinking it was supposed to confer immortality. In some accounts nectar was the food, ambrosia the drink.

NECTAR, a solution of sugars that is a secretion of the nectaries of plants. Its odor attracts insects which cross-fertilize flowers by accumulating and transfering pollen from blossom to blossom while collecting nectar as food.

NECTARINE, a smooth-skinned fruit that is a variation of the peach. The nectarine, *Prunus persica* var. *Nectarina*, is smaller than the peach and richer in quality. Two varieties of nectarines have been produced—a freestone, *P. violacea*, and a clingstone, *P. laevis*. Nectarines have grown from the seeds of peaches, and peaches have developed from nectarine seeds. Both nectarines and peaches may also be produced from the other by bud variation. Cultivation of the nectarine is the same as that of the peach. The nectarine, however, is more susceptible to some of the plant diseases affecting peaches, and the nectarine is not as popular on the market. In California alone it is planted on a commercial scale for canning and as a dried fruit, although limited breeding and selection indicate that nectarines thrive in any region where peaches can be grown.

NEEDHAM, town, E Massachusetts, Norfolk County; on the New York, New Haven, and Hartford Railroad; 10 miles WSW of Boston. The town has manufactures of knit goods, rubber products, and surgical instruments. Settled as part of Dedham, 1680, it was incorporated separately in 1711. Pop. (1960) 25,793.

NEEDLE, a small, thin, rod-shaped instrument sharpened at one end, usually perforated at the other to carry thread, and used most commonly for sewing and embroidery. Sewing needles, although available in scores of sizes and shapes, are usually straight, made of tempered steel, and about 1¼ to 3 inches in length. They are manufactured by cutting steel wire into lengths adequate for two needles; the length is sharpened at both ends, perforated on each side of the middle, and then cut in half. Two needles are thus formed. Final steps in preparing the needle for market include hardening and tempering, polishing, and packaging.

Surgical needles are used to close wounds. They are curved and have an eyelet opposite the point. The point may resemble that of an ordinary sewing needle, or it may have a triangular shape or a sharp cutting edge. Surgical needles range in size from those a fraction of an inch long, which are used in holders, to others several inches in length. Sewing-machine needles usually have the eyelet near the point, and the opposite end usually is larger in diameter and shaped to be held in the machine. Knitting needles are slender, blunt-pointed, and eyeless, commonly 9 to 12 inches long. They are made from such materials as steel, cattle bone, plastic, or hardwood; some have heads to prevent the yarn from sliding off. Crochet needles ordinarily are about 5 inches long and have a hook instead of an eye at one end to carry the thread. The styluses used in phonographs are also called needles, and although they are usually made of steel, the points often are of a more durable material such as sapphire or diamond.

Hypodermic needles are hollow and made of stainless steel; they range from 6 inches in length down to extremely small size and are attached to syringes used in most instances for injection of drugs or nutrients beneath the surface of the skin. The production of hypodermic needles involves more than a hundred operations, beginning with a tube several feet long and about 3 inches in diameter; by means of precise rolling and drawing operations under high temperature, the tube ultimately is reduced to a diameter frequently less than 1/200ths of an inch. A point is then ground and the needle made part of a device that locks onto a syringe.

NEEDLEFISH, any of the slim cylindrical fishes inhabiting moderately warm seas and comprising the family *Belonidae*. The approximately 50 species of needlefish are usually greenish with silver scales, and have long narrow jaws lined with sharp teeth. An unusual feature of the needlefish is its green bones. Some species grow to 5 feet. Needlefish, sometimes called garfish, swim near the surface catching small fish, their main food. Two major species are the Atlantic needlefish, *Strongylura marina*, and the California needlefish, *S. exilis*. Needlefish are edible but not prized as food. Although the needlefish and the fresh-water gars resemble each other and are sometimes equated, they are not related.

NEEDLES, city, SE California, San Bernardino County; on the Colorado River, the Santa Fe Railway, and U.S. highways 66 and 95; 220 miles ENE of Los Angeles. Founded in 1883 and incorporated in 1913, the city takes its name from three needle-like pinnacles on the Arizona side of the river. Products include fruits and vegetables. Pop. (1960) 4,590.

NEEDLES, THE. See WIGHT, ISLE OF.

NEEDLEWORK, any work done with needle and thread—either simple sewing and mending or, more frequently, decorative work such as knitting, crocheting, needle-point lace work, embroidery, and appliqué. The development of this practical and decorative art dates from prehistoric man's discovery that garments could be made by joining pelts together with thongs. It is likely that man began to decorate his garments with needlework even before spinning and weaving were developed.

Knitting, Crocheting, and Tatting are considered needlework although they require special needles or shuttles. In knitting, two or more needles are used to manufacture a fabric by drawing loops of thread or yarn through previously formed loops (see KNITTING). In crocheting, which is a type of knitting, a single, hooked needle is used to make a fabric (see CROCHETING). In tatting, linen or cotton threads are knotted into lace by means of a shuttle.

Needle-Point Lace, one of the basic types of handmade lace, is worked with one needle and one thread on a paper pattern (see LACE, *Handmade Lace*). It evolved from embroidery.

Embroidery is any ornamental needlework utilizing thread to decorate fabric or leather (see EMBROIDERY). Embroidery differs from tapestry work only in that the design is sewed, rather than woven, into the fabric. One of the most famous embroidered works, the Bayeux "tapestry," obviously is misnamed.

Popular embroidery stitches include the cross, the lazy daisy, the buttonhole, the feather, and the stem and outline stitches. Several of the many embroidery stitches are also used in other types of needlework; for instance, the feather stitch is popular for quilting, and the chain stitch is often used in appliqué work.

Types of Embroidery. Needle point as a rule is embroidery executed on canvas with diagonal stitches. When fine canvas and fine thread (or wool) are used and the stitches are short, the work is called petit point. Drawn-thread work is accomplished by withdrawing from a fabric some of the threads of which it is composed and stitching a design into the remaining threads. In drawn-fabric work the threads of the fabric are pulled apart to produce an open design. Hemstitching is a form of drawn-fabric work used to finish decoratively the edges of the material. In couching, a thick thread is attached to the surface of a fabric by a series of single stitches worked across the heavy thread at regular intervals; this ornamental work is often of intricate design, and is especially beautiful when a heavy gold thread is used.

Quilting, Patchwork, and Appliqué are types of needlework that consist essentially of sewing together pieces of material so as to form patterns. Quilting basically is the joining together, by means of a stitched design, of two pieces of material that are separated by a padding. In English quilting the entire article is padded; in Italian quilting only the areas forming the designs are padded. Patchwork is the sewing together of patches of cloth of various colors and designs, and usually of different shapes and sizes. Appliqué consists either of sewing a contrasting patch onto a background material or of cutting pieces from the background material and replacing them with contrasting material.

NEENAH, city, E central Wisconsin, Winnebago County; on Lake Winnebago at its outlet into the Fox River, and on the North Western, the Milwaukee, and the Soo Line railroads; adjacent to Menasha and 10 miles N of Oshkosh. Main products are paper, wood, machinery, butter, cheese, furnaces, flour, and textiles. The city was settled in 1843 and incorporated in 1873. Pop. (1960) 18,057.

NEGAPATTINAM, formerly Negapatam, seaport city, SE India, E central Madras State, Tanjore District; at the mouth of the Vettar River; 45 miles E of Tanjore city and 160 miles S of Madras. Because of Negapattinam's deltaic location on a shallow coast, vessels must lie 2 miles offshore; lighters service the port's wharves and long foreshore storage and landing area. Chief exports are peanuts to Europe and colored cotton piece goods, tobacco, and vegetables to the Malay Peninsula and Ceylon. Industries include textile dyeing and printing plants, a salt factory, metallurgical works, vegetable-oil extraction mills, and railway workshops. The port, called Negapatam until 1949, was one of the earliest and the most important of the Portuguese settlements along the Coromandel Coast. It was taken by the Dutch in 1660 and by the British in 1781. Pop. (1951) 57,854.

NEGAUNEE, city, Michigan, N central Upper Peninsula, Marquette County; near Lake Superior; on the North Western, the Duluth, South Shore, and Atlantic, and the Lake Shore and Ishpeming railroads and U.S. highway 41; 10 miles SW of Marquette. Production of iron ore is the major industry. Negaunee was settled in 1846 and incorporated in 1873. Pop. (1960) 6,126.

NEGEV, or Negeb, desert region, bounded on the N by the Gaza Strip and the Lydda and Jerusalem regions, E by Jordan, S by the Gulf of Aqaba, and W by Egypt; area 4,700 sq. mi. The Negev, a roughly triangular limestone plateau comprising the southern half of Israel, was once well populated and fertile but is now predominantly barren. The north Negev, which occupies three-fifths of the cultivable area of Israel, is the site of a redevelopment program to provide irrigation. The central Negev remains a desert but has potentially valuable mineral deposits. To the far south is Elath, Israel's outlet to the Red Sea. Among the region's historical features are King Solomon's Mines near the mountains of Moab, the ruins of ancient Khalasa, and the preserved Byzantine town of Subaita. The Negev was the scene of fighting between Egyptian and Israeli troops in 1948. Beersheba is the economic center of the region.

NEGLIGENCE, failure to act with the degree of forethought and intelligence that characterizes the conduct of a reasonably prudent man—in common law the foundation of civil liability for injury to person or property other than that resulting from premeditation and a formed intention. The concept of such liability is not absolute, for no man is required to insure that the results of his acts will not be harmful. Nor are those duties that are dictated merely by good morals or by humane considerations within the domain of the law. There can be no fault or negligence or breach of duty where there is no act, service, or contract that a party is bound to perform or fulfill. To constitute actionable negligence three essential elements must exist: a duty or obligation to protect another from injury; a failure to discharge that duty; and injury resulting from the failure. The foundation of liability is the negligent person's superior knowledge—or its legal equivalent, opportunity by the exercise of reasonable diligence to acquire knowledge—of the peril that subsequently results in injury.

The law, while recognizing that inevitable accident resulting from an act of providence is not the result of negligence or misconduct on the part of one who has in no way contributed to the casualty, also distinguishes degrees of negligence. Negligence may be slight, ordinary, gross, willful, or wanton; and one guilty of gross, willful, or wanton negligence may be criminally, as well as civilly, liable for injuries caused thereby. In determining liability, various factors must be considered, such as intellectual capacity, the comparative knowledge of the parties to the transaction complained of respecting its dangers, and emergency or sudden peril as affecting judgment. Society owes greater consideration and protection to persons known to be unable to care for themselves than to those who are fully able to do so.

In a majority of the American states the general rule is that a violation of a penal or criminal statute is negligence per se, or negligence as a matter of law, even though the wrongdoer be also subject to a penalty provided by the statute. To establish liability for such negligence there must be a causal connection between the unlawful act and the injury.

Liability of Property Owner. One who invites or induces others to come upon his land owes such persons the duty to have his premises in a reasonably safe condition and to give timely warning against concealed perils. No such duty, however, is owed trespassers or others who visit the premises without right or invitation. No invitation can be implied from mere toleration of such trespassers. Where, however, persons are permitted generally to use or establish a thoroughfare under such circumstances as to induce a belief that it is public in character, persons entering the premises by such thoroughfare in the interest or advantage of the owner or occupant are presumed to come by invitations.

Although everyone in a sense has an absolute right to use his property as he sees fit, the principle has been limited to hold that the maintenance of dangerous conditions is at the owner's peril, even though forces of nature such as storms have caused or contributed to such conditions. In the case of a danger that attracts children (known in law as an attractive nuisance) recovery will be allowed for negligence resulting in injury to a child trespasser if the owner of the property knew, or ought to have known, that a child would make use of the dangerous instrumentality and if he provided no safeguards against the peril.

Contributory Negligence. Under the traditional rule of the common law, if an injured person is guilty of negligence that was a contributing cause of his injury, he is without remedy, however slight be his negligence in comparison with the negligence of the person charged with primary responsibility. In some American states, as for example Wisconsin, the doctrine of comparative negligence is applied: contributory negligence of the injured person, so long as it was not the predominating cause of his injury, operates in mitigation of the amount of recovery, but does not bar recovery. In cases involving injuries to employees who have been contributorily negligent, modern statutes such as employers' liability laws allow recovery of a proportional amount bearing the same relation to the full amount as the negligence attributable to the employer bears to the entire negligence attributable to both (see EMPLOYERS' LIABILITY).

One who is aware of a danger and fails to take measures to avoid an injury therefrom is guilty of contributory negligence and may not recover. There are, however, pronounced exceptions. It is not contributory negligence for a person to risk his life or to place himself in great danger in an effort to save the life of another, or to rescue another from sudden peril or great bodily harm, unless the act was rash and reckless in the judgment of reasonably prudent persons. If the contributory negligence consists in an effort to save property that a reasonably prudent man would have undertaken under similar circumstances, most jurisdictions give the injured party redress. Similarly, if because of an emergency all that is left to the injured party is a choice of evils, he is not to blame if he chooses the greater where he is compelled to decide hurriedly. Under the doctrine of last clear chance, a person who has the opportunity to avoid causing harm to another who has negligently placed himself in a position of peril is considered in law as solely responsible for injury that results.

Agency Relationships. In the vast realm of cases dealing with agency relationships, the one for whom an agent acts is normally held responsible for the agent's conduct, so long as a connection between such conduct and the purpose for which the agent was hired is established. There is a rule exempting government agencies, acting in their governmental capacity, and public charitable corporations from liability for negligence. See AGENCY.

Rules of Evidence. In the trial of an action to recover damages for a negligently caused injury, the mere fact that an injury has been sustained will not ordinarily give rise to a presumption that the injury resulted from the negligence of the defendant. On the other hand, certain accompanying elemental facts have long been regarded as sufficient proof of negligence to establish a prima facie case. Under the doctrine known as *res ipsa loquitur* (the thing speaks for itself) negligence will be presumed where it appears that the injury was caused by an instrumentality under the defendant's control and that such an injury is not normally to be expected when the management of the instrumentality is non-negligent.

The burden of proof not only of the negligence complained of, but also of the allegation that such negligence was the proximate cause of a loss actually sustained, is on the party who seeks to recover. To support a verdict in his favor the plaintiff, in most American jurisdictions, is under no obligation to produce direct evidence to show freedom from fault on his part. That fact may be shown by circumstantial evidence or may be inferred by the jury from circumstances appearing in the proof. Negligence is generally a question of fact to be decided by a jury acting under instructions from the court as to the law applicable to the facts in issue. See MASTER AND SERVANT; TORT, Tort Liability.

ROBERT D. HURSH

NEGOTIABLE INSTRUMENT, a written security or document payable either to the bearer or to a particular person and transferable by indorsement and delivery, or in some cases delivery alone, the legal title thus vesting in the indorsee. Typical of negotiable instruments are bills of exchange, promissory notes, checks, drafts, money orders, and trade acceptances. A number of other instruments such as bills of lading, warehouse receipts, and stock certificates have similar legal characteristics of negotiability, but are not negotiable instruments in the historic sense.

Development of the Law. With the growth of trade during the Middle Ages there arose an increasing need for a system of credit instruments. Bankers and merchants adopted the use of commercial paper in an effort to satisfy this need. The law merchant, or *lex mercatorum*, a body of commercial laws administered by special courts established for the benefit of merchants and traders, was developed to regulate this system. (See LAW MERCHANT.) As commerce became more important the common law gradually incorporated more and more of the law merchant, eventually adopting it almost in its entirety; later the special commercial courts were consolidated into the common law system.

In the United States the Uniform Negotiable Instruments Act was adopted in 1896 by commissioners concerned with uniform state laws. It was the result of many years of study and effort by legal scholars, bankers, and laymen who were attempting to clarify the statutes and decisions that pertained to negotiable instruments. No radical departures from previous interpretations were included in the act, and it is essentially a codification of the law of commercial paper as found in the law merchant. The Uniform Negotiable Instruments Act was adopted by every state and territory except Pennsylvania, which adopted the Uniform Commercial Code, a broader body of law embracing much of the act.

Essentials of a Negotiable Instrument. The obligation embodied in a negotiable instrument has its basis generally in either an order or a promise to pay. The order—as contained, for example, in a bill of exchange—is a demand by one person, the drawer, upon a second person, the drawee, to pay a sum of money to a third person, the payee. The promise occurs where—as in a promissory note—one person, the promisor, agrees to pay a sum of money to a second person, the payee. Negotiability requires that an instrument be payable in a certain and fixed amount of money. The instrument must be as definite as possible; the order or promise it contains must be absolute, without contingencies, and not coupled with any independent or collateral undertaking. A negotiable instrument must be in writing; it must be signed by the maker or drawer; it must be payable either to the bearer or to a specific order, giving the payee the necessary authorization to transfer the instrument; it must identify with certainty the parties concerned with the instrument; and it must be payable on demand or at a fixed and determinable future time. Consideration is an essential factor of a negotiable instrument just as it is with other types of contracts, but a consideration need not be indicated upon the face of the instrument. See CONTRACT; CONSIDERATION.

Transfer. The transfer of an instrument payable to bearer ordinarily is accomplished by a mere delivery. An order instrument generally is transferred by requiring an indorsement along with delivery. The indorsement, which must pertain to the entire instrument and not merely to part of it, passes legal title to the transferee and makes the indorser a surety for the drawer, who has primary liability (see FIDELITY AND SURETY BONDS). Indorsers may be liable in the order of their signatures on the instrument.

Payment and Dishonor. To obtain payment, the holder of the instrument must present it at the proper time to the person liable for the obligation. A demand instrument must be presented within a reasonable time; what constitutes a reasonable time depends upon such factors as the custom of the trade or business, the relationship between the parties, and the nature of the instrument. An instrument that is not payable on demand must be presented on the day of maturity. A negotiable instrument is discharged by payment made in due course by or for the person primarily liable; by an intentional cancellation of the instrument by the holder; by any other act by the holder that would discharge any similar simple contract; and when the person primarily liable for payment is also the holder on the maturity date.

A negotiable instrument is considered to be dishonored when it is duly presented and payment is refused or cannot be obtained. Once an instrument has been dishonored, the holder gains the right of recourse against parties who are secondarily liable, such as previous indorsers—provided they are given due notice of the dishonor. See ASSIGNMENT; BILL OF EXCHANGE; BOND; CHECK; DRAFT; INDORSEMENT; PROMISSORY NOTE.

NEGRI, ADA, 1870–1945, Italian poet, was born in Lodi and taught school at Motta Visconti, 1888–92. She won fame with her *Fatalità* (1892), a protest against poverty and oppression. In 1893 she became a professor of literature in the Normal School of Milan. *Tempeste* (1895) was also a condemnation of social injustice, but the violence of her early works gave way to gentle lamentation in *Maternità* (1904) and most of her later poems including *Dal profondo* (1910), *Esilio* (1914), *Finestre alte* (1923), *Sorelle* (1929), *Il dono* (1936). She also wrote the autobiographical novel *Stella Matlutina* (1921). She was the first woman to be elected, 1940, to the Italian academy founded by the Fascist government.

NEGRIN, JUAN, 1887–1956, head of the Loyalist (republican) government during most of the Spanish Civil War, was born in Tenerife in the Canary Islands. He studied medicine and became professor of physiology at the University of Madrid. A leader of the Socialists, he was appointed minister of finance shortly after the outbreak of civil war, 1936. Negrín succeeded Francisco Largo Caballero as prime minister in 1937. His government was overthrown by a military coup d'état led by Gen. José Miaja, 1939, and Negrín was forced to flee to France. He headed España Combatiente, an organization that opposed the Spanish republican government-in-exile in Mexico. España Combatiente eventually, in 1945, recognized the government-in-exile and Negrín lived in retirement in London and Paris after that time.

NEGRI SEMBILAN, state of the Federation of Malaysia, on the W coast of the Malay Peninsula; bounded by the states of Pahang on the N, Johore on the E, Malacca on the S, and Selangor and the Strait of Malacca on the W; area 2,580 sq. mi.; pop. (1961 est.) 423,000. Negri Sembilan has a low, fertile, coastal plain and mountain spurs entering from the east; higher valleys and ranges are densely timbered. The only harbor is Port Dickson, connected by rail with Seremban, the capital, situated on the main Malayan rail line from Singapore to Penang. Rice, tapioca, rubber, coconuts, fruits, and spices are cultivated; tin mining is important, and gold and other minerals are found. The state was a part of the East Indian kingdom of Madjapahit in the fourteenth century. Negri Sembilan and other Malay states came under British protection in the late nineteenth century and with Perak, Selangor, and Pahang formed the Federated Malay States in 1895. Negri Sembilan itself is a federation of nine small states, governed by a sultan. In 1948 the state became a unit of the Federation of Malaya. There were no changes in boundaries of Malayan states when the Federation of Malaysia was formed Sept. 16, 1963.

NEGRITO, a brown-skinned Negroid pygmy found in the Philippines, Malay Peninsula, interior of New Guinea, and in the Congo Valley area of Africa. Although Negritos have an average height of less than 5 feet they are generally well proportioned. Unlike most Negroids they have round or bullet-shaped heads. Their noses are typically broad and flat, their lips thick and everted, and all possess very curly or frizzy hair.

U.P.I.

Calling for equal opportunities, more than 200,000 Negroes and whites marched in Washington in 1963.

Negrito culture is a simple one. Negritos are usually hunters and food gatherers, although in New Guinea they have engaged in agriculture. Their houses are mere shelters or windbreaks made of saplings and leaves, readily abandoned whenever food is scarce. Negritos have few furnishings other than bamboo tubes, baskets, mats, and weapons. Clothing usually consists of strips of beaten bark or leaves. Negritos use the bow and arrow, but in the Malay Peninsula they have imitated their neighbors and hunt with blowguns and poison darts. Except in the Andaman Islands and the interior of New Guinea, Negritos speak the language of their neighbors. Experts believe that their native dialects are unrelated to other languages. Wherever Negritos have come into contact with more advanced peoples they have rapidly assimilated, and anthropologists believe that they will eventually become extinct.

FAY-COOPER COLE

NEGRO, U.S. The more than 22 million Negroes in the United States are a distinct social category but are not genetically distinct enough to be considered a race or a subrace. Although the African slaves taken to the New World were of the Negroid race, there was soon considerable interbreeding with whites, in large measure through the white slave owner's taking of Negro concubines. Consequently, a majority of U.S. Negroes today have some Caucasian ancestry, and a significant minority have more Caucasian than Negroid ancestry. Because of the varying degrees of Caucasoid ancestry and because the original Negro slaves in North America were of different subraces, U.S. Negroes are quite varied in appearance, ranging in skin color from dark brown to lighter than the average European Caucasian. Hair color ranges from very dark brown to red or medium brown. Even those persons who are predominantly Caucasoid genetically and in appearance are considered Negro if their Negroid ancestry, however small, is generally known.

Because of the extensive interbreeding with whites, genetically recessive Negroid features such as marked prognathism do not characterize U.S. Negroes. However, they share a number of characteristic features with their approximately 200 million African kinsmen. These features include thick, everted lips, a broad nose, a round head, kinky hair (which is relatively flat, rather than round, in cross-section), long limbs relative to the length of the trunk of the body, and heavy (and thus dark brown) pigmentation of the skin, hair, and eyes. Some of the taller U.S. Negroes are probably related to the Nilotic peoples, who are the tallest human subrace and have oblong rather than round heads. Many U.S. Negroes resemble, but are not closely related to, the natives of Melanesia, in the South Pacific, who are classified as Negroid by many physical anthropologists.

No genetically based differences between U.S. Negroes and whites in intelligence or in other psychological characteristics have been demonstrated, and most psychologists and social scientists believe that such differences are nonexistent or too

During the period of "slave running," blacks were auctioned to plantation overseers in slave markets.

THE BETTMANN ARCHIVE

BROWN BROTHERS
Nat Turner, leader of an unsuccessful slave revolt in Virginia in 1831, is shown at the moment of his capture.

small to be of practical importance. The average intelligence test scores of white children exceed those of Negroes by several points, the difference being greater in adolescence than at younger ages. However, this difference can result from the considerable average difference in the environmental influences upon the intellectual development of Negroes and whites. Differences in community and family environments may be at least as important as the difference in average quality between Negro and white education, which is great at all levels, from the first grade through college. Intelligence test scores of Negro children are apparently unrelated to their degree of Caucasoid ancestry, when comparisons are made among children with similar social and economic backgrounds. The upper limits of measured intelligence are about the same for Negroes and whites.

Economic Status. Negroes are the largest economically disadvantaged ethnic minority in the United States, and comprise about 11 per cent of the population. The birthrate of Negroes has long been greater than that of whites; therefore, when the heavy immigration of whites to the United States was stopped by legislation in 1924, and when the difference in Negro and white death rates fell well below the difference in birthrates, Negroes began to increase slowly as a percentage of the total population. The higher birthrate of Negroes in the United States is largely the result of their lower average income and education. Poor and poorly educated people of all ethnic categories have unusually high birthrates. At the higher educational and economic levels, Negroes and whites have similar birthrates, and some comparisons have shown the birthrate of well-educated Negroes to be lower than that of whites with the same amount of education. Therefore, as Negroes approach educational and economic equality with whites, their percentage in the total population is expected to become stable, probably at less than 15 per cent.

Population. Historically, Negroes were highly concentrated in the Deep South, but since World War I, and especially since World War II, there has been heavy Negro migration to the Northeast and Midwest, and more recently to the Far West. In 1910 almost 90 per cent of all U.S. Negroes lived in the South, but the percentage declined to 77 in 1940, to 60 in 1960, and to 53 in 1968. This interregional migration has been accompanied by rapid urbanization. Whereas in 1910 just over one fourth of all Negroes, compared with half of all whites, were urban, the proportion of Negroes in towns and cities now exceeds three fourths and is slightly higher than the urban proportion of whites. Furthermore, the Negro population is highly concentrated in large metropolitan areas. In 1968, 68 per cent of all Negroes, but only 64 per cent of all whites, were metropolitan. Outside the South rural Negroes are rare, and relatively few live in small towns and suburban communities. In all regions, metropolitan Negroes are highly concentrated in the central cities. In 1968, 79 per cent of the metropolitan Negroes, but only 41 per cent of the metropolitan whites, lived in the center of cities rather than in suburbs and fringe areas. About twice as many Negroes now live in city ghettos as live in southern rural areas and small towns, where most Negroes lived as recently as 1940.

In all U.S. communities, Negroes are largely segregated from whites in place of residence. In many communities, there are practically no city blocks in which both Negroes and whites reside. In spite of recent important changes in other aspects of Negro-white relations, residential segregation has not declined appreciably in any region. In the South, where until recently well-to-do white families and their Negro household servants often lived in the same neighborhoods, residential segregation has increased measurably in recent decades and now is slightly greater than in the North and West. Unlike the partial residential segregation of some other minorities, such as the Jewish minority, the segregation of Negroes is largely involuntary–the result of resistance by whites to Negroes moving into their neighborhoods. Among its many detrimental consequences are limited housing choices and higher

Negroes were discouraged from participating in the Civil War until shortly before its end. Shown below is a Negro infantry company at Fort Lincoln in 1865.

THE BETTMANN ARCHIVE

THE BETTMANN ARCHIVE

W. E. B. DuBois

housing costs for Negroes, and perpetuation of segregation in schools.

Education. Since the beginning of World War II, U.S. Negroes have made substantial economic, occupational, and educational advances, and in several respects they have narrowed the vast socioeconomic gap between themselves and whites. For instance, in 1968 the median years of school completed by nonwhites aged 25 through 29 (more than 90 per cent of all nonwhites in the United States are Negroes) was 12.2, compared with 12.6 for whites–a difference of less than half a year. As recently as 1960 the difference was 1.5 years, and in 1940 it was about 3 years. The effects of this educational gain are mitigated, however, by the substantial difference remaining in the average quality of the education of Negroes and whites. In the fall of 1965, Negro twelfth-grade pupils averaged more than three grade levels below whites in national standardized achievement tests in reading and other school subjects. There were substantial but smaller differences at the lower grades. Therefore, a considerable educational gap still exists between Negroes and whites that is not revealed in the data on years of school completed.

There is widespread agreement among educators and social scientists that the overall inferiority of Negro education in the United States grows in large measure out of racial segregation in the schools. Northern ghetto schools as well as southern all-Negro schools often have inferior facilities and less experienced and less qualified teachers. More important, in a typical predominantly Negro school, lower-class children have contacts mainly with other lower-class children and are denied the intellectual stimulation that comes from contacts and competition with children from more privileged homes and neighborhoods. Although enforced racial segregation in the public schools has long been contrary to the U.S. Supreme Court's interpretation of the Constitution (beginning with the landmark decision in the case of *Brown* v. *Board of Education* in 1954), 87 per cent of all Negro first-grade pupils (including 72 per cent of those in the metropolitan North and West) were enrolled in predominantly Negro schools in the fall of 1965. Continued segregation results from determined resistance to school integration by many white southerners and from residential segregation in all regions.

Both discrimination and the relatively poor quality of Negro education have prevented Negro occupational gains from increasing in proportion to the gains in amount of education. Although Negro representation in highly rewarded occupations has increased steadily since the beginning of World War II (except for temporary losses immediately after the war), only 31 per cent of all employed nonwhites were in nonmanual and skilled manual occupations in 1967, compared with 63 per cent of all employed whites. Furthermore, in almost all occupations, Negro earnings average well below those of whites. Negro unemployment remained about twice the white rate throughout most of the 1950's and 1960's.

The narrowing of the income gap between Negroes and whites that might be expected from the narrowing of the educational and occupational differences has not occurred. Since the end of World War II the nonwhite family's median income has hovered around 53 or 54 per cent of the white family's median income, rising to a higher level only during the Korean and Vietnam Wars. In 1967 the percentage rose to 62, a record high, but it is not certain that this signals the beginning of a continuing upward trend. The relative economic position of Negroes did not increase from 1947 through 1963, mainly because a decrease in the demand for skilled labor widened the income difference between highly educated and poorly educated workers. Although Negroes who became well educated and moved into higher-level occupations improved their relative economic positions, the more numerous unskilled and semiskilled Negro workers, considered as a whole, lost in relative standing.

NORVAL D. GLENN

History

Slave Trade. The Portuguese slave trade began in 1441, the English in 1562; and by 1600 both were extensive. At the same time the Arabs traded in slaves, which they had acquired usually by capture rather than purchase. No accurate estimate within millions of the number of Africans involved is possible, especially since there were heavy casualties en route to the trading centers and heavier

As director of agricultural research at Tuskegee Institute, botanist George Washington Carver (1860?–1943) developed many new products from peanuts.

THE BETTMANN ARCHIVE

Negro leaders who met in 1963 to plan the March on Washington were (left to right) Whitney Young, Jr., of the National Urban League; A. Philip Randolph, of the Negro American Labor Council; the Rev. Dr. Martin Luther King, Jr., of the Southern Christian Leadership Conference; James Farmer, of the Congress of Racial Equality; and Roy Wilkins, of the National Association for the Advancement of Colored People.

WIDE WORLD PHOTOS

ones on the middle passage, or Atlantic Sea run. It is estimated that six or seven lives were lost for each slave delivered in America. Casualties were less among those sent to Europe and the Middle East.

In 1726 more than 171 ships were engaged in the West Indies slave trade out of Bristol, Liverpool, and London, and about that time the English traffic alone handled between 50,000 and 100,000 slaves a year. Between 1759 and 1803, 642,000 slaves are known to have arrived in Brazil. Slave labor in the West Indies was mainly for the rum and sugar plantations. In the Spanish colonies it served to provide mining labor and personal servants. In the United States slaves were used first for tobacco cultivation and personal service and later, in ever-increasing volume, for rice and cotton cultivation. In the United States alone the slave population increased by 200,000 between 1790 and 1800; by another 300,000 between 1800 and 1810; by 500,000 in the decade 1820–30. There were 4 million slaves in the United States at the beginning of the Civil War.

The American prohibition of the slave trade in 1808 and the British ban of the previous year checked the traffic only superficially; it continued as "slave running" until the Civil War. British emancipation in 1833 had great and immediate effect in British colonies, as did Pres. Abraham Lincoln's Emancipation Proclamation (1863) in the United States. The status of Negroes in both the colonial possessions and the states, however, was destined to reflect for generations the stigma and demoralization of the slave regime, which for some 300 years had transplanted to the United States alone an estimated total of 1.5 million persons–at least 500,000 of whom were smuggled in after the slave trade ban.

The Negro in the New World. As English colonists in the South launched upon an agricultural adventure requiring large investments of capital and laborers, the supply of white indentured servants gradually became inadequate, and the enslavement of African blacks became a convenient consequence. Negroes had been in the New World, however, more than 150 years before this happened. A black cabin boy had sailed with Columbus's fourth voyage in 1502. Blacks had shared in the explorations of Balboa and had accompanied him when he discovered the Pacific; they had been with Hernán Cortés in his conquest of the Aztecs in Mexico; and they had served Pánfilo de Narváez and Alvar Nuñez Cabeza de Vaca in their explorations of the Gulf of Mexico and the Southwest. Estevan, the most famous of such black explorers, became the first man from the Old World to visit present-day New Mexico in his search for the Seven Cities of Cibola.

Africans were introduced for the first time to an English settlement on the American mainland when a Dutch frigate landed its cargo of twenty blacks at Jamestown, Va., in 1619. Even then slavery was far away, and the gradual attrition of the rights of black indentured servants was not completed until 1662, when their status was lowered to service for life by Virginia law. Soon afterward, this prescribed status was adopted by colonists of Maryland, the Carolinas, and other territories.

Contrary to popular opinion, however, blacks were not enslaved because of their greater fitness for labor in a hot climate. Nor could justification for the enslavement of blacks be realistically based upon their savagery and need for cultivation, although this rationalization was used by southern intellectuals. For the Africans had been imported largely from West African areas, most of which possessed highly organized cultures. Their enslavement was a choice among alternatives available to the colonists to increase the economic value of the plantation economy.

Slavery. The choice meant that Europeans would abandon democratic precepts as related to blacks and reserve them only for themselves. Guided by mercantilistic economics, they organized slave labor in a manner that left no chance for personalization among black people. Characterizing every slave code in the colonies, and later in the states of the republic, were the insecurity of the black American's person, the destruction of his dignity, and the elimination of the sanctity of his family. One drop of black blood condemned him to this status, and all so condemned constituted the personal property of their owners. The owner had right to the slave's person as well as to his labor. The slave's physical and social mobility was limited by legal specifications and occurred only through the benevolence of his owner, backed by the rigidity of the system. As the institution matured, a mechanism for developing the "model slave" evolved. The slave was kept constantly under strict discipline; implanted in his mind was a belief in his personal inferiority; the enormity of his master's power was kept before him at all times; in the end, he experienced a childlike dependency upon those whom he served and all members of the class they represented. See SLAVERY.

The process of the institutionalization of slavery was not accomplished, however, without violent rebellion. More than one hundred slave mutinies

Assassinated in 1965, Malcolm X was a passionate exponent of evolving black consciousness in America. His autobiography was published posthumously.

U.P.I.

took place during the period of the slave trade. Uprising at sea eventually represented so great a risk to the slave traders that many took out insurance against it. Individually, slaves committed suicide, wounded themselves, and refused to take food in desperate efforts to reclaim their freedom. As slavery was institutionalized and spread throughout the eastern colonies, rebellion took the form of serious insurrection. In 1663 white indentured servants and blacks launched a combined insurrection against their masters in Gloucester county, Va. That colony suffered a rash of insurrections between 1687 and 1730; there were also serious insurrections in South Carolina in 1720, 1730, 1738, and 1739, and in New York in 1712 and 1741.

The philosophy that revolutionary American colonists used to justify their independence from Great Britain stimulated blacks to institute petitions for their freedom, to file court cases to gain their emancipation, and finally to take up arms in defense of the colonies' aspiration. At this time many revolutionary intellectuals and leaders recognized the inconsistency in their position as oppressed colonists and their role as slaveholders. John Woolman, Anthony Benezet, Benjamin Franklin, and Benjamin Rush were among the first white Americans to undertake antislavery activities.

A serious campaign for their freedom was launched by slaves in Boston, Mass., on Apr. 20, 1773. Acting in behalf of their fellow slaves, Peter Bestes, Sambo Freeman, Felix Holbrook, and Chester Joie petitioned the assembly for their emancipation so that they could transport themselves "to some part of the coast of Africa" to settle. Another group submitted a petition on May 25, 1774; basing their request for freedom upon their natural rights, they appealed in behalf of their children, whom they requested be freed at the age of 21. Other blacks in Massachusetts sued their masters in courts, demanding that their owners show by what right they held title to the blacks. An early case was that of John Siffin, who in 1701 sued for his freedom on the grounds that his master had promised to free him. In 1766 Jenny Slew, another slave, brought suit against her owner, John Whipple, on the grounds that he was restraining her liberties. Though practically all of these cases were won by the slaves, the litigation process was too slow and expensive to constitute a major force toward emancipation. Both the petitions and the freedom suits, however, served to foster antislavery activities and to bring emancipation closer for slaves in New England and the Middle Antlantic regions.

Undaunted by the slow process of litigation and devoted to the colonial revolutionary cause, which they had come to define in terms of their own freedom, black Americans joined in combat against the English crown. The first occasion for involvement came on Mar. 5, 1770, when Crispus Attucks, supposedly a Boston Negro, became the first American to die for independence during the Boston Massacre. Blacks followed Attucks in combat, reinforcing the slaves' claim of a role in the Revolutionary War. Peter Salem, a slave at Farmingham, Mass., and Salem Poor, another Negro, distinguished themselves in the Revolutionary army. See Attucks, Crispus; Boston Massacre.

Despite much official vacillation that delayed the large-scale use of Negroes in the war effort, Lord Dunmore's proclamation of Nov. 23, 1775, facilitated the official enlistment of blacks as legitimate members of the Continental forces. Their enlistment grew rapidly, and they eventually constituted about 3,000 out of 300,00 American soldiers. They participated in practically every battle between 1775 and 1781. Black soldiers Prince Whipple and Oliver Cromwell were with George Washington when he crossed the Delaware. Lemuel Haynes, later a distinguished minister, participated in the Battle of Lexington; and the American victory at Stony Point in 1779 was considerably influenced by the espionage activities of the black soldier Pompey.

ERNEST RESHOVSKY-PIX

Winner of the Nobel peace prize in 1964, the Rev. Dr. Martin Luther King, Jr. was the most influential U.S. Negro leader since Booker T. Washington.

The black contribution to the war was not in vain. After independence was gained, slavery was virtually eliminated in the North, and the Northwest Ordinance of 1787 curtailed the spread of slavery to the new territories that were being added to the infant republic.

Another form of pressure against slavery was the achievement of individual blacks, who, despite the limitations placed upon their development by the slave regime, managed to rise in the social order. The slave girl Phyllis Wheatley was an admired colonial poetess, who went to England and was entertained in literary circles and at court. By the time the nation was founded, Benjamin Banneker, another slave, had become a prominent astronomer, and in 1791 he was appointed to assist in the survey of Washington, D.C. Paul Cuffe, a slave who became a successful shipbuilder, participated in many of the petitions for freedom that the slaves presented to the Massachusetts Assembly and began a movement for colonizing Negroes in Africa. A southerner, John Chavis, became a noted minister under the official guidance of the Presbyterian Church. He developed private schools for whites and blacks and taught some of the South's leading statesmen.

Abolitionism and the Civil War. At the beginning of the nineteenth century there developed an abolitionist movement sponsored by various antislavery societies. Several forces contributed to its effectiveness: the growing body of antislavery writings, the gradual development of a free Negro population, and the political conflicts that were generated around the slavery question as new territories were added to the Union. Manumission and antislavery societies, which had been relatively ineffective before the Revolutionary War, grew in size and influence after independence. The earliest such society was founded in Pennsylvania in 1775. Although these groups met strong resistance from the southern states, their influence grew rapidly. Through private manumission, self-purchase, northern emancipation, and escape via underground railroad, a large free Negro population had developed by 1800. Despite the laws of southern states that restricted the teaching of slaves, a corps of black in-

STEVE SCHAPIRO-BLACK STAR

Among many important modern U.S. Negro authors are Langston Hughes (right), 1902–67, a leading American poet; and prose writers James Baldwin (top left), 1924– , and Ralph Ellison (bottom left), 1914– . Baldwin wrote novels and eloquent essays on the black urban experience. Ellison's novel *Invisible Man* was acclaimed a masterpiece of fiction, winning the 1953 National Book Award.

HENRI CARTIER-BRESSON

U.P.I.

tellectuals sprouted within the slave regime. Some, such as Norbert Rillieux of New Orleans, who perfected an evaporating pan that revolutionized the sugar-refining industry, were inventors. Many, such as Daniel A. Payne of South Carolina, David Walker of North Carolina, and Nat Turner of Virginia, had acquired a high degree of literacy. Walker, through his *Appeal*, which was published in 1829, stimulated the slaves to rebel. Turner led the South's most threatening insurrection in 1831. Probably the greatest antislavery influence originating among blacks, however, was created by those who had gained literacy within the slave regime and then escaped to the North. The autobiographies of Thomas H. Jones, the Reverend Richard Sinquefield, Josiah Henson, and many others were used by abolitionist societies to dramatize the evils of slavery. Frederick Douglass, the most eloquent of this group, wielded the greatest influence. A vital force in the antislavery society founded by William Lloyd Garrison in 1832, Douglass published the widely circulated Negro newspaper *North Star* beginning in 1847. *The Liberator*, organized by Garrison, was another important abolitionist publication. Other blacks who played significant roles in the abolitionist movement were William Wells Brown, Frances Ellen Watkins Harper, and Robert Purvis. See ABOLITIONIST; TURNER, NAT.

The question of slavery was a major U.S. political issue in the 1850's and 1860's and an important cause of the Civil War. Despite the Dred Scott decision of 1857 and other federal attempts to avoid a rift in the nation, determined abolitionists continued to assist the escape of runaway slaves. They debated the issue so essential to the election of 1860, and chose Abraham Lincoln and the Republican party as the least of several evils. Some even turned to Gerrit Smith as the candidate who most directly expressed their aspiration to eliminate slavery at whatever cost to national unity. After the start of the Civil War the abolitionists kept the issue of slavery before President Lincoln and supported each instance when Union generals attempted to emancipate refugee slaves seeking the protection of Union armies as they cut across the South. The Emancipation Proclamation issued on Sept. 22, 1862, to take effect Jan. 1, 1863, was a product of the tenacity of militant abolitionists as much as of the military conditions in the field. While it was Lincoln's signature that eventually freed the slaves, it was the persistent efforts of abolitionists that helped the president to make up his mind. See EMANCIPATION PROCLAMATION; SMITH, GERRIT.

In the struggle for their emancipation the black masses were not inactive. As in the case of the Revolutionary War, they sought to play an active military role but were faced with opposition to their participation until the circumstance of war compelled the Union to reverse its policy. The South incorporated its slaves as combatants. Acting out of self-defense, the North retaliated with large-scale enlistment of blacks, many of whom distinguished themselves in combat. Sgt. William Carney won the Congressional Medal of Honor for his heroism at Fort Wagner; Joachim Pease, a seaman, was awarded the Navy Medal of Honor; Harriet Tubman, an ex-slave and active abolitionist, who had conducted more than 300 slaves to freedom via the underground railroad, was a valuable spy for the Union side; and Robert Smalls, the black pilot of a Confederate gunboat, rendered significant service to the Union when he surrendered his vessel to the Union fleet. All together, more than 186,000 Negroes served on the Union side.

Reconstruction. After the war the dislocations suffered by 4 million freed slaves posed the largest problem of social welfare the United States had yet experienced. By necessity, these people found themselves virtual wards of the federal government. On June 13, 1866, Congress passed the Fourteenth Amendment, which made Negroes citizens of the United States and reinforced this citizenship with a clause that gave them equal protection of the laws. It sent the Fifteenth Amendment to the states in February, 1869, and on Mar. 30, 1870, made the voting rights of the black man part of constitutional law. Blacks arose to political prominence in the South. P.B.S. Pinchback became lieutenant-governor of Louisiana; Joseph Rainey was a South Carolina congressman; B. K. Bruce, a former slave, was a Mississippi senator. In the period 1870–76, 14 Negroes entered Congress as representatives of southern states. During these years, black representatives at state constitutional conventions and

CULVER PICTURES

PUBLIFOTO-PIX

The black contribution to the American musical heritage has been vast. Blues singer Bessie Smith (left), 1900?–1937, influenced generations of jazz singers. Duke Ellington (top right), 1899– , was the twentieth century's greatest jazz conductor-composer. Lyric soprano Leontyne Price (shown dressed as Cleopatra, bottom right), 1927– , became one of the world's leading opera stars.

GARY RENAUD-PIX

in the legislative halls helped fashion the South's public school system. Black political ascendancy was soon erased, however, as other issues claimed the attention of the federal government.

The reassertion of southern white supremacy was accomplished by a series of legal maneuvers that were upheld by the Supreme Court. In the Slaughterhouse cases of 1873, the Supreme Court in effect limited the extent of the fourteenth amendment as it applied to Negroes, differentiating between U.S. and state citizenship. It exposed blacks to the discriminatory will of private individuals in the cases of *U.S.* v. *Reese*, *U.S.* v. *Cruikshank*, and *Hall* v. *De Cuir;* and it virtually deprived them of many of their rights of citizenship in the civil rights cases of 1883. By the close of the century, practically every southern state had enacted laws that created a system of racial segregation.

Segregation and Negro Education. Segregation, constituted by law at the beginning of the twentieth century, created two separate community orders wherever blacks and whites resided in the same towns, installed rules of interracial etiquette that placed blacks in a position permanently inferior to that of whites, promoted a racial division of labor through which the occupational mobility of black people was limited, and muted the voice of the black voter so as to render the Negro American politically impotent. A significant force in the socialization of inferiority was the system of public education, which Negro Americans had helped to develop in the South during its period of Reconstruction. Public barriers to the education of Negroes developed as early as 1885, and when writers such as Thomas Dixon, Jr., expressed the white southern view of blacks as alien and unassimilable, it became clear that the South would tolerate only the kind of education for freedmen that would prepare them for a condition of separation and inferiority.

The leader of the compromise effort in behalf of freedman education was Gen. S. C. Armstrong, an officer of Negro troops during the Civil War. He founded Hampton Normal and Agricultural Institute for Negroes in 1868 under the auspices of the American Missionary Association. In 1872 he presented his program of industrial education for Negroes to the National Education Association, and he succeeded in winning strong converts for his educational policies at the First Mohonk Conference on the Negro question in 1890. Booker T. Washington, General Armstrong's chief disciple, extended the concept of Negro industrial education. Having entered Hampton in 1872, he gained direct access to the general's ideas, won his confidence, and in 1881 founded and became head of Tuskegee Institute. In 1884, when Washington spoke before a meeting of the National Education Association in Madison, Wis., he showed that Tuskegee had been organized according to Armstrong's concept of white and black coexistence and mutual aid. Washington's presentation of his formally structured ideology of industrial education at the Atlanta Exposition in 1895 established him as chief spokesman for the Negro American. Washington recommended that blacks surrender their aspiration to have automatic equality and seek to win white respect by achieving excellence in every endeavor they were permitted to pursue within the caste system. Since blacks were allowed to be farmers, domestic servants, and laborers, Washington advocated that their education be geared to make them more proficient in these occupations. Since they lived in separate communities, he suggested strongly that their commercial education be shaped to help them develop and operate their own business institutions, and that their higher education provide professional services for their own schools, hospitals, and other segregated institutions. See ARMSTRONG, SAMUEL CHAPMAN; WASHINGTON, BOOKER TALIAFERRO.

The position that Washington advocated was consistent with that of other leaders and agencies that had begun to support Negro schools and colleges. The George Peabody Fund, established in 1867, supported black schools in the South. John F. Slater, a Connecticut textile industrialist, founded in 1882 the Slater Fund for the development and support of Negro industrial training schools in the rural South. John D. Rockefeller established the General Education Board in 1902 to promote education without distinction of race, sex, or creed. In 1905 Anna T. Jeanes, the Quaker daughter of a Philadelphia merchant, began the Jeanes Fund to develop rural elementary schools, and a group of black women known as Jeanes Supervisors carried the idea of industrial education to the homes and schools under their jurisdiction. All of these philanthropic efforts reflected Washington's philosophy of education. His position, however, was not unchallenged.

Opposition to his educational philosophy grew as he became more famous, and it eventually polarized black leadership in the United States. Serious opposition began with attacks on Washington by Monroe Trotter, owner of the *Boston Guardian*. The strongest opposition came from W. E. B. DuBois, who had attended Fisk University, taken a Ph.D. at Harvard, and studied at the University of Berlin. After spending his early youth in Massachusetts, DuBois gained his earliest experiences of segregation at Fisk and later as a teacher of sociology at Atlanta University. In his book *Souls of Black Folk* (1903), DuBois countered Washington's philosophy. He extolled the virtues of higher education and the need to educate "the talented tenth," proposed the development of sympathy and knowledge of the world as it involves human relations, and charged that Washington's ideology sacrificed men for workers. "If we make technical skill the object of education," he contended, "we may possess artisans but not, in nature, men." While Washington placed his confidence in the benevolence of southern people and the goal of success in business, DuBois believed in the intellectual and leadership potential of a Negro elite that would place the destiny of black people in their own hands. See DUBOIS, WILLIAM EDWARD BURGHARDT.

The Negro Organizes. During the controversy, economic conditions and educational opportunities for Negroes deteriorated, philanthropic support waned, and discrimination in the apportionment of public funds hindered their most advantageous use. The deprivation of black sharecroppers caused many to seek refuge in the large industrial cities of the North. Beginning around 1880, and reaching a peak during World War I, blacks from the South made a great exodus to northern cities, which rapidly became as segregated as those in the South.

As discrimination and deprivation grew around them, black Americans became polarized in their defense strategies. One group, aimed at finding equality within the general society, pursued its goals through the strength of the constitutional rights left to them, through the development of a new image for black people, and through the formation of a national social service agency to facilitate the normal adjustment of southern rural Negroes to the northern urban environment. The other group sought to develop a separate black society.

The most important element of the first group was led by DuBois, who in 1905 established the Niagara Movement, which gained the support of several Negro organizations working toward equality. It directed its attention toward the problems of disfranchisement, inadequate housing and educational opportunities, job discrimination, and slum conditions in which black children were raised. The Niagara Movement later merged with the National Association for the Advancement of Colored People, which was created in 1910 under the leadership of Mary White Ovington. Accepting the aspirations of the Niagara Movement, the NAACP developed a system of national branches through which it came to function as the most potent effort to assimilate black people. Using the strategy of court litigation built around the equal protection clause of the Constitution, the NAACP moved strongly against disfranchisement and inadequate educational opportunities, and mildly against segregated housing. Beginning in 1918, it moved through such cases as *Chandler* v. *Neff* (1924), *Nixon* v. *Herndon* (1927), and *U.S.* v. *Classic* (1941), to win complete Negro voting rights with the *Smith* v. *Allwright* decision (1944). About 1936, the NAACP launched its campaign to win for black teachers salaries equivalent to those of white teachers. By 1950, after placing more than 30 cases before the federal courts, the campaign was successfully completed. A bid for school desegregation, begun in 1935 with the case of *Donald G. Murray* v. *The University of Maryland*, resulted in the desegregation of higher education at the professional and graduate levels, and in 1954, with the case of *Brown* v. *Board of Education*, it succeeded in destroying all legal basis for public school segregation. See NATIONAL ASSOCIATION FOR THE ADVANCEMENT OF COLORED PEOPLE.

BERT ANDREWS

Lonne Elder III's play *Ceremonies in Dark Old Men* was a powerful Negro drama of the 1960's.

While the NAACP challenged segregation in the courts, a group of black intellectuals attempted to refurbish the black image. Carter G. Woodson, a Harvard-trained black historian, founded in 1915 the Association for the Study of Negro Life and History. Through its *Journal of Negro History* and the many excellent historical and social science works that grew out of this movement, the history of the Negro American was revived. Influenced by James Weldon Johnson and a sophisticated group of white intellectuals who sponsored the works of black writers, poets such as Langston Hughes, Countee Cullen, and Claude McKay gained prominence. Black novelists and dramatists won equal fame, and both groups fostered a self-pride that was badly needed among blacks.

Next, organizations were formed to speak directly to the mass of the black poor. Founded in 1911, the National Urban League played an important role in facilitating the expansion of Negro job opportunities. Another movement, operated through the Universal Negro Improvement Association (U.N.I.A.) was founded in 1914 by Marcus Garvey, a Jamaican. It sought the establishment of a new nation in Africa; the revival of the opulence and nobility of the black heritage, which subservience under whites had erased; and the development of economic programs that would render blacks secure in a separate economy. Although Garvey estimated that he had a following of approximately 6 million, there is evidence that his following reached only one fifth of that number. Though blacks had previously manifested the aspiration to be apart from American society and culture, never before had the enthusiasm for such a movement been so great. During the Depression years a second separatist design for the black urban masses was created. Elijah Poole (later Elijah Muhammad) and Wali Farad founded the Nation of Islam, commonly called the Black Muslims. Incorporating many elements of Islam, the movement, which represented an emotional alienation from all that was white, sought to create a black state within the United States. Strictly regulating the behavior of its members, it constituted a large number of urban blacks as a separate community—alienated from whites and unafraid of them. Malcolm X, one of Elijah Muhammad's chief disciples, embraced the faith on his release from prison and became the sect's most articulate spokesman. Mainly through his speeches the sect gained the image of a "hate white" movement, and his influence stimulated a more general orientation toward separatism between black and white. See GARVEY, MARCUS.

In 1960 a sit-in movement started by students of North Carolina Agricultural and Technical College, a Negro institution, spread rapidly to include students in black colleges throughout the South. It was inspired by the Montgomery, Ala., bus boycott of 1955, whose leader, the Rev. Dr. Martin Luther King, developed a new order in race relations. The nonviolent methods inspired by King shaped the Southern Christian Leadership Conference, which he founded. Faithful to the nonviolent strategy until his assassination in 1967, King made a greater impact upon the American conscience in the area of race relations than any other American since Booker T. Washington. Although the goals of the sit-ins were limited, they succeeded in ending segregation in public places in practically every southern city. See KING, MARTIN LUTHER.

Black Power. The slow process of desegregation that followed the Supreme Court's decision of 1954 sparked other and more militant black movements. One of these movements was launched by the Student Nonviolent Coordinating Committee (SNCC), a group of students who first came together to direct the sit-ins more efficiently. This group also experienced frustration, especially as it sought to increase the southern Negro's political power in response to an opportunity afforded by the Civil Rights Act of 1964. The frustrations led to greater aggression and the development of the concept of Black Power. As postulated by the leader of this movement, Stokely Carmichael, Black Power was an effort to restore into their own hands the power and destiny of black people by electing black public officials and by reconstructing the economics of black communities through cooperatives and new economic arrangements. In this movement, separatism was conceived of as a withdrawal to last only as long as it would take for blacks to gain enough power to deal with the white world. In 1970 this movement continued to be important. The movement toward black nationalism also continued through the Black Muslims; and black writers such as LeRoi Jones and Eldridge Cleaver emerged as passionate exponents of the awakened black consciousness. See CIVIL LIBERTIES AND RIGHTS; DEMOCRACY. HENRY ALLEN BULLOCK

BIBLIOG.–Albert P. Blaustein and Clarence C. Ferguson, Jr., *Desegregation and the Law* (1957); Leonard Broom and Norval D. Glenn, *Transformation of the Negro American* (1965); Henry Allen Bullock, *A History of Negro Education in the South from 1619 to the Present* (1967); W. Haywood Burns, *The Voices of Negro Protest in America* (1963); Kenneth B. Clark, *Dark Ghetto: Dilemmas of Social Power* (1965); Bertram Doyle, *The Etiquette of Race Relations in the South* (1937); Stanley M. Elkins, *Slavery: A Problem in American Institutional and Intellectual Life* (1962); Essien U. Essien-Udom, *Black Nationalism: A Search for an Identity in America* (1962); John Hope Franklin, *From Slavery to Freedom: A History of Negro Americans* (1967); Lorenzo J. Green, *The Negro in Colonial New England* (1968); Louis R. Harlan, *Separate and Unequal: Public School Campaigns and Racism in the Southern Seaboard States, 1901–1915* (1968); William L. Katz, *Eyewitness: The Negro in American History* (1967); Ullin W. Leavell, *Philanthropy in Negro Education* (1930); Louis E. Lomax, *The Negro Revolt* (1962); Milton Meltzer, ed., *In Their Own Words: A History of the American Negro, 1619–1865; 1865–1916; 1619–1966* (1967); Loren Miller, *The Petitioners: The Story of the Supreme Court of the United States and the Negro* (1967); Pauli Murray, ed., *States' Laws on Race and Color* (1951); Gunnar Myrdal, *An American Dilemma* (1944); Talcott Parsons and Kenneth B. Clark, eds., *The Negro American* (1966); Thomas F. Pettigrew, *A Profile of the Negro American* (1964); Benjamin Quarles, *The Negro in the Civil War* (1953); Kenneth M. Stampp, *The Peculiar Institution* (1956); Karl E. Taeuber and Alma F. Taeuber, *Negroes in Cities* (1965).

NEGRO RIVER, N South America, a major tributary of the Amazon River; rises along the Venezuela-Colombia border, flows for 1,400 miles S into Brazil and then SE to its junction with the Amazon at Manaus. Most of the river's tributaries come from the north. The largest is the Branco. The Negro's headwaters are connected via a natural waterway, the Casiquiare River, to the Orinoco River. River boats and hydroplanes serve as the chief transportation means along the river. The Negro largely flows through tropical rain forest. Some rubber, nuts, and other forest products are gathered, and there is some lumbering in its valley. Grassland areas, away from the river, are used for cattle grazing.

NEGROS, island, fourth largest in the Philippines, in the Visayan group between Panay on the NW and Cebu on the E; maximum length and width 135 and about 50 miles respectively; the area is 4,905 square miles. Negros is quite mountainous, the main range running north-south along the eastern length and reaching an elevation of over 8,000 feet near the center of the island. Although there are no large rivers Negros is well drained, and the interior is heavily forested. The central forest area is thinly inhabited by tribes thought to be Negritos. The coastal areas are densely populated by Visayans, an intelligent and vigorous people whose chief occupation is agriculture. Sugarcane, rice, tobacco, coconuts, hemp, and corn are produced; some livestock is raised; and fishing, lumbering, and copper mining are engaged in. Industries include distilling, and the manufacturing of handicraft, sugar products, pulp and paper, chemicals, nails, and fabrics. The island is divided into two provinces, Negros Occidental and Negros Oriental. The largest city on the island is Bacolod, capital of Negros Occidental province. (For population, see Philippines map in Atlas.)

NEGROS OCCIDENTAL, province, Philippines, NW Negros Island; area, 2,989 square miles. Apart from the extreme north and northwest, the province is mountainous; the highest point is Mt. Canlaon (over 8,000 ft.). The interior is forested. The densely populated coastal plain is one of the major agricultural areas of the Philippines, producing rice, corn, and sugarcane. Bacolod is the capital and chief city. (For population, see Philippines map in Atlas.)

NEGROS ORIENTAL, province, Philippines; SE Negros Island and including the adjacent Siquijor Island; area, 2,053 square miles. The Negros portion of the province—the major part—consists almost entirely of forest-covered mountains; the highest point is Cuernos de Negros (more than 6,000 ft.). Population is concentrated on the narrow, eastern coastal plain, where corn and abaca are chief crops. Siquijor is also a densely populated agricultural area. Negros Oriental became a separate province in 1890 when the military district of Negros was divided. Dumaguete is the capital city. (For population, see Philippines map in Atlas.)

NEHEMIAH, Hebrew leader, the colleague of Ezra in rebuilding Jerusalem and reorganizing the Jewish nation after the Exile. He was the son of Hachaliah, and one brother, Hanani, is mentioned (Neh. 1:1–2). As cupbearer to Artaxerxes I (Longimanus) in Shushan, the capital of Persia, he won his master's favor and was commissioned to go to Jerusalem as governor (about 445 B.C.). In the face of strong opposition from their neighbors, he led the Jews in rebuilding the walls of the city in 52 days (Neh. 6:15). He instructed Ezra to read the Law of

Moses to the people, who rallied to the support of its requirements regarding observance of the Sabbath, the institutions of the Temple, and foreign marriages. After 12 years as governor, Nehemiah returned to his old post in Persia but, possibly during the next year, obtained leave to go again to Jerusalem. There he found that many abuses had gained a foothold, but these he rectified by immediately instituting reforms. During his governorship Nehemiah accepted no pay. In addition, he entertained regularly at his table 150 Jewish leaders and others.

The Book of Nehemiah. Modern scholars generally agree that the books of Ezra and Nehemiah were originally one book and that, together with I and II Chronicles, they were written by "the chronicler." Jewish tradition attributes the book to Nehemiah, and the evidence of his personal memoirs is seen in several passages (Neh. 1:1–7, 5; 12:27–43; 13:4–31). Earlier documents, such as the list of those who had returned first to Jerusalem, were also incorporated (Neh. 7:6–73); the rest of the book was based on historical sources. Its date is placed as early as the latter half of the fifth century B.C. and as late as 330 B.C. The Book of Nehemiah is organized as follows: (1) Chapters 1–7, Nehemiah's return and rebuilding of the walls of Jerusalem; (2) 8–10, promulgation of the Law of Moses by Ezra, and its results; (3) 11:1–12:26, list of the families to dwell in Jerusalem and in other cities; (4) 12:27–13:3, dedication of the wall of Jerusalem; (5) 13:4–31, Nehemiah's second governorship and further reforms.

NEHRU, JAWAHARLAL, 1889–1964, Indian statesman and first prime minister of India, born in Allahabad to an affluent Brahman family. Nehru was privately tutored until 1905, when he was sent to Harrow, the English public school. In 1907 he entered Trinity College, Cambridge, to study science. He afterward studied law at the Inner Temple in London.

After passing his bar examinations in the summer of 1912, Nehru returned to India. Because his father, Motilal Nehru, was head of a successful law firm, it was assumed that the young Nehru would pursue a legal career. However, finding legal practice too confining, he turned to politics.

Political currents in India were following a nationalist course. The Indian National Congress, founded in 1885 to mobilize independence aspirations, had begun to gather momentum in the years immediately prior to World War I. In 1916 Jawaharlal attended its annual session at Lucknow. There he met Mohandas Karamchand Gandhi, who had returned in 1915 from South Africa, where his political efforts had resulted in a successful, nonviolent revolt against the policies of General Smuts. Gandhi's attendance at the 1916 session of the congress marked his formal entry into Indian politics. At this session the congress joined with the Muslim league in a new demand for self-government in India. Extremist leaders had returned to the congress after nearly a decade's exile, and the independence movement took on sudden new impetus. Nehru joined wholeheartedly.

In 1916 Nehru married Kamala, a striking and brilliant woman who died of tuberculosis in 1936. Their only child, Indira, became in 1966 the first woman prime minister of India.

In 1919 the British moved to curb mounting unrest in India with the repressive Rowlatt Act. Gandhi seized the opportunity to organize a general strike and fast to oppose the law. In Amritsar, in the Punjab, troops opened fire on demonstrators, killing about 400. The incident served to weld the sympathies of Nehru and his father to Gandhi's cause and leadership. At the 1920 session of the congress at Amritsar, Nehru's father achieved the presidency, but the initiative had clearly passed to Gandhi.

CULVER PICTURES

Jawaharlal Nehru

Much to the chagrin of his more moderate father, Nehru plunged headlong into the radical struggle initiated by Gandhi. Nehru and Gandhi worked together for most of the period until Gandhi's death, bound by an affection and respect remarkable for men of such dissimilar temperaments. Nehru was an agnostic, whereas Gandhi was deeply religious; Nehru was a revolutionary, Gandhi a conservative. Moreover, Nehru's rationalist philosophy frequently contrasted with Gandhi's fasts and his reliance on an "inner voice." Ultimately, Nehru became the leader of a faction of the National Congress party that advocated socialist reform and industrialization in opposition to Gandhi's agrarian emphasis. Notwithstanding these and other fundamental differences on ends and means, the relationship developed as one of father and son, master and disciple.

The civil disobedience movement (1919–45), under Gandhi's command and with Nehru's active support, made uneven progress. There were as many setbacks as successes, and people in tens of thousands resolutely suffered imprisonment. During this period Nehru moved steadily to the center of the national struggle. Between 1921 and 1945 he was sentenced to imprisonment nine times, and he passed nearly 10 years of his life in jail. But in the course of his repeated incarcerations he rose to a level of national eminence exceeded only by that of Gandhi. Early in his career he became secretary-general of the National Congress party and later served three times as its president.

Both Gandhi and Nehru stood squarely for the principle of separation of church and state. But the antagonism of the Hindu majority and the Muslim minority, which had flared up often during British rule in India, intensified as the prospects for self-government improved. The result was that independence was accompanied by a period of almost unprecedented bloodshed and suffering, as the Indian subcontinent was partitioned into two independent entities—Hindu India and Muslim Pakistan. Throughout, Gandhi had opposed this division of the country and held to the position that "even if the whole of India burns, we shall not concede Pakistan." But power had already slipped from Gandhi's hands and Nehru realized that independence could not wait on reconciliation. On Aug. 15, 1947, British rule in India was formally ended, and Nehru became prime minister of an independent India.

From the outset of his administration, Nehru's ambitious domestic programs were beset with difficulties. In the economic sphere he focused his attention on a series of 5-year plans, begun in 1951. The aim of Nehru's plans was socialism. However, despite gains in other areas, this proved the most elusive of goals; elements of the private sector and the bureaucracy impeded the government at every juncture.

Frequently frustrated by apathy and corruption at home, Nehru turned his energies more to foreign affairs. Under Nehru's initiative, the infant nation undertook a major innovation in the conduct of international affairs. The genius of Nehru's policy was to turn political and economic weaknesses into assets. The advantages of this policy, labeled "neutralist" in the early 1950's, were later evidenced by its adoption in a host of smaller nations in Africa and Asia.

Nehru's policy (he called it "independent" rather than "neutralist") was double-edged. He realized that India's immediate survival depended on a constant flow of food and goods from wealthier nations. He also recognized the danger to India's independence of accepting such aid from only one of the powers involved in the cold war. Nehru reasoned that, whatever her sympathies, India would do best to maintain equally friendly relations with all nations, irrespective of their international dispositions or internal systems.

Secondly Nehru's policy established India as active peacemaker among nations. This role, most clearly manifested by India's persistent refusal to enter into military alliances, was reminiscent of the method of Gandhi—nonviolence coupled with an appeal to higher morality.

During the Korean conflict, Nehru's policies gave India the chance to lead the way to negotiations. At the outset of the fighting, India had taken a position of cautious support for the UN police action but had been careful to avoid a sharp confrontation with the Communists. This restraint later enabled her to introduce a successful compromise resolution in the UN General Assembly on the exchange of war prisoners, which eventually was to form the basis for a de facto settlement of the Korean conflict. In 1956 Nehru preferred to withhold censure of the Soviet Union for its actions in Hungary, and at the same time he attacked the "colonial aggression" of Britain and France at Suez. During the late 1950's and early 1960's India's adherence to the precept of coexistence was severely tested by border tensions with China. Nehru continued to seek out the Chinese for a peaceful settlement, while maintaining a forceful defense of India's territorial rights. India's peace-loving stance was compromised by her armed conquest of Goa in 1962 and at the time of Nehru's death India and Pakistan had not yet resolved their dispute over Kashmir.

Personal diplomacy was an indispensable part of Nehru's successes. Private consultations in Washington, London, Moscow, and Peking became matters of routine during his years as prime minister. His performance earned for India a position of respect and influence in the major councils of the world.

With Nehru's death on May 27, 1964, an epoch in the history of Asia ended. As he once said of himself, "I have become a curious mixture of the East and West, out of place everywhere, at home nowhere."

Throughout his career, Nehru was a prolific writer. His most notable works include *An Autobiography* (1936), *Glimpses of World History* (1939, *The Discovery of India* (1946), *Nehru on Gandhi* (1948), and *Independence and After* (1949).

MOHAN SINHA MEHTA

BIBLIOG.–Michael Brecher, *Nehru, A Political Biography* (1959), *Nehru's Mantle: The Politics of Succession in India* (1966); K. T. Char, *Profile of Jawaharlal Nehru* (1967); W. R. Crocker, *Nehru, A Contemporary's Estimate* (1966); Michael Edwardes, *Nehru: A Pictorial Biography* (1963); Beatrice Lamb, *The Nehrus of India* (1967); Frank Moraes, *Jawaharlal Nehru* (1956); Vincent Sheean, *Nehru: The Years of Power* (1959).

NEILSON, JOHN, 1776–1848, Canadian journalist and political figure, born in Balmaghie, Kirkcudbright, Scotland. He went to Canada at the age of 14. As owner and editor of the Quebec *Gazette* after 1797 and a member of the Lower Canada legislative assembly, he vigorously opposed the reunion of Lower and Upper Canada but was finally reconciled to the plan. He was a member of the united legislative assembly after 1841.

NEILSON, WILLIAM ALLEN, 1869–1946, U.S. scholar, born in Doune, Scotland. He was professor of English at Harvard (1906–17), and president of Smith College (1917–39). Neilson was editor of the Cambridge edition of William Shakespeare's works (1906, rev. ed. 1942), and editor in chief of the second edition of *Webster's New International Dictionary* (1934). He edited many textbooks and wrote such works as *Essentials of Poetry* (1912) and *A History of English Literature* (1920).

NEISSE RIVER, Czech *Nisa*, Polish *Nysa*, either of two rivers in Czechoslovakia, East Germany, and Poland. The Lusatian (or Görlitzer) Neisse rises in northern Bohemia (Czechoslovakia), flows north through Saxony and Brandenburg, and enters the Oder River 9 miles north of Gubin, Poland; length about 140 miles. After 1945 the Lusatian Neisse, from the border of Czechoslovakia to its junction with the Oder, formed the boundary between East Germany and Poland. The Glatzer Neisse rises NE of Międzylesie, Poland, near the Czech border and flows southwest and then northeast through Poland into the Oder, near Brzeg (Brieg); length 121 miles.

NEITH, or Net, one of the most ancient of Egyptian goddesses, the chief divinity of the city of Saïs, and known as the mother of gods. She was identified by the Greeks with Athena. Neith was represented holding two crossed arrows and a shield.

NEJD, one of the two principal provinces of Saudi Arabia; bounded by Iraq and Jordan on the N, the Persian Gulf and Oman on the E, Yemen and South Yeman on the S, and the province of Hejaz on the W; area 447,000 square miles.A major oil pipeline from Hasa runs through northern Nejd province to Jordan. Only a small amount of oil has been found in Nejd proper. Dates, millet, wheat, maize, and fruits are gorwn in numerous oases, and camels, horses, donkeys, and sheep are raised. Nejd was the home of King Ibn Saud who, with his Wahabi followers, in 1926 won control over Hejaz, Hasa, and Asir to form a new consolidated kingdom, named Saudi Arabia in 1932. Riyadh is the capital of Nejd and, with Mecca, is one of Saudi Arabia's two capitals. See ARABIAN PENINSULA; SAUDI ARABIA. (For population of province, see Saudi Arabia map in Atlas.)

NEKHEB, or Nikhab, ancient city, Egypt, site of the modern village of El Kab (Al-Kab); on the E bank of the Nile River; 45 miles SSE of Luxor. Nekheb was the capital of Upper Egypt in earliest Egyptian history. Its brick wall, built by Amenemhet III about 1800 B.C., is one of the best-preserved ancient city walls.

NEKRASOV, NIKOLAI ALEKSEEVICH, 1821–78, Russian poet, born near Vinnitsa in the Ukraine. Disinherited for refusing to enter the army, he did hack literary work for a time, and in 1846 became coeditor of the journal *Sovremennik* (The Contemporary), which was suppressed in 1866 for its radical views. Nekrasov replaced it with another liberal journal, *Otechestvennye Zapiski* (The Annals of the Fatherland). Perhaps his best-known work is the long narrative poem *Who Can Live Well in Russia* (1870–74), the story of seven peasants who set out to look for a happy Russian and found only a promise of happiness for the future. Among his other poems, all reflecting compassion for the sufferings of Russia, are *Sascha* (1854), *The Red-Nosed Frost* (1863), and *Russian Women* (1873).

NELLORE, city, SE India, SE Andhra Pradesh state, capital of Nellore district; on the Penner River, on the Coromandel coast of the Bay of Bengal; 93 miles N of Madras, with which it is connected by railroad and highway. Industries include rice and oilseed milling, ceramics, and mica processing. An arts and sciences and a Sanskrit college are located in the city. (For population, see India map in Atlas.)

NELSON, HORATIO, 1758–1805, British admiral, born in Burnham Thorpe, Norfolk, where his father was the rector (parish priest). He went to local schools until the age of 12, when he joined H.M.S. *Raisonable*, a guardship in the Thames River, commanded by his maternal uncle, Maurice Suckling.

Early Adventures. Nelson saw much of the world in his youth. He made a voyage to the West Indies, later joined a polar expedition under Constantine Phipps, and spent 2 years in Far Eastern waters. His frigate was in action off the Indian coast with a vessel in the service of Tipu Sahib of Mysore, with whom Britain was at war. Nelson returned home with fever, but soon recovered and was promoted to lieutenant (1777). During the war of American independence he served in the West Indies on the *Lowestoft* and gained quick promotion. He was favored by the commander in chief, Sir Peter Parker, and gained command of the frigate *Hinchingbroke* before he had reached 21. He sailed to Nicaragua and fought against the Spaniards, allies of the American revolutionists. In 1780 he was again invalided home with fever. After convalescence in Bath he crossed the Atlantic again, but he had no further opportunities for distinction before the peace.

In 1784 he was given his one and only peacetime command, that of the frigate *Boreas*. In the West Indies he and his lifelong friend, Cuthbert Collingwood, made themselves unpopular by interfering with trade between the islands and the newly independent United States, a trade widely practiced though forbidden by British law. He returned home in 1787 with a wife, Frances Nisbet, and stepson. He lived mainly at home in Burnham Thorpe until the outbreak of war with revolutionary France in 1793.

Rise to Fame. In command of the *Agamemnon*, of 64 guns, he was sent to the Mediterranean to serve in the fleet under Lord Hood. Henceforward, he was continually in action, either at sea or ashore, for the rest of his life. He lost the sight of his right eye (though not the eye itself) at the siege of Calvi, Corsica, in July, 1794. He continued in the Mediterranean under successive commanders in chief until the British fleet was forced to withdraw to the Atlantic owing to the insecurity of the remaining British bases and to French success all over the continent.

Nelson's great chance for distinction came in February, 1797. As a commodore he was present at an action off Cape St. Vincent in which the British commander, Sir John Jervis, won an earldom for defeating a far superior naval force of Spain, France's ally. Nelson played a leading part in the capture of two of the four prizes that crowned Jervis's success. Shortly afterward, he became a rear admiral by seniority and was knighted. In July, 1797, he lost his right arm in an unsuccessful night attack on Tenerife.

The Battle of the Nile and World Fame. Nelson recovered quickly, and early in 1798 he was given

CULVER PICTURES

Horatio Nelson

charge of a independent squadron sent to destroy a French expedition to Egypt, commanded by Bonaparte. After a frustrating search, he discovered the French fleet anchored in Aboukir Bay, near the mouth of the Nile. In the course of a night action he annihilated almost the entire French force. "Victory is not a name strong enough for such a scene!" exclaimed Nelson next day. The French army was marooned in Egypt. Naples became Nelson's base until he returned home in 1800, a peer of the realm and a duke of the Kingdom of Naples, whose sovereign he had supported.

In 1801 Nelson led an attack on the Danish fleet at Copenhagen to prevent its use in the service of France. For this difficult enterprise he was made a viscount and, 2 years later, commander in chief, Mediterranean. At the Battle of Trafalgar (Oct. 21, 1805), Admiral Lord Nelson destroyed the main Franco-Spanish fleet and died in the hour of victory. His life was one of utter dedication to his country, his death an irreplaceable loss but also an inspiration. In tactical mastery he has never been excelled, and he was a superb leader of men. His private life was less happy. His marriage broke up, and he lived latterly with Lady Hamilton, widow of an old friend. It is through his deeds that he is best remembered. OLIVER WARNER

BIBLIOG:–G. P. B. Naish, ed., *Nelson's Letters to His Wife and Other Documents* (1958); Sir Harris Nicolas, ed., *The Dispatches and Letters of Lord Nelson* (1844–46); Oliver Warner, *Victory: the Life of Lord Nelson* (1958), *Nelson's Battles* (1965).

NELSON, SAMUEL, 1792–1873, U.S. jurist, born in Hebron, N.Y. He was graduated from Middlebury College, Vermont, in 1813, and was admitted to the bar (opening an office in Cortland, N.Y.) in 1817. In 1831 he became associate justice of the state supreme court, and in 1837 chief justice. In 1845 Pres. John Tyler appointed him to the U.S. Supreme Court. As a strict constructionist in interpreting the Constitution, Nelson concurred in the Dred Scott decision and during the Civil War disapproved of expanding the power of the executive branch of the government. An authority on admiralty and maritime law, Nelson was a member of the joint high commission for settlement of the *Alabama* claims in 1871. He resigned from the Supreme Court in 1872.

NELSON, THOMAS, 1738–89, colonial American patriot, and a signer of the Declaration of Independence, born in Yorktown, Va. He was a member of the provincial conventions in Virginia in 1774, 1775, and 1776, becoming colonel of the 2nd Virginia regiment at the outbreak of the Revolutionary War in 1775; but he resigned the same year to become a member of the Continental Congress. He was in command of the Virginia state militia during the siege of Yorktown in 1781, where it is said he ordered the bombardment of his own house because it was believed to be Gen. Charles Cornwallis' headquarters. He became governor of Virginia in 1781.

NELSON, THOMAS, 1822–92, Scottish publisher, born in Edinburgh, the son of Thomas Nelson (1780–1861). He entered his father's publishing house in 1839 and established a London branch in 1844. Head of the manufacturing department of the Edinburgh office from 1846, he invented a rotary press in 1850, and was largely responsible for the accuracy and clarity of the firm's typography. He extended the scope of Nelson and Sons' publications to include juveniles, travel and adventure books, and textbooks.

NELSON, city, SE British Columbia; on the west arm of Kootenay Lake; about 300 miles E of Vancouver. The city has manufactures of woodworking machinery, boats, and dairy products. Nelson was settled in 1887 and incorporated in 1897. (For population, see British Columbia map in Atlas.)

NELSON, municipal borough, NW England, E Lancashire; on a tributary of the Ribble River; 25 miles N of Manchester, with which it is connected by highway and railroad. Cotton and other textile milling is the chief industry of Nelson. (For population, see England map in Atlas.)

NELSON RIVER, central Canada, Manitoba province; flows NE from the NE corner of Lake Winnipeg into Hudson Bay at Port Nelson; length 400 miles. It is navigable 127 miles above its mouth. The Bow and Saskatchewan rivers, Lake Winnipeg, and the Nelson form a continuous, 1,660-mile-long watercourse. The Nelson was discovered in 1612 by an English explorer, Sir Thomas Button. A Hudson's Bay Company post was established at its mouth in 1670, and for many years the river was an important fur-trading route.

NEMAN RIVER, or Nemunas, also Niemen, U.S.S.R.; rises in Minsk region of Byelorussia, follows a westerly course to Grodno, then flows N through Lithuania to Kaunas and again W to the Kurskiy Zaliv of the Baltic Sea; length about 585 miles. The river is used for logging in its upper course and is navigable from Grodno to its mouth, a distance of about 375 miles.

NEMEA, valley and town in Argolis province of ancient Greece, and in mythology the scene of Hercules' slaying of the Nemean lion. Games in honor of Adrastus were held at Neméa following the expulsion of the cult of Adrastus from Sicyon by the tyrant Cleisthenes (600–570 B.C.), and about the same time Neméa became one of several sites of Panhellenic games held in honor of Zeus, Apollo, and Poseidon. In 394 B.C. Sparta decisively defeated Corinth and Argos at Neméa.

NEMESIS, in Greek mythology, a goddess of justice and divine retribution, especially associated with the equalizing of fortune and misfortune and with the punishing of pride and wrongdoing. She was the daughter of Night and was worshiped at Rhamnus in Attica. According to some legends, Nemesis wss loved by Zeus, from whom she tried to flee by transforming herself into various animals. Zeus was at last able to approach her by taking the form of a swan, and as a result she brought forth an egg from which Helen of Troy was hatched.

NEMI, LAKE, central Italy, 17 miles SE of Rome. In an extinct crater in the Alban Hills, the oval, mile-long lake is noted for its beauty. At the northeast edge are an ancient temple and sacred grove dedicated to Diana, whose priest was a runaway slave who, according to tradition, won office by challenging the reigning priest to mortal combat. Lake Nemi has yielded many objects of archaeological interest, including two Roman galleons which were destroyed by the Germans in 1944.

NEMOURS, LOUIS CHARLES PHILIPPE RAPHAEL d'ORLEANS, Duc de, 1814–96, French prince, born in Paris. The second son of King Louis Philippe, Nemours in 1826 was made a cavalry colonel and later took part in three Algerian expeditions (1836, 1837, 1841). In 1831 he was elected king of the Belgians by the Belgian national congress, but his father, fearful of antagonizing Great Britain, forced him to decline the throne. A conservative who encountered considerable liberal opposition, he left the country for England during the revolution in 1848. Working from exile to unite various royalist factions, Nemours returned to France in 1871, but failed to realize his hopes for a Bourbon restoration. He died in 1896 at Versailles.

NENETS NATIONAL OKRUG, U.S.S.R., Russian Soviet Federated Socialist Republic, NE Archangel oblast, above the Arctic Circle; bounded by the Yamal-Nenets National Okrug on the E, Archangel oblast and Komi Autonomous Soviet Socialist Republic on the S, and the Barents Sea on the W and N; area 82,797 square miles. The Nentsi, formerly known as the Samoyeds, are of a chiefly Mongoloid ethnic strain. The district's economy is dominated by fishing, reindeer raising, and seal hunting. Sawmilling, tanning, dairy and truck farming, and coal and fluorspar mining have been introduced on a small scale. The capital of the Nenets National Okrug is Naryan-Mar, at the mouth of the Pechora River. The area was organized as a national district in 1929. (For population, see U.S.S.R. map in Atlas.)

NENNIUS, late eighth-century Welsh historian, a native of Mercia. He is the traditional author of the *Historia britonum*, the first work to identify King Arthur as a historical figure. The history gives an account of the origin of the Britons, the Roman occupation, and the arrival of the Saxons—closing with the 12 battles of King Arthur. Goeffrey of Monmouth drew upon the work in writing his *Historia regum britanniae*, which in turn became a source of the medieval poetic cycles dealing with the Arthurian legend. Versions exist in Latin, Welsh, Irish, and English. Internal evidence suggests that Nennius merely compiled or revised already existing accounts.

NEODYMIUM, chemical element; symbol Nd; atomic number 60; atomic weight 144.24; melting point 1,024°C; boiling point 3,027°C; specific gravity 6.80 and 7.004, depending on allotropic form; valence 3. It is a silvery-white metal of the rare earth series. It rapidly tarnishes in air to form an oxide that spalls off and exposes fresh metal. It should be stored under mineral oil or wrapped in a closed plastic bag. Its name is derived from the Greek *neos* (new) and *didymos* (twin). Neodymium was first isolated by Baron Carl Auer von Welsbach in 1885, but it was not obtained in highly pure form until 1925. Its oxide is blue, and neodymium salt solutions are usually blue. Neodymium is usually used as a compound with other rare-earth compounds rather than as an element. The element is often used as a constituent of a didymium mixture, whose chief substances are lanthanum, praseodymium, and neodymium compounds. Didymium materials are used in the waterproofing of textiles, in paint driers, in the glass and ceramic industry, and as dielectrics in condensers. Neodymium salts of comparatively high purity are used to color porcelain and glass. Glass so treated may transmit either red or blue light, depending on the direction (see DICHROISM) of the beam. See RARE EARTHS.

NEO-KANTIANISM, a philosophical movement prominent in Germany during the late nineteenth and early twentieth centuries, was a continuation and development of the philosophy of Immanuel Kant, particularly of his theory of knowledge. As expressed by Kant in his *Critique of Pure Reason* (1781), the theory maintains that no knowledge is possible apart from the organizing activity of the human mind; while the senses furnish the materials of all human knowledge, it is mind that arranges them. This being so, all the order and law man thinks to discover in the world around him is, in reality, only such as is imparted to the world by mind itself. The end result is the limitation of knowledge to that multitude of phenomena that can be organized by mind. The external cause of the phenomena, the thing-in-itself, must remain forever unknown, although Kant thinks man is justified in believing such things-in-themselves to exist.

The impetus to the revival of this Kantian view, which had been eclipsed earlier by the philosophy of Georg W. F. Hegel, was provided by F. A. Lange (1828–75) in his famous *History of Materialism* (1865). Following Kant, Lange found the world, as studied by physical science, to be a world dependent upon man's modes of perception and not a world existing independently on its own account. He concluded that any valid philosophy of science must be based on the Kantian theory of knowledge. This connection between Kantian philosophy and science was further emphasized by Hermann Cohen (1842–1918). Arguing that the real is what can be thought, and that apart from thought no reality is given or discoverable, Cohen denied the existence of the thing-in-itself and stressed the importance of the laws of thought. A similar position was maintained by Paul Natorp (1854–1924), for whom the laws of thought were the criteria of all truth. The significance of Neo-Kantianism as the basis of the twentieth century scientific world view was developed in detail by Ernst Cassirer (1874–1945) in his monumental *Philosophy of Symbolic Forms* and by Sir Arthur Eddington (1882–1944) in his *Philosophy of Physical Science* (1939). ROBERT C. WHITTEMORE

NEOMYCIN, an antibiotic produced by certain strains of *Streptomyces fradiae*, an organism belonging to the actinomycetes and found abundantly in various soils. Neomycin was discovered in 1949 by Dr. Selman A. Waksman and Hubert A. Lechevalier of the Rutgers University department of microbiology. It is similar to streptothricin and streptomycin, two other antibiotics isolated earlier. See ANTIBIOTIC; STREPTOMYCIN.

Neomycin is an alkaline chemical substance, highly resistant to the action of heat and to the effect of different microorganisms. It is readily soluble in water and is soluble in organic solvents. There appear to be several closely related neomycins. Neomycin is active against various Gram-positive and Gram-negative bacteria, including also streptomycin resistant forms. It is highly active against the tuberculosis organism and the bacteria that inhabit the digestive tract, but not against fungi and viruses. It is highly effective in urinary tract infections. Its optimum activity is at a slightly alkaline reaction. Neomycin can be administered by mouth, into the skin, or into the peritoneum. It is most toxic when given intravenously and least when given orally. It is not readily absorbed from the digestive tract and is an ideal intestinal antiseptic. SELMAN A. WAKSMAN

NEON, a rare gaseous element present in the atmosphere in a ratio of 18 parts of neon to 1 million parts of air. Neon, which appears in Group O of the periodic table (see PERIODIC TABLE), with the other rare gases, is colorless, odorless, and tasteless, and is chemically inert, forming no compounds. The element, discovered in 1898 by Sir William Ramsay and Morris W. Travers, has a normal boiling point of −245.9°C (−410°F) and a normal freezing point of −248.5°C (−415°F) at 1 atmosphere of pressure. Its density is 0.9004 grams per liter at 0°C (32°F). Neon has three naturally stable isotopes of mass numbers 20, 21, and 22. Radioactive isotopes of this element have also been produced artificially. Neon is produced in commercial quantities as a by-product of the fractional distillation of air used in making oxygen.

Neon Tubes. The neon tube was first designed by Georges Claude, a French engineer, in 1915. Because of the unique red-orange color emitted, and because of their low operational costs, neon tubes are used widely in advertising signs—being shaped into letters or designs. They became so popular that the term "neon sign" came to designate all modern luminous signs, including those filled with substances other than neon and emitting lights of different colors. Because a neon light can be turned on or extinguished instantaneously, neon tubes found use in high-speed equipment such as stroboscopes, where it is vital that there be no afterglow. A neon tube becomes luminous by passing through it a high-voltage electric current that excites electrons in the atoms of gas; the energy created by the movement of electrons is manifested as visible light. See ELECTRIC LAMP.

NEOPLATONISM, a school of philosophy that revived the doctrines of Platonism and attempted to reconcile them with Aristotelianism and Oriental concepts (see PLATO). Specifically, Neoplatonism is identified with the teachings of the last school of pagan philosophy that flourished in Alexandria and Athens in the early Christian Era; the Italian humanists of the Renaissance are also known as Neoplatonists, as are in general the members of any philosophical group espousing a doctrine founded upon Plato's metaphysical and ethical principles.

The Neoplatonic schools of Alexandria and Athens marked both the consummation and the collapse of ancient philosophy. As Plato's teachings developed in the early centuries of the Christian Era, they acquired a heavy religious tinge, for they were the basis on which the last of the pagan thinkers hoped to raise a system to combat Christianity.

Neoplatonic Doctrine. There exists as a supreme principle over and beyond all reality a suprarational principle, the One, which contains all perfections and is without limitations. From the self-contemplation of the One there arises a second principle, Mind, which contemplates the perfections and beauty of the One. Through this contemplation is begotten a life principle, Universal Soul, from which derive all forms, both animate and inanimate, that make up the universe. Individual souls are emanations from the Universal Soul. They possess freedom and responsibility and are thus able to turn aside from the Universal Soul and descend into corporeality. The period spent in connection with the body is a time of trial for the soul, as it has cut itself off from the only real existence (the One) and has been forced to assume a false existence. The soul therefore, strives to return to its true being. It must first return to itself through the practice of virtue; but to be free of sin and the material world is not enough: the soul seeks a higher reunion with the One. This is accomplished by contemplation of the One; the result of this contemplation is that the soul (in ecstasy) loses itself in the source of all being and all good.

The Ethical Ideal was paramount for the Neoplatonists. Yet, in their desire to combat Christianity, they transformed their ethical doctrine into a religion. Although the Neoplatonists failed to create a stable and enduring religion, their effect on later ethical development was great. Neoplatonism failed as a religion because its appeal was limited to the intellectually elite. The summit of religious activity for the Neoplatonist was an inward peace to be obtained by speculative activity. But the doctrine could not teach a method of making this inward peace and blessedness permanent, nor could it appeal to the mass of people not endowed with the necessary speculative ability to comprehend such a lofty and esoteric ideal.

Schools. The Alexandrian school of Neoplatonism was founded by Ammonius Saccas (175?–?242), but the best known and most acute of the Alexandrian Neoplatonists was Ammonius' pupil Plotinus (205?–270) who elaborated the Neoplatonic teachings in his *Enneads*. The title of this work, the Greek word for *nine*, derives from the fact that each of the six major sections of the work is divided into nine tractates. These writings of Plotinus were collected and edited by his pupil Porphyry (232?–?304) who appended to them a life of Plotinus.

Porphyry spent most of his time combating Christianity. He stressed ascetic practice, holding that evil arises not from the body but from the "untamed desires" of the soul. With the advent of Porphyry's pupil Iamblichus (died ?333), Neoplatonism dropped all pretentions of being merely a philosophical doctrine and interested itself in theological matters.

At Athens the most distinguished leaders of Neoplatonism were Plutarch (350?–430), his disciple, Syrianus, and Proclus (411?–485). Proclus' numerous writings were for the most part commentaries on the *Dialogues* of Plato. Probably his most influential work was the *Elements of Theology* in which he gives a formalistic statement of Neoplatonism as it developed in the Athenian school. Proclus' influence on medieval theological and mystical writers was considerable, both by reason of what he himself said and because he served as a bridge for medieval thinkers to reach Aristotle and Plato. Among early Christian thinkers, such as St. Augustine (354–430), Neoplatonic doctrines were influential and served as the first basis for the growth of theology and scholastic philosophy. WILLIAM A. GERHARD

BIBLIOG.–C. Bigg, *Neoplatonism* (1895); G. Santayana, *Platonism and the Spiritual Life* (1927); T. Whittaker, *Neo-Platonists* (ed. 1928); P. Shorey, *Platonism, Ancient and Modern* (1938); B. Switalski, *Neoplatonism and the Ethics of St. Augustine* (1946); E. Cassirer and others, eds., *Renaissance Philosophy of Man* (1949); P. V. Pistorius, *Plotinus and Neoplatonism* (1952).

NEOPRENE. See RUBBER, Synthetic Rubber Compounding, *Chloroprene Rubber*.

NEOPTOLEMUS, also called Pyrrhus, in Greek legend a son of Achilles. He was taken to Troy by Odysseus because oracles said that Troy could not be captured without his aid. He was one of the heroes in the wooden horse; during the sack of Troy he killed Priam, and after the capture of the city he officiated at the sacrifice of Priam's daughter, Polyxena, on Achilles' tomb. The captive Andromache, wife of Hector, fell to Neoptolemus' lot in the distribution of the spoils. By some accounts, he afterward reigned at Phthia in Thessaly, married Menelaus' daughter, Hermione, and was slain by Orestes, the former lover of Hermione. According to other accounts he settled in Epirus, where Molossus, his son by Andromache, founded the dynasty of the Molossian kings. Neoptolemus was buried at Delphi and was worshiped there as a hero.

NEO-PYTHAGOREANISM, a Greco-Alexandrian school of philosophy that revived Pythagorean doctrines, appearing in the first century B.C. and lasting until it was absorbed into Neoplatonism in the third century A.D. The movement was an attempt to combine religious elements with pagan philosophy. It emphasized the duality between the soul and the body. God was conceived of as being wholly spiritual, and matter was thought to be the source of evil from which men must free themselves by ascetic practices. The chief exponent of Neo-Pythagoreanism was Apollonius of Tyana (died A.D. ?97). See PYTHAGORAS.

NEOSCHOLASTICISM, a twentieth century philosophical movement whose aims are to reinvestigate, reassert, and adapt to modern life the principles and systems of medieval Scholasticism. Beginning late in the nineteenth century, its adherents attempted to revise and expand the medieval system in a way that would take into account modern science and the challenges to Scholasticism presented by later philosophical modes of thought, especially (after World War I) those associated with existentialism.

With the coming of the Reformation and the growth of interest in natural science and later in the social sciences, especially economics, Scholasticism fell into disrepute. With the revolt against Roman Catholicism, many philosophic principles—including Scholasticism—associated with that theology were rejected as being concerned not with truth but rather with defense of a particular faith. Furthermore, certain Scholastic principles—those dealing with the philosophy of nature, and those dealing with ethics such as might be applied to politics and business—seemed inadequate in the light of political, economic, and technological changes taking place in Europe. Since most Scholastics were clergymen, and since the attacks of reformers were felt to be dangerous to the church, Scholastic speculations became centered on religious polemics and apologetics. From the sixteenth to the late nineteenth century, therefore, Scholasticism was a dormant tradition in European thought, except when revived by Roman Catholic scholars such as Giacomo Cajetan (1469–1534) and Francisco Suárez (1548–1617).

In the bull, *Aeterni Patris* (1879), Pope Leo XIII strongly recommended the study of Scholastic philosophy, especially that of St. Thomas Aquinas (1225?–74). Leo established, 1894, the Institut Supérieur de Philosophie at the University of Louvain, Belgium, to foster the study of Scholasticism. Under the direction of Désiré Joseph (later Cardinal) Mercier, the institute became a leading center of Neoscholasticism. Besides the traditional courses in metaphysics, epistemology, and ethics, the institute also offered courses in cosmology, physics, and sociology and published the influential *Revue néo-scholastique* (after 1946, *Revue philosophique de Louvain*).

The movement soon assumed major proportions in Great Britain, Italy, the United States, Canada, and especially France. The most outstanding French exponents were Reginald Garrigou-Lagrange (1877–), Étienne Gilson (1884–), and Jacques Maritain (1882–), whose writings represent the most extensive application of the philosophy of St. Thomas to twentieth century political and moral problems. Gilson was more independent of the Thomistic synthesis than was Maritain. Both Gilson and Maritain taught at the Pontifical Institute of Medieval Studies of the University of Toronto, Canada. In the United States the movement was adopted by Catholic schools, and there was a revival of interest in the Aristotelic-Thomistic tradition among a number of non-Catholic educators, among them Mortimer Adler (1902–), who taught at the University of Chicago, 1930–52, and was head of the Institute for Philosophical Research, 1952– . The journals *Thomist* and *New Scholasticism* became prominent organs of the movement in the United States.

BIBLIOG.–C. R. Baschab, ed., *Manual of Neo-scholastic Philosophy* (ed. 1937); M. J. Adler, *Problems for Thomists* (1940); R. E. Brennan, *Essays in Thomism* (1942); A. C. Pegis, ed., *Essays in Modern Scholasticism* (1944); D. F. F. J.

Mercier, *Manual of Modern Scholastic Philosophy* (2 vols. ed. 1938–50); M. Picard, *Human Face* (1930), *Flight from God* (1951), *World of Silence* (1952); E. H. Gilson, *Reason and Revelation in the Middle Ages* (ed. 1950), *Unity of Philosophical Experience* (1950), *God and Philosophy* (ed. 1951), *Being and Some Philosophers* (ed. 1952), *Spirit of Medieval Philosophy* (ed. 1953), *History of Christian Philosophy in the Middle Ages* (1955), *Christian Philosophy of St. Thomas Aquinas* (1956); M. M. C. J. de Wulf, *Introduction to Scholastic Philosophy, Medieval and Modern* (1956); J. Maritain, *Freedom in the Modern World* (1936), *Scholasticism and Politics* (ed. 1945), *Range of Reason* (1952), *Approaches to God* (1954), *Existence and the Existent* (1957).

NEOSHO, city, SW Missouri, seat of Newton County; on the Frisco and the Kansas City Southern railroads and U.S. highways 60 and 71; in the Ozark Mountain region 20 miles SE of Joplin. Neosho is the trade center of a dairy and berry-growing area; its main industries are dairying and the production of flour and feed. The city was founded in 1839 and incorporated in 1855. Pop. (1960) 7,452.

NEOSHO RIVER, SE Kansas and NE Oklahoma; rises in Morris County, Kansas, and flows SE past Emporia and Chanute into NE Oklahoma, where it flows SSW into the Arkansas River near Muskogee; length about 460 miles. In Oklahoma the Neosho frequently is called the Grand.

NEOSTIGMINE, a bitter white powder of synthetic origin that is used as a drug. Its action resembles that of physostigmine (see ESERINE). Neostigmine increases peristalsis of the digestive tract and is useful in relieving sluggish conditions of the bowel. It also produces increased tone in the smooth muscle of the urinary tract. Neostigmine is used in the treatment of myasthenia gravis (see MUSCLE), a disease characterized by progressive fatigue in the muscles; administration of neostigmine restores some of the muscle power. Atropine is an antidote for overdoses.

NEPAL, kingdom, S central Asia; bounded by China on the N, Sikkim on the NE, and India on the E, S, and W; maximum length and width 520 and 150 miles respectively; area about 56,000 sq. mi.; pop. (1961) 9,387,661. The capital is Katmandu.

Physical Factors. Nepal, situated between the main ridge of the Himalayas with its tremendous peaks and the Ganges Plain with its low flat terrain, has a variety of physical characteristics. The country may be divided into three geographical zones, roughly parallel with the main southeast-northwest axis: the region of the Main Himalayas, that of the Outer Himalayas, and the foothills descending to the Ganges Plain.

The northernmost zone consists of the main ridge of the Himalayas with its numerous peaks, including the world's highest, Mount Everest (29,028 ft.), and such other giants as Kanchenjunga (28,146 ft.), Makalu (27,790 ft.), and Dhaulagiri (26,810 ft.). The climate of this great crystalline uplift may best be described as arctic and subarctic with a permanent cover of snow and ice in all areas above 17,000 feet. Just below this permanently icy area is a zone of mountain meadows at elevations of 13,000 to 17,000 feet which may be utilized as grazing areas during the brief summer period. Within those portions of the valleys and basins where elevations are below 13,000 feet, are woodlands and forests—scrubby and sparse on unexposed slopes where rainfall is low, luxuriant and dense on exposed slopes where rainfall is heavy. These forests consist of a variety of conifers including spruce, fir, and juniper.

South of the Main Himalayas is the middle zone of complexly folded sedimentary rocks often referred to as the Outer Himalayas, where again a parallel arrangement of ridges and peaks is dominant. Spurs from the main range and local uplifts and folding have to a large extent compartmentalized this zone into four areas each of which is the headwater region for one of the four major river systems of Nepal—from west to east, the Sarda, Karnali, Gandak, and Kosi. All these streams flow generally southward and empty into the Ganges. One of the most important areas in this zone is the Vale of Katmandu, a former lake basin—the largest area of flat land in interior Nepal and therefore one of the few sections of the country where wheeled vehicles can replace pack animals and porters. Much of this zone, having a fairly abundant rainfall, was originally covered with evergreen forests containing both coniferous and deciduous species such as cheer pine and evergreen oak.

UPI

Snow-covered peaks and steep rock gorges rise above the confluence of two large glaciers in the Nepal Himalaya. The distant peaks, about 19,000 feet high, are unnamed.

The third physical region of Nepal is the zone of gently folded ranges in the foothills where elevations are generally below 4,000 feet. These foothills are covered with dense stands of the valuable sal and other subtropical monsoon forest species interspersed with jungle-like grasslands and shrublands. Big game animals—notably elephant, tiger, wild boar, and rhinoceros—inhabit this area. The foothills merge gradually along the southern boundary of Nepal with the Terai—the swampy, jungle-covered northern outer edge of the Ganges Plain.

Social and Economic Factors. The population comprises an aboriginal Mongoloid people, who speak Sinitic dialects of the Tibeto-Burmese type and profess Buddhism, and an Aryan element (originally from Rajputana) including the Gurkhas, who use languages largely Sanskritic in grammar and vocabulary and adhere to Brahmanism. Outside of Katmandu and nearby Bhadgaon and Patan, there are few large towns. Average population density is 150 persons per square mile.

Rice, wheat, jute, tobacco, and linseed are produced in the Terai, and there is extensive cutting of lumber in the foothills. The heart of agricultural activity in Nepal is in the valleys and basins of the Outer Himalayas where the scarcity of level land makes extensive terracing of slopes necessary. In the more favorable areas of this region population is extremely dense (more than 2,000 per sq. mi.). Because of the wide variety of environments many different crops are produced, ranging from irrigated rice in the flat lowlands to spring-sown barley and buckwheat in forest clearings on the slopes of the upper valleys. Cottage industry, featuring the production of coarse cloth, brass and copper articles, and household goods, is carried on in this section of the country. In the high Himalayas economic activities are limited to nomadic herding of sheep and yaks and some grain production in the more sheltered areas.

Although there is some trade with India, commerce plays a minor part in the economy of Nepal, which follows a policy of regulated isolation. Another barrier to trade has been a poor transportation and communications system, hindered by the rugged terrain. The first railway into Nepal, a narrow-gauge line from Raxaul, a border village in Bihar, was built in 1927. Since then other lines have been constructed to the borders of the country. A highway connects Katmandu with Raxaul. A rope railway, operated by electricity from a valley power station, is in service between Bhimphedi and Katmandu, a distance of 15 miles. Eastern Tarai, a district about 300 miles in length, is linked with the capital by a telephone network.

Government and History. Nepal is a constitutional monarchy under the rule of a king, assisted by a cabinet headed by the premier. The judicial system includes a supreme court, composed of a chief justice and four judges, and of special courts.

Nepal was parceled into small kingdoms under Newar kings until the Gurkhas, led by Prithvi Narayan Shah, conquered the country in the last half of the eighteenth century. Soon after the conquest the Gurkhas fought two wars with Tibet, losing the first to Tibet's ally, China, and winning the second—a victory by which Nepal gained trade rights in Lhasa. The treaty signed in 1816 at the conclusion of the Nepalese campaign regulated the subsequently amicable relations of Nepal and India. In 1923 Britain recognized the complete independence of Nepal. During World War II, however, Nepal aided the British with money and troops. An agreement to foster commerce and friendly relations between Nepal and the United States was signed in 1947, and economic aid treaties were concluded in 1951 and 1957.

Constitutional reforms were introduced in 1949 but political power was still wielded by the hereditary prime minister. In November, 1950, King Tribhuvana was temporarily deposed by the prime minister and the former's son became ruler. Upon the king's return in February, 1951, he proclaimed a constitutional monarchy, and in November of that year the prime minister was deposed and a cabinet formed. Crown Prince Mehendra Bir Birkram Shah Deva succeeded his father as King Mehendra, in March, 1955. The government was administered by King Mehendra and Premier Kunwar Indergit Singh until the premier resigned in November, 1957. King Mehendra was in sole control of the government until May, 1958, when he appointed Gen. Subarna Shanshere as premier. In 1959 a new constitution was adopted and Nepal's first parliamentary elections were held.

Alfred W. Booth

NEPHELITE, a mineral of the feldspathoid group, sometimes appearing as small, glassy crystals but generally occurring in massive, compact, imbedded grains. It is usually gray but may be white, yellowish, or red; it is transparent to translucent. Nephelite, or nepheline, is a sodium-potassium aluminum silicate with a formula of $(Na, K)\ (Al, Si)_2O_4$, a hardness of 5.5 to 6, and a specific gravity of 2.55 to 2.65. The massive variety is often called eleolite because of its greasy luster. The glassy crystalline variety, which is rare, is found in the lavas of Mount Vesuvius; the massive variety occurs in older rocks such as phonolite, nepheline syenite, and nephelene basalt. Nephelite is found in Maine, New Jersey, and Arkansas in the United States, on the Kola Peninsula in the U.S.S.R., in Norway, and in sections of South Africa.

NEPHI, city, central Utah, seat of Juab County; on the Union Pacific Railroad and U.S. highway 91; 50 miles SSW of Provo. Nephi is a grain and livestock shipping center, and has manufactures of rubber goods, flour, and plaster. The city was settled by Mormons in 1851. Pop. (1960) 2,566.

NEPHRITE, a mineral that is a fibrous variety of actinolite or tremolite of the amphibole group. It is a calcium magnesium ferrous silicate, usually pale to dark green but sometimes nearly white; it is transparent to translucent. Nephrite, with a hardness of 6 and a specific gravity of 3, is a hard and tough mineral because of the matted interwoven texture of its fibers. It is sometimes classed as jade, together with jadeite. When polished, nephrite has a beautiful luster that makes it valuable, especially in the Orient, for ornamental purposes. Nephrite is found in Turkistan, Siberia, New Zealand, and Germany.

NEPHRITIS. See Kidney, Common Diseases of the Kidney, *Bright's Disease*.

NEPOS, CORNELIUS, 99?–?24 B.C., Roman historian, was born probably in Verona. He was a friend of Cicero, Atticus, and Catullus. A universal history, a collection of anecdotes, *Chronica*, and other works are lost. *De excellentibus ducibus exterarum gentium* —a section of *De viris illustribus*, a collection of lives of distinguished Romans and foreigners—is his only major extant work. Though full of errors, the biographies contain information not found elsewhere and are noted for their excellent style.

NEPTUNE, in Roman mythology the god of the sea. He was originally a water god but came to be identified with the Greek god, Poseidon. His attribute was the trident. His festival, the Neptunalia, was celebrated July 23.

NEPTUNE, eighth planet from the sun and one of the four huge major planets of the solar system. Neptune is not visible to the naked eye, being only as bright as an eighth magnitude star (see Magnitude). It was identified in 1846, but the elements of its orbit had been determined before that.

Orbit, Physical Data. The mean distance of Neptune from the sun is 2,797 million miles, which is 30.07 times that of the earth. The orbit is nearly circular, the eccentricity being only 0.0086 (the earth's eccentricity is 0.016), and the plane of the orbit is tilted a little less than 1°47′ from the plane of the ecliptic, which is the plane of the earth's orbit. Neptune makes its orbit at an average speed of 3.4 miles per second in a period of 164.783 sidereal years (164.788 tropical years), the interval between two consecutive alignments of the sun and planet with the same star. Since the planet's eastward motion on the celestial sphere is slow, the synodic period—the average interval between two consecutive alignments of the sun, earth, and Neptune—is only 367.4 mean solar days, exceeding the earth year by only slightly more than two days.

The mass of Neptune is 17.26 times that of the earth, as determined from the gravitational effects on its satellites and on Uranus (see Orbit, *Satellite Orbits*). Neptune's diameter is 31,100 miles (3.9 times

MCDONALD OBS.

Neptune with its satellites—Triton, bottom, and Nereid, arrow—as seen with an 82-inch telescope in prime focus. The insert is a Cassegrain focus view of Neptune and Triton.

the earth's), the mean density is 1.6 times that of water, and the surface gravity is 1.1 times the earth's. From observations of shifts in position of its spectrum lines, the planet was found to have an eastward rotation about its axis with a period of 15.8 hours (see DOPPLER EFFECT). The polar flattening, or oblateness, is therefore large, the ratio $\frac{(a-b)}{a}$ being 1/45, where *a* and *b* are the equatorial and polar radii, respectively.

Atmosphere. Like other planets, Neptune shines by reflected sunlight, the average fraction reflected (albedo) being 0.62 (see ALBEDO). Sunlight penetrates the atmosphere, with the result that the spectrum observed is the solar spectrum, but modified—chiefly in the yellow, red, and infrared—by the presence of absorption bands of ammonia (NH_3) and strong bands of methane (CH_4). (See BAND SPECTRUM.) It is this absorption of the reds from the solar light that gives Neptune its green color. From the strength of these bands it can be concluded that the atmosphere must be very extensive. The surface temperature cannot be much above 300° below 0°F.

Satellites. Neptune has two satellites: Triton, which was discovered in 1846 shortly after the discovery of the planet itself, and Nereid, discovered in 1949. Triton revolves in the retrograde direction (westward) at a mean distance of 220,000 miles from its primary in a period of 5 days and 21 hours; the plane of the orbit is inclined about 35° to the ecliptic. The diameter of Triton is uncertain, but probably about 3,300 miles, and its mass is nearly twice that of the earth's moon. The second satellite, Nereid, ranges from 828,000 miles to more than 6,000,000 miles from Neptune and requires 359 days for one complete revolution. It is much smaller than Triton, with an approximate diameter of 200 miles and a mass that is 4,000 times smaller than that of Triton. See SATELLITE; PLANET.

BIBLIOG. F. L. Whipple, *Earth, Moon and Planets* (1952); R. H. Baker, *Astronomy* (ed. 1959); Patrick Moore, *A Guide to the Planets* (1960).

NEPTUNIUM, a metallic, transuranic, radioactive element with atomic number 93, an atomic weight of 293, and the symbol Np. Since its valence may be 3, 4, 5, or 6, it is active chemically. It has a melting point of 640°C (1184°F). There are at least three structural modifications of the element. Neptunium was discovered in 1940 by E. M. McMillan and P. H. Abelson at the University of California upon bombarding uranium-238 with neutrons from a cyclotron. Neptunium-237, the parent of the neptunium family ultimately formed by the bombardment of U-238, exists only in very small quantities in nature. Neptunium isotopes with mass numbers which vary from 231 to 241 were also discovered by using similar methods.

NEREIDS, in Greek mythology, 50 sea nymphs, daughters of Nereus and Doris. They were supposedly beautiful maidens who were helpful to voyagers, and were often represented riding on sea monsters and sporting with the Tritons. Among the most famous of the Nereids were Thetis, the mother of Achilles; Amphitrite, the wife of Poseidon; and Galatea who was beloved by Polyphemus. See NYMPHAE.

NEREUS, in Greek mythology, a sea-god, the son of Pontus and Gaea, and the father (by the sea-goddess, Doris) of the 50 Nereids. He was supposedly friendly and helpful, possessing infallible prophetic powers, and had the ability to assume various shapes. The Mediterranean, and more particularly the Aegean Sea, was Nereus' special province. He bore the trident as the sign of his authority.

NERGAL, Babylonian and Assyrian god, a solar deity who later came to be especially associated with the burning, destructive aspect of the sun, and as such was the god of war, pestilence, and the chase. He was represented on the gates of Babylonian temples by the figure of a lion.

NERI, SAN FILIPPO DE', Saint Philip Neri, 1515–95, Italian founder of the Oratorians, was born in Florence. In 1533 he went to Rome, where he studied theology and philosophy for about three years and thereafter devoted himself to visiting the sick and to public preaching. With his confessor, Persiano Rosa, he founded, 1548, the Confraternity of the Most Holy Trinity to assist pilgrims and convalescents. In 1551 he was ordained a priest and entered a community of priests at the Church of San Girolamo where he organized, 1564, the Oratorians—a communal congregation of secular priests who conducted daily spiritual exercises in the oratories of San Girolamo and other churches—services that included sacred music dramas which were subsequently called oratorios. The Oratorians were recognized by Pope Gregory XIII in 1575. Neri was canonized in 1622; his feast day is May 26.

NERNST, WALTHER HERMANN, 1864–1941, German Nobel prize-winning physical chemist, was born in Briesen, West Prussia; studied at the universities of Zürich, Berlin, Graz, and Würzburg; became professor of physics at Göttingen, 1891, and founded its institute for physical and electrochemistry, 1895. He went to the University of Berlin, 1905, became president of the Physical-Technical Institute at Berlin-Charlottenburg, 1922, and director of the physical institute at the University of Berlin, 1925. His heat theorem, dealing with the entropy of matter as it approaches absolute zero, was incorporated in the third law of thermodynamics and won for him the 1920 Nobel prize in chemistry. He invented a microscale and the Nernst electric lamp equipped with a metal oxide filament, which when heated becomes a conductor of electricity.

NERO, GAIUS CLAUDIUS, third century B.C., Roman general and consul in 207 B.C. By his march from the south of Italy to join Marcus Livius Salinator in Umbria, he enabled the Roman army to defeat Hasdrubal in the Battle of the Metaurus, 207 B.C., which virtually decided the second Punic War.

NERO CLAUDIUS CAESAR, A.D. 37–68, emperor of Rome, was born in Antium to Gnaeus Domitius Ahenobarbus and Agrippina the Younger. Originally called Lucius Domitius Ahenobarbus, his name was changed when he was adopted by the Emperor Claudius, A.D. 50, after Claudius' marriage to Agrippina. Nero's childhood had been rather obscure (his mother had long been out of favor at court), but his adoption brought him close to the throne, for he was older than Claudius' own son, Britannicus. In 54 Claudius died suddenly, probably poisoned by Agrippina, who suppressed her husband's will and had Nero proclaimed emperor. As Claudius' wife, Agrippina had had great influence; after his death she planned that she would be the real ruler, assisted by the councilors she had chosen for her son—the philosopher Seneca, and Burrus, commander of the imperial guards. The two men, however, found it easy within a few months of Nero's accession to persuade him to reject his mother's influence. When Agrippina threatened to replace Nero with his stepbrother Britannicus through intrigues similar to those she had used to overthrow Claudius, Nero had Britannicus murdered. Eventually, to end Agrippina's opposition to his marriage with Poppaea Sabina, the emperor had his mother murdered, A.D. 59.

Nero's Reign was distinguished by successful wars fought by his generals in Britain, where the conquest of the island continued, and in the east, where the Parthians were prevented from seizing Armenia, which was given to a Parthian prince as vassal of Rome. At home Nero's rule was less fortunate. During his first years imperial policy was moderate and wise, but after the death of Burrus in 59 and the retirement of Seneca in 62 Nero slipped ever more into folly and extravagance. He resorted to wholesale confiscations and executions among the aristocracy as well as to debasement of the coinage. Conservative circles were horrified by his appearance as a singer on the stage and his indulgence, under the name of art, in the decadent excesses of the Greek culture of his day. After the discovery and suppression of a widespread conspiracy in 65, his tyranny was reinforced by hatred and fear. Although he had won the liking of the people, he lost it as a result of the great fire of Rome, 64, which was widely credited to him—although he attempted to divert suspicion by his notorious persecution of the Christians, some of whom he had coated with pitch and burned as living torches in his gardens. His unwar-like character and effeminacy finally alienated the armies, which revolted, first in Gaul and then in Spain where Galba was proclaimed emperor. When Galba was accepted by the imperial guards in Rome, Nero stabbed himself (June 9, A.D. 68) exclaiming, it is said, "What an artist dies in me."

STEWART IRWIN OOST

BIBLIOG.–A. E. P. B. Weigall, *Nero: Emperor of Rome* (ed. 1947); C. M. Franzero, *Life and Times of Nero* (1956); R. Graves, trans., *Suetonius: Twelve Caesars* (1957); G. Walter, *Nero* (1957).

NERUDA, JAN, 1834–91, Czech writer, was born in Prague. He was a member of the staff of the journal *Národní Listy*, 1865–91, and a cofounder of *Květy*, 1866, an organ influential in the Czech literary revival. He was best known for literary criticism, *Collected Feuilletons* (1876–77), and for lofty, romantic verse as in *Churchyard Blossoms* (1857), *Songs of the Cosmos* (1878), and *Ballads and Romances* (1883).

NERVA, MARCUS COCCEIUS, A.D. 35?–98, emperor of Rome, A.D. 96–98, was born in Umbria. He was consul under Vespasian in 71, and under Domitian in 90. On the assassination of the latter in 96, Nerva was declared emperor by the senate and army, and his just administration restored order and tranquillity to the Roman world.

NERVAL, GÉRARD DE, pseudonym of Gérard Labrunie, 1808–55, French writer, who was born in Paris. His *Élegies nationales* (1826) was followed by a translation of Johann Wolfgang von Goethe's *Faust* (1828), and by the age of 21 Nerval had acquired a considerable literary reputation. A trip to the Middle East in 1843 was recorded in his *Voyage en Orient* (1848–50). He wrote several plays, including *Piquillo* (with Alexandre Dumas, 1837), *Léo Burckart* (1839), and *L'imagier de Harlem* (1851); but his most original work was his bizarre sonnets, *Les chimères*, in which he appears as a forerunner of Charles Baudelaire and Stéphane Mallarmé. Nerval was one of the most versatile talents of the romantic period, but his life of dissipation and incessant wandering ended in insanity and suicide.

NERVI, PIER LUIGI, 1891– , Italian architect, renowned as an innovator in the use of reinforced concrete, was born in Sondrio, and studied at the University of Bologna. In addition to many industrial buildings, Nervi designed the United Nations Educational, Scientific and Cultural Organization (UNESCO) buildings in Paris and the *Palazzo dello Sport* in Rome. Nervi's design, 1960, for the Turin *Palazzo del Lavoro* (Labor Palace) calls for a roof consisting of 16 square slabs of concrete, each of which is supported at its center by a tapering column 75 feet high; the independence of each unit is emphasized by the presence of glass strips between each slab.

NERVII, an ancient Gallic tribe belonging to the Belgic Gauls. Their territory extended from the Sabis (Sambre) River to the North Sea, and corresponded roughly to the modern province of Hainaut in southwest Belgium and the French Department of Nord. They were defeated by Julius Caesar in 57 B.C.

NERVOUS BREAKDOWN, a state of being incapable of facing one's problems and dealing with them adequately. Nervous breakdown is not a scientific diagnosis; it is a popular description of a variety of emotional disturbances requiring withdrawal from social activity for a time. Usually the individual no longer feels capable of making his own decisions and carrying on daily activities. Psychiatric guidance is needed; treatment is aimed at helping the individual to gain insight into his problems. See PSYCHIATRY; PSYCHONEUROSIS.

NERVOUSNESS, mental agitation and tension sometimes accompanied by physical restlessness. Occasionally nervousness is manifested by trembling, rapid heart rate, and profuse perspiration.

Nervousness may be a symptom of illness. It occurs classically in toxic goiter, in which the entire body metabolism is accelerated by excessive secretion of the thyroid gland (see GOITER, *Toxic Goiter;* THYROID GLAND). Nervousness is often a prominent symptom of the inner conflicts of emotional illness (see MENTAL ILLNESS).

Lay persons, however, ascribe to nervousness any state of tenseness and unrest. The word is popularly used to describe the psychoneuroses (see PSYCHONEUROSIS). Nervousness is a normal reaction to danger. It is almost universally experienced by soldiers before battle and is a prominent manifestation of stage fright.

MARC H. HOLLENDER, M.D.

NERVOUS SYSTEM, the structures of the body that together give the organism the quality of irritability. The nervous system of multicellular animals is a complex group of tissues and structures that regulate and control the activities of the animal both voluntarily and automatically. The nervous system not only acts to keep the organs operating co-operatively, but helps the organism to react adaptively to changes outside the body. In man, and probably to some extent in other higher animals, adaptive behavior includes thinking, reasoning, and feeling, and these functions are performed by the nervous system.

The nervous system may be compared to an extensive communications system. It transmits impulses (messages) from sense organs (receivers) to a central switchboard (the brain). An impulse may be caused by a stimulus within or without the body and may pass through several local switchboards (lower centers) before reaching the brain. The impulse is transmitted from the brain or the lower centers to the proper regions or organs in such a way that an action appropriate to the stimulus is initiated. The nervous system does no work in the sense that the muscular system works; it simply connects various parts of the body with one another and with the outside environment.

Anatomical Divisions. The nervous system is regarded as composed of the following major divisions:

- I. Central nervous system
  - A. Brain
  - B. Spinal cord
- II. Peripheral nervous system
  - A. Cerebrospinal nervous system
    - 1. Cranial nerves
    - 2. Spinal nerves
  - B. Autonomic nervous system
    - 1. Sympathetic division
    - 2. Parasympathetic division

The brain is the largest and most complicated single structure in the nervous system. (See BRAIN.) It controls the vital activities of the body and is the center of thinking, remembering, feeling, and voluntary action. One part of the brain, the cerebellum, is most important in co-ordination. Twelve pairs of cranial nerves emerge from the brain (see BRAIN, Cranial Nerves) and carry impulses of sight, hearing, smell, and taste as well as those for control of the internal organs. They also supply nerves to the skin, muscles, and glands of the head and neck.

Descending from the base of the brain and continuous with it is a large tubular structure, the spinal cord. (See SPINAL CORD.) In man the spinal cord extends from the lower end of the medulla oblongata to the level of the first or second lumbar vertebra, and is 40 to 45 centimeters (about 16 to 18 in.) in length. It lies within but does not fill a tubular space which, because it is surrounded by the vertebrae, is

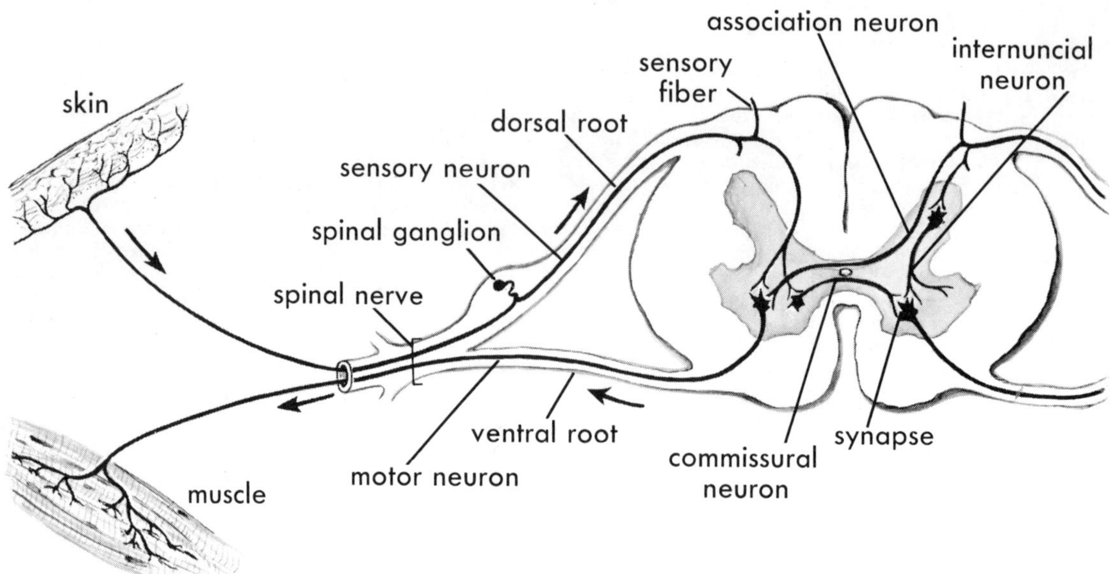

Diagrammatic Cross Section of Spinal Cord, Illustrating Nerve Connections of Reflex Arc

called the vertebral canal. The spinal cord is covered by the same type of protective membranes, or meninges, that surround the brain and is bathed in cerebrospinal fluid. (See CEREBROSPINAL FLUID.) The 31 pairs of spinal nerves that arise from the cord and emerge from the canal through the intervertebral foramina, or openings, carry impulses to and from the muscles, skin, and other structures. They and the cranial nerves constitute the cerebrospinal nervous system, and the brain and spinal cord form the central nervous system.

The peripheral nervous system includes the cerebrospinal nervous system, which is under voluntary and conscious control, and the autonomic nervous system, which is not. The autonomic nervous system regulates blood pressure, heart beat, digestion, and similar functions and is connected to the cerebrospinal nervous system by small branches. (See AUTONOMIC NERVOUS SYSTEM.) The peripheral nervous system is made up of nerves and ganglia. Nerves are bundles of conducting fibers. Those that carry impulses into the central nervous system are afferent, or sensory, fibers; those that carry impulses from the central nervous system are efferent, or motor, fibers. Ganglia are small groups of nerve cells the conducting fibers of which travel along the nerves. Ganglia of sensory cells, such as dorsal root ganglia and spinal ganglia, are associated with the spinal nerves and are located near the nerves' entry into the cord. The autonomic nervous system has many ganglia, some lying along the front of the vertebral column, or spine, and others placed among the internal organs.

In some regions the nerves form plexuses, or networks. Those of the autonomic system lie along blood vessels and in the walls of the internal organs. Those of the cerebrospinal system are large and are composed of spinal nerves from which arise the individual nerves that go to the limbs: the brachial plexuses go to the arms; the sacral plexuses to the legs. An individual nerve in the arms and legs, therefore, is composed of sensory fibers, which carry impulses to the spinal cord, motor fibers, which carry impulses to the muscles; and autonomic fibers, which go to the blood vessels and sweat glands.

MICROSCOPIC STRUCTURE OF NERVOUS TISSUE

The nervous system is made up of nerve cells (see CELL), called neurons, and supporting cells, called neuroglia. Cell bodies of neurons are found only in the central nervous system and in ganglia. Neuroglia, of which there are four types, are found in the central nervous system only. Neurons in various parts of the central nervous system vary so much in form, size, and arrangement that different regions can be identified by their characteristic microscopic appearance. Most cells give off two kinds of processes: one axon and, usually, many dendrites. Axons, which are the actual nerve fibers, may be up to 3 feet long and may have side branches called collaterals, which connect with other cells. Axons are thin and have a uniform diameter and a cytoplasmic matrix made up of threadlike neurofibrils. Dendrites are thicker and irregular in contour; they taper rapidly and branch frequently. They are much shorter than the axons and form a feltlike meshwork around the neuron cell bodies. See CONNECTIVE TISSUE; TISSUE.

Many of the axons in the central nervous system are naked. The axons of spinal nerves have a relatively thick myelin sheath, around which is a thin membrane called the neurilemma. Myelin is a fatty substance which, because it is highly refractile, gives nerves their white color. Axons within the central nervous system do not have a neurilemma but are surrounded by neuroglia cells instead. Some axons of the autonomic nervous system have a neurilemma but no myelin sheath.

There are two types of tissue within the central nervous system. The first is white matter, which is made up of bundles of myelinated axons with the supporting cells. The second is gray matter, which is made up of neuron cell bodies, unmyelinated axons, the feltwork of dendrites, and the neuroglia. Within the gray matter there are accumulations of neuron cell bodies; depending on their arrangement these congregations are called nuclei, columns, or centers. In the brain the gray matter, except for some deep-buried masses, is on the surface; the white matter is underneath. In the spinal cord, on the other hand, the gray matter is in the center, surrounded by white matter. The main connecting link between the brain and the rest of the body, the spinal cord carries nervous impulses to and from the brain; it also contains centers that route some impulses automatically from one part of the body to another without sending them first to the brain. These centers, which operate what are called spinal reflex actions, are located in the central part of the cord, or the part made up of gray matter; whereas most of the fibers connecting the brain with the nerves are on the outer surface of the cord and form its white matter. The spinal nerves are more regular in structure and function than the cranial nerves; some spinal nerves, however, have the same functions as cranial nerves. Each spinal nerve has two roots, or legs: the dorsal, or posterior, root contains sensory fibers; the ventral, or anterior, root carries motor fibers.

Conduction of Nerve Impulses

The mechanism of conduction of the nerve impulse along the axon, a complex physicochemical phenomenon, has been only partially explained. It is known that electrical changes accompany the transmission of the nerve impulse, since these changes can be measured and timed. In addition the release and removal of the chemical substance acetylcholine appears to be an essential characteristic of the process.

Synapses. After passing along the axon the impulse comes to the junction between one neuron and the next, or the synapse, which connects the axon of one neuron with the cell body or dendrite of another. There is no continuity between one neuron and the next, however, since neurofibrils do not go across the synapse. Thus, one cell activates another in the nervous system because the impulse passes across the synapse, a process taking a small measurable period of time. One important property of the synapse is that it transmits impulses in one direction only, from the axon of one cell to the dendrite of the next cell. Since the axons are capable of transmitting an impulse in either direction, it is the synapse that makes it possible for nerve paths to exist with a definite direction of conduction. Without this provision incoming impulses would produce a chaotic response in the entire nervous system.

Reflexes. In some of the lower animals, such as the coelenterates (see Coelenterata), there are specialized nerve cells in the skin that come into immediate contact with a muscle fiber, so that the sensory cell is simply a trigger that serves to activate the underlying muscle. In slightly higher animal forms there are interposed ganglion cells that serve to activate more than one muscle fiber when the sensory cell is stimulated. In even higher forms, such as the earthworm, the ganglion cells become massed in a chain of ganglia, and some cells develop into motor cells. Thus the path from stimulation to effect is as follows: An impulse arises as the result of stimulation of an end organ, is conducted by way of an axon to the central nervous tissue, and then passes over a synapse to one or more motor cells that conduct it through their axons to the muscle. Such a path is called a reflex arc.

In the vertebrates this pathway is less prominent. Furthermore, many reflex arcs of vertebrates are much more complicated. The incoming sensory impulse may pass through many intermediate neurons before reaching the motor cells that will set the muscles into action; it may be transmitted up or down the cord, across it, to the lower centers of the brain, or to the cortex. In turn, the cells of the motor pathways, or descending tracts, connect with the motor neurons of the cord, which send the impulse to the muscle fibers.

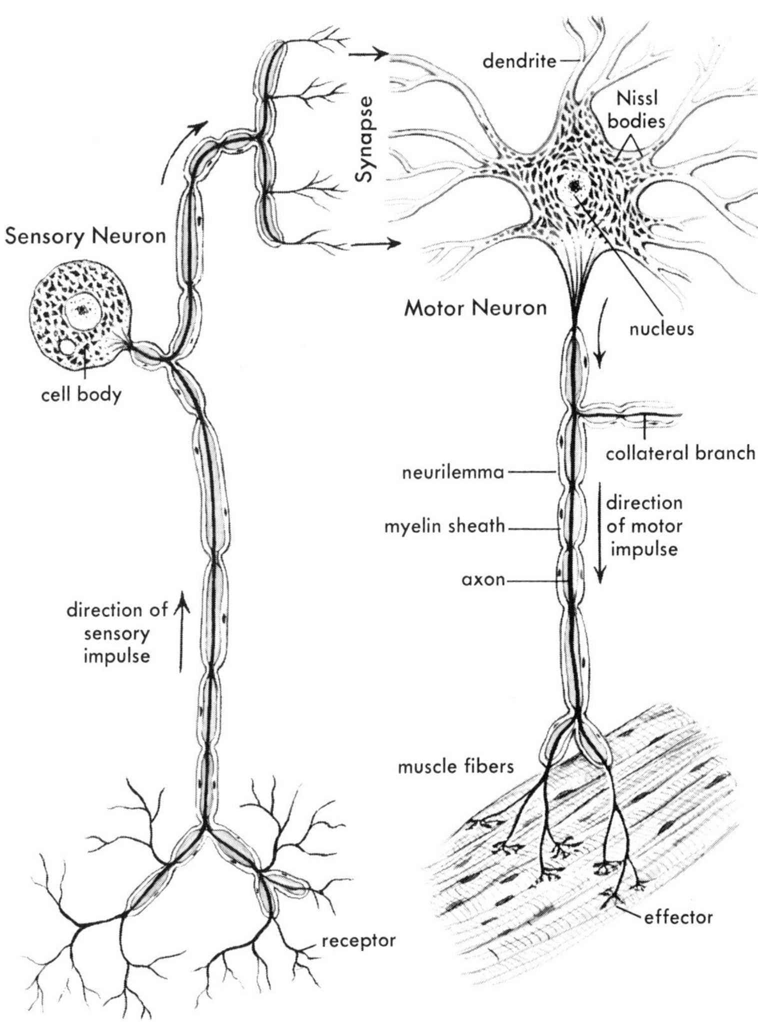

Diagram of Synapse Between Sensory and Motor Neuron

Reflexes mediated by the cranial nerves operate in the same way, but because of the complexity and specialization in the brain, their paths are not so well traced. There are simple protective reflexes such as that manifested by blinking, more complex ones that result in such actions as ducking from a flying object, and other extremely complex ones involving maintenance of muscle tension, balance, and circulatory efficiency.

Levels of Integration

In the nervous system specialized cells receive stimuli from within and without the body and send their impulses into the central nervous system by way of their axons. In the central nervous system the incoming impulses connect with motor cells through chains of neurons and through centers of varying complexity, the highest functional units of which include those of consciousness and thinking. The motor neuron receives impulses from all levels—from adjacent levels of the spinal cord, from lower centers in the brain, and from the cortex. The motor neuron sends out such impulses as are determined by the total combined effects of the impulses it receives by way of the various pathways.

The spinal cord in man is much like a primitive type of nervous system. On the other hand, the higher the animal in

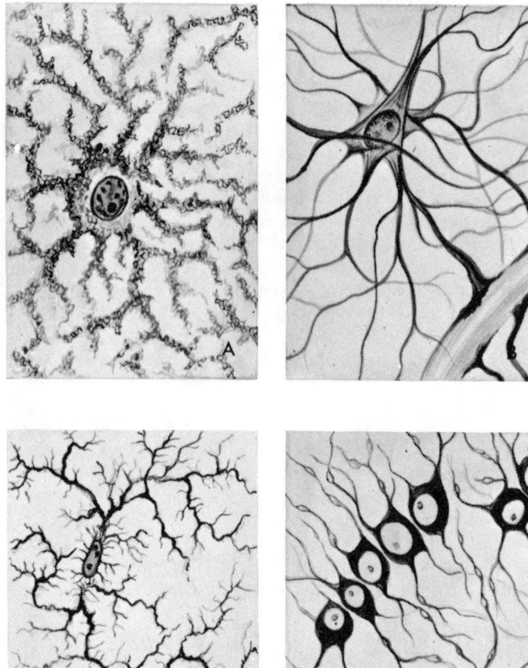

Neuroglia Cells: *A*, protoplasmic astrocytes, found chiefly in gray matter of the brain and spinal cord; *B*, fibrous astrocytes, found chiefly in white matter of the brain and spinal cord; *C*, microglia, found chiefly in gray matter, some in white matter (they function as protective agents by ingesting harmful material); *D*, oligodendroglia, found in both gray and white matter of the brain and spinal cord.

the phylogenetic scale, the greater the number of complex structures—such as the thalamus, red nucleus, and cerebellum—it has and the larger and more important they are. The cerebrum represents the highest level and most complex structure in the nervous system.

Some pathways and centers perform functions that do not reach the level of consciousness and therefore are not under willful control. For instance, the fibers of the spinocerebellar tracts transmit to the cerebellum impulses coming from the organs, and these impulses are then acted upon without conscious control. At the same time they are transmitted to the cortex and thus into consciousness. The cortex can then consciously alter an otherwise inevitable reflex response (for example, one that would throw a person off balance). The greater complexity of the nervous path to the cerebrum, with the greater number of synapses involved, helps explain why reflex actions are faster than those requiring thought.

Embryological Development

The central nervous system develops from the neural plate, a thickened area of the ectoderm, or outer layer of cells. (See Embryology of Man.) The edges of this plate thicken more rapidly than does the center, and the groove thus formed becomes deeper and deeper and finally becomes the neural tube as the thickened edges fold in over it and fuse in the mid-line. As the embryo grows older, constrictions divide the front end of the tube into a forebrain, midbrain, and hindbrain. The tube then bends forward in the region of the midbrain. At the front end of the tube two lateral bulges appear, which increase greatly in size and eventually form the cerebral hemispheres. The portion of the forebrain from which they grow remains as the diencephalon, almost surrounded by the hemispheres.

In the midbrain the walls of the tube thicken and cells differentiate into the various structures of this portion of the brain. Two sets of thickenings appear prominently in the hindbrain. The lower come together beneath the tube and eventually form the pons. The lateral ones grow upward to form the cerebellum. The rear portion of the hindbrain undergoes thickening of its walls and becomes the medulla oblongata; the long, lower portion of the tube also thickens, to form the spinal cord.

During the formation of the neural tube a thickened band of epithelium, the neural crest, comes to lie at each side of it. Cells migrate out from this crest alongside the neural tube. Some of these stay close to the tube, forming the dorsal root ganglia of the spinal nerves. These cells send fibers out to the sensory organs and in to the central nervous system. Other cells migrate out farther from the central nervous system and eventually come to lie in the various ganglia of the autonomic nervous system. Cells remaining in the neural tube send motor fibers out to the muscles and other organs. Spinal nerves are formed by groups of motor and sensory fibers.

In lower animals, such as the earthworm, each body segment, or metamere, has its own feeding and excreting mechanisms as well as its own nerve supply. The tendency to anatomical arrangement according to metameres is also seen in higher animals, and is particularly prominent in the nervous system. In man the craniospinal nerves are arranged in 43 pairs; they are referred to by number, the first pair being nearest the top of the spinal cord and the 43rd nearest the end of it. Each of the sensory roots supplies a definite area of skin, and the motor fibers of each root activate definite groups of muscles. In general the skin and muscles supplied are derived from the same metamere in the embryo from which the nerve grows. The relation between the nerve and the area supplied is most evident in the trunk, where it is not distorted by outgrowth of limbs. In the sensory sphere the distribution of any given root overlaps that of adjacent roots, so that at least two roots must be interrupted in order to produce an area of lost sensation. Likewise, fibers from several roots activate most of the muscles, so that damage to one root rarely causes complete paralysis. See Neurology; Learning; Mind; Psychology; Comparative Psychology; Psychiatry; Psychosis; Psychoneurosis.

John S. Garvin, M.D.

Bibliog.–American Assn. for the Advancement of Science, *Evolution of Nervous Control from Primitive Organisms to Man* (1959); F. Brücke, ed., *Biochemistry of the Central Nervous System* (1959); Archibald R. Buchanan, *Functional Neuro-Anatomy* (1961); Loyal Davis, *Principles of Neurological Surgery* (1953); John Grayson, *Nerves, Brain and Man* (1961); Roy R. Grinker and Others, *Neurology* (1960); Ira J. Jackson and Ray K. Thompson, *Pediatric Neurosurgery* (1959); Albert Kuntz, *Autonomic Nervous System* (1953); Fletcher McDowell and Harold G. Wolff, *Handbook of Neurological Diagnostic Methods* (1960); Mayo Clinic, *Clinical Examinations in Neurology* (1956); Sir Charles S. Sherrington, *Integrative Action of the Nervous System* (1961); George M. Wyburn, *Nervous System: An Outline of the Structure and Function of the Human Nervous System* (1961).

NESS, LOCH, lake, N central Scotland, Inverness-shire, extending 24 miles SW-NE along the Great Glen of Scotland; maximum width 2 miles, maximum depth 751 feet. Loch Ness is part of the Caledonian Canal, and empties through the 7-mile-long River Ness into Moray Firth at Inverness. It receives the rivers Oich and Glentarff at Fort Augustus and the river Moriston at Invermoriston. Since 1933 Loch Ness has received considerable publicity as the home of a reputed monster or sea serpent. The lake remains free of ice throughout the winter.

NESSELRODE, COUNT KARL ROBERT, 1780–1862, Russian government official, was born in Lisbon. As a member of the diplomatic corps of Alexander I he took a prominent part in the negotiations preceding the Peace of Paris, 1814, and in the Congress of Vienna. He was minister of foreign affairs, 1816–56, supported the Holy Alliance, became chancellor, 1844, and concluded the Treaty of Paris, 1856, after the Crimean War. He was the creator of Nesselrode pudding, a frozen dessert consisting of a custard and candied fruit, raisins, and chestnuts.

NESSUS, in Greek legend a centaur who carried travelers across the River Evenos. Hercules entrusted his wife Deianira to Nessus; when the centaur tried to make off with her, Hercules shot him with a poisoned arrow. In revenge the dying Nessus told Deianira that she might use some of his blood to make her husband love her exclusively; Deianira dipped Hercules' robe in the centaur's blood and gave it to her husband. Hercules was tortured by the poisonous blood and threw himself on a burning funeral pyre.

NEST, the site where an animal may live, rest, deposit its eggs for incubation, rear its young, or store food. The nest may be merely a sheltered space, a quickly scooped shallow depression such as is favored by trout and salmon, or an intricate and elaborate form such as the honeybee constructs. A nest used as an abode is usually built for an individual family, but in some cases many nests are connected by tunnels to form a complex community. Among the animals using communal dwellings are the prairie dog, ant, and termite. Nest building has been best developed among birds. Materials that birds use to construct nests include grass, leaves, twigs, downy or breast feathers, fur, and mud. Plant cotton, grass, or twigs bound together by saliva are sometimes used by swifts.

A nest may be situated underground, exposed or sheltered on the ground, in a cave, on a rocky ledge, on a tree limb or within a tree cavity, and even on the site of the nest of another species. Most animals begin to build their nests only after the establishment of a territory for the family food supply and after courtship. The nest is used primarily for depositing eggs for incubation and as a place to raise the young. Some animals such as the sea turtle occupy the nest only during the laying of the eggs; others, as the bear and the ground hog, occupy their nests the year around. Some nests may be used for only one season.

NESTOR, in Greek legend king of Pylos, a son of Neleus and the only one left alive by Hercules when he captured Pylos. Nestor took part in the war of the Lapithae against the Centaurs, in the hunt of the Caledonian boar, and in the Argonautic expedition. In Homer's *Iliad* and *Odyssey* Nestor appears as a kindly and wise old man, renowned for his good advice and his admiration of the past.

NESTORIAN, one of a fifth century sect that emphasized the distinction between the two natures of Jesus Christ, the divine and the human, to such an extent that its teachings implied two separate persons. Nestorius, for whom the group was named, in 428 received his appointment from Emperor Theodosius II as patriarch of Constantinople. As a result of coming under the influence of Theodore of Mopsuestia (see Theodore of Mopsuestia) and the Antiochian school, Nestorius held the view that the Virgin Mary was the mother of Christ only in His human nature and that God was Christ's father in His divine nature. Specifically, he rejected the title Theotokos, or Mother of God, that was increasingly being applied to Mary as a form of reverence. Cyril of Alexandria championed the orthodox viewpoint, and a bitter controversy followed (see Cyril of Alexandria, Saint). In December, 430, in line with action taken the preceding August at a council in Rome, Cyril hurled 12 anathemas at Nestorius and led the Council of Ephesus, which convened June 22, 431, at the call of Emperor Theodosius II, to pronounce sentence of deposition on Nestorius before the arrival of his chief supporter, John of Antioch. John convened an opposition council that a few days later condemned Cyril and vindicated Nestorius. In a compromise theological formula, the two parties represented by John and Cyril were reconciled in 433; Nestorius was first returned to his monastery in Antioch, 435, and then banished to Upper Egypt, where his death occurred probably about 451. Other irreconcilables took refuge in Persia, India, and China but did not prove to be successful missionaries. See Council of Ephesus.

Nestorians who survived persecution through the centuries are today represented by the Assyrian Christians, sometimes called the Assyrian, East Syrian, or Nestorian church, with followers in Iraq, Iran, and Malabar, India. They venerate Nestorius as a saint and refuse to call the Virgin Mary the Mother of God. They do not recognize the primacy of Rome and refuse to recognize the validity of the general church councils after the second because the third, at Ephesus, condemned Nestorius. Their liturgy is of the Antiochene family and is said in Syriac; the rite is called Chaldean or East Syrian. Although a small, isolated body, the church has relations with some Jacobites and some Anglicans. Their number in 1958 was estimated at 275,000. Living among the Nestorian or Assyrian Christians, and outnumbering them, are the Uniats, commonly called Chaldean Catholics who maintain ties with Rome. They have been a separate church organization since splitting from the Nestorians in the sixteenth century, although they still observe many of the same rites and practices. The largest of the Uniat groups, the Malabar Chaldean Catholic, developed during the time of the early Nestorian missions to India. In 1958 the Uniat membership was estimated at 350,000.

Bibliog.–J. W. Etheridge, *Syrian Churches* (1846); G. P. Badger, *Nestorians and Their Rituals* (1852); G. M. Rae, *Syrian Church in India* (1892); J. F. Bethune-Baker, *Nestorius and His Teaching* (1908); W. A. Wigram, *Introduction to the Assyrian Church, 100–640 A.D.* (1910); F. Loofs, *Nestorius and His Place in History* (1914); W. F. Adeney, *Greek and Eastern Churches* (ed. 1923); B. J. Kidd, *Churches of Eastern Christendom from A.D. 451 to the Present Time* (1927); A. R. Vine, *Nestorian Churches* (1937).

NET, an openwork fabric usually manufactured of threads or twine so plaited, looped, or knotted together as to intersect one another at regular intervals. The meshes, or openings may be of any size or shape.

Practical applications of netting are diverse. Netting is used in the production of such articles as curtains, wearing apparel, and various forms of protection against small pests such as mosquitoes and flies; these items are often made of closely woven nylon, rayon, cotton, or silk. (See Lace.) Various types of nets are employed extensively in the fishing industry. (See Fisheries, *Methods of Fishing.*) Nets are also used to capture birds and butterflies. Nets constitute part of the equipment needed in tennis, volleyball, badminton, and similar games. Fabricated of steel, nets were sunk in numerous harbors in World Wars I and II as antisubmarine devices.

NET, in accounting, the amount remaining after deducting from the gross receipts all costs, outlays, and losses. In a commercial enterprise net assets are equivalent to the book value (or the market value) of assets after liabilities are deducted—in other words, the actual value of the proprietary interest in the business. Net profit is the monetary gain realized from an investment after deducting the applicable losses and expenses. In a business transaction net profit is the amount of the difference between the selling price of an asset and the cost of the asset sold, including the operating expenses. Net loss occurs from an excess of gross expenses and costs of a business operation above total income. Net income is the balance that remains after all expenses and losses—including the cost of disposing of capital assets—have been deducted from the total income for any given period. Net price signifies a price that is not subject to deductions or discounts. See Accounting; Bookkeeping; Profit.

NETHERLANDS INFORMATION SERVICE

To preserve its lowlands this kingdom wages a constant battle with the encroaching sea.

NETHERLANDS, or Holland, kingdom, NW Europe; bounded by the North Sea on the W and N, Germany on the E, and Belgium on the S; maximum length (NE-SW) and width (E-W) 190 and 125 miles respectively; area (1957), including interior water, 15,588 sq. mi., of which 12,258 sq. mi. is land; pop. (1961 est.) 11,554,794. The seat of the government is The Hague ('s Gravenhage), but the states-general, or parliament, is in Amsterdam. See map in Atlas, Vol. 20. For the national flag in color, see FLAG.

PHYSICAL FACTORS

Geology. This low-lying country is a western extension of the North German glaciated plain. Sedimentary rocks basic to this geologic division of Europe are covered in the Netherlands either by delta deposits of the Rhine, Meuse (Maas), and Scheldt rivers or by glacial materials deposited during the Ice Age. Only in extreme southeast Limburg is bedrock exposed.

Topography. The Netherlands has three distinct physiographic bands extending northeast-southwest. The name Holland (hollow land) designates a low central trough that lies between upland regions on the east and west. The narrow, sandy coastal area on the west is characterized by dunes, some fixed and some shifting. The central trough or hollow is polder area, once sea bottom but now rich agricultural land, often as much as 20 feet below sea level. The area is protected from the sea by dikes.

The eastern upland, which comprises most of the provinces of Drenthe, Overijssel, Gelderland, North Brabant, and Limburg, is the highest area of the Netherlands, but even there seldom averages more than 300 feet above sea level. In the northern part of the upland is an area of glacier moraine. In the central part of the elevated area is the delta of the Rhine and Meuse rivers. In southern Limburg are loess hills; on the German border near Aachen the Netherlands rises to a height of 1,057 feet.

Coasts. The coast line of the Netherlands is extremely irregular. In the north an arc of islands, the West Frisians, mark a once-continuous offshore sand bar, ruptured by severe storms during the thirteenth century. Behind these islands are wide, mud flats, which are submerged during high tide. Zeeland, in the south, is a series of low-lying islands of sediment deposited by the Scheldt and the Rhine.

Rivers and Lakes. The Netherlands is a riverine state, for it literally sits astride and controls the outlets of some of the most important rivers of Europe. As the Rhine enters the Netherlands it divides into two main branches, the Lek and the Waal. The Meuse, coming from France, through Belgium, flows through the southern Netherlands and empties into the sea south of Rotterdam. The estuary of the Scheldt, basically a Belgian waterway, is in the Netherlands. In the north is the IJsselmeer, a small remnant of what was the Zuider Zee. With the closing of the Afsluit Dike, the salt-water bay became a fresh-water lake. Four large areas have been drained and have become rich polder agricultural land.

Canals link the rivers to provide an excellent network of water transportation in central and southern Netherlands. The North Sea Canal, built in 1876, has been enlarged twice and now accommodates the largest vessels. It runs from IJmuiden on the sea to Amsterdam, which had been closed from the ocean by the dike on the Zuider Zee. The Juliana Canal was built from the Belgian border near Liège and runs through Limburg along the Meuse, bypassing long sections where the river curves sharply.

Climate. The combination of westerly winds and the warming waters of the North Atlantic Drift produces a marine climate for the Netherlands. Rainfall, distributed evenly throughout the year, averages approximately 28 inches. Humidity is high, and sea fogs are common. In spite of a latitudinal position the same as that of Labrador, temperatures in the Netherlands are not extreme. January is the coldest month, with temperatures averaging 34°F. The summer average is a moderate 62°.

Soils and Natural Vegetation. In its original state the Netherlands did not have especially good soil. In the north and east, sands, gravels, and clays deposited during the Ice Age were conducive to the formation of peat bogs. Because of the shortage of good agricultural land, sandy lands were enriched with marls and fertilizer, and the peat bogs were drained. The dune land of the western coastal area is composed of sand and is the location for many of the important cities. In some of the dune lands the Dutch experimented with forestation techniques similar to those used in the Landes dune section of France.

The most important agricultural areas are the polders. Marshes that once filled brackish lagoons have accumulated quantities of humus, and when these areas are drained and leached of salt for several years the soils are rich. The water table is quite high, however, often restricting the kinds of crops that can be produced. Natural vegetation—heath in the north and east, hardwood forests in the south—has given way to agricultural land, but large areas have been reforested, chiefly with softwoods.

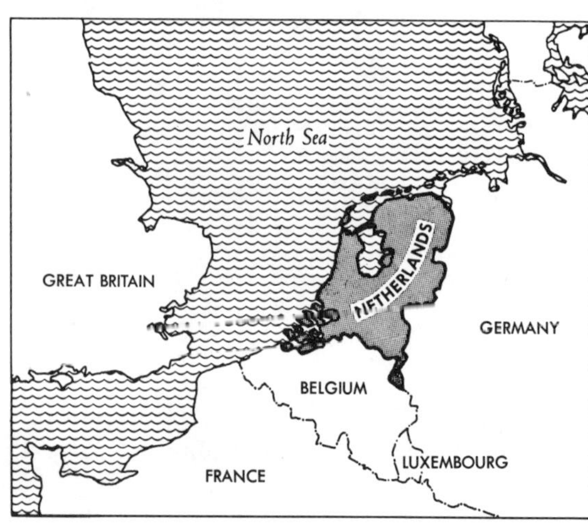

Location Map of the Netherlands

NETHERLANDS

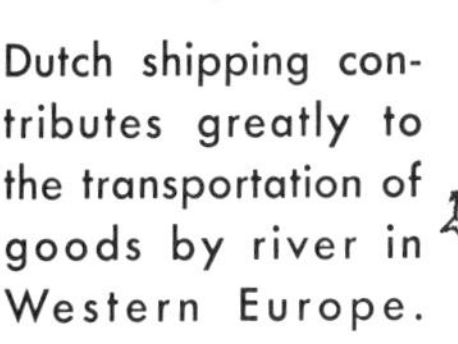

Dutch shipping contributes greatly to the transportation of goods by river in Western Europe.

Dairy products are exported.

Factories where diamonds are cut and polished are concentrated in Amsterdam, whose workmen are internationally famous for their fine craftsmanship.

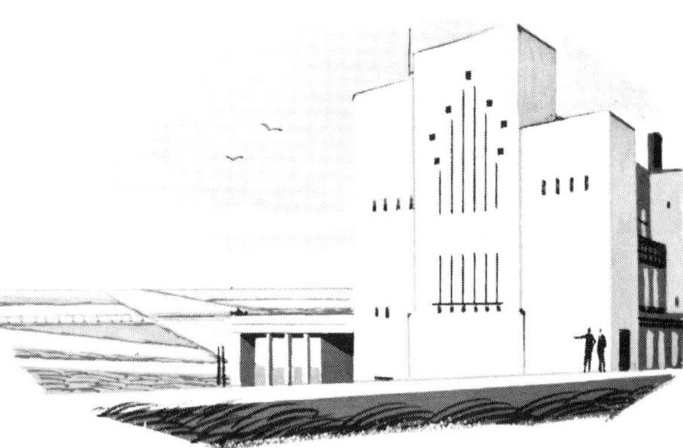

New polders are kept dry by electrical and diesel pumping stations which pump excess water into wide drainage canals. Windmills are used in the older polders.

All the coal mined in the Netherlands is from the Limburg area and is domestically consumed. Small amounts of lignite, clay, and salt also are produced in the country.

PRINCIPAL RESOURCES, INDUSTRIES, AND PRODUCTS

- Aluminum refining
- Apples
- Barley
- Beets
- Cattle
- Cement
- Chemicals
- Coal
- Dairy products
- Diamond cutting
- Diversified manufacturing
- Fish
- Flax
- Flower bulbs
- Hogs
- Horses
- Leather goods
- Oats
- Petroleum
- Potatoes
- Poultry
- Salt
- Sheep
- Shipbuilding
- Steel
- Textiles
- Vegetables
- Wheat

Animals. Wild animals, though not abundant, include the usual small varieties: hare, badger, beaver, weasel, ermine, fox, and deer. The stork is so common that it is characteristic of the Netherlands.

Social Factors

Population. With an estimated 928 people per square mile in 1961, the Netherlands had a problem of overpopulation greater than that of any other country of northwestern Europe. An annual increase of more than 150,000 people indicated that population was growing far too fast for land capacity, nevertheless the declaration of independence in Indonesia in 1950 caused the transfer of 235,000 Dutch and 150,000 Eurasians from former island possessions to an already overcrowded country.

PRINCIPAL CITIES

City	Population 1947 Census	Population 1959 (Official Estimate)
Amsterdam	803,847	872,428
Rotterdam	646,248	731,047
Hague, The (capital)	532,998	606,825
Utrecht	185,246	252,104
Haarlem	156,856	168,863
Eindhoven	134,527	163,083
Groningen	132,021	143,996
Tilburg	114,312	134,974
Nijmegen	106,523	127,110
Arnhem	97,350	123,238
Enschede	80,346	121,981
Breda	81,873	105,531

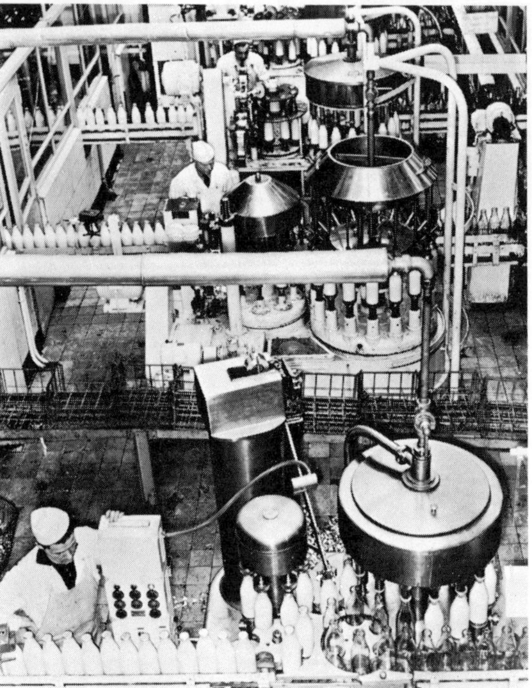

NETHERLANDS INFORMATION SERVICE

Production of dairy products, a leading part of the economy of the Netherlands, is concentrated in the polders. Gouda, Edam, and Alkmaar are noted for butter and cheese.

Language, Religion, and Education. Two Teutonic languages are used in the Netherlands. Dutch is the official language, but Frisian is spoken in a small area in the extreme north.

Protestantism is the predominant religion of the Netherlands, followed rather closely by Roman Catholicism. The 1947 census showed the following percentages: Dutch Reformed, 31; other Protestant, 13.3; Roman Catholic, 38.5; Jewish, 0.2; others and no creed, 17.

Education is compulsory and free to the age of 15. Sixty-seven per cent of the elementary schools in 1955 were private. Secondary schools include gymnasiums, municipal high schools, and technical schools. Public universities are located at Leiden (founded 1575), Utrecht (1636), Groningen (1614), and Amsterdam (1632). The Roman Catholic University of Nijmegen and the Calvinist University of Amsterdam are private institutions.

Economic Factors

Perhaps the most significant natural resource of the country is the initiative of the Dutch people. Where there was little agricultural land, the Dutch created it. Where there is little mineral resource, they import commodities that make manufacturing possible.

Agriculture in the Netherlands is highly intensified. Farm products are among the leading exports of the country, but only 20 per cent of the population is engaged in farming. Dutch farms are quite small, seldom larger than 250 acres. Dairying is more important than crops, and many polders are meadowland because the water table is too near the surface to allow the growing of crops. Milk, butter, and eggs rank high as export items, and Dutch Gouda, Edam, and Alkmaar cheeses and Dutch chocolate are famous throughout the Western world. The production of these items is regulated by the government, and their quality is high. The raising of tulip, hyacinth, and other bulbs is almost as important as dairying, and utilizes about 17,000 acres in the area between the dune lands and the polder area, from Haarlem south to The Hague. Other important crops are potatoes, sugar and fodder beets, turnips, wheat, rye, oats, barley, carrots, peas, and flax.

Fisheries. The North Sea, 4,800 miles of canals, and hundreds of miles of rivers provide the Netherlands with a fishing industry of considerable importance for both home consumption and export. Although herring is the most important catch, plaice, haddock, cod, and sole are taken from areas as far away as the Lofoten Islands and the Irish Sea. Fresh-water fishing in the IJsselmeer is notable for eels, which helped to destroy the mosquito blight after the sea became a fresh-water lake. Nearly two-thirds of the Netherlands' annual catch of fish is exported.

Mining. The bedrock of the Netherlands is submerged under deep, unconsolidated layers of alluvium and glacial deposits; mining cannot therefore be an important industry. There are small amounts of coal, crude petroleum, lignite, salt, and clay in the country. Limburg, an extension of the German coal fields, is the source of limited supplies of coal. The mines are modern and well equipped but produced only 13,091,760 tons in 1958—all needed for local consumption. Salt deposits are found near Boekelo in Gelderland, and clays along the river beds. Fine clays are used in producing the famous blue delft china. Oil wells at Oud Schoonebeek supply almost 25 per cent of the Netherlands' petroleum requirements.

Manufacturing. Industrialization in the Netherlands can be attributed to population pressures, for until the nineteenth century the nation was commercial and agricultural. Shipbuilding is one of the leading industries in the Netherlands, and engages more than 40,000 workers. The major centers include Rotterdam, Amsterdam, and Dordrecht, which are supplied by the steel-producing center at Velsen. Agricultural industries, whose products include cheese, condensed milk, potato flour, beet sugar, and canned foods, are mainly in southern and eastern Holland. The processing of vegetable oils, cocoa, tobacco, and quinine from products of the Netherlands' colonies is primarily carried on near the main ports of entry, Amsterdam and Rotterdam; many such processing plants line the two maritime canals—

BLACK STAR

Dutch Farmer

NETHERLANDS INFORMATION SERVICE

Windmills drain the land by use of canals in the polders.

NATIONAAL FOTO PERSBUREAU

Maiden of Marken

NETHERLANDS INFORMATION SERVICE

Similar homes line a street on the Island of Marken.

EWING GALLOWAY

Diamond Polisher

EWING GALLOWAY

A large diamond-cutting factory is located in Amsterdam.

BLACK STAR

Volendam Fisherman

NETHERLANDS INFORMATION SERVICE

Fishermen mend nets in a boat at harbor at Volendam.

NETHERLANDS INFORMATION SERVICE

This ceramic shop in Limburg is characteristic of the many small craft trades for which the Netherlands is famous. Delft is one of the notable centers of china production.

the North Sea Canal and the New Waterway—that serve those cities. Except for the processing of the country's own agricultural products, manufacturing in the Netherlands is dependent on raw materials from colonies and other countries. The iron and steel industry was a late development, but a small, efficient smelting and steel plant at Velsen, near Haarlem, produced 728,000 tons of pig iron and 1,150,000 tons of steel in 1956—a little more than one-third of the country's needs. Coal for this production is derived from the Limburg area, and iron ore is imported from Sweden. Aluminum is produced at factories along the New Waterway and the North Sea Canal because the necessary bauxite is imported largely from Surinam in South America. Manufacture of shoes and leather goods is concentrated in the southern part of the country, especially at Breda, and there are textile mills at Tilburg in the southern Netherlands and at Hengelo and Enschede on the eastern border. With the exception of flax, raw materials for the textile industries are imported.

Eindhoven, in the south, is the center of the electrotechnical industry; and Amsterdam is noted for diamond cutting. This location for so specialized an industry is related to early connections of the Netherlands and the Union of South Africa and to early

NETHERLANDS INFORMATION SERVICE

Production of the motorized bicycle, accelerated in the 1950's, has resulted in heavy traffic problems in already bicycle-clogged Dutch cities. Exports are also expanding.

exploration of areas that are still major sources of diamonds. Before World War II the diamond-cutting industry in Amsterdam employed 13,000 skilled workers.

Commerce. The early mercantile policy of the Netherlands created dependence on other countries for both raw materials and markets; lack of self-sufficiency became critical to the Dutch economy when colonies in South Africa and Ceylon were lost in the late eighteenth and early nineteenth centuries and Indonesia (see INDONESIA) established independence in 1950. Although Surinam and Dutch possessions in the Caribbean remained sources of raw materials, markets were considerably diminished.

Benelux, an economic union formed by Belgium, Luxembourg, and the Netherlands after World War II, facilitates the movement of goods between the three member countries. The Netherlands is also a member of the European Coal and Steel Community and the European Economic Community, both of which also include Belgium, France, West Germany, Italy, and Luxembourg. The role of the European Coal and Steel Community, an outgrowth of the Schuman Plan, is to seek a common market for raw materials, iron, and steel. It calls for relaxed tariff barriers and free migration of labor to bolster industrial production in western Europe. The Netherlands and the other nations of the European Economic Community participate in a common market established to remove all customs restrictions on the free movement of goods, capital, and persons by 1972.

In 1959 the major Dutch markets were the German Federal Republic (21 per cent), Belgium (14 per cent), Great Britain (10 per cent), the United States (5 per cent), and France (5 per cent). Chief exports are petroleum and coal-tar products, eggs and dairy products, bulbs and flowers, electrical machinery and apparatus, fabric and clothing, and cut and polished diamonds. Imports include timber, coal, uncut diamonds, textiles, cereals, and iron and steel.

Transportation. The Netherlands, historically a maritime country because of its situation at the gateway to northwestern Europe, has the seventh largest merchant marine in the world. It had 1,766 seagoing vessels (100 tons and more) in 1959, and river carriers and barges exceeded sea tonnage by 160,000 tons. Approximately 4,500 miles of excellent navigable inland waterway provide cheap transportation; 2,850 miles of railroads are operated by a government-owned company; and there are approximately 2,500 miles of primary highways. The Royal Dutch Airlines (KLM) provide services to North Sea and Scandinavian countries, Indonesia, and America.

Tourist Attractions. Because of its extreme flatness, the Netherlands could be scenically uninteresting if Dutch initiative had not created orderly landscapes characterized by neat brick villages and picturesque windmills. During late spring and early summer acres of blooming tulips and other flowers draw tourists to the Haarlem area. On the island of Marken in western Holland, connected to the mainland until the end of the thirteenth century, many old Dutch traditions have been preserved. Ferry service links Marken with the mainland, and every year numerous tourists visit the island to see the ancient costumes and customs. WILLIAM KOWITZ

ADMINISTRATION

Government. The Netherlands is a constitutional monarchy divided into 11 provinces, each with its own representative body having considerable power of local legislation. Collectively these local bodies are known as the provincial states. The national executive power belongs to the sovereign, and the legislative authority rests with the sovereign and the states-general, which consists of two chambers: the upper or first, composed of 50 members elected by the provincial states for six-year terms, one half being renewed every three years; and the second, composed of 100 members elected directly for four-year terms. Elections are based on universal suffrage and proportional representation. In practice the government is parliamentary with real power in the hands of a ministry responsible to the states-general. The sovereign appoints a premier, who represents a majority in the states-general and selects the ministers of his cabinet. The upper chamber does not have the power to introduce legislation or to amend bills submitted to it. In addition to the provincial states there are 1,015 municipalities, each with its own municipal council empowered to pass bylaws. The municipal burgomasters are appointed by the sovereign for six years. The polder boards, elected by the landowners of each polder, maintain the dikes and apportion local taxes. Justice is administered by the high council of the Netherlands, 5 courts of justice, 19 district tribunals, and 62 cantonal courts. Judges are appointed for life by the sovereign. There is no trial by jury.

Netherlands Coat of Arms

Armed Forces. The army is composed of both volunteers and draftees. By an act of 1922 every male Dutch citizen is liable to service in the armed forces between the ages of 20 and 40. The navy consists of 1 escort carrier, 2 cruisers, 12 destroyers, 5 submarines, and 154 smaller vessels. The army and the navy each has its own air force.

History

Early History. The lowlands about the mouths of the Scheldt, Meuse, and Rhine were formerly inhabited by the Frisii, Batavi, and Belgae, all of whom came under Roman dominion in the first century. The Batavi supplied the Roman armies with a body of cavalry but revolted against them under Julius Civilis (A.D. 69–70). After Roman rule ended in the fifth century, Frisians occupied the north and west coasts; Franks settled in districts south of the Rhine, displacing or mingling with the Frisians; and Saxons occupied the interior that lies beyond the present Zuider Zee.

Middle Ages. With the division of Charlemagne's dominions in 843, the Netherlands became part of Lotharingia, the borderland between Germany and Gaul, which from 879 onward was associated with the German kingdom, and Flanders became an unruly fief of France. The feudal system never took root in Friesland, but split the remaining districts into small semi-independent states—duchies, counties, bishoprics—which became grouped together through the marriages and the wars of their lords during the thirteenth and fourteenth centuries. In the fifteenth century the groups were gradually united under the dukes of Burgundy. Throughout the Middle Ages trade flourished among Flanders, England, and Scandinavia—and society became urbanized in self-governing towns.

Spanish Domination. When Charles the Bold died in 1477 the territory passed to his son-in-law, Maximilian of Austria, and became part of the Circle of Burgundy. Philip the Fair, son of Maximilian, linked the Netherlands with Spain by marriage; and Philip's son, Charles V, the future emperor, was born in Ghent. With the addition of the northeastern provinces, 17 provinces were grouped together under Charles, and the combination was confirmed by the Pragmatic Sanction of 1549. The sovereign was represented in each province by a stadholder. At least for the southern provinces, his reign was a golden one. On his abdication in 1555 the Netherlands passed to his son, Philip II of Spain. During the latter part of his reign Charles had taken measures to check the spread of the reformed doctrines in his dominions; but after the accession of Philip II the matter was taken in hand with greater energy, and vigorous efforts were made to suppress heresy.

Protestant Revolt. Philip, on his departure for Spain in 1559, left his half-sister Margaret, duchess of Parma, as regent of the Netherlands. Both populace and nobility were alienated by Margaret's choice of a foreign ecclesiastic, Cardinal de Granvelle, as her adviser, by the continued presence of Spanish garrisons, and by the religious persecutions. The nobility, after vainly petitioning the duchess for a suspension of the king's edicts against Protestantism, founded in 1566 the party of the *Gueux*, or Beggars, pledged to side with the people against Spanish tyranny and the Inquisition. Prominent among the petitioners were Comte Lamoral d'Egmont and Philip de Montmorency, count of Horn. Fortified by the attitude of the nobles, the Protestant leaders took new courage; the numbers of their followers swelled and broke in a burst of anti-Catholic iconoclasm that tumbled down statues, wrecked altars, and damaged cathedrals.

Spanish Oppression. Philip's reply to the outbreak was to dispatch Alvarez de Toledo, duke of Alva, renowned for his cruelties, to the Netherlands with 10,000 Spanish troops. Vengeance was swift and terrible. Aided by the Council of Blood, a special court instituted for the speedy trial of all whose fidelity to the king was suspect, Alva carried on a relentless campaign for the suppression of Protestantism. Thousands were put to death, among them Egmont and Horn, and thousands more fled the country. In 1568 William, prince of Orange and count of Nassau, after fruitless attempts at negotiation, formed a small army to oppose the Spanish oppressors. At first the ill-equipped Dutch army met with little success before Alva's splendidly equipped forces, but with characteristic persistence they refused to recognize defeat; Brielle was captured by the *Gueux de Mer*, Dutch freebooters, in 1572, and Flushing and Enkhuizen were also taken. See INQUISITION.

William of Orange. Heartened by these successes, many of the northern towns acknowledged William's leadership, and on July 18, 1572, the League of Dordrecht recognized William of Orange as stadholder, or governor, in lieu of the duke of Alva, over the provinces of Holland, Zeeland, and Utrecht, and leader of the defensive league. In September, 1572, William's army was routed before Mons; Haarlem fell after a glorious siege; Leiden saved itself by cutting the dikes; but the successful defense of Alkmaar and a Spanish naval defeat on the Zuider Zee led to Alva's recall.

Efforts Toward Independence. In 1576 the estates of Holland and Zeeland were summoned to meet at Delft with a view to closer union; an act of federation was drawn up, and William was acknowledged supreme ruler. A short time later the southern provinces joined with the Hollanders and Zeelanders and the treaty known as the Pacification of Ghent, later confirmed by the Union of Brussels, was agreed upon. Don John of Austria was made governor general in 1577 and was forced to accept the terms of the Pacification of Ghent by signing the Perpetual Edict, which confirmed the authority of the prince of Orange in Holland and Zeeland in the name of the king. Don John was succeeded in 1578 by Alessandro Farnese, duke of Parma, who at length won back the southern provinces for Spain. But the following year the seven northern provinces entered into a union, the Union of Utrecht, which in 1581 declared its independence. William of Orange became the ruler of Holland and Zeeland, and François, duke of Anjou, obtained the sovereignty of Gelderland, Utrecht, Groningen, Overijssel, and Friesland. Anjou later left the country after a treacherous attempt at usurpation. William was assassinated at the instance of the Spanish king in 1584, and in the following year Antwerp surrendered to the duke of Parma.

Aid from England. Long-hoped-for aid came from England. Queen Elizabeth I sent an army under Robert Dudley, duke of Leicester, in 1585, and although this was not immediately successful it served Holland well by distracting Philip's attention to England, to the conquest of which he turned his efforts, with a conspicuous lack of success. Dutch victories under the leadership of William's son, Maurice of Nassau, and Jan van Olden Barneveldt, leader of the Dutch Republicans, led to a truce in 1609.

Expansion of the Netherlands. The provinces had meanwhile been ceded to Isabella, Philip's daughter and archduchess of Austria. Many refugees came from the more cultured southern provinces and countries intolerant of intellectual minorities, and the next 80 years were the most brilliant in Dutch cultural life. The East India Company was founded in 1602 by Barneveldt. Trade with the Indians at the site of New York was opened in 1610, and a settlement was made there in 1624. Settlements were also established in Java; Ceylon was cleared of Portuguese in 1658; and Dutch colonists settled in the West Indies and Brazil. Navigators like Willem Barents, Willem Cornelis Schouten, and Jakob Le Maire explored the arctic seas and the far south.

The provinces at that time differed in character and constituted seven republics rather than a single one. Each sent delegates to the states-general at The Hague; but each state had only one vote, and for important decisions unanimity was requisite. There was a council of state, in which the representation was less unequal, and the members of which voted individually. Until 1747 the stadholder technically did not hold office in all provinces at once, but he was *de facto* president of the confederation, controlled its navy and army, and had two votes in the council. Dependencies of various kinds, such as lands acquired from the Roman Catholic south, had no representation.

Conflict of Republicans and Monarchists. The history of the period 1609–1747 is largely concerned with the conflict of the monarchical and republican elements in the constitution. Before 1609 the Calvinist and Remonstrant theological controversy had begun between Franciscus Gomarus and Jacobus Arminius, professors at the University of Leiden, which had been founded in 1575. Maurice and Barneveldt, already at variance, took opposite sides. The Gomarists triumphed; Barneveldt was executed, and the great jurist, Hugo Grotius, was sentenced to life imprisonment.

Wars with Spain and England. The war with Spain, renewed in 1621, was brought to an end by the Treaty of Westphalia in 1648, by which Spain recognized the independence of the United Provinces and their conquests in the Far East. Prince Maurice had been succeeded in 1625 by his brother, Frederick Henry, who insisted on religious peace but made no effort to increase his powers. William II, his son, sought to elevate himself to the rank of sovereign, but died in 1650 after a reign of three years. During the long minority of his posthumous son, William III, afterward king of England, the power rested with Holland and its pensionary, Jan De Witt. Commercial rivalry with England led to great naval wars, 1652–54 and 1664–67. During the latter a Dutch fleet under Michel de Ruyter and Cornelis De Witt sailed up the Medway River and burned the English fleet as it lay at anchor. The Peace of Breda, July 31, 1667, gave Surinam to Holland and New Netherlands, on the North American continent, to England.

Triple Alliance. In 1668 Holland joined England and Sweden in a triple alliance to check the growing power of France. The English king, Charles II, however, concluded a secret treaty with Louis XIV of France, and in 1672 Holland found itself facing a French invasion from the south and an allied English and French attack at sea. De Ruyter's fleet offered effective resistance to the allied squadrons, but land forces were less successful. Town after town surrendered to the French armies, whose advance was checked only by the opening of the sluices in the dikes which flooded the country. The English, wearied with the war, signed the Treaty of Westminster in 1674, and concluded the Peace of Nijmegen with France in 1678.

In the meantime a popular reaction set in against De Witt, the grand pensionary, and he was murdered by an infuriated mob. The Perpetual Edict of 1667, which had been modified by De Witt to curb the power of the Orange family, had been repealed, and the stadholdership had been re-established in 1672 in the young prince of Orange, who was called to the English throne as William III in 1688.

Decline of Dutch Power. The Dutch were parties to the Grand Alliance in 1689 and joined in the wars of William III and the Spanish Succession, settled by the Treaty of Utrecht in 1714, but gained little by either. Their industries were crippled by the consequent heavy taxation, especially customs and excise duties, which fell heavily on the necessities of life and on raw materials, combined with the adoption of the mercantile system. The growth of navigation lost the Dutch their trade, and the cessation of religious warfare brought in greater nations as competitors. Hence they declined throughout the eighteenth century. The Belgian provinces passed, at the Peace of Rastatt, to the house of Austria in 1714. After William's death without issue, 1702, the Republican or oligarchical element ruled until 1747, when the French invasion caused its overthrow and the election of William Henry (William IV), son of John William, prince of Orange, as hereditary stadholder of all seven provinces. He died in 1751, and his son, William V, came of age in 1766.

Foreign Intervention. When the provinces joined the armed neutrality during the American Revolution, Great Britain attacked them, and William V was deposed by the patriot party in 1786. He was restored by Prussia, which jointly with Great Britain guaranteed his rule. He was dethroned again nine years later by the patriots and an invasion by French republican armies, whereupon the Batavian republic was set up. Napoleon I, because of the republic's failure to respond to his demands for money and to conform to his plans of empire, sent his brother Louis Bonaparte to be king in 1806. More interested in his subjects than his brother was, Napoleon deposed Louis in 1810 and united the country with France. In 1813 an anti-French revolution set up William of Orange, son of William V, for whom the Congress of Vienna created the kingdom of the Netherlands, including Belgium. The Belgians revolted in 1830, and the Treaty of London, signed in the following year, guaranteed the neutrality of the new kingdom. See BELGIUM, History, *Independence Movement*.

Late Nineteenth and Early Twentieth Century. Abdicating in 1840, William I was followed by his son, William II, who granted a more parliamentary constitution in 1848. William II was succeeded in 1849 by his son William III. After his accession the country became occupied with colonial and internal affairs and took little part in European politics.

William III appointed Jan Rudolf Thorbecke, an old line liberal, Prime Minister; the Netherlands subsequently embarked upon a period of economic liberalism. Thorbecke also was responsible for reorganizing local government so that the provinces and municipalities became autonomous. He was deposed during a power-conflict between Protestants and Catholics and was succeeded by Conservative F. A. Van Hall. Under Hall, the Netherlands Trading Company, the modern continuation of the East India Company, was deprived of its monopolistic position, and customs and local tariffs were gradually abolished;

the Dutch railroad system was expanded, and the harbors at Rotterdam and Amsterdam were modernized.

Thorbecke returned to power in 1862 and instituted plans to greatly extend public secondary education. The period, 1862–1870, was also a time of cultural renascence, and expanded sea trade, as Dutch ports became outlets for German manufactures. In 1890 William III died and was succeeded by his daughter Wilhelmina, with her mother, Princess Emma, as regent. Wilhelmina was married in 1901 to Prince Henry of Mecklenburg-Schwerin.

The period preceding World War I was marked by rapid industrialization, especially in the south around Tilburg and Eindhoven. Expanding industries pointed up the need for labor reform as early as 1866, when the first labor union was organized. The General Netherlands Workers Union was formed in 1871, and by 1878 the Social Democratic party was gaining political importance.

Dutch political differences between 1870 and 1920 were based chiefly upon different conceptions of the attitude of the state toward religion, the Liberals believing in complete separation while the Anti-Liberals, or Clericals, both Protestant and Catholic, advocated religious instruction in the schools. Bitter controversies were waged over the question, which was settled in 1917 with a complete victory for the clerical parties. The 1917 constitutional revision, which incorporated this change, also included universal male suffrage and proportional party representation. Just 70 years earlier, voting rights in the Netherlands had belonged only to men who owned a substantial amount of property. Later, in 1884, suffrage had been extended a little further. Complete universal suffrage was accomplished by 1922.

After the Franco-Prussian War, the Netherlands' foreign policy was based on a desire for complete political neutrality, so as to free its foreign trade from any interruption. When World War I broke out the country's army was kept in constant readiness, but military conflicts were deftly side-stepped. Although Netherlands shipping was preyed upon by German submarines her ports remained open to all foreign trade. In 1918, the deposed German Kaiser was accorded asylum in Doorn. A project to reclaim the Zuider Zee was begun in 1920; in 1932 the waters of the Zee were cut off from the North Sea and converted into the IJsselmeer.

Between World Wars I and II Rotterdam became a major world port and Amsterdam became the principal distribution center of products from the East Indies. The export trade consumed 60 per cent of the country's manufactures, and large amounts of diamonds, food products, chemicals, textiles, and steel were sent overseas. The Depression seriously affected Dutch industry and commerce, but the critical international situation of the late 1930's led to increased armaments orders and employment.

World War II and After. On May 10, 1940, German forces suddenly attacked the Low Countries. Within four days the Netherlands was completely overrun and its army surrendered. Rotterdam was severely bombed as a warning against further resistance. The royal family and chief government officials escaped to England, where they set up a provisional Dutch government that continued to rule the colonies and carried on the war against Germany (see WORLD WAR II, *Invasion of the Low Countries*). The Dutch never acquiesced in the German occupation; they engaged in acts of sabotage that the Germans tried to repress. Dutch forces took part in the Allied invasion of Europe. After the liberation of the Netherlands, the wartime cabinet resigned and a provisional government was created in 1946. The task of the new government was hampered by the revolt of the Netherlands Indies. After several years of alternate truce and warfare, the Republic of the United States of Indonesia, later renamed the Republic of Indonesia, was formed in 1949. Queen Wilhelmina retired from the throne in 1948 and was succeeded by her daughter Juliana, whose consort was Prince Bernhard of Lippe-Biesterfeld.

The years following World War II were characterized by increased participation in international economic and political organizations. The Netherlands was a founding member of the United Nations. Foreseeing economic extinction in standing alone, the governments of the Netherlands, Belgium, and Luxembourg banded together in 1948 in an economic alliance known as Benelux. In a wider sphere, the Netherlands joined the supranational European Coal and Steel Community and the European Council for Nuclear Research in 1952, and shortly afterward the European Payments Union, the Western European Union and NATO, and in 1957, the European Economic Community. The Netherlands suffered serious losses when the Indonesian government ordered the expulsion of all Dutch nationals and the seizure of Dutch property in the republic in 1957. Rejecting a Dutch claim to Netherlands New Guinea, Indonesia broke off diplomatic relations in 1961 and subsequently, apparently with UN connivance, established complete control over what was thereafter called West Irian.

The sea broke through the dikes in 1953, inundating one-sixth of the country, a disaster that threatened to wreck the newly established economy, but the Dutch set to work to reclaim the land they had lost, and more. Drainage of the IJsselmeer, an area of 860 square miles, was continued, and the polders brought under cultivation. Another vast engineering scheme called the Delta Project, was begun in the southwest to end the danger of flooding in Zeeland and to open that relatively thinly populated area to industrial development.

BIBLIOG.–Adriaan J. Barnouw, *Pageant of Netherlands History* (1952); Sydney Clark, *All the Best in Holland* (1960); Sigfried J. De Laet, *Low Countries* (1959); Willem de G. van Embden, *Life in Europe: The Netherlands* (1960); Albert Hyma, *History of the Dutch in the Far East* (1953); Bartholomew Landheer, ed., *Netherlands* (1946); Doré Ogrizek, *Netherlands* (1951); Sacheverell Sitwell, *Netherlands* (1955); Jan J. M. Timmers, *History of Dutch Life and Art* (1959).

NETHERLANDS ANTILLES, also Netherlands West Indies, two groups of islands about 550 miles apart, in the Lesser Antilles, Caribbean Sea; including in the southern group Aruba, Bonaire, and Curaçao off the NW coast of Venezuela and in the northern group the Leeward Islands of Saba, Saint Eustatius, and the southern part of Saint Martin; area 366 sq. mi.; pop. (1961) 187,041, Negroes and mulattoes comprising more than 80 per cent. Aruba, Bonaire, and Curaçao are rocky islands with a tropical, semi-arid climate modified by the northeast trade winds; the northern group are volcanic and have a more humid tropical climate. Although Dutch is the official language, Papiamento—a mixture of Dutch, Spanish, English, and French—is commonly spoken in the southern group of islands, and English in the northern group. The principal cities are Willemstad, the capital, in Curaçao, and Oranjestad and Sint Nicolaas in Aruba.

Oil refining, established in 1916, is the major industry of the Netherlands Antilles. The refineries, which are located in Aruba and Curaçao—the largest of the islands—and receive their crude oil mainly from the Lake Maracaibo region of Venezuela, produced more than 750,000 barrels of refined oil per day in 1957. Other industries, also concentrated in Aruba and Curaçao, include the mining of calcium phosphate for fertilizer, shipbuilding, and the manufacture of straw hats, tile, and cement. Bonaire and the Leeward group are economically unimportant; stock raising and subsistence farming are the chief occupations.

Curaçao, discovered by Alonso de Ojeda in 1499 and first settled by Spaniards in 1527, was taken by the Dutch, along with Aruba and Bonaire, in 1634.

The northern islands were settled by the Dutch in the middle and late seventeenth century. The British took the islands and occupied Curaçao during the Napoleonic Wars, but all were returned to the Netherlands in 1816 and have been part of the kingdom of the Netherlands since 1922. In 1954 each island was given autonomy in internal affairs, but external affairs such as foreign relations and defense are controlled by the council of ministers of the kingdom.

NETSCHER, CASPAR, 1639–84, Dutch portrait and genre painter, was born in Heidelberg, Germany. He went to Holland as a youth, studied painting with Gerard Terborch, and after 1661 lived in The Hague. He is best known for paintings of conversation pieces and scenes from mythology for small cabinets.

NETTLE, a herbaceous plant of the genus *Urtica*, belonging to the nettle family, *Urticaceae*, and characterized by stinging hairs that grow on the stems and leaves. The plants grow 2 to 4 feet high and bear oppositely toothed or cut leaves; the flowers usually are small and greenish. The great, common, or stinging nettle, *U. dioica*, is a perennial with heart-shaped leaves and is found in North America, Europe, and Asia. The Roman nettle, *U. pilulifera*, grows as an annual in southern Europe.

NEUBRANDENBURG, town, NE Germany, in the East German state of Mecklenburg; on the Tollense River and Tollense Lake; 70 miles N of Berlin. Industries include iron smelting and the manufacture of chemicals, paper, machinery, and lumber. The old portion of the town, founded in 1248 by the margraves of Brandenburg, contains ruins of fourteenth century walls and towers. The city passed to Mecklenburg in 1292. (For population, see Germany map in Atlas.)

NEUCHATEL, canton, W Switzerland; bounded by France on the W and NW, the cantons of Bern on the NE and Vaud on the S, and Lake Neuchâtel on the E; total area equals 309 square miles. The canton, largely within the Jura, has numerous forests and some meadow and pasture lands. There are large asphalt deposits in the Val de Travers. Dairying and the production of meat and hides are important activities. The chief industry is watchmaking, concentrated at Neuchâtel, the capital, and at Le Locle and La Chaux-de-Fonds. Other manufactures are cotton fabrics, hosiery, electrical appliances, cutlery, and wood products. The canton was admitted to the Swiss Confederation in 1815, but was at the same time a principality under Prussian suzerainty—from which it revolted in 1848. The population is largely French-speaking and Protestant.

NEUCHATEL, town, W Switzerland, capital of the canton of Neuchâtel; on the NW shore of Lake Neuchâtel, on the slopes of the Jura; 25 miles NW of Bern. Neuchâtel has manufactures of watches, lace, jewelry, electrical appliances, and chocolate. The town is an educational center and has a famous university founded in 1838. The twelfth century castle houses government offices. (For population, see Switzerland map in Atlas.)

NEUCHATEL, LAKE, W Switzerland, bordering on the cantons of Neuchâtel, Bern, Fribourg, and Vaud; area about 92½ sq. mi.; maximum depth 502 feet; elevation 1,417 feet. Lake Neuchâtel is the third-largest Swiss lake, and the largest entirely within Switzerland.

NEUILLY, TREATY OF, an agreement concluded between the Allied powers and Bulgaria in November, 1919, at Neuilly-sur-Seine, France. The treaty imposed an indemnity from Bulgaria of $450 million and established a reparations commission to supervise its payment. Bulgaria lost western Thrace to Greece, its only direct access to the Aegean Sea, and to Yugoslavia three small areas on its western boundary. Bulgaria's army was reduced to 20,000 men, and the country was obliged to surrender its navy and war materials. See BULGARIA.

NEUILLY-SUR-SEINE, town, N central France, Seine Department; E of the Seine River, at the N edge of the Bois de Boulogne; a fashionable residential suburb immediately NW of Paris. Its chief industry is automobile manufacturing; other products include carpets, perfumes, dyes, rubber, and varnish. The town was the site of a château, built in 1740, that became the favorite residence of Louis Philippe and was burned in the Revolution of 1848. (For population, see France map in Atlas.)

NEUMANN, JOHN VON, 1903–57, Hungarian-American mathematician, born in Budapest. He early distinguished himself by his prodigious grasp of mathematics and physical science. He took the Ph.D. in mathematics at 23 in the University of Budapest and subsequently taught there and at Göttingen, Berlin, and Hamburg. He went to the United States in 1930 as lecturer at Princeton University, where he was made professor of mathematics in 1933. Three years later, he joined the Institute for Advanced Study, where he stayed for the rest of his life.

Von Neumann had, in 1933, published *Mathematical Foundations of Quantum Mechanics* and during World War II his profound knowledge of physics made him one of the government's most valued advisers.

During the early 1950's, in the midst of a drive to end government employment of communists and security risks, Von Neumann insisted on the right of the accused to confront his accuser. In 1954 he was named Atomic Energy Commissioner. In 1956 Von Neumann was awarded the Medal of Freedom, the Presidential Medal of Merit, and the $50,000 Fermi Prize.

Though perhaps best known for his work in quantum theory, computer theory and game theory (with Oskar Morgenstern he had, in 1944, published a mathematical consideration of strategy in poker, business, war and love entitled *Theory of Games and Economic Behavior*), Von Neumann's greatest invention is probably the theory of operator rings, which ties together the three main strands of twentieth century mathematics: function theory, algebra, and geometry.

NEUMUNSTER, city, NW Germany, in the West German State of Schleswig-Holstein, 35 miles N of Hamburg. It is a railroad center and has manufactures of machinery, furniture, textiles, leather, and paper. Neumünster was founded about 1127 and chartered as a city in 1870. (For population, see Germany map in Atlas.)

NEUNKIRCHEN, town, W Germany, in the West German State of Saar; on the Blies River; 15 miles NE of Saarbrücken. Neunkirchen has important coal mines, sandstone quarries, iron and steel works, coking plants, and distilleries. (For population, see Germany map in Atlas.)

NEUQUEN, province, W Argentina; bounded by the provinces of Mendoza on the N and Río Negro on the E and S and by the Republic of Chile on the W; area 36,429 square miles. The western part of Neuquén lies in the Andes Mountains, the eastern half in rolling plains. Parts of Argentina's lake district and most of Nahuel Huapí National Park are in the southwest. The capital is Neuquén city. Grain, fruit, livestock, and some oil are produced. (For population, see Argentina map in Atlas.)

NEURALGIA, a term derived from the Greek words *neuron* and *algos* (meaning nerve pain), used to describe throbbing, lancinating, shooting, burning, or stabbing pain, of unknown cause, that follows the anatomical course or distribution of a nerve. Among a number of separate and distinct neuralgias, one of the most common is trigeminal neuralgia, or *tic douloureux*, which affects one side of the face and is confined to the area of cutaneous distribution of one of the three major branches of the trigeminal nerve. The pain, which is often triggered by movements of the face, by pressure on certain parts of the skin of the face, or by drinking hot or cold liquids, characteristically comes on suddenly and is excruciating and of a stabbing nature, lasting seconds and recurring frequently. It is usually a periodic disorder; bouts last from several weeks to several months, with variable frequency and severity. The condition, though intensely distressing, is benign and does not in itself shorten life. Although its cause is usually undetermined, trigeminal neuralgia on rare occasions may be a symptom of multiple sclerosis or of a tumor involving the nerve within the cranial cavity. The treatment of this neuralgia has included the use of analgesic and anticonvulsant drugs (phenylhydantoins), alcohol injections into the Gasserian ganglion, and severing of the involved nerve root.

Glossopharyngeal neuralgia is a rare condition with symptoms similar to those of trigeminal neuralgia but in which pain involves the region of the tonsil in the back of the throat, the larynx, and occasionally the ear. Talking and swallowing produce intense pain. *Atypical facial neuralgia* is a condition characterized by long-lasting, aching pain affecting the region of one of the cheeks and part of the upper jaw. It is usually a manifestation of psychiatric disease, such as anxiety neurosis, hysteria, or depression. *Postherpetic neuralgia* is characterized by severe, continuous, burning pain in the distribution of any nerve previously afflicted with herpes zoster (shingles). This condition usually improves spontaneously. Neuralgias involving the nerves to the diaphragm, rib muscles and extremities can also be distinguished. Often these may be due to ruptured intervertebral discs, diabetes, or small tumors attached to the nerve (neuromas). Neuralgia can occur when the nerve is subject to pressure, injury, inflammation, or decreased blood supply. It is incorrect to use the term neuralgia to describe any vague, ill-defined ache or pain.

Pierre M. Dreyfus, M.D.

Bibliog.—J. C. White and W. H. Sweet, *Pain, Its Mechanisms and Neurosurgical Control* (1955); H. G. Wolff, *Headache and Other Head Pain* (1948).

NEURASTHENIA, chronic weakness and weariness having no organic cause. According to one theory, it results when mental energy is bound up in repressing needs which cannot be faced or desires (sexual or aggressive) which cannot be satisfied. Neurasthenia protects profoundly depressed people from suicide, for they cannot summon up even enough energy to kill themselves. It is therefore not wise to cure a neurasthenia, which is but a symptom, without setting aright the deeper disorder which is its cause.

NEURITIS, inflammation of a peripheral nerve. Cold; pressure by tumor; poisoning by lead; arsenic and alcohol; deficiency of vitamin B_1; diabetes mellitus, diphtheria, typhoid fever, and mononucleosis may cause it, and treatment of the cause may cure it.

NEUROLOGY, the branch of medicine that deals with afflictions of the nervous system. Neurology must be distinguished from the related medical specialties of psychiatry, which deals with disorders of the mind and with behavioral aberrations, and neurological surgery, a subspecialty of surgery, which deals with the surgical treatment of disorders of the nervous system. Within the field of neurology itself are found a number of subspecialties, such as neurophysiology, neuropathology, and neurochemistry.

Neurological Symptoms and Signs. Diseases of the nervous system manifest themselves in a variety of ways. Partial or complete paralysis of limb or facial musculature may indicate derangement of some part of the motor system. In motor paralysis, specific changes and abnormalities of reflexes can be detected. A failure to smell, see, or taste, or a failure to feel pain, vibration, or touch hints at a lesion in some part of the sensory system. Numbness and tingling in the extremities are symptoms associated with disease of the sensory system, either central or peripheral. Difficulty with gait or balance, or incoordination of arms or legs suggests a lesion of the cerebellar system. Convulsions, delirium, and alterations in the state of consciousness are signs of deranged cerebral function. Disturbances of memory and orientation or of reading, writing, calculation, speech, and other acquired skills are also associated with lesions of the cerebrum. Headaches are a common neurological symptom. However, frequently they are not due to structural disease of the brain; they may have their basis in a malfunctioning of some other system of the body, or they may be caused by emotional stress.

Neurological Diagnosis. A neurological examination usually includes a complete physical examination and a detailed examination of the tendon reflexes, the sensory system, the mental status, coordination, and the function of each cranial nerve and the motor system. More complicated diagnostic tests include a number of X-ray procedures, the making of an electroencephalogram, and the microscopic and chemical examination of the cerebrospinal fluid. The X-rays range from plain views of the skull and bony spine to special X-rays that outline the brain within the skull after air or contrast material has been injected into the spaces surrounding the brain and spinal cord (subarachnoid space) or into the arteries that supply the brain. New radioisotopic scanning devices can also detect the presence of brain tumors.

Neurological Diseases. Diseases of the nervous system can be arbitrarily classified into nine different and broad categories: (1) *vascular diseases*, which involve the nervous system by affecting its blood supply ("strokes" and cerebral hemorrhages); (2) *neoplastic diseases*, which encompass a large variety of tumors that originate in or invade the nervous system from other parts; (3) *traumatic diseases* caused by direct injury to the brain, the spinal cord, or the peripheral nerves; (4) *degenerative diseases*, which are illnesses of totally unknown cause, such as senile dementia and Parkinson's disease; (5) *developmental diseases*, which are the result of deformities of the nervous system that have occurred during its development before birth (mongolism and various forms of mental retardation); (6) *infectious diseases* such as meningitis, encephalitis, and poliomyelitis, which are caused by bacterial, viral, or fungal invasion of the nervous system; (7) *metabolic and nutritional diseases*, which are due to fundamental and sometimes generalized biochemical abnormalities, or to a lack of specific vitamins, or to malnutrition, and which affect the brain secondarily; (8) *demyelinating diseases*, such as multiple sclerosis, which are due to inflammation and gradual dissolution of myelin, a chemical substance that is part of the nerve sheath; (9) *muscle diseases* such as muscular dystrophy.

Recent Advances in Neurology have been much enhanced by the development of refined diagnostic techniques. The discovery of a large number of antibiotics has considerably reduced the mortality from infectious diseases involving the nervous system. The development of new and powerful anticonvulsant drugs has aided in the treatment of seizure disorders. In fact, a majority of patients suffering from epilepsy now can be enabled to live perfectly normal lives through the use of these drugs. The most significant recent advance in neurology has been the development of a poliomyelitis vaccine made of live, attenuated virus. The widespread use of this vaccine has virtually eradicated the dreaded disease.

Pierre M. Dreyfus, M.D.

Bibliog.—W. R. Brain, ed., *Diseases of the Nervous System*, (6th ed. 1962); T. R. Harrison et al., *Principles of Internal Medicine* (1962); Webb Haymaker, ed., *The Founders of Neurology* (1953); S. A. Wilson and A. N. Bruce, *Neurology* (1955).

NEUSE RIVER, E North Carolina; formed by the junction, NE of Durham, of the Little, Eno, and Flat rivers; flows mainly SE to New Bern, where an estuary 5 miles wide and 40 miles long opens into Pamlico Sound. The length is about 275 miles.

NEUSIEDLER LAKE, Hungarian Fertö tó, SE Austria, Burgenland Province, and NE Hungary; 25 miles SE of Vienna. It varies in width from 4 to 8 miles and is about 20 miles long. A canal connects the lake to the Repce River. The reeds that surround the Neusiedler Lake are used by Austrian cellulose manufacturers.

NEUSS, city W Germany, in the West German State of North Rhine-Westphalia; in the Ruhr Basin near the Rhine River, with which it is connected by the Erft Canal; 4 miles SW of Düsseldorf. It is a railroad junction and a river port. Manufactures include machinery, tools, chemicals, flour, oil, textiles, paper, soap, and metalware. Neuss was chartered as a city in the twelfth century. It was sacked by Alexander of Parma in 1586 and annexed by Prussia in 1816. Pop. (1951) 83,930.

NEUSTRIA, the western part of the kingdom of the Franks under the Merovingian dynasty. It corresponded to the area of N central and NW France, and its principal city was Soissons. Neustria was created in 511 when the domain of Clovis I was partitioned among his sons. During the sixth century Neustria fought sporadically with Austrasia, with which it was twice temporarily united during the reigns of Clotaire I and Clotaire II. Mayors of the palace rather than kings ruled during and after the seventh century, and in 687, Pepin II of Hérstal, then mayor of Austrasia, reunited the kingdoms. By 720 Charles Martel, illegitimate son of Pepin II, was ruler in fact of all Frankish kingdoms; in 751 Martel's son, Pepin III, the Short, became king of all the Franks and established the Carolingian dynasty.

NEUTRALITY is the status under international law of a state that remains at peace in time of war between other states. Neutrality is thus an attitude of impartiality toward belligerents, which at times has included equal grants of assistance to both sides. In the early days of international law there was a belief in benevolent neutrality; under that concept individual states felt bound to render aid promised by pre-existing treaties. Later it was found that formal impartiality was not enough, and that complete abstention was required for neutrality. Under that strict concept prior agreements did not excuse any aid from a neutral to a belligerent.

Another type of neutrality is so-called permanent neutrality. In the past certain states and territories have been neutralized, so that each was obliged to maintain its neutrality during wartime, usually in return for an agreement by other states to respect its nonbelligerent status. In other cases a piece of territory or a body of water has been internationalized. Switzerland is an example of a neutralized state. Germany's attack on the perpetually neutral state of Belgium in 1914 occasioned Great Britain's entry into World War I. The Dardanelles is a partially neutralized body of water. Armed neutrality is the position assumed by a state that announces to belligerents that it is prepared to protect its neutral rights by force. In 1780, for example, a league of states was formed to compel Great Britain to respect the neutral rights of each state.

Development. Neutrality as a legal institution appeared relatively late in the development of international law. (See INTERNATIONAL LAW, *Content of International Law*.) As long as princes and political units of different grades were involved with one another by the obligations of the feudal system there was not much opportunity for any community to remain neutral if an affiliated political unit became involved in war. With the weakening of feudal bonds and the establishment of strong national states this situation changed. Hugo Grotius, who laid the basis for international law, visualized neutrality quite clearly (see GROTIUS, HUGO); after the Peace of Westphalia in 1648 the position was still more practicable; and by the eighteenth century the time was opportune for the development of the system.

The United States, beginning in 1793–94, worked out the theory and practice of neutrality most completely—in part as a result of the desire of the young nation to remain aloof from the quarrels and wars involving other (and stronger) powers, in part because of its desire to remain friendly (and a profitable purveyor) to both sides in any war. By 1825 the pattern of neutrality was firmly established in international law, with other countries following the precedent set by the United States. American leadership in neutrality persisted until 1917 and was resumed to a certain extent in the period 1921–41. The Neutrality Acts of 1935–37 forbade Americans to sell arms or make loans to foreign belligerents or to travel on belligerent vessels.

Principles of Neutrality. The basis of the law of neutrality was the right of a state to refrain from participation in any war involving other states. Before the development of this law the assumption was that in any war every outside power affected would line up on one side or the other; thus in the Nootka Sound (see NOOTKA SOUND) controversy between Great Britain and Spain the two powers assumed that the United States would inevitably take sides in the quarrel over conflicting claims to the region, an expectation that was not fulfilled. Once the right of a state to remain at peace in case of war between other countries was established, there followed the right of the neutral state to have its neutrality (chiefly its territorial neutrality) respected by the belligerents; there followed also the obligation on the part of the neutral to refrain from interfering in the conduct of the war—the right to be neutral was matched by the obligation so to act. The law of neutrality was thus a complicated system of rights and obligations, concerned largely with maritime commerce; it dealt with blockade, contraband of war, and right of search. See BLOCKADE; CONTRABAND OF WAR; FREEDOM OF THE SEAS; SEARCH AND SEIZURE.

Breakdown of Neutrality. An attempt was made to codify the law of neutrality in maritime warfare in the Declaration of London of 1909, and although that convention was never ratified it stated the law as of that time. (See DECLARATION OF LONDON.) During World War I attempts were made by the United States and other neutrals, at least before 1917, to promote observation of the rules of the declaration; and some belligerents did more or less fully adhere to it. As the war progressed, however, the terms of the declaration became less suitable for the conditions of the war; and after the entry of the United States into the war there was no strong neutral to insist on the observance of the old rules. By the end of the war in 1918 the law of neutrality was about as uncertain as the law of land warfare. During the years of peace nothing was done to review, revise, or restate the antiquated law, so that when World War II broke out in 1939 the law was not clear on numerous points. In the postwar period, because of the many technological and social changes affecting the international community and the nature of war itself, the rights and obligations of neutral states were less clear than ever before.

Another factor that undermined the old law of neutrality was the doubt concerning the ethical and practical value of that position. Neutrality implied unconcern about the issues at stake in the particular war; or it implied an obligation to regard both parties as morally and socially on a par, or at least an obligation not to raise any questions about the matter. In the eighteenth century, when wars frequently arose over nothing more than colonial rivalries and possessions, the neutral attitude was quite tolerable, and indeed seemed to embody a certain moral dignity and superiority. After the latter part of the nineteenth century, however, the issues involved took on a more general and serious character, and when any resort to war except for defensive purposes came to have the appearance of aggression and to stand condemned as such, the moral basis for neutrality disappeared.

The Future of Neutrality. It cannot be assumed that there will be no recurrence of war. If war should come it is essential that the activities of the belligerents be regulated and restricted by law. Neither can it be assumed that neutrality will entirely disappear; for although neutrality is incompatible morally and logically with the principle of international solidarity and with the principles of such systems as the League of Nations and the United Nations, or of any system of collective security, there is no assurance that all states will be included or completely involved in such systems. Since nonmember states must be reckoned with politically, arrangements may be made permitting them to retain a certain degree of neutrality. However exceptional and even absurd this situation, it cannot be ignored any more than can the incompatibility between collective security and neutrality as general principles.

There are two possible solutions for the problem of neutrality, neither entirely satisfactory but both holding some promise. One is for the neutral or potentially neutral state or states to recognize that the objects of neutrality—peace and security—may be better attained in certain circumstances by co-operative action to prevent or suppress war than by individual nonbelligerent action. Such a change of attitude would be difficult for a neutral state. The second is a grant from the collective organization of special immunity for one or more states (such as Switzerland) in view of their historic traditions and especially in view of the services they can render to the international community in their neutral role. The easiest solution—abolition of neutrality and all its implications—is highly debatable both as to its possibility and as to its moral and political value. See BELLIGERENCY; PEACE; WAR. PITMAN B. POTTER

BIBLIOG.-Columbia University, *Neutrality: Its History, Economics, and Law* (4 vols. 1935); World Peace Foundation, *Collective Security* (1936); G. Cohn, *Neo-Neutrality* (1939); N. Orvik, *Decline of Neutrality, 1914–1941* (1953); Royal Institute of International Affairs, *War and the Neutrals* (1956); J. B. Oakes, *The Edge of Freedom* (1961).

NEUTRALIZATION, the reaction between an acid and a base to make an acidic solution more basic, or a basic solution more acidic. The change from an acidic to a neutral or basic solution, or from a basic to a neutral or acidic solution, can easily be observed by the use of indicators, or compounds that have one color in an acid solution and a different color in a basic solution.

When an acid such as hydrochloric acid, HCl, is mixed with a base such as sodium hydroxide, NaOH, the hydrogen and the hydroxyl ions react as follows: $H^+ + OH^- \rightarrow H_2O$. If the solution is evaporated to dryness, neutral sodium chloride remains. Using the classical definitions of an acid, a base, and a salt, one may say that neutralization is the reaction of an acid and a base to yield a salt and water. Considerable heat is liberated in neutralization reactions between strong acids and bases.

The degree of acidity or alkalinity of a substance is important in such fields as medicine, electroplating, and food processing. A scale has been developed to express this factor, and the solution is said to have a certain *p*H. Water which is neutral has a *p*H value of 7. A solution with a *p*H less than 7 is acidic and a solution with a *p*H greater than 7 is basic or alkaline. Blood has a *p*H of 7.3 and is therefore slightly alkaline. (*p*H is mathematically defined as the logarithm of the reciprocal of hydrogen ions expressed in moles per liter.) See PH.

In many chemical and physiological processes it is necessary to maintain the acidity or alkalinity within very narrow limits (fairly constant *p*H). This rather constant *p*H may be accomplished by the use of buffer solutions. Buffer solutions tend to resist changes in acidity or alkalinity and generally consist of a salt of a weak acid in the presence of the free acid or the salt of the weak base in the presence of the free base. Thus a mixture of sodium acetate and acetic acid or a mixture of ammonium hydroxide and ammonium chloride would constitute such a buffer solution. See BUFFER SOLUTION.

Modern Theories. Discussion of acids and bases generally relates to water solutions of these substances, but of course other solvents are possible and frequently desirable. Chemists were forced under these circumstances to broaden and generalize their definition of acids and bases. For advanced technical aspects the broader definition, postulated independently by J. N. Brönsted and T. M. Lowry in 1923, of an acid as a proton donor and a base as a proton acceptor may be advantageous. Gilbert N. Lewis has further broadened the definition of an acid to include any substance that can accept an electron pair to form a co-ordinate bond; a base is any substance that can donate an electron pair to form a co-ordinate bond. According to these theories, neutralization is the formation of a co-ordinate bond between acid and base. These advanced theories answer difficulties that chemists encounter in dealing with substances in solvents other than water, such as benzene, liquid ammonia, and pyridine. See ACID; BASE; BRÖNSTED THEORY. F. P. CASSARETTO

NEUTRINO, a particle that, with beta particles, is assumed to be emitted from atomic nuclei, in order to account for otherwise unexplainable energy and momentum losses. Its existence was suggested in 1931 by the Austrian-Swiss physicist Wolfgang Pauli, and its role in beta decay, that is, in neutron-proton interconversion within the nucleus, was elaborated by the U.S. physicist Enrico Fermi in 1934. The neutrino is believed to have no measurable mass when at rest, no electrical charge, and negligible magnetic properties and, therefore, is believed capable of tremendous penetration of matter. At least two types of neutrinos exist, each type also having its antiparticle or antineutrino. One type of neutrino is associated with beta decay in which the neutrino is emitted in positive beta decay (positron) or electron capture, and the antineutrino in negative beta decay (negatron). Another type of neutrino is associated with pi-meson decay in which the neutrino is emitted in the decay of a positive pi-meson, and the antineutrino in the decay of a negative pi-meson. GLENN T. SEABORG

NEUTRON, a neutral particle that has an atomic weight of approximately unity (precisely 1.00898 on the scale on which the atomic weight of oxygen-16 is 16). Closely packed neutrons and protons (nucleons) make up the nuclei of all atoms. The neutron is slightly heavier than the proton; in the free state it decays, yielding a proton with a half life of about 13 minutes. It has a negative magnetic moment. As in the case of other elementary particles, the neutron has an antiparticle that has been artificially produced.

The neutron was discovered in 1932 by the English physicist Sir James Chadwick, as a product of the bombardment of beryllium nuclei with alpha particles (helium ions) from the natural radioactive element polonium. Neutrons were produced subsequently in many artificially-induced nuclear reactions; these are now the more important sources.

After a number of collisions with nuclei, the speed of a fast neutron is reduced to such an extent that it has approximately the same average kinetic energy as the atoms of the medium in which it underwent such nuclear collisions; the resulting neutrons are then known as thermal, or slow, neutrons. Thermal neutrons are readily captured by nuclei because of their slow speed and absence of electrical charge. Both fast and slow neutrons are important as projectiles in fundamental nuclear investigations.

Neutrons have an especially important application in the nuclear fission of heavy elements such as uranium and plutonium. The energy released may be utilized in a controlled manner in chain reactors (piles) for nuclear (atomic) power production or in nuclear weapons. Reactors are also important sources of neutrons and of fissionable material such as plutonium. GLENN T. SEABORG

NEVADA, state, W United States; bounded by Oregon and Idaho on the N, Utah and Arizona on the E, and California on the S and W; extreme measurements 484 miles N–S and 321 miles E–W; area 110,540 sq. mi., including 751 sq. mi. of inland water; pop. (1960) 285,278. It ranks seventh among the states in area and 50th in population. Nevada's name is a Spanish word meaning snow-clad; a familiar name, Sagebrush state, refers to the prevalence of several varieties of this plant. Another nickname is Silver state, referring to Nevada's once celebrated silver mines. The state tree is the piñon; the state flower is the sagebrush; and the bird is the mountain bluebird. The state motto is "All for Our Country." Nevada was the 36th state to enter the Union. Reno is the largest city, Carson City the capital. See map in Atlas, Vol. 20. For the state flag in color, see FLAG.

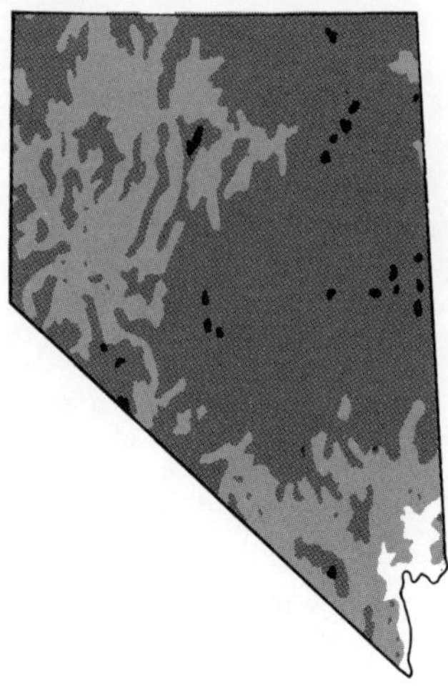

Elevation Map. White area indicates sea level to 2,000 feet; light gray, 2,000-5,000 feet; dark gray, 5,000-10,000 feet; black, over 10,000 feet.

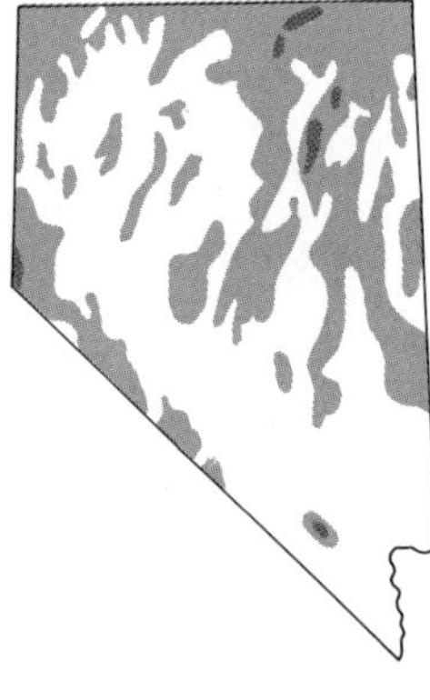

Precipitation Map. White area indicates under 10 inches annually; light gray, 10-20 inches; dark gray, 20-30 inches.

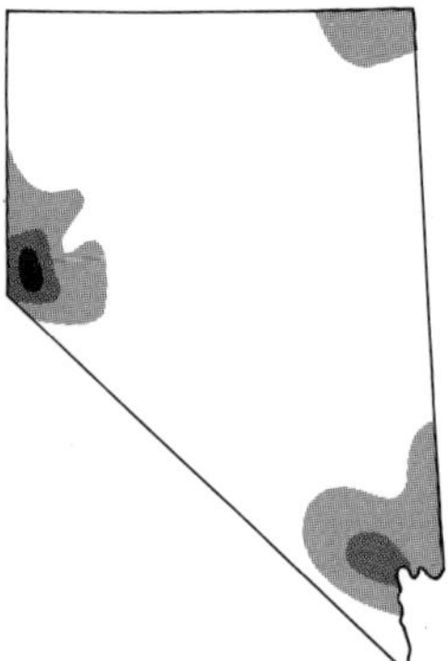

Population Density Map. Black area indicates 20-60 people per square mile; dark gray, 10-20; light gray, 2-10; white, less than 2.

PHYSICAL FACTORS

Topography. Most of Nevada lies within the Great Basin between the Sierra Nevada and the Wasatch Mountains. Its average elevation is 5,500 feet. The state's highest mountain is Boundary Peak (13,145 ft.) on the Nevada-California border. Mount Wheeler (13,058 ft.), the second highest peak, is in the Snake Range in eastern central Nevada. Parallel mountain ridges are separated by canyons, valleys, and plains, many of which are deserts. Almost all of the region has interior drainage; most streams rising within its borders flow into sinks or lakes, or lose themselves in deserts. In summer, sun-baked mud deserts result from evaporation of shallow lakes. The Truckee, Carson, and Walker rivers empty into Pyramid, Carson, and Walker lakes, respectively. Nevada's most important river, the 290-mile-long Humboldt, rises in the northeast, flows west and south, and discharges into Humboldt Sink. Part of Lake Tahoe and most of Lake Mead lie within the state, and the Colorado River forms Nevada's southeastern boundary for about 15 miles. With its tributaries the Colorado drains the extreme southern portion of the state.

Climate. Nevada's climate is variable. The annual temperature over a period of 56 years averaged 49.9°F, with extremes of 122° and −50°. In general the days are dry and clear, with long periods of sunshine; cloud-free days average 193 per year. Annual precipitation, falling mostly in winter and spring, averages 9.05 inches. The eastern slope of the Sierra Nevada is the wettest part of the state. Snowfall there averages 37.4 inches, mostly falling on the peaks. Prevailing winds are from the south, southwest, and west. The growing season extends from the end of May to the end of September.

Soils and Natural Vegetation. Nevada's mountain ranges have scanty soil and little or no vegetation. Soils are mostly sedimentary in the southern and eastern parts of the state but in the northern section have their origin in lava, porphyries, and sedimentaries of ancient Lake Lahontan. Much of the soil, when reclaimed through irrigation, can be adapted to farming.

Plants range from alpine to desert varieties. Just below the snow line grow blue lupine, Indian paintbrush, red snow plant, scrub willow, and alder. In river valleys are aspen and wild peach trees and elderberry, currant, and gooseberry bushes. Meadowlands are carpeted with blue iris and rue; ferns, dogwood, pine, and juniper are common. The deserts of Nevada produce 28 varieties of cacti. In the north sagebrush abounds, and in the southwest the creosote bush flourishes. The Joshua tree is common in the desert, as are the mesquite, sweet fern, and yucca.

Animals. Wild game refuges in Nevada preserve mule deer, pronghorn antelope, and desert bighorn sheep, and herds of wild horses forage on the plains. Smaller animals include badger, beaver, skunk, jack rabbit, cottontail, desert coyote, raccoon, porcupine, bobcat, squirrel, chipmunk, and gopher. Common birds are sage hen, partridge, plover, pheasant, snipe, duck, bald eagle, turkey vulture, crow, raven, jay, lark, wren, robin, magpie, owl, heron, and crane.

Nevada's lakes and streams have rainbow, brook

On the Nevada state seal the plow and the sheaf of wheat represent the state's agricultural resources. The quartz mill, mine tunnel, and carload of ore symbolize Nevada's mineral wealth. The seal was adopted in 1866.

BIRD	Mountain bluebird
FLOWER	Sagebrush
TREE	Single-leaf piñon
CAPITAL	Carson City
MOTTO	All for Our Country
ENTERED THE UNION	Oct. 31, 1864
ORDER OF ENTRY	36th

ROTKIN, P. F. I.

Lake Tahoe, Nevada's famous resort, lies on the California border, 6,000 feet above sea level.

and cutthroat trout, black bass, catfish, green sunfish, bluegill, and black crappie. Lizards, including the poisonous gila monster, snakes, amphibians, and freshwater crustaceans are common.

PRINCIPAL CITIES

	Population 1950 Census	1960 Census
Las Vegas	24,624	64,405
Reno	32,497	51,470
North Las Vegas	3,643	18,422
Sparks	8,203	16,618
Henderson	3,903	12,525
Elko	5,393	6,298
Carson City (capital)	3,082	5,163
Boulder City	3,875	4,059
Ely	3,558	4,018
Winnemucca	2,847	3,453

Social Factors

Population. From 1960 to 1967 Nevada accounted for the highest population growth rate of any of the 50 states. Since the 1960 census was taken, its population has increased by over 55 per cent to an estimated 444,000. Most of this population live in urban areas, of which the two largest are Las Vegas and Reno. The great majority are native-born citizens of the United States. Religious affiliations include Roman Catholics, Mormons, Baptists, and Episcopalians. In 1960 there were 6,681 Indians in Nevada, mostly Paiute, Shoshoni, and Washo. There are several Indian reservations.

Public Institutions. Nevada has a state board of education consisting of the governor, the superintendent of public instruction, and one member from each of the five supervisory districts. School attendance is compulsory for children 7 to 18 years of age. The state university is situated at Reno. A state hospital for mental diseases is maintained at Reno, a state penitentiary and an orphans' home are located at Carson City, and Elko has a men's reformatory. Old age assistance is available to those who meet the state's requirements.

Economic Factors

Agriculture. Stock raising, the most important branch of the state's agriculture, accounts for more than two thirds of Nevada's agricultural income. Large ranches are chiefly in Elko, White Pine, Humboldt, and Eureka counties. Nearly all grazing area is public domain; privately owned lands amount to

Reno is known for its gambling and quick divorces, but it is also a cultural and university center.

HERBERT LANKS—PIX

Surrounded by desert, Las Vegas is a round-the-clock city of casinos, clubs, and luxury hotels.

ROTKIN, P. F. I

only about one-seventh of the total. Seven national forests in the state cover 5 million acres and provide pasturage for cattle and sheep during 9 to 12 months of the year. Large numbers of shorthorn and Hereford cattle are raised. In some counties sheep raising is as important as cattle raising, and wool is a valuable item in the state's economy. Dairying and poultry raising also are profitable industries in certain parts of the state.

Nevada's major crops are barley, wheat, potatoes, oats, corn, and hay. They are almost wholly dependent on irrigation, 90 per cent of the cropland being irrigated—mainly in the western part of the state and along the Humboldt River. Nevada also shares irrigation waters impounded by Hoover Dam in the Colorado River. In 1962 Nevada had 2,400 farms with a total area of 8,700,000 acres; acreage per farm averaged 3,625. The value of farm marketings in 1962 totaled $46.4 million: $7.1 million for crops and $39.3 million for livestock and livestock products.

PRINCIPAL CROPS

Crop	Unit	Annual Average 1951-60
Barley	bushel	619,000
Cotton lint	500-lb. bale	3,200
Hay	short ton	606,000
Oats	bushel	203,000
Potatoes	100 lbs.	304,000
Wheat	bushel	509,000

Department of Commerce

Mining. For many years gold and silver mining were the leading mineral industries of Nevada. The Comstock Lode, discovered in 1859, yielded gold and silver valued at $340 million during the first 30 years it was worked, but by 1953 gold was the third-ranking mineral produced in the state and the silver yield was at one of the lowest levels in Nevada's history. Copper and tungsten concentrates are the state's leading mineral products. In 1963 Nevada ranked 32nd among the states in mineral production with an output valued at $83,733,000.

MINERAL PRODUCTION

Mineral	Unit	1950	1960
Barite	short ton	47,608	137,727 *
Copper	short ton	52,569	77,485
Gold	fine ounce	170,000	66,000
Gypsum	short ton	495,229	802,395
Iron ore (usable)	long ton	—	733,610
Lead	short ton	9,408	987
Manganese ore	short ton	—	49,076
Mercury	76-lb. flask	680	7,821
Sand and gravel	short ton	1,346,608	4,084,984
Silver	fine ounce	1,634,000	703,000
Stone	short ton	1,611,942†	579,000
Zinc	short ton	21,606	420

*1962 †1955

Manufactures. The principal manufactures are products of mines and forest; other important industries are dairying, printing and publishing, the making of bread and other bakery products, and railroad shop construction and repairs. There are about 5,000 people employed in manufacturing in just over 200 manufacturing establishments.

Transportation. Nevada is crossed by three transcontinental railroads: the Southern Pacific and the Western Pacific in the north and the Union Pacific in the south. Smaller lines serve mining regions: the Virginia and Truckee, which once served the Comstock area, operates between Reno and Minden; the Nevada Northern serves the Ely district; and the Tonopah and Goldfield serves the Goldfield district. Three transcontinental highways—U.S. 6, 40, and 50—cross the state from east to west; and U.S. 93, 95, 91, and 395 run north and south. Airlines serve Reno, Elko, Las Vegas, and Boulder City.

Tourist Attractions. Fine highways wind through Nevada's magnificent mountains and national forests. There are five state parks: Cathedral Gorge, Kershaw Canyon, and the Valley of Fire have unusual eroded cliffs and spires; Fort Churchill preserves the state's first military post (1860–71); and Beaver Dam is a recreational center and hunting base. Part of the Hoover Dam and Lake Mead recreational area lies within the state, offering a fine view of magnificent gorges, jagged Black Canyon, and the dam. In southwestern Nevada is a part of Death Valley National Monument; Lehman Caves National Monument, along the eastern border, possesses spectacular limestone formations. Eastern Lake Tahoe, lying among the forested hills on the west boundary of Nevada, is a famed year-round resort. Sportsmen are drawn to game refuges and vacationists to dude ranches. Gambling is licensed (and taxed) by the state, and the Nevada divorce requirement of six weeks' residence accounts for a constant influx of persons from other states.

GOVERNMENT

The Constitution of Nevada was adopted in 1864 and has been amended over 60 times. Amendments may be initiated by either the legislature or the voters, and must be approved by majorities of both legislative houses within two consecutive sessions and by a majority of the popular vote.

Executive Officers include the governor, lieutenant governor, secretary of state, attorney general, and comptroller—all elected to four-year terms. The governor may succeed himself in office. Although he appoints important administrative officials, his actual control over administrative affairs is checked by a number of independent boards and commissions.

The Legislature consists of a senate, elected for four years, and an assembly elected for two years. The constitution limits both houses to 75 members, and stipulates that the membership of the senate may not be less than one-third nor more than one-half that of the assembly. Regular sessions convene in January of odd years and are limited to 60 days. The governor's veto can be overridden by a two-thirds vote of the members of each house.

Judicial Authority is vested in a supreme court of three members, who serve six years; eight district courts whose judges serve four years; municipal courts whose judges serve four years; and police courts whose judges serve two years. All members of the Nevada judiciary are popularly elected by nonpartisan ballot.

Other Factors. To be qualified to vote in Nevada, a person must be at least 21 years of age and have

The Capitol at Carson City was built in 1870, six years after Nevada joined the Union. Named for Kit Carson, the city is the smallest state capital in the United States.

NEVADA STATE HIGHWAY DEPT.

NEVADA

LAS VEGAS NEWS BUR.

Hoover Dam, one of the highest dams ever built, impounds the waters of the Colorado River to form famed Lake Mead.

NEVADA STATE HIST. SOC.

Chief feature of Lehman Caves National Monument is this lavishly adorned natural cavern of metamorphic limestone.

Liberty Mine at Ruth, one of the world's largest open pit mines, produces large quantities of copper and some gold.

RENO C. OF C.

Skiing, Nevada's most popular winter sport, is conducted by enthusiasts at the Reno and Mount Rose ski bowls a few miles north of Lake Tahoe.

USAF

A cloud from a nuclear test shot rises 40,000 feet above the Nevada desert at the Yucca Flat atomic proving grounds northwest of Las Vegas.

NEVADA
Highlights of History

John C. Frémont explored Nevada first on a trip to the Great Basin in 1843-44. He later led an expedition to Sierra Nevada.
ANHEUSER-BUSCH

"Mining on the Comstock" is the title of this lithograph done in 1876. It includes an interior of a mine shaft and mine buildings.
LIB. OF CONGRESS

The oldest permanent settlement in Nevada is Genoa, once called Mormon Station. A museum is a reminder of the past.

CARSON CITY DAILY APPEAL
On Nov. 25, 1861, Carson City was declared the permanent capital of Nevada. The first capitol was a log building.

The first concrete for Hoover Dam was poured on June 6, 1933, and the last May 29, 1935. President Coolidge approved the project, but construction began when Hoover was in office.
NEVADA HISTORICAL SOC.

resided in the state for six months, in the same county for 30 days, and in the same election district for 10 days. In 1904 the initiative and referendum were adopted.

Nevada is represented in Congress by two senators and one representative.

History

Exploration. There is no record of European exploration of the Nevada region before the nineteenth century, although the Spanish at Santa Fe, N.M., may well have crossed the southern part en route to California in 1776. In 1822 the region became part of Mexico, but in the following decade it was extensively explored by Peter Skene Ogden of the Hudson's Bay Company, and by U.S. trappers (see BONNEVILLE, BENJAMIN LOUIS EULALIE DE; SMITH, JEDEDIAH STRONG). Between 1843 and 1845 the region was mapped by Lt. John C. Frémont of the U.S. Army; in 1848 it was ceded to the United States by the Treaty of Guadalupe Hidalgo.

Territory and State. The region was then organized as part of Utah Territory, and was called Western Utah. In 1849 settlements were established by Mormons in the Carson Valley. There was little further settlement until the discovery of silver in 1859 (see COMSTOCK LODE). Friction developed between the Mormons and the miners, who resented Mormon ways and being governed from the distant territorial capital of Salt Lake City. This situation led to a petition to Congress for annexation of the region to California; the petition was denied, but resulted in the organization of Nevada Territory in 1861. During the Civil War, because of pro-Union, antislavery sentiment prevailing in the territory, Nevada was admitted to statehood on Oct. 31, 1864, ahead of other territories having larger populations.

As the output of the Comstock Lode diminished, and with the demonetization of silver in the late 1800's, Nevada went into an economic decline; more than one-third of its population moved elsewhere. Early in the 1900's, however, mining was revived somewhat; the development of sheep raising, irrigation, and railroads led to further economic improvement. For many years Nevada laws attracted divorce seekers, and the state legislature has encouraged this source of commerce by reducing residence requirements and generally simplifying divorce procedure. In 1931 gambling was legalized, and it became the major industry of such cities as Las Vegas and Reno. Since 1951 atomic weapons have been intermittently tested near Las Vegas. In 1954 oil was discovered in the state. During the 1950's Nevada's proportional population increase was one of the greatest of any state.

BIBLIOG.-J. G. Scrugham, *History of Nevada* (3 vols. 1935); Writers' Program, *Nevada: A Guide to the Silver State* (1940); E. M. Mack and B. W. Sawyer, *Our State: Nevada* (ed. 1946); H. Arthur, *Nevada* (1949).

NEVADA, city, central Iowa, seat of Story County; on the North Western and Rock Island railroads and U.S. highway 30; 32 miles NNE of Des Moines. The city is a livestock-shipping center and has manufactures of brooms and feeds. It was established about 1853 and incorporated in 1869. Pop. (1960) 1,773.

NEVADA, city, SW Missouri, seat of Vernon County; on the Missouri-Kansas-Texas and the Missouri Pacific railroads and U.S. highways 54 and 71; 50 miles N of Joplin. Cheese, brick, and tile are manufactured in the city, and there are coal mines in the vicinity. Nevada was settled in 1855 and was named for Nevada City, Calif. In 1863, during the Civil War, the city was burned to the ground. Pop. (1960) 8,416.

NEVADA, UNIVERSITY OF, a coeducational, land-grant, state-controlled institution of higher learning at Reno. The school was established in 1874, and collegiate instruction was first offered in 1886. Colleges of agriculture, engineering, and liberal arts were founded in 1885. The Mackay School of Mines became a college of the university in 1950; and the normal school, founded in 1888, became the college of education in 1954. The college of agriculture includes schools of agriculture and home economics, and the college of engineering has schools of mechanical, civil, and electrical engineering. A junior college branch is maintained at Las Vegas. The university offers the bachelor's degree, and the master's degree is offered by the college of education, by most departments of the college of liberal arts, and in selected fields in the other colleges. The university library contains a special collection on Nevada. See COLLEGES AND UNIVERSITIES.

NEVADA CITY, city, NE central California, seat of Nevada County; on the western slope of the Sierra Nevada. In mid-nineteenth century it became the center of a thriving mining area, and lode gold is still processed in the region. The city was platted in 1849 and incorporated in 1851. Pop. (1960) 2,353.

NEVA RIVER, U.S.S.R., NW Russian Soviet Federated Socialist Republic, Leningrad Region; rises at the S end of Lake Ladoga, flows SW then NW, and empties into the Gulf of Finland of the Baltic Sea at Leningrad; length 45 miles. It drains an area of more than 115,000 square miles, and is connected by canal systems with the Volga and Northern Dvina rivers. The Neva is ice-free for an average of 218 days annually between April and November; during that time its lower course is navigable by large vessels. Alexander Nevsky, prince of Novgorod, defeated the Swedes at the Neva near the site of Leningrad in 1240.

NEVERS, ERNEST, known as Ernie, 1903- , U.S. football player, was born in Willow River, Minn., attended Stanford University (All-America fullback, 1925), and after graduation played professionally with the Duluth Eskimos and Chicago Cardinals. He was coach of the Cardinals, 1929–31, 1939; was All-Professional fullback, 1931; and was elected to the Football Hall of Fame, 1951.

NEVERS, Roman Noviodunum and Nebirnum, town, central France, capital of Nièvre Department; at the confluence of the Loire and Nièvre rivers; 159 miles SE of Paris. Nevers is noted for the manufacture of decorative earthenware (faïence). Other products include porcelain, chemicals, agricultural equipment, and woodworking machines. The town dates from Roman times, and among the notable old buildings are the Cathedral of St. Cyr; the Romanesque Church of St. Étienne; the ducal palace; and the Convent of St. Gildard—burial place of Bernadette of Lourdes. Pop. (1954) 35,183.

NEVES, city, SE Brazil, Rio de Janeiro State; on Guanabara Bay; 9 miles ENE of Rio de Janeiro, of which it is a suburb. Neves has shipyards and metalworks. Pop. (1950) 52,424.

NEVILLE'S CROSS, locality, England, 1 mile SW of Durham, was the scene of a battle between the English and Scots, fought on Oct. 27, 1346. Taking advantage of Edward III's preoccupation with the wars in France, the Scots invaded England. Their defeat and the capture of their king, David Bruce, resulted from a military innovation—the use of massed English bowmen in offense.

NEVIN, ETHELBERT WOODBRIDGE, 1862–1901, U.S. musician, was born in Edgeworth, Pa., and studied music in Pittsburgh, Boston, and Berlin. He made his debut as a pianist in Pittsburgh, 1886, but soon turned to composing. His piano suite *Water Scenes* (1891) included "Narcissus" which became world famous. After his health began to fail, he and his family lived in Italy, where he composed the suites *In Arcady* (1892), *May in Tuscany* (1896), and *A Day in Venice* (1898). Returning to New York, he wrote his most famous song, *The Rosary*, in 1898.

NEVINS, ALLAN, 1890- , U.S. historian noted especially as a biographer, winner of two Pulitzer prizes, was born in Camp Point, Ill., and studied at the University of Illinois. He was a staff writer for various New York papers, including the *Evening Post*,

1913–23, the *Sun*, 1924–25, and the *World*, 1925–27, 1928–31. In 1931 he became professor of American history at Columbia University. He wrote *The Emergence of Modern America* (1927); *Frémont: The West's Greatest Adventure* (1927); *Grover Cleveland—A Study in Courage* (1932; Pulitzer prize); *Hamilton Fish: The Inner History of the Grant Administration* (1936; Pulitzer prize); *John D. Rockefeller* (1940); *A Brief History of Britain* (1943); *Ordeal of the Union* (2 vols. 1947); *New Deal and World Affairs* (1950); *Emergence of Lincoln* (2 vols. 1950); and with Frank Hill, *Ford: The Times, the Man, the Company* (1954) and *Ford: Expansion and Challenge* (1957).

NEVIS, island in the West Indies, belonging to the St. Kitts-Nevis-Anguilla presidency of the Leeward Islands; its total area is about 36 square miles. Lying in the Caribbean Sea, Nevis is separated from the island of St. Kitts by a strait about 2 miles wide. The island is an extinct, almost circular volcano rising to 3,596 feet, on whose fertile slopes grow sea-island cotton, sugar cane, limes, oranges, and other fruit. The principal export is cotton lint, grown by the inhabitants on 4,500 acres and marketed through a government ginnery. Nevis was discovered by Columbus in 1493, colonized by the British in 1628, captured by the French in 1782, and returned to the British the following year. The island belonged to the West Indies Federation from 1958 until 1962, when the federation was dissolved. Pending the formation of a new West Indies Federation, the island was again placed under the direct control of the British Colonial Office. The capital city of Nevis is Charlestown. (For population, see West Indies map in Atlas.)

Alfred W. Booth

NEVIS, BEN, mountain, W central Scotland, Inverness County; 4 miles ESE of Fort William. Ben Nevis (4,406 ft.) is the highest peak in Great Britain. It is not a striking mountain as it lacks a distinct peak, but it affords a fine view from its precipitous northeastern slopes.

NEVSEHIR, province, central Turkey; bounded by the provinces of Yozgat on the NE, Kayseri on the SE, Niğde on the S and SW, and Ankara on the W and NW. The province of Nevşehir is drained by the Kizil Irmak River. Chief centers are Nevşehir, the capital, and Kirşehir. The province is essentially agricultural, and the main products are grain, vegetables, and Angora goats, from whose fleece mohair is made. The province was created in 1954 from the former Kirşehir Province and parts of neighboring provinces. (For population, see table in article on Turkey.)

NEW, HARRY STEWART, 1858–1937, U.S. public official, was born in Indianapolis, Ind., and educated at Butler University. He was on the staff of the Indianapolis *Journal*, 1878–1903; was a state senator, 1896–1900; a member of the Republican National Committee, 1900–12, chairman, 1907–08; and was U.S. senator from Indiana, 1917–23. As postmaster general under U.S. Presidents Warren Harding and Calvin Coolidge, 1923–29, he expanded the airmail service.

NEW ALBANY, city, S Indiana, seat of Floyd County; on the N bank of the Ohio River; on the Baltimore and Ohio, the Monon, the Pennsylvania, and the Southern railroads and U.S. highways 460, 150, and 31; 4 miles NW of Louisville, Ky. New Albany is a manufacturing center in an agricultural area. Manufactures include veneer, plywood, clothing, stoves, furnaces, fertilizer, leather, furniture, foundry products, and prefabricated houses. New Albany was settled about 1800 and incorporated as a city in 1838. (For population, see Indiana map in Atlas.)

NEW AMSTERDAM, seaport, NE British Guiana, seat of Berbice County and District; on the Atlantic Coast, at the mouth of the Berbice River; 55 miles SE of Georgetown. New Amsterdam is a market center for the coastal region, which produces sugar, rice, and cattle. The city, built in 1740 as a Dutch fort, was captured by the British in 1803. (For population, see Guianas map in Atlas.)

NEWARK, village, W California, Alameda County; on the Southern Pacific Railroad; 22 miles SSE of Oakland. The village has chemical industries and dairies. (For population, see California map in Atlas.)

NEWARK, city, NW Delaware, New Castle County; on the Baltimore and Ohio and the Pennsylvania railroads; 12 miles WSW of Wilmington. The chief products of the city are fiber, paper, concrete blocks, and buttons. Newark is the seat of the University of Delaware. The city was settled in the late seventeenth century and incorporated in 1852. (For population, see Delaware map in Atlas.)

NEWARK, city, NE New Jersey, seat of Essex County; on the Passaic River and Newark Bay; on the New Jersey Central, the Lackawanna, the Erie, the Hudson and Manhattan, the Lehigh Valley, and the Pennsylvania railroads; on U.S. highways 1, 9, and 22, the New Jersey Turnpike, and the Garden State Parkway; a scheduled airline stop; 11 miles WSW of New York, N.Y. The largest city in New Jersey, Newark is in the center of one of the nation's most intensely developed industrial, commercial, and financial areas. About 45 per cent of all the persons in New Jersey live within 10 miles of Newark. (For population, see New Jersey map in Atlas.)

Newark is an important port of entry with a large deep-water harbor and extensive docking, loading, and warehousing facilities. Port Newark, on Newark Bay, was transformed after World War I from a marsh to a terminal for ocean-going vessels that represented a public and private investment of more than $90 million. In 1956 about 2.7 million tons of foreign and domestic cargo passed through the port. Together with Newark Airport, which was the leading East Coast air terminal until the opening of La Guardia Airport, New York, N.Y., in 1939, Port Newark after 1948 comprised one of the units of the bistate Port of New York Authority. Part of the metropolitan area of New York City, Newark is served by major transcontinental and international airlines and scores of bus and trucking lines. The Hudson and Manhattan Railroad, known as the tubes, connects Newark with Manhattan via a tunnel that passes beneath the Hudson River.

Setting. Downtown Newark lies close to the site of the original settlement. The nucleus of the commercial district is at the intersection of the two main business thoroughfares, Market and Broad streets. Buildings of interest in the city include the First Presbyterian Church, built in 1787 as the successor to the original church of Newark's Puritan Congregationalist founders; Trinity Episcopal Church, dating in part from 1743; the 35-story National Newark Building, erected in 1931, one of the tallest in New Jersey; the John Plume House, probably the oldest in the city (built about 1710); the municipal stadium, seating 14,000; the New Jersey Historical Society, founded in 1845 and housing a valuable collection of early documents; and the city hall and the county courthouse, both built in 1906.

Newark is the site of the colleges of arts and sciences, pharmacy, business administration, and law of Rutgers, The State University (1766). These colleges of Rutgers in Newark formerly made up the University of Newark, which was created in 1935. Other state-supported institutions of higher learning in the city are one of New Jersey's six teachers' colleges (1855) and the Newark College of Engineering (1881)—the latter co-supported by the city of Newark. Seton Hall University, a Roman Catholic institution founded in 1856, has its colleges of arts and sciences, education, business administration, law, and nursing in Newark.

The Newark Public Library was founded in 1888. Under John Cotton Dana, librarian from 1902 to 1929, the business branch, the first of its kind, was established in 1904. The Newark Museum was founded by Dana in 1909 to foster the study of art, science, and industry.

Newark has an extensive system of fine parks. Military Park, near the business section, was laid out by the city's founders as a military training ground and was known as the lower common. Gutzon Borglum's bronze sculpture *Wars of America*, depicting soldiers of the conflicts from the Revolutionary War through World War I, is in the park. Washington Park, set aside as a market place in 1767 and later known as the Upper Green, contains the equestrian statue of George Washington by Massey Rhind and a memorial, marking the site of the colonial market place, with the carved figure of an Indian and a Puritan, also by Borglum. Branch Rook and Weequahic parks are each more than 300 acres in area.

Economic Factors. Newark's industry produces a wide diversity of manufactured articles: shoes and other leather goods, electrical equipment, foundry and machine-shop products, paints and varnishes, malt liquors, chemicals, automobile bodies and parts, jewelry, celluloid, drugs, fountain pens, cutlery, clothing, dyed furs, food products, cigars and cigarettes, aircraft, cosmetics, wire, furniture, ink, printed matter, paper products, and dynamos. In 1954 there were 1,889 manufacturing establishments in the city employing 90,157 workers and paying $384,894,000 in wages; value added by manufacture was $688,013,000.

Newark is New Jersey's principal retail and wholesale center. In 1954 there were 6,055 retail establishments having 29,132 employees and paying wages of $81,766,000. The retail sales for that year amounted to $660,971,000. In the same year there were 1,433 wholesale establishments with 17,844 employees receiving $86,800,000 in wages. The city is also the leading financial center of the state and a national insurance center.

History. Newark was settled in 1666 by a band of 30 Puritan Congregationalist families from the New Haven colony in Connecticut, led by Robert Treat. Land for the settlement was bought from the Hackensack Indians. The origin of the name of the city is uncertain, but some scholars believe that it was originally New Ark or New Work—signifying a new project. As a theocracy, Newark was strictly supervised and managed by the church. Spinning, weaving, sawmilling, tanning, and iron forging were the early industries. From 1746 to 1756 the town was the seat of the College of New Jersey, later renamed Princeton University. During the Revolutionary War Newark was used by George Washington as a supply base for his retreat across the state in 1776.

After the Revolution new factories sprang up, and with industrial prosperity came release from severe religious supervision. About 1790 Moses Combs founded Newark's shoe industry, which soon after employed a large part of the town's workers. The manufacture of jewelry was introduced in 1801, the first bank was organized in 1804, and the first insurance company in 1810. By 1831 brewing and hatmaking were major industries. In 1836 Newark was incorporated as a city. The Civil War caused industry to boom, and the invention of such products as celluloid, and electrical instruments in the late nineteenth century resulted in a great diversification of industrial activity. Newark became a recognized part of the New York City metropolitan area, with many residents commuting daily across the Hudson to earn their living. With the creation of Newark Airport in 1929 and the development and enlargement of Port Newark, the city became a great distributing center. Newark had a commission form of government from 1917 to 1953, when a mayor-council form was adopted.

NEWARK, village, W New York, Wayne County; on the New York Barge Canal and the New York Central and the Pennsylvania railroads; 27 miles ESE of Rochester. Newark has rose nurseries and manufactures of paper containers, canned goods, furniture, and chemicals. It was settled about 1820 and incorporated as a village in 1839. Pop. (1960) 12,868.

NEWARK, city, central Ohio, seat of Licking County; on the Licking River and the Baltimore and Ohio and the Pennsylvania railroads; 32 miles ENE of Columbus. In the vicinity are extensive deposits of natural gas, oil, bituminous coal, sand, and clay. Main products include glass, aluminum, wire goods, and golf equipment. Newark was incorporated as a city in 1860. Pop. (1960) 41,790.

NEWARK, officially Newark-upon-Trent, municipal borough, E central England, Nottingham County; near the Trent River; 16 miles NE of Nottingham. Newark is a railroad and highway junction. It has manufactures of plaster, farm machinery, iron and brass products, and malt. Gypsum and limestone deposits are nearby. It is the site of the castle in which King John died in 1216 and of a grammar school founded in 1529. Pop. (1955 est.) 23,940.

NEW AUGUSTA, village, SE Mississippi, seat of Perry County; near the Okatoma River, on the Bonhomie and Hattiesburg Railroad and U.S. highway 98; 18 miles SE of Hattiesburg. The village mills process lumber from nearby forests. Pop. (1960) 275.

NEW BEDFORD, city, SE Massachusetts, one of three seats of Bristol County; on Buzzards Bay, the New Haven Railroad, and U.S. highway 6; a scheduled airline stop; 13 miles ESE of Fall River. New Bedford is one of the leading U.S. cities in the manufacture of textiles and a trade center for the numerous summer resorts in its vicinity. Formerly one of the world's greatest whaling ports, it remains an important fishing center and has steamer connections with Boston, New York, and other coastal ports. The principal manufactures are cotton, silk, and rayon textiles, tools, machinery, rubber goods, glass products, clothing, hardware, boats, lubricating oils, textile mill supplies, electrical equipment, plastics, golf balls, and brass and iron products. New Bedford is the site of a textile institute and a school of design. Its public library, established in 1852 and one of the oldest in the United States, contains a collection of whaling logs and items from early Quaker settlements. The Bourne Whaling Museum exhibits a half-size model whaling ship and other relics and reproductions of objects from the whaling era. The Seamen's Bethel, erected in 1832 to give moral and religious inspiration to the many sailors who visited the city, was immortalized in Herman Melville's *Moby Dick*. Settled in 1640, New Bedford was known as Bedford village, a part of Dartmouth, until its incorporation as a town in 1787. During the Revolutionary War the New Bedford Harbor became a base for the American privateers who preyed on British shipping. As a result the city was partially destroyed by the British in 1778. It was incorporated as a city in 1847. Pop. (1960) 102,477.

NEWBERG, city, NW Oregon, Yamhill County; on the Southern Pacific Railroad and U.S. highway 99W; 22 miles SW of Portland. Newberg has pulp, lumber, and flour mills. The city was settled by Quakers and incorporated in 1893. Pop. (1960) 4,204.

NEW BERN, city, E North Carolina, seat of Craven County; on the Neuse River; on the Atlantic Coast Line, the Norfolk Southern, and the Southern railroads and U.S. highways 70 and 17; a scheduled airline stop; 98 miles SE of Raleigh. Main products are men's clothing, fertilizer, lumber, and canned oysters. New Bern was settled in 1710 and incorporated as a city in 1723. Pop. (1960) 15,717.

NEWBERRY, TRUMAN HANDY, 1864–1945, U.S. public official, was born in Detroit. He was in the railway, steel, and banking businesses in Detroit, was assistant secretary of the navy, 1905–08, and secretary of the navy, 1908–09. In 1918 he was elected to the U.S. Senate, but resigned in 1922, after he had been convicted in the Michigan courts for corruption in obtaining the nomination. The case was dismissed by the Supreme Court, and he was exonerated by the U.S. Senate Committee on Privileges and Elections.

NEWBERRY, town, NW central South Carolina, seat of Newberry County. Newberry's chief manufacturers are cottonseed products, hospital supplies, lumber, and flour. Cotton and timber are produced in the area. The town was founded about 1830 and is the site of Newberry College, a coeducational, liberal arts college established in 1856. (For population, see South Carolina map in Atlas.)

NEWBERRY LIBRARY, a free public reference library in Chicago, Ill., which was established in 1887 with $2 million provided in the will of Walter Loomis Newberry (1804–68), pioneer merchant. Its quarters, a fine Spanish-Romanesque building of Connecticut marble, occupy the site of the historic Mahlon Ogden Home which survived the Chicago fire. Originally planned as a general collection in all fields of knowledge, Newberry has restricted its collections to the field of humanities since 1894 by agreement with other Chicago libraries. Accessions number more than 800,000 books, manuscripts, and bound pamphlets. Widely known private collections acquired include the Wing collection of typographical history, the philological library of Prince Louis Lucien Bonaparte, the Silver collection of English and continental history and literature, and the Ayer collection of Americana and literature on the American Indian. Fine collections are also assembled in cartography, genealogy, English literature, history, medieval and Renaissance manuscripts, history of printing, art, and music.

NEWBERY, JOHN, 1713–67, English publisher, born in Waltham St. Lawrence, Berkshire. He began publishing in London in 1744. Although he published works by such writers as Oliver Goldsmith, Tobias Smollett, and Samuel Johnson, he is most noted as a publisher of books especially for children. His original, freshly illustrated children's books, some of which he may have written himself, include *Goody Two Shoes*, *Giles Gingerbread*, and *Mother Goose's Melodies*. The Newbery Medal award in his honor was established in 1922 to be granted annually to the U.S. author making the outstanding contribution to children's literature. See CHILDREN'S LITERATURE.

NEWBERY MEDAL, an annual award given to the author of the most distinguished contribution to American literature for children published in the United States the preceding year. The award was first presented in 1922 by Frederic G. Melcher (1879–1963) who named it after John Newbery, eighteenth-century London publisher and bookseller. Selection of the book and presentation of the award are made by the Children's Services Division of the American Library Association. The first Newbery Medal went to Hendrik van Loon for his *The Story of Mankind* (1921). WINIFRED C. LADLEY

NEWBOLT, Sir HENRY JOHN, 1862–1938, English poet and author, born at Bilston, Staffordshire. He was graduated from Oxford and practiced law for twelve years. His first work of fiction, *Taken From the Enemy*, appeared in 1892, but it was a volume of ballads, *Admirals All* (1897), that first brought him literary renown. In addition to numerous volumes of poetry and fiction, he published, in 1920, a history of naval operations during World War I.

NEW BRAUNFELS, city, S central Texas, seat of Comal County, on the Guadalupe River; 30 miles NE of San Antonio and 45 miles S of Austin. Among the city's industries are textiles, furniture, wool, lime, and leather. Cold-water springs in the city are the source of Comal River, which enters the Guadalupe River within the city limits. New Braunfels was settled by Germans in 1845 and incorporated in 1847. (For population, see Texas map in Atlas.)

NEW BRIGHTON, residential community in Richmond Borough, New York City, on the NE shore of Staten Island. Sailors' Snug Harbor, a home for retired seamen, is near New Brighton.

NEW BRIGHTON, borough W Pennsylvania, Beaver County; 29 miles NW of Pittsburgh. New Brighton has manufactures of pottery, bricks, and metal products. The borough was settled in 1789 and incorporated in 1838. (For population, see Pennsylvania map in Atlas.)

NEW BRITAIN, largest island of the Bismarck Archipelago, part of the Australian territory of Papua–New Guinea; in the SW Pacific Ocean, between the Bismarck Sea on the N and the Solomon Sea on the S, 52 miles NE of New Guinea; about 300 miles long with an average width of 50 miles; area with adjacent islands 14,100 square miles. The crescent-shaped island is composed of a string of volcanic mountains which culminate with Ulawan, or the Father (7,546 ft.), on the north side of the island. There are a few coastal roads and many excellent harbors, notably at Rabaul, chief center and former capital of the New Guinea territory. The natives are of Melanesian origin. Agriculture is an occupation chiefly in the northeast, and the principal products are tropical fruits, cocoa, and coffee. New Britain was discovered by William Dampier, in 1700, on his exploratory voyage of the South Pacific. St. Georges Channel, between New Britain and New Ireland, was discovered in 1766 by Philip Carteret. New Britain became a German protectorate in 1884 under the name of Neu Pommern (New Pomerania). Earlier, in 1872, the government of New South Wales had favored British annexation of New Britain; in 1914 it was taken by Australian forces, ostensibly to protect the mainland from German invasion. The island was mandated to Australia as part of the New Guinea territory in 1921. Japanese forces took the island in 1942 and although U.S. troops landed there in 1943, Japan controlled part of New Britain until the end of the war. Rabaul, destroyed early in the war, was rebuilt. (For population, see Southeast Asia map in Atlas.)

NEW BRITAIN, city, central Connecticut, Hartford County; 9 miles SW of Hartford. New Britain is called the hardware city because nearly half the builders' hardware made in the state is produced here. It also has manufactures of electrical appliances, ball bearings, clothing, knit goods, and wood products. The city is the site of Central Connecticut State College, a coeducational, state-supported teachers' college. The Institute Museum houses art, historical, and natural history exhibits. Settled in 1686, the city was incorporated as a town in 1850. Part of the town was incorporated as a city in 1870, and in 1905 the town and city were incorporated together. (For population, see Connecticut map in Atlas.)

NEW BRUNSWICK, one of the four original Canadian provinces in the Confederation of 1867, bounded on the N by the province of Quebec, on the W by the state of Maine, on the E by the Gulf of St. Lawrence, and on the S by the Bay of Fundy. In the southeast it joins the province of Nova Scotia on a 17-mile isthmus. The province measures approximately 160 miles in width and 193 miles in length and covers an area of 28,354 square

NATIONAL FILM BOARD

St. John, New Brunswick's chief city, sprawls at the mouth of the St. John River on the Bay of Fundy. Shipping and a dry dock are the major industries.

miles. It has a coastline of approximately 600 miles. Pop. (1965) 625,000. The capital is Fredericton. See map in Atlas, Vol. 20.

Physical Features

Geology. New Brunswick is part of the Appalachian region which extends up the eastern side of North America. Along the Bay of Fundy in the south of the province are the Southern Uplands, underlain by the oldest rocks in the province, Pre-Cambrian granites. From the southeast to the northwest of the province extends a broad band of igneous and metamorphic rocks culminating in Mount Carleton (elevation 2,690 feet). Associated with these central highlands in the northwest are large bodies of valuable base metal ores, and still farther northwest are the northern uplands, which are underlain by folded Paleozoic sedimentary rocks. The extensive lowland in the eastern section of the province is developed on flat carboniferous sandstones. Associated with this are the coal seams in the Chipman area and the natural gas in the Moncton vicinity.

Lakes and Rivers. Nearly all the major river valleys follow the southwest to northeast physiographic trend. The most important of these are the Restigouche and the Nepisiguit which flow into Chaleur Bay, the Miramichi which flows into the Gulf of Saint Lawrence, and the upper section of the Petitcodiac which flows into Shepody Bay. Many of these rivers have shallow tidal estuaries and the exceptionally high tides of the Bay of Fundy (they are over 50 feet) cause the most peculiar phenomena of the reversing falls at the mouth of the Saint John River and the tidal bore which rushes up the Petitcodiac River, past the city of Moncton.

Climate. As is true of the other Canadian Maritime provinces, New Brunswick has a climate characteristic of an inland rather than of a seacoast region. The prevailing westerly winds carry weather systems passing from the continent off to the North Atlantic. At Saint John, the average summer and winter temperatures differ by 42 degrees (January average being 19° and July 61°), while even farther inland the summer high temperatures can exceed 90° F. In the highland regions, winter readings of 30° below zero have been recorded. The annual average precipitation is about 40 inches. About one third occurs in the form of snow. The average length of the frost-free season varies from 150 days at Saint John on the coast to 115 days in the upper Saint John Valley and to fewer than 90 days at higher interior elevations.

Soil and Vegetation. Over four fifths of the province of New Brunswick are forested (about 14,055,600 acres). Exploited since the early days of settlement the forests are today largely secondary growth. About two thirds are needle-leaved trees in the following order of importance: spruce (3 species), balsam fir, pine (3 species), cedar, hemlock, and tamarack. Broadleaved species (hardwood) comprise the other third. These hardwoods are mainly birch, maple, beech, and poplar, with small quantities of elm, oak, basswood, and butternut. The hardwood species grow in the highlands, while the conifers are to be found in the river valleys and on the lower slopes. There are large areas of peat bog in the coastal areas in the northeast of the province where there is very poor drainage. This has made the extraction of peat moss a very important industry. Along the estuaries of the rivers flowing into the head of the Bay of Fundy there are large tidal marshlands developed on the huge accumulation of silts washed in and deposited there by the tides. This area was originally covered by broadleaf and other salt marsh grasses, but recently much of the land has been reclaimed for agricultural use.

Animal Life. The tremendous amount of wildlife in New Brunswick attracts sportsmen from all over the world. Deer are especially common; moose, though once almost extinct, have been restored through very strict regulations. New Brunswick is home to a great number of fur-bearing animals including bear, otter, lynx, beaver, muskrat, raccoon, fox, marten, woodchuck, rabbit, and red squirrel. There are over 200 species of birds of which grouse, duck, and Hungarian partridge are the most popular for game. The Saint John, Miramichi, and Restigouche rivers are renowned as a habitat for the Atlantic salmon. Trout are abundant in nearly all the brooks and streams of the province.

The lion of England appears in gold upon a red background on the shield of New Brunswick. Below the lion, a silver schooner with red flags is represented, symbolic of the province's maritime interests.

FLOWER	**Purple violet**
CAPITAL	**Fredericton**
ENTERED FEDERATION	**July 1, 1867**
ORDER OF ENTRY	**One of original four**

Economic Features

Until 1900, agriculture, fishing, and forestry in New Brunswick were mainly a subsistence operation. Since 1900 there have been vast changes, with the opening of many fish packing and freezing plants and the construction of pulp and paper mills to make use of readily accessible hydroelectric power.

Agriculture. From the earliest settlement until 1900, mixed farming was carried on, with much trading of products among farmers as a means of subsistence. Cash income was derived principally from winter lumbering or from fishing. In the early 1900's, the tremendous expansion of industry in other Canadian provinces and in the United States provided job opportunities away from New Brunswick, thus resulting in a large decrease in farm population and production. The improvement in farm acreage came almost to a standstill, and has since been increasingly confined to the most favorable areas. About one third of the farm industry in New Brunswick today is involved with the potato crop, but more than half the total cropland (approximately 600,000 acres) is normally in hay, with additional acreage in pasture. Apples are an important crop in the Saint John River valley, and other small fruits and vegetables are also grown there commercially. Dairying is extensive.

Forestry. Timber and its by-products are still the province's economic mainstay. The industry's gradual conversion from long lumber to pulp and paper is the most far-reaching transition in the economic history of the province. Pulp and paper mills are located in Edmundston, Campbellton, Dalhousie, Bathurst, Newcastle, Saint George, and Saint John. The provincial government owns nearly half of the forest lands and disposes of cutting rights in the form of timber licenses and stumpage permits. Over half the remaining acreage is in small wood lots and other small holdings from which pulpwood and saw logs are sold to the highest bidders. The balance of privately owned land is held mainly by operators of forest industries.

Secondary Industries. There are a number of prosperous secondary industries in New Brunswick. Saint John has foundries, a sugar refinery, a drydock, a pulp mill, an oil refinery, and other manufacturing plants. Fredericton has boot and shoe factories and a brick and tile plant. Heating appliances made at Sackville are nationally distributed. Saint Stephen has a long established confectionery industry and a more recently developed flake-board plant. An electronics industry at Atholville, near Campbellton, employs many women in the area. Bayside, just south of Saint Stephen, is the site of a large tuna packing plant.

New Brunswick elevation: white areas 0 to 500 feet; gray areas 500 to 1,000 feet; dark gray areas 1,000 to 2,000 feet; black areas over 2,000 feet.

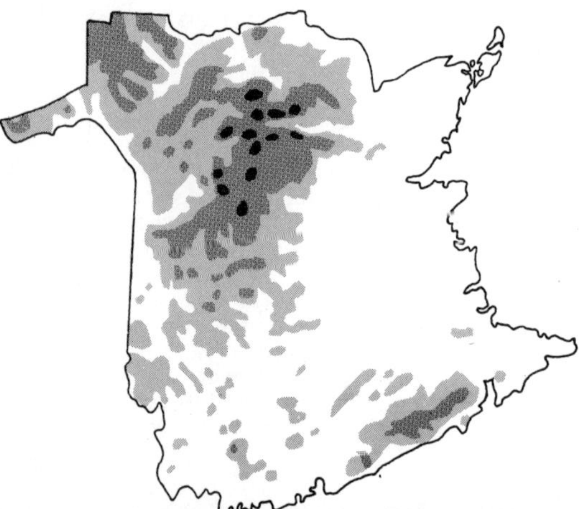

Fisheries. The two areas of concentration of the fishing industry are the island parishes of the Bay of Fundy and the northeastern triangle about Shippegan Island. The oysters of Kent County and the lobsters of Shediac are renowned for their quality. There are more than 30 commercial species of fish caught in coastal waters; four of these species (lobsters, sardines, cod, and herring—in that order of importance) account for over 80 per cent of the total catch. There are approximately 11,000 fishermen and over 125 fish processing plants in the province.

Mining. Extensive surveys in the Bathurst-Newcastle area of northeastern New Brunswick have revealed vast deposits of copper, nickel, lead, zinc, and silver, and a large mine-mill-smelter-chemicals complex is being developed near Bathurst. Coal is mined in the Grand Lake Basin. Elsewhere in the province there have been discoveries of antimony, tungsten, manganese, uranium, and tin. Gypsum, used primarily in the production of cement, is found at Havelock.

Electric Power. The development of hydroelectric facilities in New Brunswick proceeded rapidly after the end of World War II. By the early 1960's there were a total installed hydroelectric turbine capacity of more than 300,000 horsepower and a thermoelectric generating capacity of 300,000 kilowatts. The possible use of tidal power in Passamaquoddy Bay (where the United States started and abandoned a project in the 1930's) is again under consideration by the provincial and federal governments.

Communications and Service Industries have greatly improved in recent years. A hard-surfacing program for the roads of the province, begun in the mid-1930's, has been extended to all the great highways. The Trans-Canada Highway runs diagonally across the face of the province and over the Princess Margaret Bridge at Fredericton. Air Canada serves Fredericton, Moncton, and Saint John, supplementing the more local services of Eastern Provincial Airways. Tourism is a major industry, and more than 700,000 tourist vehicles visit the province annually. The province is serviced by many privately owned radio and television stations in addition to the nationwide facilities of the Canadian Broadcasting Corporation. Sackville is also the location of the Corporation's overseas radio transmitter. At Dorchester is situated a large federal penetentiary. The largest army training center in Canada is Camp Gagetown; it extends almost 40 miles along the western bank of the Saint John River from Oromocto in the north to Welsford in the south and is laid out for the full-scale maneuvers of an infantry division, with artillery ranges and space for the movement of armored fighting vehicles. Each summer thousands of troops from all over Canada arrive for training. The name is derived from Gagetown, a village enclosed between the training area and the river and originally named after General Gage who commanded the British troops at Bunker Hill. Rivaling its neighbor, Fredericton, in population, the new town of Oromocto has been crated from the old village and the surrounding forest of the same name.

Social Features

Religion. New Brunswick's population reflects great religious diversity. From the earliest days of settlement Roman Catholic priests labored among the Acadian parishes, while Baptist and Congregational churches appeared as the centers of community life for New England settlers. Scots brought their national Presbyterian faith. Wesleyanism was established on the Chignecto marshlands and spread rapidly.

The lieutenant-governor and the leading officials for the most part belonged to the Church of Eng-

NATIONAL FILM BOARD

A major New Brunswick industry is the manufacture of pulp and paper. Mills are located mostly in the northern part of the province and in St. John.

NATIONAL FILM BOARD

Students aboard a trawler receive advice from the crew on fishing gear. New Brunswick ranks fourth among Canadian provinces in value of fish catch.

land, which at the time of the province's founding acquired official status as the established church. But as its communicants never numbered more than one fifth of the population this privileged position was frequently the cause of great bitterness. The provincial laws which in the beginning gave licenses to perform the marriage ceremony only to ministers of the Anglican and Presbyterian churches and to Roman Catholic priests, represented only one of the ways in which religion and politics were dangerously enmeshed.

All important Canadian religious denominations have been active and have prospered in New Brunswick since colonial days. In 1845 Fredericton became the see of the first Church of England bishop, the Right Reverend John Medley. Christ Church Cathedral, which is one of the architectural attractions of the province, was constructed as a consequence of his untiring effort. It is a fine example of late Gothic architecture, being an almost exact replica of St. Mary's Church at Snettisham, Norfolk, England. At the head of the Roman Catholic Church in New Brunswick is the Archbishop of Moncton. There are also Anglican parishes at Saint John, Bathurst, and Edmundston.

Education. The only institution of higher learning that has direct affiliation with the provincial government is the University of New Brunswick, which stands on a commanding hill within the southwestern city limit of Fredericton. It was originally founded as the College of New Brunswick in 1800. In 1824 it was elevated to university status, and in 1828 its name was changed by Royal Charter to Kings College, and the Arts Building, one of the finest and oldest stone structures in Canada, was erected. In 1859, owing chiefly to criticisms based on the privileges of the Church of England in its administration, the college was recognized as the University of New Brunswick, and its management was changed to accommodate the requirements of all the people of the province. Subsequently it as steadily extended its facilities, offering courses in forestry, engineering, and law, as well as the conventional university studies.

Denominational institutions of higher education have also been established. From 1864 the University of St. Josephs at Memramcook has served as a cultural rallying point for citizens of Acadian extraction. After extending its facilities into Moncton it became in 1963 the University of Moncton with a status comparable to that of the University of New Brunswick at Fredericton, drawing upon the human resources of smaller Roman Catholic colleges, St. Louis at Edmundston and Sacred Heart at Bathurst. St. Thomas University, and English language Roman Catholic college at Chatham, was moved to the campus of the University of New Brunswick in 1964 though it remained completely independent. At Saint John a junior college of the University of New Brunswick came into existence in the same year. These changes came about in consequence of the report of a Royal Commission on Higher Education in 1962.

At Sackville is located the Mount Allison University, dating from 1840. It is under partial control of the United Church of Canada. The public school system of the province has developed along lines uniform with those of the other Canadian provinces. New Brunswick Teachers' College at Fredericton, center of professional instruction for teachers, is closely identified with the University of New Brunswick. JUDITH DUNCANSON

History

The history of New Brunswick may be divided into the French, the British colonial, and the national peiods.

Under the French regime from 1604 to 1763 New Brunswick was part of the French province of Acadia. Samuel de Champlain made his first settlement at the mouth of the Saint Croix River in 1604, and in the course of the next century a number of fur traders and missionaries worked among the Indian population. Although the Saint John River valley was divided into seigniories, few settlers were ever brought to the region, and it remained an almost unbroken wilderness.

By the Treaty of Utrecht in 1713 France lost the peninsula of Acadia which the English renamed Nova Scotia. The New Brunswick area now assumed a far greater prominence as a French frontier. At the Isthmus of Chignecto the French constructed Fort Beauséjour as a first line of defense against the English menace at Halifax. To populate their barren frontier the French administration at Quebec mounted a propaganda campaign to entice the French Acadians living under British rule in Nova Scotia to migrate to French territory. A number of Acadians did migrate, but in 1755 on the outbreak of the Seven Years' War Beauséjour was taken by an English force. This event was followed by the expulsion of the Acadians from Nova Scotia.

At the conclusion of the war New Brunswick was ceded to England and incorporated into the colony of Nova Scotia. The imperial problems of the two decades following 1763 gave England little opportunity to exploit her newly acquired territory, and it was not until the American Revolution that any attempt at organized settlement was made.

Between 1783 and 1785 more than 20,000 United Empire Loyalists, mostly from New York, New Jersey, and Pennsylvania, made permanent settlement in Nova Scotia. About two thirds of these settled along the lower Saint John River and the Passamaquoddy Bay. In 1784 they petitioned the British government for the creation of a distinctive Loyalist colony. The petition was granted and the new colony, New Brunswick, was named in honor of the German dominion of George III. The new colony contained about 12,000 Loyalists centered on the Saint John River; about 1,000 "Old Inhabitants"—pre-Loyalist Americans—settled in the same area; and perhaps 5,000 Acadians, mostly refugees from Nova Scotia, who were given land on the eastern coast.

It was the Loyalists for whom the colony had been created, and it was they who were to provide the political and social leadership of the province in its first century. It was their intention to create in the New World a British colony, firmly based upon monarchical and conservative principles, which would be the envy of the continent. The early government consisted of a governor appointed from London, an elected legislative assembly, an appointed legislative council, and an appointed executive council. The major source of political conflict was later to arise from the fact that the ministers of the crown held office at the pleasure of the governor rather than of the assembly.

The New Brunswick economy thrived under the aegis of British mercantilism. From 1809 until 1845 the colony prospered on the proceeds of its shipbuilding and timber trade with Great Britain and the British West Indies. More than any other North American colony New Brunswick suffered from the loss of British commercial protection after 1846. The post-Napoleonic period also witnessed a substantial change in the basic constituency of the colony's population. The old Loyalist element was augmented by the arrival of tens of thousands of British immigrants, mostly of Irish origin. These caused considerable social friction, for not only did they usually fill roles at the lower end of the social scale, but about two thirds of them were Ulster Protestants, and the four decades after 1840 witnessed numerous conflicts between Orangemen and Irish Roman Catholics. Paralleling these economic and social changes was an increasing demand for "responsible" government (i.e., that the executive council be made responsible for its actions to the legislative assembly).

A popular tourist attraction of New Brunswick is the Hopewell Rocks, created by frost, winds, and high tides. They tower 100 feet above the Bay of Fundy.
CANADIAN GOVERNMENT TRAVEL BUREAU

With the development of a free trade policy by Great Britain after 1845 the timber economy began a rapid decline. A brief respite was granted between 1854 and 1866 by the Reciprocity Agreement with the United States, but after its abrogation the colony entered a period of economic decline that continued into the twentieth century. The loss of British economic favor was followed by the granting of responsible government as the British Liberal movement reached its zenith. By 1860 the major question in New Brunswick was that of its ultimate destiny. The colony could either remain a crown colony, become part of an Atlantic community, or join the United States. The question was answered in 1864 with the proposal for a union of all the British North American colonies. Despite considerable opposition the Confederation was accomplished in 1867, and New Brunswick became one of the four original provinces of the Dominion of Canada.

The national period of New Brunswick history has been marked by depression. In 1879 Prime Minister MacDonald introduced his National Policy designed to protect and thus develop Canadian manufacturing industry. The policy largely succeeded in the central provinces, but in New Brunswick it was disastrous to an area whose commercial base was the sale of timber and fish on the American market. The depression induced emigration on a massive scale. The population was 321,233 in 1881 and only 351,889 in 1911. Most of the emigration occurred among the English-speaking population, and the result was a startling rise in the proportion of French-Canadians in the province (from less than one fifth to nearly one third of the population). The period was marked by several bitter religious and ethnic struggles. In 1871 the Protestant majority forced upon the Roman Catholic minority a free, public, non-sectarian school system. Although extensively modified this act has remained a focal point of strife. Similar struggles ensued over liquor legislation and wartime conscription.

The most marked development of the twentieth century has been the emergence of dual cultures within the province. The southern and western regions remain English-speaking and Protestant, the stronghold of the Progressive Conservative party, with an educational system centered on the University of New Brunswick and Mount Allison University. The northern and eastern areas remain French-speaking and Roman Catholic, the principal base of the Liberal party, with an educational system centered on l'Université de Moncton.

After 1918 there was some improvement in economic conditions with the development of the pulp and paper industry in several provincial centers. The result was a combination of a few comparatively flourishing urban areas and large, very poor rural areas where more than half the population lived. Poverty is still particularly acute in the French rural districts where large families, low incomes, and very low educational standards have combined to create a generational cycle of economic destitution.

Government

The government of New Brunswick, as constituted by the British North American Act of 1876, is vested in the lieutenant governor and a unicameral legislature of 52 members. The former is appointed by the governor general in council, and the latter is elected by universal suffrage. The executive function is exercised by the executive council headed by the premier.

THOMAS WILLIAM ACHESON

BIBLIOG.–*The Canada Yearbook* (Annual); *The Canadian Almanac and Directory* (Annual); *The Canadian Annual Review* (Annual); The Department of Industry and Development (New Brunswick), *Annual Report;* James Hannay, *The History of New Brunswick* (1909); W. S. MacNutt, *New Brunswick* (1963); D. F. Putnam, *Canadian Regions, A Geography of Canada* (1952).

NEW BRUNSWICK, city, E New Jersey, seat of Middlesex County; at the head of navigation on the S bank of the Raritan River; 22 miles SW of Newark. New Brunswick is a manufacturing center of surgical supplies and pharmaceuticals; other manufactures include needles, steel strings, cigars, and clothing. The city is the site of Rutgers, The State University, founded in 1766 as Queens College. Divisions of the university include Douglass College (formerly the New Jersey College for Women). Rutgers has a broad program in the liberal arts and sciences, with colleges of engineering, agriculture, nursing, and law. Rutgers is a university and a land-grant college, under both state and private control. The Agricultural Experiment Station and the New Brunswick Theological Seminary, founded in 1784, are also located in the city. Joyce Kilmer was born in New Brunswick, and the U.S. Army Camp Kilmer is nearby. The first permanent settlement was made in 1681 by a group of English colonists from Long Island. The city was named in honor of George I, king of Great Britain and duke of Brunswick. During the American Revolution, New Brunswick was occupied successively by American and British troops, and from New Brunswick George Washington began the march south that ended in the final American victory at Yorktown (1781). (For population, see New Jersey map in Atlas.)

NEW BRUNSWICK, UNIVERSITY OF, a nonsectarian, coeducational institution of higher learning at Fredericton, New Brunswick. It was founded in 1800 as the College of New Brunswick, later became King's College, and in 1859 acquired its present name. The first degree was awarded in 1828. It has faculties in arts, science, engineering, law, and forestry. The university is governed by provincial authority. The university library contains the Rufus Hathaway collection of Canadian literature, the Earl Lloyd George papers, and a Kipling atlas.

NEWBURGH, city, SE New York, Orange County; on the W bank of the Hudson River; 60 miles N of New York City. Now a shipping center, Newburgh was a whaling port before the Revolutionary War. The city has tugboat- and barge-building industries; other manufactures include carpets, machinery, textiles, tile, and pharmaceuticals. Hasbrouck House, Gen. Washington's headquarters from April, 1782, to August, 1783, is a state museum. Crawford House is a museum of the history, art, and culture of the Hudson River area. Germans from the Rhenish Palatinate settled there in 1709. In 1865, Newburgh was incorporated as a city. (For population, see New York map in Atlas.)

NEWBURY, municipal borough, Berkshire county, England, located about 50 miles WSW of London. The borough is an agricultural market and has manufactures of pharmaceuticals and aircraft. It contains a twelfth-century church, a fourteenth-century castle, and a thirteenth-century hospital. Two civil war battles were fought there in 1643 and 1644. (For population, see England map in Atlas.)

NEWBURYPORT, city, NE Massachusetts, one of the seats of Essex County; at the mouth of the Merrimack River, 37 miles NNE of Boston. Newburyport was a highly prosperous commercial center in the mid-nineteenth century, but declined with the passage of the Jefferson Embargo Act. The city has produced rum and silverware since early colonial times, and also has manufactures of shoes, electrical supplies, and tools. Newburyport was settled in 1635 as a part of Newbury; it became a separate community in 1764, and was incorporated as a city in 1851. (For population, see Massachusetts map in Atlas.)

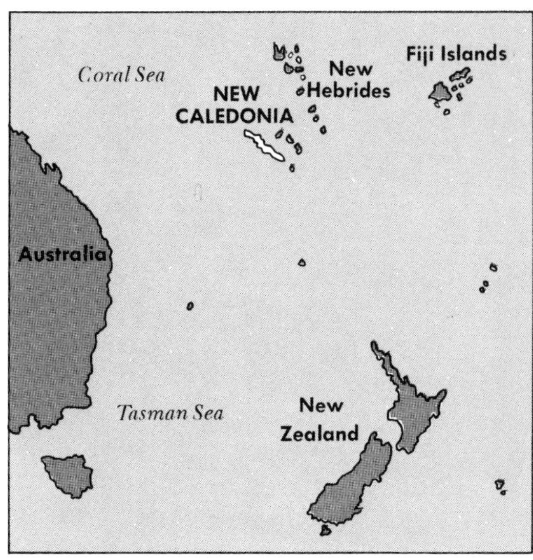

Location Map of New Caledonia

NEW CALEDONIA, island of the SW Pacific, forming with its dependencies an overseas territory of the French Union; located 750 miles ENE of Australia. The island has an area of 7,324 square miles and is 250 miles long by 31 miles wide. Nearby dependent islands are the Isle of Pines, the Loyalty Group, the Huon Islands, Belep Archipelago, Chesterfield Island, and Walpole Island. See Pacific Ocean map in Atlas, Vol. 20.

Physical Features. The island, of continental origin, is large, elongated, and almost completely surrounded by 400 miles of coral reef. The interior is mountainous and irregular, yet the island has a significant area of lower land with subdued relief. The highest point is 5,413 feet above sea level. Inland streams flow to the highly indented coastline.

Climate is subtropical, occasionally influenced by the tropical easterlies. Dry west coasts contrast with wet eastern districts. Precipitation ranges from 40 to 70 inches per year, with a January to June maximum. Mean monthly temperatures vary from 65° to 72° F.

Vegetation consists of scrubby forest and grazed grassland in the interior, and coconut palms on the coastal lowlands. Useful coniferous trees thrive in the moister valleys. With increased elevation vegetation tends to become stunted. As on most Pacific islands, the majority of the plant species is endemic.

Social and Economic Features. The population of the territory in 1963 was 86,519, including 35,000 Europeans, 44,000 Melanesians, 1,200 Vietnamese, 3,700 Indonesians, and 4,600 Polynesians. The indigenous inhabitants of the area are the Kanakas, a Melanesian people of muscular, wooly-haired, Negroid stock. The impact of French occupation and administration of the island has been most marked on the indigenes, who have lost their former social organization and control of land. Reduced to little more than half the total population, they are now mostly confined to reserves. The territory has the largest "alien" group of any island area in the

THE NEW YORK TIMES

The near-extinct kagu (or cagou), the symbolic bird of New Caledonia, dwells in forested mountains.

southwest Pacific, and of the Europeans, 34,000 are French. Approximately 35,000 people reside in Nouméa, the capital city, largest port, and center of French administration in the Pacific. There are 50 smaller towns and villages, mostly strung out along the coast.

New Caledonia's economic problems are those common to all developing countries in the tropics, including distance from overseas markets, poor interior communication, small internal market and labor force, and lack of resources and capital. Although only six per cent of the land area is cultivable, coffee, coconuts, and corn are raised commercially. On suitable pastoral land 105,000 cattle are grazed. By far the most important economic enterprise is mining. Nickel, chrome, and iron ores are the leading exports in addition to smelted nickel matte. New Caledonia has the largest deposits of nickel ore in the world; 1964 production was 58,200 short tons, behind only Canada and the U.S.S.R. Other important exports include coffee, mother-of-pearl, trochus shell, and preserved meat. Manufactured goods, petroleum, coal, and coke are the chief imports. In 1963, 56 per cent of imports and 66 per cent of exports were from and to France and the French Union.

Government and History. New Caledonia is administered by a governor, who is also high commissioner for French Pacific territories. The governor is assisted by a privy council and a territorial assembly.

New Caledonia was discovered by Capt. James Cook in 1774, annexed by France in 1853, and became an independent French colony in 1860. Between 1863 and 1898 the territory was a notorious French penal settlement. Large numbers of indentured laborers, mostly from Southeast Asia, were introduced to work on plantations and mines but the majority were repatriated between 1960 and 1963. During World War II, New Caledonia served as headquarters of the U.S. armed forces in the South Pacific area. In 1958 it elected to remain an overseas territory within the French Republic.

BRYAN H. FARRELL

BIBLIOG.–J. Bourgeau, *La France du Pacifique* (1954); W. G. Burchett, *Pacific Treasure Island: New Caledonia* (1942); H. Deschamps and J. Guiart, *Tahiti, Nouvelle Calédonie, Nouvelles Hebrides* (1957); J. P. Faivre, J. Poirier, and P. Routhier, *Géographie de la Nouvelle Calédonie* (1955).

NEW CANAAN, town, SW Connecticut, Fairfield County; about 20 miles ESE of Bridgeport. New Canaan is chiefly a residential town and summer resort area. It manufactures dairy and wood products and has nurseries. The town was incorporated in 1801. (For population, see Connecticut map in Atlas.)

NEWCASTLE, DUKES OF, four successive creations of British dukes between 1665 and 1756. The first creation was William Cavendish (1592–1676), an English royalist leader, who commanded royalist forces south of the Tweed during the Civil War. After defeat at the Battle of Marston Moor (1644), he retired to the Continent until the Restoration (1660). He was created first duke of Newcastle in 1665.

His son Henry (1630–91) succeeded to the title. One of Henry's daughters married John Holles (1662–1711), earl of Clare, who received the title in 1694.

The estates of John Holles were left, in 1711, to his nephew, Thomas Pelham (1693–1768), who added the name Holles to his own. On the death of Queen Anne (1714), Pelham-Holles, one of the richest Whigs in England, supported the accession of George I. In gratitude, he was created earl of Clare (1714) and duke of Newcastle-upon-Tyne (1715). From 1724 to 1748, he was secretary of state for the southern department under Sir Robert Walpole. In 1754 he succeeded his brother, Henry Pelham, as prime minister. Difficulties of the Seven Years' War led to his resignation in 1756, whereupon he was created duke of Newcastle-under-Lyme. He was recalled to head the coalition ministry (1757–62), dominated by William Pitt.

NEWCASTLE, city, SE Australia, New South Wales; on the Tasman Sea, at the mouth of the Hunter River; about 100 miles NNE of Sydney. Newcastle is situated in Australia's richest coal-mining district. It is the continent's third busiest port; its exports include coal, iron and steel, textiles, chemical products, timber, wool, meat, wheat, and dairy products. The city was originally a penal colony, established in 1797. During the twentieth century, with the establishment of its coal, iron, and steel industries, Newcastle became one of the most important industrial centers of the southern hemisphere. (For population, see Australia map in Atlas.)

NEW CASTLE, city, N Delaware, in New Castle County; on the W bank of the Delaware River, 5 miles SW of Wilmington. Plastics and foundry products are manufactured. New Castle was settled by the Dutch in 1651 and was the colonial capital and the first state capital. The city was incorporated in 1875. (For population, see Delaware map in Atlas.)

NEW CASTLE, city, E central Indiana, seat of Henry County; on the Big Blue River, 48 miles NE of Indianapolis. It is a manufacturing and trade center for the surrounding area. New Castle was founded in 1819 and incorporated in 1839. (For population, see Indiana map in Atlas.)

NEW CASTLE, city, W Pennsylvania, seat of Lawrence County; at the confluence of the Shenango and Mahoning rivers; 45 miles NNW of Pittsburgh.

New Castle is in an area of bituminous coal mines and limestone quarries. Steel and pottery are manufactured. Before white settlement in 1798, New Castle was an Indian trading center. It was incorporated as a borough in 1825 and as a city in 1869. (For population, see Pennsylvania map in Atlas.)

NEWCASTLE-UNDER-LYME, municipal borough, central England, Staffordshire; about 40 miles NNW of Birmingham. It is one of the centers of an important coal-mining and pottery-manufacturing district. Other products include textiles, clothing, paper, and tiles. The town was chartered in 1173. In 1932 the borough absorbed nearby areas, including Wolstanton. The thirteenth-century parish church of St. Giles was rebuilt in 1876. (For population, see England map in Atlas.)

NEWCASTLE-UPON-TYNE, city and county borough, NE England, county town of Northumberland; 8 miles from the mouth of the Tyne River; about 260 miles NNW of London. The city is connected with Gateshead, across the river, by five bridges.

Since the seventeenth century, coal exports have been the foundation of the city's industrial expansion. It has long been an important shipbuilding and ship repairing center. Other manufactures include heavy ordnance, mining equipment, locomotives, marine engines, turbines, heavy iron and steel goods, glass, lead and copper wares, pottery, chemicals, cigarettes, and cotton and woolen textiles. The city is also an important railway communications center.

The castle from which the city takes its name was originally built by Robert of Normandy in 1080; the keep, dating from 1172, has been preserved. The Church of St. Nicholas, since 1882 the Cathedral of Newcastle, dates from the fourteenth century and has a beautiful fifteenth-century spire. All Saints', St. Andrew's, and St. John's are also ancient churches. A natural history museum, an art gallery, libraries, and King's College of the University of Durham are located in the city.

In early times a military station on the Roman wall, *Pons Aelii*, occupied the site of the city. In 1644, Newcastle was garrisoned by the Royalists, but fell 10 weeks later to the Scots. Charles I was held prisoner in Newcastle after his surrender to the Scots in 1646. Newcastle has been the see of a bishop since 1882. (For population, see England map in Atlas.)

NEWCHWANG, city, NE China, S Liaoning province, on the Liao River, 30 miles above its mouth. The oldest port of the Liao valley, Newchwang was an important trading center during the eighteenth century but in the nineteenth, it was supplanted by Yingkow and Dairen (now Talien). During the Russo-Japanese war, Newchwang was occupied by both Japan and Russia; it was restored to China at the end of the war. Important manufactures at Newchwang are salt, pulp material, and cotton goods.

NEWCOMB, SIMON, 1835–1909, U.S. astronomer, born in Wallace, Nova Scotia. He went to the United States in 1853, and was graduated from Harvard University in 1858. He was an assistant in the *American Nautical Almanac* office, 1857–61, became a professor of mathematics in the U.S. Navy in 1861, and was assigned to the Naval Observatory. In 1877 he was made director of the *American Ephemeris and Nautical Almanac*, a position he resigned when he retired from the navy in 1897. He was also professor of mathematics and astronomy at Johns Hopkins University, 1884–94 and 1898–1900.

The results of his most important early research were presented in a paper (1860) proving that the asteroids could not be fragments of a larger planet. In Paris he found unpublished lunar occultations and extended lunar observations back from 1750 to about 1645. His investigations of the orbits of Neptune and Uranus won for him the gold medal of the Royal Astronomical Society of London in 1874.

In 1877 Newcomb began to restudy the fundamental data involved in calculation of the positions of celestial bodies, an enormous task that he had largely completed at the time of his death. He supervised the building of the Naval Observatory's 26-inch telescope and helped establish Lick Observatory. EVERETT I. YOWELL

NEWCOMEN, THOMAS, 1663–1792, English engineer and co-inventor of a steam pump or "atmospheric" steam engine, was born in Dartmouth, Devon. Newcomen's experiments coincided with those of Thomas Savery, who first obtained a patent in 1698. Newcomen went into partnership with Savery and made notable improvements upon Savery's engine, inventing the internal condensing jet and the automatic valve gear. Newcomen's first known engine (1712) was superseded in importance only by Watt's engine of 1769.

NEW CRITICISM, a movement in twentieth-century American criticism introduced in Joel E. Spingarn's address, delivered at Columbia University in 1910, entitled *The New Criticism*; a popularization of the aesthetics of Benedetto Croce. Not until 1941 did the term become well-known with the publication of a book of essays, *The New Criticism*, by the poet John Crowe Ransom. The New Criticism insists upon a close structural analysis of a work of art and asserts that it must be considered, in Ransom's words, as "independent of morality or any other useful set of ideas." Major figures associated with the New Criticism were Yvor Winters, R. P. Blackmur, Cleanth Brooks, and Allen Tate. Critical writings by I. A. Richards and T. S. Eliot also bear affinities to the New Criticism.

BIBLIOG.–John Crowe Ransom, *The New Criticism* (1941); Allen Tate, *Collected Essays* (1959).

NEW CUMBERLAND, borough, SE Pennsylvania, Cumberland County; on the Susquehanna River, 3 miles S of Harrisburg. New Cumberland has an army depot. Originally an Indian village, it was settled by whites in 1810 and incorporated as a borough in 1831. (For population, see Pennsylvania map in Atlas.)

NEW DEAL, a phrase used by Franklin D. Roosevelt in 1932 to describe his platform as Democratic presidential candidate—"I pledge you . . . a new deal for the American people." Subsequently New Deal became a label for the social and economic reform policies of the Roosevelt administrations. The initial phase of the New Deal was effected in legislation enacted during the "Hundred Days" (March 9–June 16) emergency session of the 73rd Congress called by President Roosevelt in 1933. This legislation, designed to provide immediate relief from the economic distress caused by the Depression, to effect financial reform, and to speed agricultural and industrial recovery, included the Emergency Banking Relief Act (March 9), the Economy Act (March 20), the Federal Emergency Relief Act (May 12), the Agricultural Adjustment Act (May 12), the Federal Securities Act (May 27), the Banking Act of 1933 (Glass-Steagall Act, June 16), and the National Industrial Recovery Act (NIRA, June 16). The Civilian Conservation Corps Reforestation Relief Act (March 31) established the Civilian Conservation Corps to provide immediate jobs for the unemployed, and the Tennessee Valley Authority was established (May 18) as a part of a broad conservation program. Further legislation enacted in 1934 established the Securities and Exchange Commission and the Federal Communications Commission.

The New Deal generally is divided into two phases, since in 1935 Roosevelt shifted abruptly from his concern with economic recovery and agrarian reform to an emphasis on social and economic legislation aimed largely at labor and other urban groups. The second New Deal emanated from legislation proposed by the President in his Message to Congress in January, 1935, much of which was subsequently enacted. The National Labor Relations Act (Wagner-Connery Act) of 1935 created the National Labor Relations Board; the Social Security Act established the Social Security Board; the Revenue Act of 1935 opened a series of "soak the rich" taxes; the Revenue Act of 1936 introduced the undistributed profits tax; the Walsh-Healy Government Contracts Act of 1936 provided the first federal minimum wages and hours legislation; the Bankhead-Jones Farm Tenant Act, 1937, established the Farm Security Administration; the National Housing Act of 1937 (Wagner-Steagall Act) created the U.S. Housing Authority; and the Fair Labor Standards Act (Wages and Hours Law, 1938) and the Agricultural Adjustment Act of 1938 authorized payments for soil conservation as well as commodity loans to farmers and established parity prices.

Conflict arose between the Supreme Court and the Roosevelt administration. Some of the early New Deal legislation was invalidated, including the National Industrial Recovery Act and the Railroad Retirement Act. Roosevelt proposed legislation to alter the composition of the court which became known as the "court-packing" bill. Although this measure was defeated, the controversy was finally resolved by legislation increasing retirement pay, the retirement of three justices between 1937–39, and the court's validation of several acts. New Deal legislation waned with the approach of World War II, as the government shifted its attention to foreign affairs. However, Roosevelt's reforms have had lasting effects.

BIBLIOG.–D. R. Fusfeld, *Economic Thought of Franklin D. Roosevelt and the Origin of the New Deal* (1956); Charles Hurd, *When the New Deal Was Young and Gay* (1965); Dexter Perkins, *New Age of Franklin Roosevelt: 1932–1945* (1957).

NEW DELHI, capital of India, situated in the north, between the west bank of the Jumna River and outliers of the Aravelli Range. The city occupies part of a low divide that historically controlled the principal gateway for cultural invasions of India. Ruins of seven or more capitals of former Indian empires are found in the vicinity. Old Delhi, the last of these still in use, is a heavily populated adjunct to the north of New Delhi. Both cities are situated within the Union territory of Delhi, a federal district similar to the District of Columbia in the United States. New Delhi is the central focus of Indian political life.

With the transfer of the Indian capital from Calcutta to Delhi in 1911, the British initiated plans for New Delhi, which was constructed during the 1920–30 period. New Delhi, designed by Sir Edwin Lutyens and Sir Herbert Baker, has the geometric form of planned modern capitals. The city is laid out along an east-west axis, Rajpath, a wide, triple-laned boulevard that connects the National Stadium and War Memorial Arch with the Secretariat, Parliament, and the President's House. Other parts of New Delhi display intricate patterns of intersecting roads, which link dispersed government areas, residential, shopping, and recreational areas, and a foreign diplomatic enclave.

Connaught Place, the central business district, has a circular street pattern, curved buildings to match, and covered walks. It contains some of the most fashionable shops, restaurants, and cinemas in India, and it is also the principal location of banks, auto showrooms, bookstores, and newspaper publishers. Light manufacturing industries are found north of New Delhi proper and in Old Delhi, where flour milling, printing, metalworking, and a variety of handicrafts are important sources of employment.

Numerous ruins of fortresses, tombs, and monuments are scattered throughout the New Delhi area, especially in the south. These include Purana Qila, a fortress-palace; the tomb of Humayun; and Tughluqabad, an imposing fourteenth-century fort. Other striking monuments are Qutb Minar, a stone tower 234 feet high (thirteenth-century), and the Iron Pillar, a single piece of wrought iron 23 feet high, attributed to the Guptas in the fifth century. In Old Delhi, the Red Fort, built by Emperor Shah Jahan in the seventeenth century represents one of the most magnificent fortress-palaces in the world. The Jama Masjid, which faces the fort, is another important architectural gem, with its striped domes and graceful minarets. The population of New Delhi proper is 294,565 (1964 est.). The New Delhi-Delhi metropolitan region numbers 2,630,485 (1964 est.). See DELHI. DAVID FIRMAN

The Jama Masjid, a mosque built in the 1600's, is one of New Delhi's architectural treasures.
FRITZ HENLE—PHOTO RESEARCHERS

In the early morning, fruit and vegetable vendors hawk their wares on Old Delhi's streets and sidewalks.
VAN BUCHER—PHOTO RESEARCHERS

BIBLIOG.–John Hill, *The Indian Sub-Continent* (1963); Martin Hürlimann, *Delhi, Agra, Fatehpur Sikri* (1965); Emily Polk, *Delhi, Old and New* (1963); Vincent Smith, *The Oxford History of India* (1958); L. Dudley Stamp, *Asia—A Regional and Economic Geography* (ed. 1962).

NEW ECHOTA MARKER NATIONAL MEMORIAL, NW Georgia, Gordon County, near Calhoun. The memorial comprises slightly less than an acre at the site of the last Cherokee Indian capital in Georgia. Although their government was recognized by the U.S. government, an estimated 13,000 Cherokees were forced by federal and state troops, in 1838, to surrender their land to the state of Georgia and move westward. The memorial was established in 1930.

NEW ECONOMIC POLICY (NEP), a political and economic program of the Soviet Union instituted by Lenin in 1921, when the decline of industry threatened to bring about famine and peasant rebellion. By the NEP, peasants were permitted to pay the government a tax based on a percentage of their agricultural production, and to sell the remainder of their produce on the free market. During the following two years, the NEP was extended into other areas; factories were handed over to trusts or even to individuals. In 1928–9, under Stalin, the policy was abruptly discontinued. Farms were collectivized, and the cautious individualism authorized by the NEP was ended.

NEWELL, FREDERICK HAYNES, 1862–1932, U.S. civil engineer, born in Bradford, Pa. He was instrumental in preparing the Reclamation Act in 1902 and served, first as chief engineer, then as director, of the Reclamation Service. Newell was head of the department of civil engineering at the University of Illinois from 1915 until 1920, and in 1919 he became president of the American Association of Engineers. He published many works on hydrography and irrigation.

NEWELL, PETER SCHEAF, 1862–1924, U.S. cartoonist and illustrator, born near Bushnell, Ill. He achieved popularity through his illustrations in *Harper's Weekly* and *Harper's Bazaar*. He also illustrated children's books and contemporary fiction, notably *Alice In Wonderland* (1901).

NEW ENGLAND, region NE United States, comprising the states of Connecticut, Maine, Massachusetts, New Hampshire, Rhode Island, and Vermont; bounded on the N by Canada, on the E by the Atlantic Ocean, on the S by Long Island Sound, and on the W by the state of New York; area 66,608 square miles, including 3,476 square miles of inland water. (For population, see maps of individual states in Atlas.)

The terrain of New England rises abruptly from a thin coastal plain to the northeast extremity of the Appalachian Mountain system, the Green and the White Mountains and the Berkshire Hills being the principal ranges. The region is dotted with glacial lakes and is drained by the Connecticut, Merrimack, Kennebec, and Penobscot rivers and a number of lesser streams. Chief cities are Boston, Worcester, and Springfield, Mass.; Hartford, Conn.; and Providence, R.I. The climate is characterized by mild summers and cold winters. Principal industries are manufacturing, diversified farming, fishing, and tourism.

Sectionalism. Early driven to commerce and shipbuilding for lack of adequate agriculture, most of New England was dependent on shipping by the mid-seventeenth century. Of particular significance in the prosperity of New England shipping, and ultimately in the region's economic estrangement from Britain, was the triangle or three-cornered trade developed in the early eighteenth century. In this trade cycle, rum carried to Africa in New England ships was exchanged for slaves, who were exchanged in the West Indies for molasses and sugar, which were in turn converted to rum in New England. After the British Parliament in 1733 placed a tax on French-made molasses (the Molasses Act) to protect British West Indian planters who were being undersold by the French, New England shipowners increasingly engaged in illicit trade to obtain cheap mollasses and to avoid other restrictions of British mercantilism. Although New England independence and intellect contributed to the breach between the American colonies and Britain, and to the political foundation of the republic, the region was virtually untouched by the fighting in the Revolutionary War after 1776.

After the Revolution, New England was beset by economic hardships that were to cause some sharp political differences with the rest of the nation. These difficulties, which continued until the Civil War, can be attributed to the loss of commercial advantages New England possessed as part of the British Commonwealth, trade restrictions imposed by the federal government as a result of differences with England and France, the Napoleonic Wars, and the abolition of the slave trade by Congress in 1807. With undisguised opposition to the War of 1812, which virtually closed their shipping outlets, the New England states limited their participation in the conflict to shipbuilding and the outfitting of privateers. Much smuggling existed between New England and Canada.

The rise of New England as the nation's manufacturing center after the War of 1812 created a sectional paradox during the slavery crisis. Driven on the one hand by Puritan tradition and rising liberalism to condemn slavery on moral grounds, and on the other to demand raw cotton for New England mills and factories, New England leaders were led to compromise with proslavery leaders on many issues.

After 1800 New England declined somewhat in economic importance in relation to other sections of the country, partly because of the lack of a frontier, the westward expansion of the middle and southern states that enticed many men from New England, and the growing importance of seaports in other sections of the United States. This decline was in some measure offset by the development in New England of the insurance and textile industries. Expanding from marine insurance that had been introduced in Boston in the early 1700's, New England underwriters developed successfully life and fire insurance companies by the mid-nineteenth century.

Before the Revolutionary War the making of textiles in the American colonies had been largely confined to the home. In 1789 Samuel Slater (1768–1835) founded the first spinning mill in New England at Pawtucket, R.I., and in 1814 Francis Cabot Lowell (1775–1817) with the aid of Paul Moody (1779–1831) opened the first combined spinning and weaving factory in the United States at Waltham, Mass. The early success of the New England textile industry was partly a result of the abundance of inexpensive female labor. The opportunity of marriage for many women having dwindled with the large migration of men to the West, many women sought their livelihood in the mills of factory towns.

The Puritan Tradition. A common cultural force originally united the New England states when, as English colonies, they subscribed in large measure to the tenets of Puritanism. Thus was provided the foundation for the intellectual leadership that represents New England's chief contribution to American culture and kept the region the nation's cultural center into the nineteenth century. See PURITANISM.

Modern Cultural Trends. By the late seventeenth century the tenets of the early Puritans were modified as a result of new scientific thought and a general reaction against the severity of the code. The more liberal forces of eighteenth-century theories of reason, the writings of such social theorists as Voltaire and Jean-Jacques Rousseau, and the rise of Romanticism in Europe further modified the Puritan tradition, and resulted in the so-called flowering of New England literature during the nineteenth century. Predominant in the Transcendentalist school, which advocated a supremacy of the spirit over matter and logic, were Ralph Waldo Emerson and Henry David Thoreau. Other New England figures notable in the development of Romantic prose and poetry were William Cullen Bryant, Nathaniel Hawthorne, Oliver Wendell Holmes, Henry Wadsworth Longfellow, James Russell Lowell, Herman Melville, and John Greenleaf Whittier. See UNITED STATES LITERATURE.

Social Change. America's westward growth tapped New England, as New England had tapped old England, and young men deserted the towns and farms for opportunities in the West. When the Erie Canal was opened in 1825, northern New England suffered a severe economic blow as it was then blocked off from the central avenues of trade that linked East to Midwest by land and water. Meanwhile eastern Connecticut, the Providence area of Rhode Island, and the Boston-Worcester-Springfield arc of Massachusetts became important industrial centers and lost many of the earlier regional ties with Maine, New Hampshire, and Vermont.

The New England Character. The businessman and farmer of the nineteenth century were models for the Yankee that came to be widely accepted as typical of New England. Although characterizations of New England business sagacity as depicted by the Canadian jurist and humorist Thomas Chandler Haliburton (1796–1865) are exaggerated, such qualities as industriousness, initiative, and an outward reserve are common to a people living in a harsh environment and faced with keen competition.

BIBLIOG.–J. T. Adams, *Founding of New England* (1963); Arthur Griffin and D. McCord, *New England Revisited* (1966); Andrew Hepburn, *Complete Guide to New England* (1962); L. K. Mathews, *Expansion of New England* (1962); Perry Miller, *The New England Mind* (1953).

NEW ENGLAND CONFEDERATION, a union of the colonies of Massachusetts Bay, Plymouth, Connecticut, and New Haven, formed in 1643 to meet common problems such as disputes with the Indians, the French, and with the Dutch of New Netherland, and boundary controversies among themselves. The confederation was officially known as the United Colonies of New England. Its articles of agreement provided that all members respect the territory and government of the others, that no member colonies might consolidate without the consent of the others, and that a new member colony could be admitted only by common consent. A board of eight commissioners was authorized to declare war, although the confederation was largely advisory. Rhode Island, Maine, and New Hampshire were excluded because of religious and political nonconformity. The confederation was dissolved in 1684.

NEW ENGLAND CONSERVATORY OF MUSIC, a private, professional school, located in Boston, Mass. Established in 1867, the conservatory began college-level instruction in 1870, with the first baccalaureate degree awarded in 1927. The school offers Bachelor's and Master's degrees in music and Artists Diplomas for excellence in applied music. The conservatory is accredited, coeducational, and nonsectarian.

NEW ENGLAND PRIMER, a popular schoolbook, first published in Boston, Mass., about 1683, by Benjamin Harris. It became the standard beginner's schoolbook in the New England colonies. The contents of the primer included woodcuts illustrating the alphabet, a syllabary, the Lord's Prayer, Creed, a child's prayer ("Now I lay me down to sleep"), the Shorter Catechism, and a poetic exhortation by the martyr John Rogers.

NEW FOREST, woodland region, s England, Hampshire; roughly bounded by Wiltshire on the N, Southampton Water on the E, the Solent on the S, and the Avon River on the W; area about 140 square miles. The forest is primarily oak and beech, with scattered marshy wasteland. About two thirds of the New Forest is maintained by the government as a national park. The New Forest was so named in 1079 by William I, who used it as a royal hunting preserve.

NEWFOUNDLAND AND LABRADOR, the easternmost province of Canada, formerly known as the province of Newfoundland only. It includes the island of Newfoundland (area 43,359 square miles; population 444,319 in 1961) and Labrador (area 112,826 square miles; population 13,534 in 1961), which is part of the Canadian mainland. It is one of four eastern provinces of Canada that are collectively known as the Atlantic Provinces. The capital is the City of St. John's on the east coast of the island. See LABRADOR; see also map in Atlas, Vol. 20.

Physical Features

Topography and Drainage. Newfoundland island is triangular-shaped and separated from the Canadian mainland by the Strait of Belle Isle to the north, 10 miles and more in width, and by Cabot Strait to the southwest, about 60 miles across. The western part of the island is the highest; the Long Range has rounded peaks of about 2,000 feet altitude. The south central section is a rolling, often barren plateau about 1,000 feet above sea level; it slopes toward an island-fringed, low, fiorded northeast coast. The longest rivers, such as the Exploits and Gander, flow to the northeast; the Humber River breaks through the Long Range to reach the west coast. A few of the interior lakes are large and deep (Grand Lake, 205 square miles; Red Indian Lake, 70 square miles), but in addition there are many small lakes, bogs, and swamps in the interior —remnants of the glacial age. The south coast is particularly steep and rocky; the rest of the coast has low hills and very little coastal plain.

Climate. Newfoundland island has a cool and wet climate, as it is surrounded by the cold water of the Labrador Current. The southeast coast is the mildest in winter, with an average January temperature of 25° F; the northwest peninsula is 10 degrees colder. Summers are cool along the coast,

Newfoundland has one of the oldest arms of Canada's provinces. Two Indians bear a shield on which the lions of England have been quartered with white horses; the shield is red and divided by a cross.

FLOWER	**Pitcher plant or Indian cup**
CAPITAL	**St. John's**
ENTERED FEDERATION	**March 31, 1949**
ORDER OF ENTRY	**10th**

GEORGE WHITELEY—PHOTO RESEARCHERS

At Carbonear, a fishing and trading center on Conception Bay in southeastern Newfoundland, a settlement has existed since the mid-seventeenth century.

averaging only about 55° F in July, but some western interior valleys record average July temperatures of about 60° F.

The south coast receives heaviest average annual precipitation, more than 50 inches, owing to the warmer air masses that bring moisture from the Gulf Stream offshore to the southeast. Precipitation of about 30 inches annually is recorded in the northwestern peninsula. Snowfall, averaging 120 inches, is heaviest on the northeast coast. Fog is common over the fishing banks to the south and southeast of Newfoundland island, but is rare in the interior of the island.

Flora and Fauna. The island's forests are mainly coniferous, consisting largely of white and black spruce, balsam fir, and tamarack; there are also some birch and poplar. As much of the surface is bare rock or bogs, only 35 per cent of the island is forested and only half of that amount (about 9,000 square miles) is productive growth. Animal life is similar to that of the nearby provinces and is not abundant. Caribou, moose, and bear live in the forested interior. Birds are plentiful, particularly sea birds. There are a few small fur-bearing animals, but trapping is no longer of much economic significance.

Fish, particularly cod, are abundant off the coasts, especially to the east and northeast, where the shallow water above the continental shelf adjoining Newfoundland favors the growth of plankton and other fish food. Small white whales appear during the summer and occasionally the larger whales are seen off the Labrador coast.

Social Features

Population grew slowly early in this century, but it increased rapidly after 1945, to 457,853 in 1961. About half of the population lives in urban centers of more than 1,000 persons. About 98 per cent of the people are of British origin, the descendants of British fishing families who settled the northeast and east coasts a few centuries ago. Labrador has remained sparsely inhabited, with only three per cent of the population in 1961. At one time there was a major migration of fishermen from Newfoundland island to Labrador during the summer, but this movement is no longer significant.

About 90 per cent of Newfoundland's population lives on or near the coast, and about 65 per cent are on the east and northeast coasts. About half the people live on Avalon peninsula, which juts out from the east coast, where St. John's, the capital and main port, is the largest city (90,838 population est., 1964). The only other sizable city is Corner Brook, a pulp and paper city on the west coast. Some of the larger fishing centers, especially those with filleting or freezing plants, have 3,000 to 5,000 persons. There are about 1,000 fishing villages, called outports, of a few hundred persons each, scattered around the coasts. The number and size of these outports are declining as fishermen obtain modern gear and move toward the larger towns.

Religion and Education. Newfoundland's population adhered to three main churches in 1961: Roman Catholic (163,618), Anglican (130,618), and United (97,886). There were more Salvation Army members than in any other Canadian province (36,258).

The administration of education is similar to that of other Canadian provinces, under an elected

Elevation Map of Newfoundland and Labrador. White areas 0-500 feet; light gray areas 500-1,000 feet; dark gray areas 1,000-2,000 feet; black areas 2,000-5,000 feet.

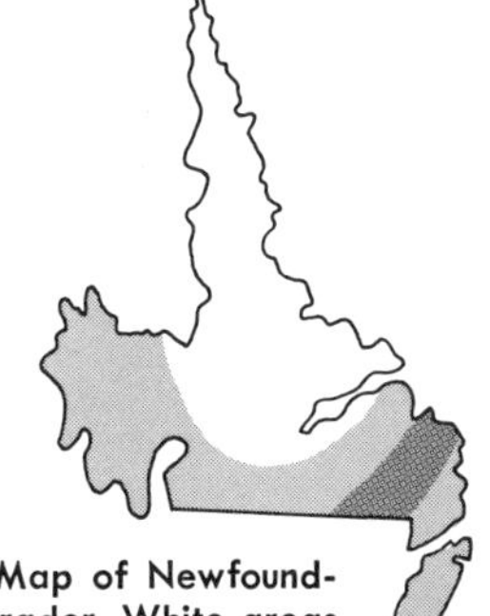

Precipitation Map of Newfoundland and Labrador. White areas 20-30"; light gray 30-40"; dark gray 40-50"; black 50-60".

Population Density Map of Newfoundland and Labrador. White areas less than 1 person per square mile; gray areas 1 to 30 per square mile; black areas, over 30.

PETER WERLE—PHOTO RESEARCHERS

Gander is one of several cities in Newfoundland with an air terminal. Development of transportation facilities in the province, however, has been limited. The lack of roads especially has impeded economic development. Among the Canadian provinces, Newfoundland and Labrador also has the smallest number of telephones in proportion to population. The traditional means of communication in Newfoundland has been, and still is, by water.

minister and a civil service deputy-minister. Because the population was scattered in small centers, education levels were not so high as in other provinces and teachers were often lacking. Educational facilities were improved rapidly after about 1950 and became more available as people moved into the larger towns and cities. The provincial university is Memorial University on the western edge of St. John's.

Economic Features

Fishing is still the main occupation of Newfoundlanders, but it has declined steadily in relative significance since 1945. Although there are fewer fishermen each year, production is greater and the value of the fish and fish products has increased considerably. The Newfoundland fishing industry, like that of Nova Scotia, has changed gradually during the 1950's and 1960's from its traditional methods. Cod, dried on open-air curing "flakes," is difficult to market, and more and more curing, processing, filleting, and freezing plants are being established in the larger fishing villages. The picturesque Newfoundland schooner which sailed to the Grand Banks has disappeared from the fishery, and has been replaced by a modern fleet of trawlers and draggers based on St. John's and the southern towns. The Banks fishery to the south and southeast of Newfoundland is shared with fishermen from several European nations. There is still much inshore fishing along the northeast coast, largely dependent upon the cod migrations during the summer. Inshore fishing is mainly a family enterprise of small boats and nets set off the islands or headlands. Some of the larger fishing vessels may travel to the Labrador coast for the summer fishing, but they bring their catch back to Newfoundland curing plants. The chief market for Newfoundland frozen or filleted fish is in the United States. The seal hunt in early spring in the Gulf of St. Lawrence is shared with other Atlantic Provinces fishermen. The hunt amid the ice floes off the coast of Labrador is of minor importance.

Forestry. The relatively small, coniferous trees of Newfoundland are valuable as pulpwood. Much of the forest of the Humber and Exploits river valleys is owned by two large pulp and paper companies, with modern mills at Corner Brook and Grand Falls. Pulpwood is towed along the coasts toward the two mills or transported on the rivers in the interior. There is also increasing use of the railway and new roads for the transport of pulp logs. Newsprint and other pulp or paper products are exported mainly to the United States or to western Europe. Pulp and paper rank along with fish products as leading exports. Many small sawmills in Newfoundland produce lumber for local use, but they are not of significant value to the province. Because the largest forest areas are in the northern half of the island, near the greatest number of fishermen, the two occupations are often combined. Many men cut pulpwood in the forest during the winter and return to fishing from their small coastal villages in summer.

Mining. Iron ore has been the main product of Newfoundland's mining industry since 1900. Production from the Wabana deposits on Bell Island ceased in 1966, but by that time iron ore production had increased from the deposits in western Labrador, notably at Labrador City, Wabush Lake, and from the ore bodies near Schefferville which are shared with Quebec. The interior of Newfoundland island has not been thoroughly prospected, despite the large deposit of lead-copper-zinc that has been worked at Buchans since 1927. The new mines, discovered in the 1950's and 1960's, are on or near the coasts. Fluorspar, mined at St. Lawrence on Burin peninsula, is important as a flux in the aluminum industry on mainland North America. Copper and asbestos are produced on the northeast coast at Tilt Cove and Baie Verte respectively. These mines have helped to diversify the occupation possibilities of the coastal fishermen.

Agriculture. Owing to the cool summer climate and the lack of large areas of fertile soil, there is little farming in Newfoundland. There are, however, small gardens at most fishing villages where fish is often used as fertilizer. In 1961 Newfoundland recorded 1,752 farms, and only 21,000 cultivated acres. Most farms raise feed grains, pasture, or root crops. Cultivation is scattered in small pockets along the coasts of Avalon and Burin peninsulas, and in some of the warmer narrow valleys of western Newfoundland such as the Codroy and Humber. The island imports much of its basic food supply.

Water Power. Newfoundland uses some of its water resources to produce electric power. The natural environment of the island favors widespread distribution of small water power sites: there is natural storage in the many lakes of the interior plateau; ample precipitation throughout the year provides volume; rapids and small falls are near the coast where the population is heaviest. The largest developed sites are on the longest rivers, the Exploits and Humber, and are used mainly by the pulp and paper mills. The newest power plant is at Baie d'Espoir on the south coast. Plans have been announced for harnessing one of the largest undeveloped water power sites in eastern North America, located in Labrador at Churchill Falls (formerly called Grand Falls) on the Churchill River (formerly Hamilton River).

Manufactures and Commerce. There is little manufacturing in Newfoundland, except for consumer goods used by the City of St. John's. Pulp and paper products from Corner Brook and Grand

Falls are the most valuable manufactures of the island. The value of fish products is increasing. Most of Newfoundland's ores are exported without final processing, and are significant mainly as export values. Newsprint, ores, and fish are sent to the United States; pulp and ores are sent to Britain; and small amounts of lower quality fish go to the Caribbean region.

Transportation and Communication. The Trans-Island Railway, now part of the Canadian National Railways, crosses the north central part of the island. Much of the freight carried along the railway is pulpwood or newsprint. St. John's, Canada's most easterly port, is the eastern terminal. The railway passes through Gander, Grand Falls and Corner Brook to its southwestern terminal at Port-aux-Basques, whence federal government ferries run to Sydney, N.S. Branch lines connect to Lewisporte, Bonavista, Carbonear, and Argentina. The Trans Canada Highway follows a similar route across the island, but is farther north occasionally and nearer the coast. Numerous branch roads were built after 1955 to give greater accessibility to many of the isolated outport villages. With the exception of the south-central coast, one of the main changes in post-war Newfoundland has been the increase in mobility and accessibility, which is related to increased transport facilities.

Because of its position, jutting eastward into the Atlantic, Newfoundland was important in early transatlantic flying and had several large air bases during World War II. These bases and airports became less significant in the post-war years when long range aircraft became more common and Newfoundland could be flown over. Major air fields are at Gander and at Goose Bay at the head of Lake Melville in Labrador. Newfoundland is the terminal for transatlantic submarine cables.

Tourist Attractions. The tourist trade has played a minor role in the past economy of Newfoundland, because of the island's distance from centers of population in North America and its lack of paved roads. With the continual improvement of transportation facilities in the 1960's, the distinctive fishing communities, sheltered harbors, places with quaint names, and the lake fishing are all becoming known to the tourist. The first national park on Newfoundland island, Terra Nova Park, was established in 1957 on the shores of Bonavista Bay.

J. Lewis Robinson

History

Discovery and Settlement. The rich fishing grounds of Newfoundland were probably discovered by Bristol sailors shortly after 1480 but the official discoverer was John Cabot, who reached either Newfoundland or Labrador in 1497. Thereafter, fishermen from Spain, Portugal, and France joined West Country Englishmen in exploiting the cod fishery. By the end of the sixteenth century France and England were chief rivals for control of Newfoundland.

During the first half of the seventeenth century a number of attempts were made to colonize Newfoundland. All ended in failure—mainly because of the inveterate hostility of the transient fishermen from the West Country who feared that colonists would eventually monopolize the fishery.

After 1634 the transients obtained the support of the crown in their struggle with the colonists, and in 1699 parliament enacted anti-settlement legislation which remained the basic law of Newfoundland for more than 150 years. The rationale for this anti-settlement policy was twofold: mercantilist theory dictated that fishing, a mother country industry, was not a suitable field for colonial enterprise and that the transient fishery was an invaluable "nursery for seamen."

The latter idea also dominated the thinking of the French, who, in 1662, garrisoned Placentia as the seat of a royal governor and a base of operations in Newfoundland waters. From this base they attacked and destroyed virtually every English settlement in Newfoundland in 1696, in 1705, and again in 1708. However, the Treaty of Utrecht in 1713 recognized British sovereignty in Newfoundland. The French retained the right to land and dry fish on the coast between Cape Bonavista on the east and Pointe Riche on the west passing by the north. The Treaty of Versailles in 1783 moved the French limits on the east coast northward to Cape St. John and on the west coast southward to Cape Ray. Thereafter, for a period of 121 years, the French Shore problem was a crucial one to Newfoundland.

While the French demanded an exclusive fishery, and the British government wavered but usually insisted on the principle of concurrent rights, the Newfoundland government demanded that its sovereignty over all of Newfoundland should be recognized. It was not until the signing of the *Entente*

In the Wabana mine under the ocean floor near Bell Island off Newfoundland's east coast, a mechanical loader fills waiting shuttle cars with iron ore.

GEORGE HUNTER

This paper mill located in Grand Falls is one of the two great paper mills of Newfoundland. The other, at Humber Arm, is the largest of its kind in the world.

NATIONAL FILM BOARD PHOTO BY CHRIS LUND

NATIONAL FILM BOARD

Petty Harbour, a fishing village near St. John's, was settled in the sixteenth century. It generates hydroelectric power for most of St. John's.

Cordiale in 1904 that France gave up her claim to any rights in Newfoundland. Meanwhile, development in the entire northern peninsula and west coast of the island had been stultified as these areas were without even the modicum of administrative and social service that had been provided elsewhere in the island.

Throughout the seventeenth and eighteenth centuries the population of Newfoundland slowly increased despite repressive legislation, deportation and threat of deportation, the denial of property rights, the lack of any social services, and the operation of a particularly vicious judicial system managed by the captains of fishing ships. By 1729 the British government found it necessary to appoint a naval governor, and in 1792 a supreme court of civil and criminal jurisdiction was established. However, both governor and court remained in Newfoundland only during the summer months when the transient fishermen were present. It was not until 1825 after the existence of a settled colony was finally acknowledged, that a government, consisting of a governor and an appointed council, was established. In 1832 the government was made representative by the addition of an elected house of 15 members chosen from nine districts on the basis of virtually universal male suffrage.

Self-Government. The assembly was driven to exasperation by the obstructionist tactics of the council until finally the struggle for control of finances resulted in deadlock. To break the deadlock the constitution was suspended in 1842 and an amalgamated legislature of three elected members for every two appointed councilors was inaugurated.

The old constitution was restored in 1848 and almost immediately thereafter the assembly demanded full responsible government—that is, the form of government in which the governor chooses executive advisers who are responsible to and have the confidence of the elected assembly.

The campaign for responsible government aroused bitter sectarianism as Irish Catholics took the position of fighting for the rights of fishermen and servants against the exploitation of the Protestant merchants and government office holders. But the result was victory for liberals and the inauguration of responsible government in 1855. Sectarianism continued, however, to be a feature of Newfoundland political life into the twentieth century.

Between 1864 and 1869 Newfoundland was involved in the discussions that led to the confederation of Canada. The island continued, however, to look eastward toward Britain, and the idea of confederation was rejected at the polls. In 1895 negotiations for union with Canada were re-opened but once again Newfoundlanders chose to continue their independent course.

Twentieth Century. The first two decades of the twentieth century saw the emergence of new political forces in Newfoundland dedicated to more radical social policies than those thitherto practiced. The first evidence of this tendency appeared in 1907 with the formation of the Peoples' party, which by 1913 had acquired political control of the entire southern half of the island. It was prevented from expanding to the north, however, by the extremely rapid growth of the Fishermen's Protective Union, led by William Ford Coaker, which originated at Herring Neck in 1908 and spread quickly along the northeast coast.

One part of Coaker's plan to assist the fishermen, loggers, and other laborers was to educate them politically so that they might choose their representatives in the assembly from among themselves. So successful was he, that following the election of 1913, the F.P.U. formed the effective opposition. Following the outbreak of war in 1914 Coaker led his followers into a coalition National government in which he assumed cabinet rank. With the dissolution of the coalition at the end of the war he reverted to an alliance with the Liberals.

The Statute of Westminster, enacted by the British parliament in 1931, recognized the fact that Newfoundland had obtained full Dominion status. However, complete political independence did not lessen the degree of economic dependence which grew out of reliance on one or two basic commodities whose prices were subject periodically to severe fluctuations on the world market. Thus, the depression of 1929 completely overwhelmed Newfoundland's economy.

The immediate consequence was the election in 1932 of a conservative United Newfoundland party with a mandate from the people to seek appointment of a royal commission by the British government to examine Newfoundland's plight and to suggest remedies. The royal commission was appointed in 1933 and recommended the suspension of responsible government and the inauguration of government by a commission of six members appointed by and responsible to the government of the United Kingdom. In 1934 Newfoundland came under the rule of such a government.

Portuguese have fished off Newfoundland coasts for 400 years. Their three-masted ships carry 100 men.
GEORGE WHITELEY—PHOTO RESEARCHERS

The commission of government implemented a fisheries policy which had been outlined by Coaker but which he had failed to carry over the opposition of local merchants. Vast improvements were made in health, education, and other social services, the railway was brought up to standard, and customs duties were reduced. The spoils system, blatant political patronage, and nepotism were almost eliminated by a reorganization of the civil service. The commission's accomplishments can be attributed in part to the boom conditions created by World War II. In the new type of war Newfoundland attained great strategical significance and benefited immensely from the establishment of Canadian and U.S. military bases on her soil, as well as from the high demand and unprecedented prices paid for her staple commodities.

Following the war, the British Labour government decided that steps should be taken to restore some form of self-government to Newfoundland. The first step was the election of a national convention to recommend "possible forms of future government to be put before the people at a national referendum."

In the beginning the convention gave serious consideration to only two alternatives: the continuation of government by commisssion or the reversion to responsible government as it existed in 1932. But there emerged in the convention an able politician and a convinced exponent of confederation with Canada, the journalist Joseph Roberts Smallwood. Smallwood had been much influenced by Coaker and the early policies of the F.P.U. He now showed himself to be a remarkably effective orator and a shrewd tactician.

Despite Smallwood's best efforts the convention failed to recommend any form of government other than a continuation of that in existence or a return to the old constitution. Nevertheless, the British government decided to add confederation with Canada to the ballot choices and Smallwood, who had failed to convert the national convention, took his proposition directly to the electorate.

Confederation. The referendum was held in June of 1948. The vote was approximately 14 per cent for a continuation of government by commission; 45 per cent for restoration of the constitution of 1832; and 41 per cent for confederation. When a second referendum was held with only responsible government and confederation on the ballot paper, 52 per cent of the electorate chose confederation, 48 per cent a return to responsible government. The campaign had been a bitter one, with anti-confederate strength concentrated in the Avalon Peninsula. One factor in deciding the outcome had been the campaign by certain anti-confederates for economic union with the United States. Such a union at least hinted at the dissolution of ties with Britain and the Commonwealth, which would not be considered by those who held the balance of power and who had previously voted for retention of commission of government. Moreover, Britain herself had been most anxious that Newfoundland should enter confederation.

Following the referendum a delegation was sent to Ottawa to work out the terms of union. Finally, on Mar. 31, 1949, Newfoundland became the tenth province of Canada and Prime Minister John A. MacDonald's idea of a nation stretching from sea to sea was fully realized. Representative and responsible government was restored to Newfoundland, though now in a unicameral form. Moreover, Newfoundland now sent seven members to the house of commons at Ottawa and six members to the senate of Canada. Smallwood became the first premier of the province, a position in which he repeatedly succeeded himself.

Newfoundland's economy quickly felt the impact of Canadian taxes, Canadian tariffs, Canadian subsidies and subventions, and of Canadian social services. These changes, together with improved communications, the revision of trade patterns, the introduction to the island of Canadian business and, to a lesser extent, industry, have resulted in what amounts to an economic revolution. Newfoundland has enjoyed, since confederation, unprecedented prosperity and growth. In 1964 the name of the province was officially changed to Newfoundland and Labrador. LESLIE HARRIS

BIBLIOG.–Canada, Department of Trade and Commerce, *Newfoundland, an Introduction to Canada's New Province* (1950); Parzival Copes, *St. John's and Newfoundland—An Economic Survey* (1961); C. R. Fay, *Life and Labour in Newfoundland* (1956); G. E. Gunn, *The Political History of Newfoundland, 1832–1864* (1966); A. H. McClintock, *The Development of Constitutional Government in Newfoundland* (1941); J. R. Smallwood, ed., *The Book of Newfoundland* (2 vols., 1937); Vaino Tanner, *Newfoundland-Labrador* (1947).

NEWFOUNDLAND DOG, a large, physically powerful working dog, believed to have been developed in Newfoundland in the sixteenth century. The Newfoundland dog stands 26 to 28 inches high and weighs 110 to 150 pounds. It has a wide back, deep chest, and short neck. The head is broad, and the coat is coarse, dense, and water repellent; it usually is black, occasionally with some spots of white on the chest.

Newfoundland Dog

WM. BROWN

NEW FRANCE, the French colony in North America from the end of the sixteenth century to the middle of the eighteenth century. Its center was the St. Lawrence Valley, and it extended into much of southern Canada, the Great Lakes region, and the Mississippi Valley.

Early Exploration and Settlement. Recorded French explorations of the New World began in 1524 with the Florentine navigator Giovanni da Verrazano, who explored much of the North Atlantic coast in search of areas for settlement. Ten years later, Jacques Cartier's three voyages up the St. Lawrence River established the basis of French knowledge of the country.

The first permanent foundation was made at Quebec in 1608 by Samuel de Champlain, known as the "Father of New France." He established or supervised such posts as Montreal and Trois Rivières, and directed exploration of the St. Lawrence Valley and of the area around lakes Huron and Ontario. The Company of New France was formed in 1627 and given control of trade in the colony. Quebec was surrendered to the British in 1629, but was reacquired in 1632.

The French early allied themselves with the Hurons and with Algonquian tribes of the area, thus incurring the enmity of the powerful Iroquois Confederacy, which became the ally of the British. French efforts were directed to the fur trade with the Indians, and to their conversion to Catholicism.

King Louis XIV in 1663 revoked the powers of the company and established direct royal control over the colony. Governmental power in New France was vested in the governor, the intendant, the bishop of Quebec, and appointed councilors.

Expansion and Conflict. Exploration, the fur trade, and missionary work took the French along the Great Lakes, where they established posts. Jacques Marquette and Louis Jolliet in 1673 portaged from the lakes to the Mississippi and went down much of the great river. Sieur de La Salle founded posts on the lakes and on the St. Joseph and Illinois rivers. In 1682 he went down the Mississippi to its mouth. By the end of the century the French had established settlements in the Illinois country and at Biloxi; shortly thereafter Detroit and New Orleans were founded. There were eighteenth-century explorations of what are now western Canada and the United States, and claims were made to the upper Ohio Valley.

This expansion brought the French into conflict with the other colonial powers. By the mid-eighteenth century the English confronted the French in the Hudson Bay region, on the New England frontier, and in the Ohio Valley. Border raids and Indian alliances were continuous, and colonial rivalry merged with other French-English differences to bring on a series of wars.

The wars were for the most part inconclusive, and usually ended in a return to the prewar situation. The French loss of Acadia (Nova Scotia) in Queen Anne's War, confirmed by the Treaty of Utrecht in 1713, was an exception. The last of the wars between Britain and France in North America (1754–63) originated in conflicting claims to the Ohio Valley. In New France, after early French success, the losses of Quebec in 1759 and of Montreal the following year were decisive. New France was ceded to Britain by the Treaty of Paris in 1763. See CANADA; FRENCH AND INDIAN WAR; MONTREAL; QUEBEC.

GEORGE J. FLEMING, JR.

BIBLIOG.–P. F. X. de Charlevoix, *History and General Description of New France* (6 vols., 1962); D. G. Creighton, *Empire of the St. Lawrence* (1957); N. E. Dionne, *Champlain* (1963); William J. Eccles, *Canada under Louis XIV, 1663–1701* (1964); Harold A. Innis, *Fur Trade in Canada* (ed. 1956); G. M. Wrong, *Rise and Fall of New France* (1928).

NEW FRONTIER, in U.S. history, the slogan of the 1960 Democratic presidential campaign and subsequently the motto of Pres. John F. Kennedy's administration, similar to Pres. Franklin D. Roosevelt's "New Deal." The slogan was introduced by President Kennedy upon his acceptance of the Democratic presidential nomination, July 15, 1960. The goals of the New Frontier called for "more sacrifice, instead of more security," and "courage—not complacency"; these goals for the future were "not a set of promises" but "a set of challenges." In domestic affairs, New Frontier programs sought to stabilize the economy while increasing productivity, and to expand civil rights legislation. New Frontier goals were expressed in global affairs by the establishment of the Peace Corps, the expansion of the Food-for-Peace Program, and the pursuit of a foreign policy sympathetic to struggling young nations.

NEWGATE, former prison, London, England. Originally a gatehouse dating from the twelfth century, the prison was burned down by rioting peasants in 1381, and damaged by fire in 1666. It was rebuilt in 1780 and partially destroyed by mob violence that same year. After the prison reform acts of 1877, Newgate was no longer used as a penal institution. The edifice was finally town down in 1902.

NEW GEORGIA ISLANDS, South Pacific Ocean, a group of the Solomon Islands that includes New Georgia (50 mi. long, 5 to 28 mi. wide) and the smaller islands Rendova, Gizo, Kolombangara, and Vangunu; extending NW–SE in an area about 130 miles long and 40 miles wide; total island area about 2,000 square miles. The population is comprised primarily of Melanesians. Copra is the chief export. New Georgia is part of the British Solomon Islands protectorate. (For population, see Pacific Ocean map in Atlas.) OTIS W. FREEMAN

NEW GLASGOW, town, N Nova Scotia; near the mouth of the East River; about 90 miles NE of Halifax. Founded in 1809, it soon became a noted shipbuilding port. New Glasgow is located in a coal-mining district and its industries include steel-casting and rolling works, potteries, and foundries. It was incorporated in 1875. (For population, see Atlantic Provinces map in Atlas.)

NEW GRANADA, former name for the present-day republic of Colombia. The province of New Granada was created by the Spanish crown in 1549 to be governed by Peru. In 1717, New Granada was created a viceroyalty. After the colonial wars of independence, the territory was named the Republic of Gran Colombia and included Colombia, Ecuador, Venezuela, and Panama. When Ecuador and Venezuela seceded, it became the Republic of New Granada. This evolved into the Republic of Colombia in 1885. In 1903, Panama seceded to become a separate republic. See COLOMBIA.

NEW GUINEA, the world's largest island after Greenland, located in the SW Pacific Ocean between 0°21′ and 10°41′ S lat. and 130°56′ and 150°53′ E long. It has an area of 330,000 square miles and an estimated population of 3,000,000 (1966). The island has two main political divisions. West Irian, lying west of 141° E long., was formerly administered by the Netherlands, but was ceded to Indonesia in 1962 under an agreement with the United Nations requiring Indonesia to seek the wishes of the inhabitants before 1969 on their ultimate future. The eastern part of the island consists of the combined territories of Papua and New Guinea, administered as a single political unit by Australia. The Territory of New Guinea was German from 1884

Location Map of New Guinea

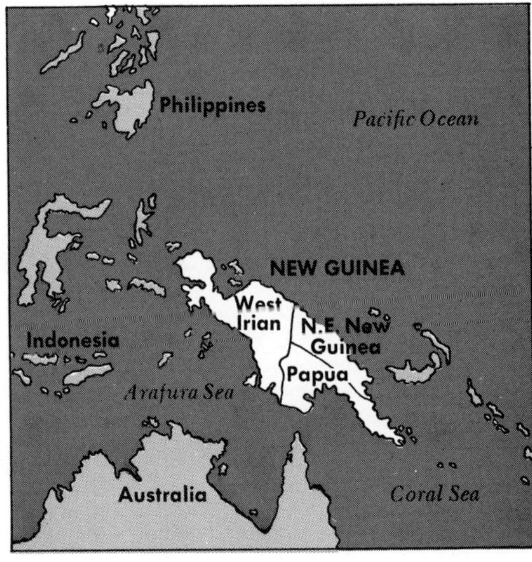

DIANE RAWSON—PHOTO RESEARCHERS

Most Papuan natives live in villages such as this one. Villages seldom number more than 50 families.

until 1914; now Australia holds it as a Trust Territory from the United Nations. Papua, which was claimed by Britain in 1884, has been a Territory of the Australian Commonwealth since 1906. See Pacific Ocean map in Atlas, Vol. 20.

Physical Features

Terrain and Drainage. In shape, New Guinea is sometimes likened to a giant bird, and the western peninsula of the island is named the Vogelkop, or Bird's Head. The island is mountainous and of recent geological formation. Mountain building culminated in the Tertiary era and has not yet ceased; the whole northern coastline seems to be undergoing uplift, while the southern coastline is sinking. The backbone of the island is the central cordillera, a chain of mountains running almost the full length of the island. The ranges rise very steeply from the lowlands on both sides, but especially in the south where a mighty escarpment called the Limestone Barrier rises 6,000 to 10,000 feet from the southern plain over a length of some 400 miles. In West Irian the Trikora (Carstensz) Mountains rise to more than 16,000 feet and carry glaciers covering several square miles. Other high points are Mt. Sukarno (Wilhelmina), reaching 15,585 feet, and Mt. Wilhelm, the highest point in the Australian territory, which reaches 15,400 feet. The Owen Stanley range in the eastern peninsula of Papua is continuous with, but geologically older than, the central cordillera; here Mt. Victoria reaches a maximum height of 13,363 feet. Within the central mountains are a number of wide valleys lying between 5,000 and 7,000 feet above sea level; these valleys are inhabited by about one million people.

South of the central cordillera is an extensive plain occupied in part by the swampy lowlands of the Fly and Digul river systems. A deep trough north of the ranges is occupied by the valleys of the Mamberamo, Sepik, Ramu, and Markham rivers, and north of this region lies a discontinuous series of mountains reaching 13,000 feet in the Saruwaged chain. Off the north coast are a number of islands, most of them volcanic. To the northeast lie the curving chains of the Bismarck and Solomon archipelagoes, which are the emergent portions of young mountain chains. There are numerous volcanoes, several of which are active, both on these islands and on part of the mainland. When Mt. Lamington in Papua erupted violently in 1951, 3,000 people were killed. Earthquakes are frequent except near the south coast of the island.

The drainage of the central cordillera is collected into a number of large river systems, and the lower Purari, Fly, Sepik, Ramu, Digul, Eilanden, and Mamberamo rivers carry great quantities of water to the sea. The Fly and Sepik are navigable for several hundred miles by launches and barges. Flooding is a problem in populated low-lying areas near their banks.

Climate. Though New Guinea lies wholly within the tropics, its climate is far from uniform. At the coast there is no cold season, yet temperatures in the mid-year months on the south coast may remain at an average of 10 degrees cooler than in January-February. Daily mean temperatures on the coast range between 65° and 88° F, but in the mountains there is a much greater range, so that at 5,000 feet nights may be as cool as 50° F, even though daytime temperatures may still reach the 80's. Frost has been recorded in sheltered basins as low as 5,500 feet, but generally is rare at altitudes below 7,500 feet. The snow-line lies around 15,500 feet, but is rising, and the four remaining ice caps on West Irian mountains have all shrunk greatly since they were first visited by explorers early in the twentieth century.

Rainfall varies widely. Except in a few areas where the seasons are reversed, or which have no seasonality, January to March is the wettest period and June to September the driest. Only the coastal area around Port Moresby and a few isolated pockets elsewhere receive less than 50 inches in a normal year, but large areas in the lowlands north and south of the ranges and in the valleys within the central cordillera receive an average of less than 125 inches. The heaviest rainfall occurs in a belt lying along the southern face of the central cordillera, in southern and central New Britain, and in the south-central Vogelkop; here, recorded mean amounts generally exceed 175 inches, and in places annual rainfalls of over 250 inches have been measured. Exceptional years occur: in July, 1965, some areas in the Bismarcks and Solomons received more than 100 inches in one month. But quite large areas in the south and in the northern inland are liable to drought conditions during part of the year; Port Moresby has recorded a spell of 100 days without significant rainfall.

Vegetation and Soil. Most of New Guinea is forested, though the composition of the forest varies widely. Swamp forests and dense tropical rain forests mantle most of the lowlands; these forests have some valuable hardwood timbers. The montane forests have less floristic variety, and the highest forests are often completely dominated by *Nothofagus* beech. The high mountains of New Guinea are particularly interesting to the botanist because of the mingling of flora of Indo-Malayan and Australian types. Above about 11,000 feet, forest gives way to alpine tundra. In the drier areas at lower and middle altitudes are extensive grasslands, some of which have been created by man, largely through the agency of fire. The southern plains, near Torres Strait, are mantled by savanna woodland very similar to that of northern Australia.

Soils differ widely. On steep slopes they are generally young and frequently rejuvenated, since landslipping is very common, while on areas above river flood levels in the lowlands are some very old, deeply leached, and infertile soils. Some soils on young volcanic deposits are of high fertility, and soils in some limestone areas are also of good quality, where the rainfall is not excessive.

Fauna. Animal life is related to Australian rather than to Indo-Malayan types, and there are a number of marsupials. There are no large fauna, other than introduced deer, and virtually no carnivores. Dangerous saltwater crocodiles inhabit the estuaries, but the freshwater crocodiles are less aggressive. Except in the dry areas on the southern side of the island, poisonous snakes are relatively scarce, though snakes in general are very plentiful. There is a diverse bird fauna, including several varieties of the brilliantly plumed bird of paradise, and the large, flightless cassowary.

Social Features

Mainly on linguistic grounds, the dark-skinned and woolly-haired people of New Guinea are divided into two main groups. The Papuans, who occupy the whole inland area, the larger islands, and some coastal regions, are distinguished from the Melanesians, who are more recent arrivals and occupy a number of smaller islands and coastal locations. Some Malay-speaking people have been settled in the far west for several hundred years, and on two atolls north of the Bismarck islands are Polynesian-speaking people. The people of New Guinea are predominantly agriculturists who grow root crops (especially the yam, taro and sweet potato) for subsistence by cultivation that varies from the rudimentary slash-and-burn methods of some lowland groups, to the elaborate ridging, ditching, and draining methods used by some people in the central highlands, many of whom have a good understanding of the value of mulching, and who even burn peat for potash. In some areas these methods are still carried on with only stone and wood tools, as they were everywhere before discovery and exploration. Some people in lowland areas depend for food largely on the pith of the sago palm (*Metroxylon sagu*), and some coastal people depend largely on fishing and collecting reef fauna.

Except in part of the central highlands where houses are dispersed, people live in villages, but these show a wide range of size and form. In most "Papuan" areas men live in club houses apart from the women, but in "Melanesian" areas family houses are more common. Pigs are everywhere important, and in much of the island women share houses with their pigs. There is a complete absence of organized political groups larger than a few thousand persons, and of any hereditary or elected leadership empowered to settle disputes. Leadership over a village or descent group is achieved by personality, prowess in warfare and oratory, and skill in manipulating the system of reciprocal exchange and aid between persons. This system is everywhere present, though its form changes: in the Sepik area the main items of "gift" are carefully-grown long yams, while the highlanders give pigs in colorful ceremonies. Membership in a group, which carries with it rights to land and to mutual aid, is generally reckoned by descent in either the male or female line. Warfare between small groups was endemic in New Guinea until suppressed by the colonial administrations, and in some outlying areas intergroup fighting continues even today.

Administration, Religion, and Education. Administration and missions have by now penetrated almost the whole island except some remote parts of West Irian. There is a great variety of mission groups, but about half the Christian population is Roman Catholic. Education still reaches only a minority of school-age children, and at the primary level is still provided largely by the missions. The administration, and some missions, also provide a limited amount of secondary and technical education, and some promising students are sent to Australia or Java for higher schooling. There are two infant universities—colleges in the American sense

River and ocean settlements of New Guinea fish for subsistence. The island's fresh and salt water resources have undergone little commercial exploitation.

CHRISTA ARMSTRONG—RAPHO GUILLUMETTE

A simple island schoolhouse is hung with religious symbols that are supposed to ward off evil spirits.

DIANE RAWSON—PHOTO RESEARCHERS

DIANE RAWSON—PHOTO RESEARCHERS

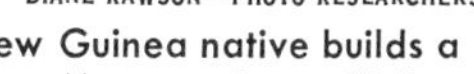

A New Guinea native builds a canoe. Many natives still live much as their ancestors did.

CHRISTA ARMSTRONG—RAPHO GUILLUMETTE

At this high school in Mount Hagen classes last from 8 a.m. to 6 p.m. without breaks. Students walk several miles to and from school.

—at Sukarnapura (1963) and Port Moresby (1967). There have been many changes as a result of administration and mission influence, and a monetary economy is now grafted onto the subsistence economy over much of the island. Clothing is widely adopted in the larger cities, and tools and some foodstuffs are bought from trade stores. In some coastal areas there is now an elite possessing some education and skills, adopting a range of European customs, and possessing a limited knowledge of the outside world. The political leaders of the 1960's came mainly from this group.

Economic Features

Agriculture. From the earliest days of development, the copra industry has been the basis of the economy. There is an annual production of over 120,000 tons, the overwhelming bulk of it from the Australian territory. About 75 per cent is produced on European-owned plantations, the balance on native small-holdings. There are also old established rubber plantations in Papua, and since 1945 cocoa and coffee plantations have been established as new rural industries, both by European and native growers. These latter industries are in a highly expansionist phase, but there are problems of marketing the crops. A tea industry has recently been started in the central highlands, and less successful attempts have been made to establish rice, groundnuts, and passion-fruit as cash crops. An old established nutmeg industry in the Vogelkop has expanded in recent years.

The plantations are mainly located in the Bismarck archipelago, on the north coast between Lae and Madang, and around Port Moresby. Coffee is grown mainly in the highlands. Plantations are the main employers of labor, and over 100,000 indigenes (90,000 in the Australian territory and between 15,000 and 20,000 in West Irian) are employed. Native cash-cropping is more widely dispersed, but the most productive areas are close to the centers of plantation development. For relatively large populations in remote areas there is virtually no possibility of earning money except by working as migrant labor. Though some areas are densely populated—especially the valleys of the central highlands—there is nowhere much shortage of food. Diets, however, are lacking in protein, and attempts are now being made to set up a cattle industry.

Extractive Industries. Gold mining has been important historically, especially around Bulolo and Wau in Australian New Guinea, but output has declined greatly in recent years. Oil was produced around Sorong and Steenkool in the Vogelkop from 1948 until 1962, but efforts to locate an economic field elsewhere in the island, especially around the Gulf of Papua, were unsuccessful. Natural gas has been found, but not exploited. Nickel deposits in West Irian also remain unworked. Recently there have been investigations into the feasibility of reworking long-unused copper deposits near Port Moresby. There is abundant limestone suitable for cement making, though the market is insufficient to warrant development. There are very large potential reserves of hydroelectric power, and preliminary work on a dam on the Ramu river west of Lae was begun in 1966.

The most promising new industry is forestry, which, in the Australian territory, has greatly increased its production since 1960. A small industry making plywood was set up at Bulolo in 1953, and since 1960 large new concessions have been opened up, in New Britain, Bougainville, and elsewhere. Great quantities of fine hardwood timber exist.

Industry, Communications, and Towns. With only a limited market, the potential for industrial development is small, but brewing, cigarette manufacture, and various service industries have been added to a base of coconut-oil extraction, coffee-drying and grading, and similar agricultural processing industries. The mountainous nature of the terrain has inhibited the growth of a network of good roads, and internal markets are compartmented into small areas, each focusing on one of the principal ports—Port Moresby, Rabaul, Lae, Madang, Sukarnapura, Manokwari, and Merauke. A road system penetrates the highlands from Lae for more than 400 miles, but much of the road is fit only for small four-wheel-drive vehicles. Coastal shipping services focus on the overseas ports. A large proportion of cargo, especially between the highlands and Madang and Lae, goes by air.

The only large town is Port Moresby (population about 45,000), the main center for administration in the Australian area and the port for almost the whole of Papua. Rabaul and Sukarnapura each have over 10,000 people. Most of the expatriate population—Australian and Indonesian—is centered in the towns.

H. C. BROOKFIELD

Papua—New Guinea

History. The earliest European contact was made in 1512 by Antonio d'Abreu from Portugal. The naming of islands by Dutch, English, French, and Spanish navigators continued intermittently to 1871 without involving settlement or exploration. Early exploration by Russian and German scientists occurred in the north and by British and Australian expeditions in the south. The inland Highlands were explored on foot only after 1933.

German interests in New Guinea increased after the Franco-Prussian War. Private companies, recognized by the German government, established interests in New Britain, New Ireland, and the Duke of York islands by 1884. Great Britain, attempting to avoid costly administration, used the Fiji-based Western Pacific High Commission to keep law and order over British subjects without annexing land. Australian colonies, particularly Queensland, pressed Britain to annex the southeast coast to forestall German expansion.

In April, 1883, Queensland unilaterally took possession of the southeast coast, but Britain, expecting negotiation with Germany, refused to sanction it. In May, 1884, a syndicate of German bankers under von Hansemann founded the *Neu Guinea Kompagnie* and secretly sent Otto Finsch to the northeast coast to acquire land for plantations. Australian suspicions were aroused. On Nov. 6, 1884, Commodore Erskine proclaimed British New Guinea a protectorate; this was followed in 1888 by formal annexation. Germany announced annexation of the north in November, 1884.

From 1885 to 1899 German New Guinea was administered from Madang by the *Neu Guinea Kompagnie* under charter. Plantation development was rapid. The imperial government, on assuming responsibility, moved the capital to Kokopo in New Britain and extended German influence to Micronesia, Nauru, and the islands of Bougainville and Buka. German Lutheran and Roman Catholic missions were established. On Sept. 11, 1914, an Australian expeditionary force landed at Kokopo, took possession of the country, and ended German influence.

In British New Guinea an unhappy joint administrative arrangement between the Australian colonies (the Commonwealth Government assumed responsibility in 1902) and the Western Pacific High Commission lasted until 1905. The first administrator, Sir William McGregor, initiated land and native policies effective thereafter. The Papua Act, 1905, formally brought British New Guinea under Australian control and initiated the new name, Papua. This legal position lasted until the Japanese invasion in 1942. New Guinea became a Mandate under the League of Nations in 1921, and its administration by Australia was kept separate from Papua until the introduction in 1942 of the Australian New Guinea Administrative Unit (ANGAU), which governed both territories as the Japanese retreated, until 1946. New Guinea became a United Nations Trust Territory after the war. Its administration was united with that of Papua in 1945 and a common legislative council was established in 1949.

Sir Hubert Murray administered Papua from 1907 to 1940. His native policy of peaceful conquest and control by village constables was considered exemplary at the time. It was made possible by the absence of large, centrally controlled tribes among the indigenous inhabitants. Murray received little financial assistance from Australia. Peace, law, and order, rather than development of native peoples, characterized his administration. Education was a mission responsibility. New Guinea's natural resources and the discovery of gold deposits in the Bulolo Valley in 1921 provided the mandate with money for limited development that was aided also by Australian funds. Income tax was introduced in 1959. An outright grant from Australia to the Papua–New Guinea Administration provides the balance. The house of assembly approves an annual budget. In addition to the grant, Australia provides defense, civil aviation, and some public works independently of the New Guinea budget.

Government. The constitutional authority to administer the country is provided by the New Guinea Act, 1949–63, of the Commonwealth of Australia. This government delegates authority to the Minister and Department of Territories in Canberra which in turn delegates authority to the administrator, resident in Port Moresby.

International considerations and the Trusteeship Agreement have encouraged Australian policy to aim at self-government or independence as and when the indigenous inhabitants request it. No nationalist movement pressing for independence has emerged.

The 1963 amendments to the Act provide for a house of assembly of 64 members. Ten are reserved official seats; ten are special seats reserved for non-indigenous members, and 44 are open seats for which any race may stand. All persons vote for both open and special seats on a modified preferential system. Compulsory registration of adults on a common roll was introduced in 1963 and voluntary voting for both kinds of seat was provided. The house elects its speaker. The administrator and, in limited instances, the governor-general retain power of assent.

The February-March election of 1964 resulted in a majority of indigenous members, though non-indigenous candidates won six open seats in addition to the ten special seats. There was a 72.3 per-cent poll.

Some attempts by indigenous and non-indigenous people to form political parties have occurred, but with as yet uncertain influence. No parties emerged in the 1964 election.

The administrator may appoint up to fifteen members to serve as departmental under-secretaries. To date these have all been indigenous appointments. Their duty is to understudy departmental heads with a view to eventual cabinet responsibilities. The policy making instrument is currently the administrator's council, consisting of the administrator, three official members, and seven elected members of the house.

The country is divided into 15 administrative districts, six in Papua and nine in New Guinea. These are administered by a district commissioner responsible to the Department of the Administrator in Port Moresby. The commissioners chair their districts, co-ordinating committees of public servants representing specialized services such as education, agriculture, and health. They also chair a district advisory council of about 20 appointed members, mixed racially, and representing varied local interests.

Districts are divided geographically and each subdistrict is administered by a subordinate officer with specialized staff corresponding broadly to the district level. Local government councils, co-operative societies, rural development committees, and other statutory instruments are regulated and encouraged at this level. Towns of importance have urban advisory boards. Legislation is pending to introduce an elected system of urban local government.

Judicial functions are executed by a central legal department with independent judges appointed by the governor-general of Australia. The supreme court is presided over by the chief justice and up to three other judges. Appeals are heard by the High Court of Australia. District courts are presided over by stipendiary magistrates, and in remote areas administrative officers apply limited judicial powers.

The training of indigenous magistrates is proceeding. The Native Lands Commission, warden's courts for mining matters, and other agencies are independent authorities with judicial powers.

Local taxation raises about one third of annual governmental and administrative funds for both territories in increasing amounts after 1948. The Australian grant to Papua-New Guinea exceeded $78 million in 1966–67. Much of this was for health, educational, and agricultural development.

D. G. Bettison

Bibliog.–D. G. Bettison and others, eds., *The Papua-New Guinea Elections, 1964* (1965); H. C. Brookfield and Paula Brown, *Struggle for Land* (1963); A. P. Elkin, *Social Anthropology in Melanesia* (1954); Brian Essai, *Papua and New Guinea* (1961); E. K. Fisk, ed., *New Guinea on the Threshold: Aspects of Social, Political and Economic Development* (1966); International Bank for Reconstruction and Development, *The Economic Development of the Territory of Papua and New Guinea* (1965); S. W. Reed, *The Making of Modern New Guinea* (1943); Colin Simpson, *Adam with Arrows* (1954), *Islands of Men* (1956); Gavin Souter, *New Guinea: The Last Unknown* (1963); Judy Tudor, *Handbook of Papua and New Guinea* (1964).

NEW HAMPSHIRE, state in the northeastern part of New England, bounded on the N by Quebec, on the E by Maine and the Atlantic Ocean, on the SE and S by Massachusetts, and on the W and NW by Vermont and Quebec. Narrow at the N but widening toward the S, New Hampshire is about 180 miles long and, in the southeast part, about 90 miles wide; area, 9,304 square miles, of which 280 square miles are inland water. The state's western boundary is the low water mark on the west bank of the Connecticut River. The seacoast is only 18 miles in length. The population (1960) was 606,921, an increase of 13.8 per cent over 1950. Concord, a city in the south central section, on the Merrimack River, is the capital. There are ten counties in the state. See map in Atlas, Vol. 20. For state flag in color, see FLAG.

Physical Features

A mountainous ridge a few miles east of the Connecticut River and the White Mountains in the north separate the state into four distinct areas. The southeastern section contains most of the cities and the manufacturing centers. In general, the surface of the state is uneven, marked by forest-covered mountains, long fertile valleys, and numerous lakes. Mount Washington, 6,288 feet, in the Presidential range of the White Mountains, is the highest elevation. The Androscoggin, Connecticut, Merrimack, Piscataqua, and Saco rivers, with their many tributaries, drain the five major watershed areas.

Climate. The state has cold winters, especially in the north, and hot summers, particularly in the central and southern sections. In normal years precipitation ranges from 35 to 50 inches and is well distributed over the four seasons. Snowfall varies from an average of 50 inches near the coast to 150 inches in the mountains. The mean summer temperature is 75° F in the mountains and 80° F elsewhere. In the cooler northern part the average for the year is 41° F—66.5° F in the summer and 17° F in the winter. For brief periods temperatures as low as −38° F have been recorded in the central and northern sections. The growing season is usually less than three months in the north and nearly twice as long in the south.

Soils. Less than 2,500 acres of land are classified as suitable for intensive cultivation and these are chiefly in the Connecticut and Merrimack river valleys. The glacial debris is about 95 per cent sandy and rocky loam requiring heavy fertilization to produce a crop. Although upwards of 2,300,000 acres were listed as improved land for agricultural purposes in 1860, most of this has reverted to forest growth.

Inland Waters and Coastal Areas. There are over 1,300 lakes or ponds in New Hampshire. The largest is Winnipesaukee, some 22 miles long and from one to ten miles wide. It contains 274 islands. Other lakes are Squam, Winnisquam, Ossipee, Newfound, Mascoma, and Sunapee. The short seacoast has five sandy beaches: Seabrook, Hampton, Rye, Jeness, and Rye North, and two rocky headlands, Great Boar's Head and Little Boar's Head. Nine miles offshore are the Isles of Shoals, of which three, Star, White, and Lunging, belong to New Hampshire.

Flora and Fauna. New Hampshire is one of the most wooded states. Nearly 85 per cent of the area is covered by trees. A few small areas of primeval forests still exist, chiefly in the White Mountains

The New Hampshire seal portrays the sun rising over the ocean and the frigate Raleigh ringed in laurel. Encircling the field is the inscription "Seal of the State of New Hampshire." It was adopted in 1931.

BIRD	**Purple finch**
FLOWER	**Purple lilac**
TREE	**White (or paper) birch**
CAPITAL	**Concord**
MOTTO	**Live Free or Die**
ENTERED THE UNION	**June 21, 1788**
ORDER OF ENTRY	**9th**

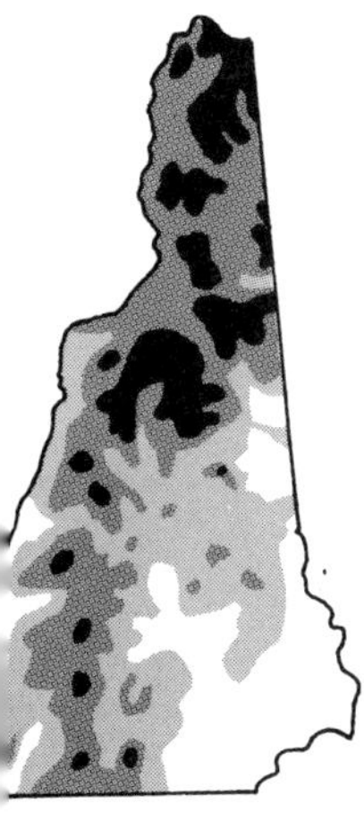

Elevation Map of New Hampshire. White areas 0-500 feet; light gray areas 500-1,000 feet; dark gray areas 1,000-2,000 feet; black areas over 2,000 feet. Mount Washington in the White Mountains is the state's highest elevation.

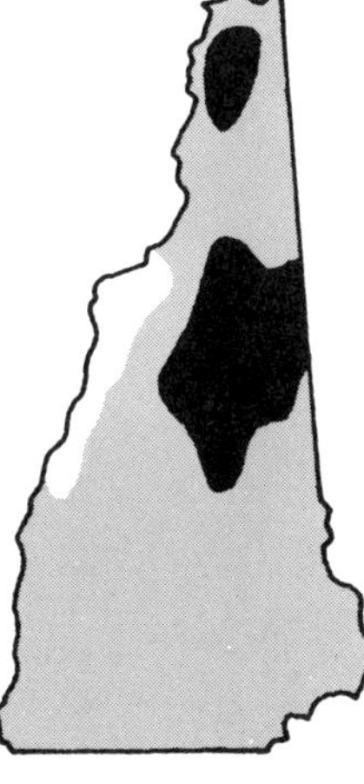

Precipitation Map of New Hampshire. White areas 28 to 36 inches; gray areas 36-44 inches; black areas 44-52 inches. Snowfall is heaviest in the mountains, averaging 185 inches atop Mount Washington.

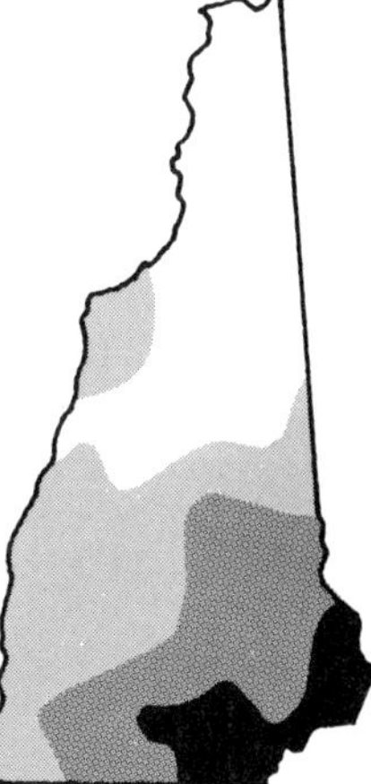

Population Density Map of New Hampshire. White areas 15-30 inhabitants per square mile; light gray areas 30-70; dark gray areas 70-150; black areas 150-200. The largest city is Manchester. Other cities are Nashua, Concord, and Portsmouth.

Beautiful Echo Lake lies at the bottom of Franconia Notch, one of New Hampshire's most stunning geological formations. The lake is surrounded by peaks of the Kinsman and Franconia ranges of the White Mountains that rise to altitudes of from 2,000 feet to over 5,000 feet. Franconia Notch, which is about six miles long, contains several natural wonders, a stream (the Pemigewasset), and another lake (the Profile). It was created by a moving glacier.

DOUGLAS GRUNDY—FPG

but also in the College Woods at Durham. Birch, beech, white pine, spruce, fir, and sugar maple grow in the northern part. In the central and southeastern areas the white pine is common while beech, birch, hemlock, maple, oak, and pine are most common in the southern section. Ash, cedar, elm, hickory, and willow are native to the state. The federal government and the state or towns own some 805,000 acres of forest land. The White Mountains National Forest of about 670,000 acres is the largest tract. In the colonial period the white pines of New Hampshire were in demand for masts for the royal navy. Today the forest products are used in several industries, of which paper making is one of the most important.

Many varieties of wild flowers are found in the state. Among the most common are trailing arbutus, black-eyed Susans, asters, paint-brush, blue and yellow violets, goldenrod, fringed gentian, painted and purple trilliums, wild iris, daisies, Indian pipe, lilies, lady-slippers, several kinds of honeysuckle, and fireweed. In most areas brakes and ferns are common. The flowering dogwood grows chiefly in the southwestern section while mountain laurel is abundant in the Monadnock region. On the higher elevations of the Presidential range in the White Mountains many alpine plants are found. Among the native flowering shrubs and vines are the elderberries, dwarf and highbush blueberries, blackberries, wild raspberries, wild grapes, pin and choke cherries, sweet fern, red-osier, sumacs, sheep laurel or lambkill, and American alder. There is an important growth of wild rhododendrons in the Peterborough area.

No species of wild animals are of economic importance in New Hampshire. The state obtains a small amount of income from licenses and there is a little trapping for furs. Deer are the most common larger wild animals and are found everywhere in the state but chiefly in the north where bear are also the most plentiful. The few moose are chiefly in the Ossipee region. There is a herd of elk in Pillsbury Game Sanctuary in Washington. Privately owned Corbin's Park in Croydon has elk, antelopes, buffalo, moose, Himalayan goats, deer, and wild boar. Among other animals native to the state are foxes, red and grey squirrels, shrews, moles, striped chipmunks, wood and field mice, porcupines, fishercats, skunks, rabbits, Canada lynx, otter, mink, beaver, pine martens, wildcats, raccoons, woodchucks, and muskrats. The wolverine was once commonly found but seems to have disappeared.

Only about half of the more than 280 different species of birds that have been recorded regularly nest in the state. Those which are most often seen are sparrows, bluebirds, robins, woodpeckers, thrushes, and vireos. Less common are chickadees, red-winged blackbirds, purple finches, warblers, grackles, barn swallows, bluejays, cedar waxwings, juncos, and chimney-swifts. Loons, gulls, and ducks are the most frequently noted of the over 100 species of water birds on record. Migratory water fowl, such as the Canada goose, coots, and the brant, frequent Great Bay near Portsmouth. The chief game birds are woodcock, quail, ruffled grouse, and pheasant.

There is little salt water fishing except for lobsters, but in the rivers and lakes almost 100 species of fish are found. Brook trout and black bass are the favorites but among the other game fish are pickerel, perch, landlocked salmon, horned pout, lake trout, and rainbow and brown trout. The aureolus, or golden trout, is native to Lake Sunapee but many have been transplanted elsewhere. There are six known species of turtles of which the snapping and the painted are most often found. Of the 20 different kinds of snakes, only the copperhead and the rattlesnake, rarely found, are poisonous. Over 20 different kinds of toads and frogs have been identified as well as several kinds of salamanders.

Social Features

Population. In 1623, when the first white men settled in New Hampshire, the different Indian tribes formed part of the Pennacook Confederacy. By the end of the colonial period few Indians remained in the state. The population of 1790, numbering 141,885, was composed chiefly of Welsh or English stock with a small number of Scotch-Irish, Irish, Scotch, Dutch, German, and French, and a few Negro slaves. The composition of the population remained fairly static for about 40 years and reached 269,328 in 1830. Thereafter immigration of foreign white stock coupled with emigration of descendants of the original settlers resulted in a marked change in the ethnic composition of the population. After 1860 the change became even more marked when emigration resulted in the first and only decrease in the population, about 2.4 per cent between 1860 and 1870. In the last part of the nineteenth century and the early years of the twentieth, immigation of foreign white stock increased significantly, and French-Canadians became the largest ethnic group.

In 1910 the population was 430,572, of which 22.4 per cent were foreign born—the highest percentage of foreign born ever recorded for the state. Today at least 50 foreign countries are represented in the population. In addition to the French-Canadians, there are sizable numbers of people of British, Irish, Polish, Scandinavian, Italian, German, Russian, Austrian, Czech, Hungarian, and Greek origin. The present population is concentrated in the southeastern part of the state. The three counties of Hillsborough, Rockingham, and Strafford have over half of the residents. There are 13 incorporated cities. They are (in descending order of size): Manchester, Nashua, Concord, Portsmouth, Dover, Keene, Berlin, Rochester, Laconia, Claremont, Lebanon, Somersworth, and Franklin. The population of the 13 cities is just over half the total population of the state. There are some towns with populations larger than the smaller cities so that urban population of New Hampshire in 1960 was set at 353,766.

Religion. Roman Catholics constitute the largest religious group in New Hampshire. The leading churches among the Protestant denominations are the Congregational, Episcopal, Methodist, and Baptist.

Labor. New Hampshire had a work force of about 262,000 in 1965, of which about 154,000 were employed in industry. The state is the second most highly industrialized one in the nation. Nonmanufacturing employed about 69,000 and some 13,000 are employed in different services. Agricultural employment is not significant. Wages are below the national average, but family income is increased because so many married women are employed. Unemployment is considerably below the national average and in some occupations there is a labor shortage.

Education. Public education in New Hampshire dates from 1647 when the state was a part of Massachusetts. District schools were authorized by a law of 1827 and were the characteristic form of elementary education in the nineteenth century. Private academies provided secondary education in the first half of the same century after which public high schools were established. In 1919 there was a reorganization of public education with the establishment of a seven-member State Board of Education, appointed by the governor and Executive Council, which has general oversight of the tax-supported elementary and secondary schools. The board appoints the commissioner of education. Attendance is compulsory for all children between the ages of eight and 16. Most pupils attend public schools and the rest private or parochial schools. The state university, chartered in 1866, is now at Durham. There are several vocational institutes with more being planned. Among the many private colleges, most of which have been established recently, the best-known is Dartmouth, at Hanover, which was founded in 1769. Since 1964, profits from a sweepstakes have been paid to public schools.

Economic Features

Over 1,000 companies in New Hampshire are engaged in manufacturing. Many employ only a few workers but others employ up to as many as 3,400. The list of products produced is close to 400, of which the following are the chief manufactured items: leather and leather products, especially shoes; electrical products; machinery; textiles; lumber and wood including furniture and fixtures; paper and allied products; printing and publishing; apparel; food; fabricated metal products; primary metal products; stone and clay products. The Industrial Park Authority was created in 1955 to help in the establishment of new industries, a function in which the Division of Economic Development is also concerned.

Agriculture. Until after the Revolution, the economic life of New Hampshire was dominated by agriculture, with commerce in second place. Self-sufficient farming was characteristic until the 1830's when wool production became important, followed later by dairying. Between 1830 and 1930 the percentage of the population engaged in agriculture declined from 83 to 11, while between 1860 and 1900 the number of acres of improved land decreased from 2,367,034 to 1,076,879. There are about 10,000 farms at present. Most farm income is derived from livestock and poultry and their products. The main crops are hay, apples, and potatoes. The Agricultural Experiment Station of the University of New Hampshire has developed many varieties of agricultural products for the state.

Fisheries. In the colonial period, fishing and the related shipbuilding industry contributed significantly to the economic life of New Hampshire. The major rivers were sources of migratory fish, especially salmon and shad, but these disappeared with the building of dams in the nineteenth century and the pollution of the waterways. The state now ranks fifth in yield of fish among the five New England states with fishing fleets.

Mining. Although about 200 minerals are known to occur in New Hampshire, only a few have proven profitable to extract. In the early nineteenth century the state led in the production of mica. Later granite was the leading mineral product but today sand and gravel head the list. The most important mineral products at present are clay, feldspar, sand and gravel, and stone.

Transportation and Communication. New Hampshire's system of planned roads began before the Revolution. Private toll roads or turnpikes were built after the Revolution and well into the next century. The locks and canals on the Merrimack River provided for water transportation, by way of the Middlesex Canal, to Boston. This system was abandoned after the railroads were built from the 1830's on. Most of the state's remaining railroads provide chiefly freight service. The excellent system of public roads, noted for the efficiency with which they are kept cleared in the winter, is a product of the twentieth century. The roads are continually being improved or expanded either as town, state, or federal highways.

There are several airfields, most with limited use. Year-round air service is available only at the largest cities. Bus service has replaced railroad passenger service, which has been almost completely curtailed. Freighters and tankers dock at Portsmouth, the only seaport.

Telephone service is available generally throughout the state. The New England Telephone and Telegraph Company services most of the state,

Dartmouth College in Hanover, founded in 1769, is one of America's most distinguished men's schools.
WARD ALAN HOWE—FPG

supplemented by several affiliated local companies. The Western Union Telegraph Company provides telegraph service.

Commerce and Trade. Colonial exports from New Hampshire were chiefly forest products, boards, staves, and masts. Wooden ships were built for export into the nineteenth century. Starting as the products of small home industries in the colonial period, boots, shoes, and textiles became the chief exports of the nineteenth century. The Amoskeag Mills, at Manchester, chartered in 1831, were the biggest cotton textile factory in the world before the Depression of the 1930's, when the mills were sold and converted for a variety of industries. In the nineteenth century the wagons and coaches manufactured at Concord by the Abbot and Downing Company were world famous. Exports from New Hampshire at present are representative of the great variety of products manufactured, among which are shoes, textiles, paper and other lumber products, machinery, and electronic devices, as well as agricultural products.

Recreation. The tourist business, which now accounts for a significant part of the state's income, became important in the last half of the nineteenth century. Large hotels in the White Mountains and in the Lakes Region did a thriving business during the summer months. Most of these have now been replaced by other types of accommodations, and year-round recreation facilities are available. Out-of-state residents own about two thirds of the summer homes and provide most of the patrons of the boys' and girls' camps. The State Division of Parks maintains numerous parks and camping areas in addition to those run by private interests. Skiers have a choice of state-owned facilities, as at Sunapee, or private ones. Scenic tours, such as the Kancamagus Highway through the White Mountain National Forest, natural wonders, museums, horse racing, fishing, hunting, and motor boating are among the many tourist attractions.

Forests. Towns were the first political units in New Hampshire to own forest areas. The state began purchasing forests after 1871, the year in which the first gift of such land was made. A forestry commission was established in 1893 with functions similar to those now carried on by the Division of Resources Development. Over the years additional areas were acquired, such as Crawford Notch and Franconia Notch. The Society for the Protection of New Hampshire Forests and the Appalachian Mountain Club have been active in the state's acquisition of such natural resources. The federal government, in 1911, purchased the White Mountain National Forest, of which the greater part is in Carroll, Coos, and Grafton counties. About one sixth of the commercial forest lands is publicly owned.

The state maintains lookouts and fire towers to detect and control forest fires. It has a nursery near Concord to help in reforesting. Research is carried on with the objective of converting submarginal farm lands to forests. Forest conservation is fostered as a means of flood control and to prevent soil erosion. The New Hampshire Conservation and Taxation Act of 1949, one of the first laws of its kind in the nation, provides for a severance tax on lumber when it is cut, in place of a property tax each year on standing timber, and permits a tax abatement when the cutting is done according to good forestry practices.

Government

New Hampshire was the first of the original 13 colonies to adopt a constitution. Drawn up by a provincial congress at Exeter on Jan. 5, 1776, this temporary constitution served until a permanent one went into effect on June 2, 1784. The latter, although amended many times, is still in use. Amendments can be proposed by the legislature or by a constitutional convention.

The legislature, known as the General Court, consists of a senate of 30 and a house of representatives of not over 400 members, elected biennially for two-year terms. It meets on the first Wednesday in January in odd-numbered years. As a rule only one session is held but special sessions may be called. Both houses are chosen on a population basis. The regular session is limited to 90 legislative days or July 1, whichever comes first. No compensation is paid thereafter except for the special sessions and these are limited to 15 days. The constitution prohibits the legislature from levying a graduated income tax. A veto may be overridden by a two-thirds vote of both houses. Any bill not returned by the governor in five days, not counting Sundays, becomes a law unless the legislature has adjourned during that time.

The executive branch consists of a governor, a popularly-executed Executive Council of five, and a large number of administrative agencies. Most of the members of the latter are appointed by the governor with the advice and consent of the council. The governor must be at least 30 years old and a resident of the state for at least seven years before being elected. The governor and council are chosen for two-year terms. Consent of the council is not required for approving or vetoing bills but is for nearly all other functions of the governor. In the absence from the state of the governor, except on official business, the acting governor is the president of the senate, and after him, the speaker of the house. The state treasurer and the secretary of state are elected by joint ballot of the senators and representatives.

The judicial system consists of a supreme court with a chief justice and four associate justices; a superior court with a chief justice and seven associate justices; a probate court in each of the counties; and 37 district courts. Each district court has a justice and a special justice and in many district courts there are one or more municipal courts each with a justice and a special justice. The supreme court is the state's highest court of appeals on questions of law. The superior court tries civil and criminal cases of a serious nature and the district courts try minor cases.

Every two years the counties elect a sheriff, a county attorney, a treasurer, a register of deeds,

New Hampshire's State House at Concord was built in 1819 and remodeled in 1864 and 1910. It is fronted by a statue of a native son, Daniel Webster.
NEW HAMPSHIRE STATE PLANNING AND DEVELOPMENT COMMISSION

FPG

The tiny mountain village of Jackson, New Hampshire, is a summer hotel and ski center. It is enclosed, within a radius of 10 miles, by 20 mountain peaks.

a register of probate, and three commissioners. The County Convention, composed of representatives to the legislature, makes the appropriations for the county.

Cities are governed by mayors and aldermen but may vote to adopt a city-manager form of government. Towns usually have government by elected officials but a few use the town-manager form of administration. The 22 unincorporated places in New Hampshire have no local government but their residents can vote in state elections.

Finances. The major sources of state government income aside from federal funds are: profit from state liquor stores, racing revenue, tobacco tax, insurance companies tax, telephone companies tax, legacy tax, and beer tax. A gasoline tax is ear-marked for the highway fund. There is no general sales tax nor graduated income tax. Local property taxes support town, city, and county governments.

History

No white men are known to have been in New Hampshire until after 1600. Among the early visitors to the coast were Samuel de Champlain in 1605 and Captain John Smith in 1614. The state's area was included in the grant made in 1620 by James I of England to the Council for New England. The Council made several grants between 1622 and 1631 to Captain John Mason on which the Masonian claims to New Hampshire were based.

The Colonial Period. The first settlement in New Hampshire was made in 1623, at what is now the town of Rye, by David Thomson. He left in 1626 and the settlement was taken over by the Laconia Company, in which John Mason was a partner. The company expanded to include "Strawberry Banke," later named Portsmouth. Also in 1623 Edward Hilton settled in Dover at Hilton's Point, six miles up the Piscataqua River. Hampton was settled in 1638 under the authority of Massachusetts and the same year the Reverend John Wheelwright settled Exeter.

John Mason died in 1635. Massachusetts claimed that her 1629 charter included the four New Hampshire settlements and that Massachusetts' northern boundary was three miles north of the Merrimack River, a claim which she interpreted by 1652 to be three miles north of the outlet of Lake Winnipesaukee. By 1642 the four New Hampshire towns were taken under the jurisdiction of Massachusetts.

Robert Tufton Mason, grandson of the original grantee, succeeded in 1677 in gaining title to all unsettled lands in New Hampshire while the local courts were to determine the title to settled lands. Two years later New Hampshire was made a royal province, or crown colony, and separated from Massachusetts, but no charter was issued. The new government of New Hampshire became effective in January, 1680, with John Cutt as president. From 1686 to 1689 the colony was a part of the Dominion of New England, then rejoined Massachusetts briefly until 1692, when it became a separate political entity and continued as such thereafter. From 1699 to 1741 New Hampshire and Massachusetts had the same royal governor but were, at the same time, separate and distinct colonies.

The Mason claims were a source of continued controversy until they were sold in 1746 to a group known as the Masonian Proprietors. The boundary dispute with Massachusetts was not settled until 1741, the same year in which the eastern boundary was established. New Hampshire's claim to Vermont, under which township grants were made, was ruled invalid in 1764 and the boundary was set at the west bank of the Connecticut River. The northern boundary of the state was settled by the Webster-Ashburton Treaty of 1842.

During all four French and Indian wars, New Hampshire was subjected to Indian raids. Men from the colony helped to destroy Norridgewock in 1721–22; served in Lovewell's attack on the Pigwacket Indians in 1724–25; defended Old Fort No. 4, or Charlestown, in King George's War; and were at the capture of Louisburg in the same conflict.

Benning Wentworth became governor of New Hampshire in 1741, and for the first time in the eighteenth century a governor was not shared with Massachusetts. He chartered many towns during his administration, especially after 1760. His home at Little Harbor became the center of the administration of the colony.

John Wentworth succeeded his uncle in 1767, and was the last royal governor. Under him the colony was divided, in 1771, into five counties (Cheshire, Grafton, Hillsborough, Rockingham, and Strafford), a system of roads was planned, and in 1769 Dartmouth College was chartered.

Revolution and Statehood. New Hampshire men seized the powder and arms at Fort William and Mary (now Fort Constitution) in December, 1774. The following June royal government ended when John Wentworth fled. A provisional government was set up and in January, 1776, a provisional constitution was adopted. Meshech Weare became the chief executive officer. Independence was voted on June 15, 1776. New Hampshire was represented in the Continental Congress by such men as Nathaniel Folsom, John Langdon, John Sullivan, and Matthew Thornton. The state built the *Ranger* for John Paul Jones and sent three regiments of the state militia into the Continental Army. Privateers operated out of Portsmouth. John Stark was in command of New Hampshire troops at the Battle of Bennington.

After the Revolution, the state had a large debt and demands for an issue of paper money arose. An armed revolt was put down in September, 1786, when John Sullivan was president of the state. By a vote of 57 to 47 New Hampshire, in 1788, was the ninth state to vote for ratification of the federal constitution.

Politics in the state were at first dominated by the Federalists, who, however, soon lost out to the Democratic party led by William Plumer. The Congregational Church ceased to be tax-supported in 1819. Concord became the capital in 1808 and the State House was built in 1816. The Democratic party in the state was split in 1846 with one faction supporting John P. Hale and the Jacksonian Democrats backing Franklin Pierce. New Hampshire-born political figures who gained national prominence in this period included Lewis Cass, Horace Greeley, and Daniel Webster.

In the Civil War, New Hampshire had about 32,500 men engaged in military activities while another 6,500 were in other organizations connected with the conflict. Franklin Pierce, a Democrat, elected in 1852, was the only New Hampshire man to become president of the United States. Henry Wilson, born in the state, was elected vice-president in 1872. Since the Civil War, the Republican party has generally controlled the state government.

Farming and lumbering were the chief sources of income in the early nineteenth century, but gradually manufacturing took over. Antislavery and temperance organizations attracted a considerable following before the Civil War and a prohibition law was enacted in 1855. The second half of the nineteenth century saw industrial expansion, the growth of cities, better means of transportation and communication, and increased state responsibility for public health and public education.

Significant twentieth-century events for New Hampshire have been the signing of the Treaty of Portsmouth (N.H.) in 1905 ending the Russo-Japanese War; the success of the progressive Republicans who elected Robert P. Bass governor in 1910; and the Depression of the 1930's, when the Amoskeag Mills in Manchester were closed. In 1944 the New Hampshire resort of Bretton Woods was the site of the historic International Monetary Conference that helped lay the foundations of the United Nations. About 20,000 New Hampshire men served in World War I and about 60,000 men and women in World War II. In 1963, New Hampshire adopted the first legal state lottery in the United States since 1894. PHILIP M. MARSTON

BIBLIOG.–Jeremy Belknap, *History of New Hampshire* (1831 ed.); E. S. Bowles, *Let Me Show You New Hampshire* (1938); R. N. Hill, *Yankee Kingdom: Vermont and New Hampshire* (1960); L. S. Morrison, *Government of New Hampshire* (1952); J. D. Squires, *Granite State of the United States* (4 vols., 1956); L. W. Turner, *William Plumer of New Hampshire, 1759–1850* (1962).

NEW HAMPSHIRE, UNIVERSITY OF, a coeducational, partly state-supported, land grant institution of higher learning at Durham, administered by a board of trustees, some appointed and some elected by alumni. Chartered by the state in 1866, under the provisions of the Morrill Act, The New Hampshire College of Agriculture and the Mechanic Arts was opened in 1868, in Hanover, as an independent institution co-operating with Dartmouth College. Moved to Durham in 1893, it became the University of New Hampshire in 1923. Divisions of the University are the agricultural experiment station (1887); agricultural extension service (1911); summer school (1922); separate colleges of liberal arts, technology, and agriculture (1923); graduate school (1928); engineering experiment station (1929); university extension service (1948); and The Whittemore School of Business and Economics (1962). The University offers the bachelor's degree; most departments offer the master's degree, and several offer the doctor of philosophy degree.

In 1963 Plymouth and Keene Teachers' colleges were made state colleges and became part of the enlarged University of New Hampshire.

PHILIP M. MARSTON

NEW HAMPSHIRE GRANTS, the early name for present-day Vermont. From 1749 to 1764, 131 township charters were granted by the governor of New Hampshire in an area also claimed by New York. In 1764, King George III declared in favor of New York with resulting conflicts between charters. The New Hampshire grantees, organized under Ethan Allen as the Green Mountain Boys, successfully opposed the New York claimants, and in 1777 declared their independence. In 1791, the Grants became the state of Vermont. See VERMONT.

NEW HARMONY, town SW Indiana, Posey County; on the Wabash River, 22 miles WNW of Evansville. New Harmony is a trade center within a short distance of oil wells and sand and gravel pits. Originally called Harmonie, it was founded in 1815 by George Rapp as a communal settlement. In 1825 the town was sold to Robert Owen, and continued as a communal settlement until 1828. Many of the original buildings are still standing. The ideas of its leaders led to the development in the United States of free tax-supported schools, the library system, and the liberation of women. For many years it was the principal center of research in the Middle West and produced many geological books. The headquarters of the U.S. Geological Survey was established in New Harmony in 1839. (For population, see Indiana map in Atlas.)

NEW HAVEN, city SE Connecticut, port of entry, seat of New Haven County, situated on Long Island Sound, 34 miles SSW of Hartford. The city is the seat of Yale University, the home of many industries, and a pioneer in urban redevelopment. Its harbor ranks third in importance in New England, and overseas shipping has been a contributing factor to the city's growth.

New Haven occupies approximately 18 square miles at the head of New Haven Bay, into which empty the Quinnipiac, Mill, and West rivers. The city is centered in picturesque New Haven Green,

ROBERT PERRON—PHOTO RESEARCHERS

Yale University's striking modern architecture and New Haven's massive urban renewal programs have totally transformed the face of this once-drab city.

within which stand three churches: Trinity Episcopal, United Congregational, and Center Congregational. Besides the Green, there are more than 2,000 acres of parks, playgrounds, and squares in the city.

History. In 1638, a group of Puritans from England, attracted by the splendid harbor, decided to settle in the town of Quinnipiac, so named from the tribe of Indians who occupied the land. The Quinnipiacs were a friendly, rather weak tribe, who sold the land to the settlers for certain tools and utensils, reserving the right to hunt and fish on much of the territory. Furthermore, they were glad to have the protection of the English against their more powerful enemies, the Mohawks. These Puritans represented the best blood of England, many of them being men of considerable wealth and education. They sought to escape the persecution which was being visited upon all who failed to accept the complete authority of the established church. Prominent in the group were John Davenport, an Oxford graduate; Theophilus Eaton, a merchant of wide reputation; Edward Hopkins, later governor of the Connecticut Colony; and the family of David Yale, grandfather of Elihu Yale. The town was laid out in nine original squares, each square containing approximately 16 acres, the central square being reserved for a "marketplace," now called the Green. In 1643, New Haven became an independent jurisdiction or colony, including the towns of Guilford, Branford, Milford, Stamford, and Southold, Long Island. In 1665, however, the colony was annexed to the Connecticut colony, after Governor Winthrop had secured one charter from Charles II of England, embracing the entire territory along Long Island Sound.

Education. From the very beginning, the Puritans gave great importance to education. In 1657, Edward Hopkins, governor of the colony of Connecticut, died, leaving an estate of £1,400 "for the breeding up of hopefull youths both at the grammar school and colledge for the publique service of their country in future tymes." In 1701, a group of ministers gave some books for the founding of a college, which in 1718 received a gift from Elihu Yale, resulting in the name Yale College. New Haven has four other colleges, all actively growing and each serving its own special purpose: Southern Connecticut State College, New Haven College, Albertus Magnus College, and Quinnipiac College.

Industry. In industry New Haven has many "firsts." There, Eli Whitney not only invented the cotton gin, thus revolutionizing the cotton industry, but realized the idea of mass production of rifles by his invention of interchangeable parts. In 1878, the first commercial telephone exchange was started there. Such names as Charles Goodyear (vulcanizer of rubber), Winchester (maker of repeating rifles), and Elihu Root (inventor of machine tools) testify to the inventiveness of the city's inhabitants.

From its beginning New Haven also had an important shipbuilding industry. From these first industries stem many of the city's present manufactures. Among these are metal products, transportation equipment, firearms and ammunition, clocks and watches, rubber goods, machinery, electrical equipment, paper products, marine specialties, furniture, lamps, and textiles.

Urban Redevelopment. Since 1953, New Haven, with the help of state and federal grants, has spent more than 300 million dollars to clear out existing slums and to provide new housing and industrial facilities. Pop. (1960) of city proper, 152,048; of urban area, 278,794. GEORGE B. LOVELL

BIBLIOG.–H. T. Blake, *Chronicles of New Haven Green* (Papers from the New Haven Colony Historical Society, 1898); Isabel Calder, *The New Haven Colony* (1934); Rollin Osterweis, *Three Centuries of New Haven* (1953).

NEW HEBRIDES, archipelago, SW Pacific Ocean; about 1,000 miles NE of Brisbane, Australia; area about 5,700 square miles. The islands extend 450 miles from south to north in a rough Y formation. The New Hebrides are mostly volcanic islands. The major islands are Espiritu Santo, Malekula, Erromanga, Efate, Ambrym, Tanna, Pentecost, Aoba, Epi, Maewa, Aneityum, Malo, and Paama. The Banks and Torres islands are the northernmost islands of the archipelago. There are active volcanoes on Ambrym, Tanna, and Lopevi. The climate of the New Hebrides is tropical and humid and the soil is fertile. Forests yield sandalwood and cabinet woods, and plantations produce copra—the chief export—and cacao, coffee, and cotton. Fruits, sago, yams, and other vegetables are grown for local use. The people are mostly Melanesians. Vila on Efate Island is the port of entry and administrative center. Most people reach the New Hebrides by plane, although ocean vessels provide service to France, Australia, New Caledonia, Hong Kong, New Guinea, and the Solomon Islands.

In 1606 Pedro Fernandes de Queirós, a Portuguese navigator, discovered the group. They were forgotten until 1768 when they were explored by the Frenchman Louis Antoine de Bougainville. Captain James Cook charted the islands in 1773 and gave them the name New Hebrides. Thereafter, numerous traders reached the islands, and missionaries arrived in 1830. Conflicting British and French interests led to an agreement in 1887 for dual government of the islands, and a formal condominium was agreed upon in 1906 and ratified in 1914 and 1922. Under this form of government, unique in the South Pacific, both French and British are represented by resident commissioners. (For population, see Pacific Ocean map in Atlas.)

OTIS W. FREEMAN

NEW HUMANISM (or neo-humanism), a movement in American literary criticism that flourished in the late 1920's and early 1930's. Originated as a reaction to the nineteenth-century romantic tradition, its leaders were Irving Babbitt and Paul Elmer More. The aesthetic principles of the New Humanists were conservative and directed toward the social and moral aspects of literature. A collection of essays, *Humanism and America* (1930), edited by Norman Foerster, is representative of the movement.

NEW HYDE PARK, village, New York, Nassau County; residential suburb, 16 miles E of New York City. It was named Hyde Park in 1817, re-named New Hyde Park in 1871, and incorporated in 1927. (For population, see New York map in Atlas.)

NEW IBERIA, city, S central Louisiana; on navigable Bayou Teche; 20 miles SE of Lafayette. New Iberia is a processing center for agricultural products from the area and has manufactures of bricks, paper, machine tools, and wood products. There are oil wells and salt mines on nearby Avery Island, as well as a bird sanctuary and a pepper sauce (Tabasco) factory. Points of interest include St. Peter's College. Settled by Canary Islanders in 1779, the city was incorporated in 1839 as Iberia and renamed New Iberia in 1868. (For population, see Louisiana map in Atlas.)

NEWINGTON, town, W central Connecticut, 5 miles SSW of Hartford. Newington has manufacturers of tools and concrete products. It was settled in 1670 and incorporated in 1871. (For population, see Connecticut map in Atlas.)

NEW IRELAND, second-largest island in the Bismarck Archipelago, SW Pacific Ocean; about 230 miles long and 10 miles wide except near the S end where it widens to 40 miles; area 3,340 square miles

(3,800 including offshore islands). The population are mostly Melanesian natives. New Ireland is mountainous and well forested and has a hot, humid climate. Kavieng, near the north point of the island, is the chief port and local administrative center. Nearby are the principal copra plantations. New Ireland is included in the Trust Territory of New Guinea, administered by Australia. The island was discovered in 1616 by Dutch navigators Willem Schouten and Jakob Lemaire. A group of Italian, French, and Belgian colonists attempted settlement on the island in 1880, but were driven out. New Ireland was occupied by the Germans in 1885, and was named Neu Mecklenburg; Kavieng was settled in the early 1900's. The island was taken by Australian forces in 1914 and renamed New Ireland. Early in World War II it was captured by the Japanese, who held it until the end of the war. (For population, see Pacific Ocean map in Atlas.)

OTIS W. FREEMAN

BIBLIOG.–C. A. Borden, *South Sea Islands* (1961); Sir Harry Luke, *Islands of the South Pacific* (1962); *Pacific Islands Year Book and Who's Who* (Annual).

NEW JERSEY, a Middle Atlantic state of the United States; bounded by New York on the N and NE, the Atlantic Ocean on the E, Delaware Bay on the S, and Delaware and Pennsylvania on the W; area 7,836 square miles, including 314 square miles of inland water; population (1965 est.) 6,774,000. The state ranks forty-sixth among the states in area and eighth in population. New Jersey was one of the original thirteen states. Newark is the largest city; Trenton the capital. See map in Atlas, Vol. 20. For the state flag in color, see FLAG.

Physical Features

Physiography. Portions of two of the major physiographic provinces of the United States, the Appalachian Highlands and the Atlantic Coastal Plain are represented in New Jersey. In relief the state reaches from seal level at Cape May, the southernmost point, to 1,803 feet in elevation at High Point in the Kittatinny Mountains. Three subdivisions of the Appalachian Highlands extend diagonally from southwest to northeast across the state and are separated from the Atlantic Coastal Plain along a line known as the Fall Line from Trenton to New Brunswick to Perth Amboy.

The northernmost of these subdivisions is the Ridge and Valley Province consisting of a belt of fertile valleys and steep-sided forest-crested ridges lying chiefly in Warren and Sussex counties. The broad Kittatinny Valley, drained by the Paulins Kill and Walkill rivers is the home of many dairy farms. The hillsides support fruit orchards and woodlands while the level lands provide acres of wheat, corn, oats, rye, hay, and soy beans for the dairy herds. To the north the Kittatinny Mountains separate this valley from the Delaware Valley and River which form the western boundary of the state. The strikingly beautiful Delaware River eroded these mountains to form the Delaware Water Gap, the entrance to attractive recreational lands on both sides of the river.

To the southeast, paralleling the Ridge and Valley Province, is the Reading Prong, known in New Jersey as the Highlands. In a belt 10 to 25 miles wide are many flat-topped broad ridges separated from one another by narrow fertile valleys. There are also transverse valleys such as the Rockaway, Pequannock, and Spruce, which provide east-west routes across the Highland belt, while the broader northeast-southwest valleys supply locations for prosperous dairy and crop farms and apple and peach orchards. Many beautiful streams and pretty lakes make this one of the most attractive sections of the state.

A generous section of the Piedmont Plateau completes the northern half of the state. A lowland of gently rolling hills and broad valleys, it is occasionally interrupted by high steep-sided hills of trap rock of volcanic origin. The best known of these are the Palisades along the Hudson River, the Watchung Mountains extending from the north of Paterson in Passaic County southward to Bound Brook in Somerset County, and the Sourland Mountains in southern Hunterdon County. Usually forested, they are attractive sites for homes, parks, and recreational areas. The New Jersey Piedmont covers about one fifth of the state and is the great metropolitan area of northern New Jersey.

Southern New Jersey is part of the Atlantic Coastal Plain. This plain, comprising three fifths of the land surface of New Jersey, has a gentle slope stretching southeastward from the Piedmont to the Atlantic shoreline. An area of gently rolling surfaces, much of it is less than 100 feet above sea level. A cuesta, beginning at the Atlantic Highlands, rises sharply to 235 feet above Sandy Hook and overlooks Lower New York Bay. It extends through Monmouth County past Mount Holly and Mullica Hill to the Delaware Bay and sets the pattern for river drainage in South Jersey. To the north and west of the cuesta's steep slope, rivers flow to the Delaware, the Raritan, and New York bays. This area is called the Inner Coastal Plain. The cuesta's very gentle southeastern slope reaches to the salt marshes of the Atlantic Ocean and the Delaware Bay, and forms the Outer Coastal Plain.

Southward from Sandy Hook for 125 miles stretch numerous sand bars, sand reefs, and islands backed by inlets, lagoons, and back bays. Due to the shallow waters of the continental shelf this section of New Jersey has no harbors for big ships, but there are many splendid marinas for fishing and pleasure craft. Sandy Hook is the northern point of a long finger of land beginning at Long Branch. Another such sliver of land reaches from Point Pleasant to Barnegat Inlet. These as well as the islands to the south provide excellent sites for residential towns and cities such as Atlantic City, Asbury Park, and Wildwood.

Inland from the salt marshes, beaches, and back bays, the pine barrens extend westward for miles. Pine trees, scrub oak, huckleberries, and swamp cedars grow there in some of the poorest agricultural soil in the United States. The better drained areas support thinly scattered residential areas, state forests, chicken farms, and blueberry and cranberry bogs. In contrast to this excellent greensand, marl soils support the productive market gardening areas of the Inner Coastal Plain. Growing, processing and marketing of more than a dozen different fruits and vegetables as well as dairy farming are leading industries. Two of the larger cities in New Jersey, Trenton, the capital, and Camden, a leading

New Jersey's state seal was adopted in 1928. The three plows, the horse's head, and the goddess Ceres holding a horn of plenty represent the agricultural importance of the state. Liberty is at left.

BIRD	**Eastern goldfinch**
FLOWER	**Purple violet**
TREE	**Red oak**
CAPITAL	**Trenton**
MOTTO	**Liberty and Prosperity**
ENTERED THE UNION	**Dec. 18, 1787**
ORDER OF ENTRY	**3rd**

Despite its small size, New Jersey ranks seventh among the leading industrial states. It is sometimes called the *Workshop of the Nation,* because of the thousands of varied goods manufactured and processed in its factories. In chemical production, New Jersey leads the nation. This chemical plant at Linden is only one of more than 800 located throughout the state, whose products include basic chemicals, drugs and vitamins, cleaning solutions, explosives, paints and varnishes, plastics, and soaps.

D. JORDAN WILSON—PIX

industrial center, are located on the Delaware River.

New Jersey is almost surrounded by water. Only the northern boundary, which extends 48 miles from the Delaware River to the Hudson River, is land. The remaining 432 miles of boundaries are either Delaware River and Bay on the west or the Atlantic seacoast and the Hudson River and New York Bay on the east. In addition there are more than one hundred rivers and creeks and more than 800 lakes and ponds in New Jersey. Most of these are in the northern half of the state. Among the best-known lakes are Hopatcong, Greenwood, Budd, Culvers, and Swartswood.

The Delaware River is of major importance to the state. Not only does it supply water for houses and factories but it is navigable for ocean-going ships as far as Camden. The Hudson also has played an important role in the economic development of the state because of the excellent harbor it has at its mouth, where Jersey City and Hoboken are located. Three other rivers in north Jersey are also of especial importance in supplying industrial and domestic water and hydroelectric power. The Passaic River, which rises near Morristown, flows northeastward to Paterson where it plunges over a 72-foot fall into a steep-walled gorge. Here it turns southward and flows into Newark Bay, another well-developed harbor area. Between the Passaic and the Hudson is the Hackensack River. The third of New Jersey's other significant rivers is the Raritan, the longest river entirely within the state. Through carefully planned conservation practices, this river is regaining its former beauty. Its valley is a densely populated part of the state and serves both agricultural and manufacturing activities.

The southern half of the state has many smaller rivers, of which the better known are the Maurice, the Great Egg Harbor, the Mullica, and the Navesink.

Climate. One of the most valuable resources of the state is its humid temperate climate. Central New Jersey is located in a transitional zone characterized by climatic elements found in Humid Continental, Warm Summer, and Humid Subtropical types of climate. Accordingly, although New Jersey is less than 170 miles in length, there are decided differences between north and south Jersey. The narrow coastal strip, which is affected by sea breezes, can be considered a marine climate. At Riverdale, 10 miles north of Paterson, –34° F has been recorded and 110° F has been registered at Runyon in Middlesex County, but extremes of temperature are rare. The average July weather for the state is in the low 70's; Sussex County averages 72° F, Cape May averages 74° F.

The average winter temperature for the whole state is 30° F for January, with an average of 26° F in the northern highlands and 35° F in Cape May County. The growing season accordingly varies from 140 days in the Kittatinny Mountains to 220 in Cape May County.

New Jersey's rainfall averages three to four inches per month throughout the year. Northern New Jersey averages 46 inches of rainfall per year; the Highlands receive as much as 50 inches. About one fourth of the winter precipitation falls as snow. Southern New Jersey averages 45 inches annually. Snow seldom occurs in Cumberland, Cape May, and Atlantic counties. The length of the growing season, the even distribution of precipitation, and the great extent of level lands account for the vari-

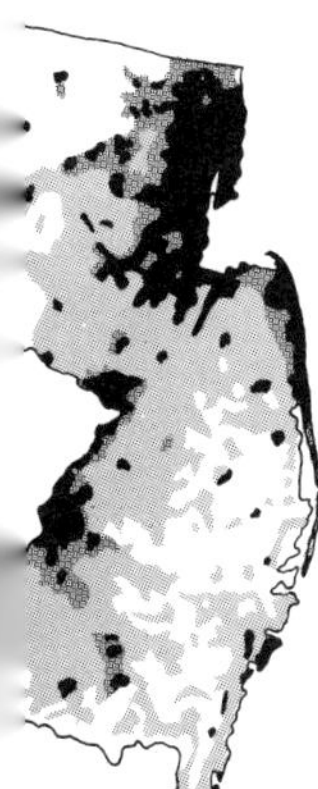

New Jersey's population density (per square mile) is shown on map at left: 0-50 (white); 50-200 (gray); 200-1,000 (dark gray); over 1,000 (black).

Average annual rainfall in the state is shown by map at right: under 44 inches (white); 44-46 inches (gray); 46-48 inches (dark gray); 48-50 inches (black).

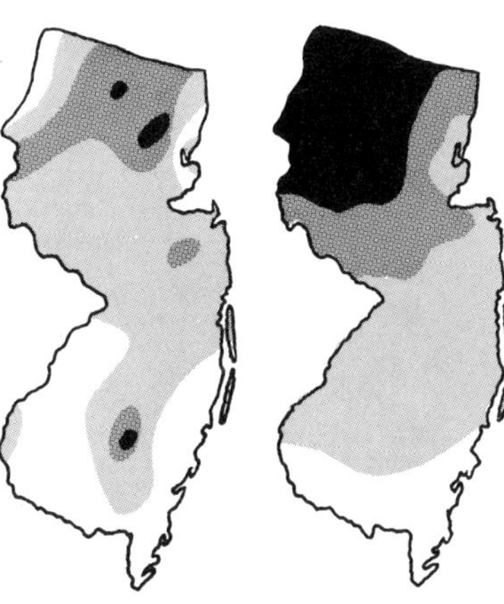

At left, average January temperatures are shown: over 34° F (white); 32-34° (gray); 30-32° (dark gray); under 30° (black). Average July temperatures are shown at right: 70-72° F (white); 72-74° (gray); 74-76° (dark gray); 76-78° (black).

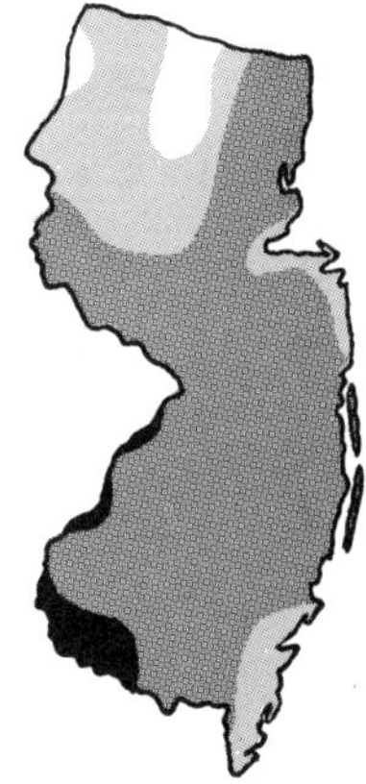

ety and amount of fresh produce marketed in the nearby urban centers of Philadelphia and New York.

Flora and Fauna. At the time of colonial settlement the land in New Jersey was nine-tenths forested. The Highlands were covered with forests of oak, hickory, birch, chestnut, maple, and other hardwoods. Southern New Jersey had chiefly softwoods such as pines and cedars and various types of oaks. Even today, 46 per cent of the state is in forest, most of it under private ownership. A unique forest is that of holly on Sandy Hook where trees attain a height of 20 to 30 feet, with trunks 30 inches in diameter.

Along the shore and in the pine barrens are found bayberry, wild orchids, gentians, beach plum, sand cherry, dune grass, and salt hay. An outstanding area of wild flowers is found in the vicinity of Morristown, where 80 species of flowering plants and shrubs including swamp azalea, buttonwood, mountain laurel, and dogwood are found. Throughout the state there are bittersweet, dogwood, bayberry, laurel, wild roses, asters, and goldenrod.

Unexpectedly in such an urbanized area many animals, migratory fowl, birds, and fish are found. White tail deer, mink, otter, fox, opossum, muskrat and chipmunk, as well as water and land snakes, turtles and frogs, abound in the forested hills, marsh lands, and state forests throughout the state. There are state game farms such as that near Forked River, the State Quail Farm near Van Hiseville, and fish hatcheries at Hancock's Bridge and Hackettstown.

Both salt and fresh water fish abound in the state. Salt water fish include flounder, sea and striped bass, bluefish, and tuna. Trout, bass, pickerel, and perch are found in fresh water streams and lakes. Clam digging is carried on from Barnegat Bay to Cape May. The chief oyster beds are located in Delaware and Barnegat bays. Crabs and lobsters are taken from New Jersey's back bays and offshore fisheries. The most important fish in order of the value of the catch are oysters, clams, menhaden, porgy, bass, fluke, shad, bluefish and mackerel. More than 75 species of sea food are taken from the coastal waters of New Jersey. Menhaden is the leading fish not used for food. These go to factories where they are converted to oils and fish meal for paints, varnishes, and insect sprays; and into vitamin feeds for poultry and pigs.

Social Features

Population. New Jersey is one of the most densely populated and highly urbanized states in the United States. Industrial and professional opportunities attract foreign immigrants as well as out-of-state migrants. Since the 1940's, New Jersey has had a boom in population. With few exceptions much of this growth is suburban rather than urban. By 1960 the population had passed the six million mark and in 1965 there were more than 899.5 persons per square mile in the state. Density figures for 1960 showed that densities varied from 39,497 per square mile in West New York, to 16,786 in Newark, to 3.1 persons per square mile in some sections of the pine barrens. Even though the scenic charms of rural New Jersey have long attracted the Philadelphia and New York commuter, the rapidity of settlement in suburbia has prevented the planning that would keep it natural. In areas of urban sprawl unattractive highways, monotonously designed housing developments, and inefficient shopping centers have taken the place of former appealing landscapes.

The geographic distribution of population is extremely uneven. The largest concentration is in the northeastern area adjacent to the Hudson River. In the counties of Essex, Bergen, Hudson, Union, and Middlesex live more than 60 per cent of the people. Another 15 per cent are concentrated along the Delaware from Trenton to Camden. The state population is 90 per cent urban. Of the remaining 10 per cent only 2 per cent actually can be called farmers. Large stretches of land in the pine barrens have few or no inhabitants. Along the shore the greatest area of population concentration is the Atlantic City region and the stretch from Point Pleasant to Long Branch. Many summer homes on the shore have been converted into year-round dwellings for commuters to Trenton, Philadelphia, and New York.

Of about 606,000 foreign-born who lived in New Jersey in 1960, the leading nationalities—Italian, German, Polish, British, Russian, and Hungarian—comprised about 70 percent.

Education. Responsibility for the public schools is shared by the state and by individual localities. Public schools serve more than one million pupils in the elementary and secondary divisions. There are also thousands of students enrolled in the state's colleges and universities. In addition to 379 public secondary schools in 1966, there were also 142 private and parochial secondary schools. Vocational schools provide training in skilled trades, agriculture, and business.

Higher education today in New Jersey is a cooperative venture. The state publicly supports such institutions as Rutgers, the State University; Newark College of Engineering; six state colleges located at Montclair, Paterson, Glassboro, Jersey City, Trenton and Newark; and the Trenton Junior College. County and community colleges, three of which began operation in 1967, are planned for all counties. Of the 89,400 secondary school graduates in 1966, 59.8 per cent entered college.

In addition there are 34 private colleges and universities in the state. In 1965 the private institutions enrolled nearly 35,000 full-time students of whom 24,400 were from New Jersey. Publicly sponsored

D. JORDAN WILSON—PIX

Founded in 1746, Princeton University was the fourth college established in the colonies. The borough of Princeton was once the capital of the United States.

institutions served approximately 36,000 New Jersey boys and girls in widely-diversified programs of study in teacher training, liberal arts, dentistry, engineering, law, medicine, chemistry, electronics, and religion.

Among the well-known accredited private colleges and universities are the Institute for Advanced Study in Princeton and Princeton University, Fairleigh Dickinson University, Seton Hall University, Rider College in Trenton, Westminister Choir College in Princeton, Upsala College in East Orange, Stevens Institute of Technology in Hoboken, St. Peter's College in Jersey City, Edward Williams College in Hackensack, and Drew University in Madison.

Religion. More than two thirds of the citizens of New Jersey are affiliated with some religious institution. The Roman Catholic population in 1965 was 2,726,870 and the estimated Jewish population was 350,000. The largest Protestant churches are Presbyterian, Methodist, Episcopalian, United Lutheran, the American Baptist Convention, and the Reformed Church of America.

Economic Features

Manufacturing Industries. Ranking seventh among states in industrial production New Jersey owes its industrial importance to its location at the center of a great domestic market. Within 250 miles of New Jersey's factories live more than 55 million cunsumers with a buying power of more than $121 billion. New Jersey also plays a vital role in the trade of the world. The U.S. Department of Commerce reports that New Jersey sells an estimated $897 million worth of manufactured products annually.

New Jersey has the most diversified industrial structure in the nation. Surprisingly, few of the plants have more than 2,500 employees, and only 24 firms out of 14,000 can be classified as large-scale employers. One third employ fewer than five people. At the same time 86 of the leading 100 industries in the United States function within the state. Chemicals and allied products rank first, electrical equipment ranks second, and food products rank third among the industries in the state. Non-electrical machinery, transportation equipment, and fabricated metals are next in importance. Apparel and textiles hold seventh and twelfth places in value added by manufacture.

Outside of the food and lumber industries, stone, clay, and glass products are the only ones utilizing natural resources found in the state.

It is likely that more than one half of New Jersey's manufactured products are never seen or used by individual consumers, since they can be characterized as durable goods utilized by factories as special tools, machine parts, or raw materials used for processing other types of products.

While manufacturing today is spread throughout the state, greatest concentration is in two areas. Three fourths of all the factory workers are employed in the seven counties of northeastern New Jersey. Chemicals, food processing, electrical goods, and textile and pharmaceutical production are important in this area. The second area is along the Delaware River from Penns Grove to Trenton. Food processing, petroleum products, electrical machinery, and stone and glass products are important here. Chemicals, shipbuilding and apparel manufacture are also of consequence in this section.

Agriculture. Although less than 40 per cent of the land is used for agriculture, New Jersey is one of the nation's important agricultural states. In 1964, 13,000 farms utilizing 1,330,000 acres produced $271,057,000 worth of livestock and poultry and their allied products, field crops, vegetables for fresh market and for processing, fruits, forest products, and greenhouse and nursery products. With the exception of egg and potato production in Monmouth County and dairy production in Sussex and Warren counties, much of the market gardening is done in Burlington, Cumberland, and Gloucester counties. Asparagus, several varieties of beans, tomatoes, peppers, sweet corn, potatoes (both white and sweet), apples, and peaches are among the main crops. New Jersey leads the nation in blueberry production and is also a major grower of strawberries, peaches, and cranberries. Tomatoes, more than 70 per cent of which are processed, are the leading crop in dollar value. They earned $13,770,000, or 27 per cent of total farm value. Asparagus contributed $9,756,000; lettuce, $4,639,-000; and sweet corn, $3,451,000. In 1963 milk ranked first among individual farm products, and provided $59,034,000 of farm income. Specialty crops such as shade trees, shrubbery and plants for ornamental purposes, roses, carnations, potted plants for city markets, race horses, charolais beef cattle, and Christmas greenery all contribute much to farm income. The best known farm in New Jersey is Seabrook Farms in Cumberland County. It is the site of the largest processing plant in the United States, freezing vegetables from 55,000 acres in New Jersey, Pennsylvania, Maryland, and Delaware.

Fisheries. On a tonnage basis, New Jersey ranks fourth among the fishing states. In 1960 the total catch was 373 million pounds. Since the largest catch—menhaden—is inedible, the rank by value of all fish, $9,607,000, placed New Jersey in eleventh place. The three processing plants for menhaden are at Port Monmouth, Tuckerton, and Wildwood, all close to the Atlantic shore. Oysters, clams, lobsters, and scallops contributed $4,125,000.

Tourism. New Jersey's landscape of quiet beaches, forested mountains, streams, and lakes gives the state a $2 million resort industry. Many

Grazing horses feed in a rich pasture in the gently rolling Piedmont region of north-central New Jersey. Poultry and vegetables are the chief farm products.

HERBERT LANKS—PIX

PHOTO RESEARCHERS

The Pulaski Skyway, spanning the industrial environs between Jersey City and Newark, is used by thousands of New Jersey commuters who work in New York.

historic spots also attract millions of visitors throughout the year. Well known are Washington Crossing Park on the Delaware, Morristown National Historic Park, and Menlo Park, associated with Thomas A. Edison. New Jersey offers motels, hotels, and camp sites from Atlantic City to Stokes State Forest in the Kittatinny Mountains.

Transportation. The most important railroads, highways, and airways of New Jersey stretch from Philadelphia and Camden to Jersey City, Newark, and New York City and serve three fourths of New Jersey's citizens and industrial plants. This heavy-density traffic links the most modern port facilities in the world. Camden-Philadelphia port, the world's largest fresh-water port, handles the nation's largest import tonnage, valued at approximately $1 billion. Six high-level bridges and two low-level bridges between Camden and Philadelphia initiate the traffic carried eastward on U.S. Highway 1 and the New Jersey Turnpike. At the opposite end of this corridor are Newark, Elizabeth, Hoboken, Kearney, and Bayonne. This is the busiest section of the Port of New York; in 1965, it handled 9 million tons valued at $57 million. The George Washington and Verrazano bridges and the Holland and Lincoln tunnels link New Jersey with New York City. The 173-mile Garden State Parkway, longest superhighway in New Jersey, runs from Cape May to the New York State Thruway. It also connects directly with the New Jersey Turnpike at Woodbridge. These three highways are the major roads in a skein of 32,374 miles of roads, including 1,887 miles of state roads. Passenger cars and trucks utilize these highways. Newark Truck Terminal is one of the largest in the world.

New Jersey is served by 130 airports. These include Newark Airport, which served 4,867,800 passengers in 1965, and handles about 110 million pounds of cargo and 21 million pounds of mail annually. Other airports are McGuire Air Force Base, a military field; Teterboro air terminal for business, training and personal flying; and the National Aviation Facilities Experimental Services at Pomona.

Major railroads in New Jersey are the Pennsylvania, the Reading, the Pennsylvania-Reading Seashore Lines, and the Lehigh and New England lines. These railroads carry annually 14 million tons of New Jersey products to points outside the state and bring in 40 million tons for sale and processing by business and industries. They also carry, on an average day, 100,000 commuters.

Research. New Jersey leads the nation in research facilities available to agriculture, industry, health, education, and business. Today more than 625 research facilities contribute to the scientific and technological advancement of the state. It is estimated that 10 per cent of the national funds expended on research and development are spent in New Jersey. Outstanding research plants are RCA's David Sarnoff Research Center in electronic research, Princeton University's Institute for Advanced Study, and the James Forrestal Research center devoted to peacetime use of nuclear power. Chemical, pharmaceutical, and electronics industries have attracted research facilities to Middlesex, Union, Hudson, Essex, Passaic, Bergen, Morris, Monmouth, and Camden counties. Outstanding facilities are those of the Standard Oil Company at Linden; the Bell Telephone Company (electronics) at Whippany, Murray Hill, and Holmdel; and the E. I. du Pont Company (chemicals and plastics) at Deepwater in Salem County. Rutgers University is a leader in agricultural research.

Altogether, research facilities employ nearly 25,000 scientists and contribute one half billion dollars annually to the state's economy.

BERENICE CASPER

History

The original inhabitants of New Jersey were the *Lenni Lenape*, or Delaware Indians. Within a century of the coming of the white man, these aborigines had either perished or migrated westward. The explorer Giovanni da Verrazano, sailing on behalf of France, was the first European to sight the Jersey coast, in 1524. Almost a century later, in 1609, Henry Hudson set foot ashore at Sandy Hook and claimed the region for the Netherlands. Soon thereafter, the Dutch West India Company established fur trading posts on the Hudson and Delaware rivers. The Dutch town of Bergen (now Jersey City) was the first permanent settlement in New Jersey. In the late 1630's, the New Sweden Company began to compete with the Dutch for the fur trade in the Delaware Valley. Although several hundred Swedes and Finns were brought over, this Swedish venture in colonization was short-lived. In 1655 Dutch forces led by Gov. Peter Stuyvesant captured the few Swedish forts on the Delaware.

Acting on English claims in the New World, Charles II in 1664 granted to his brother, James, the Duke of York, the territory between the Delaware and Connecticut rivers. The conquest of New Netherland in the same year brought this region under the English Crown. James then presented the lands between the Hudson and Delaware rivers to Sir George Carteret and John, Lord Berkeley. Since Carteret had sheltered James from the Puritans on the Isle of Jersey in 1650, the new colony was called New Jersey. In order to attract settlers, the proprietors offered generous land grants and issued the "Concessions and Agreements" of the Lords Proprietors in 1665 which provided for liberty of conscience and a representative assembly. In 1676 the colony was divided into the provinces of East Jersey and West Jersey and the latter portion was settled by English Quakers. The West Jersey Laws, Concessions, and Agreements of 1677 was a very liberal document for its time, insuring religious freedom, an elected legislature, trial by jury, and other legal guarantees. English Quakers and Scots then purchased East Jersey from Carteret's widow in 1682.

New Jersey's early years were troubled by conflicts between proprietors and settlers over land titles and taxes. The political unrest led to the uniting of West and East Jersey as a royal colony in 1702. Although the governor was now appointed by the Crown, the colonial assembly retained control over policies through its power to levy taxes. Strife between governor and assembly was chronic. Continuing disputes between absentee landlords and farmers culminated in the land riots of 1745.

British imperial policies after 1763 aroused widespread resentment in New Jersey. Jerseymen protested vigorously against the Currency Act, the Stamp Act, and the Townshend Duties; in 1774 they held their own "tea party" at Greenwich. In response to the Intolerable Acts of 1774 committees of correspondence were formed and a delegation was sent to the First Continental Congress. On July 2, 1776, the Provincial Congress asserted its independence of British authority by adopting a new constitution for New Jersey. Distrust of executive power was reflected in this charter which gave the legislature extraordinary authority, including the election of the governor and judges. The first governor, William Livingston, was re-elected annually from 1776 to 1790.

In the Revolutionary War, New Jersey earned the title "Cockpit of the Revolution" since several major campaigns were fought over its countryside. The Battles of Trenton, Princeton, and Monmouth were the most important of these. While many Jerseymen were ardent Patriots, a considerable number were Loyalists, some of whom served in Tory regiments. Guerrilla warfare and atrocities embittered feelings between Patriot and Tory, and at the end of the war many Loyalists fled into exile.

New Jersey played a leading role in the movement to strengthen the central government of the United States. The state was actively represented at the Annapolis Convention of 1786 and the Constitutional Convention of 1787. At Philadelphia its delegates proposed the "New Jersey Plan" by which each state was to have an equal vote in the Congress. On Dec. 18, 1787, the New Jersey ratifying convention voted unanimously in favor of the new Constitution.

The Federalists enjoyed a brief period of dominance in New Jersey politics until the party of Jefferson, the Democratic-Republicans, came to power in 1801. While the unpopularity of the War of 1812 brought the Federalists back into office temporarily, the Democrats otherwise retained control until 1826. With the emergence of the Whig and Democratic parties in the late 1820's, closely contested elections came to characterize the state's politics. Although the Whigs and their successors, the Republicans, occasionally won state and national elections, until 1892 New Jersey was usually in the Democratic column. Regardless of party, transportation interests, first the Camden and Amboy Railroad and later the Pennsylvania Railroad, ruled the state legislature through most of the nineteenth century.

The constitutional convention of 1844 sought to correct the deficiencies of the state constitution of 1776. The supremacy of the legislature was replaced by a government based on the separation of powers, with a popularly elected governor and independent judiciary. The new Constitution also included a bill of rights and removed all property qualifications on voting while denying the ballot to Negroes and women.

Commercial interest and ideas of states' rights, created a strong pro-Southern sympathy in New Jersey. There was a noticeable lack of enthusiasm in much of the state for the Civil War and especially for such measures as the Emancipation Proclamation. New Jersey, which had split its electoral vote between Lincoln and Douglas in 1860, gave its support to the Democratic candidate, George B. McClellan, in 1864. Despite the antiwar feeling, 88,000 Jerseymen served in the Union forces. Following the war, New Jersey largely opposed the Radical Reconstruction policies and only reluctantly ratified the Thirteenth, Fourteenth, and Fifteenth amendments.

The "Gilded Age" in New Jersey was one of industrial achievement and political corruption. The inventions of Thomas A. Edison were only the most spectacular of the technological contributions of Jerseymen. Chemicals, oil refining, and electrical goods joined the older industries, textiles, pottery, and iron goods, in an era of rapid expansion. Meanwhile, hundreds of thousands of European immigrants arrived to man the mills and factories. Low wages and other forms of exploitation caused the industrial workers to resort to frequent strikes. These protests were often forcibly suppressed by the combined powers of employers and government.

Through lobbying and corruption a political climate favorable to business was maintained in New Jersey. So permissive were the state's incorporation laws that it became known as the "Mother of Trusts." The downfall of the corrupt Democratic regime in 1893 brought the Republicans to power, but it brought no sharp departure from these conservative policies. New Jersey had a mild case of Progressivism early in the twentieth century which produced limited gains in political reform, labor and social legislation, and business regulation. While much reform legislation was enacted during Gov. Woodrow Wilson's term of office (1911–1913),

A planetarium forms part of the New Jersey State Museum in Trenton. The State Library is located nearby.

J. W. CELLA—PHOTO RESEARCHERS

The State Capitol, built in 1792, is situated in Trenton, which became New Jersey's capital in 1790.

J. W. CELLA—PHOTO RESEARCHERS

the spadework had been done by Progressives of both parties in the preceding decade.

World War I brought an industrial boom to New Jersey, with munitions plants and shipyards operating at full capacity. The war also brought an era of political intolerance to the state with the persecution of German-Americans and "radicals." Over 150,000 Jerseymen entered the armed services, but the failure of the Democratic party to carry the state in 1916 and again in 1920 indicated the unpopularity of President Wilson's war policies.

Since 1920 the normal condition of New Jersey politics has been one of deadlock. Because the distribution of seats in the legislature favored the rural counties, the Republicans have had a majority in the Senate and sometimes in the Assembly, while the governor has more often than not been a Democrat. The overrepresentation of sparsely populated country districts has meant conservative fiscal policies and the inability of the state to provide the services and facilities required for a burgeoning urban and suburban population. For several decades the most powerful figure on the New Jersey political scene was Frank Hague, Democratic boss of Hudson County. By producing great pluralities in his county, Hague was consistently able to elect his candidates to the governorship.

The impact of the Great Depression was particularly severe in industrial New Jersey with hundreds of thousands unemployed and destitute. The New Deal programs of relief and recovery provided assistance to the needy, spurred the organization of labor unions, and had a liberalizing influence on the state's political complexion. New Jersey, which had voted Republican in the 1920's, voted for Franklin D. Roosevelt in the next four elections (1932–1944). Not until World War II did prosperity return to the state. Once more New Jersey served as an arsenal of war materials; nearly a million workers were employed in its industries. In addition, the state sent 560,000 men and women into the armed forces.

In the postwar decades, New Jersey has vacillated in its political allegiance between the two major parties. Republican Thomas E. Dewey carried the state in the presidential election of 1948, while Dwight D. Eisenhower won by large pluralities in the two following elections. New Jersey returned to the Democratic column in 1960, supporting John F. Kennedy by a slight margin, and in 1964, giving Lyndon B. Johnson a substantial plurality. Meanwhile, Jersey voters were electing Alfred E. Driscoll, Republican, and Robert B. Meyner, Democrat, each to two terms as governor. In 1965, Democrat Richard J. Hughes was re-elected governor with a Democratic majority in both houses of the legislature. Efforts to bring about legislative reapportionment and to enact a broad-based state tax indicated that the deadlock in New Jersey politics might at last be broken.

Government

The constitutional convention of 1947 brought much needed reforms to the state government of New Jersey. It greatly increased the power of the governor and thoroughly reorganized the judiciary. The new constitution also expanded the Bill of Rights to guarantee the right of employees to collective bargaining and to prohibit discrimination or segregation "because of religious principles, race, color, ancestry or national origin."

As the chief executive, the governor is the only state official elected on a statewide basis. With the advice and consent of the senate, he appoints the top officials of the state agencies and the judges of the state and county courts. The governor recommends legislation and may veto bills. A two-thirds majority of each house is required to override the veto. The governor's term of office is four years, and he may not serve more than two successive terms.

The New Jersey legislature consists of a senate and a general assembly. The senate has 21 members, one from each county, who are elected for four years. The 60 members of the general assembly are apportioned among the counties on the basis of population (each county has at least one representative); their term of office is two years. The legislature meets each year on the second Tuesday in January. Unlike most legislatures, the majority of all the members of each house is required for the approval of a bill.

The judicial system of New Jersey is composed of a supreme court, a superior court, and county courts. The supreme court is the state's highest tribunal which hears appeals from the lower courts. The superior court has both original and appellate jurisdiction, while the county courts are courts of the first instance for both civil and criminal cases.

Each of New Jersey's 21 counties is governed by a Board of Chosen Freeholders which exercises both legislative and executive functions. Other county officials include a sheriff, clerk, prosecutor of pleas, and coroner. The state's 567 incorporated municipalities have various forms of government, including mayor-council, commission, and council-manager. A merit system for public employment and promotion is in effect for many positions in the state, county, and municipal governments. Competitive examinations are administered by the State Civil Service Commission.

To qualify to vote in New Jersey one must be an American citizen, 21 years of age, be properly registered, and have resided in the state for six months and in the county for 40 days prior to election day. All candidates for public office in partisan elections are nominated in primary elections. Only voters who are registered party members may vote in the primary of their party.

RUDOLPH J. VECOLI

BIBLIOG.–J. E. Bebout and R. J. Grele, *Where Cities Meet: The Urbanization of New Jersey*, Vol. 22, The New Jersey Historical Series (1964); S. J. Flink, ed., *The Economy of New Jersey* (1958); L. B. Irwin and H. I. Ellis, *New Jersey the Garden State* (1962); S. M. Kennedy, et al., *The New Jersey Almanac 1964–1965, Tercentenary Edition* (1963); R. P. McCormick, *New Jersey: A Students' Guide to Localized History* (1965); J. R. Pierce and A. G. Tressler, *The Research State: A History of Science in New Jersey*, Vol. 15, The New Jersey Historical Series (1964); B. M. Rich, *The Government and Administration of New Jersey* (1957); R. J. Vecoli, *The People of New Jersey* (1965); Kemble Widmer, *The Geology and Geography of New Jersey*, Vol. 19, The New Jersey Historical Series (1964); H. F. Wilson, et al., *Outline History of New Jersey* (1950).

NEW JERSEY TEA, *Ceanothus americanus*, a North American shrub of the buckthorn family, also known as redroot. It grows from 1 to 3 feet high and produces clusters of white or blue flowers. The three-ribbed leaves were used as tea by American troops during the Revolutionary War.

NEW KENSINGTON, city, SW Pennsylvania, Westmoreland County; on the Allegheny River; 15 miles NE of Pittsburgh. An industrial city, New Kensington has manufactures of aluminum, magnesium, glass, and electrical and metal products. It was established in 1891 on the site of Fort Crawford and incorporated as a borough in 1892. It was consolidated with Parnassus in 1931 and incorporated as a city in 1934. (For population, see Pennsylvania map in Atlas.)

NEWLANDS, FRANCIS GRIFFITH, 1848–1917, U.S. lawyer and Congressman born in Natchez, Miss. Admitted to the bar in 1869, he became a successful corporation lawyer in San Francisco. In 1893, he was elected, on the Silver Party ticket, to the House of Representatives from Nevada and served until 1903. From 1903 to 1917, he was U.S.

Democratic Senator from Nevada. Newman was the author of legislation that encouraged land reclamation through irrigation. The Newlands Act of 1913 sought to promote labor mediation.

NEWLANDS, JOHN ALEXANDER, 1838–98, British chemist,born in Southwark. In his early twenties Newlands fought under Garibaldi for Italian freedom. Returning to England, he worked as an industrial chemist. He was one of the first scientists to discover the importance of atomic weights and published his theory of periodicity and the law of octaves in 1864. Newlands's discoveries were ridiculed by his colleagues, and it was many years before the importance of his work was fully recognized. *The Discovery of the Periodic Law* (1884) contains Newlands's collected papers on the elements.

NEW LONDON, city, SE Connecticut, New London County; at the mouth of the Thames River on its W bank; 45 miles E of New Haven.

New London is a port of entry with an excellent deep-water harbor and a popular summer resort. Ship-building, marine construction, and the manufacture of textiles, dentifrices, turbines, collapsible tubes, printing presses, and paper products are major industries. The U.S. Coast Guard Academy and the Connecticut College for women are located in the city, and a U.S. Navy submarine base and officers training school are 4 miles north. Historical points of interest include the county courthouse (1784); the Joshua Hempstead House, oldest residence in the city; the Lyman Allyn Whaling Museum and the old New London Lighthouse (1760).

The city was settled as part of the Massachusetts Bay colony by John Winthrop the younger in 1646. In 1658 the community's name, Pequot, was changed to New London. Maritime interests have dominated throughout New London's history. (For population, see Connecticut map in Atlas.)

NEW MADRID, city, SE Missouri, county seat of New Madrid County, about 20 miles S of Sikeston. New Madrid has cotton gins and a sawmill and is situated in an agricultural region. The city was settled by Col. George Morgan in 1789 on the site of a French trading post. Originally the capital of a buffer territory lying between Spanish and American colonies, New Madrid passed into U.S. hands as part of the Louisiana Purchase. During the Civil War the town was occupied by the Confederate army in 1862 and recaptured in the same year by Union forces. (For population, see Missouri map in Atlas.)

NEWMAN, ERNEST, 1868–1959, British music critic and biographer, born in Liverpool. He was a music critic for the Birmingham *Daily Post* from 1906 to 1919 and for the London Sunday *Times*, 1920–58. Newman is best-known for his distinguished four-volume critical biography of Richard Wagner (1933–47). He also wrote three other books about Wagner, including an analytic study of the composer's operas. Newman also published books on Gluck, Wolf, Strauss, J. S. Bach, Beethoven, and Liszt.

NEWMAN, FRANCIS WILLIAM, 1805–97, English scholar, younger brother of John Henry Newman, born in London and graduated from Worcester College, Oxford. He was professor of classical literature at Manchester New College (1840–46) and professor of Latin at University College, London (1846–69). While he remained deistic in his beliefs, he rejected the historical basis of Christianity. He wrote *The Soul: Its Sorrows and Aspirations* (1849) and *Phases of Faith* (1850). He also wrote on mathematics, language, economics, and medicine.

CULVER

Cardinal Newman

NEWMAN, JOHN HENRY CARDINAL, 1801–90, British clergyman and writer, born in London, eldest of six children of banker John Newman and Jemima Fourdrinier, daughter of paper-makers of Huguenot descent. In 1808 he was sent to a school at Ealing. He did well at his studies, acted in Latin comedies, ran a society and a paper, and learned the violin. After reading David Hume's *Essays*, he became skeptical of Christianity but in 1816 found faith in God and studied religion under an evangelical clergyman, reading John Milner's church history, which taught him to love the Fathers of the first centuries. Although his father's income was depleted by a bank failure, Newman was entered for Trinity College, Oxford, and went into residence in the fall of 1817. He failed to gain honors in 1820, owing to overwork and nerves, but in April, 1822, was elected to a fellowship at Oriel College, then the intellectual center of the university. Even before his father died in 1824, Newman took responsibility for his family, earning money by coaching pupils. Ordained deacon in 1824, he took a curacy in a poor parish, visiting the sick and teaching children. At Whitsun in 1825 he was ordained priest in the Church of England and next year became a tutor at Oriel; in 1828 he became the Vicar of St. Mary-the-Virgin, the university church. New friends and experiences led him toward a more Catholic idea of the Church, and his sermons became the spiritual motive force of the Oxford (Tractarian) Movement, launched in 1833 with the first *Tracts for the Times*, designed to demonstrate that the authority of the clergy rested not on the State but on the teaching of the Apostles. From then till 1841, Newman was the active leader of the Catholic revival in the Church of England, while John Keble remained its inspiration and adviser. Newman edited the *British Critic* and cooperated with Edward Bouverie Pusey in producing translations of the works of the Fathers. Opposition had been growing, and when Newman in 1841 published "Tract 90," which interpreted the 39 Articles in a Catholic sense, the storm broke. Nearly all the bishops (24) condemned it, and the series was suspended. Newman retired to an outlying village, Littlemore, attached to his parish, where he had built a church and converted some stables into a miniature monastery. Since 1839 his historical reading had led him to suspect that Rome was "the divinely appointed center of unity" and that the Church of England was in schism. He resigned St. Mary's in 1843 and his Oriel fellowship two years later and was received into the Catholic and

Roman Church by Fr. Dominic Barberi, an Italian Passionist, on Oct. 9, 1845.

Newman left for Rome in September, 1846, and studied at the College of Propaganda. He was ordained a priest on May 30, 1847, and said his first mass on the feast of Corpus Christi. With a group of younger friends he joined the Congregation of the Oratory, founded in the sixteenth century by St. Philip Neri for secular priests who lived together without monastic vows. Newman returned to England at Christmas and set up the English Oratory on Feb. 2, 1848, at Maryvale, a Catholic college then outside Birmingham. A year later a foundation was made in a disused gin-distillery in the back streets of the town, and a flourishing parish built up from half-heathen factory workers. The same year a house was opened in London under Frederick (Wilfrid) Faber, which later moved to Brompton. Newman moved his own Oratory to its present home in Edgbaston, a new suburb of Birmingham, in 1853, at the conclusion of a famous trial in which he was unjustly convicted of libeling Achilli, a renegade Italian priest. At the same time he was appointed by papal brief to start and become rector of a Catholic university in Dublin, but after many difficulties was forced to resign in 1858. Newman next became involved in the internal controversies of the Catholic Church. While loyal to the pope as successor of St. Peter, he disapproved the extremism of the Ultramontanes who relied on secular arms to defend the temporal sovereignty and exalted the authority of the pope by exaggerated opinions on the extent of his infallibility. The London Oratory aligned with this dominant party, and the two houses became estranged. Newman became an object of suspicion in London and Rome and his plans for Catholic education were crushed by the ecclesiastical leaders. But his reputation with the bulk of Protestant Englishmen underwent a change for the better in 1864 when, as a result of a passing attack by the popular novelist Charles Kingsley, Newman wrote the history of his religious opinions in a series of pamphlets afterward published as *Apologia Pro Vita Sua*. This book won him respect and esteem on a world-wide scale but he continued to be regarded with suspicion by some Catholics until, after the death of Pius IX, the liberal Leo XIII made him a cardinal in 1879. For the last years of his life, Newman enjoyed honor and affection from people of all ranks and nations, and he died in peace at the age of 89.

Newman's influence has been complex and has affected ordinary people as well as the learned, since he wrote a fine classical English intelligible to almost anybody. But as he did not use the technical terms of the scholastic theology current among Catholics in the nineteenth century, it is only recently that his influence has been felt among theologians, especially on the European continent. Now it is realized that his Biblical and Patristic formation gave him an approach free of narrow legalism, while his psychological penetration and historical understanding make him congenial to those interested in personalist and existentialist philosophies, though Newman himself adopted no particular philosophy, but accepted the British empiricist tradition. Perhaps the deepest reason for his present influence is his realization of the importance of situating theology in history. His treatise on this theme, *An Essay on the Development of Christian Doctrine* (1845), was a pioneer study and is still a stimulating source of ideas. Newman wrote his own religious opinions as a personal history, the *Apologia*, and preferred historical studies of saints to the hagiography then common, which analyzed them as patterns of perfection. In *The Church of the Fathers* (1840), his sketches of the Greek Fathers were of lively realism. His humor is evident in his novel of Oxford, *Loss and Gain* (1848), and in his lectures published in 1851 as *The Present Position of Catholics*, in which he uses ridicule to dispel the wilder prejudices then held against Catholics. In his *Letter to Dr. Pusey* (1866), he used the historical approach to distinguish the traditional place of Mary in the Church from the aberrations of popular superstition. Similarly, in his *Letter to the Duke of Norfolk* (1875), written to answer an attack made by Gladstone on the Vatican decree of papal infallibility, Newman defended the function of the pope while repudiating the exaggerations of infallibilist fanatics, and he reasserted Catholic teaching on the supremacy of conscience. Newman's views on education, learning, and Christianity, finely expressed in *The Idea of a University* (1852) are still of interest to educators, while certain related opinions are brilliantly and amusingly sketched in *The Tamworth Reading Room* (1841), originally written as letters to *The Times* and reprinted in *Discussions and Arguments* (1872). Perhaps of the greatest interest to theologians now are Newman's views on the relation between Faith and Reason, first expressed in the series of *University Sermons* (1843) and finally elaborated in *A Grammar of Assent* (1870). Newman's methods were not understood by theologians of the nineteenth century, and in the early decades of the twentieth he was sometimes suspected to be "the father of Modernism." This showed a misunderstanding of his position, for it is from the tradition which he represented that the new theology of Vatican Council II, avoiding the mistakes of the Modernists, is building an understanding between the ancient faith and the modern world. The great intention behind most of Newman's work was to develop the minds of Christians so that by a full and modern understanding of their faith they could meet the challenge of skepticism and make Christianity credible to the doubtful. But this intellectual education must always go with faithful prayer and action, and Newman's greatest influence in his lifetime was perhaps exercised through his sermons. *Parochial and Plain Sermons* (1834–1843) contains expositions of a Christianity in a broad Catholic tradition, psychologically perceptive and with a deep understanding of the reality of the Gospel. Newman's spirituality was essentially Scriptural, centered on Christ, practical and austere without being unfeeling. His narrative poem *The Dream of Gerontius* (1866), treating of the soul on its way to God after death, has found many lovers, especially in the musical setting of Sir Edward Elgar. His novel *Callista* (1855) tells the story of the conversion and martyrdom of a Greek girl in third-century Africa and has a haunting poetic quality alongside a surprising realism. Newman's many-sided personality, his numerous friends, and the fact that he was the unwilling center of so many controversies, make his correspondence fascinating reading. Six volumes, covering 1845–1855, of *The Letters and Diaries of John Henry Newman* have appeared under the editorship of Charles Stephen Dessain of the Birmingham Oratory.

In considering Newman's writings as a whole it must be remembered that he wrote in response to particular challenges and that a large part of his time and energy was devoted to his pastoral ministry. He was the head of his small community and took his turn at preaching and hearing confessions till old age prevented him; he was greatly loved by his parishioners, many of them almost illiterate. In all his larger ventures, including the school he founded, he was associated with laymen, for he disliked the artificial barrier between laity and clergy then very marked in the Catholic Church. In all his dealings with people his manner was natural and without pretense, noted by many observers in that age of pretension.

MERIOL TREVOR

BIBLIOG.–V. F. Blehl, S. J., ed., *Realizations* (1964); Louis Bouyer, *Newman: His Life and Spirituality* (1958); John Coulson, ed., *On Consulting the Faithful in Matters of Doc-*

trine (1961); Hugh MacDougall, O.M.I., *The Acton-Newman Relations* (1962); Fergal McGrath, S.J., *Newman's University: Idea and Reality* (1951); Meriol Trevor, *Newman: The Pillar of the Cloud* (1962) and *Newman: Light in Winter* (1962); Jan Walgrave, O.P., *Newman the Theologian* (1960).

NEWMARKET, town, SE Ontario; on the Holland River; 25 miles N of Toronto. Newmarket is primarily a trade cneter for the surrounding area. Woodenware, leather goods, and clothing are manufactured here. (For population, see southern Ontario map in Atlas.)

NEWMARKET, urban district, E England, in Suffolk County, on the Cambridgeshire border, 13 miles ENE of Cambridge. Newmarket is a trade center for agricultural products and manufactures trailers and electronic and magnetic devices. Newmarket has been one of the major horse racing centers in England since the seventeenth century. Charles I instituted the first cup race there in 1643. (For population, see England map in Atlas.)

NEW MARKET, BATTLE OF, U.S. Civil War battle, fought on May 15, 1864, between Union forces under Maj. Gen. Franz Sigel and Confederate forces under John Daniel Imboden and Maj. Gen. John Cabell Breckinridge. Union forces moved down the Shenandoah Valley to New Market, Va., where the battle was fought in a heavy rain. The engagement was a decisive victory for the Confederates. Out of the 5,150 men engaged in combat, the Union forces lost 831 men to the Confederates' 577. The Confederate victory was helped by a charge of cadets from the Virginia Military Institute.

NEW MATH, a program introduced in the United States, intended to help students develop an understanding of the basic concepts of mathematics without rigorously memorizing meaningless sets of rules. It includes new methods of teaching that emphasize the unity of mathematics and the interdependence of its various areas. It helps students to reason each step in working problems and to discover their meanings and solutions, gives them systematic practice so as to develop skill and efficiency, and formulates a corrective program to help them overcome difficulties in understanding and solving problems. See ALGEBRA; ARITHMETIC.

NEW MEXICO, a southwestern state of the United States, bounded by Colorado on the N, Texas and Oklahoma on the E, Texas and Mexico on the S, and Arizona on the W. New Mexico extends about 390 miles from north to south, and 350 miles from east to west; area 121,666 square miles, including vast areas of semiarid grazing land but only 155 square miles of water. It is the fifth largest state; population (1965 est.) 1,029,000. The capital is Santa Fe, a city in the north central part of the state at the foot of the Sangre de Cristo Mountains. See map in Atlas, Vol. 20. For the state flag in color, see FLAG.

On the state seal, adopted in 1913, the American eagle shields a small Mexican eagle, representing the annexation of New Mexico by the United States. The scroll is inscribed with the state motto.

BIRD	**Road runner**
FLOWER	**Yucca**
TREE	**Pinon**
CAPITAL	**Santa Fe**
MOTTO	**Crescit Eundo (It Grows As It Goes)**
ENTERED THE UNION	**Jan. 6, 1912**
ORDER OF ENTRY	**47th**

Physical Features

Topography. The Rocky Mountains extend southward into New Mexico from Colorado, and include the Sangre de Cristo range on the eastern side of the Rio Grande and the Jemez and San Juan ranges on the western side of the river. Each of these ranges has several peaks above 11,000 feet. The highest mountain in the state is Wheeler Peak, near Taos, with an altitude of 13,160 feet.

More than 50 other mountain ranges are found in southern and western New Mexico, most of them narrow, rugged, fault-block ridges oriented in parallel from north to south. The higher of these ranges are forested on their upper slopes, but the lower ones have only scattered trees or none at all.

Between these fault-block ranges lie wide arid basins, some of which are drained by the Rio Grande, while others have no drainage to the sea. These basins are gradually filling up with gravel, sand, and soil washed down from the mountains.

Northwestern New Mexico is a part of the Colorado Plateaus region, and is dominated by mesas, buttes, cliffs, and canyons eroded from horizontal layers of sandstone, limestone, and shale. Much of this land is only thinly covered by soils, and the vegetation is sparse. Numerous flows of black lava and old volcanic peaks such as Shiprock are found in the area.

The eastern portion of the state is part of the Great Plains, and consists of rolling grassland broken occasionally by canyons, wide valleys, and

Elevation in New Mexico: 2,000–5,000 feet (white); 5,000–10,000 feet (gray); over 10,000 feet (black).

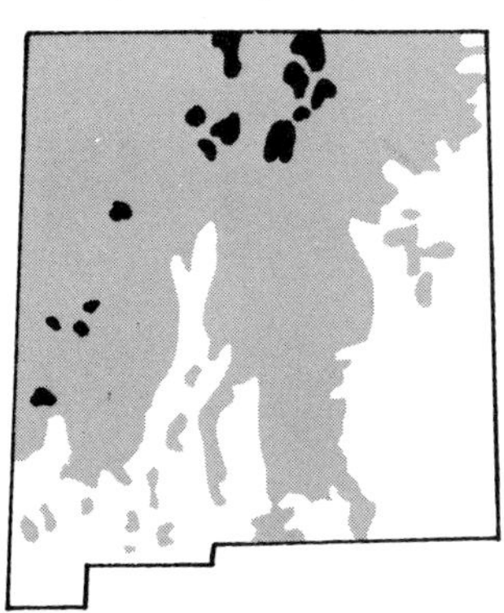

Average annual rainfall is indicated by white and gray areas on the map: 0–12 inches (white); 12–24 inches (gray).

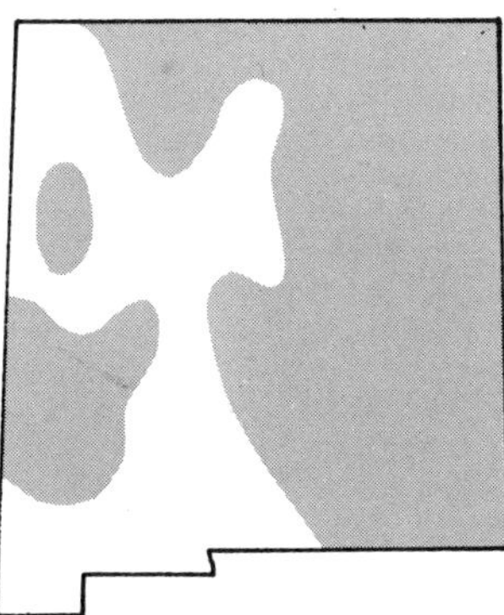

Population density (per square mile) in New Mexico: 0–3 (white); 3–10 (gray); 10–90 (dark gray); 90–250 (black).

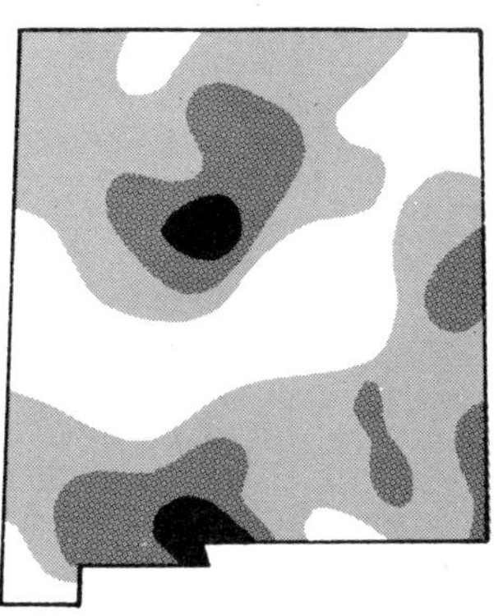

HERBERT LANKS—PIX

Pueblo Indian villages, some of prehistoric origin, found along the Rio Grande in New Mexico, housed the original inhabitants of the state.

isolated hills and buttes. An especially flat portion of the plains, between Clovis and Hobbs, is known as the Llano Estacado.

Climate. New Mexico is mostly arid to semiarid and has a mild, sunny climate. The state is located in the desert part of North America, but because it is near the cooler and moister margins of that area, it has moderate winters and summer temperatures that in some localities are only moderately warm. Annual mean temperatures are about 60° F in the south and 50° F in the north.

Average annual precipitation is about 15 inches, half of which falls during brief summer thunderstorms. Winter precipitation includes as much as 30 inches of snow in the northern mountains, but only light rains in the southern desert areas. Elevation differences account for sharp variations in climate; the mountains have a much cooler and wetter climate than the lower areas. In the south the growing season is as long as 220 days.

Soils. Much of the southern part of the state is covered with thin, light-colored, coarse-textured, desert soils. The soils on the plains and plateaus are darker and slightly richer in organic matter, while in the mountains there is a great variety of soils, ranging from rich, moist soil to barren rock. The best soils for agriculture are those on the bottomlands, or floodplains, of the larger rivers.

Rivers. The main river is the Rio Grande, which begins in Colorado and runs south through the middle of New Mexico. Most of its water is used for industrial, municipal, and irrigation purposes in several valleys along its route—especially in the Albuquerque and Mesilla valleys.

The Pecos River drains eastern New Mexico and eventually joins the Rio Grande in southern Texas. The Canadian and Cimarron rivers drain eastward from New Mexico into the Arkansas River. The San Juan, San Francisco, and Gila rivers flow westward into the Colorado River. But all of New Mexico's rivers are comparatively small, and the greater part of the state is drained only by dry washes—arroyos—that flow only briefly after rain showers.

There are few lakes, and the largest bodies of water are reservoirs impounded behind dams. These include Navajo Reservoir on the San Juan River, Elephant Butte and Caballo reservoirs on the Rio Grande, and smaller reservoirs on the Canadian, Chama, and Pecos rivers.

Flora and Fauna. The higher mountains of New Mexico are densely forested with white fir, Douglas fir, Engelmann spruce, blue spruce, alpine fir, and quaking aspen. On peaks above 12,000 feet are cool meadows of alpine tundra, composed of short grasses and tiny flowers. At intermediate elevations—between 7,000 and 10,000 feet—the forests are composed largely of ponderosa pine, the principal tree cut for lumber. In these forests are mule deer, white-tailed deer, black bears, elk, bighorn sheep, mountain lions, bobcats, foxes, muskrats, marmots, and beavers. Some of the more common birds of the forests are Steller's jays, mountain chickadees, mountain bluebirds, and spotted and green towhees. There are also numerous mourning doves, grouse, and wild turkeys. Mountain streams contain rainbow, brown, brook, and native cutthroat trout.

At the base of the mountains and on the rolling hills and higher plateaus of the state are woodlands of piñon pine and one-seed juniper. These trees are low and shrublike, providing only a pygmy forest—one of the most typical features of the southwestern landscape. A cover of short and medium-high grasses covers the lower plains and plateaus, mixed here and there with sagebrush, snakeweed, rabbit brush, and Russian thistle ("tumbleweed"). In arid southern New Mexico the dominant plant is creosote bush, although mesquite, cactus, yucca, sotol, ocotillo, century plants, and several species of grass also occur. Cottonwood trees are common along the few rivers.

The woodland, desert, and grassland areas support many small animals, including jackrabbits, prairie dogs, ground squirrels, pack rats, skunks, lizards, rattlesnakes, scorpions, tarantulas, armadillos, and peccaries. Coyotes are especially common; pronghorn antelope are rather uncommon. Roadrunners, scaled quail, mockingbirds, cactus wrens, and hawks are representative of a surprisingly large number of birds that live in the arid areas.

Social Features

Population. The people of New Mexico comprise three general groups: "Anglo-Americans," Spanish-Americans, and Indians. The term Anglo-American is applied to anyone not of Spanish or Indian ancestry. Though considerable numbers of Anglo-Americans came to New Mexico during the railroad-building period of the nineteenth century, most of them came after 1945. They now number approximately 700,000.

Immigration since World War II has caused the total population to grow rapidly. In 1950 the population was 681,187; by 1960 it 951,023. This increase constituted a ten-year rate of 39.6 per cent, in contrast to the national growth rate for the same period of 18.5 per cent.

New Mexico's population is not evenly distributed. Sixty-six per cent of the people live in cities and towns, and almost 25 per cent of the entire population lives in the one city of Alburquerque. The rural dwellers live on farms and ranches, and some in small villages along the streams and valleys. The eastern plains have the largest number of small and medium-sized cities.

JOE MONROE—PHOTO RESEARCHERS

A symbol of Spanish conquest and customs, this mission in Rancho de Taos, New Mexico, built over 250 years ago, was a fort and place of worship.

JOE MONROE—PHOTO RESEARCHERS

Adobe bricks, introduced by the Spanish, remain the building blocks for many New Mexican homes. Made of clay and hay, the bricks are hardened in the sun.

In the villages of the north central part of the state, particularly, Spanish-American people remain in the majority. These people are descended from the original sixteenth-century explorers and colonists of New Mexico. The dominant language is still Spanish, and traditional Spanish or Mexican attitudes and ways of life distinguish the area from all other parts of the United States. These villages are declining in population, however, owing to insufficient farmlands and employment opportunities. Many people have moved to Albuquerque, Santa Fe, Española, and other towns as part of an increasing trend toward urbanization. Population is declining in 16 of the state's 32 counties.

Indians. The population of New Mexico in 1960 included 56,255 Indians, of three general groups: Pueblo, Navajo, and Apache.

The 25,000 Pueblo Indians live in 18 adobe villages ("pueblos"). Most of these villages are along the Rio Grande in northern New Mexico, where water and land are available for farming. Some of these people are employed in towns near the pueblos, while others produce jewelry, pottery, and other craft items. The Pueblos emphasize community life, which features many religious and ceremonial practices. The people of the Hopi pueblos, in Arizona, are closely related to the New Mexico Pueblo Indians.

The Navajo Indians constitute the largest tribe in the United States, numbering about 100,000. Most of them live on a reservation that extends across northwestern New Mexico and adjacent parts of Arizona and Utah; some 33,000 of the tribal members live in New Mexico. Although they are still widely scattered over the land, an increasing number of Navajos are building modern homes to replace the traditional hogans. Sheep raising and farming are important occupations of the Navajos, as is wage labor. The tribe as a whole has interests in lumbering, mining, and petroleum production, and in a few manufacturing plants.

The Apache Indians live on two separate reservations, named for the Jicarilla and Mescalero branches of the tribe. The Jicarilla group, in the north, numbers about 1,600; and the Mescalero group, in the south, numbers 1,520. Though famed in past times for their war-making abilities, the Apaches are now engaged largely in cattle raising.

Religion. Because of its Spanish history, New Mexico is the oldest center of Roman Catholicism in the United States. About 32 per cent of the people are Roman Catholic, whereas the fewer numbers of Protestants are mainly of the Baptist, Methodist, and Presbyterian denominations.

Education. There are six state-supported, four-year co-educational colleges and universities. The largest is the University of New Mexico at Albuquerque, and others are New Mexico State University, New Mexico Highlands University, Eastern New Mexico University, Western New Mexico University, and the New Mexico Institute of Mining and Technology. All of these schools are accredited. State junior colleges, vocational schools, and schools and hospitals for the handicapped are also established in the state.

Other colleges include the College of Santa Fe, a Catholic school, and Saint John's College of Santa Fe and the College of the Southwest (both private). The federal government operates many Indian schools, some in cooperation with local school boards and systems.

Economic Features

Agriculture. Farming and livestock ranching are of chief importance in the greater part of the state. Because of the general aridity, however, agricultural production is small in comparison with that of many other states. In 1965 the value of crops produced was $109,813,000; the value of livestock and livestock products was $164,684,000.

About two million acres of land, much of it in the extreme eastern part of the state, are farmed without irrigation. But the most productive farmlands are along the few river valleys where irrigation water can be provided. Irrigated cropland totals about 873,000 acres, and produces more than half the value of crop output.

The principal crop is cotton, which is grown mostly in the Mesilla Valley near Las Cruces, and in other areas near Carlsbad, Deming, and Roswell. In most years about 220,000 acres are harvested and 290,000 bales are ginned, with the crop having a gross value of about $50,000,000.

The second-ranking crop is hay, principally alfalfa hay. Wheat is also important, as are grain sorghums, pecans, beans, fruits, and corn. Production of most of these crops is greatest in southern and eastern New Mexico. In the northern areas farming is more general and varied, and is practiced less intensively.

Sheep raising is important chiefly in the northeastern plains and in the northern mountains, though there is also a considerable production in the Navajo reservation of the northwest. Cattle ranching is important in almost all parts of the state, especially in the eastern plains. In 1965 there were 1,106,000 cattle and 969,000 sheep. Although the number of animals has diminished over the years, the quality of stock and production methods have been improved. The livestock are sold largely in

Kansas City, in California, and within the state itself. Dairying is of little importance.

Forest Industries. About 250,000 board feet of lumber are produced each year, mostly ponderosa pine and Douglas fir. Sixty per cent of the saw-timber is cut from private lands, 30 per cent from national forest lands, and the rest from Indian lands. The gathering of nuts from the piñon pines is a minor industry in most parts of the state.

Mining. Mining is New Mexico's most important industry: the state ranks seventh nationally in mineral output. In 1965 the production value reached $781,882,000. The most valuable minerals produced are petroleum, natural gas, potash, copper, and uranium. Petroleum and gas are produced in separate areas in the southeastern and northwestern corners of the state. New Mexico's production of petroleum ranks fifth among petroleum-producing states, while its natural gas production ranks sixth.

Since 1950 approximately half the uranium produced each year in the United States has been mined and milled in New Mexico. The mines are all in the northwestern part, mostly near Grants. About 90 per cent of the nation's potash is mined in southeastern New Mexico, with an annual production of about 2,800,000 tons.

The state ranks fourth in production of copper and molybdenum, and there is a small production of gold, silver, lead, zinc, tin, manganese, beryllium, columbite, and vanadium. The production of non-metals includes the following minerals, listed in approximate order of annual value: coal, sand and gravel, marble and other building stones, perlite, helium, pumice, salt, lime, sulfur, clay, mica, carbon dioxide gas, turquoise, gypsum, barite, and calcite.

Transportation. Major transcontinental highways, railroads, and airline routes cross New Mexico from east to west. The most important highway is U.S. 66 (Interstate 40), through Albuquerque, but there are over 65,000 miles of public roads. About 15,000 of these miles are hard-surfaced. The major railroads are the Santa Fe Railway in the north and the Southern Pacific in the south, and there are four other connecting railroads.

Manufacturing and Trade. Manufacturing is a relatively minor industry in New Mexico, limited mostly to food processing, petroleum refining, construction materials, railroad maintenance, and smelting. There are also some metal fabrication and manufacture of electronic equipment.

Albuquerque is the state's major manufacturing and trade center, and the hub of transportation routes. It and numerous other communities in the state have well developed facilities and services for tourists. Tourism ranks as a major industry of the state.

In 1965, employment in trade, commerce, finance, and services accounted for 43 per cent of the personal income of the state's residents, or $820,000,000. In addition, a large governmental employment accounted for 29 per cent of the personal income. Governmental and defense-related employment totaled 72,000 persons, whereas total employment in the state was almost 350,000.

Nuclear and Space Research. New Mexico has a major role in research and development in the fields of atomic energy, space exploration, and ballistic rocketry. Basic nuclear research is carried on at Los Alamos Scientific Laboratory, and atomic weapons incorporating the findings of this research are designed, tested, and maintained at Sandia Military Base in Albuquerque. Non-weapon uses of nuclear energy are also being developed to an increasing extent. At White Sands Missile Range, near Alamogordo, the National Aeronautics and Space Administration and the U.S. Army Ordnance Corps test short- and medium-range ballistic missiles and space exploration equipment. Additional research is carried on at Kirtland Air Force Base and Holloman Air Development Center.

Recreation. Residents and visitors to New Mexico find many attractions in climate and scenery, in historic and prehistoric landmarks, and in the present-day Spanish and Indian atmosphere. The southern desert is inviting in winter, the northern mountains are in summer. Among the many developed recreation areas and winter sports areas in the seven national forests, the most scenic places are Sandia Crest, the Pecos Valley, and the Wheeler Peak area. Other scenic places in the mountains include Philmont Scout Ranch, Cimarron Palisades, the Moreno-Eagle Nest Valley, the Valle Grande, Ruidoso Canyon, and the Hondo Valley.

In and around Santa Fe and Taos are numerous historic buildings dating from New Mexico's Spanish past, including the Palace of the Governors, the Church of San Miguel, and the churches of Ranchos de Taos, Chimayó, and Las Trampas.

The Indian pueblos of Taos and Acoma are especially interesting, and both here and throughout the state Indian dances and festivals are held at various times of year. In addition the Inter-tribal Indian Ceremonial, held at Gallup in August, brings together Indians of most U.S. tribes for ceremonial performances. During the Labor Day weekend Santa Fe holds its annual fiesta, and the State Fair in Albuquerque is presented in late September.

The ruined dwellings of the prehistoric Pueblo Indians are numerous in the state, and the more notable ones are included in national monuments—Aztec Ruins, Chaco Canyon, Bandelier, Gran Quivira, Pecos, and Gila Cliff Dwellings. In addition there are White Sands, Capulin Mountain, El Morro, and Fort Union national monuments.

The state's most visited scenic attraction is Carlsbad Caverns National Park, which makes available to the public the world's largest known underground caverns. The full extent of the huge and beautifully decorated series of caves is still unknown. JEROLD G. WIDDISON

Government

State government, as developed under the constitution of 1911, consists of a legislature of 37 members serving four-year terms in the upper house and 70 members of the lower house elected for two years. Since 1964 the legislature meets in annual sessions. Elective officials are the governor, lieutenant governor, secretary of state, auditor, treasurer, attorney general, commissioner of public lands, three corporation commissioners, and superintendent of public instruction. All are elected for two years and are subject to re-election, but must then wait two years before being eligible again. Five State Supreme Court justices serve staggered eight-year terms, while 12 district judges (in ten districts) are elected for six years each. For local government, the state is divided into 32 counties, each administered by a board of three commissioners elected for two-year terms.

History

Exploration. Advanced Indian civilization coupled with attractive tales of great wealth in the North American interior stimulated early Spanish advance into the area of New Mexico. An itinerant castaway, Alvar Núñez Cabeza de Vaca, shipwrecked with several companions on the Texas coast, wandered from there to Culiacán, Sinaloa, possibly setting foot on New Mexican soil near its southern boundary. His accounts, promising great riches as yet unseen, prompted the Spanish viceroy in Mexico City to send a follow-up expedition under Fray Marcos de Niza, a Franciscan. Accompanied by a member of the Cabeza de Vaca group, the new sortie of 1539 arrived at the Zuñi villages of northwestern New Mexico, where a hostile reception forced its return.

The Spanish next determined to send a large-scale exploring expedition under command of Francisco Vásquez de Coronado and guided by Fray Marcos. From 1540 to 1542 this expedition explored the southwest, with particular attention to New Mexico. Though the enterprise was an exploratory success, it was an economic failure and interest in New Mexico lapsed.

Missionary activity motivated the Rodríguez-Chamuscado expedition in 1580, and its disappearance, combined with hope of economic gain, led Antonio de Espejo, in company with Brother Bernardino Beltrán, to make the northward trip as a rescue operation in 1582–83. The latter group largely duplicated the exploratory activities of the Vásquez de Coronado expedition. By this time the term *Nuevo México* was applied permanently to the area along the upper Rio Grande.

Two unauthorized expeditions, by Gaspar Castaño de Sosa (1590–91) northward via the Pecos River and by Humaña and Bonilla (1593–94), gave evidence of sustained interest in the exploration of the area, though neither was successful in finding wealth or establishing a permanent settlement. This interest did lead, however, to final colonization of New Mexico. Leadership and funds were provided by a wealthy Creole mine owner, Don Juan de Oñate of Zacatecas. After frustrating delays, a colony consisting of over 400 people, 7,000 head of livestock, and a large supply train marched northward. En route, on Apr. 30, 1598, a symbolic act of Spanish possession was celebrated near El Paso. Farther north headquarters were established at the Tewa Indian pueblo, which was christened San Juan de los Caballeros, the second permanent white settlement in the United States. From this point mission-building under Franciscan auspices was begun.

Spanish Rule. Lack of food, the hostility of Indians, lack of exploitable wealth, and great isolation were difficulties that beset the colonizing group. The Acoma Indians, emboldened by the fancied impregnability of their sky city atop a stone mesa, were harshly subdued after a temporarily successful resistance to Spanish control. By 1607, worn out from extensive explorations and administrative activities and impoverished by the continued expense of his unprofitable colony, Oñate submitted his resignation, though his successor, Pedro de Peralta, did not arrive for two years. The new governor was charged with the founding of a new capital which he established in the winter of 1609–10 at Santa Fe, a more strategic site.

Spanish life settled down to an almost uneventful course in New Mexico, but Indian life was changed greatly by Spanish culture, which brought with it beasts of burden, new technology, new religion, and new obligations. During this period the Catholic church vied with the lay population for control of local affairs. A regular supply route was established linking Mexico City with Santa Fe by means of periodic trading caravans.

Repeated hostility between the Spanish and the Indians culminated in an uprising of the Pueblo Indians aided by Apaches. Under the leadership of a San Juan medicine man named Po-pé, the natives staged the Pueblo Revolt on Aug. 10, 1680, and forced the Spanish to abandon New Mexico temporarily. Survivors took refuge several hundred miles south at San Lorenzo near El Paso. Over 400 Spaniards were killed and 21 Franciscans became martyrs in the successful revolt, and it was twelve years before a reconquest could be attempted. Under the leadership of Governor Don Diego de Vargas the re-establishment of control began in 1692 and was totally completed by 1696.

Albuquerque was founded in 1706. The ensuing period was punctuated by occasional contacts with French traders who were becoming increasingly active in the trans-Mississippi West, and was concluded by sporadic attempts to connect New Mexico with Spanish outposts in both Texas and the newly-established colony of California. Efforts to this end were conducted by the Franciscan fathers Dominguez and Escalante, whose expedition of 1776 extended geographical knowledge northwestward into Utah.

The Mexican Period. In 1807, U.S. Army Lieut. Zebulon M. Pike, exploring the extreme limits of the Louisiana Purchase, was captured by the Spanish on the Conejos River, a tributary of the upper Rio Grande, and taken to Santa Fe. Subsequently he was transferred under guard to Chihuahua and later escorted back to the United States. Pike was the vanguard of increasing U.S. interest in New Mexico in the late Spanish period,

DICK KENT

Albuquerque, at the foot of the Sandia Mountains, is the major manufacturing and trade center of New Mexico, and the hub of transportation routes.

but such interlopers received hostile treatment. However, after Mexico won independence from Spain in 1821, frontier traders were accepted with enthusiasm in New Mexico. A new commercial route between New Mexico and Missouri was opened in 1822 by William Becknell, who became the "Father of the Santa Fe Trail." Trade and fur gathering brought prominent frontiersmen to the area, among them James Ohio Pattie, Ceran St. Vrain, the Bent Brothers, and Kit Carson. During the same period the territory was neglected by the home government.

As a phase of the U.S.-Mexican War, New Mexico was invaded in August, 1846, by a U.S. military force commanded by Brig. Gen. Stephen W. Kearny. A bloodless conquest resulted in the proclamation of U.S. military government. When many of these invading troops moved on to conquer California and Chihuahua, leaving a reduced occupation force, a band of malcontents revolted at Taos, where Civil Governor Charles Bent was murdered along with several other citizens. Col. Sterling Price quelled the rebellion.

Territorial Status. The Treaty of Guadalupe Hidalgo, signed Feb. 2, 1848, ended the war and gave New Mexico to the United States as part of the Mexican Cession. By 1850 the area was organized as a territory and a boundary controversy with Texas was satisfactorily settled. The following year the first territorial governor, James C. Calhoun, was inaugurated, the first legislative assembly met, and the first Bishop of Santa Fe, John B. Lamy, took charge of the newly-created diocese. Western railroad surveys in 1853 brought about two government reconnaissances of New Mexico, while a boundary dispute with Mexico resulted in U.S. purchase in 1853 of a strip of northern Mexico (the Gadsden Purchase), which added to the territory's area. Organization of Colorado Territory in 1861 had the opposite effect: it reduced the northward extent of New Mexico Territory.

During the Civil War the Confederate army of Gen. H. H. Sibley penetrated New Mexico from the south to as far north as Santa Fe. Following battles at Glorieta and Pigeon's Ranch, the Confederates began a withdrawal that was complete by mid-1862. Local Indians, under reduced restraint during the Civil War, became troublesome to the authorities and Col. Kit Carson was instrumental in the defeat of Navajo and Apache groups.

Statehood. The period after the Civil War was marked by the Lincoln County War, which gave rise to the fame of Billy the Kid (William H. Bonney), and by the coming of the railroad in 1878, which reduced New Mexico's isolation and increased local prosperity. A protracted and unsuccessful struggle for statehood toward the end of the century kept New Mexico in a territorial status for an unduly long period—until congressional passage of an enabling act in 1910. New Mexico was admitted to the Union on Jan. 6, 1912, as the forty-seventh state. Nine days later William C. McDonald was inaugurated as first governor.

On Mar. 9, 1916, Francisco Pancho Villa, the Mexican revolutionary chieftain, attacked the border town of Columbus, and provoked the prompt arrival of a U.S. punitive expedition under Brig. Gen. John J. Pershing.

World War II training requirements and subsequent defense spending brought new industry and population to New Mexico and a corresponding increase in urbanization, particularly in Albuquerque. Production of the first atomic bomb at Los Alamos and its explosion at the Trinity Site brought the world into the atomic age. Ordnance work, military bases, and increasing tourism have been added to mineral production, ranching, and irrigated agriculture to become the economic bases of the modern era.

DONALD C. CUTTER

BIBLIOG.–W. A. Beck, *New Mexico: A History of Four Centuries* (1962); Federal Writers Project, *New Mexico: A Guide to the Colorful State* (ed. 1953); Erna Fergusson, *New Mexico* (ed. 1964); George Fitzpatrick, ed., *This Is New Mexico* (ed. 1962); E. B. Mann and F. E. Harvey, *New Mexico, Land of Enchantment* (1955).

NEW MEXICO, UNIVERSITY OF, a coeducational, state-controlled institution of higher learning at Albuquerque established in 1889. Instruction was first offered in 1892, in the colleges of arts and sciences. There are schools of engineering, education, fine arts, inter-American affairs, pharmacy, business administration, law, and nursing; divisions of government research and development; a bureau of business research; and an institute of meteoritics. The university offers the bachelor's degree, the master's degree in most departments, and the doctor's degree in selected fields. The university library contains special collections pertaining to southwestern United States and to Mexico and Spain.

NEW MEXICO STATE UNIVERSITY, a coeducational, land-grant, state-controlled institution of higher learning located at University Park. The school began in 1888 as Las Cruces College and became the New Mexico College of Agriculture and Mechanic Arts, its name until 1958. Divisions of the university include colleges of arts and sciences, business administration, economics, engineering, teacher education, and agriculture and home economics. The university offers a bachelor's degree in all departments and a master's degree in most.

NEW MILFORD, town, W Connecticut, Litchfield County, on the Housatonic River, 16 miles N of Danbury. Electrical equipment and food and paper products are manufactured here. New Milford was settled in 1707 and incorporated in 1712. (For population, see Connecticut map in Atlas.)

NEW MILFORD, borough, Bergen County, NE New Jersey; on the Hackensack River; 18 miles N of Jersey City. Incorporated in 1922, New Milford is primarily a residential center. (For population, see New Jersey map in Atlas.)

NEWNAN, city, NW Georgia, seat of Coweta County; about 35 miles SW of Atlanta. Newnan manufactures textiles and wood products and is also a livestock center in a rich agricultural area of diversified farming. It is one of the richest cities in the United States on a per capita basis. Newnan was founded in 1827 as Bullsboro. (For population, see Georgia map in Atlas.)

NEW NATIONS. Of the 122 members of the United Nations in 1967, less than half were independant, autonomous states a century earlier. The great majority of the new nations appeared after World War II, when the powers of Europe, voluntarily or involuntarily, surrendered sovereignty over the territories they had acquired in the era of imperialism.

In many cases, especially in Africa, the boundaries of the new nations were the result of competition among the imperialist powers and bore little relation to the ethnic structure of the area. Other countries, like India or Morocco, boasted cultural traditions as old as or older than the European powers that had exercised dominion over them.

Below are listed the nations that gained full independence after 1940, with their former name or status in parentheses and the date of their independence.

Algeria (French)........................1962
Barbados (British)........................1966
Botswana (Bechuanaland, British)...........1966
Burma (British from 1886)................1948

Burundi (part of Ruanda-Urundi, Belgian)...1962
Cambodia (French from 1863)..............1949
Cameroun (German colony of Kamerun occupied by British and French, 1916; British portion later joined the Federation of Nigeria)....................1960
Central African Republic (as Ubangi Shari, part of French Equatorial Africa)..................................1960
Ceylon (British from 1802)..................1948
Chad (part of French Equatorial Africa).....1960
Congo-Brazzaville (as Middle Congo, part of French Equatorial Africa)..............1960
Congo-Kinshasa (Belgian Congo)...........1960
Cyprus (British from 1914; formerly within Ottoman Empire)........................1961
Dahomey (French).........................1960
Gabon (part of French Equatorial Africa)....1960
Gambia (British)...........................1965
Ghana (Gold Coast, British).................1957
Guinea (French Guinea)....................1958
Guyana (British Guiana)....................1966
India (British from the eighteenth century)...1947
Indonesia (Dutch from the seventeenth century)................................1949
Israel (part of Palestine)....................1948
Ivory Coast (French).......................1960
Jamaica (British)..........................1962
Jordan (Transjordan, part of Palestine, British mandate from 1916; formerly within Ottoman Empire)................1946
Kenya (British)............................1963
Laos (French from 1893)....................1949
Lebanon (French mandate from 1920; formerly within Ottoman Empire).........1941
Lesotho (Basutoland, British)...............1966
Malagasy (Madagascar, French)............1960
Malawi (Nyasaland, British)...............1964
Malaysia (Malaya, North Borneo, and Sarawak, British)........................1963
Maldive Islands (British)...................1965
Mali (French Sudan).......................1960
Malta (British from 1814)..................1964
Mauritania (French).......................1960
Morocco (French and Spanish from 1912)....1956
Niger (French)............................1960
Nigeria (British)..........................1960
Pakistan (part of British India).............1947
Philippines (U.S. from 1898)...............1946
Rwanda (part of Ruanda-Urundi, Belgian)..1962
Senegal (French)..........................1960
Sierra Leone (British).....................1961
Somalia (British and Italian)...............1960
Sudan (Egyptian and British)...............1956
Syria (French mandate from 1920; formerly within Ottoman Empire).................1944
Tanzania (Tanganyika and Zanzibar, British)...........................1961–63
Togo (French and British from 1914; formerly German protectorate; British portion joined Ghana)...................1960
Trinidad and Tobago (British)..............1962
Uganda (British)..........................1962
Upper Volta (French)......................1960
Vietnam (French from 1862–93)............1954
Zambia (Northern Rhodesia, British)........1964

For detailed histories, see articles on individual countries.

NEW NETHERLAND, the name of the Dutch colony in America in the seventeenth century. The Dutch West India Company established its first permanent settlement in 1624 at Fort Orange (present-day Albany). A second settlement was established at the southern tip of Manhattan Island in 1625. The Dutch colony came into conflict with Swedish and English colonists, and, in 1664, after three years of warfare, the English captured New Netherland and renamed it New York.

NEW ORLEANS, city, Louisiana, on the Mississippi River, about 110 miles above its entry into the Gulf of Mexico; area 363.5 square miles, of which 164.1 are water; pop. (1960) 627,525. New Orleans is the fifteenth largest city in the United States with a metropolitan area population of more than one million. The city covers the entire Orleans parish (county). About 40 per cent of New Orleans is below sea level; the city is also below the flood stages of the Mississippi. The *Bonnet Carré* spillway, 20 miles above the city, and the levee system maintained by the U. S. Corps of Engineers protect New Orleans from the three and one half million gallons of water that flow past the city every second.

The Mississippi River has been the backbone of the economy of New Orleans from its founding in 1718. The port of New Orleans, owned by the state of Louisiana and operated by a commission of businessmen appointed by the governor, contains nearly 10 miles of docks and approximately 10 million square feet of facilities for the handling of cargo. On an average, 5,000 ships a year enter the port, bringing in cargo worth approximately $650 million and taking out cargo valued at more than $1.5 billion. In 1965 (U.S. Department of Commerce figures), 15.88 million tons of cargo passed through New Orleans; of this total, 11.87 million tons were exported. New Orleans ranks as the greatest port in the world in the exportation of grain. Twenty-five per cent of all U.S. grain exports—430 million bushels—was shipped from New Orleans in 1965. In the value of its foreign cargo, New Orleans is second only to New York among U.S. ports. Its principal exports, other than grain, include agricultural implements, heavy construction equipment, petroleum and petroleum products, edible oils, carbon black, and forest products. Through the port of New Orleans comes a great variety of imports, chief of which are coffee, bananas, sugar, various ores, bagging, and crude rubber.

Industry was a negligible part of the economic life of New Orleans prior to the 1920's, and although much progress was made between the two wars, it was only after World War II that the city's industrial boom really began. New Orleans' proximity to Louisiana's vast reserves of natural gas, oil, sulfur, and salt; the abundant availability of limeshell and sand; and the Mississippi's inexhaustible supply of water accounted for the tremendous industrial development in the New Orleans area. Between 1946 and 1964, industrial construction or expansion required an investment of $1.32 billion. Greatest development in the 1960's was in the petro-chemical industry, and in the establishment in 1961 of the Michoud Assembly Facility by the National Aeronautics and Space Administration for the construction of first-stage boosters in the Saturn space project.

History. New Orleans was established in 1718 by Jean-Baptiste LeMoyne, Sieur de Bienville, brother of Iberville, who settled Louisiana for France in 1699. From its earliest days, New Orleans existed under the threat of floods, epidemics, and hurricanes. Yellow fever was a regular visitant from late in the eighteenth century to 1905. Ten times, during a space of 110 years, New Orleans' yellow fever death toll exceeded 1,000 a year, while in 1853, the worst epidemic to strike an American city carried off nearly 8,000 people before it finally burned itself out. Only after 1927, when major control measures were taken by U.S. engineers, did New Orleans become safe from floods. Of the three nineteenth-century scourges, only hurricanes remain. Hurricane Betsy, which struck in September, 1965, was the most devastating in New Orleans' history, with total damage in Louisiana estimated at close to $1 billion.

The first revolution in America against a European monarch was launched in New Orleans in

VAN BUCHER—PHOTO RESEARCHERS

New Orleans is Louisiana's largest city and the United States' second seaport. This view (above), taken from the roof of the Monteleone Hotel in the Vieux Carré, includes the International Trade Mart (the skyscraper, center) and the distant Greater New Orleans Bridge, spanning the Mississippi River.

J. ALLAN CASH—RAPHO GUILLUMETTE

The roomy mansions and manicured grounds of the city's Garden District (right) reflect its ante-bellum origin as the favored residence of the wealthy. Originally the separate town of Lafayette, it is now part of "Uptown" New Orleans.

1768, when the Créoles expelled Spanish Governor Antonio de Ulloa. The revolution was crushed the following year, the leaders executed, and Spanish rule firmly established. The flag of Bourbon Spain flew over New Orleans until Nov. 30, 1803, when Louisiana was transferred to France, just 20 days before France transferred it to the United States. In order to secure commercial rights in New Orleans, Pres. Thomas Jefferson wished to buy the city from Napoleon Bonaparte. But the American negotiators in Paris, Robert R. Livingston and James Monroe, acquired for $15 million not only New Orleans but also the vast mid-continental wilderness of Louisiana.

In the War of 1812, New Orleans was the target of a British expedition which sailed from Jamaica late in 1814. After a series of engagements, leading up to the main British attack, General Andrew Jackson won a great victory on the plains of Chalmette, below the city. The Battle of New Orleans, fought on Jan. 8, 1815, cost the British commander, Gen. Sir Edward Pakenham, his life.

Following peace, New Orleans became a boom town. The coming of the steamboat on the Mississippi brought growth and wealth to the city which, in 1840, joined New York and Baltimore as the only cities in the United States with 100,000 population.

A severe blow to the Confederate States of America was the fall of New Orleans to the Union fleet of David G. Farragut in late April, 1862. Thus in the second year of the Civil War, the South's largest city was in Union hands, and New Orleans became the first major American city to be occupied by "enemy" troops. For 15 years, Union soldiers remained in New Orleans, and Reconstruction did not end for the city until 1877 when Pres. Rutherford B. Hayes ordered the Federal forces to depart, thus restoring full home rule to Louisiana.

Although the Civil War crushed the economy of New Orleans and undoubtedly delayed industrial development, the city continued a steady, if not spectacular, growth up to World War I.

Architecture. The original French city is known today as the *Vieux Carré* (old square), or the French Quarter. Because of two severe fires in 1788 and 1794 during the Spanish regime, there is only one authentic French building in the French Quarter. This is the old Ursuline Convent, completed in 1751 and reportedly the oldest building in the Mississippi Valley. Some of the old houses in the *Vieux Carré* were built by the Spaniards, but most of them were built after the American flag was raised in the *Place d'Armes*, now Jackson Square. This is not only the historic heart of old New Orleans but the center of one of the most architecturally picturesque areas in the United States. Facing Jackson Square are three historic structures: Cabildo (1795), seat of the Spanish government; St. Louis Cathedral (1850), on which site a church has stood since 1727; and the Presbytere (1795), designed as a residence for the clergy attached to the church. Flanking Jackson Square on each side are the Pontalba buildings, handsome block-long row houses of red brick whose balconies have beautiful iron rails and trimming. These were built in 1850 by the New Orleans-born Baroness de Pontalba. Wrought iron and cast iron balconies are a characteristic of the *Vieux Carré*'s old structures which are built flush with the sidewalk and have rear courtyards hidden from the street.

In contrast to the *Vieux Carré*, the Garden District features large Italianate mansions with Greek revival influences, set in spacious grounds filled with trees, flowers, and shrubs. Americans who made fortunes in ante-bellum New Orleans built their homes in the then suburban town of Lafayette, where large lots were readily available.

Education and Health. New Orleans has six universities: Tulane University, privately endowed; Loyola University, operated by Jesuits; Louisiana State in New Orleans, a branch of the state university in Baton Rouge; and three Negro institutions: Dillard University, privately endowed; Xavier University, operated by the Sisters of the Blessed Sacrament; and Southern University in New Orleans, a branch of Southern University. In addition there are two colleges: Newcomb College, women's division of Tulane; and St. Mary's Dominican College, operated for women by the Dominican Order of nuns. With medical schools operated by Tulane University and Louisiana State and a dental school operated by Loyola, New Orleans is an important center of medical education.

Culture. New Orleans was one of the first established homes of grand opera in the United States, and from the 1820's resident opera troupes, recruited in Paris, performed regularly until the Civil War interrupted the city's opera continuity. Through concerts by the New Orleans Philharmonic-Symphony Orchestra and the New Orleans Opera House Association and other subscription musical series, New Orleans audiences are offered about 50 musical events each season. New Orleans was also the birthplace of jazz and authentic New Orleans jazz is being preserved by many of the city's jazz bands. A Jazz Museum is maintained in the *Vieux Carré*. Isaac Delgado Museum of Art in City Park is the city's only art gallery. The Louisiana State Museum occupies the Cabildo, Presbytere, and part of one of the Pontalba Buildings. Memorial Hall of the Louisiana Historical Association exhibits Confederate relics and artifacts.

Mardi Gras. The highlight of any year for natives or tourists is *Mardi Gras*, the Shrove Tuesday culmination of the pre-Lenten festival of Carnival. Although Carnival balls were known to be held during the French and Spanish regimes in New Orleans, the first recorded street pageant on *Mardi Gras* was in 1837. Throughout the nineteenth century and into the early years of the twentieth century, not more than a dozen Carnival organizations (secret clubs) staged masked balls or street parades. After World War I, Carnival began to expand, but it was only after World War II that the number of Carnival *krewes* multiplied rapidly. As many as 60 Carnival balls—sometimes more—are given annually, generally between Twelfth Night (January 6, when Carnival officially opens) and *Mardi Gras*. Because *Mardi Gras*, the day before Ash Wednesday, is related to Easter, it comes early or late as Easter comes early or late. Accordingly, the Carnival season may last barely a month or it may exceed two months. Carnival is the backbone of the social season in New Orleans, and queens and courts of the older organizations are picked from the season's debutantes. No public identification of most of the kings of Carnival balls, or of members either, is made except in the case of Rex, King of Carnival. To be named Rex is the highest civic recognition that may be bestowed upon a New Orleanian. The oldest Carnival groups, still active today, are the Mistick Krewe of Comus (1857); Twelfth Night Revelers (1870); Rex (1872); Knights of Momus (1872); and the Krewe of Proteus (1882). Carnival is wholly unsubsidized; it is supported by dues paid by members of the various New Orleans Carnival organizations. It is a $6,000,000 home industry.

Two other major New Orleans attractions come early each year, and both have considerable tourist appeal. The first is the Mid-Winter Sports Association's carnival of sports (including tennis, yacht racing, track and field, and basketball) which culminates in the Sugar Bowl Football Classic on New Year's Day. The second is the Spring Fiesta, timed for the blooming of spring flowers in the patios of the *Vieux Carré* and the spacious gardens of the Garden District. For two weeks, some of the old homes, patios, and gardens are opened to visitors.

Cemeteries. Of great interest to visitors in New Orleans are the cemeteries, where most of the burial is above the ground in tombs and vaults. In the days before sub-surface drainage, it was virtually impossible to employ ground burial because the soil was so soggy. The custom of tomb burial continued long after there was a need for it. On All Saints Day, November 1, practically all the graves in the city are decorated with flowers.

The People. From its establishment, New Orleans has been a polyglot community. French, German, Acadian, Spanish, and Negro groups made up its population before the city became American; by the end of the nineteenth century, Italians, Slovenes, and many other national groups were represented in the population.

CHARLES L. DUFOUR

BIBLIOG.–Herbert Asbury, *The French Quarter* (1936); John Chase, *Frenchmen, Desire, Good, Children—and Other Streets of New Orleans* (1949); N. C. Curtis, *New Orleans, Its Old Houses, Shops and Public Buildings* (1933); A. E. Fossier, *New Orleans: The Glamour Period, 1800-1840* (1957); H. T. Kane, *Queen New Orleans* (1949); E. F. Niehaus, *The Irish in New Orleans, 1800-1860* (1965); Lyle Saxon, *Fabulous New Orleans* (1928); E. L. Tinker, *Créole City: Its Past and Its People* (1953).

NEW ORLEANS, BATTLE OF, a land battle of the War of 1812, fought on Jan. 8, 1815, near New Orleans, La., between American forces under Gen. Andrew Jackson and British forces under Gen. Sir Edward M. Pakenham. News of a secret expedition against Mobile and New Orleans was received by the Americans in October, 1814. Andrew Jackson began defense preparations in early December, and on December 14, a British fleet captured the U.S. fleet of gunboats. On December 22, a British force advanced up Bayou Bienvenu where it was attacked the next day by the schooner *Carolina* and by U.S. troops; but the approach of British reinforcements forced the Americans to fall back. The Americans constructed crude earthworks across the plain of Chalmette (south of the city). Jackson's troops were attacked by British forces under Pakenham on December 27, but could not be routed, although the *Carolina* was destroyed. Jackson's army of scarcely 5,000 militiamen was reinforced by about 2,000 Kentucky militia. Gen. David Morgan, with about 800 men, held the opposite side of the river. More troops arrived to raise the British forces to nearly 10,000, and part of them were sent to attack Morgan. On January 8, Pakenham ordered a direct frontal assault upon the American entrenchments manned by Kentucky and Tennessee militia, some armed only with squirrel rifles. When Pakenham's troops approached within 200 yards of the U.S. lines, the militia opened fire and the attacking force was shattered. Pakenham was killed, and British losses exceeded 2,000 men. On the American side there were 13 killed and 58 wounded. When the British forces withdrew, they learned that peace had been declared two weeks before, on Dec. 24 by the Treaty of Ghent.

NEW ORLEANS JAZZ, a polyphonic style of jazz that developed in New Orleans in the 1890's as an outgrowth and refinement of the traditional marches and dance tunes of Negro street bands. The classic New Orleans jazz band consisted of from five to seven pieces. These might include cornet, clarinet, valve trombone, string bass, banjo or guitar, tuba, drums, and pianoforte. Two of the earliest legendary figures in New Orleans jazz were Charles "Buddy" Bolden (1868–1931) and Joseph "King" Oliver (1885–1938), leader of the famous Olympia Band, and later of the Creole Jazz Band.

NEW PHILADELPHIA, city, E central Ohio, seat of Tuscarawas County; on the Tuscarawas River; 25 miles S of Canton. It is in a clay-producing and coal-mining area, and has metal and plastics industries. Clay products, electrical equipment, and industrial materials are also manufactured. The city was founded in 1804 and incorporated in 1833. (For population, see Ohio map in Atlas.)

NEW PLYMOUTH, borough, New Zealand, W North Island, capital of Taranaki County; on the Tasman Sea; 160 miles NNW of Wellington, with which it is connected by a railroad and a highway. A seaport, New Plymouth is a shipping center for dairy products. There are oil deposits nearby. (For population, see New Zealand map in Atlas.)

NEWPORT, CHRISTOPHER, 1565?–1617, English navigator. He served with Sir Francis Drake's expedition to Cádiz, 1587, and commanded an expedition in the West Indies, 1592. In 1606, in the employ of the Virginia Company, he sailed from London with three ships and a group of colonists (including Capt. John Smith); they founded Jamestown, Va., on May 13, 1607. In 1612 he became a navigator for the East India Company.

NEWPORT, municipal borough, S England, Hampshire, capital of the Isle of Wright; on the Medina River; 12 miles SW of Portsmouth. Located near the center of the island, Newport is connected by highways with other island towns and by small ships with the mainland. It is a resort town and a trade center for agricultural products. In 1648 it was the scene of the negotiations between Charles I and the Parliamentarians. (For population, see England map in Atlas.)

NEWPORT, county borough, SE Wales, Monmouthshire; on the Usk River, 3 miles above its junction with the Severn River estuary; 11 miles NE of Cardiff. Newport is the main railroad center for the coal-mining district of south Wales. Through its extensive port facilities are exported much of Great Britain's coal and iron and steel products. Manufactures include iron, steel, copper, aluminum, rubber, asbestos, and leather products; chemicals; and aircraft. Points of interest include a Norman cathedral dating in part from the twelfth century, and the ruins of a twelfth-century castle. In 1839 Newport was the scene of a Chartist riot. See CHARTISM. (For population, see England map in Atlas.)

NEWPORT, city, NE Arkansas, seat of Jackson County; on the White River, 85 miles NE of Little Rock. Newport is a trading center settled in 1873. Cotton and rice are raised in the vicinity. (For population, see Arkansas map in Atlas.)

NEWPORT, city, N central Kentucky, a seat of Campbell County; on the Ohio River at its confluence with the Licking River; 2 miles S of Cincinnati, of which it is a suburb. Main products are machinery, clothing, and concrete building products. Newport was laid out in 1791 and incorporated as a village in 1795. A military post was established in Newport in 1806 and moved to nearby Fort Thomas after the Ohio River flood in 1884. Newport was incorporated as a city in 1835. (For population, see Kentucky map in Atlas.)

NEWPORT, city and port of entry, SE Rhode Island, seat of Newport County; on the SW tip of Rhode Island at the entrance to Narragansett Bay, with a harbor on the bay and the Atlantic Ocean to the E and S; 25 miles SSE of Providence. Newport has shipyards, fisheries, and such manufactures as medical supplies, electrical equipment, rubber goods, precision instruments, dairy products, jewelry, and furniture; but is most important as a summer resort and naval center. The Newport Naval Base includes a naval station, the Naval War College, a naval underwater ordnance station, a naval hospital, and the Melville net and fuel depot. There is a Coast Guard Station on Castle Hill. The city is the site of Salve Regina College for Women.

Points of Interest. In the old section of Newport, contiguous to the harbor, are narrow, picturesque streets and many colonial mansions, public buildings, and churches. Center of the old town is Washington Square on which are located the old city hall (1761) and the old statehouse (1739). The synagogue on Touro Street is probably the oldest in the United States. Among the city's oldest churches are the Sabbatarian Meeting House or Seventh Day Baptist Church (1729); Trinity Church (1725), an Episcopal church which has a communion service and bell donated by Queen Anne; and Central Baptist Church (1733). The Redwood Library has an excellent collection dating from 1747.

History. Newport was founded in 1639 by William Coddington, John Clarke, and several other *émigrés* from Massachusetts who had left that colony because of their sympathy with the religious views of Anne Hutchinson. Some of the settlers became shipbuilders, and by 1675 Newport was trading with the other colonies, the West Indies, and Europe. A haven for religious refugees, the city welcomed Jewish and Quaker settlers in the 1650's, Seventh Day Baptists in the 1670's. In 1732 Benjamin Franklin's brother, James, established in Newport the first newspaper in the colony. The city reached a zenith of commercial power during 1740–75. During the Revolutionary War it suffered such reverses that after the war it soon was surpassed commercially by New York City. Newport was occupied by the British, 1776–79, and was the headquarters of French troops commanded by Comte Jean Baptiste de Rochambeau, 1780–81. It was incorporated as a city in 1784, reverted to the status of a town in 1787, and was again incorporated as a city in 1853. About 1830 Newport began to attract attention as a summer resort, and by 1890 it had become the summer mecca of the extremely wealthy—the site of unprecedentedly lavish entertaining in the palatial "cottages" of the Astors, Vanderbilts, and others. Although first World War I and then the Depression of 1929 brought an end to this luxurious way of living, Newport continued to be a popular vacation center, and in the 1960's was associated in the public mind with the annual Newport jazz and folk festivals which attracted visitors from all over the world. (For population, see Rhode Island map in Atlas.)

NEWPORT BEACH, city, S California, Orange County; on the peninsula between landlocked Newport Bay and the Pacific; 25 miles SE of Long Beach. Newport Beach, primarily a resort, has a yacht harbor as well as fisheries and boat yards. According to local legend, the bay was formerly used by smugglers as a hiding place. (For population, see California map in Atlas.)

NEWPORT NEWS, city, SE Virginia, at the head of Hampton Roads, one of the world's finest harbors; the tidewater terminus since 1882 of the Chesapeake and Ohio Railroad, 70 miles SE of Richmond. Situated at the south end of the peninsula between the James and York rivers, and on the James River estuary, it is an important port. Large dry docks and shipbuilding plants are part of the Hampton Roads port facilities. There are railroad shops in the city, as well as pulp and paper, machinery, and foundry-products industries, fisheries, and seafood-packaging plants. Transfer of goods between ships and railway provides employment for many residents. Newport News is a major center for the export of coal and tobacco. Langley Field and Fort Monroe are nearby. In nearby Hilton village is the Mariners Museum, established in 1930. Newport News is in an area once known as Kecoughtan, first settled in 1611. William and Thomas Newce patented land there in 1621, and Newport News remained a fishing village in an agricultural area until the railroad was completed in 1882. It was incorporated as a city in 1896. In 1958, the city was consolidated with Warwick County, increasing its area from 4 to 64 square miles. (For population, see Virginia map in Atlas.)

NEW PROVIDENCE, island and district, N central Bahama Islands; maximum E–W and N–S distances 21 and 7 miles respectively; 175 miles ESE of Miami; area 58 square miles. New Providence consists mainly of flat lowland, covered in part by swamps and shallow lakes. A mild equable climate and excellent beaches have enabled the island to develop into a major winter resort. The island's main resources include tomatoes, bananas, coconuts, citrus fruit, sisal, and fish. New Providence is the most populous island in the Bahamas and has a good transportation system. The port of Nassau is the principal city and resort center in the island, as well as the capital of the Bahama Islands. Settled by the British in the late seventeenth century, the island was frequently raided by the Spaniards who held it temporarily, 1782–83. (For population, see West Indies map in Atlas.)

NEW PROVIDENCE, borough, New Jersey, Union County, located on the Passaic River. Formerly a small farming community, New Providence has become a residential suburb of New York City. Settled in 1720, the town was originally named Turkey and was renamed in 1778. It was incorporated in 1899. The Murray Hill Bell Telephone research laboratories are located there. (For population, see New Jersey map in Atlas.)

NEW ROCHELLE, city, SE New York, Westchester County; on the W shore of Long Island Sound; 14 miles NNE of New York City, of which it is a residential suburb. New Rochelle is also an industrial center whose principal industries include printing and the manufacture of electrical machinery and surgical dressings. The harbor on Long Island Sound provides facilities for yachting and fishing. New Rochelle is the seat of Iona College and the College of New Rochelle. Points of interest include the Thomas Paine Memorial House and the Thomas Paine Cottage. New Rochelle, settled by Huguenots in 1688, was incorporated as a village in 1857 and became a city in 1899. (For population, see New York map in Atlas.)

NEWRY, urban district, S Northern Ireland, Down and Armagh counties; on the Newry Canal; 38 miles SSW of Belfast. Newry is a seaport, and produces farm implements, fish nets, rope, and linen textiles. It is the site of a sixteenth-century church, the oldest Protestant church in Ireland. (For population, see Ireland map in Atlas.)

NEW SALEM, restored village and state park in Menard County, central Illinois; on a bluff overlooking the Sangamon River; 2 miles S of Petersburg and 15 miles NW of Springfield. New Salem was the home of Abraham Lincoln from 1831 until he was admitted to the bar in Springfield in 1837. Settled in 1828, New Salem flourished for only eight or nine years, then declined and was abandoned in 1839 after a railroad was routed through Petersburg. In 1906 William Randolph Hearst purchased the land and transferred it in trust to the Old Salem Chautauqua Association; with his consent the area was deeded to the state in 1922, and in 1923 it was established as a state park.

NEW SCHOOL FOR SOCIAL RESEARCH, an accredited school for the continuing higher education of adults, located in New York City. Founded in 1919, the school is today divided into two divisions: the New School and the Graduate Faculty of Political and Social Science (est. 1934). The New School offers both credit and non-credit courses in the liberal arts, and the Graduate Faculty offers the master of arts and doctor of philosophy degrees.

NEW SIBERIAN ISLANDS, archipelago, U.S.S.R., Arctic Ocean between the Laptev and East Siberian seas, N of the Siberian coast between 133° and 158°E longitude; included in the Yakut Autonomous Socialist Republic of the R.S.F.S.R.; area 11,000 square miles. There are three main groups of islands: the De Longs in the northeast, the Lyakhovs in the south, and the New Siberians which include three large islands—Kotelny, Faddei, and Novaya Sibir. Siberian reindeer and wolves migrate each winter to the islands across the ice-covered straits, but only sea birds stay on the islands during the summer. The climate is severe, with an average July temperature of 38°F; annual precipitation is only 3 inches. The treeless islands are uninhabited except for the personnel of a Soviet weather station. Remnants of prehistoric mammoths were found preserved in deposits of ice in the Lyakhov group. The islands were first visited in 1712 by Merkuri Vagin, a Cossack. WILLIAM T. KOWITZ

NEW SMYRNA BEACH, city, NE Florida, Volusia County; 13 miles SSE of Daytona Beach. New Smyrna Beach, a former Indian village, is a resort and fishing center sheltered from the Atlantic Ocean by a barrier beach. It has railroad shops and citrus fruit-packing plants. Points of interest include the ruins of a Spanish mission, founded in 1696, and an old fort. Spanish land grants in 1803 established the present settlement. (For population, see Florida map in Atlas.)

NEW SOUTH WALES, state, SE Australia, bounded on the N by Queensland, on the E by the Pacific Ocean (Tasman Sea), on the S by Victoria, and on the W by South Australia. It was the first settled of the six Australian states, and remains the leading state in population, agriculture, mining, and manufacturing. The original colony of New South Wales embraced all British territory in Australia, and at one stage included all the continent save the unclaimed area now comprising Western Australia. Separate colonies were detached from New South Wales in the period 1825–59; its present area is 309,433 square miles, only 10.4 per cent of the total area of the Commonwealth of Australia; population 4,235,030 (1966). Sydney is the state capital. (See Australia map in Atlas, Vol. 20.)

Physical Features

Topography and Water Resources. The state can be divided into four major physical divisions: coastal valleys, eastern highlands, western slopes, and western plains. The coastal valleys are a discontinuous series of small alluvial plains and undulating lowlands, fronted by coastal lagoons, marshes, sandhills, and beaches, and separated from each other by ridges terminating in high, cliffed headlands. The

DIANE RAWSON—PHOTO RESEARCHERS

The Three Sisters is a noted rock formation in the Blue Mountains of New South Wales. The mountains, about 40 miles west of Sydney, are a popular resort.

eastern highlands rise sharply from the coast through a zone of broken ridges and gorges, to culminate in a series of tablelands at an elevation of 2,500 to 4,000 feet. Isolated ranges rise up to 2,000 feet above the general level of the tablelands. Westward, the highlands descend gradually through a wide zone of hills and intervening plains, known as the western slopes. These merge with the western plains, which encompass over half the area of the state. While broad expanses of featureless, level land extend around the main streams and their distributaries, there are also extensive areas of subdued "ranges," which become prominent features only in the Barrier and Grey ranges of the far west.

In the eastern highlands, the Snowy Mountains culminate in Mt. Kosciusko, Australia's highest point, with an elevation of 7,314 feet. In this area elevation combines with adequate rainfall and winter snow to provide one of the few major sites for hydroelectric power in Australia. A vast project known as the Snowy Mountains Scheme was under construction in the 1960's. Great quantities of water are stored and diverted through long tunnels to the Murray and Murrumbidgee rivers. Besides providing important new sources of power, the scheme brings water for irrigation to an expanding agricultural area. Elsewhere the state's water resources are slight, and large reservoirs have been built on the upper reaches of many streams flowing westward into the Murray-Darling system to ensure a regulated flow of water to serve towns, irrigation areas, and the needs of livestock.

The climate changes from humid along the coast to arid in the far interior. Average annual rainfall decreases westward from approximately 40-60 inches on the coast to 30 inches on the tablelands, 20 inches on the western slopes, 10 inches on the plains, and under 7 inches in the northwest. The effect of rainfall is reduced by its unreliability, by the heavy loss from direct run-off, and by high evaporation, particularly in the interior. The northern parts of the stage have a summer rainfall maximum, while in the southernmost regions there is a slight winter maximum. Most of the state experiences warm to hot summers and mild winters. In January normal daily maximum temperatures are 80° to 85° F in the east and 90° to 95° F in the west, and the normal daily maximum in July is near 60° F over all the state, except the highlands, where maximum readings of 50° to 55° F are normal. In all areas light frosts are experienced in the winter months, but the cooler tablelands have severe frosts, with a frost-free period of 150 days or less. Regular winter snow cover is found only on the Snowy Mountains and adjacent ranges.

Social Features

Population. The New South Wales population represents 38 per cent of the Australian total. The population is heavily concentrated in three cities on the central coast: Sydney, Newcastle, and Wollongong. With almost 70 per cent of its population in these three cities, New South Wales exemplifies the Australian pattern of big-city concentration of population. The state's population grew 40 per cent, 1948–64, assisted by a large number of European immigrants. Virtually all this increase was absorbed by the three main cities.

Religion and Education. The main religious groups are Anglican (44 per cent of the population), Roman Catholic (29 per cent), Presbyterian, and Methodist. The education system is state-controlled, but there are many private schools, mainly Roman Catholic. Of the five state-supported but autonomous universities, three are in Sydney. These are the universities of Sydney, New South Wales, and Macquarie (opened in 1967). There are smaller universities at Newcastle and Armidale (University of New England).

Economic Features

Agriculture. New South Wales is the leading state in rural production, accounting for a third of the net value of Australia's farm production. Sheep are widespread except in the wet coastal areas and the rugged eastern slopes. The highest densities are found in the wheat-sheep belt of the lower western slopes, where merino and crossbreed flocks are a vital sector in the mixed farming economy, which is placing increased emphasis on rotational fodder crops and pastures alternating with wheat crops. The tablelands have specialized in fine-wool merino sheep. Sheep are fewer here, but have been increasing rapidly as new pastures, fertilized from aircraft, have become available. The dry western plains remain the domain of the large pastoral "runs," leased from the crown, each covering many thousands of acres and very lightly stocked with merino sheep.

Dairy cattle are concentrated in the humid coastal valleys. The dairy industry has declined in the number of farms and in production, except in

Sydney's towering skyscrapers bear scant witness to the city's origin in 1788 as a penal colony.

JOZEF VISSEL—RAPHO GUILLUMETTE

the area supplying fresh milk to the main urban markets. The raising of beef cattle, formerly extensive in the hillier country, has replaced dairying in many northern coastal areas.

Pastoral activities still dominate, and account for over half the net value of rural production. Only four per cent of the state is under crops, though this area could be enlarged appreciably, particularly on the tablelands and western slopes. Wheat, the largest crop, is concentrated in areas receiving approximately 20 inches of rainfall annually, and in areas of red-brown earths and black earths. Other important crops include barley, oats, sorghum, maize (corn), and sugar cane, as well as a variety of fruits and vegetables. The irrigated areas of the tableland, lower western slopes, and adjacent plains give heavy yields of rice, grapes, citrus, pome and stone fruits, lucerne (alfalfa), and pastures. There was a remarkable expansion in the acreage of irrigated cotton after 1960. Over 1,000,000 acres of land are irrigated, half of this being irrigated pasture.

Forestry and fishing are minor activities. Eucalyptus forests near the coast supply the state's hardwood requirements. However, a high, though decreasing, proportion of softwood requirements is imported.

Mining. The state is rich in minerals, and accounts for nearly half the net value of mining production in Australia. Annual coal production sometimes exceeds 20,000,000 tons, fulfilling the needs of heavy industry, electricity-generation, and a growing volume of exports to Japan. Though many traditional markets for coal have disappeared, production has been increasing at a rapid pace to meet new demands. The rich lead-zinc-silver field of Broken Hill continues to create new production records, even though the ore bodies have been worked continuously since 1883. Other important minerals, such as gold, copper, and tin, have declined severely in output, but recent years have seen a rapid growth in beach-sands mining, which produces most of the world's rutile and zircon.

Manufacturing. With over a third of Australia's manufacturing employment, New South Wales is the leading industrial state. Heavy industry is concentrated at Newcastle and Wollongong-Port Kembla, which together produce over 5,000,000 tons of steel annually and also support a wide range of other metal-processing, engineering, manufacturing, and shipbuilding industries. Nevertheless, the state's manufacturing is dominated by Sydney, which makes mainly consumer goods and durables.

The Sydney Harbour Bridge (1932), spanning Australia's busiest port, connects city and northern suburbs.
EWING GALLOWAY

History

Penal Settlement, 1788–1823. New South Wales was first settled as a convict colony or prison farm for offenders sentenced to transportation. The American Revolution had forced the British government to seek elsewhere for a place of exile, and Botany Bay was selected on the evidence provided by the reports of the explorations of Capt. James Cook in 1770. The first fleet arrived in 1788, bringing a party of over 1,000 convicts and marines under the command of Capt. Arthur Phillip. Phillip rejected Botany Bay as unsuitable for settlement. On Jan. 26, 1788, he established the settlement at Sydney Cove, an inlet of Port Jackson, only six miles directly north of Botany Bay. The early colonists experienced difficulties in an unfamiliar environment, and starvation was barely averted in the first few years. Stability was further shaken by indiscipline, excessive rum-drinking, and disputes between the officers of the N.S.W. Corps and governors, particularly Governor Bligh, culminating in the Rum rebellion. Exploration and settlement of the interior were hindered by the sandstone ridges and cliffs encircling the settlement and by the disapproval of the British government, which regarded the colony primarily as a prison. However, by the end of this period free settlement was gaining momentum, aided by the appearance of wool as an export staple based on newly discovered pastoral areas on the tablelands and in the Hunter Valley.

Pastoralism and Self-Government. Official recognition that New South Wales was no longer solely a penal settlement came in 1823 with an act allowing a small nominated legislative council (with only advisory powers). Autocratic rule was eroded by the increasing numbers and wealth of free settlers and emancipists. The powers of the legislative council were progressively widened and its composition increasingly included elected members. Transportation of convicts from Britain was ended in 1841. This period saw the growing dominance of the squatter-pastoralists and resulting controversy over the leasing and alienation of crown lands. Pastoral occupancy had advanced rapidly in the interior, far outstripping official settlement, and the squatters fought for recognition of their land claims on the most favorable terms. The dominance of the squatter aristocracy was short-lived as the 1855 Constitution Act, which granted full responsible government with a bicameral legislature, also provided a broad franchise soon widened to universal adult male suffrage.

Colonial Democracy, 1855–1901. Though New South Wales was not so profoundly influenced by the gold rushes as was Victoria, the influx of population, the appearance of a vociferous landless group, and the growth of towns had a major impact upon politics and contributed to the introduction of land policies aimed at closer settlement. The Robertson Land Acts of 1861 allowed bona fide settlers to select land blocks of up to 320 acres from crown land, including leasehold land held by squatters. This led to conflict between selector and squatter. While much genuine closer settlement did occur, the squatters managed to retain most of their lands, mainly in the areas away from the coast. The comparative failure of closer settlement encouraged greater urban concentration of population, and the accompanying growth of trade unionism and radicalism. Sir Henry Parkes, the dominant political figure from 1872 to 1891, introduced free trade, established the principle of secular education, and strongly advocated federation of the six colonies. In addition, the squatters' lands were whittled away by land taxation and other measures aimed at closer settlement. The

1890's were a period of great ferment, started by severe drought and economic depression, leading to a series of major strikes and to increasing labor participation in politics. The newly created Labour Party initiated advanced legislation on income tax, land reform, old age pensions, and industrial arbitration.

Federation and Thereafter. After 1901 the inauguration of federal government and the ever-increasing powers of the central government, particularly in financial matters, steadily reduced the responsibilities of the state parliament. The early post-Federation period saw many state initiatives, particularly in extending the franchise to women (1902) and in establishing free public education (1906). Major reforms have become less frequent even though New South Wales has continued to, pioneer much social legislation in Australia, being the first state to introduce the 40-hour work week (1947) and equal pay for women (1959). See AUSTRALIA. JOHN H. HOLMES

NEW SOUTH WALES, UNIVERSITY OF, an institution of higher learning located in Kensington, New South Wales, Australia. It was founded in 1949 as the New South Wales University of Technology, and its name was changed in 1958 with the establishment of faculties of arts and medicine. The bachelor's degree is awarded in applied science, architecture, arts, commerce, engineering, medicine, and science. Other degrees awarded are D.Sc., Ph.D., and M.Tech. The university has branches at Newcastle, Wollongong, and Broken Hill.

NEWSPAPER, a publication devoted mainly to news, issued regularly under a continuous title, commonly printed on a cheap grade of paper and unbound. The title *newspaper* was seldom used before the eighteenth century, and did not supersede *gazette* and *journal* until the nineteenth century.

Beginnings. Probably the first newspaper was *Ti Chau*, founded about the eighth century as the official gazette of the Chinese government. Printed from carved wood blocks, it continued publication for some 1,100 years. Forerunners of the European newspaper include written newsletters (fifth century B.C. to eighteenth century A.D.); posted bulletins such as the *Acta diurna*, published under Julius Caesar's authorization in the Forum as early as 60 B.C.; town criers and bellmen; and ballads, broadsides, and pamphlets. Occasional news pamphlets, printed from movable types and dealing with outstanding political events, wars, catastrophes, and wonders, began to appear in various European cities during the sixteenth century. Apparently the first regularly issued news pamphlets (printed under continuous titles) appeared early in the seventeenth century in Augsburg, Frankfurt, Venice, Strasbourg, and other cities.

Early English Newspapers. The English example was the *Corante, or Weekely Newes* (London, 1621), published by N. B. (Nathaniel Butter or Nicholas Bourne) and consisting of accounts of early engagements in the Thirty Years' War as translated from Dutch or German news pamphlets. English pamphlet or "newsbook" journalism continued for about 45 years, except for 1632–38 when the Star Chamber, on complaint of the Spanish ambassador, forbade "corantos," "avisos," or "relations," as newsbooks were popularly known. During the Long Parliament (1640–60) there were many "diurnals" presenting the parliamentary side, and a little later "mercuries" on the Royalist side. Under the Commonwealth (1649–60) newsbooks were suppressed at first, but Oliver Cromwell eventually licensed two weeklies which became (in effect) a semiweekly official gazette. Licensing was progressively relaxed after the Restoration, 1660, and abandoned in 1695. The pamphlet form at length gave way to the folio sheet, with the *Oxford Gazette* (later *London Gazette*) being first in 1665. In the eighteenth century, English papers were subject to severe laws of seditious libel until the Fox Libel Act of 1792, and they were heavily taxed until the middle of the next century. Yet they flourished in numbers, variety of form and content, and influence. The first English daily was the London *Daily Courant*, founded in 1702 by Elizabeth Mallett.

U.S. Newspapers

Colonial. Although occasional newssheets appeared earlier in Mexico and in Boston, the date 1690 rightly marks the beginning of American journalism. On September 25 of that year, in Boston, *Publick Occurrences Both Foreign and Domestick*, the first American newspaper designed for regular publication, made its appearance under the aegis of Benjamin Harris; unfortunately Harris had failed to obtain the license that the Massachusetts Charter required, and his paper was suspended by the government after one issue. The first continuously published American paper was the Boston *News-Letter*, founded in 1704 by John Campbell. The first American paper outside Boston was the *American Weekly Mercury*, founded in 1719 by Andrew Bradford, whose father, William, began the New York *Gazette* (1725), that city's first newspaper. By April, 1775, at least 37 papers were being published in colonies from Portsmouth, N.H., to Savannah, Ga.

The First American Daily was Benjamin Towne's *Pennsylvania Evening Post*, which advanced from triweekly to daily publication in 1783, but soon went out of business. The first successful daily in the United States was Dunlap and Claypool's *Pennsylvania Packet and Daily Advertiser*, 1784. Under the stimulus of advertising (10 of 16 columns in the first issue of Dunlap and Claypool's paper were devoted to it), dailies grew large and prosperous in the next half century, becoming commercial and partisan journals for the middle and upper classes. Their price to the reader was upward of $10 a year (more than an average man's weekly wage in that period). It was something of a newspaper revolution, therefore, when in 1833 Benjamin H. Day founded the New York *Sun* to sell for one penny. The elder James Gordon Bennett (1795–1872) began the New York *Herald* in 1835, consolidating and becoming the leader of this penny revolution, which depended upon technological improvements of presses and papermaking, and which achieved large circulations by emphasis on sensation and human interest. Horace Greeley's New York *Tribune* (founded 1841) raised the ethics of the cheap paper and exploited reforms; Whitelaw Reid took over the paper in 1873. The *Herald* and the *Tribune* were merged in 1924. The *Sun*, purchased in 1868 by Charles A. Dana and friends, became notable for its freshness, good writing, and emphasis on human-interest news stories.

In 1883 Joseph Pulitzer, already successful with his St. Louis *Post-Dispatch* (founded 1878), bought the New York *World* and by "crusading," variety, improved format, and a Sunday edition won a large readership and influenced all U.S. daily journalism. William Randolph Hearst, heir to a great mining fortune, who had been experimenting with sensationalism in the San Francisco *Examiner*, bought the New York *Journal* in 1895 and engaged in a circulation war with the *World* that made "yellow journalism" and "comic strip" household expressions. It has been said that the Spanish-American War came about largely as a result of the Hearst-Pulitzer rivalry—each vying with the other in playing up, and even inventing, sensational events. In contrast, at about the same time (in 1896) Adolph S. Ochs took over the failing *New York Times* (founded 1851 by Henry J. Raymond) and developed it into one of the greatest and most successful of papers by following the slogan "All the News That's Fit to Print."

Chains. Earlier, in the 1880's, E. W. Scripps began developing the first modern "chain" of newspapers, which included more than 20 papers by 1931; it survived past mid-twentieth century as the Scripps-[Roy] Howard chain. Taking his cue from Scripps, and ignoring the "fit to print" part of the *New York Times'* slogan, Hearst built one of the most extensive daily newspaper chains in the United States.

After World War I the New York *Daily News* initiated a period of sensational tabloid journalism; but the tabloids eventually outgrew "gutter journalism" and took their place as a legitimate part of the press, distinguished by small page size, condensation, and copious illustration.

Western Journalism began with the Pittsburgh *Gazette* (1786) and the *Kentucky Gazette* (Lexington, 1787). Joseph Charless' *Missouri Gazette* (St. Louis, 1808) was the first paper west of the Mississippi. The first Chicago paper was John Calhoun's *Weekly Democrat* (1833), which became a daily in 1840 but was absorbed in 1861 by the Chicago *Tribune*. Founded in 1847, the *Tribune* was brought to the front in 1855 when it was purchased by Joseph Medill, Dr. Charles H. Ray, and others. The first California paper, the *Californian*, was founded at Monterey and later moved to San Francisco where it was absorbed by the *Alta California*, that city's first daily. Best known of southern papers was the New Orleans *Picayune*, founded in 1836 by George W. Kendall and Francis Lumsden.

Coverage by U.S. newspaper and magazine (and later by radio and television) correspondents was vastly expanded during World Wars I and II and after. Characteristic of the modern period (from about the time of the Mexican War, 1846–48) have been such technological developments as those in communication (wireless, teletype, telephoto), presses (speed devices, color, offset), and machine composition (multiple magazines, teletypsetting, photosetting). The camera came to be recognized as indispensable in reporting, and the amount of space devoted to illustration continued to increase. Improved reporting and editing reflected the rise in the educational level of editorial workers, growth of the professional spirit, the use of unbiased interpretation as a reporting technique, and other factors. Professionalism was fostered by the growth and improvement of schools of journalism, by the organization of professional societies, and as a result of internal and external criticism of newspaper ethics. The expansion of news services to meet the widening interests of readers resulted in more comprehensive coverage of world events, facilitated by faster means of communication.

Unionization of the mechanical forces of newspapers began late in the eighteenth century. A national union was formed in 1827, but the National (later International) Typographical Union was not organized until 1852. The American Newspaper Guild, designed for editorial and clerical workers, was formed in 1933.

Newspapers Today. In 1965 there were 1,763 daily English-language newspapers of general circulation in the United States, with a total circulation of more than 60 million. There were over 8,000 weeklies, semiweeklies, and triweeklies. As compared with 50 years before, there were about 30 per cent fewer dailies and 40 per cent fewer weeklies. The consolidations and suspensions of the intervening years were caused largely by the rise in costs of labor and materials operating to eliminate economically wasteful competition. Circulation during the same period, however, increased out of proportion to population. Newspaper price per copy doubled over the years, with many newspapers deriving half their revenue from circulation. A notable development throughout the 1960's was the continued growth of both daily and weekly papers in suburban areas and "exurban" population centers, and of free-distribution weeklies in many of the large cities. The introduction of automated processes into newspaper production became a major point of conflict between management and employees. In 1965 more than 40 U.S. newspapers were reportedly using computers in their printing operations. Labor's demand for job security in the face of automation led to long and costly strikes and the death of several major newspapers. In 1966 the New York *Herald Tribune* discontinued publication as an indirect result of a strike against New York City papers in 1965.

World Newspaper Developments

Great Britain. *The* [London] *Times*, founded in 1785 by John Walter, was continued, 1803–47, by his son and namesake. Under the editorship (1817–41) of Thomas Barnes it became known as "The Thunderer." John Thadeus Delane was editor during 1841–77. C. P. Scott was editor of the Manchester *Guardian*, most famous of English provincial dailies, 1872–1929. From his founding of the *Daily*

On the modern newspaper, taping phones are used to transcribe facts reported by "leg men" on the scene. The final story is then written by these rewrite men.
THE NEW YORK TIMES

On large metropolitan papers, the cable desk is staffed by experienced editors who assemble and evaluate international wire reports and shape the story.
THE NEW YORK TIMES

THE NEW YORK TIMES

Production begins when final copy is sent from the news room to the composing room. Mechanical typesetting machines set articles into columns of metal type.

Mail in 1896 to his death in 1922, Alfred C. W. Harmsworth, Viscount Northcliffe, was the most dynamic figure in English journalism. He bought *The Times* in 1908, and it was sold to J. J. Astor and others after his death. The *Daily Mail* became the world leader in circulation under Northcliffe but was outdistanced in the late 1930's by the *Daily Express* and the *Daily Herald*. In 1965 the tabloid *Daily Mirror* had the largest daily circulation of any English-language newspaper—about 5 million. After the 1920's the number of British dailies declined about one half while total circulation doubled; the number of provincial weeklies dropped by one fourth. By 1965 there were 130 daily newspapers of general circulation in the United Kingdom, with an aggregate circulation of about 54 million.

Australia and Canada have many prosperous and growing newspapers. The Melbourne *Sun News-Pictorial*, with more than 600,000 circulation, is the largest Australian daily paper. The *Toronto Daily Star*, with 337,000, is the largest Canadian newspaper.

France. The first newspaper in Paris was the *Gazette* (later the *Gazette de France*), which was founded in 1631 by Théophraste Renaudot and continued for more than 200 years. *Mercure de France*, begun in 1672 as *Mercure Galant* by Donneau de Vizé, continued to 1853. Many papers were started after the Revolution, but Napoleon I imposed a rigid censorship. After mid-eighteenth century, French newspapers were especially numerous; and before World War I some 1,400 were being issued in Paris alone—virtually all of them organs of parties, cliques, and factions, and supported by subsidies; 60 were political dailies. Before World War II the top circulations were held by *Paris-Soir* (2 million) and *Le Petit Parisien* (1 million). *Journal des débats*, founded during the Revolution, was the oldest. During the German occupation many papers were published "underground." After the Liberation, many new dailies came into being in Paris; by 1965 only 14 were left, of which *France-Soir*, notably nonpartisan and prone to sensational display, had the largest circulation—about one million. There were more provincial dailies than ever before—about 98 in 1965.

Germany. Journalism developed early in Germany and remained prolific. There were about 30 dailies before 1700. Leading papers were not concentrated in the capital as in England and France, although most of the modern big general-circulation papers (*Massenpresse*) such as the Ullstein family's *Morgenpost* and Alfred Hugenberg's *Lokal Anzeiger*, were in Berlin. Yet before 1933 there were about 3,300 dailies for a population of 62 million. It was, however, mainly a party or factional press (*Gruppenpresse*); it was for this reason that Adolf Hitler early in his career gave close attention to newspapers as propaganda vehicles. Chief Nazi organs were the *Völkischer Beobachter* and *Der Angriff;* many of the older papers were suspended. Under the Allied occupation from 1945 newspapers were licensed, and those under Soviet control were precensored. By the mid-1960's West German newspapers were flourishing, but only one enjoyed a large circulation—*Bild-Zeitung* (2 million), of Hamburg.

Russia. Journalism began in Russia in 1703, but never flourished. In Moscow *Pravda* and *Izvestia* remained the chief Soviet journals, both under the close supervision of government. Their circulation was said to be quite large.

Latin America. Newspapers in most Latin American countries have enjoyed a considerable degree of freedom from government control, but *La Prensa*, of Buenos Aires, founded in 1869 and long the foremost South American newspaper, was suppressed in 1951 by the Juan Perón government. It resumed publication in 1956, and once again achieved the largest circulation of any Spanish-language daily—about 300,000.

Asia. China, the country that saw the beginnings of papermaking, printing, and the newspaper, has been since about 1900 a land of many small journals. In 1916 up to 50 dailies were published at one time in Peking. The more widespread use of a simplified alphabet by some papers benefited Chinese journalism. At mid-century Shanghai was the chief newspaper center, with *Shun Pao* (founded 1872) the oldest paper. Elsewhere, most dailies were party organs. Under communism all journalism was government controlled. In Peking, *Jen Min Jih Pao* (People's Daily), with a circulation of one million, is the leading paper.

In Japan occasional newssheets were circulated from the late seventeenth century, but the first regular newspapers were begun in 1861, and with the Meiji Restoration of 1868 came a flood of newspapers. By 1965 about 121 Japanese dailies had a total circulation of nearly 57 million. In Tokyo the largest circulations were those of the *Asahi Shimbun* (the world's largest circulation), *Yomiuri*, and *Mainichi*, each with an aggregate morning-evening figure ranging from 5 to 8 million; circulations of the Osaka editions of these papers also ran into the millions.

In 1780 James A. Hicky began the first newspaper to be published in India—a weekly called *Hicky's Bengal Gazette*, which was discontinued by the English authorities two years later. William Duane, later a famous U.S. editor, was driven from India after publishing the *Indian World* in 1791. Richard Johnston's *Madras Courier* at length became the "official" paper. The first vernacular paper was *Samachar Darpan* (1821), a missionary venture at Serampore. The first Indian-owned paper was Ram Mohan Roy's Bengal *Herald;* the first Hindi paper was *Udant Martand* (1826). Despite the low literacy of the population, repressive measures by the British government, and lack of modern equipment, some 240 vernacular papers were being published by 1880. Circulations never became large, however. Papers of national circulation are nearly all published in Calcutta, Bombay, Madras, and New Delhi. English-language papers are also published in the large cities. FRANK LUTHER MOTT

Organization and Operation of U.S. Newspapers

Newspapers in the United States range from the country weekly, written, set, and printed in a single small room on the village main street, to the large metropolitan daily, whose highly specialized working force of several thousand is spread over the earth. Hence, the many papers vary greatly in organization and operating procedure. Even among newspapers similar in kind and size there is no standard plan of organization. Thus, the staff of a small-town weekly may consist of one man who collects and writes local news items, assembles advertising, sets type, makes up the pages in the print shop behind a partition, runs off the papers on a simple flatbed press, puts on the addresses, carts the issue to the post office, largely for rural-route circulation—and finally collects the profits, if any, since he owns the paper. As more readers are served in a larger community and the busy owner-editor engages in civic affairs, these varied duties might be distributed among several assistants.

As organization varies, so position, titles, and duties differ. On a large paper the title of publisher may be assumed by the owner who is in full charge, makes major decisions, and establishes policy. But that title may also be given to the local representative of the chief of a chain of newspapers, acting under an over-all nationwide management; such a "publisher" may merely apply policy directives laid down at the national headquarters of the chain. The editor of the editorial page may be a writing editor actively engaged in phrasing the newspaper's daily expression of its views, or he may be an editor who directs a staff of editorial writers but himself seldom writes for publication. Under the owner there may be a single executive editor who coordinates news and editorial page operations; or the chiefs of news and editorial page staffs may report separately to the owner. Sometimes "the business side" (circulation, advertising, purchasing and bookkeeping, and usually the newspaper's physical production) is kept scrupulously apart from editorial and news departments, and this separation promotes news and editorial vigor and independence. But on many papers, large and small, the connection between the business office and news and editorial departments is quite close, so that the news and editorial columns tend to be responsive to business-office considerations—so much so that sometimes related news and advertising will appear in suspiciously close proximity.

Newspaper organization is geared necessarily to the conception of the paper's mission held by those controlling it. One paper maintains a sizable, specialized Washington bureau; another will have no Washington correspondent, relying instead on news reported by one or more news services such as the Associated Press, United Press International, the New York Times News Service, or some similar facility. Likewise, some papers keep large staffs to handle book reviews; theater, art, and music news and criticism; travel, food, fashion, and home-equipment copy; and other special material. Other papers rely on the feature services of the co-operative news organizations and the syndicates. See NEWS SERVICE.

A newspaper may print many syndicated columns of opinion or feature writers which it and other newspapers purchase for simultaneous publication throughout the country; or it may print no syndicated columns. On most larger papers one staff member (or more) will spend his time processing the 30 or more daily comic-and-adventure strips and panels; by contrast the *New York Times* prints no comics at all. Some papers regard a strong editorial cartoonist, able to comment pictorially on local, state, national, and world situations, as a vital member of the staff. For 45 years (1913–58) the St. Louis *Post-Dispatch* had such a cartoonist in the famous Daniel R. Fitzpatrick. Many other papers use no cartoons at all, or print only those obtainable from syndicates. In the 1960's Herbert Block (Herblock) of the Washington *Post* remained pre-eminent among nationally syndicated cartoonists.

THE NEW YORK TIMES

Makeup men, following layouts prepared by newsroom editors, assemble columns of solid type into final page form, along with headlines and illustrations.

As these extensive variations in intent, service, and procedure indicate, no one newspaper typifies U.S. journalism. Yet it is possible to describe an imaginary newspaper whose internal organization would be recognized as not basically inaccurate by a large number of U.S. newspapermen.

A "Typical" Newspaper

Top Echelon. Assuming local ownership, it would in all likelihood have a board of directors, probably consisting of some of the paper's own executives. The chief owner may well serve as company president and also as the guiding force in both editorial and business matters. Under him an executive editor supervises the news and editorial departments, while a business or production manager directs departments that bring in the paper's revenue through circulation and advertising and handles its daily commercial and mechanical operations. Mechanical activities (photoengraving, typesetting, press work) may be under a subexecutive or in a third "side" of the newspaper organization.

Departments. Under the executive editor, a managing editor ("M.E." in newspaper parlance) directs news gathering, writing, editing, and processing. He is assisted by a city editor responsible for the local and area news; a telegraph editor who handles the news from over the nation and around the world (there may also be a foreign news editor); a sports editor; a financial news editor; a picture editor who makes selections among the hundreds of photographs that come in every day by camera negative, by mail, or by wirephoto; and a society editor who keeps abreast of locally important engagements, weddings, parties, trips, club meetings, and the like.

A feature editor is in charge of a page (or a section of several pages) devoted to articles and features of special interest to women, and including a "children's corner." Other editors handle such specialties as political, church, realty, garden, motion picture, theater, art, literary, music, and radio and television news. An "outstate" editor supervises a special edition emphasizing news from small towns in the outlying territory and agricultural news.

The City Editor and His Staff. Of the subordinate editors, the city editor is most important, since a newspaper's primary function is to report the news of its immediate community. His local or city staff is

THE NEW YORK TIMES

Type impressions of page forms are made on paperboard mats from which metal plates are cast. Each curved plate is then locked on the press in printing position.

organized into groups of reporters who handle "runs," are on "general assignments," or who do "rewrite." The "run" men are those assigned to established news "runs" or "beats"—the police department, hospitals, city, state and federal courts, municipal and other governmental offices, school board, museums, transportation facilities, civic, labor and religious headquarters, and the larger suburbs. The paper's correspondent at the state capital usually operates under the city editor, and is essentially a member of the local news staff permanently assigned to the capital and living there. Most reporters stay on their runs for long periods, since they develop news contacts that are valuable to them in obtaining news exclusively for their newspapers. News photographers are at the service of the city editor, although they may take their assignments from the head of the photographic department. Staff artists also work closely with the news department in preparing layouts of pictures and other illustrations, touching up photographs, and drawing original sketches and maps as the news may require. In addition to the daily picture editor there may be another picture editor with a staff who produce a Sunday section.

How a Story is Handled. A "story" is a news event written as a newspaper narrative. Not all events can be printed in the papers, of course. One that would appear might be a large fire started by an arsonist and causing injuries to many victims. Producing a story about this fire would involve reporters on the police, fire, and hospital runs, as well as general assignment reporters and staff photographers dispatched to the scene by the city editor. Since time is usually at a premium (particularly on an afternoon newspaper), the reporters telephone the facts they gather to the city editor, who assesses the relative importance of the news and refers the reporters to a rewrite man who will put the relevant facts into an organized, accurate, readable news account. Thus, the rewrite man is the reporter who usually does the writing, as distinguished from the "leg man" who gathers the facts outside the office. On some papers the same person may act in both capacities, gathering the facts and then coming in to the office to write the story. From the city desk the news story goes—in short "takes" of a paragraph at a time if necessary—to the copy desk where it is processed for the composing room by a copy editor or copyreader, who also prepares a headline and accompanying subheads. On a "developing story" (with additional details becoming available over a period of time) changes may be required; these are processed much as is the original story, and appear in later editions of the paper. When possible the same staff members stay on a story to facilitate rapid and accurate handling through newsroom channels.

In the composing room—where news copy is composed (set in type) by compositors at mechanical (keyboard) typesetting machines—several compositors may work simultaneously on the takes in order to speed the story into page forms in time to meet an edition deadline. Meanwhile, the city editor, the telegraph editor, and any special news editors needed, confer with the managing editor on the relative merits of the news stories they have handled. The editor in charge decides which are to be placed in the major positions on the front page and other leading news pages. Then a dummy page showing the respective placings of the stories and their headlines is prepared by the makeup editor for use by a liaison editor, who directs the actual assembly of the type in the pages by the makeup men in the composing room.

After the many hundreds of solid lines of type have been assembled in the page forms, along with headlines, illustrations, and advertisements, each page is rolled away (on a table fitted with rollers) at a scheduled time to the stereotyping machine which fashions a matrix, or mat, of the page through the application of weight to impressionable paperboard material. The mat becomes the mold into which molten metal is cast into a plate, from which a page will be printed. These plates (each one curved as a half cylinder) are locked around a press roller over which the newsprint passes in rapid, continuous flow. If several presses are used to run an edition, additional curved plates are cast from the same mat and locked on rollers of other presses.

Business Side. When the presses have yielded up the papers, with pages cut and sections assembled, the circulation department quickly dispatches bundles of the newspapers to downtown street corners and other points of distribution. The circulation department is divided into sections that handle sales and subscriptions of various sorts. Daily distribution is maintained and enlarged by door-to-door salesmen, telephone and mail appeals, and often through a variety of puzzle contests and other promotional devices ranging from providing inexpensive accident insurance for subscribers to offering a wide assortment of prizes and awards.

Since the single-copy price of a large metropolitan newspaper rarely pays for the paper on which it is printed, publishers rely on advertising to meet the high cost of operation. Advertising is the responsibility of a many-sided and highly competitive department. One staff handles national advertising, another local advertising (with emphasis on department and other retail stores and services), another the "want ads" and other brief listings of things to be bought and sold, or traded through "swap columns." An advertising promotion department with artists and copywriters prepares advertisements for businesses too small to maintain their own advertising writers, and develops special seasonal advertising sections on travel, apparel, household appliances, automobiles, garden equipment, gifts, boats, investments, real estate, and many other such things in which readers may be induced to put their money. A few newspapers maintain an advertising censor.

Administrative offices on the business side purchase newsprint, ink, metal, photographic materials, machinery, and other supplies and equipment. Disbursing personnel keep the payroll with its multiplicity of deductions for taxes, dues, and assorted benefits; they also pay the bills. These operations require staffs of clerical employees whose daily work is almost indistinguishable from that in any other large business. This is also true of the credit manager, who extends credit to advertisers (or withholds it) and undertakes collection of outstanding accounts.

The Editorial Page. The larger the newspaper the more subdivided it is, and an editorial page department with a staff of five or six writers usually has specialists in local, state, national, and international subjects, and in business, scientific, educational, cultural, and military affairs. Editorial page policy on any subject grows out of pro and con discussion in staff meetings led by the editorial page editor. Major positions, such as the announcement of the paper's choice in a presidential election, are worked out in consultation with the owner or publisher, or are taken according to his direct instructions. The staff editorial cartoonist works closely with the editorial page editor, who ordinarily passes judgment on the cartoon idea and execution and not infrequently makes suggestions. Letters from readers intended for publication are also the editor's concern, since they are often chosen in terms of other material on the editorial page.

The Morgue. An important facility under the managing editor is the "morgue," the library or reference department, where clippings are filed under subject headings, along with photographs, reports, pamphlets, and books. Obituary material prepared in advance and filed alphabetically enables a paper to present a fully illustrated account of the life of a prominent figure within minutes after word of his death.

Employees and the Public. Although each department normally employs its own news staff members, larger newspapers maintain a personnel department to assist in employment, keep records on employees, and supervise health services and other employee benefits. Inevitably the newspaper and its staff engage in community relations in a variety of ways. Some newspaper executives regard public relations as an important personal responsibility and serve on civic boards and committees. Others avoid identification with public or community groups whose activities might subsequently conflict with their journalistic responsibilities. The tendency is for staff members to exercise a considerable freedom as individual citizens, but to avoid connections that might embarrass the newspaper in its functions of public critic and example. In the twentieth century more and more papers have maintained a special public relations staff whose activities include printing-plant tours, cooking schools, talks before civic and service groups and clubs, and sponsorship of science fairs for high school students, forums on world issues for adults, and folklore and musical festivals for all ages. See CENSORSHIP; FREEDOM OF THE PRESS; JOURNALISM; MAGAZINE.

IRVING DILLIARD

BIBLIOG.–E. M. Bartow, *News and These United States* (1952); Meyer Berger, *Story of the New York Times* (1951); F. F. Bond, *An Introduction to Journalism* (ed. 1961); T. C. Bray, *Newspaper's Role in Modern Society* (1965); Editor and Publisher, *International Yearbook;* E. H. Ford and E. Emery, eds., *Highlights in the History of the American Press* (1954); J. C. Merrill and others, *Foreign Press* (ed. 1963); F. L. Mott, *American Journalism: a History, 1690–1960* (ed. 1962); R. M. Neal, *News Gathering and News Writing* (ed. 1949); F. W. Rucker and H. L. Williams, *Newspaper Organization and Management* (1955); K. N. Stewart and John Tebbel, *Makers of Modern Journalism* (1952); Allan Woods, *Modern Newspaper Production* (1963).

When the papers have left the press, pages cut and folded, they are sent to the circulation room, where they are assembled, bundled, and marked for delivery.

THE NEW YORK TIMES

NEWS SERVICE, an agency that collects and distributes the news of the world, in word and picture, to newspapers, radio and television stations, news magazines, and other media.

To report daily news events adequately and with the necessary facility, a publication would need a full-time or part-time correspondent in virtually every populated area of the world. The cost of maintaining so enormous a staff is prohibitive for even the wealthiest newspaper or broadcasting station. Therefore, thousands of newspapers and broadcasting stations support news service organizations to obtain economical and effective coverage. Some broadcasting networks and large newspapers do maintain permanent staff correspondents in principal cities of the world, and other correspondents who move from place to place as news developments warrant, but except for local news, all news-disseminating media rely on the news services for the bulk of news reporting.

The Associated Press (AP) is the largest and oldest of the world's important news gathering agencies. It was founded in 1848 by six New York City newspapers that banded together to share the cost of collecting news outside the metropolitan area.

AP supplies news and pictures to more than 8,500 newspapers, news magazines, and radio and television stations in more than 100 nations. It also supplies its members with comic strips, serial fiction, fashion and home-making articles, book reviews, and stamp and camera columns. In the United States, AP leases some 800,000 miles of telephone or telegraph wire to serve more than 1,750 newspapers and 2,900 broadcast outlets. It maintains 111 offices in the United States and 58 offices in other nations.

In addition to its own personnel, AP indirectly has on its staff the personnel of the newspapers and stations it serves since it is a nonprofit co-operative whose members exchange news and share the cost of maintaining the organization of exchange.

Because it is a co-operative, AP spends all its revenue for gathering and distributing news and its members share the cost on the basis of their ability to pay. Each member is assessed according to a formula that has as its factors the population of the city served by the member and the circulation figure of the member's publication.

Until 1945, members of the AP, operating like a social club, were able to withhold the service from competitors by voting against the admission of new members. A U.S. Supreme Court decision forced the association to abandon this procedure.

United Press International (UPI) was formed in 1958 through the purchase by United Press Associations (UP) of the news and pictures of International News Service (INS). UP was founded in 1907 by E. W. Scripps; INS in 1909 by William Randolph Hearst.

In 1966 UPI had 6,267 clients in 114 countries and territories; employed more than 10,000 editors, photographers, and technicians; and maintained over 250 news and picture bureaus, 141 of which were in the United States. It leased more than 500,000 miles of wire throughout the world for news and picture transmission. In the United States UPI served 1,200 newspapers, 2,662 radio stations, and 374 television stations. Abroad it supplied its service to 988 papers and agencies, and 404 radio and television stations.

Unlike the Associated Press, UPI is a stock corporation that sells its service as a marketable commodity. UPI's field of operation is not so restricted as AP's; it serves special clients such as magazines, commentators in radio and television, ocean liners, and business executives desiring immediate telegraphic access to the day's news. UPI's subsidiary, Ocean Press, transmits news bulletins to ships at sea. UPI operates UPI Newsfilm, Inc., a daily news film service for television. UPI also supplies newspapers with comic strips, serials, and feature material through its subsidiary United Features Syndicate.

United Press International (British United Press) is a Canadian affiliate of UPI. It provides Canadian news for world distribution, as well as for 163 subscribers in Canada.

Reuters is a worldwide news agency founded in London, England, in 1851 by Paul Julius von Reuter, a German who in 1849 had begun sending financial news by carrier pigeon between Brussels, Belgium, and Aachen, Germany. In England, Reuter's agency grew with the expansion of telegraphic and cable facilities and of the British Empire, and after World War I became a co-operative owned by the British Press Association. Reuters maintains news exchange arrangements with the Associated Press, the Canadian Press, and the South African Press Association.

Tass. Telegrafnoje Agentstwo Ssojusa (Telegraphic Agency of the Soviet States) is the Soviet Union's official news bureau, founded in 1925. It collects all foreign and some domestic news for Soviet papers and exchanges its news with agencies serving other nations.

The Canadian Press (CP) is a co-operative that operates in much the same was as AP. It is owned and operated by about 100 Canadian daily newspapers, and the cost of editing and transmission is divided among them according to the population of the cities in which they publish. CP also serves weekly newspapers and radio and television stations. It gets world news from AP and Reuters, which have reciprocal agreements with CP for their coverage of Canada.

Other News Services. Until World War II the leading international service of France was Agence Havas, established in 1836 by Charles Havas, a Portuguese living in Paris. Since World War II, Agence France-Presse has been dominant. Other foreign services include Aneta of Holland, Israeli News Agency, Ltd., Jewish Telegraphic Agency, Press Trust of India, Swiss Telegraph Agency, and Stampa of Italy.

Progress in News Transmission. Both AP and UPI have introduced to the newspaper industry the latest scientific developments in the transmission of the written word and illustration. Before World War II they replaced the slow, manually operated Morse key and sounder with the automatic teletypewriter. Later they put into use the teletypesetter, a machine that enables an operator in a central office to work at the keyboard of a sending machine which activates mechanisms in printing plants thousands of miles away to set the news in type. In 1965 UPI introduced a computer system whereby its wire service would be transmitted to newspapers in coded tape that would automatically produce type for printing.

Transmission of pictures by wire is commonplace. After AP introduced the wirephoto technique in 1935, UP brought out its telephoto and INS its soundphoto. These methods deliver a photographic negative at the receiving end. After World War II the services inaugurated a facsimile method by which a positive picture is delivered ready for photoengraving in a newspaper plant or for immediate telecasting by a television station.

CARROLL ARIMOND

BIBLIOG.–Oliver Granling, *AP, the Story of News* (1940); R Jones, *Life in Reuters* (1942); J. A. Morris, *Deadline Every Minute* (1957); UNESCO, *World Press Newspapers and News Agencies.*

NEWSTED ABBEY, located about 9 miles NW of Nottingham, England, on the border of Sherwood Forest. The abbey was founded in 1170 by Henry II in atonement for the murder of Thomas Becket. In 1540 it was granted to Sir John Byron by Henry VIII. From 1798 it was the property of the poet Lord Byron, who sold it after he left England. Byron's relics and manuscripts are preserved there today.

NEW SWEDEN, a Swedish colony established on the Delaware River in 1638, when two ships brought to America a band of Swedish and Dutch soldiers headed by Peter Minuit. Fort Christina, named for the Swedish queen, was built within the present city limits of Wilmington, Del.; an extensive tract of land, extending from Cape Henlopen at the mouth of Delaware Bay up the west coast to Sankikan (opposite the site of Trenton, N.J.), was purchased from the Indians and named New Sweden. In 1643, the new governor, Johan Printz, built small forts at Tinicum, near the present site of Philadelphia, at Upland, near Chester, Pa., and at the mouth of the Schuylkill River. Printz maintained the independence of his tiny colony, which grew into a prosperous community of some 400 persons, comprising Swedes, Finns, and a few Poles. In 1653 Printz's successor, Johan Rising, attacked and captured Fort Casimir, which the Dutch had constructed on the site of present-day New Castle, Del. In retaliation, Gov. Peter Stuyvesant of New Netherland led an expedition against the Delaware colony in the following year; the New Swedes were overwhelmed and forced to surrender. In 1664 the Swedish settlements came under English sovereignty, and eventually the people were absorbed into the British community.

BIBLIOG.–A. B. Benson and Naboth Hedin, *Americans From Sweden* (1950). A. C. Myers, ed., *Narratives of Early Pennsylvania, West New Jersey and Delaware 1630–1707* (1912); C. L. Ward, *Dutch and Swedes on the Delaware* (1930), *New Sweden on the Delaware* (1938).

NEWT, an amphibian usually classed in the family *Salamandridae*, but sometimes put in a distinct family, *Pleurodel idae*, that resembles the salamander except for a laterally flattened tail used as a swimming organ during part of its life cycle. The newt is found throughout the world—in ponds, in warm, damp crevices of logs, and among leaf debris in forests. It eats insects, worms, centipedes, and snails. Although members of various species vary in coloration, the newt generally has a black-spotted body, dark brown back, and light brown or yellow belly. The common newt, *Trituris viridescens*, ranges in eastern North America. It is dull green during its life in water and red while it lives on land. The adult is about 3 inches long. After mating in the spring the female fastens a few eggs each day to the leaves of water plants until 200 or more eggs have been deposited. The eggs hatch about a month later, and the larvae grow from a length of about one-half inch upon hatching to 1½ inches two months later. During this time they breathe through gills and skin, but after two months lungs develop and the skin thickens, becomes rough, and changes from brown to red. At this stage the newt emerges onto land, and is known as an eft. For the next three to five years it dwells in cool, damp, wooded areas. The land phase ends in the fall, when the newt reverts to a water environment and prepares to mate. Its skin softens and changes color, and its tail, which was slender while the newt was on land, becomes flattened. Mating occurs the following spring.

NEW TESTAMENT, the collection of 27 books (including Gospels, letters, and tracts) recognized as the authoritative record of the beginnings of Christianity. The name given the Christian religion in Hebrews 8:6–8 (*The New Testament: An American Translation*), which itself was taken from one of the prophets (Jer. 31:31), was the "new testament"—the new covenant or agreement between God and Israel—exemplified in the life of Christ and the acts of His followers. The record itself became known as the "new testament." Although at least nine of the Apostle Paul's letters had been collected and put into circulation soon after A.D. 90, the first books read in Christian public worship were the four Gospels. Such reading was the practice of the church at Rome at least by A.D. 150. The addition of Paul's letters, the Acts of the Apostles, with three or four other letters and Revelation, had increased the collection to 22 books by the year 200. In Alexandria the churches of the third century further increased the number to 30 or 31, but by 367 the Greek and Latin churches had settled on a Christian scripture of the 27 books that are accepted today. The Syrian churches, on the other hand, still clung to 22 books only, while the Ethiopic New Testament increased to 35.

The Gospel of Matthew. Although the first writings of the Christian faith were the letters of the Apostle Paul, the New Testament as we know it begins with the Gospel of Matthew, to which various dates between A.D. 42 and 95 have been assigned. It is a life of Jesus the Messiah, from His birth to His resurrection. It was largely based on the earlier Gospel of Mark, supplemented by a body of Jesus' teachings drawn from other written sources. One of these, a hypothetical document composed perhaps about A.D. 50, and also used by Luke, was chiefly a collection of the teachings of Jesus. It may be that the whole Gospel received its name from a form of this document that was attributed to Matthew by Papias of Hierapolis (c. 140). These teachings form the chief feature of this Gospel, being arranged in six sermons, which establish the figure of Jesus as a great teacher of morals and religion. They are: first, the Sermon on the Mount (ch. 5–7), setting forth the standards of uprightness that must prevail in the Kingdom of God, contrasted with those of contemporary Judaism; the second sermon (ch. 10), telling how the Kingdom of Heaven is to be preached; the third (ch. 13), dealing with the growth of the Kingdom and its worth; the fourth (ch. 18), telling of life in the Kingdom; the fifth (ch. 23), a vigorous attack upon contemporary Jewish religious practices; the sixth (ch. 24–25), foretelling the downfall of Jerusalem and the end of the age. After Jesus' day the Jews actually did revolt against the Roman Empire, A.D. 66–70, and Jerusalem was destroyed, with fearful slaughter, by the Roman armies. In that disaster which put an end to the Jewish nation, some scholars say, the writer of the book of Matthew saw the punishment of the Jews for their refusal of Jesus' teachings and for His death. The book closes with the arrest, trial, and crucifixion of Jesus and His subsequent reunion with His 11 disciples in Galilee, where He commissioned them to teach all nations, and promised to remain with them always. The Gospel of Matthew presents Jesus as pre-eminently a teacher. Besides the Sermon on the Mount, it contains the Lord's Prayer, the Beatitudes, and the Golden Rule, and has always been cherished and influential. The great French historian and philologist Joseph Ernest Renan (1823–92) called it the most important book in the world.

The Gospel of Mark. A tradition (dating from Papias of Hierapolis) declares that when Peter preached among the Greeks, Mark acted as his interpreter and translated his Aramaic discourses into Greek, so that after Peter died Mark was able to write down all of Peter's memorabilia of Jesus, as recounted in the apostle's sermons. In like manner many other stories and sayings of the Gospels originally were circulated in oral form. Amid the stirring events and expectations in the early church there was at first little time or need for written records. The words and deeds of Jesus were remembered and used in the proclamation of the Christian message and in the settlement of church problems (I Cor. 7:10, 11:23–25; Acts 20:35). When written accounts began to appear, some Christians still preferred the "living and abiding voice." But as the original leaders and eyewitnesses died, the need for written memoirs became evident, and many, as Luke wrote, sought to compose accounts of "the movement that has developed among us" (Luke 1:1, *The New Testament: An American Translation*). One of these accounts was the Gospel of Mark, written after the death of Peter and just before or after the destruction of Jerusalem, A.D. 70, an event which, in prospect or reality, was vividly in the author's mind. This Gospel presents the simple story of the appearance of Jesus in Galilee declaring the coming of the Kingdom of God, arousing the animosity of the Pharisees, gathering a little group of close followers, his "apostles," preaching in parables, or stories, and curing the sick and the mad wherever He found them. After His life had been threatened three times, Jesus decided to visit Jerusalem at the great annual Passover festival, and there to present His gospel to the whole people and its leaders, in a way that could never be forgotten. What followed is one of the world's great pieces of heroic tragedy, chapters 11 to 16. Though harsh and obscure in some respects, Mark's is still the pattern gospel, which directly or indirectly underlies all the subsequent gospels, in or out of the New Testament, and actually presents the closest observance of Christ's experiences and movements. It describes Jesus pre-eminently as a man of action, undertaking to set up the Kingdom of God on earth.

The Gospel of Luke. As the progress of Christianity in the Greco-Roman world caused many to believe that the new religion had before it a worldwide future and might even dominate the Roman Empire, a Greek physician named Luke, who had been a companion and lieutenant of Paul, undertook to set forth its story from the promise of the birth of Jesus' forerunner, John the Baptist, down to the establishment of Christianity in Rome, the center and capital of the ancient world. He organized his orderly account in two volumes, the first of which we know as the Gospel of Luke and the second as the Acts of the Apostles. For the first, Luke used the same sources that Matthew had used, with additional materials, written and oral. For the second, his long stay in Palestine, when he went there with Paul after the third missionary journey, gave him abundant material for chapters 1–12, and his association and travels with Paul enabled Luke to produce the detailed record of the beginning and progress of the mission to the gentiles that forms the rest of the book. Some scholars hold that the optimistic note with which the Gospel closes indicates that it was written before the Neronian persecution of A.D. 64. Others see the weathering of initial persecutions and progress made afterward as the causes of this optimism and date the Gospel around A.D. 90, before the persecutions by Domitian. Luke's Gospel is especially rich in parables, and shows a strong social and humanitarian interest. In the two-volume work taken as a whole, Jesus appears as the author of a new religion and the founder of the Christian church. Acts is of special value as it relates the work of Paul to the earlier progress of Christianity.

The Gospel of John presents Jesus not so much as the Messiah expected by the Jews but rather as the embodiment of the wisdom of God, the bread of life, and the Saviour and Light of the World. It was written possibly in the region of Ephesus about A.D. 90–110, and shows the influence of some of the earlier Gospels and perhaps of the letters of Paul. The traditional authorship assigned to John the Disciple is believed to be correct by many scholars despite the striking differences between this and the other (synoptic) Gospels. Other scholars see more plausibility in the idea that the author was a certain John the Elder, mentioned as living in Ephesus at this time and named in II and III John. Certain primitive elements and traditions in the Gospel are then regarded as coming from the apostle through the Elder. By the end of the first century it had become clear that the future of the Christian movement lay not among the Jews but in the Greek world (the entire New Testament was written in Greek), and the Book of John was written to present the heart of the Christian message not in the Jewish terms of the other Gospels, but in ways that should be immediately intelligible to Greeks everywhere. Thus his Gospel cast the great realities of Christian experience in terms that do not grow old—its great words are Light, Love, Life, Truth, Knowledge, Freedom, words which still describe the best hopes and ideals of mankind. John is really more a dialogue than a Gospel in the usual sense, for it is full of Jesus' conversations with His friends and foes. It conceives Christianity as a deep spiritual experience of the love of God, who loved the world so much that He gave His Son to bring eternal life to mankind. And into a dark, cruel, pagan world it had brought a new kind of life, of sonship to God and friendship with Christ. Soon after the Gospel of John was published it was combined (by 120) with the three earlier Gospels into the fourfold Gospel collection which has proved to be the most influential literary unit in the world.

The Acts of the Apostles is really the second volume of Luke's work on the beginnings of Christianity. It takes up the narrative where the Gospel of Luke leaves off, and goes on to tell how Christianity gradually developed from a sect of Judaism into a world religion; how it was carried by believers throughout Palestine, and on into Syria and Antioch, where it began to reach Greeks; and how it spread westward through the provinces of the Roman Empire until it was established at Rome itself. Peter is the hero of the earlier part of the book, but Paul dominates the later chapters, and the story is told of his remarkable conversion to the Christian faith, his great missionary journeys, and finally of his voyage to Rome and his shipwreck on the way. It is a dramatic and varied narrative that relates the perils and adventures through which the first believers passed in the 30 eventful years that followed the death of Christ.

The Letters of Paul. As Paul traveled among the great cities of the empire, preaching the Gospel to the Greeks, he wrote a number of letters to the churches he had founded, to answer questions that arose among them or to correct their mistakes in doctrine or conduct. Of the letters bearing his name in the New Testament nine are regarded beyond any reasonable doubt as actually dictated by him, between A.D. 50 and 62. Many scholars hold that he is author of all 13 letters traditionally ascribed to him. They are historical sources of the first order, for they are contemporary records.

Romans. Toward the close of Paul's third missionary journey, A.D. 56–57, he wrote from Corinth his greatest letter, Romans. He had hoped to go on from Corinth to Rome, but he found himself obliged to turn east to carry the funds his gentile church had raised for the poor in Jerusalem. So he wrote to the Christians of Rome, to set forth to them the heart of the Christian message. Greek and Jew alike, he declared, had fallen short of true uprightness and acceptance with God (ch. 1–2), but a way of attaining it had been revealed through Christ: it was the way of faith (ch. 3–5), which frees the believer from sin, law, and fear (ch. 6–8). Paul went on to explain why the Jewish people had not accepted Christ (ch. 9–11), and then told how a Christian should conduct himself in the world, the state, and the church (ch. 12:1–15:13). After an account of Paul's personal plans and movements, a letter of introduction for a Christian woman named Phoebe ends the book.

I Corinthians. While Paul was settled at Ephesus, early in what is called his third missionary journey, he was visited by three men from the church at Corinth, just across the Aegean, who brought him a letter from that church. It contained a number of questions that had arisen at Corinth—concerning marriage and the sexes, buying meat at the markets of the heathen temples, behavior in church, what women should wear in church, how the Lord's Supper should be observed, and what should be done about the disturbances in their meetings produced by people who broke out into excited babbling, which they called "speaking with tongues." Paul had already been told of factions and lawsuits in the Corinthian church, and he began his reply to their letter by correcting these practices (ch. 1–6); went on to take up the questions raised in their letter (ch. 7–14); and then discussed the Christian's hope of resurrection (ch. 15). He spoke (ch. 16) of the collection his churches had been taking, and his own plans. In the 13th chapter he told them of the supreme importance of Christian love.

II Corinthians. The two parts of this letter, chapters 1–9 and 10–13, are so different in tone and attitude toward the Corinthians that they appear to have been written at different times, at different stages of the Corinthian controversy. The factions at Corinth seem to have taken offense at the tone of I Corinthians and united against Paul, and he at length wrote a spirited and caustic defense of himself, telling of all the hardships he had endured in his missionary work (11:16–33). This letter was probably written in Macedonia and sent to Corinth by the hand of Titus, while Paul remained in Macedonia visiting the communities he had established there. Titus brought him the good news that the Corinthians had seen their mistake and greatly regretted it. Paul then wrote (about A.D. 57) II Cor. 1–9, a letter of reconciliation, rejoicing in the renewed loyalty of the Corinthians (1:1–2:11), reviewing in a gentler spirit the things he had said in the previous letter (ch. 7), and setting forth the methods and motives of his missionary work (2:12–6:10). II Corinthians has preserved for us a remarkable self-portrait of Paul, for in it he has laid bare his heart.

Galatians. Following the second missionary journey, or soon thereafter, Paul heard disturbing news from the churches in Galatia, which he had established on his first missionary journey and had recently revisited. They were being persuaded that they ought to accept the Jewish law, or at least some elements of it, such as circumcision. Paul saw that this would make the Christian movement just another Jewish sect and would threaten the great spiritual attitude of faith, which he considered the central and essential thing in religion. He immediately wrote (about A.D. 53) a fiery letter to the

Galatian churches protesting against their course. Christian faith, he maintained, could not be combined with a system of legalistic observances, such as they contemplated; it was sufficient without these and incompatible with them. Christ had freed the Galatians from that old servitude, and they must never lose their freedom.

Ephesians. After Paul's death, about A.D. 62, his letters probably were neglected and forgotten. They still lay in the chests of his churches and were only occasionally read or consulted for they all had been addressed to immediate, pressing, local situations, mostly forgotten. No one had seen them all, or even those nine preserved in the New Testament; even fewer had read them. Paul himself had told the Colossians (4:15–16) to get the letter from Laodicea (meaning Philemon) to read among them and to send his letter to the Laodicean church; accordingly, both churches had doubtless preserved those two short letters. But Acts, with its vivid account of Paul, might well have stirred someone to set about collecting any letters of his that had survived, and probably it was someone in Asia who already knew these two letters who began to collect them. Certainly by A.D. 92 or 93 nine letters had been collected. Probably to introduce these collected letters to the churches, Ephesians was written, addressed to all believers (1:1), calling attention to the great doctrines of the letters (1:3–14) and urging Christians to read them (3:1–4). Many still regard the letter as coming directly from Paul, despite the striking differences between it and his other letters. It was probably intended to show the values that the old letters possessed for the new times in which its writer and his readers lived; new content is put into the old words as the great Pauline teachings are summed up in terms of divine purpose, the foundations of the faith, and the life of the Christian believer within the church universal. Because the ideas and almost all of the phraseology of the letter were drawn from the letters written by Paul, it was credited to him and placed at the beginning of the collected letters as an introduction.

Philippians. In 59–60 Paul was in prison at Rome, awaiting trial. His old friends in Philippi sent a man to him to look after him and his case, and to supply him with money. In 4:10–20 Paul thanks them for doing this. The man they had sent fell sick and almost died, and when he was well enough Paul sent him home to Philippi (2:25–30). The letter or possibly two letters, 3:2–4:23 and 1:1–3:1, commend the Philippians for their faith, encourage them in Christian virtues and the imitation of Christ, and warn them, as he had the Galatians, against the Judaizers. They reveal forcefully Paul's state of mind in his imprisonment and the tranquility of spirit Paul had achieved through Christ (4:10–12).

Colossians. Some Christians at Colossae held the ancient idea that between man and God a hierarchy of intermediary beings or "ideas" existed, and that by ascetic practices and communion with these beings man could scale the heights and reach the presence of God. These Colossians consequently thought of Christ as simply one of these intermediaries, though doubtless the greatest of them. It is likely that while Paul was imprisoned he was told of the problems arising from these beliefs and (A.D. 59–60) wrote this letter to clarify his position on ascetic practices and the omnipotence of Christ. Paul gives here his most exalted picture of the cosmic Christ, but he also discloses his usual concern for the ethical and religious duties of the individual Christian in his mundane relationships.

I, II Thessalonians. It was probably in the spring of A.D. 50 that Paul reached Corinth, on his second missionary journey, having preached in the cities of Macedonia and been forced to leave them after a short stay in each. He was anxious to know whether his converts had held to their new faith in spite of his sometimes hasty departures; and he sent his companions Silvanus and Timothy back to find out. Timothy returned from Thessalonica with the good news that the church there had kept true to the gospel of faith and love, and was eager to see Paul again. In joyful acknowledgment of this news and to answer some of their questions, Paul wrote I Thessalonians. The rise in this church of a group of people who believed the day of the Lord's return was near, and who had given up working for a living in order to prepare for that return, led Paul to write another letter, II Thessalonians, a few months later, to correct their mistake and urge them to earn their living once more.

I, II Timothy, Titus. These three "pastoral letters," as they are called because of their concern with the duties and qualifications of church leaders, or "shepherds," are traditionally ascribed to Paul, but some modern scholars give them a probable date in the early second century. This view holds that the historical and ecclesiastical situation which they reflect, and their strong differences from the other letters of Paul make it difficult to ascribe them to the apostle in their present form. Yet many feel that they contain genuine fragments of Pauline correspondence; the traditional view holds that Paul actually did write these letters to Timothy and Titus, his "sons in the ministry." Christian leaders had become aware of the need of better church organization, of the menace of the rising sects, Marcionism and Gnosticism, of the appropriation of Paul by the Marcionites, and of their attempted renunciation of the Old Testament scripture. To meet these problems the letters were composed as we have them, in the name of Paul, and came to supplement the old collection of 10 letters. The situation reflected in them assumes that Paul was released from prison at Rome and made further journeys in the course of which he wrote I Timothy on his way from Macedonia to Greece, to Timothy at Ephesus; then Titus, when Paul was planning to pass the winter in Nicopolis; and II Timothy when he was again in prison in Rome, evidently for the last time. The letters protest against the vagaries of the sects; undertake to standardize church organization by a twofold ministry, overseers (or presbyters) and deacons; reassert the inspiration of the Jewish scriptures (the Old Testament); and denounce those who would make Paul's letters the main part of the Christian scripture.

Philemon, a Christian in Laodicea had a slave, a young man named Onesimus, who had run away from him. In Rome he had fallen under Paul's influence and become a Christian. Paul sent him back to his master, asking him to receive the young man as a Christian brother and to make sure he was humanely treated. Paul addressed his letter to the church Philemon belonged to—"the church that meets in your house"—and told the neighboring church at Colossae to read the letter (Col. 4:16). He thus did all he possibly could to insure the safety of the returning runaway.

Hebrews. About A.D. 95 Christians of the second generation were in danger of taking Christianity as a matter of course, so that when persecution arose in the last years of Domitian, 93–96, Christians were in no condition to withstand it. To revive their appreciation of their faith and to fortify them against the temptation of apostasy, Hebrews was written, probably to the Christians of Rome, reminding them of their heroic behavior in times of earlier persecution (10:32–34). To show them the supreme worth of Christianity, the writer compares it to Judaism, showing point by point how the new revelation surpasses the old and, in particular, how Jesus is the perfect high priest offering Himself as a perfect sacrifice for the sins of His people. So much was thus made of Judaism that the letter was later supposed to have been written to the "Hebrews," that is, to Jewish Christians. But the author's Hellenistic modes of thought and his use of the Greek Old Testament, known to all Christians, make this assumption questionable. The epistle has been dated by many scholars at the time of Nero's persecution rather than Domitian's. This would bring it into closer association with Paul; but the letter is anonymous and differs radically in style and argument from those written by Paul. However, the author shares Paul's ethical concerns, and he digresses several times from his main theme to call for a Christian perfection of faith and life.

James. Traditionally associated with the Apostle James and sometimes dated as early as A.D. 45, this letter is regarded by most scholars as an ancient sermon, written about A.D. 100, and published as a letter to all believers. It says very little about Christ, but gives practical warnings against a wide range of human weaknesses and failings—doubt, partiality, sham, a vicious tongue, selfishness, pleasure seeking, greed, and heartlessness. Its message is cast in the bold conversational style used by Stoic street preachers of the first and second centuries.

I Peter. There are three suggested settings for the book: first, the time when the demand for emperor worship as a test of loyalty to the Roman Empire in Domitian's reign put Christians in a fearful position; another is the time of Nero's persecutions three decades earlier; a third is the popular, unorganized persecution of early Christians. The writer of I Peter saw that the Christian must not meet hate with hate; there was a nobler way of meeting persecution. So when the writer of Hebrews called on the church at Rome to teach the churches (Heb. 5:12), the Roman church replied to the revolutionary note struck by the Book of Revelation with a gentler one, in the name of Peter (2:13–17; 4:12–19). The traditional view, which sees Peter himself as the author and refers the letter to the Neronian period, attributes the quality of the Greek and the reminiscences of Paul to the scribe Silvanus (5:12). But the destination of the letter is here still a difficulty; for just as the Revelation was sent to the churches of Asia, so this heroic statement of the true Christian attitude in the face of persecution was sent out to all the Christians of the province of Asia, and to the four adjacent provinces of Asia Minor, to correct what would have been a seditious tendency in Christian teaching during times of persecution.

II Peter. This letter, to which dates as early as A.D. 66 and as late as 160 have been assigned, reaffirms the primitive Christian doctrine of the second coming of Christ, taking over most of Jude's attack upon the Docetists and turning it against those who denied the second coming. Some scholars believe the heretics whom the letter attacks so vigorously are probably the Marcionites, who were characterized by just the faults it emphasizes—depravity, love of money, fantastic doctrines, and magical pretensions. The letter reveals acquaintance with the whole library of Christian books—the four Gospels, Paul's letters, Hebrews, Jude, and I Peter. It even describes the letters of Paul as scripture, and says that they are being twisted by some (regarded by proponents of the late date for the book as the Marcionites) to their own destruction.

I, II, III John. There are differing views as to the authorship and dates of these three letters. One view holds that they were given the name John because the second and third are written in the name of "the Elder," or "Presbyter," who lived in Ephesus and whose name was John; that the letters deal with the earliest of Christian heresies, the early-second-century Docetic idea that Christ's sufferings were not real but only apparent; and that the letters were written about 110. Other scholars hold that the Apostle John wrote the three letters, between 95 and 100, to combat Cerinthian Gnosticism which taught doctrines akin to those of the Docetists. The letters were part of a movement to extend the Christian faith over the province of Asia. The third letter was to a Christian named Gaius; the second to "an elect lady" and the church to which she belonged; and the first was a general letter to be read in all the churches visited by the missionaries. This first epistle was written very much in the style of the Gospel of John, and it describes the Christian life as a great spiritual fellowship of love, because God is love and has been truly revealed in Christ's incarnation.

Jude. This short letter or tract has been traditionally assigned to Jude, the brother of James the Apostle (Mark 6:3), and in this case would date before A.D. 80. Some scholars, however, believe that its contents and late admission to the collection of New Testament books made a later situation likely. The document seems to be aimed, as were the Johannine letters, at the Docetists of the second century or at others who believed, as they did, that Christ's sufferings were not real. Their views had led them into all kinds of moral laxity and so this group and its doctrines and practices are assailed vehemently.

The Revelation. Revelation, or apocalyptic literature, was a favorite form of late Jewish writing, exemplified in parts of the Book of Daniel and in the Book of Enoch. The Apostle John, or an Elder John of Ephesus, made use of this form in the Book of Revelation during the times when Domitian demanded emperor worship as a test of loyalty to the Roman Empire in his later years, A.D. 90–96. The Book of Revelation consequently took a bitterly hostile view of the empire, and gloated over the prospect of its destruction (Rev. 18:20). John directed his Revelation to the churches of seven flourishing cities in Asia, addressing one letter to the whole group and following it with a letter to each of the seven in turn (ch. 1–3). Then, in a series of three great visions (ch. 4–22) he set forth the certainty of final triumph by the Kingdom of God, regardless of what disasters and sufferings might attend its onward march. The whole book is cast in the mysterious and often grotesque vocabulary of the apocalyptic, so stimulating to the imagination. But basically the Revelation is a great plea for unshakable faith in God and in the ultimate triumph of His cause.

See individual articles on New Testament books; JESUS CHRIST; PAUL, SAINT.

EDGAR J. GOODSPEED; ALLEN WIKGREN

BIBLIOG.–H. A. Anderson and W. Barclay, eds., *The New Testament in Historical and Contemporary Perspective* (1965); Albert Barnes, *Barnes' Notes On the New Testament* (1962); F. R. Crownfield, *Historical Approach to the New Testament* (1960); Edgar Goodspeed and others, eds., *Rockefeller McCormick New Testament* (1965); G. E. Ladd, *The New Testament and Criticism* (1966); A. F. Loisy, *Birth of the Christian Religion, and Origins of the New Testament* (1962); B. M. Newman, *Meaning of the New Testament* (1966); F. B. Rhein, *Analytical Approach to the New Testament* (1966); J. W. Russell, ed., *Compact Commentary on the New Testament* (1964).

NEW THOUGHT, a nineteenth-century religious movement in the United States. Begun by Phineas P. Quimby (1802–66), a faith healer, and later propagated in writing by Warren Felt Evans (1817–89), the ideology of the New Thought is a combination of diverse elements ranging from the writings of Ralph Waldo Emerson to some aspects of Buddhist teaching. The basis of the New Thought is faith healing and the concept of divinity as contained in the mind. A number of religious sects have developed out of this movement.

NEWTON, ALFRED, 1829–1907, English ornithologist, born in Geneva, Switzerland, and educated at Magdalene College, Cambridge, where from 1877 to 1907 he was professor of zoology and comparative anatomy. He traveled extensively and promoted the study of comparative anatomy of birds as well as the protection of birds by government legislation. He wrote *The Zoology of Ancient Europe* (1862) and *Dictionary of Birds* (1893–6).

NEWTON, Sir CHARLES THOMAS, 1816–94, English archaeologist, born in Bredwardine, Herefordshire. He studied at Christ Church, Oxford, and in 1840 became assistant curator of antiquities in the British Museum. He was made vice-consul at Mytilene in Asia Minor in 1852 and four years later discovered the ruins of the mausoleum at Halicarnassus, one of the seven wonders of the ancient world. He was keeper of Greek and Roman antiquities at the British Museum (1861–85) and professor of archaeology at University College, London (1880–88).

NEWTON, GILBERT STUART, 1794–1835, English painter, born in Halifax, N.S. He studied with his uncle, the U.S. portrait painter Gilbert Stuart, and also at the Royal Academy in London, where he exhibited his work. His painting was skillful and academic and influenced by the seventeenth-century Dutch tradition. His works included portraits of Sir Walter Scott and Washington Irving.

NEWTON, HUBERT ANSON, 1830–96, U.S. mathematician and astronomer, born in Sherburne, N.Y., and educated at Yale, where he became a professor of mathematics at age 25. As a mathematician he was an authority on transcendental curves. In astronomy he published important articles on meteors.

NEWTON, Sir ISAAC, 1642–1727, English scientist and mathematician, born on Christmas Day (old style) in Woolsthorpe, Lincolnshire. As a youth he was shy and sickly, and his academic career at Trinity College, Cambridge, 1661–65, was undistinguished; he became a fellow at the college in 1667. He was absent from Cambridge because of the plague during the year 1665–66; from this period came four of his outstanding achievements—the calculus, the binomial theorem, the law of universal gravitation, and the discovery of the composite nature of white light—even though the results of these discoveries were not, in some instances, to be published for some years.

Calculus. The expansion of $(x+y)^n$ for positive integral values of n had long been known; but Newton extended the expansion of the equation to include all rational exponents. This binomial theorem was useful in the generalization of problems leading to the calculus. Pierre de Fermat had found tangents to algebraic curves, and Archimedes long before had determined the areas of certain curved figures. Newton fashioned these problems into an algorithm (algorism) and noted their inverse relationship. Between 1669 and 1676 he wrote out several accounts of his procedures, but the chief of these, the *Methodus fluxionum*, appeared posthumously in 1736. The delay in publication led to the notorious priority controversy with Gottfried Wilhelm von Leibniz, who was known to have seen some of Newton's manuscripts in 1673; but evidence indicates that the invention of the differential calculus by Leibniz in 1676 was independent of Newton's fluxions. See BINOMIAL THEORUM; CALCULUS.

Gravitation. Newton's discovery that particles attract each other with a force varying inversely as the square of the distance between them brought under a single formulation both terrestrial and celestial motions—the fall of an apple toward the earth as well as the revolution of a planet about the sun. Newton hesitated to publish, apparently for want (at first) of an adequate proof that distances

THE GRANGER COLLECTION

Isaac Newton

are, at least for spheroids, to be measured from their centers. But in 1684 a friend, Edmund Halley, prevailed upon him to write up his results in the celebrated *Philosophiae naturalis principia mathematica* (1687), published at Halley's expense. The *Principia* centers upon "The System of the World" as derived from Newton's laws of motion and the principle of gravitation, but also includes a wide array of other topics—theorems on conics, the velocity of sound, motion in a resisting medium, and a cryptic note on his infinitesimal methods of experimentation. See GRAVITATION.

Optics In 1666 Newton purchased a glass prism, and with it soon detected one of the most curious of the operations of nature. He found that white light is not pure and homogeneous; rather, that it is a congeries of colors, each characterized by its own index of refraction—from red, which is bent the least, to violet, the most "refrangible." His analysis of light through dispersion was followed by the crucial experiment in which he synthesized white light by recombining the colors. In 1672 and 1675 Newton presented a brief account of his conclusions to the Royal Society, to which he was elected, 1672, in recognition of his construction of a reflecting telescope, 1668; but the ensuing controversies so disturbed him that he resolved thereafter to withhold publication of his discoveries. Thus it was that his comprehensive treatise, *Opticks*, did not appear until 1704, the year following the death of Robert Hooke, his sharpest critic (whose criticisms helped shape the final form of Newton's theory). See DISPERSION; REFRACTION.

Here Newton speculated freely on the nature of light. He preferred to think of it as corpuscular; but he believed that the particles set up periodic disturbances in the ether surrounding transparent bodies. This theory of "fits" enabled him to explain the production, by thin plates, of colors in "Newton's rings," and he computed the frequencies of the undulations for the various components. See NEWTON RINGS.

The *Opticks* was supplemented by two mathematical appendices: the *Enumeration of Cubic Curves* and the *Quadrature of Curves*. Three years later Newton also published a treatise on algebra, entitled *Arithmetica Universalis*, which included such topics as "Newton's method" for solving equations, "Newton's identities" relating the coefficients of polynomials and the sums of the powers of the roots, and "Newton's interpolation formula." See LIGHT; OPTICS.

Other Interests. In 1669 Newton succeeded Barrow as Lucasian professor at Cambridge, and thenceforth was recognized as without peer in mathematics. In 1697 he solved overnight the difficult brachystochrone problem proposed by the Bernoulli brothers (Jacques and Jean); and somewhat later he easily met the challenge of Leibniz to find the trajectories of a family of curves. See CALCULUS OF VARIATIONS.

Newton also conducted chemical experiments; and he valued highly his studies in Biblical chronology. Of a sensitive nature, shunning controversy yet suspicious lest his discoveries be appropriated by others, he suffered a mental depression in 1692. Three years later he left academic life to become warden, later master (in 1699), of the mint.

Honors continued to be showered upon him. He served in Parliament, 1689–90 and 1701–05. He was knighted by Queen Anne in 1705. He was president of the Royal Society from 1703 until his death at Kensington on Mar. 20, 1727. Among those at his funeral was Voltaire who returned to France to champion Newtonianism against the Cartesians (followers of René Descartes). Ultimately the success of Newtonian science in France (as elsewhere), inspired the *philosophes* to attempt a comparable "science of society," thus ushering in the Enlightenment. CARL B. BOYER

The standard edition of Newton's works is the *Opera quae exstant omnia* (ed. by Horsley, 5 vols. 1779–85); the standard biography is Sir David Brewster's *Memoirs of the Life, Writings, and Discoveries of Sir Isaac Newton* (2 vols., Edinburgh, 1855). CARL B. BOYER

BIBLIOG.–E. N. de C. Andrade, *Sir Isaac Newton* (1954); H. D. Anthony, *Sir Isaac Newton* (1960); I. B. Cohen, *Franklin and Newton* (1956); I. B. Cohen, ed., *Isaac Newton's Papers and Letters on Natural Philosophy* (1958); A. De Morgan, *Essays on the Life and Work of Newton* (1914); M. H. Nicolson, *Newton Demands the Muse: Newton's Opticks and the 18th Century Poets* (1966); H. W. Turnbull, *Mathematical Discoveries of Newton* (1945).

NEWTON, JOHN, 1725–1807, English clergyman and hymn writer, born in London. After being a sailor and a slave trader, he became a tide surveyor at Liverpool in 1755. He was ordained a deacon in the Church of England in 1764 and became curate of Olney, Buckinghamshire. There he formed a friendship with the poet William Cowper, and with him wrote the *Olney Hymns* (1779).

NEWTON, JOHN, 1823–95, U.S. soldier and engineer, born in Norfolk, Va., and graduated from West Point in 1842. Made brigadier-general of volunteers in 1861, he was in charge of constructing the defenses of Washington during the Civil War. In 1865, he was made brigadier-general of the regular army. In 1886, two years after he was made chief of engineers, he retired and became commissioner of public works in New York City. After 1888 he was president of the Panama Railroad Company.

NEWTON, city, S central Kansas; seat of Harvey County; 24 miles N of Wichita. Newton is a trade and shipping center for the surrounding agricultural area. It has a rail mill, flour mills, and a mobile home-trailer manufacturing plant. The Mennonite-owned Bethel College is in nearby North Newton. Founded in 1871 and incorporated in 1872, Newton was a cattle town and the railhead at the end of the Chisholm Trail until 1873. (For population, see Kansas map in Atlas.)

NEWTON, city, E Massachusetts, Middlesex County; on the Charles River; 8 miles W of Boston. Although primarily a residential city, Newton has manufacturers of yarn and knit goods, fastening devices, radio and signal apparatus, machinery, rubber and paper goods, tractors, and precision instruments. The city is the seat of Boston College, Andover Newton Theological School, Newton College of the Sacred Heart, and Newton Junior College. Newton, settled before 1639 and incorporated as a city in 1873, is an aggregate of 14 villages. (For population, see Massachusetts map in Atlas.)

NEWTON, town, NW New Jersey; seat of Sussex County; 35 miles WNW of Paterson. Newton is the center of a dairying area and has textile-and food-processing plants. It is the seat of Don Bosco College. Newton was founded in 1760 and incorporated as a city in 1864. (For population, see New Jersey map in Atlas.)

NEWTON ABBOT, urban district, SW England, Devonshire; 5 miles from the English Channel and 14 miles SW of Exeter. Newton Abbot is a trade center for an agricultural area. Points of interest include. the Tudor-style Ford House (1610). (For population, see England map in Atlas.)

NEWTON-LE-WILLOWS, town, Lancashire, England; 15 miles W of Manchester. Paper and glass are manufactured; the town also contains an iron foundry. (For population, see England map in Atlas.)

NEWTON'S RINGS, in optics, a phenomenon that results when light is passed through a convex lens resting on a flat piece of glass.

Although for many purposes light can be described in simple geometrical terms (traveling in straight lines), it is actually a wave phenomenon and as such is able to exhibit interference. That is, if two rays of light from a single source can later reach another common point (by means of reflections, etc.) and if the crests of each wave arrive at the same time, then a very bright effect is produced; but if a crest of one wave arrives with a trough of the other, they cancel one another and if they have the same intensity complete darkness results. Newton devised an ingenious method of exhibiting this phenomenon, by laying a lens of long focus on a flat plate of glass. The film of air between the two is now of varying thickness so that, if the apparatus is illuminated from below, the light passing through the film of air has varying path-lengths, sometimes different by a whole wavelength, sometimes by a half. One sees, then, a central black spot surrounded by successive bright and dark rings, which are very numerous if light of only one wavelength is used. In white light only a few rings can be seen, since the location of the rings for any wavelength depends on the wavelength. For the mixture of wavelengths in white light each component produces its own rings so that blurring results. See INTERFERENCE; WAVE. C. W. KILMISTER

NEW TORONTO, town, SE Ontario; located on the northwest shore of Lake Ontario between the towns of Mimico and Long Branch, 8 miles SW of Toronto, of which it is an industrial suburb. Rubber products and automobile tires are manufactured. New Toronto was incorporated in 1913, and became a part of the municipality of metropolitan Toronto in 1953. (For population, see southern Ontario map in Atlas.)

NEWTOWN, town SW Connecticut, Fairfield County; on the Housatonic River, 17 miles N of Bridgeport. Settled in 1705 and incorporated in 1711, Newtown is the site of a state mental hospital. Industrial equipment is manufactured. (For population, see Connecticut map in Atlas.)

NEW ULM, city, S Minnesota, seat of Brown County; on the Minnesota River; 75 miles SW of

Minneapolis. It is a food-processing center in a rich region of variegated agriculture. Founded in 1854 and incorporated as a village in 1857, the city, during the Sioux uprising of 1862, sheltered refugees and frightened away two Indian raiding parties with the aid of stovepipe cannon. The city was nearly destroyed, but was rebuilt, and incorporated as a city in 1876. It is the site of Dr. Martin Luther College. (For population, see Minnesota map in Atlas.)

NEW WATERFORD, town, NE Nova Scotia; on the NE coast of Cape Breton Island; 10 miles NE of Sidney. New Waterford is located in an important coal-mining region. The town is also the base of a fishing fleet. New Waterford was incorporated, 1913, and named for Waterford, Ireland. (For population, see Atlantic Provinces map in Atlas.)

NEW WESTMINSTER, city, SW British Columbia; on the N bank of the Fraser River; 9 miles ESE of Vancouver. New Westminster is an important ice-free port and the base of the Fraser River fishing fleet. The city has paper and lumber mills, an oil refinery, distilleries, a large grain elevator, and manufacturing and food-processing plants. St. Louis and Columbia colleges are the city's leading educational institutions. Founded in 1859, New Westminster was the capital of British Columbia until Vancouver Island and British Columbia colonies were united in 1866. The city was partially destroyed by fire in 1898. (For population, see British Columbia map in Atlas.)

NEW YEAR'S DAY, the first day of the calendar year, occurs January 1 in the United States and the Western world, although the date was generally recognized in Europe only after the Gregorian calendar reform in the sixteenth century, and in England and the American colonies after 1752. The custom of celebrating the first day of the year appears to be almost universal among all peoples—ancient and modern, preliterate and civilized. The date, however, has varied with the system of reckoning time and has fallen in different seasons. The Jewish Rosh Hashana and the Coptic Egyptian New Year are autumn festivals; among Hindus and the ancient Romans the festival fell at the time of the winter solstice; the Persian New Year was celebrated in the spring, and the ancient Greek New Year during the summer solstice. The traditional Chinese New Year festival begins with the new moon in January and lasts until the full moon. As well as being the beginning of the new civic year, January 1 has the additional significance for many Christians of being a holy day for one or more of the liturgical festivals of the Circumcision of Our Lord, Octave of the Nativity, and the Holy Name.

In New York's state seal, a shield picturing river commerce is flanked by Justice (holding a sword to strike down tyranny) and Liberty (at whose feet a crown, representing royal British rule, is overturned).

BIRD	**Bluebird**
FLOWER	**Rose**
TREE	**Sugar maple**
CAPITAL	**Albany**
MOTTO	**Excelsior (Higher)**
ENTERED THE UNION	**July 26, 1788**
ORDER OF ENTRY	**11th**

NEW YORK, a Middle Atlantic state of the United States; bounded on the N and W by lakes Erie and Ontario and by the Canadian provinces of Quebec and Ontario; on the S by Pennsylvania and New Jersey; and on the E by Vermont, Massachusetts, and Connecticut; area 49,576 square miles, including 1,637 square miles of inland water; population (1965) 18,073,000. Excluding Long Island and adjacent Atlantic islands, New York's maximum dimensions are about 310 miles north to south and 320 miles east to west. Among the states, New York ranks thirtieth in geographical size, and until 1963, when it was superseded by California, New York was the most populous state. New York was one of the original thirteen states. Albany is the capital. See map in Atlas, Vol. 20. For the state flag in color, see FLAG.

Physical Features

Geology. All of New York, with the exception of a small western area, was covered by the continental glacier. The results were the broadening and deepening of the valleys, rounding of the hills, and the turning aside of numerous streams, which altered the drainage of the area and caused many waterfalls as well as rapids. Thousands of lakes of all sizes were formed and, as the ice receded, it stopped here and there, piling up in hilly deposits called moraines. As a consequence, nearly all of the state's soil derives from glacial activity. The Adirondack Mountains in northeastern New York are a mass of Pre-Cambrian rocks. To the south, the Devonian rock strata of the Palaeozoic age are mainly horizontal. A belt of

HERBERT LANKS—PIX

Bear Mountain Bridge crosses the Hudson about 25 miles north of New York City. Bear Mountain is popular with day trippers, many of whom arrive by boat.

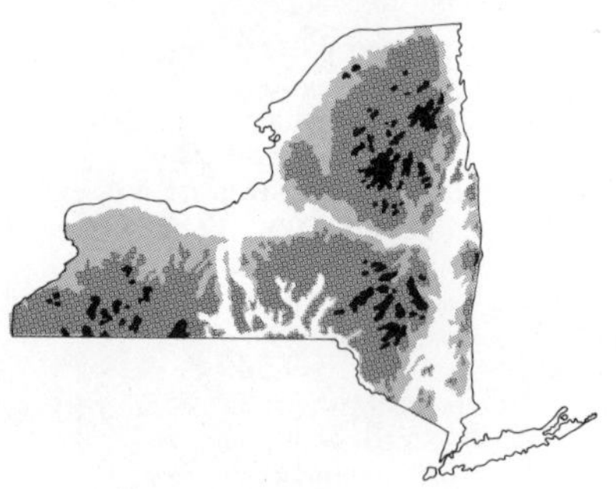

Elevation: under 500 feet (white); 500–1,000 feet (gray); 1,000–2,000 feet (dark gray); over 2,000 feet (black).

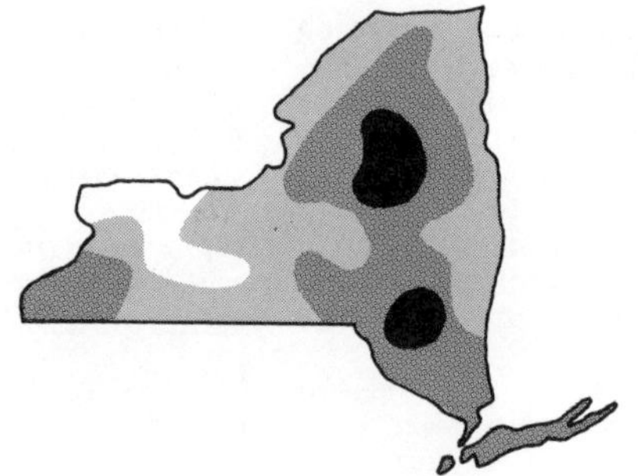

Precipitation: 24–32 inches (white); 32–40 inches (light gray); 40–48 inches (dark gray); 48–56 inches (black).

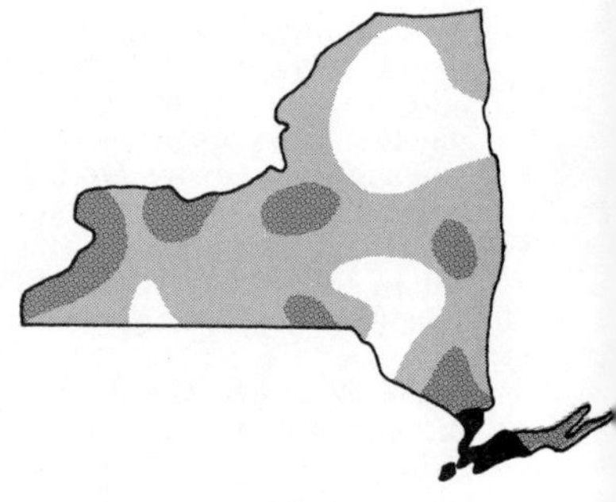

Population density: under 50 (white); 50–200 (light gray); 200–1,000 (dark gray); 1,000–77,000 (black).

Pre-Cambrian crystalline rocks extends from southern New York northeastward into Connecticut and Massachusetts and southeastward to New Jersey. A belt of Triassic sandstone with intrusions of trap rock forms the picturesque Palisades on the lower Hudson River.

Topography. Along with Pennsylvania, New York has the distinction of touching both the Great Lakes and the Atlantic Ocean. But New York is unique in the fact that both these waterways are linked within the state by lowlands and river valleys which furnish excellent routes through the lofty Appalachian range. Adorning the valleys are farms, villages, and industrial cities, with spacious wilderness prevailing in the upland country. There are several natural regions in the state of New York. One is the Adirondack Mountains, which occupy about 8,500 square miles in the northern part of the state. This scenic region is marked by clear lakes, rushing streams, waterfalls, and woodland trails. The Adirondacks contain the highest point in the state, Mount Marcy, 5,344 feet high. South of the Adirondacks are the Catskill Mountains, which extend west from the Hudson River and rise to as much as 4,000 feet above sea level. The Allegheny Plateau fans out east from the Catskills with many extended hills which are some 2,000 feet above sea level. Between them are verdant valleys with fine grazing lands that help make this one of the richest dairy sections in the nation. On the northern edge of this plateau stretch the Finger Lakes. North of the Allegheny Plateau are the lowlands called the Great Lakes Plain, which has a swampy surface but many hills, some as high as 150 feet, left by the glaciers of the Ice Age. The most prominent of these are located near Syracuse and Rochester. A ridge of solid limestone rock forms the Niagra Falls where the waters of Lake Erie drop sharply into Lake Ontario. Similarly, the St. Lawrence Lowlands south of the St. Lawrence River are about 18 miles in width and reach from the Thousand Islands to the Canadian border. To the south of the Adirondack Mountains lies the lovely Mohawk Valley, the main lowland separating the Adirondacks from the Appalachians and an important portion of the Great Lakes-Atlantic Ocean route. Old rocks jut upward on both sides of the Mohawk River. From Lake Champlain to New York City flows the Hudson River, its valley projecting into the northern reaches of the Appalachian section. As far as 150 miles up the river is the passage where the Atlantic tide meets the river current. Below the Hudson Falls at Troy a wide valley divides the Adirondacks and the Allegheny Plateau on the west from the Taconic Hills on the east. This region connects the Green Mountains of Vermont and the highland part of southern New York and northern New Jersey. Thus the state drains to the sea in various tangents. The sources of the St. Lawrence river system are mostly small plateau streams from the Adirondacks. Part of the western portion of the state drains via the Ohio River to the Mississippi, and thence to the Gulf of Mexico. A larger area drains into the Susquehanna River and thence to Chesapeake Bay, while other sections of the state send their waters through the Delaware River to the Atlantic Ocean.

Lakes and Rivers. In New York State there are over 8,000 lakes of varying size. The majority of these are small, and all of them, including Lake Erie and Lake Ontario, were caused by action of the early glaciers. Aside from these two major inland bodies of water, Lake Champlain is the state's largest lake. Scenic Lake George drains into it. Other significant bodies of water inside the state are lakes Oneida, Chautauqua, and the Finger Lakes (Cayuga, Seneca, Keuka, Canandaigua, Owasco and Skaneateles—designations of Indian origin). In the Finger Lakes region is located the picturesque Watkins Glen State Park. Falls and rapids abound in New York, the chief of these being Niagara Falls, a mile wide and 167 feet high.

The New York coastline extends for 200 miles along Lake Ontario and 75 miles along Lake Erie. Largest of the lake ports is Buffalo, which is strategically located at the headwaters of the Niagara River. Here boats from the west transfer their cargoes to rail or canal for the trip eastward. Boats also sail from this important port-center into Lake Ontario and from there to the St. Lawrence River. Although the activity on these northern lakes and rivers is important, by far the most vital coastline is that on the Atlantic. Most of this coastline is on Long Island, winding through summer resorts and fishing villages. New York City is acknowledged to be the finest harbor in the world. Touching on some 600 miles of water front, it is the world's most active international port.

Climate. Due to the state's wide range of altitude, its large bodies of inland water, and the generally humid weather which covers the northeastern part of the United States, New York has a varied climate. The mean annual temperature of the state is around 50° F, ranging from 40° in the Adirondacks to 50° in New York City. In the Adirondacks, the winters are chilly, temperatures sometimes dropping to 40 degrees below zero, but in most parts of the state, sub-zero temperatures seldom occur. The lowest temperature ever recorded was 52° below zero in Herkimer County on Feb. 9, 1934; and the highest recorded was 108° at Troy on July 22, 1926. Lake Erie, Lake Ontario, and the Finger Lakes influence temperatures in the areas adjoining them, and lakes Erie and Ontario never freeze over. Snowfall in the northern regions is significant. Usually rainfall is abundant in New York with the exception of 1961–66 in which a serious drought occurred. Average precipitation is about 40 inches, with snow accumulations ranging from 30 inches downstate to 75 inches upstate. The period of greatest rain is ordinarily between May and September, precipitation being heaviest in the southeastern part of the state and along the western slopes of the Adirondacks. The driest areas are in the Champlain Valley and west of Seneca Lake; some communities there receive less than 30 inches of rainfall a year. There is generally plentiful snow for winter sports in the mountains, the heaviest fall deriving from winds off lakes Erie and Ontario. In Herkimer, Lewis, and Jefferson counties, the average snowfall is about 160 inches, the greatest in the nation east of the Rocky Mountains. Growing seasons are most favorable around New York City and south of Lake Ontario.

Soil, Vegetation, and Animal Life. In general the surface soil is made up of sand and clay deposits left by the glacial drift. The soil of Long Island consists mostly of rocky and sandy loams used for garden produce, while soil at higher altitudes is often poor and not good for the growing of crops. Especially rich are the soils of the Genesee and Mohawk valleys. Shrubs and flowering plants abound. In the forests there are goldthread, trillium, wild sarsaparilla, and other such vegetation. Meadow plants include dandelions, daisies, goldenrod, and Queen Anne's lace. Around the edge of the woodlands are violets and clover interspersed with buttercups. In the waters grow alder, cattails, iris, and water lilies.

Rats and mice are the most numerous animals in the state. Other animals that inhabit New York are fox, rabbit, deer, chipmunk, squirrel, skunk, porcupine, raccoon, woodchuck, beaver, bear, mink, and otter. Snakes and other such reptiles exist in fairly large numbers. Birds of many kinds are in profusion. There are hawks, ruffled grouse, horned larks, pheasants, nuthatch, golden-crowned kinglet, chickadee, sparrow, blue jay, swallow, catbird, robin, wren, woodpecker, blackbird, cardinal, and oriole.

Economic Features

New York has an immense supply of skilled and unskilled labor, excellent transportation facilities, and plentiful power. The state is a center of industrial and business growth and scientific research, with excellent employment opportunities and a generally high standard of living. It is estimated that New York provides a half-million more jobs for its people than any other state. As a center for banking and finance and wholesale and retail trade, it is the most important state in the country. The state is a center of fashion, advertising, publishing, music, art, and drama. In colonial times there was an influx of people of all economic backgrounds from Europe, and after the Revolution, economic opportunities continued to draw immigrants. Since World War II, New York's economy has been highlighted by the rise of the durable-goods industry and the impressive growth of the manufacturing industries.

Agriculture. Almost half the large area of New York is farmland, and until 1890, New York was the first state in the nation in the value of its agricultural production. New York today has more than 100,000 farms, almost all of them with electrical power and 90 per cent of them with telephone service. The average yearly farm income for the state is nearly one billion dollars. Until 1830, the major agricultural products were wheat and corn, but by 1850, dairying had surpassed wheat production. Today, milk is the source of over one half of the state's total farm income. Livestock ranks second and poultry and eggs and truck crops are third. The largest duck farms in the nation are located on Long Island. Among the states, in 1964 New York ranked first in the production of maple syrup, ice cream, cabbage, and dried whole milk; and second in the production of apples, cauliflower, cottage cheese, buckwheat, and snap beans. Potatoes, onions, corn, lima beans, beets, grapes, cherries, berries, and peaches are also important crops. Important agricultural industries are processing and distributing facilities such as milk plants, canneries, dehydrators, cold storage establishments, and rail and truck transportation. The first state agriculture experiment station was built in New York, at Geneva in 1881. The agriculture of New York today is influenced by the growth of population and the expansion of suburbs. Over one fourth of the farms in New York are part-time projects, and many farms have been given over to real estate developments.

Forestry. Almost half of the state of New York is forest, located particularly in the Adirondack and Catskill mountains. The principal kinds of trees are the red and white pine, hemlock, spruce, balsam, ash, and red cedar. In the southern part of the state oak, maple, and laurel trees flourish. Other trees are hardwoods, elm, chestnut, dogwood, basswood, and sycamore.

Fisheries. Fishing is an important industry. There are 500 varieties of fish in New York waters—among them bluefish, sucker, sea bass, bullhead, flounder, yellow perch, chain pickerel, pike, and brook trout. Clams, lobsters, oysters, and scallops are found off Long Island.

Mining. Although New York leads all other states in the production of rock salt, garnet, wollastonite, emery, and talc and produces 25 other types of minerals, its commercial wealth in this respect is limited by its lack of coal and petroleum deposits. Iron and silver are abundant, especially in the Adirondacks. Near Buffalo there are gypsum

D. JORDAN WILSON—PIX

Niagara Falls, one of New York State's greatest tourist attractions, is located between Lake Erie and Lake Ontario. The photograph at right shows both the American Falls (foreground), and the Horseshoe Falls, which are on the Canadian side of the border. They are separated by Goat Island. The American Falls are about 167 feet high, 1,000 feet wide, and have a flow of about six million gallons per minute.

deposits. Elsewhere in the state are zinc, brick and other clay products, and much sand and gravel. Old salt beds once used by Indians are located not far from Syracuse. Since 1950, the value of mineral production in New York has increased from 156 to over 260 million dollars.

Electric Power. The Niagara Power Project, which was completed in 1962 by the New York State Power Authority, has a total kilowatt capacity of 2,190,000; it is the largest hydroelectric development in the United States. The energy created by Niagara Falls is utilized by thirteen giant generators. The international St. Lawrence power development, also a publicly owned project, began operation in 1960. Conducted jointly with the province of Ontario, this operation is the third largest on the continent. High voltage transmission grid wires extend from Niagara Falls to New York City. In addition, there is private utility expansion in the state, power companies having spent over three billion dollars on development between 1955 and 1965. The nation's largest privately owned atomic power plant is at Indian Point in the lower Hudson River Valley. Electricity is particularly needed in such industries as the primary metals (aluminum and steel) and in fabricated metals.

Manufacturing. Since 1840, New York has ranked first among the states in the value of its manufactured products. Its geographic position combined with its natural resources have helped it to maintain this leadership. The great commercial possibilities of New York were recognized by its earliest settlers, who quickly developed transportation facilities and lumber and grist mills. During the half-century after the American Revolution, the state remained mostly agricultural. Then the merchants of New York City gradually surpassed their rivals in Philadelphia and Boston; the opening of the Erie Canal created a demand for western wheat and other goods. For a century after 1840, New York handled more than half of the nation's imports and a third of its exports. As railroads transported more and more goods to and from New York the state became a leading center of foreign trade. New York's proportion of national commerce has since declined with the development of western transportation, but the Port of New York is still the busiest port of the world. The apparel industry is the largest manufacturing employer in the state. The total manufacturing payroll of the state is over ten billion dollars a year. The one and a quarter million persons locally employed produce almost 15 per cent of the national output. One fourth of the country's printing and publishing is done in New York state.

Service Industries. The fluctuating construction industry declined in the early 1960's but rose again in the spring of 1966. Although the number of retail and wholesale trade establishments has decreased in the past decade, the volume of trade in both categories has increased to some extent. The World's Fair of 1964–65 saw the tourist trade grow markedly, bringing millions of new visitors to New York City. In New York there is an intense concentration of service trades dealing with everything from automobile repairs to insurance, securities, banking and finance, the latter three activities being concentrated in the financial district of New York City, where over three fourths of the nation's stocks and bonds are handled.

Social Features

Population. From its beginning as a colony, New York has been distinguished by the variety of its people. The Dutch settlers encouraged immigrants from any nation, so that by 1664, when the English gained control of the colony, the people were already cosmopolitan. During the next century, however, the rate of immigration was slowed because of conflict between the British and the French and Indians. During this time French, Germans, Scots, Irish, and Negroes settled in New York. During the Revolution the population fluctuated because of the change in local government from American to British and back to American. The census of 1790 gave New York's population as 340,120. But soon a flood of New Englanders and others increased the population until a century later the population exceeded five million. Between 1845 and 1860 another influx of immigration had occurred when Irish and German immigrants poured into the state, the former because of the failure of the potato crop, the latter because of the failure of the Revolution of 1848. Increased industrialization and urbanization following the Civil War concentrated industrial and commercial activities in established population centers at strategic points along the state's main transportation routes and hastened the movement of people from rural areas to these centers. After 1890 the sources of immigration shifted from northwestern Europe to southern and eastern Europe, and many Italians, Poles, Russians, and Greeks came to New York. After World War I, such immigration was slowed down not only by the war itself but by limitations imposed by Congress in the 1920's, the Depression, and World War II. During this period, a new trend developed. People began to move in large numbers from the cities into the suburbs as automobiles enabled more people to live farther from their places of work. As suburban areas grew, population expanded farther into the surrounding rural sections which in turn became suburban. The state population has increased steadily in the first half of the twentieth century. Since 1945, a contributory factor to New York's population growth has been the resumption of immigration from Europe and the influx of many southern Negroes and Puerto Ricans. Negroes and Puerto Ricans now number about one million each.

In 1960, 78.3 per cent of the population was native white, 13 per cent was foreign-born white, and 8.5 per cent was Negro. The period between 1940 and 1960 was marked mainly by tremendous suburbanization. While New York City decreased in population, two counties, Nassau and Suffolk, tripled their populations, and Putnam and Rockland counties doubled theirs.

Religion and Education. Every major faith and many minor ones are represented in New York. Roman Catholics make up about one third of the population of the state, and Jews comprise some 15 per cent. About one half of the Jews in the United States live in New York. Headquarters of many Protestant organizations are in New York City, in particular, the National Council of Churches which has as its members most Protestant churches. The largest Catholic university in the nation, St. John's, is located in Jamaica, Queens, New York City.

In the earliest stages of settlement, only a fraction of the children in New York received any formal education. But by the close of the Dutch period, there was a free elementary school in nearly every settlement. After the Revolution, steps were taken to establish a comprehensive educational system under state control. The Board of Regents was created in 1784 to supervise education within the state, having authority to incorporate new academies and colleges. The free high school movement, however, was not widespread until after the Civil War. About 150 communities manage their own school districts under supervision of the State Education Department. Most of the school systems in rural areas have been consolidated into central school districts. Compulsory attendance, which began in 1874, requires that all children between the ages of seven and sixteen attend school. Teachers are protected by tenure and minimum salary laws and a retirement system.

NEW YORK STATE DEPT. OF COMMERCE
Construction began on the New York State Capitol at Albany in 1867 but was not completed for 30 years.

New York has 203 colleges and universities, more than any other state. The University of the State of New York includes all secondary and higher educational institutions which are tax-supported in New York State, as well as libraries, museums, historical societies, and other such institutions. Enrollment in higher education totals more than half a million students and 48,000 teachers. In 1965, 65,000 masters', doctors' and professional degrees were awarded, as well as 10,000 associate degrees. The main universities include Columbia, New York University (the largest private university in the nation), Fordham, St. John's, and City University of New York (all located in New York City); and Cornell, Union, Syracuse, Rochester, Buffalo, Colgate, Hamilton, Russell Sage, Skidmore, and Union University in the upstate regions. The U.S. Military Academy is on the Hudson River at West Point and the U.S. Merchant Marine Academy is at King's Point.

Transport and Communication. The first people to explore New York were seeking trade routes to the Orient, so the fine facilities of such rivers as the Hudson and St. Lawrence caught the fancy of Henry Hudson and Samuel de Champlain as natural arteries of transportation. Completion of the Erie Canal in 1825 stimulated canal building in the state between the Great Lakes and the Atlantic Ocean, but during the 1850's the Erie began to lose cargo to the New York Central and Erie railroads which had come to outclass the canals as freight carriers. By 1890, the Erie Canal had lost nearly all its business. Even so, 13 years later it was decided to construct another canal from Albany to Buffalo, so the Barge Canal was opened in 1916. Along with the Champlain, Cayuga, Seneca, and Oswego canals, it forms the New York State Barge Canal System, some 800 miles in length. Railroad transportation began in New York in 1831 when the Mohawk and Hudson Railroad from Albany to Schenectady was completed. It was the second railroad to begin operation in the United States. In 1853 the New York Central Railroad linking New York and Albany was organized. By 1962, 39 railroads covered some 6,255 miles of track in the state. Other important rail lines were the Delaware and Hudson, the Erie, Lehigh Valley, Delaware, Lackawanna and Western, and the Long Island.

Highways in the state total about 110,000 miles. The New York Thruway stretches some 560 miles from New York City to Buffalo, and is the world's longest toll expressway. It is a multi-lane road without traffic lights or grade crossings. In 1965 the state had 300 airports, 30 seaplane bases, and 22 heliports.

The first newspaper to be published in the state was the *New York Gazette*, established in 1725 by William Bradford who was also the official printer for the colonial government. Today some 680 newspapers (including 535 weeklies) and about 2,000 periodicals are published in the state. New York has a network of telegraph and telephone cables and microwave systems. In 1963 there were almost 7 million residential and 3 million business telephones operating in the state.

Cultural Features

Museums and Theaters. More museums are located in New York than in any other state. Notable among them are the Metropolitan Museum of Art, the American Museum of Natural History, and the Museum of Modern Art, all located in New York City. Other important museums are the State Museum in Albany, the Albright-Knox Art Gallery in Buffalo, the Remington Art Memorial in Ogdensburg, the Munson-Williams Proctor Institute in Utica, and the Glass Museum in Corning.

There are also numerous historical societies. In Cooperstown, once the home of James Fenimore Cooper, are located the New York State Historical Association, the Baseball Hall of Fame, and the Farmers' Museum. The New-York Historical Society in New York City maintains a constructive program of commemoration and publishes a quarterly. At Fort Ticonderoga on Lake George, the original fort has been restored and is a popular attraction for tourists. Other historical organizations include the Rochester Historical Society, the Albany Institute of History and Art, and the Westchester County Historical Society.

The cultural capital of the United States is New York City. The Metropolitan Opera moved in 1966 from its old home to the new Lincoln Center for the Performing Arts. Lincoln Center also houses the New York Philharmonic Orchestra, theater and ballet groups, the Juilliard School of Music, a part of Fordham University, and other cultural activities. Synonymous with Broadway in New York City is the theater, most houses of which are located off of that thoroughfare. The distinguished Eastman School of Music is located in Rochester, and Rochester, Syracuse, Buffalo, and Utica all have symphony orchestras. In recent years, the U.S. government, the state, and private foundations have contributed to the support of local entertainment programs.

Libraries in New York have been state-supported since 1796, though the present wide access to free libraries did not come about until the twentieth century. The state library was established at Albany in 1818 as a reference for the legislature and the citizenry. The world-renowned New York Public Library in Manhattan has 70 branches. New York City also provides outstanding private libraries and collections. The libraries of Columbia University, New York University, and the University of Rochester, among others, also afford fine facilities for research. The state library lends books to 1,500 registered libraries and high schools and maintains a system of mobile collections for camps, clubs, and rural areas.

Press, Radio, and Television. As journalism evolved in New York, a popular organ known as the *New York Weekly Journal* was established in 1733 under John Peter Zenger. In a famous trial in 1735 Zenger was charged with libel against local British government officials; he was acquitted when the judge ruled that his statements were truthful. This marked the beginning of freedom of the press in the nation. *The New York Sun*, which began as a penny newspaper in 1833, lasted for over a century. *The New York Tribune*, which was founded by Horace Greeley eight years later, became the first national newspaper. It ceased publication in 1966. *The New York Times*, which prospered after the Civil War, now holds an eminent national status and is known as the newspaper of record.

The first radio station in the state was WGY in Schenectady in 1922. Four years later the first coast-to-coast network was established in New York by the National Broadcasting Company. The same company started the first commercial television station in 1941. Today the national radio and television networks, the Columbia Broadcasting System, the American Broadcasting Company, and the Mutual Broadcasting System, along with NBC, all have headquarters in New York City.

Research and Development. In various parts of the state are some 1,200 private and commercial research testing laboratories which employ about 50,000 professional scientists, engineers, and technicians, and thousands of supporting personnel who develop new techniques and products. About 25,000 engineering students attend the state's universities and colleges, representing over one eighth of all such students in the nation. Many firms have set up research facilities in the cities. The New York State Atomic and Space Development Authority was established in 1962 for research in industrial progress. Large atomic installations have been built by the federal Atomic Energy Commission in New York, the most important being the Brookhaven National Laboratory on Long Island and the Knolls Atomic Power Laboratory at Niskayuna.

Social Welfare. Since the turn of the century, New York has been a leader among the states in such economic and social legislation as the regulation of labor for women and children, workmen's compensation, unemployment insurance, and old age security. State welfare agencies have widely expanded their activities. There has been a continual emphasis upon anti-discrimination legislation and, more recently, upon school and housing programs designed to implement the laws. Conservation has received increased emphasis as the state has acquired larger areas for public parks.

The charitable institutions of the state are under the supervision of such departments as Health and Social Welfare, which visit and inspect the organizations concerned. These include private and church homes; county almshouses; and schools for the deaf, blind, and feeble-minded. The State Department of Health supervises the work of all local health activities outside of New York City. These include three tuberculosis hospitals, a cancer institute, and a rehabilitation center. Employers in New York contribute the equal of 2.7 per cent of each employee's salary for unemployment insurance. Workers can collect benefits of from $2 to $50 per week, depending on their wages, for up to 26 weeks in a benefit year. The Department of Corrections has charge of state prisons, reformatories and county jails. Institutions are maintained for the criminally insane, and there is a state farm maintained for women prisoners. NORTH CALLAHAN

Government

New York State has had several constitutions. The first one, which transformed New York from a colony into a state, was adopted on April 20, 1777. New York became one of the original thirteen states on July 26, 1788. The present constitution was adopted in 1894 and amended extensively in 1938. The 1894 constitution now has 133 amendments. The chief articles under it are: bill of rights; freedom of worship; religious freedom; habeas corpus; freedom of speech and of the press; right to assemble and petition; equal protection of the law; security against unreasonable searches; universal suffrage. Proposed amendments must be approved by two successive legislatures and by a majority of the state electorate.

The government is divided into three branches: the executive, the legislative, and the judicial. The governor, lieutenant-governor, comptroller, and attorney general of the state are elected to four-year terms. The heads of the major executive departments are appointed by the governor and are subject to senate approval. The governor prepares the annual budget and submits it to the legislature. He has veto powers that may be overridden by a two-thirds vote of both houses.

The legislative branch consists of two houses, a senate and an assembly. In 1966 the senate had 65 members, and the assembly had 165 members, all elected for two-year terms. The lieutenant-governor, though not a member of the senate, is its president and presiding officer. The senate, however, elects from among its members for two years a temporary president to direct and guide its business. The assembly is presided over by a speaker, elected from and by its membership for two years. The legislature convenes annually on the first Wednesday after the first Monday in January and remains in session until it has concluded its business. The lawmaking powers of the legislature are practically limitless. It enacts or amends laws relating to the government of the state; appropriates funds for the operation of the various agencies and provides revenues to operate the judicial system; and promotes the public welfare, including the state's indigent, mentally ill, and unemployed.

The judicial system is headed by the Court of Appeals made up of a chief judge and six associates, all elected by the people for fourteen years. The state Supreme Court is composed of 141 judges elected for fourteen years from each of New York's eleven judicial districts. In each judicial department of the supreme court, there is an appellate division. The governor designates the presiding judge as well as the other judges who constitute the various appellate divisions. Other courts provided for by law are county, surrogate, city, justices', and children's courts. There is also a court of claims composed of twelve judges appointed for nine years by the governor, with advice and consent of the senate. New York State's governmental activities are divided into 20 departments. Three departments have elective executives. They are the executive, under the supervision of the governor; the department of audit and control, under the supervision of the state comptroller; and the department of law, under the direction of the attorney-general. The heads of all the other departments are appointed by the governor with the advice and consent of the senate, except the commissioner of education, who is elected by the regents of the state university, and the commissioner of social welfare, who is elected by the board of social welfare.

On the local level, the state is divided into 62 counties. With the exception of New York City counties, each has a county board of supervisors. Other officials are the county judge, the county surrogate, the treasurer, clerk, district attorney, sheriff, and coroners. Below the county level is the township. Cities are divided into three classes: the first class with a population exceeding 175,000; the second class between 50,000 and 175,000; and the third class under 50,000. Each is incorporated by charter. For a description of the government of New York City, see NEW YORK CITY.

To be eligible to vote in New York, residency in the state for one year, in the same county for four months, and in the same election district for 30 days, is required. New York is represented in the U.S. Congress by two senators and 41 representatives.

PAUL ELDRIDGE

History

Indian history in the state falls into two periods: the prehistoric, from about 3500 B.C. to A.D. 1600, and the historic period thereafter. Archaeologists have excavated several prehistoric sites, chiefly in the Finger Lakes region, from which have come important collections of artifacts. The historic period produced one of the most powerful of American Indian tribes, the Iroquois, whose confederacy of five tribes (Mohawk, Oneida, Onondaga, Seneca, and Cayuga) dominated eastern North America from Delaware into Canada. The tribes played an important role as middlemen in the fur trade and as allies or enemies of the French and English empire builders.

Exploration. In the late fifteenth century Spanish, French, Portuguese, and English explorers laid claims to the region for their respective countries. In 1609 the English sea captain, Henry Hudson, sailing for the Dutch, laid the basis for the Dutch claim. Six weeks before, Samuel de Champlain had entered the state from the north under the flag of France.

Dutch Settlement. In 1614 the private New Netherland Company was given a three-year monopoly of the fur trade. In 1621 the Dutch West India Company was given full political and economic authority in the Dutch possessions in America.

Colonization was begun with a settlement of Walloons under Cornelius May in 1624, mostly around Fort Orange (Albany). Peter Minuit became director general in 1626, purchasing Manhattan Island from Indians for a small sum, and introducing the patroon system in 1629. Although much publicized, the patroon system was not successful in attracting settlers to New Amsterdam or other areas of the colony. The administrations of the next governors, Wouter van Twiller (1633–38) and William Kieft (1638–46), were marked by Indian uprisings. After 1647, when a dour but competent governor, Peter Stuyvesant, began his administration, the colony flourished until taken by the English as a prize of war in 1664. See MINUIT, PETER; PATROON; STUYVESANT, PETER.

British Rule. During a war between England and Holland (1664–67), Charles II granted New Netherland to his brother James, duke of York. An English force under Col. Richard Nicolls, first governor of New York (1664–68), compelled Stuyvesant to surrender, and New Netherland became New York. During another war (1672–78) the Dutch recaptured the colony in 1673, but restored it to the English by a treaty of peace the next year. Thomas Dongan, who became governor in 1681, convened the first provincial assembly in 1683; this body was dissolved a few years later under James II, but was revived in 1689. When the Duke of York succeeded to the throne in 1685, New York became a royal province. In 1686 it was united with other English colonies to form the Dominion of New England under Gov. Edmund Andros. When news was received of the overthrow of James II, 1689–90, and of the succession of William and Mary, Andros was overthrown and the consolidated province came to an end. In the same year, Capt. Jacob Leisler led an uprising and took control of the government, but his regime was suppressed two years later; Leisler and a lieutenant were hanged for treason.

When New York was established in 1664 its boundaries were ill defined. In 1664 the Duke of York transferred New Jersey to Lord John Berkeley and Sir George Carteret, and in 1682 he gave Delaware to William Penn. The New York colony had claims to Maine and adjacent islands, but these regions were annexed to Massachusetts Bay Colony in 1686 and 1691. Other boundary disputes with the New England colonies remained unsettled until after the Revolutionary War. It was not until 1786 that Massachusetts recognized New York's sovereignty over 19,000 square miles of territory in the western part of the state. In 1790 New York surrendered its claim to Vermont for the sum of $30,000, thus enabling that state to enter the new Union in 1791.

During the various intercolonial wars the colony suffered an undue share of violence, its frontier being pillaged by the French and their Indian allies. The Iroquois, however, who earlier had been angered by Champlain's aid to the Hurons, remained implacable enemies of the French and valuable defenders of the New York frontier. In 1690 Schenectady was taken by the French and Indians, and most of its 250 inhabitants were killed or captured. A colonial congress met in 1690 to make common cause with the Iroquois against New France. A second, the Albany Congress, convened at Albany in 1754 to "confirm and establish the ancient friendship of the Six Nations" and to consider plans of permanent union among the colonies. See ALBANY CONGRESS; IROQUOIS.

Revolutionary War. The Stamp Act Congress of 1765 met in New York City. Two years later the New York assembly refused to vote supplies for British troops, and was promptly suspended by the crown. After the first provincial congress met in 1775, however, the mother country permitted the assembly to reconvene as a conciliatory move to stave off the impending rebellion. In January, 1774, the revolutionary party appointed a committee of correspondence to keep in touch with the other colonies. On July 9, 1776, the provincial congress ratified the Declaration of Independence, and the next day declared itself "the Convention of the Representatives of the State of New York." Patriots and loyalists were fairly evenly divided in the state; it is estimated that during and after the war about 40,000 Tories left New York, many going to Canada.

The state had a prominent role in the military history of the war; of 308 battles and engagements, 92 took place in New York territory. Early in 1775 Gens. Ethan Allen and Benedict Arnold took Ticonderoga, and Seth Warner captured Crown Point. Later the same year Gens. Richard Montgomery and Arnold launched an unsuccessful invasion of Canada from New York. In 1776 the British commander, Sir William Howe, defeated Gen. George Washington in the battles of Long Island and White Plains and gained possession of New York City,

STANDARD OIL CO. (N.J.)

Fine pastureland in the foothills of the Adirondack Mountains supports a thriving dairy industry. Until 1890 New York ranked first of all the states in agricultural production, and is still, despite the demands of industry and real-estate development, an important producer of such foods as milk, cheese, apples, beans, potatoes, grapes, eggs, and poultry.

which remained British headquarters throughout the war. In 1777 Gen. John Burgoyne embarked on an expedition from Canada, the objective being to unite with Howe and split the northern states from those in the south; the surrender of Burgoyne's forces at Saratoga prompted the French to come to the aid of the Americans. After the final treaty of peace the American Army marched into New York City late in 1783. See REVOLUTIONARY WAR.

Statehood in the New Union. In the drafting of the federal Constitution, New York exercised little more than a negative influence. As one of the larger states, it was opposed to the concessions made to the smaller ones; moreover, the strong New York faction of DeWitt Clinton feared the control of a strong central government. During the campaign for ratification, *The Federalist Papers* of Alexander Hamilton, James Madison, and John Jay won much support for the Constitution. When the ratifying convention was elected by universal manhood suffrage, about two thirds of the delegates were opposed to ratification; yet the final vote was 30 to 27 in favor. This shift resulted from the fact that after 10 states had ratified the document, New York did not dare stand outside the new Union. Thus on July 26, 1788, New York became the 11th state to ratify the Constitution. New York City was made the national capital in 1789; the following year, however, the seat of federal government was moved to Philadelphia.

Organization of the state government began with the meeting of a popular convention at White Plains in 1776. The first state constitution, adopted in 1777, remained in force 45 years. One of its noteworthy features was the establishment of a council of appointment, a committee designed to limit the power of the governor. The second constitution was adopted in 1822. It abolished property qualifications for suffrage for all male citizens except Negroes. The third constitution, adopted in 1846, marked a reaction against centralized power. The fourth constitution dates from 1894.

Later History. Slavery began under Dutch rule and persisted for a time under the English until, in 1799, a state emancipation act was passed that provided for the gradual freeing of slaves. By 1827 slavery had been abolished in the state. Before the Civil War there were many in New York who sympathized with the South, and most of its people were believers in states' rights. But when hostilities broke out, New York rallied to the defense of the Union and became in many ways a leader of the Union cause. That leadership stemmed in large part from the activities of New York newspapers, and occurred notwithstanding the so-called Draft Riots of July 13–16, 1863, in New York City, that were occasioned by the draftings of citizens for military service, and despite the fact that Horatio Seymour, the Democratic governor elected in 1862, denounced the war and its leaders. The state furnished 467,047 men to the Union military services.

The Tammany Society, organized in New York City in 1789 as a social and patriotic body, became identified with the Democratic-Republican party in 1798 and long exerted a strong and sometime pernicious influence on the politics of New York City. Especially in the period 1869–71, when it was controlled by the so-called Tweed Ring, Tammany contributed little to the social and moral uplift of the city. Another political ring, the so-called Albany Regency, flourished in the state from 1820 to 1850. See TAMMANY HALL; TWEED, WILLIAM MARCY.

The national influence of New York State, always prominent, increased considerably after the Civil War—largely as a result of the rapid growth of New York City, which as the nation's principal port of entry became by the late nineteenth century one of the world's cosmopolitan cities. Between 1870 and 1950 the state population increased by 10.5 million. This increase was an impetus to the state's creative energies in material and cultural matters that continue to dominate the nation. Although the state administration has often been dominated by political machines with such accompanying abuses as the spoils system and mediocre government, it has also brought forward many individuals of ability who have achieved outstanding state and national importance. Elihu Root (1845–1937), New York lawyer, was prominent in the drafting of the 1894 constitution, and as U.S. secretary of war, 1905–09, reorganized the War Department. Samuel Tilden (1814–86), Democratic politician and bitter opponent of the Tweed Ring, resigned the state governorship in 1876 to run for the U.S. presidency against Rutherford B. Hayes, and narrowly missed being elected. Other New York governors who became President after the Civil War were Chester A. Arthur (1881–85), Grover Cleveland (1885–89 and 1893–97), Theodore Roosevelt (1901–09), and Franklin D. Roosevelt (1933–45). Others of noted ability whose administrations promoted social reform were Herbert E. Lehman (1932–42) and Thomas E. Dewey (1942–54). A simplified code of civil procedure and an insurance law, promulgated by the New York bar and adopted by the state legislature, have served as models for legal reform in many states.

In 1950 a state authority was created by legislative act to build and operate a 404-mile superhighway between New York and Buffalo. The New York Thruway was completed in 1960. In 1954, after serving 12 years as governor, Dewey declined to run again. The Democrats then gained control of the state government when W. Averell Harriman won a close victory over Sen. Irving M. Ives. In the 1958 elections, however, when the Democrats won heavily throughout much of the nation, Harriman lost the state governorship to Republican Nelson Aldrich Rockefeller, who had served as assistant secretary of state of the United States, 1944–45. Rockefeller was subsequently re-elected in 1962 and 1966. During his first term of office, he reorganized the departments of state government and introduced legislation which re-organized the state's court system. In 1965 a bill was passed that virtually abolished capital punishment in New York. Two of the most controversial issues in the 1960's were civil rights and legislative re-apportionment of voting districts. The Metcalf-Baker law of 1963 banned discrimination in the sale or rental of private housing, and the following year another bill was passed curbing discrimination in apprenticeship training programs. A continuing problem was the issue of *de facto* segregation in public schools. In 1964, for the first time in 30 years, Democrats gained control of the state legislature. In the election former U.S. attorney general Robert F. Kennedy was elected by a great plurality over Republican Kenneth Keating to become New York's new junior senator. Both Kennedy and Republican Senator Jacob Javits emerged as important national political figures with presidential or vice-presidential possibilities. In 1965 the Democrats lost control of the state senate but retained a majority in the assembly. ERIC BRUNGER

BIBLIOG.–Abraham Bompey, *New York Story* (1965); L. K. Caldwell, *Government and Administration of New York* (1954); Carl Carmer, *The Hudson River* (1962); Paul Eldridge, *Crown of Empire: The Story of the State of New York* (1962); David Ellis and others, *New York: The Empire State* (ed. 1964); A. C. Flick, ed., *History of the State of New York* (1935); Michael Glassman, *New York State and New York City History, Geography, and Government* (ed. 1965); Stewart Holbrook, *The Old Post Road* (1962); W. A. Ritchie, *Archaeology of New York State* (1965); D. C. Sowers, *The Financial History of New York State from 1789 to 1912* (1914); R. A. Straetz and F. J. Munger, *New York Politics* (1960); R. S. Tarr, *Physical Geography of New York State* (1902); J. H. Thompson, ed., *Geography of New York State* (1966); WPA Project, *A Guide to the Empire State* (1940).

LOUIS MELANCON

New York's modern Lincoln Center for the Performing Arts includes the New York State Theater (left), the Metropolitan Opera House (center), the Vivian Beaumont Theater (right background), and the Philharmonic Hall (right).

NEW YORK, city, SE New York State; most populous city in the United States; a major American port of entry; the most important financial, educational, cultural, and trade center on the North American continent; situated at 40°42′N, 74°W at the junction of the Hudson River with New York Bay and the Atlantic Ocean; on the major U.S. highways and railroads and national and international air and shipping lines; 188 airline miles from Boston, 713 from Chicago, 2,697 from San Francisco, 3,459 from London, 4,662 from Moscow; land area 319.8 square miles; pop. (1965 est.) 7,993,000.

Physical Features

Five Boroughs. Since 1898 when Greater New York was created by charter it has been composed of five boroughs, which coincide with five New York State counties. The oldest and most crowded is the island borough of Manhattan (land area 22.6 sq. mi.) constituting New York County. The other boroughs are Brooklyn (78.5 sq. mi.), constituting Kings County at the west end of Long Island; Bronx (43.1 sq. mi.), the only borough located on the mainland, constituting Bronx County; Queens (114.7 sq. mi.), east of Kings County on Long Island, constituting Queens County; and Richmond, also known as Staten Island (60.9 sq. mi.), constituting Richmond County.

Setting. The best-known part of the city is Manhattan Island, 13.4 miles long and ranging from 1 to 2.3 miles in width, trending northeast to southwest, the Hudson River on its west side (and New Jersey across the river), the East River to the east and the Harlem River to the northeast and north. At its northerly end the island is separated from the mainland by Spuyten Duyvil Creek, connecting with the Harlem River; in 1895 a more direct canal was cut from the Spuyten Duyvil to the Harlem, so that there is deep-water navigation along the entire shore line of the island. The New York State Barge Canal uses the Spuyten Duyvil–Harlem River in its New York City section, having its terminus at Mott Haven in the southwest Bronx. At its southern end, the East River joins the Hudson to form the Upper Bay, located between Brooklyn, Manhattan, and Richmond. A strait called the Narrows, 1¼ miles wide, separates the Upper and Lower Bays, with the Lower Bay forming the passageway to the ocean. Brooklyn and Richmond face each other across the Narrows. To the east of the East River lie Brooklyn and Queens. Newtown Creek forms part of the boundary between them. Northwest of Queens the East River widens to join Long Island Sound, which then extends northeast between Long Island the the New England mainland. To the north and east of the city line are Westchester and Nassau counties respectively. To the west, Kill Van Kull and Arthur Kill separate Staten Island from New Jersey.

Located in the bays and the East River are several small islands. In the Upper Bay, the most famous are Governor's Island (173 acres) with Coast Guard installations; Liberty Island, formerly Bedloe's Island (12 acres) with the Statue of Liberty; and Ellis Island (27.5 acres), formerly a U.S. immigration station. Randall's Island (194 acres), Welfare Island (120 acres), Ward's Island (254 acres), North Brother Island (13 acres), and Riker's Island (400 acres) in the East River are used by the city for public developments such as parks, hospitals, prisons, and sewage disposal plants.

Harbor. Excellent natural harbor conditions have made New York Harbor one of the busiest ports in the world. The long shore line (about 771 miles of water front) and the deep waters, in addition to the many transit links with the interior of the nation, have contributed to the development of the city as a harbor. Along both east and west lower sides of Manhattan, along the Brooklyn water front of the Upper Bay and the East River, in south Bronx along the Harlem, in Queens along the East River, and on those parts of Staten Island facing on the Upper Bay and Kill Van Kull there are numerous piers with facilities to handle freighters and passenger ships from all over the world. Most of the large transatlantic liners dock at the piers along the Hudson on Manhattan's west side, while freighters concentrate at the Erie Basin and Bush Terminal, Greenpoint and Williamsburg in Brooklyn, Staten Island, and along the lower east side of Manhattan.

Climate. The city's climate is generally moderate. Average temperature in summer is 75°F, in winter 32°; average annual temperature is 54.4°. During heat waves temperatures may rise to 90°–95° (a high of 106° has been recorded), and during cold spells the temperature may drop to 4° or 5° above zero (minimum 15° below zero). Average annual precipitation is 42 inches, with the summer months having slightly more than the others. Situated on the Atlantic Ocean, New York is prone to high relative humidities, local seasonal fogs, and northeasterly and southeasterly storms, with the result that daily weather conditions are frequently quite variable.

Geology. Most of New York is built on bedrock. Manhattan, Bronx, and part of Richmond are underlain by metamorphic rock of great age, and in the two Long Island boroughs glacial deposits cover sedimentary rock. Glacially carried boulders and occasional glacial deposits also occur in the metamorphic rock areas. In Manhattan and the Bronx the surface is composed of northeast-southwest trending ridges separated by valleys, and therefore there are many streets with steep slopes in both boroughs. The valleys are used for major transit routes. Highest elevation in the city is Todt Hill on Staten Island (409 ft.).

Streets. Manhattan's street pattern is the simplest of the five boroughs. Its main artery is Broadway, which runs the length of the borough and through the Bronx. North-south avenues such as Broadway, Fifth, Park, and Madison intersect numbered streets with directions east if east of Fifth Avenue, and otherwise west. Beginning with First Street on the east side and 14th Street on the west side, the city plan adopted in 1807, places these broad avenues 800 to 1,000 feet apart. Below First Street to the tip of Manhattan Island the pattern of the original Dutch town of New Amsterdam is seen in the tangle of narrow, crooked streets that follow no definite plan and have old names given by the early Dutch and English settlers—Pine, Wall, Canal, Grand, and Maiden Lane. Instead of north-south numbered avenues there are the Bowery, Pearl, South and West streets, and so forth.

The Bronx street pattern is most irregular, with numbered streets beginning at 132nd Street in the South and extending to 263rd Street in the Riverdale section in the northeast. The streets are labeled east or west in reference to Jerome Avenue as the dividing line. All other streets (trending in a variety of directions, making it difficult to find one's way) have descriptive names, frequently after early landowners and settlements. In all of the boroughs each original small community contributed local street names and patterns, and local neighborhood names such as (in the Bronx) Williamsbridge, Fordham, Morrisania, and Mott Haven.

In Brooklyn and Queens similar confusion results from peculiar arrangements of some numbered streets and avenues cutting across descriptively named roads. In Brooklyn there are numbered streets preceded with East, West, Bay, South—all in different parts of the same borough. Richmond streets are arranged in individual neighborhoods.

Major retail business streets in Manhattan are 14th, 34th, 42nd, and 57th streets, Madison and Fifth avenues, and the Avenue of the Americas (Sixth Avenue); in Brooklyn—Fulton Street and Flatbush and Church avenues; in the Bronx—149th Street, Fordham Road, and Tremont Avenue; and in Queens—Jamaica and Queens boulevards.

Social Factors

Population. The total population of New York City, according to the 1960 census, was 7,781,984—divided among the five boroughs as follows: Brooklyn, 2,627,319; Manhattan, 1,698,281; Queens, 1,809,578; the Bronx, 1,424,815; and Richmond, 221,991. Based on this census, population density per square mile was about 34,600 in Brooklyn, 76,150 in Manhattan, 16,010 in Queens, 32,830 in the Bronx, and 3,630 in Richmond.

Of New York City's population in 1950, 3,758,142 were male and 4,037,329 female; 6,699,734 were of the white race and 1,095,737 were of other races. Among nonwhites, females usually outnumbered males in a larger ratio than among whites. Of the 1,095,737 nonwhites, 948,196 were classified as Negro; of these, 434,038 were male and 514,158 female. Nonwhites of other races totaled 147,541; only in this category did males (77,558) outnumber females (69,983).

Melting Pot. A large proportion of the people of New York are foreign born, or of foreign-born or mixed parentage. Estimates as to the exact numbers vary greatly. Official 1950 figures indicated that there were 2,659,935 foreign born and 1,972,200 of foreign-born or mixed parentage—not including Puerto Ricans. About 3 million considered some language other than English as the mother tongue, and of these a large proportion did not speak English at all.

Many aspects of New York life reflect the city's polyglot population, particularly the network of neighborhoods following national, racial, and cultural origins. After the 1920's the old-world neighborhood patterns began to break up as a result of slum clearance projects, new housing developments, other civic programs, and the great drop in numbers of new immigrants. In 1960, however, it was still possible to walk through many sections of New York without seeing or hearing a word of English.

The Italians comprise the largest single foreign language group, numbering more than 1 million. Other groups as estimated in 1950 included 2,000 Albanians, 20,000 Armenians, 293,500 Austrians, 3,000 Basques, 11,000 Belgians, 3,000 Brazilians, 190,000 British, 1,130 Bulgarians, a few thousand Catalans, 30,000 Chinese (95 per cent Cantonese), 2,000 Croatians, 64,500 Czechs, 14,500 Danes, 14,500 Dutch, 4,000 Filipinos, 14,000 Finnish, 51,000 French (11,000 from Canada), 15,000 Galicians, almost 500,000 Germans, 57,000 Greeks, more than 115,000 Hungarians, fewer than 1,500 Indians and Pakistani, 500 Indonesians, 500 Iranians, 456,500 Irish, 2,500 Japanese, 9,000 Latvians, 33,000 Lithuanians, 5,000 Maltese, 5,600 Mexicans, 50,000 Norwegians, 400,000 Poles, 5,200 Portuguese, 70,000 Rumanians, 800,000 Russians, 540 Serbians, 18,000 Slovaks, 4,060 Slovenes, 43,700 Swedes, 48,000 Swiss, 1,000 Turks, more than 10,000 Ukrainians, 12,250 Yugoslavs, and a few hundred each of such national or linguistic groups as Polynesians, West Indians, Carpatho-Russians, Estonians, and Ethiopians. There were also about 30,000 New Yorkers from Near Eastern countries including Syria, Jordan, Iraq, and Egypt.

In the late 1950's there were perhaps more than 700,000 Spanish-speaking residents of New York—about 90 per cent of them from Puerto Rico. Each year during the 1950's about 35,000 Puerto Ricans came to New York, where they constituted 7 to 10 per cent of the city's total population, an even larger percentage of the school-age population (more than 14 per cent in 1955), and one of the largest segments of the lower-income portion of the population.

Population Trends. In 1790 New York's people numbered 33,131. The city grew rapidly and steadily until 1930, with the largest percentage increase (126 per cent) in the period 1890–1900. After 1930 the rate of increase diminished until in the period of 1940–50 it was 5.7 per cent. In 1950 the U.S. census put the city's total population at 7,891,957. The decline of 96,486 in total population revealed by the special census of 1957 came as a surprise to many; in 1956 the city department of health had estimated the population at 8,074,000. Since all 1951–55 figures had also been estimates, it was not certain when, after 1950, the population had begun to decline. The 1950 population of the 17-county New York standard metropolitan area (as defined by the U.S. census) was 12,911,994; that of the New York urbanized area, 12,296,117. Estimates in the late 1950's placed the metropolitan area population around 15,000,000. Sharp population increases in the counties surrounding New York City created serious fiscal and administrative problems for those areas as well as for New York City, where many of those who moved their residences elsewhere still continued to derive their incomes. In the late 1950's there began a population shift toward Staten Island, where in less than a decade average property values rose from $500 to $1,500 an acre. Much of the island remained undeveloped in the late 1950's, and it was estimated that 62 per cent of New York's vacant land was in Richmond. A bridge across the Narrows (connecting Fort Hamilton in Brooklyn with Fort Wadsworth in Richmond), scheduled for completion in 1962, was expected to accelerate development of the area.

Buildings and Neighborhoods. In New York are found many of the world's famous office buildings, large banks, busy department stores, fashionable

Dazzling marquees and billboards illuminate Times Square, the heart of New York City's theater district, in midtown Manhattan.
B. NAGELSMITH

The United Nations Secretariat, 39 stories high, flanked by the General Assembly Building and Library (foreground), overlooks the East River.
UNITED NATIONS

The television antenna atop the Empire State Building, the world's tallest structure, towers 1,472 feet above the street.
A DEVANEY, INC., N. Y.

The world's great ocean liners moor in a succession of piers along the Hudson River, on Manhattan's west side.
B. NAGELSMITH

EWING GALLOWAY

The 20-story Flatiron Building, one of New York's first skyscrapers to be constructed of steel, had its walls put on from the top down after the steel work was completed.

specialty shops, and outstanding museums, concert halls, and recreational facilities. Intermingled with skyscrapers, administrative offices, small factory plants, varied retail shops, food stores, and supermarkets are residential areas ranging from skyscraper apartments and hotels in mid-Manhattan to single family dwellings in outlying parts. In the period after World War II and into the 1960's, many luxury dwellings on Park and Madison avenues were replaced by modern office buildings, and vast and numerous slum-clearance projects in some areas made way for new, medium-income, multiple-storied apartment houses.

In the lower, or southern, end of Manhattan is the banking and exchange district around Wall Street, where the New York and American stock exchanges and the cotton, coffee, sugar, and other exchanges constitute the financial heart of the country. The executive offices of many large shipping, communications, and marine insurance firms are in the vicinity. The Federal Hall Memorial Museum with its exhibit on the life of Peter Zenger is located in the Subtreasury Building at Wall and Nassau streets. To the north, in the little triangular park at Broadway and Park Row, stands the city hall, architecturally one of the most beautiful buildings in New York. North and east of the city hall is a civic center that includes the hall of records, the 24-story municipal office building, the taller U.S. courthouse, the county courthouse, the New York State office building, the building of the departments of health, hospitals, and sanitation, and the huge criminal courts building. Formerly along the narrow streets by the East River in lower Manhattan, the old cold-water tenements, occupied since the late 1800's primarily by Jewish and Irish immigrant groups, were in the 1950's being gradually replaced by city-sponsored apartment dwellings for low-income families, and by co-operatively owned apartment buildings for middle-income groups. Nearby areas of tenements are occupied by Chinese and Italian immigrants. Little Italy, just north of Chinatown, partly merges with it. The colorful Chinese quarter centered in Mott, Doyers, Pell, and Bayard streets is the cultural meeting place of the Chinese workers scattered throughout the city and a major tourist attraction.

Adjacent to the financial district, on the west side of Manhattan and extending northward, is a great produce section—fruits, vegetables, butter, eggs, and the like—whose business day is mostly between 2 and 10 A.M. North on Broadway from the municipal center are wholesale dry goods, clothing, and hosiery concentrations spreading from Broadway into the cross streets; further northward to 40th Street is the famous garment district. On the west side of Manhattan, southward from 59th Street, is a great and varied manufacturing and warehouse area, interspersed with slums and two residential nuclei in the Chelsea and Greenwich Village neighborhoods. The Coliseum, at 59th Street and Broadway, is a convention and exposition hall that can accommodate 35,000 people and up to four simultaneous expositions. Fifth Avenue, formerly lined with the individual homes of wealthy citizens, has lost nearly all of them, except at its extreme southern end in Washington Square; around 59th Street are some luxury hotels and clubs. Stretching farther north along Fifth Avenue are rows of large apartment buildings and fine residences. Along Park Avenue in the 50's many apartments were being replaced at mid-century by the office buildings of large national companies, such as the famous Lever House. In this area also are a few of the city's many large hotels, including the renowned Waldorf-Astoria. Third Avenue, formerly covered by the tracks of an elevated train, was in the 1950's being converted into a broad, tree-lined thoroughfare with tall luxury apartment buildings, offices, and shops. Third Avenue in the 50's is noted for its many antique dealers. North of 42nd Street, for six blocks between First Avenue and the East River, is the United Nations Headquarters, completed in 1951. It includes a 39-story secretariat building and conference, assembly, and library buildings on 18 acres valued at $85 million. From 59th Street northward, Manhattan is largely residential, with fine apartments bordering the western edge of Central Park and Riverside Drive, which overlooks the Hudson. In the streets between, residents are crowded into former one-family houses and apartments. A large medical center and two collegiate groupings (Columbia University and the College of the City of New York) are in this area. North of 110th Street, in the old Harlem district, is the principal Negro and Puerto Rican section of Manhattan; there are other large concentrations in Brooklyn, Bronx, and Queens.

A 130-acre civic center was being built in the late 1950's in downtown Brooklyn, at an estimated cost of $130 million. In Brooklyn are the headquarters of the New York City board of education and transit authority, as well as numerous banks and a busy retail shopping district. There are concentrations of buildings for businesses and services in the Jamaica, Long Island City, Astoria, Flushing, and Forest Hills sections of Queens. The major concentrations of nonresidential buildings in the Bronx are in the Fordham section and in the factories and offices at 149th Street in south Bronx, Mott Haven, and along lower Bruckner Boulevard. At 155th Street and the Grand Concourse are the county government buildings and the major Bronx hotels. On Staten Island the St. George Ferry gateway building houses Richmond's leading civic, business, and cultural activities.

Skyscrapers. The 10-story Tower Building (1888–89), at 50 Broadway, was one of the first steel frame skyscrapers. Its height was surpassed in 1890 by the 26-story New York World Building, since demolished, and then by the 27-story Singer Building and the 60-story Woolworth Building. There are two major areas of skyscrapers. One, in the financial district, includes the 71-story Chase Manhattan Bank, the 66-story 60 Wall Street Tower, the 54-story City Bank–Farmers Trust, and the 50-story Irving Trust. The other area is in mid-Manhattan where a magnificent panorama of the city may be seen from the 86th and

102nd observation floors of the world's tallest skyscraper—the Empire State Building, whose 102 stories rise 1,250 feet. Among other mid-town skyscrapers are the 77-story Chrysler Building, the 50-story Chanin Building, the Metropolitan Life Insurance Building with its huge tower clock, and Rockefeller Center. The latter is a group of buildings on 12½ acres between 48th and 52nd streets, the largest privately owned business and entertainment center in the world. Through it runs a private street, Rockefeller Plaza. An immense theater, the Music Hall, is included in the Center.

On the east side, between 42nd and 57th streets, are Lever House and other tall structures such as those of Colgate-Palmolive, Universal Pictures, Arabian-American Oil, and the Seagram Company. In Brooklyn the tallest building in the business section that fans out from the Boro Hall is the Williamsburg Bank Building, 512 feet tall. See SKYSCRAPER.

Parks in the five boroughs (not including many tiny squares and triangles at street intersections) and the 926 miles of parkways within the city are administered by the park department, which operates and manages within its parks 18 golf courses, 500 tennis courts, 17 swimming pools, 16 miles of beaches, and numerous baseball fields, boat basins, and zoos. Even in lower Manhattan there are several small parks, such as Battery and Bowling Green. Union Square was formerly a favorite forum for political orators. The city's most frequented park is the 840-acre Central Park, stretching 2½ miles from 59th to 110th Street between Fifth and Eighth avenues. It contains a zoo, botanic gardens, bridle paths, boating facilities, an ice-skating rink, an ancient Egyptian obelisk (see CLEOPATRA'S NEEDLES), and numerous memorials ranging from great bronze plaques to individual statues and busts. At two Revolutionary War sites on a high rugged ridge in northern Manhattan, are Fort Washington Park and Fort Tryon Park, in which is located the Cloisters, a branch of the Metropolitan Museum. Among many parks in the Bronx are Van Cortlandt Park, with huge playgrounds, golf courses, and other sports and recreational facilities: Mosholu and Pelham Bay parks, both with golf courses, and the latter with a bathing beach and picnic facilities; and Bronx Park (721 acres), containing the largest U.S. zoological park and an outstanding botanic garden. Of the 21 principal parks in Brooklyn, Prospect is the largest and finest, with extensive recreational facilities, a zoo, and botanical garden. In Queens, Flushing Meadow Park (1,259 acres), a reclaimed marsh, was the site in 1939–40 of the New York World's Fair, one of whose remaining buildings, having been used as a United Nations meeting place for a time, has roller- and ice-skating rinks. Great Kills Park is the largest in Richmond; La Tourette and Silver Lake parks have golf courses.

The Bronx Zoo, famous for its zoological rarities, has more than 2,500 specimens of mammals, birds, reptiles, and amphibians. A herd of Nyala antelope is among them.

NEW YORK CONVENTION AND VISITORS BUR.

NEW YORK CONVENTION AND VISITORS BUR.

New York Public Library at Fifth Avenue and 42nd Street has one of the largest reference libraries in the world. Building was constructed in 1911 at cost of $9 million.

Randall's Island is the site of Downing Stadium (seating 21,441), used for sports events and concerts. The city's park system also provides facilities for archery, bicycling, cricket, football, hockey, and running. In addition there are large privately owned stadiums, such as Yankee Stadium (seating 80,000) in the Bronx, home of the New York American League baseball team; the Polo Grounds (66,000) in Manhattan, and Ebbets Field (40,000) in Brooklyn. Baker Field (33,000) is Columbia University's athletic stadium, Lewisohn, the stadium of City College. Two noted race tracks, Aqueduct and Jamaica, are in Queens, and Belmont is just outside the city line in Elmont, Nassau County.

Libraries. Three public library systems, with a total of 180 branch libraries, serve the city. The New York Public Library, second only to the Library of Congress in holdings, maintains reading rooms and circulations in Manhattan, Bronx, and Richmond. The main building at 42nd Street and Fifth Avenue contains a variety of reference rooms—including the map, prints, theater, and music collections and the Oriental, Slavonic, and Jewish divisions. Special collections are located in the Library for the Blind, the municipal reference library, and the Schomburg collection of Negro literature and history. The Brooklyn public library, organized in 1896, has its main collection in the beautiful Ingersoll Building facing Prospect Park, completed in 1941. The main building of the Queens public library system is in Jamaica. In addition the city has more than 1,000 specialized libraries, most of them open to the public under certain conditions. These include those affiliated with the colleges and universities (usually available to students only), those maintained by professional associations, and those of private research units.

Museums. The city is rich in art, scientific, and historical museums—most of them supported by private endowments. The Metropolitan Museum of Art at Fifth Avenue and 82nd Street houses one of the world's largest collections of paintings, sculptures, antiquities, porcelains, pottery, jewels, armor, and early firearms; its branch in Fort Tryon Park, the Cloisters, is devoted to medieval art. The American Museum of Natural History and Hayden Planetarium, on the west side of Central Park, are equally eminent in natural science collections, displays, lectures, publications, and worldwide research. The New York Historical Society maintains an important library and an extensive museum of Americana with special emphasis on New York history; it owns nearly all of John James Audubon's original bird paintings. The Museum of the City of New York concentrates on city history, and sponsors public exhibitions and lectures. The collections in the museum of the Brooklyn Institute of Arts and Sciences, the Whitney Museum of American Art, the Museum of Modern Art, the American Jewish Historical Society, the Museum of Primitive Art, and the Museum of Contemporary Arts are noteworthy. In a cluster at 156th Street

EZRA STOLLER

The Solomon R. Guggenheim Museum on Fifth Avenue, one of the later works of architect Frank Lloyd Wright, has as its nucleus the Guggenheim Collection of modern paintings.

and Broadway are the museums and libraries of the American Academy of Arts and Letters and the American Indian, the American Numismatic, the Hispanic, and the American Geographical societies. The art gallery of Henry C. Frick, open to the public in his former house on Fifth Avenue, contains one of the finest of small art collections, and the J. P. Morgan Library and the Guggenheim Museum contain priceless art collections. There are numerous privately owned art galleries in New York whose special exhibits are usually open to the public.

Many of New York's historically important buildings are maintained, publicly or privately, as museums. A few among these are Fraunces Tavern at Pearl and Broad streets, where Gen. George Washington bade farewell to his officers at the close of the Revolutionary War; the Theodore Roosevelt Birthplace on 28th Street; the Alexander Hamilton Home and the Stephen Jumel Mansion in Washington Heights; the Dyckman Cottage, an eighteenth century Dutch farmhouse at Broadway and 204th Street in Manhattan; the Frederick van Cortlandt Mansion (1748) and the Edgar Allan Poe Cottage (about 1815) in the Bronx; the John Bowne Homestead (1660), where the Society of Friends first met in the area, at Bowne Street and Fox Lane in Flushing, Queens; the home of Rufus King, an early statesman, at Jamaica Avenue and 152nd Street, Queens; the gray-shingled Old Quaker Meeting House (1696) on Northern Boulevard in Flushing, Queens; and the Christopher Billop Homestead (1688) on Staten Island, where in 1776 Benjamin Franklin, John Adams, and Edward Rutledge met Earl Richard Howe, British admiral, in an effort to end the Revolutionary War (hence it is often referred to as Conference House).

Churches. A Dutch Reformed congregation, said to have been organized in 1628, erected a church within Fort Amsterdam in 1642. A small colony of Spanish and Portuguese Jews that came to New York in 1654 was the oldest Jewish congregation in North America. This congregation, Shearith Israel, worships in a beautiful temple at 70th Street and Central Park West. The meeting house of an early Quaker settlement in Flushing still stands on Northern Boulevard. The old John Street Methodist Church, built originally in 1841, is regarded as the cradle of that denomination in America. The city's oldest and richest church is Trinity (Protestant Episcopal, chartered 1679), on Broadway at the head of Wall Street; the present building, erected in 1846, is the third on the site. In its churchyard are buried Alexander Hamilton, Robert Fulton, Albert Gallatin, and other famous persons. It maintains eight chapels, the oldest of which is St. Paul's, formerly a parish church (erected in 1764 at Broadway, Fulton, and Vesey streets) where Earl Richard Howe worshiped during the Revolution, and in which George Washington's pew is preserved. Under the wall of St. Marks-in-the-Bouwerie (Bowery) at Second Avenue and East 10th Street, the early Dutch governor Peter Stuyvesant is buried. The Episcopal Cathedral of St. John the Divine, a Gothic-style building at 112th Street and Amsterdam Avenue in Morningside Heights, has been under construction since 1892 as funds have become available (estimated total cost to be $30 million). St. Thomas', St. Bartholomew's, and the Church of the Heavenly Rest are fashionable mid-town churches. The Episcopal Church of the Transfiguration, built in 1870 at 1 East 29th Street, is affectionately known as the Little Church Around the Corner; it shares the loyalty of the theatrical profession with St. Malachy's Roman Catholic Church on 49th Street. Of more than 1,000 Jewish synagogues in the city, the most renowned are in Manhattan. Especially notable are the graceful Temple Emanu-El (1929) at Fifth Avenue and 65th Street and Central Synagogue at Lexington Avenue and 55th Street, the city's oldest house of worship in continuous use (1872). St. Patrick's Cathedral (1879) at Fifth Avenue and 50th Street is the seat of the Roman Catholic diocese of New York. It is an imposing structure in Gothic style whose twin spires are 330 feet high; it has 70 stained-glass windows, many of them by the French artisans, Nicholas Lorin and Henri Ely. Another important Catholic church is old St. Peter's at Church and Barclay streets, built first as a chapel in 1786 and rebuilt in 1838; it serves the city's oldest Roman Catholic parish. Armenian, Greek, and Russian Orthodox bishops also have their seats in the city. The famous Riverside Church (formerly Park Avenue Baptist), at Riverside Drive and 122nd Street, is an impressive 22-story Gothic structure with a 72-bell carillon in its tall tower. The leading Presbyterian churches are the First (1716), the Fifth Avenue, and the Brick Church at 91st Street and Park Avenue. The two most famous Dutch Reformed churches are the Marble Collegiate and St. Nicholas, both on Fifth Avenue. The Methodist denomination's largest structure is Christ Church at Park Avenue and 60th Street. The headquarters of the Ethical Culture Movement are at 64th Street and Central Park West. Christian Science is represented in many local neighborhood units. See CHURCH ARCHITECTURE.

DIOCESE OF NEW YORK

The Cathedral Church of St. John the Divine, which has been under construction since 1892, will be the largest Gothic-style cathedral in the world when it is completed.

Education. The board of education, consisting of nine unpaid members drawn from all boroughs, is responsible for the administration of educational programs in the public elementary and secondary schools of the city. The board selects its own president and vice-president. It constructs and maintains school buildings, and staffs and supervises all schools. The board of superintendents, consisting of the city superintendent of schools and eight associates elected by the board of education for a six-year term, has jurisdiction over teachers and courses of study. There are also district superintendents in charge of schools within specific areas of each borough. Fifty-four local school boards work in conjunction with the city board.

New York maintained 623 elementary schools, 126 junior high schools, 57 high schools, 29 vocational high schools, and 96 evening schools in 1960, when total registration was 1,078,883. There are day classes for adults in English and citizenship; classes for children physically and mentally handicapped; and evening academic, commercial, and trade schools. In addition the board maintains and supervises after-school recreational and educational programs in afternoon centers for children of elementary and junior high school ages, and community centers during evening hours for high school students and adults.

The board of higher education (consisting of the president of the board of education and 21 citizens appointed for a nine-year term) administers seven municipal colleges—the City College (1847), Hunter College (1870), Brooklyn College (1930), Queens College (1937), and the two-year community colleges of Staten Island (1955), the Bronx (1957), and Queensborough (1958). Since 1961 these are collectively known as the City University of New York. Total enrollment for 1960 was 91,450 students. The City University offers graduate work leading to the master's degree in a variety of fields. Several Ph.D. programs are also available.

Privately supported institutions of higher learning in New York include Columbia University, founded in 1754 as Kings College in lower Manhattan, and now situated on Morningside Heights. New York University is composed of 14 colleges, schools, and divisions at five centers in Manhattan and one in the Bronx on the 43-acre campus for men at University Heights. The Hall of Fame is situated on the latter campus. Fordham University (1841), a Roman Catholic institution sponsored by the Society of Jesus, is located on a beautiful 75-acre campus in the Bronx. Among other colleges and universities are Manhattan College; Long Island University; St. John's University; Cooper Union, which offers tuition-free adult education; New York City Community College of Applied Arts and Sciences; Pace College; Polytechnic Institute of Brooklyn; Pratt Institute; Brooklyn Law School; and Juilliard School of Music. Among the city's theological schools are Union Theological Seminary, Jewish Theological Seminary, General Theological Seminary of the Protestant Episcopal Church, Hebrew Union College–Jewish Institute of Religion, and Yeshiva University. See COLLEGES AND UNIVERSITIES.

Hospitals and Medical Schools. Of the more than 400 hospitals and clinics in New York, the city sponsors 28, of which the most notable is the enormous Bellevue Hospital. Other city hospitals and clinics are located on Welfare Island and in all the boroughs. The Columbia-Presbyterian Medical Center between Broadway and Riverside Drive at 168th Street includes the Presbyterian Hospital, hospitals for women and babies, Vanderbilt Clinic, Columbia University's colleges of physicians and surgeons and of oral and dental surgery, the neurological and psychiatric institutes, and a school of nursing. A similar affiliated group overlooking the East River between 68th and 71st streets includes Cornell University Medical College, a hospital for special surgery, New York Hospital, and a nurses school. The New York University–Bellevue Medical Center, on First Avenue between 26th and 30th streets, has a college, a postgraduate medical school, and an institute of physical medicine and rehabilitation. Along Fifth Avenue between 98th and 106th streets are the large Mt. Sinai Hospital with its associated schools and clinics; the New York Academy of Medicine; and the Fifth Avenue–Flower Hospital. Other large hospitals in Manhattan include St. Luke's and the Women's Hospital on Morningside Heights, St. Vincent's on West 11th Street, Lenox Hill and Roosevelt in mid-town. Hospitals in the Bronx include a U.S. veterans hospital, Montefiore, Misericordia, and several smaller units. Among Brooklyn's many hospitals are the Jewish, Methodist, Brooklyn, and Long Island College hospitals. In Queens, St. Anthony's and the Booth Memorial hospitals are most notable.

Newspapers. New York's first newspaper was the *Gazette* (1725). Predecessors of the city's present daily newspapers were the *Evening Post*, founded in 1801 by William Coleman (today's *Post*); the *Sun*, founded in 1833 by Benjamin Day, and the *World*, founded in 1860 by Manton Marble—both taken over by Joseph Pulitzer in 1883 (today's *World Telegram and Sun*); the *Herald*, founded in 1835 by James Gordon Bennett, and the *Tribune*, founded in 1841 by Horace Greeley (today's *Herald Tribune*); and the *Times*, founded in 1850 by Henry J. Raymond. Other New York daily newspapers are the *Journal-American*, the *Daily News*, the *Brooklyn Daily*, The *Wall St. Journal*, and the *Journal of Commerce*. There are also several smaller community and foreign-language dailies. See NEWSPAPER.

Theaters. The history of New York's theatrical life dates to the mid-eighteenth century. George Washington was a patron of the John Street Theater, which was opened in 1767. In the course of time the main theatrical district moved progressively northward from the Bowery to Madison Square at 23rd Street, and thence to Herald Square (34th Street). By the mid-twentieth century most of the city's 32 legitimate theaters were concentrated in the area between 40th and 52nd streets, from Eighth Avenue to the Avenue of the Americas (Sixth Avenue). This area comprises the heart of U.S. theater—the principal source of original and road companies that tour the major cities of the country. After 1950, the so-called off-Broadway theaters, many of them in Greenwich Village and other downtown neighborhoods, attracted enthusiastic audiences by presenting new and often experimental plays and revivals. All types of theatrical productions attract many out-of-town visitors as well as New Yorkers. See AMERICAN DRAMA; DRAMA; ACTING AND ACTORS.

The Metropolitan Opera House (seating capacity 3,300) is one of the world's leading centers of grand opera. Other opera, as well as drama and ballet, is frequently staged at the municipally owned City Center, opened in 1943. Carnegie Hall (seating capacity 2,632) is perhaps America's most famous auditorium for concert music; also in the building are many music studios for teaching and rehearsing. Town Hall on 43rd Street is known for concerts and lectures. In the mid-1960's a modern music, art, and educational center with an opera house and concert hall was being completed for Lincoln Square at 66th Street and Broadway.

The largest motion picture theater is Radio City Music Hall, which seats 6,200 people. Other prominent motion-picture houses presenting first-run showings are centered along Broadway from 42nd to 51st streets.

Many New York theaters once devoted to legitimate stage presentations have been converted to radio and television broadcasting. The large radio-television networks and a number of smaller organizations operate 25 radio stations (one of them sponsored by the board of education, another municipally owned) and 7 television channels. Madison Square

Garden (seating capacity 20,000), bounded by Eighth and Ninth avenues, 49th and 50th streets, is used primarily for sporting events. It has moved uptown from its former location at Madison Avenue and 26th Street.

Hotels and Restaurants. The Astor House, opened in 1836 on Broadway between Vesey and Barclay streets, was New York's first great hotel. The building was not razed until after 1920, but long before that a new Hotel Astor had risen on Times Square. Many of the major hotels are located near the Grand Central and Pennsylvania railroad stations and in mid-town theatrical and business areas. They include the New Yorker, Commodore, Roosevelt, Hilton, Americana, Biltmore, Victoria, Manhattan, Taft, Edison, and Governor Clinton. Most of the hotels catering to socially prominent persons, and whose facilities are used for major social occasions, are along Park, Madison, and Fifth avenues at Central Park South and in the 50's. These include the Waldorf-Astoria (2,200 rooms), the Plaza (1,060), Gotham, St. Regis, Pierre, Savoy-Plaza, Ambassador, St. Moritz, and Sherry-Netherland. The St. George on Brooklyn Heights (2,632 rooms) is the largest hotel in the city. The hotels located in the other boroughs are generally smaller and fewer in number. See HOTEL.

The city offers a great selection of nationality-group eating places including Austrian, German, Italian, Swiss, Chinese, Mexican, Japanese, Indian, Hawaiian, Spanish, Swedish, and Turkish. The city's chief night club areas are on Broadway, 52nd Street, on the east side along Second and Third avenues, and in Greenwich Village.

ECONOMIC FACTORS

Manufactures. New York is the leading manufacturing city of the United States. Manufacturing leads all other activities in number of people employed—almost 30 per cent of the total in 1963. After World War II many of the larger companies decided to move their plants to nearby suburban centers, but there was no lessening in the importance of manufacturing in the city itself, whose many plants produce a wide diversity of manufactured articles. Although there are many areas of industrial concentration such as those in parts of lower and mid-Manhattan, in Long Island City, and in downtown Brooklyn, manufacturing is citywide. Even in many residential areas, stores and upper floors of structures have been put to use by smaller manufacturers. In 1961 there were about 39,000 manufacturing establishments in New York employing 1,189,775 workers and paying about $3.32 billion in wages. Value added by manufacture was $10.8 billion. About two-thirds of the plants were in Manhattan; and the next largest number were in Brooklyn.

Most of the manufactures of the city are nondurable, consumer goods. In Manhattan there are several sections known for specific products, such as the garment district on the west side from 34th to 40th streets. (See GARMENT INDUSTRY.) Ladies' hats are made in the district bounded by 37th and 39th streets and Fifth and Sixth avenues. The fur district centers around West 30th Street. In 1961, 30 per cent or 334,000 of the city's manufacturing establishment employees worked in the clothing industry. The almost $2.42 billion in value added by manufacture in that industry was more than one-fifth of the total for the entire country. New York City was also the leading U.S. printing and publishing center, with more than $2.06 billion in value added by manufacture—one-fifth the nation's total. (See PUBLISHING, United States.) Food industries were third in importance with 83,000 employees and $1.18 billion in value added by manufacture. Their plants were mostly in Long Island City, in other parts of Queens, and in the upper Bronx and in Brooklyn. In lower Manhattan small and diversified plants prevail, especially machine shops and factories producing leather and plastic items. Other manufactures include scientific instruments, cosmetics, watches, bank notes, electrical machinery, appliances, chemicals, and telephone and electronic equipment. There are hundreds of small concerns specializing in diamond cutting and setting.

Commerce. New York ranks first in retail and wholesale trade in the United States. The executive offices of many of the nation's largest firms are located there. The commercial pre-eminence of the city is based largely on the fact that it is the major U.S. port. By mid-twentieth century the Port of New York had at least 650 miles of developed shore facilities, including 200 piers. In addition to the water-level route to the Great Lakes via the Hudson and Mohawk valleys, the city makes use of the semiprotected coastal navigation to New England ports and to the south. Half of the nation's imports and exports, as well as a high percentage of its coastal shipping, moves through the harbor. Major cargo items are petroleum products, coal, sand and gravel, steel scrap, bananas, coffee, and newsprint.

In 1958 there were 115,643 retail and about 30,000 wholesale establishments in New York. Total retail sales amounted to $13.6 billion—about 6.8 per cent of the national total. The New York City area alone in that year did more retail business than any single state in the union except New York State itself and California. Of the total retail sales for New York State, the New York City area was responsible for 65 per cent. Grocery stores had the largest volume of sales, with restaurants and drinking places close behind—a reflection of the city's huge population. New York's commercial stature was further advanced in the post-World War II years by the fact that more and more national concerns chose the city as the site of their main offices—many of them erecting their own buildings. As a result the proportion of clerical workers in the city labor market increased until in the mid-1960's they rivaled the manufacturing workers in numbers.

Closely allied with New York's commercial supremacy is its financial leadership of the United States. Wall Street has long been a synonym for national finance, for the heart of the national stock market is the New York Stock Exchange and, dealing in fewer and less active stocks, the American Exchange. (See STOCK EXCHANGE.) The commercial banking of the city is distributed almost equally between national banks and trust companies, which also do general banking. The giant banking concerns of the city have their headquarters in the Wall Street district. About two-thirds of the country's total clearinghouse transactions pass through New York City's banks. Under the state law savings banks are organized under the mutual system and have no capital stock. The majority of the nation's life insurance companies have administrative offices in New York and vicinity.

Transportation. Beginning in 1832 horse-drawn buses constituted the major means of public surface transportation in New York. In time they were superseded by cable cars, which in turn gave way to electrically powered vehicles. The famous two-level, gasoline-motored buses of the Fifth Avenue line were used from 1907 until the early 1950's. In the period after World War II the electric trolley lines were almost completely superseded by motor buses. The elevated railroads (the "el") date from 1867 when a quarter-mile, experimental, cable-operated elevated railroad was built in lower Manhattan. It was extended northward on Ninth Avenue to 29th Street. In 1871 the cables were exchanged for steam operation, and within the following decade steam-operated lines were constructed along Second, Third, and Sixth avenues, and later (with the Ninth Avenue line) extended far into the Bronx. The "el" lines were electrified in 1902–03. While this made them somewhat less dirty, they remained noisy and still blocked off the sky. By 1960 all the "el" tracks in Manhattan had been razed. The first elevated line in Brooklyn was opened in 1885, followed by others built by many companies; these were eventually consolidated into the Brooklyn-Manhattan Transit Company, reaching Coney Island, Jamaica, Canarsie, and many other areas.

There are three subway systems in the city, linking all the boroughs via tunnels and bridges, providing transit to all parts of the city (except Richmond). The earliest line, begun in 1900, was built by the Interborough Rapid Transit Company. Via east and west side routes, the IRT has several lines that connect Manhattan by specially built tunnels with Brooklyn and the Bronx, terminating at Flatbush and New Lots avenues; extends into the Bronx with termini at Van Cortlandt Park, Woodlawn Cemetery, and Bronx and Pelham Bay parks; and crosses the East River to Flushing, in Queens. The BMT System has many lines in Brooklyn and traverses lower Manhattan to enter Queens; its different lines terminate in Brooklyn, at Coney Island, Bay Ridge, and Canarsie; and in Queens at Jamaica and Astoria. The Independent System, city built, extends its main lines up Sixth and Eighth avenues, Manhattan, northward to 207th Street in Manhattan and 205th Street in the Bronx; some tracks pass under the East River to 179th Street, Jamaica; others serve Brooklyn with roads to Coney Island and East New York; a cross line leaves Queens Plaza to pass through Williamsburg to join the East New York Line in downtown Brooklyn. The city purchased all three systems in 1940 and operates them through a transit commission of three members. The city also operates the trolley and bus lines in Queens. The Hudson and Manhattan Railroad operates underground lines from Herald Square and Cortlandt Street in Manhattan under the Hudson River to Newark, N.J. The Long Island, the New York Central, and the New York, New Haven and Hartford railroads provide commuter services to certain parts of the city population, as well as to the suburbs.

The first ferry service in the area was instituted by the Dutch between New Amsterdam and the Brooklyn shore. In the nineteenth century, ferries between the various boroughs were numerous—some owned by the city, others by railroads and private concerns. In the twentieth century most of the ferries were replaced by bridges and tunnels, but at mid-century the city still maintained the ferry from the Battery to Staten Island—as it had since 1905—and some railroads terminating on the New Jersey shore still provided ferry service to the city.

New York City is served by U.S. highways 1 and 9 as well as by a network of expressways offering rapid highway travel without grade crossings or traffic lights. These include the West Side Elevated Highway, Henry Hudson Parkway, Franklin D. Roosevelt Drive, Major Deegan Expressway, Bronx River Parkway, Cross-Bronx Expressway, Hutchinson River Parkway, Grand Central Parkway, Long Island Expressway, Cross Island Parkway, Interborough Parkway, Whitestone Parkway, Brooklyn-Queens Expressway, Shore Parkway, and Southern Parkway.

Railroads. Most railroads approaching the city from the west send passengers and freight by ferry across the Hudson. The only lines having tracks and passenger stations in the city are the Pennsylvania, the New York Central, the New Haven, and the Long Island. The Pennsylvania passes under the Hudson to enter its station. The famous Doric-front edifice was razed in 1963 to make way for the new home of Madison Square Garden. However, the passenger terminal below street level remains in use. Pennsylvania's leased system, the Long Island, which has several lines and stations of its own in Brooklyn and Queens, tunnels under the East River to share Pennsylvania Station. The Grand Central Station is the depot of the New

BANK OF MANHATTAN CO.

The main trading floor of the New York Stock Exchange is the site where 1,375 member firms trade the largest dollar volume of securities of any stock exchange in the world.

York Central, which enters it via a 2½-mile tunnel under Park Avenue. The New York, New Haven and Hartford Railroad also uses that station. The New York Central is the only company operating a freight line into Manhattan—a highly important track extending down the west side as far as the market district. A New York, New Haven and Hartford freight line extends into south Bronx. Lighters, which ferry freight cars between New Jersey terminals and Brooklyn, Queens, and south Bronx, represent about 28 per cent of the city's harbor traffic. The Sunnyside yards of the Pennsylvania Railroad in Long Island City, reached by tunnel from Pennsylvania Station, are among the largest passenger railroad yards in the world.

Bridges and Tunnels. There are many bridges and tunnels traversing the Hudson, East, and Harlem rivers—linking Manhattan Island with the other boroughs and with New Jersey. The first bridge was the Brooklyn Suspension Bridge, completed in 1883, from Park Row, at the city hall, across the East River to Brooklyn; it is 5,889 feet long, and its stone towers rise 272 feet above low water. Other bridges soon followed: The Williamsburg Bridge (suspension, 7,308 ft.), 1904, from Delancey Street, Manhattan, to Brooklyn; the Manhattan Bridge (suspension, 6,855 ft.), 1909, from Canal Street to Brooklyn; the Queensborough Bridge (cantilever, 8,601 ft.), 1909, from 60th Street, Manhattan, to Long Island City, Queens; and Hell Gate Bridge (steel arch channel span, 1,017 ft.), 1917, with a total length of 3 miles and constructed by the New York Connecting Railroad to link the Pennsylvania and Long Island railroads with the New York, New Haven and Hartford tracks. There are many low bridges across the Harlem River; and two high steel arches, the Washington (1888) and Henry Hudson (1936) bridges, connect northern Manhattan with the Bronx. The Triborough Bridge (1936) connects Manhattan, the Bronx, and Queens; it crosses Ward's and Randall's islands by viaducts, the East and Harlem rivers by a suspension span of 1,380 feet and a vertical lift bridge. The George Washington Bridge (1931) extends from 178th Street, Manhattan, to the cliffs of Fort Lee, N.J. It has a suspension span of 3,500 feet, 215 feet above the water, and is hung from steel towers 635 feet tall. The Bronx-Whitestone Suspension Bridge between the Bronx and Queens (1939) has a channel span of 2,300 feet. The Throgs Neck Bridge (1961) spans 1,800 feet across the Long Island Sound. The longest, heaviest suspension bridge in the world is the Verrazano-Narrows Bridge (1964) connecting Brooklyn and Staten Island. Three bridges connect Staten Island with New Jersey: the Outerbridge Crossing (1928) to Perth Amboy; the Goethals Bridge (1928) to Elizabeth; and the Bayonne Bridge (1931), a 1,675-foot steel arch that is one of the longest in the world, to Bayonne across Kill Van Kull. See BRIDGE.

Passing under the Hudson are the Holland Tunnel (1927), twin tubes 9,250 feet long extending from Canal Street, Manhattan, to Jersey City, N.J.; and the Lincoln Tunnel (1937), extending 8,000 feet from 38th Street, Manhattan, to Weehawken, N.J. The Queens-Midtown Tunnel (1940) runs for 3,055 feet from 36th Street, Manhattan, to Long Island City, Queens, and connects with Long Island parkways. The 9,117-foot Brooklyn-Battery Tunnel (1950) extends under the harbor from Battery Park to Red Hook, Brooklyn. See TUNNEL.

Port of New York Authority is a self-supporting corporate agency created in 1921 by the states of New Jersey and New York to deal with the planning and development of terminal and transportation facilities of the area, and to foster the commerce of the New York–New Jersey Port District. The authority administers the Lincoln and Holland tunnels; the George Washington, Goethals, and Bayonne bridges; and the Outerbridge Crossing. It operates a grain terminal along the Brooklyn water front; the New York Union Motor Truck Terminal in lower Manhattan that was designed to reduce traffic congestion and to provide modern, rapid, truck cargo-handling facilities; and a commuter-bus terminal at 40th Street between Eighth and Ninth avenues. It is sponsoring a world trade center in lower Manhattan and pier construction in Brooklyn, as well as extensive development of port facilities in New Jersey. Under the terms of a 50-year lease with the city, the Port of New York Authority is also responsible for the city's airports. La Guardia, or New York Municipal, Airport, built in 1939, underwent a $115 million rehabilitation in the 1960s. La Guardia handles domestic air traffic and many private and business flights. Most overseas air traffic is handled by the 5,070-acre John F. Kennedy International Airport. Both Kennedy and La Guardia are in Queens. The authority also operates the West 30th Street and Downtown heliports. In all, the Port of New York Authority operates 23 facilities representing an investment of $1.45 billion.

ADMINISTRATION

Government. New York is governed under a charter that was adopted by popular referendum in 1961 and went into effect in 1963. There are three branches of administrative and legislative authority in the government: mayor, city council, and board of estimate. The mayor is the chief executive officer responsible for all municipal administration. He has the power of appointment and removal of the heads of the city's various departments and boards, and that of veto over ordinances passed by the council. The council consists of 36 members, including the council president who is elected on a citywide basis. The council may override the mayor's veto of legislation by a two-thirds majority vote, and the president of the council acts as mayor in the event the office is vacated. The board of estimate is composed of eight members: president (mayor), comptroller, president of the city council, and presidents of the five boroughs. It has legislative and administrative duties and oversees matters of finance, including the expense and capital budgets, zoning, and franchises. The mayor and members of the council and board of estimate are elected for terms of four years.

Subordinate Departments. In 1954 the office of city administrator was created to assist the mayor in the direction of the city's many agencies, boards, commissions, and departments—including the department of city planning, transit authority, board of education, fire department, police department, department of labor, department of sanitation, department of traffic, department of public works, department of parks, law department, department of correction, department of welfare, department of investigation, housing authority, air pollution control, board of elections, department of hospitals, department of health, department of licenses, department of commerce and industrial development, department of marine and aviation, department of purchase, human rights commission, department of markets, art commission, and department of water supply, gas, and electricity.

Judicial System. The New York City courts include the Civil Court, which tries civil cases, and the Criminal Court, which deals with criminal cases. In addition, there is Surrogates' Court, which handles wills, estates, and related matters, and the Family Court (part of the state Family Court system) which concerns itself with adoption, family support, and related matters. Civil and Surrogates' court judges are elected for 10 and 14 years respectively; criminal and family court judges are appointed by the mayor for 10 years.

HISTORY

Dutch Settlement. The environs of what is today New York City were visited by the Florentine navigator Giovanni da Verrazano in 1524, but there is no evidence of further exploration of the area during the sixteenth century. Henry Hudson, seeking a northwest passage from the Atlantic to the Pacific, entered New York Bay on Sept. 3, 1609, and anchored off Manhattan Island before proceeding up the Hudson River. Hudson reported the possibility of a profitable fur trade with the Indians, and by 1614 Dutch commercial interests had induced the kingdom of the United Netherlands to charter the New Netherland Company to engage in the fur trade. The company's charter was not renewed in 1618, but in 1621 the privately owned Dutch West India Company was established to engage in trade from New France to the Strait of Magellan (see NEW FRANCE). The enterprise encouraged the United Netherlands to view the region between New France and Virginia as a colony, which was called New Netherland. When 30 Walloon families arrived in New Netherland to settle on the Delaware River and at Fort Orange (Albany), eight men located on Manhattan Island, 1624. They were later joined by 45 settlers who brought household goods, farm tools, and cattle. In 1626 Peter Minuit, director-general of the New Netherland colony, cleared the colony's title to Manhattan Island by purchasing it from the Canarsee Indians—a Delaware tribe—for trinkets and beads worth 60 guilders (about $24). Minuit built a fort on the island and named the settlement New Amsterdam. See MINUIT, PETER.

Colonial Period. The city and colony were renamed New York in honor of the British proprietor, the Duke of York, later James II of England. The duke's representative, Sir Richard Nicolls, became the first British governor of New York; though immediately instituting English offices in the city civil administration, he generally permitted a gradual change from Dutch to English practices. In 1673 New York was recaptured by the Dutch and renamed New Amsterdam; but on Feb. 9, 1674, Britain regained control of the city. The early British administration was not without friction. In 1689 the German-born merchant Jacob Leisler led an insurrection against the colonial administrators, who he believed favored the rich; and in 1735 the trial and acquittal of John Peter Zenger, publisher of the New York *Journal*, who had been prosecuted for criticism of the gover-

Historic Fraunces Tavern was the scene of General Washington's farewell to the officers of the Continental Army.

nor, was a marked precedent in the development of freedom of the press in America. See ZENGER, JOHN PETER.

William Bradford (1663–1752) set up the first printing press in the city in 1693; and the first newspaper in New York, the *Gazette*, appeared in 1725. By 1772 the first regular stagecoach was operating between New York and Boston.

Revolutionary War. On Oct. 7, 1765, representatives of the 13 colonies met at New York to consider measures against the Stamp Act. The Sons of Liberty were organized, and largely through their efforts the Stamp Act was rendered practically ineffective. (See SONS OF LIBERTY; STAMP ACT.) The fight that resulted when British soldiers felled a liberty pole on Jan. 18, 1770—known as the Battle of Golden Hill—in which one citizen was killed and several wounded, is considered by some to have been the first bloodshed of the American Revolution. In 1775 a committee of public safety took over the city government, displacing the British. After the battle of Long Island, in August, 1776, colonial forces under Gen. George Washington that were guarding the city and the lower Hudson River valley were forced to retreat to New Jersey, thereby permitting occupations of the city, which continued until 1783. See LONG ISLAND, BATTLE OF.

The first American city government in New York was set up Feb. 5, 1784, when James Duane became mayor. From 1785 to 1790 New York was the young nation's capital. Federal Hall, built in 1700 at the corner of Wall and Nassau streets (on the site of the present subtreasury building built in 1842), was the seat of government. Washington was sworn in on its balcony as the first President under the new Constitution, Apr. 30, 1789. The capital was moved to Philadelphia a year later. New York remained the capital of New York State until superseded by Albany in 1797.

Nineteenth Century. In 1796, on a pond near the present site of the Civic Center near Broadway and Park Row, John Fitch exhibited the nation's first steamboat with a screw propeller. A steam ferry to Long Island was established in 1812, and in 1818 steam vessels began plying Long Island Sound. In 1819 the *Savannah* left New York on the first voyage made by a steamship across the Atlantic. The commerce of the city grew rapidly in those years, especially after the completion of the Erie Canal in 1825, giving the city an efficient transportation route to the West. See ERIE CANAL.

Epidemics of cholera in 1832 and other years took many lives. In 1835 a great fire in the business district caused damage estimated at $20 million. There was much disorder in the lower east side tenement districts—flaring into numerous race riots, the Astor Place Riot in 1849, and the Gang Riots of 1857. New York in general was highly loyal during the Civil War, contributing more than 100,000 soldiers to the Union cause; there were, however, disloyal elements who caused the destructive Draft Riots in 1863. See DRAFT RIOT.

In 1789 the Society of St. Tammany was founded as a benevolent organization, but soon became political in character and, as Tammany Hall, controlled the city's government for more than a century. Under William Marcy Tweed it became most corrupt. Tweed's power was broken in 1873, but Tammany regained control the following year and continued under bosses almost as vicious as Tweed. An occasional "reform" mayor held office for a single term, only to be quickly replaced by a Tammany choice. See BURR, AARON; TAMMANY HALL; TWEED, WILLIAM MARCY.

By 1870 New York was the nation's chief financial center; the panics of 1837, 1857, and 1873 were therefore felt more severely there than elsewhere (see PANIC). Nevertheless physical expansion continued. Elevated lines were built through Manhattan between 1870 and 1880 and, with the Brooklyn Bridge (1883) and other local transportation facilities, gave further impetus to the city's growth and prosperity. Greater New York, a consolidation of the various boroughs, came into being in 1898. Seth Low, president of Columbia University, served one term as mayor, 1901–03—then the usual reversion to Tammany rule immediately followed.

Twentieth Century. The Greater New York Charter of 1898 was amended, 1901, and again, 1905, extending the authority of the Board of Estimate and increasing the mayor's term of office from two to four years. The reform administration of Democratic Mayor John Purroy Mitchel, 1914–17, was marked by nonpartisan political appointments and administrative improvements such as the standardization of the salaries of city employees and a "pay as you go" system for the city budget. There followed, however, a series of Tammany controlled mayors, under whom city spending reached such a level that banks refused further loans to the city. A state investigation resulted in the resignation, 1932, of Mayor James J. Walker, under charges of misconduct. The next year a fusion ticket supported by Republicans, Socialists, and some Democrats brought in Fiorello H. La Guardia as a reform mayor. Tammany Hall control of city politics declined further when La Guardia was re-elected, 1937 and 1941. The La Guardia administration was responsible for the 1936 city charter, more persistent and thorough law enforcement, city purchase of many transit lines, and physical improvements such as extensive slum clearance, construction of low-cost housing, a new municipal airport, and new highways and parks.

William O'Dwyer succeeded La Guardia, 1946. The city's traditional 5-cent subway fare was raised to 10 cents, 1948, and to 15 cents, 1953. O'Dwyer was re-elected mayor, 1949, but under charges of corruption, resigned, 1950, to become U.S. ambassador to Mexico. Vincent Impellitteri was appointed interim mayor and, at a special election, 1950, was returned to office. In 1954 Impellitteri was succeeded as mayor by Robert F. Wagner, who was re-elected, 1957. Wagner was democratic candidate again in 1961, and was reelected to a third term.

Notable physical changes in New York during the 1950's included the razing of the Third Avenue "El", 1955, and the completion, 1956, of the Coliseum and Convention Hall and the third tube of the Lincoln Tunnel. The name of Bedloe's Island, on which stands the Statue of Liberty, was changed to Liberty Island by the U.S. Congress, 1956. Construction was begun, 1959, on a bridge across the Narrows of New York Bay to connect Brooklyn and Staten Island, and a lower deck was added to the George Washington Bridge in 1960. See BRONX, THE; BROOKLYN; LONG ISLAND; MANHATTAN; QUEENS; STATEN ISLAND.

PHOTO BY KLAUS SCHNITZER

A common terrace joins 13 buildings designed by Edward Durell Stone at State University of New York at Albany.

NEW YORK, STATE UNIVERSITY OF, a state coordinating and integrating body for various state-supported institutions of higher learning located throughout the state of New York. The title was adopted by the New York State legislature in 1948. The university has no campus of its own. Its component members are 4 university centers, 2 medical centers, 17 state colleges, 6 agricultural and technical institutes, and 30 community colleges. The university centers are located at Albany, Binghamton, Buffalo, and Stony Brook. The other learning centers, such as colleges of arts and sciences (formerly teachers colleges), are located at Brockport, Buffalo, Cortland, Fredonia, Geneseo, New Paltz, Oneonta, Oswego, Plattsburgh, and Potsdam. Specialized centers, colleges, and schools include the Upstate Medical Center, Syracuse; the Downstate Medical Center, Brooklyn; The Maritime College, in the Bronx; the College of Ceramics at Alfred University, Alfred; the College of Forestry at Syracuse University, Syracuse; and the colleges of agriculture and home economics, the School of Industrial and Labor Relations, and the Veterinary College, at Cornell University, Ithaca; and the two-year agricultural and technical institutes located at Alfred, Canton, Cobleskill, Delhi, Farmingdale, and Morrisville.

The State University of New York also supervises locally operated community colleges: Adirondack Community College, Glens Falls; Auburn Community College, Auburn; Borough of Manhattan Community College, New York City; Bronx Community College, Bronx; Broome Technical Community College, Binghamton; Corning Community College, Corning; Dutchess Community College, Poughkeepsie; Erie County Technical Institute, Buffalo; Fashion Institute of Technology, New York City; Fulton Montgomery Community College, Johnstown; Genesee Community College, Batavia; Herkimer County Community College, Ilion; Hudson Valley Community College, Troy; Jamestown Community College, Jamestown; Jefferson Community College, Watertown; Kingsborough Community College, Brooklyn; Mohawk Valley Community College, Utica; Monroe Community College, Rochester; Nassau Community College, Garden City; New York City Community College, Brooklyn; Niagara County Community College, Niagara Falls; Onondaga Community College, Syracuse; Orange County Community College, Middletown; Queensborough Community College, Queens; Rockland Community College, Suffern; Staten Island Community College, Staten Island; Suffolk County Community College, Selden; Sullivan County Community College, South Fallsburg; Ulster County Community College, Stone Ridge; and Westchester Community College, Valhalla. See COLLEGES AND UNIVERSITIES.

NEW YORK PHILHARMONIC, the oldest symphonic orchestra in the United States and the third oldest in the world. The Philharmonic Society of New York was founded in New York City in 1842 by Ureli Hill and gave its first concert that year in Apollo Hall. The orchestra was incorporated in 1853. During the course of its history, the Philharmonic absorbed a number of orchestras: the National Symphony in 1921, the City Symphony in 1923, the American Orchestral Society, and, most important, the New York Symphony Society (founded by Leopold Damrosch, 1878) in 1928. It then became known as the Philharmonic-Symphony Society of New York. Its finances, originally handled by the musicians themselves, were backed by a group of guarantors after 1909. The Philharmonic's Young People's Concerts, inaugurated by Walter Damrosch with the New York Symphony in 1891, are still popular today. The orchestra plays in the new Philharmonic Hall in Lincoln Center. The Philharmonic has had a host of world-known guest maestros to conduct it, among them Richard Strauss, Igor Stravinsky, Arthur Honegger, Bruno Walter, and Leopold Stokowski. The list of its permanent conductors is equally impressive. Among the best known are Anton Seidl (1892–98), Walter Damrosch (1902–03), Gustav Mahler (1909–11), Arturo Toscanini (1926–36), Sir John Barbirolli (1937–42), Artur Rodzinski (1943–47), Dimitri Mitropoulos (1950–57), and Leonard Bernstein (1957–69).

NEW YORK PUBLIC LIBRARY, founded in 1895, has the largest collection of volumes of any public library in the United States. It was established in New York City by combining the private libraries of John Jacob Astor, merchant (1763–1848), James Lenox, philanthropist (1800–80), and Samuel J. Tilden, political leader (1814–86). The gifts of Astor and his descendants amounted to about $1.7 million. At the time of consolidation the Astor library contained more than 250,000 volumes and the Lenox library about 86,000. Aside from his private library, Tilden left an endowment of $2 million to the New York Public Library. In 1901 Andrew Carnegie granted $5.2 million to the library for the erection of circulating libraries throughout New York City, and in 1909 John S. Kennedy left a bequest of $3.5 million.

The New York Public Library serves the inhabitants of Manhattan, the Bronx, and Richmond. Queens borough is served by the Queens Public Library and Brooklyn borough by the Brooklyn Public Library, both of which are supported by New York City taxes. The central building of the New York Public Library is in Manhattan. In 1899 the Croton distributing reservoir was removed and the modern Renaissance-style building was opened to the public in 1911. Work in the central building is carried on with private funds, whereas the support of the branch libraries that make up the circulation department comes from annual appropriations from the city and state. The library has 156 leading agencies, including bookmobiles to reach outlying districts. The reference department contains more volumes than any other library in the United States with the exception of the Library of Congress.

Included in the library's collection of famous rare items are the Tickhill Psalter, written by John Tickhill about 1310 and noted for its illustrations and artistic work; Gutenberg Bible, the first major work produced after the invention of movable type; the Columbus Letter, the first printing and only known copy of Christopher Columbus's announcement of the discovery of the New World; the Bay Psalm Book, the first book printed in what is now the United States; the Olive Branch Petition, signed by members of the Continental Congress on July 8, 1775, and sent to George III of England in a final hope of heading off the American Revolution; the Jefferson Declaration, one of five drafts in Thomas Jefferson's handwriting of the Declaration of Independence; and Washington's Farewell Address, the final form of the manuscript in George Washington's handwriting.

NEW YORK STATE BARGE CANAL, canal system, composed of the old Erie, the Champlain, the Oswego, and the Cayuga and Seneca canals. It connects the Hudson River with Lake Erie and has branches to Lake Ontario, Lake Champlain, and Cayuga and Seneca lakes; it is 12 feet deep, has a minimum bottom width of 75 feet, a minimum surface width of 123 feet, and is 525 miles long. The main canal extends from Troy on the Hudson River to Tonawanda on the Niagara River, which flows into Lake Erie. This waterway follows the canalized Mohawk River west to Rome in Oneida county, then follows the route, but not always the bed, of the old Erie Canal. At Waterford the Champlain section joins and follows the canalized Hudson River to Fort Edward. A land cut completes the branch to Lake Champlain, which is connected with the St. Lawrence by the Richelieu River. The Oswego section follows the canalized Oswego River to Lake Ontario. The Cayuga and Seneca Canal follows the Seneca River to Cayuga and Seneca lakes. An improvement of the Erie Canal system, the barge canal was authorized in 1903 by public vote; work was begun in 1905 and completed in 1918. The barge canal system has numerous connected reservoirs and dams, which provide waterpower and also control floods, particularly in the Mohawk and Hudson valleys. The canal provides drainage for central New York.

NEW YORK UNIVERSITY, a privately controlled, coeducational institution of higher learning in New York, N.Y. The school was established in 1831 as the University of the City of New York, and instruction was first offered in 1832. The name was changed in 1896. Divisions of the university include the University College of Arts and Science, and the School of Engineering and Science (both located at the University Heights Center in the Bronx); the School of Commerce, Institute of Retail Management, School of Education, School of Continuing Education and Extension Services, Graduate School of Arts and Science, Graduate School of Public Administration, School of Law, Washington Square College of Arts and Science, Graduate School of Social Work, and School of the Arts (all located at the university's Washington Square Center in Manhattan); and the School of Medicine, Post-Graduate Medical School, College of Dentistry, and Graduate School of Business Administration (all located in Manhattan). The Hall of Fame for Great Americans, established in 1900, is located at the University Heights Center. The Institute of Fine Arts, located in Manhattan, is a division of the Graduate School of Arts and Science. Town Hall, a concert hall, is also part of the university. The university has a system of the libraries that include many special collections. See COLLEGES AND UNIVERSITIES; HALL OF FAME FOR GREAT AMERICANS.

NEW ZEALAND, independent state and member of the Commonwealth of Nations, in the South Pacific Ocean about 1,200 miles SE of Australia. It consists of two large islands (the North Island,

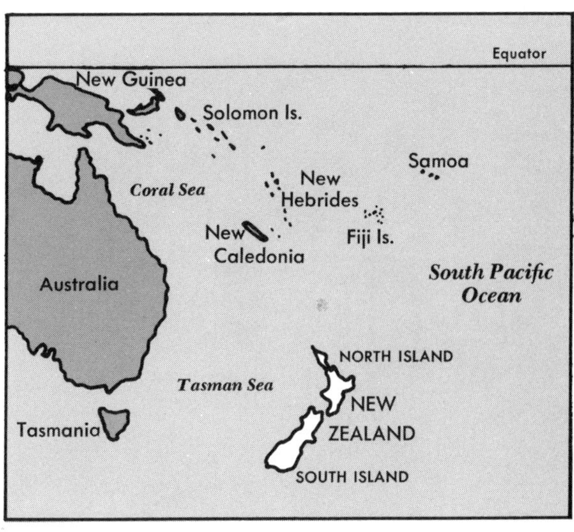

Location Map of New Zealand

44,281 square miles; and the South Island, 58,093 square miles), with the smaller islands, Stewart and Chatham, as well as various minor islands and outlying territories in the South Pacific. These minor islands within the boundaries of New Zealand are the Kermadec Islands, Three Kings Islands, Auckland Islands, Campbell Island, Antipodes Islands, Bounty Islands, Snares Islands, and Solander Island. Only Campbell Island is permanently inhabited. Overseas territories administered by New Zealand are Niue Island, the Tokelau Islands, and the Ross Dependency (a part of Antarctica); total area (exclusive of overseas territories) 103,736 square miles; population (1970 est.) 2,806,000. The population includes 230,000 Maoris (1968 est.). New Zealand's three largest cities in order of size are Auckland, Christchurch, and Wellington, the capital. See map in Atlas, Vol. 20. For flag in color, see FLAG.

Physical Features

Physiography. New Zealand is structurally part of the girdle of the recently disrupted crust of the earth that fringes the Pacific. It is still disturbed by frequent earthquake shocks, and its active volcanoes and thermal regions indicate the thinness of the crust in this region and the persistence of structural deformation. The country is broken and mountainous. The Southern Alps and their extensions span the entire length of the South Island and are bor-

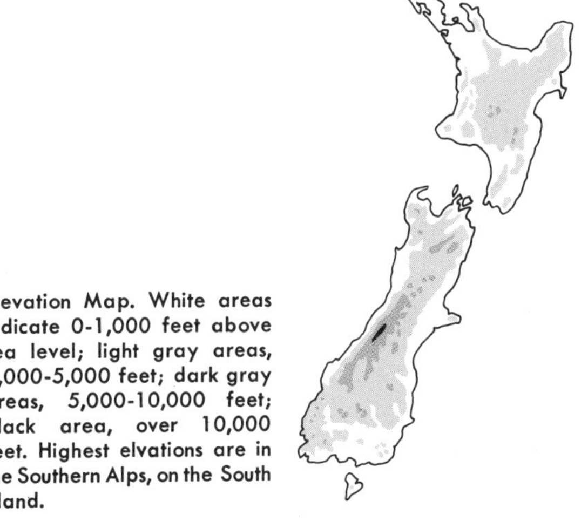

Elevation Map. White areas indicate 0-1,000 feet above sea level; light gray areas, 1,000-5,000 feet; dark gray areas, 5,000-10,000 feet; black area, over 10,000 feet. Highest elevations are in the Southern Alps, on the South Island.

CONSULATE GENERAL OF NEW ZEALAND, NEW YORK

The volcanic cone of Mt. Ngauruhoe rises above the desolate landscape of Tongariro National Park.

dered to the west by the giant Alpine fault. Numerous peaks reach above 10,000 feet. The mountains of the North Island are narrower, lower, and still forested. They parallel the east coast and overlook a southwestern extension of the Kermadec Trench, in the ocean east of the island. Elsewhere the general surface of both islands is finely dissected hill country. Plains and rolling low hills are rare, but they accommodate all the cities and towns and most of the population.

The country has roughly the shape of a reversed letter "S," inclined to the east in the North Island and to the west in the South Island. Cook Strait, a frequently stormy stretch of ocean, separates the two main islands. The rocks and structure of the South Island are older—mainly schists and graywackes of the Triassic and Jurassic periods. They rise as gaunt, gray, rocky, snow-capped ranges, faulted and glaciated. Mount Cook rises to 12,349 feet, and its range is the source of the largest glaciers. Those that plunge westward from the divide descend into subtropical forest to within a few hundred feet above the Tasman Sea, which in the far southwest penetrates the deep, forest-fringed, ice-cut valleys of Fiordland. In the northeast, the drowned coast of the Marlborough district has many miles of sheltered waterways and narrow inlets.

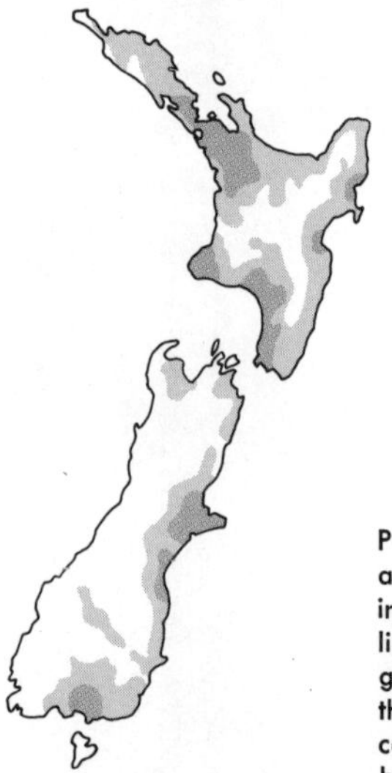

Population Density Map. White areas indicate less than 1 inhabitant per square mile; light gray areas, 1-10; dark gray areas, 10-50. By far the largest population concentration is the Auckland urban area, on the North Island.

With its active volcanoes and frequent deep-seated earthquake shocks, the North Island is, by comparison, geologically young. Except where the axial ranges and other minor elevations project through it, the island is deeply mantled in soft, weak Tertiary and Cretaceous rocks—sandstone, clay stone, and mudstone. These are widely coated with Quaternary volcanic rocks or unconsolidated ashfall. The pumice ash has been spread and deposited frequently in the last two or three thousand years. The most widespread bed of volcanic ash had its origin in a massive shower in the vicinity of Lake Taupo in the Volcanic Plateau region in the center of the North Island. The plateau is horizontal except where faulted and interrupted by geysers, geothermal steam vents, boiling mud pools, and solfataras. But around this plateau, the thickly bedded Cretaceous and Tertiary rocks have been deeply dissected into a jumble of hill country with steep slopes, razorback ridges and frequent papa (bluish clay) gorges. The deceptively smooth-looking cone of Mt. Egmont (8,260 feet) stands apart from the other remnants of Tertiary and Quaternary volcanic activity; surrounded by green pasture, the volcano is responsible for the westward projection of the North Island in the Taranaki salient.

The basement strata of Triassic-Jurassic graywackes occur north of the Volcanic Plateau and represent the northern projection of the structural arc of the island, curving away to the northwest. Here again they bear a Tertiary cover of sediments and are interrupted by volcanic masses or are studded by gentle scoria cones of Quaternary age. The west coast of the North Island is smoothed by massive wave deposits of iron sand. They sweep from the mouth of the Waikato River almost to Cape Maria van Dieman, and are broken only by the narrow, shallow entrances to the Manukau, Kaipara, and Hokianga harbors. Sheltered from the prevailing westerlies, the northeastern coast of the North Island is picturesquely broken and rocky and studded with little beaches and spectacular offshore islands. With its mild climate, warm ocean waters, and deep-sea fishing, its coastline is fast becoming an important tourist attraction.

Climate. Though marked by sharp regional contrasts, New Zealand's climate is generally mild and equable, as a result of its mid-latitude and mid-oceanic location. Except in the lee of the Southern Alps and at high elevations, winters are extraordinarily mild. Coastal localities in most of the North Island are almost free of frost. Summers are warm and sunny. Outdoor activities can be enjoyed during most of the year, and the open-air bathing season is 5 or 6 months in the south, longer in the north. Variations in elevation over short distances, however, provide conditions for winter sports on both islands for more than half the year. At sea level, snow is rare and occurs only on the South Island.

Precipitation is almost everywhere abundant. Most of the country has between 40 and 80 inches a year; exposed coastlands and mountain slopes record from 100 inches to 300 inches a year. Less than 40 inches are recorded in a few sheltered areas, mainly in the east coast lowlands of the South Island. In Central Otago, on the South Island, only 50 miles from Milford Sound (where annual precipitation exceeds 250 inches) only 15 inches are recorded annually. Almost the whole country has over 1,900 hours of sunshine annually, and some areas enjoy more than 2,400 hours; even on the west coast of the South Island (where annual precipitation averages more than 100 inches) 1,800 to 1,900 hours of bright sunshine are recorded annually.

Flora. Originally, New Zealand was profusely forested from shoreline to snow line. The first European explorers, however, found extensive areas of bunched tussock grasses on the plains and in the shelter of the Southern Alps; it is now thought that this grassland may have been induced when the primeval forest was destroyed by fires set by hunters of the moa bird in the eleventh and twelfth centuries.

The vegetation of New Zealand was mostly indigenous. The rest had either Malaysian, Australian, Antarctic, or South American affinities. The mixed subtropical hardwood forests of the North Island were often characterized by tawa (*Beilschmiedia tawa*), a type of evergreen, but also contained valuable timber trees. The subantarctic forests of the higher elevations of the North Island and the southern parts of the South Island, were characterized by one or another of five species of southern beech (*Nothofagus*).

Perhaps the most striking physical achievement of the European in New Zealand has been the large-scale replacement of the indigenous vegetation with an alien, exotic plant cover derived from various parts of the world. Today New Zealand is essentially pastureland, predominantly European grasses and clovers which have been improved by careful, scientific selection. In addition there are some Australian, African, and North American grasses. The bases of the country's forest industries are North American species. Monterey pine (*Pinus radiata*) from California is the principal element in what is one of the world's largest man-made forests; it comprises almost a million acres on the pumice lands of the Volcanic Plateau.

Fauna. Because of its lengthy geological isolation, New Zealand appears to have had no land mammals in prehuman times, apart from bats. It did have, however, birds—especially sea birds and forest birds. Many of the birds were flightless and bulky, notably the different genera of ratite moas, now extinct; the kiwi; and the takahe (*Notornis*). The latter were recently rediscovered; they had been believed extinct for at least a century. It also had unusual reptiles including the tuatara (*Sphenodon punctatum*), today regarded as a living fossil.

The Polynesians brought to New Zealand the dog and rat. Europeans have subsequently naturalized a large number of different animals from stoats and weasels to rabbits, deer, Australian opossums, moose, wapiti, and tahrs. They have also richly stocked New Zealand rivers and lakes with brown and rainbow trout and Atlantic and quinnat salmon. Today, the man-made pastures of New Zealand support a heavier concentration of domesticated hoofed mammals (including more than 60 million sheep), than any comparable land area in the world.

Social Features

Population. The first human beings to reach New Zealand were Polynesians who built an economy and culture based on hunting the several species of moa birds. They are called moa hunters to distinguish them from the Maori, who after the extinction of the moa practiced an economy based partly on the cultivation of kumaras, taros, and gourds, but principally on gathering the indigenous resources of forest, stream, sea, and shore. The moa hunters probably never numbered more than 25,000. The Maori population may have reached 250,000 in the eighteenth century.

With the coming of European explorers, and especially after British annexation in 1840, the Maori population declined rapidly. In 1890 there were only 38,000 Maoris, and their extinction was considered certain. Today, however, they comprise a rapidly increasing proportion of the population and number 230,000. The Polynesian element in the New Zealand population is also being reinforced by the immigration of Cook Islanders, Tongans, Samoans, and Niueans. More Polynesians live in Auckland than in any other city in the world.

In 1970 the population of New Zealand reached 2,800,000. Its growth has been recently slowed by an outflow of emigrants. During the 1950's and early 1960's, however, the annual average rate of growth exceeded 2 percent. Of the total population, 86 percent is New Zealand-born, and only 9 percent were born in the United Kingdom.

CAMERA PRESS-PIX

With a sheep population of many millions, New Zealand is a leading exporter of wool, lamb, and mutton.

CONSULATE GENERAL OF NEW ZEALAND, NEW YORK

Cattle enter a milking shed on a farm in the Waikato Valley, a center of the dairy industry.

For a country that is so dependent economically on agriculture, the population is heavily urbanized. Almost 80 percent live in urban areas, boroughs, and townships with populations of more than 1,000, and 46 percent live in the four main urban centers—Auckland, Wellington-Hutt, Christchurch, and Dunedin. Some 71 percent live in the North Island, including 95 percent of all Maoris.

Education. In New Zealand education is free, secular, and compulsory for children (including Maoris) between the ages of 7 and 15. There are six independent universities—the University of Auckland, University of Waikato (at Hamilton), Victoria University of Wellington, Massey University (at Palmerston North), the University of Canterbury (at Christchurch), and the University of Otago (at Dunedin). Lincoln College, an agricultural institution, forms part of the University of Canterbury. College enrollment in 1970 numbered more than 30,000. There are also nine teachers colleges.

Religion. There is no state religion. The four most important religious denominations, in order of number of adherents, are Church of England, Presbyterian, Roman Catholic, and Methodist.

Social Welfare. A social security act passed in 1938 provides for retirement, unemployment, medical care, hospitalization, and other welfare measures. Financed by general taxation, it is one of the world's most complete systems of social security. As a result, there is no real poverty in New Zealand.

Economic Features

Agriculture. New Zealand's high standard of living rests heavily on agricultural exports, especially livestock products. Agriculture provides employment for about 14 percent of the employed population, and although there are only 66,000 separate farm units, averaging 630 acres in size, the value of per capita agricultural production is the highest in the world. In 1970, the value of farm exports reached almost a billion dollars, 90 percent of the value of all exports. Meat and its by-products accounted for 41.3 percent of the value of all exports; wool for 21.7 percent; and dairy products for 20.8 percent.

The highly specialized pastoral agriculture is based on the intensive care and management of livestock and pasture swards (principally of ryegrass and white clover), established in the nineteenth century in place of the indigenous forest. In addition to 60 million sheep, there are 8.6 million cattle, including 2.3 million dairy cows. These are practically all raised on less than 20 million acres of improved grassland. The country's 13 million acres of indigenous tussock grazing land carry very few livestock. Dairying is heavily concentrated on the North Island. Sheelp raising is more evenly divided between the two isands.

The raising of crops and fruits is, in comparison with livestock, relatively insignificant, although New Zealand satisfies its own requirements of wheat, barley, oats, maize, fruits of various kinds, and has a growing export of apples, pears, tinned peaches and apricots, fresh strawberries, Chinese gooseberries (kiwi fruit), tamarillos, and vegetables of many kinds. Arable cropland is largely confined to the eastern, lowland areas of the South Island, especially to the Canterbury plains. The heaviest concentrations of intensive cropping, market gardening, orcharding, viticulture, and hop and tobacco growing are in the areas of Hawkes Bay, Nelson, suburban Auckland, Poverty Bay, and Central Otago.

More than a million acres of forest—especially on the Volcanic Plateau—supply a rapidly expanding timber, pulp, and paper industry, which is the basis of a growing export trade. Australia and Japan are the principal markets.

Minerals. The recent discovery of natural gas and petroleum, at Kapuni in Taranaki and beneath Cook Strait, promises to satisfy local requirements and to prove much more valuable than coal, which has been the most important mineral used since the 1890's. In 1969 New Zealand first began to quarry some of its 3 billion tons of coastal iron sand deposits just north of the mouth of the Waikato River; the iron sand is smelted in Glenbrook or exported, untreated, to Japan.

Power. In addition to coal, coal gas, natural gas, and petroleum condensates as energy sources, New Zealand has long exploited its water resources for cheap hydroelectric energy. Water power is the basis for an aluminum-smelting plant near Invercargill; the plant is backed by British, Australian, and Japanese interests, and uses bauxite from Queensland, Australia. At Wairakei, near Lake Taupo, geothermal steam generates electric energy. Though New Zealand's considerable geothermal heat resources remain mostly untapped, it is thought that they may be capable of supplying as much energy as is presently generated by hydroelectricity. In 1969 more than 12 billion kilowatt-hours of electric power were generated by public utilities, 85 percent of these by water power.

Manufacturing. Unlike agriculture, manufacturing is carried on largely for the domestic market. However, with the threat posed to agricultural exports by Great Britain's endeavor to join the European Economic Community, strong attempts are being made to find other foreign markets for manufactured goods. Over 25 percent of the working population are employed in manufacturing; nevertheless, the contribution of manufacturing to the gross national product is only a little more than that of farm industries, which employ far fewer people.

Manufacturing for the domestic market is protected by duties and tariffs and by import and exchange licensing. The ranking industries, in terms of employment, are as follows: food processing, transportation equipment, textiles and apparel, machinery, and timber and paper.

Transportation. Transport, both internal and external, is particularly important to New Zealand, since the country depends so heavily on international trade. Though the country is small, its towns and cities are scattered and separated from each other by difficult terrain, and the existence of Cook Strait increases the cost of internal transport.

After the United States and Canada, New Zealand has more motor vehicles per capita than any other country. New Zealand has a network of first-class highways, and there are modern urban ex-

CONSULATE GENERAL OF NEW ZEALAND, NEW YORK
Pulp and paper manufacture dominates Kawerau, one of many modern single-industry towns in New Zealand.

pressways. Rail transportation is relatively undeveloped, but practically all towns and cities with more than 20,000 people have air services operated by the New Zealand National Airways Corporation.

External shipping services are operated by foreign companies. The country's international airline, Air New Zealand, operates to North America, Australia, and Southeast Asia as well as to island destinations in the Pacific. Several foreign airlines also connect New Zealand to all parts of the world.

KENNETH B. CUMBERLAND

Auckland, New Zealand's manufacturing center, has diversified industries, including automobile assembly.
CONSULATE GENERAL OF NEW ZEALAND, NEW YORK

Government

New Zealand is a monarchical state within the Commonwealth of Nations. It is governed by a prime minister and cabinet who are members of the majority party in Parliament. The functions of the crown are performed by a Governor-General, nominated by the New Zealand government and appointed for a 5-year term. The Governor-General and an elected House of Representatives together constitute Parliament, which has unrestricted legislative powers and can amend the constitution and determine the forms and structure of the courts of law. Parliamentary election districts are redrawn after each census, every 5 years, by an independent Representation Commission, first instituted in 1887. The Commission also determines the number of members in the House, at present 80, plus four separately elected Maori representatives. Members are elected by a simple majority. Universal suffrage has existed since 1893; the secret ballot was introduced in 1870, and triennial elections in 1879.

History

Prehistory. New Zealand has probably been settled for more than a thousand years. The indigenous Maori population is thought to be descended from eastern Polynesian voyagers who lost their way, or were driven out of their homeland. By the eighteenth century there were probably more than 200,000 Maoris in New Zealand, mostly on the North Island. A seminomadic polytheistic people, they achieved a high state of neolithic culture.

European Settlement. The first recorded sighting of New Zealand by Europeans was made in 1642, by the Dutch explorer, Abel Janszoon Tasman, who touched on the west coast of the South Island. Subsequently the name New Zealand, after the Dutch province, was applied to this coast. In 1769 the English naval explorer James Cook circumnavigated and charted New Zealand; at the same time French and other explorers started visiting the islands. The establishment of a British convict settlement in eastern Australia in 1788 brought New Zealand into more direct contact with Europe, through missionaries, whalers, sealers, and traders. By the 1830's there was a flourishing settlement in the Bay of Islands, in the extreme north. Meanwhile in Great Britain there were pressures on the government to occupy the territory. Humanitarians stressed the need to protect the native peoples from European settlers, while an influential group of colonial reformers and speculators founded the New Zealand Company (1839) to organize settlements, each reproducing a cross section of English society, as advocated by the colonizer Edward Gibbon Wakefield (1796–1862). In 1839 Capt. William Hobson was appointed by the British government to take possession of part or all of New Zealand. Arriving at the Bay of Islands in January, 1840, he and his assistants in the following months concluded the Treaty of Waitangi with groups of Maoris, whereby the latter ceded sovereignty to Britain's Queen Victoria in return for having the rights and privileges of British subjects. In May, 1840, learning that a Wakefield settlement had been formed at Wellington, Hobson proclaimed British sovereignty over all New Zealand. This precipitated many years of wrangling between the government and the New Zealand Company over rights and land claims.

Constitutional History and External Relations. Demands by settlers for self-government were met by the British with the New Zealand Constitution Act of 1852. The scattered nature of the early settlements—the government-sponsored town of Auckland and a string of Wakefield colonies established in the 1840's—led to a quasi-federal system in which powers were shared between a central government and parliament, and six (later nine) provinces. In 1876, however, the provinces were abolished. In 1950, the ineffective upper house of Parliament was also abolished. Fears of the unrestricted powers now possessed by the House of Representatives led to the provision in 1956 that basic clauses of the electoral law could be amended only by a two-thirds majority of Parliament. In 1962 New Zealand was the first country outside Scandinavia to appoint an ombudsman to investigate private citizens' complaints against governmental decisions.

In its gradual evolution toward full independence from Great Britain, New Zealand followed Canada's example. It remained formally dependent, however, until the adoption in 1947 of the 1931 Statute of Westminster, by which the British parliament gave complete autonomy to self-governing colonies. Although New Zealand was a founding member of the League of Nations and participated in the Boer War and in World Wars I and II, it was only during World War II that formal diplomatic relations were established with foreign countries.

New Zealand is a member of various southeast Asian regional pacts and organizations. It has a special interest in the South Pacific, administering Niue and the Tokelau Islands, and retaining responsibility for the defense and external relations of the Cook Islands, which gained internal self-government in 1965. New Zealand administered the trust territory of Western Samoa from 1920 until it became an independent state in 1962. The recent decline of Great Britain as a major power has led New Zealand to look instead toward the United States for protection, a relationship exemplified by the 1951 ANZUS pact among Australia, New Zealand, and the United States, by New Zealand's membership in SEATO, and by its token participation in the Vietnam War. Economically, however, New Zealand remains closely linked to Great Britain, which is the chief market for its exports.

Race Relations. There was sporadic racial conflict from the first days of European contact, and minor wars occurred between the British and the Maoris in the 1840's. The final conquest of the Maoris came in the 1860's. Facing continuing European expansion and growing pressure for land, a group of tribes in the center of the North Island, united loosely under a Maori "king" in the late 1850's. In 1860 war broke out over a disputed land purchase at Taranaki on the west coast. Although the affair ended in a truce in 1861, the colonials became convinced of the need to crush the king movement as the focus of Maori independence and of their resistance to further settlement; in a brief campaign in 1863 the King Maoris were defeated by the British army. The war was then carried to the east and west coasts of the North Island. Between 1864 and 1867 large tracts of Maori land were confiscated and opened to settlement. Land laws of the 1860's broke up the Maoris' communal system of tenure and permitted settlers to purchase land directly from the Maoris. European dominance was now assured, and the way was opened for the formation of a biracial society in which the Maoris would be a minority partner. The country's predominantly British character has been fostered by immigration policies aimed at keeping out Asians and at maintaining a controlled flow of British-born immigrants.

For many years it was assumed that the Maoris would completely die out. The effects upon them of European contacts had been devastating. With the aid of the white man's guns they had decimated their number in the 1820's and the 1830's, while new diseases had brought sweeping epidemics. By the mid-nineteenth century the Maori population had dropped by about 40 percent, and it continued to decline until the end of the nineteenth century.

ALLYN BAUM FROM RAPHO-GUILLUMETTE

ALLYN BAUM FROM RAPHO-GUILLUMETTE

The majestic scenery of Milford Sound (top) is characteristic of the South Island's rugged Fiordland, comprising one of the world's largest national parks. The business section of Wellington (above), New Zealand's capital, on the southern tip of the North Island, is built on reclaimed land. Cable cars climb steep slopes to the suburbs. Shown below is the Parliament House, in the heart of the city.

CONSULATE GENERAL OF NEW ZEALAND, NEW YORK

Thereafter it started to rise again, and new leaders sought to rehabilitate the Maoris into a European society. After World War I government programs of social and economic development were initiated. Despite New Zealand's continuing progress toward becoming a genuinely biracial society, however, Maoris remain an underprivileged race. They attain generally poorer standards of health and education than the rest of the community, and are disproportionately engaged in unskilled labor.

Political and Economic History. While the development of the North Island was retarded by difficult terrain and warfare, the South Island in the early 1860's boomed with the expansion of pastoral farming and with the discovery of gold in 1861. Depression in the late 1860's, however, prompted Julius Vogel, colonial treasurer, to initiate in 1870 a major expansion of central government activity. By massive overseas borrowing, Vogel sought to finance a program of immigration and public works. Facing opposition from provincial interests, he led the successful movement to have the provinces abolished (1876). Among other provincial functions, the central government took over control of education, establishing a primary school system of free, compulsory, secular education in 1877. A brief spell of prosperity in the early 1870's was followed by almost 20 years of depression. Conditions improved in the 1890's, with better world farm prices and with the introduction after 1882 of refrigerated shipping. Refrigeration added meat and dairy products to wool as New Zealand's staple exports.

In 1890 New Zealand trade unionists were defeated in a major inter-Australian maritime strike, but they gained a political victory with the election of a Liberal government, New Zealand's first effective party government, which held office from 1891 to 1912. This government encouraged small farm settlement, opening up new land, subdividing old estates, and providing loans to new settlers. A detailed system of laws to regulate labor conditions was introduced, and a labor department created to police the new legislation. The Industrial Conciliation and Arbitration Act of 1894 sought to prevent strikes and to encourage trade unionism. Industrial disputes were to be settled by conciliation boards or by compulsory arbitration. The Liberal government was also partly responsible for impressive decreases in infant mortality in the early twentieth century. Acts of 1901 and 1904 provided for the registration of nurses and of midwives. Richard John Seddon, Liberal prime minister from 1893 to 1906, was one of the most powerful political figures in New Zealand history. A man of tremendous humanitarian drive, dictatorial, unabashedly using public works for political purposes, he achieved a remarkable rapport with the electorate.

By 1912 the bases of Liberal support were drawing apart—small farmers turning to the new Reform (conservative) party, and urban working classes to the Labour movement. The Reform party held power from 1912 to 1928, headed until 1925 by Prime Minister Ferguson Massey. It ended political abuses in the public service by placing most departments of state under a commission. Although the Reform party had a passive concept of government activity in both domestic and foreign affairs, it placed major agricultural exports (excluding wool) under marketing boards dominated by producer representatives. Faced by world depression in the late 1920's, coalition governments drastically cut back government expenditure, while at the same time increasing state control over the economy.

With the advent of a Labour party government in 1935 under Michael Joseph Savage, a rapid acceleration of state activity was initiated. Import and exchange controls were imposed, and a number of key concerns were nationalized. A system of guaranteed prices for dairy products was introduced. The Social Security Act of 1938 extended, consolidated, and renamed the forms of state charity and assistance that had developed in previous decades. New Zealand had been one of the first countries to have old age pensions which, on a noncontributory basis, had been introduced by the Liberals in 1898. Pensions were added for widows in 1911, for miners in 1915, a family allowance in 1926, and unemployment relief in 1930. These pensions and allowances were increased in 1938, and there were added orphan, disability, and sickness benefits, universal superannuation, and subsidized doctors' fees and prescription charges. The government also instituted an elaborate system of controls and subsidies to stabilize prices. By the time it left office in 1949 (including a period during World War II when it was in coalition, 1940–45) the Labour government had transformed New Zealand into a welfare state.

Labour was succeeded in 1949 by Sidney George Holland's National party (an amalgamation of the former Reform and Liberal parties). Holland's government remained in office until 1957, achieving its greatest political success by crushing the 1951 wharf strike; the economy boomed, thanks to high wool prices. The Labour government that followed was faced, however, with falling overseas prices, and its stringent budgetary measures led to its defeat in 1960, and the return to power of the National party under (Sir) Keith J. Holyoake. In recent years this government has encouraged local industry and a diversified economy, with the result that there has been a striking increase in the export of manufactured goods. G. A. Wood

BIBLIOG.–R. M. Chapman, W. K. Jackson and A. V. Mitchell, *New Zealand Politics In Action: the 1960 General Election* (1962); L. Cockayne, *New Zealand Plants and Their Story* (1967 ed.); J. B. Condliffe, *New Zealand In the Making* (1959 ed.); K. B. Cumberland, *This Is New Zealand: a Pictorial Description* (1964 ed.); K. B. Cumberland and J. W. Fox, *New Zealand: a Regional Geography* (1964 ed.); K. B. Cumberland and J. S. Whitelaw, *The World's Landscapes: New Zealand* (1970); B. H. Farrell, *Power In New Zealand: A Geography of Energy Resources* (1962); R. W. Firth, *Economics of the New Zealand Maori* (1959 ed.); B. J. Garnier, *The Climate of New Zealand* (1958); A. H. McLintock, ed., *An Encyclopedia of New Zealand* (1966); Joan Metge, *The Maoris of New Zealand* (1967); R. S. Milne, *Political Parties in New Zealand* (1966); *New Zealand Official Yearbook* (annual); W. H. Oliver, *The Story of New Zealand* (1963 ed.); R. J. Polaschek, *Government Administration In New Zealand* (1961); J. W. Rowe and M. A. Rowe, *New Zealand* (1967); K. J. Scott, *The New Zealand Constitution* (1962); Keith Sinclair, *A History of New Zealand* (1969 ed.); W. B. Sutch, *The Quest For Security In New Zealand, 1840 to 1966* (1967); F. L. W. Wood, *New Zealand In the World* (1940).

NEXT FRIEND, in law, one who, without being legally appointed as guardian, takes some legal action in the name and for the benefit of an infant or other person who is not legally competent to act. A person of unsound mind, even though he has not been adjudged incompetent, may be represented by a responsible friend in most states. The next friend should have no pecuniary or other interest in the suit, and he is usually a relative. Courts are generally careful to prevent an abuse of this right and in some cases appoint a guardian *ad litem* (for the suit) to supersede the next friend. A next friend is answerable for the costs of the proceeding, but he may recover the amount expended if the action was well founded.

NEY, MICHEL, duc d'Elchingen and prince de La Moskova, 1769–1815, French marshal, born in Saarlouis, Saar. He became a noncommissioned officer in the hussars in 1788. During the French Revolution he was promoted to general of brigade and served as interim commander of the Army of the Rhine in 1799. In 1804, after the establishment of the French Empire, Napoleon Bonaparte appointed Ney marshal of France. He won a series of victories—Elchingen in 1805 (which won him the title duc d'Elchingen); Jena in 1806; Eylau (Bagrationovsk) and Friedland (Pravdinsk) in 1807—and was called "the bravest of the brave" by Napoleon. In 1812 Ney led the III Corps, Grand Army, to victory at Smolensk and Borodino and was created prince de La Moskova. He commanded the rear guard in the retreat from Moscow. Ney led the French to victory at Lützen and Bautzen in 1813, and to defeat at Dennewitz. After Napoleon abdicated in 1814, Ney became an officer of LOUIS XVIII, and on Napoleon's return from Elba he was sent to capture his former commander, but rejoined him instead. He commanded the I and II Corps at Quatre-Bras, June 16, and led the Old Guard at Waterloo, June 18, 1815. He was sentenced to death for treason by the French house of peers, and was shot in the Luxembourg Gardens, Paris.

NEZ PERCÉ, one of a North American Indian tribe of the Shahaptian linguistic family, formerly living in regions of the Pacific Northwest corresponding to central Idaho, SE Washington, and NE Oregon. Although Nez Percé, a name first given to a number of Indian groups in the northwest by early French explorers, means "pierced nose," it is believed that the Nez Percé tribe did not commonly indulge in this practice. Lewis and Clark reported them to be a friendly people in 1805 (see Lewis and Clark Expedition). In 1831 a party of Nez Percés went to St. Louis to learn about Christianity, and as a result of their interest several missions were later established among them. In 1855 and in 1863 large tracts of Nez Percé territory were ceded by treaty to the United States. Uncertainty over hunting restrictions caused some Nez Percés to revolt, and in 1877 a U.S. Army force was sent to subdue them. Under the able leadership of Chief Joseph, a group of Nez Percés defeated one army detachment and evaded other army units in a 2,000-mile retreat through sections of Idaho, Wyoming, and Montana before surrendering near the Canadian border. The survivors were settled in Indian Territory in 1878, but suffered from the climate and from disease, and were resettled in 1885 at the Colville Reservation in northern Washington, where they merged with other groups.

The Nez Percés subsisted by hunting, fishing, and food gathering. They are believed to have acquired the horse about 1700. Their traditional dwelling was a long house inhabited by many families; hunting parties lived in tepees. Men wore the breechcloth, leggings, moccasins, and blankets; women wore gowns of skins. The Nez Percé population, reported by Lewis and Clark to be about 6,000 in 1805, was estimated at 1,700 in 1853. In 1950 a total of 1,090 Indians were living on the Nez Percé Reservation in Idaho.

NEZPERCE, village, W Idaho, seat of Lewis County; 39 miles ESE of Lewiston. Nezperce, a milling center for flour and lumber, is in a wheat-producing region. Pop. (1960) 667.

NGAMI, LAKE, a shallow reed-covered lake in the Okovanggo Basin, NW Bechuanaland, S central Africa, at the N edge of the Kalahari Desert. It receives the Okovanggo River and varies greatly in size, depending on variations in rainfall; it averages about 40 miles long and 5 miles wide. Lake Ngami was discovered in 1849 by David Livingstone, who described it as an inland sea.

NGAOUNDÉRÉ, town and market center, W central Africa, Adamaoua Region, N central Cameroun; altitude 3,670 feet; 275 miles NE of Yaoundé. Its facilities include a hospital, hydroelectric plant, and meteorological station. The principal agricultural products of the area are coffee, cattle, sheep, and goats.

NIAGARA, BATTLE OF. See Lundy's Lane, Battle of.

NIAGARA FALLS, city, W New York, Niagara County, on the E side of the Niagara River at the falls; on the Erie, the Lehigh Valley, the New York Central, and the Canadian National railroads and U.S. highway 62; 17 miles NNW of Buffalo. It is a famed resort city for tourists, who are attracted by the spectacle of the falls. One of the oldest museums in the country was moved to Niagara Falls in 1864 from Ontario. Niagara University is situated nearby. Extensive local development of hydroelectrical power has made Niagara Falls an important industrial center. The city is also a major electrochemical and electrometallurgical center. Products manufactured there include chemicals, aircraft, machinery, abrasives, grease and graphite, metal and steel products, and electrical equipment.

The falls region was visited by Father Louis Hennepin in 1678. Control of this region was strategic during the colonial era because the portage around the falls was the only break in the all-water journey between the St. Lawrence River and the upper Great Lakes. French forts were built there in 1745 and 1750, but the region was captured by the British in 1759. The area's first settlement, Manchester, was burned by British forces in 1813. Construction of the Erie Canal ended the profitable business from portage around the falls. Efforts were made to harness the falls and by 1881 Niagara power was turning the first generator. The present city was formed in 1892 by the union of Niagara Falls and Suspension Bridge villages. Pop. (1960) 102,394.

NIAGARA FALLS, city, S central Canada, Ontario, Welland County; at the Falls of the Niagara River and on the Canadian National, the New York Central, and the Wabash railroads; 18 miles NW of Buffalo, N.Y. Niagara Falls, a port of entry, utilizes hydroelectric power for paper and pulp milling, food canning, and manufacturing industrial machinery, railroad and electrical equipment, domestic appliances, leather, clothing, graphite, silverware, toilet articles, batteries, castings, and cereal foods. Many U.S. firms have plants there. The city is the seat of Queen Victoria Park, which extends 2½ miles along the gorge of the Niagara River. Niagara Falls became important in 1855 when a bridge was built connecting the city with its U.S. counterpart, Niagara Falls, N.Y. The city was incorporated in 1903. Pop. (1956) 23,563. See Niagara River.

NIAGARAN SERIES, sedimentary rocks laid down in the middle Silurian period. (See Geologic Time.) Two formations of the series are recognized, the Clinton and the Niagaran. The Clinton, the lower of the two, includes beds of shale, limestone, and iron ore generally in the form of hematite. This ore probably was formed by a replacement process that involved chemical precipitation. In some places it is called "flaxseed ore," because of the size and shape of the small concretions. It is found in scattered locations from Alabama to New York and west to Wisconsin. The Niagaran formation is mainly limestone and dolomite. It covers the eastern part of the United States, and extends slightly beyond the Mississippi north of the Missouri River and into Missouri, Arkansas, Oklahoma, and Texas in the south. The Niagaran formation also is found on the north coast of Greenland and on arctic islands. In the east the limestone is 100 to 300 feet thick, but in Wisconsin and Illinois it attains a thickness of 400 to 500 feet. The Niagara River falls over a cliff of this limestone. The formation is notable for the occurrence within it of circular or elliptic coral reefs and plainly evident coral growths embedded in the central portions of the reefs. These fossil corals are commonly found in the Hudson Bay region and in Illinois, Indiana, and Wisconsin.

NIAGARA-ON-THE-LAKE, or Niagara, town, Canada, S Ontario, Lincoln County; on Lake Ontario at the mouth of the Niagara River, on the New York Central Railroad; 27 miles NNW of Buffalo, N.Y. It is across the border from New York's Fort Niagara State Park. Niagara's industries include fruit and vegetable canning, jam making, and basket weaving. The town is a summer resort and the seat of a historical museum. Niagara's Fort George, built in 1790, was the scene of a battle during the War of 1812. The town was originally settled in 1780 by United Empire loyalists from the American colonies, and during the period 1792 to 1796 was the capital of Upper Canada. Pop. (1956) 2,740.

NIAGARA RIVER, NW New York and S Ontario, forms part of the international boundary between the United States and Canada; flows N out of E Lake Erie between Fort Erie, Ont., and Buffalo, N.Y., around Grand Island (in the United States), over Niagara Falls, and into Lake Ontario; length 34 miles. During its course the river descends about 326 feet, about half of this at Niagara Falls. The river is navigable for about 20 miles above the falls and for about 7 miles below the falls between Lewiston, N.Y., and Lake Ontario. The broad, smooth stream is converted into a series of rapids about ½ mile above the cataract. For about 2 miles below the falls the current is smooth. The stream then churns through the Whirlpool Rapids into the Whirlpool, where the waters hurl against the Canadian side and sweep around in a great eddy. Below the Whirlpool the Niagara is again broad and calm. The composition of the river bed at the falls—soft shale and sandstone overlaid with hard limestone—accounts for the change in shape and location of the falls through the centuries.

Niagara Falls. At one time, perhaps between 25,000 and 50,000 years ago, there probably were five Niagara falls in the vicinity of Syracuse, N.Y. Those falls disappeared when the level of the northern Great Lakes decreased and the overflow of Lake Erie was collected into one stream, the present Niagara River. Upon reaching an escarpment at the site of Lewiston (7 miles north of the present location of the falls) the waters pitched over into the valley below. The pounding of the water at the bottom of the falls wore away the soft material under the limestone lip of the cataract, causing the limestone to break off and the falls to move slowly upstream.

Beginning in 1953 a joint U.S.–Canadian project was undertaken to control the continuing erosion of the falls so that their beauty might be preserved and their power best utilized for the generation of electricity. A control dam was constructed about a mile upstream to distribute more evenly the flow of water over the falls, and provide power plants with the proper volume of water. The project also included deepening the bed of the Horseshoe (Canadian) Falls and eliminating small, stray flows. It was hoped that this work would prevent the recurrence of large-scale cave-ins which have occurred from time to time.

Luna and Goat islands divide the cataract into three falls: the American, the Luna (or Bridal Veil), and the Horseshoe. Luna Falls, which is in the United States, is much the smallest of the three. American falls are about 1,000 feet wide and fall about 167 feet. Behind them is a series of cavernous recesses, one of which, the Cave of the Winds, is accessible to tourists. The Horseshoe Falls, so named because of their inward curve, are about 2,500 feet wide and drop about 160 feet. The beauty of the falls annually attracts great numbers of tourists, particularly honeymooners. Parks and reservations on both sides provide pleasant drives and vantage points. The New York reservation includes Prospect, Devil's Hole, and Whirlpool state parks and Goat, Luna, and several smaller islands. Queen Victoria Park, on the Canadian side, offers the best view of both cataracts. Rainbow Bridge, below the falls, was completed in 1941. It replaces a steel arch that was built in 1898 and destroyed by an ice jam in 1938. A 1950 U.S.–Canadian treaty governs the diversion of water for power production.

History. The falls were visited by many early French explorers and missionaries. Father Louis Hennepin, who accompanied Cavelier, Sieur de La Salle's expedition of 1678, wrote what is probably the first account of the spectacle in *Description de la Louisiane* (1683). The region about the falls played an important part in the early settlement of the colonies; trading posts and forts were built along the river, and skirmishes with the Indians took place on both sides of the stream. Several battles of the War of 1812 took place in the vicinity, and for a time during the Canadian uprising of 1837–38 William Lyon Mackenzie's forces held Navy Island, 2 miles above the falls.

The falls were for many years a mecca for daredevils until stringent regulations prohibited further feats of daring. Charles Blondin (original name Jean François Gravelet) was probably the most famous of the acrobats who walked a tightrope above the river. In 1859 he astounded onlookers not only by making his own way across the chasm, but by carrying another man on his shoulders. The first person to go over the falls in a barrel was Mrs. Annie Edson Taylor, who observed in 1901, after her terrifying ride in a wooden barrel, "Nobody ought ever to do that again." But others did—in wood, steel, and rubber contrivances. Some did not live to pass on to others Mrs. Taylor's advice.

NIAMEY, city, W Africa, capital of the republic of Niger; on the Niger River and the Tanezrouft trans-Sahara motor route; a scheduled airline stop; 495 miles NNW of Lagos. Niamey is a government administrative center and an agricultural market center for millet, corn, manioc, and rice. Hides, onions, livestock, skins, and mats are exported from Niamey, primarily to Nigeria. The city also has plants for processing lime and leather, and for manufacturing pottery, rugs, and charcoal. Pop. (1964 est.) 41,975.

HARRISON FORMAN WORLD TRAVEL

Niamey is built on hills above the left bank of the Niger River. Most of its trade is carried on by women.

NIAS ISLAND, Indonesia, North Sumatra Province, 65 miles W of Sumatra. The area is 1,569 sq. mi. Nias is the largest island off the west coast of Sumatra; it is roughly rectangular in shape, and hilly, The highest elevation, in the south central part, is 2,907 feet. The soil is fertile, and coconuts, pepper, rice, tobacco, and sugar cane are grown. The island natives are proto-Malay, related in physical type and language to the Batak of Sumatra. For long periods they were isolated on their island, but there are definite cultural signs of contact with Indians and other peoples. They live in large towns on hilltops, connected by stone pathways through the jungle. Nias is one of the few places in the world where great stone columns, or megaliths, are still constructed. (For population, see Southeast Asia map in Atlas.)

FAY-COOPER COLE

NIBELUNGENLIED, or Song of the Nibelungs, is a heroic epic in Middle High German, written about 1200 by an unknown poet. The narrative is based on lays of earlier Frankish origin, and fuses historical and legendary elements. The historical foundation of the epic was the overthrow of the Burgundian Kingdom by Attila in 436; this was fused with the legend of Siegfried and Brunhild. Long forgotten, the poem was revived as a German national epic during the Napoleonic Wars. It has been the subject of numerous critical studies, the first by Karl Lachmann in 1816. In *Der Ring des Nibelungen* the composer Richard Wagner used some material from the *Nibelungenlied*, although his principal source was the Icelandic ***Volsunga Saga.***

Story. Siegfried, possessor of the Nibelung treasure, sets out to woo the beautiful Kriemhild, sister of King Gunther of Burgundy. Gunther promises his sister to Siegfried, but first Siegfried must help Gunther to win Brunhild, queen of Iceland, who will marry only a man who can defeat her in three trials of strength. With a magic cloak that makes him invisible, Siegfried wins the contest for Gunther, and the two couples are married. Several years later Siegfried and Kriemhild visit Gunther and Brunhild, and jealousy develops between the queens. Brunhild learns that it was Siegfried who had won her; furious at the deception she seeks revenge and has Siegfried treacherously slain by Hagen, Gunther's henchman. Then for many years Kriemhild mourns Siegfried and plots her own revenge. She marries Etzel (Attila), king of the Huns, and invites Gunther, Hagen, and their followers to Etzel's court, where she provokes the slaughter of all the Burgundians and is in turn killed by the magician Hildebrand.

Die Klage, the Lament of the Survivors, continues the *Nibelungenlied.* It was written in the twelfth century in Middle High German. The poet of *Die Klage* states that the story is based on a Latin work written by one Konrad, at the request of Bishop Pilgrim of Passau. Technically and imaginatively inferior to the *Nibelungenlied*, the *Klage* nevertheless has an appealing simplicity and sincerity.

NICAEA, ancient city, W Asia Minor, in Bithynia, on the E shore of Lake Ascanius. The modern town is Iznik, Bursa Province, Turkey. Nicaea was founded by the Macedonians about 300 B.C., and the kings of Bithynia frequently resided there. Two ecclesiastical councils were held in the city, 325 and 787 (see COUNCILS OF NICAEA). Nicaea was captured by Crusaders in 1097 during the first Crusade (see CRUSADES, *The First Crusade*), but it reached the height of its importance about 100 years later when, after Constantinople had fallen to the armies of the fourth Crusade, the Byzantine aristocracy fled to Nicaea. Theodore I Lascaris, son-in-law of the deposed Emperor Alexius III (1195–1203), was crowned in 1206 and established an empire that was to last until the Byzantine Empire was restored in 1261. See BYZANTINE EMPIRE, *Constantinople Captured and Regained*.

NICARAGUA, republic, Central America; bounded on the N by Honduras, on the E by the Caribbean Sea (coast line 336 miles), on the S by Costa Rica, and on the W by the Pacific Ocean (coast line 219 miles); area 57,143 sq. mi., including 3,475 sq. mi. of water; population (1963 est.) 1,606,000.

The country is shaped roughly like a triangle with the apex pointing to the southeast. Nicaragua's largest city, Managua, is also its capital. The city is located in the southwest portion of the country on Lake Managua, about 30 miles inland from the Pacific Ocean.

The national flower of Nicaragua is the heliotrope. For the national flag in color, see Flag. For a map of Nicaragua, see Atlas.

PHYSICAL FACTORS

Topography. The Central American cordillera forms the backbone of the country. It trends from northwest to southeast at a distance of 12 to 30 miles from the Pacific Coast, reaching average heights of 4,000 to 5,000 feet, with an occasional peak of 6,000 feet.

The land may be divided into five zones, each with its distinctive characteristics: (1) The Mosquito coast—the low, flat, swampy, tropical jungle region of the Carribbean coast—is lined with coral reefs and lagoons. (2) The broken plateaus west of the coast, with some interspersed mountains and lowlands, comprise one-third of the area of Nicaragua, and contain almost all the country's mineral wealth. (3) The eastern part of the Central American cordillera is parallel with the lake region, and is bounded on the west by a steep escarpment. (4) The lake basin, which includes most of the country's 3,475 miles of water surface, is the heart of the country in number of cities, population density, and economic activity. There are two large lakes, Managua and Nicaragua. In the north Lake Managua drains through the narrow, rapids-filled Tipitapa River or channel into the larger Lake Nicaragua. Lake Nicaragua drains to the southeast through the San Juan River into the Caribbean. Some of the extinct volcanoes associated with the western volcanic chain are scattered through this region. Several islands in the lakes, such as Ometepe, are extinct volcanoes. A cluster of extinct volcanoes lies at the northern end of the lake basin, between Lake Managua and the Gulf of Fonseca. (5) The western part of the cordillera is primarily a chain of volcanic peaks fronting on the Pacific. The several active volcanoes in this zone are subject to frequent eruptions; some are constantly giving off smoke or vapor, and earthquakes are not uncommon.

Location Map of Nicaragua

Since the Nicaraguan uplands are in the westernmost portion of the country, the longer rivers flow to the east coast. These are the Coco (Segovia), navigable for 150 miles, which forms the boundary with Honduras; the Río Grande; the Escondido (Bluefields); and the San Juan, navigable from Lake Nicaragua to the rapids at its mouth.

Climate. The three climatic zones of Nicaragua range from the tropical rain forest zone of the east coast to the tropical savanna on the west. Between them is the drier, more temperate, interior plateau area. The east coastal climate extends inland 50 to 100 miles depending on the nearness of the mountains and plateaus to the coast. The annual temperature in this region is about 75°F, with less than a 5° range; rainfall, however, varies widely between the coastal towns of Bluefields (more than 127 inches) and San Juan del Norte (almost 260 inches). The period of least rain is January through April, and the maximum occurs from July through August, a period of thunderstorms. In the interior there are high temperatures only at midday; rainfall averages about 60 inches. The hot west coast has wet and dry seasons and receives almost all of its rainfall, which can vary between 60 and 100 inches, within the period of June to October.

Plants and Animals. Forests cover almost 50 per cent of the land area with variations according to altitude ranging from the oak, fir, and pine trees of the uplands to the tropical fruits, bananas, oranges, pineapples, and coconuts of the tropical coast. In addition to fruits, the forests provide dyewoods, gums, resins, rubber, camphor and other medicinal products, spices, and mahogany and other cabinet woods.

There is an abundant and varied tropical fauna including monkeys, pumas, alligators, armadillos, jaguars, anteaters, snakes, spiders, parrots, macaws, hummingbirds, buzzards, wild turkeys, and water fowl.

SOCIAL FACTORS

Population. Nicaragua is the largest country in Central America, but the most thinly populated. Average population density is 27 persons per square mile. About 80 per cent of the inhabitants live in the western half of the country. Most of them are either of mixed Spanish or Indian extraction.

Nicaragua

There are some of pure Spanish descent and a number of Indians. Most of the population of the eastern half of Nicaragua are Mosquito, Zambo, or other Indians, and Negroes from Jamaica and other Caribbean islands. The two areas differ in many respects and there is little communication between them.

Since 1930 Nicaragua has made use of a restricted immigration policy toward Chinese, Turks, Negroes, Arabs, and Jews. There are 123 town sites in Nicaragua of which at least 98 have populations between 2,000 and 50,000.

PRINCIPAL CITIES

	Population*
Managua (capital)	236,000
León	49,612
Matagalpa	14,702
Jinotepe	15,342
Granada	32,441
Masaya	30,103
Chinandega	19,025
Bluefields	11,376

*1960 figures

Religion and Education. Roman Catholicism is the official state religion of Nicaragua, but there is freedom of worship. The republic consists of one archbishopric, the ecclesiastical province of Nicaragua, and five bishoprics with headquarters at León, Granada, Matagalpa, Juigalpa, and Puerto Cabezas.

Secondary schools are neither compulsory nor free, and the compulsory attendance law for ages 6 to 14 is not enforced. The illiteracy rate is high—more than 65 per cent of the population. In 1947 all schools of higher education were combined into the National University of Nicaragua at León, with branches at Managua and Granada. Its professional schools include medicine, chemistry and pharmacy, law, dentistry, and engineering. The Military Academy of Nicaragua is located in Managua.

Economic Factors

Agriculture is the chief economic activity of Nicaragua. It employs 65 per cent of the labor force and in 1961 furnished more than 37 per cent of the gross national product. Little more than 1 million acres, less than 5 per cent of the total land area, is devoted to crops—about equally divided between annual crops such as corn, cotton, and rice and perennial crops such as sugar cane and coffee. Much of the national prosperity depends on the coffee crop, which leads all others in gross value and which has been the principal export crop since 1947. The coffee plantations are located chiefly in the upland departments of Carazo, Chinandega, Jinotega, Managua, and Matagalpa. In 1961–62 the coffee crop, produced on 155,000 acres, reached an all-time high of 59,000 tons, but it usually averages about 22,500 tons. Sugar production, employing about 75,000 people, is centered around Chinandega. Bananas were for many years the leading crop of the east coast but, because of plant diseases and insects, production was vastly curtailed and many banana plantations were relocated on the west coast. Among other export crops are cotton, sesame seed, cacao, ipecac root, and rice. The western portion of Nicaragua raises most of its own food, while the east imports. Most of the tobacco, corn, beans, plantains, oranges, pineapples, and yucca or cassava produced is for domestic consumption. Tobacco is raised largely in the region around Masaya.

Cattle are raised successfully in the western lowlands, the central highlands, and the eastern coastal areas, especially in Chinandega, Chontales, and Rivas. Nicaragua's first modern packing plant was established in 1955. There is some export of live cattle to Peru. Hides and skins are usually sold to domestic buyers, and dairy production has an almost wholly local market.

PAN AMERICAN UNION

Coffee is grown at altitudes ranging from 1,500 to 3,000 feet in the uplands of Nicaragua, and is the country's chief export. Coffee beans are usually dried in the sun.

Fishing provides an important subsistence activity on the Atlantic Coast. Only turtles are a significant export item; 1,600 were exported in 1961.

Natural Resources. Nicaragua's forests are reasonably rich, containing mahogany, cedar, dyewoods, gumwoods, and medicinal plants; but primarily because of labor shortages, timber production was in decline at mid-century.

Of the total land area of some 36.5 million acres, about 17.5 million acres are under timber, about 2.1 million acres of land are arable, and 900,000 acres are used for grazing.

Nicaragua is the leading gold mining and exporting nation in Central America. The most important deposits are in Madríz, Chontales, and Matagalpa in the northeast and León in the northwest. Silver is also mined. Mining activity increased with the introduction of air transport for the moving of mining equipment into the mining areas and the carrying out of the products of the mines. From 1938 to 1961 the production of gold rose from 44,500 to 226,250 fine ounces. As most gold is mined under foreign concession, only about 30 per cent of the proceeds remains in the country. Among the country's mineral resources that remained undeveloped at mid-century were copper, lead, zinc, tin, nickel, antimony, iron, mercury, limestone, coal, lignite, sulfur, salt, petroleum, and precious stones.

Manufacturing is restricted to the processing of agricultural products and the production of the more basic consumer goods for local markets. Coffee cleaning and processing is the largest industry and is centered in the urban areas. There are more than 20 sugar mills—half of them in Chinandega, the rest scattered through the departments of León, Granada, Managua, and Rivas. Among other manufactures are shoes, cotton and silk textiles, soap, cigarettes, matches, furniture, leatherware, dairy products, bread, hard and soft beverages, pharmaceuticals, turpentine, sesame oil, metalware, construction materials including cement, and electrical power. Expansion of industrial production has been checked by lack of fuels and raw materials and the low purchasing power of the people.

Commerce. From 1937 to 1953 and again in 1955, 1958, and 1959 Nicaragua had a favorable balance of trade, but in 1954, 1956, 1957, 1960, and 1961 the balance was unfavorable. In 1961 the deficit was $6 million, with imports of $74.4 million and exports of $68.4 million. In 1947 about 85 per cent of Nicaragua's imports were provided by the United States; in 1961 the percentage was about 49 per cent. The remaining 51 per cent of the country's imports come from West Germany, Japan, the United Kingdom, and the Netherlands Antilles.

JUNTA NACIONAL DE TURISMO

A park and monument in Managua honor the genius of Rubén Darío, Nicaragua's poet laureate. His country won international literary fame in 1888 when *Azul* was published.

Nicaraguan exports go mainly to the United States, West Germany, Japan, the United Kingdom, the Netherlands, and other Central American countries.

Principal imports are machinery, vehicles, iron and steel products, chemicals and drugs, and various foodstuffs. Major exports include coffee, cotton, gold, timber, sugar, and livestock. At one time bananas were an important export. During World War II rubber was a major export (a million pounds in 1944), but after the war its importance dwindled.

Transportation. Nicaragua is greatly handicapped by its lack of good transportation facilities. Primary overland transportation routes run north-south; there is little overland connection between the east and west coasts. Most of the roads are mere trails over which only oxcarts can be driven in the wet season, although at mid-century efforts were being made to improve the highway system, in some instances with the aid of U.S. capital. Among the major paved highways are the Pan American, about 240 miles of which are in Nicaragua. This highway is of great value for tourist traffic and for the shipping of coffee and grains. Railroads are government-owned and operated as the Pacific Railroad of Nicaragua. The principal line runs primarily through the coffee districts from El Viejo in the north to Granada in the south, a distance of 230 miles. There is a 20-mile connection from Puerto Morazán to Chinandega. All railroads are single track.

Aside from some small government-owned vessels that use Lakes Managua and Nicaragua, the country has a negligible merchant marine. Corinto, the principal seaport of Nicaragua, situated on a small island connected by bridge with the west coast of the mainland, handles about 70 per cent of the nation's foreign trade. The cities of Managua, León, Granada, and Chinandega in the lake basin or associated lowlands have access by rail to the port. Other important west coast ports are San Juan del Sur and Puerto Morazán. El Bluff near Bluefields on the Escondido River is the major Caribbean port. San Juan del Norte, Cabo Gracias a Dios, and Puerto Cabezas are the other Caribbean ports. Other water-borne traffic is carried by the San Juan River from Lake Nicaragua to a point near its mouth, where rapids obstruct navigation. This river is looked upon as a future route for a trans-Nicaragua canal. The only other navigable stream is the Coco, navigable for about 150 miles upstream from its mouth on the Caribbean and giving access to several towns and a large portion of the mining region of eastern Nicaragua.

Much travel and a considerable amount of freight shipment moves by air, including gold and silver. Besides a local system of freight and passenger transport, there is daily air service to the United States and South America and to other parts of Central America.

ROBERT D. LORING

ADMINISTRATION AND HISTORY

Government. The president of Nicaragua, 3 vice presidents, 16 senators, 42 deputies, and local council members are directly elected by secret ballot to four-year terms. All persons over 21 are eligible to vote, as are those over 18 who can read or write or are married, and those under 18 who meet certain educational requirements. Nicaragua is divided into 16 departments and one *comarca* (district), the heads of which are appointed by the president. The departments have 123 *municipios*, each headed by a mayor. There is no Nicaraguan army; the national guard functions as both police force and army. Enlistment is for three years and military service can be made compulsory at any time. A coast guard is maintained to combat smuggling.

Prehistoric Period. The pre-Columbian Indians who inhabited Nicaragua were of Mayan stock, and formed a part of the Mayan culture which extended to the border of Costa Rica. Some sculptured monoliths on the islands in the Nicaraguan lakes are the scant relics of the former high civilization. See MAYA.

Colonial Period. Columbus sighted the land in 1502 on his fourth voyage and named several points, among them Cabo Gracias a Dios (see COLUMBUS, CHRISTOPHER, *Fourth Voyage*). The interior was first explored by Gil González Dávila (died 1543), who in 1522 led an expedition from Panama into the western part of the country. He had been sent out by Pedrarias Dávila (1440–1531), governor of Panama, who wished to forestall any conquest of the land from the north by Cortés in Mexico (see CORTÉS, HERNÁN). Pedrarias became suspicious of González and sent out Francisco Fernández de Córdoba (1475–1526) to take his place. Córdoba built the cities of León and Granada in 1524 and subsequently revolted against Pedrarias. In the same year González, avoiding the territories of Pedrarias, landed in Nicaragua to take possession of the land he had discovered, but failed to do so. Pedrarias himself advanced into Nicaragua and overthrew Córdoba in a surprise attack. Deprived of his command in Panama by royal mandate, Pedrarias was instead given the governorship of Nicaragua, where he ruled until his death in 1531. The whole of Central America was at that time included in the captaincy general of Guatemala.

Failing to find the gold that was their sole reason for being in the New World, the Spaniards did not settle in large numbers during the sixteenth century—there were scarcely 500 in all the land by the century's end—but those who did settle in Nicaragua developed a profitable commerce with Panama and the West Indies that attracted the attention of English pirates. Settlement of the east coast by the English in the seventeenth century marked the beginning of a long dispute that lasted until the end of the nineteenth century. Great Britain in 1786 recognized the sovereignty of Spain over the east coast, and in 1860 decided to give up its claims to the protectorate of the Mosquito coast.

End of European Control. The Revolution of 1820 in Spain brought a revised colonial policy under which provincial deputations were elected and Gavino Gainza (1760–1824) was appointed captain general of Guatemala. The reforms could not counteract the effect of poor communications with Spain, which were essentially the same as in the time of the conquistadors. The increasing wealth of the country accorded ill with the monopolistic practices of Spain's colonial policy; as a result, smuggling increased considerably, while the decline of Spanish sea power rendered the system of convoys unworkable. Because of inherent economic and political disadvantages in the Spanish system of colonial rule, a weak central government in Spain, and burgeoning political liberalism inspired by the American and French revolutions, a spirit of revolt developed throughout Central America. In 1821 Agustín de Iturbide, then leading a successful Mexican revolt against Spain, suggested the union of Central America with Mexico. (See ITURBIDE, AGUSTÍN COSME DAMÍAN DE.) The suggestion was adopted by a majority of the delegates, but a number of towns in Nicaragua refused to recognize the union. Their opposition was crushed by Iturbide's general, Vicente Filísola. With the dethronement of Iturbide as emperor in 1823, Filísola convoked a congress of the Central American provinces which proclaimed the Republic of Central America. The republic struggled on until 1838 when, disrupted by the centrifugal tendencies of the provinces, it separated into the five countries of which Nicaragua is one.

Internal Conflicts. The intense rivalry that developed between León and Granada, causing political disturbances, was not allayed by the choice of Managua as capital in 1835. The nineteenth century was a period of continual turmoil in which the conservatives were for the most part predominant. In 1856 the Liberal party enlisted the aid of William Walker in an attempt to gain supremacy. Walker, an adventurer from the United States, attacked Granada with a band of 58 followers and quickly had himself proclaimed president. During this period the international importance of Nicaragua was greatly enhanced by the establishment of a regular transport route across the country by way of the San Juan River and Lake Nicaragua. The route was operated by Cornelius Vanderbilt, who resented Walker's interference and cut off his reinforcements and supplies. Aided by Vanderbilt, the forces of Nicaragua, Honduras, and Costa Rica drove Walker from the country in 1857. See WALKER, WILLIAM.

Thirty years of conservative predominance came to an end in 1893 with the election of José Santos Zelaya to the presidency. In an attempt to form a Central American federation with himself as president, Zelaya invaded Honduras and overthrew the government, and tried to start a revolution in El Salvador. As a result of his aggressive attitude the United States supported a revolution against him, and he was forced to resign in 1909. See ZELAYA, JOSÉ SANTOS.

Zelaya's successors, José Madriz in 1909–10 and Juan J. Estrada in 1910–11, were unable to restore order. When the provisional president, Adolfo Díaz (1874–), found himself unable to cope with the worsening political situation in 1911–12, he appealed to the United States for help. A detachment of marines was sent, which maintained order in the country until 1925, when it was withdrawn. Immediately disorder flared up again, and the marines returned the following year, remaining until 1933.

Somoza Regime. In 1937 Gen. Anastasio Somoza (1896–1956) became president, setting up a dictatorial government. In 1947 he retired from the presidency, continuing as minister of war, but the following year he was re-elected president.

International relations took a turn for the worse in 1948, when Nicaragua accused Costa Rica, Guatemala, and Venezuela of plotting to overthrow the governments of Nicaragua, Honduras, and the Dominican Republic. Costa Rica retorted by charging the Nicaraguan government with giving aid and comfort to Costa Rican rebels. Under the pacifying influence of the Organization of American States the matter was allowed to lapse (see ORGANIZATION OF AMERICAN STATES), but flared up again in 1955 when Pres. José Figueres of Costa Rica accused Nicaragua of training and arming an invasion force of Costa Rican rebels. These charges were vigorously denied by Nicaragua, although the activities of the revolutionary army, which was busily engaged on the Costa Rican border, proved somewhat embarrassing. The Organization of American States after investigating the matter concluded that the rebels had indeed come from Nicaragua. In the interests of international peace four war planes were sold to the Costa Rican government and a buffer zone was created between the two countries in which the rebel army could be defeated without damage to Nicaraguan neutrality.

The Somoza regime aroused some opposition in certain segments of the population and Somoza, though professing disdain for the many attempts on his life, had taken to wearing pistols. An attempted assassination in 1954 resulted in the declaration of a state of siege throughout the country. In 1956 Somoza was assassinated and was succeeded in office by his son, Col. Luis Somoza Debayle (1922–). The new administration appeared more liberal than the previous government. A number of press restrictions were lifted and public criticism of the government was tolerated. Luis Somoza also asked for a law to bar a president from succeeding himself in the next term. The law, approved in 1959, also extended to members of the president's family.

Nicaragua was plagued by several revolution attempts and a number of border raids from Costa Rica and Honduras during Luis Somoza's seven-year term of office, including an airborne invasion by a small group of Costa Rican exiles in 1959. The president claimed that that raid as well as others was inspired by the Cuban government of Fidel Castro.

U.S. naval units were ordered into the area on Nov. 17, 1960, at the request of Guatemalan and Nicaraguan officials who feared an invasion "from abroad." The units were recalled three weeks later after the invasion threat subsided.

Dr. René Schick Gutierrez was elected president by an overwhelming majority Feb. 3, 1963. The election was marked by antigovernment demonstrations in which at least four persons died. Although he was a candidate of the government's Liberal party, the new president claimed he would conduct his government independent of the Somoza family influence that had monopolized the government since 1937.

BIBLIOG.–I. J. Cox, *Nicaragua and the United States, 1909–1927* (1927); A. F. Carr, *High Jungles and Low* (1953); Gerard Colvin, *Central America* (1962); E. P. Hanson, ed., *New World Guide to Latin American Republics* (1950 ed.)

NICARAGUA, LAKE, SW Nicaragua, maximum NW–SE and NE–SW distances 103 and 45 miles respectively; separated from the Pacific Ocean by a 12-mile-wide isthmus. Lake Nicaragua is the largest lake in Central America and is 110 feet above sea level. It drains into the Caribbean Sea through the San Juan River on the southeast and is joined with Lake Managua on the northwest by the Tipitapa River. It contains several large islands. Granada is the chief port.

NICARAGUA CANAL, a proposed alternative to the Panama Canal to run by way of the San Juan River and Lake Nicaragua. Although frequently discussed since 1826, the project was never realized. During the California gold rush of 1848 the need for a canal was emphasized when miners from the eastern United States used the Nicaragua route, covering the last part by stagecoach. Surveys were conducted in 1850 and again during 1870–75, with no resulting action. The prospect of an international Panama Canal projected by the French engineer Ferdinand de Lesseps was distasteful to the U.S. Congress, and in 1884 a treaty was concluded with Nicaragua that provided for joint U.S.–Nicaraguan ownership; when Lesseps' company collapsed into bankruptcy in 1889 the treaty no longer seemed necessary and it was never ratified. A private concern, the Nicaragua

Location Map of the Proposed Nicaragua Canal

Canal Company, began work in 1889, but the depression of 1893 forced it to cease operations. Three commissions appointed by the U.S. government in 1895, 1897, and 1899 recommended the Nicaragua route, but the offer of the reorganized Lesseps company in 1901 to sell its property interests to the United States reawakened interest in the Panama scheme—an interest further aroused by a revolution in Colombia, 1903, as a result of which Panama came into existence and concluded a treaty favorable to the United States in the same year. The Nicaragua plan was not entirely abandoned, however, and a treaty ratified in 1916 gave the United States the right to construct an alternative route through Nicaragua. See PANAMA CANAL; HAY-PAUNCEFOTE TREATY.

NICCOLINI, GIOVANNI BATTISTA, 1782–1861, Italian man of letters, was born in San Giuliano, near Pisa, and was educated at Florence and at the University of Pisa. In 1807 he became professor of history and mythology, secretary, and librarian at the Florence Academy of Fine Arts. His dramas, chiefly of political and patriotic character, include *Antonio Foscarini* (1827); *Lodovico Sforza* (1834); *Beatrice Cenci* (1838–44); *Arnaldo da Brescia* (1843), considered his masterpiece; and *Filippo Strozzi* (1847). Niccolini also wrote several volumes of verse and translated from Aeschylus, Euripides, and Ovid.

NICCOLITE, a metallic mineral sulfide, sometimes called copper nickel because of its characteristic pale copper-red color. It is opaque and, like silver, tarnishes to gray or black. Niccolite, a nickel arsenide, has the formula NiAs. Its hardness is 5 to 5.5 and its specific gravity is 7.78. The mineral is usually found with a massive structure and occasionally as a crystal. Niccolite ore is a minor source of nickel and is found in Germany and in Ontario, Canada.

NICCOLÒ D'AREZZO, also known as Niccolò di Piero de' Lamberti, 1350?–?1417, Italian sculptor and architect, was born in Arezzo. He worked on the decoration of the cathedral in Florence, and did much to free Venetian art from Byzantine tradition.

NICCOLÒ DE' NICCOLI, 1363–1437, Italian antiquary, was born in Florence and became associated with Cosimo de' Medici. He collected Greek and Latin manuscripts, coins, and medals. His manuscripts formed the foundation of the Laurentian Library in Florence.

NICE, Italian Nizza, city, SE France, capital of Alpes-Maritimes Department; on the Mediterranean coast at the mouth of the Paillon River; 15 miles from the Italian border and 650 miles SE of Paris. The beauty of its setting with the Maritime Alps in the background and the mild Mediterranean climate (mean temperature 60°F) make it a popular resort, and the tourist trade is a principal industry. Manufactures include silk, tobacco, perfume, furniture, and soap. Flowers, fruits, and olives are grown. The old town, with its narrow, crooked streets and tall stone houses, lies on the east bank of the Paillon; the new town, with wide avenues and luxurious hotels and villas, is on the north and west. The main avenue, the Promenade des Anglais, extends for 4 miles along the Mediterranean shore. Nice has a casino; an art museum; a seventeenth century Roman Catholic cathedral; and a nineteenth century Gothic church, Notre Dame du Voeu. To the north of Nice is the town of Cimiez, which has interesting Roman ruins, gardens, and fine hotels. Nice, the ancient Nicaea, is believed to have been founded by Phocaean settlers who came from Massilia (Marseilles), probably in the fifth century B.C. During the Middle Ages, Nice was frequently in dispute and was held by the Saracens and later by Provence. In the fourteenth century it passed to Savoy, was taken by France, 1792, but was restored to Sardinia, 1814. In 1860 it was ceded to France. Pop. (1954) 244,360.

NICE, county and former division in the duchy of Savoy and the kingdom of Sardinia, corresponding to the E part of Alpes-Maritimes Department, SE France; principal city, Nice. Between the eleventh and the fourteenth century the region was a part of the Holy Roman Empire and was ruled by the kingdom of Arles and Burgundy and the counts of Provence. In 1388 Nice became a countship under the suzerainty of Count Amadeus VII of Savoy, whose successor, Amadeus VIII, was made Duke of Savoy in 1416. In the early sixteenth century Nice was contested by the armies of King Francis I of France and Holy Roman Emperor Charles V, and in 1543 the city of Nice was sacked by the Algerian corsair, Barbarossa II. During the seventeenth century the county flourished under the liberal policies of Charles Emmanuel I and II, dukes of Savoy, but again became a prize in wars with France in 1690 and 1705. Nice was restored to Savoy by the Treaty of Utrecht, 1713, and after 1720 was ruled by the kingdom of Sardinia (then the name for the domains of the house of Savoy). In 1796 it was ceded by Sardinia to France, but was restored to Sardinia in 1814 by the Congress of Vienna. When, by the Treaty of Villafranca, 1859, Savoy was permitted to decide by plebiscite whether to merge with Italy, Nice elected to join France. See FRANCE, History, *Napoleon III;* ITALY, Modern Italy, *Napoleonic Invasions;* SAVOY.

NICEPHORUS I, died 811, Byzantine emperor, was minister of finance under the Empress Irene, 797–802. Raised to emperor by a palace revolution in 802, he abandoned Irene's toleration of holy images in the

Crowded with tourists, the Promenade des Anglais follows the Mediterranean shore line in Nice. Across the avenue from the sea are many of the more popular resort hotels.
FRENCH GOVT. TOURIST OFFICE

churches and returned to iconoclasm. Several plots to dethrone him were successfully crushed, and the death in 809 of the great caliph, Harun al-Rashid, rid him of a dangerous foe in the east. The Bulgarian king, Krum, however, in July 811 defeated the emperor and his army. JOHN R. WILLIAMS

NICEPHORUS II, surnamed Phocas, 912?–69, Byzantine emperor, began his career as a general in Asia Minor. In 960 he commanded an expedition that drove the Moslems from Crete. On the death of Romanus II, 963, Nicephorus was proclaimed emperor. His six-year reign was one of the most glorious in the military annals of Byzantium. The Moslems were conquered in Cilicia and Cyprus, Mesopotamia and Syria were overrun, and in 969 Antioch and Aleppo fell. In Sicily and Italy, however, the Byzantines suffered serious reverses. Nicephorus was murdered in a palace conspiracy, 969 and was succeeded by one of the conspirators, his nephew, John Tzimisces. JOHN R. WILLIAMS

NICEPHORUS III, surnamed Botaniates, died 1081, Byzantine emperor, is significant mainly as the last ruler of "the time of troubles" (1056–81). A general in Asia Minor, Nicephorus in 1078 overthrew Michael VII and was proclaimed emperor. He enlisted the support of Alexius Comnenus and overcame his rivals. Later, however, he quarreled with Alexius, who deposed him in 1081 and initiated the strong rule of the Comneni dynasty. JOHN R. WILLIAMS

NICHOLAS I, SAINT, called Nicholas the Great, died 867, pope, was born in Rome, Italy. His election to the papal throne as successor to Benedict III, 858, was supported by the Holy Roman Emperor Louis II, but Nicholas let it be known that he would not let that compromise him. When the emperor's brother, Lothair of Lorraine, sought to marry his mistress after divorcing his wife, Nicholas declared that the divorce was invalid. The resulting quarrel with Louis did not sway Nicholas, who deposed the prelates siding with Lothair. In this and other instances Nicholas insisted on the right of the papacy to intervene in disputes involving members of the hierarchy and on the right of any bishop to appeal over his superior directly to the papacy—policies that were to influence the relation of the papacy to the various Christian European rulers during the Middle Ages. Nicholas dealt, as well, with the deposition of Ignatius, patriarch of Constantinople, by the Byzantine Emperor Michael III. Nicholas refused to recognize the usurper patriarch Photius and eventually secured, 867, the restoration of Ignatius to his see. Nicholas wrote the *Responsa Nicolai ad consulta Bulgarorum* as a reply to the Bulgarian King Boris' request for information on Christian beliefs. The feast day of St. Nicholas is November 13.

NICHOLAS II, original name Gerard of Burgundy, died 1061, pope, was born in Savoy and was elected to succeed Stephen X in 1058. He deposed the antipope Benedict X and presided over a synod that reformed the laws governing papal elections. Throughout his pontificate Nicholas was advised by Hildebrand (later Gregory VII).

NICHOLAS III, original name Giovanni Gaetano Orsini, 1216?–80, pope, was born in Rome, and succeeded John XXI in 1277. By passing laws that forbade foreigners to hold public office in Rome and arranging treaties with Emperor Rudolf I of Hapsburg and Charles I (of Anjou) Nicholas considerably weakened foreign control over Rome. He failed in his efforts to reunite Roman and Eastern churches. Nicholas was strongly criticized for nepotism.

NICHOLAS IV, original name Girolamo Masci d'Ascoli, died 1292, pope, was born in Ascoli. Elected to succeed Honorius IV, 1288, Nicholas became the first Franciscan pope. He sent missionaries to the Far East and attempted without success to launch a decisive crusade against the Moslems.

NICHOLAS V, original name Pietro Rainalducci, died 1333, antipope from 1328 to 1330, was born in Corvaro, Italy. A Franciscan, he was elected antipope during the pontificate of John XXII, at the instigation of the Holy Roman Emperor Louis IV. Nicholas was excommunicated by John, 1330, and in the same year made his submission to him.

NICHOLAS V, original name Tommaso Parentucelli, 1397–1455, pope from 1447, was born in Sarzana, Italy. As successor to Eugenius IV he was patron of countless scholars and artists who flocked to Rome seeking employment in his projects for translating the Greek classics and restoring and beautifying the city. He undertook the rebuilding of St. Peter's Basilica and enriched the Vatican Library with a large number of original manuscripts and copies of documents brought to Rome from all over Europe by his agents. Nicholas arranged the resignation of the last antipope, Felix V, and crowned Frederick III, last Holy Roman emperor crowned in Rome. CHARLES R. MEYER, S.T.D.

NICHOLAS I, or Nikolai Pavlovich, 1796–1855, czar of Russia, third son of Paul I, was born in Tsarsko-selo. He ascended the throne in December, 1825, when his brother Constantine declined it on the death of their eldest brother, Alexander I. Initial uncertainty over succession was seized upon by military conspirators (later called Decembrists) in St. Petersburg and the south as an opportunity for a revolt demanding a constitutional monarchy. The revolt was quelled by Nicholas who thereupon centralized the administration and inaugurated a secret police system to suppress revolutionary ideas. He put down a Polish uprising, 1830–31, and began the Russification of Poland. When the Revolution of 1848 spread across Europe Nicholas volunteered his help to other rulers, and in 1849 sent his troops into Hungary to suppress the Magyar uprising against the emperor of Austria. Nicholas' reign was also marked by wars in the east and a gradual conquest of the Caucasus. In a campaign against Persia he gained new lands in Armenia, 1828, and in a costly war with Turkey, 1828, he obtained freedom of navigation on the Danube, in the Black Sea, and through the Dardanelles, and a protectorate over Wallachia and Moldavia (Treaty of Adrianople, 1829). In 1853 he provoked another war with Turkey, but England and France joined Turkey, and in the ensuing Crimean War, 1853–56, Russia was defeated. Nicholas I died in the midst of the war, and was succeeded by his son Alexander II.

NICHOLAS II, 1868–1918, czar of Russia, son of Alexander III and the last of the Romanov dynasty, was born in St. Petersburg. He was given a predominantly military education and little opportunity to acquaint himself with world affairs except for a trip through the Far East, 1890–91. In Japan he narrowly escaped death when a Japanese fanatic attacked him with a saber.

Nicholas ascended the throne, Nov. 1, 1894, and the same month married Princess Alix of Hesse (Empress Alexandra Feodorovna). He attempted to continue his father's absolutist policy in internal affairs and to carry out a policy of peace in foreign affairs. Endeavoring to maintain a balance of power in Europe, Nicholas acknowledged the military alliance between Russia and France that was concluded in 1893, and in 1899 called the first Hague Peace Conference. He let Russia drift, however, into a war with Japan, 1904–05, in which unpreparedness and corruption in the government resulted in Russia's disastrous defeat. To meet growing criticism of the government, the czar was forced in October, 1905, to grant several reforms, among them the summoning of

Czar Nicholas II

the duma (parliament). When the revolution subsided the czar's government began to curtail the reforms, and under Premier Pëtr Stolypin (1863–1911) strong repressions were resumed. The outbreak of World War I in 1914 briefly rallied various factions in Russia to the support of the government, but heavy Russian losses at the front, economic privations at home, and the weak and irresolute administration of Nicholas brought renewed unrest among many elements of society. In 1915 Nicholas assumed command of the army and left the Empress Alexandra to run the government. A mystic, and an easy prey to spiritual influences, Alexandra was dominated by a monk of sorts, Grigori Rasputin (1873–1916), a dissolute quack. The rift between the populace and the government made revolution almost inevitable, and in March, 1917, Nicholas II abdicated both for himself and his 13-year-old son, Alexis Nikolaevich.

The imperial family was placed under arrest in the palace at Tsarsko-selo and then removed, first to Tobolsk in Siberia and then to Ekaterinburg (later Sverdlovsk) in the Urals. On the night of July 16, 1918, local Bolsheviks, acting with the approval of the central Soviet government in Moscow, put to death Nicholas, Alexandra, their son, and their four daughters.

NICHOLAS I, 1841–1921, king of Montenegro, was born in Njeguš, and in 1860 succeeded Danilo I as prince of Montenegro. During his reign Nicholas obtained from the European powers recognition of Montenegro's independence, 1878; and assumed the title of king, 1910. He supported the Balkan allies in the war against Turkey, 1912, and when World War I broke out, 1914, he entered on the side of Serbia. He opposed the union of Montenegro and Serbia and was deposed by a national assembly, 1918. Nicholas, a writer of considerable talent, was the author of a number of poems and dramas.

NICHOLAS OF CUSA, Nikolaus von Cusa, Latinized as Nicolaus Cusanus, 1401–64, philosopher, astronomer, mathematician, mystic, and cardinal, was born in Kues (Cusa), western Germany. He received his early education in the famous school of the Brethren of the Common Life at Deventer in the Netherlands. Later he entered the University of Heidelberg, but he soon left to enter that of Padua, where in 1423 he became doctor of canon law. He next studied theology at Cologne and was ordained priest.

Nicholas attended the early sessions of the Council of Basel, 1431–49, where he attracted attention as a champion of the council's claim to superiority over the pope. By 1435, however, he had abandoned this position and become a stanch supporter of Pope Eugene IV, who sent him in 1437 to Constantinople to escort a Greek delegation to Italy to discuss the reunion of the Western and Eastern churches. He was next sent to Germany to win adherents for Eugene against the Council of Basel. In 1448 Nicholas was created cardinal, and two years later he was also made bishop of Brixen, in the Tyrol. In the latter role he strove to reform his diocese, but his opponents proved too strong for him and drove him from his see. Just as peace was about to be re-established in 1464 Nicholas died.

As astronomer and mathematician Nicholas advocated reform of the calendar, claimed to have squared the circle, and anticipated Copernicus in holding that the earth moves. As a historical critic, he cast serious doubts on the authenticity of the Donation of Constantine (see CRITICISM, Literary Criticism, *Criticism in History and Philosophy;* DONATION OF CONSTANTINE.) His principal mystical work is *The Vision of God.* His most famous work, however, is the philosophical treatise *De docta ignorantia* (On Learned Ignorance). JOHN R. WILLIAMS

NICHOLAS OF MYRA, SAINT, died ?345 or 352, was born in Asia Minor. All that is certainly known of him is that he was bishop of Myra in Lycia in the fourth century. Numerous legends made him a popular saint in both Eastern and Western churches: he was patròn saint of Russia, and of mariners, merchants, travelers, and children. St. Nicholas was looked upon as a wonder-worker, and many miracles were attributed to him. The legend that he gave purses of gold to the three daughters of an impoverished nobleman to serve as dowries, and thereby keep them from lives of prostitution, gave rise to the custom of giving gifts to children on St. Nicholas' feast day, December 6, and attributing the gifts to St. Nicholas. In some countries the custom came to be associated with Christmas; and in the United States, St. Nicholas became identified with Santa Claus, a corruption of the Dutch name for Saint Nicholas.

NICHOLASVILLE, city, central Kentucky, seat of Jessamine County; on the Southern Railway and U.S. highway 27; 11 miles SSW of Lexington. The main industry is the manufacture of shoes. Nicholasville was settled in 1798 and incorporated as a city in 1890. Pop. (1960) 4,275.

NICHOLS, CHARLES AUGUSTUS, called Kid, 1869–1953, U.S. baseball player, was born in Madison, Wis. As a pitching star for the Boston Braves, 1890–1901, he won 332 games and lost 181. He retired in 1906, and in 1950 was elected to the Baseball Hall of Fame.

MANCHESTER ART GALLERY

***The Landlord,* a satirical portrait in oil, is by William Nicholson. A popular caricaturist, book illustrator, and poster designer, versatile Nicholson was knighted in 1936.**

NICHOLSON, SIR WILLIAM, 1872–1949, English artist, was born in Newark-upon-Trent. He first attracted attention with a series of posters that he designed in collaboration with his brother-in-law, James Pryde, under the pseudonym of Beggarstaff Brothers. Nicholson produced many woodcuts, including those in *The Square Book of Animals* (1896), *An Alphabet*, and *An Almanac of Twelve Sports* (with Rudyard Kipling, 1898). Nicholson manifested able technique in such paintings as *The Black Pansy*, *The Landlord*, *Fish*, *The Master of Jesus*, and *The First Communion Day*. He was also noted for his portrait wood engravings, verging on caricature, of Queen Victoria, Kipling, Henry James, James McNeill Whistler, and others.

NICIAS, 470?–413 B.C., Athenian general and political leader, was a member of the aristocratic party, and after the death of Pericles, 429 B.C., became one of the leaders of the conservative faction during the Peloponnesian War. He opposed war with Sparta, but served as a general during the first part of the war, 431–421. In 427 he captured the island of Minoa; in 426 ravaged Mílos; in 425 defeated the Corinthians; and in 424 captured Cythera. In 421 he was chiefly responsible for bringing about peace with Sparta, known as the Peace of Nicias. Soon afterward he came into rivalry with Alcibiades, leader of the democracy, who wished to renew the war. Against his will Nicias was appointed joint commander with Alcibiades, and Lamachus of the expedition against Syracuse in 415. Alcibiades was recalled, Lamachus was killed, and Nicias was left in sole command. His irresolute strategy ended in disaster; he was captured and executed by the Syracusans, 413.

NICKEL, a metallic element, symbol Ni, of Group VIII of the periodic table (see PERIODIC TABLE). The element has an atomic weight of 58.71 and the atomic number 28 (see ATOMIC AND MOLECULAR WEIGHTS) and is known to have five stable isotopes with mass numbers 58, 60, 61, 62, and 64. Nickel was discovered in 1751 by the Swedish mineralogist, Alex F. Cronstedt (1722–65). The element is characterized by its ability to impart its own properties to its alloys. Occurring in amounts equal to one part in 10,000 of the earth's crust, nickel is primarily found in sulfide and silicate ores. The largest known deposits of sulfide ores are in the Sudbury area of Ontario, Canada; New Caledonia is the site of the largest known deposits of silicate ores.

INTERNATL. NICKEL CO.

After cooling from the molten state, nickel alloy ingots are removed from ingot molds for processing into various forms such as bars, tubes, sheets, and special shapes.

Properties. Nickel is a hard, white, malleable, ductile, and corrosion-resistant metal capable of taking a brilliant polish. Thus the metal can be used extensively in the electroplating industry as an ornamental covering for metals with less resistance to corrosion, in the manufacture of kitchen utensils and other food processing equipment, and in the manufacture of marine and chemical laboratory equipment. These same properties also permit the use of nickel in coins of small denominations. The element has a melting point of 1455°C (2651°F) and a specific gravity of 8.9. The low coefficient of linear expansion of nickel permits its use, primarily in the alloy invar, in measuring devices such as surveyor's tapes, pendulums, and bimetallic thermostats. Nickel also is a good conductor of heat, has fair electrical conductivity, and is ferromagnetic. It is capable of absorbing large quantities of hydrogen—a property which probably accounts for the fact that the metal, in a finely divided state, is an excellent catalyst for the hydrogenation and dehydrogenation of organic compounds.

Preparation. The Orford process is a method of extracting nickel from its sulfide ores, used particularly on pentlandite from Sudbury. The metal is first crushed and ground. It is then subjected to two flotation processes: the first yields a sulfide concentrate containing nickel, iron, and copper, and the second separates the copper from the nickel-iron concentrate. The latter concentrate is then roasted to effect partial oxidation of the iron remaining in the concentrate and removal of some of the sulfur. The concentrate is then smelted with a flux to remove all the rock and additional quantities of iron in the form of a slag (see SMELTING). Smelting yields a nickel-iron matte containing trace amounts of copper, and largely composed of sulfides of these metals. The matte is placed in a Bessemer converter (see BESSEMER STEEL, *Process Description*) for further separation of the iron and sulfur from the nickel. The final separation of nickel from the copper and other metals in the matte is obtained by controlled cooling, fine grinding, magnetic separation, and differential flotation. The resulting product, nickel sulfide, is converted to nickel oxide by a roasting process, and the oxide is then reduced by carbon to yield a 96 per cent pure nickel. Electrolytic refining in a sulfate bath results in 99.98 per cent pure nickel being deposited on the cathode of an electrolysis device, while platinum and other precious metals are recovered in the anode sludge. See ELECTROMETALLURGY.

A melter taps molten nickel alloy into a ladle from an electric induction furnace. The alloy is then made into forms and shapes that may in turn become useful products.

INTERNATL. NICKEL CO.

Nickel may also be recovered from certain sulfide ores by the Mond process, which involves roasting the iron-nickel matte containing copper and removing the copper portion by leaching with dilute sulfuric acid. The resulting oxides are reduced by water gas (hydrogen and carbon monoxide). The metallic mixture is then heated to 50°C (122°F) and treated with carbon monoxide to yield nickel tetracarbonyl gas, $Ni(CO)_4$, which is a poisonous, volatile, unpleasant-smelling gas that at 200°C (392°F) decomposes to 99.9 per cent pure nickel and carbon monoxide.

Silicate ores such as garnerite, the New Caledonian ore, are refined by first drying and briquetting the ore with calcium sulfates and limestone fluxes, and then smelting with coal or coke. The resulting nickel sulfide matte is subjected to the Bessemer process, which produces nickel sulfide with a low iron content. The nickel sulfide is ground and roasted to remove the sulfur, briquetted with a carbonaceous material, and reduced by heating to the metallic form.

Compounds. Nickel has valences of 2 and 3, but may occur in compounds with a valence of 1 or even zero—for example, the cyanide complexes $K_3Ni(CN)_4$ or $K_4Ni(CN)_4$. Nickel, however, occurs in compounds most often in a bivalent state. Nickel monoxide, NiO, its most common oxide, is a green to grayish green solid. The nickel oxides are important in the production of ferrous and nonferrous alloys, in ceramic glazes as coloring agents, in the manufacture of glass as colorizers and decolorizers, and in the production of ferrites. Nickel hydroxide, $Ni(OH)_2$, is used in electroplating and as a constituent of the positive plates of storage batteries. Nickel sulfate, $NiSO_4 \cdot 6H_2O$, the cheapest and most widely used nickel compound, is employed as an important constituent of nickel plating baths, as an enameling dip, and as a catalyst. Nickel acetate, $Ni(C_2H_3O_2) \cdot 4H_2O$, is used as a sealing agent for anodized aluminum, as a reagent in the preparation of metallized dyes, and as a catalyst in homogeneous systems. A basic nickel carbonate, $NiCO_3 \cdot 2Ni(OH)_2 \cdot 4H_2O$, occurring in nature as the mineral zaratite, is also used extensively as a catalyst. Nickel nitrate, $Ni(NO_3)_2 \cdot 6H_2O$, finds only limited use as a catalyst because of its high cost. Nickel formate, usually occurring as $Ni(HCOO)_2 \cdot 2H_2O$, is used in the preparation of organic catalysts. Nickel sulfide, NiS, occurs in nature as the mineral millerite. Nickel chloride is a bright green compound, usually found as the hexahydrate $NiCl_2 \cdot 6H_2O$, which is employed as a reagent in the preparation of other nickel compounds and catalysts, and most frequently in electroplating.

Alloys. Nickel-chromium alloys are widely used in the manufacture of corrosion-resistant stainless steel, which has numerous uses in many major industries. An alloy, alnico, composed of varying percentages of nickel, iron, aluminum, and sometimes cobalt and copper, is frequently employed in permanent magnets. Monel metal is an important nickel-base alloy that finds extensive use in home appliances, marine equipment, food processing equipment, and other apparatus requiring high-strength corrosion-resistant materials. Permalloy and Hipernik are representative of the nickel-base alloys that are commercially important by virtue of their magnetic properties. Permalloy, which also has an extremely high permeability in low magnetic fields in addition to an outstanding ability to withstand corrosion, is used in electrical equipment for the transmission and reproduction of sound. Hipernik, which also has great permeability but at higher fields, is used in the cores of transformers. Other alloys used as corrosion-resistant materials include those of nickel, molybdenum, and iron; nickel, molybdenum, chromium, and iron; and nickel and silicon. Nickel is added to wrought and cast steels in order to produce a stronger ferrite and a finer perlite, and to improve the hardenability, strength, ductility, fatigue resistance, and ease of carburizing (surface hardening). Clad steels—steels covered with a layer of nickel or a nickel alloy—provide the same resistance to corrosion on the clad surface as do the nickel bearing materials, and at considerably less cost.

BIBLIOG.–N. V. Sidgwick, *Chemical Elements and Their Compounds* (1950); A. M. Hall, *Nickel in Iron and Steel* (1954); O. W. Main, *Canadian Nickel Industry* (1955); H. B. Director, ed., *Nickel Handbook and Commercial Outlook for 1957* (1956).

NICKEL PLATING. See ELECTROPLATING.

NICKEL STEEL. See STEEL.

NICOBAR ISLANDS. See ANDAMAN AND NICOBAR ISLANDS.

NICOLAI, CHRISTOPH FRIEDRICH, 1733–1811, German writer and bookseller, was born in Berlin. With Moses Mendelssohn he established the periodical *Bibliothek der Schönen Wissenschaften*, 1757, and with Mendelssohn and Gotthold Lessing collaborated in publishing the literary review *Briefe, die Neueste Literatur Betreffend*, 1759–65. Nicolai was a leader of the opposition to the critical school and the romantic movement. He wrote *Anekdoten von Friedrich II* (1788–92); a novel, *Sebaldus Nothanker* (1773); biographies of eighteenth century writers; and satirical attacks on the works of Goethe, on the leaders of the romantic school, and on the philosophy of Immanuel Kant and Johann Fichte.

NICOLAI, OTTO, in full Carl Otto Ehrenfried Nicolai, 1810–49, German operatic composer, was born at Königsberg. He was *Kapellmeister*, 1841–47, of court opera in Vienna where he founded the Philharmonic concerts, 1842. He wrote several operas, a symphony, a mass, and piano pieces. His best known work is *Die lustigen Weiber von Windsor* (*The Merry Wives of Windsor*), produced in 1849.

NICOLAY, JOHN GEORGE, 1832–1901, U.S. biographer, was born in Essingen, Bavaria, and was brought to the United States in 1838. On Abraham Lincoln's nomination for the presidency, Nicolay became his private secretary, with John Hay as assistant secretary. Nicolay and Hay wrote *Abraham Lincoln: A History* (10 vols. 1890) and edited *Lincoln's Complete Works* (2 vols. 1894; rev. ed., 12 vols. 1905). Nicolay was U.S. consul at Paris, 1865–69, and marshal of the Supreme Court, 1872–87.

NICOLE, PIERRE, 1625–95, French author, was born in Chartres. He went to Port Royal, 1649, and taught there for several years. An able controversialist, he promoted the cause of Jansenism. He wrote *Les Visionnaires* (1666) and *Essais de morale* (14 vols. 1671 *et seq.*). In 1679 he fled to Belgium to escape persecution. Four years later he returned to Paris and was a leader in the attack on quietism.

NICOLET, JEAN, 1598–1642, French explorer in North America, was born in Cherbourg and was brought to New France by Samuel de Champlain, 1618, to be trained as an Indian interpreter and explorer. Stationed at first on Allumette Island in the Ottawa River, where he learned the language and craft of the Indians, in 1624 he was made translator to the Nipissing Indians, and in 1633 became interpreter at the Trois Rivières settlement in Québec. In 1634 he set out to discover a northwest passage to the orient. He journeyed across Lake Huron into Georgian Bay, then into the Straits of Mackinac, and along the coast of Lake Michigan to Green Bay, where he discovered Winnebago Indians instead of Orientals. After his return to Trois Rivières he was drowned in the St. Lawrence River. The importance of Nicolet's voyages through the Great Lakes region first became known to historians during the mid-nineteenth century through study of the missionary reports known as the *Jesuit Relations*, which make it clear that Nicolet was the first known white explorer of the Lake Michigan–Wisconsin area. HARVEY WISH

NICOLET, town, Canada, S Québec Province; on the Nicolet River near its junction with the St. Lawrence, on the Canadian National Railway; 9 miles SSW of Trois Rivières. Nicolet has manufactures of hosiery, knit goods, optical supplies, and furniture. In 1955 part of the town was destroyed by a landslide. Pop. (1956) 3,771.

NICOLLE, CHARLES JEAN HENRI, 1866–1936, Nobel prize-winning French scientist, was born in Rouen, studied medicine in Paris, and was professor of microbiology at the Rouen school of medicine, 1895–1903. He became director of the Pasteur Institute in Tunis, 1903, and after 1932 taught at the Collège de France. He was awarded the 1928 Nobel prize in physiology and medicine for discovering that typhus is transmitted by body lice. Nicolle also pioneered in the prophylaxis of measles, undulant fever, and other infectious diseases.

NICOLLET, JOSEPH NICOLAS, 1786–1843, French mathematician and explorer in America, was born in Cluses Savoy, was educated in the Collège de Cluses, was appointed secretary and librarian in the Paris Observatory, 1817, and later became professor of mathematics in the Collège Louis-le-Grand, Paris. He came to the United States, 1832, and in 1836 explored the headwaters of the Mississippi, acquiring considerable ethnological data regarding the Indians and recording valuable scientific observations. In 1838 and 1839 he led expeditions that explored the upper regions of the Missouri River. Nicollet wrote *Report Intended to Illustrate a Map of the Hydrographical Basin of the Upper Mississippi River* (1843) and other books.

NICOLLS, RICHARD, 1624–72, English colonial governor, was born in Ampthill, Bedfordshire. He commanded a troop of horse in the Royalist army during the civil war and went into exile after the defeat of Charles I. At the Restoration, 1660, he became groom of the bedchamber to the Duke of York, and in 1664 was appointed to a commission to settle disputes among the New England colonies and to conquer New Netherland from the Dutch. Peter Stuyvesant was forced to surrender New Amsterdam to Nicolls, Aug. 26, 1664, and the English authority soon included the whole territory; Nicolls changed the name of the province and its chief town to New York, won the friendship of the Dutch population by the fairness of his rule, and acquired the good will of the Iroquois Indians. He promulgated the Duke's Laws, 1665, and granted a charter incorporating New York as a city the same year. He was governor until 1668. He returned to England and was killed in a naval battle during the Anglo-Dutch War.

UPI

Nicosia's one-time church of St. Sophia, now a mosque, contains the tombs of the Lusignan kings, a dynasty that ruled the island of Cyprus during the later Middle Ages.

NICOSIA, or Levkosia, city, N central Cyprus, capital of the Republic of Cyprus and also of Nicosia District; a scheduled airline stop; 32 miles W of its port, Famagusta. Hub of the island's highway system, Nicosia is a trade center for wheat, wine, olive oil, citrus fruit, and livestock. Its manufactures include leather goods, textiles, pottery, and bricks. The city is the site of St. Sophia Church, built in the thirteenth century and later converted into a mosque, which contains the tombs of the Lusignan kings. Other points of interest include a women's training college and the Cyprus Museum, founded in 1883 and famous for its collections of antiquities and for its archaeological library. In 1191 Nicosia was taken by King Richard I of England, who gave it to Guy de Lusignan, a French nobleman, the following year. The city fell to the Venetians in 1489 and to the Turks in 1571. It contains the remains of fortified walls built by the Venetians. Nicosia came under British control in 1878. Cyprus gained independence in 1960. (For population, see Near and Middle East map in Atlas.)

NICOT, JEAN, sieur de Villemain, 1530?–1600, French scholar, was born in Nîmes, and was ambassador to Portugal, 1559–61. While there he obtained from a Flemish merchant seeds of the tobacco plant, which he took back to France; the plant was named *Nicotiana* in his honor. He wrote a *Historia francorum* (1566) and compiled one of the first French dictionaries (1606).

NICOTIANA, a genus of mostly herbaceous plants belonging to the nightshade family, *Solanaceae*, and generally known for their rapid growth and large foliage covered with soft, sticky hairs. The always simple leaves are large, alternate, and lanceolate, and contain the poisonous substance nicotine (see NICOTINE). The small, fragrant, sometimes showy, funnel-shaped flowers grow in terminal clusters and may be yellow, white, or purple; in many cases they open only at night. Some species are grown as ornamental border plants. The genus contains both annuals and perennials and is native to tropical America but ranges into North and South America, and one species, *Nicotiana suaveolens*, is found in Australia. The most important species of the genus is tobacco, *N. Tabacum*, from which the commercial product is obtained (see TOBACCO). A few of the better known species are jasmine tobacco, *N. alata* var. *grandiflora*, which has large flowers; *N. Bigelovii*, the Indian tobacco of the southwestern United States; tree tobacco, *N. glauca*, which may grow 20 feet high; and *N. tomentosa*, the giant nicotiana, which may be woody.

NICOTINE, a rapidly acting and highly poisonous alkaloid, $C_{10}H_{14}N_2$, of the tobacco plant, *Nicotiana Tabacum*. It is an oily colorless liquid that turns yellowish brown when exposed to air; its sharp taste and odor are associated with tobacco. Although nicotine is not used as a drug because of its harmful side effects, various preparations of it have proved valuable as research tools—knowledge of the physiology of the nervous system, for example, has been increased by studies employing nicotine preparations.

When nicotine is absorbed through the skin or mucous membranes, it first stimulates and then paralyzes all sympathetic and parasympathetic ganglia (see AUTONOMIC NERVOUS SYSTEM). Some of the effects of nicotine are unpredictable because of the conflicting actions of the sympathetic and parasympathetic division of the autonomic nervous system and because of the complex actions of the drug on the body. Most of these effects, however, can be divided into two phases. In the first phase the usual effects of nicotine include a slowing of the heart, a rise in blood pressure, and constriction of the peripheral blood vessels. The alimentary canal may be so stimulated that diarrhea occurs, and in addition vomiting may ensue from the stimulation of the central nervous system. In the second phase the action of nicotine causes the heart to beat faster and the blood pressure to fall, and may cause dilation of the peripheral blood vessels. The motility of the alimentary tract is inhibited and the skeletal muscles are paralyzed. See CURARE; MUSCLE.

Poisoning. Nicotine is extremely toxic; about 1 grain may constitute a fatal dose for an adult. The drug is an active ingredient in many insecticide sprays and accidental swallowing of them may cause death. In some instances prolonged contact with tobacco or its dust has resulted in nicotine poisoning. When tobacco is swallowed, vomiting usually ejects it before a dangerous amount of nicotine is absorbed. See BUERGER'S DISEASE.

Symptoms of nicotine poisoning include weakness, nausea, and abdominal cramps, usually followed by vomiting and diarrhea. In severe poisoning, consciousness is lost, convulsions may occur, and as the muscles of respiration become paralyzed death follows.

No specific antidote for nicotine poisoning is known. As soon as the poisoning is discovered, the stomach should be pumped in order to remove as much nicotine as possible before it is absorbed. Since nicotine is quickly destroyed in the body, artificial respiration can sometimes support life until the worst effects of the poison subside.

NIDWALDEN, demi-canton, central Switzerland, a subdivision of Unterwalden Canton; area 106 square miles. The region is generally mountainous and forested. It supports a thriving tourist industry. There are woodworking, glass, and cement factories. The capital is Stans. (For population, see Switzerland map in Atlas.)

NIEBUHR, BARTHOLD GEORG, 1776–1831, German historian, was born in Copenhagen. He entered the Prussian civil service, 1806; became royal historiographer and professor at the University of Berlin, 1808; and was ambassador to the Vatican, 1816–23. In 1812 he compiled from his lectures the first two volumes of his masterwork *Römische Geschichte* (*History of Rome*); the third volume was published posthumously, 1832. This work, epoch-making in its scientific and critical spirit, revolutionized the study of Roman history with its rejection of the legendary element in early Roman history and its reconstruction of early social and political developments.

NIEBUHR, REINHOLD, 1892–   , U.S. Protestant theologian, born in Wright City, Mo. He studied at the Eden Theological Seminary, St. Louis, and at the Yale Divinity School, and was ordained in the ministry of the Evangelical Synod of North America, 1915. As a pastor in Detroit, Mich., 1915–28, and subsequently as a professor at Union Theological Seminary, Niebuhr applied neo-orthodox Protestant Christian doctrine to social and political issues. Calling himself a Christian realist, Niebuhr strongly criticized those who considered Christianity other worldly and "only for Sundays," saying that Christians can and must apply their faith to everyday questions of living. He edited the periodicals *Christianity and Society* and *Christianity and Crisis* and wrote a number of books, among them *Moral Man and Immoral Society* (1932); *Christianity and Power Politics* (1940); *The Nature and Destiny of Man* (Gifford Lectures, 2 vols. 1941, 1943); *The Self and the Dramas of History* (1955); *Resurrection and Historical Reason* (1957); *The Structure of Nations and Empires* (1959); and *Man's Nature and His Communities* (1965). His brother Helmut Richard Niebuhr (1894–1962), a minister of the Evangelical and Reformed Church, taught at the Yale Divinity School after 1931 and wrote *The Social Sources of Denominationalism* (1929), *Christ and Culture* (1951), *The Purpose of the Church and Its Ministry* (1956), and *Radical Monotheism and Western Culture* (1960).

NIELLO, the process of filling furrows incised upon a metallic surface (usually silver) with a metallic amalgam so as to produce a dark design on a bright surface. The process of incised engraving may have developed directly from the practice of taking an impression of the carved-out metallic surface before filling the furrows with the amalgam. The niello process dates from the Middle Ages, and was highly developed by fifteenth-century Italian craftsmen. It is still in use in India.

NIELSEN, CARL AUGUST, 1865–1931, Danish composer. He was professor at the Copenhagen Conservatory, where he had studied under Niels Gade, and director of the Musical Society. His great works are six symphonies, though his chamber music is often played. His experiments in polytonality aroused opposition, but by his death his music was universally accepted.

NIEMEYER, OSCAR, 1907–   , Brazilian architect, influenced by Le Corbusier with whom he worked on the Ministry of Education building, Rio de Janeiro, in 1936. He served on the UN headquarters design committee (1947) and was the chief architect in the creation of the capital city of Brasília.

NIEMOLLER, MARTIN, in full Friedrich Gustav Emil Martin Niemöller, 1892–   , German Protestant churchman, born in Lippstadt, entered the German navy at 18, and became a submarine commander. He was ordained a Lutheran minister in 1924. Assigned to a church in Berlin-Dahlem in 1931, Niemöller at first championed national socialism, but in 1933 turned against the Nazi party and in 1935 founded the Confessional church, which opposed Adolf Hitler. Niemöller was imprisoned in concentration camps from 1937 to 1945. After World War II he became president of the Evangelical church in Hesse and Nassau, and head of a union of all German Protestant churches.

NIEPCE, JOSEPH NICEPHORE, 1765–1833, French pioneer in photography, born in Châlon-sur-Saône. He discovered that a sun-printed image could be permanently fixed by coating a metal plate with bitumen before placing it in the camera—the first process by which a camera picture was made. After 1829 he worked with Louis J. M. Daguerre to improve the process, particularly to shorten the exposure time. Daguerre made public the daguerreotype process six years after Niepce's death.

NIETZSCHE, FRIEDRICH, 1844–1900, German philosopher, born in Röcken, Prussia, the son of a Lutheran minister. Nietzsche studied classical philology at the universities of Bonn and Leipzig and published scholarly papers while still a graduate student. When the professorship of classical philology at the University of Basel, Switzerland, fell vacant, he was recommended so highly that he was offered the chair, although he was only 24. Leipzig conferred the doctorate on him without any thesis or examination, and in April, 1869, Nietzsche became an associate professor and a Swiss subject. The following year he was promoted to full professor.

In August, 1870, he volunteered to serve as a medical orderly in the Franco-Prussian War, but returned to Germany in September with dysentery and diphtheria. In 1879 he retired for reasons of health and received a modest pension. He continued to suffer from severe migraine headaches, his very shortsighted eyes gave him a great deal of trouble, and he was in pain much of the time. During the next ten years he spent most of his summers in the Swiss Alps and his winters in Italy while devoting all his energies to his books. He

Nietzsche

CULVER

generally published a book a year, but in 1888 he completed five books. In January, 1889, he suffered a complete mental and physical collapse, and henceforth wrote nothing.

Early Works. His first book, *The Birth of Tragedy* (1872), proposed that the then still prevalent conception of Greek culture as characterized by serenity, harmony, and restraint was one-sided. In addition to this "Apollinian" genius, Nietzsche postulated a "Dionysian" tendency that found expression in the festivals of Dionysus and in Euripides' tragedy, *The Bacchae:* a dark, cruel undercurrent of boundless passion. Greek tragedy was born of the fusion of these two tendencies, but soon succumbed to unpoetic rationalism. After celebrating the music dramas of Richard Wagner (whom he later criticized sharply) as a rebirth of tragedy, Nietzsche looked forward to an "artistic Socrates"—a symbol of his own ambition to fuse poetry and philosophy, the spirit of criticism and the vision of tragedy.

The four *Untimely Meditations* (1873–76) that followed did not yet project a distinctive philosophy of his own, neither did the five brilliant collections of aphorisms that he published between 1878 and 1882. Even these books, however, would ensure his inclusion in any history of German literature.

The Major Works. Nietzsche's mature philosophy is presented in somewhat poetical form in *Thus Spoke Zarathustra* (published in four parts, beginning in 1883), in more systematic fashion in *Beyond Good and Evil* (1886), in the three essays comprising his *Genealogy of Morals* (1887), and in the books written in 1888: *The Case of Wagner*, *The Twilight of the Idols*, *The Antichrist*, *Ecce Homo*, and *Nietzsche contra Wagner*. Many of his posthumously published notes are also of considerable philosophical interest, especially a selection issued under the title *The Will to Power*.

Troubled by the rising tide of nihilism—the loss of faith in all traditional values and a growing sense of futility—Nietzsche proposed that man needs to give himself new goals and new values. The former are summed up in a single word in *Zarathustra*, "the overman"; the latter are discussed at far greater length in many chapters, and again in *Beyond Good and Evil* where they are epitomized by the word "nobility." The term "overman" (*Ubermensch*; G.B. Shaw popularized "superman") was very rarely used by Nietzsche, except in the Prologue of *Zarathustra:* it stands for a goal that man might try to realize on earth, without any faith in another world—a higher state of being, characterized by a creative employment of the passions. The Darwinistic misinterpretation of the concept, to the effect that Nietzsche was pinning his hopes on evolution, was unequivocally condemned by him in *Ecce Homo*, but gained wide currency nevertheless.

Nietzsche came to believe that the very same events recur eternally at gigantic intervals, as the power quanta that constitute the world eventually repeat their configurations. He found this idea terrifying but thought that anyone who has given his life form and content might actually welcome its eternal recurrence. Few of Nietzsche's interpreters have taken this doctrine seriously.

Nietzsche's conception of the will to power as man's fundamental motive force was closely associated with his idea of sublimation: he deprecated crude forms of power, including political and military power, and found the highest degree of power in art and philosophy. Nietzsche's comments on the German Empire of Bismarck, and on the Germans generally, are almost unsurpassed in their harshness. In some passages he suggested that the will to power might characterize all life; even that it might be the basic force of the universe. But it is mainly the psychological explanations Nietzsche based on this conception that have elicited wide interest; e.g., his attempt to show that the values of Christianity were largely created by resentment and by the will to power of the weak and impotent.

Influence. No other philosopher since Kant and Hegel has had a comparable influence on philosophy, psychology, theology, and literature. His impact has been especially notable in Germany and France, where many of the leading novelists and poets, psychoanalysts and existentialists have paid lavish tribute to him. WALTER KAUFMANN

BIBLIOG.–A.C. Danto, *Nietzsche as a Philosopher* (1965); R.J. Hollingdale, *Nietzsche, The Man and His Philosophy* (1965); Karl Jaspers, *Nietzsche* (1936; Eng. tr., 1965); Walter Kaufmann, *Nietzsche* (1950; rev. ed., 1956); G.A. Morgan, Jr., *What Nietzsche Means* (1941).

NIEUWLAND, JULIUS ARTHUR, 1878–1936, U.S. chemist and botanist, born in Hansbeke, Belgium. He was taken to the United States about 1881 and educated at Notre Dame and the Catholic University of America. Following his ordination as a Roman Catholic priest, 1903, he taught first botany and then organic chemistry at Notre Dame (1904–36). After 1925 Nieuwland conducted research with Du Pont chemists that led to Duprene, one of the first commercially successful synthetic rubbers, and lewisite, a deadly gas.

NIEUWPOORT, or Nieuport, town, W Belgium, West Flanders province; on the Yser River; 10 miles SW of Ostend. The chief industries are fishing and the manufacture of bricks and chemicals. Nieuwpoort was a strong fortress in the Middle Ages. In 1488–89 it resisted a siege by the French, and in 1600 it was the scene of a Dutch victory over the Spaniards. The town was destroyed during World War I. It was rebuilt and was again the scene of heavy fighting in World War II. (For population, see Belgium map in Atlas.)

NIEVRE, department, central France; bounded by the departments of Yonne on the N, Côte d'Or and Saône et Loire on the E, Allier on the S, and Cher on the W; area 2,659 square miles. The Morvan Mountains occupy the eastern part, plateaus the central region, and fertile plains the south and west. The principal rivers are the Loire and the Yonne, which is connected to the Loire by the Nivernais Canal. Chemical, lumber, and metal industries are important, and pottery and woodenware are produced in large quantities. There are important coal deposists and many vineyards in the area. Stock raising is the chief agricultural pursuit. The chief towns are Nevers (the capital), Clamecy, and Decize. The department was formed in 1791—mainly from the former province of Nivernais. (For population, see France map in Atlas.)

NIGDE, province and city, S central Turkey. The province is bounded by the provinces of Nevşehir and Kayseri on the NE, Adana on the SE, Içel on the S, Konya on the SW and W, and Ankara on the NW; Lake Tuz is situated on Niğde's northwest border. Principal agricultural products are rye, vegetables, and mohair goats.

Niğde is the capital. Located 75 miles NNW of Adana, it is an agricultural trade center. Occupied by the Seljuk Turks from the eleventh through the fourteenth centuries, it was taken by the Ottoman Turks in the fifteenth century. (For population, see Turkey map in Atlas.)

NIGER, republic, Africa, formerly an overseas territory of France, bounded on the N by Algeria and Libya, on the E by Chad, on the S by Nigeria and Dahomey, and on the W by Upper Volta and Mali; area about 450,000 square miles; population

3,200,000 (1964 est.). The name Niger is derived from the French word for the great river which, ironically, flows for less than 150 miles through the extreme southwestern corner of the country. The capital is Niamey. For flag in color, see FLAG. See also northern Africa map in Atlas, Vol. 20.

PIX

Much of Niger is desert or near-desert; the burnoose and the mud-walled house are both designed to protect man from the sun.

Physical Features

The dominating physical characteristic of Niger is its aridity. Only the southern fourth of the land receives sufficient annual rainfall (about 20 inches) to support agriculture. Northward, a band of grassy savanna and steppe lands stretches from Niamey to Lake Chad and supports most of the population. The savanna gives way to desert as the average rainfall diminishes to the vanishing point in the Sahara. Thus the greater part of the country is a vast rocky and sandy tract, sparsely dotted with oases which serve as bases for Niger's widely scattered nomadic populations. The most important relief on this landscape is the Air massif, a volcanic plateau which rises a few thousand feet from the surrounding plain. Precipitation occurs during a rainy season that arrives in June and lasts until October. This is followed by a dry season of dust storms (the harmattan winds) which sweep down from the Sahara. The daily temperature high of 105° F in the humid months descends to 82° F during the dry season.

Social Features

In part, the social fabric of Niger has been shaped by geographical influences. These have given rise to two distinct groups of peoples: the nomadic pastoralists who inhabit the desert oases and roam the great dry stretches, and the agriculturists who have settled the southern grasslands, the riverbanks, and the shores of Lake Chad. The two major groups of nomads are the Tuareg, camel pastoralists who live in the northwest, and the Teda, who inhabit the Air massif and lands to the east and southeast. Together these nomads account for no more than one quarter of the total population. The farming peoples are represented by the Hausa, the largest ethnic group in the country, the Songhai and Zerma (Djerma) who are settled near the Niger River, and numerous smaller groups in the Lake Chad region. An immigrant people, the Fulbe (better known by their Hausa name, Fulani), came originally from the west. They were cattle keepers, but many among them have intermarried with the farmers. Each of these peoples belongs to cultural units which extend far beyond Niger's borders; and in many cases, particularly with the Hausa, their brother populations in neighboring countries are numerically much larger. This fact underscores one of the central problems that the government now faces in welding together a modern nation-state. While in some ways their languages are historically related, each group speaks a tongue which is not understood by the others. Partly for this reason, French has been made the national language. A final group, the Europeans, have never numbered more than 3,000.

Islam is the religion of over two thirds of the population. The remainder either practice traditional religions or are Christian (about 10,000). Education on the European pattern has been introduced at primary (50,000 pupils) and secondary (1,750) levels; there are teachers training colleges and technical schools, but no university.

Economic Features

The economic picture of Niger similarly reflects geographic conditions. In earlier times trade caravans crossed the land between Mediterranean North Africa and the market cities of the western Sudan. In the twentieth century, the focus of trade has been reoriented southward to the West African coast. Niger thus finds itself placed far from shipping ports; transport costs seriously reduce the values of exports and raise the prices of imports. Roads of varying quality provide the only transport network, since the river is difficult to navigate. There are no railway lines except those reached by road in Dahomey, the Upper Volta, and Nigeria.

More than 85 per cent of the population is engaged in farming or stock-raising. Most produce is still consumed within the country; but since the French occupation various cash-producing crops have been introduced. The most important among these crops is peanuts, purchased by France. An increasingly important export crop is cotton. The main foods raised for local consumption are millet, sorghum, beans, and rice; small amounts of these are traded to neighboring countries. Stock-raising is the other major sector of the agricultural economy. Relatively large numbers of cattle, sheep, and goats are exported, primarily to Nigeria. Animal hides and skins are similarly important. Mining of tin and tungsten in the Air massif brings a little revenue.

Like other developing countries, Niger has drawn up long-range economic development plans which began to have an effect in the 1960's. Such plans depend heavily upon foreign assistance, mostly supplied by France. Niger remains within the franc

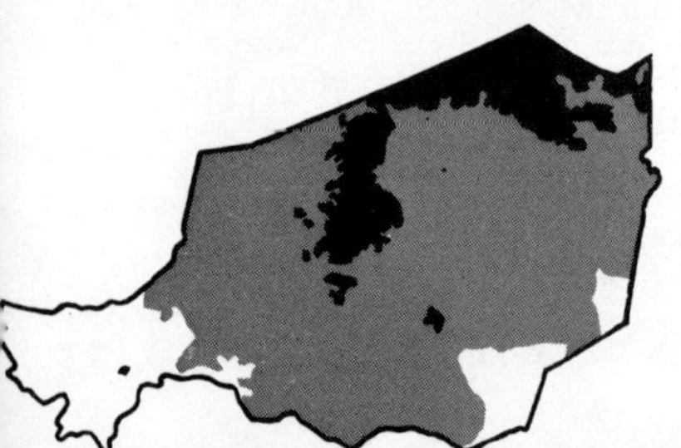

Niger: elevation. Black areas, over 2,000 feet above sea level; gray areas, 1,000-2,000; white areas, under 1,000.

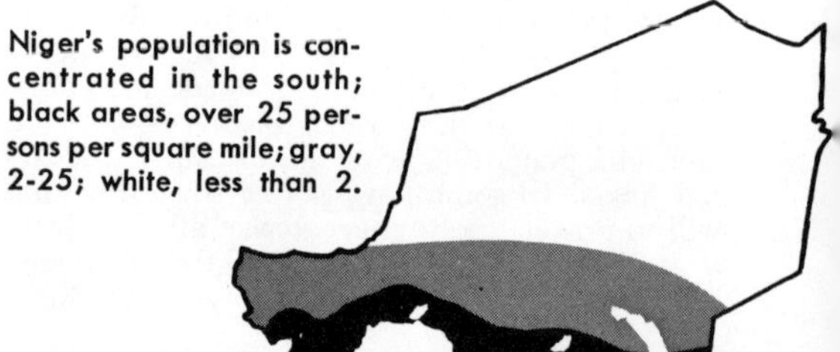

Niger's population is concentrated in the south; black areas, over 25 persons per square mile; gray, 2-25; white, less than 2.

bloc and uses the standard West African currency, the CFA franc (CFA 250 = $US 1, 1966).

History

Since the boundaries of Niger were drawn without regard to the ethnic groups which came to form parts of it, the precolonial history of the country must necessarily take into account what occurred far beyond its borders. Therefore, the Tuareg can be understood properly only if one is aware that the Niger segment of their numbers belongs to a loose federation of tribes extending through Mali and Mauritania, and into Algeria. Similarly, the Songhai and Zerma were once the powerful leaders of a great empire (fifteenth and sixteenth centuries) which controlled the Niger River; the Hausa were part of an important city-state complex centered in what is now Northern Nigeria, which was taken over by the Fulani during the Islamic revolution of the early nineteenth century; the Teda may have provided the first ruling class which founded the empire of Kanem-Bornu around Lake Chad. See AFRICA.

Following the era of the caravan trade, the first Europeans to visit Niger were Mungo Park, 1805–6, and Heinrich Barth, in the 1850's. Barth has left us much information about the Fulani rulers in the southwest and about the Kanembu rulers in the southeast. In 1890 the French were pushing into the area from the west, and the British from the south. These two powers agreed upon a line of division between their two spheres, which became Niger's southern boundary. The actual conquest and pacification of the territory required almost 30 years until, in 1919, the nomadic peoples of Air finally submitted to French authority.

For a long while Niger was classed as a military territory. In 1922 it became a colony under civilian authority as a part of Afrique Occidentale Française, governed from Dakar. At the time of the colonial referendum in 1958, Niger voted by a 78 per-cent majority to remain a member of the French Community. On Feb. 25, 1959, a new constitution was proclaimed which resulted in Niger declaring itself an independent republic on Aug. 3, 1960. Legislative power was invested in a national assembly, and executive authority was given to a president.

The consolidation of power under Pres. M. Hamani Diori and the single legal political party (Parti Progressiste Nigérien) proved difficult. An early split between Diori and a co-founder of the P.P.N., Djibo Bakary, resulted in the latter's creation of an opposition group called Sawaba (Freedom) and his subsequent exile from the country. Djibo created a government-in-exile which President Diori charged with responsibility for local unrest and an attempt at his assassination in April, 1965. The government sought support in a variety of external alliances, the most important of which is the Council of the Entente (linking Niger to the neighboring states of Dahomey, Upper Volta, and Ivory Coast). Similarly, Diori elicited the cooperation of Hausa emirs in Northern Nigeria against the banned Sawaba. On the international scene, Niger sought to preserve a position of strict neutrality, although its strongest links are still with France and the primarily Western-oriented nations of West Africa. The most pressing problems of nationhood are yet to be resolved: national integration of the many cultural groups which make up the population and successful bids for outside aid to support development programs. ROBERT R. GRIFFETH

BIBLIOG.–L. K. Jakande, "Niger Republic" in *West Africa Annual* (ed. 1964); Ruth S. Morgenthau, *Political Parties in French-Speaking West Africa* (1964); E. Séré de Rivières, *Le Niger* (1952); Virginia Thompson, "Niger" in *National Unity and Regionalism in Eight African States* (ed. G. M. Carter, 1966).

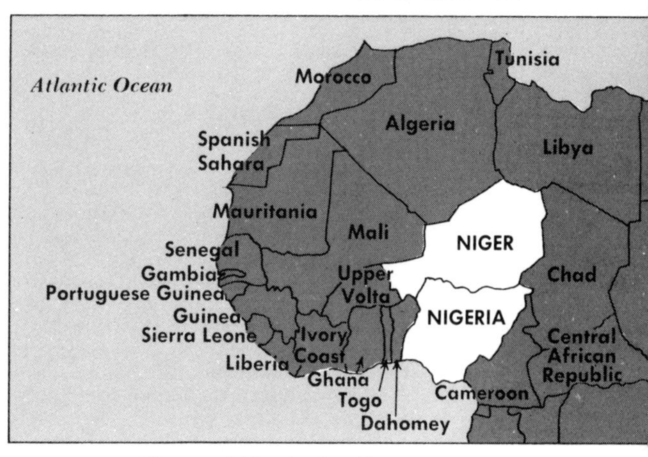

Niger and Nigeria: Location

NIGERIA, republic, W Africa, bounded on the N by Niger, on the NE by Chad, on the E by Cameroun, on the S by the Bight of Benin (Gulf of Guinea), and on the W by Dahomey; about 356,669 square miles in area; population (1963 census) 55,653,821. The capital is Lagos; the capitals of Nigeria's four regions are Kaduna (North), Ibadan (West), Enugu (East), and Benin City (Midwest). For flag in color, see FLAG. See also northern Africa map in Atlas, Vol. 20.

Physical Features

The natural regions of Nigeria, from south to north, include a lagoon and swamp coastal belt up to 60 miles wide, a zone of high forest and wooded plains, and scrub savanna merging into desert in the north. Above the forest belt the general elevation is only about 2,000 feet, though parts of the central plateau rise above 6,000 feet.

Climate. The climate is tropical in the north with a maximum mean temperature of 94° F, and equatorial in the south with a maximum mean temperature of 84° F and high humidity. Between November and April prevailing dry winds from the northeast (*harmattan*) bring cooler air and dust to much of the country, while in the south there is a rainy season from May to October with as much as 170 inches in the eastern sector of the coast. In the extreme north annual rainfall may be less than 25 inches.

Drainage. The country is aptly named after the Niger—the third largest river of Africa—which flows down from the northwest and joins the Benue River 340 miles from the sea. Together, these two drainage systems sustain life over immense areas. Secondary rivers run from the central plateau to Lake Chad; and in the west the Ogun River links the Yoruba region with the coastal lagoon complex, which is the most prominent feature of the low-lying delta of the Niger.

Despite the great volume of the main river systems, many parts of Nigeria are chronically short of water for most of the dry season and suffer from flooding and erosion during the short, heavy rains. Water conservation and control is a major problem for improvement of agriculture and com-

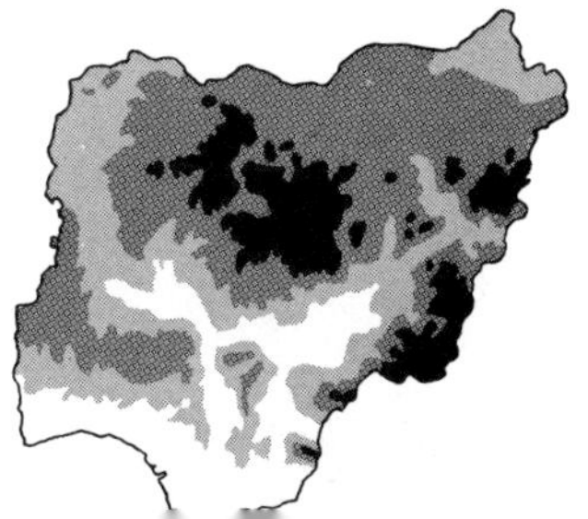

Nigeria: elevation. Black areas, over 2,000 feet above sea level; dark gray areas, 1,000-2,000; light gray areas, 500-1,000; white areas, below 500 feet.

munications. The Niger is navigable as far as Onitsha for most of the year; the Benue is open to Makurdi from June to November.

Social Features

Population. Compared with other countries of Africa, Nigeria has a high average density of 150 persons per square mile, though the population is unevenly distributed. This large population is a mosaic of tribes and languages in which there are several dominant groups: the Sudan people of the north, in the main Hausa farmers and townsmen of Kano, Sokoto, and Zaria; the sedentary and pastoral Fulani who live throughout the western Sudan; the Kanuri founders of Bornu, settled mainly in the Chad basin; and the Nupe, who inhabit the Niger area above the Benue confluence. Most of these peoples are Muslims or deeply influenced by long contact with Islam. Secondly there are the great families of the Guinea forest: the Yoruba who make up almost the entire population of the Western region and extend over the border into Dahomey; the Edo, or Bini, of the Benin area with strong cultural affinities with the Yoruba; the Ibo who inhabit the Eastern region, particularly around Onitsha, Owerri, and Ogoja; the Ibibio and Efik of Calabar; and the Ijaw of the Delta. An important pagan group of Benue province is the Tiv, who have long resisted control by African neighbors or by Europeans.

Language. The languages of the Northern region belong to the Chadic branch of the Afro-Asiatic group, Hausa and Kanuri predominating. Toward the south the Kwa language group is spoken by most peoples of the middle belt. In the east the central branch of the Niger-Congo language family is spoken—particularly Ibibio. Throughout the Northern region Hausa is a *lingua franca* and is also a written language with Arabic script. Many of the southern languages have been reduced to written form. English is the language of trade and administration in all areas. Local dialects of the main languages number as many as 250—the most important being spoken by as many as 5,000,000 people and the least significant by no more than a few hundred. See AFRICAN LANGUAGES.

Society. Nigeria has been occupied by man for over 2,000 years and has absorbed many migrations from the north and east, producing a series of flourishing civilizations whose early history is at last being revealed through archaeology and written and oral history. Social and political structures have, therefore, been profoundly modified by population movements over long periods of time. Before the nineteenth century, they ranged from highly centralized Islamic states in the north, to the Yoruba kingdoms of the west, the village-centered age-grade societies of the Eastern region, the trading states of the Niger Delta, and several small pockets of "chiefless" societies in the middle belt and the eastern Benue.

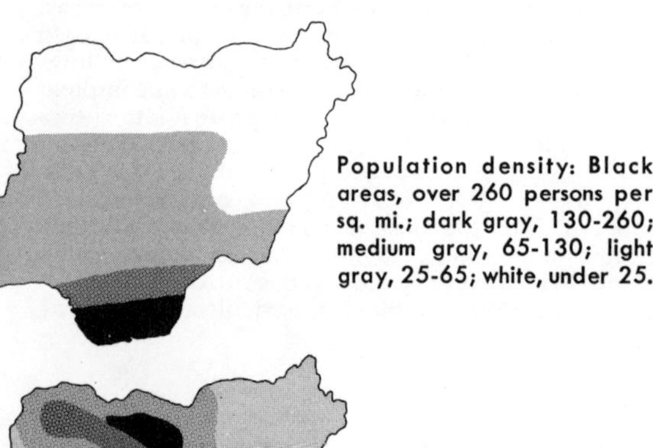

Population density: Black areas, over 260 persons per sq. mi.; dark gray, 130-260; medium gray, 65-130; light gray, 25-65; white, under 25.

Nigeria: annual average rainfall. Black areas, over 80 inches; dark gray, 60-80; light gray, 40-60; white, 20-40.

MARC AND EVELYNE BERNHEIM—RAPHO GUILLUMETTE

Lagos, Nigeria's capital, is a city of contrasts: high-rise apartments, neo-Gothic churches, and shanties.

All these populations have been for the most part agriculturalist and pastoralist, specializing in the production of grain (sorghum, rice, millet) in the northern savanna zone and root crops (yams) and fruits in the region of the forest. The early introduction of iron-smelting techniques and trading contacts with North Africa gave rise to a great variety of crafts, markets, and commercial exchange in the Niger area. The population has been unusually urbanized, even in pre-European times, as witness the ancient cities of Kano, Katsina, Benin, and Abeokuta. Today such new centers as Lagos and Ibadan (founded about 1830) are the largest cities in West Africa; and many smaller towns and villages shelter predominantly farming populations whose fields lie outside the town walls.

The historic commercial connections between Nigerian peoples and the outside world made currency familiar from early times, but literacy was limited to those converted to Islam in the Hausa states, or to European missionary pupils from the mid-nineteenth century onwards. Technologically backward, the African society of the region has managed to cope with climatic and ecological disadvantages and produce complex forms of social and political organization at a highly sophisticated level. It is not surprising that many of the more recently introduced methods of modern government have been adapted to older and sometimes more autocratic forms of control.

The Nigerians have proved most adaptable to European patterns of wage labor since the nineteenth century. The occupational structure of most Nigerian towns is similar to all societies undergoing change from rural to urban-based employment. Wage earners still form a relatively small proportion of the total work force of the country; but the mobility of labor and the demand for education are encouraging rapid demographic growth in the centers of commerce and administration.

Education. Until the end of World War II, education was very much the responsibility of mission schools which were, however, excluded from the Northern region. Since 1955, all the regions have invested heavily in primary education and in universities. Today, about three fifths of the country's small children attend primary schools. Secondary education has lagged behind this advance. The University of Ibadan was founded in 1948 to teach the humanities, sciences, medicine, and agriculture. It was followed by universities at Lagos, Nsukka, Ife, and Zaria, as well as a number of technical colleges.

NIGERIAN CONSULATE

The glistening mosque of Kano stands in splendid isolation from the city's close-packed dwellings.

MARC AND EVELYNE BERNHEIM—RAPHO GUILLUMETTE

Neatly stacked bags of peanuts make avenues of pyramids in Northern Nigeria.

Religion. Christian missions have made serious inroads into the wide variety of pagan beliefs in the south, but very little headway with the Muslim populations of the north. Protestants predominate among the Yoruba, Ibibio, and Efik (the Anglican Church claims 1,000,000 adherents); some 2,000,000 Ibos have been converted to Roman Catholicism. There are several important African churches, founded at the end of the nineteenth century, and since 1964 attempts have been made to unite them.

Health. The more serious diseases found in Nigeria are sleeping sickness, malaria, and diseases associated with nutritional deficiencies. There is only one qualified doctor to about every 40,000 inhabitants. See AFRICA.

Economic Features

Production. Agriculture employs some 80 per cent of the working population and accounts for 85 per cent of the country's total exports. Given a great stimulus by European trade in the nineteenth century, production of tropical exports is limited to palm oil and kernels, cotton, groundnuts, rubber, cocoa, and hardwoods. The traditional growth and sale of vegetables for internal consumption has increased over the last century, but is today insufficient to feed the expanding population and is supplemented by the imported rice and wheat. Both groundnuts and palm oil are sold for the domestic market, as well as being exported abroad. Minerals such as tin, iron, limestone, columbite, gold, coal, lead, zinc, and wolfram are exploited on the plateau, and in the Delta important oil deposits were opened up in 1964.

Trade and Economic Development. All together, Nigeria's total exports were valued at some £164,000,000 by 1962 and imports at £203,000,000. The main countries trading with Nigeria are the United Kingdom, followed by the Benelux countries, the United States, and West Germany.

After World War II Nigerian industries were developed on a small scale—particularly cement, textiles, tobacco, and food processing. There was heavy investment in the production of electric power and the construction of a dam at Jebba on the Niger. Two investment plans, involving £339,000,000 and £676,000,000, were administered by both the regional and federal governments and divided among agriculture, industry, ports, and railways. The country's budget is heavily dependent on indirect taxes obtained from duties on imports.

History and Government

Some of the earliest evidence of human occupation of Nigeria consists of neolithic stone tools, widely distributed throughout the country. Discovery of terra-cotta heads of the "Nok" culture dated at between 500 B.C. and A.D. 200 provided stylistic and technical antecedents for the famous Benin bronzes which are remarkable for their verisimilitude. Archaeological evidence cannot yet be fully related with the political and economic history of the western Sudan of which Nigeria forms a part. But it is clear that the early expansion of human settlement between the Niger and Lake Chad, following the arrival of desert nomads of Berber origins in the seventh and eighth centuries, is closely linked with the formation of political units of large dimensions based on peasant agriculture and external trade. Arab chronicles of the eighth century indicate the origins of the empire of Kanem (on the northern boundary of modern Nigeria), which was to rival the Negro empires of Ghana and Mali 400 years later. In the fourteenth century Kanem fell to the founders of the Bornu empire; the Hausa states grew, traded with North Africa, and were partly converted to Islam in the same period. Father south the Oyo empire of the Yoruba, founded by the early fifteenth century, began to expand over the vast region between the Niger and Togo. In the sixteenth century there were close links between northern Nigeria and the Songhai empire of the Upper Niger, before Songhai power was broken by Morocco. Internal conflicts between the Hausa states and pressure from the pagan Jukun of the southern Benue area prevented the rise of a rival to Oyo.

Contact with Europeans on the coast began in the fifteenth century, when the Portuguese traded with Benin. As Benin declined and the Atlantic slave trade began, other European rivals—English, Dutch, and French—struggled for a lucrative commerce in men, ivory, and spices, which resulted in the export of at least 11,000,000 Africans from this area of the coast by the end of the eighteenth century. The internal effects of the slave trade have yet to be fully assessed—some African states prospered, others were ruined. But by the end of the eighteenth century the Oyo empire was in decline; the Islamic revolutions of the western Sudan led to the conquest of the Hausa states by the Fulani under Usman dan Fodio; and in the 1830's Oyo was destroyed and the great Yoruba empire broke up into a series of warring successor states.

European commercial and humanitarian interests grew steadily in the nineteenth century. The mystery of the course and outlet of the Niger was solved by 1830, and steam vessels went up the great river in 1841. The campaign against the slave trade and the development of trade in palm oil led to the foundation of a British colony at Lagos in 1861, after a decade of consular rule, and the active intervention of consuls and the Royal Navy in the affairs of the Delta and Lower Niger markets. Thereafter, the two main avenues of British expansion were from Lagos and along the Niger. In 1886 the Royal Niger Company began to consolidate British monopoly of the Niger markets as far north as Rabba; in 1892 Lagos Colony began to expand territorially by establishing protectorates over the Yoruba states. Conflicts with France and Germany were settled as part of the general partition of Africa (1892–1906).

The administrative system that emerged from British occupation was a mixture of the older pragmatism and direct control exercised by early governors on the coast and the encouragement of a measure of provincial autonomy, first begun by Lord Lugard among the emirates of the north. In 1914 a semblance of unity was given to the country by the amalgamation of the Colony and Protectorate of Southern Nigeria with the Northern Protectorate, which had passed from the control of the Royal Niger Company in 1900. This unity was fostered to a great extent by the construction of railways after 1898 between Lagos and Kano, via Ibadan; but for a long time the only constitutional link was the person of the governor-general.

This division between north and south, which to some extent reflected the great ethnic and historical divisions of Nigeria, was perpetuated by the relatively swift pace of social, economic, and political change in the Yoruba, Ibo, and Ijaw areas in the interwar period. Exposed longer to European contact and in touch with proto-nationalist groups elsewhere in British West Africa, educated southern Nigerians agitated for reform of the Legislative Council, easier access to administrative posts, higher education, and the end of indirect rule which widened the gulf between traditional chiefs and an emergent literate leadership. From 1922, when representation was widened to include unofficial elected members of the Legislative Council, agitation against British rule was limited mainly to the urban centers. Under Sir Donald Cameron in the 1930's, a High Court was introduced for the whole country, native councils were set up in Western Nigeria, and the powers of customary courts were limited. But Northern Nigeria remained outside the responsibility of the Legislative Council.

After World War II, the example of India and the formation of an Ibo political party—the National Council of Nigeria and the Cameroons—in 1944 contradicted the assumption that British rule would last for decades. The Yoruba quickly formed their own party, later called the Action Group, in 1945, and in the north the Northern People's Congress, formed in 1949, represented the essentially conservative views of the emirate authorities. These three political parties, under the leadership respectively of Dr. Nnamdi Azikiwe, Obafemi Awolowo, and the northern emirs began to contest power as constitutional changes, begun in 1946, set up regional houses of assembly and a house of chiefs for the north and, from 1953, progressively widened the franchise. The constitution of 1951 gave the north half the seats in a central legislature, while the old executive council was gradually transformed into a council of ministers at Lagos. After 1956, when the Federation was inaugurated, the three regions became internally self-governing. A series of constitutional conferences guided the Federation toward complete independence on Oct. 1, 1960, when Nigeria joined the Commonwealth.

Independence was followed by several political developments that altered the balance of power between the federal government and the regions. Federal politicians from the north and east kept control at the expense of the western opposition.

In 1963, Nigeria became a republic with Dr. Azikiwe as its first president. But regional strife was not quelled, and serious new tensions began to develop as an outgrowth of eastern resentment of the northern consolidation of federal power. On Jan. 15, 1966, a group of eastern Ibo army officers overthrew the federal government; in the wake of the coup, Prime Minister Balewa and several key government leaders were murdered. By January 17, however, the army commander-in-chief, Major-General Johnson Aguiyi-Ironsi, an Ibo, suppressed the uprising and assumed command of the government. General Ironsi moved immediately to suspend the constitution, disband the parliament, and enforce military rule.

The Ironsi government, however, was short-lived. On July 29, 1966, dissident army elements from the north staged a countercoup, killing General Ironsi and replacing him with Lieutenant-Colonel Yakubu Gowon. The coup led to the exodus of nearly 2 million Ibos from the northern region. Thousands of Ibos, meanwhile, were massacred by northern mobs, abetted by government troops. As the pressure for civil war mounted, Colonel Gowon continued efforts to forge a new federal constitution. By April, 1967, however, these efforts had been all but abandoned.

On May 30, the Military Governor of the Eastern region, Lieutenant-Colonel Odumegwu Ojukwu, announced the secession of the region from the federation and its independence as the Republic of Biafra. Colonel Gowon's government immediately branded the secession as an act of rebellion. A prolonged civil war ensued, during which the Ibos suffered heavy losses through combat and starvation. The conflict officially ended on Jan. 12, 1970, with the surrender of Biafra to the federal government. C. W. NEWBURY

BIBLIOG.–James S. Coleman, *Nigeria: Background to Nationalism* (1958); Michael Crowder, *A Short History of Nigeria* (1966 ed.); Frederick Forsyth, *Biafra Story* (1969); Thomas Hodgkin, *Nigerian Perspectives* (1960); C. W. Newbury, *The West African Commonwealth* (1964); Walter Schwartz, *Nigeria* (1968).

NIGER RIVER, W Africa, rising in the Futa Jallon upland near the Sierra Leone-Guinea border about 175 miles from the Atlantic, and flowing NE and E through Mali, then SE into Nigeria and S into the Gulf of Guinea; length 2,600 miles. It is the third longest river in Africa.

The upper Niger, called the Joliba, flows past Kouroussa and Siguiri in Guinea to Bamako and Ségou in Mali. Below Ségou stands the 8,600-foot-wide Sansanding Dam, completed in 1946. The Niger separates into several braided arms in the Macina and receives the Bani River at Mopti. The river then passes Timbuktu in the southern fringe of the Sahara Desert and reaches its most distant point from the ocean (780 miles) before turning southeast at Bourem. Then, as the middle Niger, it continues past Niamey in Niger Republic into Nigeria and past the mouth of the Kebbi River to the Bussa Rapids. There the river becomes the lower Niger, called the Kworra, and passes Jebba and Lokoja where it receives the Benue River, its largest tributary. Below Onitsha, which is 120 miles from the coast, there begins the 15,000-square-mile mangrove-dotted Niger Delta. The Niger has a great potential for irrigation; it is generally unsuited for commercial shipping.

NIGHT BLINDNESS, *Nyctalopia,* the inability to see in dim light. When a normal person passes from bright light to darkness he can at first see nothing, but his eyes gradually become accustomed to the darkness as visual purple (a pigment in the rod cells of the retina) is built up. Inability to build up visual purple in the retina results in night blindness. It may be caused by a deficiency of vitamin A, by certain drugs or diseases, or it may be inherited. See EYE.

NIGHT-BLOOMING PLANT, one whose flowers are closed most of the daylight hours but open during the night; examples are bindweed, morning-glory, moonvine, evening primrose, various species of *Mentzelia*, and night-blooming cereus. The flowers of these plants are pollinated principally by night-flying insects such as moths. See CEREUS.

H. J. FULLER

NIGHTHAWK, a slim-winged, ample-tailed, gray bird mottled and patterned with black and brown, belonging to the goatsucker family, *Caprimulgidae*. The nighthawk, *Chordeiles minor*, has a wingspan of about 18 inches. It feeds mostly on flying insects and hunts in the evenings. As it swoops vigorously about, distinctive white markings can be seen on the wings. Otherwise it closely resembles the whip-poorwill. The nighthawk builds no nest for its clutch of two eggs, but lays them on the ground. The nighthawk ranges throughout eastern North America but spends its winters in South America. SEE GOATSUCKER.

NIGHTINGALE, FLORENCE, 1820–1910, English nurse and reformer, known as the Lady with the Lamp, born in Florence, Italy, daughter of wealthy William Edward and Frances Nightingale.

Unwilling to abide by the social and legal conventions of the time, when women were under the tutelage of their husbands or fathers, Miss Nightingale was determined to find a career among the sick. She gained her early nursing experience in France and Germany.

Shortly after the outbreak of the Crimean War in 1854, she volunteered her services. Even as she was volunteering, public criticism of the treatment of sick and wounded English troops in the Crimea and in the hospital at Scutari, across the straits from Constantinople, roused her old friend Sidney Herbert, Secretary of War, into sending a letter asking her for her help. Her official appointment to head a delegation of nurses caused a sensation since she was the first woman to serve in such a capacity. She arrived at Scutari in November, 1854, with some 38 women, only to run into opposition from the medical authorities, many of whom were hostile to the idea of women in military hospitals. By biding her time and doing nothing until requested, she was finally allowed into the hospital. She and her nurses gradually assumed control not only of nursing duties, but of the kitchen, the laundry, recreation for the patients, and care of the wives of the troops. Her concern for the troops caused her to be almost worshiped by the soldiers at Scutari and the newspapers carried her reputation to England where she quickly became a heroic figure.

Upon leaving Scutari in 1856, she deliberately avoided the receptions planned for her and slipped quietly into England where she sought obscurity in order to work on two major projects: bettering the conditions in British military hospitals and reforming nursing. Her first effort was a series of unpublished studies in 1858 entitled *Notes on Matters Affecting the Health, Efficiency, and Hospital Administration of the British Army*, which eventually led to major reforms in the army medical and statistical systems. This was followed in 1859 by the *Notes on Hospitals* and *Notes on Nursing* (1860). The first was influential in changing hospital construction. She started a training school at St. Thomas' Hospital in London, and the reforms made there were soon imitated throughout Europe and America. Exhausted by her labors she retired to her bedroom where she spent most of her last 50 years.

Florence Nightingale

She still kept active, however. As a member of the Royal Sanitary Commission on the Health of the Army in India she was instrumental in modifying public health conditions in India, and she also assisted William Rathbone (1819–1902) in establishing the visiting nurse system in Liverpool. In 1867 she wrote the influential pamphlet, *Suggestions for the Improvement of the Nursing Service for the Sick Poor*. Never an easy person to work with, Miss Nightingale in her old age attempted to prevent the formation of the British Nurses' Association because it departed from some of her ideas on nursing education. In 1907 she was recognized as one of the pioneer founders of the International Red Cross and was also given the Order of Merit, the first woman to be so honored by the British government.

VERN L. BULLOUGH

BIBLIOG.–Bonnie and Vern Bullough, *The Emergence of Modern Nursing* (1964); Sir Edward Cook, *Life of Florence Nightingale* (1913); Cecil Woodham-Smith, *Florence Nightingale, 1820–1910* (1950).

NIGHTINGALE, a European songbird of the thrush family, *Turdidae*, about 6½ inches long, with brown back, plain white breast, and chestnut tail. Both sexes are alike in plumage. The nightingale, *Luscinia megarhynchos*, inhabits woods, thickets, and hedges near meadows and water throughout Europe. During the winter it migrates to Africa. It builds a well-hidden nest near the ground among thickets and lays four to six eggs. A solitary bird, the nightingale is remarkable for its song, an intricate melody of superb clarity.

NIGHTSHADE, a family of plants (*Solanaceae*) of which the genus *Solanum* is also called nightshade. They are mostly herbs or shrubs, with alternate leaves and various-colored fruit—usually berries. Members of the genus are numerous and include plants cultivated for medicine or food, some that are poisonous, and others that are decorative. See BELLADONNA; BITTERSWEET; POTATO; TOMATO.

Black nightshade, *S. nigrum*, growing to about 15 inches, with white flowers and black berries, is a common (and poisonous) weed in eastern North America. Other members include Jerusalem cherry, *S. pseudo-capsicum*; African holly, *S. giganteum*, which comes from Asia; and *S. integrifolium*, the scarlet or tomato eggplant, native to Africa.

NIHILISM, in political theory, the doctrine that conditions are so bad that destruction of the social organization is necessary. It was primarily a Russian phenomenon; formulation of the doctrine can be ascribed to Ivan Turgenev's novel, *Fathers and Sons* (1862).

Nihilism (Latin *nihil*, nothing), originating as a purely theoretical expression of a radical political philosophy, was early transformed by its followers into action as anarchism and terrorism. The temper of the times is most accurately reflected in the career and writings of the anarchist, Michael Bakunin (1814–76). The climax of decades of revolutionary activity came with the assassination of Tsar Alexander II in March, 1881. Nihilism in all its forms was ruthlessly suppressed thereafter, by the government of Alexander III and his son, the ill-fated Nicholas II, until the moment of its final triumph in the October Revolution of 1917.

Among Philosophers nihilism has been the denial of the validity of all distinctions of metaphysical or moral value. Hence Gorgias, the sophist (fifth century B.C.) argues that our recognition of the ceaseless flux of all things, combined with our awareness that the truth revealed in sense perception is in fact no truth because men's sensations differ, impels the conclusion that nothing exists—if it did exist it could not be known and if it were known it could not be communicated. According to Sankara (Indian, ninth century), all diversity being illusion, the duty of man is through yoga to achieve oblivion (nirvana). Arthur Schopenhauer's doctrine of salvation as the denial of the will is but the developed expression of this nihilist idea: ". . . to those in whom the will has turned and has denied itself, this our world, which is so real, with all its suns and milky ways—is nothing."

ROBERT C. WHITTEMORE

NIIGATA, city, Japan, NW Honshu, capital of Niigata Prefecture; at the mouth of the Shinano River; 160 miles NNW of Tokyo. Niigata is Japan's principal west coast port and an important industrial center producing refined oil, machinery, textiles, chemicals, and metalwork. An excellent grade of rice is grown in the area, accounting for 5 per cent of Japanese consumption of that commodity. Since 1868, when Niigata was opened to foreign trade, it has handled exports of iron ore, fertilizer, beans, marine products, machinery, paper, textiles, and gold; and imports of cement, oil, wheat, lumber, and salt. In winter, because of the severe weather, the city utilizes the port in Ryotsu on Sado Island, thus being able to carry on a year-round trade in the produce of the fertile Shinano Valley. Japanese coastal vessels stop at Niigata on their way to and from Vladivostok and other Siberian ports, or Rashin and Seishin and other Korean ports. Occasionally foreign vessels also stop there, but because of limited harbor facilities Niigata's direct foreign trade is not extensive. The city's important buildings include Niigata University, a private university founded in 1949, and government buildings such as the prefectural office and governor's residence, commercial museum, meteorological observatory, export rice inspection office, and rice exchange. (For population, see Japan map in Atlas.)

PAUL YUNG

NIJINSKY, WASLAW, 1890–1950, Russian ballet dancer and choreographer, was born in Kiev of Polish parents, both dancers. At the age of nine Nijinsky was accepted at the Imperial School of Dancing, St. Petersburg. He seemed slow-witted in many ways (perhaps because of a fall on his head that resulted in a brain concussion) but despite this handicap developed so rapidly as a dancer that in 1907, while still in school, he made his debut at the Maryinsky Theater in the Mozart ballet, *Don Juan*.

MUS. OF MODERN ART, N.Y.
Nijinsky

His highly successful career with the Imperial Russian Ballet was cut short in 1911, when he was dismissed for wearing an improper costume in a performance for the dowager empress. Nijinsky had met Sergei Diaghilev during his first season with the Imperial Ballet, and in 1911 Diaghilev took Nijinsky to Paris to head his new company, the Ballet Russe.

In 1912 Nijinsky achieved great success with his first composition as a choreographer to the tone poem *L'Après-midi d'un faune* (Afternoon of a Faun) by Claude Debussy. The unconventional conception of the piece created a sensation, as did his second composition, choreographed to Igor Stravinsky's *Le Sacre du printemps* (The Rite of Spring).

In 1913 the Diaghilev company went on tour of South America, Diaghilev remaining in Europe. In Buenos Aires, Nijinsky married a Hungarian dancer in the company, Romola de Pulszky. Diaghilev, furious, dismissed them both. Nijinsky then organized a small company which appeared at the Palace Theater, London. He had little talent for business, however, and the company disbanded after two weeks. In Austria at the outbreak of World War I, Nijinsky, as a Russian, was interned, first in Budapest and later in Vienna. The internment is thought to have aggravated Nijinsky's already noticeable mental illness. He was released in 1916 and toured South and North America, triumphing everywhere, but developed a more and more acute persecution complex. Returning to Europe he and his wife settled in Switzerland, where it became necessary to confine him for a long period in the Sanatorium Bellevue at Kreuzlingen. He never fully recovered, but was able to spend his last years in England under his wife's care.

In addition to *L'Après-midi d'un faune* and *Le Sacre du printemps*, Nijinsky's large repertory included *Le Spectre de la rose*, *Schéhérazade*, *Narcisse*, *Till Eulenspiegel*, *Pétrouchka*, and *Les sylphides*.

CLARENCE JOSEPH BULLIET

NIJMEGEN, or Nijmwegen, formerly Nimeguen, city, E Netherlands, Gelderland Province; on the Waal River; 59 miles E of Rotterdam. Nijmegen has manufactures of textiles, shoes, clothing, and machinery. The city contains the eighth century Valkhof, thirteenth century Groote Kerk, sixteenth century town hall and Latin school, seventeenth century weighhouse, and a modern Roman Catholic university. Settled and named Noviomagus by the Romans, Nijmegen was chartered as a town in 1184. It was a member of the Hanseatic League. The city suffered heavy damage during the fighting between Allied airborne troops and the Germans, September, 1944. (For population, see Netherlands map in Atlas.)

NIKA RIOTS, an insurrection against the Emperor Justinian I at Constantinople in 532. Two hostile factions—the Blues, representing orthodox Christianity, and the Greens, representing monophysitism—joined forces in a popular uprising, with "Nika" (Victory) as their slogan. The city was filled with fire and bloodshed; many public buildings were burned, including the church of Hagia Sophia and much of the palace. Finally Belisarius attacked the rioters, who had fortified themselves in the Hippodrome, and killed more than 30,000 of them.

NIKE, in Greek mythology, the goddess of victory (in Roman mythology, Victoria). She was represented as a winged maiden, often with a garland in one hand and a palm branch in the other, or a fillet in both hands. The *Nike* (or *Winged Victory*) *of Samothrace*, in the Louvre, Paris—a statue discovered on Samothrace, 1863–dates probably from about 200 B.C.

NIKKO, town, central Japan, Honshu, Tochigi Prefecture; in Nikko National Park; 75 miles N of Tokyo. Primarily a tourist resort and religious center, Nikko is reached by railroad or by a scenic highway lined for miles with giant cryptomeria trees. Among the places of interest in the city are the mausoleums of Ieyasu and Iemitsu, first and third shoguns of the Tokugawa dynasty, and the seventeenth century shrine of Tosho-gu. They are characterized by elaborate wood carving and brilliant lacquer work. Surrounding scenery includes such waterfalls as Kegon Falls that serve as outlet for Lake Chuzenji. (For population, see Japan map in Atlas.)

NIKOLAYEV, region, U.S.S.R., S Ukrainian Soviet Socialist Republic; bounded by the regions of Kirovograd on the N, Odessa on the W, Dnepropetrovsk and Kherson on the E, and by the Black Sea on the S; area 9,600 sq. mi.; pop. (1956 est.) 996,000. The main rivers are the Bug and the Ingul. The region is noted for its grain, agricultural machinery, and shipbuilding. The capital is Nikolayev.

THEODORE SHABAD

NIKOLAYEV, city U.S.S.R., S central Ukrainian Soviet Socialist Republic, capital of Nikolayev Region; at the confluence of the Ingul and the Bug rivers, on the Black Sea; 65 miles NE of Odessa. The "Black Sea Pompeii," site of the ancient Greek city of Olbia, is in the vicinity. Nikolayev is the foremost shipbuilding center on the Black Sea, engaged primarily in constructing vessels for the Black Sea mercantile fleet. In addition the city produces road-building machines, farm machinery, glass, canned fish, and flour. It has a large ship-engineering school. Nikolayev was founded in 1784. During World Wars I and II it was occupied by the Germans. (For population, see U.S.S.R. map in Atlas.) THEODORE SHABAD

NIKON, 1605–81, Russian religious reformer, was born in Valmanovo near Nizhni Novgorod (later Gorkiy. A priest and monk, he became metropolitan of Novgorod, 1648, and patriarch of Moscow, 1652—a position he accepted only after an agreement that his will would be followed in all things concerning the Russian Orthodox church. His reforms aimed at ridding the Russian rites of additions and ancient peculiarities. He convened a synod at Moscow, 1654, to revise the church service books. His reforms were largely successful, but Nikon's rigorous methods of enforcement led to a schism in the church and the founding of the sect of Raskolniks (Old Believers) who returned to the earlier practices. In 1658, having lost the favor of Czar Alexis Mikhailovich, Nikon retired to a monastery. He was deposed and degraded, 1666, but his reforms were confirmed.

NIKOPOL, town, N Bulgaria, Pleven Province; on the Danube River opposite Turnu-Magurele, Rumania; terminus of a railroad leading to the Danube; 25 miles NE of Pleven. The city's main industry is its activity as a river-rail transshipment center. Founded in 629 by Emperor Heraclius, Nikopol was the scene of a major victory by Sultan Bajazet I of Turkey over King Sigismund of Hungary in 1396. It became one of the leading cultural centers in the Balkan Peninsula. THEODORE SHABAD

NIKOPOL, city, SW U.S.S.R., Ukrainian Soviet Socialist Republic, Dnepropetrovsk Region; on the Dnepr River; 190 miles NE of Odessa. Nikopol has approximately half of the world's known deposits of manganese, as well as an important steel pipe industry. During World War II the Germans captured and destroyed most of the city but it was rebuilt after the war. (For population, see U.S.S.R. map in Atlas.) THEODORE SHABAD

NILE, BATTLE OF THE, was fought in Aboukir Bay on Aug. 1, 1798, during Napoleon's invasion of Eygpt, between a British fleet of 14 ships under Horatio Nelson and Napoleon's French fleet of 17 ships. The French fleet was drawn up in the bay, about 15 miles NE of Alexandria, in two lines meeting to form an obtuse angle to seaward. Nelson sent half his fleet to penetrate the French lines and attack from the landward or windward side, and the other half to the seaward or leeward side to prevent the French from escaping. By attacking from the windward, Nelson's ships were able to move from one French ship to another, while the French ships were forced to await their coming. The maneuver was highly successful, all but two battleships of the French fleet being captured or destroyed. See NAPOLEON I.

Carloads of manganese ore move through the mining city of Nikopol. The city, situated in the Dnepr River basin in the Ukraine, is a great center of manganese production.
SOVFOTO

NILE RIVER, Arabic Bahr el Nil, African River, about 4,160 miles in length from its most remote source, is the second longest—perhaps the longest—river in the world. Flowing generally from south to north, its system drains an area of more than 1.1 million square miles of east central and northeast Africa. Its major tributaries are the Blue Nile (Bahr el Azraq) and the White Nile (Bahr el Abyad and Bahr el Jebel). The Blue Nile drains the highlands of Ethiopia; the White's waters come from the lake region of Uganda, Rwanda, Burundi, and Tanganyika. The two Niles unite at Khartoum to form the main river, which flows from this point about 1,700 miles to the Mediterranean Sea, receiving no other tributaries than the Atbara River. In northern Egypt the Nile forms a large delta before its waters reach the sea. The White Nile flows out of Lake Victoria (sections of it in Uganda being called the Victoria Nile and the Albert Nile). The Nile's most distant source is in the Rwanda and Burundi region near Lake Tanganyika at the headwaters of the Luvironza, a tributary of the Ruvuvu. This stream then flows into the Kagera River, which empties into Lake Victoria. If the Nile is measured from this lake, considered by some its source, the river's length is still considerable—3,485 miles. The Blue Nile has its source in Lake Tana and the headwaters of the Abbai, a river entering the lake. The Atbara rises in the Ethiopian highlands not far from Lake Tana. See RIVER; DELTA.

Location Map of the Nile River

The Nile flow is fed by the heavy, seasonal rainfalls of the tropical highlands of northeast Africa. Some of the water gathered there is lost through evaporation or percolation, but each year more than 21,000 billion gallons of water flows northward past Wadi Halfa in Sudan into Egypt. Much of this is lost to the sea in time of flood. At other times the demands of irrigation reduce the flow so much that dams are required at the mouths of the Nile to keep out the sea. This is the purpose served by the Edfina Diversion Dam on the Rosetta branch of the Nile Delta and a temporary log-and-earth structure, the Faraskour Dam, erected each year across the Damietta branch. Compared with other rivers, the Nile is regular in its habits of flow, rising to flood peak about the beginning of September—about six months after the start of the heavy seasonal rains in the highlands of Ethiopia. Accurate prediction of flood heights has long been difficult but important—in earlier times because the amount of overflow determined the amount of land to be worked, in modern times for determining the availability of storage water and anticipating the possibilities of damaging overflow.

In ancient times the economy of Egypt and its government, religion, and art were greatly influenced by the river's habits. Indeed, the central event of the

HAMILTON WRIGHT

Houseboats and other watercraft anchor along the banks of the Nile at Cairo, Egypt. From here the river flows north through the Nile Delta channels into the Mediterranean.

political calendar in ancient Egypt was the symbolic annual voyage of the Pharaoh along the river. The Greek historian, Herodotus (484?–?424 B.C.), termed Egypt "the gift of the Nile"; and the Roman poet, Tibullus (54?–?18 B.C.), addressing the river as "Father Nile," observed that "because of thee Egypt never sues for showers." Despite modern technology, Egypt remains basically dependent upon the river, as does much of Sudan. See EGYPT.

Early Methods of Irrigation. Until modern times, the people of the lower Nile depended upon some form of basin irrigation—a system in which flood waters are carried over the fields and retained long enough to saturate the soil and drop a load of silt. This method, in use by 4000 B.C., permits but one cropping a year except when supplemented in limited areas by other means of irrigation in which water is raised by human, animal, or machine-powered devices. At mid-twentieth century about 700,000 acres in upper (southern) Egypt were watered by basin irrigation. Supplemental irrigation often is carried on by means of the shadoof, a pail or jar suspended from one end of a counterbalanced pole; the *saqia*, or water wheel; and the Archimedean screw. Occasionally power pumps are used. See IRRIGATION, History, *Ancient Times;* DAM, History.

Control and Utilization in Modern Times. The effort to meet the demands of increasing populations in the area by extending the growing seasons and providing sources of electric power began the development, in the nineteenth century, of a modern system of irrigation and power works along the Nile. Since the interests of Egypt, Sudan, Ethiopia, and Uganda are directly involved, control and use of the river are a subject of international concern and negotiation. Egypt's interests and needs long were dominant; but those of Sudan and Ethiopia, because they control the water sources, have also become influential.

The modern system of Nile control, based on perennial irrigation, originated in projects inaugurated by Mohammed Ali Pasha (1769?–1849), and culminated in the Mohammed Ali Dam, which was not completed and in good working order until 1890. This dam, constructed across the two Nile branches at the head of the delta, was designed to raise the water level about 13 feet for gravity-flow irrigation; its function was taken over by a new dam built on the downstream side in 1939. Other important structures on the Egyptian Nile are the Aswan, Esna, Nag Hammadi, Zifta, and Assiut dams, designed to raise the water levels; and the Edfina and Faraskour dams, barriers to invasion by the Mediterranean Sea at times of low water in the river. Aswan Dam, used mainly for storage of water, was completed in 1902 and heightened in 1912 and 1933. Its sluices are closed after the mud-laden flood crest has passed, to avoid silting of the reservoir; waters retained are later released for irrigation.

Outside Egypt a number of major works on the Nile had been completed by the mid-1950's and others were planned. In Sudan the Gebel Aulia Dam, on the White Nile, stores water for use in Egypt, and the Sennar Dam on the Blue Nile provides for irrigation of about 1 million acres of land in the Gezira District. Owens Falls Dam in Uganda, part of a great hydroelectric project, was built during 1949–54 by agreement with Egypt; this project raised the level of Lake Victoria about 3 feet and provides water to be released for use in Egypt in time of shortage. Proposed were a Jonglei diversion canal to bypass the swampy sudd region and thus reduce water losses by evaporation; a Lake Tana Dam to create further storage; and a high dam (*Sadd el Aali*) to be built some 5 miles above Aswan. It was estimated that this dam would allow an additional 1.3 million acres to be cultivated, permit the remaining basin lands to be converted to perennial irrigation, and eventually provide for the yearly production of 8.3 billion kilowatt-hours of electricity.

Navigation. The Nile carries many thousands of boats over its surface yearly. Because of cataracts at several points along the river, there is no uninterrupted service from the sea to the highlands, but all of the Egyptian Nile is navigable. The bulk of the carriers are freight vessels, most of them sail-propelled or towed from the bank against the current when winds fail. River passenger service remains a tourist attraction, but has declined in importance because of increased air travel. FRED W. FOSTER

BIBLIOG.–R. F. Burton, *Lake Regions of Central Africa* (1860); J. H. Speke, *Journal of the Discovery of the Source of the Nile* (1864); H. H. Johnston, *Nile Quest* (1903); E. Ludwig, *Nile* (1937); H. E. Hurst, *Nile* (1952).

NILES, HEZEKIAH, 1777–1839, U.S. journalist, was born in East Bradford, Chester County, Pennsylvania. A printer by trade, he entered the publishing business in Wilmington, Del. Moving to Baltimore he became an editor of the *Evening Post*, 1805, and in 1811 established the *Weekly Register* (later *Niles' Weekly Register* and *Niles' National Register*), continued after his death to 1849 by his son. Later a source book of American political history, the *Register* exercised great influence in its day.

NILES, village, NE Illinois, Cook County; a NW suburb of Chicago. Niles is primarily residential but has manufactures of radio equipment, tools and dies, and duplicating machinery. The village was incorporated in 1899. Pop. (1960) 20,393.

NILES, city, SW Michigan, Berrien County; on the St. Joseph River, the New York Central Railroad, and U.S. highways 112, 31, and 33; 11 miles N of South Bend, Ind. Principal industries are the canning of mushrooms and the manufacture of paper, refrigerators, wires and cables, and furniture. In 1690 a Jesuit mission was established on the site of Niles, and 1697 the French built Fort St. Joseph there. The fort was captured by the British, 1761; the Indians, 1763; and Spaniards and Indians, 1780–81. It was abandoned for a time, and was resettled in 1827. Niles was incorporated as a village in 1838 and as a city in 1859. Ring Lardner, the writer, and Montgomery Ward, the mail-order merchant, were born there. Pop. (1960) 13,842.

NILES, city, NE Ohio, Trumbull County; on the Mahoning River and the Baltimore and Ohio, the Pennsylvania, and the Erie railroads; 8 miles NW of Youngstown. Niles is an iron and steel center and has manufactures of electric light bulbs, pressed steel products, chemicals, structural steel, metal laths, tin plate, and bricks. The city has a memorial to Pres. William McKinley, who was born there. It was settled in 1806. Pop. (1960) 19,545.

NILES CENTER. See SKOKIE.

NILGIRI HILLS, or Neilgherry Hills, meaning blue mountains, S India, Madras State, an almost isolated plateau more than 6,000 feet above sea level, connecting the Eastern Ghats with the Western

Ghats. The highest point is Mount Dodabetta (8,640 ft.). The Nilgiri Hills contain numerous plantations and estates producing cinchona, tea, coffee, and eucalyptus. A number of primitive tribes live on its forested slopes. Ootacamund, a famous resort city and the summer capital of Madras State, is located in the hills. ALFRED W. BOOTH

NIMES, city, S France, capital of Gard Department; at the foot of outlying hills of the Cévennes Mountains; between Montpellier and Avignon. There are foundries and metalworks, plants that manufacture silk textiles, hosiery, clothing, and carpets, and trade in alcohol, wine, and grains. Nîmes was developed under the Roman Emperor Augustus, and the city (called Nemausus by the Romans) is famous for well preserved Gallo-Roman remains. The arena, an elliptical amphitheater seating about 24,000 spectators, dates from the second century. The city's best preserved Roman monument is the Maison Carrée (Square House), a first century Corinthian temple, which later became a museum of antiquities. Other remains include the Tour Magne, a watchtower built about 50 B.C.; two Roman gates, the Porte d'Auguste and the Porte de France; and an eighteenth century park, Jardin de la Fontaine, which contains the temple of Diana. The Pont du Gard aqueduct is nearby. After being ravaged by Saracens, Vandals, and Visigoths, Nîmes was ceded to France in the thirteenth century. It was a Protestant stronghold during the sixteenth century religious wars. The author Alphonse Daudet was born here. (For population, see France map in Atlas.)

NIMITZ, CHESTER WILLIAM, 1885–1966, U.S. Navy officer, was born in Fredericksburg, Tex., was graduated from the U.S. Naval Academy, and served with the submarine force in World War I. He was assistant chief of the Bureau of Navigation, 1935–38; commander of Battleship Division 1, Battle Force, 1938–39; and chief of the Bureau of Navigation, 1939–41. During World War II, as commander in chief of the Pacific Fleet, 1941–45, he directed naval operations against Japan; he was made fleet admiral 1944. He was chief of naval operations, 1945–47, and on retiring, 1947, was made special assistant to the secretary of the navy. In 1949 he was chosen to head a United Nations commission that investigated the Kashmir dispute between India and Pakistan, and in 1951 he served as chairman of the presidential commission on internal security and individual rights.

NIMZOWITSCH, ARON, 1886–1935, European chess master, was born in Riga, Latvia. He gained first prize in tournaments at Dresden, 1926; Berlin, 1928; and Karlovy Vary, 1929—and equal first at Mariánské Lázně, 1925; Niendorf, 1927; and London, 1927. Nimzowitsch was a founder of the "hypermodern" chess school and wrote *Mein System* (1927) and *Die Praxis meines Systems* (1930).

NIN, ANAIS, 1914– , U.S. writer, was born in Paris, the daughter of Joaquín Nin y Castellano, and was brought to the United States as a child. Unable to find a publisher for her early manuscripts, she bought a press and printed her own books: *Winter of Artifice* (1939), *Under a Glass Bell* (1944), *This Hunger* (1945), and *The House of Incest* (1949). These and her commercially published novels and short stories, which include *The Four-Chambered Heart* (1950), *A Spy in the House of Love* (1954), *Seduction of the Minotaur* (1961), and *Collages* (1964), are dreamlike chronicles of the subconscious in which can be found reflections of her own atypical life. In all Nin's works there is no distinction made between the inner and outer selves of her main characters—who are always women —or between reality and the world of dreams.

NINETY SIX, town, NW South Carolina, Greenwood County; 8 miles E of Greenwood. The town has brick plants and textile, cottonseed oil, and lumber mills. It was settled in 1730 as the first outpost in the South Carolina piedmont and moved to its present site in 1855. Legend states that an Indian girl rode 96 miles to this spot to warn of an attack by her people. This distance became the name of the town. Nearby Star Fort was captured by the British during the Revolutionary War, and besieged without success in 1781 by Gen. Nathanael Greene. (For population, see South Carolina map in Atlas.)

NINEVEH, ancient city, N Iraq, on the E bank of the Tigris River, opposite modern Mosul. The city has been extensively investigated by archaeologists. The earliest settlement unearthed dates from about 5500 B.C., and the first written record dates from the early second millennium B.C. during the reign of Hammurabi. The city was linked by roads with Carchemish, Arbela, and Egypt. Shalmaneser IV made Nineveh the capital of the Assyrian Empire in about 725 B.C. and Sargon II restored the temple to the gods Nebo and Marduk, but it was to Sargon's son, Sennacherib (ruled about 705–681 B.C.), that the city owed its first period of splendor. He ringed the city with a moated double wall of hewn limestone 80 feet high, 7½ miles in circumference, and pierced by 15 gates. His palace was decorated with friezes depicting his conquests, such as the Siege of Lachish. Sennacherib's son Esarhaddon completed the armory begun by his father and built a palace for himself on the southernmost of the two mounds, the Nebi Yunus. His son Assurbanipal restored the walls and temple of Ishtar (or Ninni), and built a palace with gardens nearby. The sculptured reliefs of a lion hunt that adorned its walls represent the apex of Assyrian art. An invaluable library discovered in the two palaces includes religious and medical texts and historical records. In 612 B.C. Nineveh was besieged by the armies of Cyaxares, king of Media, who reduced it to a heap of rubble. See ASSYRIA; BABYLONIAN AND ASSYRIAN ART AND ARCHITECTURE.

NINE WORTHIES, nine heroes of ancient and medieval legend, frequently alluded to in English literature and depicted in medieval tapestries and paintings. Medieval Welsh literature identifies them as heroes of the pagan, Jewish, and Christian peoples: Hector, Alexander, and Julius Caesar; Joshua, David, and Judas Maccabaeus; and Arthur, Charlemagne, and Godfrey de Bouillon (Guy of Warwich is sometimes substituted for Godfrey). The preface to William Caxton's printing of the *Morte d'Arthur* (1485) enumerates the same Nine Worthies. In the late medieval (probably fourteenth century) English poem *Parlement of the Thre Ages*, the histories of the Worthies are given. In the amusing masque of the Nine Worthies presented in William Shakespeare's *Love's Labour's Lost*, only five Worthies are impersonated—Hector, Alexander, Judas Maccabaeus, and (uniquely) Pompey the Great and Hercules.

NINGPO, city, E China, NE Chekiang Province; at the head of the Yung River delta; 90 miles ESE of Hangchow and 100 miles S of Shanghai. Ningpo exports cotton, jute, fruits, tea, rice, and lumber, and is the base of one of the principal fishing fleets of China. The city was founded in the eighth century and during the Ming Dynasty was known as Chingyüan. The Portuguese established a settlement there in 1533, but it was abandoned in 1545 as commercially unsuccessful. Three centuries later Ningpo was one of the Chinese ports opened to foreign trade by treaty with Great Britain (see OPIUM WAR). In 1911 the city became the capital of Ninghsien and took the name of that country; in 1949 it reverted to its original name. (For population, see China map in Atlas.)

NINGSIA, or Ning-hsia, former province, NW China, NE Kansu Province; bounded by the Mongolian People's Republic on the N, Kansu on the S, Shensi on the SE, and the Inner Mongolian Autonomous Region on the E; on the Mongolian Plateau, crossed by the Yellow River (Hwang Ho) in the SE and the Etsin Gol (river) in the NW; area 100,000 sq. mi. Ningsia occupies the irrigated Ningsia Plain and the Ala Shan Desert. The area was settled by the

Chinese in the thirteenth century and protected by the Great Wall. In early Chinese history it was known as Hsia, whence the name Ningsia (peaceful Hsia). It was part of the Tangut (or Torgot) kingdom, governed by Tangut viceroys. Genghis Khan (1162–1227) used it as a proving ground for his invasion and conquest of China proper. It continued to exist as a Chinese satellite and after 1914 became a part of Kansu as the military district of Sitao. In 1928 this district was set up as Ningsia Province, and Yinchwan, formerly also known as Ningsia, was made its capital. In September, 1954, the province was abolished and Ningsia became part of Kansu Province.

The Ala Shan Desert region, inhabited by about 40,000 Mongols, consists of autonomous units, or banners. The most important of these is the Ala Shan Banner, set up in 1949 with Tingyüanying as its capital; its people are chiefly the Alashan Eleut (Ölöt) tribe. To the west, on the Etsin Gol, the Etsin Banner is composed of the Torgot tribe. PAUL YUNG

NINIAN, SAINT, died about 432, British missionary, was born in Cumberland and lived for a number of years in Rome, where he was consecrated bishop. He established his diocese at Withern or Whithorn in Galloway, Scotland, and from that center worked to convert the southern Picts. His feast day is September 16.

NIN Y CASTELLANO, JOAQUÍN, 1879–1949, Cuban pianist, was born in Havana, of Spanish parents, and studied and taught for a time at the Schola Cantorum, Paris. After 1939 he lived in Havana. In piano concerts throughout Europe and South America, Nin presented both the works of early keyboard composers and those of contemporary Spaniards. His compositions include *Quatre chants d'Espagne* (1937) and *Rapsodie Ibérienne* (1930) for violin and pianoforte; and *Chaîne de valses* (1929) for piano. He edited collections of early music, including 33 *Pianoforte Sonatas by Old Spanish Composers* (2 vols. 1925) and 7 *Old Spanish Picaresque Songs* (1926).

NIO. See CYCLADES.

NIOBE, in Greek legend, was the daughter of Tantalus and the wife of Amphion, king of Thebes. She had many children (12 to 20 according to various accounts) and haughtily boasted of them to the goddess Leto, who had given birth only to Apollo and Artemis. To punish Niobe, Apollo and Artemis slew her children. Moved by pity, the gods transformed Niobe into a stone on Mount Sipylus in Lydia, in which form she wept forever. The story of Niobe was the subject of a group of statues attributed to the Greek sculptor, Scopas (fourth century B.C.). Roman copies are in the Uffizi at Florence.

NIOBIUM, formerly columbium, a rare metallic element with an atomic number of 41, atomic weight of 92.91, and a specific gravity of 8.7. Niobium, symbol Nb, is a hard, gray metal with a boiling point of 2415°C (4379°F) and a melting point of 3300°C (5972°F). Most of its stable compounds show a valence of 5, the pentoxide Nb_2O_5 and the pentchloride $NbCl_5$ being typical; the less stable compounds show a valence of 3. The metal is active at high temperatures, reacting with all nonmetallic elements except the rare gases, and having a special affinity for oxygen and nitrogen. These properties make niobium valuable in producing alloys, especially steel alloys, although not until the 1950's had sufficient quantities of the ore been discovered and mined to make commercial use feasible. Niobium resists tarnishing and corrosion at high temperatures, and small amounts of it are added to stainless steel to increase corrosion resistance and to make the steel stronger and more easily welded. Niobium is also added to alloys used in making the blades of gas turbines and jet engines to provide strength to the parts while exposed to the high operating temperatures.

Niobium was discovered in 1801 by Charles Hatchett, an English chemist, who named the element columbium. In 1864 C. W. Blomstrand became the first to prepare the metal. Niobium ores, mainly columbite, are found in Nigeria, The Congo, Canada, Malagasy, and Brazil.

NIOBRARA RIVER, SE Wyoming and N Nebraska; rises in Niobrara County, Wyoming, flows E into and across Nebraska, and enters the Missouri River at Niobrara; length about 430 miles. The Box Butte Dam irrigates the area near Marsland, Neb.

NIORT, town, W France, capital of Deux-Sèvres Department; on the Sèvre Niortaise River; 225 miles SW of Paris. Industries include flour milling and the manufacture of leather goods (especially gloves and shoes), metal goods, textiles, and pharmaceuticals. It is a center of fruit and vegetable production. Niort grew up around a castle built in 1155 by Henry II of England. In 1226 it was captured by Louis VIII of France. In 1360 it was restored to the English by the Peace of Brétigny, but was returned to France in 1373. Niort was a Protestant stronghold in the sixteenth and seventeenth centuries, and suffered greatly during the religious wars (1562–98). It was the birthplace of Madame de Maintenon, one of the mistresses of Louis XIV. Pop. (1954) 33,167.

NIPIGON, LAKE, Canada, W central Ontario, 30 miles N of Lake Superior. It is about 65 miles long and 45 miles wide and is dotted with many islands, including Kelvin, Geikie, and Shakespeare. Lake Nipigon is drained into Lake Superior by the Nipigon River.

NIPISSING, LAKE, Canada, SE central Ontario, NE of Lake Huron, nearly midway between Lake Huron and the headwaters of the Ottawa River. About 50 miles long, the lake extends westward from North Bay on the northeastern shore. It is separated by a short portage from Turtle Lake on the east and is drained from the SW by the French River, which flows into Georgian Bay. Lake Nipissing was once part of the route followed by fur traders traveling west from Montreal.

NIRVANA, the state of perfect peace and enlightenment that is the goal of Buddhism. It is the perfect condition a Buddhist attains when he has conquered his passions and is able to view the sins and turmoil of the world with calm detachment. To attain nirvana the Buddhist is required to live—not merely to believe—the teachings of Buddha (see BUDDHISM). Nirvana is not synonymous with either the Christian ideal of a future life after death or the theory that beyond the grave lies annihilation. It is a state which the Buddhist may attain in this life by advancement through the successive stages of Buddha's teachings.

NIŠ, town, E Yugoslavia, Serbian People's Republic; on the Nisava River; 130 miles SE of Belgrade. It is an important railway junction, with connections to Belgrade, Sofia, and Salonika. The Turkish part of the town is on the north bank of the river and the Serbian town is on the south bank. The Turkish quarter contains several mosques and an old fort; the Serbian quarter is more modern, and houses government buildings and most of the industrial establishments. Coal fields near Niš have facilitated the development of manufacturing, and the town has railway repair shops; engine, motor, and vehicle works; iron foundries; and flour mills.

Niš was known in Roman times as Naissus, and was the birthplace of the Roman Emperor Constantine the Great. The Goths were defeated in the vicinity of the town by Claudius II in 268. From the ninth to the twelfth century Niš fell successively to the Bulgarian, Hungarian, Byzantine, and Serbian empires. In 1456 it fell to the Turks, who held it for three centuries, except during the period from 1689 to 1737 when it was under Austrian occupation. The Serbians captured the town from the Turks during the Russo-Turkish War, 1877–78, and Niš was permanently awarded to Serbia by the Treaty of Berlin (1878). After the outbreak of World War I it was briefly the capital of Serbia, following the occupation of Belgrade by the Austrians. The town was occupied by the Bulgarians from 1915 to 1918. In April, 1941, it was taken by the Germans, who were expelled by the Yugoslav, Russian, and Bulgarian forces in October, 1944. (For population, see Balkan States map in Atlas.) THEODORE SHABAD

NISHAPUR, or Neyshapur, town, NE Iran, in the Ninth Province, near the Kuh-i-Binalud Mountain Range; 43 miles W of Meshed, with which it is connected by a railroad and a highway. Nishapur is a trade center for an agricultural area that produces cotton and wheat. Its industries include cotton ginning, cottonseed oil milling, tanning, rug weaving, and pottery making. Some 30 miles northwest of the town are famed turquoise mines. Nishapur was the birthplace and contains the tombs of the Persian poets Omar Khayyám and Ferid ed-Din Attar. The town was founded during the third and fourth centuries by kings of the Sassanid Dynasty. It was one of the important centers of Khurasan until it was demolished by two earthquakes and a Mongol invasion in the thirteenth century. (For population, see Near and Middle East map in Atlas.)

NISHINOMIYA, city, Japan, central Honshu, Hyogo Prefecture; on Osaka Bay; 10 miles NW of Osaka. Nishinomiya is part of the heavily industrialized Osaka-Kōbe metropolitan area. Its main products are sake, beer, vegetable oil, foodstuffs, metal products, machinery, cosmetics, and chemicals. Its port has modern facilities to handle freight. The city is also famous for its hot springs. During World War II, Nishinomiya manufactured airplane parts; it was partly destroyed by aerial bombings. (For population, see Japan map in Atlas.)

NISUS, in Greek mythology, king of the city of Nisa. During the siege of Nisa by the Cretan king, Minos, Nisus' daughter Scylla became enamored of Minos, cut from her father's head the lock of hair on which his life depended, and offered it to Minos in return for his love. Minos accepted her offer and captured the city. According to some versions of the legend Nisus died when the lock was removed; according to others he only lost his throne.

NITER, a mineral of the nitrate class usually appearing as a thin incrustation or in crystalline form. It is white and translucent and has a vitreous luster. Niter, commonly called saltpeter, is a potassium nitrate with the formula KNO_3. Its hardness is 2, its specific gravity 2.09 to 2.14. The mineral is used as a source of nitrogen compounds and is usually found as an incrustation of soils in hot dry climates such as are found in Spain, Italy, Egypt, Iran, and India. See NITROGEN, Chemistry, *Nitrates.*

NITEROI, city, SE Brazil, capital of Rio de Janeiro State; on Guanabara Bay; 5 miles E of Rio de Janeiro, of which it is a residential suburb and with which it is connected by ferry. Niterói is a popular bathing resort. It is the seat of colleges of nursing, law, pharmacy and dentistry, veterinary medicine, economics, philosophy, and medicine. It is a railroad terminal and has shipbuilding, textile, and food-processing industries. Its manufactures also include flat glass, matches, tobacco products, furniture, chemicals, and pharmaceuticals. (For population, see Brazil map in Atlas.)

NITHARD, 795–?844, Frankish historian, illegitimate son of St. Angilbert and of Bertha, daughter of Charlemagne. Nithard wrote historical accounts of the division of the Carolingian Empire among the sons of Louis the Pious. Nithard served Charles the Bald, who won control of the western part of the empire. See CAROLINGIANS.

NITRA, town, E Czechoslovakia, in Zapadoslovensky Region, about 45 miles ENE of Bratislava. The city is an agricultural processing center. A ninth-century castle and a cathedral dating in part from the thirteenth century are the noted structures. Nitra was the capital of Nitra Region from 1949 until the territorial reorganization in 1960. (For population see Czechoslovakia map in Atlas.)

NITRATION, the chemical process that employs the reaction of nitric acid, or one of its derivatives, on an organic compound to introduce one or more nitro, $(-NO_2)$ groups into the organic compound. The mechanism of nitration is believed to depend on the formation of the nitronium ion, NO_2^+. A strongly acid solution favors the formation of this ion. Thus the greater effectiveness in nitration of such reagents as fuming nitric acid, a mixture of nitric and sulfuric acids, when compared with nitric acid alone is believed to be caused by the fact that such a mixture contains a great concentration of nitronium ions. The sulfuric acid, in addition, acts as a dehydrating agent and tends to remove any excess water. A simple example of nitration using nitric acid as reagent is:

$$\underset{\text{ethane}}{C_2H_6} + \underset{\text{nitric acid}}{HNO_3} \longrightarrow \underset{\text{ethyl group}}{C_2H_5^+} + \underset{\text{hydrogen ion}}{H^+} + \underset{\text{hydroxyl ion}}{OH^-} +$$

$$\underset{\text{nitronium ion}}{NO_2^+} \longrightarrow \underset{\text{nitroethane}}{C_2H_5NO_2} + \underset{\text{water}}{HOH}$$

In general, a nitro group will tend to attach itself to a tertiary carbon atom, H—C— (with single bonds above and below the C) (one to which only one hydrogen atom has been attached), rather than to a secondary carbon atom, H—C—H (with single bonds above and below the C) (one that has been directly united with two hydrogen atoms). It tends also to attach itself to a secondary carbon atom in preference to a primary carbon atom,

```
   H
   |
H—C—H
   |
```

(one that has three hydrogen atoms attached). It is easier, furthermore, to introduce the first nitro group into a compound than it is to introduce a succeeding group. For example toluene, $C_6H_5CH_3$, may be nitrated to nitrotoluene at a temperature of 30°C (86°F); but a temperature of 50°C (122°F) must be used to nitrate the nitrotoluene to dinitrotoluene, and a temperature of 100°C (212°F) to nitrate the dinitrotoluene to trinitrotoluene.

Nitro compounds are rather easily reduced to amines, and are often produced as intermediates in the production of amines. Almost all the nitrobenzene produced, for example, is converted to aniline. The addition of a nitro group to a compound frequently affects a neighboring group; thus nitrophenol is more acidic than phenol, and the introduction of a nitro group into chlorobenzene results in a compound in which the chlorine is much more reactive and can be easily replaced by other groups.

Nitro compounds tend to be oxidizing agents; compounds that contain two or more nitro groups such as trinitrotoluene (TNT) and picric acid (trinitrophenol) may be highly explosive. In addition to their use as explosives and as chemical intermediates, nitro compounds are employed in dyes, in chemical analyses, in perfume, and as solvents. Nitro compounds often are poisonous and trichloronitromethane (chloropicrin) has been used as a fumigant and soil disinfectant.

NITRIC ACID, a colorless, strong mineral acid widely used in industry. The pure acid, whose chemical formula is HNO_3, freezes at −41.6°C (−42.9°F), boils at 83°C (181°F), and is 1.5 times as heavy as water. Nitric acid and water are miscible in all proportions. A mixture of nitric acid and water when heated has a boiling point that changes until the solution contains about 68 per cent nitric acid; at this composition the two liquids form a constant-boiling mixture that has a boiling point of 120°C (248°F). (See AZEOTROPIC MIXTURE.) Although pure nitric acid is colorless, the concentrated acid usually seen in the laboratory is somewhat yellow. The color is caused by the presence of nitrogen dioxide, NO_2, that is formed from nitric acid under light or heat: $4HNO_3 \rightarrow 4NO_2 + 2H_2O + O_2$. To minimize this reaction, nitric acid is kept in amber glass bottles.

Chemical Reactions. Nitric acid takes part in three different types of reaction: it may act as an acid, as an oxidizing agent, and as a nitrating agent. Thus nitric acid, like any other acid, may react with metallic oxides or hydroxides to form salts: $MgO + 2HNO_3 \rightarrow H_2O + Mg(NO_3)_2$. It may also react with metals to yield hydrogen; however, unless the acid is highly diluted, little or no hydrogen is actually obtained because any hydrogen that is formed tends to be immediately oxidized by the remaining acid.

Nitric acid is a powerful oxidizing agent. Thus it can oxidize active metals such as zinc, inactive metals such as silver, nonmetallic elements such as sulfur and carbon, and many organic and inorganic compounds. The oxidizing action of the acid is increased by the action of oxides of nitrogen. The chemical reactions that take place may vary with the temperature and the concentration of the acid. For example, dilute nitric acid reacts with hydrogen sulfide to give free sulfur, but the concentrated acid oxidizes hydrogen sulfide to sulfuric acid. When nitric acid acts as an oxidizing agent, the nitrogen products formed must have a lower valence than the nitrogen in nitric acid (see NITROGEN; OXIDATION AND REDUCTION), and the nature of the products also depends on the conditions of the reaction. For example, when zinc reacts with nitric acid, zinc nitrate is always produced, but other reaction products may include ammonium nitrate, NH_4NO_3; free nitrogen, N_2; or nitrous oxide, N_2O. Similarly, when dilute nitric acid reacts with copper, nitric oxide is produced; but when concentrated nitric acid reacts with copper, nitrogen dioxide is found: $3Cu + 8HNO_3$(dilute) $\rightarrow 3Cu(NO_3)_2 + 2NO + 4H_2O$; but $Cu + 4HNO_3$ (concentrated) $\rightarrow Cu(NO_3)_2 + 2NO_2 + 2H_2O$.

As a nitrating agent, nitric acid acts to introduce the nitro (NO_2) group into organic compounds. See NITRATION.

Physiological Effects. Nitric acid produces yellow stains in contact with the skin. If not removed promptly by washing with water, the acid may cause painful burns. Nitric acid, its vapors, and its fumes—the nitrogen oxides—are also harmful to the mucous membranes and the digestive system, and particularly dangerous because often when they are first inhaled only mild discomfort results and more serious symptoms may not appear for several hours. Inhalation of the fumes may cause death.

MANUFACTURE

Originally the alchemists prepared nitric acid by heating niter (saltpeter, KNO_3) or soda niter (Chile saltpeter, $NaNO_3$) with sulfuric acid, and this method is still convenient for the preparation of 100 per cent nitric acid: $NaNO_3 + H_2SO_4 \rightarrow NaHSO_4 + HNO_3 \uparrow$. The sodium acid sulfate formed serves as the starting material for the manufacture of sodium sulfate.

Arc Process. The arc process, in which air is passed through powerful electric arcs to induce a reaction between the oxygen and nitrogen of the air, is little used in the United States. In the arc process the nitrogen and oxygen combine to form nitric oxide which is immediately oxidized to nitrogen dioxide. The nitrogen dioxide then reacts with water to form nitric acid.

Ostwald Process. About 90 per cent of all the nitric acid manufactured in the United States is produced by the Ostwald process, which oxidizes ammonia to nitric acid. The process was developed by Wilhelm Ostwald in the early part of the twentieth century, about the time that Fritz Haber perfected the Haber process for the manufacture of ammonia. (See AMMONIA, *Synthesis*.) There are two main variations of this process: one is carried out at ordinary air pressure, the other at a pressure of about 100 pounds per square inch. In both variations a mixture of about 9 parts air and 1 part ammonia is passed over a rhodium-platinum catalyst at a temperature of about 1000°C (1800°F), and nitric oxide is formed: $4NH_3 + 5O_2 \rightarrow 4NO + 6H_2O$. The nitric oxide promptly reacts with more oxygen of the air to give nitrogen dioxide: $2NO + O_2 \rightarrow 2NO_2$. The gases are passed through a spray of water in one or more absorption towers, where nitric acid is formed: $3NO_2 + H_2O \rightarrow 2HNO_3 + NO$. The nitric oxide is again oxidized to nitrogen dioxide when it passes up the absorption tower with excess oxygen from the air, and reacts with more water to yield more nitric acid. A nitric acid solution containing about 60 per cent nitric acid is produced by this process; the concentration can be increased to about 68 per cent by distillation. Customarily nitric acid has been marketed in three concentrations: that with specific gravity 1.330 or 36°Bé (Baumé), containing 52.3 per cent nitric acid; that with specific gravity 1.381 or 40°Bé, containing 61.4 per cent nitric acid; and that with specific gravity 1.408 or 42°Bé, containing 67.2° nitric acid.

Wisconsin Thermal Process, developed in 1947, produces highly concentrated nitric acid. Unlike the niter-sulfuric acid and Ostwald processes, the Wisconsin, or pebble-bed, process, is independent of any source of nitrogen other than that of the atmosphere. Essentially, nitrogen is oxidized by oxygen of the air upon heating for a fraction of a second to about 4000°F during its passage through heated pebble beds. Water is then removed from the mixture and the nitric oxide formed is catalytically oxidized to nitrogen dioxide. Fluidized silica gel is used to aid in the separation of the nitrogen dioxide and the removal of water. The nitrogen dioxide is then converted to nitric acid.

Other methods that have been used to obtain a highly concentrated acid include the distillation of the nitric acid solution in the presence of sulfuric acid, the use of dilute nitric acid rather than water to convert the nitrogen dioxide to nitric acid, and the oxidation of ammonia by pure oxygen rather than air.

Fuming Nitric Acid contains various nitrogen oxides and has a concentration greater than 86 per cent; red fuming nitric acid contains especially large amounts of nitrogen dioxide. Fuming nitric acid may be prepared by passing nitrogen dioxide through nitric acid, by adding a small amount of a reducing agent to highly concentrated nitric acid, or by distilling nitric acid with sulfuric acid.

USES

The explosives and fertilizer industries use the greatest volume of nitric acid. (See EXPLOSIVE; FERTILIZER.) In the fertilizer industry it is used largely in the production of ammonium nitrate, NH_4NO_3, sometimes in the manufacture of various types of phosphate fertilizers. In the explosives industry nitric acid is used to manufacture inorganic nitrates such as potassium nitrate, the oxidizing agent of black gunpowder; organic nitrates such as glyceryl trinitrate, or nitroglycerin, the active ingredient of dynamite; and organic nitro compounds such as picric acid and trinitrotoluene (TNT). Because of its oxidizing properties, nitric acid is also well suited for use in rocket and missile fuels.

Nitric acid is used in the metal-processing industry for pickling to remove scale and surface oxides, and in the passivating of stainless alloy sheets to dissolve iron particles from the stainless surface. For many years nitric acid has played an important part in the textile industry, particularly before World War II when cellulose nitrates were the basis of rayon manufacture. That process was later changed, but nitric acid is used in the production of some synthethic fibers. Cellulose nitrates are used extensively in the production of lacquers for automobile and furniture finishes. They are also used for the plastic coating of fabrics such as artificial leather. Nitric is one of the most important acids used in analytical and research chemistry throughout the laboratories of the world.

Production of nitric acid in the United States rose from less than 100,000 tons in 1935 to more than 3.0 million tons in 1960.

NITRIDING, a process for producing a hard surface on steel, using nitrogen as the hardening agent. The process is used extensively for the surface hardening or casehardening of machined steel parts that have been previously heat-treated. Successful nitriding is usually accomplished on a special class of alloy steels known as nitralloys, which contain 0.85 to 1.2 per cent of aluminum and varying combinations of chromium, molybdenum, and vanadium, for which nitrogen has a strong affinity. Nitriding is also used for casehardening some of the chrome-nickel stainless steels and medium alloys of the chrome-molybdenum-nickel group.

The machined parts to be nitrided are first stress-relieved; they are then loaded into a gastight batch or continuous furnace into which ammonia is introduced under pressure. The furnace temperature is kept between about 930°F and 1100°F for a long period of time. Hardening to a depth of 0.02 inch is imparted to an average nitralloy specimen in approximately 25 hours.

Nitriding imparts a harder surface to alloy steels than does any other process known, without objectional distortion and growth and without the necessity for further heat treatment of the nitrided parts. The process is widely used for such parts as piston pins, in which great wear resistance and retention of hardness at elevated temperatures are demanded. Nitriding also improves the corrosion resistance of steels. See CASEHARDENING; ANTICORROSION PROTECTION, *Surface alloying;* HEAT-TREATING.

NITRILE, an organic compound that may be regarded as either an ammonia derivative or a derivative of hydrogen cyanide, HCN. It is characterized by the formula R–C≡N, where R may stand for an alkyl group such as the ethyl group (C_2H_5) or for an aromatic group such as the phenyl group (C_6H_5). Nitriles may be prepared by several means, including the dehydration of an amide and the reaction of an organic halide with a metal cyanide. For example, methyl iodide reacts with sodium cyanide to yield acetonitrile and sodium iodide: $CH_3I + NaCN \rightarrow CH_3CN + NaI$. This method of preparing a nitrile may be used to add a carbon atom to a carbon chain, and frequently is an intermediate step in the preparation of other compounds. Nitriles are highly reactive and are rather easily hydrolized to amides and acids, converted to aldehydes and ketones, and reduced to amines. Nitriles are isomeric with isonitriles, compounds that have the type formula RNC, in which the nitrogen is joined to the end carbon as well as to one of the carbons contained in the R group. See ORGANIC CHEMISTRY, *Amines and Amides.*

NITRITE. See NITROGEN, Chemistry, *Nitrites.*

NITROBENZENE, or oil of mirbane, an organic compound obtained by treating benzene, C_6H_6, with a mixture of nitric and sulfuric acids and purifying it by washing in water and by distillation. The compound, which has a formula of $C_6H_5NO_2$, is a pale yellow liquid with a strong characteristic odor comparable to that of bitter almonds—and is poisonous. Nitrobenzene is 1.89 times as heavy as water and has a boiling point of 210.9°C (428°F) and a melting point of 5.7°C (42°F). Although insoluble in water, nitrobenzene is a good solvent itself, and is used as such and as a mild oxidizing agent industrially. It is also used in black shoe polishes, but it finds its most important use in the form of analine—to which it is reduced industrially with scrap iron and hydrochloric acid—in the manufacture of dyestuffs and pharmaceuticals.

NITROGEN, the odorless, colorless, tasteless, and rather inert gas that constitutes about four-fifths of the earth's atmosphere. Specifically, nitrogen makes up about 78 per cent of the air by volume, a little more than 75 per cent by weight. It is a nonmetallic chemical element (symbol N) that occurs in the form of diatomic molecules (formula N_2). Its atomic weight is 14.008, its atomic number is 7, and it is in period 2, group VA, of the periodic table. (See PERIODIC TABLE.) Two isotopes of nitrogen occur in nature. Neither is radioactive and the lighter isotope, N-14, accounts for 99.64 of all nitrogen atoms. Although nitrogen is a gas at ordinary temperatures, it may be cooled to a liquid that boils at −195.8°C (−320.4°F) and freezes at −209.8°C (−345.6°F). The density of the gas at standard pressure and temperature is 1.2506 grams per liter, a little less than that of air; liquid nitrogen near its boiling point has a density of 0.808 grams per cubic centimeter and solid nitrogen at −252°C (−422°F) has a density of 1.206 grams per cubic centimeter.

History. Daniel Rutherford (1749–1819) is usually credited with discovering nitrogen in 1772. The element apparently was also discovered independently about the same time by Karl Wilhelm Scheele (1742–86), Joseph Priestley (1733–1804), and Henry Cavendish (1731–1810), all of whom were working on the properties of air and other gases. Antoine-Laurent Lavoisier suggested the name *azote* (without life) for the newly discovered element, because its most striking property seemed to be the fact that air from which the oxygen had been removed by burning some substance or by other means (and from which the carbon dioxide had likewise been removed by absorption with an alkali) no longer would support life. Although the French still call the element azote and although the root of that word has persisted in such terms as *azo* and *hydrazoic*, the name *nitrogen* (niter former) was adopted by the English-speaking peoples because nitrogen is a constituent of niter and because if in the presence of potash an electric spark is passed through air to which excess oxygen has been added, potassium nitrate results.

Nitrogen that has been obtained from air by the removal of oxygen, water vapor, and carbon dioxide still contains argon and other noble gases as impurities. Although Cavendish had hinted at the possibility that a little more than 1 per cent of the air might not consist of the gases known in his time, no definitive evidence was obtained until John William Strutt, 3rd Baron Rayleigh (1842–1919) conducted some highly accurate density determinations on nitrogen obtained from air and on nitrogen obtained by the decomposition of ammonia, and found that nitrogen from ammonia was distinctly lighter than that from air. Rayleigh and Sir William Ramsay (1852–1916) co-operated in further research that resulted in the discovery of argon and other noble gases.

CHEMISTRY

Although nitrogen is nonreactive at ordinary temperatures, it can be made to react with other substances either by raising the temperature or by electrical activation, particularly by passing a glow discharge through the gas at reduced pressure. After such a discharge, the nitrogen itself retains a greenish glow for some time, and is highly reactive even after its glow has disappeared. Some bacteria are able to convert atmospheric nitrogen into nitrogen compounds at ordinary temperatures and without the presence of an electric discharge. Once a nitrogen compound has been formed, it can easily be converted into some other nitrogen compound, and nitrogen is found to exhibit a bewildering number of real and apparent valences. See VALENCE.

Nitrogen Oxides in which the nitrogen exhibits valences of 1 to 5 are known, and there are probably two additional nitrogen oxides in which the nitrogen has an apparent valence of 6. The nitrogen oxides include nitrous oxide or laughing gas, N_2O; nitric oxide, NO; nitrogen sesquioxide, or dinitrogen trioxide, often known as nitrogen trioxide, N_2O_3; nitrogen dioxide, NO_2; nitrogen tetroxide, N_2O_4, often derived from the polymerization of nitrogen dioxide; and nitrogen pentoxide, N_2O_5. The oxides in which the nitrogen seems to have a valence of 6 are nitrogen trioxide, NO_3, and nitrogen hexaoxide, N_2O_6. Nitrogen sesquioxide and nitrogen pentoxide are the anhydrides of nitrous acid, HNO_2, and nitric acid, HNO_3, respectively, but the three oxides of most industrial importance are nitrous oxide, nitric oxide, and nitrogen dioxide.

Nitrous oxide may be prepared by heating ammonium nitrate. Since nitrous oxide breaks up readily into nitrogen and oxygen, it supports combustion and will cause a glowing splinter to burst into flame. See NITROUS OXIDE.

Nitric oxide is unexpectedly stable; a piece of phosphorus that has just begun to burn can be extinguished by thrusting it into a jar of nitric oxide. If the phosphorus has been burning vigorously, however —that is, if it is at a sufficiently high temperature—it will decompose the nitric oxide and continue to burn. In the laboratory nitric oxide may conveniently be prepared by treating copper with dilute nitric acid. Commercially nitric oxide is obtained by the oxidation of ammonia or by direct reaction with oxygen. See NITRIC ACID, Manufacture.

Nitric oxide readily unites with the oxygen of the air to form nitrogen dioxide, NO_2. Nitrogen dioxide is a reddish-brown gas with an unpleasant odor. As it is cooled its color fades and it is gradually converted into the colorless nitrogen tetroxide, N_2O_4. In the laboratory it may be prepared by treating copper with concentrated nitric acid or by heating a heavy metal nitrate. For example, lead nitrate yields lead monoxide, nitrogen dioxide, and oxygen: $2Pb(NO_3)_2 \rightarrow 2PbO + 4NO_2 + O_2$. On a large scale, nitrogen dioxide is produced by exposing nitric oxide to the oxygen of the air.

All the nitrogen oxides can act as oxidizing agents, and all except nitrogen pentoxide can act as reducing agents. They form various oxyacids of nitrogen. By far the most important of these is nitric acid. Nitrous acid is relatively unimportant as an acid, but is useful as the parent compound of the nitrites, or salts of nitrous acid.

Nitrogen-Hydrogen Compounds. Commercially the most important compound of nitrogen and hydrogen is ammonia, NH_3. Other nitrogen-hydrogen compounds include hydrazine, $NH_2 \cdot NH_2$ (see HYDRAZINE) and hydrazoic acid, HN_3, an unstable compound that is readily oxidized to nitrogen or reduced to hydrazine or ammonia. Hydroxylamine, NH_2OH, may be considered a compound in which a hydroxyl group has been substituted for one of the amine groups. It is a base that has about the same strength as hydrazine and ammonia, and, like them, forms salts with acids such as hydrochloric acid.

Nitrides. The nitrogen oxides and the hydrogen-nitrogen and halogen-nitrogen compounds are nitrides; generally, however, only metallic nitrides are called by that name. The metallic nitrides fall into three general classes: those in which the bond between the metal and the nitrogen is ionic, so that the crystal actually consists of metal ions and nitride ions; those in which the metal and the nitrogen share electrons by covalent bonds; and those in which the bond between the metal and nitrogen most closely resembles a metallic one. The ionic nitrides, formed especially by the alkali and alkaline earth metals, are unique in that they probably are the only compounds that contain a simple negative trivalent ion, the N^{-3} ion. The covalent nitrides generally are formed between nitrogen and a metal of the boron group, and resemble carbon in structure. One of them, boron nitride, has attracted considerable attention because by the use of high temperature and pressure it has been possible to convert this compound from a graphite-like to a diamond-like structure. Boron nitride that has been treated in this fashion is harder than diamond and is known as borazon. Metallic nitrides in which the bond resembles a metallic one may be made by heating in nitrogen certain metal powders such as those of molybdenum, scandium, or manganese. These nitrides resemble metals in their conductivity and metallic luster, but tend to be much harder and have much higher melting points than the corresponding metals.

Nitrites. Metal nitrites may be formed indirectly by the oxidation of ammonia and directly by the reduction of a metallic nitrate. They contain the NO_2^- ion and are often used as oxidizing agents, although they themselves can be oxidized, particularly in an alkaline medium. They are also chemical intermediates, and some of the organic nitrites are used in medicine.

Nitrates. Despite the increasing importance of anhydrous ammonia and other nitrogen materials, the inorganic nitrates are probably still the most important inorganic nitrogen compounds and are essential to the present-day practice of agriculture. They are the salts of nitric acid and contain the nitrate ion NO_3^-. All known metal nitrates are soluble in water. Nitrates are good oxidizing agents and often act as explosives. They decompose on heating, the products depending on the type of nitrate and on the presence and kind of reducing agent. If ammonium nitrate is gently heated, it decomposes into nitrous oxide and water: $NH_4NO_3 \rightarrow N_2O + 2H_2O$. If an alkali nitrate such as sodium nitrate is heated, the corresponding nitrite is produced: $2NaNO_3 \rightarrow 2NaNO_2 + O_2$. If an inactive metal nitrate is heated, it decomposes into the metal oxide, oxygen, and nitrogen dioxide: $2Cu(NO_3)_2 \rightarrow 2CuO + 4NO_2 + O_2$.

Some nitrates are obtained from natural mineral sources, such as Chile saltpeter (sodium nitrate); much of the nitrogen in the soil is continuously produced by the nitrogen-fixing bacteria, and it is probable that the deposits of natural nitrates were originally also obtained from this source. Most of the nitrates produced by chemical means, however, are derived from atmospheric nitrogen and are obtained by the action of nitric acid on metal oxides, hydroxides, or carbonates. Sometimes the finished acid is used for this purpose, at other times the dissolved nitrogen oxides react directly with the metallic compounds.

Other Compounds. Nitrogen forms compounds with many other elements. Among the more important compounds are calcium cyanamide, used as a fertilizer, and the metal cyanides, containing the CN group, used in metallurgy. Besides being a part of many inorganic compounds, nitrogen also exists as a part of many organic compounds, such as the amides, the amines, the amino acids, the azo compounds, the nitro compounds, and the esters of nitrous and nitric acids. The first organic compound ever synthesized from an inorganic compound was a nitrogen compound (see UREA), and nitrogen is a constituent of all proteins.

Nitrogen Fixation is the conversion of atmospheric nitrogen into nitrogen compounds. (See AMMONIA; NITRIC ACID.) Nitrogen fixation by the aid of lightning is chemically analogous to nitrogen fixation by the electric arc process. A tremendous amount of nitrogen, however, is fixed biologically. See NITROGEN CYCLE.

PRODUCTION AND USES

If very pure nitrogen is desired it may be produced by the decomposition of ammonium nitrite or other nitrogen compounds; but since these compounds were made from atmospheric nitrogen in the first place, this method of preparation is not desirable except for special cases. Most nitrogen produced is made by removing the water vapor, carbon dioxide, oxygen, and at times the noble gases from the air. The oxygen may be removed chemically but is more frequently removed by first liquefying the air and then separating the various gases by means of fractional distillation, a method that supplies not only nitrogen but also oxygen and the noble gases. The nitrogen may be used as an element to provide an inert atmosphere, as in light bulbs, thermometers, and some canned foods; or it may be converted into nitrogen compounds, particularly ammonia and ammonium salts, nitric acid and the nitrates, and the organic nitrogen compounds.

Nitrogen is one of the elements necessary to all plant and animal life, and the nitrogen balance—the amount of nitrogen assimilated by the body as against the amount of nitrogen eliminated—is an important factor in maintaining life. See AMINO ACIDS; CHEMISTRY; ELEMENT; EXPLOSIVE; FERTILIZER; METABOLISM; NUTRITION; PROTEIN.

BIBLIOG.-E. F. Degering and others, *Outline of Organic Nitrogen Compounds* (ed. 1950); N. V. Sidgwick, *Chemical Elements and Their Compounds* (2 vols. 1950); D. N. Prianshikov, *Nitrogen in the Life of Plants* (1951); Air Pollution Foundation, *Catalytic Decomposition of Nitric Oxide* (1957).

NITROGEN CYCLE, a series of chemical reactions that change the nitrogen of the air into inorganic and organic compounds, make it a part of plant and animal proteins, and eventually decompose the compounds into free atmospheric nitrogen. The processes that incorporate nitrogen into compounds are known as nitrogen fixation and nitrification and those that break down such compounds, as denitrification. The nitrogen cycle is essential to plant and animal life because nitrogen is part of all proteins and because most living things are unable to utilize atmospheric nitrogen directly.

Nitrogen is converted into compounds by lightning that induces the union of the oxygen and the nitrogen of the air, by chemical synthesis, and by bacterial action. Lightning causes the formation of nitrogen oxides that are converted into nitrites and nitrates; chemical synthesis is used to produce either ammonia or nitrogen oxides; bacterial action may cause the formation of ammonia or of nitrites and nitrates. Some bacteria live free in the soil; others have a symbiotic relationship with legumes, which are therefore often grown to enhance soil fertility.

Part of the ammonia formed may be decomposed by bacteria and revert to nitrogen. Other bacteria, and to a lesser extent chemical synthesis, convert the rest of the ammonia into nitrites and nitrates. Some of these compounds may again be broken down into ammonia or atmospheric nitrogen, but a large fraction of them is used by growing plants and is incorporated into plant proteins. These plants may be eaten by animals and form animal proteins, they may decay into ammonia, or they may be decomposed directly into atmospheric nitrogen by bacterial action and burning. Similarly the animal proteins may be oxidized to nitrates and nitrites, they may decompose into ammonia, they may be converted to atmospheric nitrogen by bacterial decomposition and decay, or they may be converted into nitrogen waste compounds, such as urea, that are later converted to nitrogen or ammonia. See BACTERIA, *Bacteria in Soil and Silage;* NITROGEN; NITRIC ACID, Manufacture.

NITROGEN MUSTARD, a powerful local vesicant, or blistering agent, that affects all exposed tissue, including the eyes, skin, and respiratory tract. As a tertiary amine it is a relatively stable oily substance; the crystalline form reacts readily when dissolved in water (see AMINE). Nitrogen mustard is the nitrogen analogue of sulfur mustard, or mustard gas, and much of the early research with the substance, especially in World War II, concerned its use as a poisonous gas for chemical warfare.

From the skin or respiratory tract nitrogen mustard rapidly gains access to the circulatory system and is carried throughout the body. Its most important action as a drug is to inhibit mitosis, or cell division, especially in bone marrow and lymphoid tissue. Nitrogen mustard is sometimes used to cause regression of diseases characterized by an abnormal increase in the number of certain cells, such as Hodgkin's disease and chronic leukemia (see HODGKIN'S DISEASE; LEUKEMIA). Therapeutically nitrogen mustard is administered intravenously in aqueous solution—commonly in the form of mechlorethamine. Great care must be exercised in its use because it has access to and may damage normal tissue. Like X ray, nitrogen mustard can produce changes in genes (see GENE). Large doses of nitrogen mustard affect the central nervous system and may cause death.

NITROGLYCERIN, or glyceryl trinitrate, $C_3H_5(NO_3)_3$, an organic chemical compound derived from glycerin, $C_3H_5(OH)_3$. Nitroglycerin is a colorless liquid when pure; otherwise it is pale yellow. It has a sweet taste but is poisonous. Nitroglycerin has a specific gravity of 1.6, and is practically insoluble in water. The liquid freezes at 8°C (46.4°F) and evaporates upon gentle heating. It is not easily set afire but will explode when heated to 180°C (356°F). Nitroglycerin is manufactured commercially by adding a glycerin to a concentrated mixture of nitric and sulfuric acids. When the nitration of the glycerin has been completed, the mixture is run off into a vessel and allowed to stand until the separation of the nitroglycerin is complete. After washing, the nitroglycerin is suitable for industrial use.

Nitroglycerin's most important use is as an explosive. It is rarely employed by itself because of its tendency to detonate upon the slightest jarring; it is usually combined with a porous material such as silica, thus becoming a relatively safe and powerful explosive which ordinarily can be set off only by a detonator. Alfred Nobel (1833–96) discovered the method of insuring the safe handling of nitroglycerin, thus opening the way for its extensive use. It is also combined with guncotton to form blasting gelatin. (See EXPLOSIVE.) Since nitroglycerin quickly relaxes the blood vessels supplying the heart when taken internally, it is used medically to relieve the pain of angina pectoris, which is caused by the spasm of these vessels.

NITROMERSOL, a compound of mercury that is used as an antiseptic. It is an effective inhibitor of bacterial growth, but is relatively ineffective against spores. Nitromersol (Metaphen) occurs as brownish yellow powder or crystals that lack a distinct smell and taste. Since it is relatively nonirritating to the skin and mucous membranes, it is widely used in first-aid treatment of minor cuts and scratches and as a disinfectant before surgery. It may also be used as an irrigating solution and as a disinfectant for surgical instruments. Nitromersol is marketed in such forms as tinctures, solutions, suppositories, and ophthalmic ointments.

NITROSOBENZENE, C_6H_5NO, one of two intermediate products in the reduction of nitrobenzene to an aniline, the other being phenylhydroxylamine, C_6H_5NHOH. Nitrosobenzene melts at 68°C (154°F), and is a colorless, crystalline substance that yields a greenish solution having an odor resembling cyanic acid. It is chemically unstable, but can be used as an intermediate in the preparation of dyes.

NITROUS OXIDE, or N_2O, the only inorganic gas that is useful as an anesthetic agent. It is colorless and odorless and is marketed in steel cylinders as a liquid under pressure. When the pressure is released nitrous oxide again becomes a gas. The gas is heavier than air and will support combustion, but is not explosive.

The American dentist, Horace Wells, first recognized the anesthetic value of nitrous oxide in 1844. Since its effect lasts for only a short time, it is usually used only for operations done quickly, such as opening abscesses and extracting teeth. When nitrous oxide is inhaled, it produces laughter and hilarity before the unconscious state is reached and as its anesthetic effects wear off; hence its popular name—laughing gas. This peculiar effect is not often produced, because nitrous oxide alone is not employed as an anesthetic agent. Oxygen must be used with nitrous oxide to prevent asphyxia, which would occur rapidly otherwise. Recovery from the anesthetic is rapid, complete, and usually without ill effects. Nitrous oxide may be effectively combined with some other anesthetics such as ether. See ANESTHESIA.

NITTI, FRANCESCO SAVERIO, 1868–1953, Italian public official, born in Melfi. A professor of finance at the University of Naples, he entered parliament as a Liberal deputy (1904) and served as minister of commerce and agriculture (1911–17) and of finance (1917–19). In 1919 Nitti became premier of Italy, serving for about a year, during which he was twice forced to resign and reconstruct his cabinet. When the Fascists came to power, Nitti went into exile in France. He returned to Italy in 1945 and in 1947 made an unsuccessful effort to form a democratic cabinet.

NITZSCH, KARL IMMANUEL, 1787–1868, German Lutheran theologian, born in Borna, Saxony. He studied at the University of Wittenberg and taught there and at the universities of Bonn and Berlin. In *System der christlichen Lehre* (1829; English trans., 1849), *Praktische Theologie* (3 vols., 1847–67), and in other works he adopted much of the theological system of Friedrich Schleiermacher. See SCHLEIERMACHER, FRIEDRICH ERNST DANIEL.

NIUE, also Savage Island, s Pacific, at 19°2′ s lat., 169°52′ w long.; a dependency of New Zealand; one of the Cook Islands but under separate administration; area about 100 square miles. The population consists mainly of Polynesians. The island is of coral rising to an elevation of 200 feet in the central fertile plateau. Alofi, on the west coast, is the chief town and port. Despite poor harbors, copra and bananas are exported. Yams and fruits are among the subsistence crops. OTIS W. FREEMAN

NIVELLE, ROBERT GEORGES, 1856–1924, French military leader, born at Tulle, Corrèze. In World War I he became division commander (1915), commander of the 2nd army (May, 1916), and commander in chief of French forces (December, 1916). He was removed from command after the failure of the April, 1917, offensive, but was exonerated by a committee of inquiry (1917). He held a North African command in 1917 and retired in 1921.

NIVENITE, a mineral of the uraninite variety containing yttrium, thorium, and lead; velvet black in color and occurring in massive forms. It has a specific gravity of 8.01 and a hardness of 5.5, but it is more soluble than the other varieties of uraninite. Nivenite was discovered in 1889 in Llano County, Tex., by William Niven (1850–1937), a U.S. mineralogist.

NIVERNAIS, region and former province, central France, corresponding to the modern department of Nièvre; bounded by Orléanais on the N, Burgundy on the E, Bourbonnais on the S, and Berry on the W; the principal city is Nevers. The counts of Nivernais, or Nevers, were created in the tenth century as vassals of the dukes of Burgundy. About 1250 Nivernais was united by marriage with the houses of Bourbon, Burgundy, and Flanders and gained the counties of Auxerre and Tonnerre. Louis of Flanders, count of Nivernais, was defeated by Philip IV of France in 1312, but maintained the independence of his county. In 1384 Nivernais passed by inheritance to Philip, third son of Philip the Bold of Burgundy. A century later it became a fief of the Germanic house of Cleves. As a reward for military aid, Francis I elevated the county to a dukedom in 1539. In 1565 the houses of Cleves and Gonzaga (Italian) were united by marriage, and in 1659 the duchy of Nivernais was sold by Gonzaga descendants to Jules Cardinal Mazarin. In 1669 Louis XIV made Nivernais a royal province. In 1793 Louis Jules Mancini Mazarini, duke of Nivernais, was forced to relinquish his domain to the republic of France. See NEVERS; NIÈVRE.

NIXON, RICHARD MILHOUS, 1913– , 37th president of the United States and vice-president during the two administrations of Pres. Dwight D. Eisenhower; born in Yorba Linda, Calif., near Los Angeles, the son of Francis Anthony and Hannah Milhous Nixon. A Quaker, he studied at Whittier College (a Quaker school) and at Duke University Law School. In 1937 he began to practice law with the firm of Wingert and Bewley in Whittier, Calif.; the firm name soon was changed to Bewley, Knoop, and Nixon. In 1940 he married Patricia Ryan; they had two children, Patricia and Julie. After the outbreak of World War II Nixon worked as an attorney with the office of emergency management (January–August, 1942), then served in the Navy until January, 1946, when he was mustered out with the rank of lieutenant commander.

In Congress. In the 1946 elections Nixon successfully opposed the Democratic incumbent, Jerry Voorhis, for the office of U.S. representative from the 12th California district. Nixon was re-elected in 1948. As a member of the 80th and 81st Congresses he became nationally known for his work with the House Committee on Un-American Activities, particularly in connection with the controversial Alger Hiss–Whittaker Chambers case. Ultimately, in large measure because of Nixon's persistence, Hiss was convicted on charges of perjury in denying that he had known Chambers or had given governmental secrets to him as a Soviet agent. Nixon was co-author, with Rep. Karl Mundt, of a subversive activities control bill, which although not passed by the 80th Congress was partly incorporated in the (Patrick) McCarran Internal Security Act of 1950. In 1950, campaigning on a platform that condemned the Democratic administration's policies toward China and Korea and that urged prolonging the

Richard M. Nixon

President Nixon is flanked by his two daughters, Julie and Patricia, and his wife Pat.

work of the Un-American Activities Committee, Nixon easily won election as U.S. senator from California, defeating Helen G. Douglas.

An Active Vice-President. Nominated as Dwight D. Eisenhower's running mate on the Republican ticket in the 1952 presidential election, Nixon played an important but unspectacular part in the campaigning until shortly before the election, when he was accused of improperly accepting (from southern California businessmen) a donation of some $18,000 to cover his extra campaign expenses. He made a nationally televised speech to defend himself against charges of impropriety in his finances. Nixon was elected vice-president in 1952 and was re-elected in 1956. After the latter Republican victory, Nixon was regarded as a leading contender for the 1960 Republican presidential nomination.

Nixon became one of the most active vice-presidents in U.S. history, handling liaison work between the White House and Congress, presiding over cabinet meetings during the president's absence (the first vice-president to do so), and undertaking a series of good-will trips around the world. He was chosen by President Eisenhower to do most of the administration's campaigning for Republican congressional candidates, and during President Eisenhower's illnesses in 1955, 1956, and 1957, Nixon conducted cabinet meetings, received White House staff reports, and assumed many routine presidential duties. Eisenhower in 1958 announced the terms of an agreement between himself and Nixon stipulating how the latter would take over the former's powers if the president were to become disabled. In 1959 Nixon visited the U.S.S.R. and spoke at length with Premier Nikita Khrushchev. These talks included the widely publicized (and televised) "kitchen debate" at a U.S. exhibition of American life in Moscow. He won the Republican nomination for the U.S. presidency in 1960, running with Henry Cabot Lodge. He campaigned vigorously but unsuccessfully against Sen. John F. Kennedy, who won by the narrow margin of 118,574 popular votes (electoral vote: 303 to 219). The campaign was highlighted by a series of televised debates between the two candidates, debates which some observers felt contributed to Nixon's defeat. Two years later he ran for governor of California but lost that race also, to incumbent Gov. Pat Brown. He then entered a law firm in New York City.

The Presidency. For the next 6 years, although Nixon did not seek public office, he traveled extensively around the country, maintained his contacts with Republican leaders, and remained an important spokesman for the party. In 1964 he campaigned for the unsuccessful Republican candidate Barry Goldwater. In 1968 he announced that he would once again seek the presidency and embarked on the presidential primary circuit, outdistancing his two most prominent Republican rivals, Gov. George Romney of Michigan and Gov. Nelson Rockefeller of New York. His nomination at the party convention in Miami Beach was in itself a remarkable political achievement and testimony to Nixon's tenacity and political skill. He chose as his running mate Gov. Spiro T. Agnew of Maryland.

Nixon's Democratic opponent was Vice-President Hubert Humphrey (President Johnson declined to run). Nixon managed a majority in the Electoral College against both his Democratic opponent and against American Independent party candidate George Wallace, who carried the Deep South. Nixon's popular plurality, however, was only several hundred thousand votes, and he faced Democratic majorities in both houses of Congress. As president, Nixon reduced U.S. forces in Indochina from a level of 542,000 men in 1969 to 284,000 in 1971. He and the vice-president campaigned extensively for the 1970 Congressional elections. The major issues were an inflationary economy, an increasing crime rate, and radical student dissent. The elections did not significantly alter the previous party balance in Congress.

BIBLIOG.–W. Costello, *The Facts About Nixon* (1960); Ralph De Toledano, *Nixon* (1960 ed.); Sidney Kraus, ed., *The Great Debates* (1962); Earl Mazo and Stephen Hess, *Nixon: A Political Portrait* (1968); Richard Nixon, *Six Crises* (1962); Garry Wills, *Nixon Agonistes* (1970).

NIZHNI TAGIL, city, W central U.S.S.R., Russian Soviet Federated Socialist Republic, Sverdlovsk oblast; on the eastern slope of the Ural Mountains, near the confluence of the Tagil and the Tura rivers; 75 miles N of Sverdlovsk. A giant iron and steel center, Nizhni Tagil has two steel mills, one originally founded in 1725. The city also has railroad-car shops, a coke-chemical industry, and machinery plants. Nearby is the iron mine of Vysokaya Mountain. The city developed in 1725 around the old ironworks. (For population, see U.S.S.R. map in Atlas.) THEODORE SHABAD

NJORD, the sea-god in Scandinavian mythology who ruled the wind and calmed the sea and was especially worshiped by sailors and fishermen. Njörd was father of Freyr and Freya, gods of fertility.

NKRUMAH, KWAME, 1909– , first president of Ghana, born in Nkroful, Gold Coast (later Ghana). He attended Achimota College and then went to the United States, where he was graduated from Lincoln University in Pennsylvania. In 1947 he returned to the Gold Coast to serve as general secretary to the nationalistic United Gold Coast Convention. He formed the Convention People's party in 1949, which won a sweeping victory in the general election of 1951. Nkrumah, in prison for sedition, was released to head the new government. He continued as prime minister after the Gold Coast became the independent state of Ghana in 1957, and became president of Ghana when the republic was declared in 1960. He was an advocate of Pan-Africanism, and his enterprise helped create the African Charter in 1961. Gradually his rule became dictatorial and Communist-oriented. While Nkrumah was on a visit to Communist China in 1966, his government was overthrown, and he became an exile in Guinea, where Guinean president Sékou Touré declared Nkrumah joint president of Guinea. His writings include *Towards Colonial Freedom* (1946), *Ghana* (1957), *Africa Must Unite* (1963), and *Challenge of the Congo* (1967).

NOAH, Biblical character (Genesis, 5), tenth in descent from Adam, chosen by God to preserve the human race and animals from the flood with which God proposed to inundate the world. Following God's instructions, Noah built an ark of gopher wood and installed therein his family and representatives of every kind of animal. When the flood receded the ark landed on Mount Ararat. By Noah's sons the world was repeopled.

NOAILLES, a distinguished French family dating from the eleventh century. Antoine de Noailles (1504–62) was admiral and ambassador to England in 1553–56. His great-grandson, Duc Anne Jules de Noailles (1650–1708), born in Paris, became a marshal of France in 1693. Anne Jules's son, Duc Adrien Maurice de Noailles (1678–1766), served in the later wars of Louis XIV and in the early wars of Louis XV, becoming marshal in 1734. His son, Duc Louis de Noailles (1713–93), born in Versailles, was marshal of France after 1766. Louis's son, Duc Jean François Paul de Noailles (1739–1824), lieutenant general, emigrated to Switzerland during the French Revolution. Jean's cousin, Vicomte Louis Marie de Noailles (1756–1804), born in Paris, served with Marquis Marie Joseph de Lafayette, his brother-in-law, during the American Revolution, and as a member of the States-General (1789), proposed the abolition of titles and privileges. A great-grandson of Louis, Duc Paul de Noailles (1802–85), born in Paris, was a peer of France and wrote *Histoire de Mme. de Maintenon* (1848–58). Paul's son, Duc Jules Charles Victurnien de Noailles (1826–95), born in Paris, was an economist and author. Jules's brother, Marquis Emmanuel Henri Victurnien de Noailles (1830–1909), born in Maintenon, entered the diplomatic service in 1871. Comtesse Anne Elisabeth Mathieu de Noailles (1876–1933), Princesse Brancovan, born in Paris and wife of a grandson of Duc Jules de Noailles, was a poet and novelist.

NOBEL, ALFRED BERNHARD, 1833–96, Swedish chemist and philanthropist, born in Stockholm and educated in St. Petersburg, Russia, and in the United States. Returning to Sweden he worked with his father, Emanuel Nobel, in the development of torpedoes and submarine mines, and experimented with the manufacture of nitroglycerin for commercial use. In 1867 he patented dynamite, nitroglycerin compound with kieselguhr, which could be safely handled and transported. Among Nobel's other inventions were an early smokeless powder (ballistite), artificial gutta-percha, a gas meter, a liquid-measuring device, and a barometer. In his will he established the Nobel prizes. See Nobel prize.

NOBELIUM, chemical element number 102, named for Alfred Nobel; symbol No, atomic weight 254. It is not found in nature. In 1957 a group of British, Swedish, and U.S. scientists working at the Nobel Institute for Physics in Stockholm reported its synthesis from curium-244. In 1958 scientists at the University of California prepared nobelium from curium-246.

NOBEL PRIZE, an award made at least once every 5 years (and as a rule annually) for important discoveries or inventions in each of six categories of knowledge, from a fund bequeathed for this purpose by Alfred B. Nobel. By mid-twentieth century the original bequest of $8 million had grown to about $12 million and the cash awards varied from approximately $30,000 to $50,000 each. The six groups in which the prizes are awarded are physics; chemistry; medicine and physiology; literary work of "an idealistic tendency" that has proved itself of "the greatest benefit to mankind"; important services in the interest of peace; and economic science. In physics, chemistry, and economic science the prizes are awarded by the Swedish Royal Academy of Sciences; in medicine and physiology, by the Royal Caroline Medico-Chirurgical Institute in Stockholm; in literature, by the Swedish Academy in Stockholm; in peace, by a committee of five members selected by the Norwegian Storting (parliament).

NOBEL PRIZE WINNERS

YEAR	PHYSICS	CHEMISTRY	PHYSIOLOGY AND MEDICINE	LITERATURE	PEACE
1901	W. Röntgen (Ger)	J. H. van't Hoff (Neth)	E. A. von Behring (Ger)	R. F. A. Sully Prudhomme (Fr)	J. H. Dunant (Swi) Frédéric Passy (Fr)
1902	H. A. Lorentz (Neth) P. Zeeman (Neth)	Emil Fischer (Ger)	Sir Ronald Ross (UK)	T. Mommsen (Ger)	E. Ducommun (Swi) C. A. Gobat (Swi)
1903	A. H. Becquerel (Fr) Pierre Curie (Fr) Marie Curie (Fr)	S. A. Arrhenius (Swe)	N. R. Finsen (Den)	B. Björnson (Nor)	Sir William R. Cremer (UK)
1904	Lord Rayleigh (UK)	Sir William Ramsay (UK)	I. P. Pavlov (USSR)	F. Mistral (Fr) J. Echegaray y Eizaguirre (Sp)	Institute of International Law
1905	P. Lenard (Ger)	A. von Baeyer (Ger)	Robert Koch (Ger)	H. Sienkiewicz (Pol)	Baroness Bertha von Suttner (A)
1906	J. J. Thomson (UK)	H. Moissan (Fr)	Camillo Golgi (It) S. Ramón y Cajal (Sp)	G. Carducci (It)	Theodore Roosevelt (US)
1907	A. A. Michelson (US)	E. Buchner (Ger)	C. L. A. Laveran (Fr)	Rudyard Kipling (UK)	E. T. Moneta (It) L. Renault (Fr)
1908	G. Lippmann (Fr)	Lord Rutherford (UK)	P. Ehrlich (Ger) E. Metchnikoff (USSR)	R. Eucken (Ger)	K. P. Arnoldson (Swe) Fredrik Bajer (Den)
1909	G. Marconi (It) K. F. Braun (Ger)	W. Ostwald (Ger)	E. T. Kocher (Swi)	Selma Lagerlöf (Swe)	A. M. F. Beernaert (Bel) Baron Paul d'Estournelles (Fr)

A	Austria	Ch	China	Gr	Greece	Jap	Japan	Sp	Spain
Aus	Australia	Cz	Czechoslovakia	Hun	Hungary	Neth	Netherlands	Swe	Sweden
Arg	Argentina	Den	Denmark	Ice	Iceland	Nor	Norway	Swi	Switzerland
Bel	Belgium	Fin	Finland	Ind	India	Pol	Poland	UK	United Kingdom
Can	Canada	Fr	France	Ire	Ireland	Port	Portugal	US	United States
C	Chile	Ger	Germany	It	Italy	SA	South Africa	USSR	Soviet Union
								Yug	Yugoslavia

NOBEL PRIZE WINNERS (continued)

YEAR	PHYSICS	CHEMISTRY	PHYSIOLOGY AND MEDICINE	LITERATURE	PEACE
1910....	J. D. van der Waals (Neth)	O. Wallach (Ger)	A. Kossel (Ger)	Paul von Heyse (Ger)	International Peace Bureau
1911....	Wilhelm Wien (Ger)	Marie Curie (Fr)	A. Gullstrand (Swe)	Count Maurice Maeterlinck (Bel)	T. M. C. Asser (Neth) A. H. Fried (A)
1912....	N. G. Dalén (Swe)	V. Grignard (Fr) P. Sabatier (Fr)	Alexis Carrel (Fr)	Gerhart Hauptmann (Ger)	Elihu Root (US)
1913....	H. Kamerlingh Onnes (Neth)	A. Werner (Swi)	Charles Richet (Fr)	Sir Rabindranath Tagore (Ind)	H. Lafontaine (Bel)
1914....	M. von Laue (Ger)	T. W. Richards (US)	R. Bárány (A)	No award	No award
1915....	Sir William H. Bragg (UK) Sir William L. Bragg (UK)	R. Willstätter (Ger)	No award	Romain Rolland (Fr)	No award
1916....	No award	No award	No award	V. von Heidenstam (Swe)	No award
1917....	C. G. Barkla (UK)	No award	No award	K. Gjellerup (Den) H. Pontoppidan (Den)	International Red Cross
1918....	Max Planck (Ger)	Fritz Haber (Ger)	No award	No award	No award
1919....	Johannes Stark (Ger)	No award	Jules Bordet (Bel)	C. Spitteler (Swi)	Woodrow Wilson (US)
1920....	C. Guillaume (Fr)	W. H. Nernst (Ger)	August Krogh (Den)	Knut Hamsun (Nor)	Léon Bourgeois (Fr)
1921....	Albert Einstein (Ger)	F. Soddy (UK)	No award	Anatole France (Fr)	K. H. Branting (Swe) C. L. Lange (Nor)
1922....	Niels Bohr (Den)	F. W. Aston (UK)	A. V. Hill (UK) O. Meyerhof (Ger)	J. Benavente y Martínez (Sp)	Fridtjof Nansen (Nor)
1923....	R. A. Millikan (US)	Fritz Pregl (A)	Sir Frederick Banting (Can) J. J. R. Macleod (UK)	W. B. Yeats (Ire)	No award
1924....	K. Siegbahn (Swe)	No award	W. Einthoven (Neth)	W. Reymont (Pol)	No award
1925....	James Franck (Ger) Gustav Hertz (Ger)	R. Zsigmondy (Ger)	No award	G. B. Shaw (UK)	Charles G. Dawes (US) Sir Austen Chamberlain (UK)
1926....	J. B. Perrin (Fr)	T. Svedberg (Swe)	J. Fibiger (Den)	G. Deledda (It)	A. Briand (Fr) G. Stresemann (Ger)
1927....	A. H. Compton (US) C. T. R. Wilson (UK)	H. Wieland (Ger)	J. Wagner-Jauregg (A)	Henri Bergson (Fr)	L. Quidde (Ger) F. Buisson (Fr)
1928....	Sir Owen Richardson (UK)	A. Windaus (Ger)	C. Nicolle (Fr)	Sigrid Undset (Nor)	No award
1929....	L. V. de Broglie (Fr)	Sir Arthur Harden UK H. von Euler-Chelpin (Swe)	Sir Frederick G. Hopkins (UK) C. Eijkman (Neth)	Thomas Mann (Ger)	F. B. Kellogg (US)
1930....	Sir Chandrasekhara Raman (Ind)	Hans Fischer (Ger)	K. Landsteiner (US)	Sinclair Lewis (US)	N. Söderblom (Swe)
1931....	No award	F. Bergius (Ger) Karl Bosch (Ger)	O. H. Warburg (Ger)	E. A. Karlfeldt (Swe)	Jane Addams (US) N. M. Butler (US)
1932....	W. Heisenberg (Ger)	I. Langmuir (US)	E. D. Adrian (UK) Sir Charles Sherrington (UK)	John Galsworthy (UK)	No award
1933....	P. A. M. Dirac (UK) E. Schrödinger (Ger)	No award	T. H. Morgan (US)	Ivan Bunin (USSR)	Sir Norman Angell (UK)
1934....	No award	H. C. Urey (US)	George Minot (US) W. Murphy (US) G. Whipple (US)	Luigi Pirandello (It)	Arthur Henderson (UK)
1935....	Sir James Chadwick (UK)	F. and I. Joliot-Curie (Fr)	H. Spemann (Ger)	No award	C. von Ossietzky (Ger)
1936....	C. D. Anderson (US) V. F. Hess (US)	P. J. Debye (Neth)	Sir Henry H. Dale (UK) Otto Loewi (Ger)	Eugene O'Neill (US)	C. Saavedra Lamas (Arg)
1937....	C. J. Davisson (US) G. P. Thomson (UK)	Sir Walter N. Haworth (UK) P. Karrer (Swi)	A. von Szent-Györgyi von Nagyrapolt (Hun)	R. Martin du Gard (Fr)	Viscount Cecil of Chelwood (UK)
1938....	Enrico Fermi (It)	Richard Kuhn (Ger) (accepted, 1949)	C. Heymans (Bel)	Pearl Buck (US)	Nansen International Office for Refugees
1939....	E. O. Lawrence (US)	L. Ružička (Swi) A. Butenandt (Ger) (accepted, 1949)	G. Domagk (Ger) (accepted, 1947)	F. E. Sillanpää (Fin)	No award
1940–42	No award	No award	No award	No award	No award
1943....	Otto Stern (US)	G. de Hevesy (Hun)	E. A. Doisy (US) Henrik Dam (Den)	No award	No award
1944....	I. I. Rabi (US)	Otto Hahn (Ger)	J. Erlanger (US) H. S. Gasser (US)	J. V. Jensen (Den)	International Red Cross
1945....	Wolfgang Pauli (A)	A. Virtanen (Fin)	Sir Alexander Fleming (UK) E. B. Chain (UK) Sir Howard W. Florey (Aus)	Gabriela Mistral (C)	Cordell Hull (US)
1946....	P. W. Bridgman (US)	J. B. Sumner (US) W. M. Stanley (US) J. H. Northrop (US)	H. J. Muller (US)	Hermann Hesse (Swi)	J. R. Mott (US) E. G. Balch (US)

NOBEL PRIZE WINNERS (continued)

YEAR	PHYSICS	CHEMISTRY	PHYSIOLOGY AND MEDICINE	LITERATURE	PEACE
1947....	Sir Edward Appleton (UK)	Sir Robert Robinson (UK)	C. F. Cori (US) G. T. Cori (US) B. A. Houssay (Arg)	André Gide (Fr)	American Friends Service Committee and (British) Friends Service Council
1948....	P. M. S. Blackett (UK)	A. Tiselius (Swe)	P. H. Müller (Swi)	T. S. Eliot (UK)	No award
1949....	H. Yukawa (Jap)	W. F. Giauque (US)	W. R. Hess (Swi) A. C. Egas Moniz (Port)	William Faulkner (US)	Lord John Boyd-Orr (UK)
1950....	Cecil F. Powell (UK)	Otto Diels (Ger) Kurt Alder (Ger)	Philip S. Hench (US) E. C. Kendall (US) Tadeus Reichstein (Swi)	Lord Bertrand Russell (UK)	Ralph J. Bunche (US)
1951....	Sir John Cockcroft (UK) E. T. S. Walton (Ire)	E. M. McMillan (US) G. T. Seaborg (US)	Max Theiler (SA)	Pär Lagerkvist (Swe)	Léon Jouhaux (Fr)
1952....	Felix Bloch (US) E. M. Purcell (US)	Richard Synge (UK) Archer Martin (UK)	Selman Waksman (US)	François Mauriac (Fr)	Albert Schweitzer (Ger)
1953....	Fritz Zernike (Neth)	H. Staudinger (Ger)	Fritz Lipmann (US) Hans Krebs (UK)	Sir Winston Churchill (UK)	Gen. George Marshall (US)
1954....	Max Born (UK) Walter Bothe (Ger)	Linus Pauling (US)	J. F. Enders (US) T. H. Weller (US) F. C. Robbins (US)	Ernest Hemingway (US)	Office of the United Nations High Commissioner for Refugees
1955....	Polykarp Kusch (US) Willis E. Lamb (US)	Vincent du Vigneaud (US)	Hugo Theorell (Swe)	Halldór Kiljan Laxness (Ice)	No award
1956....	John Bardeen (US) Walter H. Brattain (US) William Shockley (US)	Sir Cyril N. Hinshelwood (UK) Nikolai N. Semenov (USSR)	André F. Cournand (US) W. Forssmann (Ger) Dickinson W. Richards Jr. (US)	Juan Ramón Jiménez (Sp)	No award
1957....	Tsung-Dao Lee (Ch) Chen Ning Yang (Ch)	Sir Alexander R. Todd (UK)	Daniel Bovet (It)	Albert Camus (Fr)	Lester B. Pearson (Can)
1958....	P. A. Cherenkov (USSR) I. M. Frank (USSR) I. E. Tamm (USSR)	Frederick Sanger (UK)	G. W. Beadle (US) Joshua Lederberg (US) E. L. Tatum (US)	Boris Pasternak (USSR) (declined)	Dominique Pire (Bel)
1959....	Emilio Segrè (US) Owen Chamberlain (US)	Jaroslav Heyrovský (Cz)	Severo Ochoa (US) Arthur Kornberg (US)	Salvatore Quasimodo (It)	Philip Noel-Baker (UK)
1960....	Donald A. Glaser (US)	Willard F. Libby (US)	Sir F. M. Burnet (Aus) P. B. Medawar (UK)	Saint-John Perse (Fr)	Albert John Luthuli (SA) (awarded, 1961)
1961....	Rudolf L. Mössbauer (Ger) Robert Hofstadter (US)	Melvin Calvin (US)	Georg von Békèsy (US)	Ivo Andric (Yug)	Dag Hammarskjöld (Swe)
1962....	Lev Landau (USSR)	Max Perutz (UK) John Kendrew (UK)	Maurice Wilkins (UK) Francis Crick (UK) J. D. Watson (US)	John Steinbeck (US)	Linus Pauling (US)
1963....	Eugene Wigner (US) Maria Goeppert Mayer (US) Hans Jensen (Ger)	Carl Ziegler (Ger) Giulio Natta (It)	Andrew Huxley (UK) Sir John Eccles (Aus) Alan Hodgkin (UK)	Giorgos Seferiades (Gr)	International Red Cross committee and League of Red Cross Societies
1964....	Charles Townes (US) Nikolai Basov (USSR) A. Prochorov (USSR)	Dorothy Crowfoot Hodgkin (UK)	Konrad E. Bloch (US) Feodor Lynen (Ger)	Jean-Paul Sartre (Fr) (declined)	Martin Luther King (US)
1965....	R. P. Feynman (US) J. S. Schwinger (US) Shinichiro Tomonaga (Jap)	Robert B. Woodward (US)	André Lwoff (Fr) Jacques Monod (Fr) François Jacob (Fr)	Mikhail Sholokhov (USSR)	United Nations Children's Fund
1966....	Alfred Kastler (Fr)	Robert Mulliken (US)	Charles Huggins (US) Francis Rous (US)	Shmuel Agnon (Israel) Nelly Sachs (Swe)	No award
1967....	Hans A. Bethe (US)	Manfred Eigen (Ger) Ronald G. W. Norrish (UK) George Porter (UK)	Halden K. Hartline (US) Georg Wald (US) Ragnar Granit (Swe)	Miguel A. Asturias (Guatemala)	No award
1968....	Luis W. Alvarez (US)	Lars Onsager (US)	Robert W. Holley (US) H. Gobind Khorana (US) Marshall W. Nirenberg (US)	Yasunari Kawabata (Jap)	René Cassin (Fr)
1969....	Murray Gell-Mann (US)	Odd Hassel (Nor) Derek Barton (UK)	Max Delbruck (US) Alfred Hershey (US) Salvador Luria (US)	Samuel Beckett (Ire)	International Labor Organization
1970....	Hannes Alfvén (Swe) Louis Néel (Fr)	Luis Leloir (Arg)	Julius Axelrod (US) Sir Bernard Katz (UK) Ulf von Euler (Swe)	Aleksandr I. Solzhenitsyn (USSR)	Norman Borlaug (US)

YEAR	ECONOMIC SCIENCE
1969....	Ragnar Frisch (Nor) Jan Tinbergen (Neth)
1970....	Paul A. Samuelson (US)

The Nobel Foundation was established in 1900 to administer the prize money. The foundation set up four Nobel institutes to aid in the selection of the winners. The first prizes were awarded in 1901. The cash awards, diplomas, and gold medals are awarded annually on December 10.

NOBILE, UMBERTO, 1885– , Italian Arctic explorer, born near Salerno. He piloted the dirigible *Norge* in the 1926 Roald Amundsen-Lincoln Ellsworth transpolar flight and later became involved in a disagreement with Amundsen and Ellsworth as to who deserved most credit for the flight's success. Nobile was made a general in the Italian air force by Benito Mussolini and led a transpolar flight in the dirigible *Italia*, which flew across the North Pole on May 25, 1928, and was wrecked on the return flight. Held responsible for the crash, Nobile resigned his commission. He was an adviser on airship construction in the U.S.S.R. and later taught in the United States. After World War II he returned to Italy.

NOBILITY, a group or class possessing distinction or a privileged position by law or custom, who ordinarily hand the position on by inheritance; also, the position of distinction possessed. *Nobilis* in Latin meant known, or recognized, and also excellent; in societies where nobility as an institution was strong, there was usually the feeling that the class was gifted with special qualities of leadership or excellence, which were recognized in its privileged position. Privileged classes existed in some form in most historic societies and were commonly associated with wealth—particularly landed wealth—and with military or political office or power.

Ancient and Feudal Nobility. The *eupatridae*, or wellborn, in ancient Athens and the patricians of republican Rome are instances of classes with hereditary privileges in classical civilization.

The German tribes had a nobel warrior class, from whom priests and kings were chosen; claims to distinction within it were mainly based on skill and bravery in war.

In most of Europe feudal nobility was a powerful class, legally dependent on the monarch and hereditary in practice. It came to be identified with the knights, or mounted warriors, because of the nature of feudal society. In the city of Venice, however, a class of families distinguished by commercial wealth became increasingly powerful under the republican constitution.

In the later Middle Ages in most European countries, the privileges and position of the nobility became more definitely fixed. The possession of coats of arms, rules governing dress and precedence, and codes of etiquette were marks of this development, as were greater concern for noble ancestry and the prohibition, by custom if not by law, of engagement in trade and other pursuits by those of noble birth. A hierarchy of titles became fixed, and in many countries those without titles were distinguished as nobles by names including the prefix "of" (von, *de*).

Modern Development. In England, although the nobility remained and retained some of its position and power into the twentieth century, it was distinguished in several ways from the typical nobility of the continent. The different position of the "gentry" from that of the lesser nobility of Europe was one such difference. The greater flexibility of the system was another. Only the eldest son of a peer inherited title and position normally, so that other descendants might lose legal distinction. At the same time, by marriage or by royal creation, members of other classes might move into the peerage.

The French *noblesse* came in the late Middle Ages to include higher royal officials, members of the law courts, and higher military officers—the *noblesse de robe* and *noblesse d'épée*—legally ranking with the elder hereditary nobility, though socially quite different. The development of royal power in France especially deprived the older nobility of much of its function and power, although its privileges remained. The Revolution in 1790 abolished all titles and privileges. Napoleon I reinstituted a nobility, as did the restored monarchy in 1815, but it was abolished in law once more by the Third Republic.

The German nobility was divided into the high, which was held to rank with the sovereign princes, and the low. After about 1356 *Briefadel*, nobility by diploma, was common. With the consolidation of many of the German states after the Napoleonic Wars, a number of nobles lost power, though retaining titles and privileges. In both the Austrian and later German empires, the nobility commonly held the high military and civil offices.

The Spanish nobility was marked by a special insistence on purity of blood and by the class of grandees, with special privileges at court. The Polish nobility of the eighteenth century, with its constitutional power—extending to election of the king—was among the most politically powerful. The Japanese constitutional changes in the late nineteenth century included the substitution for the old feudal nobility of a peerage with titles equivalent to those of Europe. The growth of democratic institutions and ideas in most of the world in the twentieth century was marked by the legal and often the practical abolition or decline of nobility in most nations. See FEUDAL SOCIETY; KNIGHTHOOD.

GEORGE J. FLEMING, JR.

BIBLIOG.–A. Goodwin, ed., *European Nobility in the Eighteenth Century* (1953); F. L. Ford, *Robe and Sword* (1953); G. de Morant, *World Nobility and Peerage* (1954 ed.); J. B. Burke, *Genealogical and Heraldic History of the Peerage, Baronetage, and Knightage* (1967 ed.).

NOBLE, JOHN WILLOCK, 1831–1912, U.S. government official, born in Lancaster, Ohio. He studied at Yale University and Cincinnati Law School. He served as U.S. district attorney for the eastern district of Missouri (1867–70). As secretary of the interior in Pres. Benjamin Harrison's cabinet (1889–93), he was responsible for the formation of national forest lands (1891).

NOBLE GASES, a group of six gaseous elements with filled valence electron shells, which were once thought to be inert. These gases are, in order of increasing density, helium, neon, argon, krypton, xenon, and radon. In 1868 a new yellow line in the spectrum, differing from the sodium line, was discovered during a solar eclipse by Pierre Janssen, a French astronomer. The line was interpreted as being a new element that occurred in the solar disk, and was named helium. It was not until 1895, however, that Sir William Ramsay, in experiments with radioactive minerals, was able to isolate the element helium. By 1900 the presence of all the noble gases had been detected.

Although early attempts were made at preparing compounds from the noble gases, as late as 1962 no compound had been isolated and the gases were still referred to as inert gases. This inertness seemed logical because of the stable octet (duet in the case of helium) of electrons that fills the outer shell of the atoms of the group. In June, 1962, Neil Bartlett, a British Columbian chemist, reported the preparation of xenon-platinum hexafluoride, a red crystalline solid, $Xe\ (PtF_6)_x\ [1 \leq x \leq 2]$, by direct interaction of xenon with PtF_6. This discovery led to increased interest in noble gas chemistry and to the rapid development of the field.

The ability of the noble gases to form compounds is inversely proportional to ionization potential and energy differences in internal energy levels. Therefore the reactivities of the gases increase from helium to radon in the group. Most of the present chemistry is concerned with xenon because krypton is quite unreactive to present chemical techniques and radon is radioactive and therefore difficult to work with.

The noble gases are minor constituents of the atmosphere and most are obtained commercially from liquid air. Helium occurs in relatively high content in some natural gas and can be isolated from it. The principle value of noble gases is their relative inertness. They are often utilized in producing an unreactive atmosphere in chemistry and manufacture. The gases are also valuable for their specific properties. Helium is used in lighter-than-air rafts for buoyancy, argon and neon are used in electric discharge-type lamps, and radon is used as a source of radioactivity in the treatment of cancer. JOSEPH S. FOOS

BIBLIOG.–Cedric L. Chernick, *Record of Chemical Progress 24, 139* (1963); Gerhard A. Cook, *Argon, Helium, and the Rare Gases* (1961); F. A. Cotton and G. Wilkinson, *Advanced Inorganic Chemistry* (1966); G. J. Moody and J. D. R. Thomas, *Noble Gases and Their Compounds* (1964).

NOBLE METALS, metallic elements whose surfaces are not oxidized in the atmosphere. They include gold, iridium, osmium, palladium, platinum, rhodium, ruthenium, and silver. The resistance of the noble metals to oxidation has made them well suited, individually or alloyed with each other, for use in jewelry, electrical contacts, and some types of laboratory equipment. Noble metals are often applied to base metals as a thin layer, or cladding.

NOCERA INFERIORE, town, S Italy, Campania Region, Salerno Province; 8 miles NW of Salerno. It has textile factories, lumber mills, and tomato canneries. Known to the ancients as Nuceria Alfaterna, the town was occupied by the Romans in 307 B.C.; destroyed by Hannibal in 216 B.C., and then rebuilt; and sacked during the Social War of 90–88 B.C., and again by revolting slaves under Spartacus in 73 B.C. It was recolonized by military veterans during the reigns of Augustus and Nero (first century A.D.) (For population, see Italy map in Atlas.)

NOCTURNE, a musical composition of light, sentimental, and reflective nature, thought appropriate for evening or night listening, and usually written for the pianoforte. It owes its origin to the Irish composer John Field, and its chief exponent was Frédéric Chopin.

NODDY, any one of the several species of terns in the genus Anoüs. Its distinctive features are the round tail, brown or dark-gray color, and white crown. The noddy breeds on islands throughout the tropical and subtropical seas. It was named for its apparent stupidity, for it can often be caught by hand.

NODE, a point in a vibrating body at which there is essentially no vibration, or at which the amplitude is zero. Nodes occur at points on a stationary wave, which is composed of at least two waves of identical amplitude (displacement) and frequency traveling in opposite directions in the same medium. Such a wave may result from any kind of wave disturbance and is called a stationary wave because its movements, if rapid enough, cause the vibrating body to appear motionless. After a taut rope or string is plucked, it produces a standing wave.

The meeting, or interference, of the crest of one wave with the trough of another so cancels the effects of each wave that at certain points zero amplitude, or a node, results. When the crests of the waves correspond, the maximum displacement of the standing wave is equal to the sum of the amplitudes of the individual waves. The point of maximum displacement is the antinode. Nodes and antinodes are of musical significance. The sounds made by most musical instruments depend on vibrating strings or air columns. A violinist produces a node wherever he places his finger on a violin string, thereby stopping vibrations at that point. Antinodes are present at points of maximum air movement, such as at the open end of a whistle. See WAVE.

NODIER, CHARLES, 1780–1844, French writer, was born in Besançon. His satire on Napoleon Bonaparte resulted in his imprisonment in 1803, after which he spent several years in the Jura and Switzerland. He went to Paris in 1814 and in 1824 was appointed librarian of the Bibliothèque de l'Arsenal. Nodier gathered around him many young literary men and did much to encourage the growth of Romanticism. His novels and short stories include *Thérèse Aubert* (1819), *Smarra* (1821), *Trilby* (1822), *Histoire du roi de Bohême* (1830), *La Fée aux miettes* (1832), and *Le Chien de Brisquet* (1844).

NOEL-BAKER, PHILIP JOHN, 1889– , British statesman and author, born in London and educated in England and the U.S. He began his lifelong involvement in the cause of peace in 1919, when he became a member of the British delegation to the Paris Peace Conference, which established the League of Nations. He was also a member of the league's secretariat and helped to draft the covenant of the league. After teaching international relations at the University of London, he became a Labor member of Parliament. In 1932 he was the principal assistant to the president of the Disarmament Conference at Geneva. At the close of World War II he helped to draft the United Nations Charter and was a delegate to the General Assembly. In 1959 he was awarded the Nobel peace prize in recognition of his services and writings. The Albert Schweitzer book prize was awarded to him in 1960. He was the author of *The Arms Race: A Program for World Disarmament* (1958) and *World Disarmament Now* (1964).

NOGALES, city, S Arizona, seat of Santa Cruz County, a port of entry contiguous with Nogales, Mexico; 60 miles S of Tucson. In a mining and livestock raising area, Nogales has a large export-import trade with Mexico. The city was settled in 1880 and incorporated in 1893. (For population, see Arizona map in Atlas.)

NOGALES, city, NW Mexico, Sonora State, a port of entry contiguous with Nogales, Ariz.; 62 miles S of Tucson, Ariz. In a cattle-raising and mining region, Nogales is an important port of international trade. Its pleasant climate has made the city an increasingly popular health resort. (For population, see Mexico map in Atlas.)

NOGENT-SUR-MARNE, town, N central France, Seine Department; E of the Bois de Vincennes; 6 miles SE of Paris, of which it is a residential suburb. Nogent has large stone quarries and its industries manufacture chemicals, tools, and optical instruments and process food products. Points of interest include an old Gothic church with a Romanesque tower. Because of its beautiful location, the town was called Beauté, and was the site of a castle built by King Charles V and given by King Charles VII to his mistress, Agnès Sorel, who became known as the Dame de Beauté. The castle was destroyed in the eighteenth century.

NOGI, Count MARESUKE, 1849–1912, Japanese soldier, born near Tokyo. He was a captain in the imperial army in the Civil War (1877); and in the Sino-Japanese War (1894–95) he commanded a brigade at the battles of Chinchow and Port Arthur. Later he was created a baron of the empire. A general in the Russo-Japanese War (1904–05), he captured Port Arthur on Jan. 1, 1905, and commanded a corps at the Battle of Mukden. On Sept. 13, 1912, bereaved by the death of Emperor Mutsuhito, Nogi and his wife committed hara-kiri.

NOGUCHI, HIDEYO, 1876–1928, Japanese bacteriologist, born in Inawashiro, Fukushima. He was graduated from Tokyo Medical College in 1897. He went to the United States to teach at the University of Pennsylvania in 1900 and became associated with the Rockefeller Institute for Medical Research in 1904. He made notable contributions to the study of poliomyelitis, serpent venoms, and trachoma, but he was best known for work on syphilis and yellow fever. He was among the first to isolate in a pure culture the *Treponema pallidum*, the causative organism of syphilis, and to demonstrate its presence in the brain in cases of general paresis and in the spinal cord in cases of locomotor ataxia. He also devised a method of diagnosis, the Noguchi luetin reaction. He then turned his attention to the study of the yellow fever virus. While working on this study in Accra, Gold Coast (Ghana), he contracted the disease and died.

NOGUCHI, ISAMU, 1904– , U.S. sculptor, born in Los Angeles, Calif., son of the Japanese poet Yone Noguchi (1875–1947). Noguchi studied with Gutzon Borglum before beginning premedical studies at Columbia University. He returned to art, however, studying at the Leonardo da Vinci School in New York. He was an assistant to Constantin Brancusi in Paris through a Guggenheim fellowship in 1927–28, and he studied in China and Japan in 1929–31. Combining ancient and modern styles of both the Eastern and Western art traditions, Noguchi has used many different materials and textures in his sculpture. He has also gained recognition for his furniture designs, his stage sets for the Martha Graham dance company, and the gardens of UNESCO in Paris.

NOISE, because of its undesirable physiological and psychological effects upon people, is considered to be any unwanted or disturbing sound. Noise is of interest as a sound to be eliminated.

Measurement. Since the relative importance of a noise is strongly dependent upon circumstances, scientific methods of specifying the amount of noise are essential. Only in terms of scientific measurements is it possible to specify the tolerable limits of noise in any particular situation.

The basic physical yardstick for the measurement of the loudness of noise is the decibel—essentially the unit of sound energy. The scale measuring the level of noise (high or low) in decibels ranges from the threshold of audibility (at zero) to levels that will cause the ear to experience sensations of tickling (at 125) or of actual pain (at 140). Continuous exposure over a number of years to noise levels above 90 to 100 decibels often may cause loss in hearing. An increase in noise level by 10 decibels, which corresponds to a tenfold increase in sound energy, will just double the apparent loudness of the noise. A change of 1 decibel, on the other hand, is scarcely noticeable except under the most favorable listening conditions.

The overall level of noise, however, is only part of the picture; knowledge of the frequencies, or pitches, of the sounds involved in the noise is also essential. Most of the energy of pure tones, such as are generated by a well-played musical instrument, is concentrated at a single frequency. Conversely, confused or discordant sounds, like those from a jet aircraft or railroad train, are not characterized by any particular frequency. A sound of this sort is called broad-band noise because its energy is distributed over a wide band of the audible frequency range. This distribution, however, is seldom uni-

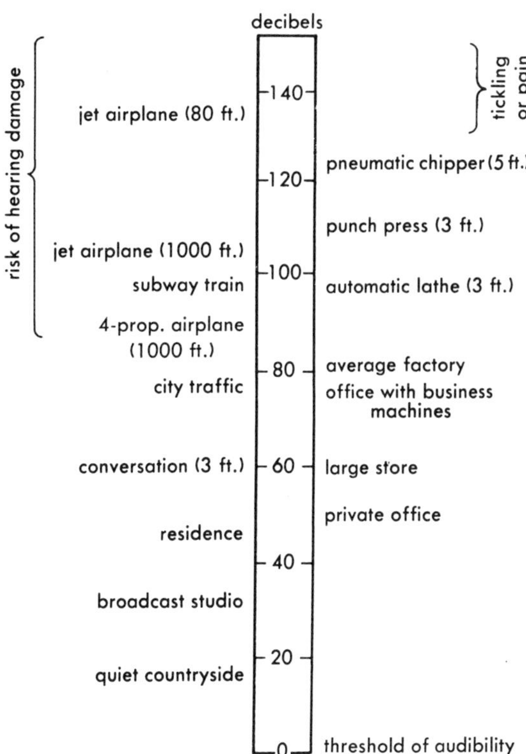

Decibel Scale of Common Noises

form; for example, the noise of a propeller-driven airplane is principally low in frequency, whereas most of the noise caused by a riveting machine is high in frequency. The spectrum of a broad-band noise can be represented by a graph showing the amount of energy in the various frequency bands. Many of the effects of noise are strongly dependent upon the shape of the spectrum. A noise that is predominantly low in frequency, for example, does not interfere with the audibility of speech as much as one whose energy is concentrated at a high frequency.

Causes. Noise may originate in any mechanism that sets the air into fluctuating motion. Although at times it appears that the sources of noise are diverse, the basic cause can be traced in nearly every case to one of the five methods of generating fluctuating forces.

When a stream of air jets from a nozzle, it quickly becomes turbulent. The fluctuating motions of the particles of air in this turbulent stream are the direct cause of the noise that radiates away from such a jet. This principle operates in the exhaust from a jet airplane or in the stream of compressed air escaping from an air hose. Additional noise is created when a jet of air strikes the edge of a solid object, thus bringing other aerodynamic forces into play.

In other cases, various mechanical forces acting upon a solid object make it vibrate. The motion of that object causes vibrations in the surrounding air, just as a loudspeaker does; this motion of the air spreads out from the source and is the noise that is heard. Mechanical impact is the original source of some of the most annoying noises—hammering, riveting, drop forges, footsteps, and the like. Friction is the source of other noises such as those from unoiled door hinges, squeaking automobile brakes, or fingernails scratched over blackboards. In most machines there are either reciprocating or eccentrically rotating parts that cannot be completely balanced. The unbalanced forces from these parts cause the whole machine to vibrate and thereby create noise. Such noises are usually more or less pure tones. The humming sounds given off by electric motors and transformers are another kind of noise. Fluctuating magnetic forces—an inherent part of the operation of such equipment—cause motion that is eventually transmitted to the air and then to the ear.

Effects on Man. As the level of a noise is increased, various effects on man can be observed. These effects range from annoyance, interference with speech communication, decreased efficiency, and increased fatigue, to more or less permanent loss of hearing. The most common effect of noise is annoyance. Individual sensitivity to a given noise varies widely and depends markedly on the situation in which the noise is heard.

At a level of about 60 decibels a noise begins to interfere with the understanding of speech. Since low-frequency noises seldom interfere with communication, the interference depends primarily on the amount of sound energy in the higher-frequency range. This interference is quite common and disturbing in large offices containing many machines.

When speech communication is not a consideration, a steady loud noise will seldom have any marked effect upon the efficiency of routine work. Unusual and unexpected noises can be the cause of startled reactions that will affect efficiency; but if the noise continues until the novelty wears away, work efficiency is usually recovered. Work efficiency is not recovered under such conditions, however, when the tasks involve complex judgments or decisions or are paced by a machine production line. In these cases continuous loud noise can greatly affect the efficiency of work by causing an occasional extra mistake.

The loss of hearing earlier mentioned has become a matter of great concern in many noisy manufacturing plants. There is little evidence, however, that any other physiological effect from loud noise occurs except at the most extreme levels of noise when a physical sensation of tickling or of pain may occur in the ear. Such occasions are rare; those extreme levels would be encountered only in extremely close proximity to the exhaust from jet engines, for example, and few individuals have the opportunity or inclination to remain in such an environment.

Effects on Materials. Extremely intense noise can rip apart thin panels of metal—that is, can cause fatigue failures. Fatigue occurs in a piece of metal when it is repeatedly subjected to large stresses. No single application of such stress is sufficient to cause failure, but after many applications, perhaps millions, the metal fractures. If a thin metal panel is exposed to the intense noise that occurs quite close to the exhaust of a jet engine, it may vibrate like a drumhead with such large amplitude that fatigue failure results. Aircraft designers take great care to insure that this situation does not occur in airplanes.

Noise control usually implies a reduction in the overall level of noise, but a change (in the spectrum) that eliminates high frequencies and permits additional low-frequency noise could result in greater comfort and increased understanding of speech. In some circumstances, moreover, the elimination of a loud, steady noise may uncover weaker intermittent noises that can then be more disturbing than the steady one was.

The first consideration in noise control is the attempt to locate the sources of intense noise far from people. Busy airports, for example, should not be close to residential areas; it is not always possible, however, to make good use of distance in this fashion. The next important step is the redesign of the machinery causing the noise, for if the fundamental source of the particular noise is understood, it is frequently possible to find other methods of performing the job that will not create so much disturbance. As a simple example, a jet of air will cause much less noise if it is allowed to escape with lower velocity from a larger nozzle, even though the same amount of air flows through the nozzle. This solution is not feasible in jet airplanes that depend upon the high velocity of the jet for the thrust that moves the plane. Intensive investigations have been carried out in the attempt to muffle the sound from jet airplanes without causing a loss of thrust. Research in this area has met with some success, and noise-suppression devices have been put on jet craft.

There are two fundamental ways to protect people from a noise once it has been created. Sound insulation is afforded by solid walls and closed windows. Although any barrier of this sort will reflect much of the sound that strikes it, satisfactory reduction of intense levels of noise may require exceedingly heavy structures—two 8-inch-thick concrete walls separated by several inches of air, for example. Because even small cracks and openings destroy the effectiveness of sound insulation, enclosures designed to stop sound usually must be airtight. The second approach to reducing levels of noise is that of sound absorption. A sound wave that strikes a porous, fibrous material will penetrate into the cavities and dissipate much of its energy there because of friction between the air and the material. Acoustical tiles and blankets of glass fibers are common examples of materials that will absorb noise. Such materials are used to line ventilation ducts so that the noise produced by the fan is gradually absorbed along the duct until the level is too low to cause a disturbance. Sound-absorbent materials covering ceilings also strongly reduce the noise levels at a distance from the source of noise in a room. P. W. SMITH, JR.

BIBLIOG.–Philip H. Beales, *Noise, Hearing, and Deafness* (1965); John J. Downing, *Modulation Systems and Noise* (1964); D. K. C. MacDonald, *Noise and Fluctuations* (1962); M. Rodda, *Noise and Society* (1967).

NOLA, town, s Italy, Campania Region, Naples Province, 15 miles NE of Naples. It is an agricultural center and has macaroni and glass factories. One of the most ancient towns of Campania, Nola fell to the Romans in 313 B.C. St. Paulinus is said to have introduced at Nola the use of church bells. The emperor Augustus died there in A.D. 14, and the free-thinker Giordano Bruno was born there in 1548. (For population, see Italy map in Atlas.)

NOLDE, EMIL, real name Emil Hansen, 1867–1956, German expressionist painter and graphic artist, born in Nolde, Schleswig. He studied in Munich, Copenhagen, and Paris, where he was attracted by the work of the French Impressionists. Seeking a style that would express powerful concepts and emotions, he broke with the Impressionists, about 1904, and aligned himself briefly with the German expressionist painters of the *Brücke* (Bridge) group. Too individualistic to remain long within any school, Nolde worked independently after 1907. He began a series of religious paintings (*The Last Supper*, *Pentecost*, *Triptych of St. Mary of Egypt*, and others) distinguished by their violent and frightening feeling as well as by the artist's typically brilliant coloration. Later, after a trip to Russia and the Far East, Nolde executed watercolors, engravings, and paintings that explored the nature of primitive societies.

NOLLE PROSEQUI, from the Latin meaning "unwilling to prosecute," an entry of record made by the plaintiff in a civil suit or the prosecuting officer in a criminal action, declaring that he will proceed no further as to some or all of the counts, or some or all of the defendants. In a criminal action nolle prosequi does not have the effect of acquittal, since the defendant can be reindicted; and in civil cases it does not bar future actions. In many jurisdictions nolle prosequi may be entered without the consent of a defendant before a jury is impaneled, but his consent is necessary if a jury has been impaneled.

NOME, city, Alaska, sw Seward Peninsula; on the N shore of Norton Sound; 525 miles w of Fairbanks. The city is in a gold-mining, fur-trapping, and fur-farming area, and is the supply center for northwestern Alaska. Its port, open from June to November, has steamer service to Seattle. Mark Field, a commercial and military air base, is nearby. Natives of the region produce needlework and ivory carving that are among the finest Eskimo craftwork. In 1898–99 gold was discovered in the vicinity and by 1900 Nome was the center of a gold rush. The population of the city reached more than 12,000 before it was sharply reduced by the dwindling number of gold strikes and the harshness of the climate. After a devastating fire in 1934 Nome was largely rebuilt. (For population, see Alaska map in Atlas.)

NOMINALISM, that philosophical viewpoint which insists that human language does not have in fact, and cannot have in theory, any necessary connection with ultimate reality. Metaphysically, nominalism assumes that a world of ideas such as postulated by Plato does not in fact exist. Plato believed that all particular things and qualities are imperfect reflections of perfect, ideal forms (universals), which exist in the realm of ideas; for example, any particular cow is a more or less imperfect copy of the perfect, universal cow in the world of ideas. This universal cow is ultimately real, and such reality as any particular cow may have devolves upon it through its relation to the universal cow. The word *cow* as applied to particular cows is more real than these particular cows, since the word's ultimate referent is the universal cow. During the Middle Ages this doctrine came to be known as realism.

Since for nominalism there is no realm of ideal forms (or, if there is such a realm, human beings cannot know of it), it follows that words cannot refer to or derive their meaning from ideal forms, or universals; therefore such meaning as words may have must derive entirely from the particular objects to which they refer—such, at least, is the "either/or" upon which nominalism depends. Carried to its logical conclusion, nominalism asserts that all words (*cow*, *truth*, *God*) are accidental, arbitrary, and based at best upon customary, conventional usage. Thus, even if the word *cow* is used without reference to a postulated ideal cow, the word is unreal as a designation for all particular cows since, despite apparent similarities, no two cows are exactly alike. Since only this or that particular object is real, the nominalists' references to seemingly similar particulars by common names is entirely a matter of social convention—perhaps useful if recognized and discounted as such, but harmful if accepted literally.

Although the tendency to think in this way existed in ancient philosophy, it did not achieve prominence (nor was it called nominalism) until the Middle Ages, when nominalists such as the French ecclesiastic Berenger de Tours (998–1088) and the scholastic theologian Roscellinus (died after 1120) disputed with realists such as Guillaume (William) de Champeaux (1070?–1121). The greatest theologian of the twelfth century, Peter Abelard (1079–1142), brilliantly concorded the two views in his philosophy of conceptualism. In the fourteenth century the English "Doctor Invincibilis" William of Ockham, or Occam (1300–49?), fostered nominalism, stressing its virtues as a conceptual aid in the development of natural science. A tendency among many later thinkers and scientists was to regard the natural order of things in terms of nominalism while remaining realists in matters affecting faith and morals. The various positivist schools were nominalistic in their assumptions, as were most schools of philology, linguistics, and language reform in the nineteenth and twentieth centuries. See CONCEPTUALISM; POSITIVISM; REALISM.

NONCOMMISSIONED OFFICER, an enlisted person in military and naval service who holds a grade or rating conferred by special order of a local commanding officer authorized to confer or withdraw such ratings. A noncommissioned officer does not have rank as do commissioned officers, or a warrant of the type granted warrant officers. Hence, he can never issue a command, only an order. In the U.S. Navy noncommissioned officers are called petty officers.

NONCONFORMITY, refusal to comply with established rules or ceremonies, especially religious rules or ceremonies. Historically notable nonconformists were those members of the Church of England who refused to attend the church's services, and clergymen who denied obedience to the Act of Uniformity of 1662, which required the use of the Book of Common Prayer in public worship. At the time of the passage of Queen Elizabeth's Act of Uniformity (1559), which required kneeling at the altar and wearing specified vestments, there were nonconforming bishops. The climax of nonconformity came in the "great ejectment" (1662), when 2,000 Puritan clergymen resigned rather than comply with the Act of Uniformity. The Religious Toleration Act of 1689 brought relief to nonconformists. In England all non-Anglican communions are technically nonconformist. Nonconformity is possible in any country with an established national church, but in countries where church and state are separate, such as the United States and France, nonconformity cannot exist. See CHURCH; PURITANISM; TOLERATION ACT.

JAMES D. MOSTELLER

NONFEASANCE, the nonperformance of some act that ought to be done. It generally does not indicate breach of contract, but rather failure to perform a duty, whereby some individual sustains damages. When a legislative act requires a person to do a thing, nonfeasance subjects that person to punishment. For example, if a statute requires supervisors of highways to make repairs, supervisors who neglect to do so may be punished.

NONIMPORTATION, a policy adopted on several occasions by American colonists and later by the United States as a retaliation against measures of the British government. As a gesture of protest against the Stamp Act, several colonies agreed in 1765 to refrain from importing British goods. The refusal of the colonies to import from Britain in 1770 caused the repeal of all of the Townshend Acts of 1767 except the tax on tea. A nonimportation resolution by the first Continental Congress in September, 1774, failed to win concessions. After the ensuing Revolutionary War the policy of nonimportation was revived by the United States in 1806 to discourage Britain from seizing U.S. vessels and seamen. The trade restrictions were unpopular in New England, however, and the policy was abandoned the same year.

NONINTERCOURSE ACT, a U.S. law that became effective beginning Mar. 1, 1809, designed to induce Great Britain and France to repeal measures restricting free trade. It replaced the unpopular Embargo Act of 1807 by forbidding relations only with Britain and France, and provided that relations would be reopened with the warring nation first to remove its restrictions on neutral trade. The act failed to impress either belligerent, and expired in 1810. It was followed on May 1, 1810, by Macon's Bill Number Two, which reopened direct trade with both Britain and France but offered to renew the restrictions against either country if the other would withdraw its trade restrictions.

NONJURORS, the clergy and laymen, principally of the Anglican church, who refused to give the oath of allegiance demanded by William III when he came to the throne of England after the Revolution of 1688. The objections of the nonjurors were twofold. One, the "state point," denied William's title to the crown; the other, the "church point," declared that no sovereign had the right to deprive a bishop of his see without ecclesiastical sanction. The nonjurors were supplanted in their sees and benefices by members of the clergy who could accept an oath of allegiance. See DIVINE RIGHT OF KINGS; ENGLAND, History, *The Glorious Revolution*.

NONMETAL, an element whose physical and chemical properties are generally opposite to those of metals. Nonmetals are essentially different from metals because they readily complete electron shells by sharing electrons (see PERIODIC TABLE). Typical nonmetals are gases or powdery solids, which are easily vaporized, have no luster, and thus are poor reflectors of light. Nonmetals also have low specific gravity, are brittle, and make good insulators because of their low heat and electrical conductivity. These elements form compounds with both metals and other nonmetals. They also form acidic compounds with oxygen and hydrogen, and are set free at the anode in electrolysis. Some typical nonmetallic elements are bromine, carbon, chlorine, fluorine, iodine, nitrogen, oxygen, phosphorus, silicon, and sulfur.

NONNUS, early fifth century Greek poet, was a native of Panopolis (later Akhmim), Egypt. His epic *Dionysiaca* tells of Dionysus' expedition to India. Nonnus' metrical paraphrase of the Gospel of St. John was written after he became converted to Christianity.

NONPARTISAN LEAGUE, a farmer's organization, founded in North Dakota in 1915, that advocated state ownership and operation of grain elevators, flour mills, and packing plants, state hail insurance, and rural credit banks operated at cost. The league's philosophy was that the state government should operate as a co-operative agency to prevent excessive charges by railroads, grain buyers, millers, and out-of-state agents. The group was headed by Arthur C. Townley, a former Socialist party organizer.

By 1916 some 40,000 farmers had joined the organization. League members controlled the Republican party organization in North Dakota and through it by 1918 controlled the North Dakota state government. The league meanwhile had established national headquarters in St. Paul, Minn., and had started organizations in Colorado, Idaho, Iowa, Kansas, Minnesota, Montana, Nebraska, Oklahoma, South Dakota, Texas, Washington, and Wisconsin. State organizations generally used the method employed in North Dakota—gaining control of a major party in primary elections—but not so successfully in other states as in North Dakota.

By 1919 the league had about 200,000 members, mostly in Minnesota, Montana, North Dakota, and South Dakota. After 1924, however, the league's importance declined. In North Dakota, state-operated banks, grain elevators, mills, and other ventures placed a heavy burden upon the taxpayers because Eastern bankers refused to take $6 million in bonds intended to finance state enterprises. The league was criticized for mismanagement and extravagance, but it was an important faction in the Republican party until 1956, when it gave its support to the Democratic party. In Minnesota the league developed into the Farmer-Labor party, a coalition of city workers and farmers. See FARMER-LABOR PARTY.

NONSUIT, a judgment rendered against a plaintiff in an action in which he refuses or neglects to proceed, or in which he is unable to make out a prima facie case after trial has begun. Before a trial the plaintiff may have a voluntary nonsuit at any time, but after he has put in his evidence only the discretion of the court may grant or refuse an application for nonsuit. A nonsuit does not bar another action upon the same facts as it does not determine the merits of the case; but if trial proceeds to a verdict, the cause becomes *res judicata* (matter adjudged) and a nonsuit cannot be permitted.

NOODLE, a food made of wheat flour and egg. It is retailed in various sizes and shapes; ribbonlike forms and those cut into letters of the alphabet are most common. This product originated in Germany. See MACARONI; SPAGHETTI.

NOOTKA, one of two main divisions of the Wakashan linguistic stock of North American Indians, the other being Kwakiutl. Most Nootka occupy Vancouver Island, British Columbia, from Cape Cook south to Port San Juan. The Nootka region was explored by Juan de Fuca in 1592, and during the seventeenth and eighteenth centuries other Spaniards visited the Indians there. Captain James Cook gave the first thorough account of the Nootka in 1778 when mapping the Pacific Coast of North America; thereafter the British were in constant contact with the Indians. Relations between the Nootka and whites were friendly except for a ship massacre in 1803, and many of the Indians accepted Christianity. The Nootka originally lived in communal cedar houses in small villages. Both sexes wore shells suspended from their pierced noses. Their religious ceremonials included sacred dramas based on mythological legends. They subsist on fishing and whale hunting, and are noted for seamanship. The Nootka are closely related to the Makah of northwest Washington and to the extinct Ozette. More distantly related are the Bellabella and the Bellacoola, also living on Vancouver Island. The Nootka population is estimated to have been 8,000 in 1780, 2,500 in 1906, and about 1,500 in 1950. Some Nootka merged with the Makah, of whom there were 489 in 1950 on Near Bay Reservation in Washington.

NOOTKA SOUND, an inlet of the Pacific Ocean on the W coast of Vancouver Island, SW Canada, British Columbia. Nootka Island is to the west. Two lengthy arms, the Tahsis and Muchalat inlets, reach inland from the sound. A Spaniard, Juan Pérez, reached the sound in 1774, and the English explorer Capt. James Cook visited and named it in 1778. A Spanish-British conflict over the sound was resolved by the Nootka Convention of 1790, whereby Spain relinquished its claims.

NO PLAY, an ancient form of Japanese drama evolved from serious pantomimic dances introduced in Shinto ritual about the year 600. Later, under Chinese influence, intoned dramatic dialogue was added to the mimicry, then called *Dengaku no No*. Under the patronage of the shogun, Yoshimitzu (about 1350), two dancer-dramatists, Kwan-nami and his son Seami, were inspired to raise No drama to classic form which, with the refinements of the seventeenth century, remained basic to Japanese religious drama. As a Zen (contemplative) Buddhist, Seami imbued his subtle art with *yugen* (what is beneath the surface), thus evading banal actuality. Hence the *shite* (star actor) and his all-male subordinates, gorgeously costumed and masked, often appear as ghosts to re-enact their legendary, supernatural, or worldly romances. No is enacted on a bare stage extending into the audience (as the Elizabethan stage did), with only a painted tree as background. Drummers, flutists, and chorus accent the recitative. A program of several No plays is interspersed with lighter entertainment (*kyogen*) for contrast and to insure public enjoyment of No.

E. BRADLEE WATSON

NORANDA, city, Canada, W Québec Province; on Osisko Lake and the Canadian National and the Ontario Northland railways; immediately NW of Rouyn and 135 miles NNE of North Bay. Noranda is in a region rich with copper, zinc, and gold mines and has a sizable smelting plant. Pop. (1956) 10,323.

NORD, department, N France; bounded by the North Sea on the N, Belgium on the NE and E, and the departments of Aisne and Somme on the S and Pas-de-Calais on the SW and W; area 2,229 sq. mi. The northern part is a lowland with a sandy coast, the central regions are also flat, but in the south the terrain is more hilly. Navigable rivers are the Scheldt (Escaut), Lys, Sambre, Scarpe, and Yser. Nord is one of France's major industrial departments, and one of the most densely populated. The chief crops are wheat, barley, sugar beets, potatoes, chicory, tobacco, and forage grasses. Dairy and beef cattle are raised, and there are cod and herring fisheries. The most important coal fields of France lie in the Valenciennes Basin. Textile industries, especially wool, are operated on a large scale in the Lille-Roubaix-Tourcoing area. Metalworking plants are numerous, and other manufactures include glass, chemicals, sugar, and pottery. The chief cities are Lille, the capital, and Roubaix, Tourcoing, Valenciennes, Douai, Wattrelos, Cambrai, Denain, Armentières, Marcq-en-Baroeul, Maubeuge, Lomme, La Madeleine, and Dunkirk. The area was the scene of severe fighting during World War I, and again in World War II when British and French forces were evacuated from the continent through Dunkirk. Under German occupation the region suffered both from the occupation forces and from numerous Allied air attacks. Pop. (1954) 2,098,545.

NORDAU, MAX SIMON, originally Max Simon Südfeld, 1849–1923, German writer and physician, was born in Budapest of Jewish parentage. After travel in Europe, he began the practice of medicine in Budapest, 1878, and in 1880 moved to Paris. Nordau's literary activity began with his *Conventional Lies of Civilization* (1884). His other works, mainly ethical and cultural studies in a satiric vein, include *Paradoxes* (1885); *Degeneration* (1892–93), a much criticized study of the relation between genius and degeneracy based on the theories of the criminologist, Cesare Lombroso; *The Right to Love* (1894); *The Interpretation of History* (1909); and *Biology of Ethics* (1921). He also wrote novels including *The Malady of the Century* (1888), *A Comedy of Sentiment* (1891), and *Morganatic* (1904); and a number of volumes of essays, travel sketches, and fairy tales. Nordau was a prominent Zionist and initiated a bitter controversy when, with Theodor Herzl, he urged that Zionists accept East Africa for Jewish settlement.

NORDENSKJÖLD, BARON NILS ADOLF ERIK, 1832–1901, Swedish Arctic explorer, was born in Helsingfors (Helsinki), Finland, and was educated at the university there, but left Finland for political reasons and after 1857 made Sweden his adopted country. He was geologist on several expeditions to Spitsbergen, became director of the Royal National Museum in Stockholm, 1858, and led an Arctic expedition, 1868, which reached latitude 81°42′. After voyages to the Yenisey River, Siberia, in 1875 and 1876, he sailed from Sweden, 1878, to seek a Northeast Passage; reached China, 1879, and completed the circumnavigation of Eurasia in 1880, the year in which he was made a baron. He explored the interior of Greenland, 1883, and visited Spitsbergen, 1890. His son, Nils Erland Herbert Nordenskjöld (1877–1932), an ethnologist, traveled extensively in South America; and his nephew, Nils Otto Gustaf Nordenskjöld (1869–1928), explored the Antarctic regions.

NORDERNEY, one of the East Frisian Islands, in the North Sea, off the NW coast of Germany, 23 miles NNW of Emden; maximum E-W and N-S distances 8 and 2 miles respectively; area 9 sq. mi.; pop. 6,452. The town of Nordseebad Norderney at the southwestern tip of the island is a popular seaside resort. See FRISIAN ISLANDS.

NORDHAUSEN, town, central Germany, in the West German state of Thuringia; at the foot of the Harz Mountains; 51 miles W of Halle. Its industries include oil refining, distilling, and woodworking. The old town has walls and towers dating from the fifteenth century, a Gothic cathedral, the thirteenth century Church of St. Blasius, and a town hall that dates from 1610. Nordhausen was founded early in the tenth century. It became a free imperial city in 1253, and belonged to the kingdom of Westphalia from 1807 until 1813 when it was taken by Prussia. In World War II the town manufactured V-2 rockets. Pop. (1956) 38,759.

NORDHOFF, CHARLES, 1830–1901, U.S. journalist and author, was born in Erwitte, Westphalia, Prussia, and was brought to the United States by his parents in 1835. He served in the U.S. Navy, 1844–47, and in the merchant service until 1853. He was an editor with the Harper publications, 1857–61; was managing editor of the New York *Evening Post*, 1861–71; traveled in the West and the Pacific for two years; and after 1874 was associated with the New York *Herald*. He wrote *Man-of-War Life* (1855), *Whaling and Fishing* (1856), *Nine Years a Sailor* (1857), *The Freedman of South Carolina* (1863), *America for the Working Men* (1865), *The Communistic Societies of the United States* (1875), *Politics for Young Americans* (1875), *God and the Future Life* (1881), and other works.

NORDHOFF, CHARLES BERNARD, 1887–1947, U.S. writer, was born in London of American parents; studied at Harvard University, and served with the Lafayette Escadrille in World War I. He became well known as coauthor with James Norman Hall of *Mutiny on the Bounty* (1932) and other tales of adventure in the Pacific, including *Men Against the Sea* (1933), *Pitcairn's Island* (1934)—sequels to *Mutiny on the Bounty*—and *The Hurricane* (1935). Nordhoff alone wrote *The Fledgling* (1919), *The Pearl Lagoon* (1924), *Picaró* (1924), and *The Derelict* (1928).

NORDICA, LILLIAN, stage name of Lillian Norton, 1859–1914, U.S. soprano, born in Farmington, Me. She made her operatic debut in *La Traviata* in Brescia, Italy, 1879, and first appeared in opera in New York in 1883. She sang at Covent Garden, London, 1887–93, and during most of the period 1896–1907 was associated with the Metropolitan Opera in New York.

NORDKYN, or Kinnarodden, cape, NE Norway, Finmark County; on Barents Sea; 95 miles ENE of Hammerfest. Nordkyn is the most northerly point of the European mainland.

NORDLAND, county, N central Norway; bounded on the N by Troms County, on the E by Sweden, on the S by Nord-Tröndelag County, and on the W by the Norwegian Sea; area 14,797 sq. mi.; pop. (1958 est.) 235,844. A little more than half of Nordland lies north of the Arctic Circle. The county includes the Lofoten Islands, the southern part of the Vesteraalen Islands, and many scattered islands. The coast line is broken by many fiords, such as Ofot, Folda, Vest and Salt. The terrain is generally mountainous, and culminates in the Sulitjelma Range (6,279 ft.). The chief cities are the ports of Narvik and Bodö, the capital. Major resources are fishing, lumbering, mining, quarrying, steelmaking, and livestock raising.

NORD-TRÖNDELAG, county, central Norway; bounded by Nordland County on the N, Sweden on the E, Sör-Tröndelag County on the S, and the Norwegian Sea on the W; area 8,657 sq. mi.; pop. (1958 est.) 115,914. Nord-Tröndelag's coast line is island studded, and indented by many fiords such as Trondheim and Folda, and by inlets. There are also a number of lakes and short rivers. The capital is Steinkjer and the largest town Namsos. The county is chiefly agricultural; hay, rye, potatoes, cattle, sheep, goats, and hogs are the major products.

Fishing, lumbering, and the mining of pyrites are also important. Before 1918 the county was named Nordre Trondhjem.

NORE, THE, a sandbank and its surrounding anchorage, SE England, in the Thames Estuary, midway between the Essex and Kent coasts, 40 miles E of London. It is marked by a lightship.

NORFOLK. The 1st earl of Norfolk was Ralph the Staller (1011?–69), who was created earl of Norfolk and Suffolk possibly by William the Conqueror. His son Ralph de Guader (1040?–98) succeeded him, but forfeited the earldom in 1075 when he revolted against William. The 1st earl of the second creation was Hugh Bigod (1095?–1177), who was made earl of Norfolk by King Stephen in return for his support, 1140 or 1141. The Bigod family held the earldom until the 5th earl, Roger Bigod (1245–1306), died without an heir. The 1st earl of the third creation was Thomas of Brotherton, the fifth son of Edward I, who was created earl of Norfolk in 1312 by his half-brother Edward II. When Thomas died the title passed to his daughter Joan (died 1399), who became countess of Norfolk. In 1397 she was created duchess of Norfolk; on the same day her grandson and heir, Thomas Mowbray (1366–99), was created 1st duke of Norfolk. Both titles remained in the Mowbray family until the death of the 4th duke, John Mowbray (1444–76), when the dukedom lapsed. The earldom was inheritable through the female line, however, and passed to John Mowbray's daughter Anne (1472–81), who became countess of Norfolk. In 1478 Anne was married to Richard, duke of York (1472–83), the second son of Edward IV—Richard having been created duke of Norfolk the previous year in anticipation of the marriage. On Anne's death the earldom of Norfolk became dormant; and when Richard was murdered the dukedom again lapsed.

In 1483 John Howard (1430?–85), who was coheir to Anne Mowbray's estates through his mother (the daughter of Thomas Mowbray, the 1st duke), was created duke of Norfolk by Richard III. He thus became the 1st duke of the third creation. Norfolk led Richard's vanguard at Bosworth Field and died in the battle. Henry VII, the victor of Bosworth, had Norfolk attainted in his first parliament, and all Norfolk's honors were forfeited. Norfolk's son, Thomas Howard I (1443–1524), had been created earl of Surrey on the same day his father was created duke of Norfolk. Surrey, too, had fought against Henry VII; but he managed to gain the royal favor and was restored to his earldom, though not to his father's title. In 1513 he defeated the Scots at the Battle of Flodden, and as a reward was created duke of Norfolk by Henry VIII, 1514. The dukedom remained with the Howards (except for one interval during the lifetime of the 3rd duke, Thomas Howard II, 1473–1554, when the title was forfeited) until 1572, when the 4th duke, Thomas Howard III (1536–72), was attainted and executed (see Mary, Queen of Scots). The 4th duke's grandson, Thomas Howard, earl of Arundel, Surrey, and Norfolk (1622–77), was restored to the dukedom of Norfolk in 1660. Both titles remained with the Howard family thereafter.

The duke of Norfolk is the premier duke of England; that is, he holds the oldest ducal title and is therefore the first duke in order of precedence. And since 1672 the duke of Norfolk has also been the hereditary earl marshal. The duke of Norfolk's oldest son is called by his father's second title—the earl of Arundel and Surrey. In 1960 the duke and earl of Norfolk was Bernard Marmaduke Fitzalan-Howard (1908–), the 16th duke in the Howard line.

Thomas Howard II, 3rd Howard Duke of Norfolk (1473–1554), led the English vanguard at Flodden in 1513 and was rewarded by being created earl of Surrey, 1514. He succeeded his father as duke of Norfolk in 1524. Norfolk led the opposition to Cardinal Wolsey and favored Henry VIII's divorce from Catherine of Aragon. He was "chief adviser" to his niece Anne Boleyn and his fortunes rose with hers. Norfolk became president of the privy council in 1529 and earl marshal in 1533. In 1536 he presided at Anne's trial. Norfolk was the leading English soldier of his day; he suppressed the Pilgrimage of Grace, 1536–37, and commanded the army in Scotland, 1542, and France, 1544. Although Norfolk for family reasons had favored the break with Rome and had received large grants of monastic property, he opposed the reformed faith and its champion, Thomas Cromwell. On Cromwell's fall he arranged the marriage of his niece Catherine Howard to the king, 1540. Queen Catherine's disgrace and execution weakened Norfolk's position. Norfolk, in 1546, was superseded in the king's favor by his enemy Edward Seymour, earl of Hertford, and in 1547 was attainted and condemned to death. He was saved by Henry VIII's death, but remained in the Tower until 1553, when Mary restored him to his dukedom.

Robin S. Oggins

NORFOLK, city, NE Nebraska, Madison County; on a branch of the Elkhorn River, on the North Western and the Union Pacific railroads and U.S. highways 81 and 275; 90 miles NW of Omaha. The city is situated in a prosperous grain and livestock raising area and has manufactures of cereals, flour, beverages, and serum. Norfolk was settled in 1866 and incorporated in 1881. Pop. (1960) 13,111.

NORFOLK, city, SE Virginia, within but administratively independent of Norfolk County; on the Elizabeth River at Hampton Roads; on the Atlantic and Danville, the Chesapeake and Ohio, the Atlantic Coast Line, the Norfolk and Western, the Seaboard Air Line, the Norfolk Southern, the Southern, the Pennsylvania, and the Virginian railroads and U.S. highways 58, 13, 460, and 60; a scheduled airline stop; forming with Newport News on the NW and Portsmouth on the W the Port of Hampton Roads. Norfolk is also at the northern boundary of two sections of the Intracoastal Waterway—the Albemarle and Chesapeake and the Dismal Swamp canals—and has numerous coastal and foreign shipping connections.

Norfolk is the second largest city in Virginia (Richmond is the largest) and is a major seaport, port of entry, headquarters of naval operations, and industrial center. A U.S. Naval Air Station and supply center and the Atlantic Fleet headquarters are at Norfolk; the Norfolk Naval Shipyard is at nearby Portsmouth. Textiles, seafood, farm products, coal, minerals, and chemicals are among the products shipped out of Norfolk. Imports include coffee, timber, oil, hides, and wood products. The city has an automobile assembly plant, shipyards, and foundries, and manufactures of food and lumber products, fertilizers, cement, textiles, clothing, drugs, bags, and agricultural equipment. Norfolk is a distribution center for the truck farms of the region.

Separated by branching Elizabeth River, Norfolk, left and rear center, and Portsmouth, right, are part of the large metropolitan area that has grown up about Hampton Roads.

PHOTO CRAFTSMEN, INC.

Among the buildings of special historic interest in Norfolk are the Myers House, built 1789–91, an excellent example of the Adam style; and St. Paul's (Episcopal) Church, built in 1739, the only building to survive the bombardment and fire of 1776. Ocean View, within the city, and nearby Virginia Beach and Cape Henry are popular summer resorts. At Cape Henry, in 1607, a group of English colonists came ashore briefly before continuing on to Jamestown, where they established the first permanent English settlement.

The original site of Norfolk consisted of 50 acres purchased in 1682 by the trustees of Lower Norfolk County. The settlement built up a flourishing trade with the West Indies, and in 1736 it was incorporated as a borough. Much of Norfolk was destroyed during the Revolutionary War when in 1776 John Murray, earl of Dunmore, the British governor of Virginia, ordered the bombardment of the town. Later the occupying colonial forces burned what remained of the town in order to drive the tory residents from the vicinity. Rebuilt at the end of the war, Norfolk regained its commercial prestige and in 1845 was incorporated as a city. The Civil War naval engagement between the *Monitor* and the *Merrimac* took place off Norfolk on Mar. 9, 1862. During World Wars I and II Norfolk was an important troop embarkation port and supply center. The continuing naval importance of the city was revealed by the U.S. Navy's expenditure of more than a quarter of a billion dollars for construction work in the Norfolk area during 1950–54. A 3½-mile tunnel and trestle crossing Hampton Roads from Norfolk to Hampton on the north was completed in 1957. Pop. (1960) 305,872.

NORFOLK, maritime county, E England, ranking fourth in size among English counties; bounded on the N and E by the North Sea, on the S by Suffolk, on the SW by Cambridgeshire, and on the W by Lincolnshire; area 2,178 sq. mi. The coast is low and flat, subject to the encroaching sea, and is bordered in part by dangerous sandbanks, in part by low cliffs or dunes. There are no good harbors. Yarmouth is the chief port, with King's Lynn second in volume of trade. The principal rivers are the Nene and the Ouse, emptying into the Wash, and the Yare, Bure, and Waveney, all of which flow into the sea near Yarmouth. The Yare is navigable to seagoing craft west to Norwich. The county is generally an undulating plain, the western part a low fen marked by drainage ditches and dikes. East of the Ouse lies the northeast extension of the English chalk hills; there are tracts of heath along the Suffolk border, and in the southeast the land is fertile and wooded. In the northeast are the Broads, consisting of numerous shallow lakes formed in the river courses—a resort for boating, fishing, and duck hunting, and a sanctuary for bittern and other wildlife. Norfolk is one of the chief wheat-growing counties of England and also produces large crops of barley, oats, rye, potatoes, clover, and hay. Market garden produce and sugar beets are grown on the reclaimed fen. Small fruits are cultivated and dairy farming is an important occupation. The herring fisheries of Yarmouth are extensive; and fish-canning and processing plants in the city form a large industry. Norfolk industries include also the manufacture of silk, worsted, boots and shoes, agricultural implements, flour, and bricks, as well as malting, brewing, and tanning.

Evidences of neolithic man have been found in the chalk and gravel deposits of the county. In early times Norfolk was a part of the region occupied by the Iceni. The Romans located several stations there, including Caistor near Norwich; and later the region formed part of East Anglia. Pop. (1951) 546,550.

NORFOLK ISLAND, part of the Commonwealth of Australia, about 930 miles NE of Sydney at 29°2′S lat. and 167°57′E long.; area 13 sq. mi.; pop. (1954) 954. The island is of volcanic origin and rises to an elevation of 1,050 feet (Mount Pitt). Fertile, humid, and subtropical, it has luxuriant vegetation including many fruits and Norfolk Island pine, used widely abroad as an ornamental tree. Norfolk Island was discovered by Capt. James Cook in 1774 and at two periods between 1788 and 1855 was used as a penal station. In 1856 descendants of the mutineers of H.M.S. *Bounty* and their Tahitian women were brought in from their small Pitcairn Island; most of the present inhabitants of Norfolk are descended from these people. See BOUNTY, MUTINY ON THE.

OTIS W. FREEMAN

NORFOLK ISLAND PINE. See ARAUCARIA.

NORICUM, a former kingdom and later a Roman province, south of the Danube River, which corresponded approximately to modern Austria. The Taurisci were the dominant Celtic tribe in Noricum. During the time of Julius Caesar the kingdom of Noricum was an independent ally of Rome, and was later peacefully incorporated into the Roman Empire. During the reign of Diocletian, Noricum was divided in two parts, Noricum Mediterraneum in the south and Noricum Ripense on the Danube. It was overrun in the fifth century by the Goths and the Franks, and in the sixth century by the Slavs.

NORILSK, city, U.S.S.R., N Russian Soviet Federated Socialist Republic, Krasnoyarsk Territory, 1,300 miles N of the city of Krasnoyarsk. Norilsk is well within the Arctic Circle, at 69°20′N lat. and is the northernmost large industrial city in the world. Its industry is based on a large complex of mines and smelters that produce copper, nickel, cobalt, platinum, and rare metals such as palladium. The city is linked by a short railroad with the Yenisey River port of Dudinka. Norilsk's development began in 1942 and was speeded after World War II. Pop. (1956 est.) 92,000.

THEODORE SHABAD

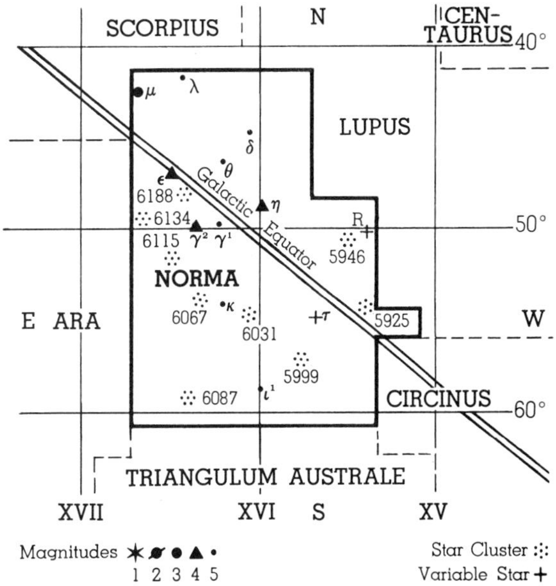

The Constellation Norma

NORMA, the Level, a modern southern constellation that contains no star brighter than the fourth magnitude. It extends from about the 42° to just beyond 60° south declination and straddles the 16th hour circle, so that it appears on the meridian about 10 P.M. on June 22. The galactic equator passes through this constellation and Norma is comparatively rich in nebulae and star clusters. NGC 6067, a rich cluster 20′ in diameter, can be seen from the southern part of the United States by means of even a small telescope. The star shown as R Normae in the drawing appeared as a nova in 1893; at its brightest its magnitude was 7. See CONSTELLATION.

NORMAL, town, central Illinois, McLean County; on the Gulf, Mobile, and Ohio and the Illinois Central railroads and U.S. highways 51 and 66; adjacent to Bloomington. The town is located in rich corn country and has several canneries. It is the seat of the state's oldest teachers college—Illinois State Normal University, founded in 1857. Originally called North Bloomington, Normal was incorporated in 1865. Pop. (1960) 13,357.

NORMAL CURVE, a bell-shaped symmetric curve representing the relative frequencies of the occurrence of events in a special type of frequency distribution called normal—in which the center, when it has the value of x corresponding to the maximum value of y, is the point of coincidence of mean, median, and mode. See FREQUENCY DISTRIBUTION; MEAN; MEDIAN; MODE.

Standard Form of Normal Curve

In the above figure of the standard form of the normal frequency curve, M is the point of coincidence. The equation of the standard form of the curve is $y = (1/\sqrt{2\pi})\, e - x^2/2$. Here x is the number of standard deviations by which a single observation t departs from the mean (algebraic average) μ: $x = \frac{t-\mu}{\sigma}$ (e is the base of natural logarithms). The relative frequency of occurrence of x is given by y. More than 99 per cent of the area of a normal curve lies within 3 standard deviations of the mean, which means that an item drawn at random from a normally distributed series has a probability of less than one in 100 of falling 3 or more standard deviations from the mean. In the standard form of the normal curve the total area under the curve is unity. By algebraic inspection one can determine that the curve trails off indefinitely in the x direction, plus or minus, with y always decreasing but never reaching zero.

The normal curve has uses in every branch of science where experimentation and statistical sampling techniques are utilized—as in the measurement of intelligence. An important assumption underlying the scoring systems for many of the tests that measure intelligence quotients (IQ) of individuals is that their distribution follows the normal curve. Similarly in the control of quality of manufactured articles, specifications for mass production of items such as radio tubes are drawn up with the assumption that deviations from specifications will follow the normal curve. On that assumption scientifically constructed sampling schemes are devised to prevent materials that vary too much from passing inspection.

For a long time it was considered axiomatic that any statistical distribution would naturally approach the normal if enough cases were measured accurately, but it is generally believed today that such a certainty is possible only if the original conditions are properly qualified. See STATISTICS; STANDARD DEVIATION.

NORMALIZING, a form of annealing used to produce a finer and stronger grain structure in ferrous steels and alloys. It is accomplished by heating steel containing less than 0.83 per cent of carbon to temperatures between 50° and 100°F above the critical or transformation range, holding at that temperature for an adequate time, and then slow cooling in still air at normal temperature. The result is a fine-grained, strong pearlitic structure mixed with ferrite in the low-carbon steels, and fine pearlitic grains having a minimum of cementite at the grain boundaries of the high-carbon steels. Similar to annealing, normalizing also relieves strains and, with the improved grain structure, makes the steel or ferrous alloy more adaptable for subsequent operations such as machining or cold-working. See ANNEALING.

NORMAL SCHOOL, an educational institution that prepares teachers mainly for elementary school work but does not necessarily confer degrees. In the history of teacher education in the United States, normal schools were important primarily between 1865 and the early 1900's. Since 1920 they have declined in both number and importance as teacher education has been assumed by teachers colleges and by departments of education in many other colleges and universities.

The word *normal* derives from the Latin word meaning model or rule, and thus it was conceived to be the purpose of a normal school to provide rules for teaching. At the opening of the nineteenth century, U.S. education was largely private, and until about 1865 most teachers were trained in academies. As the concern for public education grew, teachers were needed in larger numbers and with more adequate training than the academies could provide. The idea of public education and publicly supported institutions for training teachers took definite form in Massachusetts under the leadership of James G. Carter (1795–1849), Horace Mann (1796–1859), and others. Normal schools in Prussia and France attracted the attention of American educational reformers who went abroad, and they recommended similar state programs for training teachers in America.

Early U.S. Normal Schools. The first normal school in the United States was a private institution at Concord, Vt., founded by Samuel Hall in 1823. The first public normal school was founded at Lexington, Mass., in 1839. Thereafter, similar schools were established in Massachusetts and other states.

The early normal schools, preparing teachers for elementary schools, were on a secondary school level. The program included elementary school subjects as well as methods and history of education, philosophy, and psychology, and varied from one to three years.

Development of Teachers Colleges. By 1900 most normal schools required two years of high school for entrance, and usually offered a two-year course of study. In 1900 there were about 300 normal schools, of which more than half were private. All states had some type of public normal school. Shortly after 1900, teachers colleges began to replace normal schools as institutions for training teachers, and this movement was accelerated especially after 1920, with the demand for higher standards of teacher preparation. By the late 1950's the number of normal schools had declined to about 20, whereas teachers' colleges had increased to more than 200. The change was actually greater, but beginning in the 1940's many teachers colleges became liberal arts colleges. See TEACHER TRAINING.

CHARLES A. HARPER